DAY FIGHTERS

IN DEFENCE OF THE REICH

DAY FIGHTERS
IN DEFENCE OF THE REICH
A War Diary, 1942–45

Donald Caldwell

FRONTLINE BOOKS

First published in Great Britain in 2011 by
Frontline Books
an imprint of
Pen & Sword Books Ltd,
47 Church Street,
Barnsley,
South Yorkshire.
S70 2AS

A CIP record for this book is available from the British Library.

ISBN: 978-1-84832-525-8

Designed and typeset by Ian Hughes, www.mousematdesign.com

Printed and bound in China through Printworks Int. Ltd.

Pen & Sword Books Ltd incorporates the Imprints of
Pen & Sword Aviation, Pen & Sword Maritime, Pen & Sword Military,
Wharncliffe Local History, Pen & Sword Select, Pen & Sword Military
Classics, Leo Cooper, Remember When, Seaforth Publishing and
Frontline Publishing.

For a complete list of Pen & Sword titles please contact
Pen & Sword Books Limited
47 Church Street, Barnsley, South Yorkshire, S70 2AS, England
e-mail: enquiries@pen-and-sword.co.uk
website: www.pen-and-sword.co.uk

CONTENTS

INTRODUCTION AND ACKNOWLEDGEMENTS

This book is intended to be a detailed, comprehensive daily reference to the air operations flown by the Luftwaffe in response to daylight strategic missions by the United States Army Air Force against the German Reich and the western zone occupied by Germany. It is a natural complement to *The Luftwaffe over Germany: Defense of the Reich*, a narrative history of the day *Reichsluftverteidigung* (Air Defence of the Reich) by myself and Dr Richard Muller. The present book contains a brief narrative and a table of statistics detailing every mission of every Luftwaffe unit defending the prescribed area against daylight strategic raids by the USAAF and RAF, and a summary of every 8th and 15th US Army Air Force strategic mission over this area in which the Luftwaffe was encountered, beginning with the first numbered 8th Air Force raid in August 1942 and ending in May 1945. Many specially prepared mission maps are included, as well as tables summarising strengths, victory claims and losses of the Luftwaffe and the Allies in this campaign. I have called it a 'War Diary' because its contents are as close as possible to those of a conventional, official unit war diary.

Most people picking up this book will understand the challenges facing any serious Luftwaffe historian owing to the lack of primary documentation. I accumulated the data needed from more than 1,000 sources over a period of 25 years. The tables are inevitably incomplete; I found the lack of some important official data, especially unit mission strengths prior to 1944, especially galling. Since each table in this book might contain data from 100 sources, conventional footnotes for the tables have been passed up in favour of a general discussion of sources and an extensive bibliography. Direct quotes are, however, referenced as they appear.

I first solicited the help of Luftwaffe veterans when I began serious research in 1985, and their generous assistance proved invaluable. Their numbers are unfortunately but inevitably growing fewer by the year, but here are all of the men who provided material that I eventually used in this book: Willi Andiel, Hans Berger, Karl Boehm-Tettelbach, Hans-Ekkehard Bob, Walter Bohatsch, Oskar Bösch, Hans Bott, Hermann Buchner, Eberhard Burath, J. E. Clade, Peter Crump, Martin Drewes, Georg-Peter Eder, Günther Ehrlich, Fritz Engau, Wolf Falck, Richard Franz, Adolf Galland, Georg Genth, Adolf Glunz, Heinz Gomann, Alfred Grislawski, Klaus Hahn, Alois Höhn, Hans-Joachim Jabs, Robert Jung, Jörg Kiefner, Otto Kleinert, Gerhard Kroll, Ottomar Kruse, Heinz-Günter Kuring, Erwin Leykauf, Fritz Marktscheffel, Wilhelm Mittag, Werner Molge, Theo Nau, Johannes Naumann, Karl-Heinz Ossenkop, Dietrich Peltz, Horst Petzschler, Douglas Pitcairn, Günther Rall, Willi Reschke, Arno Rose, Wolfgang Schenck, Ernst Scheufele, Jan Schild, Dieter Schmidt–Barbo, Gerhard Schöpfel, Ernst Schröder, Erich Schwarz, Günther Sinnecker, Georg Spies, Peter Spoden, Otto Stammberger, Heinrich Staniwoga, Karl-Heinz von den Steinen, Fritz Ungar, Willi Unger, Hans Weik, Berthold Wendler, Gerd Wiegand, Günther Wolf, Helmut Zittier and Paul Zorner.

Next, special thanks are owed to Les Butler for the maps and to Rich Muller for his frequent encouraging words, many helpful suggestions, editing of the text and tracking down of references, many at very short notice.

Luftwaffe memorabilia are considered collectibles, which presents another challenge to the serious researcher. Photo albums and documents that were shared freely in the 1980s and 1990s now appear on eBay® to be sold to wealthy collectors, frequently never to be seen again by the general public. The small band of serious air war historians and enthusiasts has fought this pernicious trend by freely sharing their material, aided by Internet discussion boards such as *12 O'Clock High* (http://forum.12oclockhigh.net). I wish to acknowledge the following men and women for their generous gifts of time, information, leads, photographs, documents and/or photographic assistance: Arno Abendroth, Remi Badru, E. J. Bakker, Bernd Barbas, Nick Beale, John Beaman, Csaba Becze, Paul Berg, Dénes Bernád, Christer Bergström, Steve Blake, Jan Bobek, Winfried Bock, Manfred Boehme, Theo Boiten, Andreas Brekken, Jerry Brewer, David Brown, Eric Brown, Edwina Campbell, Sven Carlsen, Carl Charles, Steven Coates, Jerry Crandall, A. J. Cranston, Jim Crow, Ferdinando D'Amico, Curt Deatrick, Arie De Jong, Ivo De Jong, Wim de Meester, Linda Dewey, Larry deZeng, C. J. Ehrengardt, Russ Fahey, Bob Fletcher, Stephen Fochuk, John Foreman, Jim Forsyth, Robert Forsyth, Norman Franks, Garry Fry, Carl Geust, Bob Gill, Chris Goss, Steve Gotts, Richard Goyat, Timothy Gravelle, John Gray, Lewis Griffith, Russell Guest, Tomislav Haramincic, Ian Hawkins, Bill Hess, Larry Hickey, Michael Holm, Kevin Holzimmer, George Hopp, Bertrand Hugot, Budd Jones, Peter Kassak, Jim Kitchens, Werner Kock, Bob Korkuc, Harold Lake, Malcolm Laing, Bruce Lander, Gerd Lanio, Eric Larger, Joss LeClerq, Jean-Yves Lorant, Rod MacKenzie, John Manrho, Bill Marshall, Lex McAulay, Ian McLachlan, Michael Meyer, Robert Michulec, Kenneth Minor, Kees Mol, Eric Mombeek, George Morrison, Williamson Murray, Wesley Newton, Frank Olynyk, Neil Page, Mack Palmer, Evgeniy Pavlenko, Don Pearson, Robert Peczkowski, Doug Peifer, Gordon Permann, Jim Perry, Toni Petito, Peter Petrick, Gert Poelchau, Dick Powers, Dr Alfred Price, Dr Jochen Prien, Ron Putz, Lorenz Rasse, Jean-Louis Roba, Peter Rodeike, Barry Rosch, Brown Ryle, Tom Semenza, Chris Shores, Barry Smith, Evelyn Smith, Sam Sox, Christian Stopsack, Klaes Sundin, Günter Sundermann, Lothair Vanoverbeke, John Vasco, Leon Venter, Luc Vervoort, Dave Wadman, Walter Waiss, Edward Westermann, Dan Williams, Tony Wood and Ad van Zantvoort. I apologise for any inadvertent omissions; however, anyone who posts to Internet discussion boards using pseudonyms has chosen not to be acknowledged.

The Bundesarchiv–Bildarchiv (Koblenz) has granted permission to reprint photographs from its collection. Permission has been received from Motorbuch Verlag, Helios Verlags- und Buchvertriebsgesellschaft, the Gemeinschaft der Flieger Deutsche Streitkräfte e.V. and the Kassel Mission Memorial Association, Inc., to reproduce pilot's accounts from published works.

I wish to acknowledge the help received from the professional staffs of the British National Archives (Public Record Office), the Bundesarchiv–Militärarchiv (Freiburg), the Military Archives Division of the National Archives and the United States Air Force Historical Research Agency.

I take responsibility for the book's inevitable errors of omission and commission. I wish to state further that I translated all quotations in the book that were originally written in the German language. The responsibility for any consequent errors in fact or tone is my own.

Donald Caldwell
Lake Jackson, Texas
June 2010

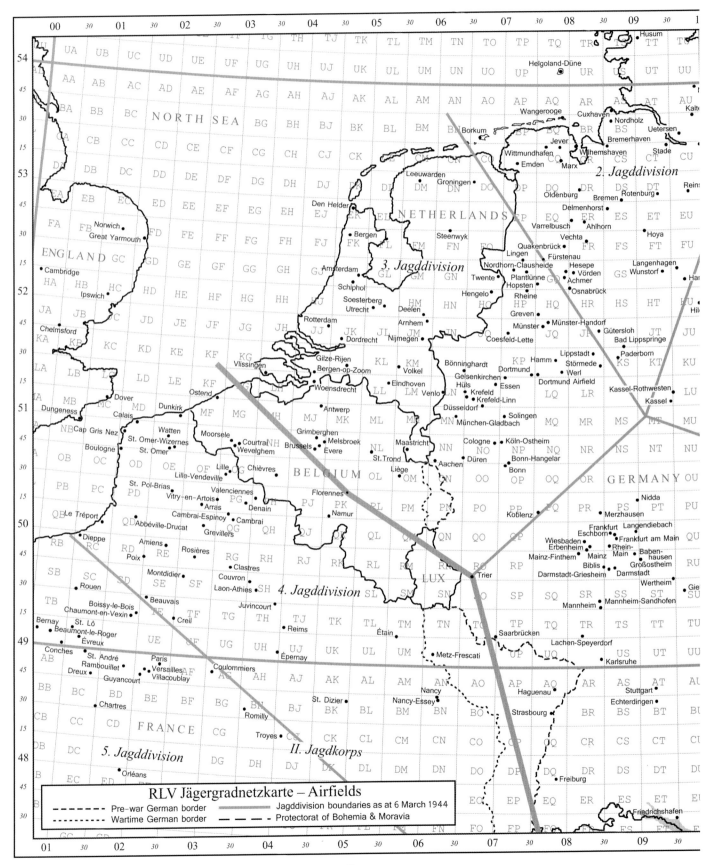

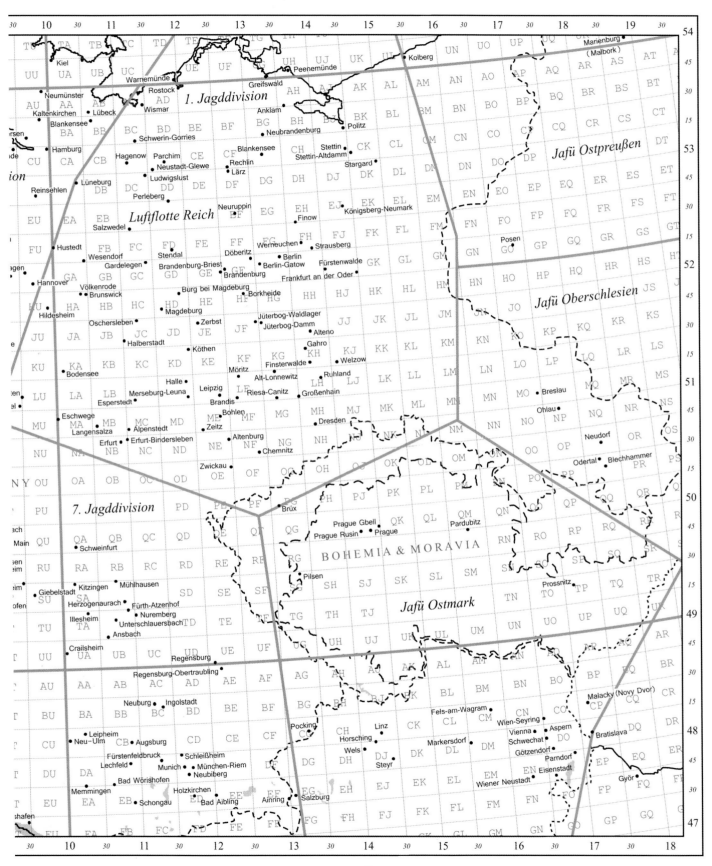

CHAPTER 1

AUGUST – DECEMBER 1942

August 1942

Eight months after Germany declared war on the USA, American heavy bombers were arriving in the United Kingdom. The Luftwaffe leaders knew this, and that United States Army Air Forces (USAAF) doctrine called for high-altitude daylight strategic bombing, but the mere threat of an American bombing campaign did not warrant the reinforcement or centralisation of Germany's day fighter defences. The Luftwaffe itself had failed to defeat the United Kingdom with daylight bombing in 1940, and the Royal Air Force's small day attacks on German targets since the beginning of the war had failed likewise, at

high cost. Confidence that the forces on hand could meet the American threat was high. For more than a year, the day fighter defences had comprised three *Jagdgeschwader* (Fighter Wings), spread thinly near the coast from Cherbourg along the English Channel and the North Sea coast to Denmark and southern Norway. The authorised strength of these three Geschwader was 442 fighters; their operational strength on 27 July was 333. Almost all were Focke-Wulf Fw 190s, the nimble radial-engine fighter whose performance had shocked the RAF when it entered service on the *Kanalfront* (English Channel front) in 1941. Bombers penetrating the coastal crust would be

Four Fw 190As of 11./JG 1, photographed in their net-covered boxes at Deelen in the summer of 1942. *(Burath)*

taken care of by Flak, aircraft factory defence flights, and the operational flights maintained by each advanced flight training school.

The wing defending the most territory was Major Erich von Selle's Jagdgeschwader 1 (JG 1), whose four Gruppen, or groups, were stationed along the North Sea coast from Norway to the Netherlands. It was part of the air defence command responsible for the Reich proper, *Luftwaffenbefehlshaber Mitte* (Central Air Command; Lw Bfh Mitte), which was commanded by a Flak officer and contained only a single *Fliegerkorps* (Flying Corps) led by a night fighter specialist. Operational control of the day fighters rested with two *Jagdfliegerführer* (Fighter Commands; Jafü) who were part of two *Jagddivisionen* (Fighter Divisions). This complex command structure was not tested by day in 1942. The Americans did not cross the German border, and JG 1 encountered the American 8th Air Force over the Netherlands on only a few occasions. It did counter a few raids by RAF tactical forces, but most of its operational flights were routine coastal patrols and convoy escorts.

The two Jagdgeschwader based nearest to the English Channel and nicknamed the *Kanalgeschwader*

were thus the first to face the Americans. They belonged to a front-line air force, *Luftflotte 3* (3rd Air Fleet). This force had been left in the western occupied zone (France and the Low Countries) in mid-1941 when most of the Luftwaffe was transferred east to support the German invasion of the Soviet Union. Its bombers had conducted the night Blitz on England, and the task of its fighters was to maintain air superiority above the region against the fighters and light bombers of the RAF. They had performed this task with great success; they were now to face a different challenge.

In August 1942, the Fw 190s of Major Walter Oesau's JG 2 'Richthofen' were based in northwestern France, under the command and control of Jafü 3. The Stab and I./JG 2 were at Triqueville, II./JG 2 was at Beaumont–le–Roger, and III./JG 2 was at Théville, less one Staffel which was guarding the U-boat bases in Brittany. Major Gerhard Schöpfel's JG 26 'Schlageter' was under Jafü 2 and deployed as follows: the Stab and I./JG 26 at St. Omer in the Pas de Calais; II./JG 26, the 'Abbéville Boys', at Abbéville-Drucat on the lower Somme, and III./JG 26 at Wevelghem, in western Belgium. In addition to these Fw 190 units,

Mechanics sit on the cowling of a 12./JG 1 Fw 190A-4 at Deelen in the autumn of 1942. Note the presence of both Geschwader and Gruppe emblems and the dark colour of the lower cowl panel. *(Burath)*

Major Walter Oesau, JG 2 Kommodore (left), with Hptm. Siegfried Schnell, one of his successful Staffelkapitäne, on the Kanalfront in 1942. Oesau was killed on 11 May 1944 as JG 1 Kommodore. Schnell became Kommandeur of III./JG 54 in the RLV force on 1 May 1943 and transferred to IV./JG 54 on the Eastern Front in February 1944. He was killed in combat that same month. *(Author's collection)*

Major Gerhard Schöpfel. A pre-war JG 26 pilot and Staffelkapitän, Schöpfel was Kommodore of JG 26 for all of 1942. He was replaced by Hptm. Josef Priller in January 1943 and spent the rest of the war in various mid-level staff and combat leadership positions. *(Schöpfel)*

17 August

8th Air Force VIII BC (VIII BC) Mission #1: 12 97th Bomb Group (97th BG) B 17s bomb Rouen–Sotteville rail yards, TOT 1839-1846 – lose 0-0-2 [lost-cat E (scrapped)-damaged], claim 0-0-1 [downed-probable-damaged]. Close escort of 4 sqds RAF Spitfire IX claims 1-5-4, loses 3-0-1.

The VIII BC's first heavy bomber mission sent a mere dozen Boeing B-17 Flying Fortresses to Rouen in late afternoon. Supermarine Spitfires of RAF Fighter Command provided the escort. Most were Spitfire Vs, which were markedly inferior to the Fw 190A. The new Spitfire IX, which equipped one fighter wing, would prove to be the Focke-Wulf fighter's equal. After patrolling the Channel coast in the morning, at least one JG 2 Gruppe and all three JG 26 Gruppen were scrambled against a late raid that proved to contain the B-17s. Hptm. Erich Leie's I./JG 2 and Hptm. Conny Meyer's II./JG 26 reached the Allied formation, but not until it had already dropped its bombs and turned for England. The Focke-Wulfs did not attack the bombers, but did draw their fire. Instead, they tangled with the RAF escort and claimed four Spitfires for the loss of one I./JG 2 Fw 190 and pilot. Three Spitfire IXs were, in fact, shot down, and a fourth was seriously damaged. The German pilots identified the bombers as RAF Short Stirlings and Handley-Page Halifaxes and were reportedly impressed by their close formation and heavy defensive fire.

The Fw 190A-3 of Oblt. Wilhelm-Ferdinand 'Wutz' Galland, Kapitän of the 5. Staffel of II.//JG 26, at Abbéville in 1942. Galland was killed by P-47s on 17 August 1943, the second brother of Adolf Galland to die in JG 26. *(Crump)*

there were two independent Staffeln, 11.(Höhen)/JG 2 and 11.(Höhen)/JG 26, which were equipped with the high-altitude Bf 109G-1. These were based at Ligescourt and Norrent–Fontes, nominally under JG 26. The two Jafü reported directly to Luftflotte 3. Its command structure was thus quite flat, not typical for the Luftwaffe, but the overlapping territories of the two controllers did lead to occasional problems, and the quick reaction times necessitated by the closeness of the American bases prevented the assembly of the large combat formations that later became common over the Reich. The standard interception unit in Luftflotte 3 would remain the Gruppe, nothing larger.

This II./JG 26 Fw 190A-3 is a typical example of the aircraft equipping the three air defence Jagdgeschwader in late 1942 and early 1943. Obfw. Werner Gerhardt was killed in it off Dieppe on 19 August. *(Crump)*

19 August

8th Air Force VIII BC Mission #2: 22 of 24 B-17s bomb Abbéville–Drucat airfield, TOT 1132-1140 – lose 0-0-3, claim 0-0-0.

The Americans' second raid was an attack on the II./JG 26 base at Abbéville–Drucat, which was ignored by the Luftwaffe. The Kanalgeschwader were fully occupied elsewhere; this was the day of Operation JUBILEE, the ill-fated Allied raid on Dieppe.

20 August

8th Air Force VIII BC Mission #3: 11 of 12 B-17s bomb Amiens–Longeau rail yards, TOT 1901 – lose 0, claim 0. Close escort of 4 sqds RAF Spitfire IX claims 1-1-1, loses 0-0-1.

The VIII BC sent 12 B-17s to Amiens. One JG 2 Gruppe and the three JG 26 Gruppen were scrambled against this raid, but the Spitfire escort kept all formations away from the bombers.

21 August

8th Air Force VIII BC Mission #4: 12 B-17s target Rotterdam shipyard (recalled) – lose 0-0-1, claim 2-5-6. Close escort of 8 sqds RAF Spitfires claims 0, loses 0.

The VIII BC ordered its first raid on a target outside France. The RAF's diversionary raids on the Pas de Calais occupied JG 26, leaving the defence to Oblt. Detlev Rohwer's Woensdrecht-based II./JG 1. The bombers were recalled after missing rendezvous with their escort (1 squadron of USAAF and 8 squadrons of RAF Spitfires) and were attacked on withdrawal by nine II./JG 1 Fw 190s. These damaged one B-17 severely, costing the VIII BC its first fatality. One Axis fighter force-landed with combat damage.

24 August

8th Air Force VIII BC Mission #5: 12 B-17s bomb LeTrait shipyard, TOT 1716-1723 – lose 0-0-5 (to Flak), claim 0-0-0. Escort of 10 sqds RAF Spitfires claims 3-1-4 Fw 190s, loses 2-0-3.

The VIII BC sent a dozen B-17s to Le Trait. II./JG 26 and I./JG 2 were scrambled, but only II./JG 26 made contact and was kept from the bombers by the escort. The Gruppe claimed five Spitfires without loss. Two Spitfire IXs were shot down; two more force-landed in England with wounded pilots.

Luftwaffe defensive activity – 17 August 1942

Unit	Type	Gruppe up			Gruppe down		Claims	Losses				
		Base	No	Time	Base	Time		Dest	Dam	KIA	MIA	WIA
Luftflotte 3												
Jafü 2:												
I./JG 26	Fw 190A	St. Omer–Arques		1820	St. Omer–Arques	1853	0	0	0	0	0	0
II./JG 26	Fw 190A	Abbéville		1837	Abbéville	1920	4 Spitfire	0	0	0	0	0
III./JG 26	Fw 190A	Wevelghem		1827	Wevelghem	1902	0	0	0	0	0	0
Jafü 3:												
I./JG 2	Fw 190A	Triqueville		1831	Triqueville	1903	0	1	0	1	0	0

Luftwaffe defensive activity – 20 August 1942

Unit	Type	Gruppe up			Gruppe down		Claims	Losses				
		Base	No	Time	Base	Time		Dest	Dam	KIA	MIA	WIA
Luftflotte 3												
Jafü 2:												
I./JG 26	Fw 190A	St. Omer–Arques		1802	St. Omer–Arques	1836	0	0	0	0	0	0
II./JG 26	Fw 190A	Abbéville		1756	Abbéville	1838	0	0	0	0	0	0
III./JG 26	Fw 190A	Wevelghem		1844	Wevelghem	1948	0	0	0	0	0	0
Jafü 3:												
I./JG 2	Fw 190A	Triqueville		1837	Triqueville	1928	2 Spitfire	0	0	0	0	0

Luftwaffe defensive activity – 21 August 1942

Unit	Type	Gruppe up			Gruppe down		Claims	Losses				
		Base	No	Time	Base	Time		Dest	Dam	KIA	MIA	WIA
Lw Bfh Mitte												
XII. Fliegerkorps												
Jagddivision 1												
Jafü Holland-Ruhr:												
II./JG 1	Fw 190A	Woensdrecht	9	?	Woensdrecht	?	0	0	1	0	0	0

Luftwaffe defensive activity – 24 August 1942

Unit	Type	Gruppe up			Gruppe down		Claims	Losses				
		Base	No	Time	Base	Time		Dest	Dam	KIA	MIA	WIA
Luftflotte 3												
Jafü 2:												
II./JG 26	Fw 190A	Abbéville		1710	Abbéville	1800	5 Spitfire	0	0	0	0	0
Jafü 3:												
I./JG 2	Fw 190A	Triqueville		1706	Triqueville	1759	0	1	0	0	0	1

27 August

8th Air Force VIII BC Mission #6: 7 of 9 97th Bomb Group B-17s bomb Rotterdam shipyard, TOT 1840 – sight no e/a, lose 0-0-3 (to Flak). Escort of 7 sqds RAF + 12 US Spitfires claims 0, loses 0.

The VIII BC sent a small force to Rotterdam in late afternoon. The Channel units had spent the early afternoon battling RAF Spitfires escorting a raid by Bostons on Abbéville-Drucat airfield. They had landed for the day when the heavy bombers were detected, and the Luftwaffe fighters were not scrambled again to oppose them.

28 August

8th Air Force VIII BC Mission #7: 11 of 14 97th BG B-17s bomb Méaulte–Potez aircraft factory, TOT 1437-44 – sight no e/a, lose 0-0-3, one KIA (to Flak). Escort of 8 sqds RAF Spitfires claims 1 Bf 109, 0-3-3 Fw 190s, loses 1-0-2.

The VIII BC B-17s bombed Méaulte in mid-afternoon. The Channel units had spent the early afternoon chasing RAF feints and diversions, and only II./JG 26 and one or both of the two Luftflotte 3 high-altitude Staffeln were scrambled against what proved to be the day's true raid. The RAF close escort kept the German fighters away from the bombers, shooting down one 11.(Höhen)/JG 2 Bf 109G 1 for the loss of one Spitfire IX shot down and a second seriously damaged. II./JG 26 was credited with two Spitfires.

29 August

8th Air Force VIII BC Mission #8: 12 of 13 97th BG B-17s bomb Courtrai–Wevelghem airfield, TOT 1231-36 – lose 0-0-3, claim 1-2-0. B-17 escort of 4 sqds RAF Spitfire IX and escorts of RAF raids claim 2-2-4 e/a, lose 3 fighters and 2 pilots.

The VIII BC bombed the III./JG 26 base at Wevelghem. Much of Hptm. Josef 'Pips' Priller's Gruppe was already airborne against another raid, but the field itself sustained considerable damage. One German unit apparently succeeded in reaching the bombers, as evidenced by the Allied claims; its identity, however, is unknown.

Fw 190A-2s of the III./JG 26 Stabsschwarm stand ready for take-off from Wevelghem, Belgium, in 1942. The nearest aircraft is that of Fw. Grünlinger, wingman to the Gruppenkommandeur, Hptm. Priller; in the middle, a Gruppe staff aircraft; behind, a wingman's aircraft from the 7th Staffel. (Cranston)

September 1942

5 September

8th Air Force VIII BC Mission #9: 31 of 37 B-17s bomb Rouen–Sotteville rail yard, TOT 1130-35 – sight no e/a, lose 0-0-0. B-17 escort of 4 sqds RAF Spitfire IX claims 2-1-3, loses 6.

The VIII BC bombed a frequent target, the Rouen rail yard. Interception in the target area by JG 2 Fw 190 formations was ineffective. I./JG 2, 11.(Höhen)/JG 2 and II./JG 26 reached the withdrawing bombers, but were kept away from the B-17s by Spitfires, which were then punished severely for their success. Six Spitfires were shot down, for the loss of one I./JG 2 Fw 190A-3 and damage to one 11.(Höhen)/JG 2 Bf 109G-1.

6 September

8th Air Force VIII BC Mission #10: 43 of 64 B-17s bomb St. Omer airfields, Méaulte–Potez aircraft factory, TOT 1840-48 – lose 2-0-7, claim 4-19-20. Escort of 7 sqds RAF and 3 sqds US Spitfires claims 1-1-7 e/a, loses 3-0-0.

The VIII BC lost its first two B-17s today, on its tenth mission. The German intercept force was the largest to date – three Gruppen – and the efficient Spitfire IX wing, which had provided close escort to previous missions, missed rendezvous and was late reaching the battle. The Spitfire high cover was bounced from above and behind and dispersed by Hptm. Conny Meyer's II./JG 26, which then joined Hptm. Helmut-Felix Bolz's II./JG 2 in attacking the bombers from the French coast to the target. After numerous passes from all directions, two B-17s ultimately went down; each Jagdgruppe was credited with two Fortresses. Their claims for three Spitfires did match the true RAF losses. The II./JG 2 lost one Focke-Wulf and pilot; a I./JG 2 Focke-Wulf was damaged seriously enough to write it off. Hptm. Meyer's II./JG 26 continued its string of loss-free intercept missions.

7 September

8th Air Force VIII BC Mission #11: 9 of 29 B-17s bomb Rotterdam, Utrecht shipyards, TOT 1011-30 – lose 0-0-5 (to Flak), claim 12-10-12. Escort of 5 sqds RAF Spitfires claims 1-0-5 e/a, loses 1-1-1.

The VIII BC sent its small force to two Dutch shipyards. Two JG 1 Gruppen intercepted the bombers and were met by the Spitfire IX escort wing, which shot down two Focke-Wulfs without loss to itself or the bombers. III./JG26, the easternmost JG 26 Gruppe, was the only Luftflotte 3 unit to see combat. This Gruppe took off intending to catch the bombers on their return flight, but was quickly engaged by Spitfires sweeping the coast. One Spitfire was claimed. In fact, one crashed in Belgium, a second was abandoned over the sea, and a third crash-landed on Manston.

October 1942

2 October

8th Air Force VIII BC Mission #13: 36 of 49 B-17s bomb St. Omer–Wizernes airfield and Méaulte-Potez aircraft factory, TOT 1617-18 – lose 0-0-6, claim 9-9-5. Escort of 13 sqds RAF Spitfires claims 2-5-1 e/a, loses 5. 31 1st Fighter Group (1st FG) P-38s claims 0, loses 1; 23 4th FG Spitfires claim 4-0-2, lose 0.

The VIII BC attacked two targets, a St. Omer airfield and the Méaulte–Potez aircraft factory. Several diversionary raids and sweeps were ignored by the German controllers, but the principal diversion, a sweep of the Pas de Calais by three fighter wings, was met near Calais by Hptm. Johannes Seifert's I./JG 26, which lost two Fw 190s to the US 4th FG, flying its first mission as an American unit after its formation from the three RAF Eagle squadrons. III./JG 26 met the withdrawing Spitfires over the Channel and accounted for the sweep's two losses, while losing one Fw 190.

The St. Omer raiders faced only scattered attacks. These B-17s were escorted by the P-38s of the 1st FG, flying its first mission as a unit; one P-38 failed to return. The Spitfire IX wing escorted the Méaulte force. Hptm. Hans 'Assi' Hahn's III./JG 2, Hptm. Meyer's II./JG 26 and the two Höhenstaffeln all reached these bombers as they were coming off their bomb run, splitting the escort and making quick passes at the B-17s from all directions, damaging several but downing none. Three III./JG 2 Focke-Wulfs went down, killing two pilots. The escorts shot down one 11.(Höhen)/JG 26 Bf 109G-1, while losing one Spitfire to II./JG 26.

Luftwaffe defensive activity – 28 August 1942

Unit	Type	Gruppe up			Gruppe down		Claims	Losses				
		Base	No	Time	Base	Time		Dest	Dam	KIA	MIA	WIA
Luftflotte 3												
Jafü 2:												
11.(H)/JG 2	Bf 109G	Ligescourt		~1410	Ligescourt	1450	0	1	0	0	0	1
II./JG 26	Fw 190A	Abbéville		1405	Abbéville	1510	2 Spitfire	0	0	0	0	0
Jafü 3:												
I./JG 2	Fw 190A	Triqueville		1412	Triqueville	1453	0	0	0	0	0	0

Luftwaffe defensive activity – 5 September 1942

Unit	Type	Gruppe up			Gruppe down		Claims	Losses				
		Base	No	Time	Base	Time		Dest	Dam	KIA	MIA	WIA
Luftflotte 3												
Jafü 2:												
11.(H)/JG 2	Bf 109G	Ligescourt		~1110	Ligescourt	~1210	1 Spitfire	0	1	0	0	0
II./JG 26	Fw 190A	Abbéville		1110	Abbéville	1210	6 Spitfire	0	0	0	0	0
Jafü 3:												
I./JG 2	Fw 190A	Triqueville		1123	Triqueville	1135	0	1	0	0	0	1

Luftwaffe defensive activity – 6 September 1942

Unit	Type	Gruppe up			Gruppe down		Claims	Losses				
		Base	No	Time	Base	Time		Dest	Dam	KIA	MIA	WIA
Luftflotte 3												
Jafü 2:												
II./JG 26	Fw 190A	Abbéville		1805	Abbéville	1905	2 B-17, 1 Spitfire	0	0	0	0	0
Jafü 3:												
I./JG 2	Fw 190A	Triqueville		1803	Triqueville	1917	0	1	0	0	0	0
II./JG 2	Fw 190A	Beaumont–le–Roger		~1800	Beaumont–le–Roger	~1915	2 B-17, 2 Spitfire	1	0	1	0	0

Luftwaffe defensive activity – 7 September 1942

Unit	Type	Gruppe up			Gruppe down		Claims	Losses				
		Base	No	Time	Base	Time		Dest	Dam	KIA	MIA	WIA
XII. Fliegerkorps												
Jagddivision 1												
Jafü Holland-Ruhr:												
II./JG 1	Fw 190A	Woensdrecht		~0945	Woensdrecht	~1045	0	1	0	1	0	0
IV./JG 1	Fw 190A	München–Gladbach		0945	München–Gladbach	1045	0	1	0	1	0	0
Luftflotte 3												
Jafü 2:												
III./JG 26	Fw 190A	Wevelghem		1040	Wevelghem	1130	1 Spitfire	0	0	0	0	0

Oblt. Kurt Kranefeld (III./JG 26) cruises over the Belgian countryside in his 'Black 11' in late 1942 or early 1943. The Kanalgeschwader had many tasks in addition to bomber interceptions, including routine patrols. *(Meyer)*

9 October – Lille (see map)

8th Air Force VIII BC Mission #14: 79 of 108 B-17s and B-24s bomb Lille industrial area, TOT 1025-31 – lose 4-2-46, claim 25-38-44. 30 sqds of RAF Spitfires claim 5-1-3, lose 1. 3 sqds US P-38s claim 0, lose 0-0-1; 3 sqds US Spitfires claim 0, lose 0.

The VIII BC sortied more than 100 bombers for the first time. Their target was the Lille industrial area. The escort plan dispensed with close escort in favour of a complex scheme of sweeps and diversions, utilising 36 squadrons of Allied fighters. Hptm. Priller's III./JG 26, which led the defensive effort, encountered none of the Allied fighters and was able to attack the bombers repeatedly. The Gruppe claimed five B-17s and one B-24, matching the number of bombers lost over France or scrapped on their return to England. This was the greatest success yet against the American heavy bombers. One III./JG 26 pilot was lost to bomber fire; one III./JG 2 pilot was lost at sea under unknown circumstances.

One B-17 Fortress shot down at 1045 hours, E of Lille–Vendeville airfield
[Stammberger's victim was Capt. Olson's 306th Bomb Group B-17: DC]

This was the period in which we dispersed to small fields every evening from our operational bases because British commando attacks were expected. My Staffel had not returned from Moorsele to Wevelghem when I was ordered to lead a scramble. We were to climb in the direction of St. Omer. We were not able to assemble as planned, because we sighted a large swarm of bumblebees [heavy bombers] only three or four kilometres from St. Omer. There was no sign of a proper formation; they were at three levels up to 6,000 metres, but the individual vees were scattered. Above them were fighter condensation trails. The bombers flew just west of Lille and made a sharp left turn before we could get there. I finally reached height and position. We approached the individual vees in pairs and attacked like wild men: approach from behind, full throttle and dive away. The bombers grew larger and larger, and all our

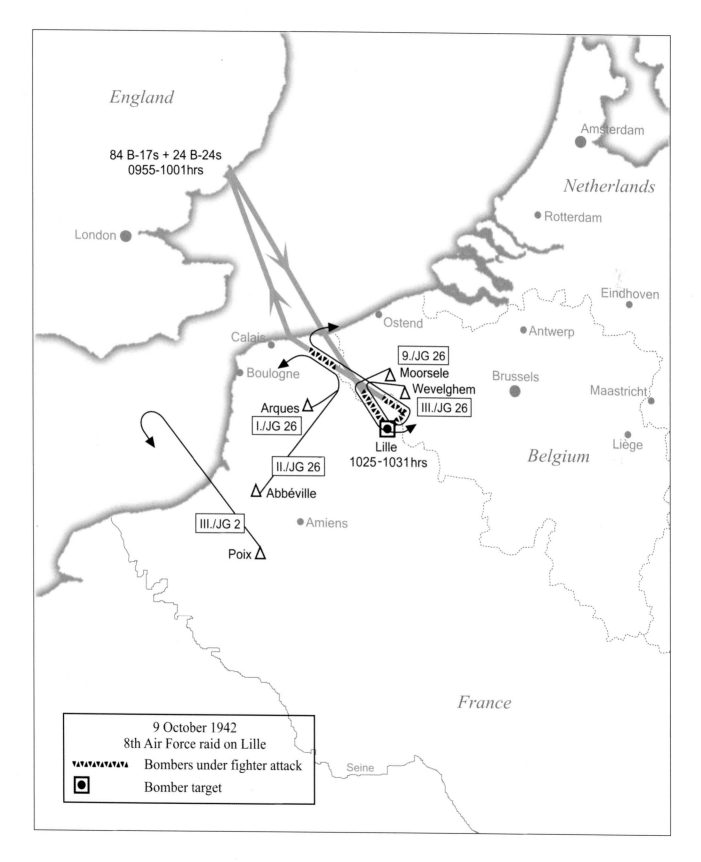

England

84 B-17s + 24 B-24s
0955-1001hrs

London

Netherlands

Amsterdam

Rotterdam

Eindhoven

Ostend

Antwerp

Calais

Boulogne

9./JG 26
Moorsele
Wevelghem
III./JG 26

Brussels

Maastricht

Arques
I./JG 26

Lille
1025-1031hrs

Liège

Belgium

II./JG 26

Abbéville

Amiens

III./JG 2

Poix

France

Seine

9 October 1942
8th Air Force raid on Lille

▼▲▼▲▼▲▼▲▼▲▼▲ Bombers under fighter attack
◉ Bomber target

attacks were begun much too soon and broken off again because we feared colliding with these barn doors. I wondered why I was scoring no hits and then realised – 40 metres wingspan! I then approached much closer and saw hits on the enemy's left wing. By my third attack, both left engines were burning, and I fired freely at the right outboard engine as the crate spiralled downhill in broad left turns. At about 2,000 metres, four or five men jumped out; the bomber struck the ground east of Vendeville. I looked up. The sky was empty. I was out of cannon ammo and slunk home. Four rear attacks on a single bomber! Amateurish and stupid!

Lt. Otto Stammberger
9./JG 26

Lt. Otto Stammberger (III./JG 26) in a Belgian salvage yard. He is standing beside the vertical tail of a B-17E 41-9018, formerly of the 92nd Bomber Group. Piloted by Lt. Chorak, the airplane was shot down by JG 26 on a raid to Lille on 9 October. *(Stammberger)*

21 October

8th Air Force VIII BC Mission #15: 23 of 107 B-17s and B-24s bomb Lorient U-boat base, TOT 1406, Cherbourg airfield, TOT 1313 – lose 3-0-6, claim 10-4-3. Escort of 2 sqds US P-38s claims 0, loses 0.

The VIII BC put up more than 100 bombers for a raid on Lorient, although most failed to bomb owing to cloud cover. The raiders were met by the dedicated defenders of the U-boat bases, 8./JG 2, which were accompanied today by members of the III./JG 2 Stab. Confirmed claims totalled four B-17s for the loss of one Fw 190 and pilot; the Americans lost three B-17s.

November 1942

The month was notable for the first major ground operation by the Western Allies, Operation TORCH, the invasion of Vichy-held northwestern Africa. The Luftwaffe quickly flew units from the western and eastern combat air forces to Tunisia. Luftflotte 3 gave up its two high-altitude Bf 109G Staffeln, which never rejoined Luftflotte 3, and the Fw 190-equipped II./JG 2,

Luftwaffe defensive activity – 2 October 1942

Unit	Type	Gruppe up			Gruppe down		Claims	Losses				
		Base	No	Time	Base	Time		Dest	Dam	KIA	MIA	WIA
Luftflotte 3												
Jafü 2:												
11.(H)/JG 2	Bf 109G	Ligescourt		~1610	Ligescourt	~1710	0	0	0	0	0	0
I./JG 26	Fw 190A	St. Omer–Arques		1607	St. Omer–Arques	~1710	1 P-38, 1 Spitfire	2	0	0	0	2
II./JG 26	Fw 190A	Abbéville		1610	Abbéville	1700	1 Spitfire	1	0	1	0	0
III./JG 26	Fw 190A	Wevelghem		1520	Wevelghem	1615	1 Spitfire	1	1	0	0	0
11.(H)/JG 26	Bf 109G	Norrent–Fontes		~1610	Norrent–Fontes	~1710	0	1	0	0	0	0
Jafü 3:												
I./JG 2	Fw 190A	Triqueville		1525	Triqueville	1623	0	0	0	0	0	0
	Fw 190A	Poix–Nord		1539	Poix–Nord	1600	1 Spitfire	0	0	0	0	0
III./JG 2	Fw 190A	Poix		~1600	Poix	~1700	1 B-17, 1 Spitfire	2	1	2	0	0

Luftwaffe defensive activity – 9 October 1942

Unit	Type	Gruppe up			Gruppe down		Claims	Losses				
		Base	No	Time	Base	Time		Dest	Dam	KIA	MIA	WIA
Luftflotte 3												
Jafü 2:												
I./JG 26	Fw 190A	St. Omer–Arques		1017	St. Omer–Arques	1030	0	0	0	0	0	0
II./JG 26	Fw 190A	Abbéville		1038	Abbéville	1130	0	0	0	0	0	0
III./JG 26	Fw 190A	Wevelghem		1024	Wevelghem	1117	3 B-17, 1 B-24	1	0	1	0	0
9./JG 26	Fw 190A	Moorsele		1025	Moorsele	1100	1 B-17, 1 B-17 HSS	0	0	0	0	0
Jafü 3:												
III./JG 2	Fw 190A	Poix		—	Poix	—	0	1	0	1	0	0

Luftwaffe defensive activity – 21 October 1942

Unit	Type	Gruppe up			Gruppe down		Claims	Losses				
		Base	No	Time	Base	Time		Dest	Dam	KIA	MIA	WIA
Luftflotte 3												
Jafü 3:												
Stab III./JG 2	Fw 190A	Brest–Guipavas?		~1315	Brest–Guipavas?	~1415	1 B-17	0	0	0	0	0
8./JG 2	Fw 190A	Brest–Guipavas		~1315	Brest–Guipavas	~1415	3 B-17	1	0	1	0	0

Left: Hptm. Egon Mayer. Mayer joined JG 2 in December 1939 and was promoted to III./JG 2 Gruppenkommandeur in November 1942. He is credited with developing the mass head-on attack technique, the most successful early tactic against American heavy bombers. He became JG 2 Kommodore on 1 July 1943, and had claimed 102 victories before he was shot down and killed by American fighters on 2 March 1944. Mayer was one of only 12 pilots with 100 confirmed victories against the Western Allies. *(Author's collection)*

which returned to France after four months. Other units, including I./JG 2, moved to southern France temporarily, but returned after the successful German occupation of southern France. The 8th Air Force was hit even harder by the need to send units to Africa. Four fighter groups and the two most experienced B-17 groups in England left permanently; the VIII BC was unable to put 100 bombers over a target until the following April. It began sending low-strength missions to the Brittany U-boat bases, a target complex that had just been declared its highest priority. Only one Staffel, 8./JG 2, defended the region until Hptm. Egon Mayer, the new Kommandeur of III./JG 2, began transferring the rest of his Gruppe to Vannes on the 22nd to bolster the defences of the vital bases. To cover Normandy in the absence of the Gruppe, 9./JG 26 moved from Wevelghem to Beaumont–le–Roger.

7 November

8th Air Force VIII BC Mission #16: 34 of 68 B-17s and B-24s bomb Brest U-boat targets, TOT 1230-39 – lose 0-1-12, claim 4-3-7. RAF sweeps claim 0, lose 1.

An unescorted raid on Brest was met by 8./JG 2, which claimed one B-24 for the loss of two Fw 190s and pilots to the bomber gunners. Part of Ergänzungs-Jagdgruppe West was also up and lost one Bf 109.

8 November

8th Air Force VIII BC Mission #17: 42 of 53 B-17s bomb Abbéville–Drucat airfield, TOT 1258; Lille-Fives locomotive factory, TOT 1310 – lose 1-0-13, claim 11-6-14. Escort of 212 RAF Spitfires claims 1-0-2 e/a, loses 7-1-2 a/c.

The VIII BC bombed a constant irritant, Abbéville airfield, as well as the Lille industrial area. II./JG 2, I./JG 26 and II./JG 26 had been scrambled in late morning versus what proved to be a large force of Spitfires, which were avoided. The two B-17 formations then brought all of JG 26 and most of JG 2 into the air. II./JG 26 took off from Abbéville–Drucat as 12 B-17s approached their field. The Focke-Wulfs climbed out to the west and returned in time to bounce the force's top cover, shooting down two Spitfires and then damaging most of the B17s.

I./JG 26 and III./JG 26 attacked the Lille force continuously from the target area to the coast. Six Spitfire squadrons were assigned as close escort, giving the bombers much better protection than they had

received on the 9 October raid. The JG 26 pilots claimed one B-17 and three Spitfires. II./JG 2 and III./JG 2 were also engaged and claimed four Spitfires from the various formations. Seven of the escorting Spitfires went down. One III./JG 2 Focke-Wulf was shot down by a Spitfire; its pilot died of his injuries. Two JG 26 Fw 190s were hit and force-landed with light damage and injury to one pilot.

17 November

8th Air Force VIII BC Mission #20: 35 of 63 B-17s and B-24s bomb St. Nazaire U-boat base, TOT 1125 – lose 0-1-16, claim 6-8-2.

The VIII BC attacked the major U-boat base at St. Nazaire. Sixteen Luftwaffe fighters engaged the bombers, but few details are available from the German records. One B-17 was scrapped in England, and one III./JG 2 Fw 190 crashed after combat; its pilot bailed out without injury.

18 November

8th Air Force VIII BC Mission #21: 53 of 65 B-17s and B-24s bomb St. Nazaire, Lorient, La Pallice U-boat bases, TOT 1203-58 – lose 1-1-27, claim 5-3-1. No escort.

The VIII BC attacked three U-boat bases. 8./JG 2 was scrambled against the unescorted raid and attacked the La Pallice force, claiming two B-17s (one was confirmed) for the loss of two Fw 190s, 1 KIA and 1 WIA. The Americans lost one B 17 shot down and one scrapped in England.

23 November

8th Air Force VIII BC Mission #23: 36 of 58 B-17s and B-24s bomb St. Nazaire locks and drydocks, TOT 1300-45 – lose 4-1-17, claim 16-2-1. No escort.

The VIII BC sent an unescorted bomber force to St. Nazaire. This long-distance raid gave the newly concentrated III./JG 2 the perfect opportunity for Hptm. Mayer to test a new mode of attack that he had been contemplating for several weeks. The bombers were greeted on their bomb run by a full Gruppe of Focke-Wulfs, attacking in Ketten of three aircraft from dead ahead. Four B 17s tumbled from the formation, victims of the Luftwaffe's most successful single pass through the heavies to date; a fifth was scrapped in England. One Focke-Wulf failed to return from its mission.

Luftwaffe defensive activity – 7 November 1942

Unit	Type	Gruppe up			Gruppe down		Claims	Losses				
		Base	No	Time	Base	Time		Dest	Dam	KIA	MIA	WIA
Luftflotte 3												
Jafü 3:												
8./JG 2	Fw 190A	Brest–Guipavas		~1145	Brest–Guipavas	~1245	1 B-24	2	0	2	0	0
Erg-JGr West	Bf 109F	Cazaux		~1200	Cazaux	~1300	0		1	0	0	0	0

Luftwaffe defensive activity – 8 November 1942

Unit	Type	Gruppe up			Gruppe down		Claims	Losses				
		Base	No	Time	Base	Time		Dest	Dam	KIA	MIA	WIA
Luftflotte 3												
Jafü 2:												
I./JG 26	Fw 190A	St. Omer–Arques		1203	St. Omer–Arques	1237	3 Spitfire	0	1	0	0	1
II./JG 26	Fw 190A	Abbéville		1215	Abbéville	1300	2 Spitfire	0	0	0	0	0
III./JG 26	Fw 190A	Wevelghem		1200	Wevelghem	1230	1 B-17	0	1	0	0	0
Jafü 3:												
II./JG 2	Fw 190A	Beaumont–le–Roger		~1200	Beaumont–le–Roger	~1300	1 Spitfire	0	0	0	0	0
III./JG 2	Fw 190A	Poix		~1200	Poix	~1300	3 Spitfire	1	0	1	0	0

Luftwaffe defensive activity – 17 November 1942

Unit	Type	Gruppe up			Gruppe down		Claims	Losses				
		Base	No	Time	Base	Time		Dest	Dam	KIA	MIA	WIA
Luftflotte 3												
Jafü 3:												
III./JG 2	Fw 190A	Brest–Guipavas?		?	Brest–Guipavas?	?	0		1	0	0	0	0

Luftwaffe defensive activity – 18 November 1942

Unit	Type	Gruppe up			Gruppe down		Claims	Losses				
		Base	No	Time	Base	Time		Dest	Dam	KIA	MIA	WIA
Luftflotte 3												
Jafü 3:												
8./JG 2	Fw 190A	Brest–Guipavas		~1145	Brest–Guipavas	~1245	1 B-17	2	0	1	1	1

Luftwaffe defensive activity – 23 November 1942

Unit	Type	Gruppe up			Gruppe down		Claims	Losses				
		Base	No	Time	Base	Time		Dest	Dam	KIA	MIA	WIA
Luftflotte 3												
Jafü 3:												
III./JG 2	Fw 190A	Vannes		~1300	Vannes	~1415	4 B-17, 1 B-24	1	0	0	1	0

December 1942

6 December

8th Air Force VIII BC Mission #24: 6 of 19 B-24s bomb Abbéville–Drucat airfield, TOT 1124; 37 of 76 B-17s bomb Lille-Fives steel factory, TOT 1208 – lose 2-0-10, claim 5-8-6 e/a. Spitfire escort (11 Group RAF) claims 3-1-1, loses 1-1-0.

The VIII BC reverted to short-range, fully escorted missions. Today's was flown in conjunction with Operation OYSTER, a large raid on Eindhoven by RAF light bombers. After an early-morning Channel patrol that downed two Spitfires, all of JG 26 was scrambled at 1100 hours on reports of strong Allied activity over the Somme Estuary. This proved to be a badly scattered B-24 formation and its escort, most of which was aborted. Six bombers pressed on and bombed Abbéville–Drucat airfield. II./JG 26 attacked the B-24s over their own field. No B-24s fell immediately. A later attack by I./JG 26 brought down one of the bombers, at a cost of two Focke-Wulfs and their pilots.

An hour later, after the JG 26 pilots had had ample time to land for refuelling and re-arming, the main B-17 force appeared on German radar. These bombers, escorted or supported by six Spitfire wings, targeted the Lille steel works. Few of the Spitfire pilots saw any German aircraft, but all three JG 26 Gruppen reached

and attacked the bombers. The only two claims for B-17s were made by II./JG 1, part of which was vectored to the B-17s after a successful attack on the RAF light bombers. It is probable that bad weather interfered with the plans of both the attackers and the defenders. No German fighters were lost to the Lille raiders.

12 December

8th Air Force VIII BC Mission #25: briefed target of Romilly–sur–Seine not bombed; 17 of 90 B 17s bomb Rouen–Sotteville motor yards, TOT 1239-41 – lose 2-0-11, claim 19-8-2. Sweeps and diversions by 23 sqds RAF, 3 sqds US Spitfires claim 4-1-6, lose 3-1-2.

The VIII BC scheduled a raid on the important aircraft supply park at Romilly–sur–Seine, southeast of Paris and thus well beyond escort range. By 1100, the air over the Channel was thick with Allied formations. A number of sweeps and diversions were flown. The three JG 26 Gruppen scrambled through a continuous cloud deck. Most sweeps were not engaged, but I./JG 26 downed one Spitfire and badly damaged a second, while II./JG 26 also claimed a Spitfire.

The main bomber formation crossed the French coast east of Dieppe shortly before noon and headed south. The JG 26 Gruppen scrambled again, but were quickly ordered to land and await the bombers' return. In the absence of I./JG 2 and II./JG 2, defensive coverage of central and western France was now very

I./JG 26 Fw 190A-4s on St. Omer in late 1942 or early 1943. *(Genth)*

weak. 9./JG 26, their partial replacement, scrambled from Beaumont–le–Roger and followed the bombers until the last of the Spitfires had turned back. The Focke-Wulfs then made their attack, shooting down two B-17s and damaging many others. Romilly–sur–Seine was covered in cloud and was not bombed; some of the B-17s dropped on Rouen on the return flight. II./JG 26 scrambled and climbed out over the Somme Estuary to attack the withdrawing bombers. Their initial pass succeeded in damaging a few more B-17s; they were then driven off by three wings of Spitfires arriving to escort the bombers back to England. The subsequent dogfights cost the RAF another Spitfire. I./JG 26 joined the battle as it was winding down, but filed no claims. Part of III./JG 26 was up, but was kept in reserve and did not make contact. The day's battles cost JG 26 no pilots or reportable damage.

20 December – Romilly–sur–Seine (see map)

8th Air Force VIII BC Mission #26: 72 of 101 B-17s and B-24s bomb Romilly–sur–Seine airfield, TOT 1240-46 – lose 6-1-30, claim 53-13-8. Sweeps by 192 RAF, 36 US Spitfires claim 0-0-1, lose 0.

The VIII BC mission plan for this raid on Romilly–sur–Seine was a near duplicate of that of the 12th, and the defenders were ready. RAF Fighter Command's (RAF FC's) four diversionary sweeps of the Pas de Calais brought up all of JG 26, which made desultory contact with one Spitfire wing. It was quickly ordered away as the main Allied force had already been detected over the Channel and heading for Fécamp. While some JG 26 fighters landed for quick service, most flew down the coast toward Dieppe. II./JG 26 and III./JG 26 were the first to arrive and paralleled the bomber formation until the Spitfire escort turned back. The fighters immediately hit the B-17s from dead ahead. Two B-17s (one claimed as a B-24) went down over Rouen. The three JG 26 Gruppen attacked continuously in relays until low fuel forced them to break off, without further loss to the Americans. The JG 2 Geschwaderstab scrambled from Beaumont–le–Roger and made a successful attack before the bombers reached the target. 9./JG 26 scrambled from the same base, reached the bombers on withdrawal and made successful head-on attacks that downed two B-17s. Part of II./JG 26 had missed the incoming bombers and had landed on Beaumont–le–Roger for refuelling. It was now the last

fresh formation to reach the bombers and shot a B-17 into the Channel off Dieppe. The JG 2 Geschwaderstab flew a quick second sortie and downed its second B-17 of the day, also off Dieppe. One of the Stab claims was by the Kommodore, Major Walter Oesau, who had been grounded after his 100th victory and had just been restored to flight status. More JG 26 fighters began to arrive from the Pas de Calais on their second sorties just as the return escort was spotted over the Channel. After a few inconclusive engagements, both sides retired to their bases.

Six B-17s went down over France, one was scrapped on return to England, and 30 more bombers sustained combat damage. JG 2 claimed two B-17s and lost one pilot. JG 26 claimed four B-17s and one B-24, and lost one plane and pilot. Many German fighters ran out of fuel in the prolonged engagement, but it is believed that only six were damaged beyond repair in their subsequent forced landings.

COMBAT REPORT[2]
20 December 1942

One B-17 Fortress shot down from 6,500 metres at 1310 hours, 5–6 km E of Meaux
[Stammberger's victim was Lt. English's 91st Bomb Group B-17: DC]

I scrambled from Beaumont–le–Roger with my 9th Staffel at 1214 hours and, after climbing through three layers of clouds and entering a clear area, made contact with heavy bombers southeast of Paris. They had already dropped their bombs on the ERLA aircraft factory at Romilly-sur-Seine, which I could see clearly. I approached from the front. The bombers were heading directly toward me, having turned left after bombing and taken up a northwestern course for England. I fired on a B-17 on the outside right of the formation and obtained hits in the cockpit and right engine. The bomber drifted out of formation to the right, and I repeated my attack, scoring hits in the same area. I recovered to the rear of the plane and saw six men bail out. The bomber crashed near Meaux, east of Paris. My Staffel was no longer with me. I put down on Le Bourget at 1305 hours to refuel and returned to Beaumont–le–Roger.

Lt. Otto Stammberger
9./JG 26

30 December

8th Air Force VIII BC Mission #27: 40 of 77 B-17s bomb Lorient U-boat base, TOT 1238-42 – lose 3-0-22, claim 29-7-3. No escort.

The VIII BC flew an unescorted raid to Lorient. Interception was left to the well-positioned III./JG 2, which flew missions against the incoming and withdrawing B-17s. Nine victory claims were confirmed, triple the true number of B-17s to go down, for the loss of one Fw 190 and pilot.

COMBAT REPORT[3]
30 December 1942

One B-17 Fortress destroyed from 5,000 metres at 1155 hours, PQ [map reference] 4857/14 West

I scrambled as a Rottenführer [element leader] against an enemy bomber formation reported at 4827/14 West. At 1148 hours, in the course of the battle that developed in 4857/14 West, I attacked a Fortress flying at 5,000 metres at the left of the formation from the left, making three passes from the front and three from the left. During the third attack I hit the Fortress between the two right engines, which burst into flames.

As I was preparing for my seventh attack, the Fortress dove forward, and its right wing broke off. It went straight down, hitting the water in 4857/West at 1155 hours. I saw no parachutes.

Lt. Georg-Peter Eder
7./JG 2

Right: Lt. Georg-Peter Eder as a member of JG 2 in 1942. Eder had an active career in JG 51, JG 2, JG 1 and JG 26 and was an early transfer to jets, ending the war in III./JG 7 after a total of 572 combat missions. He was shot down 17 times, bailed out nine times and was injured 14 times. *(Author's collection)*

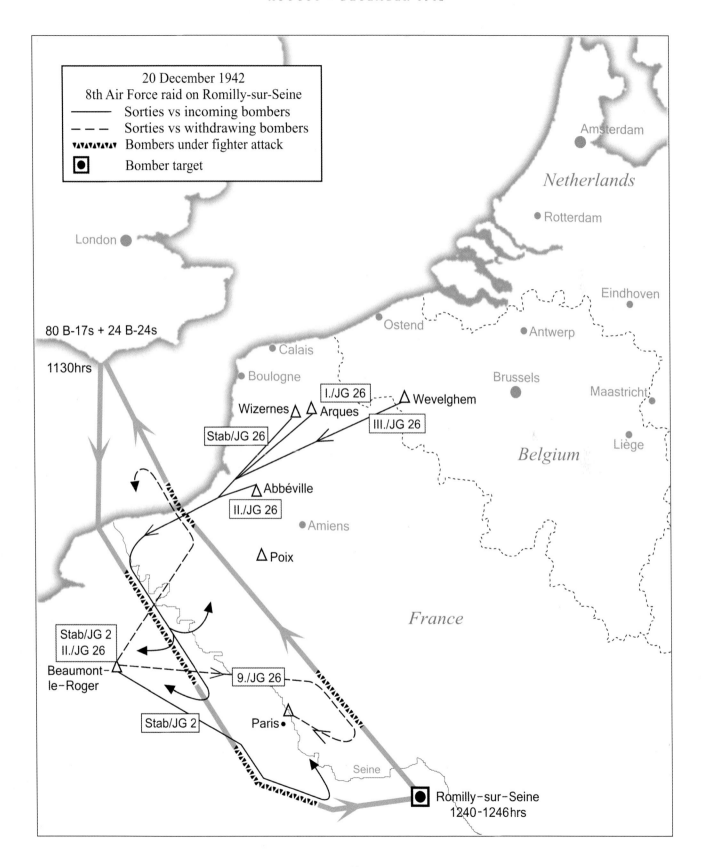

20 December 1942
8th Air Force raid on Romilly-sur-Seine
—————— Sorties vs incoming bombers
– – – – – Sorties vs withdrawing bombers
▼▲▼▲▼▲▼▲▼ Bombers under fighter attack
◉ Bomber target

Amsterdam

Netherlands

Rotterdam

London

80 B-17s + 24 B-24s

1130hrs

Ostend

Eindhoven

Antwerp

Calais

Boulogne

Brussels

Maastricht

I./JG 26

Wizernes ▲ ▲ Arques

△ Wevelghem

Liège

Stab/JG 26

III./JG 26

Belgium

△ Abbéville

II./JG 26

Amiens

△ Poix

France

Stab/JG 2
II./JG 26

Beaumont-
le-Roger △

9./JG 26

Stab/JG 2

Paris •

Seine

◉ Romilly-sur-Seine
1240-1246hrs

Luftwaffe defensive activity – 6 December 1942

Unit	Type	Gruppe up			Gruppe down		Claims	Losses				
		Base	No	Time	Base	Time		Dest	Dam	KIA	MIA	WIA
Lw Bfh Mitte												
XII. Fliegerkorps												
Jagddivision 1												
Jafü Holland-Ruhr.												
II./JG 1	Fw 190A	Woensdrecht		~1230	Woensdrecht	~1330	2 B-17, 4 Boston, 1 Ventura	0	0	0	0	0
Luftflotte 3												
Jafü 2:												
I./JG 26	Fw 190A	St. Omer–Arques		1100	St. Omer–Arques	1200	1 B-24, 1 Spitfire	2	0	1	1	0
2nd sorties	Fw 190A	St. Omer–Arques		1203	St. Omer–Arques	1237	0	0	0	0	0	0
II./JG 26	Fw 190A	Abbéville		1100	Abbéville	1150	0	0	0	0	0	0
2nd sorties	Fw 190A	Abbéville		1216	Abbéville	1307	1 Spitfire	0	1	0	0	0
III./JG 26	Fw 190A	Wevelghem		1100	Wevelghem	1217	1 Spitfire	0	0	0	0	0
2nd sorties	Fw 190A	Wevelghem		1300	Wevelghem	1347	0	0	0	0	0	0
Jafü 3:												
9./JG 26	Fw 190A	Beaumont–le–Roger		1159	Beaumont–le–Roger	1306	0	0	0	0	0	0

Luftwaffe defensive activity – 12 December 1942

Unit	Type	Gruppe up			Gruppe down		Claims	Losses				
		Base	No	Time	Base	Time		Dest	Dam	KIA	MIA	WIA
Luftflotte 3												
Jafü 2:												
I./JG 26	Fw 190A	St. Omer–Arques		1122	St. Omer–Arques	1148	2 Spitfire	0	0	0	0	0
2nd sorties	Fw 190A	St. Omer–Arques		1334	St. Omer–Arques	1430	0	0	0	0	0	0
II./JG 26	Fw 190A	Abbéville		1107	Abbéville	1147	1 Spitfire	0	0	0	0	0
2nd sorties	Fw 190A	Abbéville		1255	Abbéville	1357	1 Spitfire	0	0	0	0	0
III./JG 26	Fw 190A	Wevelghem		1120	Wevelghem	1225	n/c	0	0	0	0	0
2nd sorties	Fw 190A	Wevelghem		1410	Wevelghem	1422	n/c	0	0	0	0	0
Jafü 3:												
9./JG 26	Fw 190A	Beaumont–le–Roger		1151	Beaumont–le–Roger	1300	2 B-17	0	0	0	0	0
2nd sorties	Fw 190A	Beaumont–le–Roger		1345	Beaumont–le–Roger	1427	n/c	0	0	0	0	0

Luftwaffe defensive activity – 20 December 1942

Unit	Type	Gruppe up			Gruppe down		Claims	Losses				
		Base	No	Time	Base	Time		Dest	Dam	KIA	MIA	WIA
Luftflotte 3												
Jafü 2:												
Stab/JG 26	Fw 190A	Wizernes		~1115	Wizernes	~1200	0	0	0	0	0	0
I./JG 26	Fw 190A	St. Omer–Arques		1113	Arques, others	1135	0	0	0	0	0	0
2nd sorties	Fw 190A	St. Omer–Arques		1300	St. Omer–Arques	1412	0	1	5	1	0	0
II./JG 26	Fw 190A	Abbéville		1116	Beaumont, Poix	1149	1 B-17	0	0	0	0	0
2nd sorties	Fw 190A	Beaumont–le–Roger		1300	Beaumont–le–Roger	1417	1 B-17	3	0	0	0	0
III./JG 26	Fw 190A	Wevelghem		1110	Wevelghem, others	1220	1 B-24	1	5	0	0	0
Jafü 3:												
Stab/JG 2	Fw 190A	Beaumont–le–Roger		~1115	Beaumont–le–Roger	~1245	1 B-17 HSS	0	0	0	0	0
2nd sorties	Fw 190A	Beaumont–le–Roger		~1315	Beaumont–le–Roger	~1415	1 B-17	0	0	0	0	0
III./JG 2	Fw 190A	Vannes		~1115	Vannes	~1245	0	1	0	1	0	0
9./JG 26	Fw 190A	Beaumont–le–Roger		1116	Beaumont–le–Roger	1146	0	0	0	0	0	0
2nd sorties	Fw 190A	Beaumont–le–Roger		1214	Le Bourget	1305	2 B-17	0	0	0	0	0

Luftwaffe defensive activity – 30 December 1942

Unit	Type	Gruppe up			Gruppe down		Claims	Losses				
		Base	No	Time	Base	Time		Dest	Dam	KIA	MIA	WIA
Luftflotte 3												
Jafü 3:												
III./JG 2	Fw 190A	Vannes		~1115	Vannes	~1215	6 B-17	1	0	0	1	0
2nd sorties	Fw 190A	Vannes		~1300	Vannes	~1400	3 B-17	0	0	0	0	0

Notes:

[1] Stammberger correspondence with author, 1989.

[2] Stammberger correspondence with author, 1989.

[3] Eder Gefechtsbericht, in private collection.

CHAPTER 2

JANUARY – JUNE 1943

January 1943

The Luftwaffe air defence effort began 1943 as it had ended 1942. Control was vested in two completely independent organisations: *Luftwaffenbefehlshaber Mitte* (Central Air Command; Lw Bfh Mitte) in Germany and Holland, and Luftflotte 3 in France and Belgium. Their fighter units were engaged in a variety of tasks, but all took part in the *Reichsluftverteidigung* (air defence of the Reich; RLV). Lw Bfh Mitte, headquartered at Berlin-Dahlem and under the command of General der Flakartillerie Hubert Weise, had overall responsibility for all flying and antiaircraft forces based within the pre-war borders of the Reich and earmarked for defence. The flying units came directly under XII. Fliegerkorps with four fighter divisions: Jagddivision 1 at Berlin, Jagddivision 2 at Stade, Jagddivision 3 at Deelen and Jagddivision 4 at Döberitz. The Jagdfliegerführer (Jafü) were located within the command posts of the fighter divisions and were responsible for the conduct of day fighter operations within the fighter division areas. In early 1943, the most important of these were Jafü Holland-Ruhrgebiet under Oberst Walter Grabmann and Jafü Deutsche Bucht under Generalmajor Walter Schwabedissen.

Obstlt. Dr. Erich Mix's Jagdgeschwader 1 (JG 1) began the year as the only day fighter Geschwader in Lw Bfh Mitte. It had four Gruppen instead of the standard three, and they were stretched thinly along the North Sea coast. The Stab and the First Gruppe were at Jever on the north German coast with 4 Fw 190s and 40 Bf 109s. The Second Gruppe was at Woensdrecht in the Netherlands with 41 Fw 190s. The Third Gruppe was based in western Denmark and southern Norway with 53 Fw 190s. The Fourth Gruppe was at München-Gladbach with 41 Fw 190s. The Geschwader saw some action against RAF Fighter Command and Coastal

**Generalmajor Walter Grabmann. One of the most proficient and influential upper-level RLV commanders, Grabmann became Jafü Holland–Ruhrgebiet in August 1942 and in November 1943 was given command of Jagddivision 3, a position he retained until the last chaotic month of the war. After the war, he was a principal author of the USAF Historical Studies on the German Air Force. *(Author's collection)*

Command raids, but spent most of its time escorting convoys and flying patrols in anticipation of the arrival of the American heavy bombers.

Generalfeldmarschall Hugo Sperrle's Luftflotte 3, headquartered in Paris, was a front-line air force and had a wide variety of missions, both offensive and defensive. Its fighter units were the guardians of the Channel coast, dealing with enemy fighter sweeps, shallow penetration RAF daylight raids and reconnais-

Generalfeldmarschall Hugo Sperrle. From 1940–1944, Sperrle was commander of Luftflotte 3, the air force left with responsibility for air operations from France and the Low Countries after most of the Luftwaffe moved east for the invasion of the Soviet Union. He was reputed to be Hitler's favourite field marshal, whose mere entrance into a room could strike fear in the enemies of the Reich. Sperrle was relieved of his command and placed in the Führer Reserve when the Luftwaffe retreated to the German border with the army in September 1944 and never returned to active duty. *(Author's collection)*

sance flights, as well as providing escort for coastal convoys, reconnaissance missions and air-sea rescue operations, while maintaining their readiness for the expected expansion of the American bomber offensive. Sperrle's fighters were under the new Höherer Jagdfliegerfüher West, commanded by Oberst Max-Josef Ibel at Chantilly, which relied on the two established Jagdfliegerführer for control of operations: Jafü 2 under Obstlt. Karl Vieck at St. Pol and Jafü 3 under Major Gordon Gollob at Deauville.

The day fighter defences of the western occupied zone actually began 1943 at lower strength than the previous autumn. Jafü 3 had one day fighter wing, Obstlt. Walter Oesau's Jagdgeschwader 2 (JG 2, the Richthofen Geschwader), with which to defend the western section of the Channel coast, the Paris region and the U-boat bases on the western coast of France. Oesau's Geschwader was at less than half strength. He commanded only a strengthened Stabsschwarm, with 14 Fw 190A-4s and six Bf 109G 1s; his Third Gruppe, with 49 Fw 190A-4s; and one borrowed Staffel, 9./JG 26. The rest of his Geschwader had moved south in response to Operation TORCH, the Allied invasion of northwestern Africa. I./JG 2 returned from southern France in late January; II./JG 2 remained in Tunisia until March. A high-altitude Staffel, 11(Höhen)./JG 2, never returned from Africa, but was merged there into JG 53.

Jafü 2 had one day fighter wing, Major Gerhard Schöpfel's Jagdgeschwader 26 (JG 26, the Schlageter Geschwader) to defend the eastern Channel coast, the industrial region along the French-Belgian border and the most direct aerial route from England to the Ruhr. JG 26 was almost up to authorised strength. Its Stab had five Fw 190A-4s; the First Gruppe 33 Fw 190A-4s; the Second Gruppe 33 Fw 190A-4s and 11 Bf 109G-4s; the Third Gruppe 35 Fw 190A-4s and three Bf 109G-1s and G-4s. The Geschwader lacked only its high-altitude Staffel, 11.(Höhen)./JG 26, which had been absorbed by JG 51 in Tunisia, and the one Staffel that was on temporary loan to JG 2. During January Major Josef 'Pips' Priller replaced Schöpfel as Kommodore. Priller's first major task was to plan the transfer of his entire Geschwader to the northern sector of the Eastern Front over the next few months, in exchange for the 'Green Heart' Geschwader, JG 54. The swap was to take place by Gruppen and Staffeln, staged to permit continuity of coverage on both fronts. Only the pilots, key staff members and certain items of critical equipment were to move. Maintenance crews, aircraft and all other equipment were to remain at their original bases. In late January, I./JG 26 and 7./JG 26 left for the East by train.

Elements of JG 27, the famed Afrikageschwader, began arriving in Evreux on 2 January. In late 1942 the wing had been withdrawn to Germany for rebuilding, and its First Gruppe, I./JG 27, was deemed ready to re-enter combat. It was sent to Jafü 3 to help defend the Paris region. It soon became apparent that the Gruppe was still far from full effectiveness, especially in its tough new operational environment.

The VIII BC, the heavy bomber component of the American 8th Air Force in England, had been gutted for Operation TORCH and had fewer than 100 B-17s available for operations. It did not cross the German border until late January, and then only on the direct order of General Arnold in Washington. The four Lw Bfh Mitte fighter Gruppen continued their routine of coastal sweeps, convoy escorts and training. The Luftflotte 3 fighters were more active, contending with small raids by American B-17s and RAF fighters and light bombers. The RAF offensive campaign, which had begun in 1941, was at this time more an annoyance than a real threat, but absorbed most of Luftflotte 3's defensive efforts during the first part of

1943. As 1943 progressed, the RAF raids became very useful as screens and diversions, but they had no direct strategic value until 1944, when they became strong enough to play a role in the battle for air supremacy over the Continent. The 1943 raids on coastal targets will be ignored in this book unless they had a significant effect on the defences against a simultaneous strategic (i.e., heavy bomber) raid.

3 January
8th Air Force VIII BC Mission #28: 68 of 85 B-17s and B-24s bomb St. Nazaire U-boat base, TOT 1130-1140 – lose 7-3-47, claim 14-18-4. No escort.

A USAAF raid on the submarine pens at St. Nazaire cost seven B-17s shot down and three B-24s scrapped in England owing to damage by fighters and ground fire. The fighter opposition was provided by III./JG 2, which claimed 16 victories, 15 confirmed, for the loss of one missing pilot and three Focke-Wulfs. The two

Hptm. Bruno Stolle, Kapitän of the 8. Staffel of III./JG 2, prepares for an overwater flight in his immaculate FW 190A-4 in early 1943. *(Bundesarchiv 625-3174-16a)*

JG 26 Staffeln at Beaumont–le–Roger took off as a reserve force, but did not make contact. The JG 26 Staffeln on the Pas de Calais were held on the ground, while 8./JG 26 was scrambled from Wevelghem, probably against a diversion, but did not make contact.

13 January

8th Air Force VIII BC Mission #29: 64 of 72 B-17s bomb Lille–Fives locomotive factory, TOT 1427-1430 – claim 3-4-5, lose 3-0-15. Escort of 7 RAF Spitfire sqds claims 0-0-1, loses 0-0-2.

In the day's major raid, 72 VIII BC B-17s targeted the Fives locomotive factory in Lille. After an active morning battling RAF fighters and light bombers over the Pas de Calais, II./JG 26 cleared its Abbéville field on the approach of more RAF aircraft, but was not utilised against the B-17s. The Gruppe did lose one of its new Bf 109s and its pilot to a confused Fw 190 pilot right over the airfield, an incident that had several witnesses, but did not find its way into the official records. I./JG 26 and III./JG 26 were scrambled well before the bombers crossed over Calais and were able to form up in time to attack the leading bomber group, the 305th, before it reached the target. Fifteen B-17s were damaged, but only one went down. The fighters flew in line astern; each flight contained five

or six aircraft. All attacks were made from dead ahead and on the same level as the bombers. Most fighters attacked singly, half-rolling into a split-S upon reaching the bomber formation. Several 305th BG B-17s were damaged severely, but only one crashed in France, a fact that caused considerable discussion in Luftwaffe headquarters from Lille to Berlin. Two Fortresses from another group collided and crashed after bombing, an accident not attributable to enemy action. The bomber gunners claimed 29 Fw 190s downed. This was later reduced to three, but, in fact, no Focke-Wulf suffered reportable damage.

23 January

8th Air Force VIII BC Mission #30: 54 of 73 B-17s bomb Lorient port area, Brest U-boat base, TOT 1348-51, 1413 – lose 5-2-30, claim 7-7-5. RAF Spitfire penetration and reception escort claims 0-0-1, loses 0.

After nine days off, the VIII BC returned to action with an attack on the Lorient submarine base. The target area was obvious, and the Jafü 3 controller patiently kept his Vannes fighters, III./JG 2 and 9./JG 26, away from the RAF diversions and escorts until all of the Spitfires had turned back. The Vannes aircraft then attacked, followed by others flying from Brest. To

III./JG 2 Fw 190s in flight in 1943. *(Kleinert)*

the Americans, the German attacks seemed better co-ordinated than before and were made by formations of six aircraft instead of in pairs or singly. Attacks persisted until the bombers were again over the Channel, even after the arrival of the reception escort. Five B-17s went down, all from the 303rd BG; two more crash-landed in England. One III./JG 2 Focke-Wulf was shot down; its pilot survived with injuries.

27 January – Wilhelmshaven (see map)
8th Air Force VIII BC Mission #31: 55 of 64 B-17s bomb Wilhelmshaven naval base, TOT 1110-1113 – lose 1-0-32, claim 10-6-7; 0 of 27 B-24s bomb – lose 2-0-11, claim 12-8-6. No escort.

The 8th Air Force commanders were under great pressure from Washington to extend their raids to the Reich. This was the first day in 1943 that promised reasonably good weather over both the American bases and the prospective targets in northern Germany. A mission was ordered, and 64 B-17s and 27 B-24s were dispatched to Wilhelmshaven. JG 1 was given its first opportunity to intercept the heavies in some strength. The I./JG 1 base at Jever was directly below the B-17 wing as it approached from the North Sea, and the Gruppe apparently made a maximum-strength inter-ception. The light armament of their Bf 109G-1s had little effect on the Fortresses, however. One B-17 finally went down, but three Messerschmitts and their pilots were shot down into the North Sea; the pilot of a fourth was able to bail out and come to earth without injury. The Luftwaffe credited the Messerschmitt pilots with four victories and scored the battle as a draw. The

B-17 crewmen had won a clear-cut victory, somewhat obscured by their usual overclaiming; they were credited with 10 Luftwaffe fighters.

The small B-24 formation got lost almost from take-off and headed east across the North Sea far to the south of their ordered route. They crossed the coast of Holland near Woensdrecht, turned south and wandered above the northern Netherlands before finally turning back north to the North Sea, where they jettisoned their bombs. II./JG 1 and IV./JG 1 scrambled from Woensdrecht and München–Gladbach and flew north after this attractive target. Two II./JG 1 Staffeln landed on Schiphol to refuel and were unable to intercept. The third, 4./JG 1, pressed on and was able to make one pass at the B-24s, which shot down one of their number; its pilot was able to bail out with wounds. The Focke-Wulf pilots, in turn, claimed two Liberators. 12./JG 1, part of IV./JG 1, made an effective interception as the B-24s withdrew over Terschelling. Two B-24s were claimed; two did go down, but the second was the direct result of the Staffel's only loss. B-24 gunners shot down a Focke-Wulf, which then collided with a lower B-24, slicing off its tail. Neither the German pilot nor any of the American crewmen survived. The returning B-24 crews claimed 12 Luftwaffe fighters. The three American bombers lost cost JG 1 four KIA or MIA, one WIA and seven fighters.

The strikingly painted Fw 190A-4 of Oblt. Hans Mohr of the II./JG 1 Stab in early 1943. It carries the Gruppe *Tatzelwurm* on the cowl, a personal emblem behind that and the chevron and circle of the Gruppe Technical Officer. *(Mombeek)*

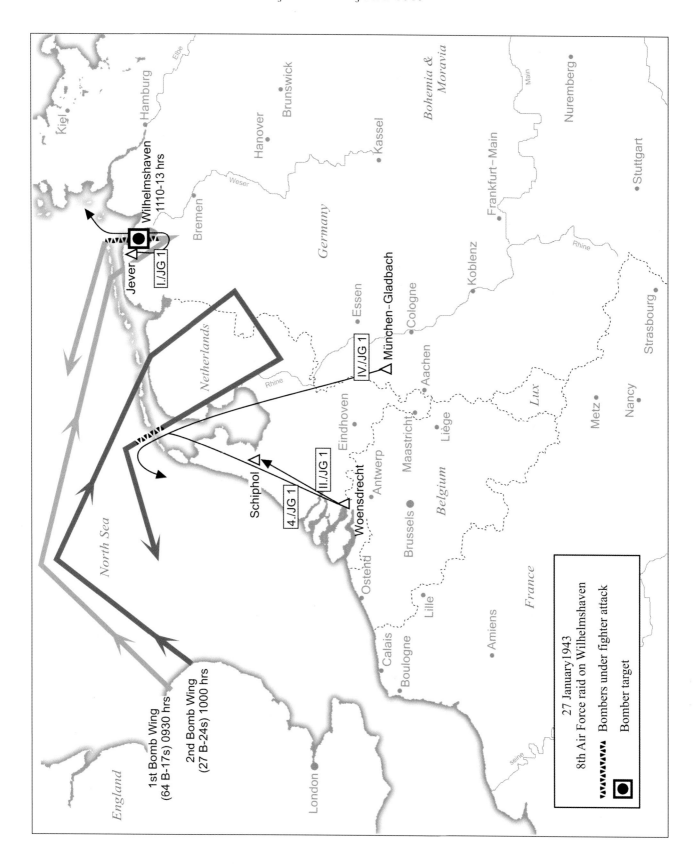

Kiel

Hamburg

Elbe

Wilhelmshaven
1110-13 hrs

Jever △ I./JG 1

Bremen

Weser

Hanover

Brunswick

Germany

Bohemia &
Moravia

Main

Nuremberg

Kassel

Frankfurt–Main

Stuttgart

Essen

München-Gladbach IV./JG 1 △

Cologne

Koblenz

Rhine

Strasbourg

Netherlands

Rhine

Aachen

Lux

Eindhoven

Maastricht

Liège

Metz

Nancy

North Sea

Schiphol

Woensdrecht II./JG 1 △

4./JG 1

Antwerp

Belgium

France

Brussels

Ostend

Lille

Amiens

Calais

Boulogne

England

London

Seine

1st Bomb Wing
(64 B-17s) 0930 hrs

2nd Bomb Wing
(27 B-24s) 1000 hrs

27 January1943
8th Air Force raid on Wilhelmshaven

▾▾▾▾▾▾▾▾ Bombers under fighter attack

◉ Bomber target

Luftwaffe defensive activity – 3 January 1943

Unit	Type	Gruppe up			Gruppe down		Claims	Losses				
		Base	No	Time	Base	Time		Dest	Dam	KIA	MIA	WIA
Luftflotte 3												
Jafü 3:												
III./JG 2	Fw 190A	Vannes	20	1109	Vannes	~1200	14 B-17	3	0	0	3	0
8/JG 2	Fw 190A	Brest–Guipavas	10	1146	Brest–Guipavas	~1200	0	0	0	0	0	0
2nd sorties	Fw 190A	Brest–Guipavas	5	1243	Brest–Guipavas	~1200	1 B-17	0	0	0	0	0
4. + 9./JG 26	Fw 190A	Beaumont–le–Roger	13	1006	Beaumont–le–Roger	1040	n/c	0	0	0	0	0
2nd sorties	Fw 190A	Beaumont–le–Roger	6	1145	Beaumont–le–Roger	1230	n/c	0	0	0	0	0

Luftwaffe defensive activity – 13 January 1943

Unit	Type	Gruppe up			Gruppe down		Claims	Losses				
		Base	No	Time	Base	Time		Dest	Dam	KIA	MIA	WIA
Luftflotte 3												
Jafü 2:												
I./JG 26	Fw 190A	St. Omer–Arques		~1410	St. Omer–Arques	~1500	1 B-17	0	0	0	0	0
II./JG 26	Fw 190A	Abbéville		1320	Abbéville	1402	0	0	0	0	0	0
5./JG 26	Bf 109G, Fw 190A	Abbéville		1320	Abbéville	1402	0	1	0	1	0	0
III./JG 26	Fw 190A	Wevelghem		1408	Wevelghem	1501	1 B-17	0	0	0	0	0

Luftwaffe defensive activity – 23 January 1943

Unit	Type	Gruppe up			Gruppe down		Claims	Losses				
		Base	No	Time	Base	Time		Dest	Dam	KIA	MIA	WIA
Luftflotte 3												
Jafü 2:												
III./JG 2	Fw 190A	Vannes	*28	1321	Vannes	~1445	4 B-17	1	0	0	0	1
9./JG 26	Fw 190A	Vannes	--	1345	Vannes	1445	2 B-17	0	0	0	0	0
8./JG 2	Fw 190A	Brest–Guipavas		~1400	Brest–Guipavas	~1445	0	0	0	0	0	0

*28 Fw 190s total up from Vannes

Luftwaffe defensive activity – 27 January 1943

Unit	Type	Gruppe up			Gruppe down		Claims	Losses				
		Base	No	Time	Base	Time		Dest	Dam	KIA	MIA	WIA
Lw Bfh Mitte												
Jafü Deutsche Bucht:												
I./JG 1	Bf 109G	Jever		~1030	Jever	~1130	4 B-17	5	0	2	1	0
Jafü Holland-Ruhr:												
4./JG 1	Fw 190A	Woensdrecht		~1100	Schiphol	~1230	2 B-24	1	0	0	0	1
IV./JG 1	Fw 190A	München–Gladbach		~1110	München–Gladbach	~1210	2 B-24	1	0	1	0	0
IV./NJG 1	Bf 110	Leeuwarden		1209	Leeuwarden	~1310	n/c	0	0	0	0	0

February 1943

The VIII BC had a lower priority for reinforcements than the air units in northwestern Africa and, for the next four months, operated with only four groups of B-17s, the 91st, 303rd, 305th and the 306th, wryly called 'The Four Horsemen'; and two groups of B-24s, the 44th and 93rd, which were so understrength that they were usually ordered to fly diversions. The VIII Fighter Command (VIII FC) contained only one group, the Spitfire-equipped 4th, which was subordinated to the RAF for operations. The Americans' top priority targets were the U-boat bases in western France. Although American bombs could not penetrate the roofs of the pens, a fact that was well known, and no submarine was ever damaged by the raids, which by all of the evidence had no effect at all on the U-boat campaign, the raids continued for political reasons. The U-boat construction yards on the North Sea were also chosen for attack. These had several advantages: they were on the U-boat target list; they met the definition of a 'strategic' target; they met the political demand for raids on Germany; and they were on the coast, thus easy to find and approachable from the North Sea, reducing the unescorted bombers' vulnerability to the Luftwaffe's short-range, single-engine interceptors.

Several components of JG 54 left Russia, picked up new Bf 109Gs in Germany and arrived on the Channel Front as part of the planned exchange with JG 26. 4./JG 54 was subordinated to III./JG 26 in Wevelghem, where it replaced 7./JG 26 smoothly and without incident. III./JG 54, containing the Green Heart Geschwader's 7th, 8th and 9th Staffeln, had more difficulty. It was too large to merge into the flying organisations already present and had to be trained to fight as a unit under the rigorous conditions of the Western Front. Its training continued until late March.

4 February – Emden (see map)
8th Air Force VIII BC Mission #33: 39 of 65 B-17s bomb Emden industrial area, TOT 1200-1215 – lose 5-?, claim 25-8-6. RAF Spitfire sweep claims 1-1-1, loses 0.

The VIII BC dispatched 65 B-17s to Hamm. After wandering over cloud-covered northern Germany for 90 minutes, 39 B-17s eventually found and bombed Emden. Twenty-one B-24s also took off, but all returned early with mechanical difficulties resulting from the extreme cold. Three JG 1 Gruppen were directed to the B-17s by Staffeln. In a prolonged battle, primarily with

fighters attacking singly from all directions, the B-17 gunners shot down six fighters, killing two pilots. The leading 91st BG lost two B-17s to II./JG 1 Fw 190s before Emden was located. A 303rd BG B-17 turned back with frozen guns and was shot into the Zuider Zee by a swarm of JG 1 fighters. The 305th BG lost two B-17s. One apparently collided with a Fw 190; the second was shot down by a new weapon in the day battle: Bf 110 night fighters. Eight IV./NJG 1 Bf 110s were ordered to scramble from Leeuwarden as the B-17s approached their base. The night fighter crews were not trained in day tactics, but today they made the only closed-formation attacks reported by the returning Americans. The two Schwärme pressed their attacks to close range from the rear. They were credited with downing three B-17s, but all eight Bf 110s were damaged by defensive fire; two of them were forced to make crash landings. The Americans lost five B-17s; Lw Bfh Mitte lost three KIA or MIA, four WIA and nine fighters.

A sweep of the Pas de Calais by RAF Spitfires provoked a massive response by JG 26 and succeeded in keeping this Geschwader in its own area, well away from the withdrawing bombers. This association with the main raid justifies its brief mention in this book. The approximately 100 Focke-Wulf pilots made no claims and lost one killed and one wounded.

14 February
8th Air Force VIII BC Mission #34: 74 B-17s target Hamm rail yards, recalled before bombing – lose 0-0-1, claim 1-0-0. RAF Spitfire sweep claims 1-1-1, loses 0.

The VIII Bomber Command dispatched another mission to Hamm; it was recalled with its bombs. One JG 1 Staffel made brief contact with the bombers between the clouds and returned to file one claim, which was not confirmed; no B-17 was lost.

15 February
8th Air Force VIII BC Mission #35: 21 of 23 B-24s bomb Dunkirk shipping, TOT 1540 – lose 2-1-7, claim 3-1-0. RAF Spitfire escort and sweeps claim 7-1-3, lose 0.

The Allied air forces mounted three raids beginning at 1300 hours in an attempt to sink the German armed merchant ship *Coronel* at Dunkirk. The first raid was not intercepted owing to slow response by the Jafü 2 controllers. The second was a repeat of the first; again, no contact was made. When a third attack force was detected, the defenders were directed not to the coast but to mid-Channel, to intercept it on its return flight. This third Circus – the RAF term for heavily escorted light bomber raids – was the largest of the day and atypically contained American heavy bombers, 22 B-24s from the 44th BG. One B-24 was shot down by the Dunkirk Flak. A second was shot down east of Dover by 7./JG 2, but the attempted interception was otherwise unsuccessful. Fighter Command claimed 11-2-5 Focke-Wulfs during the day, 7-1-3 in support of this Circus, while losing no Spitfires. The Luftflotte 3 Fw 190 units claimed four Spitfires, while losing two fighters and pilots.

16 February
8th Air Force VIII BC Mission #36: 65 of 89 B-17s and B-24s bomb St. Nazaire port, TOT 1052-55 – lose 8-0-30, claim 13-9-2. RAF Spitfire penetration escort sights nothing.

The day's major Allied mission was an attack on the St. Nazaire submarine pens by 71 B-17s and 18 B-24s. The Jafü 3 controller held his fighters away until the 11 escorting fighter squadrons turned back. 9./JG 26 was the first to attack the bombers, just as they left the target. The Staffel attacked continuously for the next 45 minutes, in head-on passes to very close range by one or two aircraft. The bombers claimed 16-11-2 of the dozen Focke-Wulfs, but only one fighter sustained reportable damage. The Staffel claimed two B-17s during their long fight. I./JG 2 had by now returned from southern France, and its three Fw 190 Staffeln, flying second sorties from St. Brieuc, attacked in groups of four to six until the bombers were halfway back across the Channel and turned back at the approach of the Spitfire withdrawal escort, which was apparently running late. I./JG 2 filed six victory claims, of which five were confirmed. The III./JG 2 Staffeln flying from Brest apparently failed to score. Some Bf 109s from a reconnaissance Staffel, 2./NAGr 13, put in a late appearance and claimed two B-17s over the Channel. Six B-17s failed to return from the mission; two B-24s collided over the Channel. JG 2 lost two Fw 190s, but no pilots.

26 February
8th Air Force VIII BC Mission #37: 65 of 93 B-17s and B-24s bomb Wilhelmshaven U-boat yard, TOT 1124-25 – lose 7-1-?, claim 21-9-5. No escort.

The day's primary target, Bremen, could not be located in the clouds, and the Americans paid a return visit to Wilhelmshaven. The four JG 1 Gruppen were scrambled in succession as the bombers flew east along the coast. I./JG 1, whose Jever base was closest to the target, made repeated attacks and was ultimately credited with two B-17s and four B-24s. The other Gruppen, some flying second sorties, claimed two B-17s and three B-24s. The Geschwader suffered no casualties. Twelve IV./NJG 1 Bf 110s scrambled from Leeuwarden against the withdrawing bombers and claimed two B-24s (one confirmed), but lost Knight's Cross holder Hptm. Ludwig Becker and his crew in the North Sea. The use of decorated, experienced night fighter crews in day interceptions was henceforth discouraged, although crews would continue to be sent up for the next year, mainly against stragglers. The Americans lost or scrapped eight bombers. Jafü Holland-Ruhr lost two MIA, two WIA and three aircraft.

PILOT'S ACCOUNT[1]
26 February 1943

Today I had my first contact with the heavies. I was flying on the far right of my formation and lost it during a left turn. I flew on alone, far out over the North Sea. Too late I noticed and tried to catch up. I eventually sighted them and headed their way at full throttle. But their silhouettes grew larger and larger – far too big for fighters. Indeed, these were heavy bombers – 60 or 70 in tight formation. How was one supposed to take them on? Fear comes as a result of experience, which I lacked. Without thinking, I changed course to meet them head on – I was flying through a cloud of bullets and tracer. I also opened fire and then, suddenly, a burst came toward me from the left, as red as a tomato. I evaded it, recrossed the formation and went in again. It was then time to head for the coast, which was 100 km away. What did the Amis think of this attack by a lone German fighter? At least they could say they had hit my Fw 190 with a good burst in the engine. I returned to base on 13 out of 14 cylinders.

Lt. Eberhard Burath
Adjutant, IV./JG 1

An exhausted Oblt. Eberhard Burath, IV./JG 1 Adjutant, in an undated photograph. (Burath)

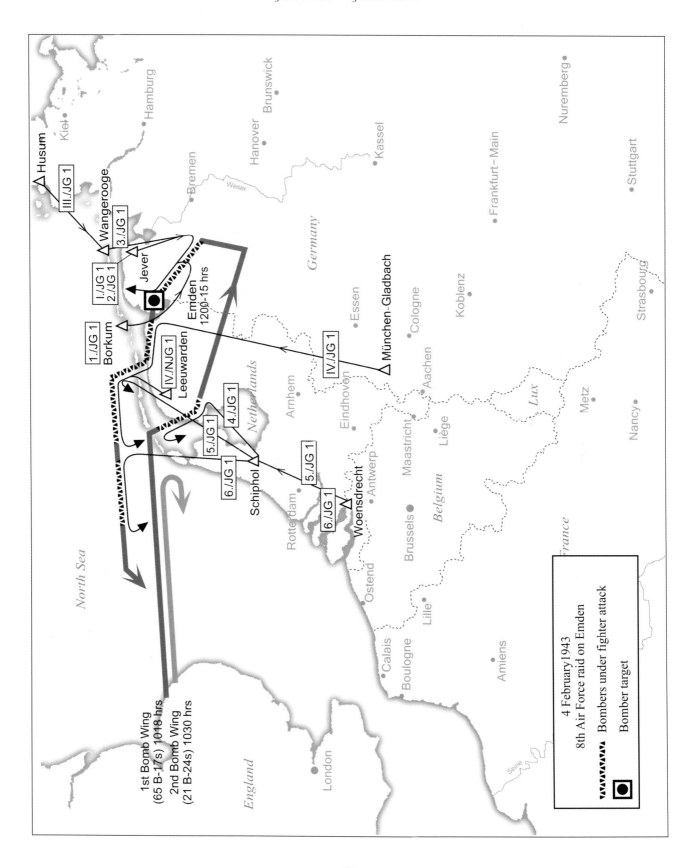

Husum

△ Husum

III./JG 1

Wangerooge

3./JG 1

Jever

1./JG 1
2./JG 1

Emden
1200–15 hrs

1./JG 1
Borkum

IV./NJG 1
Leeuwarden

München-Gladbach

IV./JG 1

4./JG 1

5./JG 1

6./JG 1

Schiphol

5./JG 1

6./JG 1
Woensdrecht

North Sea

1st Bomb Wing
(65 B-17s) 1018 hrs
2nd Bomb Wing
(21 B-24s) 1030 hrs

England

London

Kiel

Hamburg

Brunswick

Nuremberg

Hanover

Kassel

Weser

Bremen

Germany

Frankfurt–Main

Stuttgart

Essen

Cologne

Koblenz

Strasbourg

Aachen

Lux

Metz

Netherlands

Arnhem

Eindhoven

Maastricht

Liège

Belgium

Nancy

Antwerp

Rotterdam

Brussels

Ostend

France

Lille

Calais

Boulogne

Amiens

Seine

4 February 1943
8th Air Force raid on Emden

▼▼▼▼▼▼ Bombers under fighter attack

◉ Bomber target

39

27 February

8th Air Force VIII BC Mission #38: 60 of 78 B-17s and B-24s bomb Brest U-boat base, TOT 1455-1500 – lose 0-0-2, sight no e/a. RAF Spitfire penetration escort claims 0-0-1, loses 3.

An American attack on Brest was screened effectively by a simultaneous attack on Dunkirk by RAF light bombers, which held the attention of JG 26. The heavy bombers were escorted partway by RAF Spitfires, which were bounced by 8./JG 2 and lost three, although only two were claimed. One Focke-Wulf crash-landed with mechanical damage. The bomber crewmen saw no Luftwaffe fighters.

Luftwaffe defensive activity – 4 February 1943

Unit	Type	Gruppe up			Gruppe down		Claims	Losses				
		Base	No	Time	Base	Time		Dest	Dam	KIA	MIA	WIA
Lw Bfh Mitte												
Jafü Deutsche Bucht:												
Stab I./JG 1	Bf 109G	Jever		1110	Jever	1155	0	0	0	0	0	0
1./JG 1	Bf 109G	Borkum		1110	Borkum	1155	0	2	0	0	0	0
2./JG 1	Bf 109G	Jever		1110	Jever	1155	0	0	0	0	0	0
3./JG 1	Bf 109G	Wangerooge		1110	Wangerooge	1155	1 B-17	1	0	0	0	0
III./JG 1	Fw 190A	Husum		1111	Wangerooge	1252	n/c	0	0	0	0	0
Jafü H-Ruhr:												
4./JG 1	Fw 190A	Schiphol		1127	Schiphol	~1230	1 B-17	0	0	0	0	0
5./JG 1	Fw 190A	Woensdrecht	10	0909	Schiphol	1035	transfer	0	0	0	0	0
	Fw 190A	Schiphol	10	1211	Schiphol	~1330	2 B-17	0	3	0	0	0
6./JG 1	Fw 190A	Woensdrecht	7	0909	Schiphol	1035	transfer	0	0	0	0	0
	Fw 190A	Schiphol	7	1230	Schiphol	~1330	1 B-17	1	0	1	0	0
IV./JG 1	Fw 190A	München–Gladbach		1132	München–Gladbach	1250	1 B-17	3	0	1	1	0
IV./NJG 1	Bf 110	Leeuwarden	8	~1130	Leeuwarden	~1315	3 B-17	2	6	0	0	4

Luftwaffe defensive activity – 14 February 1943

Unit	Type	Gruppe up			Gruppe down		Claims	Losses				
		Base	No	Time	Base	Time		Dest	Dam	KIA	MIA	WIA
Lw Bfh Mitte												
Jafü H-Ruhr:												
4./JG 1	Fw 190A	Schiphol		~1030	Schiphol	~1130	0	0	0	0	0	0

Luftwaffe defensive activity – 15 February 1943

Unit	Type	Gruppe up			Gruppe down		Claims	Losses				
		Base	No	Time	Base	Time		Dest	Dam	KIA	MIA	WIA
Luftflotte 3												
Jafü 2:												
7./JG 2	Fw 190A	Calais–Marck		~1530	Calais–Marck	~1630	1 B-24	0	0	0	0	0
I./JG 26	Fw 190A	Lille–Vendeville		1536	Lille–Vendeville	1624	0	0	0	0	0	0
II./JG 26	Fw 190A	Vitry		1535	Vitry	1634	1 Spitfire	0	0	0	0	0
III./JG 26	Fw 190A	Wevelghem		1533	Wevelghem	1602	0	2	2	2	0	0

Luftwaffe defensive activity – 16 February 1943

Unit	Type	Gruppe up			Gruppe down		Claims	Losses				
		Base	No	Time	Base	Time		Dest	Dam	KIA	MIA	WIA
Luftflotte 3												
Jafü 3:												
I./JG 2	Fw 190A, Bf 109G	Beaumont–le–Roger		1020	St. Brieuc	1057	n/c	0	0	0	0	0
2nd sorties	Fw 190A, Bf 109G	St. Brieuc		~1115	Beaumont–le–Roger	~1215	5 B-17	2	0	0	0	0
III./JG 2	Fw 190A	Vannes		~1040	Vannes	~1140	0	0	1	0	0	0
9./JG 26	Fw 190A	Vannes		1040	Vannes	~1140	2 B-17	0	0	0	0	0
2./NaGr 13	Bf 109G	St. Brieuc		~1115	St. Brieuc	~1215	2 B-17	0	0	0	0	0

Luftwaffe defensive activity – 26 February 1943

Unit	Type	Gruppe up			Gruppe down		Claims	Losses				
		Base	No	Time	Base	Time		Dest	Dam	KIA	MIA	WIA
Lw Bfh Mitte												
Jafü Deutsche Bucht:												
I./JG 1	Bf 109G	Jever		1112	Jever	~1140	2 B-17, 4 B-24	0	0	0	0	0
III./JG 1	Fw 190A	Husum		1105	Husum	1200	1 B-24	0	0	0	0	0
Jafü H-Ruhr:												
II./JG 1	Fw 190A	Schiphol	6	1007	Schiphol	~1110	0	0	0	0	0	0
8./JG 1	Fw 190A	Deelen		1001	Leeuwarden	1117	0	0	0	0	0	0
2nd sorties	Fw 190A	Leeuwarden		1144	Leeuwarden	1247	1 B-24	0	0	0	0	0
IV./JG 1	Fw 190A	Deelen		1001	Jever	1115	1 B-17	1	0	0	0	0
2nd sorties	Fw 190A	Jever		~1130	Deelen	~1240	1 B-17, 1 B-24	0	0	0	0	0
IV./NJG 1	Bf 110	Leeuwarden	12	1150	Leeuwarden	~1350	1 B-24	2	0	0	2	2

Luftwaffe defensive activity – 27 February 1943

Unit	Type	Gruppe up			Gruppe down		Claims	Losses				
		Base	No	Time	Base	Time		Dest	Dam	KIA	MIA	WIA
Luftflotte 3												
Jafü 3:												
8./JG 2	Fw 190A	Brest–Guipavas		~1430	Brest–Guipavas	~1530	2 Spitfire	0	1	0	0	

March 1943

Hitler and thus Göring still did not consider the Reich in serious danger from the daylight bombing campaign, and March brought no reinforcement of Lw Bfh Mitte. However, the two Luftflotte 3 Jagdgeschwader were obviously being worn down, as either the Americans or the Royal Air Force could be counted on to appear over their territory on every flyable day. The western Jagdflieger began to receive reinforcements from other theatres. I./JG 27 saw its first combat from its new French base on 8 March. I./JG 3 left Russia for Döberitz on the 10th to be rebuilt to establishment strength before moving to France. On the 15th, II./JG 2 left North Africa to return to France. Its arrival at Poix would restore the Richthofen Geschwader to its full three-Gruppe establishment. III./JG 54 moved counter to this westward flow, however. Major Priller steadfastly refused to declare it suitable for operations from France, and in late March III./JG 54 was detached from JG 26 and ordered to Oldenburg, near Bremen. From this location, it could assist JG 1 in defending northern Germany against the infrequent raids of the VIII BC, while remaining outside the range of Allied fighters.

The Lw Bfh Mitte single-Gruppe attacks were unable to stop the unescorted bomber formations approaching over the North Sea. The reason was believed to be the light armament of the primary fighter in the Reich, the Bf 109G. Better weapons were promised. Erprobungskommando 25 (ErprKdo 25), a new unit formed specifically to bring new weapons into service, was now testing aerial rockets. At this time, 2./JG 1 began training to drop 250-kg bombs on bomber formations, apparently on its own initiative.

The armament of the main Luftflotte 3 fighter, the Fw 190A, was more than adequate to bring down bombers. The problems in the western zone were the presence of large Allied fighter screens and the short warning time available to scramble and form up for effective attacks on the bombers. Despite this extreme time pressure, the Jafü 2 and Jafü 3 controllers and pilots continued to refine their technique against the heavies. Combined missions by several fighter formations could eventually be co-ordinated.

4 March
8th Air Force VIII BC Mission #39: 44 of 71 B-17s bomb Hamm rail yards, Rotterdam shipyard, TOT 1020-43 – lose 5-0-24, claim 16-3-4. No escort.

Hamm was the primary target for the VIII BC raid. The 91st BG led the force of 71 B-17s across the North Sea. The three trailing groups got separated; most eventually bombed Rotterdam. The 16 B-17s of the 91st found themselves alone, reached the primary and thus became the first American force to bomb the Ruhr. A lone Bf 110 was the first German fighter to attack, 50 miles inland; then attacks by 226 Bf 109s, Fw 190s and Bf 110s began, continuing until the Dutch coast was crossed on the return flight. III./JG 26 flew from Wevelghem to Woensdrecht to reinforce Lw Bfh Mitte, but failed to find the bombers. The single-engine fighters that did attack were from the four JG 1 Gruppen, attacking in Staffeln or Schwärmen. They succeeded in downing one 91st Group B-17 and one from the aborting 306th BG, while losing two of their

number. Few of their nine victory claims were confirmed. Results by the day fighters against the small American formation were surprisingly poor. The Bf 110s, night fighters from III./NJG 1 and IV./NJG 1, did better, downing three 91st BG B-17s for the loss of one crew from each of the two Gruppen. The men of the 91st credited the survival of three-fourths of their number to their tight formation. The group received the 8th Air Force's first Distinguished Unit Citation for the mission. The Americans lost a total of five B-17s. Lw Bfh Mitte lost four MIA and four aircraft.

6 March
8th Air Force VIII BC Mission #40: 65 of 71 B-17s bomb Lorient U-boat base, TOT 1441-45 – lose 3-0-8, claim 7-2-1; 15 of 15 B-24s bomb Brest U-boat base, TOT 1416-17 – lose 0-0-3, claim 2-0-2. RAF Spitfire penetration escort claims 0-0-1, loses 2.

The USAAF returned to the Brittany U-boat bases. The B-17s attacked Lorient; the B-24s, Brest. The sole defenders were from III./JG 2: 8./JG 2 took on the penetration escort, claiming 2 Spitfires for no losses. 7./JG 2 then attacked the B-17s, claiming four while sustaining no reportable damage.

8 March
8th Air Force VIII BC Mission #41: 54 of 67 B-17s bomb Rennes rail yard, TOT 1430 – lose 2-1-9, claim 14-1-5; 13 of 16 B-24s bomb Rouen rail yard, TOT 1402-03 – lose 2-1-3, claim 14-3-3. RAF Spitfire escort claims 5-0-1, loses 2.

The VIII BC split its small force, sending 54 B-17s to Rennes in Brittany, while 16 B-24s targeted the Rouen railroad yards. The bombers were escorted by 16 RAF Spitfire squadrons and supported by a sweep by 4th FG Spitfires. Jafü 3's III./JG 2 tackled the B-17s and their escort and claimed two bombers and one fighter without loss. 3./JG 27 scrambled later on its first RLV mission and downed one B-17 for the loss of one Bf 109 and pilot. Jafü 2 defended against the Rouen raid and was able to get Major Josef 'Pips' Priller's JG 26 Stabsschwarm; Hptm. Wilhelm-Ferdinand 'Wutz' Galland's II./JG 26; Major Reinhard Seiler's III./JG 54, on its first bomber intercept mission since transferring from the Eastern Front; and Lt. Georg-Peter Eder's 12./JG 2 into position for a perfectly co-ordinated attack on the B-24s. 12./JG 2 was newly formed and was intended for II./JG 2; however, it was flying independently while its parent was in Tunisia. Priller's force and 12./JG 2 held off the escorts, allowing Galland to lead his two dozen Focke-Wulfs in a tight right bank into a devastating head-on attack. The lead bomber burst into flames, followed by the No. 2 aircraft in the leading vee. The bomber formation fell apart completely; bombs were scattered over the French countryside as the aircraft sought to evade the German fighters. The two lead B-24s crashed in France, while a third crashed after reaching England. Two Spitfires were also shot down. The Allied escorts downed two 12./JG 2 aircraft, whose pilots bailed out. III./JG 54 reported no victories or losses. JG 26 suffered no damage or loss. Its pilots took credit for forcing the bombers to turn back before reaching their target. This proved to be the only such triumph ever gained over the 8th Air Force. The USAAF lost or scrapped six bombers; the RAF lost two Spitfires. Luftflotte 3 lost two KIA or MIA, three WIA and five fighters.

A III./JG 2 Fw 190A-4 in a dramatic propaganda photograph taken in France in 1943. (Crow)

12 March
8th Air Force VIII BC Mission #42: 63 of 72 B-17s bomb Rouen–Sotteville rail yard, TOT 1241-44 – no losses, claim 1-0-0. RAF Spitfire escort claims 3-2-1, loses 0-0-1.

The four B-17 groups bombed the Rouen railroad yards shortly after noon. I./JG 2 and 12./JG 2 were engaged by the Spitfire escort, which claimed three while losing only one damaged. The B-17 crews sighted only one enemy fighter and claimed its destruction. The Messerschmitt pilot claimed a B-17; neither side's claim was accurate. No Luftwaffe fighter sustained damage or loss. Jafü 2 ordered JG 26 formations and III./JG 54 up from Lille–Vendeville and Vitry in ample time to make an interception; however, they failed to make contact. It is possible that there was a problem passing the control to Jafü 3, in whose area the target lay. Two III./JG 54 Messerschmitts made forced landings with engine damage; these were the only Luftflotte 3 losses on its fruitless mission.

13 March

8th Air Force VIII BC Mission #43: 75 of 80 B-17s bomb Amiens–Longeau rail yard and secondary targets, TOT 1515-17 – lose 0-0-11, claim 2-0-2. RAF Spitfire escort claims 5-0-4, loses 6.

The VIII BC sent 80 B-17s to Amiens. Jafü 2 and Jafü 3 plotted a large formation, including heavy bombers, east of Dieppe and got most of their fighters up to intercept: the Stab/JG 26 and III./JG 54 from Vendeville, II./JG 26 from Vitry, and 12./JG 2 and I./JG 27 from their bases west of the Somme. The bombers were late in forming up, and both bombers and escort were badly scattered. Enough Allied fighters stayed within sight of the B-17s, however, to break up most of the German attacks, and no B-17s were shot down, although 11 were damaged. The escorts claimed five Luftwaffe fighters, an exact match for German combat losses. Seven Spitfires were claimed; true losses were six. Three of the RAF fighters apparently were the victims of Hptm. Heinrich Setz, the Kommandeur of I./JG 27, which was flying its first full-strength combat mission from France. Setz was then shot down and killed. The B-17s scattered their bombs on several targets of opportunity. Luftflotte 3's six confirmed Spitfire claims cost it four KIA, one WIA and five fighters.

18 March

8th Air Force VIII BC Mission #45: 97 of 103 B-17s and B-24s bomb Vegesack U-boat yard, TOT 1531-35 – lose 2-1-23, claim 52-20-23. No escort.

Seventy-six B-27s and 27 B-24s targeted the U-boat yards at Vegesack, near Bremen. The Bf 109s of I./JG 1 reached the bombers near Helgoland and claimed two after a quick head-on attack on the B-24 box. One was downed by a III./NJG 3 Bf 110; the success of the lone black night fighter was described accurately by bomber crewmen in their post-mission interrogations. Although the German attacks continued for almost two hours, they were weak in strength, even though I./JG 1, III./JG 1, IV./JG 1, 2./JG 27 (temporarily reinforcing II./JG 1, which today was itself diverted by an RAF light bomber attack), various night fighter Schwärme and the Focke-Wulf factory protection Schwarm made contact. The German pilots were credited with four B-17s and four B-24s, while losing two pilots and four aircraft. The Americans lost only one B-24 and one B-17; a second B-17 crash-landed in England.

A pair of III./NJG 3 Bf 110G-4 night fighters patrol a bright sky over a solid German undercast. The time is probably early 1943, although they have already lost their early all-black camouflage. *(Bundesarchiv 659-6436-15)*

The Fw 190A-4 (W.Nr. 555) of the IV./JG 1 Adjutant, Lt. Eberhard Burath, after it crashed on take-off from Deelen on 11 March 1943. Burath was not hurt. *(Burath)*

22 March

8th Air Force VIII BC Mission #46: 84 of 102 B-17s and B-24s bomb Wilhelmshaven dock area, TOT 1501-10 – lose 3-0-22, claim 28-9-9. No escort.

All four JG 1 Gruppen were able to fly two missions against today's raid on Wilhelmshaven, evidence that the Lw Bfh MItte controllers and ground crews were gaining skill with experience. The fighter pilots themselves were not as effective, one bomb group mission summary stating flatly that "… these fighters were not comparable in combat to the fighters in France." Six claims for heavy bombers were confirmed, but only three failed to return to England. The American claim of 28 fighters downed was highly optimistic; no Luftwaffe fighters were lost or sustained reportable damage. There was one tactical innovation today: a 2./JG 1 pilot dropped a 250-kg bomb into the middle of a vee of B-17s and received credit for blowing the wing off one. The details in the pilot's combat report, however, do not match those for the day's only B-17 loss.

28 March

8th Air Force VIII BC Mission #47: 70 of 103 B-17s bomb Rouen–Sotteville rail yard, TOT 1248-50 – lose 1-0-9, claim 5-4-1. RAF Spitfire escort claims 0-0-0, loses 4.

The USAAF targeted Rouen in marginal weather. The small force of bombers flew a triangular course in mid-Channel awaiting their escorts, allowing the defenders ample time to get airborne. The 13 squadrons of RAF fighters were eventually recalled, but one Spitfire wing was bounced by I./JG 2 over Abbéville, losing four. II./JG 26 and 12./JG 2 had a clear shot at the unescorted B-17s and damaged nine, but only one went down, apparently the victim of Lt. Eder of 12./JG 2. Eder himself was injured by the bombers' fire, but was able to force-land his badly damaged Bf 109 on Beaumont–le–Roger. His Messerschmitt and one I./JG 2 Focke-Wulf were the only Luftwaffe combat losses on the mission.

31 March

8th Air Force VIII BC Mission #48: 33 of 102 B-17s and B-24s bomb Rotterdam shipyards, TOT 1325 – lose 4-3-5, claim 1-1-2. RAF Spitfire escort sights nothing.

Today's target for the VIII BC was Rotterdam, but the entire formation of 102 bombers was blown off course by unanticipated high winds, resulting in numerous course changes above the Channel. Four of the six bomber groups aborted the mission, and II./JG 26, the only Luftwaffe Gruppe to make contact, did not catch the other B-17s until they were halfway back across the Channel. The German pilots, all low on fuel, were ordered to make only one pass from the rear before turning for France. They downed one B-17 and one B-24, matching US records, but the claims were not confirmed because they were not witnessed.

COMBAT REPORT[2]
31 March 1943

One B-24 destroyed from 7,000 metres at 1248 hours, 100 km NW of Ostend
[Unconfirmed for lack of a witness, but victim was Lt. Williams's 93rd Bomb Goup B-24: DC]

I scrambled from Vitry–en–Artois with my 4. Staffel at 1207 hours and headed for Rotterdam. We did not reach the heavies before they dropped their bombs. We followed them out to sea. I made two attacks on a Liberator 100 km north of Ostend, the first from the side and the second from behind, hitting the right wing and the tail. The Lib fell away to the right into the clouds. No witness; I was alone. I landed on Wevelghem at 1308 hours to refuel. At 2000 hours that evening, the victory was confirmed by the watch officer at the radio listening service, whch had heard a Liberator report at 1245 hours that it was no longer controllable due to enemy action and that the crew was going to bail out. It gave its location as about 100 km north of Ostend, for the air-sea rescue service. The aircraft could only fly in a right bank; it could not reach base.

Lt. Otto Stammberger, Staffelkapitän
4./JG 26

PILOT'S ACCOUNT[3]
31 March 1943

[Crump's victim was Lt. Ashcraft's 305th Bomb Group B-17: DC]

A new tactic of the heavy formations made its first appearance. The direction of attack appeared to be over Holland into the Ruhr, and so we of the opposing defences were disposed accordingly. During their approach, they turned and left England on a southerly course, as if to attack a target in France. But the entire manœuvre was then reversed; after flying south, they then turned back east. In the meantime, we were being led this way and that, and would soon be unable to attack the enemy formation due to low fuel. Auxiliary fuel tanks were available, but we were flying this mission without them …

As our [II./JG 26] Gruppe formation flew north, almost to the coast and almost out of fuel, I spotted the bomber stream in the dusk at eleven o'clock, on a northwesterly course somewhat below us. My report to the formation leader Galland brought the reply, 'Where are they? I see nothing!' A second, more detailed report brought the same reply. Apparently no one else saw the formation – or else the Kommandeur did not want to see it, having in mind our almost empty tanks. At any rate, after a short delay he turned about to a course for home, with the comment 'Ich habe Durst', which was code for low fuel. However, the rest of us were given a free hand to do what we wanted. A glance at my fuel gauge showed me that an attack was possible; my wingman agreed with me. In a gentle climb, I turned my Rotte on a course to the northwest; as we approached the bomber stream, I swung to the right, toward the last Pulk [herd; a combat box] of B-17s. I glanced around and, to my relief, found that the bombers were without fighter escort. I attacked the nearest B-17, which was at the left of the leading vee, from the front and slightly above. It began to smoke immediately. Flames erupted between its two left engines. The bomber sheered away to the left, trailing a long stream of fire. As long as I watched, it remained on course in a shallow dive. I quickly turned my eyes away from it and the rest of the enemy formation, as it was high time we got away. My wingman had been hit in an aileron and had control problems. But thanks to our altitude, and with some luck, we made smooth landings at Coxyde, a nearby coastal airfield. I do not know to this day what happened to 'my' B-17. I know only that from that day onward I was considered to have the best eyes in the Second Gruppe.

Uffz. Peter Crump
5./JG 26

The Fw 190A-5 of Oblt. Otto Stammberger in an early 1943 line-up. The aircraft are parked in the open, clear evidence that Germany still commands the skies over the western occupied zone. (Bundesarchiv 377-2814-18)

Luftwaffe defensive activity – 4 March 1943

Unit	Type	Gruppe up			Gruppe down		Claims	Losses				
		Base	No	Time	Base	Time		Dest	Dam	KIA	MIA	WIA
Lw Bfh Mitte												
Jafü Deutsche Bucht:												
I./JG 1	Bf 109G	Jever		~0930	Jever	~1030	0	0	1	0	0	0
Jafü H-Ruhr:												
4./JG 1	Fw 190A	Schiphol		0916	Schiphol	~1030	0	0	0	0	0	0
5./JG 1	Fw 190A	Schiphol		1022	Schiphol	~1200	0	0	0	0	0	0
6./JG 1	Fw 190A	Schiphol		1002	Schiphol	~1130	0	2	0	0	0	0
8./JG 1	Fw 190A	Leeuwarden		0914	Leeuwarden	1017	n/c	0	0	0	0	0
2nd sorties	Fw 190A	Leeuwarden		1049	Leeuwarden	1159	2 B-17	0	0	0	0	0
IV./JG 1	Fw 190A	Deelen		0950	Deelen	~1015	n/c	0	0	0	0	0
2nd sorties	Fw 190A	Deelen		~1100	Deelen	~1200	1 B-17	0	0	0	0	0
III./JG 26	Fw 190A	Woensdrecht	18	1124	Wevelghem	1300	n/c	0	0	0	0	0
III./NJG 1	Bf 110	Twente	4	~1100	Twente	~1230	2 B-17	1	0	0	2	0
IV./NJG 1	Bf 110	Leeuwarden	4	1100	Leeuwarden	~1230	1 B-17	1	1	0	2	0
Luftflotte 3												
Jafü 2:												
III./JG 26	Fw 190A	Wevelghem	18	~1030	Woensdrecht	~1100	transfer	0	0	0	0	0

Luftwaffe defensive activity – 6 March 1943

Unit	Type	Gruppe up			Gruppe down		Claims	Losses				
		Base	No	Time	Base	Time		Dest	Dam	KIA	MIA	WIA
Luftflotte 3												
Jafü 3:												
III./JG 2	Fw 190A	Vannes	20	1400	Vannes	~1530	4 B-17	0	0	0	0	0
8./JG 2	Fw 190A	Brest–Guipavas	15	1415	Brest–Guipavas	~1530	2 Spitfire	0	0	0	0	0
11./JG 2	Bf 109G	Triqueville	8	~1400	Théville	~1530	n/c	0	0	0	0	0

Luftwaffe defensive activity – 8 March 1943

Unit	Type	Gruppe up			Gruppe down		Claims	Losses				
		Base	No	Time	Base	Time		Dest	Dam	KIA	MIA	WIA
Luftflotte 3												
Jafü 2:												
12./JG 2	Bf 109G	Beaumont–le–Roger		1340	Beaumont–le–Roger	1440	1 Spitfire	2	0	0	0	1
Stab/JG 26	Fw 190A	Lille–Vendeville		1337	Lille–Vendeville	1440	1 Spitfire	0	0	0	0	0
II./JG 26	Fw 190A	Vitry		1334	Vitry	1436	4 B-24	0	0	0	0	0
III./JG 26	Fw 190A	Wevelghem		1310	Wevelghem	1442	0	0	0	0	0	0
III./JG 54	Bf 109G	Lille–Vendeville		1338	Lille–Vendeville	1442	0	0	0	0	0	0
Jafü 3:												
III./JG 2	Fw 190A	Brest–Nord		1344	Brest–Nord	1448	2 B-17, 1 Spitfire	0	0	0	0	1
3./JG 27	Bf 109G	Bernay	9	~1420	Bernay	~1550	1 B-17	1	0	1	0	0
II./SKG 10	Fw 190A	Rennes–St. Jacques		~1345	Rennes–St. Jacques	~1445	0	2	0	0	1	1

Luftwaffe defensive activity – 12 March 1943

Unit	Type	Gruppe up			Gruppe down		Claims	Losses				
		Base	No	Time	Base	Time		Dest	Dam	KIA	MIA	WIA
Luftflotte 3												
Jafü 2:												
Stab/JG 26	Fw 190A	Lille–Vendeville		1123	Lille–Vendeville	1220	n/c	0	0	0	0	0
II./JG 26	Fw 190A	Vitry		1123	Vitry	1218	n/c	0	0	0	0	0
III./JG 54	Bf 109G	Lille–Vendeville		~1123	Lille–Vendeville	~1220	n/c	1	1	0	0	0
Jafü 3:												
I./JG 2	Fw 190A, Bf 109G	Triqueville		~1215	Triqueville	~1320	1 B-17, 1 Spitfire, 1 Typhoon	0	0	0	0	0
12./JG 2	Bf 109G	Beaumont–le–Roger		~1215	Beaumont–le–Roger	~1320	2 Spitfire	0	0	0	0	0

Luftwaffe defensive activity – 13 March 1943

Unit	Type	Gruppe up			Gruppe down		Claims	Losses				
		Base	No	Time	Base	Time		Dest	Dam	KIA	MIA	WIA
Luftflotte 3												
Jafü 2:												
Stab/JG 26	Fw 190A	Lille–Vendeville		1503	Lille–Vendeville	1623	0	0	0	0	0	0
II./JG 26	Fw 190A	Vitry		1454	Vitry	1545	2 Spitfire	1	0	1	0	0
III./JG 26	Fw 190A	Wevelghem		1510	Wevelghem	1600	0	0	0	0	0	0
III./JG 54	Bf 109G	Lille–Vendeville		~1510	Lille–Vendeville	~1600	0	0	2	0	0	0
Jafü 3:												
I./JG 2	Fw 190A, Bf 109G	Triqueville		~1430	Triqueville	~1545	1 Spitfire	0	0	0	0	0
12./JG 2	Bf 109G	Beaumont–le–Roger		~1430	Beaumont–le–Roger	~1545	0	1	0	1	0	0
I./JG 27	Bf 109G	Bernay		1447	Bernay	~1545	3 Spitfire	3	0	2	0	1

Luftwaffe defensive activity – 18 March 1943

Unit	Type	Gruppe up			Gruppe down		Claims	Losses				
		Base	No	Time	Base	Time		Dest	Dam	KIA	MIA	WIA
Lw Bfh Mitte												
Jafü Deutsche Bucht:												
I./JG 1	Bf 109G	Jever		1442	Jever	1530	2 B-24	2	0	1	0	1
III./JG 1	Fw 190A	Husum		1450	Jever	1555	0	0	0	0	0	0
ISS Focke-Wulf	Fw 190A	Bremen		~1500	Bremen	~1600	1 B-17	0	0	0	0	0
III./NJG 3	Bf 110	Stade		~1430	Stade	~1630	1 B-24	0	0	0	0	0
Jafü H-Ruhr:												
8./JG 1	Fw 190A	Leeuwarden		1420	Leeuwarden	1512	0	0	0	0	0	0
2nd sorties	Fw 190A	Leeuwarden		1540	Leeuwarden	1645	1 B-24	0	0	0	0	0
IV./JG 1	Fw 190A	Deelen		1524	Leeuwarden	1634	2 B-17	2	0	0	1	0
2./JG 27	Bf 109G	Schiphol		1435	Schiphol	1506	n/c	0	0	0	0	0
2nd sorties	Bf 109G	Schiphol		1549	Schiphol	1649	1 B-17	0	0	0	0	0

Luftwaffe defensive activity – 22 March 1943

Unit	Type	Gruppe up			Gruppe down		Claims	Losses				
		Base	No	Time	Base	Time		Dest	Dam	KIA	MIA	WIA
Lw Bfh Mitte												
Jafü Deutsche Bucht:												
I./JG 1	Bf 109G	Jever		1421	Jever	~1445	n/c	0	0	0	0	0
2nd sorties	Bf 109G	Jever		~1500	Jever	~1530	2 B-17, 1 B-24	0	0	0	0	0
III./JG 1	Fw 190A	Husum		1447	Husum	1554	0	0	0	0	0	0
Jafü H-Ruhr:												
II./JG 1	Fw 190A	Schiphol	17	1355	Schiphol	~1445	n/c	0	0	0	0	0
2nd sorties	Fw 190A	Schiphol	7	~1530	Schiphol	1643	n/c	0	0	0	0	0
8./JG 1	Fw 190A	Leeuwarden		1401	Leeuwarden	1501	1 B-17, 1 B-24	0	0	0	0	0
IV./JG 1	Fw 190A	Deelen		1404	Deelen	1430	0	0	0	0	0	0
2nd sorties	Fw 190A	Deelen		1505	Deelen	1618	0	0	0	0	0	0
2./JG 27	Bf 109G	Schiphol		1355	Schiphol	1450	n/c	0	0	0	0	0
2nd sorties	Bf 109G	Schiphol		1518	Schiphol	1616	n/c	0	0	0	0	0
I./NJG 3	Bf 110E	Vechta		1448	Vechta	1608	0	0	0	0	0	0

Luftwaffe defensive activity – 28 March 1943

Unit	Type	Gruppe up			Gruppe down		Claims	Losses				
		Base	No	Time	Base	Time		Dest	Dam	KIA	MIA	WIA
Luftflotte 3												
Jafü 2:												
Stab/JG 26	Fw 190A	Lille–Vendeville	*46	1150	Lille–Vendeville	1232	n/c	0	0	0	0	0
II./JG 26	Fw 190A	Vitry	—	1150	Vitry	1220	n/c	0	0	0	0	0
2nd sorties	Fw 190A	Vitry	**29	1247	Vitry	~1400	0	0	0	0	0	0
III./JG 26	Fw 190A	Wevelghem	—	1150	Vitry	1233	n/c	0	0	0	0	0
2nd sorties	Fw 190A	Wevelghem	—	1247	Vitry	~1400	0	0	0	0	0	0
3rd sorties	Fw 190A	Wevelghem	12	1252	Vitry	~1400	n/c	0	0	0	0	0
Jafü 3:												
I./JG 2	Fw 190A, Bf 109G	Triqueville		~1150	Triqueville	~1230	1 Spitfire	0	0	0	0	0
2nd sorties	Fw 190A, Bf 109G	Triqueville		~1252	Triqueville	~1400	1 B-17, 5 Spitfire	1	0	0	0	0
12./JG 2	Bf 109G	Beaumont–le–Roger		~1252	Beaumont–le–Roger	~1400	1 B-17	1	0	0	0	1

*46 Stab, II., III./JG 26 Fw 190s sortie   **29 II., IIII./JG 26 Fw 190s sortie

Luftwaffe defensive activity – 31 March 1943

Unit	Type	Gruppe up			Gruppe down		Claims	Losses				
		Base	No	Time	Base	Time		Dest	Dam	KIA	MIA	WIA
Lw Bfh Mitte												
Jafü H-Ruhr.												
IV./JG 1	Fw 190A	Deelen		1328	Woensdrecht	1440	n/c	0	0	0	0	0
2./JG 27	Bf 109G	Leeuwarden		1338	Leeuwarden	1404	n/c	0	0	0	0	0
Luftflotte 3												
Jafü 2:												
II./JG 26	Fw 190A	Vitry		1207	Vlissingen, Maldegem, Wevelghem	1308	1 B-17, 1 B-24	1	0	0	0	0
III./JG 26	Fw 190A	Wevelghem		1200	Wevelghem	1259	0	0	0	0	0	0
2nd sorties	Fw 190A	Wevelghem		1325	Wevelghem	1405	0	0	0	0	0	0

April 1943

The need to reinforce Lw Bfh Mitte was now obvious, and on 1 April, the number of day fighter Geschwader in the Reich was doubled by the simple expedient of splitting Jagdgeschwader 1 into two halves. The new unit, Jagdgeschwader 11, picked up III./JG 1 (as I./JG 11) at Husum and I./JG 1 (as II./JG 11) at Jever and took over responsibility for the defence of southern Norway, western Denmark and the northeastern sector of Germany's North Sea coast, reporting to the Jafü Deutsche Bucht in Jagddivision 2. Jagdgeschwader 1 retained IV./JG 1 (now I./JG 1) at Deelen and II./JG 1 at Woensdrecht and defended the western half of its old sector, reporting to the Jafü Holland-Ruhr in Jagddivision 1. JG 1 also received a new Kommodore. Obstlt. Hans Philipp, the popular and combat-proven Kommandeur of I./JG 54, replaced Obstlt. Dr. Erich Mix. Major Anton Mader transferred from II./JG 77 to become Kommodore of JG 11. New Third Gruppen were formed in both JG 1 and JG 11 in April and May to bring these Geschwader up to a full three-Gruppe establishment.

On 10 April, the office of the General der Jagdflieger issued an important tactical regulation codifying the governing principles and recommended attack methods for the day RLV force. Its principal objective was to drive the bombers from the target or at least hinder their planned drop. The most effective tactic was a massed head-on attack to close range. Repeat attacks could be made from any direction, but firing from high deflection angles was not recommended. Attacks were to be continued through the Flak zone. Stragglers were not to be attacked until

Hptm., later Obstlt., Hans Philipp. A successful pilot on the Eastern Front, Philipp joined the RLV force in April 1943 as Kommodore of Jagdgeschwader 1. He was shot down and killed by P-47s on 9 October 1943. His final victory total was 206. (Author's collection)

after the main formation had dropped its bombs. Withdrawing bombers could be attacked and pursued to their destruction. These recommendations were never carried out exactly. Three problems were endemic and could be attributed to the heavy defensive fire from intact combat boxes: the fighter pilots tended to open fire and break away too soon, were difficult to re-assemble for repeat attacks and often went after damaged bombers prior to the bomb drop, especially those that the pilots themselves had driven from the formation.

In mid-April, Jafü Deutsche Bucht was reinforced with Jagdstaffel (JaSta) Helgoland, a unique formation based on a small island in the middle of the German (Helgoland) Bight and equipped with the long-winged Bf 109T, a derivative of the Bf 109E originally designed for carrier operations. The 70 examples of this fighter were pulled from storage when someone realised that they had the short-field performance necessary for the island's tiny airstrips. The Bf 109T was too slow for combat with modern fighters, but the Staffel did an excellent job against 1943's unescorted raids.

The day fighter defences in the interior of Germany were at this time almost non-existent. Reichsmarschall Hermann Göring and Genobst. Hans Jeschonnek, the Luftwaffe Chief of Staff, believed in a peripheral defence: that, for morale purposes, defending fighters should be based on the coast to prevent deep penetrations of Reich airspace. The day fighter operational training Gruppen and factory test units could each be called on to put up a Schwarm or Staffel of their most experienced pilots in case of emergency. The *Industrieschutzstaffel* (Industry Protection Squadron; ISS) at the Bremen Focke-Wulf plant would be tested on 17 April. The Luftwaffe high command did not concede the need to base front-line day fighter units in the Reich interior until the second half of 1943.

Experiments with air-to-air rockets and bombs continued. ErprKdo 25 was testing both the Rheinmetall-Borsig RZ 65, which scored a few successes, but was eventually rejected, and the WGr 21, a larger rocket converted from a 21-cm infantry mortar shell, which offered more potential, but required several months of development and testing. Underwing cannon were a quicker and more conventional cure for the Bf 109's weak firepower, and these were being rushed into service. In Lw Bfh Mitte, 5./JG 11 destroyed several B-17s with its 250-kg bombs, while Luftflotte 3 fighters also experimented with

The Bf 109G-1 of Lt. Heinz Knoke, Kapitän of the 2. Staffel of I./JG 1, photographed in early 1943. Knoke was among the first pilots to suggest dropping bombs on American heavy bomber formations. His aircraft has an ETC rack for a 250-kg bomb, which was being loaded when the photo was taken. *(Prien)*

aerial bombs, using a technique developed at the Rechlin experimental station, but with little success.

In France, the transfer of III./JG 54 to Germany and the continued presence of I./JG 26 in Russia left JG 26 with only two Gruppen. Three new Staffeln, 10./JG 54, 11./JG 54 and 12./JG 54, had been established as part of a planned fourth JG 54 Gruppe. These lacked a Gruppe headquarters, though, and were at first suitable only for operational training and second-line duties. They were eventually redesignated as JG 26 Staffeln and absorbed in the existing Gruppen. Major Priller satisfied the need for a third Gruppe headquarters in his region by setting up a Geschwadergruppe under his direct command. This totally irregular formation comprised the Stabsschwarm and one or more Staffeln based with Priller at Lille–Vendeville or Lille–Nord. 8./JG 26 was a permanent member; other Staffeln attached temporarily included 6./JG 26 and 11./JG 26.

4 April

8th Air Force VIII BC Mission #49: 85 of 97 B-17s bomb Paris Renault factory, TOT 1414-17 – lose 4-0-16, claim 47-13-6. RAF Fighter Command (RAF FC) Spitfire escort, heavy bombers and several simultaneous light bomber raids claim 13-4-16, lose 13.

The VIII BC target was the Renault motor vehicle factory southeast of Paris. Several feints and diversions were flown in an attempt to disperse the German defences. One reached Rotterdam and was engaged by II./JG 1. When Jafü 2 detected the heavy bombers halfway across the North Sea from Harwich, II./JG 26 and III./JG 26 were scrambled and ordered to patrol the coast until the direction of the attack was known. The bombers turned east, then back to the southwest, and the Gruppen were quickly landed and refuelled. I./JG 2 intercepted some RAF Venturas that were bombing the Caen airfield and then had to land. II./JG 26 and III./JG 26 scrambled quickly on second sorties and headed toward Beauvais, where Jafü 3 was assembling all available fighters to attack the withdrawing B-17s in strength. In the meantime, the bombers had made their southern turn, proceeded to the Paris area unmolested and made a good bombing run.

Major Oesau, the JG 2 Kommodore, led I./JG 2 and the operational Staffel of the training unit JG 105 in the first attack on the 85 unescorted B-17s north of Paris. They made several passes before the formation reached the Rouen area. At this point, the JG 26 Gruppen began making concentrated head-on attacks to close range. Spacing between the German attacking units was much closer than previously, only 900–1,400 metres (1,000–1,500 yards), catching bombers out of position when they jinked to evade the previous fighters. The Spitfires of the bombers' withdrawal cover arrived shortly thereafter. They were well above the bombers and were fended off for a while by the two JG 26 Gruppen. The battle eventually degenerated into a general fighter mêlée over the Channel, from which the bombers escaped after losing four of their number; 16 others were damaged. Thirteen RAF Spitfires failed to return from their various escort missions; Luftflotte 3 lost three pilots killed or missing and four fighters.

5 April – Antwerp (see map)

8th Air Force VIII BC Mission #50: 64 of 79 B-17s and 18 of 25 B-24s bomb Antwerp industrial area, TOT 1530-37 – lose 4-0-13, claim 23-8-4. RAF Spitfire escort claims 2-1-5, loses 1.

The VIII BC targeted the Erla aircraft repair facility at Antwerp. The B-17s and B-24s feinted toward Abbéville before reversing course. They then flew southeast before finally turning northeast toward Antwerp. Major Priller led his Stabsschwarm and 8./JG 26 in a head-on attack while the bombers were still off the coast, well before the escort turned back at Ghent. The British fighters were too far above and behind the formation to intervene. The first concentrated attack, reinforced by III./JG 26, broke the cohesion of the bomber formation. Only 82 B-17s managed to bomb their target; most of the 306th BG overshot and hit the small city of Mortsel. This group, which was in the lead, was split up by the Germans' initial pass and thus bore the brunt of the rest of the attacks. The bomber gunners succeeded in fatally wounding the III./JG 26 Kommandeur, Hptm. Fritz Geisshardt, who was the day's only German fatality. The II./JG 26 pilots had burned half their fuel following the bomber feints in the Channel before racing to Antwerp at full throttle. They made a head-on attack just as the 306th turned off the target, tearing through the scattered bombers and causing several to fall away. Three B-17s crashed in Belgium and were confirmed to JG 26. II./JG 1 from Woensdrecht apparently claimed the same three B-17s, but these were not confirmed. The latter Gruppe also engaged the Spitfires off the coast, as did I./JG 2, which had flown all the way from Triqueville and had to turn back for the coastal field at Coxyde after a brief but successful combat that claimed three Spitfires. One JG 2 pilot force-landed near Ostend with severe injuries. He was the only German casualty attributable to the escorts, which were for the most part ineffective; their high altitude made them easy to plot and evade. Four B-17s were lost, all from the 306th. Thirteen more bombers returned with damage. One Spitfire failed to return. Today was the first time that fighters from three different commands – Jafü 2 and Jafü 3 from Luftflotte 3 and Jafü Holland-Ruhr from Luftwaffenbefehlshaber Mitte – had combined forces for an interception. Their losses totalled one KIA, two WIA and six fighters.

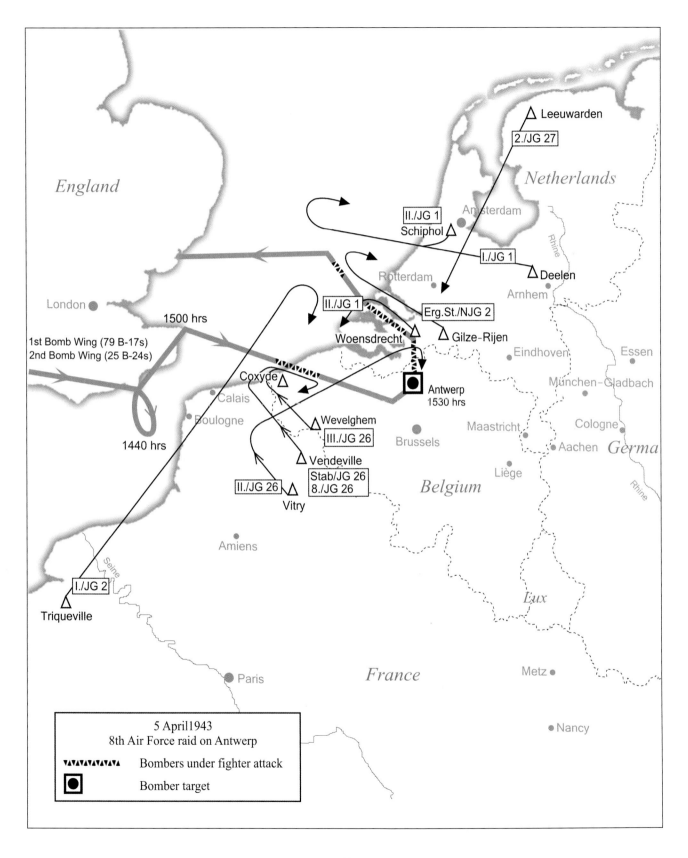

England

Netherlands

Leeuwarden

2./JG 27

II./JG 1
Schiphol

Amsterdam

I./JG 1

Rotterdam

Deelen

Arnhem

London

1500 hrs

II./JG 1

Erg.St./NJG 2

Woensdrecht

Gilze-Rijen

Eindhoven

Essen

1st Bomb Wing (79 B-17s)
2nd Bomb Wing (25 B-24s)

München–Gladbach

Coxyde

Antwerp
1530 hrs

Maastricht

Cologne

Calais

Germa

1440 hrs

Boulogne

Wevelghem

III./JG 26

Brussels

Aachen

Liège

Vendeville

Stab/JG 26
8./JG 26

Belgium

II./JG 26

Vitry

Amiens

Lux

Seine

I./JG 2

Triqueville

France

Metz

Paris

Nancy

5 April1943
8th Air Force raid on Antwerp

▼▲▼▲▼▲▼▲▼▲▼▲   Bombers under fighter attack

◉   Bomber target

PILOT'S ACCOUNT[4]
5 April 1943

[Stammberger's victim was Lt. Seelos's 306th Bomb Group B-17: DC]

At about 1430 hours, a report was received at Vitry that many bombers were assembling over southeastern England. Neither the direction of the attack nor its target could yet be determined. Our Gruppe was called to cockpit readiness; at this command, 30 pilots climbed into their aircraft and made ready to take off. We received running reports over the loudspeakers of the movements of the aircraft, which were now identified as heavy bombers – about one hundred of them. They were still circling while assembling. At 1445 hours, we were sent off into the air, first to wait over Amiens and then over Bethune. The bomber stream took a southeastern course toward Dunkirk, and we were sent to Dunkirk. The heavies had now reached the coast near Ostend and flew in the direction of Ghent–Brussels. We turned and rushed toward Brussels. Past Ghent, the stream suddenly turned east toward Antwerp. We had already been in the air more than a half hour and had used up over half our fuel, as we had been flying at high speed trying to catch up to the bombers.

After about 45 minutes, we saw the bombers far ahead on an easterly course; we were to their north. Now we took out after them at full throttle, climbing at a slight angle in order to be able to storm through the formation from the front. Suddenly, we saw the bomb carpet of the first formation strike on the southern edge of Antwerp, with large explosions and clouds of smoke. We had just reached a good attack position and broke to the right, diving on the first Pulk, which made a left turn away from us. But the Pulk following it was in just the right position for our attack. Just as this formation dropped its bombs, I found a Boeing squarely in my sights. Everything now took place in fractions of a second. The salvo from my four cannon and two machine guns hit squarely in the bomber's cockpit; I had to pull up quickly, as the bomber suddenly tipped forward – the pilot had probably been hit. The aircraft entered a spin to the left. Most of the crew bailed out. The B-17 continued flying, pilotless, for some distance; it finally crashed at about 1535 hours. After my victory, I still had enough fuel for 10 or 15 minutes of flight and returned to base with as many of my companions as were still with me.

Oblt. Otto Stammberger, Staffelkapitän
4./JG 26

Oblt. Otto Stammberger, Kapitän of the 4. Staffel of II./JG 26 until severely wounded by Spitfires on 13 May 1943. (Stammberger)

Luftwaffe defensive activity – 4 April 1943

Unit	Type	Gruppe up			Gruppe down		Claims	Losses				
		Base	No	Time	Base	Time		Dest	Dam	KIA	MIA	WIA
Luftflotte 3												
Jafü 2:												
II./JG 26	Fw 190A	Vitry	*42	1244	Vitry	1354	n/c	0	0	0	0	0
2nd sorties	Fw 190A	Vitry		1410	Vitry	1507	1 B-17, 4 Spitfire	1	1	1	0	0
III./JG 26	Fw 190A	Wevelghem	—	1250	Wevelghem	1311	0	0	0	0	0	0
2nd sorties	Fw 190A	Wevelghem	21	1350	Dieppe, Abbéville, Wevelghem	1505	1 B-17, 2 Spitfire	1	2	0	0	1
4./JG 54	Bf 109G	Wevelghem	8	1244	Wevelghem	~1330	0	0	0	0	0	0
2nd sorties	Bf 109G	Wevelghem	8	1350	Wevelghem	~1500	0	1	1	1	0	0
Jafü 3:												
Stab/JG 2	Fw 190A	Beaumont–le–Roger	5	1349	Beaumont–le–Roger	~1500	1 B-17	0	0	0	0	0
I./JG 2	Fw 190A, Bf 109G	Triqueville	14 **34	1315	Triqueville	~1415	5 Spitfire	1	1	0	1	1
2nd sorties	Fw 190A, Bf 109G	Triqueville	14 ***27	1431	Triqueville	~1500	1 Spitfire	0	0	0	0	0
12./JG 2	Bf 109G	Beaumont–le–Roger	—	~1430	Beaumont–le–Roger	~1500		0	0	0	0	0
I./JG 27	Bf 109G	Bernay	—	1315	Bernay	~1415	1 Spitfire	0	0	0	0	0
JG 105	Fw 190A	Villacoublay–Nord	8	~1400	Villacoublay–Nord	~1500	1 B-17	0	0	0	0	0
JLÜberpr Gr	Fw 190A	Paris region	4	~1400	Paris region	~1500	0	0	0	0	0	0

*42 II., III./JG 26 Fw 190s sortie   **34 I./JG 2, I./JG 27 Bf 109s sortie   ***27 I., 12./JG 2 Bf 109s sortie

Luftwaffe defensive activity – 5 April 1943

Unit	Type	Gruppe up			Gruppe down		Claims	Losses				
		Base	No	Time	Base	Time		Dest	Dam	KIA	MIA	WIA
Lw Bfh Mitte												
Jafü H-Ruhr.												
I./JG 1	Fw 190A	Deelen		1529	Woensdrecht	1632	0	0	0	0	0	0
II./JG 1	Fw 190A	Woensdrecht	10	1540	Woensdrecht	1642	0	1	1	0	0	0
	Fw 190A	Schiphol		1540	Schiphol	1622	0	0	0	0	0	0
2./JG 27	Bf 109G	Leeuwarden		1532	Woensdrecht	1643	n/c	0	0	0	0	0
Erg. St./NJG 2	Bf 110	Gilze–Rijen		1525	Gilze–Rijen	1553	0	0	0	0	0	0
Luftflotte 3												
Jafü 2:												
Stab/JG 26	Fw 190A	Lille–Vendeville		1434	Antwerp	~1545	1 B-17	1	0	0	0	0
II./JG 26	Fw 190A	Vitry	30	1444	Vitry, Antwerp, Vlissingen, Woensdrecht, Lille–Vendeville	1555	2 B-17	0	1	0	0	0
8./JG 26	Fw 190A	Lille–Vendeville		1436	Wevelghem	1545	0	1	1	0	0	1
III./JG 26	Fw 190A	Wevelghem		~1435	Wevelghem	~1545	1 B-17	2	0	1	0	0
Jafü 3:												
I./JG 2	Fw 190A, Bf 109G	Triqueville		1520	Coxyde	1610	3 Spitfire	1	0	0	0	1

16 April

8th Air Force VIII BC Mission #51: 59 of 83 B-17s bomb Lorient U-boat base, TOT 1412-14 – lose 1-0-8, claim 0-4-2; 19 of 29 B-24s bomb Brest U-boat base, TOT 1337-38 – lose 3-1-9, claim 2-3-1. RAF Spitfire escort claims 0-1-0, loses 2.

Today's raid on the Brittany U-boat bases was screened by a RAF raid on Ostend, which drew up II./JG 1 and killed its Kommandeur Major Herbert Kijewski and a member of the Gruppenstab for the loss of one Spitfire. The heavy bombers were escorted part-way by RAF fighters, which engaged part of I./JG 2 north of Brest and lost two Spitfires. III./JG 2 at Vannes and its 8th Staffel, which was now based at Brest, were able to attack the bombers on both the penetration and withdrawal legs, downing four and damaging another beyond repair. A Fw 190 ground attack Staffel, 6./SKG 10, was ordered to drop bombs on the bomber formation, without success. Luftflotte 3 lost two MIA and three Focke-Wulfs on its intercept mission.

17 April

8th Air Force VIII BC Mission #52: 107 of 115 B-17s bomb Bremen aircraft factory, TOT 1259-1303 – lose 16-0-39, claim 63-15-17. No escort.

The largest bomber force yet sent to a single target, 115 B-17s in six combat boxes, took off in the morning to bomb the Bremen Focke-Wulf factory. Their course was due east across the North Sea, out of range of the Luftflotte 3 fighters, which were nonetheless pinned in their area by several RAF diversionary missions. The defence was entirely up to Lw Bfh Mitte's Jafü Deutsche Bucht, which, with the aid of the Bremen Flak, inflicted the worst defeat yet on the American bombers. The Jafü borrowed two units from Jafü Holland-Ruhr – I./JG 1 at Deelen and 2./JG 27, flying from Leeuwarden – and employed all of its own: I./JG 11; II./JG 11; NJG 1; NJG 3; the Focke-Wulf Industrieschwarm; III./JG 54, now based in Germany; and Jagdstaffel Helgoland, which saw its first RLV action today.

The Deutsche Bucht controller kept his fighters on the ground at full alert until the bombers were fully committed to crossing the German coast and timed his interception to disrupt their bomb run. After attacking continuously for nearly an hour, JG 11 filed 13 victory claims, of which five were confirmed as full

victories and three as Herausschüsse, a new category for aircraft seen to drop from formation due to combat damage. These are shown in the tables as HSS; a useful English synonym is 'culls'. Every German formation fed into the battle claimed victories. Only one German pilot was killed; five fighters crashed. The Focke-Wulf factory was severely damaged in one of the most accurate American raids to date, losing 50 per cent of its capacity and 30 burned-out Fw 190s. But this success came at the highest cost to date, sixteen B-17s, 14 per cent of the 115 dispatched. The leading combat wing, comprising three combat boxes with B-17s from two groups, the 91st and the 306th, sustained all of the losses. This wing was hit hard by Flak on the bomb run, loosening the formation and creating tempting targets for the persistent fighters.

I./JG 1 painted black and white stripes on its cowlings when it was redesignated from IV./JG 1 in April 1943. This is the Fw 190A-4 of Lt. Eberhard Burath, the Gruppenadjutant. *(Mombeek)*

Two Fw 190A-4/Ys of 1./JG 1 – ex-10./JG 1 – in April 1943. The IV. Gruppe circle has recently been painted out. *(Mombeek)*

Luftwaffe defensive activity – 16 April 1943

Unit	Type	Gruppe up			Gruppe down		Claims	Losses				
		Base	No	Time	Base	Time		Dest	Dam	KIA	MIA	WIA
Luftflotte 3												
Jafü 3:												
I./JG 2	Fw 190A, Bf 109G	Triqueville		~1300	Triqueville	~1400	0	1	0	0	1	0
Jafü 4:												
1./JG 2	Fw 190A	Vannes		~1300	Vannes	~1430	2 Spitfire	0	0	0	0	0
III./JG 2	Fw 190A	Vannes		~1300	Vannes	~1430	4 B-17	1	0	0	0	0
2nd sorties	Fw 190A	Vannes		~1500	Vannes	~1530	0	0	0	0	0	0
8./JG 2	Fw 190A	Brest–Nord		1315	Brest-Nord	1407	3 B-24	0	0	0	0	0
2nd sorties	Fw 190A	Brest–Nord		1438	Brest-Nord	1533	1 B-17	1	0	0	1	0
6./SKG 10	Fw 190A	Rennes–St. Jacques	11	~1330	Rennes–St. Jacques	~1430	0	0	0	0	0	0

Luftwaffe defensive activity – 17 April 1943

Unit	Type	Gruppe up			Gruppe down		Claims	Losses				
		Base	No	Time	Base	Time		Dest	Dam	KIA	MIA	WIA
Lw Bfh Mitte												
Jafü Deutsche Bucht:												
I./JG 11	Fw 190A	Husum		1230	Vechta, Marx, Zwischenahn	1335	3 B-17	1	3	0	0	0
II./JG 11	Bf 109G	Jever		1231	Jever	1332	2 B-17, 3 B-17 HSS	0	0	0	0	0
III./JG 54	Bf 109G	Oldenburg		1229	Oldenburg, Ahlhorn	1335	4 B-17	1	4	0	0	0
JaSta Helgoland	Bf 109T	Helgoland–Düne	4	1315	Helgoland–Düne	~1415	1 B-17	1	0	0	0	0
I./NJG 3	Bf 110	Grove, Vechta		1237	Grove, Vechta	~1400	1 B-17	1	0	0	0	0
II./NJG 3	Bf 110	Schleswig		1245	Schleswig	~1400	0	0	0	0	0	0
III./NJG 3	Bf 110	Stade		1250	Stade	~1400	0	0	0	0	0	0
ISS Focke-Wulf	Fw 190A	Hannover–Langenhagen	3	1243	Jever	~1345	0	0	0	0	0	0
Jafü H. Ruhr:												
I./JG 1	Fw 190A	Deelen		1220	Twente	~1330	2 B-17	1	1	1	0	0
2./JG 27	Bf 109G	Leeuwarden		1239	Wittmundhafen	1340	1 B-17	0	0	0	0	0
IV./NJG 1	Bf 110	Leeuwarden		~1245	Leeuwarden	~1415	2 B-17	0	0	0	0	0

May 1943

Lw Bfh Mitte continued its slow expansion. The new III./JG 1 was moved to Leeuwarden as a 'far-forward' defender of the Bight and the German interior. I./JG 3 completed its retraining and moved to München–Gladbach, where it joined Jagddivision 5, which was not yet under attack by day. This Gruppe was among the first to receive Bf 109G-6/R6s with *Gondeln*, underwing tubs each containing a single MG 151/20 machine cannon. The JG 3 Stab left Russia for München–Gladbach and Reich defence duty, but did not receive any aircraft until October. The new III./JG 11 was established at Neumünster, but did not become operational until June. The 23rd brought a powerful reinforcement for the Reich defenders when III./JG 26 left its familiar surroundings on the Channel Front and joined Jagddivision 2 at Cuxhaven–Nordholz. The new underwing cannon enhanced the effectiveness of the Lw Bfh Mitte fighters as bomber destroyers. WGr 21 rockets promised an even greater impact; Hptm. Eduard Tratt, the commander of an

ErprKdo 25 detachment, scored his first success on the 21st. Later in 1943, this powerful rocket would become the weapon of choice for breaking up the bomber boxes.

The African campaign concluded with an Allied victory, and the Americans again gave the 8th Air Force top priority for reinforcements. New heavy bomber groups began arriving in England at an ever-increasing rate. The losses of the VIII BC were also increasing, however: they averaged 7 per cent per mission when not escorted, although only 1.6 per cent when escorted. The VIII FC was sweeping the French coast at high altitude almost every day in its new P-47s, but had to date claimed only 15 Luftwaffe fighters shot down, 11 of these on short-range escort missions. The P-47s still had no auxiliary fuel tanks; incredibly, these were only in fourth place on the 8th Air Force's priority list of needed supplies. There was an evident disconnect between the men actually flying combat missions and the top 8th Air Force commanders who obviously still believed in the 'self-defending' bomber. The errors of the Luftwaffe High Command are well documented; American errors are less frequently acknowledged. Their commanders' willful blindness to the need for escort persisted for far too long and could well have cost the Allies the strategic daylight air campaign.

1 May

8th Air Force VIII BC Mission #53: 29 of 78 B-17s bomb St. Nazaire U-boat base, TOT 1125-31 – lose 7-2-20, claim 18-6-8. RAF FC Spitfire escorts report no encounters.

Today's battles took place far to the west as the VIII BC once again targeted the St. Nazaire submarine pens. The new Jafü Bretagne (Brittany) held off its fighters until the escorting Spitfires had turned back and then unleashed them. III./JG 2 flew two missions and claimed six of the 78 B-17s dispatched, aided by the Flak. I./JG 2 and the recce unit NaGr. 13 reached the withdrawing bombers; each of these units claimed one. Nine B-17s were lost or written off on the mission; Luftflotte 3 losses totalled one KIA and three aircraft.

Below left: Major Eduard Tratt. After recovering from serious injuries received on the Eastern Front, Tratt joined Erprobungskommando 25 in 1943, testing rockets for use against heavy bomber formations. When the Zerstörer force was rebuilt for RLV duties in late 1943, Tratt became Kommandeur of II./ZG 26, flying Me 410s. He and his air gunner were shot down and killed by American escort fighters on 22 February 1944. Tratt was the highest scoring Zerstörer pilot of the war, with 38 victories in more than 350 missions. *(Author's collection)*

Below right: In June, Hptm. Tratt brought a small detachment of men to I./JG 1 to test WGr 21 aerial mortars under operational conditions. Here is a Fw 190A-5 with a mortar rocket in its underwing tube. *(Mombeek)*

4 May

8th Air Force VIII BC Mission #54: 65 of 79 B-17s bomb Antwerp industrial area, TOT 1839-43 – lose 0, claim 0; 117 VIII FC P 47 escorts (3 FGs) report 0 claims, 1 loss. RAF Spitfire escorts claim 1-1-4, lose 3.

Seventy-nine B-17s of the VIII BC attacked Antwerp industrial targets in late afternoon. After American feints in the Channel drew the Jafü 3 fighters up prematurely, Jafü 2 scrambled 59 JG 26 fighters to defend Antwerp. Major Priller led the JG 26 Geschwadergruppe up from Vendeville, formed up with II./JG 26 from Vitry and III./JG 26 from Wevelghem and headed east, sighting the Allied formation near Vlissingen. The close escort Spitfire wings were well positioned and succeeded in keeping the fighters away from the bombers until the formation was back over the Scheldt Estuary. II./JG 1 arrived from Woensdrecht, but had apparently been given too low an altitude by the controller. They were pounced on by the Spitfires and had to dive away. The Germans lost no fighters in this engagement, while claiming five Spitfires, only one of which was apparently confirmed, and one B-17, which was not confirmed. The Erla factory defence Schwarm claimed one Spitfire for the loss of one Messerschmitt, but did not reach the bombers. Three Spitfires and one P-47 were in fact lost, but this was a definite victory for the RAF escorts.

13 May

8th Air Force VIII BC Mission #55: 88 of 97 B-17s bomb Méaulte airfield, TOT 1628-30 – lose 3-0-11, claim 11-3-1. RAF Spitfire escorts claim 4-3-7, lose 5. 31 of 72 B-17s bomb St. Omer–Longuenesse airfield, TOT 1637-38 – claim 0, lose 1-1-0; 124 VIII FC P 47 escorts (3 FGs) claim 0, lose 0.

In mid-afternoon, the four B-17 groups of the VIII BC's 1st Bomb Wing (1st BW) made the day's major attack, on the Potez repair facility at Méaulte. The four B-17 groups of the new 4th BW provided the principal diversion by bombing St. Omer, covered by the three P-47 groups. JG 26 rose from all three of its airfields. II./JG 2, which had returned from Tunisia and converted to Bf 109s, and I./JG 2 were also scrambled. The 4th BW attack was ignored by the Jafü, which kept close watch on the larger 1st BW formation as it reversed course several times over the Channel. When it finally turned for France, JG 26 and the low-strength I./JG 27 were able to attack it before the Spitfires,

which were again too high, could intervene. The first attack came as the leading group crossed the French coast, and frontal attacks continued until the formation reached the coast on its way back to England. Two B-17s were shot down by the fighters, one B-17 was lost to Flak, and 11 others were hit by fighters and/or Flak – one was severely damaged by a bomb dropped by a II./JG 26 Fw 190, but reached its home base. The Spitfire escorts claimed 4-3-7 fighters, while losing five of their own. The Germans lost five pilots and nine aircraft in combat. The newly arrived II./JG 2 was especially hard hit, losing four of the pilots and writing off five new Messerschmitts.

COMBAT REPORT[5]
13 May 1943

One P-47 destroyed from 3,000 metres at 1635 hours, PQ 1139/05 East

I scrambled at 1606 hours as 12./JG 2 Staffelführer in a Bf 109G-6 'gunboat' with three MG 151/20 cannon and two MG 131 machine guns. At 1620 hours, I contacted 60–80 B-17s and more than 120 escorts flying at 6,000–8,000 metres in map quadrant 118/05 East. In the course of the resulting air battle, I made a rear attack on a Thunderbolt from above at 3,000 metres. I fired a burst from 100–150 metres distance and immediately observed flames and a white plume from the right wing. The Thunderbolt dove straight down, smoking and burning heavily. My element leader observed its crash in the sea. I saw no parachute. Landing followed at 1710 hours.
[Note: The Thunderbolt was described as 'English, with cocardes' and was apparently a Spitfire: DC]

Lt. Georg-Peter Eder, Staffelführer
12./JG 2

14 May

8th Air Force VIII BC Mission #56: 109 of 115 1st BW B-17s bomb Kiel shipyard, TOT 1200-03 – lose 3-0-27, claim 41-11-26; 17 of 21 B-24s bomb Kiel shipyard, TOT 1200-03 – lose 5-1-9, claim 21-13-1; 72 of 81 4th BW B-17s (new) bomb Antwerp industrial area and Wevelghem airfield, TOT 1320 – lose 3-0-25, claim 5-1-5. 118 VIII FC P-47 escorts (Antwerp) claim 5-3-8, lose 3; RAF Spitfire escorts (Antwerp and Courtrai) claim 8-1-5, lose 1.

The VIII BC attacked three separate targets with its small heavy bomber force. The experienced 1st BW and one B-24 group made a successful attack on the Kiel shipyards, writing off nine bombers to fighters and Flak. The Jafü Deutsche Bucht interceptors flew 114 sorties. Of this force, III./JG 54 was hardest hit, losing four Bf 109s and two pilots; a third pilot lost an eye. Losses totalled three KIA, three WIA and six fighters.

JG 26 and JG 1 were directed to attack the new 4th BW, which sent two groups against each of two targets, the automotive plants in Antwerp and the Wevelghem base of III./JG 26. The bomb groups assigned to take out Wevelghem did an effective job, killing and wounding a number of ground personnel and pilots, destroying and damaging aircraft, and carpeting the landing ground with craters. For the first time, a JG 26 airfield was left unserviceable by an air raid; III./JG 26 and 12./JG 54, a new Staffel that was soon to be redesignated 12./JG 26, were forced to move to the small Lille–Nord field. Three B-17s, three P-47s and one Spitfire were lost. German fighter losses to the gunners in the new B-17 groups were unusually high. The bombers and escorts shot down 10 fighters and damaged at least seven more, killing three pilots and wounding five.

PILOT'S ACCOUNT[6]
14 May 1943

I was returning in the morning from an unsuccessful mission against intruding bombers. As I approached the field at Vlissingen, on the Scheldt Estuary, I spotted an outbound B-17 over the coast, about 8–10 km away and at a favorable altitude. It was coming right at me. Although I was flying on empty, I took up a pursuit curve. I could not tell if it was in trouble. After my approach I attacked it from about 800 metres altitude from behind and below and just to the left. A thin flame shot from the left wing tanks. At the same time something hit my cockpit. Trash whirled around, and I tasted gunpowder on my tongue. Convinced that there was an enemy fighter behind me, I broke around brutally. But nothing – only an Fw 190 from another Geschwader appeared suddenly on my left rear; it bore markings that were unknown to me. Its large radial engine was encircled in black and white checks [and thus belonged to I./JG 1: DC]. So I must have been hit by defensive fire. But where? After

a last glance at the Boeing, which was descending in a steep left bank, trailing flames, I made my way back to Vlissingen without delay. I could not tell where I had been hit. During the landing attempt it became apparent that the entire electrical system had gone out. It was good that at least the landing gear could be extended mechanically, but I had to do without the flaps and trim tabs. It was a tight fit, anyway; the landing ground was damned short.

The search for the damaging hit brought a surprise. Expecting a dollar-size hole, I discovered in the right side of the fuselage an entrance hole about 10 mm across. The shell had then turned at an acute angle and tore up the cable harness behind the instrument bank on the right side of the cockpit when it exploded. A hands-width higher and the shell would have hit me in the abdomen, probably ending my life. A matter of luck!

Fw. Peter Crump
5./JG 26

15 May
8th Air Force VIII BC Mission #57: 76 of 113 B-17s bomb Helgoland, other targets of opportunity, TOT 1050-55 – lose 5-1-26, claim 29-20-30; 59 of 80 B-17s bomb Emden industrial area, TOT 1056-1103 – lose 1-0-9, claim 14-3-1. No escort.

The Americans attempted a full strength B-17 raid on Emden, but most bombers dropped on targets of opportunity. Jafü Deutsche Bucht got up all of its fighters (some on two missions, but totalling only 102 sorties) and intercepted successfully for the loss of four Bf 109s and three pilots, all from III./JG 54. Its unfortunate Gruppenkommandeur was sent back to the Russian Front; his replacement was Hptm. Siegfried Schnell, an experienced leader from the Channel front. Jafü Holland-Ruhr sent I./JG 1 out to sea after the withdrawing bombers, but Jafü 2 and Jafü 3 were kept busy all day chasing (or avoiding) sweeps by Spitfires and P-47s and raids by RAF light bombers – a pattern that would become the norm and that does not need to be coverered in detail in this study. The Americans lost or scrapped seven B-17s after this raid. The Germans lost the three III./JG 54 pilots and one Bf 110 crew KIA or MIA, two WIA and a total of six aircraft.

17 May

8th Air Force VIII BC Mission #58: 118 of 159 B-17s bomb Lorient U-boat base, TOT 1213-17 – lose 6-1-27, claim 47-8-29; 34 of 39 B-24s bomb Bordeaux U-boat base, TOT 1238-44 – lose 1-0-1, claim 0-1-0. RAF Spitfire penetration escort claims 2-0-1, loses 0.

The VIII BC returned to the U-boat campaign. The B-17s bombed the Lorient U-boat base, while the B-24s went to Bordeaux. JG 2 was again operating at full strength from western France. Jafü 3 and Jafü 4 scrambled 59 fighters from all three Gruppen against the Lorient raiders. III./JG 2 made a successful interception from Vannes, claiming nine B-17s, and was joined by I./JG 2 flying a second mission. II./SKG 10 was ordered to drop bombs on the bomber formation, losing one Fw 190 and pilot without success. Bordeaux was defended by only 10 fighters from JGr West, which had no success. The RAF kept much of Jafü 3 busy with Rodeos (fighter sweeps) along the western Channel coast. Jafü 2 held its fighters back. The Americans wrote off eight heavy bombers; the Germans lost six aircraft and three pilots.

The Bf 109G-6/R6 of Hptm. Hans-Ekkehard Bob, Kapitän of the 9. Staffel of III./JG 54, photographed at Oldenburg in June. Worth noting are the Third Gruppe wave and a yellow rudder with 56 red victory bars. (Bob)

Luftwaffe defensive activity – 1 May 1943

Unit	Type	Gruppe up			Gruppe down		Claims	Losses				
		Base	No	Time	Base	Time		Dest	Dam	KIA	MIA	WIA
Luftflotte 3												
Jafü 4:												
I./JG 2	Fw 190A, Bf 109G	Vannes		1018	Vannes	1143	0	0	0	0	0	0
2nd sorties	Fw 190A, Bf 109G	Vannes		1422	St. Brieuc	1508	1 B-17	0	0	0	0	0
III./JG 2	Fw 190A	Vannes		~1100	Vannes	~1200	2 B-17, 1 B-17 HSS	1	1	0	0	0
2nd sorties	Fw 190A	Vannes		~1430	Vannes	~1530	0	0	0	0	0	0
8./JG 2	Fw 190A	Brest–Nord		1133	Brest–Nord	1237	0	0	0	0	0	0
2nd sorties	Fw 190A	Brest–Nord		1346	Brest–Nord	1418	4 B-17	2	0	1	0	0
2./NaGr 13	Bf 109	St. Brieuc		~1430	St. Brieuc	~1530	1 B-17	0	0	0	0	0
II./SKG 10	Fw 190	Rennes–St. Jacques	7	~1100	Rennes–St. Jacques	~1200	0	0	0	0	0	0

Luftwaffe defensive activity – 4 May 1943

Unit	Type	Gruppe up			Gruppe down		Claims	Losses				
		Base	No	Time	Base	Time		Dest	Dam	KIA	MIA	WIA
Lw Bfh Mitte												
Jafü H-Ruhr:												
II./JG 1	Fw 190A	Woensdrecht	17	1844	Woensdrecht	1951	0	0	0	0	0	0
2./JG 27	Bf 109G	Schiphol		1840	Schiphol	1948	n/c	1	0	0	0	1
ISS Erla	Bf 109F	Antwerp	3	1830	Antwerp	1930	1 Spitfire	1	0	0	0	0
Luftflotte 3												
Jafü 2:												
Stab/JG 26	Fw 190A	Lille–Vendeville	*35	1820	Lille–Vendeville	1918	1 Spitfire	0	0	0	0	0
6./JG 26	Fw 190A	Lille–Vendeville	—	1822	Lille–Vendeville	1920	0	0	0	0	0	0
8./JG 26	Fw 190A	Lille–Vendeville	—	1820	Lille–Vendeville	1918	0	0	0	0	0	0
II./JG 26	Fw 190A	Vitry, Ligescourt	21	1710	Vitry, Ligescourt	1730	0	0	0	0	0	0
2nd sorties	Fw 190A	Vitry, Ligescourt	—	1816	Vitry, Ligescourt, Lille–Vendeville	1915	0	0	0	0	0	0
III./JG 26	Fw 190A	Wevelghem	—	1812	Wevelghem	~1920	0	0	0	0	0	0
11./JG 54	Bf 109G	Wevelghem	**24	1812	Wevelghem	~1920	0	0	0	0	0	0
12./JG 54	Bf 109G	Wevelghem	—	1812	Wevelghem	~1920	0	0	0	0	0	0
Jafü 3:												
12./JG 2	Bf 109G	Beaumont–le–Roger	***42	1712	Beaumont–le–Roger	~1730	n/c	0	0	0	0	0
2nd sorties	Bf 109G	Beaumont–le–Roger	****33	1712	Beaumont–le–Roger	~1730	n/c	0	0	0	0	0
I./JG 27	Bf 109G	Poix	—	1702	Poix	~1730	n/c	0	0	0	0	0
2nd sorties	Bf 109G	Poix	—	1702	Poix	~1730	n/c	0	0	0	0	0

*35 total Fw 190s sortie (JG 26)   **24 total Bf 109s sortie (JG 54)   ***42 total Bf 109s sortie (12./JG 2 and I./JG 27)   ****33 total Bf 109s sortie (12./JG 2 and I./JG 27)

Luftwaffe defensive activity – 13 May 1943

Unit	Type	Gruppe up			Gruppe down		Claims	Losses				
		Base	No	Time	Base	Time		Dest	Dam	KIA	MIA	WIA
Luftflotte 3												
Jafü 2:												
Stab/JG 26	Fw 190A	Lille–Vendeville		1600	Lille–Vendeville	1705	1 Spitfire, 1 B-17	0	0	0	0	0
6./JG 26	Fw 190A	Lille–Vendeville		1601	Merville	1700	1 Spitfire	1	0	1	0	0
8./JG 26	Fw 190A	Lille–Vendeville		~1600	Lille–Vendeville	~1700	0	0	0	0	0	0
II./JG 26	Fw 190A	Vitry		1604	Vitry, Abbéville	1714	1 B-17	1	0	0	0	1
III./JG 26	Fw 190A	Wevelghem		1603	Wevelghem	1713	1 Spitfire	0	0	0	0	0
11./JG 54	Bf 109G	Wevelghem		1603	Wevelghem	1713	0	1	0	0	0	0
12./JG 54	Bf 109G	Wevelghem		1603	Wevelghem	1713	0	0	0	0	0	0
Jafü 3:												
I./JG 2	Fw 190A, Bf 109G	Triqueville		~1605	Triqueville	~1710	0	1	1	0	0	0
II./JG 2	Bf 109G	Beaumont–le–Roger		1606	Beaumont–le–Roger	1711	0	2	0	0	2	0
12./JG 2	Bf 109G	Beaumont–le–Roger		1606	Beaumont–le–Roger	1711	1 Spitfire, 1 P-47	3	0	1	1	0
I./JG 27	Bf 109G	Poix		1602	Poix	~1700	3 B-17	1	0	0	0	0

Luftwaffe defensive activity vs. Kiel raid – 14 May 1943

Unit	Type	Gruppe up			Gruppe down		Claims	Losses				
		Base	No	Time	Base	Time		Dest	Dam	KIA	MIA	WIA
Lw Bfh Mitte												
Jafü Deutsche Bucht:												
Stab/JG 11	Bf 109G	Husum	4	1130	Husum	1230	0	0	0	0	0	0
I./JG 11	Fw 190A	Husum	17	1150	Husum	1230	1 B-17	1	1	1	0	0
II./JG 11	Bf 109G	Jever		1001	Jever	1143	3 B-24	1	1	0	0	1
III./JG 54	Bf 109G	Oldenburg		1129	Oldenburg, Husum	1252	3 B-24	4	1	2	0	2
JaSta Helgoland	Bf 109T	Helgoland–Düne		1139	Helgoland–Düne	1248	0	0	0	0	0	0
II./NJG 3	Bf 110	Schleswig		~1145	Schleswig	~1300	1 B-17	0	0	0	0	0

Luftwaffe defensive activity vs. raids on Belgium – 14 May 1943

Unit	Type	Gruppe up			Gruppe down		Claims	Losses				
		Base	No	Time	Base	Time		Dest	Dam	KIA	MIA	WIA
Lw Bfh Mitte												
Jafü H-Ruhr:												
I./JG 1	Fw 190A	Deelen		~1250	Deelen	~1350	0	2	1	1	0	0
II./JG 1	Fw 190A	Woensdrecht	29	1251	Woensdrecht	1405	1 B-17	1	2	0	0	1
Luftflotte 3												
Jafü 2:												
Stab/JG 26	Fw 190A	Lille–Vendeville		1214	Lille–Vendeville	1259	0	0	0	0	0	0
6./JG 26	Fw 190A	Lille–Vendeville		1214	Lille–Vendeville	1259	1 B-17	1	0	0	0	1
8./JG 26	Fw 190A	Lille–Vendeville		1214	Lille–Vendeville	1259	0	2	0	0	0	2
II./JG 26	Fw 190A	Vitry		1250	Vitry, Woensdrecht	1350	2 B-17, 1 P-47, 1 Spitfire	2	2	2	0	0
III./JG 26	Fw 190A	Wevelghem		1215	Wevelghem	~1300	1 Spitfire	1	1	0	0	1
12./JG 54	Bf 109G	Wevelghem		1215	Wevelghem	~1300	0	1	1	0	0	0

Luftwaffe defensive activity – 15 May 1943

Unit	Type	Gruppe up			Gruppe down		Claims	Losses				
		Base	No	Time	Base	Time		Dest	Dam	KIA	MIA	WIA
Lw Bfh Mitte												
Jafü Deutsche Bucht:												
Stab/JG 11	Bf 109G	Jever	4	~0945	Jever	~1100	0	0	0	0	0	0
I./JG 11	Fw 190A	Husum	16	1008	Stade, Jever, Husum	1120	2 B-17	0	0	0	0	0
	Fw 190A	Husum		1048	Stade, Husum	1130	0	0	0	0	0	0
II./JG 11	Bf 109G	Jever		0948	Jever	1109	4 B-17	0	0	0	0	0
III./JG 54	Bf 109G	Oldenburg		1005	Oldenburg, Nordholz	1103	3 B-17	4	0	1	2	0
JaSta Helgoland	Bf 109T	Helgoland–Düne		1021	Wangerooge	1127	0	0	0	0	0	0
III./NJG 3	Bf 110	Schleswig		~1000	Schleswig	~1130	0	1	1	0	2	0
Jafü H-Ruhr:												
I./JG 1	Fw 190A	Deelen		1048	Deelen	~1215	3 B-17	1	1	0	0	2

Luftwaffe defensive activity – 17 May 1943

Unit	Type	Gruppe up			Gruppe down		Claims	Losses				
		Base	No	Time	Base	Time		Dest	Dam	KIA	MIA	WIA
Luftflotte 3												
Jafü 3:												
I./JG 2	Fw 190A, Bf 109G	Triqueville		~1030	Triqueville	~1115	1 Spitfire, 1 Typhoon	0	0	0	0	0
II./JG 2	Bf 109G	Beaumont–le–Roger		~1030	Beaumont–le–Roger	~1200	1 Spitfire	0	1	0	0	0
2nd sorties	Bf 109G	Beaumont–le–Roger		~1230	Beaumont–le–Roger	~1300	1 Spitfire	3	0	0	2	1
Jafü 4:												
I./JG 2	Fw 190A	Vannes		1123	Vannes	1243	2 B-17	1	0	0	0	1
III./JG 2	Fw 190A	Vannes		~1145	Vannes	~1300	9 B-17	1	0	0	0	1
II./SKG 10	Fw 190A	Rennes–St. Jacques	10	~1125	Rennes–St. Jacques	~1245	0	1	0	1	0	0
5./BFGr 196	Fw 190A	Brest–Hourtin		~1125	Brest–Hourtin	~1245	0	0	0	0	0	0
JGr West	Bf 109	Cazaux	10	~1200	Cazaux	~1300	0	0	0	0	0	0

19 May

8th Air Force VIII BC Mission #59: 103 of 123 1st BW B-17s bomb Kiel U-boat yard, TOT 1329-33 – lose 6-0-28, claim 48-7-21; 55 of 64 4th BW B-17s bomb Flensburg U-boat yard, TOT 1325-28 – lose 0-0-9, claim 12-4-14. No escort.

Today's raid on north German U-boat yards was met by the full strength of Jafü Deutsche Bucht. The 87 defenders shot down six B-17s after a series of attacks that saw twice that many claims confirmed – the lightly armed Bf 109Gs that dominated the north German defences had great difficulty in forcing the rugged B-17s to crash. Once again, III./JG 54 sustained all of the Luftwaffe's day fighter losses; two Gruppe Bf 109s were shot down with serious injuries to their pilots.

21 May

8th Air Force VIII BC Mission #60: 77 of 98 1st BW B-17s bomb Wilhelmshaven U-boat yard, TOT 1244-45 – lose 7-0-24, claim 47-5-17; 46 of 63 4th BW B-17s bomb Emden U-boat yard, TOT 1244-46 – lose 5-2-9, claim 31-6-6. No escort.

The VIII BC continued its campaign against the U-boats with a raid on two north German shipyards. Jafü Deutsche Bucht sent up all of its day units, including a detachment from Erprobungskommando 25, the experimental unit tasked with developing new air-to-air weapons, which was credited with bringing down a B-17 with rockets. The other Deutsche Bucht units were credited with 11 B-17s. Jafü Holland-Ruhr was able to

help out today, possibly due to a bomber route that was farther to the south than usual. I./JG 1 attempted but failed to reach the incoming stream, but flew a second mission against the withdrawing bombers and downed one. 2./JG 27 reached the Emden bombers near the target and claimed three. The German defenders lost five fighters today; 10 more sustained reportable damage, several in dry-fuel tank forced landings. Americans losses totalled 14 destroyed or scrapped bombers out of 123 effective sorties, for a ruinous 11.4 per cent loss rate.

29 May

8th Air Force VIII BC Mission #61: 147 of 169 1st BW B-17s bomb St. Nazaire U boat base, TOT 1706-11 – lose 8-1-58, claim 6-0-1; 57 of 72 4th BW B-17s bomb Rennes U boat base, TOT 1601-05 – lose 6-1-30, claim 19-5-14; 34 of 38 2nd BW B-24s bomb La Pallice U boat base – no losses or claims. RAF FC Spitfire escorts report no encounters.

The VIII BC attacked the Brittany U-boat bases at Rennes, La Pallice and Lorient. Jafü 3 and Jafü 4 employed every JG 2 fighter. No assistance was requested of Jafü 2, and JG 26 stayed on the ground, although I./JG 27 made a brief, unsuccessful sortie. The airborne defenders did not close in until the RAF escorts turned back and then attacked in waves for almost two hours. Most flew two missions. The prolonged, vicious combat resulted in many duplicate claims; 19 B-17 shootdowns and three Herausschüsse were confirmed for the loss of four pilots and seven fighters. True American losses were bad enough: 16 B-17s were lost or scrapped.

Luftwaffe defensive activity – 19 May 1943

Unit	Type	Gruppe up			Gruppe down		Claims	Losses				
		Base	No	Time	Base	Time		Dest	Dam	KIA	MIA	WIA
Lw Bfh Mitte												
Jafü Deutsche Bucht:												
Stab/JG 11	Bf 109G	Jever		1243	Jever	~1345	1 B-17	0	0	0	0	0
I./JG 11	Fw 190A	Husum	20	1243	Husum	1334	0	0	0	0	0	0
II./JG 11	Bf 109G	Jever		1244	Jever, Husum	1351	5 B-17	0	0	0	0	0
III./JG 54	Bf 109G	Oldenburg		1243	Oldenburg, Husum	1350	2 B-17	0	0	0	0	0
2nd sorties	Bf 109G	Husum		~1430	Oldenburg	~1530	1 B-17	2	1	0	0	2
JaSta Helgoland	Bf 109T	Helgoland–Düne		1302	Helgoland–Düne, Wangerooge	1403	3 B-17	0	0	0	0	0
II./NJG 3	Bf 110	Schleswig	4	1310	Schleswig	~1430	0	0	0	0	0	0
III./NJG 3	Bf 110	Stade	4	~1300	Stade	~1430	1 B-17	0	0	0	0	0
Jafü H-Ruhr:												
I./JG 1	Fw 190A	Deelen		1018	Gilze–Rijen	1039	transfer	0	0	0	0	0
	Fw 190A	Gilze–Rijen		1144	Gilze–Rijen	1245	0	0	0	0	0	0

Luftwaffe defensive activity – 21 May 1943

Unit	Type	Gruppe up			Gruppe down		Claims	Losses				
		Base	No	Time	Base	Time		Dest	Dam	KIA	MIA	WIA
Lw Bfh Mitte												
Jafü Deutsche Bucht:												
Stab/JG 11	Bf 109G	Jever		1220	Jever	1320	1 B-17	0	0	0	0	0
I./JG 11	Fw 190A	Husum	19	1220	Husum	1318	2 B-17	1	0	0	0	0
II./JG 11	Bf 109G	Jever		1220	Jever, Husum	1351	4 B-17	3	1	0	1	1
III./JG 54	Bf 109G	Oldenburg		1220	Oldenburg	1324	4 B-17	0	4	0	0	1
JaSta Helgoland	Bf 109T	Helgoland–Düne		1134	Helgoland–Düne, Langeoog	1402	0	0	0	0	0	0
ErprKdo 25	Bf 109F, Bf 110G	Wittmundhafen		1230	Wittmundhafen	~1330	1 B-17	0	0	0	0	0
II./NJG 5	Bf 110	Greifswald		1316	Greifswald	1347	n/c	0	0	0	0	0
Jafü H-Ruhr:												
I./JG 1	Fw 190A	Deelen		1029	Schiphol	1113	n/c	0	0	0	0	0
2nd sorties	Fw 190A	Schiphol		1221	Leeuwarden	1330	1 B-17	1	1	1	0	1
II./JG 1	Fw 190A	Woensdrecht	23	~1220	Woensdrecht	~1330	n/c	0	1	0	0	0
2./JG 27	Bf 109G	Leeuwarden	9	1200	Leeuwarden	1300	3 B-17	°0	4	0	0	1

Luftwaffe defensive activity – 29 May 1943

Unit	Type	Gruppe up			Gruppe down		Claims	Losses				
		Base	No	Time	Base	Time		Dest	Dam	KIA	MIA	WIA
Luftflotte 3												
Jafü 2:												
I./JG 27	Bf 109G	Poix		1507	Poix	1531	n/c	0	0	0	0	0
Jafü 3:												
Stab/JG 2	Fw 190A	Beaumont-le-Roger		~1645	Vannes	~1800	1 B-17	0	0	0	0	0
2./JG 2	Fw 190A	Triqueville		1506	Dinard	1630	2 B-17	2	0	0	1	1
2nd sorties	Fw 190A	Dinard		1735	Dinard	1820	1 B-17	0	0	0	0	0
II./JG 2	Bf 109G	Beaumont-le-Roger		1526	Dinan	~1630	0	0	0	0	0	0
2nd sorties	Bf 109G	Dinan		~1700	Beaumont-le-Roger	~1830	3 B-17	0	1	0	0	0
Jafü 4:												
I./JG 2	Fw 190A, Bf 109G	Vannes		1544	Vannes	1655	2 B-17	2	3	1	0	0
2nd sorties	Fw 190A, Bf 109G	Vannes		1729	Vannes	1805	1 B-17	0	0	0	0	0
III./JG 2	Fw 190A	Vannes		~1530	Vannes	~1645	11 B-17	3	2	2	0	1
2nd sorties	Fw 190A	Vannes		~1700	Vannes	~1800	4 B-17	0	0	0	0	0

June 1943

Several new fighter units were formed in the Reich in June, but none had an immediate impact on day operations. The only conventional day fighter unit

Oberst Herbert Ihlefeld. After transferring from the Eastern Front to the RLV force in mid-1943, Ihlefeld commanded in succession JG 25, JG 11 and JG 1, holding the latter position from May 1944 to the end of the war. *(Author's collection)*

among these was IV./JG 3, which began forming at Neubiberg at the start of the month. JG 3 was being given a fourth Gruppe, outside the normal table of organisation. Although documentation is lacking, it is possible that the intent was to make an enlarged JG 3 the core of a defence force for the Reich interior. However, when IV./JG 3 became operational, it was sent to Italy. Two minor units, JG 25 and JG 50, were formed on stripped-down Bf 109s, with the task of bringing down RAF Mosquitoes, whose reconaissance and special-operations missions over the Reich at all hours were a personal affront to Göring. The units were commanded by two famous Eastern Front Experten, Obstlt. Herbert Ihlefeld and Major Hermann Graf, and received much publicity, but failed in their role and, in the third quarter, were added to the conventional RLV order of battle.

The last new fighter Geschwader would ultimately play a prominent role in the day RLV, but in 1943 was only a drain on the day fighters' resources. This was Obstlt. Hajo Herrmann's Jagdgeschwader 300 (JG 300), a night fighter unit flying conventional single-engine fighters which were not controlled from the ground, but located targets with the aid of searchlights and burning cities – the so-called *Wilde Sau* (Wild Sow) technique. Initially successful, their non-combat losses became unacceptably high in the winter of 1943–44, and the Wilde Sau units were turned over to the day

Fw. Josef Kehrle's III./JG 1 Bf 109G-6/R6 on Leeuwarden in June. It carries two unit emblems: one for his Rotte and one for his 8. Staffel. (Mombeek)

RLV force. Their effect on this force in 1943 was entirely negative: at first, JG 300 did not possess its own aircraft, but flew its missions in fighters borrowed from the day units, reducing the operational readiness of the latter for their own tasks.

The Luftflotte 3 day fighter order of battle saw a few changes in June. The Allies had cleared North Africa of the Axis. The site of their next landing was unknown. The Stab and First and Second Staffeln of I./JG 27 were ordered to leave Poix and transfer to Marignane in southern France to help protect that region. 3./JG 27 was alone at Poix for no more than a week when I./JG 26 began arriving on the base from the USSR. Their transfer to the Eastern Front had proved temporary; their experience was badly needed back on their home grounds in the west.

The strength of the VIII BC continued to grow, while that of the VIII FC was still limited to three groups of short-range P-47s. In what proved to be a last gasp of the 'self-defending bomber' concept, 11 YB-40s made their debut on the 22nd. The YB-40 'battle cruiser' was a B-17 modified to carry extra guns, ammunition and armour in place of bombs. The YB-40s could not keep up with standard B-17s once the latter had dropped their bombs, thus becoming good targets themselves for the German interceptors. They did not remain on the front lines for long, but bequeathed their effective nose armament (chin turrets with twin .50" machine guns) to the next standardised model Flying Fortress to come off the assembly lines, the B-17G.

11 June

8th Air Force VIII BC Mission #62: 218 of 252 B-17s bomb Wilhelmshaven U-boat yard, TOT 1525-1800, and Cuxhaven port, TOT ca. 1840 (secondaries) – lose 8-0-62, claim 85-20-24. RAF FC Spitfires escort medium bomber diversion to Gosnay claims 3-0-2, loses 1.

The growing VIII BC directed 10 B-17 groups to Bremen; all bombed secondary targets owing to cloud cover. Luftwaffenbefehlshaber Mitte, which was also growing, met this unescorted force with 218 fighters, primarily Bf 109s. Most Gruppen flew two missions, targeting the approaching and withdrawing streams. Results were mediocre: 15 claims for B-17s were confirmed, against true losses of eight. American bomber gunners claimed the destruction of 85 German fighters, but in fact only four were lost; all four pilots survived.

13 June

8th Air Force VIII BC Mission #63: 122 of 151 1st BW B-17s bomb Bremen, TOT 0950-56, and targets of opportunity – lose 4-0-31, claim 2-2-1; 60 of 76 4th BW B-17s bomb Kiel, TOT 0930-40, and targets of opportunity – lose 22-1-23, claim 39-5-14. No escort.

The VIII BC B-17s targeted Bremen again, but clouds caused the diversion of most bombers to Kiel and targets of opportunity. Results were poor, and the cost was high. The 1st BW saw little opposition and lost only four B-17s; the 4th BW was attacked by an estimated 100 fighters from landfall to the targets and back out to sea and lost or scrapped 23 B-17s, 20 from the 94th and 95th BGs. The wing crossed the coast in an experimental formation that proved to be fatally flawed. Many bombers could not fire directly ahead, which was the direction of most of the German attacks. The Luftwaffenbefehlshaber Mitte fighters, which flew 163 credited sorties, claimed 26 B-17s for the loss of seven fighters and two pilots, one of whom was the III./JG 26 Kommandeur, Hptm. Kurt Ruppert.

22 June – Hüls and Antwerp (see map)

8th Air Force VIII BC Mission #64: 183 of 235 1st + 4th BW B-17s bomb Hüls rubber industry, TOT 0942 – lose 16-0-75, claim 46-21-35; 39 of 42 4th BW B-17s bomb Antwerp industrial area, TOT 0911 – lose 4-1-17, claim 1-2-9. 136 VIII FC P-47 escorts (Antwerp) claim 7-0-0, lose 0; RAF FC Spitfires escorts (Hüls withdrawal) claim 0-2-6, lose 4.

The VIII BC succeeded in sending a mission to the Ruhr. Two hundred and thirty-five B-17s were dispatched to the synthetic rubber plant at Hüls. The bomber route caused the Luftwaffe some initial confusion, but Jafü Holland-Ruhr got up most of its day fighters, including for the first time today I./JG 3, which had been recalled from the Eastern Front. II./JG 1 was up very early to defend Rotterdam against a raid by RAF North American Mitchell bombers and downed two Spitfires; it was reserviced in time to attack the withdrawing Hüls bombers. Jafü Deutsche Bucht scrambled its fighters, but only III./JG 54 flew a successful mission; JG 11 and III./JG 26 proved to be

out of range. The Holland-Ruhr fighters, together with the extensive Ruhr flak belt, shot down 16 B-17s and damaged 75, but could not prevent extensive damage at Hüls. The few formations sent up against the withdrawing bombers included I./JG 26, which downed a Spitfire from the withdrawal escort for its first victory since returning from the Eastern Front. Luftwaffe losses to the experienced 1st BW gunners totalled two KIA, two WIA and nine fighters.

The major Allied diversion was an attack on the Antwerp automobile plants by two new B-17 groups, the 381st and 384th. The target was chosen specifically to keep JG 26 away from the main force. That plan worked successfully, even though the new B-17 units were 30 minutes late owing to difficulty in forming up. The three American P-47 groups were even later, due to confusing orders, and did not meet the bombers until they reached Walcheren on their return flight. The two airborne JG 26 formations, II./JG 26 and the JG 26 Geschwadergruppe (the Stabsschwarm, 6./JG 26 and 8./JG 26), made several co-ordinated attacks before the Thunderbolts arrived. The two B-17 groups lost four B-17s over the Continent and into the sea, and a fifth that crashed in England. Major Priller was able to lead his force in a quick second mission against the withdrawing Hüls B-17s and claimed another Flying Fortress before being tied up by the P-47s. JG 26 lost two Focke-Wulfs and three injured pilots, most on this second mission.

A II./JG 26 pilot sits forlornly by his obviously unready Fw 190A-4, ignored by the lunching groundcrewmen. *(Bundesarchiv 377-2814-22)*

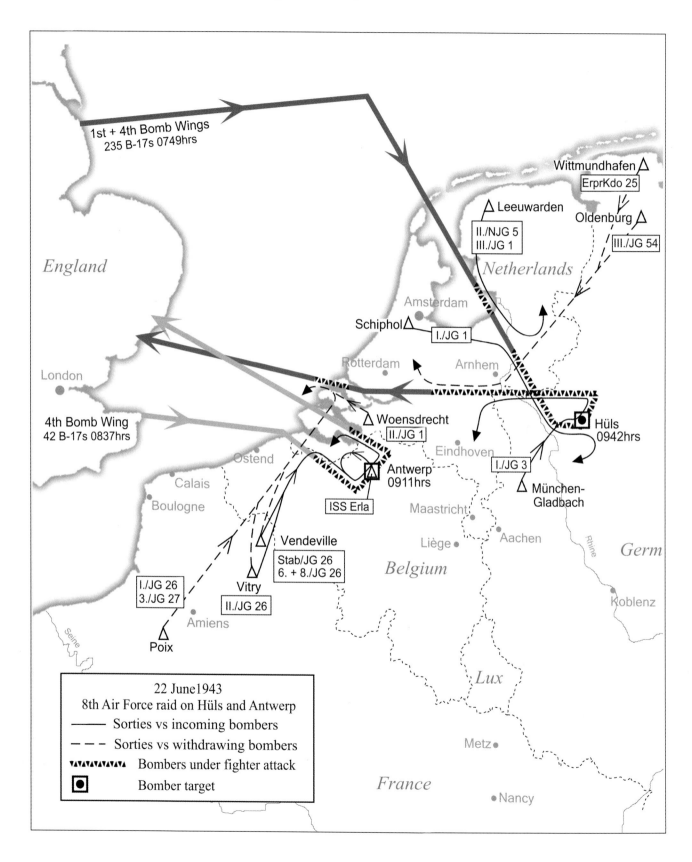

4th Bomb Wing
42 B-17s 0837hrs

1st + 4th Bomb Wings
235 B-17s 0749hrs

Wittmundhafen △
ErprKdo 25

Leeuwarden △
Oldenburg △

II./NJG 5
III./JG 1

III./JG 54

Netherlands

Amsterdam

Schiphol △
I./JG 1

Rotterdam

Arnhem

Woensdrecht △
II./JG 1

Eindhoven

Hüls
0942hrs

Antwerp
0911hrs

ISS Erla

I./JG 3

München-
Gladbach △

England

London

Belgium

Maastricht

Liège

Aachen

Germ

Koblenz

Ostend

Calais

Boulogne

Vendeville △
Stab/JG 26
6. + 8./JG 26

Vitry △
II./JG 26

I./JG 26
3./JG 27

Poix △

Amiens

Seine

Lux

France

Metz

Nancy

22 June 1943
8th Air Force raid on Hüls and Antwerp

—— Sorties vs incoming bombers
- - - Sorties vs withdrawing bombers
▼▲▼▲▼▲▼▲▼▲ Bombers under fighter attack
◉ Bomber target

Luftwaffe defensive activity – 11 June 1943

Unit	Type	Gruppe up			Gruppe down		Claims	Losses				
		Base	No	Time	Base	Time		Dest	Dam	KIA	MIA	WIA
Lw Bfh Mitte												
Jafü Deutsche Bucht:												
Stab/JG 11	Bf 109G	Husum		~1730	Jever	~1830	0	0	0	0	0	0
I./JG 11	Fw 190A	Husum	28	1730	Jever	~1830	0	0	0	0	0	0
2nd sorties	Fw 190A	Jever		~1900	Husum	~2000	0	1	0	0	0	0
II./JG 11	Bf 109G	Jever		1730	Jever	1806	4 B-17	0	0	0	0	0
2nd sorties	Bf 109G	Jever		1851	Jever	2000	2 B-17	0	1	0	0	0
III./JG 11	Bf 109G	Neumünster	19	1730	Neumünster	1835	0	0	0	0	0	1
III./JG 26	Bf 109G	Nordholz		~1730	Nordholz	~1830	2 B-17	0	0	0	0	0
4./JG 54	Bf 109G	Nordholz		~1730	Nordholz	~1830	0	1	0	0	0	1
III./JG 54	Bf 109G	Oldenburg		1730	Oldenburg	1841	4 B-17	1	2	0	0	1
JaSta Helgoland	Bf 109T	Helgoland–Düne		1732	Wangerooge	1825	0	0	0	0	0	0
2nd sorties	Bf 109T	Wangerooge		1842	Helgoland–Düne	1940	0	0	0	0	0	0
ErprKdo 25	Bf 109F, Me 410A	Wittmundhafen		1730	Wittmundhafen	1836	0	1	0	0	0	1
I./NJG 5	Bf 110	Greifswald?		~1830	Greifswald?	~2000	0	0	0	0	0	0
Jafü H-Ruhr:												
I./JG 1	Fw 190A	Schiphol		1700	Schiphol	1732	0	0	0	0	0	0
2nd sorties	Fw 190A	Schiphol		1816	Borkum, Schiphol	1910	1 B-17	0	0	0	0	0
III./JG 1	Bf 109G	Leeuwarden		~1800	Leeuwarden	~1900	1 B-17	0	0	0	0	0
IV./NJG 1	Bf 110	Leeuwarden		~1830	Leeuwarden	~2000	1 B-17	0	0	0	0	0

Luftwaffe defensive activity – 13 June 1943

Unit	Type	Gruppe up			Gruppe down		Claims	Losses				
		Base	No	Time	Base	Time		Dest	Dam	KIA	MIA	WIA
Lw Bfh Mitte												
Jafü Deutsche Bucht:												
Stab/JG 11	Bf 109G	Jever		~0845	Jever	~0950	0	0	0	0	0	1
I./JG 11	Fw 190A	Husum	22	0854	Jever	~1000	2 B-17	2	0	0	1	0
2nd sorties	Fw 190A	Jever		~1045	Husum	~1200	n/c	0	0	0	0	0
II./JG 11	Bf 109G	Jever		0854	Jever	0950	7 B-17	1	0	0	0	1
2nd sorties	Bf 109G	Jever		~1045	Jever	~1200	1 B-17	0	0	0	0	0
III./JG 11	Bf 109G	Neumünster	15	~0900	Neumünster	~1000	0	0	0	0	0	0
III./JG 26	Bf 109G	Nordholz	32	0853	Nordholz	1019	4 B-17	1	0	1	0	0
III./JG 54	Bf 109G	Oldenburg		0835	Oldenburg, Husum	1029	6 B-17	2	1	0	0	2
JaSta Helgoland	Bf 109T	Helgoland–Düne	4	0903	Helgoland–Düne	1020	1 B-17	1	1	0	0	1
	Bf 109T	Helgoland–Düne	2	0948	Helgoland–Düne	~1100	n/c	0	0	0	0	0
ErprKdo 25	Bf 109F, Bf 110	Wittmundhafen	4	~1100	Wittmundhafen	~1200	1 B-17	0	0	0	0	0
I./NJG 3	Bf 110	Zwischenahn		0943	Zwischenahn	1042	1 B-17	0	0	0	0	0
II./NJG 3	Bf 110	Jever		0902	Jever	0950	1 B-17	0	0	0	0	0
	Bf 110	Jever		1020	Jever	1112	0	0	0	0	0	0
Jafü H-Ruhr:												
I./JG 1	Fw 190A	Schiphol		0935	Schiphol	1026	0	0	0	0	0	0
2nd sorties	Fw 190A	Schiphol		1104	Schiphol	~1220	2 B-17	0	0	0	0	0
III./JG 1	Bf 109G	Leeuwarden		~0930	Leeuwarden	~1030	0	0	1	0	0	0

Luftwaffe defensive activity vs. Antwerp raid – 22 June 1943

Unit	Type	Gruppe up			Gruppe down		Claims	Losses				
		Base	No	Time	Base	Time		Dest	Dam	KIA	MIA	WIA
Lw Bfh Mitte												
Jafü H-Ruhr.												
ISS Erla	Bf 109G	Antwerp–Deurne		~0850	Antwerp–Deurne	~0950	1 B-17	0	0	0	0	0
Luftflotte 3												
Jafü 2:												
Stab/JG 26	Fw 190A	Lille–Vendeville		0843	Lille–Vendeville	0940	1 B-17	0	0	0	0	0
6./JG 26	Fw 190A	Lille–Vendeville		0843	Lille–Vendeville	0936	2 B-17	0	1	0	0	1
8./JG 26	Fw 190A	Lille–Vendeville		0843	Lille–Vendeville	0935	0	1	0	0	0	1
II./JG 26	Fw 190A	Vitry		0850	Vitry, Vlissingen	0949	3 B-17, 1 P-47	1	3	0	0	1

Luftwaffe defensive activity vs. Hüls raid – 22 June 1943

Unit	Type	Gruppe up			Gruppe down		Claims	Losses				
		Base	No	Time	Base	Time		Dest	Dam	KIA	MIA	WIA
Lw Bfh Mitte												
Jafü Deutsche Bucht:												
I./JG 11	Fw 190A	Husum		1001	Husum	1024	n/c	0	0	0	0	0
II./JG 11	Bf 109G	Jever		1003	Jever	1034	n/c	0	0	0	0	0
III./JG 11	Bf 109G	Neumünster		1002	Neumünster	1024	n/c	0	0	0	0	0
III./JG 26	Bf 109G	Nordholz		1010	Nordholz	1021	n/c	0	0	0	0	0
III./JG 54	Bf 109G	Oldenburg		0930	Schiphol, Oldenburg	1042	1 B-17	1	1	1	0	0
ErprKdo 25	Bf 109, Bf 110	Wittmundhafen		1006	Wittmundhafen	1036	0	1	0	0	0	1
Jafü H-Ruhr.												
I./JG 1	Fw 190A	Schiphol		0911	Schiphol	1032	10 B-17	1	4	0	0	0
II./JG 1	Fw 190A	Woensdrecht	20	~0820	Woensdrecht	~0900	2 Spitfire (diversion)	0	0	0	0	0
2nd sorties	Fw 190A	Woensdrecht		0930	Woensdrecht	1030	1 B-17, 1 Spitfire	0	0	0	0	0
III./JG 1	Bf 109G	Leeuwarden		~0830	Leeuwarden	~0930	1 B-17	3	7	0	0	1
I./JG 3	Bf 109G	München–Gladbach		0920	München–Gladbach	~1030	2 B-17	3	4	1	0	0
II./NJG 5	Bf 110	Leeuwarden		1006	Leeuwarden	1120	0	0	0	0	0	0
Luftflotte 3												
Jafü 2:												
St/JG 26 (2nd sorties)	Fw 190A	Lille–Vendeville		1017	Lille–Vendeville	1100	0	0	0	0	0	0
I./JG 26	Fw 190A	Poix		0946	Lille–Vendeville	1100	1 Spitfire	0	0	0	0	0
6./JG 26 (2nd sorties)	Fw 190A	Lille–Vendeville		1023	Lille–Vendeville	1104	1 B-17	0	0	0	0	0
8./JG 26 (2nd sorties)	Fw 190A	Lille–Vendeville		~1020	Lille–Vendeville	~1100	0	0	0	0	0	0
II./JG 26 (2nd sorties)	Fw 190A	Vitry		1010	Vitry	1101	0	0	0	0	0	0
3./JG 27	Bf 109G	Poix		0940	Vendeville, Maldegem	1046	1 Spitfire	0	1	0	0	0

25 June
8th Air Force VIII BC Mission #67: 167 of 275 B-17s bomb convoy off Wangerooge I., TOT 0820-0905, ~0930 – lose 18-1-61, claim 62-11-40. No escort.

The VIII BC sent its B-17s after a convoy, but bad weather forced most formations to seek out targets near the German North Sea coast. Jafü Deutsche Bucht and Jafü Holland-Ruhr ordered up 216 day fighters, which attacked whenever and wherever the bombers could be located. Twenty-one claims for downed or culled B-17s were filed, close to the true losses of 18 downed and one scrapped. German losses were high: 15 fighters were lost, and 10 pilots were killed or lost in the North Sea.

26 June
8th Air Force VIII BC Mission #68: 56 of 246 B-17s bomb Villacoublay, Poissy, Tricqueville, Le Mans airfields, TOT 1829-33 – lose 5-0-4, claim 17-5-10. 130 VIII FC P-47

escorts claim 3-3-2, lose 5-1-5. RAF FC Spitfire escort claims 0, loses 2.

The VIII BC targeted Villacoublay airfield near Paris, despite poor weather over France. There was no target escort, as the American P-47s could not yet reach Paris. The first diversionary raids by Douglas Bostons and Hawker Typhoons brought up the Jafü 2 fighters (JG 26) only briefly. Next came a low-strength B-17 raid on Triqueville, escorted by so many Spitfires that the Jafü 3 fighters (JG 2) could not get to the bombers. The fighters finally disengaged, regrouped and attacked the main force, but not until it had bombed Villacoublay. The fighters concentrated on one group, the new 384th, which was in the vulnerable low position in the lead wing. Four bombers went down, and several others dropped from formation, one of which later crashed. Jafü 2 scrambled its fighters on a second mission against a large force off Le Touquet, which proved to be 48 56th Fighter Group P-47s. Most of the German fighters avoided the Thunderbolts and continued west to engage in several small-scale combats. II./JG 26 doubled back and took the P-47s completely by surprise. The American unit lost five destroyed, one damaged beyond repair and five seriously damaged. Seven II./JG 26 claims were confirmed, for no losses. During the day, Luftflotte 3 lost a total of seven fighters and one missing pilot.

The upper level of the command-and-control side of the Jagddivision 2 command bunker (Sokrates), which was located at Schwarzenberg near Stade and played an important role in the defence of the Reich from the time it was completed in mid-1943. Designed to control the night defences, it was perhaps too large and unwieldy for the day defences, but it remained in use into 1945. This photograph was taken from the 14-metre-high frosted-glass map that split the 'Battle Opera House' down the middle. The balcony contained special-purpose maps; behind these are a row of lamps that showed the course of the battle by projecting lines and arrows on the battle map. *(Cranston)*

II./JG 11 pilots at readiness on Vörden in June are entertained by musicians from the unit. From left: Oblt. Gerhard Sommer (StaKa 4./JG 11), Hptm. Günther Specht (GrKdr. II./JG 11) (from rear), Lt. Heinz Rose (4./JG 11), Uffz. Herbert Klotz (later a Leutnant and StaKa of 4./JG 11). *(Rose)*

COMBAT REPORT[7]
26 June 1943

One P-47 destroyed at 8,000 metres at 1852 hours,
N of Neufchâtel
[Galland's victim was a 56th Fighter Group P-47: DC]

Approaching from over the sea and out of the sun at 7,000–8,000 metres, I attacked a formation of Thunderbolts that had just arrived to take over the escort of the enemy bomber formation. The Gruppe was able to approach the Thunderbolt formation unnoticed to very close range from behind and below. I fired at a Thunderbolt on the left side of the formation and observed cannon strikes. The second burst of fire, from the rear and side up to ca. 50 metres, shredded the Thunderbolt. Parts of the wings, fuselage and tail came off, and I could see large holes in the wings and fuselage. The Thunderbolt fell away out of control; it entered a spin and burst into flames. I did not observe the crash because its destruction was certain, and I went on to attack a second Thunderbolt.

Hptm. Wilhelm-Ferdinand Galland,
Gruppenkommandeur
Stab II./JG 26

28 June

8th Air Force VIII BC Mission #69: 158 of 191 B-17s bomb St. Nazaire lock gates, TOT 1655-1713 – lose 8-0-57, claim 28-6-8. 130 VIII FC P-47 escorts claim 0, lose 0-3-0. 43 of 50 B-17s bomb Beaumont-le-Roger airfield, TOT 1736-40 – lose 0-0-6, claim 0. RAF FC Spitfire escort reports no encounters.

The VIII BC again targeted the naval base at St.

A formation of 56th Fighter Group P-47s over England in mid-1943. The 56th was fully trained on the P-47 before coming overseas to join the 8th Air Force, contained a number of outstanding pilots and combat leaders and did much to win air supremacy for the Allies. *(USAAF)*

Nazaire, screened by a small B-17 raid on the major JG 2 airfield at Beaumont–le–Roger that caused considerable damage and apparently reduced the effectiveness of the northern JG 2 units. The JG 26 fighters at Vendeville and Vitry were scrambled, but landed as the Allied formations passed out of range; their later missions located nothing. Jafü 4 ordered III./JG 2 not to make contact until the Spitfire escort had turned back and then unleashed them. Berlin confirmed nine victories to the Gruppe, but awarded full credits to 13 pilots. How common was the practice of awarding full credits for shared victories, which violated the RLM's own policies, is unknown, and at this date unknowable. Eight of the 191 attacking B-17s were in fact lost, and another 57 were damaged. JG 2 lost four fighters and one pilot.

29 June

8th Air Force VIII BC Mission #70: 0 of 148 B-17s bomb Villacoublay, Triqueville airfields – lose 0-0-14, claim 0-3-3; 76 of 84 B-17s bomb Le Mans aviation industry, rail yard; TOT 1959-2003 – no losses or claims. 126 VIII FC P-47 escorts claim 2-0-0, lose 0; RAF FC Spitfire escorts claim 0-1-0, lose 0.

The VIII BC attempted to attack several French targets late in the day. The defenders comprised only the two JG 2 Gruppen in northern France and part of I./JG 27. These were scrambled and attempted to attack the bombers over the coast, but few pilots could penetrate the heavy screen of P-47s and Spitfires. The cloud cover was thick, and most of the B-17s returned to England with their bombs. JG 2 filed one claim for a B-17 (see Eder's combat report), for the loss of four pilots and their aircraft; the Allies reported no losses.

COMBAT REPORT[8]
29 June 1943

One B-17 destroyed from 7,000 metres at 2039 hours, PQ 0168/05 East

I scrambled with nine Bf 109s at 1947 hours as 12./JG 2 Staffelführer in a Bf 109G-6 'gunboat' with three MG 151/20 cannon and two MG 131 machine guns. At 2020 hours, I contacted 60–70 B-17s, 10–15 P 47s and 20–30 Spitfires in map quadrant 103/05 East. I immediately attacked the Boeing on the far left of the bomber formation from slightly above and diagonally from the left, firing from 500–300 metres. I saw hits in both left engines and the fuselage; all showed flames and smoke plumes. The Fortress sheered from the formation and dove away. I followed from above and attacked from the rear, observing strikes in the tail and fuselage. The plane was now engulfed in flames. I was now attacked by a Thunderbolt and had to engage it. After a short exchange of fire it pulled away. I returned to the Fortress I had set on fire and attacked it for a third time. Parts of the left wing flew off. The plane was still burning fiercely. It dropped back still further and dove straight down, completely in flames. Three crewmen bailed out. It crashed into the sea at 2039 hours. My wingman and I observed it clearly. Landing followed at 2110 hours.

Lt. Georg-Peter Eder, Staffelführer
12./JG 2

Luftwaffe defensive activity – 25 June 1943

Unit	Type	Gruppe up			Gruppe down		Claims	Losses				
		Base	No	Time	Base	Time		Dest	Dam	KIA	MIA	WIA
Lw Bfh Mitte												
Jafü Deutsche Bucht:												
Stab/JG 11	Bf 109G	Jever	4	0811	Husum, Langeoog	0947	2 B-17	0	0	0	0	0
I./JG 11	Fw 190A	Husum		0812	Husum	0930	5 B-17	2	1	1	0	0
II./JG 11	Bf 109G	Jever	40	0811	Jever	~0915	5 B-17	0	3	0	0	1
III./JG 11	Bf 109G	Neumünster		0813	Varel	0915	0	1	0	1	0	0
III./JG 26	Bf 109G	Nordholz		0815	Wittmundhafen, Nordholz	0922	2 B-17	4	0	2	2	0
4./JG 54	Bf 109G	Nordholz		~0815	Nordholz	~0922	0	1	0	0	0	0
III./JG 54	Bf 109G	Oldenburg		~0820	Oldenburg	~0920	1 B-17	0	0	0	0	0
JaSta Helgoland	Bf 109T	Helgoland–Düne		0820	Helgoland–Düne	0912	0	0	0	0	0	0
ErprKdo 25	Fw 190A, Bf 110G	Wittmundhafen		0823	Wittmundhafen	0953	1 B-17	1	0	2	0	0
I./NJG 3	Bf 110	Vechta		~0845	Vechta	~0945	0	0	0	0	0	0
II./NJG 3?	Bf 110	Jever		0830	Jever	~0945	0	0	0	0	0	0
Jafü H-Ruhr:												
I./JG 1	Fw 190A	Schiphol		0828	Jever	0931	2 B-17	0	0	0	0	0
III./JG 1	Bf 109G	Leeuwarden		0815	Leeuwarden	~0915	1 B-17 HSS	6	2	1	1	3
I./JG 26	Fw 190A	Rheine		0820	Rheine	~0920	2 B-17	0	1	0	0	0

Luftwaffe defensive activity – 26 June 1943

Unit	Type	Gruppe up			Gruppe down		Claims	Losses				
		Base	No	Time	Base	Time		Dest	Dam	KIA	MIA	WIA
Luftflotte 3												
Jafü 2:												
Stab/JG 26	Fw 190A	Lille–Vendeville		1739	Lille–Vendeville	1758	n/c	0	0	0	0	0
2nd sorties	Fw 190A	Lille–Vendeville		1824	Lille–Vendeville	1930	1 B-17	0	0	0	0	0
6./JG 26	Fw 190A	Lille–Vendeville		1825	Lille–Vendeville	1915	0	0	0	0	0	0
8./JG 26	Fw 190A	Lille–Vendeville		~1825	Lille–Vendeville	~1915	0	1	0	0	0	0
II./JG 26	Fw 190A	Vitry		1741	Vitry	1803	n/c	0	0	0	0	0
2nd sorties	Fw 190A	Vitry		1826	Vitry	1931	7 P-47	0	0	0	0	0
II./JG 26	Bf 109G	Lille–Vendeville		1741	Lille–Vendeville	1802	1	0	0	0	0	1
I./JG 27	Bf 109G	Poix		1702	Beaumont–le–Roger, Poix	1812	0	0	0	0	0	0
2nd sorties	Bf 109G	Beaumont–le–Roger		1827	Poix	1914	0	0	0	0	0	0
Jafü 3:												
Stab/JG 2	Fw 190A	Beaumont–le–Roger		~1730	Beaumont–le–Roger	~1830	0	0	1	0	0	0
I./JG 2	Fw 190A, Bf 109G	Triqueville		~1730	Triqueville	~1830	1 B-17	3	2	0	1	0
II./JG 2	Bf 109G	Beaumont–le–Roger		~1730	Beaumont–le–Roger	~1830	2 B-17, 2 Spitfire	2	0	0	0	2
2nd sorties	Bf 109G	Beaumont–le–Roger		~1845	Beaumont–le–Roger	~1930	1 B-17, 1 P-47	0	0	0	0	0
2./JG 105	Bf 109G	Villacoublay–Nord		~1830	Villacoublay–Nord	~1930	1 B-17	0	0	0	0	0
JLÜberprGr	Fw 190A	Orléans–Bricy		1823	Orléans–Bricy	1906	0	?	?	?	?	?

Luftwaffe defensive activity – 28 June 1943

Unit	Type	Gruppe up			Gruppe down		Claims	Losses				
		Base	No	Time	Base	Time		Dest	Dam	KIA	MIA	WIA
Luftflotte 3												
Jafü 2:												
Stab/JG 26	Fw 190A	Lille–Vendeville		1610	Lille–Vendeville	1710	n/c	0	0	0	0	0
6./JG 26	Fw 190A	Lille–Vendeville		1610	Lille–Vendeville	1710	n/c	0	0	0	0	0
8./JG 26	Fw 190A	Lille–Vendeville		1640	Lille–Vendeville	1710	n/c	0	0	0	0	0
2nd sorties	Fw 190A	Lille–Vendeville		1740	Lille–Vendeville	1810	n/c	0	0	0	0	0
11./JG 26	Bf 109G	Lille–Vendeville		1640	Lille–Vendeville	1710	n/c	0	0	0	0	0
2nd sorties	Bf 109G	Lille–Vendeville		1740	Lille–Vendeville	1812	n/c	0	0	0	0	0
II./JG 26	Fw 190A	Vitry		1630	Poix	1715	n/c	0	0	0	0	0
2nd sorties	Fw 190A	Poix		1730	Ligescourt	1745	n/c	0	0	0	0	0
I./JG 27	Bf 109G	Poix		1638	Beaumont–le–Roger	1710	n/c	0	0	0	0	0
2nd sorties	Bf 109G	Beaumont–le–Roger		1717	Poix	1823	0	0	0	0	0	0
Jafü 3:												
Stab/JG 2	Fw 190A	Beaumont–le–Roger		~1710	Beaumont–le–Roger?	~1750	0	0	0	0	0	0
I./JG 2	Fw 190A, Bf 109G	Bernay		~1710	Bernay	~1750	0	1	1	0	0	0
II./JG 2	Bf 109G	Beaumont–le–Roger		~1530	Vannes	~1600	transfer	0	0	0	0	0
	Bf 109G	Vannes		1630	Beaumont–le–Roger	1800	0	2	0	0	0	1
JLÜberprGr	Fw 190A	Orléans–Bricy		1740	Orléans–Bricy	1808	0	?	?	?	?	?
Jafü 4:												
III./JG 2	Fw 190A	Vannes		1630	Vannes	~1810	9 B-17	1	0	1	0	0

Luftwaffe defensive activity – 29 June 1943

Unit	Type	Gruppe up			Gruppe down		Claims	Losses				
		Base	No	Time	Base	Time		Dest	Dam	KIA	MIA	WIA
Luftflotte 3												
Jafü 2:												
I./JG 27	Bf 109G	Poix		1936	Poix	2005	0	0	1	0	0	0
Jafü 3:												
I./JG 2	Fw 190A, Bf 109G	Bernay		~1945	Bernay	~2100	0	1	0	1	0	0
II./JG 2	Bf 109G	Beaumont–le–Roger		1947	Beaumont–le–Roger	~2100	1 B-17	3	1	3	0	1

Notes:

[1] Burath correspondence with author, 1999.

[2] Stammberger correspondence with author, 1989.

[3] Crump correspondence with author, 1987.

[4] Stammberger correspondence with author, 1989.

[5] Eder Gefechtsbericht, in private collection.

[6] Crump correspondence with author, 1987.

[7] Galland Gefechtsbericht, in Renner, *Wilhelm-Ferdinand Galland*, 1943.

[8] Eder Gefechtsbericht, in private collection.

CHAPTER 3

JULY – SEPTEMBER 1943

July 1943

The Reichsluftverteidigung force continued its slow build-up. The Gruppen of two highly successful Jagdgeschwader, JG 3 and JG 27, were ordered back to the Reich from various combat fronts to re-equip and retrain as air defence units. The three *Zerstörergeschwader* [heavy fighter wings], ZG 1, ZG 26 and ZG 76, were now to be resurrected for Reich defence. Several Zerstörergruppen were brought home from secondary fronts; others had to be formed anew with nuclei from reconnaissance and training units. Their equipment would be either the tried-and-true Bf 110 or the new Me 410 *Hornisse*, a politically favoured, multipurpose twin-engine craft that was having a hard time finding a role to justify its high developmental expense.

There were no new single-engine fighters in the pipeline, but improvements in radio equipment and armament were being implemented. The FuG 16ZY radio apparatus was unique for the period. It permitted ground control of large formations and was first installed in the aircraft of formation leaders; it later served as a useful navigation aid. The 30-mm MK 108 cannon was replacing the 20-mm MG 151/20 as the nose armament in many Bf 109Gs and proved to be an effective bomber destroyer. A few units continued to experiment with aerial bombs, but this technique never caught on. However, RLV fighter units did use aerial rockets for the first time late in the month. The WGr 21 was converted from a 21-cm mortar shell and was launched from an underwing 'stovepipe'. The Bf 109 and Fw 190 carried two; the Bf 110 later carried four. They were wildly inaccurate, but were intended to break up the bombers' tight formations, for which purpose a near miss was as good as a hit.

One of the two American heavy bomber types, the

Consolidated B-24 Liberator, had disappeared from the VIII Bomber Command (VIII BC) order of battle, and would not be encountered again by the Reich defenders until mid-August. The three B-24 groups had flown to North Africa, from where they would take off on the famous low-altitude raid on the Romanian Ploesti petrochemical complex on 1 August.

4 July – French targets (see map)
8th Air Force VIII BC Mission #71: 105 of 121 1st Bomb Wing (1st BW) B-17s bomb LeMans air industry, TOT 1240-43 – lose 4-0-29, claim 24-5-15. Escort of 8 sqds of RAF Spitfires claim 2-1-0, lose 0. 61 of 71 1st BW B-17s bomb Nantes aviation industry, TOT 1246-49 – lose 3-1-34, claim 28-9-7. No escort. 71 of 83 4th BW B-17s bomb La Pallice lock gates, TOT 1201-04 – lose 1-0-1, claim 0-1-0. No escort.

The VIII BC attacked three widely separated French targets: aircraft factories at Nantes and Le Mans and the U-boat base at La Pallice. The Jafü 3 controller got up the JG 2 Stabsschwarm and part of II./JG 2 in time to attack the Le Mans force prior to bombing. The Jafü 4 (Brittany) controller was late in scrambling his aircraft, but these then made prolonged attacks on the withdrawing Nantes bombers. A few JG 2 pilots flew to the Channel coast and had some success against the withdrawal escort and straggling Le Mans bombers. The pilots claimed, and were credited with, 21 B-17s destroyed or shot from formation; actual B-17 losses were eight shot down, one scrapped and 54 damaged. JG 2 lost one pilot killed, one missing and four injured; 21 of its fighters were destroyed or damaged, most by the bombers after the escorts turned back, but some in dead-stick landings after their long missions. Jafü 2 kept its fighters in its own area and then vectored them to Le Havre to await the bombers' return. There they encountered a large number of

Spitfires and were unable to reach the bombers. They kept patrolling, looking for an opening in the screen, but were unable to find one, and finally had to break off owing to low fuel. The Americans considered their operational plan (divergent paths and targets) to have been a great success and documented it in detail.

10 July

8th Air Force VIII BC Mission #72: 70 of 286 B-17s bomb Abbéville and Caen airfields, TOT 0729-35, 0832 – lose 3-0-49, claim 41-15-13. Escort of 18 sqds RAF Spitfires claims 1-0-2, loses 0; 128 VIII Fighter Command (VIII FC) P-47 escorts claim 0, lose 0.

The VIII BC dispatched 286 B-17s to targets in northern France. Bad weather prevented most from bombing, but 31 aircraft dropped on Caen, and 36 bombed Abbéville with fair results. The large RAF and USAAF escort to these short-range targets was considered excellent. Despite the many Luftflotte 3 fighters in the area, only three B-17s were shot down. JG 2 fought an extended combat from Rouen to Paris, where a bomber force targeting Le Bourget aborted and lost one pilot and one fighter while claiming six B-17s and one Spitfire. II./JG 26 reached the Somme Estuary in time to see the bombers withdrawing from Abbéville, but they were already out of range, and Jafü 2 directed the Focke-Wulfs west, against the Caen force. The Gruppe downed one B-17 on its first pass and continued attacking for 10 more minutes until low fuel forced it to break off. The JG 26 Geschwadergruppe (today the JG 26 Stabsschwarm, 6., 8. and 11. Staffeln) made contact in the Rouen area, but filed no claims. JG 26 pilots landed on Amiens, Rouen, Octeville, Le

This photograph from a well-known but often misidentified series shows Bf 109G-6 'Black 6' (W. Nr. 27083) of 5./JG 2 in the summer or autumn of 1943, after the return of II./JG 2 from North Africa and its conversion from Fw 190s to Bf 109s. This example is typical of the period: it is a 'Kanonenboot' (gunboat) variation with two MG 151/20 machine cannon in underwing gondolas; a short radio mast; an external DF loop; and 'Galland' armour attached to the canopy. Uffz. Hünig was shot down and killed in this airplane on 20 October. *(Bundesarchiv 487-3066-7)*

Havre and Poix, in addition to their Vendeville and Vitry bases. No JG 26 fighter sustained reportable damage.

Fw 190A-5s of 8./JG 2 on Brest–Nord in the summer of 1943. *(Cranston)*

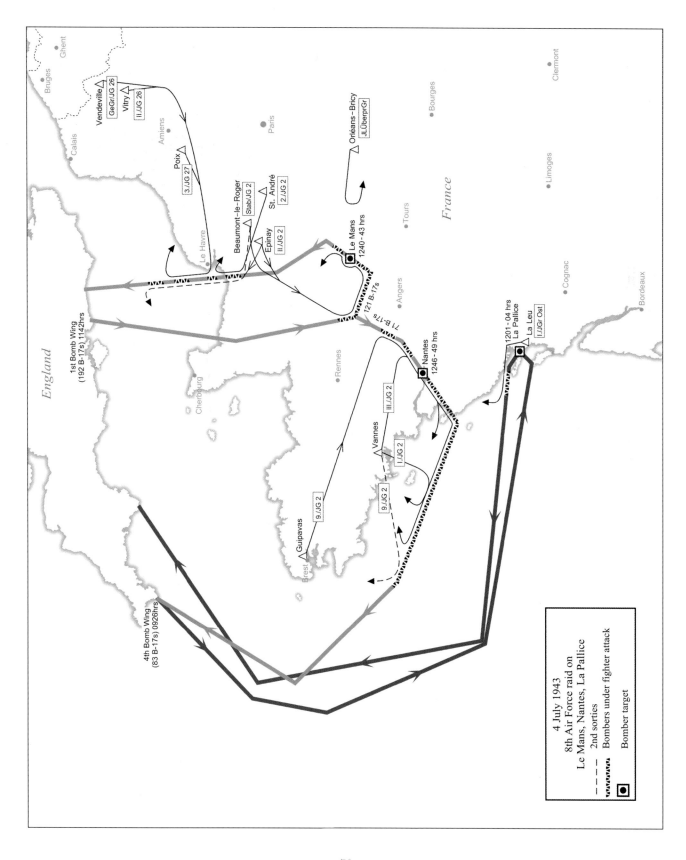

Vendeville △ GeGr/JG 26
Vitry △ II./JG 26
Poix △ 3./JG 27
Beaumont-le-Roger △ Stab/JG 2
St. André △ 2./JG 2
Epinay △ II./JG 2
Orléans – Bricy △ JLÜberprGr

Le Mans 1240 - 43 hrs

1st Bomb Wing
(192 B-17's) 1142hrs

121 B-17's
71 B-17's

Nantes 1246 - 49 hrs

Vannes △ III./JG 2
I./JG 2
9./JG 2
9./JG 2

La Pallice 1201 - 04 hrs
La Leu △ I./JGr Ost

Guipavas △

4th Bomb Wing
(83 B-17's) 0926hrs

England
France

4 July 1943
8th Air Force raid on
Le Mans, Nantes, La Pallice

—————— 2nd sorties
▲▲▲▲▲ Bombers under fighter attack
◉ Bomber target

COMBAT REPORT[1]
10 July 1943

One Spitfire IX shot down from 7,000 metres at 0828 hours, quadrant 0013/05 East (over sea)
One B-17 Fortress shot down from 7,000 metres at 0832 hours, quadrant 0186/05 East (over sea)

I scrambled with two Bf 109G-6s at 0800 hours as 12./JG 2 Staffelführer in a Bf 109G-6 'gunboat' with three MG 151/20 cannon and two MG 131 machine guns. At 0820 hours, I contacted ca. 80 B-17s and 80–100 Spitfires in map quadrant 004/05 East. In the course of the ensuing air battle, I was attacked from behind by two Spitfire IXs. I immediately banked away and, after a further turn, found myself in firing position behind one of the two Spitfires. The Spitfire attempted to reverse its turn, but I fired in my turn from 80–100 metres. It was hit in the fuselage and fell off immediately over its right wing, burning brightly. It crashed in the sea at 0828 hours. I did not see a parachute.

At 0829 hours, after shooting down the Spitfire, I attacked a B-17 from behind and below. The enemy bomber immediately dropped away in a spin. I made two further attacks from the rear. Its tail and part of the fuselage came off during the dive. It crashed straight into the sea at 0832 hours. I saw four parachutes. The radio service confirmed the crash of a B-17 and a Spitfire at my reported location. Both crashes were observed by my wingman, Uffz. Vater. We landed at Abbéville at 0840 hours.

Oblt. Georg-Peter Eder, Staffelführer
12./JG 2

14 July
8th Air Force VIII BC Mission #73: 53 of 64 1st BW B-17s bomb Amiens airfield, TOT 0742 – lose 1-3-34, claim 9-0-2. 128 VIII FC P 47 escorts claim 3-0-3, lose 3-1-1. 101 of 116 1st BW B-17s bomb Villacoublay air depot, TOT 0811-15 – lose 3-0-67, claim 15-7-16. 52 of 84 4th BW B-17s bomb Le Bourget airfield, TOT 0750-0820 – lose 4-1-50, claim 41-27-32. RAF Fighter Command (RAF FC) Spitfire escorts claim 1-3-3, lose 3-1.

The VIII BC targeted Amiens, Villacoublay and Le Bourget. The Amiens raiding force was smaller and earlier than the others and served to shield the main force from the Jafü 2 fighters. The Amiens bombers were escorted by all three American P-47 groups; the target was well within their range. Jafü 2 scrambled the JG 26 Geschwadergruppe, II./JG 26 and 3./JG 27 just as the Amiens force was crossing the French coast. The three German formations attacked the bombers for 20 minutes before the P-47s were able to divert them. Only one B-17 went down, the victim of a JG 27 Messerschmitt, but three more crash-landed in England. In the meantime, Jafü 3 directed the JG 2 Focke-Wulfs and Messerschmitts against the two forces raiding the Paris region. Eight of the unescorted B-17s were claimed, a perfect match for the seven downed and one later scrapped. The Luftwaffe also claimed four Spitfires and three P 47s, while losing a total of seven fighters and two pilots. The defensive mission was a victory by their criterion. However, the raid on Villacoublay was an outstanding success for the Allies; the hangars containing the Luftflotte 3 Fw 190 repair facility were destroyed, along with 70 Fw 190s belonging to a number of fighter, bomber, reconnaissance, headquarters and training units.

17 July
8th Air Force VIII BC Mission #74: 34 of 291 B-17s bomb N German t/os, convoy – lose 2-3-80, claim 60-16-36. Escort recalled. 21 of 41 4th BW B-17s bomb Amsterdam aviation industry – lose 0-0-11, no claims. Escort recalled.

The VIII BC dispatched 332 B-17s in the morning to bomb targets in northern Germany and Holland. Poor weather prevented the combat wings from forming up properly, and the mission was eventually recalled. Twenty-one bombers attacked Amsterdam with poor results, and another 34 bombed scattered German targets. The dispersed formations presented such a large number of targets to the Jafü Holland-Ruhr and Jafü Deutsche Bucht controllers that they were unable to concentrate their fighters in any one area, and the opportunity to score heavily against unescorted bombers flying in poor formations was wasted. Units were sent after the incoming or withdrawing streams; a few Gruppen flew separate missions after both. Only 110 sorties were credited. Claims for 10 B-17s were confirmed, but in fact only five were shot down or scrapped. Eleven German fighters and five pilots were lost to bomber fire, bad weather or poor navigation over the North Sea.

Luftwaffe defensive activity – 4 July 1943

Unit	Type	Gruppe up			Gruppe down		Claims	Losses (—: included in 1st sortie)				
		Base	No	Time	Base	Time		Dest	Dam	KIA	MIA	WIA
Lw Bfh Mitte												
Jafü H-Ruhr:												
I./JG 26	Fw 190A	Woensdrecht		1215	Woensdrecht	1245	n/c	0	0	0	0	0
Luftflotte 3												
Jafü 2:												
GeschGr/ JG 26	Fw 190A	Lille–Vendeville	30	1241	Abbéville, Poix, Vendeville, Caen	1347	0	0	0	0	0	0
II./JG 26	Fw 190A	Vitry	30	1244	Vitry, Octeville, Ligescourt, Amiens	1353	0	0	1	0	0	0
3./JG 27	Bf 109G	Poix	20	1234	Poix	1345	0	0	0	0	0	0
Jafü 3:												
Stab/JG 2	Fw 190A	Beaumont–le–Roger	4	1216	Beaumont–le–Roger	~1245	3 B-17	0	0	0	0	0
2nd sorties	Fw 190A	Beaumont–le–Roger		~1300	Beaumont–le–Roger	~1400	1 B-17 HSS	0	0	0	0	0
2./JG 2	Fw 190A	St. André		1244	St. André	1334	0	0	0	0	0	0
II./JG 2	Bf 109G	Evreux	26	1207	Evreux	1315	3 B-17	2	5	1	0	1
2nd sorties	Bf 109G	Evreux		~1300	Evreux	~1400	1 P47, 1 Spitfire	—	—	—	—	—
JLÜberprGr	Fw 190A	Orléans–Bricy		1230	Orléans–Bricy	1240	0	?	?	?	?	?
Jafü 4:												
I./JG 2	Fw 190A, Bf 109G	Vannes	*40	1310	Vannes	1345	2 B-17, 2 B-17 HSS	3	3	0	0	2
III./JG 2	Fw 190A	Vannes	—	1232	Vannes	1330	4 B-17	1	0	0	0	1
9./JG 2	Fw 190A	Brest–Guipavas	15	1210	Vannes, Nantes	1320	2 B-17, 2 B-17 HSS	4	3	0	1	0
2nd sorties	Fw 190A	Vannes	10	1340	Brest–Guipavas	1432	2 B-17	—	—	—	—	—
JGr Ost	Bf 109G	La Leu	30	1205	La Leu	~1305	1 B-17	0	0	0	0	0

*40 I./JG 2 and III./JG 2 fighters up from Vannes on 1st sorties

Luftwaffe defensive activity – 10 July 1943

Unit	Type	Gruppe up			Gruppe down		Claims	Losses				
		Base	No	Time	Base	Time		Dest	Dam	KIA	MIA	WIA
Luftflotte 3												
Jafü 2:												
II./JG 2	Bf 109G	Poix	*25	0728	Poix	0824	2 B-17	0	0	0	0	0
Stab/JG 26	Fw 190A	Lille–Vendeville	2	0738	Lille–Vendeville	~0840	0	0	0	0	0	0
6./JG 26	Fw 190A	Lille–Vendeville	6	0728	Vendeville, Amiens	0837	0	0	0	0	0	0
8./JG 26	Fw 190A	Lille–Vendeville	6	0738	Vendeville, Le Havre	0834	0	0	0	0	0	0
11./JG 26	Bf 109G	Lille–Vendeville	7	0728	Vendeville, others	~0840	0	0	0	0	0	0
II./JG 26	Fw 190A	Vitry–en–Artois	21	0732	Vitry, Rouen, Poix	0845	1 B-17	0	0	0	0	0
3./JG 27	Bf 109G	Poix	—	0729	Poix	0824	0	0	0	0	0	0
Jafü 3:												
Stab/JG 2	Fw 190A	Beaumont–le–Roger?	4	~0745	Beaumont–le–Roger?	~0845	0	0	0	0	0	0
I./JG 2	Fw 190A	Conches	21	0749	Conches	~0845	1 B-17	0	1	0	0	1
6./JG 2	Bf 109G	Evreux	7	0740	Evreux	~0845	2 B-17	0	0	0	0	0
11./JG 2	Bf 109G	Evreux	7	0740	Evreux	~0845	0	0	1	0	0	0
12./JG 2	Bf 109G	Evreux	8	0740	Evreux	~0845	1 B-17, 1 Spitfire	1	0	1	0	0
Jafü 4:												
III./JG 2	Fw 190A	Vannes	22	~0745	Vannes	~0845	0	0	0	0	0	0

*25 Bf 109s (Stab II/JG 2, 5./JG 2, 3./JG 27) sortie from Poix

Luftwaffe defensive activity – 14 July 1943

Unit	Type	Gruppe up			Gruppe down		Claims	Losses				
		Base	No	Time	Base	Time		Dest	Dam	KIA	MIA	WIA
Luftflotte 3												
Jafü 2:												
GeschGr	Fw 190A	Lille–Vendeville		0733	Lille–Vendeville, Poix	0830	0	0	0	0	0	0
JG 26	Fw 190A	Lille–Vendeville, Poix, Maldegem		0807	Lille–Vendeville, Poix, Octeville	0908	0	0	0	0	0	0
II./JG 26	Fw 190A	Vitry		0731	Vitry, Ligescourt, Poix	0820	2 P-47	1	0	0	0	1
2nd sorties	Fw 190A	Vitry, Poix, Ligescourt		0820	Vitry, Ligescourt	0920	0	0	0	0	0	0
3/JG 27	Bf 109G	Poix		0725	Poix	0810	1 B-17	1	0	0	0	1
2nd sorties	Bf 109G	Poix		0817	Poix	0933	0	0	0	0	0	0
Jafü 3:												
Stab/JG 2	Fw 190A	Beaumont-le-Roger?		~0730	Beaumont-le-Roger?	~0830	2 B-17	0	0	0	0	0
I./JG 2	Fw 190A, Bf 109G	Bernay, St. André		0728	Bernay, St. André	0823	2 B-17	3	0	1	0	1
II./JG 2	Bf 109G	Poix		0845	Poix	~0930	4 Spitfire, 1 P-47	1	0	1	0	0
6./JG 2	Bf 109G	Evreux		0723	Evreux, Rouen	~0815	1 B-17	0	0	0	0	0
12./JG 2	Bf 109G	Evreux		0723	Evreux, Rouen	~0815	1 B-17, 1 B-17 HSS	1	1	0	0	0
I./JG 105	Bf 109G	Villacoublay–Nord		~0745	Villacoublay–Nord	~0845	1 B-17	0	0	0	0	0
JLÜberprGr	Bf 109F	Orléans–Bricy		0732	Orléans–Bricy	0745	0	?	?	?	?	?

Oblt. Gerhard Sommer (Kapitän of the 4. Staffel of II,/JG 11) greets a car of inspectors at Jever in July. *(Rose)*

Fw. Hans-Gerd Wennekers (II./JG 11) poses in a captured B-17 at Jever in July. *(Rose)*

COMBAT REPORT[2]
17 July 1943

One B-17 destroyed from 7,500 metres at 0912 hours, PQ UQ-7/05 East S, 32 km N of Spiekeroog [Hondt's victim was Lt. Powledge's 94th Bomb Group B-17: DC]

I scrambled with four Bf 109Ts at 0848 hours as Staffelführer and quickly made contact with the enemy flying at 7,500 metres just west of Helgoland. We flew in a northerly direction alongside the formation for 5–10 minutes, climbing from 6,500 metres. At ca. 0910 hours, we turned into the formation and attacked head on. I shot at the third machine from the right in the middle of a Pulk and saw hits in the left inner engine and the fuselage. My left aileron was then shot away. Despite heavy control forces I attacked a Pulk flying to the lower left behind the first before returning to land. According to my witness, Uffz. Turowski, my B-17 went down trailing a light plume of smoke, just NNW of Helgoland.

Lt. Erich Hondt
Jagdstaffel Helgoland

The long-winged Bf 109T 'Toni', originally designed for service on the aircraft carrier *Graf Zeppelin*, served in several specialised units, most notably the Jagdstaffel Helgoland, which needed its short take-off capability for its tiny airstrip. This example is equipped with smoke-generating apparatus, probably for testing its efficacy in protecting naval units or ground operations. *(Crow)*

24 July

8th Air Force VIII BC Mission #75: 208 of 309 B-17s bomb Norwegian ports, industry, TOT 1317-1414 – lose 1-1-64, claim 13-4-3. No escort.

This was the first day of the VIII BC's 'Blitz week', its first sustained campaign. Its objective was to extend and weaken the German fighter defences by flying seven bombing missions in seven consecutive days. Today's targets were aluminium, magnesium and nitrate plants under construction in Heroya, Norway. The defences were taken completely by surprise. 10./JG 11, the only day fighter Staffel in southern Norway, lost two pilots to B-17 defensive fire. One bomber was interned in Sweden, and a second was scrapped in England; both had been hit by Flak.

25 July

8th Air Force VIII BC Mission #76: 100 of 182 1st BW B-17s bomb Hamburg shipyard and t/os, TOT 1630-45 – lose 15-0-67, claim 38-6-27. No escort. 118 of 141 4th BW B-17s bomb Kiel shipyard and t/os, TOT 1630-1700 – lose 4-1-50, claim 6-0-0. No escort.

'Blitz week' continued with a complex VIII BC attack on northern Germany following a massive RAF Bomber Command night raid on Hamburg. Most of the 1st BW targeted Hamburg, but cloud cover and intense smoke from the previous night's fires caused problems in target recognition, and only 100 B-17s bombed Hamburg or the surrounding area. The rest of the wing was to bomb Kiel, but aborted, while the longer-range 4th BW was to bomb the Focke-Wulf factory at Warnemünde, near Rostock, but owing to cloud cover was forced to bomb its secondary target, Kiel. The Jafü Deutsche Bucht wasted some effort chasing the Warnemünde force before identifying the day's main target as Hamburg. It got all of its fighters into the air, most on two missions, with varying success. Help was requested from Jafü Holland-Ruhr, and I./JG 1 and

II./JG 1 were sent north to Jever, from which the latter flew a successful mission against the withdrawing 1st BW, along with III./JG 1 from Leeuwarden. The rest of the Holland-Ruhr fighters and those of Jafü 2 were kept busy in their own areas by RAF light bombers and fighter bombers. III./JG 54 had recently transferred from Germany to Amsterdam-Schiphol and proved an unwelcome surprise to the RAF over the Netherlands. Twenty B-17s were lost or scrapped in the main show. Proof of confirmation for many of today's Luftwaffe claims is lacking, but following this book's normal procedure, those claims believed in condition for confirmation are tabulated here. Luftwaffe losses to the B-17s were relatively light. Only one pilot, Major Karl-Heinz Leesmann, the III./JG 11 Kommandeur, was killed. The crew of one IV./NJG 1 Bf 110 was rescued from the sea and taken prisoner by a Royal Navy torpedo boat crew. Seven fighters were lost or damaged beyond repair, and five pilots were injured.

The Bf 109G-1 of Lt. Heinz Rose (II./JG 11) after a forced landing in the Lankersee near Preetz on 25 July. The ripped-off oil cooler is lying on the wing. Note the Geschwader emblem of JG 11 (formerly JG 1): a map of the Deutsche Bucht, covered by a hunter's bow and arrow. *(Rose)*

Below: **Hptm. Klaus Mietusch's III./JG 26 scrambles from Nordholz on 25 July.** *(de Jong)*

Obfw. Georg Fröhlich (III./JG 1) and his Bf 109G-6 at Leeuwarden in the summer. The airplane carries the 8. Staffel emblem and the pilot's own heart emblem. *(Mombeek)*

Luftwaffe defensive activity – 17 July 1943

Unit	Type	Gruppe up			Gruppe down		Claims	Losses				
		Base	No	Time	Base	Time		Dest	Dam	KIA	MIA	WIA
Lw Bfh Mitte												
Jafü Deutsche Bucht:												
Stab/JG 11	Bf 109G	Jever		0841	Jever	0940	0	0	0	0	0	0
I./JG 11	Fw 190A	Husum		0844	Husum	0948	1 B-17	3	0	1	0	2
II./JG 11	Bf 109G	Jever		0841	Jever	0940	2 B-17	2	1	0	0	0
2nd sorties	Bf 109G	Jever		1010	Jever	1037	n/c	0	0	0	0	0
III./JG 11	Bf 109G	Oldenburg		0845	Oldenburg	0900	n/c	0	0	0	0	0
III./JG 26	Bf 109G	Nordholz		0850	Nordholz	1005	2 B-17	2	1	0	1	1
JaSta Helgoland	Bf 109T	Helgoland–Düne	5	0848	Helgoland–Düne	0949	2 B-17	1	0	0	1	0
ErprKdo 25	Bf 109G, Bf 110	Wittmundhafen		0849	Wittmundhafen	1001	0	0	0	0	0	0
2nd sorties	Bf 109G, Bf 110	Wittmundhafen		1010	Wittmundhafen	1053	0	0	0	0	0	0
I./NJG 3	Bf 110	Vechta		0953	Vechta	~1100	0	0	0	0	0	0
Jafü H-Ruhr:												
Stab/JG 1	Fw 190A	Rheine		1000	Rheine	~1100	n/c	0	0	0	0	0
I./JG 1	Fw 190A	Arnhem, Deelen		0844	Arnhem, Deelen	0935	n/c	0	0	0	0	0
2nd sorties	Fw 190A	Arnhem, Deelen		1023	Arnhem, Deelen	1127	0	0	0	0	0	0
II./JG 1	Fw 190A	Rheine	15	1023	Rheine	~1100	0	0	1	0	0	0
III./JG 1	Bf 109G	Leeuwarden		1000	Leeuwarden	~1100	0	2	0	1	1	0
I./JG 3	Bf 109G	München–Gladbach		~1000	München–Gladbach	~1100	3 B-17	1	1	0	0	0
I./JG 26	Fw 190A	Woensdrecht		1024	Woensdrecht	1118	0	0	2	0	0	0
III./JG 54	Bf 109G	Schiphol		0838	Schiphol, Waalhaven	0948	0	0	0	0	0	0
2nd sorties	Bf 109G	Schiphol, Waalhaven		1038	Schiphol	1117	0	0	1	0	0	1
III./NJG 1	Bf 110	Twente		1010	Twente	1113	n/c	0	0	0	0	0

Luftwaffe defensive activity – 24 July 1943

Unit	Type	Gruppe up			Gruppe down		Claims	Losses				
		Base	No	Time	Base	Time		Dest	Dam	KIA	MIA	WIA
Lw Bfh Mitte												
Jafü Deutsche Bucht:												
10./JG 11	Fw 190A	Lister		~1200	Lister	~1300	0	2	0	2	0	0

Luftwaffe defensive activity – 25 July 1943

Unit	Type	Gruppe up			Gruppe down		Claims	Losses				
		Base	No	Time	Base	Time		Dest	Dam	KIA	MIA	WIA
Lw Bfh Mitte												
Jafü Deutsche Bucht:												
I./JG 1	Fw 190A	Deelen		1540	Jever	1524	transfer	0	0	0	0	0
	Fw 190A	Jever		1705	Jever	1804	n/c	0	0	0	0	0
II./JG 1	Fw 190A	Rheine	21	1521	Jever	1548	transfer	0	0	0	0	0
	Fw 190A	Jever	21	1559	Jever	~1700	2 B-17	0	0	0	0	0
Stab/JG 11	Bf 109G	Jever		~1450	Jever	~1520	n/c	0	0	0	0	0
I./JG 11	Fw 190A	Husum		1446	Husum	1526	n/c	0	0	0	0	0
2nd sorties	Fw 190A	Husum		1545	Husum	1638	0	0	0	0	0	0
3rd sorties	Fw 190A	Husum		1651	Husum	1740	2 B-17	0	0	0	0	0
II./JG 11	Bf 109G	Jever		1454	Jever	1516	0	0	0	0	0	0
2nd sorties	Bf 109G	Jever		1600	Jever	1715	2 B-17	3	2	0	0	4
III./JG 11	Bf 109G	Oldenburg		1458	Oldenburg	1514	n/c	0	0	0	0	0
2nd sorties	Bf 109G	Oldenburg		1612	Schleswig a/fs	~1715	1 B-17	0	0	0	0	0
III./JG 26	Bf 109G	Nordholz		1622	Nordholz	~1715	3 B-17	2	1	0	0	0
JaSta Helgoland	Bf 109T	Helgoland–Düne	5	1454	Helgoland–Düne	1527	n/c	0	0	0	0	0
2nd sorties	Bf 109T	Helgoland–Düne	5	1608	Helgoland–Düne	1740	2 B-17	0	0	0	0	0
ErprKdo 25	Fw 190A, Bf 110	Wittmundhafen		1457	Wittmundhafen	1541	0	0	0	0	0	0
2nd sorties	Fw 190A, Bf 110	Wittmundhafen		1603	Wittmundhafen	1715	2 B-17	1	0	1	0	0
Jafü H-Ruhr:												
III./JG 1	Bf 109G	Leeuwarden		1400	Leeuwarden	1430	n/c	0	0	0	0	0
2nd sorties	Bf 109G	Leeuwarden		1655	Leeuwarden	~1815	1 B-17 HSS	1	3	1	0	1
IV./NJG 1	Bf 110	Leeuwarden	16	~1700	Leeuwarden	~1900	1 B-17	1	0	0	2	0
I./NJG 4	Bf 110	Florennes		~1700	Florennes	~1900	0	0	0	0	0	0
Jafü Mitteldeutschland:												
I./NJG 5	Bf 110	Stendal		~1700	Stendal	~1900	0	0	0	0	0	0

26 July

8th Air Force VIII BC Mission #77: 199 of 303 B-17s bomb Hannover rubber industry, Hamburg U-boat yard, t/os, TOT 1159-1243 – lose 24-3-86, claim 60-10-36. No escort.

Today's 'Blitz week' targets were two synthetic rubber factories in Hannover and the U-boat yards in Hamburg. As on the previous day, the plan proved excessively complex. Bad weather over the Continent forced most of the 303 B-17s to bomb targets of opportunity. Jafü 2 and Jafü 3 handled the RAF diversions, while the Jafü Holland-Ruhr and Jafü Deutsche Bucht fighters were directed to the scattered, unescorted *dicke Autos* (fat cars, the Luftwaffe code word for heavy bombers). Most of the defenders were able to fly two missions. The Americans lost 24 B-17s downed and three scrapped. Eight German fighters were downed by the bomber gunners; five pilots were killed.

28 July

8th Air Force VIII BC Mission #78: 95 of 302 B-17s bomb Kassel and Oschersleben air industry, t/os, TOT 1027-54 – lose 22-5-118, claim 83-34-63. 123 VIII FC P-47s claim 9-1-6, lose 1-0-1.

Although the weather remained bad, 'Blitz week' resumed today with maximum-strength attacks on the Focke-Wulf factories at Kassel and Oschersleben. Few bombers attacked the briefed targets. Both were far inland, and the Deutsche Bucht and Holland-Ruhrgebiet controllers were able to vector their Jagdgruppen for continuous attacks on the bomber stream on both the inbound and withdrawal phases of the mission – ca. 350 fighters took off. One ErprKdo

The pilots of 1/JG 1 gather at Deelen in early July after the award of the EK II to Uffz. Kunze and Uffz. Hübl. From left: Ofhr. Berger (WIA 29 Nov 43), Obfw. Kaiser (WIA 4 Oct 43), Lt. Lück (WIA 9 Apr 44), Uffz. Rathenow (KIA 3 Nov 43), Uffz. Hübl (WIA 8 Oct 43), Lt. Schott (KIA 27 Sep 43), Uffz. Kunze (KIA 5 Jan 44), Lt. Engleder (WIA 16 Dec 43), Uffz. Rauhaus (KIA 31 Jul 44), Uffz. Knespel (KIA 28 Jul 43). *(Berger)*

25 Schwarm carried WGr 21 rockets today, as did several Jagdgruppen, according to some reports. One full Staffel (5./JG 11) dropped 250-kg bombs. The purpose of both these powerful but inaccurate weapons was the same: to break up the tight bomber formations to facilitate attack by cannon and machine guns. American fighters introduced their own tactical innovation: the 4th FG attached droppable ferry tanks to their P-47s and penetrated to the Dutch-German border, where they broke up a promising attack on the

Hptm. Hans Naumann, the Kapitän of the 6. Staffel of II./JG 26, prepares to take off from Vitry-en-Artois in his Fw 190A-6 on 26 July. *(Bundesarchiv 482-2864-30A)*

The B-17 shot down on 28 July by Lt. Heinz Rose (II./JG 11), but not credited to him. It crash-landed near Vörden, east of Zutphen, Holland. *(Rose)*

Lt. Rüdiger von Kirchmayr runs up the engine of his II./JG 1 Fw 190A-5 in preparation for take-off in July. The yellow undercowl is a theatre marking; the cowl ring and Gruppe *Tatzelwurm* [dragon-worm; a creature from Nordic folklore] are in the 5. Staffel colour, red. *(Mombeek)*

B-17s by I./JG 3 and I./JG 26. The day's battles had gone reasonably well for the defenders prior to the appearance of the Thunderbolts. Every day unit of Jafü Holland-Ruhr and Jafü Deutsche Bucht made contact. Twenty-seven B-17s and one P-47 were lost or written off after their return, for the loss of eight German pilots KIA or MIA, 13 WIA and 23 fighters.

29 July

8th Air Force VIII BC Mission #79: 139 of 168 1st BW B-17s bomb Kiel shipyard and t/os, TOT 0901 – lose 6-2-62, claim 48-6-33. No escort. 54 of 81 4th BW B-17s bomb Warnemünde aviation industry, TOT 0922-24 – lose 4-0-7, claim 0-2-0. No escort.

The VIII BC targets were the Kiel U-boat yards and a Heinkel aircraft factory in Warnemünde. Both were on the Baltic Sea. The defenders were apparently slow to recognise the raid. Only the fighters of Jafü Deutsche Bucht could reach it, and then only as the bombers returned after bombing. Eight claims for B-17s are known to have been confirmed; 10 in fact went down, and two more were scrapped. The Luftwaffe lost seven fighters to the bomber gunners, but no pilots were killed; three were injured. The Jafü Holland-Ruhr and Jafü 2 fighters were kept occupied by the RAF FC and the American P-47s, which were becoming more aggressive as their pilots gained skill with experience.

30 July – Kassel (see map)

8th Air Force VIII BC Mission #80: 134 of 186 B-17s bomb Kassel aviation industry, TOT 0910-28 – lose 12-5-82, claim 48-13-32. 107 VIII FC P-47s claim 25-4-8, lose 7-1-0.

The final mission of 'Blitz week' was an attack on two Kassel Fw 190 factories by all 186 operational B-17s. The bombers' course across Holland in a long, single stream disclosed the target area soon enough for the Germans to concentrate fighters from four Jafü to intercept them. An

The 4./JG 11 'circus wagon', which stored the instruments of the staff band, at Jever in the summer of 1943. 'The sensation of the Continent' (painted on the other side) promises 'paradise without Eve'. *(Rose)*

Luftwaffe defensive activity – 26 July 1943

Unit	Type	Gruppe up			Gruppe down		Claims	Losses				
		Base	No	Time	Base	Time		Dest	Dam	KIA	MIA	WIA
Lw Bfh Mitte												
Jafü Deutsche Bucht:												
Stab/JG 11	Bf 109G	Jever		~1113	Husum	~1235	0	0	0	0	0	0
2nd sorties	Bf 109G	Husum		~1300	Jever	~1345	1 B-17	0	0	0	0	0
I./JG 11	Fw 190A	Husum	28	1023	Husum	1139	3 B-17	1	0	0	0	0
2nd sorties	Fw 190A	Husum		1202	Husum, Borkum	~1330	1 B-17	0	0	0	0	0
II./JG 11	Bf 109G	Jever		1030	Jever	1055	0	0	0	0	0	0
	Bf 109G	Jever		1113	Jever	1235	3 B-17	3	0	2	0	0
2nd sorties	Bf 109G	Jever		~1330	Jever	~1500	0	0	0	0	0	0
III./JG 11	Bf 109G	Oldenburg		1118	Oldenburg, Vechta	~1250	1 B-17	0	2	0	0	0
2nd sorties	Bf 109G	Oldenburg, Vechta		~1315	Oldenburg	~1430	0	0	0	0	0	0
III./JG 26	Bf 109G	Nordholz		1130	Nordholz	1250	1 B-17	0	0	0	0	0
2nd sorties	Bf 109G	Nordholz		1300	Nordholz	~1400	2 B-17	0	0	0	0	0
JaSta Helgoland	Bf 109T	Helgoland–Düne		1037	Helgoland–Düne	~1107	n/c	0	0	0	0	0
2nd sorties	Bf 109T	Helgoland–Düne	5	1123	Helgoland–Düne	1218	2 B-17	0	1	0	0	1
ErprKdo 25	Bf 109G	Wittmundhafen		1034	Wittmundhafen	1106	n/c	0	0	0	0	0
	Bf 109G, Bf 110	Wittmundhafen		1116	Langensalza, Wittmundhafen	1221	0	1	0	0	1	0
2nd sorties	Bf 109G	Langensalza		1300	Wittmundhafen	1406	n/c	0	0	0	0	0
I./NJG 3	Bf 110	Vechta		1120	Vechta	1220	1 B-17	0	0	0	0	0
III./NJG 3	Bf 110	Stade		~1200	Stade	~1400	2 B-17	0	0	0	0	0
Jafü H-Ruhr:												
Stab/JG 1	Fw 190A	Deelen		~1149	Deelen	~1305	0	0	0	0	0	0
I./JG 1	Fw 190A	Deelen		1149	Deelen, Borkum, Zwischenahn	1310	4 B-17	2	4	1	0	1
II./JG 1	Fw 190A	Rheine	17	1120	Rheine	1235	2 B-17, 1 B-17 HSS	0	5	0	0	0
III./JG 1	Bf 109G	Leeuwarden		1120	Leeuwarden	~1230	0	0	0	0	0	0
2nd sorties	Bf 109G	Leeuwarden		~1300	Leeuwarden	~1430	0	0	1	1	0	0
I./JG 3	Bf 109G	München–Gladbach		~1120	München–Gladbach	~1230	0	0	0	0	0	0
IV./NJG 1	Bf 110	Leeuwarden		1129	Leeuwarden	1219	0	0	0	0	0	0
	Bf 110	Leeuwarden		~1300	Leeuwarden	~1430	1 B-17	0	0	0	0	0

early-morning raid on Woensdrecht by medium bombers did not affect operations from this base, which serviced the Luftflotte 3 fighters all morning. The closest fighters, the JG 26 Geschwadergruppe (now the Stabsschwarm, 8., 10. and 11. Staffeln), I./JG 26, and I./JG 3, attacked the incoming stream as soon as the Spitfires turned back. The rest of the defenders were concentrated along the bombers' presumed return route to attack the B-17s as they withdrew. The German fighters flew 285 effective sorties, including 40 second sorties. JG 2 flew an outstanding mission from Poix and Woensdrecht, claiming eight B-17s and three P-47s from east of Rotterdam out over the North Sea. The day's battles with the B-17s were brought to an end by the arrival of 107 P-47s, the full strength of the VIII FC. All three P-47 groups were now equipped with drop tanks, and they had been given a new mission – close escort of the American bombers – to replace their previous high-altitude sweeps in co-operation with the RAF. The result was the largest battle to date between American and German fighters. For the day, the Americans lost 17 B-17s destroyed or scrapped; eight P-47s were lost or written off. Losses to the RLV force were high: 14 pilots were dead or missing, and 31 fighters were destroyed. The day's battle was an accurate precursor of the future for the RLV force, which would never have enough planes to defeat the American escorts in a direct confrontation.

Luftwaffe defensive activity – 28 July 1943

Unit	Type	Gruppe up			Gruppe down		Claims	Losses				
		Base	No	Time	Base	Time		Dest	Dam	KIA	MIA	WIA
Lw Bfh Mitte												
Jafü Deutsche Bucht:												
Stab/JG 11	Bf 109G	Jever		~0845	Jever	~1000	0	1	0	1	0	0
2nd sorties	Bf 109G	Jever		~1130	Jever	~1250	0	0	0	0	0	0
I./JG 11	Fw 190A	Husum		0848	Husum	1004	4 B-17	1	0	0	0	2
	Fw 190A	Husum		1037	Husum	1105	n/c	0	0	0	0	0
2nd sorties	Fw 190A	Husum		~1130	Husum	~1250	0	0	0	0	0	0
II./JG 11	Bf 109G	Jever		0835	Jever	0950	10 B-17	2	1	0	0	1
	Bf 109G	Jever		1013	Jever, Vechta	1110	1 B-17	0	0	0	0	0
2nd sorties	Bf 109G	Jever, Vechta		1130	Jever	1257	1 B-17	0	0	0	0	0
III./JG 11	Bf 109G	Oldenburg		~1000	Oldenburg	~1100	2 B-17	1	0	0	0	1
III./JG 26	Bf 109G	Nordholz		0835	Nordholz, Sylt	1006	2 B-17	2	0	1	0	0
JaSta Helgoland	Bf 109T	Helgoland–Düne		0854	Wangerooge	0925	n/c	0	1	0	0	1
2nd sorties	Bf 109T	Helgoland–Düne		0935	Helgoland–Düne	1038	1 B-17	0	0	0	0	0
ErprKdo 25	Bf 109G, Bf 110	Wittmundhafen		0842	Wittmundhafen, Wangerooge	0950	0	0	0	0	0	0
	Fw 190A	Wittmundhafen		~1000	Wittmundhafen	~1100	1 B-17	1	4	0	1	0
2nd sorties	Bf 110	Wittmundhafen		1154	Wittmundhafen	1315	n/c	0	0	0	0	0
ISS Focke-Wulf	Fw 190A	Bremen		~1000	Bremen	~1100	1 B-17	1	0	1	0	0
ISS Fieseler	Fw 190A	Kassel		~1030	Kassel	~1130	1 B-17	0	0	0	0	0
Jafü H-Ruhr:												
Stab/JG 1	Fw 190A	Deelen		~0955	Deelen	~1055	0	0	0	0	0	0
I./JG 1	Fw 190A	Deelen, Arnhem		0956	Deelen, Leeuwarden	1055	2 B-17	3	4	1	0	2
2nd sorties	Fw 190A	Deelen, Leeuwarden		1220	Deelen, Arnhem	1300	0	0	0	0	0	0
II./JG 1	Fw 190A	Rheine	13	1005	Rheine	~1100	2 B-17	1	2	0	0	1
III./JG 1	Bf 109G	Leeuwarden		0946	Leeuwarden	~1100	0	3	0	1	0	2
I./JG 3	Bf 109G	München–Gladbach		1145	München–Gladbach	~1245	1 B-17	4	3	2	0	0
I./JG 26	Fw 190A	Woensdrecht		1004	Woensdrecht, Deelen	1030	1 P-47	0	0	0	0	0
2nd sorties	Fw 190A	Woensdrecht, Deelen		1130	Woensdrecht, Deelen	1250	1 B-17, 1 P-47	3	1	0	0	3
III./JG 54	Bf 109G	Schiphol		0909	Schiphol	0938	0	0	0	0	0	0
	Bf 109G	Schiphol		1015	Schiphol	1051	0	0	0	0	0	0
2nd sorties	Bf 109G	Schiphol		~1130	Schiphol	~1250	1 B-17	0	0	0	0	0
Luftflotte 3												
Jafü 2:												
GeschGr/JG 26	Fw 190A	Lille–Vendeville		1135	Vendeville, Schiphol, Woensdrecht	1307	0	0	0	0	0	0
	Fw 190	Lille–Vendeville		1725	Venlo	1815	transfer	0	0	0	0	0
II./JG 26	Fw 190A	Vitry–en–Artois		1100	Rheine, Deelen	1220	transfer	0	0	0	0	0

Luftwaffe defensive activity – 29 July 1943

Unit	Type	Gruppe up			Gruppe down		Claims	Losses				
		Base	No	Time	Base	Time		Dest	Dam	KIA	MIA	WIA
Lw Bfh Mitte												
Jafü Deutsche Bucht:												
Stab/JG 11	Bf 109G	Jever		~0850	Jever	~0945	1 B-17	0	0	0	0	0
I./JG 11	Fw 190A	Husum		0837	Husum	0942	4 B-17	1	0	0	0	0
II./JG 11	Bf 109G	Jever		0850	Jever	0947	0	2	1	0	0	0
III./JG 11	Bf 109G	Oldenburg		~0845	Oldenburg	~0945	0	2	0	0	0	1
III./JG 26	Bf 109G	Nordholz		0845	Nordholz, Schleswig	0945	3 B-17	1	2	0	0	1
JaSta Helgoland	Bf 109T	Helgoland–Düne	3	0844	Helgoland–Düne	~0950	0	0	1	1	0	1
ErprKdo 25	Bf 109G, Fw 190A, Bf 110, Me 410	Wittmundhafen		0825	Westerland–Sylt, Wittmundhafen	1000	0	0	0	0	0	0

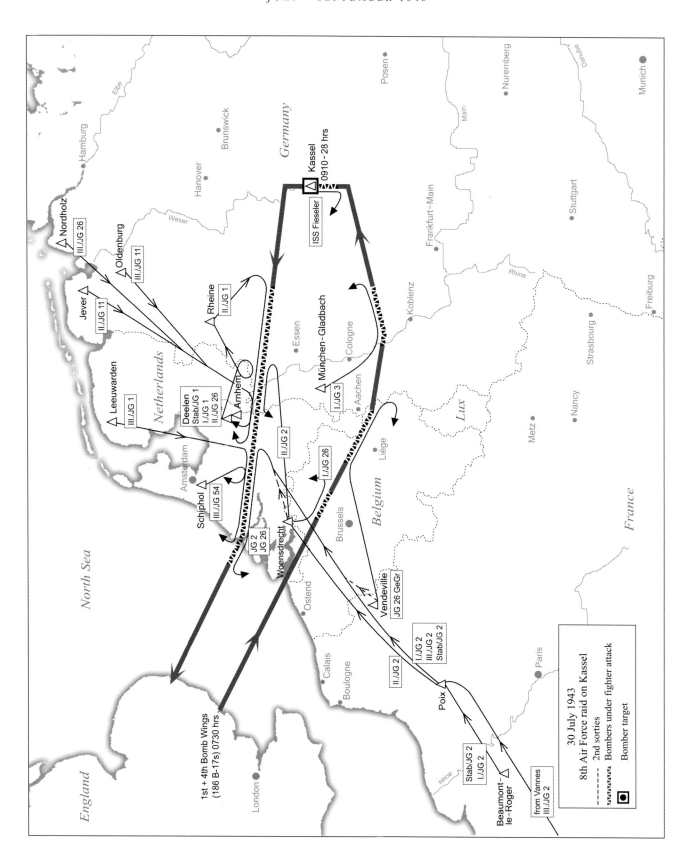

Germany

Munich

Nuremberg

Posen

Danube

Brunswick

Hanover

Hamburg

Elbe

Weser

Kassel
0910 – 28 hrs

ISS Fieseler

Frankfurt–Main

Stuttgart

Rhine

Freiburg

Koblenz

Main

Nordholz
III./JG 26

Oldenburg
III./JG 11

Jever
II./JG 11

Rheine
II./JG 1

München-Gladbach
I./JG 3

Essen

Cologne

Aachen

Strasbourg

Nancy

Metz

Lux

Leeuwarden
III./JG 1

Netherlands

Deelen
Stab/JG 1
I./JG 1
II./JG 26

Arnhem

II./JG 2

I./JG 26

Liège

Belgium

Amsterdam

Schiphol
III./JG 54

JG 2
JG 26

Woensdrecht

Brussels

Ostend

Vendeville
JG 26 GeGr

Paris

North Sea

Calais

Boulogne

Poix

II./JG 2

I./JG 2
III./JG 2
Stab/JG 2

Seine

England

London

1st + 4th Bomb Wings
(186 B-17s) 0730 hrs

Stab/JG 2
I./JG 2

Beaumont-
le-Roger

from Vannes
III./JG 2

France

30 July 1943
8th Air Force raid on Kassel
——— 2nd sorties
- - - - - Bombers under fighter attack
wwwww Bombers under fighter attack
◉ Bomber target

Luftwaffe defensive activity vs. Kassel raid – 30 July 1943

Unit	Type	Gruppe up			Gruppe down		Claims	Losses				
		Base	No	Time	Base	Time		Dest	Dam	KIA	MIA	WIA
Lw Bfh Mitte												
Jafü Deutsche Bucht:												
II./JG 11	Bf 109G	Jever		0947	Jever, Kirchhellen, Reinsehlen	1057	0	0	1	0	0	0
III./JG 11	Bf 109G	Oldenburg		0936	Oldenburg	~1045	0	2	2	1	0	1
III./JG 26	Bf 109G	Nordholz		0949	Nordholz	1045	0	0	0	0	0	0
ISS Fieseler	Fw 190A	Kassel		~0900	Kassel	~1000	0	0	0	0	0	0
Jafü H. Ruhr:												
Stab/JG 1	Fw 190A	Deelen		~0935	Deelen	~1025	0	0	0	0	0	0
I./JG 1	Fw 190A	Deelen, Arnhem		0937	Deelen, Arnhem	1030	2 B-17, 2 P-47	6	0	4	0	1
II./JG 1	Fw 190A	Rheine	6	0942	Rheine	1055	0	1	0	1	0	0
III./JG 1	Bf 109G	Leeuwarden		0950	Leeuwarden	1055	1 B-17 HSS, 1 P-47	1	2	0	0	0
I./JG 3	Bf 109G	München–Gladbach		0800	München–Gladbach, various	0930	1 B-17, 1 B-17 HSS	2	0	0	0	1
I./JG 26	Fw 190A	Woensdrecht		0812	Woensdrecht, Antwerp	0853	1 B-17 HSS	3	1	1	0	1
2nd sorties	Fw 190A	Woensdrecht		0945	Woensdrecht	1049	1 B-17, 1 P-47	1	0	1	0	0
II./JG 26	Fw 190A	Deelen		0932	Deelen	1045	2 B-17, 2 P-47	4	3	1	0	4
III./JG 54	Bf 109G	Schiphol		0949	Schiphol	1038	0	4	0	1	1	2
	Bf 109G	Schiphol		1034	Schiphol	1106	1 P-47	0	0	0	0	0
Luftflotte 3												
Jafü 2:												
GeschGr/ JG 26	Fw 190A, Bf 109G	Lille–Vendeville		0750	Lille–Vendeville, St. Trond	~0845	1 B-17	0	0	0	0	0
2nd sorties	Fw 190A	Lille–Vendeville		~0915	Lille–Vendeville	~1015	1 B-17 HSS	0	1	0	0	0
2nd sorties	Bf 109G	Lille–Vendeville		0948	Vendeville, Antwerp	1055	0	0	0	0	0	0
Jafü 3:												
Stab/JG 2	Fw 190A	Beaumont–le–Roger		0900	Poix	0915	transfer	0	0	0	0	0
	Fw 190A	Poix		0928	Woensdrecht?	~1100	1 B-17	0	1	0	0	0
I./JG 2	Fw 190A, Bf 109G	Beaumont–le–Roger		0900	Poix	0915	transfer	0	0	0	0	0
	Fw 190A, Bf 109G	Poix		0928	Woensdrecht?	~1100	2 B-17, 1 P-47	2	1	0	0	0
II./JG 2	Bf 109G	Poix		0800	Woensdrecht	0830	transfer	0	0	0	0	0
	Bf 109G	Woensdrecht		~0900	Woensdrecht	~1000	2 B-17	1	4	1	0	0
2nd sorties	Bf 109G	Woensdrecht		~1030	Poix	~1130	1 B-17, 2 P-47, 1 B-17 HSS	0	0	0	0	0
III./JG 2	Fw 190A	Vannes		~0900	Poix	~0930	transfer	0	0	0	0	0
	Fw 190A	Poix		~1000	Woensdrecht?	~1100	1 B-17	3	3	1	1	2

August 1943

The RAF Bomber Command's firestorm-inducing raid on Hamburg on the night of 27–28 July, after which the city essentially ceased to function, convinced Adolf Hitler that the Reich air defences needed massive reinforcement. The second-in-command of the Luftwaffe, Generalfeldmarschall Erhard Milch, and the General of the Fighter Arm, Adolf Galland, were worried about the growing day offensive as well as the night raids and took advantage of the opportunity presented by Hitler's concern to strengthen the day forces. Milch ordered a significant increase in the production of Bf 109, Fw 190 and Me 410 day fighters, which were the only types immediately available. The revolutionary Me 262 jet fighter, which both he and Galland supported, was not yet ready for production.

Increasing the effectiveness of the Reichsluftverteidigung called for more than just fighters: it required more pilots, more units and a more efficient organisation. Pilot training was already losing the battle for scarce fuel and received only 40 per cent of the requested amount for July. Training was a non-combat function, always short of resources. The fundamental problem of inadequate numbers of competent pilots would never be solved.

The numerical strength of the RLV force could be boosted by forming new units, enlarging the existing RLV units and transferring units from other theatres. The formation of new units was the most difficult, owing primarily to the lack of professional officers to staff them. Two new single-engine day fighter units joined the RLV force in the third quarter of 1943, JG 25 and JG 50, but these were special cases. They had been formed to catch RAF Mosquito reconnaissance aircraft and day intruders, but were unsuccessful at this mission and were added to the strength of the conventional RLV order of battle.

Expansion of the Jagdgruppen already in the RLV day force was planned, but was delayed by the demands of the southern and eastern fronts. General Galland wanted to increase the number of Staffeln in each Gruppe from three to four, to increase the number of fighters in each Staffel from 12 to 16 and, ultimately, to add a fourth Gruppe to each Jagdgeschwader. The establishment strength of each Jagdgeschwader would be increased from 124 to 208 and finally to 276 fighters. JG 2 and JG 26, the two Luftflotte 3 Jagdgeschwader, were given top priority for expansion and were enlarged to 12 Staffeln by the end of September.

The reinforcement of the RLV force with Jagdgruppen and Zerstörergruppen from the eastern and southern fronts was already underway. The three Zerstörergeschwader were reforming in the Reich. There are indications that JG 3 was to form the heart of the defences of southern Germany, while all of the Gruppen of JG 27 would eventually be concentrated in Austria, which had no first-line air defences until a raid on the Wiener Neustadt Messerschmitt factory on the 13th caused something of a panic within the Luftwaffe High Command. The Gruppen of JG 53 and JG 77 also came back from the south one at a time to rebuild, but were not fortunate enough to join the RLV force as full Geschwader; instead, they were farmed out to the Jagddivisionen as individual orphan Gruppen. Most of them had a difficult time in the RLV force, losing the majority of their original pilots in a matter of weeks or months.

The organisation of the RLV force was still fragmented and inefficient. The timely assembly of large formations was difficult, and crossing Jafü boundaries frequently resulted in loss of contact with the controller and a consequent inability to close with the enemy. Centralisation was on the way, but no real progress would be made until September.

A Bf 109G-6 of II./JG 2 crash-landed by Lt. Paul Müngersdorff near Aachen after developing engine trouble on 12 August. It was recorded as sustaining 60 per cent damage, which was equivalent to a write-off. (Prien)

Luftwaffe defensive activity – 12 August 1943

Unit	Type	Gruppe up Base	No	Time	Gruppe down Base	Time	Claims	Losses Dest	Dam	KIA	MIA	WIA
Lw Bfh Mitte												
Jafü H. Ruhr:												
Stab/JG 1	Fw 190A	Deelen		~0830	Deelen	~1000	0	0	0	0	0	0
I./JG 1	Fw 190A	Deelen		0832	Deelen, Eindhoven	0956	3 B-17	1	2	0	0	0
II./JG 1	Fw 190A	Rheine	23	0908	Rheine	~1000	4 B-17, 1 B-17 HSS	1	2	1	0	0
III./JG 1	Bf 109G	Leeuwarden		~0845	Leeuwarden	~1000	0	0	2	0	0	1
I./JG 3	Bf 109G	München–Gladbach		~0845	München–Gladbach	~0945	1 B-17	0	1	0	0	0
III./JG 3	Bf 109G	Münster–Handorf	12	0850	Münster–Handorf, Köln–Ostheim	0930	3 B-17	0	0	0	0	0
I./JG 26	Fw 190A	Woensdrecht		0814	Woensdrecht, Dwende?	0926	2 B-17, 2 B-17 HSS	2	1	0	0	1
	Fw 190A	Woensdrecht		0927	Woensdrecht	1035	1 B-17, 1 B-17 HSS		0	0	0	0
II./JG 26	Fw 190A	Volkel		0830	Volkel, München–Gladbach	0930	4 B-17	1	0	0	0	0
I./JG 27	Bf 109G	Münster–Handorf		0846	Münster–Handorf, Köln–Butzweilerhof	0937	5 B-17	2	0	0	0	0
III./JG 54	Bf 109G	Schiphol		~0815	Schiphol	~0915	1 B-17	0	2	0	0	0
Jafü Süddeutschland:												
JG 50	Bf 109G	Wiesbaden		~0900	Wiesbaden	~1000	1 B-17, 1 B-17 HSS	0	1	0	0	1
Luftflotte 3												
Jafü 2:												
GeschGr/JG 26	Fw 190A, Bf 109G	Lille–Vendeville		0805	Lille–Vendeville, Bonn–Hangelar, Brussels, St. Trond	0912	0	1	0	1	0	0
2nd sorties	Fw 190A, Bf 109G	St. Trond, Lille–Vendeville		0948	Lille–Vendeville	1049	1 B-17	0	0	0	0	0
Jafü 3:												
II./JG 2	Bf 109G	Poix		~0805	Ligescourt	~0945	2 B-17	2	1	0	0	0
2nd sorties	Bf 109G	Ligescourt		~1000	Poix	~1100	0	1	0	1	0	0
III./JG 2	Fw 190A	?		~0805	?	~0945	0	0	1	0	0	0
1./JGr Süd	Bf 109	?		~0845	?	~0945	2 B-17	0	0	0	0	0

12 August

8th Air Force VIII BC Mission #81: 243 of 330 B-17s bomb Bochum, Gelsenkirchen, Recklinghausen, Bonn, t/os, TOT 0850-0925 – lose 25-3-172, claim 29-7-13. RAF FC Spitfires claim 1-0-3, lose 1; 131 VIII FC P 47s claim 4-1-1, lose 0.

After restoring its 'Blitz week' losses, the VIII BC returned to the offensive with an early-morning attack on the Ruhr. The weather interfered with the mission, and most of the 330 B-17s bombed targets of opportunity, or none at all. The Spitfires and P-47s were ordered to escort two separate bomber streams on both penetration and withdrawal and proved too few to repeat the success of 30 July. Approximately 210 defensive sorties were flown. The Jagdgruppen nearest the coast – II./JG 2, the JG 26 Geschwadergruppe, I./JG 26 and III./JG 54 – attacked first, followed by the rest of the Jafü Holland-Ruhr fighters, including III./JG 3 and I./JG 27 on their first RLV missions as complete Gruppen. The result was the most successful interception to date. Of the 133 1st BW B-17s that did not turn back early, 25 were shot down or scrapped. The 4th BW was shielded from attack by the 1st and lost only three bombers. The RLV force lost three KIA, three WIA and 11 fighters.

Luftwaffe defensive activity – 15 August 1943

Unit	Type	Gruppe up			Gruppe down		Claims	Losses				
		Base	No	Time	Base	Time		Dest	Dam	KIA	MIA	WIA
Lw Bfh Mitte												
Jafü H. Ruhr.												
I./JG 26	Fw 190A	Woensdrecht		2016	Woensdrecht	2106	n/c	0	0	0	0	0
II./JG 26	Fw 190A	Volkel		~2015	Volkel	~2115	n/c	0	0	0	0	0
III./JG 26	Bf 109G	Schiphol		2025	Schiphol	2110	n/c	0	0	0	0	0
Luftflotte 3												
Jafü 2:												
GeschGr/JG 26	Fw 190A, Bf 109G	Lille–Vendeville		2030	Lille–Vendeville	2115	1 Spitfire	1	0	0	0	1
Jafü 3:												
Stab/JG 2	Fw 190A	Beaumont–le–Roger		~2000	Beaumont–le–Roger	~2100	0	0	0	0	0	0
I./JG 2	Fw 190A	Beaumont–le–Roger		~2000	Beaumont–le–Roger	~2100	0	0	0	0	0	1
II./JG 2	Bf 109G	Vitry–en–Artois		~2000	Vitry–en–Artois	~2100	3 B-17	3	0	3	0	0

13 August

8th Air Force VIII BC: 61 of 87 B-24s bomb Wiener Neustadt Bf 109 factory on return flight from North Africa, lose 2. 27 9th Air Force B-24s take off on mission, turn back before bombing.

The small force of B-24s returning to England after the Ploesti mission opened a new front in the air war by bombing an important Bf 109 factory in Austria from the south. Four Bf 109s of the Werkschutzstaffel provided the sole defence; these had no success. The surprise attack destroyed or severely damaged 50 complete Bf 109s and damaged the factory so severely that output did not fully recover until October.

15 August

8th Air Force VIII BC Mission #82: 290 of 327 B-17s bomb six airfields in France and Holland, TOT 2025-33 – lose 2-0-59, claim 9-0-1. RAF FC Spitfires claim 3-0-0, lose 1; 187 VIII FC P-47s claim 0, lose 0-1-0.

This was the first day of Operation STARKEY, an extended tactical exercise by the RAF and USAAF intended to convince the Wehrmacht that an invasion of the Pas de Calais was imminent. The VIII BC targeted the airfields at Amiens–Glisy, Merville, Poix, Lille–Vendeville, Vitry and Vlissingen in the late evening. Bombing results were mixed; at least one base, that of JG 26 at Lille–Vendeville, was rendered non-operational. The day's targets were all within Spitfire range, and the RAF provided effective escort.

The P-47s reverted to high-altitude sweeps of the coast and reported no encounters with the Luftwaffe. II./JG 2 made one effective attack on the heavies and claimed three B-17s (two were in fact lost) for the loss of three Messerschmitts and pilots to the Spitfires. The JG 26 Gruppen had flown two earlier missions against tactical aircraft and flew this one in low strength; they apparently never reached the bombers.

16 August

8th Air Force VIII BC Mission #83: 237 of 246 B-17s bomb Le Bourget, Poix, Abbéville airfields, TOT 1011-37 – lose 4-0-84, claim 29-3-11. RAF FC Spitfires claim 2-0-3, lose 4; 180 VIII FC P-47s claim 18-2-7, lose 3-2-0.

Operation STARKEY continued. The VIII BC pounded the Jafü 3 airfields at Poix, Abbéville and Paris–Le Bourget in the morning. The Le Bourget force was accompanied all the way to the target by P-47s equipped with pressurised belly tanks. All three JG 2 Gruppen intercepted the stream both on approach and withdrawal, but the escort was extremely effective, and only four B-17s went down. The JG 26 Geschwadergruppe in neighbouring Jafü 2 was scrambled, but its combats were inconclusive. JG 2 and all of JG 26 were up later against raids by tactical fighters and bombers. By the day's end, nine JG 2 pilots had been killed or remained missing, and 14 fighters had been lost; this would prove to be the most costly day of 1943 for the Richthofen Geschwader.

Luftwaffe defensive activity – 16 August 1943

Unit	Type	Gruppe up			Gruppe down		Claims	Losses (—: included in 1st sortie)				
		Base	No	Time	Base	Time		Dest	Dam	KIA	MIA	WIA
Luftflotte 3												
Jafü 2:												
GechGr/JG 26	Fw 190A,	Lille–Nord		0955	Lille–Nord	1100	0	0	0	0	0	0
	Bf 109G											
Jafü 3:												
Stab/JG 2	Fw 190A	Beaumont–le–Roger		~0945	Beaumont–le–Roger	~1100	0	0	0	0	0	0
I./JG 2	Fw 190A.	Beaumont–le–Roger		~0945	Beaumont–le–Roger	~1100	3 B-17, 1 P-47	8	2	4	0	4
	Bf 109G											
2nd sorties	Fw 190A.	Beaumont–le–Roger		~1130	Beaumont–le–Roger	~1230	0	—	—	—	—	—
	Bf 109G											
II./JG 2	Bf 109G	Vitry–en–Artois		~0945	Vitry–en–Artois	~1100	0	3	1	2	1	0
2nd sorties	Bf 109G	Vitry–en–Artois		~1130	Vitry–en–Artois	~1230	1 B-17	—	—	—	—	—
Jafü 4:												
III./JG 2	Fw 190A	Vannes		~0945	Evreux area	~1000	transfer	0	0	0	0	0
2nd sorties	Fw 190A	Evreux area		~1015	Vannes	~1130	2 P-47	3	2	1	1	1
Jafü Südfrankreich:												
JGr Süd	Bf 109	Orange–Caritat		?	Orange–Caritat	?	0	1	0	0	0	0
JLÜberprGr	Bf 109	Orange–Caritat		?	Orange–Caritat	?	0	2	0	2	0	0

17 August – Regensburg (see map)

8th Air Force VIII BC Mission #84a: 127 of 146 4th BW B-17s bomb Regensburg Messerschmitt factory, TOT 1248-1307 – lose 24-1-50, claim 140-19-36. Total of 240 VIII FC P-47s escort Regensburg and the later Schweinfurt mission, claim 19-3-4, lose 3-0-0; RAF FC Spitfires and Typhoons escort day's initial, final legs and diversions, claim 14-2-1, lose 3-1.

The VIII BC ordered their most ambitious operation to date: a full-strength dual mission to two widely dispersed targets, both far beyond escort range. The longer-range 4th BW would bomb the Regensburg Messerschmitt factory in southern Germany and then proceed to American bases in Tunisia. The 1st BW would follow shortly behind it, bomb the ball-bearing factories in Schweinfurt and return to England. The timing was intended to simplify the mission of the USAAF and RAF escorts and confuse the defenders. However, English weather forced a four-hour take-off delay of the Schweinfurt force and instead simplified the task of the RLV commanders. The heavy pre-dawn radio testing at the B-17 bases presaged a full-strength, deep-penetration raid. The Jafü Holland-Ruhr brought his seven Jagdgruppen to full readiness early and scrambled two of its coastal Gruppen, I./JG

26 and III./JG 26, just as the first bombers had left the English coast. These were from the 4th BW, headed for Regensburg. The two Jagdgruppen avoided the skimpy P-47 escort, which was concentrated at the head of the formation, and attacked the rear combat wings. Two other Jafü Holland-Ruhr Gruppen attacked the bombers as soon as the last P-47 turned back at Eupen. Two failed to make contact and landed to await the bombers' return; the seventh was apparently held in reserve as most of the American bombers had not yet been located. Jafü Holland-Ruhr requested support from Luftflotte 3 and Jafü Deutsche Bucht. After some skirmishes with RAF diversionary raiders, JG 2 moved east from its bases in western France. Jafü 2's two JG 26 Gruppen also did some base shuffling. JG 11 was ordered southwest from its north German bases to the Netherlands. They were too late to intercept the incoming bombers, but landed to refuel on airfields near the assumed withdrawal route.

The bombers entered southern Germany, where they were attacked by JG 50, Jafü Süddeutschland's only day fighter unit; the operational Schwärme of two nearby operational training units; various night fighter units; and, after their final turn to the target, the Regensburg factory defence Staffel. To the

Germans' great surprise, the B-17s turned south after the bombing run and proceeded to North Africa. Although 24 of the B-17s failed to reach their new base and another was scrapped there, this part of the day's combined mission was considered a success. Reconnaissance photos showed that serious damage had been done to the Messerschmitt plant. The RLV force had scrambled 404 fighters, of which 197 made contact. Losses were light: three KIA, five WIA and nine fighters.

Bf 109G-5s and G-6s are serviced at Wiesbaden–Erbenheim. These fighters were flown by I./JG 300, III./JG 300 and (possibly) JG 50 in their original delivery codes. *(Bundesarchiv 650-5438-7)*

Major Hermann Graf, Kommodore of JG 50, poses beside the highly decorated tail of his Bf 109G-6 'Red 1'. JG 50 was formed in mid-1943 to hunt RAF reconnaissance Mosquitoes. Command was given to the well-known Graf, the first pilot to claim 200 victories (all in the East). The unit was disbanded in October, its pilots being absorbed in existing Reich defence units. Graf became Kommodore of JG 11, but was eventually allowed to return to the Eastern Front as JG 52 Kommodore, with the consequence that he was imprisoned by the Soviets after the war. *(Bundesarchiv 650-5447-23)*

A JG 50 Bf 109G-6 warms up for take-off from Wiesbaden–Erbenheim. Its fuselage displays clearly the three-colour mid-war camouflage spray mottle. *(Cranston)*

Fw. Werner Möszner (III./JG 26) poses beside his Bf 109G-6 at Nordholz in August. *(Möszner via de Jong)*

Luftwaffe defensive activity vs. Regensburg raid – 17 August 1943

Unit	Type	Gruppe up			Gruppe down		Claims	Losses				
		Base	No	Time	Base	Time		Dest	Dam	KIA	MIA	WIA
Lw Bfh Mitte			404									
Jafü Deutsche Bucht:			87									
Stab/JG 11	Bf 109G	Jever		~1055	Rheine, then Gilze–Rijen	~1300	transfer	0	0	0	0	0
I./JG 11	Fw 190A	Husum	28	1245	Deelen	~1330	transfer	0	0	0	0	0
II./JG 11	Bf 109G	Jever	28	1055	Rheine	~1130	transfer	0	0	0	0	0
	Fw 190A	Rheine	28	1235	Gilze–Rijen	1310	transfer	0	0	0	0	0
III./JG 11	Bf 109G	Oldenburg	22	1107	Rheine, Münster, then St. Trond	1324	transfer	0	0	0	0	0
ErprKdo 25	Fw 190A	Wittmundhafen		1300	Deelen	1343	transfer	0	0	0	0	0
Jafü H-Ruhr:				172								
I./JG 1	Fw 190A	Arnhem, Deelen	15	1122	Ödheim, Mannheim	1300	3 B-17, 3 B-17 HSS	0	1	0	0	0
II./JG 1	Fw 190A	Rheine	21	1157	Woensdrecht	~1230	transfer	0	0	0	0	0
III./JG 1	Bf 109G	Leeuwarden	32	0840	Deelen	~0930	transfer	0	0	0	0	0
	Bf 109G	Deelen	31	1125	Mannheim, Koblenz	1230	0	1	0	0	0	1
I./JG 3	Bf 109G	München–Gladbach	20	1125	München–Gladbach	1227	1 B-17, 1 B-17 HSS	1	1	0	0	0
III./JG 3	Bf 109G	Münster–Handorf	28	1205	Woensdrecht	1305	transfer	0	0	0	0	0
I./JG 26	Fw 190A	Woensdrecht	15	1045	Woensdrecht	1141	3 B-17	1	2	1	0	1
III./JG 26	Bf 109G	Schiphol	25	1018	Schiphol	~1200	3 B-17	4	1	1	0	3
I./NJG 1	Bf 110	Venlo, Gilze–Rijen	6	~1100	Venlo, Gilze–Rijen	~1230	0	0	0	0	0	0
II./NJG 1	Bf 110	St. Trond	6	1112	St. Trond	~1330	1 B-17	0	2	0	0	0
Jagddivision 5:			179									
JG 50	Bf 109G	Wiesbaden–Erbenheim	27	1130	Wiesbaden–Erbenheim	1250	6 B-17	0	0	0	0	0
JG 101	Bf 109G	Lachen–Speyerdorf		~1130	Lachen–Speyerdorf	~1218	0	0	1	0	0	0
JG 104	Bf 109	Fürth	4	~1130	Fürth	~1245	1 B-17	0	0	0	0	0
JG 106	Bf 109E, Bf 109F	Lachen–Speyerdorf	17	~1130	Lachen–Speyerdorf	~1218	1 B-17	1	1	0	0	0
ISS R'burg	Bf 109G	Regensburg	8	~1230	Regensburg	~1257	1 B-17	0	1	0	0	0
I./NJG 6	Bf 110	Mainz–Finthen	13	~1100	Mainz–Finthen	~1230	0	0	0	0	0	0
I./NJG 101	Do 217, Bf 110	Stuttgart–Echterdingen	8	~1245	Stuttgart–Echterdingen	~1400	2 B-17	0	0	0	0	0
II./NJG101	Bf 110, Do 217	Lechfeld	16	~1230	Lechfeld	~1400	n/c	0	0	0	0	0
IV./NJG 101	Bf 110	Kitzingen	10	1230	Kitzingen	1430	0	0	0	0	0	0
II./ZG 101	Bf 110	Bad Aiblling	17	1250	Bad Aiblling	1352	0	0	0	0	0	0
Luftflotte 3												
Jafü 2:												
GeschGr/JG 26	Fw 190A, Bf 109G	Lille–Nord		1124	Lille–Nord	1230	1 Typhoon	1	0	1	0	0
Jafü 3:												
II./JG 2	Bf 109G	Vitry–en–Artois?		~1115	Vitry–en–Artois?	~1230	1 Spitfire	0	2	0	0	0

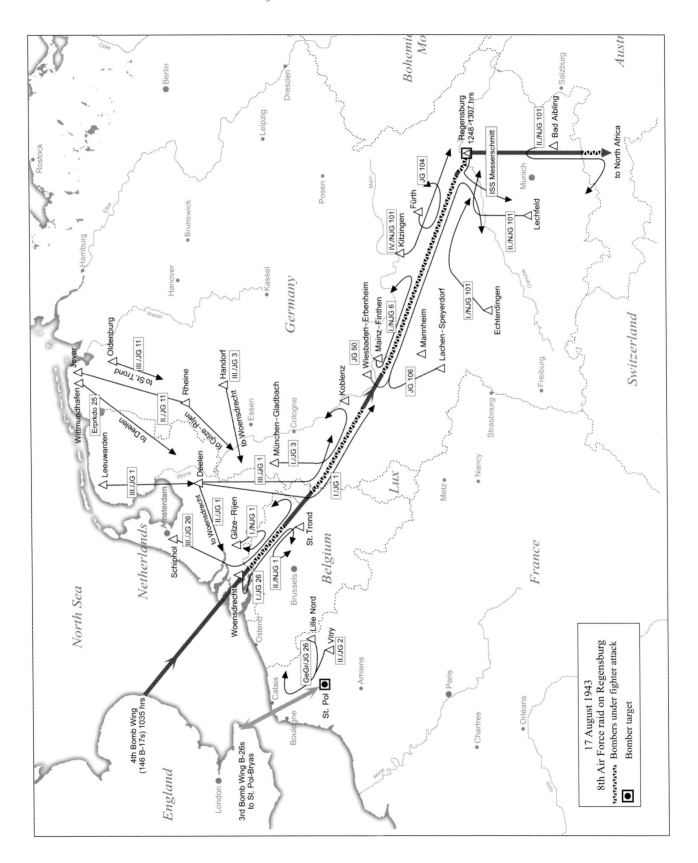

Berlin

Oder

Rostock

North Sea

Hamburg

Elbe

Oldenburg

Leeuwarden

Wittmundhafen

Jever

III./JG 11

Erprkdo 25

II./JG 11

to Deelen

to Gilze-Rijen

Deelen

Rheine

Handorf

III./JG 3

to Woensdrecht

Hanover

Weser

Brunswick

Kassel

Dresden

Leipzig

Posen

Germany

Bohemia

Austria

to St. Trond

Schiphol

Amsterdam

III./JG 26

Netherlands

II./JG 1

to Woensdrecht

Gilze-Rijen

I./NJG 1

III./JG 1

München-Gladbach

Essen

Cologne

I./JG 3

Rhine

Woensdrecht

Ostend

Calais

Boulogne

Amiens

Paris

Chartres

Orléans

Loire

Seine

England

London

3rd Bomb Wing B-26s
to St. Pol-Bryas

4th Bomb Wing
(146 B-17s) 1035 hrs

St. Pol

GeGr/JG 26

Lille Nord

Vitry

III./JG 2

Belgium

Brussels

St. Trond

II./NJG 1

I./JG 26

III./JG 1

I./JG 1

Koblenz

Wiesbaden–Erbenheim

JG 50

Mainz–Finthen

I./NJG 6

JG 106

Lachen–Speyerdorf

Mannheim

Lux.

Metz

Nancy

Strasbourg

France

Freiburg

Switzerland

Rhine

JG 104

Fürth

IV./NJG 101

Kitzingen

Regensburg
1248–1307 hrs

ISS Messerschmitt

Munich

Main

Lechfeld

II./NJG 101

I./NJG 101

Echterdingen

Danube

II./NJG 101

Bad Aibling

Salzburg

to North Africa

17 August 1943
8th Air Force raid on Regensburg
〰〰〰 Bombers under fighter attack
◼ Bomber target

17 August – Schweinfurt (see map)

8th Air Force VIII BC Mission #84b: 188 of 230 1st BW B-17s bomb Schweinfurt ball- bearing factories, TOT 1559-1611 – lose 36-3-118, claim 148-18-63. (See Mission #84a for escort totals.)

The delayed 1st BW mission to Schweinfurt entered a defensive buzz saw. The Germans had concentrated their fighters along the presumed return route of the Regensburg force, which was close to the route to Schweinfurt. In fact, of the 16 Jagdgruppen available to the RLV force, 13 were now waiting on bases within 120 km (75 miles) of the route of the new bombers as they left the English coast. The Jafü Holland-Ruhr scrambled three Jagdgruppen quickly; these found the escort strengthened from the earlier mission by the addition of Spitfires. Once these withdrew at Antwerp, the van of the stream was unprotected, and the Focke-Wulfs began to bore in, even before the P-47s at the rear turned back at Eupen. After these had left, the entire bomber stream was vulnerable, and for the next two hours, the bombers were battered by fighters from 10 Jagdgruppen, plus night fighters – an intensity of attack far greater than anything previously experienced. The day's most successful unit was JG 50, with 10 confirmed victories over the two forces; this lucky unit was based far out of range of the escorts and

Uffz. Fritz Steiner (I./JG 11) poses with his victory stick and Fw 190A-6 at Husum in August. (Rosch)

close to the routes of both bomber formations. Tied for second place were I./JG 1 and I./JG 11, each with seven claims for B-17s shot down or shot from formation.

The fighters broke away when the B-17s began their bomb run on Schweinfurt. After bombing with poor results, the surviving B-17s re-formed their defensive boxes and took up a return course to the north of their inbound route. Although night fighters kept nibbling away at the stragglers and made one ill-advised attack on the stream itself, only a few day fighters were seen at first by the bomber crews; these were in small improvised formations that had landed away from their own bases to refuel and were led in the air by the senior officer present. The last full-strength Jagdgruppe, II./JG 26, met the stream just over the German border. After one successful pass, it was surprised from the rear by P-47s of the 56th FG, which had overflown the B-17 formation and penetrated 24 km (15 miles) into Germany before wheeling around and diving on the Focke-Wulfs. The Gruppe dispersed after the quick loss of its Kommandeur, Major Wilhelm-Ferdinand Galland. The Thunderbolts then broke up the attacks of II./JG 2 and several more formations, and eventually returned to England claiming 7-0-1 Fw 190s, 4-1-1 Bf 109s and 5-0-7 twin-engine fighters for the loss of three P-47s and pilots. This was the most successful escort mission to date by an American fighter group.

The 1st BW reached its bases short of 36 B-17s; another three were scrapped. The 64 bombers lost during the day totalled 17 per cent of those dispatched and 20 per cent of those bombing, obviously a ruinous loss rate. The importance of the fighter escort was clear to all who had flown the mission, but apparently not so obvious to the American high command, who would call for more unescorted deep-penetration raids in the coming months with similar results. The Germans were, of course, pleased with the day's results. Of the 468 fighters scrambled against the second mission, 244 had made contact. Losses were within reason: 15 air crewmen were lost, and 14 were injured; ca. 38 aircraft were lost. However, there was one disquieting piece of data: the day's night fighter losses were disproportionately high. According to summary reports, 21 were lost, and 14 of their crewmen were killed. Their large size and low speed made them vulnerable to close-packed bomber formations as well as to the escorts. Their preferred targets in the future were to be straggling lone bombers, but they were still ordered to attack concentrated formations as circumstances dictated.

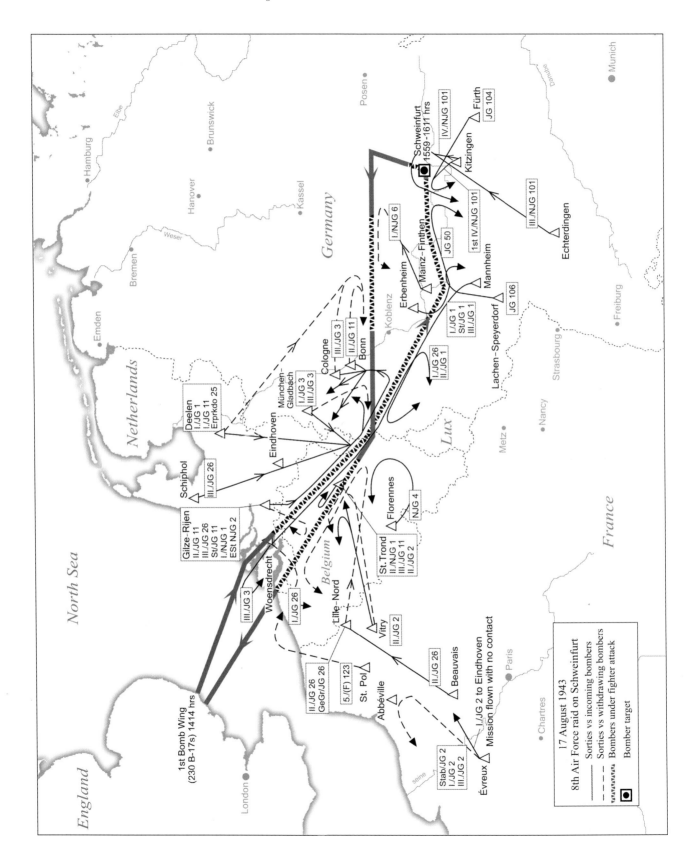

Munich

Posen

Schweinfurt
1559-1611 hrs

IV./NJG 101

Fürth
JG 104

Kitzingen

1st IV./NJG 101

III./NJG 101

Echterdingen

I./NJG 6

Mainz–Finthen

JG 50

Mannheim

Erbenheim

JG 106

Lachen-Speyerdorf

I./JG 1
St/JG 1
III./JG 1

Koblenz

III./JG 3
II./JG 11

Bonn

I./JG 26
II./JG 1

Cologne

I./JG 3
III./JG 3

München–
Gladbach

Germany

Freibrug

Strasbourg

Lux

Nancy

Metz

Hamburg

Hanover

Kassel

Brunswick

Bremen

Emden

Elbe

Weser

Deelen
I./JG 1
I./JG 11
Erprkdo 25

Eindhoven

Schiphol

III./JG 26

Netherlands

North Sea

Gilze–Rijen
II./JG 11
III./JG 26
St/JG 11
I./NJG 1
ESt NJG 2

Woensdrecht

III./JG 3

I./JG 26

Lille-Nord

Belgium

Florennes

St. Trond
II./NJG 1
III./JG 11
II./JG 2

NJG 4

Vitry

II./JG 2

II./JG 26

Beauvais

France

Paris

Chartres

1st Bomb Wing
(230 B-17s) 1414 hrs

England

London

II./JG 26
GeGr/JG 26

5./(F) 123

St. Pol

Abbéville

Stab/JG 2
I./JG 2
III./JG 2

Évreux

I./JG 2 to Eindhoven
Mission flown with no contact

seine

17 August 1943
8th Air Force raid on Schweinfurt

———— Sorties vs incoming bombers
- - - - Sorties vs withdrawing bombers
▬▬▬ Bombers under fighter attack
◙ Bomber target

———101———

Luftwaffe defensive activity vs. Schweinfurt raid – 17 August 1943

Unit	Type	Gruppe up			Gruppe down		Claims	Losses				
		Base	No	Time	Base	Time		Dest	Dam	KIA	MIA	WIA
vs. incoming stream												
Lw Bfh Mltte			*468									
Jafü H-Ruhr:												
II./JG 1	Fw 190A	Woensdrecht	19	1430	Woensdrecht, Koblenz	1545	1 B-17, 2 B-17 HSS	3	3	0	0	3
I./JG 3	Bf 109G	München–Gladbach		~1530	München–Gladbach	~1630	2 B-17	1	0	0	0	0
III./JG 3	Bf 109G	Woensdrecht	**58	1425	Köln, St. Trond, Ohlendorf	1550	0	3	2	0	0	0
Stab/JG 11	Bf 109G	Gilze–Rijen		1432	Bonn–Hangelar	~1630	0	0	0	0	0	0
I./JG 11	Fw 190A	Deelen	36	1452	Deelen	~1630	7 B-17	3	0	0	0	0
II./JG 11	Bf 109G	Gilze–Rijen	26	1432	Bonn–Hangelar, other	1530	2 B-17, 1 B-17 HSS	1	3	0	0	0
III./JG 11	Bf 109G	St. Trond		1445	Mainz–Finthen, various	1550	1 B-17	3	1	0	0	0
I./JG 26	Fw 190A	Woensdrecht	—	1434	various	~1530	3 B-17	1	0	0	0	1
III/JG 26	Bf 109G	Schiphol	15	1436	Schiphol	~1530	4 B-17	0	0	0	0	0
	Bf 109G	Gilze–Rijen		1439	Gilze–Rijen	~1600	0	0	0	0	0	0
ErprKdo 25	Fw 190A	Deelen		1430	Deelen	1530	0	0	0	0	0	0
I./NJG 1	Bf 110	St. Trond		~1430	St. Trond	~1600	1 B-17	4	0	5	0	0
ErgtSt/NJG 2	Bf 109G, Bf 110	Gilze–Rijen		~1430	Gilze–Rijen	~1600	0	1	1	0	0	1
Jagddivision 5:			*98									
Stab/JG 1	Fw 190A	Mannheim–Sandhofen		~1430	Deelen	~1545	1 B-17	0	0	0	0	0
I./JG 1	Fw 190A	Mannheim–Sandhofen		1430	Deelen	1520	1 B-17 HSS	1	1	0	0	0
III./JG 1	Bf 109G	Mannheim–Sandhofen		~1500	Mannheim–Sandhofen	~1615	2 B-17	0	0	0	0	0
JG 50	Bf 109G	Wiesbaden–Erbenheim	12	~1510	Wiesbaden–Erbenheim	~1630	4 B-17	2	0	2	0	0
JG 104	Bf 109	Fürth	7	~1500	Fürth	~1600	0	0	0	0	0	0
JG 106	Bf 109	Lachen–Speyerdorf	9	~1500	Lachen–Speyerdorf	~1600	0	0	0	0	0	0
II./NJG101	Bf 110, Do 217	Lechfeld	19	~1400	Lechfeld	~1630	n/c	0	0	0	0	0
III./NJG 101	Bf 110	Stuttgart–Echterdingen	2	~1340	Stuttgart–Echterdingen	~1630	1 B-17	0	0	0	0	0
IV./NJG 101	Bf 110	Kitzingen	10	1550	Kitzingen	1630	2 B-17	0	0	0	0	0
Luftflotte 3			*115									
Jafü 2:												
II./JG 26	Fw 190A	Beauvais		1400	Lille–Nord	1430	transfer	0	0	0	0	0
I./NJG 4	Bf 110	Florennes		1500	Florennes	1545	0	2	2	1	0	3
Jafü 3:												
I./JG 2	Fw 190A	Evreux		~1400	Eindhoven	~1500	0	0	0	0	0	0
II./JG 2	Bf 109G	Vitry-en-Artois		~1400	Vitry, St. Trond?	~1500	0	0	0	0	0	0

Luftwaffe defensive activity vs. Schweinfurt raid – 17 August 1943 Continued

Unit	Type	Gruppe up			Gruppe down		Claims	Losses				
		Base	No	Time	Base	Time		Dest	Dam	KIA	MIA	WIA
vs. withdrawing stream												
Lw Bfh MItte												
Jafü H-Ruhr:												
I./JG 1	Fw 190A	Deelen	16	1650	Deelen	~1730	2 B-17	2	2	2	0	0
I./JG 3	Bf 109G	München–Gladbach		1700	München–Gladbach	~1800	2 B-17	0	1	0	0	0
III./JG 3	Bf 109G	Köln, Ohlendorf	8	1650	München–Gladbach	1800	1 B-17, 3 P-47	0	0	0	0	0
II./JG 11	Bf 109G	Bonn–Hangelar		1700	Jever?	~1800	1 B-17	1	0	0	0	1
III./JG 11	Bf 109G	Mainz–Finthen, various		1745	Oldenburg	~1845	0	0	0	0	0	0
I./JG 26	Fw 190A	Various		1640	Woensdrecht	~1740	1 B-17	0	0	0	0	0
III./JG 26	Bf 109G	Schiphol	6	1656	Schiphol	~1800	n/c	0	0	0	0	0
	Bf 109G	Gilze–Rijen		1700	Schiphol	~1800	n/c	0	0	0	0	0
I./NJG 1	Bf 110	Venlo, Gilze–Rijen	10	1644	Venlo, Gilze–Rijen	1744	1 B-17	7	0	5	0	1
III./NJG 1	Bf 110	Twente	8	1645	Twente	1836	0	0	0	0	0	0
IV/NJG 1	Bf 110	Leeuwarden	7	1651	Leeuwarden	~1800	0	0	0	0	0	0
Jagddivision 4:												
II./NJG 5	Bf 110	Stendal		1537	Stendal	1748	n/c	0	0	0	0	0
Jagddivision 5:												
III./JG 1	Bf 109G	Mannheim–Sandhofen		1745	Leeuwarden	~1830	n/c	0	0	0	0	0
I./NJG 6	Bf 110	Mainz–Finthen	6	~1630	Mainz–Finthen	~1730	1 B-17	4	0	4	0	2
III./NJG 101	Bf 110, Do 217	Stuttgart–Echterdingen	2	~1630	Stuttgart–Echterdingen	~1750	0	0	0	0	0	0
IV./NJG 101	Bf 110, Do 217	Kitzingen		~1630	Kitzingen	~1750	1 B-17	0	0	0	0	0
II./ZG 101	Bf 110	Bad Aibling		1540	Bad Aibling	1737	0	0	0	0	0	0
Luftflotte 3												
Jafü 2:												
GeschGr/ JG 26	Fw 190A	Lille–Nord	***47	1652	Antwerp	1750	1 B-17	0	0	0	0	0
II./JG 26	Fw 190	Lille–Nord	—	1650	Antwerp, St. Trond, others	1805	2 B-17, 1 P-47, 1 Spitfire	2	4	0	1	2
5./F 123	Bf 109G	St. Pol	4	~1715	St. Pol	~1815	1 B-17	0	0	0	0	0
Jafü 3:												
Stab/JG 2	Fw 190A	Evreux	****64	1630	Evreux	~1720	n/c	0	0	0	0	0
I./JG 2	Fw 190A	Eindhoven, Évreux	—	1630	Evreux	1720	n/c	0	0	0	0	0
II./JG 2	Bf 109G	Vitry–en–Artois, St. Trond?		1640	Vitry–en–Artois	~1800	2 B-17, 1 B-17 HSS	1	1	0	0	0
III./JG 2	Fw 190A	Evreux	—	1630	Evreux	~1720	n/c	0	0	0	0	0

*total sorties vs. incoming and withdrawing streams

**58 fighters up from Woensdrecht (III./JG 3 + I./JG 26)

***47 fighters up from Lille-Nord (GeschGr/JG 26 + II./JG 26)

****64 fighters up from Evreux (Stab/JG 2, I./JG 2, III./JG 2)

II/JG 1 WAR DIARY
AND SHOOTDOWN REPORTS[3]
17 August 1943

The Gruppe scrambled 19 Fw 190s from Woensdrecht at 1430 hours. At 1445 hours, 100–120 B-17s were sighted at 6,000–7,000 metres in quadrant LQ flying SE in seven Pulks, one lagging behind. The Stab immediately began a close-formation head-on attack on the last Pulk, followed in order by the 4., 5. and 6. Staffel. The entire leading Schwarm, followed by one aircraft of the 2nd, fell away as a consequence of the strong defensive fire. Further attacks were carried out in Schwarm strength.

Claims: 5 Herausschüsse (HSS), 2 Abschüsse (Abs) submitted; 2 HSS, 1 Abs rejected by JG 1; 3 HSS filed with RLM, one Abs filed as endgültige Vernichtung (eV) [final destruction]

Losses: 2 Fw 190 total, 2 Fw 190 belly-landed with severe damage; 1 pilot into hospital; 1 pilot lightly wounded; 4 more Fw 190s hit.

Selected Abschussmeldungen (shootdown reports):

Uffz. Schönrock (4. Staffel) claims a B-17 from 6,000 metres in quadrant PP-5 at 1527 hours. A single attack was made from the front from 300–100 metres. The left inner engine burst into bright flames, and pieces broke off. Five men were seen to bail out. The B-17 crashed near Niedermendig airfield. The Fw 190A-5 of S. was hit in the engine, fuselage and wings. S. visited the crash site of B-17 124453 [91st BG] and the surviving crewmen. [Submitted to JG 1 as Abs; filed with RLM as eV; ultimate disposition unknown]

Uffz. Scharler (5. Staffel) claims a B-17 from 6,000 metres in quadrant QQ at 1528 hours. Three attacks were made from the front and side from 500–150 metres. The B-17 was last seen in a steep dive in a 45° left bank. [No damage was observed.] The crash could not be observed because of further attacks. The Fw 190A-5 of S. was hit once in the right wing. [Submitted as HSS; rejected by JG 1]

COMBAT REPORT[4]
17 August 1943

One B-17 claimed destroyed from 6,500 metres at 1524 hours in quadrant 05 Ost S/PP, Mayen-Andernach [Submitted as HSS; rejected by JG 1: DC]

At the alarm, I scrambled from Woensdrecht at 1430 hours in the Schwarm of Obfw. Beck. At 1445 in quadrant ML, we made contact with 100–120 Boeing B-17 Fortress IIs, flying to the SE. We made two close-formation attacks from the left side on the last of four Pulks. Due to the strong forces while pulling out, I went into a spin and lost my Schwarmführer. I joined up with a Rotte flying ahead of me and continued my attacks. At 1524 hours in quadrant PP, I fired at the left-most Boeing in the 4th Pulk with such effectiveness that the left inner engine showed a black smoke plume. As I pulled out, I saw the Boeing quickly drop 400–500 metres behind and 100 metres below the formation. During a new approach on the same Pulk I noticed that the Boeing I had shot from formation was under attack by one Fw 190 and two Bf 109 and was spinning down in quadrant PP. I made one more attack on the rear Pulk of the formation and landed at Koblenz at 1545 hours owing to low fuel.

Lt. Heinz Schwarz
5./JG 1

19 August

8th Air Force VIII BC Mission #85: 93 of 170 B-17s (1st BW + 4th BW) bomb Gilze–Rijen, Vlissingen airfields, TOT 1856-1914 – lose 5-1-50, claim 30-2-4. RAF FC Spitfire escorts claim 8-1-0, lose 0-1; 175 VIII FC P-47s claim 0-2-4, lose 1-0-0.

The VIII BC returned to battle with a heavily escorted late-evening raid on airfields in Holland. The tactical fighter bombers had flown four earlier missions to France to wear out the fighters of Jafü 3 and II./JG 26 and succeeded in keeping them out of the main battle. The B-17s were escorted by 10 squadrons of Spitfires on the penetration phase, two groups of P-47s over the target and two groups of P-47s on the withdrawal leg. The defence against this short-range raid was controlled by Jafü Holland-Ruhr, which ordered up all of its own fighters, the JG 26 Geschwadergruppe from neighbouring Jafü 2 and (possibly) JG 50 from

Jagddividion 5. Allied intelligence counted 136 defensive sorties. III./JG 1 was ordered to attack before the Spitfires turned back at Antwerp and was severely punished by the RAF, losing three pilots killed and five Messerschmitts destroyed for one Spitfire claim. I./JG 26 encountered first the Spitfires and then the P-47s and lost two Focke-Wulfs for no claims. I./JG 1, I./JG 3, III./JG 26 and the JG 26 Geschwadergruppe reached the bombers and claimed eight B-17s for the loss of five fighters, but no fatalities. One of the B-17 combat wings did not drop its bombs, owing to the unbroken cloud cover; the other two formations did bomb, killing a number of Dutch civilians without materially affecting Luftwaffe operations. Five B-17s were lost, and one was scrapped after the unsuccessful operation.

24 August

8th Air Force VIII BC Mission #86-I: 143 of 188 B-17s (1st BW + 4th BW) bomb Villacoublay, Conches, Evreux airfields, TOT 1900-58 – lose 1-0-79, claim 1-0-3. RAF FC Spitfire escorts claim 2-0-0, lose 0; 166 VIII FC P-47s claim 6-1-6, lose 0.

8th Air Force VIII BC Mission #86-II (return from N Africa): 58 of 85 4th BW B-17s bomb Bordeaux airfield, TOT 1257-1300 – lose 3-2-40, claim 1-0-3. No escort.

The VIII BC mounted two missions. The 4th BW B-17s returning to England from North Africa bombed Bordeaux en route. Flak was heavy; aerial opposition was limited to the operational training units Jagdgruppe West and Jagdgruppe Ost, which claimed one B-17 for the loss of one KIA, one WIA and two Bf 109s. Jafü 3 apparently held JG 2 on the ground to await the late-evening arrival of the rest of the bombers from England. These targeted three airfields in France and were heavily escorted by 166 P-47s, which covered their charges so well that only one B-17 failed to return to England. JG 2 lost four fighters and three pilots, and its two claims were apparently not confirmed. II./JG 26 and part of the JG 26 Geschwadergruppe were sent up in low strength, probably after stragglers, but there were no stragglers. One pilot noted heavy damage to one B-17 in his logbook, but no claims were filed.

27 August

8th Air Force VIII BC Mission #87: 187 of 224 B-17s (1st BW + 4th BW) bomb Watten V-2 construction sites, TOT 1946-2041 – lose 4-1-98, claim 7-0-6. RAF FC Spitfire escorts claim 8-1-3, lose 7; 173 VIII FC P-47s claim 8-1-2, lose 1.

The VIII BC was ordered to make a full-strength attack on a construction site at Watten, on the Pas de Calais between St. Omer and Dunkirk. The Allies only suspected the purpose of the site, which was, in fact, to become a V-2 rocket base. The small size of the target required the B-17s to bomb in trail, as groups or even squadrons. They were split into four task forces that took more than an hour to cross the target. The escort of 23 Spitfire squadrons and the four P-47 groups was concentrated at the head and rear of the stream, as it was felt that the defenders would have to land for servicing after their initial attacks and could not reach the stream again until late. Two JG 26 Gruppen fought through the Spitfires, but were able to claim only one B-17. I./JG 2 also claimed one Fortress. The second and third bomber waves saw no German fighters, and the fourth was so well covered by the escorts that the Jafü 2 fighters up on second sorties and I./JG 26, the lone reinforcement to arrive from Jafü Holland-Ruhr, were scattered and driven off. The Allied plan proved to be a sound one: only four B-17s were downed, and a fifth was scrapped in England. Three B-17s were definitely shot down by Flak, so only one or two were downed by the fighters.

31 August

8th Air Force VIII BC Mission #88: 106 of 319 B-17s (1st BW + 4th BW) bomb Amiens airfield, TOT 1907-24 – lose 3-1-54, claim 5-1-3. 160 VIII FC P-47s claim 2-1-1, lose 2.

The VIII BC targeted a number of Luftflotte 3 bases, including the important Romilly depot. In an effort to outwait the unpredictable weather, the raid was scheduled for late afternoon, giving the American Martin B-26 Marauders and RAF light bombers an opportunity to wear down the Luftflotte 3 fighters and Channel airfields before the B-17s took off. The Lille bases sustained such damage that the JG 26 Geschwadergruppe (the Stab, 8., 10. and 11. Staffeln) had to spend the next four days at Wevelghem. The late-arriving heavy bombers were obviously on a shallow-penetration raid across a broad front. Jafü 2 scrambled all of its fighters, and I./JG 26 took off from Woensdrecht. The only Jafü 3 unit known to have taken part was II./JG 2. The weather did not cooperate with either side; most of the bombers aborted or bombed secondary targets, and the German fighters had difficulty keeping in formation or even finding the bombers. II./JG 26 and at least part of the JG 26 Geschwadergruppe did make attacks; one claim was confirmed. Four B-17s were lost or written off; one German pilot was injured.

Luftwaffe defensive activity – 19 August 1943

Unit	Type	Gruppe up			Gruppe down		Claims	Losses				
		Base	No	Time	Base	Time		Dest	Dam	KIA	MIA	WIA
Lw Bfh Mitte												
Jafü H-Ruhr:												
I./JG 1	Fw 190A	Deelen		~1845	Deelen	~1945	4 B-17	0	0	0	0	0
III./JG 1	Fw 190A	Leeuwarden		1830	Leeuwarden	~1930	1 Spitfire	5	5	3	0	1
I./JG 3	Bf 109G	München–Gladbach		~1930	München–Gladbach	2030	1 B-17	1	0	0	0	0
III./JG 3	Bf 109G	Münster–Handorf		1930	Münster–Handorf	2025	n/c	0	0	0	0	0
I./JG 26	Fw 190A	Woensdrecht		1810	Woensdrecht	1900	0	1	1	0	0	1
III./JG 26	Bf 109G	Schiphol	20	1836	Schiphol	~1930	1 B-17 HSS	3	0	0	0	2
Jagddivision 5:												
JG 50	Bf 109G	Wiesbaden		~1800	Wiesbaden	~1900	0	1	0	1	0	0
Luftflotte 3												
Jafü 2:												
GeschGr/JG 26	Fw 190A, Bf 109G	Lille–Nord		1802	Lille–Nord, Norrent–Fontes	~1945	2 B-17	0	0	0	0	0
12./JG 26	Bf 109G	Moorsele		~1900	Moorsele	~2000	0	1	0	0	0	1
II./JG 26	Fw 190A	Beauvais–Tillé		1920	Beauvais–Tillé	2029	n/c	0	0	0	0	0

Luftwaffe defensive activity – 24 August 1943

Unit	Type	Gruppe up			Gruppe down		Claims	Losses				
		Base	No	Time	Base	Time		Dest	Dam	KIA	MIA	WIA
Luftflotte 3												
Jafü 2:												
GeschGr/JG 26	Fw 190A	Lille–Nord		1927	Lille–Nord	2038	n/c	0	0	0	0	0
II./JG 26	Fw 190A	Beauvais–Tillé		1823	St. André?, Beauvais–Tillé	1931	0	0	0	0	0	0
2nd sorties	Fw 190A	Beauvais–Tillé		1941	Beauvais–Tillé	2011	n/c	0	0	0	0	0
Jafü 3:												
I./JG 2	Fw 190A, Bf 109G	Evreux, St. André		1855	Evreux, St. André	2005	0	0	5	0	0	0
II./JG 2	Bf 109	Vitry–en–Artois		~1830	Vitry–en–Artois	~2000	0	1	1	1	0	0
Jafü 4:												
III./JG 2	Fw 190A	Vannes		~1830	Beauvais, Bernay, Conches	~2000	1 Spitfire	3	2	2	0	1
JGr Ost	Bf 109G	Toulouse–Blagnac		~1200	Toulouse–Blagnac	~1300	1 B-17	1	0	1	0	0
JGr West	Bf 109G	Cazaux, Biarritz		1301	Cazaux, Biarritz	1353	0	1	1	0	0	1

Luftwaffe defensive activity – 27 August 1943

Unit	Type	Gruppe up			Gruppe down		Claims	Losses (—: included in 1st sortie)				
		Base	No	Time	Base	Time		Dest	Dam	KIA	MIA	WIA
Lw Bfh Mitte												
Jafü H-Ruhr.												
I./JG 26	Fw 190A	Woensdrecht	20	2000	St. Omer–Arques	2059	0	2	0	0	0	0
Luftflotte 3												
Jafü 2:												
GeschGr/ JG 26	Fw 190A, Bf 109G	Lille–Nord	*70	1910	Lille–Nord	~2000	1 Spitfire	1	0	0	0	0
2nd sorties	Fw 190A	Lille–Nord	**50	2020	Lille–Nord	2055	0	—	—	—	—	—
II./JG 26	Fw 190A	Beauvais–Tillé	—	1908	Beauvais–Tillé	2012	1 B-17, 1 Spitfire	1	0	1	0	0
2nd sorties	Fw 190A	Beauvais–Tillé	—	~2030	Beauvais–Tillé	~2130	0	—	—	—	—	—
Jafü 3:												
Stab/JG 2	Fw 190A	Evreux, Beaumont–le–Roger	***40	1922	Evreux, Poix, Beaumont–le–Roger	~2030	0	1	0	0	0	0
I./JG 2	Fw 190A, Bf 109G	Evreux, Beaumont–le–Roger	—	1922	Evreux, Beaumont–le–Roger	~2030	1 B-17	1	0	1	0	0
II./JG 2	Bf 109G	Poix, Vitry–en–Artois	—	1910	Poix, Vitry–en–Artois	~2030	0	0	2	0	0	0
III./JG 2	Fw 190A	Conches?	—	1922	Conches?	~2030	0	1	1	1	0	0

*70 Jafü 2 aircraft up on 1st sorties

**50 Jafü 2 aircraft up on 2nd sorties

***40 Jafü 3 aircraft up on 1st sorties

Luftwaffe defensive activity – 31 August 1943

Unit	Type	Gruppe up			Gruppe down		Claims	Losses				
		Base	No	Time	Base	Time		Dest	Dam	KIA	MIA	WIA
Lw Bfh Mitte												
Jafü H-Ruhr.												
I./JG 26	Fw 190A	Woensdrecht		1817	St. Omer–Arques	1850	n/c	0	0	0	0	0
Luftflotte 3												
Jafü 2:												
GeschGr/JG 26	Fw 190A, Bf 109G	Lille–Nord		1810	Lille–Nord	1915	0	0	0	0	0	0
2nd sorties	Fw 190A	Lille–Nord		1940	Lille–Nord	2010	n/c	0	0	0	0	0
II./JG 26	Fw 190A	Beauvais–Tillé, Lisieux		1815	Beauvais–Tillé, Montidier	1947	1 B-17	0	2	0	0	1
Jafü 3:												
II./JG 2	Bf 109G	Poix		~1810	Poix	~1915	0	0	0	0	0	0

September 1943

The weakened VIII Bomber Command flew only six missions in the 19 days following Schweinfurt-Regensburg, all to targets in France and the Low Countries, and its next mission to Germany, on the 6th, was a disastrous failure. Strategic raids on the Reich from the south were still weak and infrequent. The fundamental reorganisation of the day defences was nevertheless long overdue. The process began early in the month, when Generalmajor Josef 'Beppo' Schmid relieved General der Flieger Josef Kammhuber as commander of XII. Fliegerkorps, which had been nominally responsible for all defensive fighters in Germany since its formation in 1941. In practice, control of day fighter operations had devolved to the Jafü staffs, while Kammhuber's XII. Fliegerkorps ran the night fighter defence operations through the air division headquarters. (The RLV Jagddivision boundaries as of 14 September are shown in the figure.) Schmid immediately began advocating a similar centralisation of the day fighters. The formal unification of the RLV fighter command within the Reich took place on the 15th, in the most significant Luftwaffe defensive reorganisation of the war. Schmid was named commander of the new I. Jagdkorps at Zeist. His mission was "direction of day and night fighter forces and activities in the northern areas of Germany, Holland and northern Belgium". The new Korps became the principal operational flying command in Lw Bfh Mitte, controlling the day and night fighters based in the geographical areas of the three Jagddivisionen in northern and western Germany. Several of the Jagddivisionen were renumbered at this time: Jagddivision 4 in Berlin became Jagddivision 1; Jagddivision 2 in Hamburg–Stade remained unchanged; Jagddivision 1 in Deelen became Jagddivision 3. In the south, Jagddivision 5, which continued to report directly to Lw Bfh Mitte, became Jagddivision 7. The Jagdfliegerführer (Jafü) that had previously served as the tactical controllers lost that authority to the Jagddivisionen, and these commands disappeared entirely by the end of the year.

Luftflotte 3 successfully resisted the trend toward defensive centralisation and retained full control of its fighters. On 15 September, they were put under a new II. Jagdkorps under Genlt. Werner Junck at Chantilly near Paris, which was given two Jagddivisionen: the 4th (ex-Jagddivision 3), headquartered at Metz, and

the 5th (ex-Jafü West, containing Jafü 2 and Jafü Bretagne), based in Paris. The line separating Luftflotte 3 from Lw Bfh Mitte ran through the middle of Belgium and then roughly along the French-German border. Allied raids on Germany from England, especially to central and southern Germany, thus crossed the territories of both air fleets, and defensive command-and-control problems persisted; these finally ended only with the expulsion of the

Genlt. Josef 'Beppo' Schmid. Commander of the I. Jagdkorps in 1943–44, Schmid held the most important operational command in the RLV, but is best known today for his miscalculations as head of the 5. Abteilung, the RLM Intelligence Section, during the Battle of Britain in 1940. He proved to be the strong leader that the RLV force needed and held his own in the political infighting that characterised the Luftwaffe high command. After the war, he was a principal author of the USAF Historical Studies on the German Air Force. *(Author's collection)*

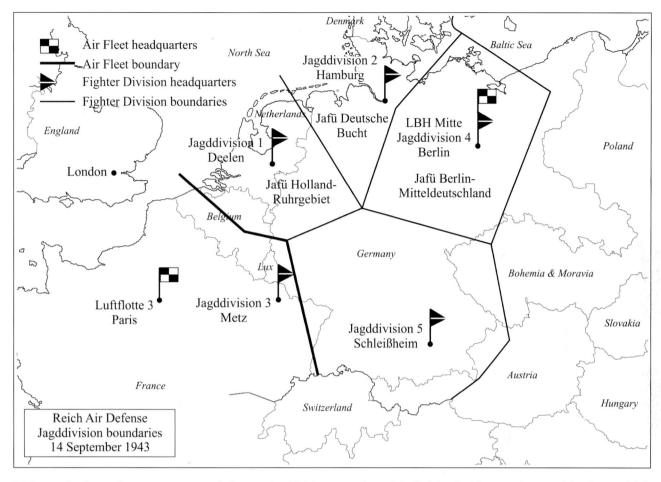

Reich Air Defense
Jagddivision boundaries
14 September 1943

Wehrmacht from the western occupied zone in 1944.

At mid-month, III./JG 26 returned to Luftflotte 3 and its home Geschwader from its attachment to Luftwaffenbefehlshaber Mitte and settled in at Lille–Vendeville. With three standard Jagdgruppen once again under his control, Obstlt. Piller disbanded his unique Geschwadergruppe and returned all of its Staffeln bar one to their home Gruppen. He kept 8./JG 26 with him at Lille–Nord as the Geschwader *Führungsstaffel* [leadership squadron], as he felt that the standard Stabsschwarm of four aircraft was too vulnerable.

One twin-engine unit entered combat with the RLV force in September, although its stay was brief. In May, the First Gruppe of Kampfgeschwader 51 (I./KG 51), a conventional Ju 88 bomber unit, had transferred from Russia to Germany without aircraft, to be retrained as a Me 410 *Hornisse* bomber destroyer unit. The aircraft it received had single-stage superchargers and a critical altitude (the maximum altitude at which the supercharger could maintain performance equal to that at sea level) of only 3,000 metres (10,000 feet), which left them completely unsuited for their planned role. The Gruppe flew only a handful of missions before being repurposed as a light night bomber unit for harassing raids on England.

The VIII BC was expanding far more rapidly than the German defences. A new layer of administrative control was established on the 13th with the activation of three Bombardment Divisions (Bomb Divisions). The First was the old 1st BW; the Second contained the B-24 units that were returning from North Africa; and the Third was the redesignated 4th BW. Newly arriving bomb groups were assigned to newly constituted bomb wings within the divisions. The VIII FC was growing far more slowly, but with experience and improved tactics its P-47 groups could now provide effective defence to the limit of their range.

2 September

8th Air Force VIII BC Mission #89: 34 of 319 B-17s bomb two French airfields, TOT 1905-22 – lose 0-0-9, no claims. 182 VIII FC P-47s claim 0, lose 3-1-4.

The VIII BC targeted French airfields for a late evening raid, but all of the 1st BW and most of the 4th BW aborted because of unbroken cloud cover over the targets. The P-47 mission was then changed to a sweep. At the same time, a raid by medium bombers to similar targets crossed the Channel, escorted by RAF Spitfires. The Jagdgruppen in northern France were scrambled, as was I./JG 26 from Grimbergen. II./JG 2 claimed one Spitfire for the loss of one Messerschmitt; III./JG 2 claimed a P-47; I./JG 26 lost one Focke-Wulf for no claims. II./JG 26 flew a successful mission against the 56th FG. The Focke-Wulfs were returning to Beauvais–Tillé from Creil and spotted two flights of P-47s in a rare clear area below them. Their bounce and the subsequent dogfights downed two P-47s and damaged several others, one of which was scrapped in England. No German fighter was hit in this combat. Hptm. Johannes Naumann and his men filed four victory claims, but only one was confirmed; the lower cloud deck prevented any other crashes from being witnessed.

3 September

8th Air Force VIII BC Mission #90: 233 of 298 B-17s bomb six targets in Paris region, TOT 0943-1055 – lose 9-0-75, claim 26-5-18. 160 VIII FC P-47s claim 4-1-0, lose 1-0-2.

The VIII BC took advantage of a predicted clear morning and sent 233 B-17s and the four P-47 groups to the important Romilly–sur–Seine air depot and several other targets in the Paris region. Jafü 2 and Jafü 3 scrambled their fighters and sent them south. The two JG 26 Gruppen converged on the 1st BW, which had targeted Romilly, southeast of Paris, while the JG 2 fighters attacked the 4th BW nearer Paris proper. The P-47s were assigned to both bomber formations and flew all the way to Paris, but apparently left gaps in the coverage. Some German fighters managed to fly two missions, and attacks on the 4th BW were almost continuous. Seven Luftflotte 3 fighters were lost, and five pilots were killed and one injured, while 11 B-17s and one P-47 were claimed. Nine B-17s and one P-47 were lost to the defences.

PILOT'S ACCOUNT[5]
3 September 1943

I scrambled from Wevelghem at 0900 hours in my mill, Fw 190A 'Black 10'. Oblt. Janda led us. We climbed to the south. A radio report: "'Dicke Ottos' [sic; actually 'Autos' – DC] Richtung Paris." We climbed to 11,000 metres. The Thunderbolts below could do nothing to us. I attacked a B-17 from the front, but fired with too little deflection. The fighter escort was then in my sights. I dove to 4,000 metres and reassembled. My fuel was low. I landed on Villaroche with Schmidtke. Janda was missing in the Orléans-Fontainebleau area. No one had seen him.

Uffz. Gerd Wiegand
8./JG 26

Fw-Fhj. Gerd Wiegand of 8./JG 26 was a favourite subject for the Propaganda Kompanie photographers, one of whom took this 'glamour shot'. *(Bundesarchiv 492-3332-13)*

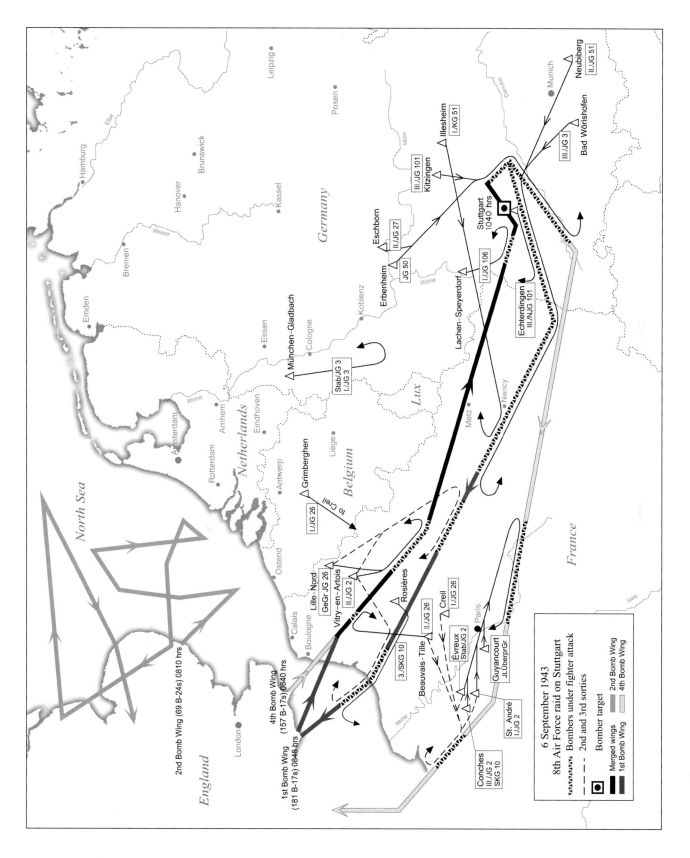

Neubiberg II./JG 51

Munich

Bad Wörishofen III./JG 3

Illesheim I./KG 51

Posen

III./JG 101 Kitzingen

Leipzig

Germany

Hamburg

Elbe

Brunswick

Hanover

Kassel

Weser

Eschborn I./JG 27

JG 50

Erbenheim

Stuttgart 1040 hrs

Lachen-Speyerdorf I./JG 106

Echterdingen III./NJG 101

Bremen

Emden

Main

Rhine

Koblenz

München-Gladbach

Essen • Cologne

Rhine

Stab/JG 3 I./JG 3

Lux

Metz

Nancy

Danube

North Sea

Amsterdam

Arnhem

Netherlands

Eindhoven

Rotterdam

Antwerp

Liège

Belgium

Grimberghen I./JG 26

to Creil

France

Ostend

Calais

Boulogne

Lille-Nord GeGr JG 26

Vitry-en-Artois II./JG 2

Rosières

Creil I./JG 26

II./JG 26

3./SKG 10

Beauvais-Tille

Évreux Stab/JG 2

Guyancourt JLÜberprGr

Paris

St. André I./JG 2

Seine

Conches III./JG 2 SKG 10

Loire

England

London

2nd Bomb Wing (69 B-24s) 0810 hrs

4th Bomb Wing (157 B-17s) 0840 hrs

1st Bomb Wing (181 B-17s) 0848 hrs

6 September 1943
8th Air Force raid on Stuttgart

▵▵▵▵▵ Bombers under fighter attack

- - - - 2nd and 3rd sorties

◉ Bomber target

◉ Merged wings

▬▬ 1st Bomb Wing

2nd Bomb Wing

4th Bomb Wing

6 September – Stuttgart (see map)

8th Air Force VIII BC Mission #91: 262 of 338 B-17s bomb Stuttgart and t/os, TOT 1040-1329 – lose 45-10-116, claim 98-20-50. RAF FC Spitfires escort (diversions and withdrawal) claim 11-0-5, lose 3; 176 VIII FC P-47s claim 1-0-0, lose 1.

The largest force yet employed by the VIII BC on a single mission, 338 B-17s, was dispatched against aircraft industry targets in Stuttgart. The mission, officially characterised by the Americans as a 'costly fiasco', was flown over the Continent despite heavy cloud cover. The formations became split up, and 45 B-17s were destroyed, either by enemy action or by ditching or crash-landing after their fuel ran out. Ten more were scrapped after their return to England. Most of the Luftflotte 3 Jagdgruppen had busy and successful days. A medium

bomber raid and a complex diversion by the B-24s of the understrength 2nd BW pinned the Channel units to their base areas, but only briefly. The B-17s took the most direct route toward Stuttgart, straight up the course of the Somme River, and the 1st BW retraced it on their return, while the longer-range 4th BW swung west of Paris to avoid some of the punishment. Many of Luftflotte 3's pilots flew several missions against the incoming and withdrawing bombers. Some of Jafü Holland-Ruhr's units were either held on the ground or failed to make contact in the clouds, but Hptm. Werner Schroer's II./JG 27 was vectored directly to the target and claimed nine B-17s (six known confirmed) on its first RLV mission, which proved to be its most productive of the war. The Luftwaffe lost 22 airplanes, but only nine aircrewmen KIA and eight WIA, on its 250 effective sorties.

A tight B-17 formation *en route* to Stuttgart under close escort by 78th Fighter Group P-47s, one of which is seen in the foreground. The date is probably 6 September 1943. *(USAAF)*

COMBAT REPORT[6]
6 September 1943

One B-17 claimed destroyed from 7,500 metres at 1132 hrs, 10 km southeast of Baden
[Filed as Herausschuss but not confirmed: DC]

I scrambled in my Bf 109G-6 'Yellow 6' gunboat [three MG 151/20, two MG 131] at 1030 hours as a Schwarmführer under the orders of the Jafü. We reached a B-17 formation flying at about 7,500 metres

in the Stuttgart area and immediately attacked. During my first attack from the front, I observed effective hits in the top turret and right inner engine. I had to break away beneath the bomber and received hits in my propeller and wing. When I pulled up, I could see that the bomber I had hit had dropped from the formation in a flat dive, trailing a long plume of white smoke. Further observations were not possible due to the solid cloud deck.

Obfw. Alfred Surau
9./JG 3

Luftwaffe defensive activity – 2 September 1943

Unit	Type	Gruppe up			Gruppe down		Claims	Losses (—: included in 1st sortie)				
		Base	No	Time	Base	Time		Dest	Dam	KIA	MIA	WIA
Lw Bfh Mitte												
Jafü H-Ruhr:												
I./JG 26	Fw 190A	Grimbergen		1912	Grimbergen, Arques	1935	n/c	0	0	0	0	0
2nd sorties	Fw 190A	Arques, Grimbergen		1955	Grimbergen	2017	0	1	1	0	0	0
Luftflotte 3												
Jafü 2:												
GeschGr/ JG 26	Fw 190A, Bf 109G	Lille–Nord		1915	Lille–Nord, Moorsele	2022	0	0	0	0	0	0
II./JG 26	Fw 190A	Beauvais–Tillé		1805	Beauvais–Tillé, Creil	1908	n/c	0	0	0	0	0
2nd sorties	Fw 190A	Creil		1945	Beauvais–Tillé	2055	1 P-47*	1	0	0	0	1
Jafü 3:												
Stab/JG 2	Fw 190A	Evreux		~1915	Evreux	~2015	0	0	0	0	0	0
I./JG 2	Fw 190A, Bf 109G	Evreux		~1915	Evreux	~2015	0	0	1	0	0	0
II./JG 2	Bf 109G	Vitry–en–Artois		~1915	Vitry–en–Artois	~2015	1 Spitfire	1	1	1	0	0
III./JG 2	Fw 190A	?		~1830	?	~1930	1 B-17, 1 Spitfire	0	0	0	0	0

*II./JG 26: + 2 P-47 claims unconfirmed (unwitnessed)

Luftwaffe defensive activity – 3 September 1943

Unit	Type	Gruppe up			Gruppe down		Claims	Losses				
		Base	No	Time	Base	Time		Dest	Dam	KIA	MIA	WIA
Luftflotte 3												
Jafü 2:												
II./JG 2	Bf 109G	Poix, Vitry–en–Artois		~0900	Poix, Vitry–en–Artois	~1010	1 B-17	0	1	0	0	1
2nd sorties	Bf 109G	Poix, Vitry–en–Artois	10	~1035	Poix, Vitry–en–Artois	1135	0	0	0	0	0	0
GeschGr/JG 26	Fw 190A, Bf 109G	Lille–Nord, Wevelghem	*86	0900	Lille–Nord, Villaroche, Cambrai–Epinoy, Rosières	1010	0	1	1	1	0	1
II./JG 26	Fw 190A	Beauvais–Tillé		0905	Beauvais–Tillé, Villaroche, Creil	1054	2 B-17, 1 P-47	4	3	2	0	2
Jafü 3:												
Stab/JG 2	Fw 190A	Evreux	**60	~0920	Evreux	~1010	0	0	0	0	0	0
2nd sorties	Fw 190A	Evreux	***20	~1030	Evreux	~1130	1 B-17****	0	0	0	0	0
I./JG 2	Fw 190A, Bf 109G	Evreux		~0920	Evreux	~1010	0	0	0	0	0	0
2nd sorties	Fw 190A, Bf 109G	Evreux		~1030	Evreux	~1010	0	1	0	1	0	0
III./JG 2	Fw 190A	Conches?		~0900	Conches?	~1010	4 B-17	0	1	0	0	0
2nd sorties	Fw 190A	Conches?		~1030	Conches?	~1130	1 B-17	1	0	1	0	0
JLÜberprGr	Fw 190A	Guyancourt		0940	Villaroche	1020	0	0	1	0	0	1
2nd sorties	Fw 190A	Villaroche		1040	Guyancourt	1055	n/c	0	0	0	0	0

*86 Jafü 2 aircraft up on 1st sorties

**60 Jafü 3 aircraft up on 1st sorties (3 Gruppen)

***20 Jafü 3 aircraft up on 2nd sorties (2 Gruppen)

****Stab/JG 2: + 2 B-17 claims unconfirmed (unwitnessed)

Luftwaffe defensive activity – 6 September 1943

Unit	Type	Gruppe up			Gruppe down		Claims	Losses				
		Base	No	Time	Base	Time		Dest	Dam	KIA	MIA	WIA
Lw Bfh Mltte												
Jafü H-Ruhr:												
I./JG 3	Bf 109G	München–Gladbach		~1030	München–Gladbach	~1145	n/c	2	0	0	0	0
III./JG 3	Bf 109G	Bad Wörishofen	25	1027	Bad Wörishofen, Echterdingen, Karlsruhe	1143	2 B-17, 7 B-17 HSS	2	1	1	0	0
I./JG 26	Fw 190A	Grimbergen		0832	Grimbergen	0929	n/c	0	0	0	0	0
	Fw 190A	Grimbergen		1117	Grimbergen, Vitry, Creil	1224	1 B-17 HSS	0	0	0	0	0
Jagddivision 5:												
II./JG 27	Bf 109G	Frankfurt–Eschborn	20	1003	Stuttgart–Echterdingen	1120	6 B-17	1	0	1	0	0
JG 50	Bf 109G	Wiesbaden–Erbenheim	12	~1030	Wiesbaden–Erbenheim	~1145	4 B-17	3	1	1	0	0
II./JG 51	Bf 109G	Neubiberg		1045	Neubiberg, Landsberg	1205	n/c	1	1	0	0	0
II./JG 106	Fw 190A	Lachen–Speyerdorf		~1030	Lachen–Speyerdorf	~1130	1 B-17	1	0	0	0	1
III./NJG 101	Bf 110F	Kitzingen		~1045	Kitzingen, Grosselfingen	~1200	2 B-17	0	0	0	0	0
I./KG 51	Me 410A	Illesheim	7	~1030	Illesheim	~1200	0	3	0	2	0	1
Luftflotte 3												
Jafü 2:												
II./JG 2	Bf 109G	Vitry–en–Artois		0828	Vitry–en–Artois	0843	n/c	0	0	0	0	0
	Bf 109G	Vitry–en–Artois		~0900	Vitry–en–Artois	~1045	2 B-17, 1 P-47	0	1	0	0	1
2nd sorties	Bf 109G	Vitry–en–Artois		~1230	Vitry–en–Artois	~1330	1 B-17 HSS	1	0	0	0	0
3rd sorties	Bf 109G	Vitry–envArtois		~1400	Vitry–en–Artois	~1615	3 B-17	0	0	0	0	0
GeschGr/JG 26	Bf 109G, Fw 190A	Lille–Nord		0828	Lille–Nord	0843	n/c	0	0	0	0	0
	Bf 109G, Fw 190A	Lille–Nord		0858	Lille–Nord, Couvron?, Cambrai–Sud	1002	0	0	0	0	0	0
2nd sorties	Fw 190A	Lille–Nord		1000	Lille–Nord	1125	0	0	0	0	0	0
2nd sorties	Bf 109G	Lille–Nord, Cambrai–Sud		1020	Lille–Nord	1102	0	1	0	0	0	0
3rd sorties	Bf 109G, Fw 190A	Lille–Nord		1145	Lille–Nord	1252	0	0	0	0	0	0
3rd sorties	Bf 109G	Lille–Nord		1227	Lille–Nord	1400	0	0	0	0	0	0
I./JG 26	Fw 190A	Creil		1300	Creil	1353	2 B-17	0	0	0	0	0
	Fw 190A	Creil		1415	Grimbergen	1455	transfer	0	0	0	0	0
II./JG 26	Fw 190A	Beauvais–Tillé		0828	Beauvais–Tillé	0904	n/c	0	0	0	0	0
	Fw 190A	Beauvais–Tillé		0925	Beauvais–Tillé	1056	0	2	4	2	0	0
2nd sorties	Fw 190A	Beauvais–Tillé		1123	Beauvais–Tillé, Romilly	1248	1 B-17, 2 B-17 HSS	0	1	0	0	1
Jafü 3:												
Stab/JG 2	Fw 190A	Evreux		0925	Evreux	0954	n/c	0	0	0	0	0
2nd sorties	Fw 190A	Evreux		~1145	Evreux	~1300	3 B-17	0	0	0	0	0
3rd sorties	Fw 190A	Evreux		~1330	Evreux	~1430	0	0	0	0	0	0
I./JG 2	Bf 109G, Fw 190A	St. André		0925	St. André	0954	n/c	0	0	0	0	0
2nd sorties	Bf 109G, Fw 190A	St. André		1124	St. André	1311	7 B-17	2	3	0	0	2
3rd sorties	Bf 109G, Fw 190A	St. André		~1330	St. André	~1430	1 B-17	0	0	0	0	0
III./JG 2	Fw 190A	Conches		~1200	Conches	~1300	3 B-17	3	0	0	0	1
3./SKG 10	Fw 190A	St. André		~1200	St. André	~1300	1 B-17	0	0	0	0	0
JLÜberPrGr	Fw 190A	Guyancourt		?	Guyancourt	?	0	1	0	1	0	0
Jafü Bretagne:												
2./NAGr 13	Bf 109G	Dinard		~1400	Dinard	~1500	1 B-17	0	0	0	0	0

7 September

8th Air Force VIII BC Mission #92: 105 of 114 1st BW B-17s bomb Brussels–Evere, TOT 0949-52 – lose 0-1-10, claim 0; 58 of 148 4th BW B-17s bomb Watten V-2 sites, TOT 0920-54 – lose 0-0-39, claim 0. 178 VIII FC P-47s claim 3-0-2, lose 1-1-1.

The weather cleared enough in the early morning for the VIII BC to send the two B-17 wings against two nearby targets, Brussels–Evere airfield and the V-2 site at Watten. Luftwaffe resistance was light, and the two Jagdgruppen to approach the bombers were kept away by the P-47s.

9 September

8th Air Force VIII BC Mission #94: 330 of 377 B-17s + B-24s bomb eight French airfields and Paris industry, TOT 0916-1016 – lose 2-0-47, claim 16-2-9. 215 VIII FC P-47s claim 1-0-0, lose 2.

The VIII BC brought Operation STARKEY to an end with fragmentation and high-explosive bomb attacks on eight Luftwaffe airfields in France. The fighters of Jafü 2 and Jafü 3 rose to defend their bases, but the four P-47 groups flew an extremely effective escort mission. A Luftwaffe report stated that the P-47s prevented any head-on attacks by turning aggressively into every German approach. JG 2 claimed two B-17s and one P-47; JG 26 filed no claims. Most of the fighter combats were not fought to conclusion; the two Geschwader lost five aircraft and three pilots.

15 September

8th Air Force VIII BC Mission #95: 273 of 308 B-17s + B-24s bomb two French airfields and Paris aviation industry, TOT 1948-2011 – lose 6-2-40, claim 15-2-4. RAF FC Spitfires claim 0-2-0, lose 1; 201 VIII FC P-47s claim 0-0-1, lose 2.

The VIII BC attacked several targets near Paris, including the Romilly air depot, late in the evening. Jafü 2 and Jafü 3 scrambled their fighters and sent them toward the presumed target area, but they became embroiled with the numerous Spitfires escorting large RAF Mitchell and USAAF B-26 medium bomber raids, which were otherwise ignored, and failed to reach the heavy bombers before the bombing. All of the German units were ordered up on a second mission against the withdrawing bombers, but successes were few. The Americans lost one bomber and wrote off two; the RAF lost one Spitfire. Luftflotte 3 lost three Focke-

II./JG 27 Bf 109G-6s on the St. Dizier apron in September. The unit had just joined Luftflotte 3 after two years in the Mediterranean theatre. The aircraft are 'gunboats' with underwing 20-mm cannon and carry the Gruppe emblem on the cowling. 'White 2' has three rows of victory bars on its rudder; its pilot is unknown. *(Prien)*

Wulfs and one pilot. JG 2 claimed five B-17s and one B-24; JG 26 claimed one Spitfire.

16 September

8th Air Force VIII BC Mission #97: 131 of 147 1st Bomb Division (1st BD) B-17s bomb Nantes port and airfield, TOT 1602-12 – lose 7-1-47, claim 22-2-5; 93 of 148 3rd BD B-17s bomb La Pallice port, La Rochelle, Cognac airfields, TOT 1831-58 – lose 4-5-17, claim 22-2-5. 79 VIII FC P-47s claim 2-0-1, lose 0.

The VIII BC B-17s left England in the evening to bomb targets in southwestern France. The reorganisation of the air defences the previous day increased only the number of Luftflotte 3 headquarters, not operational strength. Jagddivision 4 (commanding Jafü 2) and Jagddivision 5 (commanding Jafü 3) scrambled all of their fighters, but only I./JG 2 was able to penetrate the escort and make a successful attack. Once the P-47s turned back, Jafü Bretagne in Brittany sent up III./JG 2, the operational Staffeln from two advanced training Gruppen, a maritime recce Staffel, and II./ZG 1, whose usual mission was maritime support. These units claimed eight B-17s. Most of the Jagdgruppen in northern France were sent up on second sorties against the withdrawing B-17s, but the Spitfires supporting medium bomber raids in the area provided excellent if impromptu cover, and no more B-17s were lost. The Americans lost or wrote off 17 B-17s for the day; the Germans, eight aircraft and five pilots.

Luftwaffe defensive activity – 7 September 1943

Unit	Type	Gruppe up			Gruppe down		Claims	Losses				
		Base	No	Time	Base	Time		Dest	Dam	KIA	MIA	WIA
Lw Bfh Mitte												
Jafü H-Ruhr:												
I./JG 1	Fw 190A	Arnhem, Deelen		0950	Arnhem, Deelen	1050	n/c	0	0	0	0	0
III./JG 1	Bf 109G	Leeuwarden		~0915	Leeuwarden	~1015	0	1	0	0	1	0
I./JG 26	Fw 190A	Grimbergen		0920	Grimbergen	1018	1 P-47	0	0	0	0	0
Luftflotte 3												
Jafü 2:												
11./JG 26	Bf 109G	Lille–Nord		0911	Lille–Nord, Maldeghem	1014		0	0	0	0	0

Luftwaffe defensive activity – 9 September 1943

Unit	Type	Gruppe up			Gruppe down		Claims	Losses				
		Base	No	Time	Base	Time		Dest	Dam	KIA	MIA	WIA
Lw Bfh Mitte												
Jafü H-Ruhr:												
I./JG 26	Fw 190A	Grimbergen		1055	Grimbergen	1136	0	1	1	0	0	1
Luftflotte 3												
Jafü 2:												
GeschGr/ JG 26	Fw 190A, Bf 109G	Lille–Nord		0857	Lille–Nord	1013	0	0	0	0	0	0
II./JG 26	Fw 190A	Beauvais–Tillé		0852	Beauvais–Tillé	1000	0	0	0	0	0	0
12./JG 26	Bf 190G	Moorsele		0857	Moorsele	0952	0	0	0	0	0	0
Jafü 3:												
Stab/JG 2	Fw 190A	Evreux		0909	Evreux	1030		0	0	0	0	0
I./JG 2	Fw 190A, Bf 109G	Evreux		0909	Evreux	1030	2 B-17	0	1	0	0	0
II./JG 2	Bf 109G	Vitry–en–Artois		0857	Vitry–en–Artois	1013	0	2	2	1	0	0
III./JG 2	Fw 190A	Beaumont–le–Roger		~0910	Beaumont–le–Roger	~1030	1 P-47	2	2	2	0	0
1./FAGr 123	Bf 109G	Toussus–le–Buc		?	Toussus–le–Buc	?	0	1	0	0	1	0

23 September

8th Air Force VIII BC Mission #100: 154 of 247 B-17s bomb Nantes port, Vannes and Kerlin airfields, TOT 0913-26 – lose 1-2-58, claim 24-1-3. 158 VIII FC P-47s claim 4-0-1, lose 1-0-2.

8th Air Force VIII BC Mission #101: 80 of 91 B-17s bomb Nantes port, Rennes airfield, TOT 1910-34 – lose 2-1-26, claim 0. 109 VIII FC P 47s fly penetration escort; no claims or losses.

The VIII BC B-17s returned to action with two separate missions to France, one early in the morning and the other late in the afternoon. As the first force appeared to be heading for southwestern France,

Jagddivision 4 held most of its fighters on the ground, while Jagddivision 5 directed the Stab and First Gruppe of JG 2 to Brittany, where it met III./JG 2 and, much to their surprise, the Thunderbolts of the 353rd FG, which stayed with the B-17s all the way to Nantes and shot down five fighters for the loss of one P-47. Only two claims for B-17s were filed, and one of these bombers in fact made it back to Britain. Stab/JG 2 and I./JG 2 probably had to land at unfamiliar bases for servicing and were available only at low strength later in the day. In mid-afternoon, the B-26s bombed a number of airfields, including the II./JG 26 field at Beauvais–Tillé, to tie down the Jagddivision 4 fighters. Their mission was successful: three Spitfires were shot

Luftwaffe defensive activity – 15 September 1943

Unit	Type	Gruppe up			Gruppe down		Claims	Losses				
		Base	No	Time	Base	Time		Dest	Dam	KIA	MIA	WIA
Lw Bfh Mitte												
Jafü H-Ruhr.												
I./JG 26	Fw 190A	Grimbergen		1914	Grimbergen	1953	n/c	0	0	0	0	0
Luftflotte 3												
Jafü 2:												
Stab/JG 26	Fw 190A	Lille–Nord		1800	Lille–Nord	1855	0	0	0	0	0	0
2nd sorties	Fw 190A	Lille–Nord		1900	LillevNord	2030	0	0	0	0	0	0
8./JG 26	Fw 190A	Lille–Nord		1800	Lille–Nord	1855	1 Spitfire	0	1	0	0	0
2nd sorties	Fw 190A	Lille–Nord		1900	Lille–Nord	2030	0	0	0	0	0	0
II./JG 26	Fw 190A	Beauvais–Tillé, Nivillers		1808	Beauvais–Tillé, Nivillers, Creil	1919	0	2	0	0	0	2
2nd sorties	Fw 190A	Beauvais–Tillé, Nivillers		1950	Beauvais–Tillé, Nivillers	2016	0	0	0	0	0	0
III./JG 26	Bf 109G	Lille–Vendeville		1800	Lille–Vendeville	1855	0	0	0	0	0	0
2nd sorties	Bf 109G	Lille–Vendeville		1900	Lille–Vendeville	2030	0	0	0	0	0	0
12./JG 26	Bf 109G	Moorsele		1800	Moorsele	1855	0	0	0	0	0	0
II./JG 27	Bf 109G	St. Dizier		1945	St. Dizier	2015	n/c	0	0	0	0	0
Jafü 3:												
Stab/JG 2	Fw 190A	Evreux		~1900	Evreux	~2000	0	0	0	0	0	0
2nd sorties	Fw 190A	Evreux		~2015	Evreux	~2115	0	0	0	0	0	0
I./JG 2	Fw 190A, Bf 109G	Evreux		~1900	Evreux	~2000	1 B-17	0	3	0	0	1
2nd sorties	Fw 190A, Bf 109G	Evreux		~2015	Evreux	~2115	1 B-24	0	0	0	0	0
II./JG 2	Bf 109G	Vitry–en–Artois		1800	Vitry–en–Artois	1855	0	0	0	0	0	0
2nd sorties	Bf 109G	Vitry–en–Artois		1900	Vitry–en–Artois	2030	0	0	0	0	0	0
III./JG 2	Fw 190A	Beaumont–le–Roger		~1800	Beaumont–le–Roger	~1900	0	0	0	0	0	0
2nd sorties	Fw 190A	Beaumont–le–Roger		~1915	Beaumont–le–Roger	~2030	4 B-17	0	0	0	0	0
JLÜberPrGr	Fw 190A	Orléans–Bricy		1512	Orléans–Bricy	1537	0	1	0	1	0	0

down, for the loss of two II./JG 2 Messerschmitts, but none of these fighters was available to oppose the late B-17 mission, which sailed through northern France unmolested and lost only one bomber in the target area. The Spitfires and P-47s punished JG 2 severely; the Geschwader lost three KIA, seven WIA and 11 fighters. JG 26 lost one WIA and two fighters.

27 September

8th Air Force VIII BC Mission #104: 246 of 308 B-17s bomb Emden, TOT 1058-1108 – lose 7-1-78, claim 32-7-24. 262 VIII FC P-47s claim 21-2-6, lose 1-1-1.

The VIII BC's first raid on Germany in three weeks was noteworthy in two respects. The P-47 force, now expanded to six groups, all carried auxiliary tanks and, for the first time, provided escort to a target in Germany. And the attack was led by four B-17Fs of the new Pathfinder Force (PFF). These were equipped with H2S (American designation H2X), a British radar device able to distinguish large geographic features such as coastlines, but not specific targets. The force's aiming point was the city centre, and the Americans thus became full participants in the RAF's area bombing campaign. The upgraded fighter command organisation within the Reich got its first workout in daylight today. Jagddivison 2 (JD 2 – ex-Jafü Deutsche Bucht) got up all of its fighters, including for the first time two Zerstörergruppen. It identified the target early due to a radio intercept and ordered its units to join up in a single combat formation. Owing to weather and radio problems, this

Luftwaffe defensive activity – 16 September 1943

Unit	Type	Gruppe up			Gruppe down		Claims	Losses				
		Base	No	Time	Base	Time		Dest	Dam	KIA	MIA	WIA
Luftflotte 3												
II. Jagdkorps												
Jagddivision 4:												
8./JG 26	Fw 190A	Lille–Nord		1503	Beauvais–Tillé	1525	n/c	0	0	0	0	0
II./JG 26	Fw 190A	Beauvais–Tillé, Nivillers		1415	Evreux	1430	transfer	0	0	0	0	0
	Fw 190A	Evreux		1500	Rennes	1600	0	1	1	1	0	0
2nd sorties	Fw 190A	Rennes		1655	Morlaix	1755	n/c	0	0	0	0	0
2nd sorties	Fw 190A	Beauvais–Tillé		1810	Beauvais–Tillé	1938	0	0	0	0	0	0
III./JG 26	Bf 109G	Lille–Vendeville		1500	Beauvais–Tillé	1602	n/c	0	0	0	0	0
2nd sorties	Bf 109G	Beauvais–Tillé		1810	Lille–Vendeville	1938	0	0	0	0	0	0
12./JG 26	Bf 109G	Moorsele		~1505	Moorsele	~1605	0	0	1	0	0	0
Jagddivision 5:												
Stab/JG 2	Fw 190A	Evreux		1450	Evreux	1618	0	0	0	0	0	0
I./JG 2	Fw 190A,	Evreux		1450	Evreux	1618	3 B-17	0	1	0	0	1
	Bf 109G											
II./JG 2	Fw 190A	Vitry–en–Artois		1505	Beauvais–Tillé	1602	n/c	0	0	0	0	0
2nd sorties	Fw 190A	Beauvais–Tillé		1810	Vitry–en–Artois	1938	1 Spitfire	2	0	1	0	1
Jafü Bretagne:												
III./JG 2	Fw 190A	Brest–Guipavas		1532	Brestv–Guipavas	~1630	2 B-17	2	0	2	0	0
II./ZG 1	Bf 110G	Lanvéoc–Poulmic		~1800	Lanvéoc–Poulmic	~1930	3 B-17	1	1	0	0	0
2./JGr Ost	Bf 109F	La Leu		1815	La Leu	1915	1 B-17	1	0	0	0	0
4./JGr Ost	Bf 109G	La Leu		1830	La Leu	1915	2 B-17	0	0	0	0	0
JGr West	Bf 109F	La Leu		1802	La Leu	1839	0	0	0	0	0	0
SAGr 128	Fw 190A	Brest		~1800	Brest	~1900	0	0	1	0	1	0

did not happen, and II./JG 11 bore the brunt of the battle. The Gruppe claimed seven B-17s and one P-47. Of its 37 Bf 109s which took off from Oldenburg, 12 did not return; eight were lost with their pilots in the North Sea. Jagddivision 3 (JD 3 – ex-Jafü Holland-Ruhrgebiet) was called on and fed five Jagdgruppen into the battle singly. Most were split up by the P-47s, which seemed to be everywhere, but II./JG 3 distinguished itself on its first major RLV mission by claiming six B-17s for the loss of three Bf 109s and one missing pilot. As far as the American bomber generals were concerned, the PFF-guided mission was a mixed success. Although bombing results were poor, the P-47s did extremely well, and only eight B-17s were lost or scrapped. Lw Bfh Mitte flew a total of 388 sorties and lost 18 aircrewmen – most missing in the North Sea – and 28 fighters. The losses of II./JG 11 were the heaviest for any RLV Gruppe to date. The mission does not seem to have provoked the strong response in Berlin that it should have, but two Bf 109 Gruppenkommandeure are known to have removed

the drag-producing gun tubs and rocket launchers from their fighters to lower their vulnerability to the P-47s. This action was unauthorised and greatly reduced their firepower against the American heavy bombers.

Fw 190A-6 'Black 5' of II./JG 1, shown here at Rheine in the summer, was lost on a night mission on 27 September while being flown by a II./JG 300 pilot. *(Mombeek)*

UNIT COMBAT REPORT[7]
27 September 1943

1. Combat readiness was ordered by the Jafü at 1024 hours. The order to take off was given at 1044 hours, without an intermediate state of cockpit readiness. I ordered cockpit readiness at the take-off order, to make a simultaneous start-up and take-off possible.

2. I gave the take-off order myself at 1046.30 hours. One Schwarm lifted off at 1047 hours; Gruppe take-off time was 1050 hours.

3. The Gruppe assembled over the field in a left turn at 400 metres and first took up a course from the field of 180°, as there was a rainstorm to the north and west with a cloud layer between 500 and 4,500 metres. We could not fly through this cloud.

4. At the Ems-Jade Canal, the Gruppe took up a course of 270° and climbed to altitude. The 4. Staffel was to the left of the Stabsschwarm, the 6. was to the right, and the 5. was above. The Gruppe flew up to this point in a *Gruppenkeil* [Gruppe wedge], with the Staffeln aligned to the left and right.

5. While south of the Jever airfield at 1,000 metres, I saw a strong condensation trail toward Emden and then the first enemy Pulk of 40–60 Boeing Fortresses at about 7,000–7,200 metres. At this time, the Gruppe was still flying in close formation at 270°. Upon inquiring of ground control whether we should drop our auxiliary tanks, we were ordered to wait for a later formation to enter quadrant BO. Since I could see the bomber Pulks in front of me, I myself gave the order to drop tanks. I based my decision on the need to increase our rate of climb and mobility to face the attacks of the enemy escorts, which could be glimpsed above the Fortress Pulks through the contrails.

6. After reaching about 3,000 metres, the Gruppe found itself directly beneath two Boeing Pulks, which were flying east in quadrant BQ-7. This time, ground control gave us permission to attack. The Gruppe made a climbing turn toward a Pulk that was not yet under attack. The enemy formation turned to a course of 270° in quadrant CQ-6, while the Gruppe was still 1,500 metres below it. The enemy's altitude was reached in quadrant CQ-5. The prolonged turn of the enemy formation made a head-on attack impossible, so the Gruppe prepared an attack from the high rear, in which the 5. Staffel would go in first firing its 21-centimetre mortar shells. The rest of the Gruppe was in an expanded attack formation in the order Stabsschwarm, 6. Staffel and 4. Staffel. The enemy formation was now flying north in quadrant CQ-4; the Gruppe was now in position about 1,000 metres above it. The enemy fighters – recognised as Thunderbolts – were still 2,000 metres above the Boeing Pulk, which itself was at 7,000 metres. I radioed the Staffeln and ground control, 'Kleine Indianer über uns' [Small Indians (enemy fighters) above us]. It was standard practice on receipt of these code words for the 6. Staffel to drop back to give the 'shooters' cover against a surprise attack. However, the 4. Staffel, which should have been directly behind the Stabsschwarm, was trailing the formation instead, as the Staffelkapitän had been unable to drop his tank. Six more aircraft had the same problem. These pilots were under orders not to take part in dogfights, for their own safety. The Stabsschwarm made the first attack on a Pulk of 40–60 Fortresses from 1,000 metres above. The enemy escort did not disturb this attack. Uffz. Utzera shot one Fortress out of formation during this attack. A Boeing that I attacked in the left rear of the Pulk moved over to the right side. While the Stabsschwarm climbed steeply for another pass, the 6. Staffel attacked and shot down one Fortress. I then saw three Thunderbolts dropping down in a left turn from our high left side onto the 4. Staffel, flying in the rear. I gave the warning, 'Achtung! Kleine Indianer hinter uns!' [Attention! Small Indians behind us!] and, with my wingman close beside me, positioned myself behind the three Thunderbolts, which were approaching the rear 4. Staffel Schwarm. Paying no attention to the Thunderbolts, the 4. Staffel made its attack on the Boeing Pulk and shot two down. Its rear Schwarm was then approached by the Thunderbolts. To protect them, I opened fire from 500 metres behind with the left-wing cannon and one MG 131 (my other weapons were jammed). The Thunderbolts, which had already opened fire on the 4. Staffel Schwarm, pulled up in a steep left turn. At this moment the Stab formation was fired at from the rear by other Thunderbolts. I gave the signal to reverse direction to

the left and warned my No. 2 by radio. My No. 2 did not make a sharp left turn, however, but attempted to remain beside me and was hit by the Thunderbolt behind me, which was then driven away by a diving Fw 190 …

7. Some of the Schwärme were already involved with the diving Thunderbolts and split up. Some of the pilots attempted to escape the fire of the enemy fighters behind them by diving away. Most, however, stayed in the fight and tried to get at the Boeings again. A new attack on the bombers was not possible, however, since the enemy fighters, coming down in Schwärme or Rotten, forced the Gruppe into accepting dogfights. I observed that our pilots, inexperienced in fighter-versus-fighter combat, made smooth turns instead of pushing the rudder pedals hard enough to roll away from the onrushing Thunderbolts. Some pilots with Bf 109G-6/U4s [with MK 108 30-mm engine cannon] spun out and entered the clouds.

8. In my opinion, the Bf 109G-6 and G-6/U4 can turn better than the Thunderbolt at low speed. The Thunderbolts with their speed advantage will overrun them; their throttle response in climbs or dives is too slow. The *Gallandpanzer* [armoured glass headrest] with its improved vision to the high rear has proven itself. Many of the MK 108 aircraft suffered jams at the beginning of the turning combat. Out of 19 aircraft with MK 108 cannon, seven suffered jams.

9. In discussing our losses, it is important to understand that our pilots are inexperienced in the ways of fighters and were forced into individual combat without adequate knowledge of tactics or situational awareness. Also, many had to enter combat while carrying auxiliary tanks.

10. Perhaps some of the missing pilots crashed into the ground because they did not know how low the cloud deck persisted. The variable cloud cover hampered our mission from the start. Recognition of the enemy formation and especially the fighter escort was hindered by the strong condensation trails. It was not possible to see the ground over the coast and the islands …

11. Thirty-seven Bf 109s took off from Jever; all made contact with the enemy. The nine Bf 109Ts of Jagdstaffel Helgoland did not make enemy contact. Including the missing, this Gruppe sustained nine total losses. There was, in addition, one total aircraft loss, the pilot bailing out successfully; five belly-landings due to combat damage; and four aircraft with lighter damage. It can be assumed that several of those lost were shot down by the Fortresses …

12. The returning pilots reported eight certain shootdowns and Herausschüsse and one probable victory. These comprised seven Boeing Fortress IIs and two Thunderbolts.

Hptm. Günther Specht, Gruppenkommandeur II./JG 11

Major Günther Specht, II./JG 11 Gruppenkommandeur from May 1943 and JG 11 Kommodore from 15 May 1944 until his loss in Operation Bodenplatte on 1 January 1945. An outstanding combat commander, he was awarded the Oak Leaves to his Knight's Cross after his death. His final victory total was 34, including 17 heavy bombers. His 1939 duty as a Bf 110 pilot with I./ZG 26 had cost him an eye. *(Rose)*

Luftwaffe defensive activity – 23 September 1943

Unit	Type	Gruppe up			Gruppe down		Claims	Losses				
		Base	No	Time	Base	Time		Dest	Dam	KIA	MIA	WIA
Luftflotte 3												
II. Jagdkorps												
Jagddivision 4:												
8./JG 26	Fw 190A,	Lille–Nord		1615	Lille–Nord, Abbéville	1720	0	0	2	0	0	0
2nd sorties	Fw 190A	Lille–Nord, Abbéville		1736	Lille–Nord	1755	n/c	0	0	0	0	0
II./JG 26	Fw 190A	Beauvais–Tillé		0837	Beauvais–Tillé, Rouen	0916	n/c	0	0	0	0	0
2nd sorties	Fw 190A	Beauvais–Tillé		1612	Beauvais–Tillé	1716	1 Spitfire	1	0	0	0	1
III./JG 26	Bf 109G	Lille–Vendeville		1615	Lille–Vendeville	1720	1 Spitfire	0	2	0	0	0
12./JG 26	Bf 109G	Moorsele		~1615	Moorsele	~1720	0	1	1	0	0	0
Jagddivision 5:												
Stab/JG 2	Fw 190A	Evreux	*69	~0830	Vannes?	~1000	0	1	0	0	0	1
2nd sorties	Fw 190A	Vannes?		~1630	Evreux	~1730	0	0	0	0	0	0
I./JG 2	Fw 190A,	Evreux, St. André	—	~0830	Vannes?	~1000	1 P-47	3	0	0	0	2
	Bf 109G											
2nd sorties	Fw 190A,	Vannes?		~1630	Evreux, St. André	~1730	1 Spitfire	1	1	1	0	0
	Bf 109G											
II./JG 2	Bf 109G	Vitry–en–Artois	—	1615	Vitry–en–Artois	1720	0	2	2	0	0	2
Jafü Bretagne:												
III./JG 2	Fw 190A	Brest–Guipavas	—	~0900	Brest–Guipavas	~1000	1 B-17	2	1	1	0	2
2nd sorties	Fw 190A	Brest–Guipavas		~1730	Brest–Guipavas	~1900	1 B-17	2	1	1	0	0

*69 JG 2 fighters (all Gruppen) up on 1st sorties

Luftwaffe defensive activity – 27 September 1943

Unit	Type	Gruppe up			Gruppe down		Claims	Losses (—: included in 1st sortie)				
		Base	No	Time	Base	Time		Dest	Dam	KIA	MIA	WIA
Lw Bfh MItte												
I. Jagdkorps			160									
Jagddivision 1:												
III./JG 54	Bf 109G	Schwerin		1129	Schwerin, Oldenburg	1221	n/c	0	0	0	0	0
Jagddivision 2:												
Stab/JG 11	Bf 109G	Jever		~1055	Jever	~1140	0	0	0	0	0	0
I./JG 11	Fw 190A	Husum		1052	Husum	1154	1 B-17, 1 P-47	1	0	0	1	0
II./JG 11	Bf 109G	Jever	37	1055	Jever	1141	7 B-17, 1 P-47	12	3	1	8	2
III./JG 11	Fw 190A	Oldenburg		1056	Oldenburg	1203	n/c	0	0	0	0	0
JaSta Helgoland	Bf 109T	Helgoland–Düne	9	~1030	Helgoland–Düne	~1130	n/c	0	0	0	0	0
III./ZG 1	Me 410A	Hildesheim		~1045	Hildesheim	~1215	n/c	1	0	2	0	0
III./ZG 26	Bf 110G	Wunstorf, Plantlünne	37	1045	Wunstorf, Plantlünne	1215	0.	0	0	0	0	0
I./ZG 76	Bf 110G	?		?	?	?	1 B-17	1	0	0	2	0
ErprKdo 25	Ju 88C, Fw 190A, Bf 110	Achmer, Wittmundhafen		1050	Achmer, Wittmundhafen	1150	0	1	0	0	0	1
2nd sorties	Fw 190A	Achmer		1250	Achmer	1316	0	0	0	0	0	0
ISS Focke-Wulf	Fw 190A	Bremen		~1030	Bremen	~1130	n/c	0	1	0	0	0
Jagddivision 3:												
Stab/JG 1	Fw 190A	Deelen	2	~1030	Deelen	~1140	1 B-17	0	2	0	0	0
I./JG 1	Fw 190A	Arnhem, Deelen		1031	Wittmundhafen	1140	0	2	0	1	0	1
II./JG 1	Fw 190A	Woensdrecht	21	1032	Marx, Leeuwarden, Diepholz, Oldenburg, Jever, Vechta	1156	1 B-17 HSS	3	3	1	0	2
III./JG 1	Bf 109G	Leeuwarden		~1030	Leeuwarden	~1140	0	0	0	0	0	0
I./JG 3	Bf 109G	Bönninghardt		~1030	Bönninghardt	~1140	0	3	1	1	0	1
II./JG 3	Bf 109G	Schiphol		1033	Schiphol	~1215	6 B-17	3	2	0	1	2
Jagddivision 7:												
JG 50	Bf 109G	Wiesbaden–Erbenheim		?	Wiesbaden–Erbenheim	?	n/c	1	0	0	0	0
Jafü Norwegen:												
I./JG 5	Bf 109G	Herdla		~1100	Herdla	~1200	0	0	0	0	0	0
IV./JG 5	Bf 109G	Stavanger		~1100	Stavanger	~1200	1 B-17	0	0	0	0	0

Notes:

[1] Eder Gefechtsbericht, in private collection.

[2] Hondt Gefechtsbericht, in private collection.

[3] II./JG 1 Kriegstagebuch, BA-MA RL 10/483.

[4] Schwarz Gefechtsbericht, BA-MA RL 10/482.

[5] Wiegand correspondence with J.-L. Roba, 1988.

[6] Surau Gefechtsbericht, NARA T-971 roll 11.

[7] II./JG 11 Gefechtsbericht, in private collection

CHAPTER 4

OCTOBER – DECEMBER 1943

October 1943

This month represented the high point of the Reichsluftverteidigung effort against the American daylight raids. The reorganisation begun in September continued to be tweaked. Overall air defence policy and guidance were set forth at Lw Bfh Mitte. XII. Fliegerkorps was disbanded, and Generalmajor Josef 'Beppo' Schmid was given operational authority over all day and night fighter units in the I. Jagdkorps area of responsibility, which still did not include southern Germany or Austria. The boundaries between Schmid's three Jagddivisionen, Jagddivision 7 and its subordinated Jafü Ostmark, and Luftflotte 3 in the west were redrawn.

The month's tactical innovation was the introduction of six rocket-armed Zerstörergruppen to the order of battle. III./ZG 1 was renamed II./ZG 26, making Jagddivision 2's ZG 26 a full three-Gruppe Geschwader. Jagddivision 7's ZG 76 had two strong Gruppen and a weak third Gruppe that never reached full strength. II./ZG 1 remained in Austria as the lone representative of its Geschwader in the RLV force. The Bf 110s and Me 410s proved capable of smashing unescorted heavy bomber combat boxes. The USAAF was forced to suspend deep-penetration raids until the bombers could be escorted all the way to the target. America was winning the race to build up fighter strength in the theatre, however, even if their standard P-47 escort could not reach the farthest targets. The RLV force could only expand its single-engine fighter strength by withdrawing complete units from the active combat fronts. A shortage of fighters forced the postponement of the long-planned enlargement of the Jagdgeschwader in the Reich to three four-Staffel Gruppen. The two Luftflotte 3 Geschwader, JG 2 and JG 26, the guardians of the western occupied zone, were so reinforced on 1 October, however, and the anomalous JG 26 Geschwadergruppe was disbanded.

Pilots and groundcrew of II./JG 2 relax in front of Bf 109G-6 'White 1' during a low readiness state at Evreux in the autumn. The airplane is a 'gunboat' with underwing 20-mm cannon. *(Bundesarchiv 483-2897-3)*

Major Kurt Bühligen, Kommandeur of II./JG 2 (centre) in earnest conversation with the pilot of 6./JG 2 Bf 109G-4 'Yellow 4' at Evreux in the autumn. *(Bundesarchiv 483-2897-26)*

Hptm. Johannes Kiel, Kapitän of the 7. Staffel of III./ZG 26, supervises the loading of 21-cm rockets on his Bf 110G. Kiel was promoted to III./ZG 76 Kommandeur in November 1943, but was killed in action on 29 January 1944. *(Bundesarchiv 649-5371-16)*

1 October

12th Air Force XII Bomber Command (XII BC): 73 B-24s bomb Wiener Neustadt Bf 109 factory, lose 7; 42 B-17s bomb Steyr + TOs, lose 3. No escort.

The three 8th Air Force (8th AF) B-24 groups, which had gone to North Africa in September to support the Allied landings in Italy, joined the two B-24 groups of the Mediterranean Theatre's 12th Air Force in a raid on the important Messerschmitt plant at Wiener Neustadt, while the 12th AF's B-17s targeted Augsburg, but turned back early. The weak defenders in this area put up 176 sorties and performed adequately against the unescorted bombers. Confirmed heavy bomber claims totalled five for III./JG 3 and six for I./JG 27. I./KG 51 scrambled its Me 410s, and a number of Bf 110s were also up, but apparently made no claims. Known American losses to all causes were seven B-24s (all from the 8th AF units) and three B-17s. One of the latter was shot down north of Pisa by a Bf 109 from III./JG 77, which sustained no known losses. The defenders based in the Reich lost at least one KIA, two WIA and three Bf 109s.

A ZG 1 Bf 110G-2/R3 on the gun calibration stand. *(Petrick)*

2 October

8th Air Force VIII Bomber Command (VIII BC) Mission #106: 180 of 186 3rd Bomb Division (3rd BD) B-17s, 159 of 163 1st BD B-17s bomb Emden, TOT 1557-1603 – lose 1-0-11 (3rd BD), 1-0-23 (1st BD), claim 15-6-12. 227 VIII Fighter Command (VIII FC) P 47s (5 FGs) claim 5-3-1, lose 0-0-1.

This raid was another American attempt to bomb through an undercast using British H2S radar equipment. It was unsuccessful, but the bad weather also hampered the defences. Only one bomber was lost to fighter attack; the Luftwaffe pilots claimed nine and were ultimately credited with four, plus one P-47. Their losses totalled two KIA, four MIA, four WIA and 11 fighters, most to P-47s over the North Sea.

P-47D T9+FK of the 2nd Staffel of the Versuchsverband Ob.d.L., photographed on a visit to a JG 1 airfield. Its history in US service is unknown. *(Berger)*

Luftwaffe defensive activity – 1 October 1943

Unit	Type	Gruppe up			Gruppe down		Claims	Losses				
		Base	No	Time	Base	Time		Dest	Dam	KIA	MIA	WIA
Lw Bfh Mitte			**188**									
Jagddivision 7:												
III./JG 3	Bf 109G	Bad Wörishofen	29	1230	Bad Wörishofen, Friedrichshafen	1425	4 B-17, 1 B-17 HSS	0	1	0	0	0
II./JG 51	Bf 109G	Neubiberg	19	1228	Neubiberg	~1345	n/c	0	0	0	0	0
I./ZG 76	Bf 110G	Ansbach	12	1240	Ansbach	~1345	0	0	1	0	0	0
II./ZG 76	Bf 110G	Wertheim	30	1247	Wertheim	~1345	0	0	0	0	0	0
III./NJG 101	Bf 110G	Stuttgart–Echterdingen	6	1307	Stuttgart–Echterdingen	1433	n/c	0	0	0	0	0
I./ZG 101	Bf 110G	Memmingen	6	1325	Memmingen	~1430	0	0	0	0	0	0
Jafü Ostmark:												
I./JG 27	Bf 109G	Fels am Wagram	39	1232	Fels am Wagram	~1330	3 B-17, 2 B-24, 1 B-17 HSS	2	1	1	0	0
2nd sorties	Bf 109G	Fels am Wagram	13	1417	Fels am Wagram	~1530	n/c	0	0	0	0	0
1./JG 108	Bf 109F	Wiener Neustadt	8	1232	Wiener Neustadt	~1330	0	0	1	0	0	0
I./KG 51	Me 410A	Hörsching	14	1237	Hörsching	~1330	0	0	1	0	0	2

Luftwaffe defensive activity – 2 October 1943

Unit	Type	Gruppe up			Gruppe down		Claims	Losses				
		Base	No	Time	Base	Time		Dest	Dam	KIA	MIA	WIA
Lw Bfh Mitte												
I. Jagdkorps			**256**									
Jagddivision 2:												
Stab/JG 11	Fw 190A	Jever		~1230	Marx	~1300	transfer	0	0	0	0	0
	Fw 190A	Marx		~1640	Nordholz	~1735	0	0	0	0	0	0
I./JG 11	Fw 190A	Husum		1639	Husum	~1745	0	1	0	0	1	0
II./JG 11	Bf 109G	Jever		1235	Marx	1300	transfer	0	0	0	0	0
	Bf 109G	Marx		1643	Nordholz, Dordrecht	1735	0	0	1	0	0	1
III./JG 11	Bf 109G	Oldenburg		1638	Oldenburg	1740	2 B-17, 1 P-47	8	0	2	3	2
JaSta Helgoland	Bf 109T	Helgoland–Düne		1547	Nordholz	1638	0	0	0	0	0	0
I./ZG 1	Bf 110	Bad Lippspringe	*42	1720	Bad Lippspringe	1730	n/c	0	0	0	0	0
II./ZG 1	Bf 110	Hesepe	—	1716	Bad Lippspringe	1730	n/c	0	0	0	0	0
Jagddivision 3:												
I./JG 3	Bf 109G	Bönninghardt		~1630	Bönninghardt	~1730	0	0	1	0	0	1
II./JG 3	Bf 109G	Schiphol		1645	Schiphol	~1730	2 B-17	2	1	0	0	0
III./ZG 26	Bf 110G	Plantlünne	—	1335	Wunstorf	1400	transfer	0	0	0	0	0

*42 total Zerstörer sorties

4 October

8th Air Force VIII BC Mission #108: 130 of 155 1st BD B-17s bomb Frankfurt, TOT 1055-1111 – lose 8-0-80, claim 37-11-37; 152 of 168 3rd BD B-17s bomb Saarlautern, Saarguemines, Saarbrücken, TOT 1133-1145 – lose 4-2-21, claim 37-7-7; 38 2nd BD B-24s fly North Sea diversion – lose 4-0-19, claim 13-6-3. 223 VIII FC P-47s (5 FGs) claim 19-1-2, lose 0-1-15.

Clear weather allowed a successful raid on Frankfurt by the 1st BD, while the 3rd BD bombed several industrial targets in the Saar and the St. Dizier base of II./JG 27, which had just become operational in the RLV force. All attacks on the B-17s had ended before they reached their targets. B-17 losses totalled 12-2. No second sorties were flown, and no attacks were made on the withdrawing bombers. Bf 110s and Me 410s from the newly reformed ZG 76 were attacked near Düren by P-47s and lost 11 KIA, seven WIA and 10 aircraft.

A diversionary flight by two B-24 groups attracted a major part of the defences. The three JG 11 Gruppen and JaSta Helgoland reached the unescorted bombers and shot down four while claiming seven. Luftwaffe losses totalled 17 KIA (including three Gruppenkommandeure), 12 WIA and 23 aircraft on 563 sorties, 320 of which were credited with enemy contact. The day's failures brought sharp reproaches from RM Göring.

The enemy. A Pulk of B-17s as seen from a II./ZG 76 Bf 110G flying a parallel course. (*Bundesarchiv 663-6740-15*)

A flight of I./ZG 76 Bf 110s on a Reich defence mission with WGr 21 rockets. (*Petrick*)

A Schwarm of II./ZG 76 Bf 110G-2s in flight over southern Germany in late 1943. (*Bundesarchiv 658-6385-15*)

UNIT COMBAT REPORT[1]
4 October 1943

At 0915 hours, we were ordered to combat readiness by the Jafü. Shortly thereafter we were ordered to cockpit readiness. At 0926 hours, we were ordered to take off and rendezvous with the Oldenburg Gruppe [III./JG 11] over Marx at 7,000 metres. It had been arranged that 5./JG 11 would attach itself to the Oldenburg Gruppe, while the Helgoland Staffel would join II./JG 11. II./JG 11, with the Stabsschwarm, 4. and 6. Staffel, and the Helgoland Staffel, was to escort the other fighters.

The Gruppe took off with 29 aircraft at 0928 hours. The Helgoland Staffel took off from Jever with nine aircraft at 0938 hours.

After assembly, the Gruppe entered the overcast at 800 metres and left the clouds at 1,200 metres. The Oldenburg Gruppe was sighted at 2,200 metres. The 5. Staffel joined it, and the bulk of II./JG 11 fell in 300–500 metres behind. After an initial course of 360°, we turned to 270° in PQ TQ and shortly thereafter sighted an enemy formation of about 40–60 Liberators, which was then headed south and turned away to the west. The Gruppe was flying in a stepped Gruppe combat line.

Since the Liberator *Pulk* was about 1,000–2,000 metres above us (our Gruppe was at 7,200 metres), the Oldenburg Gruppe took position beneath a thin cloud layer, so that it could not be seen from above. It was in loose formation. I led my escorts beneath the same cloud, so that they were in plain sight and would not be mistaken for enemy fighters. I observed the Nebelwerfer [WGr 21 rocket mortar] attack of 5./JG 11, which, on average, fired 50 metres too short. At the same time I saw behind me, 2,000–3,000 metres above and to the left, a formation of twin-engined aircraft with single tails, which I identified on the grounds of its course paralleling the bombers and another look at the underside of the wings as a Mosquito or Beaufighter formation. I ordered the 6. Staffel to take formation above me and to the left … I then observed beneath me a Liberator that had been shot from its formation and turned back. After I had determined that no enemy fighters were around and none of our attacking unit was nearby, I asked the Jafü for permission to attack the Liberator … I attacked from behind with my Schwarm at about

4,500 metres. My first attack was unsuccessful. A pilot from the 6. Staffel then forced it to dive into the clouds. My Stabsschwarm made its second attack from the rear against the right third of the trailing Liberator Pulk, which flew nervously. Both right engines of the last machine exploded in black smoke, and it tipped over into the clouds. Shortly afterward I observed an attack by a 4. Staffel Schwarm on the rear Liberator Pulk. After the attack, a bomber sheered away from the left side of the formation with a smoking #4 engine, lost altitude and took up a course to the west at an angle of 25°. As I was pulling up to begin another attack, I saw seven Fw 190s attack the formation. They attacked from high above the right front and immediately shot two Liberators from formation. In the meantime, most of my Gruppe, especially those without external tanks, had broken off for the return flight, at my orders. I too turned back for the coast with low fuel and landed on my base at 1053 hours.

I noted, first, that the weight of fire from aircraft without wing armament was insufficient against heavy bombers; second, the effect of a battle far over the sea on the morale of the pilots cannot be simply stated.

The losses of the Gruppe have not yet been compiled.

To carry out an escort mission successfully, it is important that: (a) the escort formation does not fly too close together; and (b) an understanding is reached between the escorting and escorted formations.

During today's weather conditions of multiple cloud layers up to 10,000 metres, the escort unit must be properly located with respect to the attacking Gruppe. The controller had no understanding of this; it was a new concept for the ground control.

The pilots have been briefed on escort procedures, but no training missions have taken place.

A total of 38 Bf 109Gs and Bf 109Ts took part in the mission; 31 made contact with the enemy.

The pilots of the Gruppe claimed four certain and one probable victory. It is expected that two of these are double claims with other units.

Hptm. Günther Specht, Gruppenkommandeur
II./JG 11

Luftwaffe defensive activity – 4 October 1943

Unit	Type	Gruppe up			Gruppe down		Claims	Losses				
		Base	No	Time	Base	Time		Dest	Dam	KIA	MIA	WIA
Lw Bfh Mitte												
I. Jagdkorps			320									
Jagddivision 1:												
JG 50	Bf 109G	Gardelegen		~1100	Gardelegen	~1200	0	0	1	0	0	0
III./JG 54	Bf 109G	Schwerin		1046	Schwerin, Kassel, Göttingen	1156	n/c	0	0	0	0	0
Jagddivision 2:												
Stab/JG 11	Fw 190A	Marx		~0930	Marx	~1034	0	0	0	0	0	0
I./JG 11	Fw 190A	Husum		0934	Husum	~1034	4 B-24	2	0	2	0	0
II./JG 11	Bf 109G	Marx	29	0928	Borkum, Marx	1053	2 B-24	1	0	0	0	0
III./JG 11	Bf 109G	Oldenburg		0931	Oldenburg	1041	1 Beaufighter	0	0	0	0	0
JaSta Helgoland	Bf 109T	Helgoland-Düne	9	0938	Nordholz	1053	1 B-24	0	0	0	0	0
III./ZG 1	Me 410A	Hesepe	*89	0928	Hesepe	1140	0	0	1	1	0	0
I./ZG 26	Bf 110G	Lippspringe	—	1215	Wittmund, Lippspringe	1305	0	0	0	0	0	1
III./ZG 26	Bf 110G	Wunstorf	32	0920	Wunstorf, Bremen	1115	0	0	0	1	0	0
ErprKdo 25	Fw 190A, Me 410A	Achmer	—	0935	Achmer	1010	n/c	0	0	1	0	0
Jagddivision 3:												
Stab/JG 1	Fw 190A	Deelen		~1000	Deelen	~1150	0	0	0	0	0	0
I./JG 1	Fw 190A	Deelen		1004	Ailertchen, Deelen	1145	2 B-17	1	2	0	0	2
II./JG 1	Fw 190A	Rheine	17	1004	Odendorf, Mainz, Köln, Waren, Langendiebach, Bonn-Hangelar	~1150	2 B-17	1	6	1	0	0
III./JG 1	Bf 109G	Eelde		~1000	Eelde	~1150	0	0	0	0	0	0
I./JG 3	Bf 109G	Bönninghardt		~1200	Bönninghardt	~1330	0	0	0	0	0	0
II./JG 3	Bf 109G	Schiphol		~1200	Schiphol	~1330	2 B-17	0	0	0	0	0
Jagddivision 7:												
Stab/ZG 76	Bf 110G	Ansbach		~1040	Ansbach	~1230	1 B-17	0	0	0	0	0
I./ZG 76	Bf 110G	Ansbach		~1040	Ansbach	~1230	0	4	1	3	0	4
II./ZG 76	Bf 110G, Me 410A	Wertheim		1040	Wertheim, Bonn–Hangelar	~1141	0	6	1	8	0	3
III./NJG 101	Bf 110	Stuttgart–Echterdingen		1058	Stuttgart–Echterdingen	1252	n/c	0	0	0	0	0
IV./NJG 101	Bf 110F	Kitzingen		1050	Kitzingen	1240	1 B-17	2	0	0	0	1
Luftflotte 3												
II. Jagdkorps												
Jagddivision 4:												
II./JG 2	Bf 109G	Vitry–en–Artois?		~1100	Vitry–en–Artois?	~1200	0	2	0	2	0	0
II./JG 27	Bf 109G	St. Dizier		1055	St. Dizier	1202	2 B-17	3	2	1	0	1
II./NJG 4	Bf 110G, Do 217	Juvincourt		~1100	Juvincourt	~1230	1 B-17	0	0	0	0	0

*89 total JD 2 + JD 3 Zerstörer sorties

8 October

8th Air Force VIII BC Mission #111: 158 of 174 1st BD B-17s bomb Bremen, TOT 1505-1513 – lose 13-0-105, claim 66-9-45; 156 of 170 3rd BD B-17s bomb Bremen, TOT 1505-1527 – lose 14-2-110, claim 84-12-33; 43 of 55 2nd BD B-24s bomb Vegesack, TOT 1622-1624 – lose 3-0-21, claim 17-1-7. 274 VIII FC P 47s (6 FGs) claim 12-2-4, lose 3-0-5.

The day's targets for all of the American bombers were near Bremen. The three bomb divisions flew on divergent courses before converging in the target area. The RLV force flew 559 sorties and was able to mount strong attacks on the formations as they became concentrated in a limited area. The fighters of Jagddivision 3 (JD 3) attacked the B-17s of the 1st BD, which approached due east across the Netherlands. The Jagddivision 2 (JD 2) fighters took on the B-24s of the 2nd BD and the B-17s of the 3rd BD, which took a more circuitous route across the North Sea before crossing the Dutch coast near Groningen. One escorting P-47 group was dispersed by I./JG 3 and II./JG 3, a rare success by the forward Gruppen, but an indication of what they could have accomplished had there ever been enough of them. The Zerstörer Gruppen loitered in the target area, beyond the range of the escorts, and made successful rocket attacks on the 1st BD. The three JG 1 Gruppen attacked the B-

17s repeatedly until encountering the P-47s of the withdrawal escort, which shot down and killed the JG 1 Kommodore, Obstlt. Hans Philipp. It was an otherwise successful day for the defenders who lost 24 KIA or MIA, 14 WIA and 33 fighters; the Americans lost 32 heavy bombers and three P-47s.

9 October

8th Air Force VIII BC Mission #113: 164 of 175 1st BD B-17s bomb Anklam, Gdynia, TOT 1142-1324 – lose 20-1-76, claim 76-20-51; 147 of 152 3rd BD B-17s bomb Marienburg, Gdynia, TOT 1253-1324 – lose 6-1-50, claim 39-6-6; 41 of 51 2nd BD B-24s bomb Danzig, Gdynia, TOT 1305 – lose 2-1-19, claim 7-3-4. 153 VIII FC P-47s (4 FGs) claim 0, lose 0.

The VIII BC dispatched all of its bombers to strike targets in eastern Germany and Poland, entirely without fighter escort. Their northern route and the total absence of German day fighters in the target areas allowed them to reach and bomb their targets without being attacked by the Luftwaffe, which staged north to catch them on their return. Almost every I. Jagdkorps day and night fighter unit succeeded in making contact, aided by perfect, cloudless autumn weather; 549 sorties were logged, of which ca. 345 made contact. Bomber losses totalled 31. German losses were six aircrewmen KIA or MIA, 15 WIA and 15 aircraft destroyed. The American P-47s flew a non-productive sweep of the Netherlands.

10 October 1943 — Münster (see map)

8th Air Force VIII BC Mission #114: 119 of 133 3rd BD B-17s, 117 of 141 1st BD B-17s bomb Münster, TOT 1503-1518 – lose 29-1-56 (3rd BD), 1-2-46 (1st BD), claim 148-18-63. 216 VIII FC P-47s (5 FGs) claim 19-0-0, lose 1-2-1.

The VIII BC sent its bombers to Münster, which was close enough to England to allow escort to the target. The two B-17 bomb divisions were to attack the city centre in a single stream, while the weak B-24 division flew another diversion over the North Sea to pin the JD 2 fighters to their home areas. The good weather and late take-off of the bombers foretold a high-strength, shallow-penetration raid, and the commander of JD 3 deployed his forces accordingly. The three JG 26 Gruppen were borrowed from Luftflotte 3 and were all staged in the target area, unsuspected by the Americans. Most of the P-47s were

The **4th Bomb Wing** leaves the **Marienburg** Focke-Wulf plant on **9 October** after a raid that was touted by the USAAF as a typical example of pinpoint bombing. In fact, it was one of the most accurate raids of the war. *(USAAF)*

Luftwaffe defensive activity – 8 October 1943

Unit	Type	Gruppe up			Gruppe down		Claims	Losses				
		Base	No	Time	Base	Time		Dest	Dam	KIA	MIA	WIA
Lw Bfh MItte												
I. Jagdkorps			559									
Jagddivision 1:												
JG 25	Bf 109G	Gardelegen		~1450	Gardelegen	~1600	0	1	0	0	0	0
III./JG 54	Bf 109G	Schwerin		0946	Gardelegen	1006	transfer	0	0	0	0	0
	Bf 109G	Gardelegen		1453	Oldenburg, Gardelegen, Bergen (NL)	1610	0	0	2	0	0	1
I./NJG 5	Bf 110G	Stendal		1523	Stendal	1650	n/c	0	0	0	0	0
Jagddivision 2:												
Stab/JG 11	Fw 190A	Husum		1425	Husum	~1530	0	1	0	1	0	0
I./JG 11	Fw 190A	Husum	22	1425	Husum	1540	2 B-17	1	4	0	0	1
2nd sorties	Fw 190A	Husum		~1600	Husum	~1700	1 B-17	0	0	0	0	0
II./JG 11	Bf 109G	Marx	28	1422	Marx, Wesermünde	1548	1 B-17	1	1	1	0	0
2nd sorties	Bf 109G	Marx, various	23	1600	Marx	1700	1 B-24	0	0	0	0	0
III./JG 11	Bf 109G	Oldenburg		1420	Oldenburg	~1600	4 B-17	1	0	1	0	0
10./JG 11	Fw 190A	Jever?		~1425	Jever?	~1545	0	2	0	2	0	0
JaSta Helgoland	Bf 109T	Jever	9	1426	Jever	~1545	0	0	0	0	0	0
I./ZG 1	Bf 110G	Lippspringe		1410	Lippspringe	1609	5 B-17, 1 P-47	1	2	2	0	0
III./ZG 1	Me 410A	Hesepe, Osnabrück		1425	Hesepe, Osnabrück	1535	0	2	0	2	0	1
Stab/ZG 26	Bf 110G	Wunstorf		~1430	Wunstorf	~1615	2 B-17	0	0	0	0	0
III./ZG 26	Bf 110G	Wunstorf	35	1430	Wunstorf	1555	7 B-17	2	1	4	0	3
ErprKdo 25	Fw 190A, Me 410A	Achmer		1425	Achmer	1613	2 B-17	2	2	2	0	0
	Fw 190A, Ju 88, Bf 110G	Achmer		1626	Achmer	~1730	1 B-24	0	0	0	0	0
II./NJG 3	Bf 110G	Schleswig		~1530	Schleswig	~1730	2 B-24	0	0	0	0	0
III./NJG 3	Bf 110G	Lüneburg		1523	Lüneburg	1638	0	0	0	0	0	0
ISS Focke-Wulf	Fw 190A	Bremen		~1500	Bremen	~1600	1 B-17	1	0	1	0	0
Jagddivision 3:												
Stab/JG 1	Fw 190A	Deelen		1411	Deelen	~1545	2 B-17	2	0	1	0	1
I./JG 1	Fw 190A	Deelen		1411	Deelen, Diepholz	~1545	3 B-17	4	2	1	0	3
II./JG 1	Fw 190A,	Rheine	14	1424	Rheine	~1545	1 B-17	3	1	1	0	2
III./JG 1	Bf 109G	Leeuwarden, Eelde		~1415	Leeuwarden, Eelde	~1545	1 B-17, 1 P-47	2	3	1	0	0
11./JG 1	Bf 109G	Rheine	3	1424	Rheine	~1545	1 B-17 HSS	0	0	0	0	0
I./JG 3	Bf 109G	Bönninghardt		~1410	Bönninghardt	~1510	1 P-47	3	4	1	0	2
2nd sorties	Bf 109G	Bönninghardt		~1530	Bönninghardt	~1700	0	2	0	0	2	0
II./JG 3	Bf 109G	Schiphol		1408	Schiphol	1515	1 P-47	2	0	1	0	0
2nd sorties	Bf 109G	Schiphol		~1530	Schiphol	~1700	1 B-17	0	0	0	0	0
I./JG 26	Fw 190A	Grimbergen		1555	Deelen	1648	n/c	0	0	0	0	0
III./JG 26	Bf 109G	Vendeille		1414	Leeuwarden	1500	transfer	0	0	0	0	0
	Bf 109G	Leeuwarden		1605	Lille–Vendeville	1714	0	0	2	0	0	0

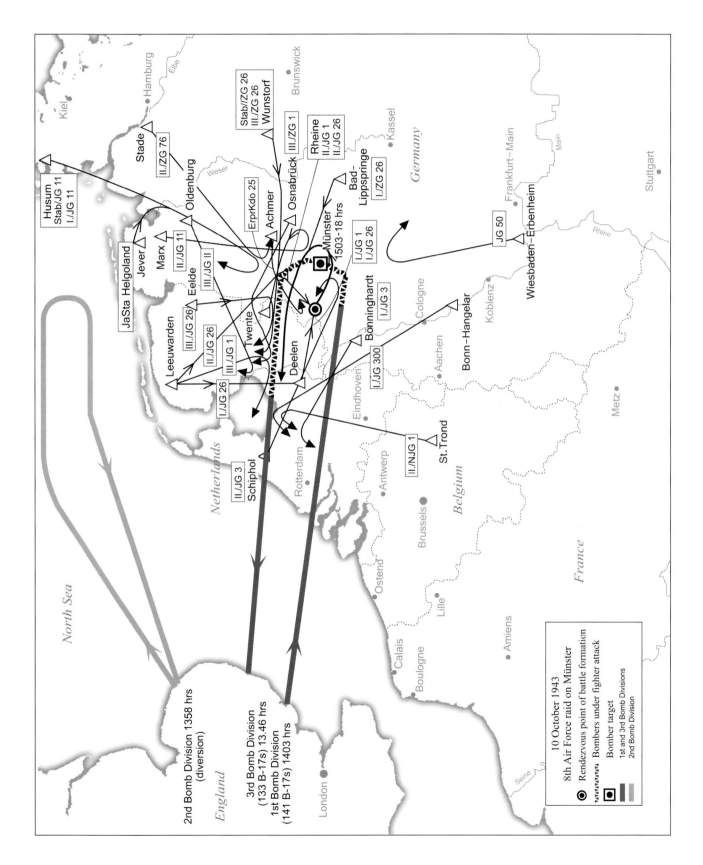

Husum
Stab/JG 11
I./JG 11

Stade

II./ZG 76

Oldenburg

JaSta Helgoland

Jever

Marx

II./JG 11

III./JG II

Eelde

Leeuwarden

III./JG 26

II./JG 26

III./JG 1

I./JG 26

Twente

Deelen

Schiphol

II./JG 3

Stab/ZG 26
III./ZG 26 Wunstorf

III./ZG 1

ErprKdo 25

Achmer

Osnabrück

Rheine
II./JG 1
II./JG 26

Bad-
Lippspringe

I./ZG 26

Münster
1503–18 hrs

I./JG 1
I./JG 26

Bönninghardt

I./JG 3

I./JG 300

Bonn–Hangelar

II./NJG 1

St. Trond

JG 50

Wiesbaden–Erbenheim

Kiel

Hamburg

Elbe

Brunswick

Weser

Kassel

Germany

Frankfurt–Main

Main

Stuttgart

Rhine

Cologne

Aachen

Eindhoven

Rotterdam

Netherlands

Antwerp

Belgium

Brussels

Ostend

Calais

Boulogne

Lille

Amiens

Metz

France

North Sea

2nd Bomb Division 1358 hrs
(diversion)

3rd Bomb Division
(133 B-17s) 13.46 hrs
1st Bomb Division
(141 B-17s) 1403 hrs

England

London

Seine

10 October 1943
8th Air Force raid on Münster

◉ Rendezvous point of battle formation
⊡ Bomber target

◢◣ Bombers under fighter attack

1st and 3rd Bomb Divisions
2nd Bomb Division

Luftwaffe defensive activity – 9 October 1943

Unit	Type	Gruppe up			Gruppe down		Claims	Losses (—: included in 1st sortie)				
		Base	No	Time	Base	Time		Dest	Dam	KIA	MIA	WIA
Lw Bfh Mitte												
I. Jagdkorps			549									
Jagddivision 1:												
JG 25	Bf 109G	Gardelegen		~1050	Gardelegen	~1200	0	0	0	0	0	0
III./JG 54	Bf 109G	Schwerin, Gardelegen		1052	Schwerin, Gardelegen, Neubrandenburg	1219	2 B-17	2	4	1	0	2
2nd sorties	Bf 109G	Schwerin, Gardelegen		1348	Schwerin, Gardelegen	1515	1 B-17	—	—	—	—	—
Stab/NJG 2	Ju 88C	Parchim		~1130	Schleswig	~1330	n/c	0	0	0	0	0
	Ju 88C	Schleswig		~1430	Parchim	~1630	1 B-17	0	0	0	0	0
I./NJG 2	Ju 88C, Bf 110G	Parchim		~1130	Schleswig	~1330	n/c	0	0	0	0	0
2nd sorties	Ju 88C, Bf 110G	Schleswig		~1430	Parchim	~1630	1 B-17	0	2	0	0	0
NJG 5	Ju 88C, Bf 110G	Döberitz, Stendal, Parchim, Neuruppin		1134	Döberitz, Stendal, Parchim, Schleswig, Neuruppin	1310	2 B-17	0	0	0	0	0
II./NJG 101	Bf 110, Do 217	?		~1130	?	~1330	2 B-17	0	0	0	0	0
Jagddivision 2:												
I./JG 5	Bf 109G	Friedrichshafen (D)		~1530	Friedrichshafen (D)	~1700	1 B-17	0	1	0	0	0
Stab/JG 11	Fw 190A	Husum		1155	Husum	~1315	0	1	0	0	0	1
I./JG 11	Fw 190A	Husum	26	0930	Husum	~1000	n/c	0	0	0	0	0
2nd sorties	Fw 190A	Husum	16	1155	Husum	1319	5 B-17	3	1	2	1	0
3rd sorties	Fw 190A	Husum	9	1445	Husum	1558	2 B-17	0	0	0	0	0
II./JG 11	Bf 109G	Jever		0637	Marx	0642	transfer	0	0	0	0	0
	Bf 109G	Marx		0934	Marx, Schleswig, Husum	1100	0	1	0	0	0	1
2nd sorties	Bf 109G	Marx, Schleswig, Husum		~1200	Marx	~1230	0	0	0	0	0	0
3rd sorties	Bf 109G	Marx		~1430	Marx	~1600	4 B-17	0	0	0	0	0
III./JG 11	Bf 109G	Oldenburg		0934	Oldenburg, Schleswig a/fs	~1100	0	0	2	0	0	0
2nd sorties	Bf 109G	Oldenburg, Schleswig a/fs		~1430	Oldenburg	~1600	0	0	0	0	0	0
JaSta Helgoland	Bf 109T	Jever		1040	Stade	1135	n/c	0	0	0	0	0
2nd sorties	Bf 109T	Stade		1235	Nordholz	1359	0	0	1	0	0	0
3rd sorties	Bf 109T	Nordholz		1458	Jever	1545	0	0	0	0	0	0
I./ZG 1	Bf 110G, Me 210	Lippspringe		0920	Lippspringe, Schleswig	1120	0	0	0	0	0	0
2nd sorties	Bf 110G, Me 210	Lippspringe		~1200	Lippspringe	~1330	4 B-17	1	1	0	0	3
3rd sorties	Bf 110G, Me 210	Lippspringe		~1430	Lippspringe	~1600	4 B-17	0	0	0	0	0
III./ZG 1	Me 410A	Hesepe		0930	Hesepe	1055	n/c	0	0	0	0	0
2nd sorties	Me 410A	Hesepe		1140	Hesepe	1420	2 B-17	0	2	0	0	0
3rd sorties	Me 410A	Hesepe		~1445	Hesepe	~1600	1 B-17	0	0	0	0	0

Luftwaffe defensive activity – 9 October 1943 Continued

Unit	Type	Gruppe up			Gruppe down		Claims	Losses (—: included in 1st sortie)				
		Base	No	Time	Base	Time		Dest	Dam	KIA	MIA	WIA
Stab/ZG 26	Bf 110G	Wunstorf		~0920	Wunstorf	~1120	0	0	0	0	0	0
2nd sorties	Bf 110G	Wunstorf		~1200	Wunstorf	~1330	1 B-17	1	0	1	0	0
III./ZG 26	Bf 110G	Wunstorf	26	0935	Leck, Schleswig	1120	n/c	0	0	0	0	0
2nd sorties	Bf 110G	Leck, Schleswig		1155	Wunstorf, Husum	~1400	9 B-17	2	1	0	0	6
3rd sorties	Bf 110G	Wunstorf		1518	Wunstorf	1640	1 B-17	0	0	0	0	0
II./ZG 76	Bf 110G	Stade		1225	Stade	1355	0	0	0	0	0	0
2nd sorties	Bf 110G	Stade		1500	Stade	1705	0	0	0	0	0	0
ErprKdo 25	Fw 190A	Achmer		0940	Achmer	~1115	0	0	0	0	0	0
2nd sorties	Fw 190A	Achmer		~1200	Achmer	~1300	1 B-17	0	0	0	0	0
3rd sorties	Fw 190A	Achmer		~1330	Achmer	1507	0	0	0	0	0	0
NJG 3	Bf 110G, Ju 88C	Grove, Stade, Lüneburg, Vechta, Aalborg, Schleswig		~1130	Grove, Stade, Lüneburg, Vechta, Aalborg, Schleswig	~1330	3 B-17	3	3	1	0	2
2nd sorties	Bf 110G, Ju 88C	Grove, Stade, Lüneburg, Vechta, Aalborg, Schleswig		1434	Grove, Stade, Lüneburg, Vechta, Aalborg, Schleswig	1631	2 B-17, 1 B-24 HSS	—	—	—	—	—
ISS Focke-Wulf	Fw 190A	Bremen		~0940	Bremen	~1115	0	0	0	0	0	0
Jagddivision 3:												
Stab/JG 1	Fw 190A	Deelen		~1130	Deelen	~1300	0	0	0	0	0	0
I./JG 1	Fw 190A	Deelen		~1130	Deelen	~1300	1 B-17	0	1	0	0	0
II./JG 1	Fw 190A	Rheine	7	0949	Rheine	1022	n/c	0	0	0	0	0
III./JG 1	Bf 109G	Leeuwarden		~1300	Leeuwarden	~1415	2 B-17	1	0	0	0	0
2nd sorties	Bf 109G	Leeuwarden		~1430	Leeuwarden	~1530	0	0	0	0	0	0
11./JG 1	Bf 109G	Rheine	3	~0950	Rheine	~1020	n/c	0	0	0	0	0
II./JG 3	Bf 109G	Schiphol		~1300	Schiphol	~1430	2 B-17	0	0	0	0	0
I./JG 26	Fw 190A	Grimbergen		1225	Leeuwarden	1308	transfer	0	0	0	0	0
Luftflotte 3:												
II. Jagdkorps:												
Jagddivision 4:												
II./JG 26	Fw 190A	Cambrai–Epinoy		1343	Leeuwarden	~1440	transfer	0	0	0	0	0
III./JG 26	Bf 109G	Lille–Vendeville		1230	Eelde	1351	transfer	0	0	0	0	0

assigned to the trailing 1st BD, in the expectation that the leading 3rd Division would achieve surprise, which was not, in fact, attained. Eight JD 3 Jagdgruppen were airborne before the leading B-17s reached the coast of Holland. The forward Gruppe, II./JG 3, took on the escorts, while the rest formed up for an attack on the head of the stream.

The diversion by the 2nd BD's B-24s was quickly detected for what it was, freeing up the fighters of Jagddivision 2 to join the battle farther south. 476 day fighters, night fighters and Zerstörer took off to engage the Americans. Attacks on the vulnerable 3rd BD alternated between head-on passes by Fw 190s and

Bf 109s and rear rocket barrages from Me 410s and Bf 110s. Most of the fighters broke away briefly over Münster before resuming their attacks, which continued until the arrival of the one P-47 group assigned to escort the 3rd BD on withdrawal.

The Luftwaffe defenders destroyed 33 B-17s and one P-47 for the loss of 20 aircrewmen KIA, 13 WIA and 34 aircraft. Ten of today's losses were twin-engine Zerstörer, emphasising their need for protection from the American escorts. German operational and tactical control and execution were otherwise quite successful. They came close to destroying the leading bomber wing; this would have totally disrupted the mission. It did not happen because of the attackers' lack of numbers, a handicap that they never overcame.

COMBAT REPORT[2]
10 October 1943

One Boeing B-17 destroyed from 7,000 metres at 1506 hours, PQ JP-3, Hohenhalte (12 km NW of Münster)

At 1431 hours, I took off in Fw 190A-6 'Red 1' with II./JG 1 and I./JG 26 against an attack on Münster. Led by Y-Führung, I sighted four *Pulks* of B-17s and B-40s at 1453 hours in PQ JP and made my first close-formation attack at 1500 hours. On my second closed attack, I attacked a B-17 from the right as the third aircraft behind the attack leader Hptm. Koch, hitting the right wing from the side, dove beneath its right wing and hit the last B-17 on the left flank in a steep bank from beneath to short range. I observed bright flames and pieces falling off the right side of the fuselage, right wing and engines. While diving away beneath the B-17, I received hits in my engine. My cockpit was immediately filled with smoke and gasoline fumes, and I bailed out. The B-17 I had attacked crashed near Hohenhalte (12 km NW of Münster) at 1506 hours (witness Fw. Reimitz). While in my parachute, another B-17 dived past me in a steep bank and crashed into pieces 80–100 m from me (victory of Uffz. Ruttau). I landed 3 km west of the two B-17s, which were 800 metres apart, and my Fw 190.

Hptm. Walter Hoeckner, Gruppenkommandeur Stab II./JG 1

---

14 October 1943 – 2nd Schweinfurt raid (see map)
8th Air Force VIII BC Mission #115: 101 of 149 1st BD, 128 of 142 3rd BD B-17s bomb Schweinfurt ball-bearing factories, TOT 1439-1457 – lose 45-5-63 (1st BD), 15-2-75 (3rd BD), claim 186-27-89. 107 of 196 VIII FC P-47s (2 FGs) escort (penetration leg only) claim 13-1-5, lose 1-4-2.

The VIII BC ordered a return trip to Schweinfurt on short notice, based on predicted favourable weather over the Continent, despite marginal conditions over England. All three bomb divisions were scheduled to fly the mission; each would be escorted by a single P-47 group on penetration and a single group on withdrawal. There would be no diversionary raids, and

the course was nearly a straight line to the target, due to the restricted range of the 1st BD B-17s. The German defences were again controlled by JD 3's Oberst Grabmann, who predicted a full-strength, deep-penetration raid from the heavy volume of radio traffic and the early take-off. Before the bombers reached the English coast, he had put his own fighter units on full alert and asked the neighbouring Jagddivisionen to bring their own fighters to readiness. The small B-24 wing never did form up and was ordered to fly a diversion in the North Sea, thus wasting one of the three airborne P-47 groups, which went with them. The B-17s and their own P-47s finally took up a course to the southeast. The 1st BD was to the east of and slightly ahead of the 3rd BD, ensuring that it would receive most of the attacks from JD 3, based right in its path. Grabmann's two forward units, I./JG 3 and II./JG 3, attacked the P-47 escort between Woensdrecht and Antwerp. The rest of his fighters, about 150 from the three JG 1 and two JG 26 Gruppen, concentrated over Düren and began attacks on the 1st BD as soon as the escorts turned back near Aachen. As the JD 3 fighters broke away from low ammunition or low fuel, they were relieved by JD 2 units, followed by those of JD 7, whose territory included Schweinfurt. German tactics were a repeat of those found successful on the 10th. III./JG 3 stayed with the B-17s all the way to Schweinfurt and was credited with the greatest success of any Jagdgruppe: 17 B-17s shot down or shot from their formations. This was the largest and most successful daylight operation ever flown by the twin-engine fighters; six Zerstörergruppen and 11 Nachtjagdgruppen were ultimately awarded victory credits.

None of the USAAF or RAF withdrawal escorts could take off because of heavy clouds over their bases. The B-17s were only saved from annihilation by the movement of the front across the Channel. None of the JD 3 units was able to fly a second mission, owing at least in part to the worsening weather. The many II. Jagdkorps fighters in this area should have had it easy against the unescorted, disorganised bomber formations, but could claim only nine B-17s; the rest managed to escape in the towering cumulus formations.

This mission, seemingly preordained to failure, marked the bloody end of the American doctrine of the self-defending heavy bomber. The Luftwaffe destroyed or fatally damaged 67 B-17s in 3 hours and 14 minutes of continuous attacks. Every Luftwaffe fighter unit in western Europe but one was ultimately employed – 882 fighters took off, and ca. 672

Luftwaffe defensive activity – 10 October 1943

Unit	Type	Gruppe up			Gruppe down		Claims	Losses				
		Base	No	Time	Base	Time		Dest	Dam	KIA	MIA	WIA
Lw Bfh Mitte			476									
I. Jagdkorps			346									
Jagddivision 1:												
JG 25	Bf 109G	Gardelegen		~1430	Gardelegen	~1530	0	2	0	1	0	0
Jagddivision 2:												
Stab/JG 11	Fw 190A	Husum		~1430	Husum	~1530	0	0	0	0	0	0
I./JG 11	Fw 190A	Husum		~1430	Husum	~1530	0	0	0	0	0	0
II./JG 11	Bf 109G	Marx		1439	Twente	1550	2 B-17, 1 P-47	1	1	0	0	0
III./JG 11	Bf 109G	Oldenburg		1455	Oldenburg	1620	n/c	0	0	0	0	0
JaSta Helgoland	Bf 109T	Jever		~1430	Jever	~1530	0	1	0	0	0	0
III./ZG 1	Me 410A	Hesepe, Osnabrück	*70	1420	Hesepe, Osnabrück	1615	0	5	1	6	0	2
Stab./ZG 26	Bf 110G	Wunstorf	—	1419	Wunstorf	~1615	1 B-17	0	0	0	0	0
I./ZG 26	Bf 110G	Lippspringe	—	1410	Lippspringe	1520	6 B-17	1	2	0	0	2
III./ZG 26	Bf 110G	Wunstorf	25	1419	Wunstorf	1619	7 B-17	4	0	6	0	2
II./ZG 76	Bf 110G	Stade	—	1430	Achmer	1640	0	0	0	0	0	0
NJG 3	Bf 110G	Stade, Vechta, Lüneburg, Aalborg, Schleswig	**103	~1430	Stade, Vechta, Lüneburg, Aalborg, Schleswig	~1630	0	0	0	0	0	0
ErprKdo 25	Fw 190A, Bf 110G	Achmer	—	~1430	Achmer	~1545	1 B-17	3	1	1	0	1
Jagddivision 3:												
Stab/JG 1	Fw 190A	Deelen		~1420	Deelen	~1530	0	0	0	0	0	0
I./JG 1	Fw 190A	Deelen		1420	Deelen	~1530	2 B-17	3	0	3	0	0
II./JG 1	Fw 190A	Rheine	13	1431	Rheine	~1530	4 B-17, 1 B-17 HSS	4	0	0	0	0
III./JG 1	Bf 109G	Leeuwarden		~1430	Leeuwarden	~1600	3 B-17	1	0	1	0	0
11./JG 1	Bf 109G	Rheine	4	1431	Rheine	1431	0	0	0	0	0	0
I./JG 3	Bf 109G	Bönninghardt		~1410	Bönninghardt	~1530	0	1	0	0	0	1
II./JG 3	Bf 109G	Schiphol		1408	Schiphol	~1530	2 B-17	2	1	1	0	1
Stab/JG 26	Fw 190A	Deelen		~1415	Bönninghardt	~1530	0	0	0	0	0	0
4./JG 26	Fw 190A	Leeuwarden		1015	Deelen	1047	transfer	0	0	0	0	0
	Fw 190A	Deelen	8	1419	Bönninghardt	1530	1 B-17	0	0	0	0	0
I./JG 26	Fw 190A	Leeuwarden		1015	Deelen	1045	transfer	0	0	0	0	0
	Fw 190A	Deelen, Grimberghen		1413	Twente, Dortmund	1535	1 B-17	0	0	0	0	0
II./JG 26	Fw 190A	Leeuwarden		1147	Rheine	1220	transfer	0	0	0	0	0
	Fw 190A	Rheine		1427	Rheine, Deelen	1540	3 B-17	1	1	0	0	1
III./JG 26	Bf 109G	Eelde		1405	Loddenheide	1520	3 B-17	2	1	0	0	2
II./NJG 1	Bf 110G	St. Trond	—	~1430	St. Trond	~1630	0	1	0	0	0	1
NJG 2	Ju 88C	Parchim, Deelen, Schiphol	—	~1430	Parchim, Deelen, Schiphol	~1630	0	0	0	0	0	0
Jagddivision 7:												
JG 50	Bf 109G	Wiesbaden–Erbenheim		~1400	Wiesbaden–Erbenheim	~1530	0	2	0	1	0	0

*70 total JD 2 Zerstörer sorties

**103 total JD 2 + JD 3 night fighter day sorties

Obfw. Alfred Surau sits on the wheel of his Bf 109G-6Y at Bad Wörishofen in the autumn. The 9./JG 3 fighter carries a full set of markings: the Geschwader emblem on the cowling; a yellow spinner, machine gun 'bump' and aircraft number, along with a large eye on the bump, all for the 9. Staffel; a vertical black Third Gruppe bar; and black victory bars on a yellow rudder. *(Prien)*

Hptm. Walther Dahl, Kommandeur of III./JG 3, exits his Bf 109G-6 at Bad Wörishofen after his unit's successful mission of 14 October. The airplane is a 'gunboat' variant, although these underwing cannon cannot be seen in this photograph. *(Bundesarchiv 652-5724-7)*

contacted the enemy. The Germans lost 53 aircraft, 29 KIA or MIA and 20 WIA, but it was obvious to both sides that the defenders had won a stunning victory.

COMBAT REPORT[3]
14 October 1943

One Boeing B-17 shot from formation from 7,200 at 1355 hours, PQ PQ (near Koblenz)

After cockpit readiness, at the alarm I took off at 1244 hours in Fw 190A-6 'Yellow 1' (550757) (two MG 17, four MG 151/20) as #2 within the 6. Staffel in the II./JG 1 Verband. We were led by Y-Führung. At 1347 hours, we sighted two escorted US HB Verbände, flying SE at 7,200–7,500 metres. Because of the escort we were compelled to drop our tanks, but that of my Rottenführer would not drop away. After a brief delay he ordered me to attack alone. As a result, I closed up on three Fw 190s flying at the same height as the 1st enemy Pulk and, with them, attacked the 1st Pulk of the Verband flying on the right, which comprised five Boeings flying alone in close formation. The attacks were carried out from the left and right sides. I attacked the last of these five Boeings from the front left side to an angle of 30° from behind. I saw hits in the fuselage and tail and saw the vertical tail break up. After I pulled away, I saw the Boeing sheer away from the Pulk and drop below. I had to depart owing

to low ammunition and fuel. Final destruction was obtained by ZG 26.

Fw. Wolfgang Brunner
6./JG 1

COMBAT REPORT[4]
14 October 1943

One Boeing B-17 shot from formation from 7,000 metres at 1440 hours, 20 km S of Schweinfurt
[Not confirmed; no witness: DC]

At 1310 hours, I took off in a Bf 109G-6 with three MG 151/20s and two MG 131s [i.e., a 'gunboat'] with Lt. Stahlberg's Staffel on a mission against Boeing B-17 Fortresses. We reached the formation in the vicinity of Frankfurt am Main. After I had twice attacked the leading Pulk of the formation from the front, I made my third attack from the low rear. At 1440 hours, I hit the left wing of a Fortress with a long burst, whereupon the enemy's plane showed two strong white smoke plumes and sheered from the formation 20 km south of Schweinfurt. The fuselage burst into flames, which soon went out. I later saw two Bf 110s attacking this airplane.

Fw. Herbert Zimmer
8./JG 3

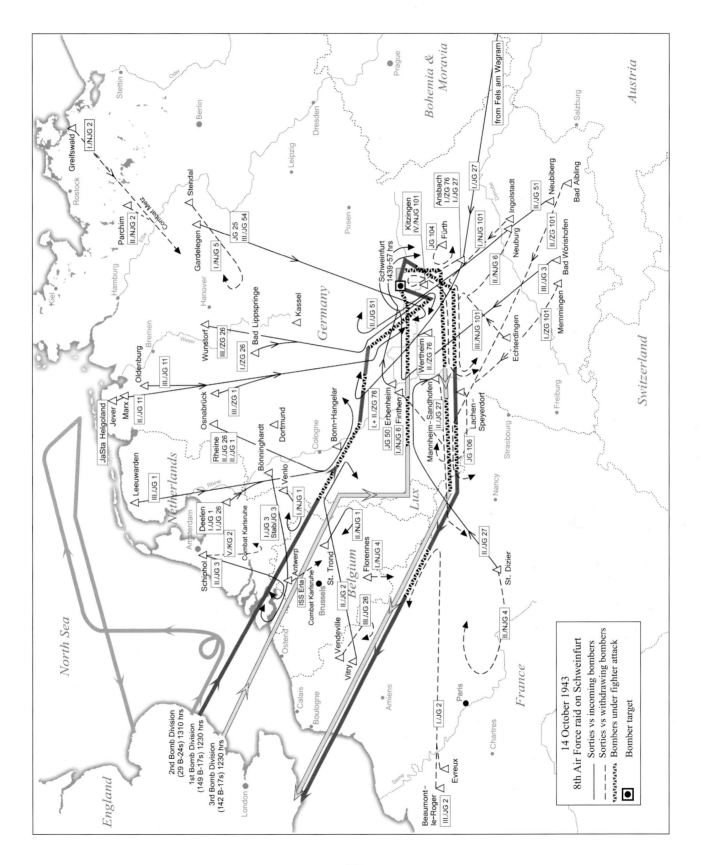

14 October 1943
8th Air Force raid on Schweinfurt

Sorties vs incoming bombers
Sorties vs withdrawing bombers
Bombers under fighter attack
Bomber target

Luftwaffe defensive activity – 14 October 1943

Unit	Type	Gruppe up			Gruppe down		Claims	Losses				
		Base	No	Time	Base	Time		Dest	Dam	KIA	MIA	WIA
Lw Bfh Mitte												
I. Jagdkorps			567									
Jagddivision 1:												
JG 25	Bf 109G	Gardelegen	7	1410	Gardelegen	~1530	1 B-17	3	0	0	0	0
III./JG 54	Bf 109G	Schwerin		1307	Gardelegen	1332	transfer	0	0	0	0	0
	Bf 109G	Gardelegen	28	1410	Schwerin, Mannheim, Kassel–Rothwesten	1545	2 B-17	3	0	1	0	1
I./NJG 2	Ju 88C	Greifswald		~1430	Greifswald	~1630	2 B-17	0	0	0	0	0
II./NJG 2	Ju 88C	Parchim		~1500	Parchim	~1630	1 B-17	0	0	0	0	0
I./NJG 5	Bf 110G	Stendal		1452	Stendal	1542	n/c	0	0	0	0	0
Jagddivison 2:												
Stab/JG 11	Bf 109G	Jever		~1310	Jever	~1415	0	0	0	0	0	0
II./JG 11	Bf 109G	Marx		1310	Bonn–Hangelar, Dortmund	1416	1 B-17	1	0	0	0	0
2nd sorties	Bf 109G	Bonn–Hangelar		1517	Wiesbaden	1610	1 B-17	0	0	0	0	0
III./JG 11	Bf 109G	Oldenburg		1315	Zellhausen	1410	0	0	0	0	0	0
	Bf 109G	Oldenburg		1400	Oldenburg	1515	2 B-17	1	1	1	0	0
JaSta Helgoand	Bf 109T	Jever		~1310	Jever	~1415	0	0	1	0	0	0
I./ZG 26	Bf 110G	Lippspringe		1255	Dortmund	1445	3 B-17	0	0	0	0	0
2nd sorties	Bf 110G	Dortmund		1505	Erfurt	1530	0	0	0	0	0	0
3rd sorties	Bf 110G	Lippspringe		1610	Dortmund	1645	0	0	0	0	0	0
II./ZG 26	Me 410A	Osnabrück		~1330	Osnabrück	~1530	3 B-17	2	0	3	0	0
III./ZG 26	Bf 110G	Wunstorf	30	1249	Wunstorf, Bonn–Hangelar	1420	3 B-17	1	1	2	0	2
2nd sorties	Bf 110G	Wunstorf	30	~1500	Wunstorf, others	1745	0	0	0	0	0	0
I./ZG 76	Bf 110G	Ansbach		~1315	Ansbach	~1530	4 B-17	0	0	0	0	0
II./ZG 76	Bf 110G	Wertheim		1315	Wertheim	1500	3 B-17	6	1	8	0	5
IV./NJG 3	Bf 110G	Grove		~1400	Grove	~1600	2 B-17	1	0	0	0	2
Jagddivison 3:												
Stab/JG 1	Fw 190A	Deelen		~1245	Deelen	~1400	0	0	0	0	0	0
I./JG 1	Fw 190A	Deelen		1240	Deelen	1354	4 B-17, 2 B-17 HSS	0	1	0	0	0
II./JG 1	Fw 190A	Rheine	14	1244	Rheine, Köln-Ostheim	~1400	1 B-17	0	2	0	0	2
III./JG 1	Bf 109G	Eelde		~1245	Eelde	~1400	2 B-17	4	1	3	0	0
11./JG 1	Bf 109G	Rheine	5	1244	Rheine	~1400	0	0	1	0	0	0
I./JG 3	Bf 109G	Bönninghardt		~1315	Bönninghardt	~1415	1 P-47	4	3	2	1	0
II./JG 3	Bf 109G	Schiphol		~1315	Schiphol	~1415	0	0	1	1	0	0
Stab/JG 26	Fw 190A	Deelen		1330	Deelen	~1430	0	0	0	0	0	0
I./JG 26	Fw 190A	Deelen		1250	Bonn–Hangelar	1405	2 B-17	2	0	1	0	1
	Fw 190A	Bonn–Hangelar		1500	Venlo	1600	transfer	0	0	0	0	0
4./JG 26	Fw 190A	Deelen		1330	Deelen–	~1430	0	1	0	0	0	0
II./JG 26	Fw 190A	Rheine		1250	Bonn–Hangelar, München–Gladbach	1420	3 B-17, 2 P-47	0	0	0	0	0
I./NJG 1	Bf 110G	Venlo		~1300	Venlo	~1500	0	0	1	0	0	0
II./NJG 1	Bf 110G	St. Trond		~1300	St. Trond	~1500	1 P-47	1	0	1	0	1
V./KG 2	Me 410A	Schiphol		?	Schiphol	?	3 B-17	0	1	0	0	1

Luftwaffe defensive activity – 14 October 1943 Continued

Unit	Type	Gruppe up			Gruppe down		Claims	Losses				
		Base	No	Time	Base	Time		Dest	Dam	KIA	MIA	WIA
ISS Erla	Fw 190A	Antwerp–Deurne		~1500	Antwerp–Deurne	~1600	1 B-17	0	0	0	0	0
Jagddivison 7:			266									
III./JG 3	Bf 109G	Bad Wörishofen	25	1310	Schweinfurt, Rhein-Main	1450	12 B-17, 5 B-17 HSS	3	3	1	0	1
JG 50	Bf 109G	Wiesbaden–Erbenheim		~1330	Wiesbaden–Erbenheim	~1530	3 B-17, 1 B-17 HSS	3	1	1	0	0
II./JG 51	Bf 109G	Neubiberg		1300	Neubiberg	~1500	3 B-17, 1 B-17 HSS	5	1	0	0	1
JG 104	Bf 109F	Fürth		~1400	Fürth	~1530	1 B-17	1	0	1	0	0
JG 106	Bf 109E	Lachen–Speyerdorf		~1430	Lachen–Speyerdorf	~1545	2 B-17	2	0	2	0	0
I./ZG 101	Bf 110	Memmingen		~1430	Memmingen	~1645	2 B-17	0	0	0	0	0
II./ZG 101	Bf 110	Bad Aibling		1505	Bad Aibling	1703	1 B-17	0	0	0	0	0
I./NJG 6	Bf 110G	Mainz–Finthen		~1430	Mainz–Finthen	~1645	1.5 B-17	0	0	0	0	0
II./NJG 6	Bf 110G	Neuburg		~1430	Neuburg	~1645	2 B-17	1	0	1	0	0
I./NJG 101	Bf 110G	Ingolstadt		~1430	Ingolstadt	~1630	3 B-17	0	0	0	0	0
6./NJG 101	Do 217N	Lechfeld		1511	Lechfeld	1611	0	0	0	0	0	0
III./NJG 101	Bf 110F	Kitzingen, Stuttgart–Echterdingen		1426	Kitzingen, Nancy	1610	2.5 B-17	0	0	0	0	0
IV./NJG 101	Bf 110F	Kitzingen		1430	Kitzingen	1630	1 B-17	0	0	0	0	0
LBeob St 7	Bf 110	Stuttgart–Echterdingen		~1600	Stuttgart–Echterdingen	~1730	1 B-17 (shadower)	0	0	0	0	0
Jafü Ostmark:												
I./JG 27	Bf 109G	Fels am Wagram		1244	Ansbach	~1400	transfer	0	0	0	0	0
	Bf 109G	Ansbach		1435	Ansbach	~1600	4 B-17, 2 B-17 HSS	3	2	0	0	1
I./KG 51	Me 410A	Hörsching		?	Hörsching	?	0	0	0	0	0	0
Luftflotte 3												
II. Jagdkorps			49									
Jagddivision 4:												
III./JG 26	Bf 109G	Lille–Vendeville	34	~1545	Lille–Vendeville	~1715	n/c	0	0	0	0	0
II./JG 27	Bf 109G	St. Dizier		1328	Mannheim	1435	0	0	0	0	0	0
	Bf 109G	Mannheim		~1515	St. Dizier	~1645	3 B-17	2	2	0	0	2
I./NJG 4	Bf 110G, Do 217	Florennes		~1400	Florennes	~1700	1 B-17	0	0	0	0	0
II./NJG 4	Bf 110G, Do 217	St. Dizier		~1400	St. Dizier	~1700	0.5 B-17	0	2	0	0	0
Jagddivision 5:												
I./JG 2	Fw 190A	Evreux		~1545	Evreux	~1715	7 B-17	0	2	0	0	0
II./JG 2	Bf 109G	Vitry–en–Artois		~1300	Vitry–en–Artois	~1400	2 B-17	0	0	0	0	0
		Vitry–en–Artois		~1545	Vitry–en–Artois	~1715	0	0	0	0	0	0
III./JG 2	Fw 190A	Beaumont–le–Roger		~1545	Beaumont–le–Roger	~1715	0	0	1	0	0	0

20 October

8th Air Force VIII BC Mission #116: 97 of 170 1st + 3rd BD B-17s bomb Düren, TOT 1413-1416 – lose 9-1-10, claim 4-1-1. VIII FC: 39 P-38s (1 FG) claim 0, lose 0; 321 P-47s (7 FGs) claim 6-0-5, lose 0-0-2.

Today's mission to Düren was the last that the weakened VIII BC would fly in October. Düren was close enough to England for full escort and was also within range of a new British navigation aid, Oboe. The first of the new Lockheed P-38 Lightning groups, the 55th FG, flew its first mission, an easy section of the withdrawal leg. The P-47s provided adequate escort to the short-range target. As predicted, the

Luftwaffe defensive activity – 20 October 1943

Unit	Type	Gruppe up			Gruppe down		Claims	Losses				
		Base	No	Time	Base	Time		Dest	Dam	KIA	MIA	WIA
Lw Bfh Mitte												
I. Jagdkorps			221									
Jagddivision 1:			20									
I./NJG 2	Ju 88C	Greifswald		~1430	Greifswald	~1530	n/c	0	0	0	0	0
Jagddivision 2:			119									
Stab/JG 11	Fw 190A	Husum		~1430	Husum	~1530	n/c	0	0	0	0	0
I./JG 11	Fw 190A	Husum		~1430	Husum	~1530	n/c	0	0	0	0	0
II./JG 11	Bf 109G	Marx		1443	Marx	1527	n/c	0	0	0	0	0
III./JG 11	Bf 109G	Oldenburg		1433	Oldenburg	1537	n/c	0	0	0	0	0
I./ZG 26	Bf 110G	Lippspringe		1410	Lippspringe	1520	n/c	0	0	0	0	0
II./ZG 26	Me 410A	Hesepe		1405	Hesepe	1540	0	0	0	0	0	0
III./ZG 26	Bf 110G	Wunstorf	23	1359	various	~1530	n/c	0	0	0	0	0
Jagddivision 3:			82									
I./JG 1	Fw 190A	Deelen		1338	Deelen	1503	n/c	1	0	1	0	0
II./JG 1	Fw 190A	Rheine	15	1405	Rheine	1529	1 B-17	1	0	0	0	0
II./JG 3	Bf 109G	Schiphol	20	1350	Schiphol, Venlo	1500	1 B-17	3	1	2	0	1
I./JG 26	Fw 190A	Grimberghen		1323	Lille–Vendeville	1447	0	1	0	1	0	0
II./NJG 1	Do 217	St. Trond		~1400	St. Trond	~1500	n/c	0	0	0	0	0
Jagddivision 7:			91									
III./JG 3	Bf 109G	Bad Wörishofen		1414	Bad Wörishofen	1525	n/c	0	0	0	0	0
II./ZG 76	Bf 110G	Wertheim		1420	Wertheim	1515	n/c	0	0	0	0	0
Luftflotte 3												
II. Jagdkorps			143									
Jagddivision 4:												
Stab/JG 26	Fw 190A	Lille–Nord	*76	~1325	Lille–Nord?	~1435	1 B-17 HSS	0	0	0	0	0
4./JG 26	Fw 190A	Lille–Nord	—	1325	Chièvres, Lille–Nord?	1402	0	1	0	1	0	0
II./JG 26	Fw 190A	Cambrai–Epinoy	—	1320	Cambrai–Epinoy, Woensdrecht, Bonn, Vogelsang	1500	0	2	0	2	0	0
III./JG 26	Bf 109G	Lille–Vendeville	—	1320	Lille–Vendeville	1500	2 B-17, 1 P-47, 1 B-17 HSS	2	0	1	0	1
12./JG 26	Bf 109G	Moorsele	—	~1320	Moorsele	~1500	0	3	0	1	0	1
Jagddivision 5:												
Stab/JG 2	Fw 190A	Evreux	**65	1320	Evreux	1427	0	0	0	0	0	0
I./JG 2	Fw 190A, Bf 109G	Evreux	—	1320	Evreux	1427	0	5	3	3	0	2
II./JG 2	Bf 109G	Vitry–en–Artois	—	1320	Vitry–en–Artois	1427	2 B-17	3	1	2	0	1
III./JG 2	Fw 190A	Beaumont–le–Roger	—	1320	Beaumont–le–Roger	1427	0	0	0	0	0	0

*76 total JG 26 sorties

**65 total JG 2 sorties

target was covered in clouds, but the Oboe failed and the bombing was poor. The day as a whole was a minor disaster for the Luftwaffe. 312 sorties were credited to I. Jagdkorps, and 141 to II. Jagdkorps, but only nine B-17s were shot down, for the loss of 20 German pilots killed or injured. Few JD 3 fighters were able to assemble, leaving the defences to the two II. Jagdkorps Jagdgeschwader, JG 2 and JG 26, which encountered the penetration escort at its strongest. Spitfires thwarted JG 2's approach to the incoming bomber stream. This Geschwader was able to claim 2 B-17s, while losing five KIA, three WIA and eight fighters. JG 26 did no better, claiming two B-17s downed and two shot from formation, plus one P-47, but losing five KIA, two WIA and eight fighters, most to the omnipresent P-47s.

P-38Js CG-H and CG-U *Texas Rebel* (flown by Capt. Gerry Leinwebber) of the 38th Fighter Squadron, 55th Fighter Group. *(Gray)*

PILOT'S ACCOUNT[5]
20 October 1943

We scrambled during poor visibility and through low-lying rain clouds. A *Krampfeinsatz* [foul-up] from take-off to landing. Even the assembly after take-off was a problem. The Gruppe formation was split up completely while penetrating the cloud deck, because the cloud tops were at widely different altitudes. The Staffeln themselves were ripped apart. Only my wingman remained with me. This armed force came face to face with the bomber formation when the two of us reached the area of Brussels; we flew to one side of it and tried to climb as high as possible. What a magnificent sight – the sun beating down; the deep blue sky above; the clouds below like cotton. And in between, the bomber formation pressed to the

southeast at 5,000–6,000 metres. There was no other aircraft from the Gruppe in sight. Two lonely planes in a special situation, of which I would try to make the best. My plan was to surprise the formation and its fighter escort from the greatest possible altitude, attacking its lead aircraft from the sun. However, two Thunderbolts intervened before we reached our favourable attack position. At this altitude – around 10,500 metres – and in this position we had to concede the superiority of the *Donnerbolzen* and their high-altitude performance. Here, our BMW radials suffered from shortness of breath. While we two little sausages hung limp and bloated in the sky – almost helpless – our two opponents stormed after us, relatively fresh. Thank God we had seen them in time and could counter their attack by breaking into them and opening fire with all weapons. We avoided further attacks with the 'emergency brake' – that is, by spinning out. That was the last best thing to try in a desperate combat situation. In this case, our manœuvre was successful.

But now a purely aeronautical problem arose. My Focke-Wulf came out of the spin in a vertical dive, at a high enough speed to cause me great concern. It began to shudder. The entire surface of the wings was covered in condensation, as is seen on the wingtips in tight banks. I did not dare load the wings further by pulling back on the stick to end the dive. Past the vertical, the plane began slowly to pull out by itself, and at 300 metres I had it back in level flight.

I am still curious today as to how fast I was going. Was I still below the sound barrier or had I broken through it? A glance at the speedometer during the critical phase showed the needle at its maximum value of 1100 km/h [660 mph]. It only dropped back slowly when I was again horizontal.

My next problem was right beneath me – the continuous cloud deck. No gap in the clouds could be seen. I would have to break through them myself. But where was I, and was the geography beneath me favourable? Recalling my scanty blind-flying training, I carefully levelled myself and dove. I caught sight of the ground: a patch of woods. That was just enough. I oriented myself with a railway line through a river valley. I was over the Ardennes, near the German border. I landed on the emergency field near Vogelsang castle. While taxiing out, I damaged my elevator on a piece of wood lying in the grass. A *Krampfeinsatz* from take-off until the end!

One piece of good news awaited me: my partner also survived the adventure in good health. He landed on Bonn–Hangelar.

Fw. Peter Crump
6./JG 26

Fw. Peter Crump (II./JG 26) and one of several 'Black 10s' that he claimed as his personal aircraft, this one a Fw 190A-6 at Vitry-en-Artois. (Crump)

24 October
12th Air Force XII BC: 23 of 25 B-24s bomb Wiener Neustadt Bf 109 factory – lose ~2; 16 of 89 B-17s bomb Ebenfurth (A) – lose ~0. 36 of 48 P-38s (1 FG) escorts claim 0, lose 0.

The XII BC flew its last mission to the Reich, in poor weather and with unknown results. Only I./JG 27 is known to have attempted an interception, but could not find the bombers in the clouds.

November 1943

The 15th Air Force was established in Tunisia on 1 November as a new strategic air force. It absorbed the long-range assets of the 12th Air Force: four B-17 groups, two B-24 groups, three P-38 groups, one P-47 group re-equipping from Curtiss P-40 Warhawks and (briefly) three B-26 medium bomber groups. The XII BC headquarters became the headquarters of the new air force, which never established a bomber command. Previous raids on Axis industry from the south had been successful, with the exception of the low-altitude Ploesti attack, and it was apparent that the German defences in southern Germany and Austria were still weak. A build-up of the strategic bombing force in Italy to the point that the Reich could be attacked from there with regularity would further stretch the forces of the RLV and, by taking advantage of the (supposedly) better Italian weather, allow missions to be mounted on days that the 8th AF in England was grounded.

The American doctrine of unescorted daylight bombing died during the second week in October. Four full-strength missions in seven days had cost the 8th AF 148 heavy bombers, 50 per cent of its average daily operational strength. The operational training of the first two groups of truly long-range American fighters, P-38 Lightnings with twin 150-gallon drop tanks, was rushed to completion. The big Lockheed fighter was returning to the ETO after a year's absence. The month also saw the arrival in England of a new version of an American fighter that had seen some service in other theatres, but was still little known in the ETO – the North American P-51 Mustang. This new plane, the longest-ranged fighter to see service in Europe, would solve the American long-range escort problem and would ultimately prove to be the best fighter of the war in most respects.

The RAF in the UK underwent a major reorganisation in November. The Allied Expeditionary Air Force (AEAF) was established to command the Allied tactical units for the forthcoming ground invasion of western Europe. The American component was the 9th US Air Force (9th AF); the RAF component was the 2nd Tactical Air Force (2nd TAF). RAF Fighter Command was divided, with part joining 2nd TAF. The AEAF began its own air campaign over France and the Low Countries. This served to occupy and wear down the Luftflotte 3 fighters (which were now part of II. Jagdkorps), but the direct involvement of the 2nd TAF fighters in escorting the strategic raids dwindled to zero, and the tactical raids will be mentioned in this book only when their timing impacted the defences against the strategic raids.

No new single-engine front-line units joined the RLV force in November, but Erprobungskommando 25 (ErprKdo 25), the experimental unit reporting to the General der Jagdflieger, Adolf Galland, is worth noting. It contained a Staffel devoted to weapons development for single-engine fighters; a similar Staffel for twin-engine fighters; Erprobungskommando 16, a small test unit for the revolutionary new Me 163 *Komet*, the world's first rocket-propelled fighter; and an experimental assault fighter unit, Sturmstaffel 1. This last-named Staffel was to comprise specially armed and armoured Fw 190s and highly motivated pilots sworn to press attacks on heavy bombers to the closest range, ramming if necessary. It was to be operational by December and undergo a six-month trial.

Generalmajor Galland with the first seven pilots of the Sturmstaffel. From left: Lt. Elser (MIA 17 Dec 44), Major von Kornatzki (KIA 12 Sep 44), Major Bacsila, Uffz. Peinemann (KIFA 28 Sep 44), Genmaj. Galland, Uffz. Röhrich (KIA 19 Jul 44), Gefr. Vivroux (DOW 25 Oct 44), Gefr. Steffen (WIA 24 Apr 44). Note the camouflaged hangar in the background – Achmer, 17 November. *(Smith)*

An RLV formation leader's school was formed, very late, and attached to I./JG 27 in Austria. It offered a six-week course to teach successful young combat pilots the bare essentials of leading fighter formations against the heavy bombers. While this course gave these pilots a brief rest from operations and provided some standardised instruction, it was widely derided as more theoretical than practical.

Oberst Hajo Herrmann's single-engine *Wilde Sau* night fighters continued to drain the strength of the day forces. The force was expanded to a full Jagddivision, containing the original JG 300 and two new Geschwader, JG 301 and JG 302. These three Geschwader were not immediately assigned their own aircraft, but borrowed fighters from the day units on their bases.

2 November

15th Air Force: 112 of 139 B-24s + B-17s bomb Wiener Neustadt Bf 109 factory – lose 5 B-24s + 6 B-17s, claim 56-27-8. 72 P-38s (2 FGs) escorts claim 0, lose 0.

The first mission of the new 15th Air Force (15th AF) was a successful attack on the Messerschmitt factory complex in Wiener Neustadt that cost the Luftwaffe several months' production of Bf 109s. Eleven of the

139 sorties were flown. II./JG 3 from Schiphol again made an early interception of the escort and dispersed one P-47 group, claiming four without loss. One Jagdgruppe thus took one American group out of the battle, but the other seven escort groups carried out their assigned missions according to plan. The problem for the Germans remained a lack of numbers. Bad weather and the numerous escorts made successful interceptions very problematic. Nine bombers and three P-47s were lost to all causes; the Luftwaffe lost 13 KIA or MIA, nine WIA and 25 fighters – III./JG 11 lost half its strength on this one mission. Spitfires escorting a late afternoon B-26 raid on Schiphol made II./JG 3 pay the price for the day's earlier success, downing eight Bf 109s and killing five pilots, including the Gruppenkommandeur, Major Kurt Brändle.

4./JG 51 Bf 109G-6/Trop 'White 12', somewhere in Italy in mid-1943. The Geschwader emblem is clearly visible on the cowling. The Second Gruppe horizontal bar is located in front of the identification numbers, a practice that was unique to this Gruppe. II./JG 51, to which this Staffel belonged, was withdrawn to Munich to rebuild and was well-placed and well-trained to meet the USAAF assault on southern Germany in late 1943. After three successful months in the RLV, the Gruppe returned to Italy, but transferred to Romania when the 15th Air Force began its campaign against Ploesti in April. The Gruppe spent the remainder of the war in the Balkans and, finally, Hungary, an anticlimactic end for a promising unit. *(Bundesarchiv 468-1422-6)*

139 bombers failed to return to Tunisia. The defenders flew 147 sorties. Three Jagdgruppen – I./JG 27, II./JG 51 and II./JG 53 – and the factory protection Schwarm claimed victories while losing two KIA, five WIA and eight Bf 109s to the bomber gunners. This result was poor enough to bring a quick inspection visit from Göring and Galland.

3 November

8th Air Force VIII BC Mission #119: 211 of 217 1st BD B-17s, 212 of 221 3rd Division B-17s, 116 of 128 2nd Division B-24s bomb Wilhelmshaven, TOT 1307-1335 – lose 7-2-47, claim 21-3-24. VIII FC: 45 P-38s (1 FG) claim 3-5-5, lose 0; 333 P-47s (7 FGs) claim 11-0-2, lose 2-1-5.

The 8th AF returned to Germany with a raid on Wilhelmshaven. The 55th FG, its only operational P-38 unit, provided the target escort and was praised by the bomber crews for an effective job. Most of the defenders were hampered by poor weather, and only

94th Bomb Group B-17s under fighter attack in late 1943. A fighter is seen behind the rear bomber. *(USAAF)*

II./JG 1 WAR DIARY[6]
3 November 1943

Two missions were flown in the course of the day. In the first, two Bf 109G/GM-1 were scrambled against a reconnaissance aircraft. In the second, 22 Fw 190s and three Bf 109s took off on a Gruppe interception mission. At 1255 hours, contact was made with 120–150 B-17s and B-40s escorted by ca. 80–100 Thunderbolts and 20–25 Lightnings. The strong escort, both close and detached, made a closed-formation attack on the Boeings impossible. Our successes were one Boeing (Obfw. Lüth) and one Lightning (Obfw. Haninger). Set against these are the following losses:

Uffz. Schieweck (5. Staffel) dead; one Fw 190 belly-landed and burned out (100 per cent damage), pilot Oblt. Kotiza uninjured; one Fw 190 belly-landed (10 per cent damage), pilot slightly injured; one Fw 190 shot down (100 per cent damage), Obfw. Lüth bailed out uninjured; one Fw 190 shot down (100 per cent damage), Fw. Sauer bailed out with light injuries; one Bf 109 shot down and burned out after force-landing, Lt. Ibing uninjured.

It was observed for the first time during this mission that the American fighter escort pursued our attacking fighters down to medium altitudes.

5 November

8th Air Force VIII BC Mission #121: 323 of 374 1st BD B-17s, 212 of 221 3rd BD B-17s bomb Gelsenkirchen, TOT 1313-1350 – lose 8-3-216, claim 5-1-3; 104 of 118 2nd BD B-24s bomb Münster, TOT 1349-1358 – lose 3-1-43, claim 21-4-7. VIII FC: 47 P-38s (1 FG) claim 5-2-2, lose 0; 336 P-47s (7 FGs) claim 13-4-1, lose 4-1-0.

The day's VIII BC targets were spaced closely to maximise escort coverage on what proved to be a cloudless day. The P-38 group flew another successful mission, and the seven P-47 groups, which were now flying slightly farther from the bombers than previously, kept most large German formations and the night fighters at a distance. Fifteen heavy bombers and five P-47s were lost or scrapped from all causes. The Luftwaffe flew 611 sorties in a maximum but generally unproductive effort and lost 23 fighters and two bombers used as interceptors. Nine aircrewmen were killed or missing, three in a friendly fire incident, and 10 were injured.

11 November

8th Air Force VIII BC Mission #127: 58 of 167 3rd BD B-17s bomb Münster, TOT 1408 – lose 4-0-28, claim 10-0-2. VIII FC: 59 P-38s (1 FG) claim 0, lose 0; 342 P-47s (7 FGs) claim 8-1-2, lose 2-0-1.

Bad weather hindered both sides today. Only 58 of the 167 3rd BD B-17s that were dispatched bombed their assigned target, Münster, while all 175 1st BD B-17s turned back at the coast because of heavy cloud which extended up to 9,800 metres (32,000 feet). The wing of B-17s that reached Münster had been unable to close up with the rest of the 3rd BD owing to the

weather over England and had missed the recall signal. Aircraft from eight Jagdgruppen were directed toward the small B-17 formation, but most found only P-47s, or nothing. II./JG 26 did locate the Pulk (herd) in a clear patch of sky south of Dordrecht and was able to attack it repeatedly. The Gruppe put down on several bases, claiming four B-17s. Three claims were confirmed; the fourth target had dived into clouds and reached England on two engines. A fourth B-17 was in fact shot down, probably by I./JG 1. These four B-17s, plus two P-47s, cost the Luftwaffe six KIA, five WIA and 14 fighters in 200 sorties.

13 November

8th Air Force VIII BC Mission #130: 143 of 272 B-17s + B-24s (all BDs) bomb Bremen, TOT 1120-1145 – lose 16-6-22, claim 20-14-13. VIII FC: 45 P-38s (1 FG) claim 7-3-5, lose 7-2-5; 345 P-47s (7 FGs) claim 3-0-1, lose 3-0-2.

Bremen was the target for the VIII BC. Bad weather forced the 1st BD to abandon the mission; most of the other B-17s and B-24s bombed unidentified 'targets of opportunity' through the clouds. Four P-47 groups failed to find their assigned bombers. The other three carried out their missions, but only the P-38 group, the 55th FG, reached the target area, and it ran into a buzz saw. The vulnerabilities of the big twin-engine fighter were becoming known to the Luftwaffe, and for the first time, the group lost as many fighters as it claimed. The three I. Jagdkorps Jagddivisionen scrambled nine Jagdgruppen, two Zerstörergruppen and parts of two Nachtjagdgruppen. The P-38s were gradually stripped away from the bomber stream during their prolonged and valiant combat, and the Gruppen directed straight to Bremen scored heavily against the heavies.

I./JG 3, now under II. Jagdkorps, attacked the withdrawing bombers over the Dutch coast, but the activity of only one Staffel of the other II. Jagdkorps fighters is known. 4./JG 26, renumbered from 8./JG 26 when JG 26 was expanded on 1 October, normally flew with the JG 26 Stabsschwarm, but the latter unit was apparently not called on today. 4./JG 26 transferred alone from Lille-Nord to München–Gladbach, from where it was scrambled against the withdrawing 3rd BD. The Focke-Wulfs downed one B-17 as well as one P-47 from the light escort, for the loss of one fighter from which the pilot bailed out without injury. The Staffel was still in the same general area half an hour later when the B-24s of the 2nd BD arrived, following

Luftwaffe defensive activity – 2 November 1943

Unit	Type	Gruppe up			Gruppe down		Claims	Losses				
		Base	No	Time	Base	Time		Dest	Dam	KIA	MIA	WIA
Lw Bfh MItte												
Jagddivision 7:			147									
III./JG 3	Bf 109G	Bad Wörishofen		1220	Vöslau, Bad Aibling	1415	n/c	0	2	0	0	0
II./JG 51	Bf 109G	Neubiberg		~1230	Neubiberg?	~1430	4 B-17	4	1	0	0	1
II./ZG 76	Bf 110G	Wertheim		1240	Graz	1410	n/c	0	0	0	0	0
Jafü Ostmark:												
I./JG 27	Bf 109G	Fels am Wagram		~1200	Fels am Wagram	~1300	1 B-17, 6 B-24	2	2	1	0	3
II./JG 53	Bf 109G	Wien–Seyring		1204	Wien–Seyring	1301	1 B-17, 1 B-24	2	4	1	0	1
ISS W-Neustadt	Bf 109G	Wiener Neustadt		~1200	Wiener Neustadt	~1300	1 B-17, 1 B-24	0	0	0	0	0

Luftwaffe defensive activity – 3 November 1943

Unit	Type	Gruppe up			Gruppe down		Claims	Losses				
		Base	No	Time	Base	Time		Dest	Dam	KIA	MIA	WIA
Lw Bfh Mitte												
I. Jagdkorps			139									
Jagddivision 2:												
I./ZG 26	Bf 110G	Lippspringe		1220	Lippspringe	1410	0	4	0	3	0	4
Jagddivision 3:												
Stab/JG 1?	Fw 190A	Deelen		~1230	Deelen	~1400	0	0	0	0	0	0
I./JG 1	Fw 190A	Deelen, Arnhem		1226	Deelen, Arnhem	1403	1 B-17	2	2	1	0	0
II./JG 1	Fw 190A	Woensdrecht	22	1255	Woensdrecht	~1400	1 B-17	4	1	1	0	2
III./JG 1	Bf 109G	Leeuwarden, Eelde		1234	Leeuwarden, Eelde	~1400	1 B-17	11	2	4	3	1
11./JG 1	Bf 109G	Rheine	3	1255	Rheine	~1400	0	1	0	0	0	0
II./JG 3	Bf 109G	Schiphol		1205	Schiphol	1310	4 P-47	0	0	0	0	0
III./JG 26	Bf 109G	Bönninghardt		1330	Bönninghardt	~1430	0	3	1	1	0	2
I./NJG 1	Bf 110G	Venlo		~1230	Venlo	~1500	0	0	1	0	0	0
II./NJG 1	Bf 110G	St. Trond		~1230	St. Trond	~1500	1 B-17	0	0	0	0	0
IV./NJG 1	Bf 110G	Leeuwarden		1310	Leeuwarden	1430	0	0	0	0	0	0
V./KG 2	Me 410A	Schiphol	7	1305	Schiphol	~1430	0	0	0	0	0	0

the same track. The Liberators' escort was also patchy: one B-24 was shot down, in exchange for one Fw 190 that belly-landed with serious damage. The rest of the Staffel landed on various Dutch bases after a successful mission. The Americans lost or scrapped 22 bombers and 12 fighters, including nine P-38s, today; the Germans lost 10 KIA or MIA, nine WIA and 21 aircraft in 355 sorties.

16 November

8th Air Force VIII BC Mission #131: 130 of 189 1st BD B-17s bomb Knaben (N), TOT 1133-1238 – lose 1-0-7, claim 2-0-4; 147 of 160 3rd BD B-17s, 29 of 39 2nd BD B-24s bomb Rjükan (N), TOT 1120-1145 – lose 1-1-3, claim 2-0-0. No escort.

An unescorted VIII BC raid on Norway was detected early enough that all of the fighters defending southern Norway – 15 Bf 109s and Fw 190s of IV./JG 5, 10./JG11, and Jagdstaffel Helgoland, plus 5 Ju 88s of IV./NJG 3 – were able to intercept. Three B-17s were lost. One IV./JG 5 Bf 109 was shot down; its pilot bailed out with injuries.

Luftwaffe defensive activity – 5 November 1943

Unit	Type	Gruppe up			Gruppe down		Claims	Losses				
		Base	No	Time	Base	Time		Dest	Dam	KIA	MIA	WIA
Lw Bfh Mitte												
I. Jagdkorps			429									
Jagddivision 1:			141									
JG 25	Bf 109G	Gardelegen		1401	Gardelegen	~1440	0	4	1	1	0	2
III./JG 54	Bf 109G	Schwerin, Gardelegen		1315	Schwerin, Münster–Handorf	1440	0	0	0	0	0	0
I./NJG 2	Ju 88C	Kassel–Rothwesten		~1300	Kassel–Rothwesten	~1430	n/c	0	0	0	0	0
I./NJG 5	Bf 110G	Stendal		1307	Stendal	~1430	n/c	0	0	0	0	0
Jagddivison 2:			205									
Stab/JG 11	Fw 190A	Husum		1305	Husum	~1415	0	0	0	0	0	0
I./JG 11	Fw 190A	Husum		1317	Husum, Ahlhorn	1425	1 B-24, 1 P-47	3	1	0	0	3
	Fw 190A	Husum		1404	Oldenburg	1450	transfer	0	0	0	0	0
II./JG 11	Bf 109G	Marx		1300	Marx	1412	n/c	0	0	0	0	0
III./JG 11	Bf 109G	Oldenburg		1303	Dortmund	1406	1 B-24	1	2	0	1	0
I./ZG 26	Bf 110G	Marx		1350	Lippspringe	1510	n/c	0	0	0	0	0
II./ZG 26	Me 410A	Hesepe		1255	Hesepe	1345	n/c	0	0	0	0	0
III./ZG 26	Bf 110G	Wunstorf	26	1245	Wunstorf	~1430	n/c	0	0	0	0	0
I./ZG 76	Bf 110G	Ansbach		1240	Ansbach	1432	n/c	0	0	0	0	0
II./ZG 76	Bf 110G	Wertheim		1240	Wertheim	1432	n/c	0	0	0	0	0
III./NJG 3	Bf 110G	Lüneburg		1308	Lüneburg	1500	n/c	0	0	0	0	0
Jagddivison 3:			83									
Stab/JG 1	Fw 190A	Deelen		~1230	Deelen	~1430	0	0	0	0	0	0
I./JG 1	Fw 190A, Me 210A	Deelen, Arnhem		1236	Deelen, Schiphol, Eindhoven	1435	1 B-17 HSS, 1 P-47	4	0	2	0	0
II./JG 1	Fw 190A	Rheine	18	1235	Rheine, Köln–Ostheim	1440	2 B-17	0	1	0	0	0
III./JG 1	Bf 109G	Leeuwarden		~1230	Leeuwarden	~1400	1 B-17	1	0	0	0	1
Stab/JG 3	Bf 109G	Bönninghardt		~1300	Bönninghardt	~1400	0	0	0	0	0	0
II./JG 3	Bf 109G	Schiphol		1220	Deelen, Venlo	1340	n/c	2	0	0	0	0
Stab/JG 26	Fw 190A	Deelen		~1230	Deelen	~1345	0	0	0	0	0	0
4./JG 26	Fw 190A	Deelen		~1230	Deelen	~1345	0	0	0	0	0	0
I./JG 26	Fw 190A	Grimbergen		1140	Köln–Ostheim	1215	transfer	0	0	0	0	0
	Fw 190A	Köln–Ostheim		1305	München–Gladbach, Deelen, Bönninghardt	1430	1 B-17	1	2	0	0	0
III./JG 26	Bf 109G	Bönninghardt		~1300	Bönninghardt	~1430	1 P-47	2	1	1	0	1
III./NJG 1	Bf 110G	Twente		~1300	Twente	~1430	0	1	0	2	0	0
IV./NJG 1	Bf 110G	Leeuwarden		1246	Leeuwarden	1436	0	0	0	0	0	0
III./NJG 2	Ju 88C	Schiphol		~1300	Schiphol	~1430	0	0	0	0	0	0
14./KG 2	Me 410A	Schiphol		1235	Schiphol	~1430	0	2	1	3	0	0
Jagddivison 7:												
III./JG 3	Bf 109G	Bad Wörishofen		1100	Oldenburg	1250	transfer	0	1	0	0	0
Luftflotte 3												
II. Jagdkorps			182									

Luftwaffe defensive activity – 5 November 1943 Continued

Unit	Type	Gruppe up			Gruppe down		Claims	Losses				
		Base	No	Time	Base	Time		Dest	Dam	KIA	MIA	WIA
Jagddivision 4:												
I./JG 3	Bf 109G	Lille–Vendeville		~1400	Lille–Vendeville	~1530	0	1	0	0	0	1
II./JG 26	Fw 190A	Cambrai–Epinoy	29	~1400	Antwerp	~1530	n/c	0	0	0	0	0
II./JG 27	Bf 109G	St. Dizier	18	~1400	St. Dizier	~1530	0	0	1	0	0	0
Jagddivision 5:												
Stab/JG 2	Fw 190A	Evreux	*26	~1300	Evreux	~1430	2 P-47	0	0	0	0	0
I./JG 2	Fw 190A	Evreux	—	~1300	Evreux	~1345	4 B-17	0	3	0	0	0
	Fw 190A	Evreux	—	~1400	Evreux	~1530	0	0	0	0	0	0
II./JG 2	Bf 109G	Vitry–en–Artois	37	~1300	Vitry–en–Artois	~1530	0	4	5	0	0	4
III./JG 2	Fw 190A	Beaumont–le–Roger	—	~1300	Beaumont–le–Roger	~1530	0	0	0	0	0	0
IX. Fliegerkorps:												
I./SKG 10	Fw 190G	Rosières	**10	~1345	Rosières	~1445	2 B-17	0	1	0	0	0
II./SKG 10	Fw 190G	Rennes	—	~1345	Rennes	~1445	0	1	0	0	1	0

*26 total JG 2 Fw 190 sorties **10 total SKG 10 sorties

Luftwaffe defensive activity – 11 November 1943

Unit	Type	Gruppe up			Gruppe down		Claims	Losses				
		Base	No	Time	Base	Time		Dest	Dam	KIA	MIA	WIA
Lw Bfh Mitte												
I. Jagdkorps			189									
Jagddivison 1:												
JG 25	Bf 109G	Gardelegen		~1330	Gardelegen	~1500	n/c	0	0	0	0	0
Jagddivison 2:												
Stab/JG 11	Fw 190A	Husum		~1330	Husum	~1500	n/c	0	0	0	0	0
I./JG 11	Fw 190A	Husum		1340	Husum	1515	n/c	0	0	0	0	0
II./JG 11	Bf 109G	Marx		1340	Marx	1505	n/c	1	0	0	0	0
III./JG 11	Bf 109G	Oldenburg		1341	Oldenburg	1504	n/c	0	0	0	0	0
II./ZG 26	Me 410A	Hesepe		~1330	Hesepe	~1500	0	0	0	0	0	0
III./ZG 26	Bf 110G	Wunstorf		1336	Wunstorf	1504	n/c	0	0	0	0	0
Jagddivison 3:												
Stab/JG 1	Fw 190A	Deelen		1320	Deelen	~1530	0	0	0	0	0	0
I./JG 1	Fw 190A	Deelen, Arnhem	12	1320	Deelen	~1530	1 P-38, 1 P-47	4	0	2	0	2
II./JG 1	Fw 190A	Rheine	19	1332	Rheine	1530	0	2	0	1	0	0
III./JG 1	Bf 109G	Volkel		1320	Volkel	~1520	1 P-47	1	0	1	0	0
II./JG 3	Bf 109G	Schiphol		1315	Deelen	1433	0	1	0	0	0	0
I./JG 26	Fw 190A	Grimbergen	25	1217	Grimbergen, Wevelghem	1329	0	3	1	1	0	2
2nd sorties	Fw 190A	Wevelghem		1420	Grimbergen	1530	n/c	0	0	0	0	0
Jagddivison 7:												
III./JG 3	Bf 109G	Bad Wörishofen		1256	Bad Wörishofen	1433	n/c	0	0	0	0	0

Luftwaffe defensive activity – 11 November 1943 Continued

Unit	Type	Gruppe up			Gruppe down		Claims	Losses				
		Base	No	Time	Base	Time		Dest	Dam	KIA	MIA	WIA
Luftflotte 3												
I. Jagdkorps												
Jagddivison 4:												
I./JG 3	Bf 109G	Lille–Vendeville	14	1221	Lille–Vendeville	1254	n/c	0	0	0	0	0
2nd sorties	Bf 109G	Lille–Vendeville	14	1424	Lille–Vendeville	~1530	0	1	0	0	0	1
4./JG 26	Fw 190A	Lille–Nord	*38	1221	Lille–Nord	1254	n/c	0	0	0	0	0
2nd sorties	Fw 190A	Lille–Nord	**36	1424	Lille–Nord	1515	0	0	0	0	0	0
II./JG 26	Fw 190A	Cambrai–Epinoy	—	1223	Cambrai–Epinoy	1302	n/c	0	0	0	0	0
2nd sorties	Fw 190A	Cambrai–Epinoy	—	1423	Vlissingen, others	1515	3 B-17	0	0	0	0	0
Jagddivison 5:												
I./JG 2	Fw 190A	Evreux		~1415	Evreux	~1530	0	1	0	1	0	0

*38 4./JG 26 + II./JG 26 Fw 190s fly 1st sorties.

**36 4./JG 26 + II./JG 26 Fw 190s fly 2nd sorties.

Luftwaffe defensive activity – 13 November 1943

Unit	Type	Gruppe up			Gruppe down		Claims	Losses				
		Base	No	Time	Base	Time		Dest	Dam	KIA	MIA	WIA
Lw Bfh Mitte												
I. Jagdkorps			314									
Jagddivision 1:												
JG 25	Bf 109G	Gardelegen		~1115	Gardelegen	~1230	1 P-38	2	0	1	1	0
III./JG 54	Bf 109G	Schwerin, Gardelegen		1115	Schwerin, Schleswig, Flensburg	1251	1 B-24	1	0	1	0	0
III./NJG 3	Bf 110G	Lüneburg		1114	Lüneburg	1255	0	0	0	0	0	0
Jagddivison 2:												
Stab/JG 11	Fw 190A	Husum		1045	Husum	~1150	0	0	0	0	0	0
I./JG 11	Fw 190A	Husum	21	1045	Husum	1150	7 B-24, 1 P-38	2	0	1	0	0
II./JG 11	Bf 109G	Vörden	28	1046	Achmer, Vörden	1208	2 P-38	4	0	1	0	2
	Bf 109G	Achmer, Vörden		~1220	Achmer	~1320	0	0	0	0	0	0
III./JG 11	Bf 109G	Oldenburg		1048	Plantlünne	1215	1 P-38	2	2	2	0	0
I./ZG 26	Bf 110G	Lippspringe		1040	Lippspringe	1250	0	0	0	0	0	0
II./ZG 26	Me 410A	Hesepe		1045	Hesepe	1230	2 P-38	4	1	3	0	5
III./ZG 26	Bf 110G	Wunstorf	25	1038	Wunstorf, various	1250	0	1	1	0	0	1
IV./NJG 3	Bf 110G	Aalborg–West		1129	Aalborg–West	1324	1 B-24	0	0	0	0	0
ErprKdo 25	Bf 110G	Achmer		1045	Achmer	1146	0	0	0	0	0	0
ISS Focke-Wulf	Fw 190A	Bremen		~1100	Bremen	~1200	0	0	0	0	0	0
Jagddivison 3:												
Stab/JG 1	Fw 190A	Deelen		~1045	Deelen	~1200	0	0	0	0	0	0
I./JG 1	Fw 190A	Deelen, Arnhem		1053	Deelen, Rheine	1159	1 B-17, 1 B-24	0	1	0	0	0
II./JG 1	Fw 190A	Rheine	11	1110	Rheine	1250	1 P-38	0	0	0	0	0
III./JG 1	Bf 109G	Volkel	10	1108	Volkel	~1230	2 P-38	2	2	0	0	1
I./JG 3	Bf 109G	Schiphol		~1130	Lille–Vendeville	~1230	1 B-17, 1 P-47	1	0	0	0	0

Luftwaffe defensive activity – 13 November 1943 Continued

Unit	Type	Gruppe up				Gruppe down		Claims	Losses				
		Base	No	Time		Base	Time		Dest	Dam	KIA	MIA	WIA
I./JG 3	Bf 109G	Schiphol		~1130		Lille–Vendeville	~1230	1 B-17, 1 P-47	1	0	0	0	0
II./JG 3	Bf 109G	Schiphol		0900		Volkel	0920	transfer	0	0	0	0	0
	Bf 109G	Volkel		1115		Schiphol	1230	n/c	0	0	0	0	0
	Bf 109G	Schiphol		~1300		Schiphol	~1400	1 B-17	0	0	0	0	0
4./JG 26	Fw 190A	München–Gladbach	—	1135		Soesterberg, others	1245	1 B-17, 1 B-24, 1 P-47	2	1	0	0	0
I./JG 26	Fw 190A	Grimbergen		~1115		Rheine	~1145	transfer	0	0	0	0	0
III./JG 26	Bf 109G	München–Gladbach		~1115		München–Gladbach	~1230	0	0	0	0	0	0
Luftflotte 3													
II. Jagdkorps													
Jagddivision 4:													
I./JG 3	Bf 109G	Lille–Vendeville	18	1040		Schiphol	~1115	transfer	0	0	0	0	0
4./JG 26	Fw 190A	Lille–Nord	*34	1040		München–Gladbach	1118	transfer	0	0	0	0	0
II./JG 26	Fw 190A	Cambrai–Epinoy	—	1040		München–Gladbach?	~1120	transfer	0	0	0	0	0

*34 4./JG 26 + II./JG 26 Fw 190s transfer France–Germany

Luftwaffe defensive activity – 16 November 1943

Unit	Type	Gruppe up				Gruppe down		Claims	Losses				
		Base	No	Time		Base	Time		Dest	Dam	KIA	MIA	WIA
Lw Bfh Mitte													
I. Jagdkorps													
Jagddivision 2:													
10./JG 11	Fw 190A	Lister	2	~1115		Lister	~1215	0	0	0	0	0	0
JaSta Helgoland	Bf 109T	Lister	5	1125		Lister	1210	0	0	0	0	0	0
	Bf 109T	Lister		1300		Lister	1400	1 B-17	0	1	0	0	0
IV./NJG 3	Ju 88C	Aalborg-West	5	1049		Lister	1245	0	0	0	0	0	0
Luftflotte 5													
Jafü Norwegen:													
IV./JG 5	Bf 109G	Sola	8	~1115		Sola	~1215	0	1	0	0	0	1

Luftwaffe defensive activity – 18 November 1943

Unit	Type	Gruppe up				Gruppe down		Claims	Losses				
		Base	No	Time		Base	Time		Dest	Dam	KIA	MIA	WIA
Lw Bfh Mitte													
I. Jagdkorps													
Jagddivision 2:													
IV./JG 5	Bf 109G	Lister		~1245		Lister	~1345	3 B-24	1	0	0	0	0
I./JG 11	Fw 190A	Husum		~1230		Husum	~1330	1 B-24	0	1	0	0	0
III./JG 11	Bf 109G	Oldenburg?		~1300		Oldenburg?	~1400	1 B-24	0	0	0	0	0
10./JG 11	Fw 190A	Lister		~1030		Lister	~1130	3 B-24	0	2	0	0	0
2nd sorties	Fw 190A	Lister		~1230		Lister	~1330	3 B-24	2	0	0	2	0
JaSta Helgoland	Bf 109T	Lister		~1000		Lister	1053	n/c	0	0	0	0	0
	Bf 109T	Lister		1136		Lister	1214	n/c	0	0	0	0	0
	Bf 109T	Lister		1243		Lister	1331	2 B-24	1	1	1	0	0
IV./NJG 3	Ju 88C	Aalborg–West, Grove		1115		Aalborg–West, Grove	1337	4 B-24	0	0	0	0	0

18 November

8th Air Force VIII BC Mission #132: 82 of 102 2nd BD B-24s bomb Oslo-Kjellar a/f (N) –lose 9-3-10, claim 10-7-5. No escort.

Reichsmarschall Hermann Göring inspects pilots of Hauptmann Karl Boehm-Tettelbach's Zerstörergeschwader 26 at the Achmer airbase on 17 November. In the left of the photo: Oberstleutnant Bernd von Brauchitsch, Göring's Chefadjutant; Generaloberst Bruno Loerzer, the Chief of the Luftwaffen-Personalamt; Hauptmann Karl Boehm-Tettelbach and Hermann Göring. *(Smith)*

A return trip to Norway by the VIII BC B-24 division found the defences better able to respond. Of the local units, 10./JG 11 attacked the incoming bombers, IV./JG 5 and JaSta Helgoland attacked on withdrawal, and the Ju 88s of IV./NJG 3 stayed with the B-24s for almost two hours. I./JG 11 and III./JG 11 raced north from Denmark and north Germany in time to attack the bombers as they withdrew. Twelve B-24s were lost: six were shot down over Norway or the North Sea, three sought refuge in Sweden, and three were scrapped in England. The Luftwaffe lost three KIA and MIA, one Bf 109T, one Bf 109G and two Fw 190s.

26 November 1943 – Bremen and Paris (see map)

8th Air Force VIII BC Mission #138: 430 of 505 1st + 3rd BD B-17s, 2nd BD B-24s bomb Bremen, TOT 1145-1228 – lose 24-5-165, claim 16-3-10; 0 of 128 3rd BD B-17s target Paris ball-bearing factory, do not bomb – lose 4-0-18, claim 8-2-3. VIII FC: 28 P 38s (1 FG) claim 0, lose 0; 353 P-47s (7 FGs) claim 36-3-9, lose 4-3-7.

The VIII BC sent seven combat wings of B-17s and

two of B-24s to Bremen in another attempt to bomb the city through clouds. Two combat wings of B-17s were sent in the other direction, to Paris. The 329 sorties flown by the defenders split as expected. I. Jagdkorps sent fighters of its three Jagddivisionen against the Bremen force, which lost 29 bombers and one P-47. Schmid lost 18 KIA, 18 WIA and 26 aircraft. Among the hardest hit were the JG 11 Stabsstaffel, which lost 3 Bf 109s; III./ZG 26, which lost 10 Bf 110s, all apparently to 56th FG Thunderbolts; and ErprKdo 25, which lost four aircraft of three different types. II. Jagdkorps defended against the Paris raiders, which returned without bombing their cloud-covered target. Five of its Jagdgruppen and one independent Staffel lost five KIA, three WIA and eight fighters to the bombers and their escorts and several others to Spitfires engaged in tactical raids. The Paris force lost four B-17s and six P-47s, all of the latter from the 78th FG, which lost three over France and three in crash landings on the English coast.

Luftwaffe defensive activity vs. Bremen raid – 26 November 1943

Unit	Type	Gruppe up				Gruppe down		Claims	Losses				
		Base	No	Time		Base	Time		Dest	Dam	KIA	MIA	WIA
Lw Bfh Mitte													
I. Jagdkorps			294										
Jagddivision 1:													
JG 25	Bf 109G	Delitzsch	20	1127		Neuruppin	1205	n/c	0	0	0	0	0
III./JG 54	Bf 109G	Schwerin, Gardelegen		1126		Schwerin, Gardelegen	1206	n/c	1	0	1	0	0
III./NJG 3	Bf 110G	Lüneburg		~1130		Lüneburg	~1245	n/c	0	0	0	0	0
I./NJG 5	Bf 110G	Stendal		1134		Stendal	1244	n/c	0	0	0	0	0
Jagddivison 2:													
Stab/JG 11	Bf 109G	Husum		1118		Husum	~1230	0	0	0	0	0	0
2nd sorties	Bf 109G	Husum		~1300		Husum	~1415	1 B-17	3	2	1	0	2
I./JG 11	Fw 190A	Husum	19	1118		Oldenburg, others	~1315	1 B-17, 1 B-24, 1 B-17 HSS	2	0	2	0	0
2nd sorties	Fw 190A	Oldenburg, others		~1330		Husum	1412	0	0	0	0	0	0
II./JG 11	Bf 109G	Plantlünne	16	1100		Quakenbrück	1230	1 B-17	2	1	1	0	0
III./JG 11	Bf 109G	Oldenburg		~1100		Oldenburg	~1230	7 B-17	1	1	0	0	1
2nd sorties	Bf 109G	Oldenburg		~1245		Oldenburg	~1330	1 P-47	0	0	0	0	0
II./ZG 26	Me 410A	Hesepe		1100		Hesepe	1141	0	0	0	0	0	0
2nd sorties	Me 410A	Hesepe		1235		Hesepe	1332	0	0	1	0	0	0
III./ZG 26	Bf 110G	Wunstorf	24	1100		Wunstorf, others	1315	4 B-17, 1 P-47	10	2	8	0	12
IV./NJG 1	Bf 110G	Quakenbrück		~1130		Quakenbrück	~1300	1 B-17	0	0	0	0	0
ErprKdo 25	Fw 190A, Bf 110G, Me 410A, Do 217	Achmer		~1200		Achmer	~1330	2 B-17	4	1	4	0	1
Jagddivison 3:													
Stab/JG 1	Fw 190A	Deelen		~1100		Deelen	~1300	0	0	0	0	0	0
I./JG 1	Fw 190A	Deelen, Arnhem		~1100		Deelen, Rheine	~1300	2 B-17	0	0	0	0	0
II./JG 1	Fw 190A, Bf 109G	Rheine	16	1105		Rheine	1250	2 B-17	2	2	1	0	0
III./JG 1	Bf 109G	Volkel		1045		Volkel	~1155	2 B-17, 1 B-24	0	0	0	0	0
11./JG 1	Bf 109G	Rheine	3	1105		Rheine	~1250	0	0	0	0	0	0
II./JG 3	Bf 109G	Schiphol		0900		Volkel	1015	transfer	0	0	0	0	0
		Volkel		1045		Volkel, Gröningen	1155	0	0	0	0	0	0
2nd sorties		Volkel		1245		Schiphol	1345	0	0	0	0	0	0
III./JG 26	Bf 109G	München–Gladbach		~1115		München–Gladbach	~1300	0	0	0	0	0	0
Jagddivison 7:			35										
II./JG 27	Bf 109G	Erbenheim	29	~1115		Rheine, Düsseldorf	1155	transfer	0	0	0	0	0
6./JG 27	Bf 109G	Düsseldorf		~1230		Erbenheim	~1400	1 B-17, 2 B-24	2	3	0	0	2
II./JG 51	Bf 109G	Neubiberg		1050		Neubiberg	1105	n/c	0	0	0	0	0
2nd sorties	Bf 109G	Neubiberg		1205		Neubiberg	1305	n/c	0	0	0	0	0

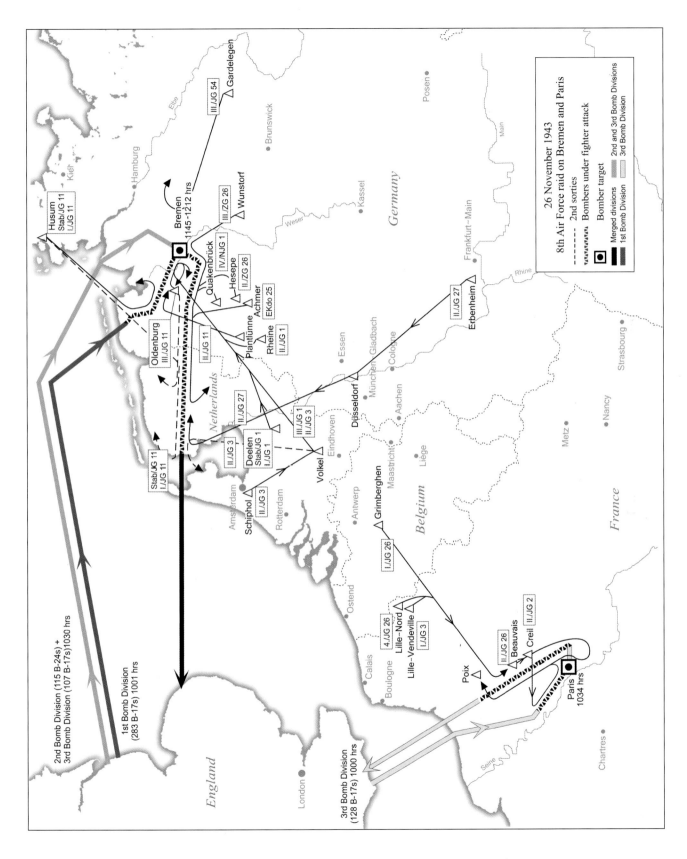

III./JG 54 — Gardelegen

Husum
Stab/JG 11
I./JG 11

Bremen
(1145–1212 hrs)

III./ZG 26 — Wunstorf

Quakenbrück
IV./NJG 1

Hesepe
II./ZG 26

Achmer
EKdo 25

Plantlünne

Rheine
II./JG 1

Oldenburg
III./JG 11

II./JG 11

II./JG 27

Stab/JG 11
I./JG 11

II./JG 3

Deelen
Stab/JG 1
I./JG 1

III./JG 1
II./JG 3

Volkel

Schiphol
II./JG 3

II./JG 27 — Erbenheim

Düsseldorf

Grimberghen
I./JG 26

4./JG 26
Lille-Nord

Lille-Vendeville
I./JG 3

Poix

II./JG 26

Beauvais
Creil
II./JG 2

Paris
1034 hrs

2nd Bomb Division (115 B-24s) +
3rd Bomb Division (107 B-17s)1030 hrs

1st Bomb Division
(283 B-17s) 1001 hrs

3rd Bomb Division
(128 B-17s) 1000 hrs

26 November 1943
8th Air Force raid on Bremen and Paris

- - - - -   2nd sorties
▲▲▲▲▲   Bombers under fighter attack
◉   Bomber target

Merged divisions
1st Bomb Division
2nd and 3rd Bomb Divisions
3rd Bomb Division

Luftwaffe defensive activity vs. Paris raid – 26 November 1943

Unit	Type	Gruppe up			Gruppe down		Claims	Losses				
		Base	No	Time	Base	Time		Dest	Dam	KIA	MIA	WIA
Lw Bfh Mitte												
I. Jagdkorps												
Jagddivision 3:												
I./JG 26	Fw 190A	Grimbergen		1012	Creil	1140	1 P-47	0	2	0	0	0
Luftflotte 3												
II. Jagdkorps												
Jagddivision 4:												
I./JG 3	Bf 109G	Lille–Vendeville		~1015	Lille–Vendeville	~1130	0	1	0	0	0	1
Stab/JG 26	Fw 190A	Lille–Nord		~1010	Creil	~1100	0	0	0	0	0	0
4./JG 26	Fw 190A	Lille–Nord		1010	Creil	1100	1 B-17, 1 B-17 HSS	0	0	0	0	0
II./JG 26	Fw 190A	Beauvais		1012	Beauvais	1117	2 B-17, 1 P-47	1	3	1	0	0
Jagddivision 5:												
II./JG 2	Bf 109G	Creil		1015	Poix	1127	4 B-17	2	3	1	0	1

COMBAT REPORT[7]
26 November 1943

One Boeing B-17 destroyed from 7,000 m at 1506 hours, PQ JP-3, Hohenhalte (12 km NW of Münster)

At 1105 hours, I took off in Fw 190A-6 'Red 1' (two MG 17, four MG 151/20) with the Gruppe on a mission to the Emden–Bremen area. Since I had no radio, the 6. StaKa took over the lead, using the Y-process. At 1147 hours, I sighted several fighters in DQ and, soon thereafter, numerous Pulks of American HBs at ca. 8,500 metres. Owing to strong icing conditions and a layer of haze, the Gruppe broke up into Rotten and Schwärme. I wanted to take the Stabsrotte up sun behind the first Pulk to gain the best attack position. I had learned that individual bombers in a formation can be attacked while in a bank, and I fired as I passed.

When in position, I first attacked a somewhat isolated B-17 from the front. After it was fired on, it disappeared into the haze and could not be found again. I again moved to the sunny side of the Verband. I was now in a good position to attack a B-17 from the side. After my attack, the right wing caught fire between the engines, but the B-17 remained in formation. I attacked again, this time from the front. The B-17 pulled up, but regained control. I immediately turned in again and attacked the B-17 once more from the low left to the closest range. The B-17 pulled up into a steep left bank and, burning, dove into the clouds at 1207 hours. The site of the Abschuss was marked exactly by a red parachute flare. The B-17 had previously jettisoned its bombs (incendiaries). The crash was witnessed by Lt. Ertmann.

Hptm. Walter Hoeckner, Gruppenkommandeur
Stab II./JG 1

29 November

8th Air Force VIII BC Mission #140: 154 of 360 1st + 3rd BD B-17s bomb Bremen, TOT 1429-1450 – lose 14-3-43, claim 15-11-10. VIII FC: 38 P-38s (1 FG) claim 2-0-2, lose 7-0-0; 314 P-47s (7 FGs) claim 13-4-4, lose 9-1-1.

The VIII BC dispatched six B-17 combat wings to bomb Bremen again, despite very bad weather over both England and Germany. Two of the wings could not form up owing to icy conditions and abandoned the mission. The rest bombed through solid cloud cover. I. Jagdkorps sent fighters of its three Jagddivisionen against them and also called on the three JD 7 Zerstörergruppen, which had no success. The II. Jagdkorps fighters could not be used as they were tied up completely by the tactical bombers of the 9th AF and

Luftwaffe defensive activity – 29 November 1943

Unit	Type	Gruppe up			Gruppe down		Claims	Losses (—: included in 1st sortie)				
		Base	No	Time	Base	Time		Dest	Dam	KIA	MIA	WIA
Lw Bfh Mitte			365									
I. Jagdkorps												
Jagddivision 1:												
III./JG 54	Bf 109G	Schwerin		0752	Döberitz	0830	transfer	0	0	0	0	0
	Bf 109G	Döberitz		~1430	Schwerin, Gardelegen	~1600	3 B-17	5	1	1	0	2
Jagddivison 2:												
Stab/JG 11	Fw 190A	Husum		1348	Husum	~1500	0	2	0	0	0	2
I./JG 11	Fw 190A	Husum		1348	Husum	1430	n/c	0	0	0	0	0
2nd sorties	Fw 190A	Husum		1600	Husum	1715	1 B-17	1	0	1	0	0
II./JG 11	Bf 109G	Plantlünne		1348	Varrelbusch	1512	2 P-47	2	1	1	0	1
III./JG 11	Bf 109G	Oldenburg		1350	Oldenburg	1523	n/c	1	1	1	0	0
Stab/ZG 26	Bf 110G	Wunstorf		~1335	Wunstorf	~1600	1 B-17	1	0	1	0	1
I./ZG 26	Bf 110G	Grove		1350	Grove	1420	n/c	0	0	0	0	0
II./ZG 26	Me 410A	Hesepe		1344	Hesepe	1510	3 B-17	1	2	3	0	1
III./ZG 26	Bf 110G	Wunstorf	14	1338	Wunstorf, Ahlhorn, others	1520	1 B-17	2	3	3	0	1
ErprKdo 25	Bf 110G, Me 410A	Achmer		~1345	Achmer	~1600	1 B-17	0	0	0	0	0
Jagddivison 3:												
Stab/JG 1	Fw 190A	Deelen		~1340	Deelen	~1500	0	1	0	0	0	1
I./JG 1	Fw 190A	Deelen, Arnhem		1338	Deelen, Rheine	~1500	2 B-17	4	0	2	0	2
II./JG 1	Fw 190A	Rheine	12	1340	Rheine, Ahlhorn	1545	2 B-17	2	1	2	0	0
III./JG 1	Bf 109G	Volkel		~1340	Volkel, various	1530	6 P-38	4	2	3	0	0
2nd sorties	Bf 109G	Volkel, various		~1545	Volkel	~1700	1 B-17, 1 P-38, 1 P-47	—	—	—	0	0
11./JG 1	Bf 109G	Rheine	2	1340	Rheine	1545	2 B-17	0	1	0	0	0
II./JG 3	Bf 109G	Schiphol		0830	Volkel	0850	transfer	0	0	0	0	0
	Bf 109G	Volkel		1330	Schiphol	1500	2 P-38	2	2	1	0	1
III./JG 26	Bf 109G	München–Gladbach		~1330	München–Gladbach	~1500	1 B-17	3	2	0	0	2
II./JG 27	Bf 109G	Erbenheim	26	1205	Rheine	1245	transfer	0	0	0	0	0
	Bf 109G	Rheine	26	1321	Hesepe	1425	0	0	0	0	0	0
	Bf 109G	Rheine		1445	Wunstorf, Rheine	1600	5 B-17	2	0	1	1	0
Jagddivison 7:												
I./ZG 76	Bf 110G	Ansbach		~1345	Rhein–Main	~1455	0	1	0	0	0	0
II./ZG 76	Bf 110G	Wertheim		1345	Rhein–Main	1455	n/c	0	1	0	0	0
III./ZG 76	Bf 110G	Öttingen		~1345	Öttingen	~1500	0	2	0	4	0	0

2nd TAF, which had recently absorbed the light bombers of No. 2 Group RAF and the tactical elements of RAF Fighter Command. The 55th FG was assigned as the target support unit, but was bounced by III./JG 1 and II./JG 3 while inbound and fought for 20 minutes to extricate itself, losing seven fighters and never coming close to Bremen. The I. Jagdkorps controllers did not realise the advantage this gave them in the target area and directed most of their fighters to attack the incoming bombers near Meppen, where there were still plenty of P-47s. The Jagdgruppen and Zerstörergruppen had to fight through them to make their attacks on the B-17s. The rockets fired by ZG 26 made a strong impression on the bomber crews. II./JG 27 distinguished itself by shooting down five B-17s. The P-47s were not especially successful today, losing 10 of

Luftwaffe defensive activity – 30 November 1943

Unit	Type	Gruppe up			Gruppe down		Claims	Losses				
		Base	No	Time	Base	Time		Dest	Dam	KIA	MIA	WIA
Lw Bfh Mitte												
I. Jagdkorps			~150									
Jagddivison 1:												
1./JG 25	Bf 109G	Delitzsch		0930	Delitzsch	1015	n/c	0	0	0	0	0
Jagddivison 2:												
Stab/JG 11	Fw 190A	Husum		1126	Husum	~1140	n/c	0	0	0	0	0
I./JG 11	Fw 190A	Husum		1126	Husum	1137	n/c	0	0	0	0	0
II./JG 11	Bf 109G	Plantlünne		1126	Plantlünne	1147	n/c	0	0	0	0	0
III./JG 11	Bf 109G	Oldenburg		1130	Oldenburg	~1200	n/c	0	0	0	0	0
Stab/ZG 26	Bf 110G	Wunstorf	1	~1100	Wunstorf	1215	n/c	0	0	0	0	0
I./ZG 26	Bf 110G	Grove	6	1055	Husum	1150	n/c	0	0	0	0	0
II./ZG 26	Me 410A	Hesepe		1120	Hesepe	1250	n/c	0	0	0	0	0
III./ZG 26	Bf 110G	Wunstorf	6	1058	Wunstorf	1215	n/c	0	0	0	0	0
ErprKdo 25	Fw 190A, Bf 110G	Achmer		1104	Achmer	1233	0	2	0	3	0	0
III./NJG 3	Bf 110G	Stade		1135	Stade	~1300	0	0	0	0	0	0
IV./NJG 3	Bf 110G, Ju 88C	Grove		1135	Grove	~1300	0	0	0	0	0	0
Jagddivison 3:												
Stab/JG 1	Fw 190A	Deelen		~1045	Deelen	~1215	0	0	0	0	0	0
I./JG 1	Fw 190A	Deelen, Arnhem		~1045	Deelen, Rheine	~1215	0	3	1	2	0	0
II./JG 1	Fw 190A	Rheine	6	1046	Rheine	~1215	0	0	0	0	0	0
III./JG 1	Bf 109G	Volkel		~1045	Volkel	~1215	n/c	0	0	0	0	0
II./JG 3	Bf 109G	Schiphol	20	0910	Volkel	0920	transfer	0	0	0	0	0
	Bf 109G	Volkel	20	1045	Schiphol	1215	1 B-17 HSS, 3 P-47	0	2	0	0	0
2nd sorties	Bf 109G	Schiphol	10	1230	Schiphol	1300	0	0	0	0	0	0
III./JG 26	Bf 109G	Mönchen–Gladbach		1042	Mönchen–Gladbach	~1200	1 B-17, 1 P-38	3	1	3	0	0
2nd sorties	Bf 109G	Mönchen–Gladbach		~1230	Mönchen–Gladbach	~1400	0	0	1	0	0	1
II./JG 27	Bf 109G	Hopsten		1000	Bönninghardt	1030	transfer	0	0	0	0	0
	Bf 109G	Bönninghardt		1205	Erbenheim	1257	1 B-17	0	0	0	0	0

their number, while 17 B-17s were lost. The RLV force flew 321 sorties and lost 25 killed or missing, 15 wounded and 36 aircraft, many due, at least in part, to the bad weather.

30 November 1943 – vs. 8th Air Force

8th Air Force VIII BC Mission #143: 80 of 381 1st + 3rd BD B-17s and 2nd BD B-24s bomb Solingen, TOT 1155-1158 – lose 3-3-9, claim 1-0-0. VIII FC: 20 P-38s (1 FG) claim 0, lose 1-0-1; 314 P-47s (7 FGs) claim 0-2-1, lose 5-0-1.

The VIII BC dispatched a medium-sized force to bomb Solingen, but most of the combat wings had to abandon the mission when clouds reaching to almost 10,000 metres (30,000 feet) made it impossible to maintain formation. The difficulties were at least as great for the German fighter pilots, most of whom were not instrument-rated. Some units were kept on the ground; others failed to make contact. 440 fighters were ordered up, but only 100 combat sorties were credited. The twin-engine fighters were recalled as soon as it was clear that this was a shallow-penetration raid. The Americans lost six bombers and five fighters. RAF Typhoons flew a supporting raid, bounced I./JG 1 scrambling from Deelen and downed three Fw 190s, killing two pilots. The Luftwaffe's total losses were eight KIA, one WIA and eight fighters.

Luftwaffe defensive activity – 1 December 1943

Unit	Type	Gruppe up			Gruppe down		Claims	Losses				
		Base	No	Time	Base	Time		Dest	Dam	KIA	MIA	WIA
Lw Bfh Mitte												
I. Jagdkorps			*184									
Jagddivison 1:												
III./JG 54	Bf 109G	Schwerin, Gardelegen		1117	Schwerin, Werl, Gardelegen	1230	n/c	1	0	0	0	1
Jagddivison 2:												
Stab/JG 11	Fw 190A	Husum		1106	Husum	~1230	0	0	0	0	0	0
I./JG 11	Fw 190A	Husum		1106	Odendorf, Husum Köln	1242	1 B-24, 1 P-47	0	0	0	0	0
II./JG 11	Bf 109G	Plantlünne		1106	Plantlünne	~1230	2 P-47	2	2	1	0	1
III./JG 11	Bf 109G	Oldenburg		1112	Krefeld, others	1236	1 B-24	0	1	0	0	0
2nd sorties		various		~1230	Oldenburg	1330	1 B-24	0	1	0	0	0
Stab/ZG 26	Bf 110G	Wunstorf		~1105	Wunstorf	~1245	1 B-24	0	0	0	0	0
I./ZG 26	Bf 110G	Grove		1145	Wunstorf	1230	n/c	0	0	0	0	0
II./ZG 26	Me 410A	Hesepe		1105	Hesepe	1320	1 B-17, 1 B-24, 1 P-47	1	2	2	0	3
III./ZG 26	Bf 110G	Wunstorf	10	1106	Köln, Dortmund, Bonn	1220	0	2	0	3	0	1
Jagddivison 3:												
Stab/JG 1	Fw 190A	Deelen		~1100	Deelen	~1230	0	0	0	0	0	0
I./JG 1	Fw 190A	Deelen, Arnhem		~1100	Deelen	~1230	3 B-17, 1 P-47	1	0	0	0	1
II./JG 1	Fw 190A	Rheine	7	1055	Rheine	1250	0	3	0	1	0	1
III./JG 1	Bf 109G	Volkel		~1100	Volkel	~1230	0	0	0	0	0	0
2nd sorties	Bf 109G	Volkel		1330	Volkel	~1430	1 B-17	3	0	1	0	1
II./JG 3	Bf 109G	Schiphol		0900	Volkel	0920	transfer	0	0	0	0	0
	Bf 109G	Volkel		1050	Schiphol	1215	n/c	1	1	0	0	1
I./JG 26	Fw 190A	Grimbergen		1055	Grimbergen, Bonn–Hangelar	1215	1 B-17	0	1	0	0	1
2nd sorties	Fw 190A	Grimbergen		1255	Grimbergen	1335	2 B-17	0	0	0	0	0
III./JG 26	Bf 109G	München–Gladbach		~1100	München–Gladbach	~1230	1 B-17. 1 P-38, 1 P-47	2	2	0	0	2
Jagddivison 7:			32									
II./JG 27	Bf 109G	Erbenheim	15	1134	Erbenheim	1245	2 B-17, 2 P-47	3	0	2	0	1
JG 106	Bf 109	Lachen–Speyerdorf		1207	Lachen–Speyerdorf	1225	n/c	0	0	0	0	0
Luftflotte 3												
II. Jagdkorps			**67									
Jagddivison 4:												
I./JG 3	Bf 109G	Lille–Vendeville		~1100	Lille–Vendeville	~1230	1 P-38, 1 P-47	2	0	2	0	0
Stab/JG 26	Fw 190A	Lille–Nord		~1045	Lille–Nord	~1200	0	0	1	0	0	0
4./JG 26	Fw 190A	Lille–Nord		1042	Lille–Nord	~1200	0	1	0	0	0	1
2nd sorties	Fw 190A	Lille–Nord		~1230	Lille–Nord	~1345	2 B-17	0	0	0	0	0
II./JG 26	Fw 190A	Grevillers, Epinoy		0946	Grevillers, Epinoy	1012	2 Spitfire	2	0	2	0	0
2nd sorties	Fw 190A	Epinoy		1044	Gilze–Rijen	1137	0	0	0	0	0	0
2nd sorties	Fw 190A	Grevillers		1200	Grevillers	1322	1 P-47, 1 Typhoon	0	2	0	0	0
Jagddivison 5:												
Stab/JG 2	Fw 190A	Cormeilles		1130	Brussels area	~1150	transfer	0	0	0	0	0
	Fw 190A	Brussels area		~1220	Cormeilles	~1330	2 P-47	1	0	0	0	0
I./JG 2	Fw 190A	Conches		1130	Brussels area	~1150	transfer	0	0	0	0	0

Luftwaffe defensive activity – 1 December 1943 Continued

Unit	Type	Gruppe up			Gruppe down		Claims	Losses				
		Base	No	Time	Base	Time		Dest	Dam	KIA	MIA	WIA
./JG 2	Fw 190A	Conches		1130	Brussels area	~1150	transfer	0	0	0	0	0
	Fw 190A	Brussels area		~1220	Conches	~1330	0	0	1	0	0	0
II./JG 2	Bf 109G	Creil		1130	Brussels area	~1150	transfer	0	0	0	0	0
	Bf 109G	Brussels area		~1220	Creil	~1330	0	0	0	0	0	0
III./JG 2	Fw 190A	Cormeilles		1130	Brussels area	1150	transfer	0	0	0	0	0
	Fw 190A	Brussels area		~1220	Cormeilles	~1330	1 B-17	2	0	1	0	1

*184 effective sorties flown by I JK vs. incoming 8th AF formations   **67 effective sorties flown by II JK vs. 8th AF formations

30 November 1943 – vs. 15th Air Force
15th Air Force: 18 B-24s target Klagenfurt airfield (Austria) – losses and claims unknown.

The information unearthed for this raid is sparse and conflicting. It is known that I./JG 27 and II./JG 53 were scrambled against it, but failed to find the bombers because of the bad weather.

December 1943

Air activity over the Reich remained at desultory levels through December. The 8th Air Force flew to France on three days and to Germany on seven. All but one of the raids on Germany were to the Ruhr, Emden or Bremen, well within P-47 range. But on the 13th, the bombers penetrated all the way to Kiel in bad weather, escorted over the target by 55th FG P-38s and 354th FG P-51s, the latter unit borrowed from the tactical 9th Air Force. This pioneer mission by the 'Pioneer Mustang Group' was not especially successful, and the presence of the new fighter was apparently not even reported to I. Jagdkorps. However, within a few months the Mustang would become well known to every member of the RLV force.

The serviceability of the RLV units improved during the month owing to the low rate of operations, but GFM Milch's plans for a dramatic expansion of the day defences came to little. The number of fighter units stationed in the Reich actually decreased in December when JG 50 and its less-successful twin, JG 25, were disbanded and II./JG 51 transferred from Munich to Italy to defend the north Italian industrial region, probably as a late replacement for IV./JG 3, which had returned from Italy to Munich in September, without aircraft. Re-equipment of IV./JG 3 went slowly at first, but was rushed to completion when it was ordered to replace II./JG 3 as a JD 3 front-line unit. The latter Gruppe was at Schiphol, where it had been pounded repeatedly by Allied tactical units. On the 13th, this Gruppe was surprised on the ground by 9th Air Force B 26s and nearly destroyed. Its shattered remnants joined III./JG 1 at Volkel, while IV./JG 3 prepared to move to Grimbergen, which was slightly farther from the North Sea coast than Schiphol.

The orders resulting in another, somewhat surprising reinforcement have not been traced. On 16 December, apparently without advance notice, the Kommandeur of I./JG 300 was ordered to lead his night Gruppe in an interception of a VIII BC day raid on Bremen after the Gruppe had been on readiness all of the previous night. Eight Bf 109s got off the ground and were led to the B-17 armada between Bremen and Oldenburg. Their rear attack claimed one bomber, but all eight fighters were damaged to some degree; one pilot was killed, and one was injured. The experiment was judged a success. Most of the *Wilde Sau* Gruppen had by now received their own aircraft and could operate independently of their former host Gruppen. These night Gruppen would soon find themselves called on regularly to fly day missions. Their success rate at night had dropped with winter, but their blind-flying skills were highhly useful for bad-weather day missions.

1 December
8th Air Force VIII BC Mission #145: 281 of 299 1st BD B-17s + 2nd BD B-24s bomb Solingen and Leverkusen, TOT 1159-1212 – lose 24-3-85, claim 4-5-5. VIII FC: 42 P-38s (1 FG) claim 0, lose 2-1-0; 374 P-47s (7 FGs) claim 20-4-7, lose 7-2-3.

The VIII BC planned a return trip to Solingen, with an early departure time to take advantage of rare morning sunshine over England. The German controllers guessed correctly that this would be a shallow penetration raid, probably to the Ruhr, and brought all units to readiness. The II. Jagdkorps fighters in the western occupied zone were well positioned to attack the bombers along their entire route. These fighters had to fight off or evade early raids on their airfields by 9th AF B 26s, but JG 26 was then able to send all of its fighters north in time to attack the incoming bombers, while JG 2 staged northeast, timed to attack the bombers on their withdrawal. Cloud cover forced the 3rd BD to abandon its mission, while the 1st BD bombed Solingen and targets of opportunity through solid clouds. The bomber formations became strung out, stretching the available escort past its limit. 283 Luftwaffe fighters got off the ground; they found it hard to stay together in the clouds, but flew the most successful defensive mission in over a month, downing 27 bombers and 12 escorts for the loss of 15 KIA, 16 WIA and 27 aircraft. The II./JG 26 casualties include two losses to RAF Spitfires escorting the early medium bomber raids. The RAF also provided part of the reception cover for the returning bombers and lost one Typhoon to II./JG 26 while performing that task, although the claim was not confirmed.

COMBAT REPORT[8]
1 December 1943

One Boeing B-17 shot down from 6,000–7,000 metres at 1220 hours, 20–30 km WSW of Aachen

I scrambled with the 6. Staffel in a Bf 109G-6 with three MG 151/20s and two MG 131s [i.e., a 'gunboat']. An air battle with several waves of Boeing bombers flying west with English escorts developed east of Aachen at 6,000–7,000 metres. During my second attack from the low rear on the left Boeing of the left rear Kette of the last Pulk, I obtained hits in the fuselage and wing. After pulling my aircraft up, I observed that the machine I had attacked broke suddenly from formation and dove away to the left. I attacked this Boeing again from the low rear and fired my last ammunition with visible effect. Since I was receiving no defensive fire, I flew about 500 metres from it as it continued to pull to the left. When the Boeing reached 3,000 metres, I was suddenly attacked from my high rear by three or four Thunderbolts. Due to canopy icing I had seen these too late. I banked away immediately and entered some clouds. At about 2,000 metres, from right above the clouds, I received hits in my engine and cockpit. I was flying in the clouds with my aircraft on fire, and it was time to bail out.

As I was under attack by the escorts, I could not observe the crash of my Boeing, which was beneath an unbroken cloud deck. It was approximately 20–30 km WSW of Aachen, in the area of Eupen–Malmedy. I landed by parachute near Eupen, in the direction of Malmedy. A Canadian landed about 5–7 km from me at the same time. He was also wounded and went with me to the Aachen hospital in the same ambulance. According to him, the crew of his shot-

Luftwaffe defensive activity – 5 December 1943

Unit	Type	Gruppe up			Gruppe down		Claims	Losses				
		Base	No	Time	Base	Time		Dest	Dam	KIA	MIA	WIA
Luftflotte 3												
II. Jagdkorps			84									
Jagddivison 5:												
I./JG 2	Fw 190A	Conches?		~1330	Conches?	~1500	2 B-17	0	0	0	0	0
Jafü Bretagne:												
JGr Ost	Bf 109G,	Biarritz, Laleu,		~1200	Biarritz, Laleu,	~1300	0	2	1	0	0	2
	Fw 190A	Bergerac			Bergerac							
JGr West	Bf 109F	St. Jean d'Angély		1145	Cazaux	1215	n/c	0	0	0	0	0
	Bf 109G,	Biarritz, Cazaux,		1215	Bordeaux, Biarritz,	1305	2 B-17	2	0	0	0	1
	Fw 190A	Corme Ecluse			Cazaux,							
					Corme Ecluse							

down Boeing received orders to bail out while just above the clouds. The time and place agree with my claim, and I assume that he was a member of the crew of my shot-down bomber. The crash took place at about 1220 hours.

Uffz. Karl Schmitz
6./JG 27

5 December

8th Air Force VIII BC Mission #149: 0 of 216 1st BD B-17s bomb W France, Paris a/fs – lose 0-1-1, claim 0; 2 of 96 2nd BD B-24s bomb Cognac a/f – lose 1-0-7, claim 0; 1 of 235 3rd BD B-17s bomb Bordeaux a/f – lose 8-0-19, claim 12-5-5. VIII FC: 34 P 38s (1 FG) claim 0, lose 0; 266 P-47s (7 FGs) claim 0, lose 1-0-0; 36 P-51s (1 FG) claim 0, lose 0.

The VIII BC mission to airfields in western France and the Paris region was disrupted badly by the weather; only three of the 548 bombers dispatched dropped

their bombs. Ten bombers were lost or scrapped upon return. The two operational training Gruppen attacked in the Bordeaux target area and claimed two B-17s for the loss of two WIA and four fighters. I./JG 2 attacked the bombers on their return flight and claimed 2 B17s without loss.

11 December

8th Air Force VIII BC Mission #151: 523 of 583 B-17s + B-24s (all BDs) bomb Emden, TOT 1220-1312 – lose 17-1-138, claim 86-22-23. 31 VIII FC P-38s (1 FG) claim 0, lose 0; 313 VIII FC P-47s (7 FGs) claim 21-0-7, lose 3-1-3; 36 IX Fighter Command (IX FC) P-51s (1 FG) claim 0, lose 1-1-0.

The VIII BC sent a large force of B-17s and B-24s to Emden. The raid is noteworthy as the first long-range escort mission for the P-51 Mustang-equipped 354th FG, which was a unit of the tactical 9th AF, as were all of the P-51 groups *en route* to the theatre. The 354th FG would be loaned to VIII FC until the latter could

---

UNIT WAR DIARY[9]
11 December 1943

The Gruppe received an order to scramble against an incoming enemy formation. At 1055 hours, 17 Bf 110s took off from Wunstorf, together with 23 Bf 110s of I./ZG 26. The formation assembled at 7,000 metres over the Dummer See. It met its fighter protection at 1120 hours. At 1130 hours, the Gruppe was ordered by Y-Führung to take a course over Wilhelmshaven–Spiekeroog to PQ AO-3. I./ZG 26 was leading.

The enemy was sighted at 1210 hours: 7 *Pulks* of Fortresses and Liberators, flying from PQ UO toward Wesermünde. The Fortresses flew in an arrow formation, staggered in altitude.

The Gruppe attacked the 4th Pulk from the rear and fired WGr 21 rockets over Wangerooge from 1,000 metres. Smoke bursts were in good position. After firing its rockets, the Gruppe, which was under attack by enemy fighters, split up. The enemy formation penetrated as far as Oldenburg and was attacked individually by the Gruppe with gunfire as far as Emden.

Very strong escort by Thunderbolts and Spitfires [Mustangs – DC], which flew above and below the formation.

Successes (III./ZG 26):	Fw. Scherkenbeck	2 B-17s shot down
	Fw. Röder	1 Spitfire shot down
	Uffz. Schubert	1 P-47 shot down
Losses (I./ZG 26):	Uffz. Bäcker	shot down; no report (2 MIA)
	Lt. Axtern	shot down; crew bails out OK
	crew unreported	belly-lands in flames; crew OK
Losses (III./ZG 26)	Uffz. Berthold	shot down; pilot KIA; gunner WIA
	Uffz. Neumann	shot down; crew KIA
	other	4 shot down; 5 WIA, 3 MIA

Major Johann Kogler, Gruppenkommandeur
III./ZG 26

Luftwaffe defensive activity – 11 December 1943

Unit	Type	Gruppe up			Gruppe down		Claims	Losses				
		Base	No	Time	Base	Time		Dest	Dam	KIA	MIA	WIA
Lw Bfh Mitte												
I. Jagdkorps			307									
Jagddivision 1:												
JG 25?	Bf 109G	Gardelegen		~1100	Gardelegen	~1230	n/c	0	0	0	0	0
III./JG 54	Bf 109G	Ludwigslust		~1100	Ludwigslust	~1230	n/c	0	0	0	0	0
IV./NJG 5	Bf 110G	Brandis		1105	Brandis	1335	n/c	0	0	0	0	0
Jagddivison 2:												
Stab/JG 11	Fw 190A	Husum		1100	Husum	~1230	1 B-17	0	0	0	0	0
I./JG 11	Fw 190A	Husum		1100	Wittmundhafen, others	1245	2 B-17, 1 B-24	2	1	1	0	1
II./JG 11	Bf 109G	Plantlünne		1102	Katwijk?, others	1309	2 P-47	3	2	1	0	1
III./JG 11	Bf 109G	Oldenburg		1100	Oldenburg	~1200	0	0	0	0	0	0
2nd sorties	Bf 109G	Oldenburg		1215	Oldenburg	~1330	2 B-17, 1 B-24, 1 B-17 HSS, 1 P-47	1	0	1	0	0
Stab/ZG 26?	Bf 110G	Wunstorf		~1055	Wunstorf	~1320	0	0	0	0	0	0
I./ZG 26	Bf 110G	Wunstorf	23	1055	Wunstorf, Wesermünde, Wilhelmshaven	1320	0	3	0	1	0	2
II./ZG 26	Me 410A	Hesepe		1115	Hesepe	1322	3 B-17	0	2	0	0	0
III./ZG 26	Bf 110G	Wunstorf	17	1055	Wunstorf, others	1320	0	5	1	6	0	6
ErprKdo 25	Fw 190A	Achmer		~1100	Achmer	~1230	0	0	2	0	0	1
I./NJG 3	Ju 88C	Grove		1210	Grove	1425	0	0	0	0	0	0
III./NJG 3	Bf 110G	Stade		1216	Stade	1410	0	0	0	0	0	0
IV./NJG 3	Bf 110G	Grove		1210	Grove	1425	0	0	0	0	0	0
Jagddivison 3:												
Stab/JG 1?	Fw 190A	Oldenburg		~1145	Oldenburg	~1300	0	0	0	0	0	0
I./JG 1	Fw 190A	Dortmund		0855	Rheine	0922	transfer	0	0	0	0	0
	Fw 190A	Rheine, Oldenburg		1122	Wittmundhaven, others	1316	3 B-17	1	0	0	0	0
II./JG 1	Fw 190A	Rheine	10	1145	Rheine	~1300	2 B-17	0	0	0	0	0
III./JG 1	Bf 109G	Volkel		~1145	Volkel	~1300	0	2	0	0	0	0
II./JG 3	Bf 109G	Schiphol		~0900	Volkel	~0920	transfer	0	0	0	0	0
	Bf 109G	Volkel		~1145	Schiphol	~1300	0	1	1	1	0	0
III./JG 26	Bf 109G	München–Gladbach		1050	Hage, others	1235	0	0	0	0	0	0
Jagddivison 7:			28									
II./JG 27	Bf 109G	Erbenheim		~1200	Erbenheim	~1330	1 B-17 HSS	3	0	1	1	1

get its own Mustang units. The Mustang's range was at least as great as that of the P-38 Lightning, which was the Allies' long-range escort fighter of choice, but the Lightning was proving to be vulnerable to the more nimble Bf 109s and Fw 190s and was also having great difficulty coping with the bad weather and low temperatures at high altitude that were typical of winter in the ETO. II. Jagdkorps kept its fighters on the ground. I. Jagdkorps sortied 335 fighters, with modest success. Eighteen bombers and six escorts were downed for the loss of 13 KIA and MIA, 12 WIA and 21 aircraft.

13 December

8th Air Force VIII BC Mission #154: 349 of 393 B-17s + B-24s (all BDs) bomb Kiel, TOT 1245-1317 – lose 3-0-105, claim 7-3-14; 171 of 182 1st BD B-17s bomb Bremen 1159-1206 – lose 0-1-30, claim 0; 114 of 123 3rd BD B-17s bomb Hamburg TOT 1300-1305 – lose 2-1-35, claim 0-0-2. 31 VIII FC P 38s (1 FG) claim 1-0-1, lose 0-1-1; 322 VIII FC P-47s (6 FGs) claim 0, lose 1-1-0; 41 IX FC P-51s (1 FG) claim 0, lose 1-0-0.

The 8th AF put 1,000 fighters and bombers in the air for

Luftwaffe defensive activity – 13 December 1943

Unit	Type	Gruppe up			Gruppe down		Claims	Losses				
		Base	No	Time	Base	Time		Dest	Dam	KIA	MIA	WIA
Lw Bfh Mitte												
I. Jagdkorps			*47									
Jagddivision 2:												
I./NJG 3	Ju 88C	Vechta		1221	Vechta	~1430	1 B-17	1	0	3	0	0
II./NJG 3	Ju 88C	Schleswig		1221	Schleswig	~1430	0	2	2	4	0	2
III./NJG 3	Bf 110G	Stade		1221	Stade	~1430	0	1	0	0	1	1
IV./NJG 3	Ju 88C	Grove, Nordholz		1221	Grove, Nordholz	~1430	1 B-17, 1 B-24	1	0	0	0	3
Jagddivision 3:												
I./JG 1	Fw 190A	Dormund		~1230	Dortmund	~1330	n/c	0	0	0	0	0
II./JG 1	Fw 190A	Rheine	7	~1230	Rheine	~1330	n/c	0	0	0	0	0
11./JG 1	Bf 109G	Rheine		~1230	Rheine	~1330	n/c	0	1	0	0	0
III./JG 1	Bf 109G	Volkel		1228	Volkel	~1330	n/c	0	1	0	0	0
III./JG 26	Bf 109G	München–Gladbach		~1230	München–Gladbach	~1330	n/c	0	1	0	0	0
III./NJG 1	Bf 110G	Twente		~1230	Twente	~1330	n/c	0	1	0	0	1

*47 sorties stated as total by I. Jagdkorps KTB

Luftwaffe defensive activity – 15 December 1943

Unit	Type	Gruppe up			Gruppe down		Claims	Losses				
		Base	No	Time	Base	Time		Dest	Dam	KIA	MIA	WIA
Luftflotte 2												
Jafü Oberitalien:			28									
III./JG 53	Bf 109G	Reggio Emilia	28	1145	Reggio Emilia	1300	0	0	0	0	0	0

the first time and bombed Bremen and Kiel against only 47 night fighters, which claimed three bombers while losing eight KIA or MIA, seven WIA and five aircraft. Some day fighters were scrambled but could find nothing in the weather and were recalled. The IX FC P-51 group joined the lone P-38 group for target support, but saw little action. II./JG 3, one of JD 3's forward Gruppen, was bombed out of its Schiphol field by B-26s and withdrew to Rothenburg, near Bremen, to rebuild. During its four months in the RLV, the unit had lost 23 pilots killed, including two Gruppenkommandeure and two Staffelkapitäne. In contrast, its previous tour on the Eastern Front had lasted 15 months and had cost the Gruppe 29 pilots killed or missing; these earlier casualties had included no formation leaders.

15 December

15th Air Force: 48 B-17s bomb Innsbruck-Main rail yards – lose 1. Escort claims 0, probably loses 0.

Part of the 15th AF bomber force, now based in Italy, targeted Innsbruck, but few details of the raid are known. The principal defenders in Austria, I./JG 27 and II./JG 53, did not respond. Apparently, the only Gruppe to intercept was III./JG 53, flying from Reggio Emilia in north Italy. The ULTRA code-breaking organisation intercepted and decoded its combat report: its 28 Bf 109s contacted the small heavy bomber formation over Ravenna. The American fighter protection was 'very good'; combat with the escort was 'unsuccessful', and the Messerschmitt pilots disengaged without loss to either side.

16 December

8th Air Force VIII BC Mission #156: 535 of 631 B-17s + B-24s (all BDs) bomb Bremen, TOT 1309-1322 – lose 10-4-155, claim 18-11-11. 31 VIII FC P-38s (1 FG) claim 0, lose 0-1-1; 131 VIII FC P-47s (3 FGs) claim 0, lose 1-0-0; 39 IX FC P-51s (1 FG) claim 0, lose 1-1-1.

Luftwaffe defensive activity – 16 December 1943

Unit	Type	Gruppe up			Gruppe down		Claims	Losses				
		Base	No	Time	Base	Time		Dest	Dam	KIA	MIA	WIA
Lw Bfh Mitte												
I. Jagdkorps			91									
Jagddivison 1:												
I./NJG 2	Ju 88R	Kassel–Rothwesten		~1200	Kassel–Rothwesten	~1400	0	1	0	3	0	0
Jagddivison 2:												
Stab/JG 11	Fw 190A	Husum		~1200	Husum	~1300	n/c	0	0	0	0	0
I./JG 11	Fw 190A	Husum		~1200	Husum	~1300	n/c	0	0	0	0	0
II./JG 11	Bf 109G	Plantlünne		1205	Plantlünne	1311	n/c	0	0	0	0	0
2nd sorties		Plantlünne		~1330	Plantlünne	1430	0	0	1	0	0	0
III./JG 11	Bf 109G	Oldenburg		~1200	Oldenburg	~1300	n/c	0	0	0	0	0
2nd sorties		Oldenburg		~1330	Oldenburg	~1430	0	1	0	0	0	1
Jagddivison 3:												
Stab/JG 1	Fw 190A	Dortmund		~1200	Dortmund	~1300	0	0	0	0	0	0
I./JG 1	Fw 190A	Dortmund		~1200	Dortmund	~1300	0	0	0	0	0	0
2nd sorties	Fw 190A	Dortmund		1326	Deelen, Dortmund	1437	9 B-17	1	2	0	0	2
II./JG 1	Fw 190A	Rheine	5	1200	Rheine	~1300	0	0	0	0	0	0
III./JG 1	Bf 109G	Volkel		~1200	Volkel	1340	n/c	0	0	0	0	0
II./JG 3	Bf 109G	Volkel		1340	Volkel	1445	n/c	0	1	0	0	0
III./JG 26	Bf 109G	München–Gladbach		~1230	München–Gladbach	~1400	0	1	0	0	0	1
I./JG 300	Bf 109G	Bonn–Hangelar	8	1220	Bonn–Hangelar	~1330	1 B-17	4	4	1	0	1

The VIII BC sent another full-strength bad-weather mission to Bremen. Of the I. Jagdkorps day fighter units, only JG 1 and JG 11 were ordered to intercept in strength, but several twin-engine night fighters were scrambled, and I./JG 300, a *Wilde Sau* single-engine night fighter unit, was also ordered up on short notice and claimed one B-17 for the loss of one pilot KIA and one WIA. One Ju 88 night fighter was shot down, and its crew of three was killed. I. Jagdkorps aircrews flew a total of 109 sorties. The day fighters lost no killed, four injured and three aircraft. I./JG 1 was the only successful day fighter unit: its performance was outstanding, resulting in claims for 13 B-17s. The Americans lost 14 bombers and four escorts.

19 December

15th Air Force: 113 of 130 B-17s + B-24s bomb Innsbruck–Main (A), Augsburg (G) – lose 6 B-17s, 5 B-24s. Apparently no escort.

The 15th AF split its small force: the B-17 wing targeted the Innsbruck rail yards, while the B-24s attacked the important Messerschmitt facilities at Augsburg. This was the first raid on Germany proper by the 15th and brought the bombers within range of JD 7, which had seen little action since the second raid on Schweinfurt. The two Bf 109 Gruppen and one Bf 110 Gruppe in Austria were not used, but the four Bf 109 Gruppen and two Bf 110 Gruppen in southern Germany were scrambled, flying 165 sorties; most made contact with the bombers, which were apparently unescorted. II./JG 51 was also up from its new base in northern Italy and reached the B-24s. Twenty-four bombers were claimed in total, at the cost of 10 KIA or MIA, four WIA and 12 aircraft to the bomber gunners or accidents.

20 December

8th Air Force VIII BC Mission #159: 472 of 546 B-17s + B-24s (all BDs) bomb Bremen, TOT 1142-1214 – lose 27-3-247, claim 21-14-23. 26 VIII FC P-38s (1 FG) claim 0, lose 0; 418 VIII FC P-47s (8 FGs) claim 13-2-2, lose 2-1-5; 47 IX FC P-51s (1 FG) claim 6-1-7, lose 4-0-0.

The VIII BC flew its third mission to Bremen in eight

Luftwaffe defensive activity – 19 December 1943

Unit	Type	Gruppe up			Gruppe down		Claims	Losses				
		Base	No	Time	Base	Time		Dest	Dam	KIA	MIA	WIA
Lw Bfh Mitte												
Jagddivision 7:			165									
III./JG 3	Bf 109G	Bad Wörishofen	30	1056	Bad Wörishofen	1255	8 B-17	1	1	0	0	0
IV./JG 3	Bf 109G	Neubiberg		1100	Neubiberg	1235	4 B-24	2	0	1	0	1
I./JG 4	Bf 109G	Bad Wörishofen	20	1108	Bad Wörishofen	~1230	n/c	1	0	0	0	1
II./JG 27	Bf 109G	Erbenheim		1047	Erbenheim	1237	2 B-17, 2 B-17 HSS	1	1	0	1	0
I./ZG 76	Bf 110G	Ansbach		~1115	Ansbach	~1245	7 B-24	4	1	6	0	1
II./ZG 76	Bf 110G	Wertheim		1115	Neubiberg	1245	0	1	1	2	0	1
I./ZG 101	Bf 110	Memmingen		~1115	Memmingen	~1300	0	0	0	0	0	0
II./ZG 101	Bf 110	Bad Aibling		1110	Bad Aibling	1302	0	0	0	0	0	0
ISS Augsburg	Bf 109G	Augsburg		~1115	Augsburg	~1215	0	0	0	0	0	0
Luftflotte 2												
Jafü Oberitalien:												
II./JG 51	Bf 109G	Udine		1130	Udine	~1230	1 B-24	2	1	0	0	1

days. Weather conditions were the best they had been all month: visibility at altitude was greater than 10 miles. The three bomb divisions attacked in a single stream, escorted by a new high of 10 fighter groups. I. Jagdkorps scrambled 346 aircraft from 11 Jagdgruppen, six Zerstörergruppen and all five twin-engine night fighter Geschwader in the Reich – evidence that I. Jagdkorps expected a deep-penetration raid, rather than one that could be fully escorted in strength. The night fighters were all ordered to land without making contact. The 220 day fighters credited with sorties were fairly effective at finding holes in the escort coverage; the Americans lost 30 bombers and seven escorts, while the Germans lost 19 KIA, nine WIA and 28 aircraft. The II. Jagdkorps fighters were fully occupied by the tactical raiders, and Schmid did not request their help.

22 December

8th Air Force VIII BC Mission #161: 234 of 346 1st BD B-17s + 2nd BD B-24s bomb Osnabrück, TOT 1356-1434 – lose 17-3-32, claim 18-8-6; 200 of 228 3rd BD B-17s bomb Münster, TOT 1353-1417 – lose 5-1-29, claim 4-0-0. 26 VIII FC P-38s (1 FG) claim 0, lose 2-0-0; 418 VIII FC P-47s (8 FGs) claim 15-1-6, lose 2-0-1; 47 IX FC P-51s (1 FG) claim 0, lose 0.

The VIII BC sent its B-17s and B-24s to Münster and Osnabrück despite the return of bad visibility over the target areas. The I. Jagdkorps defenders were hampered by the weather, but were credited with 194

Obfw. Eugen-Ludwig Zweigart sits on the cockpit sill of his III./JG 54 Bf 109G-4 in late 1943. The plane carries the nickname 'Tarzan'. *(Prien)*

Luftwaffe defensive activity – 20 December 1943

Unit	Type	Gruppe up Base	No	Time	Gruppe down Base	Time	Claims	Dest	Dam	KIA	MIA	WIA
Lw Bfh Mitte												
I. Jagdkorps			202									
Jagddivision 1:												
1./JG 25	Bf 109G	Delitzsch		1300	Döberitz	1402	n/c	0	0	0	0	0
III./JG 54	Bf 109G	Ludwigslust		1119	Ludwigslust	~1230	5 B-17, 1 P-47, 1 P-51	3	3	0	0	3
NJG 2	Ju 88C,R	Parchim, others		~1100	Parchim, others	~1250	n/c	0	0	0	0	0
NJG 5	Bf 110G	Stendal, others		1139	Stendal, others	1252	n/c	0	0	0	0	0
VschsVbd ObdL	Ju 88A	Berlin		?	Berlin	?	0	1	0	0	3	0
Jagddivison 2:												
Stab/JG 11	Fw 190A	Husum		~1100	Wunstorf	1245	0	3	0	1	0	1
II./JG 11	Bf 109G	Wunstorf		1103	Wunstorf	1245	1 P-38, 1 P-51	4	1	2	0	0
III./JG 11	Bf 109G	Oldenburg		1103	Oldenburg	~1245	3 B-17, 1 B-24	1	1	1	0	0
I./ZG 26	Bf 110G	Volkenröde		1100	Volkenröde, Wittmund	1330	1 B-17, 1 B-24	5	2	9	0	2
II./ZG 26	Me 410A	Hildesheim		1102	Hildesheim	1245	1 B-17	3	0	0	2	0
III./ZG 26	Bf 110G	Wunstorf	12	1055	Wunstorf, Zwischenahn	1230	1 B-17	1	0	1	0	0
I./ZG 76	Bf 110G	Wunstorf	4	1100	Wunstorf	1230	0	0	0	0	0	0
II./ZG 76	Bf 110G	Wunstorf	6	1100	Wunstorf	1230	0	1	0	2	0	0
NJG 3	Bf 110G	Grove, others		~1100	Grove, others	~1230	n/c	0	0	0	0	0
ErprKdo 25	Fw 190A, Bf 110G	Achmer		~1100	Achmer	~1300	1 B-17	1	0	0	0	1
Jagddivison 3:												
Stab/JG 1	Fw 190A	Dortmund		~1110	Dortmund	~1230	0	0	0	0	0	0
I./JG 1	Fw 190A	Dortmund		0846	Rheine	0910	transfer	0	0	0	0	0
	Fw 190A	Rheine		1110	Marx, others	1225	2 B 17	3	0	1	0	1
II./JG 1	Fw 190A	Rheine	12	1130	Rheine	~1230	0	0	0	0	0	0
III./JG 1	Bf 109G	Volkel		1040	Volkel	~1200	0	0	0	0	0	0
11./JG 1	Bf 109G	Rheine	2	1130	Rheine	~1230	1 B-17	1	0	0	0	0
II./JG 3	Bf 109G	Volkel		~1110	Volkel	~1230	0	0	1	0	0	0
III./JG 26	Bf 109G	München–Gladbach		~1110	München–Gladbach	~1230	5 B-17	0	0	0	0	0
2nd sorties	Bf 109G	München–Gladbach		~1245	München–Gladbach	~1400	0	0	0	0	0	0
NJG 1	Bf 110G	Venlo, others		~1115	Venlo, others	~1245	n/c	0	0	0	0	0
Erla Flzg.Werke	Do 217E	Antwerp		?	Antwerp	?	0	1	0	2	0	1
Jagddivison 7:												
II./JG 27	Bf 110G	Erbenheim		~1130	Erbenheim	~1315	1 B-17, 2 B-24	0	0	0	0	0
I./ZG 76	Bf 110G	Ansbach	4	~1000	Wunstorf	~1030	Transfer	0	0	0	0	0
II./ZG 76	Bf 110G	Frankfurt–Eschborn	6	~1000	Wunstorf	~1030	Transfer	0	0	0	0	0
III./ZG 76	Bf 110G	Frankfurt–Eschborn	3	1017	Wunstorf	1230	0	0	0	0	0	0
NJG 6	Bf 110G	Mainz–Finthen, others		1030	Vechta, Bonn, others	1130	n/c	0	0	0	0	0

Luftwaffe defensive activity – 22 December 1943

Unit	Type	Gruppe up			Gruppe down		Claims	Losses				
		Base	No	Time	Base	Time		Dest	Dam	KIA	MIA	WIA
Lw Bfh Mitte												
I. Jagdkorps			194									
Jagddivision 1:												
1./JG 25	Bf 109G	Delitzsch		~1315	Delitzsch	~1445	0	0	0	0	0	0
III./JG 54	Bf 109G	Ludwigslust		~1315	Ludwigslust	~1445	1 B-24, 2 P-47	4	0	1	0	2
Jagddivison 2:												
Stab/JG 11	Fw 190A	Husum		~1315	Wunstorf	~1445	0	0	1	0	0	0
II./JG 11	Fw 190A	Wunstorf		1321	Vechta, others	1500	0	1	0	1	0	0
III./JG 11	Bf 109G	Oldenburg		1315	Oldenburg	1438	1 B-24	1	1	0	0	1
Stab./ZG 26	Bf 110G	Völkenrode		~1315	Völkenrode	~1600	0	0	1	0	0	0
I./ZG 26	Bf 110G	Völkenrode		1320	Völkenrode, Diepholz	1545	6 B-24	1	1	1	0	0
II./ZG 26	Me 410A	Hildesheim		~1315	Hildesheim	~1600	2 B-24	2	1	3	0	1
III./ZG 26	Bf 110G	Wunstorf	11	1317	Wunstorf, others	1635	1 B-17, 1 B-24	4	1	3	0	4
NJG 3	Bf 110G	Grove, others	10	~1315	Grove, others	~1600	0	0	0	0	0	0
Jagddivison 3:												
Stab/JG 1	Fw 190A	Dortmund		~1310	Dortmund?	~1445	0	0	0	0	0	0
I./JG 1	Fw 190A	Dortmund		1315	Vörden, others	1440	2 B-17, 1 B-24, 1 P-38	0	0	0	0	0
2nd sorties	Fw 190A	Dortmund		~1530	Dortmund	~1630	0	0	0	0	0	0
II./JG 1	Fw 190A	Rheine	12	1310	Rheine	~1445	0	3	0	1	0	0
III./JG 1	Bf 109G	Volkel		1312	Volkel	~1445	1 P-38	1	0	0	0	0
II./JG 3	Bf 109G	Volkel		1310	Volkel	~1445	0	0	0	0	0	0
III./JG 26	Bf 109G	München–Gladbach		~1310	München–Gladbach	~1445	1 B-17	6	0	5	0	1
Jagddivison 7:			32									
II./JG 27	Bf 109G	Erbenheim		~1315	Erbenheim	~1445	0	0	0	0	0	0
III./JG 300	Bf 109G	Erbenheim		~1315	Erbenheim	~1445	0	2	0	1	0	0
NJG 6	Bf 110G	Mainz–Finthen, others		~1315	Bonn, others	~1600	0	0	0	0	0	0
Luftflotte 3												
II. Jagdkorps												
Jagddivision 4:												
I./JG 3	Bf 109G	Lille–Vendeville	19	1334	Volkel	~1400	transfer	0	0	0	0	0
Stab/JG 26	Fw 190A	Lille–Nord	2	1415	Rheine	~1430	transfer	0	0	0	0	0
I./JG 26	Fw 190A	Florennes	15	1403	Rheine	~1420	transfer	0	0	0	0	0
4./JG 26	Fw 190A	Lille–Nord	4	1415	Rheine	~1430	transfer	0	0	0	0	0
II./JG 26	Fw 190A	Epinoy	21	1330	Leeuwarden	~1400	transfer	0	0	0	0	0
Jagddivision 5:												
III./JG 2	Fw 190A	Cormeilles	15	1316	Rheine	~1345	transfer	0	0	0	0	0

sorties. III./JG 26 and III./JG 54, each flying alone, were overwhelmed by American escorts and lost 10 Messerschmitts for little return. The Zerstörer were escorted by II./JG 11 and were especially successful. Nine of their claims for B-24s, and one for a B-17, were confirmed, for the loss of seven aircrewmen KIA, five Bf 110s and two Me 410s. The II. Jagdkorps controllers could not ignore the heavy bombers nearby, despite the presence of 711 Allied tactical aircraft over northern France, and there is Allied radio evidence that parts of I./JG 26, II./JG 26 and I./JG 3 were sent north to refuel and wait for the withdrawing bombers, but JD 3 apparently never ordered them to scramble. American losses totaled 26 bombers and seven escorts; I. Jagdkorps lost a total of 16 KIA, nine WIA and 25 aircraft.

24 December

8th Air Force VIII BC Mission #164: 670 of 722 B-17s + B-24s (all BDs) bomb Pas de Calais V-weapons sites, TOT 1330-1510 – lose 0-2-85, claim 0. 541 VIII FC fighters claim 0, lose 0-0-2.

A full-strength raid by the VIII BC on the V-weapons sites under construction on the Pas de Calais drew no reaction from the Luftwaffe. The targets were too close to England for the defenders to form up for attacks, and the Allied fighters, both tactical and strategic, were numerous enough both to escort the bombers closely and swarm over the II. Jagdkorps airfields.

Luftwaffe defensive activity – 30 December 1943

Unit	Type	Gruppe up			Gruppe down		Claims	Losses (totals for day)				
		Base	No	Time	Base	Time		Dest	Dam	KIA	MIA	WIA
Lw Bfh Mitte												
I. Jagdkorps			128									
Jagddivison 2:												
II./JG 11	Bf 109G	Wunstorf		1151	Wunstorf	1310	n/c	0	0	0	0	0
III./JG 11	Bf 109G	Oldenburg		~1130	Oldenburg	~1300	n/c	0	1	0	0	0
I./ZG 26	Bf 110G	Völkenrode		1145	Völkenrode	1400	n/c	0	0	0	0	0
II./ZG 26	Me 410A	Hildesheim		~1130	Hildesheim	~1315	n/c	0	0	0	0	0
III./ZG 26	Bf 110G	Wunstorf	11	1135	Wunstorf	1315	n/c	0	0	0	0	0
ErprKdo 25	Fw 190G	Vörden		~1130	Vörden	~1300	n/c	0	2	1	0	0
Jagddivison 7:												
Eins/JG 106	Bf 109F	Lachen–Speyerdorf		~1130	Lachen–Speyerdorf	~1300	0	1	0	1	0	0
I./ZG 101	Bf 110	Memmingen		~1130	Memmingen	~1330	0	0	0	0	0	0
II./ZG 101	Bf 110	Bad Aibling		~1130	Bad Aibling	~1330	0	0	0	0	0	0
Luftflotte 3												
II. Jagdkorps			273									
Jagddivison 4:												
I./JG 3	Bf 109G	Lille–Vendeville		1047	Lille–Vendeville	~1200	2 P-47	3	0	3	0	0
I./JG 26	Fw 190A	Florennes		1245	Charleville	1422	2 B-17	0	1	0	0	1
4./JG 26	Fw 190A	Wevelghem		1046	Wevelghem	~1200	1 B-17, 1 P-47	0	0	0	0	0
2nd sorties	Fw 190A	Wevelghem		1250	Wevelghem	~1400	0	0	0	0	0	0
3rd sorties	Fw 190A	Wevelghem		1412	Wevelghem	~1500	1 P-47	0	0	0	0	0
II./JG 26	Fw 190A	Grevillers		1045	Grevillers	1143	1 B-24	0	0	0	0	0
2nd sorties	Fw 190A	Grevillers		1251	Grevillers, Laon	1340	0	0	0	0	0	0
3rd sorties	Fw 190A	Grevillers		~1400	Grevillers	1550	2 B-17, 2 P-47	1	0	0	0	1
I./NJG 4	Bf 110G	Florennes		~1045	Florennes	~1300	0	2	1	3	0	2
III./NJG 4	Bf 110G	Juvincourt		~1045	Juvincourt	~1300	1 B-24	1	0	0	0	2
5.(F)/123	Bf 109G	Monchy–Breton		~1230	Monchy–Breton	~1400	1 B-24	0	0	0	0	0
Jagddivison 5:												
Stab/JG 2	Fw 190A	Cormeilles		1250	Cormeilles	~1400	0	0	0	0	0	0
I./JG 2?	Fw 190A	Conches		1250	Conches	~1400	0	0	0	0	0	0
II./JG 2	Bf 109G	Creil		~1100	Montdidier, Creil	~1230	0	0	0	0	0	0
2nd sorties	Bf 109G	Montdidier, Creil		1314	Creil	1424	3 B-17, 1 P-47	5	0	4	0	1
III./JG 2	Fw 190A	Cormeilles		~1035	Montdidier	~1130	3 B-24	0	0	0	0	0
2nd sorties	Fw 190A	Montdidier		~1330	Cormeilles	~1500	1 B-17, 1 B-24	2	0	2	0	0

30 December 1943 – Ludwigshafen (see map)

8th Air Force VIII BC Mission #169: 658 of 710 B-17s + B-24s (all BDs) bomb Ludwigshafen, TOT 1156-1300 – lose 23-5-117, claim 12-4-9. 79 VIII FC P-38s (2 FGs) claim 0, lose 0; 463 VIII FC P-47s (9 FGs) claim 7-3-4, lose 11-1-5; 41 IX FC P 51s (1 FG) claim 0-1-1, lose 2-0-0. Escort of 9 sqds of 2nd TAF Spitfire IXs (penetration, withdrawal) claims 3-0-2, loses 0.

The target for VIII BC was one of the largest chemical complexes in the Third Reich: the IG Farben plant at Ludwigshafen, on the upper Rhine. The undercast was solid, but the clouds topped out at 3,000–3,700 metres (10,000–12,000 feet), with unlimited visibility above them. These were good conditions for both the bombers, which were able to maintain a tight formation while bombing a target readily identifiable by radar, and the escorts, which could keep the bombers in sight while maintaining a close watch below for any German interceptors emerging from the undercast. The 2nd BD did not yet have Pathfinder aircraft, and one wing of its B-24s followed the B-17s of the 1st BD to bomb on its markers, while two more wings followed the 3rd BD. To avoid the JD 3 fighter defences, considered to be the strongest, the bombers were routed south from England over the Seine Estuary into France and then due east to the target. The burden of the defence thus fell on the day fighters of II. Jagdkorps: the 3 Gruppen of JG 2, 2 Gruppen and 1 Staffel of JG 26, and I./JG 3. Many of these fighters flew two or even three sorties, dodging P-47s and Spitfires while looking for unescorted bombers. Most of the I. Jagdkorps fighters, on the other hand, lost their formations while climbing through the

Luftwaffe defensive activity – 31 December 1943

Unit	Type	Gruppe up			Gruppe down		Claims	Losses				
		Base	No	Time	Base	Time		Dest	Dam	KIA	MIA	WIA
Luftflotte 3												
II. Jagdkorps												
Jagddivison 4:												
II./JG 26	Fw 190A	Grevillers		1024	Tours	1135	transfer	0	0	0	0	0
	Fw 190A	Grevillers		~1230	Grevillers	~1400	1 B-17	0	0	0	0	0
	Fw 190A	Tours		1405	Vannes	1540	1 B-17	0	0	0	0	0
Jagddivison 5:												
Stab/JG 2	Fw 190A	Cormeilles		~1030	Tours	~1100	transfer	0	0	0	0	0
	Fw 190A	Tours		~1130	Tours?	~1300	1 B-24	0	0	0	0	0
I./JG 2	Fw 190A	Conches		~1030	Tours	~1100	transfer	0	0	0	0	0
	Fw 190A	Tours		~1130	Tours?	~1300	1 B-17	0	0	0	0	0
II./JG 2	Bf 109G	Creil		~1130	Tours	~1300	transfer	0	0	0	0	0
	Bf 109G	Tours		1355	St. Brieuc	1510	5 B-17	2	0	2	0	0
III./JG 2	Fw 190A	Cormeilles		~1130	Tours	~1300	transfer	0	0	0	0	0
	Fw 190A	Cormeilles		~1230	Abbéville	~1400	0	0	0	0	0	0
	Fw 190A	Tours		~1400	St. Brieuc	~1530	1 B-17	0	0	0	0	0
Jafü Bretagne:												
12./JG 2	Fw 190A	Gaël		1021	Gaël	~1200	0	2	0	1	0	1
JGr Ost	Bf 109F	Biarritz, Laleu, St. Jean d'Angély		1128	Biarritz, Laleu, St. Jean d'Angély	~1315	5 B-17, 2 B-24, 1 B-17 HSS	7	1	2	1	2
3./JGr Ost	Fw 190A	Bergerac		1128	Bergerac	1235	n/c	0	0	0	0	0
JGr West	Bf 109F	St. Jean d'Angély		1050	Bordeaux	1220	0	0	0	0	0	0
	Fw 190A, Bf 109F	Biarritz, Cazaux, Corme Ecluse		1130	Biarritz, Cazaux, Corme Ecluse	1240	3 B-17, 4 B-24	3	2	2	0	0
SAGr 128	Fw 190G	Brest	4	1120	Brest	~1230	n/c	1	0	1	0	0

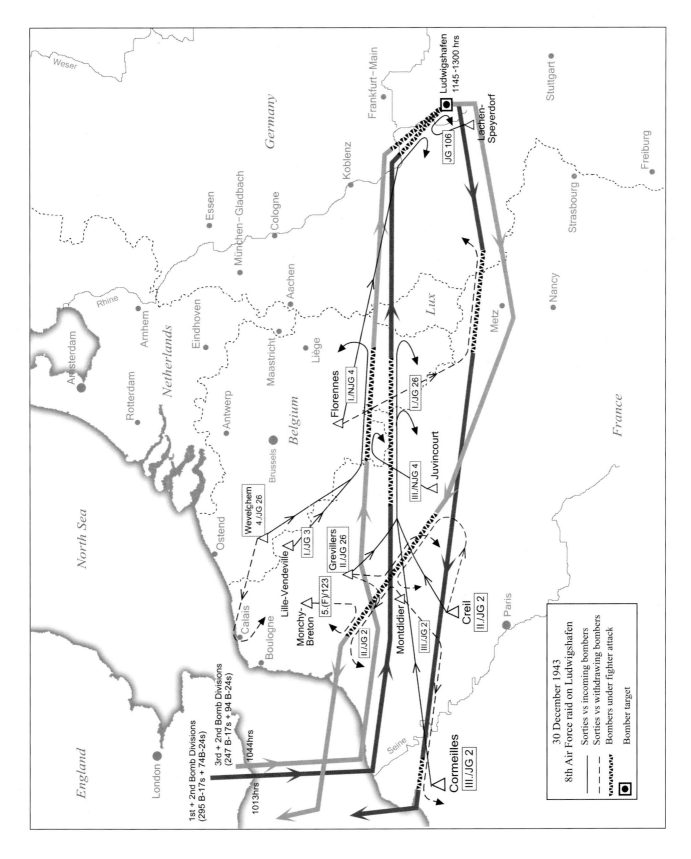

Weser

Germany

Frankfurt–Main

Ludwigshafen
1145 –1300 hrs

Stuttgart

Lachen-
Speyerdorf

JG 106

Freiburg

Koblenz

Essen

München–Gladbach

Cologne

Strasbourg

Aachen

Rhine

Netherlands

Arnhem

Eindhoven

Maastricht

Liège

Lux

Metz

Nancy

Amsterdam

Rotterdam

Antwerp

Belgium

Florennes

I./NJG 4

I./JG 26

Juvincourt

III./NJG 4

France

North Sea

Brussels

Wevelghem
4./JG 26

Ostend

Lille-Vendeville

I./JG 3

Grevillers
II./JG 26

Calais

Monchy-
Breton

5.(F)/123

II./JG 2

Montdidier

III./JG 2

Creil

II./JG 2

Paris

Boulogne

England

London

1st + 2nd Bomb Divisions
(295 B-17s + 74B-24s)

3rd + 2nd Bomb Divisions
(247 B-17s + 94 B-24s)

1044hrs

1013hrs

Seine

Cormeilles

III./JG 2

30 December 1943
8th Air Force raid on Ludwigshafen

Sorties vs incoming bombers
Sorties vs withdrawing bombers
Bombers under fighter attack
Bomber target

—169—

clouds and never came close to the bombers. Some of these flights are not included in the table – of the 386 fighters to scramble, only 128 were credited with making contact. The Americans lost 28 bombers and 14 escorts; the Luftwaffe lost 15 KIA, seven WIA and 15 aircraft, nearly all from II. Jagdkorps.

Pilots relax at Marignane, France, in late 1943. From left: Major Viktor Bauer, Jagdgruppe Ost Kommandeur; Major Heinz Bär, Jagdgruppe Süd Kommandeur, during one of his few absences from the front; and Lt. Siegfried Sy, 4./JGr Ost pilot. *(Sy)*

Lt. Siegfried Sy (4./JGr Ost) prepares for a late-1943 Mediterranean coastal mission in a Marignane-based Bf 109G 'gunboat'. *(Sy)*

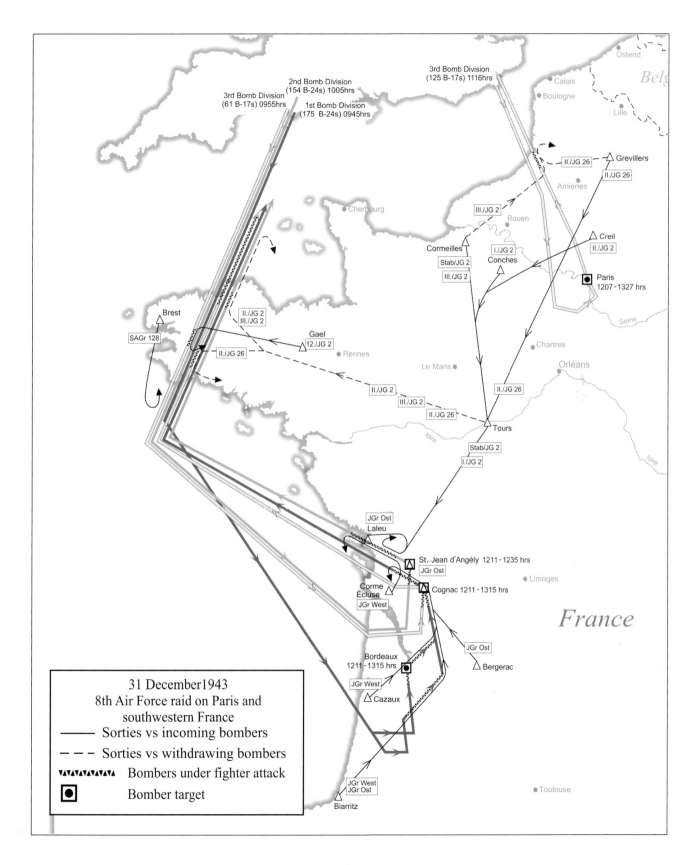

2nd Bomb Division
(154 B-24s) 1005hrs

3rd Bomb Division
(61 B-17s) 0955hrs

1st Bomb Division
(175 B-24s) 0945hrs

3rd Bomb Division
(125 B-17s) 1116hrs

Ostend

Belg

Calais

Boulogne

Lille

Grevillers

II./JG 26

II./JG 26

Amienes

III./JG 2

Rouen

Cherbourg

Creil

II./JG 2

Cormeilles

I./JG 2

Stab/JG 2

Conches

III./JG 2

Paris
1207 - 1327 hrs

Brest

II./JG 2
III./JG 2

Seine

SAGr 128

Gael

II./JG 26

12./JG 2

Chartres

Rennes

Orléans

Le Mans

II./JG 2

II./JG 26

III./JG 2

II./JG 26

Loire

Tours

Stab/JG 2

Loire

I./JG 2

JGr Ost

Laleu

France

St. Jean d'Angély 1211 - 1235 hrs

JGr Ost

Corme
Écluse

Cognac 1211 - 1315 hrs

Limoges

JGr West

JGr Ost

Bordeaux
1211 - 1315 hrs

Bergerac

JGr West

Cazaux

JGr West
JGr Ost

Toulouse

Biarritz

31 December 1943
8th Air Force raid on Paris and
southwestern France
—— Sorties vs incoming bombers
- - - Sorties vs withdrawing bombers
▼▼▼▼▼▼▼▼▼ Bombers under fighter attack
◉ Bomber target

31 December — Paris and southwestern France (see map)

8th Air Force VIII BC Mission #169: 257 of 296 B-17s + B-24s (all BDs) bomb Cognac and Bordeaux airfields, TOT 1207-1315 – lose 23-10-108, claim 17-13-27; 87 of 94 2nd BD B-24s bomb St. Jean-d'Angély a/f 1211-35 – lose 1-3-5, claim 9-1-1; 120 of 124 3rd BD B-17s bomb Paris-Ivry and Bois-Colombes industries, TOT 1207-27 – lose 1-1-49, claim 0. 74 VIII FC P-38s (2 FGs) claim 3-0-1, lose 1-1-1; 441 VIII FC P-47s (9 FGs) claim 4-1-0, lose 2-6-0; 33 IX FC P-51s (1 FG) claim 2-0-0, lose 1-0-0.

The VIII BC targeted II. Jagdkorps for the second day in a row. Two B-17 wings bombed several factories in Paris, while the rest of the bombers crossed the Brittany peninsula and made a broad swing over the Bay of Biscay to attack several airfields on the lower Atlantic French coast from the south. JD 5 and Jafü Bretagne, controlling JG 2 and two major fighter schools, were better prepared than the Americans had hoped, and the 12 American escort groups were unaccountably ineffective. Jagdgruppe Ost and Jagdgruppe West flew maximum-strength missions in defence of their own bases and claimed 17 bombers. Tours served as a staging base for all of the JG 2 Gruppen and II./JG 26, which was borrowed from JD 4, and dispatched fighters to the target area and the withdrawal track. The Americans lost 40 bombers and 11 escorts on what was supposed to be a milk run. In return, they put one training airfield out of service. Jagdgruppe Ost lost two KIA, six WIA, 17 fighters destroyed and 20 damaged on the ground at Cognac. II. Jagdkorps lost eight KIA or MIA, three WIA and 15 fighters in the air.

Notes:

[1] II./JG 11 Gefechtsbericht, in private collection.

[2] Hoeckner Gefechtsbericht, BA-MA RL 10/482.

[3] Brunner Gefechtsbericht, BA-MA RL 10/482.

[4] Zimmer Gefechtsbericht, NARA T-971, roll 11.

[5] Crump correspondence with author, 1987.

[6] II./JG 1 Kriegstagebuch, BA-MA RL 10/482.

[7] Hoeckner Gefechtsbericht, BA-MA RL 10/482.

[8] Schmitz Gefechtsbericht, BA-MA RL 10/433.

[9] III./ZG 26 Kriegstagebuch, BA-MA RL 10/256.

A 389th Bomb Group B-24 returns from a mission to Cognac, France. The date is probably 31 December 1943. *(USAAF)*

CHAPTER 5

JANUARY – MARCH 1944

January 1944

American plans to attain air superiority over Western Europe underwent a radical change at the end of 1943. Gen. H. H. Arnold took command of the 8th Air Force away from LGen. Ira Eaker and gave him a new high-level position in the Mediterranean Theatre. The strategic air war was to be run from England by LGen. Carl Spaatz in a new upper-level command, the U. S. Strategic Air Forces in Europe (USSTAF), which was to co-ordinate the efforts of the 8th and 15th Air Forces. The VIII Bomber Command was abolished, and the 8th AF absorbed its facilities and function. Gen. Dwight D. Eisenhower, the new Supreme Commander of the European Theatre, moved from the Mediterranean to England, bringing with him his own air team of generals and air marshals. These men cared little for the abstract pre-war theories of strategic bombing and had gained air superiority over the Mediterranean skies by beating down the Luftwaffe in the air and on the ground. Aided by several groups of P-51s, the fighter that Eaker had rejected, their top-priority mission was to weaken the Luftwaffe sufficiently to win the skies over Western Europe prior to the invasion of France, now scheduled for May.

By late 1943, the Nazi hierarchy and the Luftwaffe high command had finally recognised the importance of the defensive effort against the American daylight air campaign. The RLV force was not strengthened materially in January, but its organisation underwent important changes. Luftwaffenbefehlshaber Mitte was renamed Luftflotte Reich, giving it a status equivalent to the Luftflotten (Air Fleets) at the combat fronts. Genobst. Hubert Weise, a Flak general, was replaced by an experienced aviation commander, Genobst. Hans-Jürgen Stumpff. Luftflotte Reich continued to command I. Jagdkorps (which contained Jagddivisionen 1, 2, and 3) and Jagddivision 7 (which contained Jafü Österreich). In the western occupied zone, II. Jagdkorps contained the fighters of Luftflotte 3, apportioned between Jagddivision 4 and Jagddivision 5. While the Jafü still held sway in the peripheral regions, the Jagddivisionen, which were originally organised to control the night defences, now ran the day fighter operations over the Reich proper and in the Western occupied zone. As the ability of the Jagddivisionen to control large formations improved, larger formations called *Gefechtsverbände* (battle formations) were devised for them. Jagdgruppen by themselves were now too small to operate effectively in the face of the tight bomber streams and the numerous escorts. Gefechtsverbände were to be of Geschwader strength or greater and were to be commanded in the air by senior officers, preferably Kommodoren or Kommandeure. These were *ad hoc* organisations, which, in early 1944, had a semi-official status. The early Gefechtsverbände were:

Gefechtsverband	Area of operation	Controlling HQ
JG 1	Netherlands	Jagddivision 3 (JD 3)
JG 3	Rhineland	Jagddivision 3 (JD 3)
JG 11	Northern Germany	Jagddivision 2 (JD 2)
JG 27	Austria	Jafü Ostmark
JG z.b.V.	Southwestern Germany	Jagddivision 7 (JD 7)

Jagddivision 3, on the route of most 8th Air Force raids on Germany, controlled two Gefechtsverbände, while Jagddivision 1 in Berlin, which was not yet threatened by day, had none. The *Jagdgeschwader zur besonderen Verwendung* (JG z.b.V.) was not a full Geschwader but a fighter staff established 'for special use', in this case the command of a Gefechtsverband comprising several independent Jagdgruppen based in JD 7's geographic zone, since there were no 'regular' Jagdgeschwader staffs available for this duty.

Above: Genobst. Hans-Jürgen Stumpff. A successful staff officer in the First World War, Stumpff remained in the postwar Reichswehr and transferred to the Luftwaffe two years before its formation was announced. He commanded Luftflotte 5 in Norway for 3 1/2 years and became the first and only commander of Luftflotte Reich when it was established at the beginning of 1944. On 8 May 1945, Stumpff served as the Luftwaffe representative at the signing of the unconditional surrender of Germany in Berlin.

Above right: The main operations room, or 'battle opera house', of the RLV command centres was split down the centre by a huge vertical screen on which was painted the Jägergradnetz – the fighter control grid – for the area. This photo shows the backside of the screen, onto which aircraft positions were projected by a large staff of auxiliaries wielding high-intensity lamps. *(Bundesarchiv 633-3818-16)*

Right: The staff that manned the projectors in the 'battle opera houses' changed over the course of the war from uniformed Luftwaffe men to civilian women, and ultimately to Luftwaffe Helferinnen, or female auxiliaries. This photo was taken during the middle stage of the war before it was deemed acceptable to enlist German women for military service. *(Bundesarchiv 633-3818-3)*

Formation of the JG z.b.V staff was delayed, and it did not become operational until mid-April.

No Zerstörer unit was assigned to JD 3, which faced American escorts in the greatest numbers. ZG 26 was assigned to Jagddivision 2; ZG 76 was in Jagddivision 7 in southwestern Germany, although it flew a few missions from northern bases; II./ZG 1 was in Jafü Ostmark in Austria. In January, the bases of the twin-engine day fighters were thus out of range of most American escort fighters. Their Bf 110s and Me 410s were to operate in Geschwader strength under the protection of single-engine fighters if possible.

II./ZG 76 makes a maximum-strength flight over southern Germany in the winter of 1943–44. The nearest aircraft are from the 6. Staffel. (*Bundesarchiv 663-6737-26a*)

No new units joined the RLV in January, but Sturmstaffel 1 flew its first missions using its new *Sturmtaktik* – a firing approach to the rear of the bomber formations to very close range in specially armed and armoured Fw 190s. These missions were judged highly successful.

The I. Jagdkorps monthly report for January recorded its average daily operational strength as 400 single-engine fighters, 80 twin-engine fighters and 100 night fighters available for day use. The command flew 2306 operational sorties while losing 122 fighters, for a loss rate of 5.3 per cent. It estimated the number of USAAF sorties to the Reich to be 7158 for a loss of 179 bombers and escorts, a loss rate of 2.5 per cent.

The primary data used to construct the synthetic war diary that you are reading become sketchier at the beginning of 1944. The January 1944 pages of the RLM document listing victory claims and confirmations are missing, as are all of the 1944 pages of the Quartermaster General's ledger, the principal source for aircraft loss data. I have thus compiled claim and loss data from many sources, few of which agree. On

the positive side of the ledger, part of an important set of 1944 I. Jagdkorps mission maps, 'Einsatz der Fliegenden Verbände – Luftlage (eigene und feindliche Luftwaffe)' has survived in the Bundesarchiv, and I have used these as much as possible, primarily for unit mission strengths, take-off times, flight courses and combat areas.

4 January

8th Air Force Mission #174: 486 of 569 heavy bombers (from all 3 BDs) bomb Kiel port targets and t/os, TOT 1111 – lose 17-5-127; 68 of 75 3rd BD B-17s bomb Münster city, TOT 1024, lose 2-1-0 – HBs claim 4-12-4. Escort of 2 P-38 FGs, 1 P-51 FG, 9 P-47 FGs (542 sorties) claims 8-1-6, loses 2-1-1.

The 8th AF split its forces to make the best use of its escorts. All of the P-47s escorted a small B-17 force to Münster, while the rest of the bombers left 20 minutes later on a straight line for Kiel, being met in the target area by the three long-range escort groups (two P-38 and one P-51). The German defensive effort as a whole was unsuccessful. The RLV day fighters were hampered by bad weather at their bases, but the night fighters of NJG 3 and NJG 5, which were less challenged by the weather, flew one of their best day missions against the withdrawing Kiel raiders, although the details of many of their claims are today unknown. The Americans wrote off 25 bombers and three escorts. According to its War Diary, I. Jagdkorps lost seven KIA, four MIA, one WIA and 12 aircraft on 327 sorties. The present author has been unsuccessful in identifying the units to which several of these losses belonged.

5 January

8th Air Force Mission #176: 119 of 131 1st BD B-17s, 96 of 114 2nd BD B-24s bomb Kiel port targets and t/os, TOT 1125 – lose 10-1-76, claim 41-6-13; 112 of 117 3rd BD B-17s bomb Bordeaux–Mérignac a/f, TOT 1038 – lose 11-2-49, claim 50-1-9; 78 of 79 1st BD B-17s bomb Tours a/f, TOT 1144 – lose 1-0-10, claim 2-0-0; 73 of 78 3rd BD B-17s bomb Neuss, Geilenkirchen, other German t/os – lose 2-1-22, claim 2-5-2. Total escort of 2 P-38 FGs, 1 P-51 FG, 7 P-47 FGs (579 sorties) claims 33-2-10, loses 12-2-3.

In a partial reprise of the previous day's mission plan, Kiel was bombed with a small force and a target escort comprising the three long-range fighter groups. All of the northern RLV units reported fierce, heavy combat.

JG 11 shot down seven P-38s, but the 354th FG Mustangs savaged the Bf 110s of III./ZG 76 and III./NJG 5, downing 10. Eleven Kiel bombers and seven of their escorts were written off. The 350 RLV fighters to sortie lost at least 18 KIA or MIA, 12 WIA and 30 aircraft.

The rest of the bomber force was sent to three targets, the most important of which was the Bordeaux–Mérignac airfield. The P-47 escorts assigned to the Bordeaux force were too few to do the job. JG 2 had their best day against the heavies in months, and two of the operational training units in southern France were also successful. Seventeen bombers from the western forces and seven of their escorts were written off. The defenders in France lost four KIA or MIA, one WIA and eight fighters.

Luftwaffe defensive activity – 4 January 1944

Unit	Type	Gruppe up				Gruppe down		Claims	Losses				
		Base	No	Time		Base	Time		Dest	Dam	KIA	MIA	WIA
Lw Bfh Mitte													
I. Jagdkorps			316										
Jagddivision 1:													
I./NJG 5	Bf 110G	Stendal		~1130		Stendal	~1330	1 B-17, 1 B-24	0	0	0	0	0
II./NJG 5	Bf 110G	Parchim	4	~1130		Parchim	~1330	0	0	0	0	0	0
III./NJG 5	Bf 110G	Neuruppin		~1130		Neuruppin	~1330	3 B-24	0	0	0	0	0
Jagddivison 2:													
I./JG 11	Fw 190A	Husum		0917		Oldenburg	0958	transfer	0	0	0	0	0
	Fw 190A	Oldenburg		1001		Wunstorf	1155	n/c	0	3	0	0	0
2nd sorties	Fw 190A	Oldenburg		1309		Oldenburg	1341	n/c	0	0	0	0	0
II./JG 11	Fw 190A	Wunstorf		1002		Achmer	1123	0	1	0	0	0	1
2nd sorties	Fw 190A	Achmer		1233		Oldenburg	1321	n/c	0	0	0	0	0
III./JG 11	Bf 109G	Oldenburg		1020		Oldenburg	1131	n/c	0	1	0	0	0
10./JG 11	Fw 190A	Aalborg–Ost		1120		Flensburg	1212	n/c	0	0	0	0	0
I./ZG 26	Bf 110G	Völkenrode		1100		Völkenrode	~1230	0	0	1	0	0	0
II./ZG 26	Me 410A	Hildesheim		1015		Stade	1230	0	2	0	4	0	0
II./NJG 3	Bf 110G	Schleswig		~1100		Schleswig	~1300	3 B-17	0	0	0	0	0
IV./NJG 3	Ju 88C	Aalborg–West		1052		Stade	1219	1 B-17	0	0	0	0	0
ErprKdo 25	Me 410	Achmer		0957		Achmer	1206	0	0	1	0	0	0
Jagddivison 3:													
I./JG 1	Fw 190A	Dortmund		0917		Dortmund	~1000	0	0	0	0	0	0
	Fw 190A	Dortmund		1020		Plantlünne	1132	0	3	0	2	0	0
2nd sorties	Fw 190A	Plantlünne		1230		Lingen	1350	n/c	0	0	0	0	0
II./JG 1	Fw 190A, Bf 109G	Rheine	17+2	0845		Dortmund	~0900	transfer	0	3	0	0	0
	Fw 190A	Dortmund	5	0926		Rheine	~1130	1 B-17	1	0	1	0	0
2nd sorties	Fw 190A, Bf 109G	Dortmund	4+2	1233		Rheine	~1330	0	0	0	0	0	0
III./JG 1	Bf 109G	Volkel		1005		Volkel	~1130	0	2	0	1	0	0
2nd sorties	Bf 109G	Volkel		1534		Volkel	~1630	n/c	0	0	0	0	0
III./JG 26	Bf 109G	München–Gladbach		1002		München–Gladbach	1155	n/c	0	0	0	0	0

Luftwaffe defensive activity vs. 8th AF raid on Kiel – 5 January 1944

Unit	Type	Gruppe up			Gruppe down		Claims	Losses				
		Base	No	Time	Base	Time		Dest	Dam	KIA	MIA	WIA
Lw Bfh Mitte												
I. Jagdkorps			269									
Jagddivision 1:												
III./JG 54	Bf 109G	Ludwigslust		1010	Ludwigslust	1155	1 B-17, 1 P-38	1	0	0	0	0
III./JG 301	Bf 109G	Zerbst		~1015	Zerbst	~1145	0	2	1	0	0	1
I./JG 302	Bf 109G	Jüterbog		~1015	Jüterbog	~1145	0	1	2	0	0	1
I./ZG 26	Bf 110G	Völkenrode		1030	Völkenrode	1130	0	0	0	0	0	0
2nd sorties	Bf 110G	Völkenrode		~1200	Völkenrode	1315	1 B-17, 1 B-24, 1 B-24 HSS	0	0	0	0	0
II./ZG 26	Me 410A	Hildesheim		1045	HIldesheim	1235	0	0	0	0	0	0
I./NJG 5	Bf 110G	Stendal		~1200	Stendal	~1330	0	1	0	?	?	?
II./NJG 5	Bf 110G	Parchim		~1200	Parchim	~1330	0	1	0	0	0	1
III./NJG 5	Bf 110G	Neuruppin		~1200	Neuruppin	~1330	1 B-24, 1 B-24 HSS	5	0	5	0	2
Jagddivison 2:												
Stab./JG 11	Fw 190A	Oldenburg		~1000	Oldenburg	~1130	0	0	0	0	0	0
I./JG 11	Fw 190A	Oldenburg		1017	Oldenburg, Husum	1146	0	0	0	0	0	0
2nd sorties	Fw 190A	Husum		1215	Husum	~1330	2 B-17, 3 B-24, 2 P-38	0	0	0	0	0
II./JG 11	Fw 190A	Wunstorf		0951	Wunstorf	~1130	0	0	0	0	0	0
2nd sorties	Fw 190A	Wunstorf		~1200	Wunstorf	~1330	4 P-38	2	2	1	1	0
III./JG 11	Bf 109G	Oldenburg		~1000	Oldenburg	~1130	0	0	0	0	0	0
2nd sorties	Bf 109G	Oldenburg		~1200	Oldenburg	~1330	3 P-38	1	0	1	0	0
10./JG 11	Fw 190A	Husum, Aalborg–Ost		1037	Husum, Flensburg	1107	0	0	0	0	0	0
2nd sorties	Fw 190A	Husum, Flensburg		1148	Husum	~1330	0	1	0	1	0	0
III./ZG 76	Bf 110G	Wunstorf?		~1200	Wunstorf?	~1330	0	5	2	4	0	7
I./NJG 3	Bf 110G	Vechta		~1200	Vechta	~1330	1 B-17	1	0	?	?	?
II./NJG 3	Bf 110G	Schleswig		~1200	Schleswig	~1330	1 P-38	0	0	0	0	0
ErprKdo 25	Me 410	Achmer		0950	Achmer	1218	0	0	0	0	0	0
Jagddivison 3:												
Stab/JG 1	Fw 190A	Dortmund		~1000	Dortmund	~1200	2 B-24	0	0	0	0	0
I./JG 1	Fw 190A	Dortmund		~1000	Dortmund	~1145	3 B-17 HSS	0	0	0	0	0
2nd sorties	Fw 190A	Dortmund		~1200	Dortmund	~1330	1 B-17, 1 B-17 HSS	3	3	3	0	0
II./JG 1	Fw 190A	Rheine		1003	Rheine	1140	n/c	0	0	0	0	0
III./JG 1	Bf 109G	Volkel		~1000	Volkel	~1130	0	0	0	0	0	0
III./JG 26	Bf 109G	München–Gladbach		0945	München–Gladbach	1127	n/c	2	0	0	0	0
I./JG 300	Bf 109G	Bonn–Hangelar		~1030	Bonn–Hangelar	~1200	0	1	1	1	0	0
IV./NJG 1	Bf 110G	Leeuwarden		~1200	Leeuwarden	~1330	1 B-24	0	0	0	0	0
Jagddivision 7:			81									
III./JG 3	Bf 109G	Bad Wörishofen		1135	Echterdingen, Mannheim-Sandhofen	1310	n/c	0	0	0	0	0
II./JG 27	Bf 109G	Erbenheim		1115	Erbenheim	1218	1 B-17, 1 P-47	2	0	1	0	0
III./JG 300	Bf 109G	Erbenheim		~1115	Erbenheim	~1230	0	1	0	0	0	0
I./ZG 76	Bf 110G	Ansbach		~1145	Ansbach	~1300	1 B-17 HSS	0	0	0	0	0
II./ZG 76	Bf 110G	Neubiberg		1145	Neubiberg	1305	n/c	0	0	0	0	0

Luftwaffe defensive activity vs. 8th AF raid on Bordeaux – 5 January 1944

Unit	Type	Gruppe up			Gruppe down		Claims	Losses				
		Base	No	Time	Base	Time		Dest	Dam	KIA	MIA	WIA
Luftflotte 3												
II. Jagdkorps												
Jagddivision 4:												
II./JG 26	Fw 190A	Beauvais–Grevillers	4	1310	Beauvais–Grevillers	1317	1 B-17	0	0	0	0	0
2nd sorties	Fw 190A	Beauvais–Grevillers		1346	Beauvais–Grevillers	1542	n/c	0	0	0	0	0
Jagddivision 5:												
Stab/JG 2	Fw 190A	Cormeilles		~1030	Cormeilles	~1200	1 B-17, 2 P-47	0	0	0	0	0
I./JG 2	Fw 190A	Conches		~1030	Conches	~1200	10 B-17, 1 B-17 HSS	0	0	0	0	0
II./JG 2?	Bf 109G	Vitry–en–Artois		~1030	Vitry–en–Artois	~1200	0	0	0	0	0	0
III./JG 2	Fw 190A	Cormeilles		~1030	Cormeilles	~1145	1 B-17, 2 P-47	0	0	0	0	0
2nd sorties	Fw 190A	Cormeilles		~1215	Cormeilles	~1315	4 B-17	1	2	1	0	0
Jafü Bretagne:												
2./JGr Ost	Bf 109F	Laleu	1	1010	Corme Ecluse	1100	1 B-17 HSS	0	0	0	0	0
3./JGr Ost	Fw 190A	Bergerac		1039	Bergerac, St. Jean d'Angély	1209	0	4	4	1	1	1
JGr West	Fw 190A	Bergerac, Cazaux		1020	Biarritz, Bergerac, Cazaux	1210	0	4	0	1	0	0

Luftwaffe defensive activity vs. 8th Air Force – 7 January 1944

Unit	Type	Gruppe up			Gruppe down		Claims	Losses				
		Base	No	Time	Base	Time		Dest	Dam	KIA	MIA	WIA
Lw Bfh Mitte												
I. Jagdkorps												
Jagddivision 1:												
III./JG 301	Bf 109G	Zerbst?		~1110	Zerbst?	~1230	0	2	1	0	1	1
Jagddivision 7:												
III./JG 3	Bf 109G	Echterdingen		1110	Echterdingen, Bad Wörishofen	1220	n/c	0	0	0	0	0
II./JG 27	Bf 109G	Erbenheim		1111	Mannheim	1230	1 B-17, 2 P-38	1	1	0	0	0
JG 106	Bf 109E	Lachen–Speyerdorf		1145	Lachen–Speyerdorf	1220	0	0	0	0	0	0
II./ZG 76	Bf 110G	Neubiberg		1125	Neubiberg	1255	0	0	0	0	0	0
II./NJG 6	Bf 110G	Schwäbisch Hall	4	1128	Schwäbisch Hall	1230	0	0	0	0	0	0
	Bf 110G	Oedheim	4	1141	Oedheim	1330	0	0	0	0	0	0
I./NJG 102	Bf 110G	Kitzingen		1158	Kitzingen	1301	0	0	0	0	0	0
Luftflotte 3												
II. Jagdkorps												
Jagddivision 4:												
I./JG 26	Fw 190A	Florennes		1208	Creil, Gravelines	1317	3 P-47	0	0	0	0	0
II./JG 26	Fw 190A	Beauvais–Grevillers		1247	Beauvais–Grevillers	1353	3 B-17, 2 P-47	4	0	3	0	1
III./JG 26	Bf 109G	Denain		1206	Laon	1250	0	1	0	0	0	0
2nd sorties	Bf 109G	Laon		1316	Denain	~1400	0	0	0	0	0	0
I./NJG 4	Bf 110G	Florennes		1208	Florennes	1304	1 B-17	0	0	0	0	0
II./NJG 4	Bf 110G	St. Dizier		1120	Mainz–Finthen	1300	1 B-17	0	0	0	0	0

Luftwaffe defensive activity vs. 8th Air Force – 7 January 1944 Continued

Unit	Type	Gruppe up			Gruppe down		Claims	Losses				
		Base	No	Time	Base	Time		Dest	Dam	KIA	MIA	WIA
Jagddivision 5:												
Stab/JG 2	Fw 190A	Cormeilles		1255	Cormeilles	1420	1 B-17, 3 B-24	0	0	0	0	0
I./JG 2?	Fw 190A	Conches		~1240	Conches	~1400	0	0	0	0	0	0
II./JG 2?	Bf 109G	Vitry–en–Artois		~1240	Vitry–en–Artois	~1400	0	0	0	0	0	0
III./JG 2	Fw 190A	Cormeilles		1240	Cormeilles	~1400	4 B-24	1	0	1	0	0

Luftwaffe defensive activity vs. 15th Air Force – 7 January 1944

Unit	Type	Gruppe up			Gruppe down		Claims	Losses				
		Base	No	Time	Base	Time		Dest	Dam	KIA	MIA	WIA
Lw Bfh Mitte												
Jagddivision 7:			91									
Jafü Ostmark:												
I./JG 27	Bf 109G	Fels am Wagram	34	1045	Fels am Wagram	1245	n/c	0	0	0	0	0
II./JG 53	Bf 109G	Wien–Seyring	34	1041	Wien–Seyring, Steinamanger	1225	15 P-38	1	4	0	0	0
II/ZG 1	Bf 110G	Wels	38	~1045	Wels	~1245	0	0	1	0	2	0

7 January – vs. 8th Air Force

8th Air Force Mission #178: 420 of 502 heavy bombers (all BDs) bomb Ludwigshafen industrial targets and t/os, TOT 1127-57 – lose 12-4-122, claim 30-6-17. Escort of 2 P-38 FGs, 1 P-51 FG, 9 P-47 FGs (571 sorties) claims 7-0-3, loses 6-0-1.

The 8th AF flew a full-strength raid to the IG Farben chemical complex at Ludwigshafen, which was strung out along the Rhine River and made an easy target for identification by H2X, the American version of British H2S airborne radar, in the overcast winter weather. The bombers were routed due east across the Dutch coast before turning southeast toward the Ruhr. Only Jagddivision 7 (JD 7) and Luftflotte 3 intercepted, and then only shortly before the bomb run. The bombers' return route took them across France, where today JG 2 and JG 26 were ready, despite the solid cloud cover. JG 2 made effective attacks on B-24s at low cost to itself. I./JG 26 bounced the 358th FG, a new P-47 unit, and downed three Thunderbolts. II./JG 26 was surprised by both Spitfires and 4th FG P-47s while attacking seemingly unescorted B-17s and lost four Fw 190s. The Americans wrote off 16 bombers and six fighters. The Germans lost five KIA or MIA, two WIA and nine fighters on 224 sorties.

COMBAT REPORT[1]
7 January 1944

One P-47 Thunderbolt destroyed from 159 metres at 1231 hours in PQ QJ-1, 5 km SE of Maubeuge [Kiefner's victim was a 358th Fighter Group P-47: DC]

At 1208 hours, I took off in a Fw 190A-6 (four MG 151/20s and two MG 17s) with the Gruppe as wingman to Oblt. Beese on a transfer flight to quadrant TE-9. During assembly, the Gruppe made contact with five Thunderbolts which disappeared into the clouds. We took up a course toward them. At 1228 hours, we sighted three Thunderbolts and turned toward them immediately. After two had been shot down, the third pulled up in a left turn. While climbing through 150 metres, I reached firing position at a distance of 120 metres. The enemy aircraft caught fire immediately on the right side of the fuselage, about 1 metre behind the right wing, and immediately dived to earth over its right wing. By now, the entire fuselage was ablaze. I observed the crash at 1231 hours in map quadrant QJ-1 east of Colleret, 5 km southeast of Maubeuge.

Lt. Georg Kiefner
1./JG 26

7 January – vs. 15th Air Force

15th Air Force mission to Wiener Neustadt: bombers abort, 2 P-38 FGs reach target area – lose 6, claim 5-2-6.

The 15th AF bombers turned back early from Wiener Neustadt because of the weather conditions, but the P-38 escorts continued to the target area. There, the 14th FG downed a II./ZG 1 Bf 110 without loss, while the 1st FG engaged the Bf 109s of II./JG 53 in a 30-minute battle that continued to Yugoslavia. The Messerschmitt pilots claimed 15 victories; six P-38s were in fact shot down. The Americans claimed 1-1-6 Bf 109s and 3-0-0 Fw 190s, but there were no Focke-Wulfs in the area. The only Luftwaffe combat loss was apparently one II./ZG 1 Bf 110 and crew. II./JG 53 admitted to no combat losses, but one Bf 109 was destroyed and four were damaged in dead-stick landings forced by fuel exhaustion.

Uffz. Willi Maximowitz (left) and Ogfr. Gerhard Vivroux of Sturmstaffel 1 pose on Vivroux's Fw 190A-6 'White 2' at Dortmund in January. *(Smith)*

On 11 January, II./JG 1, led by Oblt. Rüdiger von Kirchmayr, carried out a successful engagement against B-17s, claiming 11. All of these pilots, seen in a posed debriefing, were successful. From left: Oblt. Wegner, Obfw. Schuhmacher, Kirchmayr, Obfw. Haninger, Oblt. Burath, Fw. Sauer, StFw. Martens and Fw. Schönrock. *(Crow)*

11 January

8th Air Force Mission #182: 266 of 291 1st BD B-17s bomb Oschersleben, Halberstadt aviation industry and t/os, TOT 1146-1200 – lose 42-3-125, claim 209-43-82. 372 2nd BD + 3rd BD B-24s + B-17s recalled, 285 bomb t/os – lose 18-2-54, claim 19-17-16. Total escort of 2 P-38 FGs, 1 P-51 FG, 11 P-47 FGs (592 sorties) claims 31-12-16, loses 5-3-6.

The three 8th AF bomb divisions took off and assembled, but worsening conditions over their home bases forced the recall of all of the 2nd BD and most of the 3rd BD, as well as much of the escort. The defenders were up early and in strength against what they believed would be a raid on Berlin, based on its departure time and course due east across Holland. The 1st BD B-17s made a successful attack on the Fw 190 factory at Oschersleben, but suffered heavily from German fighters in what the after-battle report called "the most intense opposition … since Schweinfurt". The forward units of JD 3 were up early and began attacking the bombers over the Zuider Zee. The *Fühlungshalter* (contact keeper) aircraft were quick to report the large escort gaps, and Jagddivisionen 1, 2, 3, and 4 (the last-named from Luftflotte 3) threw their fighters at them by Gruppen; no attempts were made to form Gefechtsverbände. Sturmstaffel 1 scrambled from Rheine in its Fw 190A-6s for the first test of its novel *Sturmtaktik* (assault tactics). It attacked the bomber stream alone from dead astern to very close range. Three B-17s dropped from formation as a result of their 20-mm cannon fire. The Staffel suffered no casualties on this mission, which was considered a major success. Most of the other single-engine Gruppen also flew successful missions, as did the twin-engine day and night fighters, which were directed to the American formations in full force once the shortage of escorts was confirmed. For the day, the Americans lost 65 bombers and eight fighters shot down or scrapped. 482 of the 579 defenders that scrambled were credited with enemy contact; they lost 38 KIA, 28 WIA and 58 aircraft.

Oblt. Rüdiger von Kirchmayr flew with II./JG 1 from June 1942 to October 1944 when he became Gruppenkommandeur of I./JG 11 and led it to the Eastern Front in January 1945. He joined JV 44 in April 1945 after receiving the Knight's Cross. His final total of 50 confirmed victories included 11 heavy bombers. *(Author's collection)*

COMBAT REPORT[2]
11 January 1944

One Boeing B-17 shot down from 6,500 metres at 1130 hours in PQ KA 2, 4 km SW of Osterode/Harz

After Sitzbereitschaft [cockpit readiness], I took off at the 1030 hours alarm in Fw 190A-7 'Black 1' (W. Nr. 430172; two MG 131, four MG 151/20), as the II./JG 1 formation leader. We were led by Y-Führung. At 1126 hours, the Gruppe made contact with ca. 50–60 B-17s at 6,300 metres in PQ KA. After we made a closed-formation head-on attack, I got into position in PQ KU to make a second closed attack on the first Pulk of ca. 20 B-17s. Coming out of the sun, I fired at the right outside B-17 from the front at the same altitude, from 600 metres to the closest distance. At this, the canopy and other pieces flew off the Boeing's fuselage and wing, its landing gear dropped, and it fell away to the right in a steep spiral. After the Gruppe's two closed attacks, I prepared to make a 3rd head-on attack in PQ JA. Owing to a slight course change by the Boeing formation, I had to attack at an angle of 15–20° to the right side, from the same altitude. Coming from the sun, I fired at the right upper Boeing in the first Pulk of about 20 and saw hits in engine #2, which began to show a thick cloud of black smoke. The belly turret and pieces of the canopy, fuselage and wings flew off. The Boeing dropped behind the formation and slowly began to lose altitude. It crashed at 1130 hours in PQ KA-2/4, 2–4 km SW of Osterode/Harz. The attack was witnessed by Obfw. Martens and Fw. Bauer.

Lt. Rüdiger Kirchmayr, Staffelkapitän
5./JG 1

Luftwaffe defensive activity vs. 8th Air Force – 11 January 1944

Unit	Type	Gruppe up			Gruppe down		Claims	Losses (—: included with 1st sortie)				
		Base	No	Time	Base	Time		Dest	Dam	KIA	MIA	WIA
Lw Bfh Mitte												
I. Jagdkorps			536									
Jagddivision 1:			99									
III./JG 54	Bf 109G	Ludwigslust	19	1045	Hannover	1145	2 B-17	3	1	2	0	0
III./JG 301	Bf 109G	Zerbst		~1130	Zerbst	~1300	0	0	0	0	0	0
I./JG 302	Bf 109G	Jüterbog	19	~1130	Jüterbog	~1300	1 B-17	2	1	0	0	3
II./JG 302	Fw 190A	Ludwigslust		~1045	Ludwigslust	~1130	0	0	1	0	0	1
I./ZG 26	Bf 110G	Völkenrode	*144	1030	Völkenrode	1130	5 B-17	6	5	6	0	4
2nd sorties	Bf 110G	Völkenrode		1200	Brunswick	1320	0	—	—	—	—	—
II./ZG 26	Me 410A	Hildesheim		1050	HIldesheim	~1150	?	2	3	2	0	3
II./NJG 2	Ju 88C	Parchim	**36	~1130	Parchim	~1330	0	1	1	2	0	0
I./NJG 5	Bf 110G	Stendal	—	~1130	Stendal	~1330	4 B-17	3	0	0	0	3
II./NJG 5	Bf 110G	Parchim	—	~1130	Parchim	~1330	1 B-17	0	1	0	0	0
III./NJG 5	Bf 110G	Neuruppin	—	~1130	Neuruppin	~1330	0	0	0	0	0	0
Sd Kdo OKL	?	Berlin area		~1130	Berlin area	~1300	3 B-17	0	0	0	0	0
ISS Erla	Bf 109G	Delitzsch		~1130	Delitzsch	~1300	0	2	1	1	0	2
Z ErgGruppe	Bf 110G	Brunswick		~1130	Brunswick	~1330	0	1	0	2	0	0
Jagddivison 2:			223									
Stab/JG 11	Fw 190A	Husum		1052	Oldenburg	~1150	0	1	0	0	0	1
I./JG 11	Fw 190A	Aalborg–Ost, Husum		1042	Husum, Hildesheim	1150	1 B-17, 1 B-17 HSS	1	0	0	0	0
2nd sorties	Fw 190A	Husum		1344	Husum	1405	0	0	0	0	0	0
II./JG 11	Bf 109G	Wunstorf	32	1042	Wunstorf	1200	10 B-17, 1 P-47	5	1	3	0	3
III./JG 11	Bf 109G, Fw 190A	Oldenburg		1045	Brunswick	1245	8 B-17, 1 B-17 HSS	3	1	3	0	0
Stab/ZG 26	Bf 110G	Wunstorf	—	1030	Wunstorf	1130	0	1	1	0	0	2
III./ZG 76	Bf 110G	Wunstorf?	—	~1030	Wunstorf?	~1230	0	2	0	3	0	0
I./NJG 3	Ju 88C	Grove	***62	1118	Grove	1413	0	0	0	0	0	0
II./NJG 3	Ju 88C	Schleswig	—	~1130	Schleswig	~1300	1 B-17	3	0	2	0	4
III./NJG 3	Ju 88C	Stade	—	~1130	Stade	~1300	0	1	0	0	0	0
IV./NJG 3	Ju 88C	Grove	—	~1130	?	~1245	2 B-17	4	1	7	0	1
2nd sorties	Ju 88C	?	—	~1315	Grove?	~1430	2 B-17	—	—	—	—	—
ErprKdo 25	Bf 110G	Achmer	—	1035	Achmer	1245	1 B-17	0	0	0	0	0
	Bf 110G	Achmer	—	1305	Achmer	1350	0	0	0	0	0	0
Jagddivison 3:			214									
Stab/JG 1	Fw 190A	Dortmund		~0850	Rheine	~0915	transfer	0	0	0	0	0
	Fw 190A	Rheine		~1030	Rheine	~1140	0	0	0	0	0	0
I./JG 1	Fw 190A	Dortmund		0850	Rheine	0915	transfer	4	0	0	0	0
	Fw 190A	Rheine		1030	Rheine	1140	3 B-17	1	4	0	0	1
2nd sorties	Fw 190A	Rheine		1242	Dortmund	1355	1 B-17	—	—	—	—	—
II./JG 1	Fw 190A	Rheine	15	1030	Völkenrode	1152	2 B-17	3	1	1	0	1
III./JG 1	Bf 109G	Volkel	24	1024	Volkel	~1200	0	1	0	1	0	0
2nd sorties	Bf 109G	Volkel		~1300	Volkel	~1400	1 B-17, 2 P-47	0	0	0	0	0
I./JG 3	Bf 109G	München–Gladbach		~1130	München–Gladbach	~1300	2 B-17	0	0	0	0	0

Luftwaffe defensive activity vs. 8th Air Force – 11 January 1944 Continued

Unit	Type	Gruppe up			Gruppe down		Claims	Losses (—: included with 1st sortie)				
		Base	No	Time	Base	Time		Dest	Dam	KIA	MIA	WIA
II./JG 27	Bf 109G	Eelde	13	1144	Rheine, Hopsten	1215	3 B-24	0	0	0	0	0
2nd sorties	Bf 109G	Rheine		1225	Düsseldorf	1353	1 B-24, 1 P-47, 3 B-24 HSS	0	0	0	0	0
2nd sorties	Bf 109G	Hopsten		1330	Erbenheim	1450	0	0	0	0	0	0
I./JG 300	Bf 109G	Bonn–Hangelar		~1130	Bonn–Hangelar	~1300	1 B-17	0	0	0	0	0
Sturmstaffel 1	Fw 190A	Dortmund		0850	Rheine	0915	transfer	0	0	0	0	0
	Fw 190A	Rheine		1030	Rheine	1140	3 B-17	0	0	0	0	0
2nd sorties	Fw 190A	Rheine		1242	Dortmund	1355	0	0	0	0	0	0
IV./NJG 1	Bf 110G	Leeuwarden		~1300	Leeuwarden	~1430	3 B-17	0	0	0	0	0
Jagddivision 7:												
II./JG 27	Bf 109G	Erbenheim		0913	Eelde	1030	transfer	0	0	0	0	0
I./NJG 6	Bf 110G	Mainz–Finthen	13	?	Mainz–Finthen	?	0	1	0	2	0	0
I./ZG 76	Bf 110G	Ansbach	15	1013	Ansbach	~1215	?	2	1	1	0	0
Luftflotte 3												
II. Jagdkorps			42									
Jagddivision 4:												
I./JG 26	Fw 190A	Florennes		1225	Krefeld, others	1350	6 B-17, 1 B-17 HSS	2	1	0	0	0
4./JG 26	Fw 190A	Wevelghem		0900	Florennes	0930	transfer	0	0	0	0	0
	Fw 190A	Florennes		1222	Deelen, others	~1350	2 B-17	1	0	0	0	0
II./JG 26	Fw 190A	Beauvais–Grevillers		0851	Beauvais–Grevillers	0919	n/c	0	0	0	0	0
	Fw 190A	Beauvais–Grevillers		1205	Beauvais–Grevillers	~1350	3 B-17, 1 P-47, 1 B-17 HSS	1	0	0	0	0
III./JG 26	Bf 109G	Lille–Vendeville		1205	München–Gladbach	1255	n/c	0	0	0	0	0
I./SKG 10	Fw 190G	Rosières		~1200	Rosières	~1330	1 B-17	0	0	0	0	0
Jagddivision 5:												
III./JG 2	Fw 190A	Cormeilles		~1030	Cormeilles	~1200	1 B-17	1	0	0	0	0

*144 total I. JK Zerstörer sorties **36 total JD 1 night fighter day sorties ***62 total JD 2 + JD 3 night fighter day sorties

14 January
8th Air Force Mission #183: 531 of 552 HBs (all BDs) bomb Pas de Calais V-weapon sites and t/os – lose 3-1-75, claim 8-0-1. Escort of 2 P-38 FGs, 1 P-51 FG, 9 P-47 FGs (645 sorties) claims 14-1-0, loses 3-1-10.

The weather over Germany was so bad that the 8th AF changed the target for the day to the Pas de Calais, targeting 21 V-weapon sites in the afternoon. Eight hundred and forty-four tactical aircraft had attacked these sites and other targets in northern France earlier in the day, and JG 2 and JG 26 had sparred with this morning armada with little success. They were all sent up again to oppose the heavy bomber raid. JG 2 found the bombers and downed several B-24s and P-38s for the loss of two Bf 109 Gs and their pilots. JG 26 was sent too far south by its controller who expected a deeper raid and encountered only sweeping American escorts, which downed three Fw 190s, killing two pilots and injuring the third, for the loss of two P-47s.

16 January
15th Air Force: 61 of 67 B-17s bomb Klagenfurt (A) Bf 109 component factory, TOT 1140-50 – lose 0, claim 0. P-38 escorts claim 2-2-0, lose 3.

A small raid on Klagenfurt was carried out without loss to the participating B-17s. The two Jafü Ostmark Bf 109 Gruppen did not find the bombers owing to errors by the controller or the formation leader. II./ZG 1, the local Bf 110 Gruppe, apparently attacked in strength, but was less successful than it claimed to be. P-38s warded off a full-strength attack by one of the Jagdgruppen in Italy in a vicious combat that destroyed four Bf 109s and three Lightnings.

Luftwaffe defensive activity – 14 January 1944

Unit	Type	Gruppe up			Gruppe down		Claims	Losses				
		Base	No	Time	Base	Time		Dest	Dam	KIA	MIA	WIA
Luftflotte 3												
II. Jagdkorps												
Jagddivision 4:												
I./JG 26	Fw 190A	Florennes		1445	Creil, Florennes	1606	0	1	0	1	0	0
4./JG 26?	Fw 190A	Wevelghem		~1445	Wevelghem	~1600	0	0	0	0	0	0
II./JG 26	Fw 190A	Beauvais–Grevillers		1427	Beauvais–Grevillers	1545	0	2	0	1	0	1
III./JG 26	Bf 109G	Lille–Vendeville	30	1430	Lille–Vendeville	1545	2 P-47	0	0	0	0	0
Jagddivision 5:												
Stab/JG 2	Fw 190A	Cormeilles		~1430	Cormeilles	~1545	1 P-38	0	0	0	0	0
I./JG 2?	Fw 190A	Conches		~1430	Conches	~1545	0	0	0	0	0	0
II./JG 2	Bf 109G	Creil, Evreux	30	1435	Evreux	1545	2 B-24, 2 P-38	2	0	2	0	0
III./JG 2?	Fw 190A	Cormeilles		~1430	Cormeilles	~1545	0	0	0	0	0	0

21 January

8th Air Force Mission #187: 394 of 795 HBs (all BDs) bomb Pas de Calais, Cherbourg V-1 sites and t/os, TOT 1450-152 – lose 6-3-144, claim 5-1-2. Escort of 2 P-38 FGs, 1 P-51 FG, 10 P-47 FGs (628 sorties) claims 6-0-4, loses 1-1-5.

In a near-duplicate of the 14 January mission, the 8th AF sent 795 bombers in the afternoon to bomb V-1 sites after Spitfire-escorted 9th AF B-26s had bombed targets in the same area in the morning and provoked several combats with JG 2 and JG 26. The Kanaljäger were sent up again to attack the heavy bombers. The weather was so bad that fewer than half the bombers dropped their loads; some combat boxes circled for so long that their escort had to leave them. I./JG 26 found one of these unescorted formations and downed five 44th BG B-24s. These plus two P-47s were the only successes for the Germans, who lost one KIA, one WIA and two Bf 109s.

A II./ZG 1 Bf 110G crew returns to base – probably Wels in early 1944 – to be greeted by groundcrewmen in a celebratory mood. The sign is not entirely legible, and it is not known if it refers to a round number of Gruppe air victories or combat missions. *(Bundesarchiv 676-7975-19)*

24 January

8th Air Force Mission #191: 563 HBs (all BDs) target Eschweiler, 58 B-17s bomb Zukunft t/o – lose 2-2-5, claim 1-0-3. Escort of 2 P-38 FGs, 1 P-51 FG, 10 P-47 FGs (678 sorties) claims 19-4-9, loses 9-0-6.

The Frankfurt mission that the 8th AF planned for today was fouled up completely by assembly problems over England: of the 817 bombers to take off, only 563 were dispatched; 58 completed the mission. The efforts of the German defenders were also marked by apparent confusion as Gruppen were scrambled and then recalled or sent to other bases. One German source states that 878 sorties were flown, but only 79 engaged in combat. Only four Gruppen, I./JG 1, II./JG 1, II./JG 2, and III./JG 26, plus one independent Staffel, 4./JG 26, claimed victories. The American losses of four bombers and nine fighters cost the defenders approximately eight KIA, six WIA and 21 fighters.

COMBAT REPORT[3]
24 January 1944

One P-51 Mustang shot down from 7,500 metres at 1134 hours in PQ KA 1, Saintes, 7 km SW of Hal [Haninger's victim was Capt. Giltner (POW) of the 357th FG, flying with the 354th FG: DC]

At 1023 hours, I took off in Fw 190A-6 'White 8' (W. Nr. 550872; two MG 17, three MG 151/20) with II./JG 1 on the alarm as leader of the 4. Staffel. After the Gruppe had penetrated a strong cloud deck at 1200 metres, we sighted at 1110 hours an enemy formation of 30–40 Boeings, and 150–200 Mustangs, Lightnings, Thunderbolts and Spitfires. After we had been attacked from above several times by P-47s, I climbed toward the sun with my Rotte and one a/c of 5./JG 1 (tactical sign 'Black 5') flown by Lt. Schwarz to an altitude of 8,000 metres and positioned myself behind a Staffel of 13 P-51s. I flew 800 metres behind the formation for about seven minutes, copying each movement to deceive them. I was thus able to attack them by surprise. We were first noticed when I attacked the right outside pair from 150 metres. This pair banked to the right, and the wingman thus flew right through my salvo. I observed pieces flying off the engine, cockpit and wing. The P-51 pulled sharply to the right and spun out, showing a long white smoke plume. The piot bailed out. I saw that several panels

of the parachute were ripped. The pilot fell at fairly high speed into a field on the N edge of Braine-le-Château. The airplane crashed at 1134 hours near Saintes (7 km SW of Hal) and was destroyed by the crash. The combat was witnessed by Lt. Schwarz (5./JG 1) and Ogfr. Krames (4./JG 1).

Obfw. Rudolf Haninger
4./JG 1

29 January – Frankfurt (see map)

8th Air Force Mission #198: 291 of 309 3rd BD B-17s bomb Frankfurt primary, Ludwigshafen t/o, TOT 1101 – lose 13-1-34; 345 of 366 1st BD B-17s bomb Frankfurt, TOT 1109 – lose 11-1-82; 170 of 188 2nd BD B-24s bomb Frankfurt, TOT 1140 – lose 5-3-19 – HBs claim 75-27-48. Escort of 2 P-38 FGs, 1 P-51 FG, 10 P-47 FGs (632 sorties) claims 47-6-14, loses 15-1-4.

The 8th AF judged today's full-strength raid on Frankfurt successful: 806 bombers of the 863 dispatched dropped their loads through the solid undercast. Escort was provided by 10 groups of P-47s, two groups of P-38s and one group of P 51s. American air strategy had flipped completely. A 'successful' mission was one that drew up the Luftwaffe. Bombing through overcast was now acceptable, except within the western occupied zone. Although the name was never used, this was area bombing, which the American air generals had earlier rejected. But fighters rather than bombers were now to be the

The control surfaces of a I./JG 1 Fw 190A-7 are cleaned off prior to a mission in early 1944. *(Petrick)*

Luftwaffe defensive activity – 16 January 1944

Unit	Type	Gruppe up			Gruppe down		Claims	Losses (—: included with 1st sortie)				
		Base	No	Time	Base	Time		Dest	Dam	KIA	MIA	WIA
Lw Bfh Mitte												
Jagddivision 7												
Jafü Ostmark:			109									
I./JG 27	Bf 109G	Fels am Wagram	40	1146	Fels am Wagram	1341	n/c	0	0	0	0	0
II./JG 53	Bf 109G	Wien–Seyring	35	1130	Wien–Seyring, Marburg	1355	n/c	0	0	0	0	0
II./ZG 1	Bf 110G	Wels	32	1134	Wels	~1330	3 B-17	0	0	0	0	0
Luftflotte 2												
Jafü Oberitalien:			58									
III./JG 53	Bf 109G	Villa Orba	34	1048	Villa Orba	~1200	4 P-38	4	2	2	3	1
2nd sorties	Bf 109G	Villa Orba	24	1258	Villa Orba	~1400	0	—	—	—	—	—

Luftwaffe defensive activity – 21 January 1944

Unit	Type	Gruppe up			Gruppe down		Claims	Losses				
		Base	No	Time	Base	Time		Dest	Dam	KIA	MIA	WIA
Luftflotte 3												
II. Jagdkorps												
Jagddivision 4:												
I./JG 26	Fw 190A	Florennes		1419	Abbéville, Florennes	1525	5 B-24	0	0	0	0	0
4./JG 26	Fw 190A	Wevelghem		~1415	Wevelghem	~1530	0	0	0	0	0	0
II./JG 26	Fw 190A	Beauvais–Grevillers		1415	Beauvais–Grevillers	1455	1 P-47	0	0	0	0	0
III./JG 26	Bf 109G	Lille–Vendeville		1430	Lille–Vendeville	1525	0	2	0	1	0	1
Jagddivision 5:												
Stab/JG 2	Fw 190A	Cormeilles		~1415	Cormeilles	~1530	0	0	1	0	0	1
I./JG 2?	Fw 190A	Conches		~1415	Conches	~1530	0	0	0	0	0	0
II./JG 2?	Bf 109G	Evreux		~1415	Evreux	~1530	0	0	0	0	0	0
III./JG 2	Fw 190A	Cormeilles		~1415	Cormeilles	~1530	1 P-47	0	0	0	0	0

Luftwaffe defensive activity – 24 January 1944

Unit	Type	Gruppe up			Gruppe down		Claims	Losses				
		Base	No	Time	Base	Time		Dest	Dam	KIA	MIA	WIA
Lw Bfh Mitte												
I. Jagdkorps			410									
Jagddivision 1:			83									
III./JG 54	Bf 109G	Ludwigslust		1040	Lippspringe	1145	n/c	0	1	0	0	0
2nd sorties	Bf 109G	Lippspringe		1225	Gotha	1245	n/c	0	0	0	0	0
I./ZG 26	Bf 110G	Völkenrode		1020	Völkenrode	1230	n/c	0	1	0	0	0
2nd sorties	Bf 110G	Völkenrode		1310	Völkenrode	1415	n/c	0	0	0	0	0
I./NJG 5	Bf 110G	Stendal		1114	Stendal	1331	n/c	0	0	0	0	0
JaSta Erla	Bf 109G	Delitzsch		1123	Delitzsch	1252	n/c	0	0	0	0	0
I./JG 102	Bf 109G	Zerbst		~1120	Zerbst	~1230	0	1	0	0	0	0
Jagddivison 2:			199									
Stab/JG 11	Fw 190A	Husum	?		Oldenburg	?	n/c	0	0	0	0	0
I./JG 11	Fw 190A	Aalborg-Ost		0928	Oldenburg	1050	transfer	0	0	0	0	0
	Fw 190A	Oldenburg		1128	Hesepe	1208	n/c	0	0	0	0	0
II./JG 11	Bf 109G	Wunstorf		1018	Göttingen	1212	n/c	1	0	1	0	0
2nd sorties	Bf 109G	Göttingen		1315	Wunstorf	1357	n/c	0	0	0	0	0

Luftwaffe defensive activity – 24 January 1944 Continued

Unit	Type	Gruppe up			Gruppe down		Claims	Losses				
		Base	No	Time	Base	Time		Dest	Dam	KIA	MIA	WIA
III./JG 11	Bf 109G	Oldenburg		1026	Volkel	1207	n/c	2	0	2	0	0
ErprKdo 25	Fw 190A	Achmer	8	1025	Achmer	~1230	n/c	0	0	0	0	0
	Bf 110G	Achmer	2	1025	Achmer	~1230	n/c	0	0	0	0	0
Jagddivison 3:			156									
Stab/JG 1	Fw 190A	Dortmund		~1030	Dortmund?	~1230	0	0	0	0	0	0
I./JG 1	Fw 190A	Dortmund	17	1034	Antwerp, Dortmund	1230	1 B-17, 3 B-17 HSS	2	0	1	0	1
II./JG 1	Fw 190A	Rheine	27	1023	Rheine	~1230	2 P-38, 2 P-51	6	2	3	0	2
	Fw 190A	Rheine		1110	Rheine	1208	n/c	0	0	0	0	0
2nd sorties	Fw 190A	Rheine	10	1327	Rheine	~1430	n/c	0	0	0	0	0
III./JG 1	Bf 109G	Volkel	27	1027	Volkel	~1230	n/c	0	0	0	0	0
10./JG 11	Fw 190A	Aalborg–Ost		0929	Oldenburg	1100	n/c	0	1	0	0	0
I./JG 3	Bf 109G	München–Gladbach	26	1010	München–Gladbach	~1200	0	3	0	1	0	0
Sturmstaffel 1	Fw 190A	Dortmund	15	1035	Rheine	~1215	0	1	0	0	0	0
IV./NJG 1	Bf 110G	Leeuwarden	2	1225	Leeuwarden	~1400	n/c	0	0	0	0	0
Stab/NJG 2	Ju 88C	Deelen	9	1230	Deelen	~1400	n/c	0	0	0	0	0
III./NJG 2	Ju 88C	Gilze–Rijen	16	1230	Gilze–Rijen	~1400	n/c	0	0	0	0	0
LBeob St 3	Me 210	Venlo	1	1038	Venlo	~1230	shadower	0	0	0	0	0
Jagddivision 7:			281									
III./JG 3	Bf 109G	Bad Wörishofen		1030	Bad Wörishofen	1055	n/c	0	1	0	0	0
II./JG 27	Bf 109G	Erbenheim	14	1035	Erbenheim	~1130	n/c	0	0	0	0	0
	Bf 109G	Erbenheim		1150	Erbenheim	1225	n/c	0	0	0	0	0
2nd sorties	Bf 109G	Erbenheim	8	1339	Erbenheim	1504	n/c	2	3	0	0	0
JG 106	Bf 109E	Lachen–Speyerdorf		1053	Lachen–Speyerdorf	1206	0	?	?	?	?	?
Stab/ZG 76	Bf 110G	Ansbach		~1030	Ansbach	~1230	0	1	0	0	0	0
I./ZG 76	Bf 110G	Ansbach		~1030	Ansbach	~1230	0	2	1	0	0	3
II./ZG 76	Bf 110G	Wertheim		~1030	Wertheim	~1230	0	0	3	0	0	0
I./NJG 102	Bf 110G	Kitzingen		1050	Kitzingen	1400	0	?	?	?	?	?
Luftflotte 3												
II. Jagdkorps			159									
Jagddivision 4:												
II./JG 2	Bf 109G	Reims	26	1020	München–Gladbach	1225	1 B-17	0	1	0	0	0
III./JG 2	Fw 190A	Juvincourt	10	1010	Juvincourt	~1200	n/c	0	0	0	0	0
I./JG 26	Fw 190A	Florennes	19	1018	Bonn, Florennes	1208	n/c	0	0	0	0	0
4./JG 26	Fw 190A	Florennes	4	1100	Wevelghem	~1230	1 B-17, 1 P-38	0	0	0	0	0
2nd sorties	Fw 190A	Wevelghem	4	1310	Wevelghem	1430	n/c	0	0	0	0	0
II./JG 26	Fw 190A	Epinoy	1	0930	Florennes	~1000	0	0	0	0	0	0
	Fw 190A	Beauvais–Grevillers		0937	Florennes	~1010	Transfer	0	0	0	0	0
2nd sorties	Fw 190A	Florennes	20	1051	Le Culot	1215	n/c	0	0	0	0	0
	Fw 190A	Beauvais–Grevillers	2	1311	Beauvais–Grevillers	~1400	n/c	0	0	0	0	0
JG 26	Fw 190A	Florennes	5	1259	Florennes	~1330	0	0	0	0	0	0
JG 26	Fw 190A	Florennes	7	1355	Florennes	~1415	0	0	0	0	0	0
III./JG 26	Bf 109G	Lille–Vendeville		0913	Laon–Athies	0933	Transfer	0	0	0	0	0
	Bf 109G	Laon–Athies	10	1025	Charleroi	1125	1 P-47	0	0	0	0	0
I./NJG 4	Bf 110G	Florennes	3	1130	Florennes	~1330	n/c	0	0	0	0	0
II./NJG 4	Bf 110G	St. Dizier	3	1130	St. Dizier	~1330	n/c	0	0	0	0	0
	Bf 110G	St. Dizier	2	1214	St. Dizier	~1330	n/c	0	0	0	0	0
III./NJG 4	Bf 110G	Juvincourt	5	1130	Juvincourt	~1330	n/c	0	0	0	0	0
I./SKG 10	Fw 190A	Rosières	10	1330	Rosières	~1430	n/c	0	0	0	0	0
Jagddivision 5:												
Stab/JG 2	Fw 190A	Cormeilles	3	0955	Cormeilles	~1200	n/c	0	0	0	0	0
JG 2	Fw 190A	St. Germain	8	1400	St. Germain	~1430	n/c	0	0	0	0	0

critical weapon for winning air supremacy. The day of 'bombers as bait' had arrived.

A phased escort system was instituted as part of the new, more aggressive operational plan for the American fighters. The P-47 groups covered the penetration and withdrawal phases of the mission, aided by Spitfires on withdrawal; the three long-range groups covered the target area. The fighters were ordered to cover the area over which the bombers were scheduled to fly; close escort was no longer required. For each mission, one squadron of each fighter group was designated a 'bouncing' squadron, free to pursue any approaching Luftwaffe fighter formations well beyond the visual range of the bombers.

A new route to Frankfurt was tried today. The attackers flew southeast along the boundary between Luftflotte Reich and Luftflotte 3 and then turned due east to Frankfurt. The two most prominent I. Jagdkorps units, JG 1 and JG 11, played no role in the defence; it is assumed that they were grounded by the weather. The south German units intercepted the bombers over the target, and JG 26 hit them on both their entry and withdrawal legs, with some assistance from JG 2. The RLV force flew 550 sorties, 254 of which contacted the enemy. Luftwaffe losses were 34 KIA or MIA, 18 WIA and 45 aircraft. The Americans wrote off 34 bombers and 16 fighters, a large portion of these to III./JG 3 and II./JG 26.

COMBAT REPORT[4]
29 January 1944

One Boeing B-17 shot from formation from 6,500 metres at 1114 hours in PQ TQ-3, W of Kaiserslautern [Not confirmed despite witness testimony: DC]

At 1015 hours, I took off in a Bf 109G-6 with three MG 151/20s and two MG 131s [i.e., a 'gunboat'] as Staffelführer in the Gruppe of Major Dahl against an enemy formation reported in the area of Mannheim. At 1100 hours, I saw the enemy formation near Mannheim, course east. It contained 60–70 aircraft, staggered from 6,000 to 7,000 metres. As I banked toward the formation, I saw the bombs drop, after which the bombers turned away toward the west. I made a full turn and, at 1113 hours, attacked from the front a Boeing Fortress in the middle of the formation, which was staggered higher from right to left. During my burst of fire I saw hits in the cockpit and left

engines. While pulling away to the right, I saw the aircraft I had hit pulling away in a gentle left bank, smoking heavily from the left wing and both engines and quickly losing altitude. I then attacked the airplane again, all alone, as my wingman had bugged off after the first attack. I obtained hits in the fuselage and left wing with a short burst of fire. During this attack my own airplane entered a spin owing to lack of airspeed. After I recovered, I saw that the Boeing remained behind the protection of the formation in a shallow bank, smoking heavily. Since I renewed my attack on the formation, I made no further observation of the damaged Fortress.

Lt. Ekkehard Tichy
9./JG 3

Oblt. Ekkehard Tichy joined JG 53 on the Eastern Front in 1942 after completing training and came back to the Reich with III./JG 3 in August 1943 for RLV duty, becoming 9./JG 3 Staffelkapitän in November. He lost an eye in combat with P-51s in March 1944, but returned to combat with IV.(Sturm)/JG 3 in June. During a Sturmangriff on the 91st BG on 16 August, Tichy collided with a B-17 and was killed. He was posthumously promoted to Hauptmann and awarded the Knight's Cross. (Author's collection)

30 January
8th Air Force Mission #200: 742 of 757 HBs (all BDs) bomb Brunswick primary, Hannover & other t/os – lose 20-3-115, claim 51-7-27. Escort of 2 P-38 FGs, 1 P-51 FG, 10 P-47 FGs (635 sorties) claims 45-15-31, loses 4-0-7.

Again today, the Continent was covered in cloud, and the 8th AF dropped its bombs on the signals of aircraft equipped with H_2X radar. The bombers' track took them across northern Holland on the most direct route to Brunswick. Jagddivision 3 had the main responsibility for the interception. JD 4 sent the three

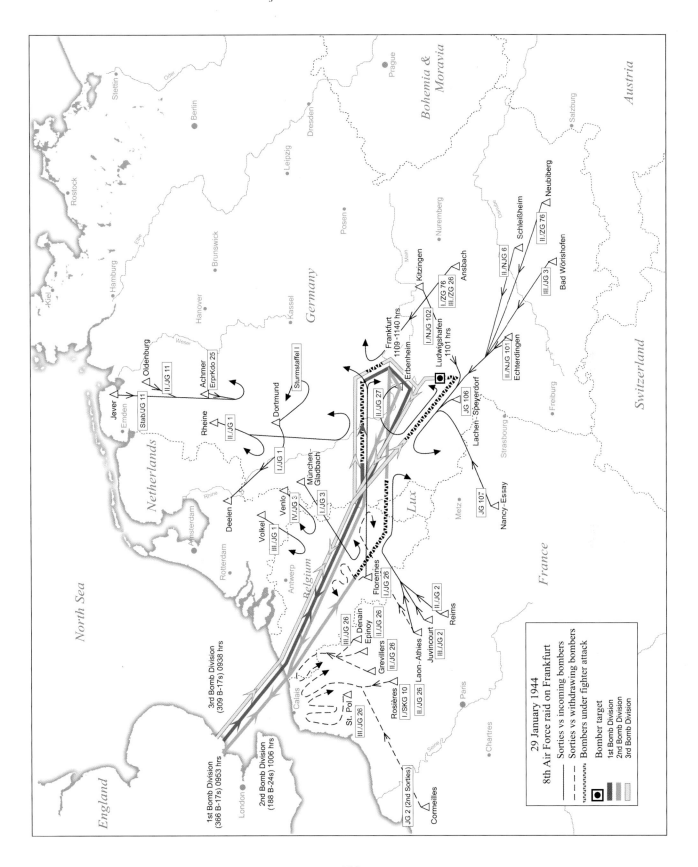

Luftwaffe defensive activity – 29 January 1944

Unit	Type	Gruppe up			Gruppe down		Claims	Losses (—: included with 1st sortie)				
		Base	No	Time	Base	Time		Dest	Dam	KIA	MIA	WIA
vs. incoming stream												
Luftflotte Reich												
I. Jagdkorps			*224									
Jagddivision 1:			*0									
I./ZG 26	Bf 110G	Volkenröde	—	1020	Oldenburg	1140	n/c	0	0	0	0	0
Jagddivision 2:			*111									
Stab/JG 11	Bf 109G	Jever	3	1019	Jever	~1110	n/c	0	0	0	0	0
II./JG 11	Bf 109G	Oldenburg	7	1020	Oldenburg	1110	n/c	0	0	0	0	0
III./JG 11	Fw 190A	Oldenburg	16	1022	Oldenburg	1111	n/c	0	0	0	0	0
ErprKdo 25	Fw 190A	Achmer	7	1022	Achmer	~1110	n/c	0	0	0	0	0
	Bf 110G	Achmer	3	1040	Achmer	~1200	n/c	0	0	0	0	0
III./NJG 3	Ju 88C	Stade	7	1037	Stade	~1200	n/c	0	0	0	0	0
Jagddivision 3:			*110									
I./JG 1	Fw 190A	Dortmund	16	1025	Deelen	1140	n/c	0	0	0	0	0
II./JG 1	Fw 190A	Rheine	14	1020	Rheine	~1140	0	0	0	0	0	0
III./JG 1	Bf 109G	Volkel	26	1009	Volkel	~1140	0	0	0	0	0	0
I./JG 3	Bf 109G	München–Gladbach	17	1015	München–Gladbach	~1140	n/c	0	0	0	0	0
IV./JG 3	Bf 109G	Venlo	25	1015	Venlo	~1140	n/c	0	0	0	0	0
Sturmstaffel 1	Fw 190A	Dortmund	12	1027	Dortmund	~1140	n/c	0	0	0	0	0
Jagddivision 7:			*196									
III./JG 3	Bf 109G	Bad Wörishofen	28	1010	Karlsruhe	1155	11 B-17, 4 B-17 HSS	6	4	2	0	1
II./JG 27	Bf 109G	Erbenheim	19	1015	Erbenheim	1140	3 B-17, 1 P-38	2	0	2	0	0
JG 106	Bf 109E	Lachen–Speyerdorf	13	1045	Lachen–Speyerdorf	1135	0	3	1	2	0	0
I/JG 301	Bf 109G	Neubiberg	3	1013	Neubiberg	~1130	0	0	0	0	0	0
I./ZG 76	Bf 110G	Ansbach	26	1018	Ansbach	~1200	0	6	1	4	0	6
II,.ZG 76	Bf 110G	Neubiberg	20	1013	Neubiberg	1110	0	4	0	1	0	5
III./ZG 76	Bf 110G	Ansbach?		1018	Ansbach?	~1200	0	2	0	3	0	0
II./NJG 6	Bf 110G	Schleißheim	18	1127	Schleißheim	~1230	1 B-17, 1 P-38, 1 P-47	6	0	11	0	1
II./NJG 101	Bf 110G	Echterdingen	14	1116	Echterdingen	~1230	0	0	0	0	0	0
I./NJG 102	Bf 110G	Kitzingen	11	1105	Kitzingen	1311	0	1	0	1	0	0
Luftflotte 3												
II. Jagdkorps			*133									
Jagddivision 4:												
II./JG 2	Bf 109G	Reims	22	1045	Reims	~1130	2 P-47	4	1	2	0	3
III./JG 2	Fw 190A	Juvincourt	13	1025	Juvincourt	~1145	1 B-24	4	0	1	2	1
I./JG 26	Fw 190A	Florennes	24	1010	Florennes, Strasbourg	1215	2 B-17, 1 P-38	0	0	0	0	0
II./JG 26	Fw 190A	Laon–Athies	20	1035	Grevillers	1205	2 B-17 HSS, 2 B-24, 2 B-24 HSS, 1 P-38	2	0	1	0	1
III./JG 26	Bf 109G	Laon–Athies	4	1030	Laon–Athies	~1145	n/c	0	0	0	0	0
I./JG 107	Bf 109E	Nancy–Essay		~1030	Nancy–Essay	~1200	0	1	0	1	0	0
III./NJG 4	Do 217	Juvincourt	1	0915	Juvincourt	~1130	shadower	0	0	0	0	0
	Bf 110G	Juvincourt	1	0940	Juvincourt	~1130	shadower	0	0	0	0	0

Luftwaffe defensive activity – 29 January 1944 Continued

Unit	Type	Gruppe up			Gruppe down		Claims	Losses (—: included with 1st sortie)				
		Base	No	Time	Base	Time		Dest	Dam	KIA	MIA	WIA
vs. withdrawing stream												
Luftflotte 3												
II. Jagdkorps												
Jagddivision 4:												
III./JG 2	Fw 190A	Juvincourt		~1200	Juvincourt	~1330	1 P-47	0	0	0	0	0
I./JG 26	Fw 190A	Florennes	5	1159	Florennes	~1330	1 B-17	1	0	1	0	0
4./JG 26	Fw 190A	Laon–Athies		~1130	Grevillers	~1300	2 B-17	1	0	0	0	0
II./JG 26	Fw 190A	Laon–Athies	8	1125	Grevillers	~1200	0	1	3	0	0	0
	Fw 190A	Epinoy	2	1219	Epinoy	~1330	1 B-17, 1 P-47	0	0	0	0	0
	Fw 190A	Grevillers	1	1220	Grevillers	1250	1 P-47	0	0	0	0	0
2nd sorties	Fw 190A	Grevillers	2	1300	Grevillers	1330	1 B-17	—	—	—	—	—
2nd sorties	Fw 190A	Epinoy	7	1300	Epinoy	~1400	1 B-17, 1 B-24	—	—	—	—	—
III./JG 26	Bf 109G	St. Pol	5	1254	St. Pol	~1400	n/c	0	1	0	0	0
	Bf 109G	Denain	4	1307	Denain	~1400	n/c	0	0	0	0	0
III./NJG 4	Bf 110G	Juvincourt	3	1232	Juvinourt	~1400	n/c	0	0	0	0	0
I./SKG 10	Fw 190A	Rosières	11	1230	Rosières	~1330	1 B -17	0	0	0	0	0
Jagddivision 5:												
Stab/JG 2	Fw 190A	Cormeilles	1	1306	Cormeilles	1400	0	1	0	0	0	0

*total sorties vs incoming + withdrawing stream

JG 26 Gruppen north to assist JD 3 in combating the bombers as they returned from the target. JD 7 split its fighters, sending some north against the 8th AF and the rest south against the 15th AF, which damaged Udine airfield in northern Italy so badly that the Luftwaffe had to move its Italian headquarters all the way to Klagenfurt in Austria. Back in the Reich, I. Jagdkorps was unable to form its Gefechtsverbände owing to the weather conditions, and its fighters were forced to fly in small, vulnerable formations. Luftwaffe personnel casualties over the Reich were very heavy, especially in the night fighters. The Ju 88 night fighters flew day missions with all three regular crewmen, including the radar operator, and often all three were killed when these aircraft were shot down by the numerous American escorts. A total of 480 contact and non-contact RLV sorties were flown, and losses in what was considered a failed defensive mission were approximately 66 KIA or MIA, 16 WIA and 75 aircraft. The 8th AF wrote off 23 bombers and four fighters. The 15th AF lost three bombers to all causes.

COMBAT REPORT[5]
30 January 1944

One Boeing B-17 shot down circa 1200 hours, PQ HQ-HR, SW of Osnabrück
[Not confirmed – crash not witnessed: DC]

I took off from Deelen with my Rotte at 1110 hours to intercept an enemy bomber formation coming in near Osnabrück on an easterly course. In the region of Zwolle, I saw the enemy and flew to the area east of Osnabrück behind three strong 4-engine formations flying 2–3 km apart, after I turned away from several strong fighter formations. The bomber formations flew directly behind one another and, making a strong condensation trail from Rheine, began to pull away from one another. During this pulling away, a B-17 turned left from the last formation and probably lost them in the heavy condensation.

As the bomber pulled away somewhat to the north, I decided to attack it, after observing that none of its own fighters were near this formation. No damage could be seen on the enemy machine, which maintained an altitude of 6,000–6,300 metres. My first attack was from directly behind. On my approach, the bomber manœuvred to the west in a large left turn. By cutting the throttle I remained directly behind it. A fairly short burst of fire set the right inner engine on fire, and I radioed my wingman, 'Get ready!' Over the radio I learned that his guns were jammed, and I thus prepared to make a second attack from an altitude of 5,500 metres. I received no defensive fire from the enemy machine, which was already burning in places. During my second attack I saw one parachute and a short burst of fire from 100 metres set the right outer engine on fire. The enemy bomber flew west; he had lost 2,000 metres in altitude during my second attack. Parts of the wing and fuselage, especially from the right half of the tail assembly, flew away, along with several parachutes. The bomber fell away burning fiercely and trailing a thick cloud of black smoke. It tipped over its right wing and went into the clouds. Lacking part of its tail and one engine, it was no longer controllable.

I could not observe the crash, which took place at about 1200 hours. Its location could not be seen owing to the closed cloud deck, but was in PQ HQ-HR. Witnessing the combat was Ufz. Schnappauf, Stab/JG 1.

Oberst Walter Oesau, Geschwaderkommodore
Stab/JG 1

31 January
8th Air Force Mission #203: 74 of 74 2nd BD B-24s bomb St. Pol/Siracourt V-1 facility – lose 0-2-0, claim 0. Escort of 2 P-47 FGs (114 sorties) claims 0, loses 0.

8th Air Force Mission #204: 209 VIII FC fighters (1 P-38 FG, 3 P-47 FGs) bomb Gilze-Rijen airfield – lose 6-1-2, claim 13-1-1.

15th Air Force: 61 of 67 B-17s bomb Klagenfurt (A) airfield – lose 0, claim 0. P-38 escorts claim 0, lose 0.

The American tactical highlight was a bombing attack on the important JD 3 base at Gilze-Rijen by 75 P-47s. Forty-seven P-38s of the 55th FG flew an accompanying sweep and lost six fighters to I./JG 1 and IV./JG 3; Jagddivision 3 sustained four operational losses.

Oberst Walter Oesau in an official portrait. An early member of the Luftwaffe and a 9-victory Condor Legion ace, Oesau was a proficient combat pilot, becoming the 3rd pilot to receive the Swords to the Knight's Cross with Oak Leaves. He was grounded after his 100th victory, but his services as a formation leader were needed so badly that he was restored to combat status in November 1943, becoming JG 1 Kommodore following Oberst Philipp's death. He continued leading the unit past the end of his endurance and was killed by P-38s on 11 May 1944. (Author's collection)

Luftwaffe defensive activity – 30 January 1944

Unit	Type	Gruppe up			Gruppe down		Claims	Losses				
		Base	No	Time	Base	Time		Dest	Dam	KIA	MIA	WIA
vs. incoming stream												
Luftflotte Reich												
I. Jagdkorps			*351									
Jagddivision 1:			*38									
I./ZG 26	Bf 110G	Volkenröde		1053	Volkenröde, Rheine	1230	0	0	0	0	0	0
II./ZG 26	Me 410A	Hildesheim	5	1102	Hildesheim	~1230	0	1	0	1	0	0
4./Zerst ErgGr	Bf 110G	Brunswick–Broitzem		1108	Brunswick–Broitzem	1255	0	0	0	0	0	0
Jagddivision 2:			*95									
II./JG 11	Bf 109G	Wunstorf	31	1103	Deelen	~1230	n/c	0	0	0	0	0
III./JG 11	Fw 190A	Oldenburg		~1115	Oldenburg	~1245	1 B-17	0	0	0	0	0
Stab/ZG 26	Bf 110G	Wunstorf	11	~1100	Wunstorf	~1230	0	1	0	0	0	0
ErprKdo 25	Bf 109G	Achmer	16	1004	Achmer	~1130	0	0	0	0	0	0
	Fw 190A	Achmer	6	1103	Achmer	~1230	0	1	3	0	0	0
	Bf 110G	Achmer	3	1057	Achmer	~1230	0	1	0	2	0	0
Jagddivision 3:			*173									
Stab/JG 1	Fw 190A	Deelen	2	1104	Deelen	~1230	1 B-17	0	0	0	0	0
I./JG 1	Fw 190A	Dortmund	17	1105	Wunstorf	1243	7 B-17	4	0	3	0	0
II./JG 1	Fw 190A	Rheine	14	1104	Rheine	1220	4 B-17	3	0	0	0	0
III./JG 1	Bf 109G	Volkel	24	1047	Volkel	~1215	0	7	3	6	0	3
I./JG 3	Bf 109G	München–Gladbach	17	1048	München–Gladbach	~1215	0	2	1	2	0	0
IV./JG 3	Bf 109G	Venlo	22	1052	Venlo	~1215	0	2	0	0	0	0
I./JG 300	Bf 109G	Bonn–Hangelar	6	1110	Bonn–Hangelar	~1230	1 B-17	2	0	1	0	0
II./JG 300	Fw 190A	Rheine	5	1104	Rheine	~1230	0	0	0	0	0	0
Sturmstaffel 1	Fw 190A	Dortmund	12	1105	Dortmund	~1240	1 B-27, 2 B-24	3	6	2	0	3
Jagddivision 7:			*125									
III./JG 3	Bf 109G	Bad Wörishofen	24	1120	Bad Wörishofen	1315	0 (vs. 15 AF)	0	0	0	0	0
II./JG 27	Bf 109G	Erbenheim	20	1150	Erbenheim	~1300	0	2	3	1	0	1
II./JG 53	Bf 109G	Wien–Seyring		1123	Klagenfurt?	1315	2 B-24 (vs. 15 AF)	4	1	2	2	0
I/JG 301	Bf 109G	Neubiberg		~1145	Neubiberg	~1300	1 B-17	1	0	0	1	0
III./ZG 76	Bf 110G	Öttingen	18	1050	Öttingen	~1230	0	1	0	0	0	0
Stab/NJG 6	Bf 110G	Schleißheim	2	1150	Schleißheim	~1230	0	0	0	0	0	0
I./NJG 6	Bf 110G	Mainz–Finthen	15	1150	Mainz–Finthen	~1230	0	1	0	2	0	0
II./NJG 6	Bf 110G	Echterdingen	11	1150	Echterdingen	~1230	0	1	0	2	0	0
LBeob St 3	Me 210	Venlo	1	1042	Venlo	~1240	shadower	0	0	0	0	0
VbdFhr Schule	Bf 109G	Fels am Wagram		1150	Ingolstadt	1325	n/c (vs. 15 AF)	0	0	0	0	0
Luftflotte 3												
II. Jagdkorps			*49									
Jagddivision 4:												
I./JG 26	Fw 190A	Florennes	16	1033	Rheine	1217	transfer	0	0	0	0	0
4./JG 26	Fw 190A	Wevelghem	5	1039	Volkel	1217	transfer	0	0	0	0	0
II./JG 26	Fw 190A	Grevillers	8	1030	München–Gladbach	~1215	Transfer	0	0	0	0	0
	Fw 190A	Cambrai–Epinoy	12	1031	Volkel?	~1215	transfer	0	0	0	0	0
III./JG 26	Bf 109G	Lille-Vendeville	8	1030	Venlo	~1215	transfer	0	0	0	0	0
	Bf 109G	Denain	8	1038	Venlo	~1215	transfer	0	0	0	0	0

Luftwaffe defensive activity – 30 January 1944 Continued

Unit	Type	Gruppe up			Gruppe down		Claims	Losses				
		Base	No	Time	Base	Time		Dest	Dam	KIA	MIA	WIA
vs. withdrawing stream												
Luftflotte Reich												
I. Jagdkorps												
Jagddivision 1:												
I./JG 302	Bf 109	Jüterbog	5	1210	Jüterbog	~1300	1 B-17	0	0	0	0	0
I./NJG 2	Ju 88C	Kassel–Rothwesten	3	1218	Kassel–Rothwesten	~1400	1 B-17	3	0	6	0	1
II./NJG 2	Bf 110G	Parchim	11	1145	Parchim	~1400	1 B-17	1	0	3	0	0
I./NJG 5	Bf 110G	Stendal	9	1157	Stendal	~1400	0	1	0	0	0	0
II./NJG 5	Bf 110G	Königsberg	4	1130	Königsberg	~1330	0	0	0	0	0	0
III./NJG 5	Bf 110G	Brandis	1	1142	Brandis	~1345	0	1	0	2	0	0
JaSta Erla	Bf 109G	Delitzsch		1230	Delitzsch	1247	n/c	0	0	0	0	0
ISS Ago	Bf 109	Oschersleben	3	1157	Oschersleben	~1300	0	0	0	0	0	0
Jagddivision 2:												
ErprKdo 25	Bf 110G	Achmer	3	1303	Achmer	~1430	0	0	0	0	0	0
	Me 410	Achmer	3	1300	Achmer	1400	0	0	0	0	0	0
I./NJG 3	Bf 110G	Vechta		~1300	Vechta	~1430	0	1	0	1	0	1
Jagddivision 3:												
II./JG 1	Fw 190A	Rheine	14	1235	Rheine	~1400	n/c	0	0	0	0	0
III./JG 1	Bf 109G	Volkel	13	1250	Volkel	1352	0	0	0	0	0	0
I./JG 3	Bf 109G	München–Gladbach	5	1240	München–Gladbach	~1400	n/c	0	0	0	0	0
IV./JG 3	Bf 109G	Venlo	14	1254	Venlo	~1400	n/c	0	0	0	0	0
II./JG 11	Bf 109G	Deelen	21	1303	Wunstorf	~1400	2 P-47	6	7	4	2	0
I./JG 26	Fw 190A	Rheine		1258	Kirchhellen	1350	1 B-17, 2 P-38	1	0	0	0	1
II./JG 26	Fw 190A	München–Gladbach	15	1234	?	1325	1 B-17, 1 P-47	1	1	1	0	1
III./JG 26	Bf 109G	Venlo		1256	München–Gladbach	1340	1 P-47	1	0	1	0	0
III./JG 301	Bf 109G	Deelen	22	1310	Deelen	~1400	0	3	1	2	0	0
I./ZG 26	Bf 110G	Rheine	6	1300	Volkenröde	~1430	1 P-51	3	0	0	0	0
II./NJG 1	Bf 110G	St. Trond	2	1237	St. Trond	~1400	n/c	0	0	0	0	0
IV./NJG 1	Bf 110G	Leeuwarden	3	1210	Leeuwarden	~1400	1 B-17	3	0	6	0	0
Stab/NJG 2	Ju 88C	Deelen	9	1218	Deelen	~1400	0	0	0	0	0	0
III./NJG 2	Ju 88C	Gilze–Rijen	11	1225	Gilze–Rijen	~1400	1 P-47	6	0	7	0	5
Jagddvision 7:												
I./ZG 76	Bf 110G	Ansbach	23	1230	Ansbach	~1400	0	1	0	0	0	0
II./ZG 76	Bf 110G	Wertheim	17	1230	Wertheim	~1400	0	0	0	0	0	0
Luftflotte 3												
II. Jagdkorps												
Jagddivision 4:												
I./JG 26	Fw 190A	Florennes	2	1224	Florennes	~1400	n/c	0	0	0	0	0
	Fw 190A	Florennes	4	1345	Florennes	~1430	n/c	0	0	0	0	0
Jagddivision 5:												
Stab/JG 2	Fw 190A	Cormeilles?		~1300	Cormeilles?	~1400	0	1	0	1	0	0
II./JG 2	Bf 109	Creil	2	1232	Creil	~1400	n/c	0	0	0	0	0
	Bf 109	Creil	3	1350	Creil	~1430	n/c	0	0	0	0	0
	Bf 109	Creil	14	1440	Lille–Vendeville	~1530	transfer	0	0	0	0	0
III.JG 2	Fw 190A	Cormeilles?		~1300	Cormeilles?	~1400	0	3	0	3	0	0

*total sorties vs. incoming + withdrawing streams

February 1944

An organisational improvement affecting the highest levels of the Luftwaffe took effect on 5 February, with the establishment of the *Oberkommando der Luftwaffe* (Luftwaffe High Command; OKL). Reichsmarschall Göring, the *Oberbefehlshaber der Luftwaffe* (Supreme Commander of the Luftwaffe; ObdL), and his Reich Air Ministry (RLM) had overseen the entire scope of aviation activities in Germany, both military and civilian. The Luftwaffe had had nothing comparable to the army and navy high commands, but the OKL now took over the general staff, the operations staff, the weapons inspectorates (including Galland's GdJ), the quartermaster branch and signals. Although more efficient than the previous bloated system, it is difficult to see any specific beneficial effect on the day RLV force, which spent a difficult month under direct attack by the USAAF.

The only Jagdgruppe to join the RLV force in February was I./JG 5 of the *Eismeer* (Arctic Ocean) Geschwader, which transferred from Bulgaria to JD 7 in southwestern Germany. One new fighter Staffel was established, 1./JG 400. This would not be operational soon, but would have the task of bringing into service the rocket-propelled Me 163. These were now concenrated in a testing unit, Erprobungskommando 16.

On the 23rd, in the middle of the Americans' 'Big Week' campaign against the aviation industry, I. Jagdkorps reorganised its three Jagddivisionen. Their day units would now comprise:

JD 1: JG 3 (4 Gruppen), ZG 26, 3 Gruppen of JG 300 and JG 302
JD 2: JG 11 (3 Gruppen), III./JG 54
JD 3: JG 1 (3 Gruppen), I./JG 300

The strategy of 'peripheral defence' had been abandoned, and the Gruppen were moved inland. The Gruppen of each Geschwader were based on separate airfields as before, but grouped closely together for quicker assembly into Gefechtsverbände. Worth noting are the listing of the *Wilde Sau* single-engine night fighter Gruppen of JG 300 and JG 302 as day units and the strengthening of Jagddivision 1. Bolstering this Jagddivision would help protect the important aviation industry targets in the Hannover and Magdeburg areas, as well as Berlin, which was expected to come under attack in the near future.

Tactical and operational highlights include:
1. Large formations (Gefechtsverbände), while

Genlt. Adolf Galland in Berlin, after he had removed his medals as a protest against Reichsmarschall Göring's insults. *(Galland)*

awkward to assemble and command in the air, especially in the prevailing weather conditions, were successful when they could be positioned properly. They were only necessary owing to the large and ever-growing number of American escorts.

2. One Gruppe of each permanent Gefechtsverband was to be equipped with Bf 109s with new high-altitude engines and designated as a *Höhengruppe* (high-altitude Gruppe), tasked with keeping the American escorts away from the Gruppen attacking the bombers. The permission of RM Göring for this deviation from standard Luftwaffe doctrine was sought and obtained.

3. The success of Sturmstaffel 1 continued, and plans were initiated to obtain equipment for one or more Sturmgruppen.

4. At the insistence of RM Göring, plans were made to increase the number and effectiveness of sorties flown against the withdrawing bombers. These included designating fully equipped assembly airfields and addressing command-and-control problems.

5. The decentralised nature of the Luftwaffe command-and-control apparatus led to problems as American strength grew and their missions increased in length and were split among multiple targets. Arguments for centralised control were raised constantly, most notably by Genlt. Schmid of I. Jagdkorps.

The I. Jagdkorps monthly report for February recorded its average daily operational strength as 350 single-engine fighters, 100 twin-engine fighters and

Men of Sturmstaffel 1 assemble for an inspection at Dortmund in February. *(Mombeek)*

The Bf 109G-6 of the 9./JG 54 Staffelkapitän, Oblt. Wilhelm Schilling, at Ludwigslust in February. Its unit markings are worth noting: a wide blue Geschwader identity band on the rear fuselage; the Geschwader emblem, a green heart, enclosing the III./JG 54 emblem beneath the cockpit; and the 9. Staffel devil's head on the cowling. *(Prien)*

50 night fighters available for day use. The command flew 2861 operational sorties while losing 299 fighters, for a loss rate of 10.3 per cent. It estimated the number of USAAF sorties to the Reich to be 10,452 for a loss of 310 to fighters, for a loss rate of 2.9 per cent.

3 February

8th Air Force Mission #206: 609 of 724 HBs (2nd BD B-24s recalled) bomb Wilhelmshaven port and Emden t/o – lose 4-1-47, claim 0-1-0. Escort of 2 P 38 FGs, 1 P-51 FG, 10 P-47 FGs (632 sorties) claims 8-0-3, loses 9-3-13.

Today, the 8th AF dropped a number of bombs in the general area of Wilhelmshaven and Emden. Few RLV fighters could get off the ground: only three Jagdgruppen and part of ErprKdo 25 made contact, and the P-47 escorts kept all of them from the bombers. The Luftwaffe lost six KIA, one WIA and 11 fighters to the P-47s or weather conditions. The 8th AF lost or scrapped five B-17s, 11 P-47s and one P-51. The seven claims by I. Jagdkorps were all for P-47s.

4 February

8th Air Force Mission #206: 633 of 748 HBs (all BDs) bomb Frankfurt rail yards and t/os, TOT 1143-1240 – lose 20-3-359, claim 4-0-1. Escort of 2 P-38 FGs, 1 P-51 FG, 10 P-47 FGs (637 sorties) claims 8-0-4, loses 1-1-9.

The 8th AF visited Frankfurt again, bombing through thick clouds that covered most of Western Europe. Only 124 defensive sorties were flown, and the only units to contact the enemy were two JG 26 Jagdgruppen from JD 4. Frankfurt was in the area defended by JD 7, whose controllers were unable to put their own fighters into contact with the bomber stream and were slow to request aid from I. Jagdkorps. I./JG 26, accompanied today by 4./JG 26, nominally a part of the Gruppe but normally operating independently, did very well, considering the odds it faced. It contacted the withdrawing bombers near Brussels, and its quick attack downed three B-17s before the arrival of P-47s forced the Fw 190s into a defensive circle, from which two were shot down with minor injuries to their pilots. The Gruppe scored a fourth victory half an hour after this combat when a straggling B-17 was located and shot down. II./JG 26 scored a victory against a B-24 attempting an early return, but its major mission against the withdrawing stream never reached the bombers; it was attacked by P-38s and P-47s in turn and lost two Focke-Wulfs. American losses totalled 23

Luftwaffe defensive activity – 3 February 1944

Unit	Type	Gruppe up			Gruppe down		Claims	Losses				
		Base	No	Time	Base	Time		Dest	Dam	KIA	MIA	WIA
Luftflotte Reich												
I. Jagdkorps			225									
Jagddivison 1:												
III./JG 54	Bf 109G	Ludwigslust		1049	Ludwigslust	1154	n/c	0	0	0	0	0
Jagdstaffel Erla	Bf 109G	Delitzsch		1108	Delitzsch	1148	n/c	0	0	0	0	0
Jagddivison 2:												
III./JG 11	Bf 109G	Oldenburg		1013	Oldenburg	~1130	3 P-47	2	1	1	0	0
ErprKdo 25	Fw 190A	Achmer		~1045	Achmer	~1200	1 P-47	1	0	0	0	1
Jagddivison 3:												
I./JG 1	Fw 190A	Dortmund		1025	Münster–Handorf, Reinsehlen	1140	n/c	0	0	0	0	0
II./JG 1	Fw 190A	Rheine	19	1038	Rheine	1238	n/c	2	0	0	0	0
III./JG 1	Bf 109G	Volkel		~1045	Volkel	~1215	0	1	0	1	0	0
I./JG 3	Bf 109G	München–Gladbach		~1045	München–Gladbach	~1215	0	1	0	0	0	0
IV./JG 3	Bf 109G	Venlo		~1045	Venlo	~1215	3 P-47	4	0	4	0	0

Luftwaffe defensive activity – 4 February 1944

Unit	Type	Gruppe up			Gruppe down		Claims	Losses				
		Base	No	Time	Base	Time		Dest	Dam	KIA	MIA	WIA
Luftflotte Reich												
I. Jagdkorps												
Jagddivision 1:												
I./7G 26	Bf 110G	Völkenrode		1100	Erfurt–Bindersleben	1250	n/c	0	0	0	0	0
Luftflotte 3												
II. Jagdkorps												
Jagddivision 4:												
I./JG 26	Fw 190A	Florennes		1241	Florennes, St. Trond	1354	3 B-17	2	1	0	0	2
4./JG 26	Fw 190A	Wevelghem		1221	Wevelghem	~1354	1 B-17	0	0	0	0	0
II./JG 26	Fw 190A	Beauvais–Grevillers	10	1144	Beauvais–Grevillers	1201	1 B-24	0	0	0	0	0
2nd sorties	Fw 190A	Beauvais–Grevillers		~1220	Beauvais–Grevillers	~1350	0	1	1	1	0	1
III./JG 26	Bf 109G	Lille–Vendeville		1305	Chièvres	1443	n/c	0	0	0	0	0

bombers and two fighters to all causes. The only Luftwaffe claims that have been located are JG 26's five; likewise, the only German losses found are JG 26's one KIA, three WIA and three Fw 190s.

5 February

8th Air Force Mission #210: 452 of 509 HBs (all BDs) bomb 6 French airfields – lose 2-4-70, claim 5-0-5. Escort of 2 P-38 FGs, 1 P-51 FG, 10 P-47 FGs (634 sorties) claims 6-0-4, loses 2-2-2.

The 8th AF sent a medium-strength raid to bomb several airfields in central France, but was unable to find most of them. JD 5 got the JG 2 Geschwaderstab and Second Gruppe airborne in time to make an interception, claiming one bomber and two fighters, but the escorts punished the small force. JD 4 sent all three JG 26 Gruppen south to assist JG 2, but its effort was futile. JG 26 made no contact with the USAAF, which wrote off six bombers and four fighters. JG 2 lost three KIA or MIA, one WIA and three fighters.

6 February

8th Air Force Mission #212: 206 of 642 HBs (all BDs) bomb 4 French airfields – lose 4-2-50, claim 3-3-0. Escort of 2 P-38 FGs, 1 P-51 FG, 10 P-47 FGs (638 sorties) claims 11-2-3, loses 4-3-2.

The 8th AF returned to France, with results similar to those of the previous day. Fewer than one-third of the bombers found targets to bomb. The understrength JG 2 (its First Gruppe was guarding southern France against an attack from the Mediterranean) flew two missions, but its successes barely matched its losses. JG 26 flew south to the Paris region, but today the P-47s were waiting. JG 26 escaped fairly lightly, but its claims were few. The Americans wrote off six bombers and seven fighters to all causes; Luftflotte 3 lost three KIA, five WIA and six fighters.

8 February

8th Air Force Mission #214: 195 of 236 1st BD + 3rd BD B-17s bomb Frankfurt rail yards and t/os, TOT 1127-58 – lose 13-2-108, claim 1-3-0. 110 of 127 2nd BD B-24s bomb Siracourt and Watten V-weapon sites, TOT 0958 – lose 0, claim 0. Total escort of 2 P-38 FGs, 1 P-51 FG, 11 P-47 FGs (642 sorties) claims 16-1-8, loses 9-1-4.

A raid on Frankfurt by the 8th AF B-17s was partially shielded by an earlier raid on the Pas de Calais by the B-24s. The Luftflotte 3 fighters were sent south in anticipation of a raid on Paris, and the B-24s escaped unscathed. The airborne German fighters were able to attack the incoming B-17s and their escorts before landing to prepare for an attack on the withdrawing stream. JD 3 was able to put JG 1 into position to make effective attacks. The Americans wrote off 15 B-17s and 10 fighters to all causes; the Germans lost 10 KIA, four WIA and 19 fighters on their 268 sorties.

10 February

8th Air Force Mission #216: 143 of 169 3rd BD B-17s bomb Brunswick industrial area and t/os, TOT 1152-1200 – lose 29-1-52, claim 42-30-61. Escort of 2 P-38 FGs, 1 P-51 FG, 8 P-47 FGs (466 sorties) claims 56-1-40, loses 9-2-6.

The 8th AF sent a small force of B-17s to Brunswick in miserable weather, screened by an even smaller formation of B-24s directed at Gilze–Rijen airfield. The B-24s drew little attention, but the Brunswick force, which appeared headed for Berlin, was attacked viciously by the north German fighter units, which

I./JG 1 Fw 190A-7 'Yellow 6' (W. Nr. 340283) is refuelled at Dortmund early in 1944. This airplane was shot down on 8 February with the loss of its pilot. (Rosch)

Luftwaffe defensive activity – 5 February 1944

Unit	Type	Gruppe up			Gruppe down		Claims	Losses				
		Base	No	Time	Base	Time		Dest	Dam	KIA	MIA	WIA
Luftflotte 3												
II. Jagdkorps												
Jagddivision 4:												
I./JG 26	Fw 190A	Florennes		1050	Florennes	1228	n/c	0	0	0	0	0
4./JG 26	Fw 190A	Wevelghem		~1100	Wevelghem	~1230	n/c	0	0	0	0	0
II./JG 26	Fw 190A	Beauvais–Grevillers		0945	Laon–Athies	1007	transfer	0	1	1	0	0
	Fw 190A	Laon–Athies		1040	Beauvais–Grevillers	1146	n/c	0	0	0	0	0
III./JG 26	Bf 109G	Lille–Vendeville		0905	Reims	0930	transfer	0	0	0	0	0
	Bf 109G	Reims		1100	Creil	1124	0	0	1	0	0	0
Jagddivision 5:												
Stab/JG 2	Fw 190A	Cormeilles		1200	Cormeilles	1300	1 P-47	1	0	1	0	0
II./JG 2	Bf 109G	Creil		~1100	Creil	~1230	1 B-24, 1 P-47	2	3	1	1	1
III./JG 2?	Fw 190A	Cormeilles		?	Cormeilles	?	0	0	0	0	0	0

Luftwaffe defensive activity – 6 February 1944

Unit	Type	Gruppe up			Gruppe down		Claims	Losses				
		Base	No	Time	Base	Time		Dest	Dam	KIA	MIA	WIA
Luftflotte 3												
II. Jagdkorps												
Jagddivision 4:												
I./JG 26	Fw 190A	Florennes		1016	Cormé	1132	1 B-17	1	0	1	0	0
4./JG 26	Fw 190A	Wevelghem		~1030	Wevelghem	~1130	0	0	0	0	0	0
II./JG 26	Fw 190A	Beauvais–Grevillers		0834	Laon–Athies	0854	transfer	0	0	0	0	0
	Fw 190A	Laon–Athies		1034	Beauvais–Grevillers	1159	1 P-47	0	0	0	0	0
III./JG 26	Bf 109G	Lille–Vendeville		~0830	Reims?	~0930	transfer	0	0	0	0	0
	Bf 109G	Reims?		~1030	Lille–Vendeville	~1200	0	1	2	1	0	2
Jagddivision 5:												
Stab/JG 2	Fw 190A	Cormeilles		~1030	Cormeilles	~1130	1 P-47	0	0	0	0	0
	Fw 190A	Cormeilles		~1200	Cormeilles	~1330	1 P-47	0	0	0	0	0
II./JG 2	Bf 109G	Reims		1010	Reims?	1130	0	2	1	1	0	2
III./JG 2	Fw 190A	Cormeilles		~1030	Cormeilles	~1130	1 B-17	1	0	0	0	1
	Fw 190A	Cormeilles		~1200	Cormeilles	~1330	1 P-38	1	0	0	0	1

formed up into three Gefechtsverbände and were directed to gaps in the escort coverage left by weather-induced take-off delays at the American fighter airfields. Thirty B-17s were lost or scrapped, 21 per cent of those credited with effective soties; 11 escorts were also written off. Fifty of the 292 Luftwaffe fighters to scramble were lost, a 17 per cent rate; at least 31 German airmen were KIA or MIA, and 20 were WIA.

11 February

8th Air Force Mission #218: 212 of 223 1st BD B-17s bomb Frankfurt rail yards, Ludwigshafen, Saarbrücken and other t/os, TOT 1218-25 – lose 5-3-124, claim 3-0-2. Escort of 2 P 38 FGs, 1 P-51 FG, 10 P-47 FGs (606 sorties) claims 30-2-28, loses 14-3-6. 94 of 201 2nd BD B-24s bomb Siracourt V-weapon site – lose 1-1-17, claim 0. Escort of 1 P-51 FG, 2 P-47 FGs (126 sorties) claim 0, lose 0.

As the foul weather continued, the 8th AF tried a near-

Luftwaffe defensive activity – 8 February 1944

Unit	Type	Gruppe up			Gruppe down		Claims	Losses (—: included with 1st sortie)				
		Base	No	Time	Base	Time		Dest	Dam	KIA	MIA	WIA
Luftflotte Reich												
I. Jagdkorps			137									
Jagddivision 1:												
I./ZG 26	Bf 110G	Völkenrode		1130	Völkenrode	1210	n/c	0	0	0	0	0
II./ZG 26	Me 410A	Hildesheim		1130	Hildesheim	1230	0	0	0	0	0	0
Jagddivision 3:												
Stab/JG 1	Fw 190A	Dortmund		~1115	Dortmund	~1300	1 P-38	0	0	0	0	0
I./JG 1	Fw 190A	Dortmund		1120	Dortmund	~1300	5 B-17	5	7	3	0	0
II./JG 1	Fw 190A	Rheine	17	1122	Rheine	~1300	1 P-47	3	1	1	0	0
III./JG 1	Bf 109G	Volkel		~1130	Volkel	~1300	0	4	1	2	0	2
IV./JG 3	Bf 109G	Venlo		1108	Venlo	~1230	0	0	0	0	0	0
Sturmstaffel 1	Fw 190A	Dortmund		~1120	Dortmund	~1300	0	0	0	0	0	0
Luftflotte 3												
II. Jagdkorps			131									
Jagddivision 4:												
I./JG 26	Fw 190A	Florennes		1050	Florennes	1145	2 P-47	0	1	0	0	0
2nd sorties	Fw 190A	Florennes		~1215	Florennes	~1330	2 P-51	0	0	0	0	0
4./JG 26	Fw 190A	Wevelghem		~1050	Wevelghem	~1145	0	1	0	0	0	1
2nd sorties	Fw 190A	Wevelghem		~1215	Wevelghem	~1330	0	0	0	0	0	0
II./JG 26	Fw 190A	Beauvais–Grevillers		0917	Beauvais–Grevillers	1042	n/c	0	0	0	0	0
	Fw 190A	Beauvais–Grevillers		~1045	Beauvais–Grevillers	~1215	1 B-17	0	0	0	0	0
2nd sorties	Fw 190A	Beauvais–Grevillers		1205	Beauvais–Grevillers	1330	0	1	0	1	0	0
III./JG 26	Bf 109G	Lille–Vendeville		0915	Lille–Vendeville	1045	0	0	1	0	0	1
I./SG 101	Fw 190A	Reims		~1300	Reims, Diedenhofen	~1430	1 B-17	0	1	0	0	0
Jagddivision 5:												
Stab/JG 2	Fw 190A	Cormeilles		~0945	Cormeilles	~1115	0	1	0	0	0	0
2nd sorties	Fw 190A	Cormeilles		~1300	Cormeilles	~1415	0	—	—	—	—	—
II./JG 2	Bf 109G	Creil		0940	Creil	1115	1 B-17	2	1	1	0	0
2nd sorties	Bf 109G	Creil		~1300	Creil	~1415	1 B-17	—	—	—	—	—
III./JG 2	Fw 190A	Cormeilles		~0945	Cormeilles	~1115	4 B-17	0	0	0	0	0
	Fw 190A	Cormeilles		~1300	Cormeilles, Gael	~1415	1 B-17	2	1	2	0	0
I./JG 101	Bf 109G?	Pau–Ouest		~1200	Pau–Ouest	~1330	1 P-51	0	0	0	0	0

COMBAT REPORT[6]
10 February 1944

One Boeing B-17 destroyed from 6,000 metres at 1255 hours, PQ FO-4, E of Zwolle
One P-47 Thunderbolt destroyed from 4,000 metres at 1300 hours, PQ FM-FN, near Zwolle

First take-off at 1031 hours. Contact made due west with two Pulks, each of 60 heavy bombers, with strong escort (Thunderbolts, Lightnings, Mustangs). Attacked by six P-47s near Rheine. Dove to 5,500 metres. Paralleled the enemy formation 10 km to the southeast. Was attacked by P-51s while attempting to approach the formation from the south. My tank could not be jettisoned, and my canopy partially iced up. No attack was possible owing to the enemy fighters. No exchange of fire owing to our poor position. The six Thunderbolts finally peeled away to the south near Osnabrück.

Second take-off at 1235 hours. Enemy sighted five minutes after take-off. Enemy formation south of

Luftwaffe defensive activity – 10 February 1944

Unit	Type	Gruppe up			Gruppe down		Claims	Losses				
		Base	No	Time	Base	Time		Dest	Dam	KIA	MIA	WIA
Luftlotte Reich												
I. Jagdkorps			303									
Jagddivision 1:												
III./JG 54	Bf 109G	Ludwigslust		1108	Ludwigslust	1254	1 B-17	3	1	2	0	2
I./JG 301	Bf 109G	Gardelegen?		~1100	Gardelegen?	~1230	1 B-17	1	0	0	0	1
I./JG 302	Bf 109G	Jüterbog		~1100	Jüterbog	~1230	0	0	0	0	0	0
I./ZG 26	Bf 110G	Völkenrode		1040	Völkenrode	1223	6 B-17	2	1	1	0	3
II./ZG 26	Me 410A	Hildesheim		~1100	HIldesheim	~1230	1 P-38	5	2	6	1	5
Jagddivison 2:												
Stab/JG 3	Bf 109G	Rotenburg?		~1145	Rotenburg?	~1330	1 P-38	0	0	0	0	0
II./JG 3	Bf 109G	Rotenburg		1154	Rotenburg	~1330	4 B-17, 1 P-47	2	3	0	0	0
Stab/JG 11	Fw 190A	Husum		~0945	Rheine	~1030	transfer	0	0	0	0	0
	Fw 190A	Rheine		~1130	Deelen	~1300	2 B-17	0	0	0	0	0
I./JG 11	Fw 190A	Husum		0952	Rheine	1045	transfer	0	0	0	0	0
	Fw 190A	Rheine		1023	Rheine	1115	transfer	0	0	0	0	0
	Fw 190A	Rheine	25	1216	Deelen	1315	4 B-17, 1 P-38, 1 B-17 HSS	8	0	4	0	2
II./JG 11	Fw 190A	Wunstorf		1038	Wunstorf	~1200	2 B-17, 1 P-47	6	2	4	1	2
III./JG 11	Bf 109G	Oldenburg		~1030	Oldenburg	~1200	7 B-17, 1 P-38, 2 P-47	6	2	4	0	2
I./NJG 3	Bf 110G	Vechta		~1130	Vechta	~1300	0	0	2	0	0	1
IV./NJG 3	Bf 110G	Grove		~1130	Grove	~1300	1 B-24	0	0	0	0	0
ErprKdo 25	Fw 190A	Achmer		~1100	Achmer	~1130	1 B-17 HSS	0	2	0	0	0
Jagddivision 3:												
Stab/JG 1	Fw 190A	Dortmund		~0910	Rheine	~0930	transfer	0	0	0	0	0
	Fw 190A	Rheine		1031	Rheine	~1145	0	0	0	0	0	0
2nd sorties	Fw 190A	Rheine		1235	Rheine	~1330	1 B-17, 1 P-47	0	0	0	0	0
I./JG 1	Fw 190A	Dortmund		0912	Rheine	0934	transfer	0	0	0	0	0
	Fw 190A	Rheine		1030	Hopsten	1145	6 B-17	1	1	0	0	0
2nd sorties	Fw 190A	Hopsten		1215	Rheine	1235	0	0	0	0	0	0
II./JG 1	Fw 190A	Rheine	19	1023	Rheine, Celle	1155	3 B-17, 2 P-47	2	3	1	0	0
	Fw 190A	Rheine		~1245	Rheine	~1245	1 B-17, 1 B-17 HSS	0	0	0	0	0
III./JG 1	Bf 109G	Volkel		~1030	Volkel	~1145	1 P-47	2	1	1	0	0
I./JG 3	Bf 109G	München–Gladbach		~1030	München–Gladbach	~1145	1 P-47	0	1	0	0	1
IV./JG 3	Bf 109G	Venlo		~1030	Venlo	~1145	1 B-17, 1 P-47	12	1	4	2	1
Sturmstaffel 1	Fw 190A	Dortmund		~0915	Rheine	~0940	transfer	0	0	0	0	0
	Fw 190A	Rheine		~1030	Rheine	~1145	1 B-17	0	0	0	0	0
IV./NJG 1	Bf 110G	Leeuwarden		~1200	Leeuwarden	~1330	1 B-17	0	1	0	0	0

withdrawal course. Contact made at 1250 hours with ca. 50 heavy bombers. From 6,000 metres attacked a single straggling bomber that had dropped back with a right inner engine that was not running at full power. Uffz. Rauhaus fired at the right engines from behind and below. Flames came from the right inner engine. While beginning his second attack, Rauhaus was attacked from above by two Thunderbolts and had to go into the clouds at 3,000 metres.

I fired at the right engines and got hits in both. The machine immediately lost altitude and gave off heavy smoke. Two men bailed out. I myself was attacked by four Thunderbolts. I attacked two that were below me, firing at one from below and behind at ca. 150 metres, and getting several hits in the fuselage. Flames appeared. The machine tipped over its left wing and dived into the clouds at 3,500 metres. I could see nothing further because I was having difficulties. After a short battle with four Thunderbolts, I was forced to evade in the clouds.

Oberst Walter Oesau, Geschwaderkommodore
Stab/JG 1

duplicate of the mission of the 8th. A B-17 raid on radar-recognisable Frankfurt was screened by a small B-24 raid on V-weapon targets. The scheme worked inasmuch as the Luftflotte 3 fighters went south to defend Paris, and the B-24s were not attacked. The fighters had to return to base and wait for the withdrawing B-17s. The large escort force did its job today. Few of the fighters from I. Jagdkorps and II. Jagdkorps reached the bombers. Their 291 sorties were smothered by the escorts, which accounted for most of the German losses of 19 KIA or MIA, 10 WIA and 29 fighters. The Americans lost or scrapped eight B-17s and 17 escorts. The small P-38 force was especially hard hit; the 20th FG lost eight Lightnings and its commander.

13 February

8th Air Force Mission #221: 140 of 192 2nd BD B-24s, 266 of 277 3rd BD B-17s bomB-17 Pas de Calais V-weapon sites and t/os – lose 4-4-131, claim 0-1-0. Escort of 1 P-51 FG, 4 P-47 FGs (232 sorties) claims 6-1-4, loses 1-0-4.

In the morning, the weather limited Allied missions from England to a few tactical sweeps, only one of which was intercepted. Radio traffic in the afternoon revealed a heavy bomber mission; from the time of day it would be targeting France. Before the bombers reached the coast, Luftflotte 3 had most of its units up and heading inland in the soupy weather, but once again the targets for the B-17s and B-24s were the Pas de Calais V-weapon sites. The German fighters missed

them, but were hit by the American escorts, which penetrated as far as Paris. Most combats were inconclusive, although II./JG 2 did suffer appreciable losses. German losses totalled two KIA, four WIA and six fighters. The Americans lost eight bombers and one P-51, none to German fighters.

20 February – 'Big Week' begins (see map)

8th Air Force Mission #226: 296 of 314 3rd BD B-17s bomb Tutow airfield, TOT 1325 – lose 6-1-37, claim 15-15-10; 340 of 417 1st BD B-17s bomb 4 aviation targets in central Germany, TOT 1325-55 – lose 7-1-161, claim 14-5-6; 244 of 272 2nd BD B-24s bomb 3 aviation targets in central Germany, TOT 1325-55 – lose 8-3-37, claim 36-13-13. Escort of 2 P-38 FGs, 2 P-51 FGs, 11 P-47 FGs (835 sorties) claims 61-7-37, loses 4-2-4.

The 8th AF mission for the first day of Operation ARGUMENT was the largest and most complex attempted at that time. Sixteen combat wings containing 1003 B-17s and B-24s took off to bomb 12 aircraft factories in central and eastern Germany and western Poland. The smaller 3rd BD crossed the English coast early and took a circuitous route to the easternmost targets. The 1st and 2nd BDs left England two hours later, escorted by all available USAAF fighters, and flew due east across Holland in a single, compact formation two combat wings abreast. It turned southeast when it reached Germany and did not split up until near its targets in central Germany. The reaction by I. Jagdkorps was slow and tentative. It eventually sortied aircraft from 18 Jagdgruppen

Luftwaffe defensive activity – 13 February 1944

Unit	Type	Gruppe up			Gruppe down		Claims	Losses				
		Base	No	Time	Base	Time		Dest	Dam	KIA	MIA	WIA
Luftflotte 3												
II. Jagdkorps												
Jagddivision 4:												
I./JG 26	Fw 190A	Florennes		~1430	Florennes	~1530	0	0	0	0	0	0
4./JG 26	Fw 190A	Wevelghem		~1430	Wevelghem	~1530	0	1	0	0	0	1
II./JG 26	Fw 190A	Beauvais–Grevillers		1425	Beauvais–Grevillers	1530	0	0	0	0	0	0
	Fw 190A	Cambrai–Epinoy		1424	Cambrai–Epinoy	1539	0	1	0	0	0	0
III./JG 26	Bf 109G	Lille–Vendeville		1429	Lille–Vendeville	~1530	0	0	3	0	0	0
Jagddivision 5:												
Stab/JG 2?	Fw 190A	Cormeilles		?	Cormeilles	?	0	0	0	0	0	0
II./JG 2	Bf 109G	Creil		1435	Creil, Orléans, Busigny	1532	1 P-47	4	1	1	1	3
III./JG 2	Fw 190A	Cormeilles, Gael		~1430	Cormeilles, Gael	~1530	0	0	1	0	0	0

Luftwaffe defensive activity – 11 February 1944

Unit	Type	Gruppe up				Gruppe down		Claims	Losses				
		Base	No	Time		Base	Time		Dest	Dam	KIA	MIA	WIA
Luftflotte Reich													
I. Jagdkorps			187										
Jagddivision 1:													
III./JG 54	Bf 109G	Ludwigslust		1040		Nancy	1215	0	2	2	2	0	1
I./ZG 26	Bf 110G	Brunswick		~1030		Brunswick	~1200	0	3	3	3	0	3
II./ZG 26	Me 410A	Hildesheim	12	1030		Wiesbaden	1245	0	0	0	0	0	0
	Me 410A	Wiesbaden		~1300		Hilldesheim	~1400	3 P-38	0	1	0	0	0
Jagddivison 2:													
II./JG 3	Bf 109G	Rotenburg		1055		Mannheim–Sandhofen	1205	transfer	0	0	0	0	0
	Bf 109G	Mannheim–Sandhofen		~1230		Rotenburg	~1400	4 P-38	1	0	0	0	0
Stab/JG 11	Fw 190A	Husum		~1020		Köln–Ostheim	~1145	transfer	0	0	0	0	0
	Fw 190A	Köln–Ostheim		~1230		Köln–Ostheim	~1415	0	0	0	0	0	0
I./JG 11	Fw 190A	Husum		1025		Köln–Ostheim	1148	transfer	0	0	0	0	0
	Fw 190A	Köln–Ostheim		1230		Köln–Ostheim	1425	1 B-17	1	1	0	0	0
II./JG 11	Bf 109G	Wunstorf		~1130		Wunstorf	~1300	3 P-51	2	1	2	0	1
III./JG 11	Bf 109G	Oldenburg		~1130		Oldenburg	~1300	0	2	1	0	1	0
ErprKdo 25	Fw 190A	Achmer		~1130		Achmer	~1130	0	1	1	1	0	0
Jagddivison 3:													
Stab/JG 1	Fw 190A	Dortmund		~1015		Rheine	~1045	transfer	0	0	0	0	0
	Fw 190A	Rheine		?		Rheine	?	0	0	0	0	0	0
I./JG 1	Fw 190A	Dortmund		1020		Rheine	1046	transfer	0	0	0	0	0
	Fw 190A	Rheine		?		Rheine	?	0	1	1	1	0	0
II./JG 1	Fw 190A	Rheine	15	1020		Rheine	1133	0	1	1	1	0	0
III./JG 1	Bf 109G	Volkel		~1030		Volkel	~1200	0	0	0	0	0	0
I./JG 3	Bf 109G	München–Gladbach		~1030		München–Gladbach	~1200	0	1	0	0	0	0
IV./JG 3	Bf 109G	Venlo		~1030		Venlo	~1200	2 B-26	1	0	1	0	0
Sturmstaffel 1	Fw 190A	Dortmund		~1025		Rheine	~1050	transfer	0	0	0	0	0
	Fw 190A	Rheine		~1200		Rheine	~1330	2 B-17, 1 B-17 HSS	1	0	0	0	0
LBeob St 3	Me 210	Venlo		~1015		Venlo	~1230	shadower	0	1	0	0	0
Jagddivision 7:													
II./JG 27	Bf 109G	Erbenheim		~1100		Erbenheim	~1230	1 P-38, 1 P-47	5	1	3	0	2
I./NJG 6	Bf 110G	Mainz–Finthen	7	~1200		Mainz–Finthen	~1400	0	0	0	0	0	0
I./NJG 102	Bf 110G	Kitzingen		1104		Kitzingen	~1230	1 P-38	1	0	1	0	0
Luftflotte 3													
II. Jagdkorps													
Jagddivision 4:													
I./JG 26	Fw 190A	Florennes		1307		Florennes	1445	1 B-17	0	0	0	0	0
4./JG 26	Fw 190A	Wevelghem		1254		Wevelghem	~1430	0.5 P-38, 2 P-47	0	0	0	0	0
II./JG 26	Fw 190A	Beauvais–Grevillers		0942		Beauvais–Grevillers	1052	0	0	0	0	0	0
2nd sorties	Fw 190A	Beauvais–Grevillers		1145		Beauvais–Grevillers	1158	0	0	0	0	0	0
3rd sorties	Fw 190A	Beauvais–Grevillers		1256		Beauvais–Grevillers	1355	1 B-17, 3 P-38	0	0	0	0	0
4th sorties	Fw 190A	Beauvais–Grevillers		1354		Beauvais–Grevillers	1430	1 B-17	0	0	0	0	0
III./JG 26	Bf 109G	Lille–Vendeville		0943		Lille–Vendeville	1015	0	0	0	0	0	0
2nd sorties	Bf 109G	Lille–Vendeville		1040		LillevVendeville	1130	0	0	0	0	0	0
3rd sorties	Bf 109G	Lille–Vendeville		1300		Lille–Vendeville	1400	0	0	0	0	0	0
III./NJG 4	Bf 110G	Juvincourt		?		Juvincourt	?	0	1	1	0	0	0
Jagddivision 5:													
II./JG 2	Bf 109G	Reims		~1230		Reims	~1400	0.5 P-38	3	3	1	0	3
III./JG 2	Fw 190A	Cormeilles, Gael		~1230		Cormeilles, Gael	~1400	0	2	0	2	0	0

Luftwaffe defensive activity – 20 February 1944

Unit	Type	Gruppe up			Gruppe down		Claims	Losses				
		Base	No	Time	Base	Time		Dest	Dam	KIA	MIA	WIA
vs. incoming 3rd BD												
Luftflotte Reich												
I. Jagdkorps			*362									
Jagddivision 1:												
II./ZG 26	Me 410A	Hildesheim	25	1040	Hildesheim	~1245	2 B-17	0	0	0	0	0
III./JG 301	Bf 109G	Zerbst		~1045	Zerbst	~1230	0	1	1	0	0	0
IV./NJG 5	Bf 110G	Brandis		?	Brandis	?	0	0	1	0	0	0
JG 110	Bf 109?	Altenburg		?	Altenburg	?	0	0	1	0	0	0
Jagddivision 2:												
Stab/JG 11	Bf 109G	Husum		0930	Oldenburg	1000	transfer	0	0	0	0	0
	Bf 109G	Oldenburg		~1100	Flensburg	~1300	1 B-17	1	0	1	0	0
I./JG 11	Fw 190A	Husum	30	0934	Oldenburg	1002	transfer	0	0	0	0	0
	Fw 190A	Oldenburg	30	1048	Flensburg, Husum	1227	2 B-17	1	7	0	0	2
II./JG 11	Bf 109G	Wunstorf		1035	Schleswig	1235	0	1	1	0	0	0
III./JG 11	Bf 109G	Oldenburg		1047	Oldenburg	1158	n/c	2	2	0	0	0
10./JG 11	Fw 190A	Aalborg-Ost		1106	Husum	1154	transfer	0	0	0	0	0
II./JG 302	Fw 190	Oldenburg		~1045	Oldenburg	~1230	0	1	0	1	0	0
III./JG 302	Bf 109G	Oldenburg		~1045	Oldenburg	~1230	0	2	0	1	0	0
III./ZG 26	Bf 110G	Wunstorf	25	1040	Wunstorf	~1130	n/c	0	0	0	0	0
II./NJG 3	Ju 88C	Schleswig		?	?	?	0	3	0	0	0	0
III./NJG 3	Bf 110G	Stade		?	?	?	0	1	0	0	0	0
IV./NJG 3	Bf 110G	Aalborg	20	1130	?	~1330	0	0	0	0	0	0
Jagddivision 3:												
II./JG 1	Fw 190A	Rheine	19	1045	Oldenburg + 4 others	~1130	n/c	0	0	0	0	0
Jagddivision 7:												
I./ZG 26	Bf 110G	Wertheim	25	1040	Volkenrode	1125	transfer	0	0	0	0	0
I./ZG 76	Bf 110G	Ansbach		1040	Delitzsch	1130	transfer	0	0	0	0	0
III./ZG 76	Bf 110G	Ansbach		1040	Delitzsch	1130	transfer	0	0	0	0	0
vs. main force												
Luftflotte Reich												
I. Jagdkorps												
Jagddivision 1:												
III./JG 54	Bf 109G	Ludwigslust		1212	Brandenburg–Briest	1340	7 B-17	8	1	2	1	3
I./JG 302	Bf 109G	Jüterbog		~1200	Jüterbog	~1330	1 B-17	5	3	0	0	2
I./ZG 26	Bf 110G	Volkenrode	20	~1200	Volkenröde	~1330	0	6	2	6	0	2
II./ZG 26	Me 410A	Hildesheim		~1200	Hildesheim	~1330	2 B-17	2	0	3	0	1
I./ZG 76	Bf 110G	Delitzsch		~1300	Delitzsch	~1500	0	1	1	2	0	0
III./ZG 76	Bf 110G	Delitzsch		~1300	Delitzsch	~1500	1 B-17	1	1	2	0	2
II./NJG 5	Bf 110G	Parchim		~1200	Parchim	~1400	0	1	0	1	0	2
III./NJG 5	Bf 110G	Neuruppin		~1200	Neuruppin	~1400	0	0	0	0	0	0
I./NJG 6	Bf 110G	Stendal–Altmark		~1200	Stendal–Altmark	~1400	1 B-17	1	0	0	0	0
II./NJG 6	Bf 110G	Stendal–Altmark		~1200	Stendal–Altmark	~1400	2 B-17	1	1	3	0	0
ISS AGO	Bf 109G	Oschersleben		~1230	Oschersleben	~1400	1 P-51	0	0	0	0	0
Jagddivision 2:												
II./JG 3	Bf 109G	Rotenburg		1135	Marx	1335	3 B-24	4	0	1	0	3

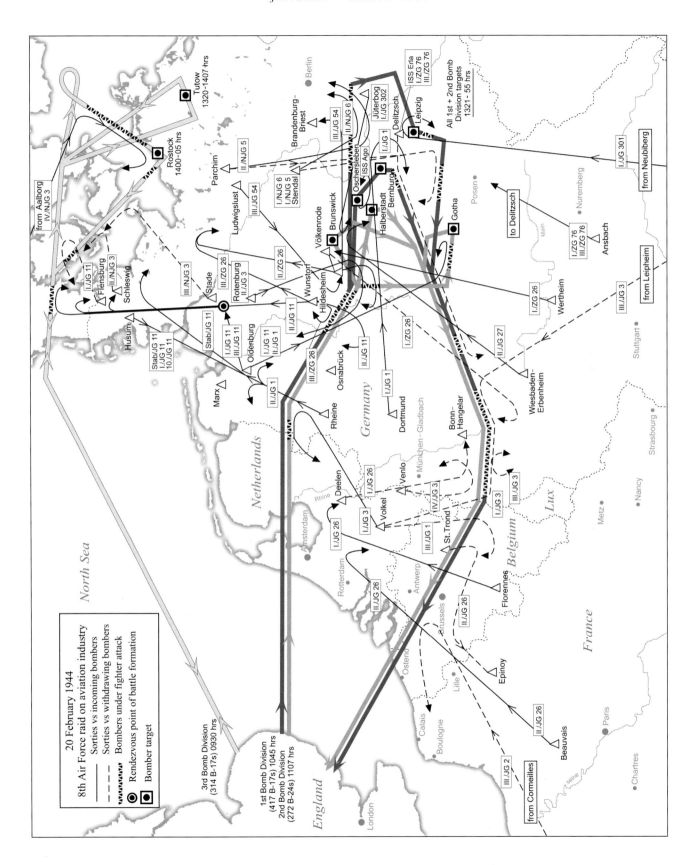

Luftwaffe defensive activity – 20 February 1944 Continued

Unit	Type	Gruppe up			Gruppe down		Claims	Losses				
		Base	No	Time	Base	Time		Dest	Dam	KIA	MIA	WIA
I./JG 11	Fw 190A	Husum		1245	Husum	1434	1 B-17, 6 B-24, 1 B-24 HSS	0	0	0	0	0
II./JG 11	Bf 109G	Wunstorf		~1300	Wunstorf	~1430	0	0	0	0	0	0
10./JG 11	Fw 190A	Husum		1258	Husum	~1430	1 B-24	0	0	0	0	0
III./ZG 26	Bf 110G	Wunstorf	13	1213	Wunstorf	1330	0	10	3	11	0	6
Jagddivision 3:												
I./JG 1	Fw 190A	Dortmund		~1300	Rheine	~1430	1 B-17, 1 P-51	3	1	2	0	1
II./JG 1	Fw 190A	Rheine	4	1152	Rheine	1255	0	0	0	0	0	0
	Fw 190A	Oldenburg	9	1300	Rheine	~1430	1 B-17, 1 P-38, 1 B-17 HSS	4	0	2	0	0
I./JG 3	Bf 109G	Volkel		~1300	Volkel	~1430	0	0	0	0	0	0
I./JG 300	Bf 109G	Bonn–Hangelar	15	~1300	Hannover	1456	1 B-24	8	2	2	0	2
II./NJG 1	Bf 110G, Do 217	St. Trond		~1300	St. Trond	~1500	0	0	1	0	0	0
LBeob St 3	Ju 88	Venlo		~1230	Venlo	~1430	shadower	1	0	0	0	2
Jagddivision 7:												
III./JG 3	Bf 109G	Leipheim		~1300	Leipheim	~1430	2 B-24	5	0	2	0	1
II./JG 27	Bf 109G	Wiesbaden–Erbenheim		~1300	Wiesbaden–Erbenheim	~1430	0	2	1	1	0	0
III./JG 300	Bf 109G	Wiesbaden–Erbenheim		~1300	Wiesbaden–Erbenheim	~1430	0	1	1	1	0	0
I./JG 301	Bf 109G	Neubiberg		~1300	Neubiberg	~1430	0	3	0	0	1	1
ISS Erla	Bf 109G	Delitzsch		1318	Nordhausen	1415	2 B-17	4	0	1	0	0
Luftflotte 3												
II. Jagdkorps												
Jagddivision 4:												
I./JG 26	Fw 190A	Florennes		1125	Deelen	1302	0	0	0	0	0	0
	Fw 190A	Florennes		1225	Deelen	1320	0	0	0	0	0	0
II./JG 26	Fw 190A	Beauvais–Grevillers	5	0910	Epinoy, Athies	0932	transfer	0	0	0	0	0
	Fw 190A	Cambrai–Epinoy, Laon–Athies	5	1125	St. Trond, Grevillers, others	1245	0	1	3	0	0	1
Jagddivision 5:												
III./JG 2	Fw 190A	Cormeilles	20	1125	?	~1200	transfer	0	0	0	0	0
vs. withdrawing stream												
Luftflotte Reich												
I. Jagdkorps												
Jagddivision 1:												
I./NJG 5	Ju 88G	Stendal–Altmark		?	Stendal-Altmark?	?	0	3	0	3	0	0
II./NJG 5	Bf 110G	Parchim		~1400	Parchim?	~1530	1 B-17	0	0	0	0	0
I./NJG 6	Bf 110G	Stendal-Altmark		~1430	Stendal-Altmark?	~1600	0	0	0	0	0	0
I./ZG 26	Bf 110G	Völkenrode		~1400	Völkenrode?	~1530	2 B-17	0	0	0	0	0
Jagddivision 2:												
I./JG 11	Fw 190A	Husum		~1330	Husum	~1500	3 B-17	0	0	0	0	0
III./JG 11	Bf 109G	Oldenburg		1445	Oldenburg	1555	n/c	0	0	0	0	0
10./JG 11	Fw 190A	Husum		1409	Esbjerg (D)	1506	1 B-17	0	0	0	0	0
	Fw 190A	Esbjerg (D)		1525	Aalborg-Ost	1628	n/c	0	0	0	0	0

Luftwaffe defensive activity – 20 February 1944 Continued

Unit	Type	Gruppe up			Gruppe down		Claims	Losses				
		Base	No	Time	Base	Time		Dest	Dam	KIA	MIA	WIA
Jagddivision 3:												
II./JG 1	Fw 190A	Rheine	4	1430	Rheine	1525	n/c	0	0	0	0	0
III./JG 1	Bf 109G	Volkel		~1430	Volkel	~1530	0	2	1	0	0	1
I./JG 3	Bf 109G	Volkel		~1430	Volkel	~1530	1 B-17	1	0	0	0	0
IV./JG 3	Bf 109G	Venlo		1405	Venlo	1600	1 P-47	1	1	0	0	1
Luftflotte 3												
II. Jagdkorps												
Jagddivision 4:												
I./JG 26	Fw 190A	Deelen		1420	Bonn–Hangelar	1514	0	0	0	0	0	0
II./JG 26	Fw 190A	St. Trond, etc.		~1430	Beauvais–Grevillers	~1600	1 B-17, 1 P-47	0	0	0	0	0
I./NJG 4	Bf 110	Florennes		~1430	Florennes	~1630	0	0	1	0	0	0
Jagddivision 5:												
III./JG 2	Fw 190A	Cormeilles?		~1500	Cormeilles	~1630	1 B-17, 1 B-24	2	0	1	0	0

*362 total sorties by I. Jagdkorps

(including seven *Wilde Sau* Gruppen), five Zerstörergruppen, 11 Nachtjagdgruppen, several specialist and training units, and five Gruppen from neighbouring II. Jagdkorps. There was no large-scale interception of the inbound formations, and the fighter attacks on the withdrawing formations were weak and poorly co-ordinated. The Americans lost or scrapped only 26 bombers and six fighters. German sortie totals conflict, but the number making contact was much lower than the Allies had expected, and recently compiled data show losses of 51 aircrew KIA or MIA, 33 WIA and 79 aircraft.

21 February

8th Air Force Mission #228: 263 of 281 3rd BD B-17s, 285 of 336 1st BD B-17s, 218 of 244 2nd BD B-24s bomb 18 aviation targets in Germany, TOT 1357-1458 – lose 16-7-105, claim 19-16-14. Escort of 2 P-38 FGs, 2 P-51 FGs, 11 P-47 FGs (679 sorties) claims 33-5-18, loses 5-3-3.

The 8th AF reverted to a simpler operational plan, flying to Germany in a single stream before splitting up to bomb targets in the Brunswick area. Heavy cloud restricted visibility, and few primaries were hit; most of the groups bombed airfields. It is believed that 331 German fighters sortied, but they were unable to form large formations, and most were unable to penetrate the large escort force to reach the bombers, which wrote off only 23. Eight escorts were lost or salvaged. The RLV force lost 27 KIA or MIA, nine WIA and 38 aircraft.

Lacking a formal service portrait, Fw. Peter Crump of II./JG 26 had this photograph taken on home leave while recovering from injuries he received when shot down by P-47s on 22 February. *(Crump)*

Luftwaffe defensive activity – 21 February 1944

Unit	Type	Gruppe up Base	No	Time	Gruppe down Base	Time	Claims	Dest	Dam	KIA	MIA	WIA
Luftflotte Reich												
I. Jagdkorps			282									
Jagddivision 1:												
III./JG 54	Bf 109G	Ludwigslust		~1300	Ludwigslust	~1430	0	4	3	4	0	0
I./ZG 26	Bf 110G	Brunswick		~1300	Brunswick	~1430	0	3	1	3	0	1
II./ZG 26	Me 410A	Hildesheim		~1300	Hilldesheim	~1430	2 B-17	1	0	1	0	1
JaSta Erla	Bf 109G	Delitzsch		1345	Nordhausen	1525	0	1	0	1	0	0
Jagddivison 2:												
II./JG 3	Bf 109G	Rotenburg		1318	Rotenburg	1513	1 P-51	2	2	1	0	1
Stab/JG 11	Fw 190A	Husum		~1300	Husum	~1430	0	0	0	0	0	0
I./JG 11	Fw 190A	Husum		1308	Husum, others	1440	1 B-17, 1 B-24, 1 P-51	0	2	0	0	0
2nd sorties	Fw 190A	Various		1515	Husum	~1615	0	0	0	0	0	0
II./JG 11	Bf 109G	Wunstorf		1308	Wunstorf	1455	1 P-47	1	0	0	1	0
2nd sorties	Bf 109G	Wunstorf		1513	Wunstorf	1553	n/c	0	0	0	0	0
III./JG 11	Bf 109G	Oldenburg		~1315	Oldenburg	~1515	1 B-17, 1 P-51	0	1	0	0	0
2nd sorties	Bf 109G	Oldenburg		~1530	Oldenburg	~1630	n/c	0	0	0	0	0
III./ZG 26	Bf 110G	Wunstorf	10	1245	Wunstorf	1530	0	0	2	0	0	0
II./NJG 3	Ju 88C	Schleswig		?	Schleswig	?	0	2	0	0	0	0
Jagddivision 3:												
Stab/JG 1	Fw 190A	Dortmund		?	Rheine	?	transfer	0	0	0	0	0
	Fw 190A	Rheine		~1245	Rheine	~1430	0	0	0	0	0	0
I./JG 1	Fw 190A	Dortmund		?	Rheine	?	transfer	0	0	0	0	0
	Fw 190A	Rheine		~1245	Rheine	~1430	1 B-17	1	0	0	0	1
II./JG 1	Fw 190A	Rheine	24	1245	Stendal, others	1425	1 B-17, 1 P-51, 1 B-17 HSS	4	2	2	0	2
2nd sorties	Fw 190A	Rheine	5	1420	Rheine	~1530	1 B-17	—	—	—	—	—
2nd sorties	Fw 190A	Stendal	—	1447	Rheine	1520	1 B-24, 1 B-24 HSS	—	—	—	—	—
III./JG 1	Bf 109G	Volkel		~1230	Volkel	~1330	0	0	0	0	0	0
2nd sorties	Bf 109G	Volkel		1415	Volkel	~1615	1 B-17, 1 P-47	6	2	3	0	1
I./JG 3	Bf 109G	München–Gladbach		~1245	München–Gladbach	~1430	0	2	1	1	0	1
IV./JG 3	Bf 109G	Venlo		1240	Hannover	1505	1 B-17 HSS	2	0	0	0	0
I./JG 26	Fw 190A	Bonn-Hangelar		1415	Rheine	1445	transfer	0	0	0	0	0
2nd sorties	Fw 190A	Rheine		1525	Melsbroek	1621	n/c	0	0	0	0	0
II./JG 26	Fw 190A	Rheine		1520	Deelen	1625	0	0	0	0	0	0
	Fw 190A	Melsbroek		1525	Melsbroek	1622	1 B-17	0	0	0	0	0
II./JG 300	Fw 190A	Rheine		~1415	Rheine	~1600	2 B-24	0	0	0	0	0
Sturmstaffel 1	Fw 190A	Langenhagen	6	1430	Langenhagen	~1600	2 B-17, 1 B-17 HSS	2	0	2	0	0
LBeob St 3	Bf 110	Venlo		~1230	Venlo	~1430	shadower	1	0	0	0	0
Jagddivision 7:												
I./JG 301	Bf 109G	Neubiberg		~1230	Neubiberg	~1400	0	2	1	0	0	0
I./ZG 76	Bf 110G	Ansbach?		~1230	Ansbach?	~1500	0	3	0	6	0	0
II./ZG 76	°Bf 110G	Ansbach?		~1230	Ansbach?	~1500	0	0	0	0	0	0
Luftflotte 3												
II. Jagdkorps												
Jagddivision 4:												
II./JG 26	Fw 190A	Grevillers		1335	Rheine	1450	transfer	0	0	0	0	0
	Fw 190A	Epinoy		1339	Melsbroek	1457	0	0	0	0	0	0
	Fw 190A	Grevillers		1425	S...burg?	1605	0	0	0	0	0	0
I./NJG 4	Bf 110G	Florennes		?	Florennes	?	0	1	0	2	0	1

22 February – vs. 8th Air Force

8th Air Force Mission #230: 181 of 289 1st BD B-17s, 74 of 177 2nd BD B-24s bomb 3 German aviation targets and 8 t/os (3rd BD recalled), TOT 1401-1516 – lose 41-4-146, claim 34-18-17. Escort of 2 P-38 FGs, 2 P-51 FGs, 12 P-47 FGs (659 sorties) claims 59-7-25, loses 11-1-21.

The 8th AF dispatched 799 bombers against a variety of targets, but once again the weather over the Continent played havoc with Allied plans. I. Jagdkorps properly identified a small diversionary force sent to Denmark, left it to the small forces on-scene and sent the north German Jagdgruppen south to join the main battle. The 2nd and 3rd BDs were recalled before bombing, and only 99 1st BD B-17s were able to bomb their primary targets. The scattered bomb groups were vulnerable to attack; 738 fighters were scrambled by I. and II. Jagdkorps against the two oncoming American air forces. The 332 to make contact with the 8th AF were responsible for most of their 45 bomber and 12 escort losses, but paid a heavy price: at least 25 aircrew KIA or MIA, as well as 12 WIA, and 54 fighters and Zerstörer lost. The fatalities included Major Eduard Tratt, the top-scoring Zerstörer pilot, and his gunner. Although bombing results were mediocre, and the Americans considered their bomber losses too high, their war of attrition against the Jagdwaffe reached new levels of success.

A line-up of I./JG 27 Bf 109G-6s on the airfield at Fels am Wagram in early 1944. JG 27 formed the heart of the day defence of Austria prior to D-Day. The Gruppe emblems, the broad green fuselage bands and the light rudders (colour unknown, but probably yellow) are noteworthy. *(Bundesarchiv 662-6658-5a)*

22 February – vs. 15th Air Force

15th Air Force: 197 of 284 B-17s + B-24s bomb Regensburg aviation industry, German + Austrian t/os, TOT 1230-58 – lose 18, claim 40-18-5. Escort of 3 P-38 FGs, 1 P-47 FG (185 sorties) claims 0, loses 2.

The USSTAF intended for Operation ARGUMENT to employ co-ordinated attacks by the 8th and 15th Air Forces. This was the first day that the ground support obligations of the 15th AF slackened enough to allow it to enter the strategic campaign. Its 284 B-24s and B-17s were assigned targets in the large Regensburg Messerschmitt factory complex. The one P-47 and three P-38 groups of the 15th AF failed to contact the German fighters. Contrary to this author's previous assertion, JD 7 opposed this raid and not that of the 8th AF, although most of the fighters of its Jafü Ostmark made contact only after long, stern chases following the bomb runs. The Americans lost 18 bombers and two fighters to all causes, while the Germans lost at least nine aircrewmen KIA, four WIA and 15 fighters and Zerstörer to the bombers' gunners.

23 February

15th Air Force: 109 of 166 B-24s bomb Steyr (A) aviation industry and t/o, TOT 1208-15 – lose 16, claim 32-8-12. Escort of 3 P-38 FGs (89 sorties) claims 1-2-0, loses 0.

The 8th AF was grounded by the weather. The 15th AF sent its bombers to Austria, but the entire B-17 wing and many of the B-24s and P-38s returned early owing to weather conditions. Only 81 B-24s bombed their primary target at Steyr, but succeeded in destroying 10 per cent of the Reich production capacity for aircraft ball bearings. The mission plan called for the P-38s to escort the bombers' withdrawal, while the penetration and target legs were unescorted. The bomber wing that reached Steyr lost 16 B-24s during a 30-minute Luftwaffe attack that started before the bomb run and ended only after the arrival of the P-38s. Although 197 fighters and Zerstörer were scrambled, only three Gruppen – III./JG 3 from Germany and I./JG 27 and II./ZG 1 from Austria – reached the bombers. Their confirmed claims for 27 B-24s and two P-38s were excessive, but their successes were considerable and came at the light cost of nine Bf 109s with three pilots KIA and two WIA to the bomber gunners, and two Bf 110s with all four of their crew KIA, plus another WIA, to the P-38s.

Luftwaffe defensive activity vs. 8th Air Force – 22 February 1944

Unit	Type	Gruppe up			Gruppe down		Claims	Losses				
		Base	No	Time	Base	Time		Dest	Dam	KIA	MIA	WIA
vs. Denmark diversion												
Luftflotte Reich												
I. Jagdkorps			*332									
Jagddivision 2:												
10./JG 11	Fw 190A	Aalborg		~1300	Aalborg	1538	0	0	0	0	0	0
11./JG 11	Bf 109T	Lister		~1300	Lister	~1500	4 B-17	2	0	2	0	0
IV./NJG 3	Ju 88C	Grove		1255	Grove	1527	2 B-17	0	0	0	0	0
vs. main raid												
Luftflotte Reich												
I. Jagdkorps												
Jagddivision 1:												
III./JG 54	Bf 109G	Ludwigslust		~1230	Ludwigslust	~1430	4 B-17	1	1	0	0	1
Stab/JG 110	Fw 190A	Altenburg		~1300	Altenburg	~1430	1 P-51	1	0	0	0	0
I./JG 300	Bf 109G	Jüterbog–Waldlager	7	1354	Jüterbog–Waldlager	1519	0	0	1	0	0	0
I./JG 302	Bf 109G	Jüterbog–Waldlager		~1400	Jüterbog–Waldlager	~1530		1	0	0	0	0
II./JG 302	Bf 109G	Ludwigslust		~1400	Ludwigslust	~1530	0	0	1	0	0	0
I./ZG 26	Bf 110G	Brunswick		~1230	Brunswick	~1445	1 B-17	2	0	0	0	2
II./ZG 26	Me 410A	Hildesheim		~1230	Hildesheim	~1430	3 B-17	1	2	2	0	0
JaSta Erla	Bf 109G	Delitzsch		~1230	Nordhausen	~1400	0	1	0	0	0	1
SKdo OKL	?	Berlin area		?	Berlin area	?	0	1	0	1	0	0
FLÜG 1	Ju 88A	?		?	?	?	0	1	0	2	0	0
4./Zerst ErgGr	Bf 110G	Brunswick–Broitzem		1245	Brunswick–Broitzem	1410	0	0	0	0	0	0
Jagddivison 2:												
II./JG 3	Bf 109G	Rotenburg		1245	Rheine	1445	2 B-17	1	2	0	0	0
Stab/JG 11	Fw 190A	Husum		~1200	Rotenburg?	~1345	0	0	0	0	0	0
	Fw 190A	Rotenburg?		~1415	Köln–Ostheim?	~1545	0	0	0	0	0	0
I./JG 11	Fw 190A	Husum		1210	Rotenburg	1315	transfer	0	0	0	0	0
	Fw 190A	Rotenburg		1424	Köln–Ostheim, Lippstadt	1544	6 B-17	0	1	0	0	0
II./JG 11	Bf 109G	Wunstorf		1254	Münster–Handorf	1508	3 B-17, 1 P-51	1	4	0	0	0
III./JG 11	Bf 109G	Wunstorf		1255	Goslar	1408	0	1	0	0	0	0
III./ZG 26	Bf 110G	Wunstorf	8	1228	Wunstorf	1410	1 B-17	8	3	4	0	3
LBeob St 2	Ju 88C	Stade		?	Stade	?	shadower	1	0	2	0	1
Jagddivison 3:												
Stab/JG 1	Fw 190A	Dortmund		~1215	Dortmund	~1345	1 B-17	0	0	0	0	0
	Fw 190A	Dortmund		~1500	Dortmund	~1600	1 B-17	0	0	0	0	0
I./JG 1	Fw 190A	Dortmund		~1215	Dortmund	~1345	2 B-17	3	0	1	0	0
II./JG 1	Fw 190A	Rheine	21	1125	Volkel	1305	2 B-17, 3 B-17 HSS	5	1	0	0	1
	Fw 190A	Volkel	1	~1345	Lippstadt	~1415	1 B-17	0	0	0	0	0
	Fw 190A	Rheine	7	1454	Rheine	~1600	1 P-47	0	0	0	0	0
III./JG 1	Bf 109G	Volkel		1455	Volkel	~1600	0	2	2	1	0	0
II./JG 2	Bf 109G	Venlo		1500	München–Gladbach, Eindhoven	1600	0	1	6	1	0	0
III./JG 2	Fw 190A	?		~1500	?	~1650	1 B-17	4	3	1	2	1
I./JG 3	Bf 109G	Volkel		~1200	Volkel	~1330	1 P-47	0	0	0	0	0
2nd sorties	Bf 109G	Volkel		~1430	Volkel	~1600	1 P-47	4	0	3	0	0

Luftwaffe defensive activity vs. 8th Air Force – 22 February 1944 Continued

Unit	Type	Gruppe up			Gruppe down		Claims	Losses				
		Base	No	Time	Base	Time		Dest	Dam	KIA	MIA	WIA
IV./JG 3	Bf 109G	Venlo		~1215	Venlo	~1400	1 B-17, 1 P-51, 1 B-17 HSS	3	0	1	0	0
2nd sorties	Bf 109G	Venlo		1500	Hannover	1534	0	0	0	0	0	0
I./JG 26	Fw 190A	Venlo		1500	München–Gladbach	1545	0	1	0	0	0	0
II./JG 26	Fw 190A	Duisburg		1340	Düsseldorf	1350	transfer	0	0	0	0	0
	Fw 190A	München–Gladbach		1355	Venlo	1405	transfer	0	0	0	0	0
	Fw 190A	Düsseldorf		1450	München–Gladbach?	~1600	0	6	2	2	0	2
	Fw 190A	Venlo		1500	München–Gladbach	1535	1 B-17, 2 P-47	0	0	0	0	0
	Fw 190A	München–Gladbach		1635	Beauvais–Grevillers	1723	transfer	0	0	0	0	0
II./JG 300	Fw 190A	Rheine		~1400	Rheine	~1530	1 B-17	0	1	0	0	0
Sturmstaffel 1	Fw 190A	Langenhagen	8	~1215	Langenhagen	~1345	1 B-17	0	0	0	0	0
Luftflotte 3												
II. Jagdkorps												
Jagddivision 4:												
I./JG 26	Fw 190A	Florennes		1135	Venlo	1320	0	0	0	0	0	0
II./JG 26	Fw 190A	Beauvais–Grevillers, Epinoy		0858	Laon–Athies	0913	transfer	0	0	0	0	0
	Fw 190A	Laon–Athies		1125	MünchenvGladbach, Duisburg	1304	2 B-17, 2 B-17 HSS	0	0	0	0	0
	Fw 190A	Beauvais–Grevillers		1355	Florennes	1430	transfer	0	0	0	0	0
	Fw 190A	Florennes		1523	St. Trond	1558	0	0	0	0	0	0
III./JG 26	Bf 109G	Lille–Vendeville?		~1500	Lille–Vendeville?	~1600	1 P-47	2	0	0	0	0
Jagddivision 5:												
II./JG 2	Bf 109G	Creil		1116	Venlo, Arnhem	1245	0	0	0	0	0	0
III./JG 2	Fw 190A	Cormeilles		~1115	?	~1245	1 B-24	0	0	0	0	0

*332 sorties by I. Jagdkorps vs. 8th AF

24 February – vs. 8th Air Force

8th Air Force Mission #233: 238 of 266 1st BD B-17s bomb Schweinfurt, TOT 1327-41 – lose 11-1-160, claim 10-1-7; 213 of 239 2nd BD B-24s bomb Gotha aviation industry and t/o, TOT 1318-30 – lose 33-1-28, claim 50-1-20; 295 of 304 3rd BD B-17s bomb Rostock and t/os, TOT 1334-1505 – lose 5-0-60, claim 23-11-15. Escort of 2 P-38 FGs, 3 P-51 FGs, 11 P-47 FGs (767 sorties) claims 38-1-14, loses 10-0-11.

With the weather predicted to be clear, the 8th AF mounted a complex full-strength, three-stream attack on Schweinfurt, Gotha and Rostock. The 1st and 2nd BDs flew directly east from England toward the German heartland, while the 3rd BD flew northeast without escort, crossed Schleswig-Holstein and attacked targets on the Baltic Sea. The southern shield again worked effectively, aided by the fact that the RLV force had no day units based in eastern Germany. The 3rd BD was opposed only by the two day Staffeln in Denmark, 10./JG 11 and 11./JG 11, and a few night fighters; it lost only five B-17s.

The leading combat wings of the main force, unaccustomed to clear weather and high winds at altitude, were ahead of schedule for most of the mission, missed most of their escorts and suffered accordingly. The 2nd BD B-24s bombed Gotha, while the trailing 1st BD B-17s split off to the south and bombed Schweinfurt. The 16 fighter groups providing escort, two flying two missions, were not enough. The B-24s proved especially vulnerable: they flew the mission well below the B-17s and below the critical altitude of the Fw 190s. JD 3 requested help early. JG 26 from neighboring JD 4 reached the bomber stream first, near the Dutch–German border. Two Gruppen found that the leading B-17 wing was unescorted and were

Luftwaffe defensive activity vs. 15th Air Force – 22 February 1944

Unit	Type	Gruppe up			Gruppe down		Claims	Losses				
		Base	No	Time	Base	Time		Dest	Dam	KIA	MIA	WIA
Luftflotte Reich												
Jagddivision 7:												
III./JG 3	Bf 109G	Leipheim		1210	Leipheim	1410	n/c	0	0	0	0	0
I./JG 5	Bf 109G	Obertraubling		~1200	Obertraubling	~1330	3 B-17	0	0	0	0	0
II./JG 27	Bf 109G	Erbenheim		~1200	Erbenheim	~1330	1 B-17, 1 P-47	2	0	0	0	1
I./JG 301	Bf 109G	Neubiberg		~1200	Neubiberg	~1330	0	2	0	0	0	1
I./JG 104	Bf 109	Fürth–Herzogenaurach		~1200	Fürth–Herzogenaurach	~1330	1 B-24	0	0	0	0	0
I./ZG 76	Bf 110G	Ansbach?		?	Ansbach?	?	0	0	0	0	0	0
II./ZG 76	Bf 110G	Ansbach?		?	Ansbach?	?	0	2	1	4	0	0
I./ZG 101	Bf 110G	Memmingen		?	Memmingen	?	0	0	0	0	0	0
Jafü Ostmark:												
I./JG 27	Bf 109G	Fels am Wagram		1200	Fels am Wagram	~1330	3 B-24, 2 B-24 HSS	3	3	2	0	1
II./JG 53	Bf 109G	Wien–Seyring		1142	Wien–Seyring, others	1340	3 B-17, 1 B-24, 1 B-24 HSS	1	4	1	0	0
II./ZG 1	Bf 110G	Wels		~1145	Wels	~1345	8 B-24	4	3	1	0	1
VbdFhr Schule	Bf 109G	Fels am Wagram		1200	Fels am Wagram	~1330	1 B-24	0	0	0	0	0
6./NJG 101	Do 217N	Parndorf		1358	Parndorf	1432	0	0	0	0	0	0
Jafü Oberschlesien:												
JGr Ost	Bf 109G, Fw 190A	Liegnitz		?	Liegnitz	?	0	1	0	1	0	0

able to make repeated head-on attacks. Both the JG 1 and JG 11 Gefechtsverbände, augmented by II./JG 3, were directed to the B-24 stream and attacked successfully, followed by the other two JG 3 Gruppen based in northern Germany and, eventually, every day fighter unit in I. and II. Jagdkorps.

Most of the German fighters landed away from their own bases, and new Luftwaffe directives on second sorties from assembly airfields were put to the test. At least two strong *ad hoc* formations were put together and attacked the withdrawing bombers. The night fighters and day Zerstörer units were also up in force. The RLV force flew 479 sorties during the day and lost at least 41 aircrew KIA or MIA, 18 WIA and 62 aircraft. The 8th AF lost 51 bombers and 10 escorts crashed or scrapped. The 11.3 per cent bomber loss rate was high, but only slightly higher than the defenders' loss rate of 11.0 per cent, and the mission counted as a victory in the Allies' war of attrition.

UNIT WAR DIARY[7]
24 February 1944

Take-off: four (total operational) Bf 110s from Wunstorf at 1201 hours

Order: scramble against incoming formations

The Gruppe formed up with 10 I./ZG 26 Bf 110s at 7,000 metres over Brunswick. II./JG 11 joined as the fighter escort over Brunswick at 1215 hours. Major Kogler led the entire formation. The Jafü transmitted instructions during the assembly. At 1315 hours, eight Pulks, each of about 15 Liberators, were sighted near Nordhausen, staggered between 4,000 and 7,000 metres and flying southeast. The enemy aircraft were jinking noticeably. Upon our approach, the enemy turned south and later southwest. We attacked near Holzminden at 1330 hours from the left and above.

III./ZG 26 scored one victory (Oblt. Meltz) and one Herausschuss (Major Kogler). Several Liberators were observed flaming brightly; others were seen to crash. No I./ZG 26 claims are available.

Luftwaffe defensive activity vs. 15th Air Force – 23 February 1944

Unit	Type	Gruppe up			Gruppe down		Claims	Losses				
		Base	No	Time	Base	Time		Dest	Dam	KIA	MIA	WIA
Luftflotte Reich												
Jagddivision 7:			*197									
III./JG 3	Bf 109G	Leipheim	24	1115	Markersdorf	1250	8 B-24, 1 P-38, 3 B-24 HSS	5	0	2	0	1
II./JG 27	Bf 109G	Erbenheim		1145	Erbenheim	1154	n/c	0	0	0	0	0
I./ZG 76?	Bf 110G	Leipheim?		~1120	Wels?	~1320	n/c	0	0	0	0	0
II./ZG 76	Bf 110G	Leipheim		1125	Wels	1325	n/c	0	0	0	0	0
II./NJG 6	Bf 110G	Schleißheim	5	?	Schleißheim	?	n/c	0	0	0	0	0
Jafü Ostmark:												
I./JG 27	Bf 109G	Fels am Wagram		1113	Fels am Wagram	1230	11 B-24, 1 P-38	4	3	1	0	1
II./JG 53	Bf 109G	Wien–Seyring		1108	Wien–Seyring	1205	n/c	0	0	0	0	0
II//ZG 1	Bf 110G	Wels		~1110	Wels	~1310	4 B-24	2	1	4	0	1
VbdFhr Schule	Bf 109G	Fels am Wagram		~1115	Fels am Wagram	~1230	1 B-24	0	0	0	0	0
6./NJG 101	Do 217N	Parndorf		1218	Parndorf	1302	0	0	0	0	0	0

*197 sorties by JD 7 + Jafü Ostmark

Landing:
2 Bf 110s land at Wunstorf at 1408 and 1414 hours.
1 Bf 110 turned back owing to cockpit damage.
1 Bf 110 – no landing report received

Additional information:
Lt. Gern was shot down over Giessen, bailed out with light injuries and returned to base claiming one Fortress.

The enemy bombers were escorted by Thunderbolts which flew above the formation. I determined that the leading Pulk, which I attacked, always turned away to the right shortly before I turned in to attack from the front. It is possible that this forced the bombers away from the target.

Major Johann Kogler, Gruppenkommandeur
III./ZG 26

A line-up of I./JG 27 aircraft on Fels am Wagram, Austria, in early 1944. 'White 25' in the foreground is a Bf 109G-4/R6 'gunboat' with 20-mm cannon in underwing gondolas. *(Prien)*

Luftwaffe defensive activity vs. 8th Air Force – 24 February 1944

Unit	Type	Gruppe up			Gruppe down		Claims	Losses (—: included with 1st sortie)				
		Base	No	Time	Base	Time		Dest	Dam	KIA	MIA	WIA
Luftflotte Reich												
I. Jagdkorps			336									
Jagddivision 1:												
Stab/JG 3	Bf 109G	Salzwedel?		~1400	Salzwedel?	~1530	1 B-24 HSS	1	1	1	0	0
III./JG 54	Bf 109G	Ludwigslust		1215	Wesendorf	1320	0	0	0	0	0	0
2nd sorties	Bf 109G	Wesendorf		1340	Wunstorf	1438	3 B-24	1	1	1	0	0
3rd sorties	Bf 109G	Wunstorf		1515	Ludwigslust	1640	1 B-17	0	0	0	0	0
I./JG 300	Bf 109G	Jüterbog–Waldlager	12	~1200	Jüterbog–Waldlager	~1330	0	1	0	0	0	0
I./JG 302	Bf 109G	Jüterbog–Waldlager		~1200	Jüterbog–Waldlager	~1330	0	0	0	0	0	0
I./ZG 26	Bf 110G	Brunswick	10	~1200	Brunswick	~1400	4 B-24	2	3	3	0	0
II./ZG 26	Me 410A	Hildesheim		~1200	Hilldesheim	~1400	2 B-17	0	1	0	0	0
I./NJG 5	Bf 110G	Stendal		~1230	Stendal	~1430	1 B-17	1	0	0	0	1
II./NJG 5	Bf 110G	Parchim		~1230	Parchim	~1430	1 B-17	0	0	0	0	0
III./NJG 5	Bf 110G	Neuruppin		~1230	Neuruppin	~1430	1 B-17	1	0	1	0	0
I./NJG 6	Bf 110G	Stendal–Altmark		~1230	Stendal–Altmark	~1430	0	3	0	5	0	0
II./NJG 6	Bf 110G	Stendal–Altmark		~1230	Stendal–Altmark	~1430	2 B-17	1	0	1	0	0
	Bf 110G	Stendal–Altmark		~1500	Stendal–Altmark	~1600	1 B-17	—	—	—	—	—
4./Zerst ErgGr	Bf 110G	Brunswick–Broitzem		1230	Brunswick--Broitzem	1345	0	0	0	0	0
ErprKdo Lärz	?	Lärz		?	Lärz	?	0	1	0	1	0	0
ESt Rechlin	Bf 109G	Rechlin		?	Rechlin	?	0	1	0	1	0	0
JaSta Erla	Bf 109G	Delitzsch		1355	Halle–Nietleben	1504	0	0	0	0	0	0
JaSta Fieseler	Fw 190A	Kassel		?	Kassel	?	0	1	0	?	?	?
Jagddivison 2:												
II./JG 3	Bf 109G	Rotenburg		1215	Köln–Ostheim	1425	8 B-24	2	0	0	0	1
Stab/JG 11	Fw 190A	Husum		~0840	Oldenburg	~0910	transfer	0	0	0	0	0
	Fw 190A	Oldenburg		~1230	Gotha?	~1400	0	0	0	0	0	0
I./JG 11	Fw 190A	Husum		0843	Oldenburg	0913	transfer	0	0	0	0	0
	Fw 190A	Oldenburg		1210	Gotha, others	~1400	9 B-24	1	2	0	0	2
II./JG 11	Bf 109G	Wunstorf		1206	Eschwege	1325	1 P-38	3	1	2	1	1
III./JG 11	Bf 109G	Oldenburg, Wunstorf		1210	Schweinfurt, others	1325	0	0	0	0	0	0
	Bf 109G	Oldenburg?		~1500	Oldenburg?	~1630	1 B-17	1	0	0	0	0
10./JG 11	Fw 190A	Aalborg–Ost		1143	Grove	1207	transfer	0	0	0	0	0
	Fw 190A	Grove		~1230	Grove?	~1400	0	0	0	0	0	0
11./JG 11	Bf 109T	Lister		?	Grove	?	transfer	0	0	0	0	0
	Bf 109T	Grove		~1130	Grove?	~1300	0	0	2	0	0	0
II./JG 302	Bf 109G	Ludwigslust	2	~1500	Ludwigslust	~1630	1 B-17	1	0	0	0	0
III./ZG 26	Bf 110G	Wunstorf	4	1201	Wunstorf	1408	1 B-17, 1 B-24	1	2	0	0	1
II./NJG 2	Ju 88C	Quakenbrück		~1330	Quakenbrück	~1530	0	0	1	?	?	?
IV./NJG 3	Ju 88C	Grove		1340	Grove	1529	3 B-17	1	0	3	0	0
LBeob St 2 (2./NJG 3 a/c)	Bf 110G	Stade		?	Stade	?	shadowers	1	0	1	0	1
Jagddivison 3:												
Stab/JG 1	Fw 190A	Deelen		?	Rheine	?	transfer	0	0	0	0	0
	Fw 190A	Rheine		~1130	Rheine	~1300	1 B-17	0	0	0	0	0
I./JG 1	Fw 190A	Dortmund		?	Rheine	?	transfer	0	0	0	0	0
	Fw 190A	Rheine		~1130	Rheine	~1300	5 B-24	5	1	3	0	2

Luftwaffe defensive activity vs. 8th Air Force – 24 February 1944 Continued

Unit	Type	Gruppe up			Gruppe down		Claims	Losses (—: included with 1st sortie)				
		Base	No	Time	Base	Time		Dest	Dam	KIA	MIA	WIA
II./JG 1	Fw 190A	Rheine	25	1130	Hannover–Langenhagen, others	1305	4 B-24	3	1	1	0	0
2nd sorties	Fw 190A	Rheine	7	1400	Rheine	~1530	1 B-24	2	0	2	0	0
III./JG 1	Bf 109G	Volkel		~1130	Volkel	~1300	0	0	0	0	0	0
2nd sorties	Bf 109G	Volkel		~1400	Volkel	~1530	0	0	1	0	0	0
II./JG 2	Bf 109G	Rheine		1058	Gütersloh	1230	1 B-17, 1 B-24, 1 P-47	5	3	2	0	2
III./JG 2	Fw 190A	?		~1130	?	~1300	0	4	0	2	0	2
I./JG 3	Bf 109G	Volkel		~1130	Volkel	~1300	1 P-47	1	1	0	1	0
IV./JG 3	Bf 109G	Venlo		1128	Venlo	1156	1 B-17	3	1	1	0	2
I./JG 26	Fw 190A	Rheine		1300	Bonn–Hangelar?	~1430	1 P-38, 1 P-47, 1 B-24 HSS	1	2	1	0	1
	Fw 190A	Varrelbusch		1335	Bonn–Hangelar	1418	0	0	0	0	0	0
	Fw 190A	Bonn–Hangelar		?	Florennes	?	transfer	0	0	0	0	0
4./JG 26	Fw 190A	Wiesbaden	2	1335	Wevelghem?	~1500	1 B-17, 2 P-47	0	0	0	0	0
II./JG 26	Fw 190A	Rheine		1300	Bonn–Hangelar?	~1430	2 B-24, 1 P-51	2	1	0	1	0
	Fw 190A	Bonn–Hangelar		?	Beauvais–Grevillers	?	transfer	0	0	0	0	0
II./JG 300	Fw 190A	Rheine	4	~1130	Rheine	~1300	0	3	0	1	0	1
Sturmstaffel 1	Fw 190A	Langenhagen		?	Langenhagen	?	0	0	0	0	0	0
Luftflotte 3												
II. Jagdkorps			143									
Jagddivision 4:												
I./JG 26	Fw 190A	Florennes		1100	Varrelbusch, Rheine	1235	2 B-24	0	0	0	0	0
4./JG 26	Fw 190A	Wevelghem		~1100	Wiesbaden	~1230	0	0	0	0	0	0
II./JG 26	Fw 190A	Beauvais–Grevillers, Epinoy		0917	Laon–Athies	0940	transfer	0	0	0	0	0
	Fw 190A	Laon–Athies		1055	Beauvais–Grevillers, Rheine	~1230	1 B-17	0	0	0	0	0
2nd sorties	Fw 190A	Beauvais–Grevillers		1517	Beauvais–Grevillers	~1700	1 B-17	0	0	0	0	0
III./JG 26	Bf 109G	Lille–Vendeville		~1100	Lille–Vendeville	~1230	4 B-17	4	0	4	0	0
	Bf 109G	St. Dizier		1443	Laon–Athies	1548	0	0	0	0	0	0
I./NJG 4	Bf 110G	Florennes		~1500	Florennes	~1500	0	1	1	?	?	?
II./NJG 4	Bf 110G	Juvincourt		~1700	Juvincourt	~1700	0	1	1	?	?	?
Jagddivision 5:												
II./JG 2	Bf 109G	Creil		~0930	Rheine	~1030	0	0	0	0	0	0
III./JG 2	Fw 190A	Cormeilles		~0930	?	~1030	0	0	0	0	0	0

24 February – vs. 15th Air Force

15th Air Force: 114 of 140 B-17s bomb Steyr (A) Bf 109 factory and t/o, TOT 1306-10 – lose 17-1, claim 24-10-2. Escort of 3 P-38 FGs + 1 P-47 FG (133 sorties) claims 12-2-3, loses 2 P-38s, 1 P-47.

The 15th AF sent its B-17 command, the 5th BW, to Steyr. The Americans were short of fighters and used the same escort plan that had worked poorly on the two previous missions: the B-17s were escorted on withdrawal only. A total of 243 fighters and Zerstörer was scrambled in defence, but not all made contact. The Jafü Ostmark controllers recognised the target early and got all three of their Gruppen – I./JG 27, II./JG 53 and II./ZG 1 – to the B-17s 100 miles from Steyr. III./JG 3 arrived from southern Germany as the target was being bombed. The defenders all concentrated on the rear of the stream and downed or wrecked 18 of the bombers in an hour of uninterrupted attacks. The P-38s then arrived and drove off the German fighters, at a cost of two of their own. The successful defenders lost six KIA, 10 WIA and 19 fighters and Zerstörer to the Italy-based attackers.

Luftwaffe defensive activity vs. 15th Air Force – 24 February 1944

Unit	Type	Gruppe up			Gruppe down		Claims	Losses				
		Base	No	Time	Base	Time		Dest	Dam	KIA	MIA	WIA
Luftflotte Reich												
Jagddivision 7:												
III./JG 3	Bf 109G	Leipheim	24	1210	Wels	1330	4 B-17, 1 B-17 HSS	2	0	0	0	0
II./JG 27	Bf 109G	Erbenheim		1138	München–Riem	1259	transfer	0	0	0	0	0
I./JG 301	Bf 109G	Leipheim		1210	Wels	1330	1 B-17	2	2	1	0	0
Stsb/ZG 76	Bf 110G	Ansbach		~0945	Ansbach?	~1100	0	1	0	0	0	0
I./ZG 76	Bf 110G	Neubiberg?		~0945	Wels?	~1100	0	0	0	0	0	0
II./ZG 76	Bf 110G	Neubiberg		0945	Wels	1055	0	1	0	0	0	0
II./ZG 101	Bf 110F	Bad Aibling		1255	Bad Aibling	1411	0	0	0	0	0	0
II./NJG 101	Do 217N	München–Riem		~1210	München–Riem	~1410	0	2	0	0	0	2
I./NJG 102	Bf 110G	Kitzingen		~1210	Kitzingen	~1410	1 B-17	0	1	0	0	1
II./NJG 102	Do 217N, Bf 110G	Stuttgart–Echterdingen		~1210	Stuttgart–Echterdingen	~1410	0	1	0	2	0	0
LBeob St 7	Bf 110G	Stuttgart–Echterdingen		~1200	Stuttgart–Echterdingen	~1400	shadower	1	0	0	0	1
Jafü Ostmark:												
I./JG 27	Bf 109G	Fels am Wagram		1200	Fels am Wagram	1335	4 B-17	4	2	0	0	3
II./JG 53	Bf 109G	Wien–Seyring		1154	Linz–Hörsching, Wien–Seyring	1338	6 B-17	3	1	1	0	2
II.//ZG 1	Bf 110G	Wels		~1130	Wels	~1400	1 B-17, 1 P-38	0	2	0	0	0
VbdFhr Schule	Bf 109G	Fels am Wagram		~1200	Fels am Wagram	~1335	1 B-17	1	0	0	0	1
Luftflotte 2												
Jafü Oberitalien:												
I./JG 77	Bf 109G	Lavariano, Italy		1150	Lavariano, Italy	1230	0	1	0	0	0	1

25 February – vs. 8th Air Force

8th Air Force Mission #233: 246 of 268 1st BD B-17s bomb Augsburg, Stuttgart industry and t/os, TOT 1352-1415 – lose 13-0-1724, claim 8-4-4; 267 of 290 3rd BD B-17s bomb Regensburg aviation industry and t/os, TOT 1350-1409 – lose 12-1-82, claim 13-1-7; 172 of 196 2nd BD B-24s bomb Fürth aviation industry and t/os, TOT 1402-20 – lose 6-2-44, claim 2-2-2. Escort of 2 P-38 FGs, 3 P-51 FGs, 12 P-47 FGs (899 sorties) claims 26-4-13, loses 3-2-6.

The German and American meteorologists all predicted clear weather over southern Germany for this day. The RLV commanders and controllers began concentrating their day fighter units early. The USSTAF sent the 8th AF on a maximum-strength raid to Regensburg, Augsburg, Stuttgart and Fürth, while the much smaller 15th AF bombed Regensburg an hour before the 8th AF arrived. The 8th AF bombers benefited today from three diversionary raids. A new B-24 group was sent across the North Sea accompanied by Mandrel aircraft, which carried radio transmitters that simulated larger formations on German radar. JG 11 was kept on the ground until the stream's direction was known. When the B-24s finally turned back, it was too late to use JG 11 against the main raid, farther south. I. Jagdkorps was able to employ only one full-strength Gefechtsverband, that of JG 1.

Another successful diversion was an unexpected bonus. The 9th AF and 2nd TAF medium bombers raided coastal targets in France and the Low Countries daily, but were usually ignored by the II. Jagdkorps controllers. Today, I./JG 26 and III./JG 2, two of the strongest Gruppen in the area, were scrambled to intercept medium bombers. They were successful, but I./JG 26 saw no action against the day's major heavy bomber raids, and III./JG 2 had to be employed against stragglers on its second mission. The other II. Jagdkorps Jagdgruppen did intercept the heavies, but in low strength.

The third 'diversion' that benefited the 8th AF was the 15th AF raid on Regensburg. JD 7 made a strenuous effort against the bombers from Italy and then had little time to service its fighters before the arrival of the 8th AF. Although the defenders

Luftwaffe defensive activity vs. 8th Air Force – 25 February 1944

Unit	Type	Gruppe up			Gruppe down		Claims	Losses (—: included with 1st sortie)				
		Base	No	Time	Base	Time		Dest	Dam	KIA	MIA	WIA
Luftflotte Reich												
I. Jagdkorps			100									
Jagddivision 1:												
Stab/JG 3	Bf 109G	Salzwedel?		~1200	Salzwedel?	~1245	n/c	0	0	0	0	0
III./JG 54	Bf 109G	Ludwigslust		1200	Ludwigslust	1245	n/c	0	0	0	0	0
I./ZG 26	Bf 110G	Brunswick		~1230	Brunswick	~1430	0	0	0	0	0	0
II./ZG 26	Me 410A	Hildesheim		~1230	Hilldesheim	~1430	2 B-24	0	0	0	0	0
Jagddivison 2:												
II./JG 3	Bf 109G	Rotenburg		~1100	Rotenburg	~1200	n/c	1	0	0	0	0
Stab/JG 11	Fw 190A	Husum		~1100	Husum	~1200	n/c – vs. diversion	0	0	0	0	0
I./JG 11	Fw 190A	Husum		~1100	Husum	~1200	n/c – vs. diversion	0	1	0	0	0
II./JG 11	Bf 109G	Wunstorf		1110	Husum	1200	n/c – vs. diversion	0	0	0	0	0
III./JG 11	Bf 109G	Oldenburg		~1100	Oldenburg	~1200	n/c – vs. diversion	0	2	0	0	0
III./ZG 26	Bf 110G	Wunstorf		~1230	Wunstorf	~1430	0	0	0	0	0	0
II./NJG 2?	Ju 88C	Quakenbrück		~1330	Quakenbrück	~1530	0	1	0	?	?	?
II./NJG 3?	Ju 88C	Schleswig		~1330	Schleswig	~1530	0	0	2	?	?	?
IV./NJG 3?	Ju 88C	Grove		~1330	Grove	~1530	0	1	0	?	?	?
ErprKdo 25	?	Achmer		?	Rechlin	?	0	0	0	0	0	0
Jagddivision 3:												
Stab/JG 1	Fw 190A	Rheine		1200	Rheine	~1330	1 B-17, 1 B-17 HSS	0	0	0	0	0
2nd sorties	Fw 190A	Rheine		~1415	Rheine	~1530	1 B-24	0	0	0	0	0
I./JG 1	Fw 190A	Dortmund		~1200	Dortmund	~1330	0	1	0	0	0	0
II./JG 1	Fw 190A	Rheine	14	1200	Echterdingen, others	1420	3 B-17 HSS	0	2	0	0	0
2nd sorties	Fw 190A	Echterdingen, others		1420	Germersheim, others	1505	1 B-24	1	0	0	0	0
III./JG 1	Bf 109G	Volkel		~1200	München–Gladbach	~1330	1 B-17	0	1	0	0	0
I./JG 3	Bf 109G	Volkel		~1250	Volkel	~1350	0	2	0	0	0	1
IV./JG 3	Bf 109G	Volkel	12	1250	Frankfurt	1350	0	1	0	0	0	1
II./JG 27	Bf 109G	München–Riem		1400	München–Riem	~1530	1 B-17	1	0	0	0	1
I./NJG 1?	Bf 110G	Venlo		?	Venlo	?	0	1	0	?	?	?
II./NJG 101?	Bf 110G	München–Riem		?	München–Riem	?	0	3	0	?	?	?
LBeob St 3	Ju 88C	Venlo		?	Venlo	?	shadower	0	0	0	0	2
Jagddivision 7:												
III./JG 3	Bf 109G	Leipheim, Echterdingen		1400	Leipheim	~1530	1 B-17, 1 P-51, 2 B-17 HSS	2	1	2	0	0
I./JG 106	Bf 109G	Lachen–Speyersdorf		1432	Lachen–Speyersdorf	1527	1 B-17, 1 B-24	0	0	0	0	0
I./ZG 76	Bf 110G	Ansbach?		~1400	Ansbach	~1600	1 B-24	0	0	0	0	0
II./ZG 76	Bf 110G	Neubiberg?		~1400	Neubiberg	~1600	0	0	0	0	0	0
I./ZG 101	Bf 110G	Memmingen		~1400	Memmingen	~1600	2 B-17	0	0	0	0	0
Luftflotte 3												
II. Jagdkorps												
Jagddivision 4:												
I./JG 26	Fw 190A	Florennes		1051	Florennes, Maldeghem	1132	2 B-26	0	1	0	0	0
	Fw 190A	Florennes		1438	Bonn–Hangelar	1550	0	0	0	0	0	0
4./JG 26	Fw 190A	Wevelghem		0800	Florennes	0842	transfer	0	0	0	0	0
	Fw 190A	Florennes		1047	Wevelghem	1138	1 B-26	0	0	0	0	0

Luftwaffe defensive activity vs. 8th Air Force – 25 February 1944 Continued

Unit	Type	Gruppe up				Gruppe down		Claims	Losses (—: included with 1st sortie)				
		Base	No	Time		Base	Time		Dest	Dam	KIA	MIA	WIA
II./JG 26	Fw 190A	Laon–Athies		1130		Cambrai–Epinoy	~1330	2 B-17	2	3	2	0	1
2nd sorties	Fw 190A	Cambrai–Epinoy		1356		Cambrai–Epinoy	1517	2 B-24	0	0	0	0	0
3rd sorties	Fw 190A	Cambrai–Epinoy		1625		Cambrai–Epinoy	1710	0	0	0	0	0	0
	Fw 190A	Beauvais–Grevillers		1747		Beauvais–Grevillers	1825	0	0	1	0	0	0
III./JG 26	Bf 109G	Laon–Athies		0943		Trier	1024	transfer	0	0	0	0	0
	Bf 109G	Trier		1130		Trier	~1330	5 B-17	1	1	0	0	0
2nd sorties	Bf 109G	Trier		1430		Lille–Vendeville?	~1600	2 B-17 HSS	0	0	0	0	0
I./JG 107	Bf 109F	Nancy–Essay		~1430		Nancy–Essay	~1600	2 B-17, 1 B-24	1	0	0	0	0
I./NJG 4?	Bf 110G	Florennes		?		Florennes	?	0	0	1	?	?	?
Jagddivision 5:													
Stab/JG 2	Fw 190A	Cormeilles		~1100		Cormeilles	~1230	0	1	1	0	0	0
II./JG 2	Bf 109G	Creil		~1200		Rheine	~1330	3 B-17	0	4	0	0	0
III./JG 2	Fw 190A	Cormeilles		~1045		Cormeilles	~1200	4 B-26	3	2	0	0	1
2nd sorties	Fw 190A	Cormeilles		~1445		Cormeilles	~1545	1 B-17	—	—	—	—	—
I./JG 101	Bf 109G	Pau–Ouest		~1130		Pau–Ouest	~1330	2 B-17, 1 B-24	1	0	0	0	1

scrambled 490 aircraft against both American air forces, including night fighters and fighter school operational flights, their success against the 8th AF did not come close to that of the previous day. The 8th AF hit all of its primary targets with reportedly excellent results while writing off 34 heavy bombers and five escorts. The RLV units employed against the 8th AF lost at least four KIA, eight WIA and 24 fighters.

25 February – vs. 15th Air Force

15th Air Force: 301 B-17s + B-24s target Regensburg aviation industry, 97 bomb target, 124 bomb t/os – lose 30-2, claim 92-16-15. Escort of 3 P-38 FGs + 1 P-47 FG (97 sorties) claims 1-1-0, loses 5.

Again today, the 15th AF provided no escort for the penetration or target legs of their mission. The bombers' route and the absence of escorts were noted soon after take-off, telegraphing their probable destination. Two Jagdgruppen in northern Italy, I./JG 53 and I./JG 77, were ordered to intercept and claimed 13 bombers for the loss of four Bf 109s. Jafü Ostmark ordered II./JG 53 to head south, and these Bf 109s met the bombers over the Alps, claiming seven B-24s for the loss of three fighters. The other Austrian units – primarily I./JG 27 and II./ZG 1 – met the unescorted bombers near Klagenfurt and also reported numerous shootdowns. The JD 7 units in southern Germany – III./JG 3, II./JG 27 and parts of ZG 76 – were well positioned, and their attacks on the

unescorted 15th AF bombers achieved great success at low cost. When the P-38s finally arrived, they were able to claim only one victory for the loss of three of their own. The 15th AF's bomber losses for the day totalled 19 B-17s and 21 B-24s, 18 per cent of the number that dropped bombs. Luftwaffe losses were at least 13 KIA, 21 WIA and 36 aircraft.

Today marked the end of 'Big Week', a signal Allied victory even though its intended goal of destroying the German aviation industry was not met. However, the Allies were well on their way to the main goal, air superiority, by making use of their large and growing quantitative superiority which the Luftwaffe could not overcome. A qualitative superiority, primarily in fighter pilots, was also becoming more evident. Big Week's day missions cost the RLV force at least 170 dead and 112 wounded aircrew and 326 aircraft. Fighter production rates could be, and were, increased to make up the material losses. Replacing the losses of skilled fighter commanders and pilots, however, proved impossible. On the American side, fighter losses were negligible. The 8th AF lost 157 bombers, 4.8 per cent of those to sortie. In comparison, RAF Bomber Command, which also took part in Operation ARGUMENT, lost 131 bombers at night, 5.7 per cent of those to sortie. The major loser among the Allied forces was the 15th AF, which lost 90 bombers, 14.6 per cent of those to sortie; it had to stop participating in deep-penetration raids on the Reich until it could obtain more long-range escort units.

Luftwaffe defensive activity vs. 15th Air Force – 25 February 1944

Unit	Type	Gruppe up			Gruppe down		Claims	Losses (—: included with 1st sortie)				
		Base	No	Time	Base	Time		Dest	Dam	KIA	MIA	WIA
Luftflotte Reich												
Jagddivision 7:												
III./JG 3	Bf 109G	Leipheim	27	1110	Leipheim, Echterdingen	1320	5 B-17, 1 B-17 HSS	0	0	0	0	0
I./JG 5	Bf 109G	Obertraubling		~1130	Herzogenaurach	~1330	3 B-17	1	0	1	0	0
II./JG 27	Bf 109G	Ingolstadt, München-Riem		1120	Schleißheim	1250	6 B-17, 2 B-17 HSS	3	2	0	0	1
I./JG 104	Bf 109E	Fürth–Herzogenaurach		~1130	Fürth–Herzogenaurach	~1330	2 B-24	5	2	1	0	3
Stab/JG 301	Bf 109G	Schleißheim		?	Schleißheim	?	0	2	0	0	0	1
I./JG 301	Bf 109G	Neubiberg		?	Neubiberg	?	1 B-24	2	0	0	0	2
I./ZG 76	Bf 110G	Ansbach		~1130	Ansbach?	~1330	4 B-17	3	1	2	0	4
II./ZG 76	Bf 110G	Neubiberg		~1130	Neubiberg?	~1330	0	2	0	3	0	0
I./ZG 101	Bf 110D	Memmingen		~1130	Memmingen	~1330	0	3	1	4	0	2
II./ZG 101	Bf 110D	Bad Aibling		~1130	Bad Aibling	~1330	0	0	0	0	0	0
I./NJG 102	Bf 110G	Kitzingen		?	Kitzingen	?	0	1	1	1	0	0
LBeob St 7	Bf 110	?		?	?	?	shadower	0	1	0	0	2
Jafü Ostmark:												
I./JG 27	Bf 109G	Fels am Wagram		1010	Wels, Fellweg, Graz	1213	8 B-17, 1 B-17 HSS	6	5	1	0	2
2nd sorties	Bf 109G	Graz?		~1300	Fels am Wagram	~1430	1 P-38	—	—	—	—	—
II./JG 53	Bf 109G	Wien–Seyring		1005	Linz–Hörsching, Wien–Seyring	1239	7 B-24	3	1	0	0	2
I./JG 108	Bf 109G	Bad Vöslau		~1100	Bad Vöslau	~1300	1 B-24	1	0	0	0	1
II./ZG 1	Bf 110G	Wels		~1100	Wels	~1330	4 B-24	0	0	0	0	0
VbdFhr Schule	Bf 109G	Fels am Wagram		~1010	Wels, Zeltweg, Graz	~1210	3 B-17	0	0	0	0	0
Luftflotte 2												
Jafü Oberitalien:												
I./JG 53	Bf 109G	Maniago, Italy		1038	Maniago, Italy	~1230	1 B-17, 6 B-24	3	0	1	0	1
2nd sorties	Bf 109G	Maniago, Italy		1320	Maniago, Italy	~1400	1 B-24	—	—	—	—	—
Stab/JG 77	Bf 109G	Povoletto, Italy	1	1040	Povoletto, Italy	1245	1 B-17 HSS	0	0	0	0	0
I./JG 77	Bf 109G	Lavariano, Italy		1040	Lavariano, Italy	1245	4 B-17	2	0	0	0	0

29 February

8th Air Force Mission #240: 218 of 226 3rd BD B-17s bomb Brunswick aviation targets and t/os – lose 1-0-54, claim 0. Escort of 2 P-38 FGs, 4 P-51 FGs, 8 P-47 FGs (554 sorties) claims 1-0-0, loses 4-0-2.

A small 8th AF raid on targets in the Brunswick area was ignored by the RLV because heavy fog enveloped all of the I. Jagdkorps bases. Bombing through cloud at a target with a poor radar return could not be expected to be effective, and the Germans reported that very little damage was in fact sustained today.

Pilots of 1./JG 1 pose around a pennant bearing their Staffel emblem at the end of February. From left to right: Uffz. Kubon (KIA 29 Mar 44), Uffz. Altenhain, Uffz. Manikowski

(KIA 11 Apr 44), Uffz. Kenzler, Uffz. Martin (KIA 20 Mar 44), Uffz. Schulze, Lt. Lück (WIA 9 Apr 44), Uffz. Talbat, Fhr. Junge (WIA 14 Aug 44), Fw. Kaiser. In the background is Fw 109A-7 'White 17'. *(Berger)*

March 1944

The authorised day fighter strength of I. Jagdkorps was augmented significantly during the month when the three single-engine night fighter Geschwader, JG 300, JG 301 and JG 302, were formally added to the day fighter order of battle. Jagddivision 30, the special headquarters set up to control their night operations, was disbanded. Many *Wilde Sau* pilots had come from the bomber arm and unlike the typical day fighter pilot were fully instrument-qualified; the nine Gruppen were put to use as 'bad weather specialists'.

Jafü Ostmark was strengthened by two Gruppen, III./JG 27 and IV./JG 27, which were brought in from peripheral theatres. All of JG 27 was eventually to be concentrated in Austria as the area's Gefechtsverband.

By the end of the month, the Luftwaffe High Command (other than Göring) no longer considered the Zerstörer to be first-line bomber interceptors. Because of its high losses, ZG 26 had moved to Königsberg–Neumark, northeast of Berlin and temporarily outside the range of American escorts.

A line-up of IV./JG 27 Bf 109G-6s on Graz–Thalerhof in March. *(Prien)*

A ZG 26 Me 410 running up its engines. Note the dramatic effect of the spiral spinners. *(Petrick)*

Incorporating the Zerstörer in the Gefechtsverbände had been difficult owing to their low cruising speed. Special mixed units were formed to provide escorts for the vulnerable twin-engine bomber destroyers, but these escorts then became unavailable for the RLV fighters' main task, attacking the bombers.

Early in the month, a new fighter control sector, Jagdabschnitt Mittelrhein, was carved from the northwestern part of Jagddivision 7 and awarded to Jagddivision 3. Simply put, this was part of the territorial squabble between I. Jagdkorps and Jagddivision 7. Finally, at the very end of March, RM Göring ordered the subordination of JD 7, including Jafü Ostmark, to I. Jagdkorps. Operational command of the Reich air defences was now vested in a single headquarters, that of Genlt. Schmid.

The campaign of attrition being waged by the USSTAF prevented any true strengthening of the RLV, despite the addition of new units. The I. Jagdkorps monthly report for March recorded its average daily operational strength (less JD 7) as 300 single-engine fighters, 60 twin-engine fighters and 50 night fighters available for day use. The command flew 2226 operational sorties while losing 240 fighters, for a loss rate of 10.9 per cent. It estimated the number of USAAF sorties to the Reich to be 16,612 for a loss of 302 to fighters, for a loss rate of only 1.8 per cent.

2 March

8th Air Force Mission #244: 375 of 481 1st BD B-17s + 2nd BD B-24s bomb Frankfurt am Main rail yard and t/os, TOT 1203-20 – lose 9-3-175, claim 2-0-2. Escort of 1 P-38 FG, 2 P 51 FGs, 10 P-47 FGs (589 sorties) claims 17-2-4, loses 4-0-10. 84 of 106 3rd BD B-17s bomb Chartres airfield, TOT 1654-1704 – lose 1-0-12, claim 0. Escort of 2 P-38 FGs, 1 P-51 FG, 3 P-47 FGs (281 sorties) claims 0, loses 0-1-0.

The 8th AF mounted two raids. The major one targeted Frankfurt, but of the 481 B-17s and B-24s that took off, only 137 were able to locate their assigned target through thick cloud cover. In the second raid, 106 B-17s attacked an airfield in France, but the Luftwaffe paid virtually no attention to it. Five I. Jagdkorps Gruppen scrambled against the major raid, but none found the bombers. The II. Jagdkorps airfields were clear, and JG 2 and JG 26 operated against both the penetration and withdrawal phases of this mission. On its 290 sorties, the Luftwaffe lost at least 18 KIA or MIA, six WIA and 25 fighters. Of these, JG 2 and JG 26 lost 10 KIA or MIA, five WIA and 14 fighters. One critical casualty was the JG 2 Kommodore, Obstlt. Egon Mayer, who was killed. Mayer had been the first Luftwaffe pilot to claim 100 victories in the west. The 8th AF came off lightly; 13 bombers and five escort fighters were written off after the two raids.

3 March

8th Air Force Mission #246: 79 of 748 B-17s + B-24s (all BDs) target Berlin, bomb Wilhelmshaven and other t/os – lose 11-0-45, claim 3-1-1. Escort of 3 P-38 FGs, 4 P-51 FGs, 10 P-47 FGs (730 sorties) claims 8-1-3, loses 7-1-14.

The number of fighters and units assigned to the RLV force could be increased only very slowly because of the Luftwaffe's other commitments. Gefechtsverbände were more effective than single Gruppen against the large American formations, and Gruppen were moved around to allow each Jagddivision in the Reich to have at least one Gefechtsverband. By today, the Stab and three of JG 3's four Gruppen, plus the independent Staffel Sturmstaffel 1, had transferred to the Berlin area as the Jagddivision 1 Gefechtsverband, in anticipation of day raids on the Reich's capital city. Today II./JG 53 moved from Austria to Frankfurt, where it would join II./JG 27 in the new *Gefechtsverband Dachs* [badger] to provide more defence to the Frankfurt basin and middle Rhine region. The region was the aforementioned Jagdabschnitt Mittelrhein, which had its own command post, further muddling command responsibilities.

The 8th AF first targeted Berlin on this date, but the mission was abandoned when dense clouds with tops above 8,500 metres (28,000 feet) were encountered. A few of the bombers dropped on targets of opportunity, and half of the 250 RLV fighters that got airborne made contact with them, but with little success. The Americans lost 11 bombers and eight fighters to all causes. The Luftwaffe lost at least 21 men KIA or MIA, three WIA and 22 aircraft.

Fw 190s 'White 1' and 'White 2' of Sturmstaffel 1, photographed from the Salzwedel hangar roof in March. *(Smith)*

PERSONAL ACCOUNT[8]

Morale of our fighter pilots was not bad [in early 1944], considering that the young pilots had little experience and a life expectancy of 10 missions. Normally, we were informed at about 0700 hours of a 'grosse Sammlung' [large assembly] over Great Yarmouth. After breakfast, we were driven to the Staffel dispersal, and about 45 minutes before the expected take-off and after determining the probable target area, 30 minutes of cockpit readiness was ordered until finally the scramble order was given. After the scramble, all units were ordered to meet at a certain point and form up in a Gefechtsverband of sometimes up to 100 aircraft before being directed to a pre-assigned attack position, from where we would separate from the main formation for our attack from the rear. The main formation would always try to overtake the bomber stream to get into position for a head-on attack.

Lt. Richard Franz, Sturmstaffel 1

Lt. Richard Franz was one of the first members of Sturmstaffel 1, joining it in February from 3./JG 77. After it was disbanded, Franz became Staffelkapitän of 7./JG 11, a position he held until the end of the war. *(Franz)*

Luftwaffe defensive activity – 2 March 1944

Unit	Type	Gruppe up			Gruppe down		Claims	Losses (—: included with 1st sortie)				
		Base	No	Time	Base	Time		Dest	Dam	KIA	MIA	WIA
Luftflotte Reich												
I. Jagdkorps			15									
Jagddivison 1:												
I./ZG 26	Bf 110G	Völkenrode		1320	Völkenrode	1350	n/c	0	0	0	0	0
	Bf 110G	Völkenrode		1530	Völkenrode	1705	n/c	0	0	0	0	0
Jagddivison 2:												
I./JG 11	Fw 190A	Rotenburg		1512	Rotenburg	~1630	0	2	0	2	0	1
Jagddivison 3:			15									
III./JG 1	Bf 109G	München–Gladbach	15	1325	München–Gladbach	~1500	1 P-47	3	0	2	0	0
I./JG 300	Fw 190A	Bonn–Hangelar	3	1330	Bonn–Hangelar	~1500	0	0	0	0	0	0
Jagddivision 7:			149									
III./JG 3	Bf 109G	Leipheim	23	1132	Leipheim	~1300	0	4	0	4	0	0
	Bf 109G	Leipheim		1220	Leipheim	1340	0	0	0	0	0	0
II./JG 27	Bf 109G	Wiesbaden–Erbenheim	34	1226	Wiesbaden–Erbenheim	1400	0	0	0	0	0	0
I./ZG 76	Bf 110G	Öttingen	21	1130	Schleißheim	~1200	n/c	0	0	0	0	0
	Bf 110G	Schleißheim	16	1220	Schleißheim	~1400	n/c	0	0	0	0	0
II./ZG 76	Bf 110G	Leipheim	12	1140	Leipheim	1320	n/c	0	0	0	0	0
Jafü Ostmark:												
I./JG 27	Bf 109G	Fels am Wagram	30	1235	Fels am Wagram	1340	n/c	0	0	0	0	0
II./JG 53	Bf 109G	Wien–Seyring	28	1225	Wien–Seyring	1300	n/c	0	0	0	0	0
Luftflotte 3												
II. Jagdkorps			126									
Jagddivision 4:												
Stab/JG 26	Fw 190A	Trier		1315	Lille–Nord	~1425	0	0	0	0	0	0
I./JG 26	Fw 190A	Florennes	13	1103	Trier	1210	1 B-17	2	0	2	0	0
2nd sorties	Fw 190A	Trier	5	1315	Florennes	1425	1 B-17	0	0	0	0	0
4./JG 26	Fw 190A	Wevelghem	6	1100	Wevelghem	~1230	0	0	0	0	0	0
II./JG 26	Fw 190A	Cambrai–Epinoy	15	1100	Cambrai–Epinoy	~1230	0	3	1	2	0	1
	Fw 190A	Beauvais–Grevillers		1100	Beauvais–Grevillers	1200	0	0	0	0	0	0
2nd sorties	Fw 190A	Beauvais–Grevillers	2	1309	Beauvais–Grevillers	1342	1 B-17	0	0	0	0	0
III./JG 26	Bf 109G	Lille–Vendeville	21	1100	Lille–Vendeville	1220	1 B-17	1	2	0	0	1
Jagddivision 5:												
Stab/JG 2	Fw 190A	Cormeilles	4	~1105	Cormeilles	~1230	0	1	0	1	0	0
II./JG 2	Bf 109G	Creil	24	1108	Reims	1210	0	3	0	1	0	2
2nd sorties	Bf 109G	Reims	13	1313	Charleroi	1442	1 B-17	—	—	—	—	—
	Bf 109G	Creil	1	1210	Creil?	~1330	0	0	0	0	0	0
	Bf 109G	Creil	2	1243	Creil?	~1330	0	0	0	0	0	0
	Bf 109G	Creil	2	1301	Creil?	~1430	0	0	0	0	0	0
III./JG 2	Fw 190A	Cormeilles	18	1106	Cormeilles	~1230	1 B-17	4	1	3	1	1
2nd sorties	Fw 190A	Reims	8	1312	Cormeilles	~1430	0	—	—	—	—	—
Jafü Bretagne:												
JGr West	Fw 190A	Biarritz		?	Biarritz	?	0	2	0	?	?	?

Luftwaffe defensive activity – 3 March 1944

Unit	Type	Gruppe up			Gruppe down		Claims	Losses				
		Base	No	Time	Base	Time		Dest	Dam	KIA	MIA	WIA
Luftflotte Reich												
I. Jagdkorps			213									
Jagddivision 1:			99									
Stab/JG 3	Bf 109G	Salzwedel		~1100	Salzwedel	~1300	0	0	0	0	0	0
I./JG 3	Bf 109G	Burg	9	1105	Burg	~1300	0	0	2	0	0	0
II./JG 3	Bf 109G	Gardelegen	16	1107	Salzwedel?	1307	0	2	0	0	0	1
IV./JG 3	Bf 109G	Salzwedel	10	1110	Salzwedel	1300	1 P-47	4	0	3	1	0
III./JG 54	Bf 109G	Lüneburg	14	1045	Lüneburg	1235	n/c	0	0	0	0	0
I./ZG 26	Bf 110G	Völkenrode	4	1055	Völkenrode	~1300	0	0	0	0	0	0
II./ZG 26	Me 410A	Hildesheim	14	1055	Hildesheim	~1300	0	1	2	2	0	0
Sturmstaffel 1	Fw 190A	Salzwedel	10	1105	Salwedel	~1300	n/c	0	0	0	0	0
ErprKdo 25	Bf 110G	Parchim	11	1114	Parchim	~1300	n/c	0	0	0	0	0
Jagddivison 2:			69									
Stab/JG 11	Bf 109G	Rotenburg	3	1047	Rotenburg	~1200	0	1	0	0	1	0
I./JG 11	Fw 190A	Hannover –Langenhagen	2	1036	Hannover –Langenhagen	~1200	0	0	0	0	0	0
	Fw 190A	Rotenburg	10	1047	Husum, others	1155	6 B-17	0	0	0	0	0
2nd sorties	Fw 190A	Rotenburg?		~1230	Rotenburg?	~1430	0	3	0	3	0	0
2nd sorties	Fw 190A	Hannover –Langenhagen	2	1240	Hannover –Langenhagen	~1400	0	0	0	0	0	0
II./JG 11	Bf 109G	Wunstorf	16	1040	Wunstorf	~1230	n/c	0	0	0	0	0
	Bf 109G	Wunstorf		1206	Lüneburg	1250	3 P-51	5	0	3	1	1
III./JG 11	Fw 190A	Oldenburg	19	1043	Oldenburg	1159	n/c	0	0	0	0	0
10./JG 11	Fw 190A	Aalborg-Ost		1108	Grove	1133	transfer	0	0	0	0	0
	Fw 190A	Grove		1145	Esbjerg (D)	1208	transfer	0	0	0	0	0
	Fw 190A	Esbjerg (D)		1403	Esbjerg (D)	1444	n/c	0	0	0	0	0
III./ZG 26	Bf 110G	Wunstorf	11	1050	Wunstorf	~1330	0	3	2	5	0	1
II./NJG 3	Ju 88C	Schleswig		~1030	Schleswig	~1230	1 B-17	0	0	0	0	0
III./NJG 3	Ju 88C	Stade		~1030	Stade	~1230	0	0	0	0	0	0
LBeob St 2	Ju 88	Stade	1	0955	Stade	~1230	shadower	0	0	0	0	0
Jagddivison 3:			38									
Stab/JG 1	Fw 190A	Rheine		~1045	Rheine?	~1245	0	0	0	0	0	0
I./JG 1	Fw 190A	Twente	14	1042	Vörden	1225	0	1	0	0	0	0
II./JG 1	Fw 190A	Rheine	15	1050	Fassberg	1248	3 P-51	2	1	2	0	0
III./JG 1	Bf 109G	München–Gladbach	9	1019	München–Gladbach	~1200	n/c	0	0	0	0	0
Jagddivision 7:			44									
III./JG 3	Bf 109G	Leipheim		~1130	Leipheim	~1300	1 B-17	0	0	0	0	0
II./JG 27	Bf 109G	Erbenheim	30	1119	Dessau	1250	2 P-38	0	0	0	0	0
ZG 76	Bf 110G	Öttingen	14	1050	Öttingen	~1300	n/c	0	0	0	0	0
Jafü Ostmark:												
II./JG 53	Bf 109G	Wien–Seyring		1505	Frankfurt–Eschborn	1700	transfer	0	0	0	0	0

4 March

8th Air Force Mission #247: 249 of 502 1st BD + 3rd BD B-17s bomb Berlin area, several t/os – lose 15-1-120, claim 6-2-3. Escort of 3 P-38 FGs, 4 P-51 FGs, 12 P-47 FGs (770 sorties) claims 8-3-4, loses 24-4-7.

Another attempt by the 8th AF to bomb Berlin ended in another recall. One combat wing of the 3rd BD failed to hear the signal and proceeded to Berlin, which it bombed through a solid undercast. The new Jagddivision 1 Gefechtsverband was able to form up despite the weather and catch the withdrawing bombers, claiming eight B-17s and two P-51s. The rest of the 246 I. Jagdkorps fighters up claimed some of the 16 bombers and 28 escorts shot down, missing or scrapped, although 11 363rd FG P-51s simply disappeared, and their fate has never been confirmed. The RLV force lost at least eight KIA, five WIA and 20 fighters on the mission.

5 March

8th Air Force Mission #246: 164 of 219 2nd BD B-24s bomb 4 airfields in SW France – lose 4-1-23, claim 14-2-5. Escort of 1 P-38 FG, 3 P-51 FGs, 3 P-47 FGs (307 sorties) claims 14-0-6, loses 5-3-1.

A raid on French airfields by the 8th AF's 2nd BD was defended by JD 5's one weak Jagdgeschwader and its school commands. The Americans wrote off five bombers and eight escorts. The Luftwaffe lost four KIA, four WIA and nine fighters. JG 2 claimed three B-24s. A massive dogfight in the target area involving Ergänzungsjagdgruppe West resulted in no known claims, although Lt. Chuck Yeager of the 357th FG was shot down by a Fw 190. Yeager evaded capture and reached Spain.

6 March – Berlin (see map)

8th Air Force Mission #250: 672 of 730 B-17s + B-24s (all BDs) bomb Berlin and several t/os, TOT 1315-1346h – lose 69-6-347, claim 97-28-60. Escort of 3 P-38 FGs, 3 P-51 FGs, 13 P-47 FGs (801 dispatched) claims 81-8-21, loses 11-3-6.

The 8th AF was finally able to put its full force over Berlin. The three bomb divisions formed into a single stream that took a straight course directly east from England over northern Holland toward Berlin. The stream then jinked to avoid known Flak belts and turned south to approach the briefed targets in the south of the city. From the American take-off, there was little doubt in I. Jagdkorps headquarters as to the intended target. As expected, the defences countered with most of their strength, putting up a total of 463 sorties, of which 332 were credited with *Feindberührung*, or enemy contact.

I. Jagdkorps command and control worked to perfection today. Two large Gefechtsverbände were formed – six Jagdgruppen in one, and four Jagdgruppen and four Zerstörergruppen in the other – and made prolonged attacks before the bomb drop. Many fighters landed from their first sorties on the newly designated assembly airfields and took off again against the withdrawing stream.

II. Jagdkorps and its two Geschwader, JG 2 and JG 26, were not so fortunate. III./JG 26 was scrambled against a tactical raid and was removed from the main battle. The orders of the other four Gruppen and one independent Staffel called for them to fly to JD 7 bases to refuel, far to the south of the bombers' incoming or withdrawal courses. They then flew low-strength missions against the withdrawing bombers.

The American escorts flew 943 sorties (three groups flew two missions), but could not always hold off the large German formations, and 75 bombers crashed or were scrapped on their return, the greatest loss on any raid of the war. However, the loss of 10 per cent of those to take off, while high, was no hindrance to further operations of the same magnitude. The loss of 14 escort fighters, was, as usual, negligible. The new large-formation tactics of the RLV had their greatest success today, but at a cost of 75 aircraft (16 per cent of those scrambled), 37 KIA or MIA and 32 WIA. Thirty-five per cent of the Zerstörer and 50 per cent of the twin-engine night fighters that engaged were lost, a strong indication that their time in the day battle was passing.

A formation of II./ZG 26 Me 410s en route from Hildesheim to attack a heavy bomber formation in early March. *(Petrick)*

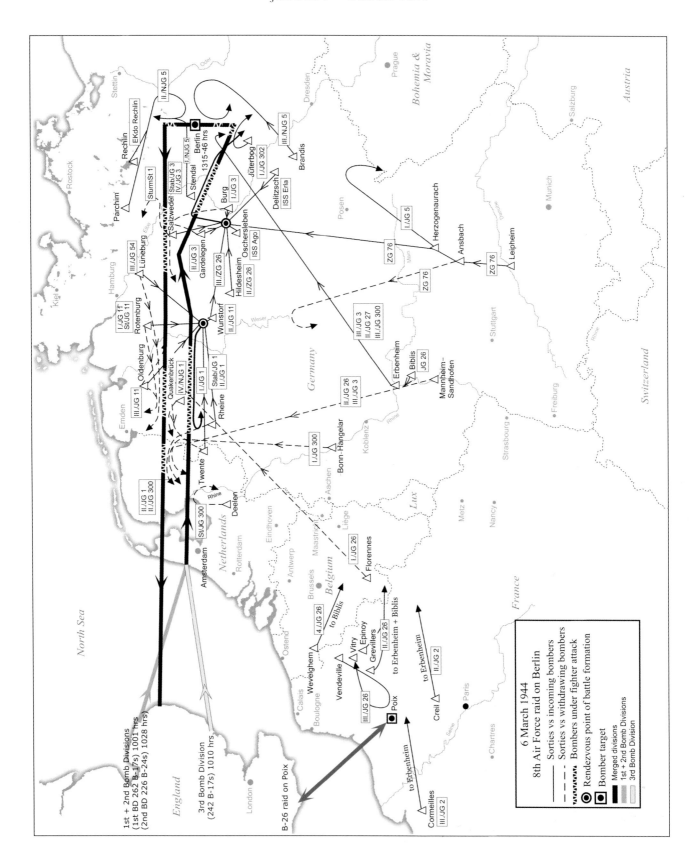

6 March 1944
8th Air Force raid on Berlin

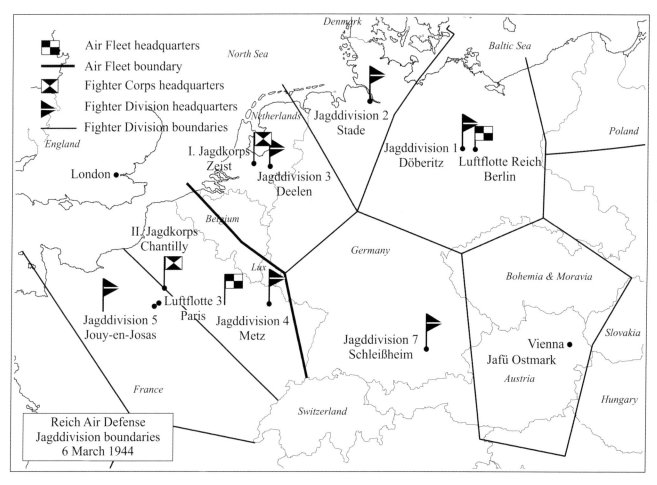

Reich Air Defense
Jagddivision boundaries
6 March 1944

COMBAT REPORT[9]
6 March 1944

One B-17 Fortress shot down from 6,800 metres at 1252 hours in PQ GE-5 W of Brandenburg

At 1137 hours, I scrambled from Salzwedel with the Gruppe in a Bf 109G-6 with three MG 151/20s and two MG 131s toward an enemy formation approaching from the west. The Gefechtsverband assembled over Magdeburg. At about 1230 hours, we sighted the escorted enemy formation approaching from the direction of Brunswick. We were at 7,500–8000 metres; the enemy formation was at 6,800–7,300 metres. After the first attack, we caught up with the enemy again. The Gruppe flew in a single file of nine aircraft. I attacked an aircraft on the left outside of the formation from exactly in front and began firing at 500 metres. I achieved several hits in the right outer engine and the right wing. I pulled away over the bomber and saw that the outer part of the right wing was totally shot up. When I came back around, I saw that the aircraft had pulled away from the formation in a steep left bank and was entering a spiral to the right. I saw two men bail out. The bomber crashed west of Brandenburg. I could not see the exact location as a cloud of smoke was covering the crash site.

Lt. Hans Weik
10./JG 3

Oblt. Hans Weik completed training and joined JG 3 on the Eastern Front in early 1943. After a tour as an instructor in which he shot down a B-24, Weik joined 9./JG 3, which was by now on Reich defence duties, in November 1943 and became Staffelkapitän of 10.(Sturm)/JG 3 in February 1944. After a productive period as a bomber destroyer, Weik was forced to bail out of his Fw 190A-8/R2 on 18 July with a serious arm injury that kept him from further combat, although he began training on Me 262s before the end of the war. Weik was credited with 36 victories, including 22 heavy bombers, in only 85 missions and was awarded the Knight's Cross. (*Author's collection*)

Left: Fw 190A-7 'White 20' (W. Nr. 642962) of Sturmstaffel 1, probably photographed at Langenhagen. Lt. Gerhard Dost was killed in this aircraft on 6 March. Its cowling machine guns have been removed, and it has not yet had a white spiral applied to its spinner. (*Smith*)

Luftwaffe defensive activity – 4 March 1944

Unit	Type	Gruppe up			Gruppe down		Claims	Losses				
		Base	No	Time	Base	Time		Dest	Dam	KIA	MIA	WIA
Luftflotte Reich												
I. Jagdkorps			149									
Jagddivision 1:			79									
Stab/JG 3	Bf 109G	Salzwedel	2	1210	Salzwedel	~1345	2 B-17, 1 B-17 HSS	0	0	0	0	0
I./JG 3	Bf 109G	Burg	14	1209	Burg	~1345	n/c	0	0	0	0	0
II./JG 3	Bf 109G	Gardelegen	16	1220	Gardelegen	1345	1 B-17. 2 P-51	2	0	1	0	1
IV./JG 3	Bf 109G	Salzwedel	8	1210	Salzwedel	1342	1 B-17	1	0	1	0	0
III./JG 54	Bf 109G	Lüneburg	15	1305	Lüneburg	1425	n/c	0	0	0	0	0
I./JG 302	Bf 109G	Jüterbog-Damm		1209	Jüterbog-Damm	~1330	1 B-17	2	0	1	0	0
Sturmstaffel 1	Fw 190A	Salzwedel	5	1235	Salzwedel	~1400	2 B-17	1	1	0	0	1
ErprKdo 25	Bf 110G	Rechlin	2	1325	Rechlin	~1430	n/c	0	0	0	0	0
EinsSt Erla	Bf 109G	Delitzsch	10	1325	Delitzsch	1434	n/c	2	0	?	?	?
LBeob St 1	Bf 110	Parchim	1	1130	Parchim	~1330	shadower	0	0	0	0	0
Jagddivison 2:			46									
Stab/JG 11?	Fw 190A	Husum		~1300	Husum	~1430	n/c	0	0	0	0	0
I./JG 11	Fw 190A	Rotenburg	5	1304	Husum, others	1410	n/c	0	0	0	0	0
	Fw 190A	Husum	2	1330	Husum?	~1430	n/c	0	0	0	0	0
II./JG 11	Bf 109G	Rotenburg	4	1304	Husum	~1315	transfer	0	0	0	0	0
	Bf 109G	Wunstorf	3	1348	Wunstorf	~1430	n/c	0	0	0	0	0
III./JG 11	Fw 190A	Oldenburg	17	1300	Husum	~1315	transfer	0	0	0	0	0
	Fw 190A	Husum	17	1330	Stade, others	1342	0	1	1	1	0	1
Jagddivison 3:			24									
Stab/JG 1?	Fw 190A	Rheine		~1300	Rheine	~1430	n/c	0	0	0	0	0
I./JG 1	Fw 190A	Twente	7	1302	Twente	~1430	n/c	0	0	0	0	0
	Fw 190A	Twente	2	1439	Twente	~1530	n/c	0	0	0	0	0
II./JG 1?	Fw 190A	Rheine		1320	Rheine	1434	n/c	0	0	0	0	0
III./JG 1	Bf 109G	Rheine	14	1308	Rheine	~1430	n/c	0	0	0	0	0
I./JG 300	Bf 109G	Bonn–Hangelar	1	1435	Bonn–Hangelar	~1530	0.5 B-17	0	0	0	0	0
Jagddivison 7:			96									
Stab/JG zbV	Bf 109G	Kassel		~1100	Kassel	~1230	0	2	0	?	?	?
III./JG 3	Bf 109G	Leipheim	18	1120	Leipheim	~1230	n/c	0	0	0	0	0
II./JG 27	Bf 109G	Erbenheim	22	1105	Erbenheim	~1230	1 B-17	4	1	2	0	1
II./JG 53	Bf 109G	Frankfurt–Eschborn	26	1105	Frankfurt–Eschborn	~1230	2 B-17, 2 P-51	4	1	2	0	1
I./JG 301	Bf 109G	Neubiberg	17	1125	Neubiberg	~1300	0	0	1	0	0	0
II./ZG 76	Bf 110G	Leipheim	13	1115	Leipheim	~1330	n/c	0	0	0	0	0
Jafü Ostmark:												
Stab/JG 27	Bf 109G	Fels am Wagram		~1100	Fels am Wagram	~1230	0	1	0	0	0	0
II./JG 53	Bf 109G	Wien–Seyring		1100	Frankfurt–Eschborn	1305	0	0	0	0	0	0
Luftflotte 3												
II. Jagdkorps			74									
Jagddivision 4:												
4./JG 26	Fw 190A	Wevelghem	2	1520	Wevelghem	~1600	1 P-38	0	0	0	0	0
III./JG 26	Bf 109G	Nancy–Essay	4	1508	Nancy–Essay	~1600	n/c	0	0	0	0	0
LBeob St 4	Me 210	Metz	1	1100	Metz	~1330	shadower	0	0	0	0	0
Jagddivision 5:												
Stab/JG 2?	Fw 190A	Cormeilles		~1225	Cormeilles	~1400	n/c	0	0	0	0	0
II./JG 2	Bf 109G	Creil	27	1240	Creil?	~1400	1 B-17	0	0	0	0	0
	Bf 109G	Creil	2	1324	Creil?	~1430	n/c	0	0	0	0	0
	Bf 109G	Creil	21	1438	Creil?	~1530	n/c	0	0	0	0	0
III./JG 2	Fw 190A	Cormeilles	13	1225	Cormeilles?	~1400	n/c	0	0	0	0	0
	Fw 190A	Cormeilles	10	1435	Cormeilles?	~1530	n/c	0	0	0	0	0
	Fw 190A	Cormeilles	1	1512	Cormeilles?	~1600	n/c		0	0	0	0

Luftwaffe defensive activity – 5 March 1944

Unit	Type	Gruppe up			Gruppe down		Claims	Losses				
		Base	No	Time	Base	Time		Dest	Dam	KIA	MIA	WIA
Luftflotte 3												
II. Jagdkorps			134									
Jagddivision 5:												
Stab/JG 2	Fw 190A	Cormeilles?		~1230	Cormeilles?	~1400	0	0	0	0	0	0
II./JG 2	Bf 109G	Tours		1237	Tours, Le Mans	1410	3 B-24	1	0	0	0	0
III./JG 2	Fw 190A	Cormeilles?		~1230	Cormeilles?	~1400	0	0	0	0	0	0
Jafü Bretagne:												
JGr West	Bf 109F,	Biarritz		~1300	Biarritz	~1430	1 P-51	6	0	4	0	2
	Fw 190A											
Jafü Südfrankreich:												
I./JG 101	Bf 109G	Pau-Ouest		~1300	Pau–Ouest	~1430	0	2	0	0	0	2

Luftwaffe defensive activity – 6 March 1944

Unit	Type	Gruppe up			Gruppe down		Claims	Losses (—: included with 1st sortie)				
		Base	No	Time	Base	Time		Dest	Dam	KIA	MIA	WIA
vs. incoming stream												
Luftflotte Reich												
I. Jagdkorps			*328									
Jagddivision 1:			*137									
Stab/JG 3	Bf 109G	Salzwedel	2	1137	Berlin–Staaken	1350	0	1	0	0	0	0
I./JG 3	Bf 109G	Burg	23	1135	Burg	~1300	0	0	0	0	0	0
II./JG 3	Bf 109G	Gardelegen	16	1136	Straußberg	1340	1 B-17	2	0	0	0	1
IV./JG 3	Bf 109G	Salzwedel	14	1137	Berlin–Staaken	1350	6 B-17, 1 P-51, 1 B-17 HSS	0	1	0	0	0
III./JG 54	Bf 109G	Lüneburg	20	1102	Lüneburg	~1300	4 B-17	8	0	3	2	3
	Bf 109G	Lüneburg	1	1256	Lüneburg	~1430	0	0	0	0	0	0
I./JG302	Bf 109G	Jüterbog	8	1137	Stendal	~1300	2 B-17	3	1	3	0	0
Sturmstaffel 1	Fw 190A	Salzwedel	7	1137	Salzwedel	~1300	4 B-17	2	0	1	0	0
II./ZG 26	Me 410A	Hildesheim	10	1125	Hildesheim	~1330	8 B-17	6	2	5	0	5
I./NJG 5	Bf 110G	Stendal	2	1210	Stendal	~1430	1 B-17	2	0	2	0	0
II./NJG 5	Bf 110G	Parchim	1	1250	Parchim	~1430	shadower	0	0	0	0	0
	Bf 110G	Parchim	9	1254	Parchim	~1430	1 B-24	5	0	4	0	0
III./NJG 5	Bf 110G	Brandis	4	1232	Brandis	1354	0	3	0	1	0	1
FLÜG 1	Fw 190A	?	1	~1200	?	~1400	1 B-17	0	0	0	0	0
Kdo F-H Tag	Fw 190A	Parchim	5	1145	Parchim	~1330	shadowers	0	0	0	0	0
EKdo Rechlin	Bf 110G	Rechlin	3	1235	Rechlin	~1400	0	1	0	1	0	1
ISS Erla	Bf 109G	Delitzsch	2	1256	Ludwigslust	1457	1 P-51	0	0	0	0	0
ISS AGO	Fw 190A	Oschersleben	3	1225	Oschersleben	~1400	0	0	0	0	0	0
III./NJG 5	Bf 110G	Königsberg–Neumark	3	1213	Brandis	~1315	transfer	0	0	0	0	0
Jagddivision 2:			*100									
Stab/JG 11	Bf 109G	Rotenburg	4	1103	Rotenburg	~1230	1 B-24 HSS	4	0	0	0	1
I./JG 11	Fw 190A	Rotenburg	17	1107	Rotenburg	1228	8 B-17, 1 P-47	5	2	1	0	1
II./JG 11	Bf 109G	Wunstorf	15	1100	Quakenbrück	~1230	3 B-17, 2 P-47	5	1	2	0	1
III./JG 11	Fw 190A	Oldenburg	18	1104	Oldenburg	1229	3 B-17	2	0	2	0	0
III./ZG 26	Bf 110G	Wunstorf	9	1126	Wunstorf	~1300	1 B-17, 1 P-51	5	1	5	0	5
IV./NJG 1	Bf 110G	Quakenbrück	1	1245	Quakenbrück	~1345	1 B-17	0	0	0	0	0
LBeob St 2	Ju 88	Stade	1	1130	Stade	~1330	shadower	0	0	0	0	0

Luftwaffe defensive activity – 6 March 1944 Continued

Unit	Type	Gruppe up			Gruppe down		Claims	Losses (—: included with 1st sortie)				
		Base	No	Time	Base	Time		Dest	Dam	KIA	MIA	WIA
Jagddivision 3:			*66									
Stab/JG 1	Fw 190A	Rheine	2	1103	Rheine	1230	1 B-17, 1 P-47	0	0	0	0	0
I./JG 1	Fw 190A	Twente	16	1045	Quakenbrück	1215	7 B-17, 1 P-47	5	2	2	0	1
	Fw 190A	Twente	1	1210	Twente	1343	1 B-17	0	0	0	0	0
II./JG 1	Fw 190A	Rheine	20	1103	Rheine	1230	6 B-17	4	2	1	0	3
Jagddivision 7:			*91									
III./JG 3	Bf 109G	Wiesbaden–Erbenheim	15	1224	Wiesbaden–Erbenheim	~1400	1 B-24	0	0	0	0	0
I./JG 5	Bf 109G	Herzogenaurach	6	1300	Herzogenaurach	~1430	n/c	0	0	0	0	0
II./JG 27	Bf 109G	Wiesbaden–Erbenheim		1117	Wiesbaden–Erbenheim	1132	n/c	0	0	0	0	0
	Bf 109G	Wiesbaden–Erbenheim	31	1224	Wiesbaden–Erbenheim	~1400	n/c	0	0	0	0	0
III./JG300	Bf 109G	Wiesbaden–Erbenheim		1224	Wiesbaden–Erbenheim	~1400	n/c	0	0	0	0	0
Stab./ZG 76	Bf 110G	Ansbach		~1100	Kassel	~1330	0	1	0	1	0	1
I.–III./ZG 76	Bf 110G	Leipheim		0835	Ansbach	1010	transfer	0	0	0	0	0
	Bf 110G	Ansbach	24	1059	Ansbach	~1330	2 B-17	3	3	3	0	6
II./ZG 76	Bf 110G	Ansbach		1250	Kassel	1435	n/c	0	0	0	0	0
Luftflotte 3												
II. Jagdkorps			*69									
Jagddivision 4:												
Stab/JG 26?	Fw 190A	Wevelghem		~1120	Biblis	~1237	transfer	0	0	0	0	0
4./JG 26	Fw 190A	Wevelghem	7	1120	Biblis	1237	transfer	0	0	0	0	0
II./JG 26	Fw 190A	Grevillers	6	1118	Biblis	1227	transfer	0	0	0	0	0
	Fw 190A	Epinoy	5	1118	Biblis	~1230	transfer	0	0	0	0	0
	Fw 190A	Epinoy	5	1215	Biblis	~1245	transfer	0	0	0	0	0
III./JG 26	Bf 109G	Lille–Vendeville		1200	Vitry	1310	1 Typhoon	0	0	0	0	0
Jagddivision 5:												
II./JG 2	Bf 109G	Creil	22	1121	Wiesbaden–Erbenheim	~1230	transfer	0	0	0	0	0
III./JG 2	Fw 190A	Cormeilles	13	1127	Mannheim–Sandhofen	~1230	transfer	0	0	0	0	0
vs. withdrawing stream												
Luftflotte Reich												
I. Jagdkorps												
Jagddivision 1:												
I./JG 3	Bf 109G	Burg	4	1356	Burg	~1530	0	—	—	—	—	—
II./JG 3	Bf 109G	Gardelegen	7	1335	Gardelegen	~1530	1 B-17, 1 P-38	—	—	—	—	—
IV./JG 3	Bf 109G	Salzwedel	1	1330	Salzwedel	~1530	1 B-17	—	—	—	—	—
III./JG 54	Bf 109G	Lüneburg	7	1409	Lüneburg	~1530	2 B-17, 1 B-24	—	—	—	—	—
II./ZG 26	Me 410A	Hildesheim	1	1354	Hildesheim	~1530	0	—	—	—	—	—
Sturmstaffel 1	Fw 190A	Salzwedel	2	1345	Salzwedel	~1530	1 B-17	—	—	—	—	—
Kdo F-H Tag	Fw 190A	Parchim	3	1300	Parchim	~1500	shadowers	0	0	0	0	0
	Fw 190A	Sorau	1	1305	Sorau	~1500	shadower	0	0	0	0	0
Jagddivision 2:												
I./JG 11	Fw 190A	Rotenburg	13	1348	Rotenburg	1419	4 B-17	—	—	—	—	—
3rd sorties	Fw 190A	Rotenburg	13	1443	Rotenburg	1456	2 B-17	—	—	—	—	—
II./JG 11	Bf 109G	Wunstorf	5	1400	Wunstorf	~1530	0	—	—	—	—	—
III./JG 11	Fw 190A	Oldenburg	7	1301	Oldenburg	~1400	0	—	—	—	—	—
	Fw 190A	Oldenburg	4	1350	Oldenburg	1530	4 B-17	—	—	—	—	—
LBeob St 2	Me 210	Stade	1	1400	Stade	~1530	1 B-24 (shadower)	0	0	0	0	0
IV./NJG 1	Bf 110G	Quakenbrück	2	1325	Quakenbrück	~1600	1 B-24	0	0	0	0	0
	Bf 110G	Quakenbrück	2	1440	Quakenbrück	~1600	1 B-17	0	0	0	0	0

Luftwaffe defensive activity – 6 March 1944 Continued

Unit	Type	Gruppe up			Gruppe down		Claims	Losses (—: included with 1st sortie)				
		Base	No	Time	Base	Time		Dest	Dam	KIA	MIA	WIA
Jagddivision 3:												
I./JG 1	Fw 190A	Twente?		~1430	Twente?	~1630	1 B-17	—	—	—	—	—
II./JG 1	Fw 190A	Rheine	4	1415	Rheine	1454	4 B-17,1 P-51, 1 B-17 HSS	—	—	—	—	—
3rd sorties	Fw 190A	Rheine	3	1526	Rheine	~1630	n/c	—	—	—	—	—
Stab/JG300	Fw 190A	Deelen	2	1408	Deelen	~1530	0	0	2	0	0	0
I./JG300	Bf 109G	Bonn–Hangelar	10	1348	Bonn–Hangelar	1545	1 B-17	3	2	1	0	0
	Bf 109G	Bonn–Hangelar	4	1505	Bonn–Hangelar	~1600	n/c	0	0	0	0	0
II./JG300	Fw 190A	Rheine		~1345	Rheine	~1530	0	1	0	1	0	0
Jagddivision 7:												
II./JG 2	Bf 109G	Wiesbaden–Erbenheim	17	1340	Wiesbaden–Erbenheim	~1530	3 B-24	2	3	0	0	2
III./JG 2	Fw 190A	Mannheim–Sandhofen	10	1346	Mannheim–Sandhofen	~1530	0	0	0	0	0	0
II./JG 26	Fw 190A	Biblis	2	1330	Biblis, Rheine	1410	0	0	0	0	0	0
	Fw 190A	Biblis	20	1340	Biblis, Rheine	~1530	1 B-17	0	0	0	0	0
4./JG 26	Fw 190A	Biblis	7	1330	Rheine	~1500	2 B-17, 1 B-24	2	1	0	0	2
I.–III./ZG 76	Bf 110G	Ansbach	15	1443	Ansbach	~1530	n/c	—	—	—	—	—
Luftflotte 3												
II. Jagdkorps												
Jagddivision 4:												
I./JG 26	Fw 190A	Florennes	13	1356	Twente	1504	1 B-17, 2 P-47	0	0	0	0	0

*total sorties vs. incoming & withdrawing streams

8 March – Berlin (see map)

8th Air Force Mission #252: 539 of 623 B-17s + B-24s (all BDs) bomb Berlin-Erkner ball- bearing factory and several t/os, TOT 1429-1502 – lose 37-3-228, claim 63-17-19. Escort of 3 P-38 FGs, 6 P-51 FGs, 10 P-47 FGs (891 sorties) claims 79-8-25, loses 18-16-7.

Keeping up the pressure on the defences, the 8th AF returned to Berlin. 623 bombers from all three divisions targeted the Erkner ball-bearing factory. Bombing conditions were good, and serious damage was both claimed and attained. The defensive effort was somewhat lower than that of the 6th, 366 sorties being flown, but was effective in two major combats. Only one Gefechtsverband was formed, that of JD 1. But other units sent up against the incoming bomber stream formed an even larger concentration, even if it was not formally called a Gefechtsverband. A full hour before the B-17s and B-24s started leaving England, JD 4 was ordered to transfer most of its fighters to Rheine, much closer to the presumed target than they were sent on the 6th. The fighters rendezvoused with five Jagdgruppen of JG 1 and JG 11, and this large force succeeded for once in overwhelming the escorts. This battle was still continuing when the JD1 Verband arrived. It contained the only Zerstörer ordered up today, seven Bf 110s of III./ZG 26. The crews of the heavy fighters found conditions to their liking and, in one of the best performances ever recorded by the Zerstörergruppen, claimed 12 B-17s and one P-51 without loss. For the day, the 8th lost or scrapped 40 bombers and a whopping 34 escorts. The RLV force lost 22 KIA or MIA, 13 WIA and 48 aircraft in a successful, if costly day.

9 March

8th Air Force Mission #253: 490 of 526 B-17s + B-24s (all BDs) bomb Berlin, 3 other secondaries – lose 8-2-221, claim 1-0-0. Escort of 3 P-38 FGs, 6 P-51 FGs, 9 P-47 FGs (808 sorties) claims 0, loses 1-3-0.

The 8th AF's third mission to Berlin in four days took the same route as the two previous raids, with no attempts at deception. The RLV commanders chose not to respond to this obvious provocation. Using bad weather as a convenient excuse, they kept their fighters on the ground. All of the Allied losses were attributable to Flak or operational factors.

11 March

8th Air Force Mission #255: 124 of 124 1st BD + 3rd BD B-17s bomb Münster rail yards and t/o – lose 1-0-24, claim 0. Escort of 1 P-51 FG, 2 P-47 FGs (140 sorties) claims 0, loses 2-0-2.

The 8th AF returned to Münster. The Luftwaffe again left their fighters on the ground, and even the Flak was ineffective: only one bomber failed to return to its base.

15 March

8th Air Force Mission #259: 330 of 344 3rd BD B-17s + 2nd BD B-24s bomb Brunswick and t/os – lose 3-0-46, claim 0-0-1. Escort of 3 P-38 FGs, 10 P-47 FGs (588 sorties) claims 38-3-13, loses 5-1-5.

The 8th AF returned to Brunswick. The German reaction was ineffective owing to the weather. Many units could not get off the ground, including the entire JD 1 Gefechtsverband, and only small formations were used, totalling 153 effective sorties. They were handled easily by the American escorts, even without the P-51s, which were grounded today. II./JG 11, one of the best units in the RLV, was treated the worst, losing seven KIA, two WIA and eight Bf 109s, and was taken off operations that evening for six weeks of rebuilding. The Americans lost only three bombers and six escorts; the RLV force lost 20 KIA or MIA, seven WIA and 29 aircraft.

16 March

8th Air Force Mission #262: 675 of 740 B-17s + B-24s (all BDs) bomb Augsburg, Friedrichshafen and t/os, TOT 1202-32 – lose 23-1-179, claim 68-32-43. Escort of 3 P-38 FGs, 4 P-51 FGs, 9 P-47 FGs (868 sorties) claims 77-7-20, loses 10-2-10.

The 8th AF targeted Augsburg and Friedrichshafen on a deep-penetration raid. All bombing was done through cloud and was largely ineffective. The RLV force was hampered greatly by weather conditions, and only Jagddivision 7 of Luftflotte Reich and Jagddivisionen 4 and 5 of Luftflotte 3 made interceptions. Of the 375 fighters to scramble, 266 were credited with enemy contact. As the bomber stream left England and prepared to cross the French coast at Le Tréport, JG 26 and possibly part of JG 2 were ordered to take off and put down quickly on Laon–Athies, where they scrambled again and assembled a fair-sized force to attack the incoming bombers. They were dispersed completely by P-47s, claiming only one B-24 before landing on several airfields for servicing before flying second sorties against the withdrawing bombers. These likewise

The operational strength of Sturmstaffel 1 – 15 Fw 190A-6s and A-7s – is parked outside the hangar at Salzwedel in mid-March. (Smith)

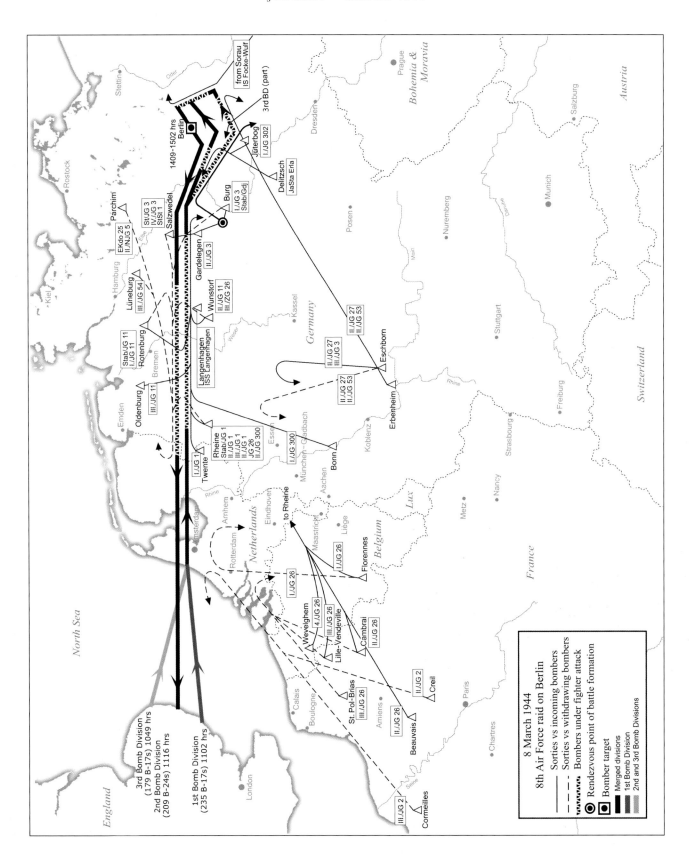

from Sorau
IS Focke-Wulf

3rd BD (part)

Prague
Bohemia &
Moravia

Salzburg

Austria

Dresden

I./JG 302

Jüterbog

Delitzsch
JaSta Erla

Munich

Berlin
1409-1502 hrs

Burg
I./JG 3
Stab/Gdj

Posen

Nuremberg

Parchim

St/JG 3
IV/JG 3
StSt 1

Gardelegen
II./JG 3

Main

Stettin

Oder

Rostock

EKdo 25
II./NJG 5

Elbe

Wunstorf
II./JG 11
III./ZG 26

II./JG 11

Kassel

II./JG 27
II./JG 53

Stuttgart

Lüneburg
III./JG 54

Kiel

Hamburg

Langenhagen
ISS Langenhagen

Weser

Germany

II./JG 27
III./JG 3

Eschborn

Freiburg

Switzerland

Stab/JG 11
I./JG 11

Rotenburg

Bremen

Emden

III./JG 11

Oldenburg

II./JG 27
II./JG 53

Erbenheim

Rhine

Rheine
Stab/JG 1
II./JG 1
III./JG 1
JG 26

I./JG 300

München–Gladbach

Essen

Koblenz

Strasbourg

Nancy

I./JG 1
Twente

Rhine

Bonn

Aachen

to Rheine

Metz

Lux

France

Arnhem

Eindhoven

Maastricht

Liège

Belgium

Amsterdam

Rotterdam

Netherlands

I./JG 26

I./JG 26
Florennes

North Sea

Weveighem
III./JG 26
4./JG 26
Lille-Vendeville

Cambrai
II./JG 26

Paris

I./JG 26

St. Pol-Brias
III./JG 26

II./JG 2
Creil

Amiens

Calais

Boulogne

Beauvais
I./JG 26

Chartres

Seine

3rd Bomb Division
(179 B-17s) 1049 hrs
2nd Bomb Division
(209 B-24s) 1116 hrs
1st Bomb Division
(235 B-17s) 1102 hrs

England

London

III./JG 2
Cormeilles

8 March 1944
8th Air Force raid on Berlin

――― Sorties vs incoming bombers
‒ ‒ ‒ Sorties vs withdrawing bombers
wwwww Bombers under fighter attack
◉ Rendezvous point of battle formation
◉ Bomber target
◻ Bomber target
▬▬ Merged divisions
▬▬ 1st Bomb Division
▬▬ 2nd and 3rd Bomb Divisions

Luftwaffe defensive activity – 8 March 1944

Unit	Type	Gruppe up			Gruppe down		Claims	Losses (—: included with 1st sortie)				
		Base	No	Time	Base	Time		Dest	Dam	KIA	MIA	WIA
Luftflotte Reich												
Luftflotte Reich												
I. Jagdkorps			*282									
Jagddivision 1:			*112									
Stab/JG 3	Bf 109G	Salzwedel	2	1248	Salzwedel?	~1430	1 B-17	0	0	0	0	0
I./JG 3	Bf 109G	Burg	17	1245	Burg	~1430	2 P-51	5	1	2	0	0
II./JG 3	Bf 109G	Gardelegen	15	1245	Gardelegen, others	1505	2 B-17	2	1	0	0	1
IV./JG 3	Bf 109G	Salzwedel	16	1248	Dessau, Jüterbog	1430	3 B-17, 1 P-38, 1 P-47, 1 P-51, 2 B-17 HSS	4	0	1	0	2
I./JG302	Bf 109G	Jüterbog	7	1255	Jüterbog	~1430	2 B-24	2	1	1	0	0
Sturmstaffel 1	Fw 190A	Salzwedel	6	1248	Salzwedel	~1430	1 B-17	0	0	0	0	0
Kdo F-H Tag	Bf 110G	Parchim	1	1237	Parchim	~1430	shadower	0	0	0	0	0
(II./NJG 5 a/c)	Bf 110G	Parchim	1	1317	Parchim	~1500	1 B-24 (shadower)	0	0	0	0	0
ISS Erla	Bf 109G	Delitzsch	3	1255	Delitzsch	1406	1 B-17	0	0	0	0	0
ISS Sorau	Fw 190A	Sorau	8	1353	Sorau	~1530	0	0	0	0	0	0
Stab/GdJ	Fw 190A	Burg	5	1349	Burg?	~1530	2 B-17	1	0	1	0	0
Jagddivision 2:			*77									
Stab/JG 11	Bf 109G	Rotenburg	3	1207	Rotenburg	~1330	1 P-51	0	1	0	0	1
I./JG 11	Fw 190A	Rotenburg	14	1207	Rotenburg	1325	4 B-17, 3 P-47	4	1	2	0	0
II./JG 11	Bf 109G	Wunstorf	19	1207	Wunstorf	~1330	1 B-17	4	0	0	2	1
III./JG 11	Fw 190A	Oldenburg	7	1205	Oldenburg	~1330	0	5	3	2	0	1
III./ZG 26	Bf 110G	Wunstorf	7	1230	Wunstorf	~1400	11 B-17, 2 P-51	0	0	0	0	0
ISS L'hagen	Fw 190A	Hannover–Langenhagen	1	1315	Hannover–Langenhagen	~1500	0	2	1	1	0	1
LBeob St 2	Bf 110G	Stade	1	1235	Stade	~1400	shadower	0	1	0	0	0
Jagddivision 3:			*93									
Stab/JG 1	Fw 190A	Rheine	2	~1200	Rheine	~1330	0	0	0	0	0	0
I./JG 1	Fw 190A	Twente	10	1155	Hannover–Langenhagen	1350	2 B-17, 3 P-47	0	0	0	0	0
II./JG 1	Fw 190A	Rheine	19	1157	Wesendorf	1330	2 B-17, 1 P-47, 1 B-17 HSS	4	2	3	0	0
4./JG 26	Fw 190A	Rheine	4	1200	Rheine	~1330	1 P-47	1	0	0	0	1
II./JG 26	Fw 190A	Rheine	11	1200	Rheine	~1330	0	0	0	0	0	0
	Fw 190A	Rheine	10	1237	Rheine	~1430	5 B-17, 1 P-51, 1 B-17 HSS	1	1	0	0	0
III./JG 26	Bf 109G	Rheine	20	1210	Zelle	1315	1 B-17 HSS	2	4	1	0	1
I./JG 300	Bf 109G	Bonn–Hangelar	6	1208	Bonn–Hangelar	~1400	1 B-17	4	0	1	0	2
Jagddivision 7:												
III./JG 3	Bf 109G	Frankfurt–Eschborn	14	1219	Frankfurt–Eschborn	~1400	n/c	0	0	0	0	0
II./JG 27	Bf 109G	Wiesbaden–Erbenheim	17	1216	Frankfurt–Eschborn	1250	n/c	0	0	0	0	0
2nd sorties	Bf 109G	Frankfurt–Eschborn		1355	Wiesbaden–Erbenheim	1415	3 B-17	2	0	2	0	0
II./JG 53	Bf 109G	Frankfurt–Eschborn		~1330	Frankfurt–Eschborn	~1500	2 B-17	3	0	2	0	1
Luftflotte 3												
II. Jagdkorps			*96									
Jagddivision 4:												
I./JG 26	Fw 190A	Florennes	—	~1000	Rheine	~1100	transfer	0	0	0	0	0
4./JG 26	Fw 190A	Wevelghem	—	~1000	Rheine	~1100	transfer	0	0	0	0	0
II./JG 26	Fw 190A	Grevillers	—	~1000	Rheine	~1100	transfer	0	0	0	0	0
	Fw 190A	Epinoy	—	~1000	Rheine	~1100	transfer	0	0	0	0	0
III./JG 26	Bf 109G	Lille–Vendeville	—	1000	Rheine	~1100	transfer	0	0	0	0	0

Luftwaffe defensive activity – 8 March 1944 Continued

Unit	Type	Gruppe up			Gruppe down		Claims	Losses (—: included with 1st sortie)				
		Base	No	Time	Base	Time		Dest	Dam	KIA	MIA	WIA
vs. withdrawing stream												
Luftflotte Reich												
I. Jagdkorps												
Jagddivision 1:												
I./JG 3	Bf 109G	Burg	1	1400	Burg	~1530	0	0	0	0	0	0
	Bf 109G	Altenburg	4	1400	Altenburg	~1530	0	0	0	0	0	0
	Bf 109G	Burg	7	1450	Burg	~1530	1 B-17	0	0	0	0	0
II./JG 3	Bf 109G	Gardelegen	9	1445	Gardelegen	~1530	0	0	0	0	0	0
IV./JG 3	Bf 109G	Altenburg	7	1400	Altenburg	~1530	0	0	0	0	0	0
	Bf 109G	Jüterbog	7	1455	Jüterbog	~1530	0	0	0	0	0	0
	Bf 109G	Salzwedel	2	1515	Salzwedel	1540	1 B-24	0	0	0	0	0
III./JG 54	Bf 109G	Lüneburg	11	1447	Lüneburg	~1615	1 B-17	5	2	2	0	0
I./JG 302	Bf 109G	Jüterbog	2	1453	Jüterbog	~1530	2 B-24	0	0	0	0	0
Ind St Erla	Bf 109G	Delitzsch	2	1450	Zerbst	1505	0	0	0	0	0	0
ErprKdo 25	Fw 190A	Parchim	5	1430	Parchim	~1530	2 B-17	0	0	0	0	0
Jagddivision 2:												
I./JG 1	Fw 190A	Hannover–Langenhagen	—	1502	Hannover–Langenhagen	1610	0	—	—	—	—	—
Stab/JG 11	Bf 109G	Rotenburg	2	1444	Rotenburg	~1600	0	—	—	—	—	—
I./JG 11	Fw 190A	Rotenburg	4	1444	Rotenburg	~1600	2 B-17, 2 B-24, 1 P-51	—	—	—	—	—
	Fw 190A	Rotenburg	—	1534	Rotenburg	1545	0	—	—	—	—	—
II./JG 11	Bf 109G	Wunstorf	2	1458	Wunstorf	~1600	0	—	—	—	—	—
III./JG 11	Fw 190A	Wunstorf	2	1506	Wunstorf	~1600	1 P-38	—	—	—	—	—
LBeob St 2	Ju 88	Stade	1	1338	Stade	~1530	shadower	0	1	0	0	0
	Ju 88	Stade	1	1400	Stade	~1600	shadower	0	1	0	0	0
II./NJG 3	Ju 88C	Schleswig	—	?	Schleswig	?	0	1	0	1	0	0
Jagddivision 3:												
II./JG 1	Fw 190A	Rheine	—	~1400	Rheine	~1530	1 B-24	—	—	—	—	—
3rd sorties:	Fw 190A	Rheine	2	1500	Rheine	~1630	0	—	—	—	—	—
III./JG 1	Bf 109G	Rheine	2	1520	Rheine	~1630	1 B-17	0	1	0	0	0
III./JG 26	Bf 109G	Rheine	2	1415	Rheine	~1630	0	—	—	—	—	—
I./JG300	Bf 109G	Bonn–Hangelar	—	~1500	Bonn–Hangelar	~1630	0	—	—	—	—	—
II./JG300	Fw 190A	Rheine	4	1502	Rheine	~1630	1 P-38	1	0	0	0	1
Jagddivision 7:												
II./JG 27	Bf 109G	Wiesbaden–Erbenheim	5	1505	Düsseldorf	1646	n/c	0	0	0	0	0
II./JG 53	Bf 109G	Frankfurt–Eschborn	7	1507	Frankfurt–Eschborn	~1645	n/c	0	0	0	0	0
Luftflotte 3												
II. Jagdkorps												
Jagddivision 4:												
I./JG 26	Fw 190A	Florennes	13	1447	Florennes	~1630	n/c	0	0	0	0	0
	Fw 190A	Florennes		1550	Deelen	1720	1 Spitfire	0	0	0	0	0
II./JG 26	Fw 190A	Cambrai–Epinoy	2	1410	Cambrai–Epinoy	~1530	n/c	0	0	0	0	0
III./JG 26	Bf 109G	St. Pol–Brias	7	1403	Lille–Vendeville	~1530	n/c	0	0	0	0	0
Jagddivision 5:												
II./JG 2	Bf 109G	Creil	25	1454	Creil	~1645	1 P-47	0	2	0	0	0
III./JG 2	Fw 190A	Cormeilles	7	1452	Cormeilles	~1645	0	0	0	0	0	0

*total sorties vs. incoming + withdrawing streams

Luftwaffe defensive activity – 15 March 1944

Unit	Type	Gruppe up			Gruppe down		Claims	Losses				
		Base	No	Time	Base	Time		Dest	Dam	KIA	MIA	WIA
Luftflotte Reich												
I. Jagdkorps			161									
Jagddivision 1:			15									
II./ZG 26	Me 410A	Hildesheim	4	1027	Hildesheim	~1200	0	0	0	0	0	0
Jagddivision 2:			71									
Stab/JG 11	Bf 109G	Rotenburg	2	0955	Rotenburg	~1200	0	0	1	0	0	0
I./JG 11	Fw 190A	Rotenburg	22	0935	Rotenburg	1155	0	0	3	0	0	0
II./JG 11	Bf 109G	Wunstorf	20	0955	Wunstorf	~1100	1 B-17, 2 P-38	8	3	6	1	2
III./JG 11	Fw 190A	Oldenburg	13	0953	Oldenburg	~1130	1 P-47	3	1	1	0	1
	Fw 190A	Oldenburg		1050	Oldenburg	1150	0	0	0	0	0	0
III./JG 54	Bf 109G	Lüneburg	13	1131	Lüneburg	~1200	0	1	0	1	0	0
III./ZG 26	Bf 110G	Wunstorf	11	1021	Wunstorf + 3 others	1215		1	0	2	0	0
Jagddivision 3:			67									
Stab/JG 1	Fw 190A	Rheine		~1000	Rheine	~1100	0	0	0	0	0	0
I./JG 1	Fw 190A	Hopsten	10	0955	Hannover–Langenhagen	~1100	1 P-38	0	1	0	0	1
II./JG 1	Fw 190A	Rheine	24	0941	Rotenburg + 9 others	1100	1 P-47	1	3	1	0	1
III./JG 1	Bf 109G	Twente	19	0952	Rotenburg	1100	0	1	0	0	0	0
I./JG 300	Bf 109G	Bonn–Hangelar		~1000	Bonn–Hangelar	~1100	1 P-38	1	0	1	0	0
II./JG300	Fw 190A	Rheine		~1000	Rheine	~1100	0	1	0	0	0	0
Jagddivision 7:			48									
III./JG 3	Bf 109G	Leipheim	18	1055	Leipheim	~1230	0	3	3	2	0	0
II./JG 27	Bf 109G	Wiesbaden–Erbenheim	5	1025	Wiesbaden–Erbenheim	~1230	0	1	0	0	0	0
II./JG 53	Bf 109G	Frankfurt–Eschborn	9	1032	several airfields	~1230	0	1	0	1	0	0
I./JG 301	Bf 109G	Neubiberg		~1030	Neubiberg	~1200	0	2	1	1	0	1
ZG 76	Bf 110G	Ansbach	30	1027	Ansbach	~1200	n/c	0	0	0	0	0
Luftflotte 3												
II. Jagdkorps			103									
Jagddivision 4:												
I./JG 26	Fw 190A	Florennes	11	1105	Rheine	1233	1 B-24	2	0	1	0	0
4./JG 26	Fw 190A	Wevelghem	5	1005	Wevelghem	~1130	0	0	0	0	0	0
II./JG 26	Fw 190A	Beauvais–Grevillers	5	1024	Rheine	1121	1 Spitfire	3	0	2	0	1
	Fw 190A	Cambrai–Epinoy	6	1100	Rheine	~1230	1 B-24	0	0	0	0	0
III./JG 26	Bf 109G	Lille–Vendeville	3	1000	Lille–Vendeville	~1130	0	0	0	0	0	0
	Bf 109G	Denain	19	1026	Denain	~1200	0	0	0	0	0	0
Jagddivision 5:												
II./JG 2	Bf 109G	Creil	31	1108	Enschede, Rheine	~1245	0	0	0	0	0	0
III./JG 2	Fw 190A	Cormeilles	18	1026	Enschede, Rheine	~1245	0	0	0	0	0	0

downed only one B-24. The parts of JG 2 remaining on their home airfields had much greater success, claiming seven B-17s and one P-47 on their two missions.

The Bf 109 units of JD 7 had some success, but this apparently came at the expense of ZG 76, the Zerstörer unit in southwestern Germany. Mustangs caught the lumbering Bf 110s as they formed up to attack the bomber stream. Their Bf 109 escorts disappeared, and the slaughter began: the P-51s shot down 23 of the 43 Bf 110s. III./ZG 76, a new unit which had just been declared operational, never flew another mission and was soon disbanded to reinforce the other units. Bases farther to the rear were sought out for the six remaining Zerstörergruppen; in the future, they were to be used only against unescorted bomber formations. The day's fighting cost the Americans 24 bombers and 12 escorts; the RLV force lost 39 KIA, 32 WIA and 67 aircraft.

17 March

15th Air Force: 213 B-17s + B-24s bomb Vienna aviation industry – claims unknown, lose at least 5. P-38 escort claims 0, loses at least 1.

The 15th AF returned to the Reich for the first time since 25 February, bombing Vienna through solid cloud. The German defenders in Italy and Austria were unable to find the bombers. The Hungarian Air Force scrambled 16 Bf 109s and 11 Me 210s which were ordered to intercept an unescorted B-24 formation over Lake Balaton. They were recalled, but one Bf 109 flight failed to receive the message and attacked. The first documented air battle between the Hungarians and the 15th AF resulted in claims for two damaged Liberators for the loss of two fighters and two KIA.

18 March

8th Air Force Mission #264: 678 of 738 B-17s + B-24s (all BDs) bomb Oberpfaffenhofen, Friedrichshafen, other aviation targets and t/os S Germany, TOT 1402 – lose 43-4-242, claim 45-10-17. Escort of 3 P-38 FGs, 5 P-51 FGs, 9 P-47 FGs (925 sorties) claims 36-4-7, loses 13-3-10.

The 8th AF mounted a major raid on aviation industry targets in southern Germany, while part of the 15th AF attacked Udine, an airfield in northern Italy. This small force fixed the Jafü Ostmark fighters near their bases until it was too late for them to intercept the larger force coming from the north. The defensive strategy of I. Jagdkorps was unique. Its fighters were sent to the large bases around Frankfurt to refuel and await the withdrawing bombers. They not only swamped the servicing facilities, but once in the air, they overwhelmed the capabilities of the small new Jagdabschnitt Mittelrhein command post. Only 152 single-engine fighters were credited with combat sorties, and none of the 27 Zerstörer airborne made contact with the enemy. The defensive mission went well, nonetheless. Several RLV formations, most notably the JG 11 Gefechtsverband, found unescorted

A Me 210 of the Hungarian Air Force. *(Price)*

bomber boxes and scored heavily: 43 bombers failed to return to England. Not all of these were shot down by the Luftwaffe: 16 of the missing airplanes headed for Switzerland, where three were shot down by the Swiss defences and the other 13 made forced landings, their crews going into internment. The Americans also scrapped four bombers in England and lost or scrapped 16 escorts. On this day, the losses of the RLV force were less than those of the 8th AF, totalling 25 KIA or MIA, eight WIA and 39 fighters. Several Gruppen were hit disproportionately hard: I./JG 5 scrambled its last seven operational fighters and lost three shot down and two force-landed away from the base. Only two returned, both damaged. The Gruppe was taken off operations. II./JG 27 was in better shape before the mission; 19 took off, but only three returned – five were shot down (with four pilots killed) and 11 belly-landed elsewhere. The two JG 300 Gruppen that saw combat were also roughed up badly.

19 March

15th Air Force: 236 of 290 B-17s + B-24s bomb Klagenfurt airfield and t/os, TOT 1335-1440; 79 of 96 B-24s bomb Graz (A) and t/os, TOT 1339-1405 – claim 28-10-3, lose 18-?-?. Escort of 3 P-38 FGs, 1 P-47 FG (115 sorties) claims 2-0-1, loses 0-1-0.

The weather forecast appeared to permit a raid on the Steyr ball-bearing plant by the 15th AF. En route to Austria, the small bomber force was pursued by the one Italian and two German fighter Gruppen of Jafü Oberitalien in northern Italy, which downed several B-17s and one P-38. The Luftwaffe units lost two KIA or MIA, one WIA and five Bf 109s; Italian losses have not been traced. The weather worsened, and Steyr could not be located. The force was split between two Austrian airfields, but the 92 B 24s ordered to bomb Graz were left unescorted. This formation was met coming off the target by 87 JG 27 Bf 109s, the entire single-engine day fighter force of the newly reinforced Jafü Ostmark, which made multiple attacks from all directions. The Geschwader lost six pilots and 10 Bf 109s to the B-24 gunners, but returned to base claiming 27 B-24s shot down; most of these claims were eventually confirmed. American losses to all causes totalled six B-17s and 12 B-24s, 5 per cent of those dispatched. This was much greater than the rate now prevailing in the 8th AF, and the 15th AF commanders attributed it directly to a shortage of escorts, especially P-51s.

20 March

8th Air Force Mission #269: 147 of 445 B-17s + B-24s (all BDs) bomb Frankfurt, several t/os – lose 7-1-165, claim 2-0-0. Escort of 1 P-38 FG, 5 P-51 FGs, 7 P-47 FGs (594 sorties) claims 4-0-1, loses 8-0-12.

The 8th AF targeted southern Germany again, but most of the bombers that completed the mission dropped on Frankfurt. The defensive effort was left to II. Jagdkorps. Several small JG 2 and JG 26 formations – a total of 67 fighters – left their bases and flew inland to Laon–Athies. One Messerschmitt pilot on his first mission lost control in the clouds and crashed to his death. The survivors scrambled from Laon–Athies, but then had to hide in the clouds from the P-47s, which shot down five more Bf 109s, killing four pilots. A III./JG 26 Staffelkapitän gained the only success for the German aviators, downing a single straggling B-17. The other American losses – seven bombers and eight fighters – were due to operational factors and Flak.

22 March

8th Air Force Mission #273: 657 of 688 B-17s + B-24s (all BDs) bomb Berlin, several t/os – lose 12-1-347, claim 0. Escort of 3 P-38 FGs, 5 P-51 FGs, 10 P-47 FGs (817 sorties) claims 0, loses 12-1-16.

The 8th AF flew a full-strength mission in bad weather, bombing Berlin through heavy clouds. The Luftwaffe kept all of its fighters on the ground; no defensive sorties were flown.

23 March

8th Air Force Mission #275: 707 of 768 B-17s + B-24s (all BDs) bomb Handorf airfield, Brunswick, Münster, several t/os, TOT 1027-1117 – lose 28-1-322, claim 33-8-11. Escort of 3 P-38 FGs, 5 P-51 FGs, 9 P-47 FGs (841 sorties) claims 20-1-6, loses 4-1-2.

A full-strength 8th AF raid on targets in north-central Germany met significant opposition despite poor weather. Strong tailwinds caused the 3rd BD to miss its penetration escorts, and it flew all the way to Brunswick without escort. The fighters of Jagddivisionen 1, 2 and 3 were scrambled and sent to Brunswick, where they made effective attacks on the 3rd BD and an unescorted 1st BD combat box before the arrival of P-51s. The two Frankfurt-area Gruppen of Gefechtsverband Dachs flew north, but apparently could not find the bombers. In the

Luftwaffe defensive activity – 16 March 1944

Unit	Type	Gruppe up			Gruppe down		Claims	Losses (—: included with 1st sortie)				
		Base	No	Time	Base	Time		Dest	Dam	KIA	MIA	WIA
Luftflotte Reich												
I. Jagdkorps			111									
Jagddivision 2:			42									
II./JG 1	Fw 190A	Oldenburg	16	1005	Rheine, Kassel, Oldenburg, others	1155	0	0	0	0	0	0
III./JG 1	Bf 109G	Oldenburg		~1000	Leipheim, others	~1155	0	1	0	0	0	0
Stab/JG 11	Bf 109G	Rotenburg	3	1015	Rotenburg	~1145	0	0	0	0	0	0
I./JG 11	Fw 190A	Rotenburg	11	1012	Stuttgart–Echterdingen	1145	0	1	0	0	0	0
	Fw 190A	Rotenburg	17	1015	Rotenburg	~1145	0	0	0	0	0	0
II./JG 11	Bf 109G	Wunstorf	12	1014	Wunstorf	~1145	0	0	0	0	0	0
III./JG 11	Fw 190A	Oldenburg	9	1011	Oldenburg	~1145	0	0	1	0	0	0
III./JG 54	Bf 109G	Lüneburg	13	1011	Lüneburg	~1200	0	0	0	0	0	0
ESt Rechlin	Do 217	Rechlin		?	Rechlin	?	0	1	0	?	?	?
Jagddivision 3:			83									
Stab/JG 1	Fw 190A	Rheine		~0800	Rheine	~0900	0	0	0	0	0	0
I./JG 1	Fw 190A	Twente		~0800	Hannover–Langenhagen	~0900	0	0	2	0	0	0
II./JG 1	Fw 190A	Rheine	20	0805	Oldenburg	~0900	transfer	0	0	0	0	0
III./JG 1	Bf 109G	München–Gladbach?		~0800	Oldenburg	~0900	transfer	0	0	0	0	0
Jagddivision 7:			86									
III./JG 3	Bf 109G	Leipheim	9	1052	Leipheim	~1230	1 B-17, 1 P-51, 4 B-17 HSS	3	2	2	0	3
	Bf 109G	Leipheim		~1200	Leipheim	~1330	0	0	0	0	0	0
I./JG 5	Bf 109G	Herzogenaurach	24	1204	Herzogenaurach	~1330	4 B-17, 1 P-51	6	9	2	0	5
II./JG 27	Bf 109G	Wiesbaden–Erbenheim	14	1051	Frankfurt–Eschborn	~1230	1 B-17	2	0	1	0	2
II./JG 53	Bf 109G	Frankfurt–Eschborn	16	1052	Frankfurt–Eschborn	~1230	0	3	0	1	0	1
I./JG 104	Bf 109G	Fürth	10	1230	Fürth	~1400	1 B-17	6	1	1	0	4
I./JG 106	Bf 109G	Lachen–Speyerdorf	7	1102	Lachen–Speyerdorf	~1215	0	0	0	0	0	0
2nd sorties	Bf 109G	Lachen–Speyerdorf	7	1240	Lachen–Speyerdorf	~1400	1 P-51	1	1	0	0	0
I./ZG 76	Bf 110G	Öttingen	~14	1120	Öttingen	~1230	1 B-17	8	2	4	0	3
II./ZG 76	Bf 110G	Leipheim	16	1045	Leipheim	~1230	0	8	1	8	0	5
III./ZG 76	Bf 110G	Öttingen	~13	1120	Öttingen	~1230	4 B-17	3	1	0	0	3
I./ZG 101	Bf 110C	Memmingen		1058	Memmingen	1240	0	4	0	7	0	0
Luftflotte 3												
II. Jagdkorps			154									
Jagddivision 4:												
I./JG 26	Fw 190A	Florennes	11	0936	Metz, Laon–Athies	1045	transfer	0	0	0	0	0
	Fw 190A	Metz	2	1242	Florennes	~1430	n/c	0	0	0	0	0
	Fw 190A	Laon–Athies	9	~1100	Couvron, St. Dizier?	~1230	0	1	0	1	0	0
2nd sorties	Fw 190A	Couvron	4	~1300	St. Dizier?	~1430	0	1	0	1	0	0
4./JG 26	Fw 190A	Wevelghem	5	1054	Laon–Athies	~1115	transfer	0	0	0	0	0
	Fw 190A	Laon–Athies	5	~1130	St. Dizier?	~1230	0	0	0	0	0	0
II./JG 26	Fw 190A	Beauvais–Grevillers, Cambrai–Epinoy	12	0930	Beauvais–Grevillers, Laon–Athies	1030	0	0	0	0	0	0
2nd sorties	Fw 190A	Laon–Athies	10	~1100	St. Dizier?	~1230	0	2	1	2	0	0

Luftwaffe defensive activity – 16 March 1944 Continued

Unit	Type	Gruppe up			Gruppe down		Claims	Losses (—: included with 1st sortie)				
		Base	No	Time	Base	Time		Dest	Dam	KIA	MIA	WIA
III./JG 26	Bf 109G	Lille–Vendeville		0950	Denain	1057	0	0	0	0	0	0
	Bf 109G	Lille–Vendeville	9	0948	Laon–Athies	~1045	transfer	0	0	0	0	0
	Bf 109G	Denain	12	0932	Laon–Athies	~1045	transfer	0	0	0	0	0
	Bf 109G	Laon–Athies	21	~1100	St. Dizier?	~1230	1 B-24	1	0	1	0	0
2nd sorties	Bf 109G	Denain, St .Dizier		~1300	St. Dizier, Reims	~1430	0	2	3	0	0	3
2nd sorties	Bf 109G	Reims	2	1304	Reims	~1430	1 B-24	1	0	0	0	1
I./JG 107	Bf 109G	Nancy–Essay	4	1040	Nancy–Essay	~1200	0	2	0	0	0	0
2nd sorties	Bf 109G	Nancy–Essay	2	1338	Nancy–Essay	~1500	0	0	0	0	0	0
Jagddivision 5:												
Stab/JG 2	Fw 190A	Cormeilles?		~0930	Cormeilles?	~1130	0	1	0	0	0	0
II./JG 2	Bf 109G	Creil	33	0945	Creil	1115	2 B-17	4	0	4	0	0
2nd sorties	Bf 109G	Creil	17	1252	Creil	~1400	0	—	—	—	—	—
3rd sorties	Bf 109G	Creil	14	1436	Creil	~1600	2 B-17	—	—	—	—	—
III./JG 2	Fw 190A	Cormeilles	17	0937	Cormeilles	~1130	3 B-17, 1 P-47	5	0	3	0	2
2nd sorties	Fw 190A	Cormeilles	5	1436	Cormeilles	~1600	0	—	—	—	—	—
I./JG 103	Bf 109G	Châteauroux–Déols		~1330	Châteauroux–Déols	~1430	1 B-17	0	0	0	0	0

Luftwaffe defensive activity – 17 March 1944

Unit	Type	Gruppe up			Gruppe down		Claims	Losses				
		Base	No	Time	Base	Time		Dest	Dam	KIA	MIA	WIA
Luftflotte Reich												
Jagddivision 7:												
Jafü Ostmark:			50									
IV./JG 27	Bf 109G	Graz–Thalerhof	26	1203	Graz–Thalerhof	~1330	0	0	0	0	0	0
Hungarian 2/1	Bf 109G	Ferihegy, Hungary	16	~1200	Ferihegy, Hungary	~1330	2 B-24 (dam)	2	2	2	0	0
Hungarian 5/1	Me 210Ca-1	Ferihegy, Hungary	11	~1200	Ferihegy, Hungary	~1330	0	0	0	0	0	0
Luftflotte 2												
Jafü Oberitalien:			85									
I./JG 53	Bf 109G	Maniago, Italy	46	1118	Maniago, Italy	~1200	n/c	0	0	0	0	0
Stab/JG 77	Bf 109G	Povoletto, Italy		1118	Povoletto, Italy	~1200	n/c	0	0	0	0	0
I./JG 77	Bf 109G	Lavariano, Italy	30	1120	Lavariano, Italy	~1200	n/c	0	0	0	0	0
	Bf 109G	Lavariano, Italy	8	1520	Lavariano, Italy	~1600	n/c	0	0	0	0	0
LBeob St Italy	?	Osoppo, Italy	1	1105	Osoppo, Italy	~1300	shadower	0	0	0	0	0

Luftwaffe defensive activity – 18 March 1944

Unit	Type	Gruppe up			Gruppe down		Claims	Losses (—: included with 1st sortie)				
		Base	No	Time	Base	Time		Dest	Dam	KIA	MIA	WIA
Luftflotte Reich												
I. Jagdkorps			133									
Jagddivision 1:												
III./JG 54	Bf 109G	Lüneburg		~1130	Frankfurt–Eschborn?	~1300	transfer	0	0	0	0	0
I./JG302	Bf 109G	Jüterbog		~1130	Frankfurt–Eschborn?	~1300	transfer	0	0	0	0	0
Jagddivision 2:												
Stab/JG 11	Bf 109G	Rotenburg		~1130	Wiesbaden–Erbenheim	~1230	transfer	0	0	0	0	0
I./JG 11	Fw 190A	Rotenburg		1132	Wiesbaden–Erbenheim	1246	transfer	0	0	0	0	0
III./JG 11	Fw 190A	Oldenburg		~1200	Wiesbaden–Erbenheim	~1300	transfer	0	0	0	0	0
Jagddivision 3:												
Stab/JG 1	Fw 190A	Rheine		~1215	Rhein–Main	~1400	0	0	0	0	0	0
I./JG 1	Fw 190A	Hopsten	17	1218	Rhein–Main, Darmstadt	1418	0	0	4	0	0	0
II./JG 1	Fw 190A	Rheine	18	1232	Rhein–Main	1412	0	0	1	0	0	0
III./JG 1	Fw 190A	Twente	13	1216	Rhein–Main	~1400	0	1	0	0	0	0
Jagdabschnitt Mittelrhein:												
III./JG 2	Fw 190A	Mannheim–Sandhofen	10	1415	Mannheim–Sandhofen	~1545	3 B-17, 1 P-51	2	0	2	0	0
Stab/JG 11	Bf 109G	Wiesbaden–Erbenheim		1415	Wiesbaden–Erbenheim?	~1600	1 B-24	0	0	0	0	0
I./JG 11	Fw 190A	Wiesbaden–Erbenheim		1415	Lahr	1525	9 B-24	0	1	0	0	0
III./JG 11	Fw 190A	Wiesbaden–Erbenheim	18	1420	Rebstock	1555	8 B-24	0	0	0	0	0
I./JG 26	Fw 190A	Mannheim–Sandhofen	5	1414	Florennes?	~1600	1 B-17	3	4	1	1	1
II./JG 27	Bf 109G	Wiesbaden–Erbenheim	19	1304	Wiesbaden–Erbenheim	1445	1 B-17, 3 P-38	5	13	4	0	0
2nd sorties	Bf 109G	Wiesbaden–Erbenheim	2	1420	Wiesbaden–Erbenheim?	~1600	1 B-24	—	—	—	—	—
II./JG 53	Bf 109G	Frankfurt–Eschborn	16	1302	Stuttgart–Echterdingen	~1445	1 B-17	1	1	1	0	0
III./JG 54	Bf 109G	Frankfurt–Eschborn?	11	1412	Frankfurt–Eschborn?	~1600	2 B-17	1	1	0	0	0
I./JG 106	Bf 109G	Lachen–Speyerdorf	6	1315	Lachen–Speyerdorf	~1430	0	0	0	0	0	0
2nd sorties	Bf 109G	Lachen–Speyerdorf	6	1445	Lachen–Speyerdorf	~1600	0	2	0	2	0	0
I./JG 300	Bf 109G	Wiesbaden–Erbenheim	7	1315	Wiesbaden–Erbenheim	~1430	0	4	0	0	0	1
III./JG 300	Bf 109G	Wiesbaden–Erbenheim		1304	Wiesbaden–Erbenheim	~1430	0	5	1	2	0	2
I./JG302	Bf 109G	Frankfurt–Eschborn?		1412	Frankfurt–Eschborn?	~1530	0	0	0	0	0	0
Jagddivision 7:												
I./JG 5	Bf 109G	Herzogenaurach	7	~1315	Herzogenaurach	~1430	0	3	4	2	0	0
III./JG 3	Bf 109G	Leipheim	19	1215	Leipheim	~1245	n/c (vs. 15AF)	0	0	0	0	0
2nd sorties	Bf 109G	Leipheim	17	1315	Leipheim	~1430	1 B-17, 1 P-51	3	2	1	0	3
3rd sorties	Bf 109G	Leipheim	3	1515	Leipheim	~1615	1 B-17	1	0	0	0	0
I./JG 301	Bf 109G	Neubiberg	14	1403	Neubiberg	~1530	0	3	2	3	0	1
I.+ II./ZG 76	Bf 110G	Leipheim	21	1327	Leipheim	~1530	0	0	0	0	0	0
I./ZG 101	Bf 110C	Memmingen		~1330	Memmingen	~1530	1 P-38	1	0	3	0	0
Jafü Ostmark:												
Stab/JG 27	Bf 109G	Fels am Wagram		0959	Fels am Wagram	1158	n/c (vs. 15AF)	0	0	0	0	0
	Bf 109G	Fels am Wagram		1353	Fels am Wagram	1451	n/c (vs. 15AF)	0	0	0	0	0
I./JG 27	Bf 109G	Fels am Wagram		0957	Fels am Wagram	1203	n/c (vs. 15AF)	0	0	0	0	0
	Bf 109G	Fels am Wagram		1359	Fels am Wagram	1500	n/c (vs. 15AF)	0	0	0	0	0
III./JG 27	Bf 109G	Wien–Seyring		~1000	Wien–Seyring	~1200	n/c (vs. 15AF)	0	0	0	0	0
	Bf 109G	Wien–Seyring		~1400	Wien–Seyring	~1500	n/c (vs. 15AF)	0	0	0	0	0
IV./JG 27	Bf 109G	Graz–Thalerhof		~1000	Graz–Thalerhof	~1200	n/c (vs. 15AF)	0	0	0	0	0
	Bf 109G	Graz–Thalerhof		~1400	Graz–Thalerhof	~1500	n/c (vs. 15AF)	0	0	0	0	0

Luftwaffe defensive activity – 18 March 1944 Continued

Unit	Type	Gruppe up			Gruppe down		Claims	Losses				
		Base	No	Time	Base	Time		Dest	Dam	KIA	MIA	WIA
II./JG 301	Bf 109G	Wien–Seyring		?	Wien–Seyring	?	0 (vs. 15AF)	3	0	1	0	0
II./ZG 1	Bf 110G	Wels		~1000	Wels	~1200	n/c (vs. 15AF)	0	0	0	0	0
	Bf 110G	Wels		~1400	Wels	~1500	n/c (vs. 15AF)	0	0	0	0	0
Luftflotte 3												
II. Jagdkorps												
Jagddivision 4:												
I./JG 26	Fw 190A	Florennes	5	1155	Mannheim–Sandhofen	~1300	transfer	0	0	0	0	0
II./JG 26	Fw 190A	Grevillers, Epinoy		?	Grevillers, Epinoy?	?	0	0	1	0	0	0
III./JG 26	Bf 109G	Denain	12	1153	Trier	~1300	transfer	0	0	0	0	0
	Bf 109G	Trier	37	1425	Trier	~1600	1 B-17	0	1	0	0	0
I./JG 107	Bf 109G	Nancy–Essay	2	1510	Nancy–Essay	~1600	0	1	0	0	0	0
Jagddivision 5:												
Stab/JG 2	Fw 190A	Aix?		~1430	Aix?	~1600	0	0	1	0	0	0
I./JG 2	Fw 190A	Aix?		~1430	Aix?	~1600	0	1	2	1	0	0
II./JG 2	Bf 109G	Creil	3	1302	Creil	~1430	1 B-24	0	0	0	0	0
	Bf 109G	Creil	14	1436	Creil	~1600	3 B-24, 1 P-51	2	0	2	0	0
2nd sorties	Bf 109G	Creil	2	1440	Creil	~1600	0	0	0	0	0	0
III./JG 2	Fw 190A	Cormeilles	10	1146	Mannheim–Sandhofen	~1230	transfer	0	0	0	0	0

meantime, their airfields were occupied by all five II. Jagdkorps Gruppen, sent north to attack the withdrawing stream. These attacks proved ineffective. The day was a mixed success for the RLV force. Of the 327 fighters to scramble, only 173 were credited with enemy contact. The Americans lost or scrapped 29 bombers and five escorts; the Germans lost 16 KIA, eight WIA and 38 fighters. Among the fatalities was the JG 3 Kommodore, Obst. Wolf-Dietrich Wilcke, who wore the Knight's Cross with Oak Leaves and Swords and had been one of the most highly decorated pilots still flying.

24 March
8th Air Force Mission #277: 222 of 230 1st BD B-17s bomb Schweinfurt, Frankfurt – lose 3-3-68, claim 0; 181 of 206 2nd BD B-24s bomb St. Dizier, Nancy-Essay airfields – lose 0-0-24, claim 0. Total escort of 2 P-38 FGs, 4 P-51 FGs, 5 P-47 FGs (540 sorties) claims 1-0-0, loses 5-0-0.

The bad weather continued. The only rational reason the USSTAF had to continue its raids was to keep up the pressure. The 1st BD targeted Frankfurt and Schweinfurt, while the 2nd BD bombed two JD 4 airfields. III./JG 1 Bf 109s had an inconclusive encounter with P-51s, but only 67 fighters, all from II.

Jagdkorps, were credited with operational sorties. Four made contact and shot down one B-17. The 8th AF wrote off six bombers and five fighters after the mission; II. Jagdkorps sustained no losses.

26 March
8th Air Force Mission #280: 500 of 573 B-17s + B-24s (all BDs) bomb 9 V-1 sites Pas de Calais, 7 V-1 sites Cherbourg – lose 5-1-236, claim 0. Escort of 6 P-47 FGs (266 sorties) claims 0, loses 1-0-5.

Five hundred 8th AF B-17s and B-24s attacked V-weapon sites on the Pas de Calais and around Cherbourg. Jagddivisionen 4 and 5 both ordered their fighters inland in anticipation of an attack on Paris. No attempt was made to intercept the bombers after they turned to bomb their coastal targets.

The 15th AF targeted Steyr, but abandoned the mission owing to the weather and dropped on the airfields in northern Italy. Jafü Ostmark scrambled some fighters, but could not catch up to the bombers; thus no RLV fighters were credited with sorties.

Axis defensive activity – 19 March 1944

Unit	Type	Gruppe up			Gruppe down		Claims	Losses				
		Base	No	Time	Base	Time		Dest	Dam	KIA	MIA	WIA
Luftflotte Reich												
Jagddivision 7:			28									
III./JG 3	Bf 109G	Leipheim	7	1316	Leipheim	~1415	n/c	0	0	0	0	0
I. + II./ZG 76	Bf 110G	Leipheim	21	1316	Leipheim	~1415	n/c	0	0	0	0	0
Jafü Ostmark:			113									
Stab/JG 27	Bf 109G	Fels am Wagram		1250	Fels am Wagram, others	1530	2 B-24	0	0	0	0	0
I./JG 27	Bf 109G	Fels am Wagram	38	1245	Agram, Graz, Marburg, Fels am Wagram	1435	6 B-24	2	1	0	0	1
III./JG 27	Bf 109G	Wien-Seyring	23	1243	Seyring, others	~1445	7 B-24	3	0	2	0	1
IV./JG 27	Bf 109G	Graz-Thalerhof	26	1243	Graz, others	~1435	5 B-24	5	0	4	0	0
II./ZG 1	Bf 110G	Wels	26	1301	Wels	~1500	n/c	0	0	0	0	0
LBeob St 7	Bf 110G	?	1	?	?	?	shadower	0	1	0	0	1
VbdFhr Schule	Bf 109G	Fels am Wagram		1245	Fels am Wagram, others	1435	1 B-24	0	0	0	0	0
Luftflotte 2												
Jafü Oberitalien:			77									
I./JG 53	Bf 109G	Maniago, Italy	19	1205	Maniago, Italy	1340	4 B-17	1	1	0	0	0
I./JG 77	Bf 109G	Lavariano, Italy	24	1208	Lavariano, Italy	1340	1 B-24 HSS, 1 P-38	4	2	1	1	0
1° Gr Caccia	Mc 205	Campformido, Italy	22	1213	Campformido, Italy	1340	0	0	0	0	0	0
2nd sorties	Mc 205	Campformido, Italy	12	1445	Campformido, Italy	~1600	n/c	0	0	0	0	0

Luftwaffe defensive activity – 20 March 1944

Unit	Type	Gruppe up			Gruppe down		Claims	Losses				
		Base	No	Time	Base	Time		Dest	Dam	KIA	MIA	WIA
Luftflotte 3												
II. Jagdkorps			67									
Jagddivision 4:												
I./JG 26?	Fw 190A	Florennes		?	Florennes	?	0	0	0	0	0	0
II./JG 26?	Fw 190A	Grevillers, Epinoy		?	Grevillers, Epinoy	?	0	0	1	0	0	0
III./JG 26	Bf 109G	Lille–Vendeville, Denain		~0900	Laon–Athies	~0945	transfer	1	0	1	0	0
	Bf 109G	Laon–Athies		~1200	Lille–Vendeville, Denain	~1330	1 B-17	1	1	1	0	0
Jagddivision 5:												
II./JG 2	Bf 109G	Creil		~0900	Laon–Athies	~0945	transfer	0	0	0	0	0
	Bf 109G	Laon–Athies		~1115	Creil	~1245	0	4	1	3	0	1
III./JG 2	Fw 190A	Cormeilles		~0900	Laon–Athies	~0945	transfer	0	0	0	0	0
	Fw 190A	Laon–Athies		~1115	Cormeilles	~1245	0	0	0	0	0	0

Luftwaffe defensive activity – 23 March 1944

Unit	Type	Gruppe up				Gruppe down		Claims	Losses (—: included with 1st sortie)				
		Base	No	Time		Base	Time		Dest	Dam	KIA	MIA	WIA
Luftflotte Reich													
I. Jagdkorps			259										
Jagddivision 1:			115										
II./JG 1	Fw 190A	Volkenrode, others		1155		Rheine	1250	transfer	0	0	0	0	0
III./JG 1	Bf 109G	Gardelegen		~1200		Twente	~1300	transfer	0	0	0	0	0
Stab/JG 3	Bf 109G	Burg	8	0950		Burg	~1145	2 B-17	1	0	1	0	0
I./JG 3	Bf 109G	Burg	28	0955		Burg	~1145	2 P-51	5	1	3	0	2
II./JG 3	Bf 109G	Gardelegen	24	0945		Gardelegen	~1145	4 B-17	3	2	1	0	1
2nd sorties	Bf 109G	Gardelegen		1255		Fassberg	1505	0	—	—	—	—	—
IV./JG 3	Bf 109G	Salzwedel	27	0944		Lippstadt, others	1145	2 B-17, 1 P-38	5	1	2	0	0
III./JG 54	Bf 109G	Lüneburg	16	0818		Lüneburg	~1030	3 B-17, 1 B-24	2	0	1	0	0
III./JG 301	Bf 109G	Zerbst	17	0944		Zerbst	~1145	0	1	0	0	0	0
I./JG302	Bf 109G	Jüterbog	8	0950		Jüterbog	~1145	0	0	0	0	0	0
Sturmstaffel 1	Fw 190A	Salzwedel	11	0943		Salzwedel	~1145	5 B-17	4	1	3	0	1
ErprKdo 25	Fw 190A?	Parchim?		?		Parchim?	?	0	1	0	1	0	0
Jagddivision 2:			62										
Stab/JG 1	Fw 190A	Hannover–Langenhagen?		~0915		Hannover–Langenhagen?	~1115	0	0	0	0	0	0
I./JG 1	Fw 190A	Hannover–Langenhagen?		0915		Hannover–Langenhagen?	1120	3 B-17	1	1	1	0	0
Stab/JG 11	Bf 109G	Rotenburg		~0915		Rotenburg	~1030	0	0	0	0	0	0
I./JG 11	Fw 190A	Rotenburg		0914		Rotenburg	1030	7 B-17	1	1	0	0	0
III./JG 11	Fw 190A	Mainz		0845		Oldenburg	1046	1 B-24	1	0	0	0	0
Jagddivision 3:			82										
Jagdabschnitt Mittelrhein:													
II./JG 1	Fw 190A	Wiesbaden–Erbenheim	19	0905		Völkenrode, others	1040	5 B-17, 1 B-17 HSS	1	5	0	0	0
III./JG 1	Bf 109G	Frankfurt–Eschborn		0912		Gardelegen	1100	1 P-47	1	3	0	0	0
II./JG 2	Bf 109G	Mainz–Finthen?		~1130		Creil	~1230	0	2	0	1	0	1
III./JG 2	Fw 190A	Mainz–Finthen?		~1130		Cormeilles	~1230	0	0	0	0	0	0
I./JG 26	Fw 190A	Mainz–Finthen		~1130		Florennes	~1230	2 B-17	1	0	0	0	1
4./JG 26	Fw 190A	Mainz–Finthen		~1130		Wevelghem	~1230	0	0	0	0	0	0
II./JG 26	Fw 190A	Mainz–Finthen		~1130		Cambrai–Epinoy	~1230	0	2	0	1	0	0
III./JG 26	Bf 109G	Mainz–Finthen		1138		München–Gladbach	1248	0	1	0	0	0	1
	Bf 109G	München–Gladbach		1425		Lille–Vendeville	1510	transfer	0	0	0	0	0
II./JG 27	Bf 109G	Wiesbaden–Erbenheim	7	0905		various NW German a/fs	~1045	0	0	1	0	0	0
	Bf 109G	various NW German a/fs		~1200		Wiesbaden–Erbenheim	~1300	transfer	1	0	1	0	0
II./JG 53	Bf 109G	Frankfurt–Eschborn	16	0907		various NW German a/fs	~1045	1 B-17, 1 B-17 HSS	1	0	0	0	1
	Bf 109G	various NW German a/fs		~1200		Frankfurt–Eschborn	~1300	transfer	0	0	0	0	0
III./JG 300	Bf 109G	Wiesbaden–Erbenheim		~0900		Wiesbaden–Erbenheim?	~1030	0	2	0	0	0	0
Jagddivision 7:			17										
I./JG 301	Bf 109G	Neubiberg?		~0945		Neubiberg?	~1145	0	1	1	0	0	0
FLÜG 1 (Süd)	Bf 109G?	Erding?		~0945		Erding?	~1145	2 B-17	0	0	0	0	0
Jafü Ostmark:													
I./JG 27	Bf 109G	Fels am Wagram		0835		Fels am Wagram	0910	n/c (vs. 15AF)	0	0	0	0	0
	Bf 109G	Fels am Wagram		0937		Fels am Wagram	1046	n/c (vs. 15AF)	0	0	0	0	0

Luftwaffe defensive activity – 23 March 1944 Continued

Unit	Type	Gruppe up			Gruppe down		Claims	Losses (—: included with 1st sortie)				
		Base	No	Time	Base	Time		Dest	Dam	KIA	MIA	WIA
Luftflotte 3												
II. Jagdkorps			51									
Jagddivision 4:												
I./JG 26	Fw 190A	Florennes	7	0830	Mainz–Finthen	~0915	transfer	0	0	0	0	0
4./JG 26	Fw 190A	Wevelghem	4	0831	Mainz–Finthen	~0915	transfer	0	0	0	0	0
II./JG 26	Fw 190A	Cambrai–Epinoy	14	0830	Mainz–Finthen	~0915	transfer	0	0	0	0	0
III./JG 26	Bf 109G	Lille–Vendeville	15	0930	Mainz–Finthen	1025	transfer	0	0	0	0	0
	Bf 109G	Denain	10	0831	Mainz–Finthen	~0915	transfer	0	0	0	0	0
	Bf 109G	Lille–Vendeville	—	1645	Charleroi	1810	0	0	0	0	0	0
Jagddivision 5:												
II./JG 2	Bf 109G	Creil	24	0820	Mainz–Finthen?	~0915	transfer	0	0	0	0	0
III./JG 2	Fw 190A	Cormeilles	7	0812	Mainz–Finthen?	~0915	transfer	0	0	0	0	0

Luftwaffe defensive activity – 24 March 1944

Unit	Type	Gruppe up			Gruppe down		Claims	Losses				
		Base	No	Time	Base	Time		Dest	Dam	KIA	MIA	WIA
Luftflotte Reich												
I. Jagdkorps			0									
Jagddivision 2:												
III./JG 11	Fw 190A	Oldenburg		~0930	Oldenburg	~1100	0	1	0	0	0	0
Jagddivision 3:												
III./JG 1	Fw 190A	Twente		~0930	Twente	~1100	n/c	0	1	0	0	0
Luftflotte 3												
II. Jagdkorps			67									
Jagddivision 4:												
I./JG 26	Fw 190A	Florennes	5	0800	Florennes	~0930	n/c	0	0	0	0	0
4./JG 26	Fw 190A	Wevelghem	4	1100	Wevelghem	~1230	1 B-17	0	0	0	0	0
II./JG 26	Fw 190A	Cambrai	4	0858	Cambrai	~1030	n/c	0	0	0	0	0
	Fw 190A	Epinoy	8	0850	Epinoy	~1030	n/c	0	0	0	0	0
III./JG 26	Bf 109G	Lille–Vendeville	7	0857	Lille–Vendeville	~1030	n/c	0	0	0	0	0
	Bf 109G	Denain	7	0857	Denain	~1030	n/c	0	0	0	0	0
Jagddivision 5:												
II./JG 2	Bf 109G	Creil	23	0845	Creil	~1030	n/c	0	0	0	0	0
III./JG 2	Fw 190A	Cormeilles	9	0849	Cormeilles	~1030	n/c	0	0	0	0	0

27 March

8th Air Force Mission #282: 701 of 714 B-17s + B-24s (all BDs) bomb 11 French airfields and 2 t/os – lose 6-5-106, claim 0. Escort of 3 P-38 FGs, 4 P-51 FGs, 11 P-47 FGs (960 sorties) claims 8-0-2, loses 10-2-5.

Eleven Luftwaffe airfields in France were bombed by 701 8th AF B-17s and B-24s. II./JG 2 managed to claim one B-17 for the loss of three Messerschmitts, but JG 26 was unable to get past the escorts. Apparently, all three JG 26 Gruppen (with a total of no more than 30 aircraft) became involved with P-47s around Chartres. Three P-47s were claimed, for the loss of one Focke-Wulf and pilot. American aircraft lost or scrapped 11 bombers and 12 fighters, but most losses were to Flak and operational causes. The two II. Jagdkorps Geschwader and Jagdgruppe West lost six KIA, two WIA and 10 fighters.

28 March

8th Air Force Mission #283: 364 of 373 1st BD + 3rd 8th Air Force Mission #283: 364 of 373 1st BD + 3rd BD B-17s bomb 4 French airfields – lose 2-1-119, claim 0. Escort of 1 P-38 FG, 3 P-51 FGs, 6 P-47 FGs (453 sorties) claims 0-0-1, loses 3-0-0.

A repetition of the previous day's attacks on French airfields brought no reaction at all from II. Jagdkorps. Flak brought down the few American aircraft lost.

29 March

8th Air Force Mission #284: 233 of 236 1st BD B-17s bomb Brunswick, various t/os, TOT 1320-1418 – lose 9-1-66, claim 8-3-6. Escort of 1 P-38 FG, 4 P-51 FGs, 5 P-47 FGs (428 sorties) claims 44-4-13, loses 12-6-12.

A mission to Brunswick by one 8th AF bomb division was countered by 258 sorties by three I. Jagdkorps Jagddivisionen. Heavy storms prevented any movement forward by Jagddivision 7 or II. Jagdkorps or any attempt to form Gefechtsverbände or concentrate for second sorties against the withdrawing bombers. JG 11 flew an outstanding mission – I./JG 11 claimed nine B-17s and two P-51s – but its Kommodore, Obstlt. Hermann Graf, the highest scoring and most highly decorated pilot on operations, had to bail out after attacking a formation of P-51s and suffered injuries that affected him for the rest of his life. Most of the Jagdgruppen encountered only escorts; I./JG 1 lost six pilots killed, and III./JG 54 lost eight. The Americans lost or scrapped 10 bombers and 18 escorts; the Germans lost 22 KIA or MIA, eight WIA and 35 fighters.

The end of March closed out Operation POINTBLANK, the Allied Combined Bomber Offensive. The 8th AF would be under General Eisenhower's command until the invasion. The heavy bombers flew missions on 23 days during the month, despite continued bad weather, at a cost of 341 aircraft. The USSTAF was clearly winning the war of attrition. During March, the German fighter force lost 22 per cent of its total pilot strength. The RLV force (Luftflotte Reich and Luftflotte 3) lost at least 265 pilots killed and missing; 121 more were wounded. The combat units were hurting. Take two examples: On 31 March, JG 1, the first Jagdgeschwader assigned to the RLV, with an establishment strength of 124 airplanes and pilots, was up to strength in aircraft, but

only 75 of these were operational. It had a surfeit of pilots on hand, bolstered by a 'probationary Staffel', but only 68 were available for duty. The neighbouring JG 26, the Luftflotte 3 stalwart, had had its establishment strength boosted to 208 airplanes and pilots, but the Geschwader reported only 57 aircraft operational out of 73 on strength. Of 175 pilots 'on the books', only 76 were available for duty; the rest were on detached duty, on leave, recuperating from injuries or too green to put on the duty roster.

Notes
[1] Kiefner correspondence with author, 1992.
[2] Kirchmayr Gefechtsbericht, BA-MA RL 10/482.
[3] Haninger Gefechtsbericht, BA-MA RL 10/482.
[4] Tichy Gefechtsbericht, NARA T-971, roll 11.
[5] Oesau Gefechtsbericht, in private collection.
[6] Oesau Gefechtsbericht, in private collection.
[7] III./ZG 26 Kriegstagebuch, BA-MA RL 10/256.
[8] Franz, correspondence with author, 2003.
[9] Weik Gefechtsbericht, in private collection.

Luftwaffe defensive activity – 27 March 1944

Unit	Type	Gruppe up			Gruppe down		Claims	Losses				
		Base	No	Time	Base	Time		Dest	Dam	KIA	MIA	WIA
Luftflotte 3												
II. Jagdkorps												
Jagddivision 4:												
I./JG 26	Fw 190A	Florennes		~1315	Florennes	~1445	1 P-47	0	0	0	0	0
4./JG 26	Fw 190A	Wevelghem		~1315	Wevelghem	~1445	0	0	0	0	0	0
II./JG 26	Fw 190A	Grevillers, Epinoy		~1315	Grevillers, Epinoy	~1445	0	1	0	1	0	0
III./JG 26	Bf 109G	Lille–Vendeville, Denain		1323	Guyancourt, others	1440	2 P-47	0	1	0	0	0
	Bf 109G	Guyancourt		1630	Guyancourt	1700	0	0	0	0	0	0
Jagddivision 5:												
II./JG 2	Bf 109G	Creil		~1500	Creil	~1630	1 B-17	3	0	0	0	2
III./JG 2	Fw 190A	Cormeilles		~1500	Cormeilles	~1630	0	0	1	0	0	0
Jafü Bretagne:												
JGr West	Bf 109G,	Biarritz		~1515	Biarritz	~1630	0	6	0	5	0	0
	Fw 190A											

Luftwaffe defensive activity – 29 March 1944

Unit	Type	Gruppe up			Gruppe down		Claims	Losses				
		Base	No	Time	Base	Time		Dest	Dam	KIA	MIA	WIA
Luftflotte Reich												
I. Jagdkorps			258									
Jagddivision 1:			79									
I./JG 3	Bf 109G	Burg	22	1233	Burg	~1400	0	2	0	0	0	0
II./JG 3	Bf 109G	Gardelegen	25	1255	Gardelegen	~1430	0	4	0	3	1	0
I./JG 301	Bf 109G	Zerbst	*12	1250	Zerbst	~1430	2 B-17	0	0	0	0	0
III./JG 301	Bf 109G	Zerbst	—	1250	Zerbst	~1430	1 P-38	3	0	1	0	2
I./JG 302	Bf 109G	Jüterbog–Damm	7	1204	Jüterbog–Damm	~1430	0	1	1	0	0	1
Jagddivison 2:			81									
IV./JG 3	Bf 109G	Salzwedel	23	1254	Hildesheim, Celle	1432	1 B-17, 1 P-51	0	0	0	0	0
Stab/JG 11	Bf 109G	Rotenburg	4	1258	Rotenburg	~1445	1 B-17, 1 P-51	1	0	0	0	1
2nd sorties	Bf 109G	Rotenburg	1	1427	Rotenburg	~1530	0	0	0	0	0	0
I./JG 11	Fw 190A	Rotenburg	24	1245	Rotenburg	~1430	7 B-17, 2 P-51, 2 B-17 HSS	3	2	1	0	2
2nd sorties	Fw 190A	Rotenburg	2	1427	Rotenburg	~1530	0	0	0	0	0	0
III./JG 11	Fw 190A	Oldenburg		1248	Magdeburg–Ost	1415	0	2	2	0	0	2
III./JG 54	Bf 109G	Lüneburg	26	1243	Lüneburg	~1430	0	9	2	8	0	0
Sturmstaffel 1	Fw 190A	Salzwedel	10	1254	Gardelegen	1410	0	0	0	0	0	0
Jagddivison 3:			78									
Stab/JG 1	Fw 190A	Hopsten?		~1235	Hopsten?	~1400	0	0	0	0	0	0
I./JG 1	Fw 190A	Hopsten	23	1235	Hannover–Langenhagen	1310	0	6	1	6	0	0
II./JG 1	Fw 190A	Rheine	30	1240	Quedlinburg	1400	3 P-51	4	0	2	0	0
III./JG 1	Bf 109G	Twente	25	1239	Twente	~1400	0	0	1	0	0	0
Jagddivision 7:												
Jafü Osterreich:												
I./JG 27	Bf 109G	Fels am Wagram		?	Fels am Wagram	?	n/c (vs. 15AF)	1	0	1	0	0

*12 sorties total for I./JG 301 + II./JG 301

CHAPTER 6

APRIL – JUNE 1944

April 1944

The Allied Combined Bomber Offensive ended temporarily on 1 April, and the heavy bomber forces in Europe were placed under General Eisenhower's Supreme Headquarters Allied Expeditionary Force (SHAEF) to prepare for the invasion. In the absence of immediate directives from SHAEF, however, the USSTAF continued its war of attrition against the Luftwaffe. The day fighter defences of the Reich and the western occupied zone (France and the Low Countries) were continuing to evolve. Luftflotte Reich under Genobst. Stumpff was an administrative head-quarters containing all of the Luftwaffe forces based in the Reich. On 1 April, Genlt. Josef Schmid added Jagddivision 7 to his I. Jagdkorps, and now had operational command of all RLV fighter forces in the Reich. Jafü Ostmark was still subordinate to Jagddivision 7, but would gain its independence as Jagddivision 8 (within I. Jagdkorps) in mid-June.

GFM Hugo Sperrle and his Luftflotte 3 continued their independent way, controlling all Luftwaffe forces in France and western Belgium. Its small fighter component was under the operational command of Genmaj. Werner Junck's II. Jagdkorps.

Only one tactical innovation had proven itself during the winter – the *Sturmangriff*, or assault attack, as practised by a single Staffel, Sturmstaffel 1. This unit gained a new fighter in April, special-build Fw 190A-8/R2 *Sturmböcke* (assault 'billy goats' or 'battering rams'), which were up-armed and up-armoured for the sole purpose of attacking the bomber Pulks. Genmaj. Adolf Galland, the General of the Fighter Arm, was responsible for new weapons and tactics and persuaded the High Command to begin converting existing RLV units to Sturmgruppen. IV./JG 3 would become the first, as IV.(Sturm)/JG 3; however, time would be needed to re-equip and retrain it for its new role.

Seven Jagdgruppen and one Stab from the three

Six Sturmstaffel 1 Fw 190A-6s warm up their engines before take-off from Salzwedel in March or April. (Smith)

Wilde Sau Geschwader (JG 300, JG 301 and JG 302) were merged smoothly into the day order of battle after disbanding two of their Geschwader staffs and two Gruppen. Many of their pilots came from the bomber arm, and their bad-weather skills were welcome, although these were cancelled out in part by their lack of training as fighter pilots.

Adolf Hitler had belatedly become convinced of the importance of air defence and ordered fighter production to be increased and new, dispersed factories to be built, underground if possible. Hitler wanted to see 2,000 operational fighters in the RLV force. However, nothing was said about expanding the training establishment, and although in late 1944 the fighter inventory approached Hitler's desired number, there were never enough qualified pilots to fly them. The size of the RLV fighter force was stagnant. The USSTAF was continuing to add new P-51 groups, and the 8th AF was converting its P-47 groups to P-51s at the rate of two per month. Although the air fighting continued to be heavy, and April saw the 8th AF sustain the greatest bomber losses of any month of the war, about 25 per cent of the force, the Luftwaffe had already lost the wars of production, training and organisation. The wastage of the Jagdwaffe continued at a ruinous pace. Luftflotte Reich lost 38 per cent of its fighter pilots; Luftflotte 3 lost 24 per cent. The entire Luftwaffe lost 489 fighter pilots in April, while completing the training of only 396. The operational strength of I. Jagdkorps remained stagnant at 400 single-engine fighters and 100 Zerstörer, but the latter could only be employed when American escorts were not expected, which was rarely.

1 April

8th Air Force Mission #287: 165 of 195 2nd BD B-24s, 0 of 245 3rd BD B-17s bomb Pforzheim, other S German t/os, TOT 1102-08 – lose 12-3-49, claim 1-1-0. Escort of 6 P-47 FGs, 5 P-51 FGs (475 sorties) claims 5-2-4, loses 4-0-14.

The 8th AF scheduled a mission to southern Germany, but poor visibility at the time of take-off and high clouds made it difficult to form up. Only the B-24s continued with the mission; they bombed, among other places, Schaffhausen, a town in Switzerland. The RLV force was also hampered by the weather and flew only 207 sorties, of which 131 made contact. These fighters were from Jagddivisonen 3, 4, 5 and 7. Only 6 B-24 claims were confirmed, and only III./JG 26 flew two successful missions, claiming one incoming and

A taxiing 11./JG 26 Bf 109G-6 'Yellow 9', in one of a series of photographs taken when III./JG 26 landed on Lille–Nord for refuelling during a transfer flight sometime between 26 March and 18 April. *(Bundesarchiv 674-7779-26a)*

one withdrawing Liberator. The Americans wrote off 15 bombers and four escorts; the Luftwaffe lost at least four KIA, four WIA and seven fighters.

2 April – Steyr, Austria (see map)

15th Air Force: 127 B-17s, 137 B-24s bomb Steyr ball-bearing factory, TOT 1202-32 – lose 8 B-17s, 13 B-24s, claim 94-20-1. 168 B-24s bomb Steyr–Puch a/c factory, TOT 1204-38 – lose 7 B-24s, claim 42-17-5. 108 P-38s (3 FGs), 45 P-47s (1 FG) escort both forces, claim 36-3-6, lose 0-1-0, 1 P-38.

The 15th AF bombed two major targets in Steyr, Austria. The escort force of three P-38 groups and one P-47 group was staged today to support the penetration leg. It is unknown whether this was due to good planning or just fortuitous, but it saved many bombers when both Jafü Oberitalien and Jagddivision 7 responded early with maximum force. Jagddivision 7 formed nine Jagdgruppen and three Zerstörergruppen into three Gefechtsverbände, which attacked before, over and after the target area. All 149 Bf 109s up over Austria made contact, as did all 60 of the Bf 110s. A Croatian unit attacked the withdrawing stream and claimed one bomber (which was unconfirmed) without loss. Jagddivision 7 lost 12 KIA or MIA, four WIA and 17 aircraft for claims of 26 bombers and two fighters. The three Jafü Oberitalien Jagdgruppen (one Italian) put up 172 Bf 109s on two missions and lost two KIA, six MIA, two WIA and 19 fighters while claiming eight bombers and two fighters. Three of the missing pilots were taken prisoner by Yugoslav partisans; one escaped, and the other two were soon exchanged. The Americans lost 28 bombers. All of their escorts returned to Italy, but one P-38 was then written off charge.

Luftwaffe defensive activity – 1 April 1944

Unit	Type	Gruppe up			Gruppe down		Claims	Losses				
		Base	No	Time	Base	Time		Dest	Dam	KIA	MIA	WIA
Luftflotte Reich												
I. Jagdkorps			150									
Jagddivision 2:												
III./JG 11	Fw 190A	Oldenburg		0856	Rotenburg	0929	0	0	0	0	0	0
Jagddivision 3:												
Stab/JG 1	Fw 190A	Rheine		~0930	Rheine	~1100	0	0	0	0	0	0
I./JG 1	Fw 190A	Hopsten	9	1000	Hopsten	1030	n/c	0	0	0	0	0
II./JG 1	Fw 190A	Rheine	4	0936	Rheine	~1100	0	0	0	0	0	0
III./JG 1	Bf 109G	Twente	4	0957	Twente	~1100	0	1	0	0	0	1
2nd sorties	Bf 109G	Twente	4	1148	Twente	~1330	n/c	0	0	0	0	0
Abschfü Mittelrhein:												
II./JG 27	Bf 109G	Wiesbaden–Erbenheim	14	0922	Wiesbaden–Erbenheim	~1100	0	2	2	2	0	0
2nd sorties	Bf 109G	Wiesbaden–Erbenheim	6	1127	Wiesbaden–Erbenheim	~1300	n/c	0	0	0	0	0
2nd sorties	Bf 109G	Karlsruhe	2	1110	Karlsruhe	~1300	n/c	0	0	0	0	0
II./JG 53	Bf 109G	Frankfurt–Eschborn	17	0923	Frankfurt–Eschborn	~1100	0	0	0	0	0	0
2nd sorties	Bf 109G	Frankfurt–Eschborn	3	1133	Frankfurt–Eschborn	~1300	n/c	0	0	0	0	0
2nd sorties	Bf 109G	Karlsruhe	3	1110	Karlsruhe	~1300	n/c	0	0	0	0	0
2nd sorties	Bf 109G	Erbenheim	1	1127	Erbenheim	~1300	n/c	0	0	0	0	0
Jagddivision 7:												
III./JG 3	Bf 109G	Leipheim	13	0940	Leipheim	~1130	1 B-24	1	0	1	0	0
	Bf 109G	Leipheim	5	1035	Leipheim	~1130	0	0	0	0	0	0
I./JG 5	Bf 109G	Herzogenaurach	13	0925	Herzogenaurach	~1130	0	0	0	0	0	0
I./JG 301	Bf 109G	Neuburg	10	1006	Neuburg	~1130	n/c	1	0	0	0	1
ZG 76	Bf 110G	Öttingen	31	1000	Öttingen	~1130	n/c	0	0	0	0	0
Luftflotte 3												
II. Jagdkorps			66									
Jagddivision 4:												
I./JG 26	Fw 190A	Florennes		0934	Florennes	~1100	0	1	0	1	0	0
4./JG 26	Fw 190A	Wevelghem		~1400	Wevelghem	~1530	1 B-24	0	0	0	0	0
II./JG 26	Fw 190A	Grevillers		~1030	Grevillers	~1200	0	0	0	0	0	0
	Fw 190A	Epinoy		~1030	Epinoy	~1200	0	0	0	0	0	0
III./JG 26	Bf 109G	Lille–Vendeville		~1030	Lille–Vendeville	~1200	1 B-24	0	0	0	0	0
2nd sorties	Bf 109G	Lille–Vendeville		~1230	Lille–Vendeville	~1400	1 B-24	0	0	0	0	0
Jagddivision 5:												
II./JG 2	Bf 109G	Creil?		~1030	Creil	~1200	2 B-24	1	1	0	0	2

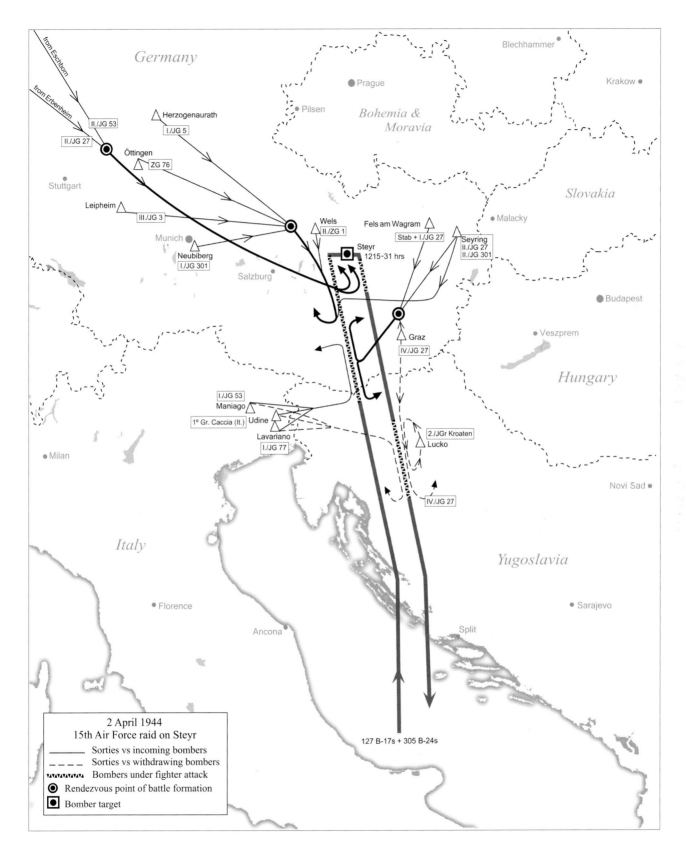

Germany

from Eschborn
from Erbenheim

II./JG 53
II./JG 27

Öttingen
ZG 76

Herzogenaurath
I./JG 5

Stuttgart

Leipheim
III./JG 3

Munich

Neubiberg
I./JG 301

Salzburg

Wels
II./ZG 1

Steyr
1215-31 hrs

Fels am Wagram

Stab + I./JG 27

Seyring
II./JG 27
II./JG 301

Graz
IV./JG 27

I./JG 53
Maniago

1° Gr. Caccia (It.) Udine

Lavariano
I./JG 77

2./JGr Kroaten
Lucko

IV./JG 27

Milan

Italy

Florence

Ancona

Split

Bohemia & Moravia

Prague

Pilsen

Blechhammer

Krakow

Slovakia

Malacky

Budapest

Veszprem

Hungary

Novi Sad

Yugoslavia

Sarajevo

127 B-17s + 305 B-24s

2 April 1944
15th Air Force raid on Steyr

———— Sorties vs incoming bombers
– – – – Sorties vs withdrawing bombers
▼▼▼▼▼ Bombers under fighter attack
◉ Rendezvous point of battle formation
▣ Bomber target

Axis defensive activity – 2 April 1944

Unit	Type	Gruppe up			Gruppe down		Claims	Losses				
		Base	No	Time	Base	Time		Dest	Dam	KIA	MIA	WIA
vs. incoming stream												
Luftflotte Reich												
I. Jagdkorps			*226									
Jagddivision 3:												
Abschfü Mlttelrheim:												
II./JG 27	Bf 109G	Wiesbaden–Erbenheim	7	1010	Wiesbaden–Erbenheim	~1200	0	0	0	0	0	0
II./JG 53	Bf 109G	Frankfurt–Eschborn	10	1015	Frankfurt–Eschborn	~1200	1 B-24	2	0	0	0	0
Jagddivision 7:												
III./JG 3	Bf 109G	Leipheim	17	0956	Leipheim	~1215	3 B-17	2	3	1	0	0
I./JG 5	Bf 109G	Herzogenaurach	12	0951	Herzogenaurach	~1200	1 B-17	0	0	0	0	0
I./JG 301	Bf 109G	Neubiberg	8	1010	Neubiberg	~1200	1 B-17	0	0	0	0	0
III./ZG 76	Bf 110G	Öttingen	28	0915	Öttingen	~1200	1 B-17	4	0	2	0	0
Jafü Ostmark:												
II./ZG 1	Bf 110G	Wels	32	0952	Wels	~1200	3 B-17, 3 B-24	5	1	5	2	2
Stab/JG 27	Bf 109G	Fels am Wagram	4	0940	Fels am Wagram	1127	1 P-47	0	0	0	0	0
I./JG 27	Bf 109G	Fels am Wagram	28	0934	Fels am Wagram	1135	3 B-24	3	1	1	0	2
III./JG 27	Bf 109G	Wien–Seyring	18	0934	Wien–Seyring	~1130	5 B-24, 2 P-38	1	0	0	1	0
IV./JG 27	Bf 109G	Graz	24	0951	Graz	~1115	3 B-24	0	0	0	0	0
II./JG 301	Bf 109G	Wien–Seyring	15	1046	Wien–Seyring	~1200	0	0	0	0	0	0
Luftflotte 2												
Jafü Oberitalien:			*95									
I./JG 53	Bf 109G	Maniago		0900	Maniago	1030	1 P-38	3	2	0	3	0
I./JG 77	Bf 109G	Lavariano		0901	Lavariano	1030	2 B-24	2	1	1	0	1
1° Gr. Ca.(It)	MC 205	Udine–Campoformido	31	~0900	Udine–Campoformido	1030	1 B-17	2	0	1	0	1
LBeob St 7	Ju 88	Villaorba		~0900	Villaorba	~1100	shadowers	0	0	0	0	0
vs. withdrawing stream												
Luftflotte Reich												
I. Jagdkorps												
Jagddivision 7:												
Jafü Ostmark:												
IV./JG 27	Bf 109G	Graz	14	1150	Graz	~1300	2 B-24	0	0	0	0	0
Luftflotte 2												
Jafü Oberitalien:												
I./JG 53	Bf 109G	Maniago		1131	Maniago	~1300	2 B-24	2	0	0	2	0
I./JG 77	Bf 109G	Lavariano		~1130	Lavariano	~1300	3 B-24	1	0	0	1	0
1° Gr. Ca. (It)	MC 205	Udine–Campoformido	31	~1130	Udine–Campoformido	1300	0	0	0	0	0	0
2./JGr (Croat)	MC 202	Lucko	2	~1100	Lucko	~1230	1 B-24 (unc)	0	0	0	0	0

*total sorties vs. incoming + withdrawing streams

Right: Fw. Helmut Zittier in the cockpit of a Hungarian Me 210. An experienced Zerstörer pilot, Zittier was ordered from 7./JG 26 to the Manfred Weiß-Fabrik in Budapest in March to factory-test Me 210s. He remained on this duty until the end of the war – reason enough for his broad smile. *(Zittier)*

Axis defensive activity – 3 April 1944

Unit	Type	Gruppe up			Gruppe down		Claims	Losses				
		Base	No	Time	Base	Time		Dest	Dam	KIA	MIA	WIA
Luftflotte Reich												
I. Jagdkorps			203									
Jagddivision 2:												
III./JG 1	Bf 109G	Oldenburg	40	?	Ingolstadt	?	transfer	0	0	0	0	0
III./JG 54	Bf 109G	Lüneburg	20	?	Neuburg	?	transfer	0	0	0	0	0
Jagddivision 3:												
Abschfü Mittelrhein:												
II./JG 27	Bf 109G	Wiesbaden–Erbenheim	*49	~1000	Wiesbaden–Erbenheim	~1130	n/c	0	0	0	0	0
II./JG 53	Bf 109G	Frankfurt–Eschborn	—	~1000	Frankfurt–Eschborn	~1130	n/c	0	0	0	0	0
Jagddivision 7:												
III./JG 3	Bf 109G	Leipheim	—	~1000	Leipheim	~1130	n/c	1	0	0	0	0
I./JG 5	Bf 109G	Herzogenaurach	—	~1000	Herzogenaurach	~1130	n/c	0	0	0	0	0
ZG 76	Bf 110G	Öttingen	**27	~1000	Öttingen	~1130	n/c	0	0	0	0	0
Jafü Ostmark:												
Stab/JG 27	Bf 109G	Fels am Wagram	4	0955	Fels am Wagram	~1145	1 B-17	0	0	0	0	0
I./JG 27	Bf 109G	Fels am Wagram	29	0955	Fels am Wagram	1146	1 B-17, 1 B-24,	0	1	0	0	0
							1 P-38	0	1	0	0	0
III./JG 27	Bf 109G	Wien–Seyring	14	0956	Wien–Seyring	~1145	0	0	0	0	0	0
IV./JG 27	Bf 109G	Graz	11	0951	Graz	~1145	1 P-38	0	0	0	0	0
II./ZG 1	Bf 110G	Wels	—	~1000	Wels	~1130	n/c	1	0	0	0	0
Abschfü Ungarn:												
1/1 FS (Hungary)	Bf 109G	Budapest–Szolnok		~1100	Budapest–Szolnok	~1200	1 B-24	2	0	1	0	0
2/1 FS (Hungary)	Bf 109G	Ferihegy		~1100	Ferihegy	~1200	1 B-17	0	0	0	0	0
5/1 NFS (Hungary)	Me 210Ca	Ferihegy		~1100	Ferihegy	~1200	0	0	0	0	0	0
Exptl Inst (Hungary)	Me 210Ca	Ferihegy		~1100	Ferihegy	~1200	0	0	0	0	0	0
ISS Danube	Me 210Ca	Budapest	1	~1100	?	~1200	0	1	0	1	0	1

*4 Jagdgruppen (49 Bf 109s) up – no contact   **3 Zerstörergruppen (27 Bf 110s) up – no contact

3 April

15th Air Force: 111 B-17s bomb Budapest Me 210 plant – lose 4, claims unknown. 358 B-24s bomb Budapest rail yards, t/os – lose 2, claims unknown. Escort of 3 P-38 FGs claims 9-0-5, losses unknown.

The 15th AF attacked a new target, Budapest, and took the defenders by surprise. The fighters and Zerstörer in southern Germany and western Austria took off in time to form a powerful Gefechtsverband, but could not reach the bombers when they turned for Budapest. Only the three JG 27 Gruppen based near Vienna and Hungary's own defenders, which totalled two squadrons of Bf 109s and two of Me 210s, made interceptions. Of a total of 194 fighters and Zerstörer to scramble, only 98 made contact. The Americans lost six bombers and few if any escorts. The Axis defenders lost a minimum of two KIA, one WIA and five aircraft.

6 April

15th Air Force: 34 HBs bomb Agram, Banja Luka airfields – lose 4, claims unknown. Escort of 3 P-38 FGs + 1 P-47 FG claims 8-2-4, loses 2 P-38s.

Agram (nowadays Zagreb), the capital of Croatia, contained a Luftwaffe airfield, was on the direct route from the American airfields in Italy to their targets in eastern Austria and could be reached by the fighters of both Jafü Östmark and Jafü Oberitalien. A small raid on this date (possibly directed at Austria, but turned back by weather) drew responses from both of these Jafü and the small, poorly equipped Croatian air force. Little damage was done by either side. The Americans lost four bombers and two escorts. The Axis defenders lost four KIA or MIA and nine fighters. The one Italian fighter group in Jafü Oberitalien engaged escorting P-47s and lost two KIA, one WIA and four Macchi MC 205s while claiming one Thunderbolt.

8 April

8th Air Force Mission #291: 611 of 664 HBs (all BDs) bomb Brunswick aviation industry, 9 German airfields, TOT 1325-1401 – lose 34-2-247, claim 58-9-32. Escort of 3 P-38 FGs, 9 P-47 FGs, 6 P-51 FGs (780 sorties) claims 88-3-46, loses 23-2-18.

The 8th AF sent its two B-17 divisions to bomb north German airfields, while the B-24-equipped 2nd BD penetrated the farthest, to aviation targets around Brunswick. The JD 1, JD 2 and JD 3 Gefechtsverbände were all ordered to the Brunswick area and were able to overwhelm the 2nd BD's escort and fall on the B-24s in the target area. The escort assigned to the B-17s was then directed to the B-24s, and the number of attacks on the bombers dwindled as the German fighters were overwhelmed in turn. The II. Jagdkorps fighters that were ordered up against the withdrawing stream accomplished little. The Luftwaffe scrambled 430 single-engine fighters, of which 313 were credited with enemy contact. Forty-two Zerstörer also took off, but were skillfully kept away from the enemy. The day's casualties were heavy. The Americans lost four B-17s (all to flak), 32 B-24s downed or scrapped and 25 escorts. The RLV force lost 43 KIA or MIA, 13 WIA and 77 fighters.

Axis defensive activity – 6 April 1944

Unit	Type	Gruppe up			Gruppe down		Claims	Losses				
		Base	No	Time	Base	Time		Dest	Dam	KIA	MIA	WIA
Luftflotte Reich												
I. Jagdkorps			150									
Jagddivision 7:												
Jafü Ostmark:												
Stab/JG 27	Bf 109G	Fels am Wagram	4	1520	Graz	1710	0	0	0	0	0	0
I./JG 27	Bf 109G	Fels am Wagram	35	1520	Graz	1710	1 B-17	0	0	0	0	0
III./JG 27	Bf 109G	Wolkersdorf	22	1522	Wolkersdorf	~1710	2 B-17, 1 P-38	1	0	1	0	0
IV./JG 27	Bf 109G	Graz	22	1547	Graz	~1710	0	0	0	0	0	0
II./ZG 1	Bf 110G	Wels	26	1606	Wels	~1715	n/c	0	0	0	0	0
Luftflotte 2												
Jafü Oberitalien:												
I./JG 53	Bf 109G	Maniago		~1500	Maniago	~1630	0	1	0	0	0	0
I./JG 77	Bf 109G	Lavariano		~1500	Lavariano	~1630	1 B-24, 1 P-47	2	0	0	1	0
1° Gr Ca (It.)	MC 205	Udine–Campoformido		~1500	Udine–Campoformido	~1630	1 P-47	4	0	2	0	1
21. LJ (Croatia)	G 50bis, MS 406c	Borongaj	2 4	~1545	Borongaj	~1645	0	2	2	0	0	0

Luftwaffe defensive activity – 8 April 1944

Unit	Type	Gruppe up			Gruppe down		Claims	Losses (—: included with 1st sortie)				
		Base	No	Time	Base	Time		Dest	Dam	KIA	MIA	WIA
Luftflotte Reich												
I. Jagdkorps			417									
Jagddivision 1:												
Stab/JG 3	Bf 109G	Salzwedel	2	1304	Salzwedel	1455	1 B-24	0	0	0	0	0
I./JG 3	Bf 109G	Burg	2	0948	Burg	~1045	0	0	0	0	0	0
	Bf 109G	Burg	26	1305	Burg	~1430	0	2	0	0	0	0
II./JG 3	Bf 109G	Gardelegen	23	1300	Gardelegen	~1430	2 P-51	3	1	1	0	0
IV./JG 3	Bf 109G	Salzwedel	25	1305	Salzwedel	1455	2 B-17, 1 B-24	1	1	1	0	0
III./JG 54	Bf 109G	Lüneburg	23	1253	Lüneburg	~1430	1 B-24	9	1	5	0	4
2nd sorties	Bf 109G	Lüneburg	8	1600	Lüneburg	~1730	2 P-38	—	—	—	—	—
I./JG 302	Bf 109G	Jüterbog	7	1301	Jüterbog	~1430	0	1	0	0	1	0
II./JG 302	Bf 109G	Ludwigslust	7	1301	Ludwigslust	~1430	0	1	0	1	0	0
II./ZG 26	Me 410A	Königsberg–Neumark	27	1310	Königsberg–Neumark	1518	0	1	1	1	0	1
III./ZG 26	Bf 110G	Königsberg–Neumark	15	1304	Königsberg–Neumark	~1515	0	0	0	0	0	0
Sturmstaffel 1	Fw 190A	Salzwedel	14	1305	Salzwedel	1504	2 B-24, 1 B-24 HSS	3	1	3	0	0
Jagddivision 2:												
Stab/JG 11	Bf 109G	Rotenburg	4	1300	Rotenburg	~1430	2 P-51	3	0	2	0	1
I./JG 11	Bf 109G	Rotenburg	1	0918	Rotenburg	~1015	0	0	0	0	0	0
	Bf 109G	Rotenburg	34	1253	Rotenburg	~1430	4 B-24, 4 P-51	6	1	5	0	2
II./JG 11	Bf 109G	Wunstorf	2	1012	Wunstorf	~1130	0	0	0	0	0	0
	Bf 109G	Wunstorf	1	1123	Wunstorf	~1300	0	0	0	0	0	0
III./JG 11	Fw 190A	Oldenburg	27	1254	Oldenburg	1435	0	11	1	6	0	0
III./JG 302	Fw 190A	Oldenburg	6	1251	Oldenburg	~1430	1 B-24, 1 P-51	4	0	3	0	0
Jagddivision 3:												
I./JG 1	Fw 190A	Lippspringe	26	1300	Hagenow	1430	4 B-24, 1 P-47, 1 P-51	5	0	1	0	2
II./JG 1	Fw 190A	Störmede	36	1256	Gardelegen	1415	5 B-24	3	0	1	0	0
III./JG 1	Bf 109G	Paderborn	26	1320	Gardelegen	1408	0	1	0	0	0	0
III./JG 3	Bf 109G	Frankfurt–Eschborn	19	1350	Frankfurt–Eschborn	~1530	0	5	1	2	0	0
Abschfü Mittelrhein:												
I./JG 5	Bf 109G	Wiesbaden–Erbenheim	8	1255	Wiesbaden–Erbenheim	~1415	2 B-24, 1 P-51	6	0	2	0	1
2nd sorties	Bf 109G	Wiesbaden–Erbenheim		~1430	Wiesbaden–Erbenheim	~1530	1 B-24	—	—	—	—	—
II./JG 27	Bf 109G	Wiesbaden–Erbenheim	23	1248	Halberstadt	~1430	1 B-17 HSS, 1 B-24, 2 P-51	5	1	3	0	2
II./JG 53	Bf 109G	Frankfurt–Eschborn	24	1249	Frankfurt–Eschborn	~1430	0	4	0	3	0	0
III./JG 300	Bf 109G	Wiesbaden–Erbenheim		~1245	Wiesbaden–Erbenheim	~1430	0	1	0	0	0	0
Jagddivision 7:												
III./JG 3	Bf 109G	Leipheim	19	?	Frankfurt–Eschborn	?	transfer	0	0	0	0	0
I./JG 5	Bf 109G	Herzogenaurach	8	?	Wiesbaden–Erbenheim	?	transfer	0	0	0	0	0
Luftflotte 3												
II. Jagdkorps												
Jagddivision 4:			*69									
I./JG 26	Fw 190A	Florennes	—	1416	Florennes	1618	1 B-24, 1 P-47	2	0	1	1	0
III./JG 26	Bf 109G	Lille–Vendeville	—	1405	Vechta	~1530	1 P-47, 1 P-51	0	1	0	0	0

*69 JG 26 sorties vs. withdrawing stream

I./JG 1 Fw 190A-7 'Black 3' is refuelled on a wet Twente airfield in April. *(Rosch)*

9 April

8th Air Force Mission #293: 402 of 542 HBs (all BDs) bomb aviation industry targets in Poland, E Germany, TOT 1145-1325 – lose 32-10-167, claim 45-8-14. Escort of 3 P-38 FGs, 9 P-47 FGs, 6 P-51 FGs (719 sorties) claims 20-1-6, loses 10-4-11.

The 8th AF sent all three bomb divisions to bomb aviation industry targets in Poland and East Prussia, on the longest-range mission for the entire force. The bombers flew east across the North Sea and Denmark before turning southeast to their targets. The two ZG 26 Gruppen at Königsberg–Neumark were poorly directed and missed a perfect chance to score heavily against the lightly escorted incoming bombers. The Jagddivisionen 1 and 2 Gefechtsverbände did reach the incoming bombers and attacked them with some success. They then flew second sorties with JD 3 fighters and II./ZG 26 Me 410s against the withdrawing bombers, which flew due west across north central Germany. The withdrawal escorts greatly outnumbered the I. Jagdkorps fighters and broke up their attacks. The JD 4 controllers did not like the odds and kept their fighters on the ground. The Americans lost 32 bombers shot down and 10 which took refuge in Sweden. 14 escorts were written off. I. Jagdkorps scrambled 356 single-engine and 56 twin-engine fighters from the three Jagddivisionen it employed;

227 and five contacted the enemy. Their losses totalled at least 14 KIA or MIA, four WIA and 27 aircraft.

10 April

8th Air Force Mission #295: 655 of 729 HBs (all BDs) bomb 11 airfields in western occupied zone – lose 3-2-121, claim 6-2-1. Escort of 1 P-38 FG, 7 P-47 FGs, 5 P-51 FGs (719 sorties) claims 8-0-1, loses 2-0-5.

The 8th AF began its new top-priority campaign – softening up the invasion coast – with an early-morning raid on 11 airfields. Jagddivisionen 3, 4 and 5 were alerted, as they were on every flyable day. A few JD 3 aircraft were apparently scrambled, but they were soon ordered to land as the raid targeted Luftflotte 3 airfields, and I. Jagdkorps aircraft did not normally cross into Luftflotte 3 territory. Two JG 2 Gruppen made an interception, with results that could be predicted given the odds they faced. The 8th AF wrote off five bombers and two escorts to all causes. The day's battles were not over for the hard-pressed Luftflotte 3 fighter pilots: the evening was spent battling the medium bombers and fighter-bombers of the American 9th AF and the RAF's 2nd Tactical Air Force. JG 2 lost four KIA, two WIA and eight fighters in the day's battles.

Luftwaffe defensive activity – 9 April 1944

Unit	Type	Gruppe up			Gruppe down		Claims	Losses (—: included with 1st sortie)				
		Base	No	Time	Base	Time		Dest	Dam	KIA	MIA	WIA
Luftflotte Reich												
I. Jagdkorps			354									
Jagddivision 1:												
Stab/JG 3	Bf 109G	Salzwedel		~1030	Salzwedel?	~1200	1 B-24, 1 B-24 HSS	0	0	0	0	0
2nd sorties	Bf 109G	Salzwedel?		~1500	Salzwedel?	~1630	0	0	0	0	0	0
I./JG 3	Bf 109G	Burg		1030	Burg	~1200	0	1	0	0	1	0
2nd sorties	Bf 109G	Burg?		~1500	Burg?	~1630	1 B-17	—	—	—	—	—
II./JG 3	Bf 109G	Gardelegen		1035	Gardelegen	1235	0	0	0	0	0	
IV./JG 3	Bf 109G	Salzwedel		1035	Salzwedel	1230	3 B-24	0	0	0	0	0
2nd sorties	Bf 109G	Salzwedel?		~1500	Salzwedel?	~1630	0	0	0	0	0	0
III./JG 54	Bf 109G	Lüneburg		~1030	Lüneburg	~1215	1 B-17	7	0	2	0	1
I./JG 302	Bf 109G	Jüterbog		~1030	Jüterbog	~1215	3 B-17. 1 B-24	1	0	0	1	0
II./JG 302	Bf 109G	Ludwigslust		~1030	Ludwigslust	~1215	2 B-24 HSS	0	0	0	0	0
II./ZG 26	Me 410A	Königsberg–Neumark		1120	Königsberg–Neumark	1400	n/c	0	0	0	0	0
2nd sorties	Me 410A	Königsberg–Neumark		~1430	Königsberg–Neumark	1600	3 B-17	2	1	1	0	0
III./ZG 26	Bf 110G	Königsberg–Neumark	18	1106	Königsberg–Neumark	~1300	n/c	0	0	0	0	0
Sturmstaffel 1	Fw 190A	Salzwedel		1055	Oranienburg	1255	0	0	0	0	0	0
2nd sorties	Fw190A	Oranienburg		~1430	Salzwedel	~1600	n/c	0	0	0	0	0
Jafü Ostpreußen:												
2./SG 152	Fw 190G	Rahmel		~1230	Rahmel	~1400	3 B-17	1	0	?	?	?
Jafü Oberschlesien:												
JGr Ost	?	Liegnitz		~1230	Liegnitz	~1400	0	1	0	0	0	0
Jagddivision 2:												
Stab/JG 11?	Bf 109G	Rotenburg		~1030	Rotenburg	~1200	0	0	0	0	0	0
I./JG 11	Bf 109G	Rotenburg		~1030	Rotenburg	~1200	1 B-24, 1 P-47	4	1	3	0	1
2nd sorties	Bf 109G	Rotenburg	8	1450	Rotenburg	~1630	5 B-17	—	—	—	—	—
III./JG 11	Fw 190A	Oldenburg		~1030	Oldenburg	~1200	0	2	1	1	1	1
2nd sorties	Fw 190A	Oldenburg		~1430	Oldenburg	~1600	2 B-17	—	—	—	—	—
III./NJG 3	Bf 110G	Stade		~1430	Stade	~1630	1 B-17	0	0	0	0	0
IV./NJG 3	Ju 88C	Westerland		~1100	Westerland	~1300	1 B-24	0	0	0	0	0
Abschfü Dänemark:												
10./JG 11	Fw 190A	Aalborg		~1000	Aalborg	~1130	0	1	0	1	0	0
Jagddivision 3:												
I./JG 1	Fw 190A	Lippspringe		1010	Wismar	1155	3 B-24, 1 B-24 HSS	2	1	1	0	1
II./JG 1	Fw 190A	Störmede	27	1005	Lübeck–Blankensee	1124	2 B-24, 1 P-47	4	3	1	0	0
2nd sorties	Fw 190A	Lübeck–Blankensee		~1500	Störmede	~1630	1 B-17	—	—	—	—	—
III./JG 1	Bf 109G	Paderborn		~1010	Paderborn	~1130	0	0	0	0	0	0
2nd sorties	Bf 109G	Paderborn?		~1500	Paderborn?	~1630	1 B-17	1	0	1	0	0

11 April

8th Air Force Mission #298: 828 of 917 HBs (all BDs) bomb aviation industry targets in E Germany, TOT 1110-1323 – lose 64-5-406, claim 73-24-33. Escort of 3 P-38 FGs, 9 P-47 FGs, 6 P-51 FGs (819 sorties) claims 51-5-25, loses 16-0-29.

The 8th AF sent a full-strength raid to six aviation targets deep in central and eastern Germany. The 3rd BD flew across the North Sea and Denmark and east over the Baltic before turning south to its targets. Its return course was approximately the reciprocal of its approach. The 1st and 2nd BDs flew due east toward Berlin on what had been nicknamed the 'Bomber Autobahn'. The 2nd BD retuned by the same route, while the 1st BD turned north and paralleled the route of the 3rd BD. The weather over northern Germany was good, and I. Jagdkorps got its forces up and concentrated in time to attack both streams effectively. The American plan was too complex for complete coverage by the escorts, and several formations paid the price, especially the 3rd BD, which was unescorted in the target area. They were opposed by the Me 410s of II./ZG 26 and the Bf 110s of III./ZG 26, all flying from Königsberg–Neumark. Many of the 33 B-17s lost by the 3rd BD were downed by these Zerstörer; nine bombers did not crash, but flew to Sweden and internment. The two Zerstörergruppen did not land to celebrate their success and prepare for second sorties, as written elsewhere, but stayed up over northern Germany for 2 1/2 hours – too long. They were surprised by the approaching 1st BD and its large escort of P-51s, which pounced on the hapless Zerstörer and downed 11. The day thus ended on a sour note for the RLV force, which could nevertheless claim a success. The Americans lost 69 bombers downed, scrapped or interned, plus 16 escorts. I. Jagdkorps scrambled 368 single-engine and 60 twin-engine fighters from its three north German Jagddivisionen; 275 and 35 contacted the enemy. Their losses totalled at least 37 KIA, 15 WIA and 53 aircraft.

I./JG 1 Fw 190A-7 'Yellow 6' prepares to move onto the Twente taxi strip in April. *(Rosch)*

COMBAT REPORT[1]
11 April 1944

One B-17 Fortress shot down from 6,000 metres at
1059 hours in PQ FB-7, 10 km NE of Fallersleben

After Sitzbereitschaft, I took off with the Gruppe at
0958 hours in Fw 190A-7 'Red 23' (two MG 151/20,
two MG 131) with orders to assemble over Paderborn
with I./JG 1 and III./JG 1 and then to meet the units of
JG 27 over the Brocken. After assembly, JG 1 flew to
the Brocken at a course of 30°, but JG 27 was not
there. After control was passed from JD 3 to JD 2,
communication was impossible, so we used the
Reichsjägerwelle [a running commentary broadcast on
a single frequency to all defenders]. In PQ GC, the
enemy was sighted – HB formations flying NE in PQ
GA. The Gruppe turned to the left and carried out a
closed frontal attack in PQ FB. I attacked the lowest B-
17 in a small Pulk on the left from the low front and
obtained hits in the fuselage and cockpit, at which the
B-17 immediately showed a bright plume. After
passing through the formation, I saw that the Boeing
had tipped over its left wing and was diving straight
down. I could not see the crash because I was in
combat with the enemy escort. Re-assembly for
further closed attacks was impossible after the Gruppe
had been split up by the very strong escort. It came
down to individual combats in Rotte and Schwarm
strength. The combat was witnessed by Obfw.
Schuhmacher, Oblt. Eder and Obfw. Bach.

Major Heinz Bär, Gruppenkommandeur
Stab II./JG 1

Obstlt. Heinz Bär, one of the dominant personalities of the
Luftwaffe fighter force, and one of the very few pilots to fly
in combat for all of World War II. His outspoken refusal to
obey orders that he considered reckless brought him a
demotion in 1943 and probably denied him the Wehrmacht's
highest award, the Diamonds to the Knight's Cross. In mid-
1944, he was given command of JG 1 and later JG 3, two of
the most successful units in the RLV force. Bär was the
highest-scoring German jet ace, with 16 claims, and the
second-highest day scorer against the western Allies, with
125 victories. (Author's collection)

Luftwaffe Defensive Activity – 10 April 1944

Unit	Type	Gruppe up			Gruppe down		Claims	Losses (—: included with 1st sortie)				
		Base	No	Time	Base	Time		Dest	Dam	KIA	MIA	WIA
Luftflotte 3												
II. Jagdkorps												
Jagddivision 5:												
II./JG 2	Bf 109G	Creil		~0900	Creil	~1130	0	1	1	1	0	1
III./JG 2	Fw 190A	Cormeilles		~0900	Cormeilles	~1130	1 B-24, 1 P-47	7	2	3	0	1

Luftwaffe defensive activity – 11 April 1944

Unit	Type	Gruppe up			Gruppe down		Claims	Losses				
		Base	No	Time	Base	Time		Dest	Dam	KIA	MIA	WIA
Luftflotte Reich												
I. Jagdkorps			*432									
Jagddivision 1:												
Stab/JG 3	Bf 109G	Salzwedel	4	1003	Salzwedel	~1130	1 B-17	0	0	0	0	0
I./JG 3	Bf 109G	Burg	22	1005	Burg	~1130	1 B-17	2	1	3	0	2
	Bf 109G	Burg	4	1125	Burg	~1300	1 P-51	0	0	0	0	0
II./JG 3	Bf 109G	Gardelegen	24	1002	Gardelegen	1207	2 B-17, 1 P-51	6	1	4	0	1
IV./JG 3	Bf 109G	Salzwedel	25	1003	Salzwedel	1145	6 B-17**, 1 P-38	4	0	1	0	3
III./JG 54	Bf 109G	Lüneburg		~1000	Rotenburg	~1130	0	4	2	0	0	0
I./JG 302	Bf 109G	Jüterbog	7	1000	Jüterbog	~1145	0	1	0	0	0	0
II./JG 302	Bf 109G	Ludwigslust	8	1004	Ludwigslust	~1145	1 B-24	0	0	0	0	0
II./ZG 26	Me 410A	Königsberg–Neumark	23	1045	Königsberg–Neumark	1300	8 B-17	8	1	13	0	2
III./ZG 26	Bf 110G	Königsberg–Neumark	13	1035	Frankfurt/Oder, Königsberg–Neumark	1300	5 B-17	3	0	3	0	1
NJGr 10	Fw 190A	Werneuchen	7	1130	Werneuchen	~1300	0	?	?	?	?	?
Sturmstaffel 1	Fw 190A	Salzwedel	6	1004	Zwickau, Salzwedel	1150	4 B-24	0	2	0	0	0
Jagddivision 2:												
Stab/JG 11?	Bf 109G	Rotenburg		~0930	Rotenburg	~1100	0	0	0	0	0	0
I./JG 11	Bf 109G	Rotenburg	17	0935	Rotenburg	~1100	1 B-24	0	0	0	0	0
III./JG 11	Fw 190A	Rotenburg	13	0935	Rotenburg, Hamburg	1045	2 B-24	7	2	4	0	1
I./NJG 3	Ju 88C	Vechta		~1030	Vechta	~1300	1 B-24	0	0	0	0	0
Abschfü Dänemark:												
10./NJG 3	Ju 88C	Grove		~1030	Grove	~1300	1 B-17	0	0	0	0	0
Jagddivision 3:												
I./JG 1	Fw 190A	Lippspringe	15	1008	Lippspringe	~1130	1 B-17, 1 P-51	2	0	1	0	0
II./JG 1	Fw 190A	Störmede	24	0958	Zerbst, Fassberg	1123	3 B-17, 2 P-51	5	1	2	0	1
III./JG 1	Bf 109G	Paderborn	21	1000	Paderborn	~1130	0	5	1	2	0	2
I./JG 300	Bf 109G	Rheine	9	1015	Rheine	~1130	n/c	0	0	0	0	0
Abschfü Mittelrhein:												
II./JG 27	Bf 109G	Königsberg–Neumark	18	0950	Königsberg–Neumark	~1130	1 B-17	1	0	0	0	1
II./JG 53	Bf 109G	Frankfurt–Eschborn	22	0956	Frankfurt–Eschborn	~1130	1 B-17	2	0	1	0	0
	Bf 109G	Goslar	1	1125	Frankfurt–Eschborn	~1300	0	0	0	0	0	0
Jagddivision 7:												
III./JG 3	Bf 109G	Leipheim	14	1000	Leipheim	~1200	4 B-24	1	0	1	0	0
I./JG 5	Bf 109G	Herzogenaurach		~1030	Herzogenaurach	~1200	1 B-24	?	?	2	0	1
ZG 76	Bf 110G	Öttingen	24	1126	Öttingen	~1330	n/c	0	0	0	0	0
vs. withdrawing stream												
Luftflotte Reich												
I. Jagdkorps												
Jagddivision 1:												
I./JG 3	Bf 109G	Burg	6	1225	Burg	~1400	0	1	0	0	0	0
II./JG 3	Bf 109G	Gardelegen	12	1235	Gardelegen	1355	0	0	0	0	0	0
	Bf 109G	Salzwedel	1	1235	Gardelegen	~1400	0	0	0	0	0	0
IV./JG 3	Bf 109G	Salzwedel	14	1235	Salzwedel, Warnemünde	1405	5 B-17	0	0	0	0	0
III.JG 54	Bf 109G	Rotenburg	3	1240	Lüneburg	~1400	0	0	0	0	0	0

Luftwaffe defensive activity – 11 April 1944 Continued

Unit	Type	Gruppe up			Gruppe down		Claims	Losses				
		Base	No	Time	Base	Time		Dest	Dam	KIA	MIA	WIA
NSGr 10	Fw 190A	Werneuchen	1	1230	Werneuchen	~1400	0	?	?	?	?	?
Sturmstaffel 1	Fw 190A	Salzwedel	2	1235	Salzwedel	~1400	0	0	0	0	0	0
Jagddivision 2:												
III./JG 1	Bf 109G	Fassberg	2	1305	Oldenburg?	~1430	0	0	0	0	0	0
I./JG 11	Bf 109G	Rotenburg	14	1245	Rotenburg	~1430	6 B-17***	1	3	0	0	0
III./JG 11	Fw 190A	Rotenburg	4	1234	Rotenburg	~1430	2 B-17	0	0	0	0	0
Jagddivision 3:												
I./JG 1	Fw 190A	Lippspringe		~1300	Lippspringe	~1430	0	0	0	0	0	0
III./JG 1	Bf 109G	Quedlinburg	2	1305	Paderborn	~1430	0	0	0	0	0	0
Abschfü Mittelrhein:												
II./JG 53	Bf 109G	Hildesheim	2	1300	Frankfurt–Eschborn	~1430	0	0	0	0	0	0

*432 total sorties vs incoming + withdrawing streams   **IV./JG 3: + 11 B-17 claims unconfirmed (unwitnessed)   ***I./JG 11: + 6 B-17 claims unconfirmed (unwitnessed)

12 April – vs. 8th Air Force

8th Air Force Mission #300: 455 HBs (all BDs) target Schweinfurt, other targets in C Germany, abandon mission – lose 6-2-26, claim 10-6-7. Escort of 3 P-38 FGs, 9 P-47 FGs, 6 P-51 FGs (766 sorties) claims 18-1-3, loses 5-2-21.

A forecast of adequate weather led USSTAF to attempt a rare joint mission of the 8th and 15th Air Forces. The target for the 8th AF was Schweinfurt, but clouds and dense contrails caused severe problems in assembly and rendezvous, and ultimately forced the cancellation of the mission. The B-24s of the 2nd BD did not turn back until they had reached the German border and ran afoul of the II. Jagdkorps fighters, which attacked the bombers after evading the escorts in cloud and contrails and downed six. The I. Jagdkorps ordered up a number of fighters which found only sweeping escorts. The Americans wrote off eight bombers and seven escorts. The RLV forces scrambled 205 fighters, of which 100 made contact, losing 12 KIA or MIA, four WIA and 24 fighters.

12 April – vs. 15th Air Force

15th Air Force: 446 HBs bomb aviation industry targets in Vienna area – lose 11, claims unknown. Escort of 3 P-38 FGs, 1 P-47 FG claims 17-2-8, loses 1.

The 15th AF mission was much more successful than that of the 8th AF, finding the skies over Vienna clear and causing severe damage to several aviation factories for very light losses. Only 11 bombers and one escort were lost to all causes. Jagddivision 7 and its subordinate commands, Jafü Ostmark and Abschnittsführer Ungarn [Air Detachment Hungary] scrambled 190 Bf 109s, 50 Bf 110s and 12 Me 210s, the last-named a new Me 210 squadron formed from the Hungarian Air Force experimental unit. Of these fighters, 127, 31 and 12 made contact. Many of their victory claims were lost in processing; their losses of at least 12 KIA or MIA, five WIA and 17 fighters, most to the four American fighter groups, were considerable.

Luftwaffe defensive activity vs. 8th Air Force – 12 April 1944

Unit	Type	Gruppe up			Gruppe down		Claims	Losses				
		Base	No	Time	Base	Time		Dest	Dam	KIA	MIA	WIA
Luftflotte Reich												
I. Jagdkorps			*421									
Jagddivision 1:												
I./JG 3	Bf 109G	Burg	14	1251	Burg	~1445	0	1	0	0	0	0
	Bf 109G	Burg	2	1401	Burg	~1500	a/f protection	0	0	0	0	0
II./JG 3	Bf 109G	Gardelegen	16	1230	Gardelegen	1442	n/c	0	0	0	0	0
	Bf 109G	Gardelegen	3	1413	Gardelegen	~1500	a/f protection	0	0	0	0	0
IV./JG 3	Bf 109G	Salzwedel	25	1245	Salzwedel, Warnemünde	1445	n/c	0	0	0	0	0
	Bf 109G	Salzwedel	2	1409	Salzwedel	~1500	a/f protection	0	0	0	0	0
	Fw 190A	Salzwedel	2	1409	Salzwedel	~1500	a/f protection	0	0	0	0	0
III./JG 301	Bf 109G	Zerbst	4	1410	Zerbst	~1500	a/f protection	0	0	0	0	0
I./JG 302	Bf 109G	Jüterbog	6	1404	Jüterbog	~1500	a/f protection	0	0	0	0	0
II./JG 302	Bf 109G	Ludwigslust	11	1420	Ludwigslust	~1500	a/f protection	0	0	0	0	0
II./ZG 26	Bf 110G	Königsberg–Neumark	11	1245	Königsberg–Neumark	~1500	n/c	0	0	0	0	0
III./ZG 26	Bf 110G	Königsberg–Neumark	13	1245	Langensalza	1510	n/c	0	0	0	0	0
Sturmstaffel 1	Fw 190A	Salzwedel	7	1245	Salzwedel	~1445	n/c	0	0	0	0	0
NJGr 10	Fw 190A	Werneuchen	4	1411	Werneuchen	~1500	a/f protection	0	0	0	0	0
JG 110	Fw 190A	Altenburg	9	1420	Altenburg	~1500	a/f protection	0	0	0	0	0
	Bf 109G	Altenburg	2	1420	Altenburg	~1500	a/f protection	0	0	0	0	0
Jagddivision 2:												
Stab/JG 11	Bf 109G	Rotenburg	2	1250	Rotenburg	~1400	n/c	0	0	0	0	0
	Bf 109G	Rotenburg	1	1428	Rotenburg	~1530	a/f protection	0	0	0	0	0
I./JG 11	Fw 190A	Rotenburg	16	1250	Rotenburg	~1400	n/c	1	2	0	0	0
	Fw 190A	Rotenburg	1	1428	Rotenburg	~1530	a/f protection	0	0	0	0	0
III./JG 11	Fw 190A	Rotenburg	12	1250	Rotenburg	~1400	n/c	1	1	0	0	0
	Fw 190A	Rotenburg	3	1428	Rotenburg	~1530	a/f protection	0	0	0	0	0
III./JG 54	Bf 109G	Rotenburg	6	1250	Rotenburg	~1445	n/c	4	0	3	0	1
	Bf 109G	Rotenburg	2	1428	Rotenburg	~1530	a/f protection	0	0	0	0	0
Jagddivision 3:												
I./JG 1	Bf 109G	Lippspringe	9	1243	Lippspringe	~1440	0	0	0	0	0	0
II./JG 1	Fw 190A	Störmede	12	1240	Wiesbaden–Erbenheim	1445	0	0	0	0	0	0
III./JG 1	Bf 109G	Paderborn	18	1243	Paderborn	~1440	0	1	0	1	0	0
Abschfü Mittelrhein:												
II./JG 27	Bf 109G	Königsberg–Neumark	13	1302	Königsberg–Neumark	~1430	0	2	0	2	0	0
II./JG 53	Bf 109G	Frankfurt–Eschborn	15	1306	Frankfurt–Eschborn	~1430	1 P-38	1	0	0	0	1
Luftflotte 3												
II. Jagdkorps												
Jagddivision 4:												
I./JG 26	Fw 190A	Florennes		~1230	Florennes	~1400	0	1	0	0	0	0
II./JG 26	Fw 190A	Cambrai		~1230	Cambrai	~1400	4 B-24**	5	3	2	1	0
III./JG 26	Bf 109G	Etain		1225	Bonn–Hangelar, Trier	1400	0	0	1	0	0	1
Jagddivision 5:												
Stab/JG 2	Fw 190A	Cormeilles		~1230	Cormeilles	~1400	0	0	1	0	0	0
II./JG 2	Bf 109G	Creil		~1230	Creil	~1400	0	2	0	1	0	1
III./JG 2	Fw 190A	Cormeilles		~1230	Cormeilles	~1400	2 B-24	5	0	2	0	0

*421 total sorties by I. JK vs. 8th + 15th AFs   **II./JG 26: + 5 B-24 claims unconfirmed (unwitnessed)

Axis defensive activity vs. 15th Air Force – 12 April 1944

Unit	Type	Gruppe up			Gruppe down		Claims	Losses				
		Base	No	Time	Base	Time		Dest	Dam	KIA	MIA	WIA
Luftflotte Reich												
I. Jagdkorps												
Jagddivision 7:												
III./JG 3	Bf 109G	Leipheim	*15	1100	Leipheim	~1300	1 B-24	1	0	1	0	0
I./JG 5	Bf 109G	Bad Wörishofen	—	1100	Bad Wörishofen		1 B-24	0	0	0	0	0
I./JG 301	Bf 109G	Neubiberg		~1130	Neubiberg	~1300	0	0	0	0	0	0
ZG 76	Bf 110G	Öttingen	19	1128	Öttingen	~1330	n/c	0	0	0	0	0
Jafü Ostmark:												
Stab/JG 27	Bf 109G	Fels am Wagram	4	1116	Fels am Wagram	~1310	0****	0	0	0	0	0
I./JG 27	Bf 109G	Fels am Wagram	**32	1116	Graz, Fels	1310	1 B-24, 1 B-24 HSS*****	0	0	0	0	0
II./JG 301	Bf 109G	Wien–Seyring	***24	1146	Wien–Seyring	~1300	0	4	0	2	0	2
III./JG 301	Bf 109G	Wien–Seyring	—	1146	Wien–Seyring	~1300	1 B-24	3	0	?	?	?
II./ZG 1	Bf 110G	Wels	31	1127	Wels	~1330	4 B-24	4	3	6	0	1
VbdFhr Schule	Bf 109G	Fels am Wagram	—	~1115	Graz, Fels	~1300	0	1	0	0	1	0
Abschfü Ungarn:												
III./JG 27	Bf 109G	Börgönd (H)	22	1105	Börgönd (H)	~1300	1 B-17******	1	0	0	0	1
IV./JG 27	Bf 109G	Vat (H)	30	1116	Vat (H)	~1300	1 P-38*******	3	0	1	0	1
Air Inst St (Hungary)	Me 210Ca	Ferihegy	12	~1115	Ferihegy	~1330	0	0	1	1	0	0

*15 sorties total for III./JG 3 + I./JG 5   **32 sorties total for I./JG 27 + VbdFhr Schule   ***24 sorties total for II./JG 301 + III./JG 301

****Stab/JG 27: 1 B-24 claim undocumented   *****I./JG 27: + 7 B-24 claims undocumented (includes VbdFhr Schule)

******III./JG 27: + 1 B-17, 4 B-24 claims undocumented   *******IV./JG 27: + 1 B-17, 1 P-47 claims undocumented

13 April – Budapest and Györ, Hungary (see map)

15th Air Force: 163 of 177 B-17s bomb Györ a/i, a/f, TOT 1147-56 – lose 5-?-?, claim 3-1-0. 338 of 362 B-24s bomb Budapest a/fs, Duna a/i, TOT 1245-58 – lose 13-?-?, claim 14-4-6. Escort of 182 P-38s (3 FGs), 46 P-47s (1 FG) claims 18-3-7, loses 2 P-47s.

A 15th AF raid on targets in the Budapest area met stiff resistance from Jagddivision 7 and its two subordinate commands, Jafü Ostmark and Abschnittsführer Ungarn. The Luftwaffe put up 185 single-engine and 44 twin-engine fighters, of which 85 singles and all 44 twins made contact. The Hungarians put up all that they had: one Bf 109G air defence squadron (two others were still forming), the Me 210 night fighter squadron and the Me 210 squadron formed from their experimental unit. The Americans lost 18 bombers and two P-47s. The Axis lost at least eight KIA, two WIA and 21 aircraft, including 13 Hungarian Me 210s. The type was immediately withdrawn from the day fighter order of battle, and the crews began retraining for the ground attack role. The Hungarian fighter pilots remaining on the Eastern Front were quickly returned to the homeland to bolster its air defences.

Axis defensive activity vs. 15th Air Force – 13 April 1944

Unit	Type	Gruppe up			Gruppe down		Claims	Losses				
		Base	No	Time	Base	Time		Dest	Dam	KIA	MIA	WIA
Luftflotte Reich												
I. Jagdkorps			185									
Jagddivision 7:												
III./JG 3	Bf 109G	Leipheim, Bad Wörishofen	14	1050	Tulln (A)	1205	n/c	0	0	0	0	0
I./JG 301	Bf 109G	Neubiberg		~1100	Neubiberg?	~1315	2 B-24	3	0	0	0	2
II./ZG 76	Bf 110G	Öttingen	20	1032	Öttingen?	~1315	4 B-24	0	0	0	0	0
Jafü Ostmark:												
Stab/JG 27	Bf 109G	Fels am Wagram	4	1103	Fels am Wagram	1250	1 B-17	0	0	0	0	0
I./JG 27	Bf 109G	Fels am Wagram	24	1105	Fels am Wagram	1215	2 B-17, 2 P-38	0	0	0	0	0
IV./JG 27	Bf 109G	Graz	18	1104	Graz	~1230	1 P-38	0	0	0	0	0
II./JG 301	Bf 109G	Wien–Seyring	11	1137	Wien–Seyring	~1315	0	2	0	1	0	0
II./ZG 1	Bf 110G	Wels		~1200	Wels	~1330	3 B-24	2	0	1	0	0
Abschfü Ungarn:												
III./JG 27	Bf 109G	Börgönd (H)	17	1112	Börgönd (H)	~1230	2 B-17	0	0	0	0	0
5./1. NJSt (Hungary)	Me 210Ca	Ferihegy		~1215	Ferihegy	~1330	1 B-24, 2 P-38	9	?	6	?	?
Air Inst St. (Hungary)	Me 210Ca	Ferihegy		~1215	Ferihegy	~1330	4 B-24, 2 P-38	4	1	?	?	?
2./1. JSt (Hungary)	Bf 109G	Ferihegy	12	1100	Ferihegy	~1230	1 B-24	1	0	0	0	0
13. St (Slovakia)	Bf 109E	Bratislava	2	~1200	Bratislava	~1300	1 LW Bf 110	?	?	?	?	?

13 April – Schweinfurt, Oberpfaffenhofen, Augsburg (see map)

8th Air Force Mission #301: 155 of 172 1st BD B-17s bomb Schweinfurt, TOT 1409h – lose 14-1-127; 184 of 211 2nd BD B-24s bomb Oberpfaffenhofen a/i and Lechfeld a/f, TOT 1509+1516h – lose 6-0-45; 227 of 243 3rd BD B-17s bomb Augsburg, TOT 1453h – lose 18-2-178; total losses include 13 interned in Switzerland. Total bomber claims 22-13-24. Escort of 3 P-38 FGs, 9 P-47 FGs, 6 P-51 FGs (871 sorties) claims 42-8-10, loses 9-2-11.

The 8th AF targets for the second joint mission in two days were deep in central Germany. Their early departure time and straight-line course telegraphed the target area and facilitated a large-scale RLV response. 403 single-engine and 31 twin-engine fighters were scrambled; 270 of the singles and all 31 of the twins made contact. The American objective of splitting the defenders between the 8th AF and 15th AF was not met, in that many Jagddivision 7 units and

some from Jafü Ostmark flew early missions against the 15th, returned to base for servicing and then flew missions against the departing 8th. As usual, these second sorties were in much lower strength than the first, but Luftwaffe command and control procedures worked well. The 8th AF bomber losses were 25 downed, 3 scrapped and 13 interned in Switzerland; escort losses totalled 11. The RLV forces lost 11 KIA, at least 13 WIA and 45 aircraft.

COMBAT REPORT[2]
13 April 1944

One Fortress destroyed from 6,000 metres at 1504 hours, 20–30 km NW of Augsburg
One Fortress shot from formation from 6,000 metres at 1508 hours, 30 km N of Augsburg
[Latter claim not confirmed: DC]

After transferring to Austria in the morning, I

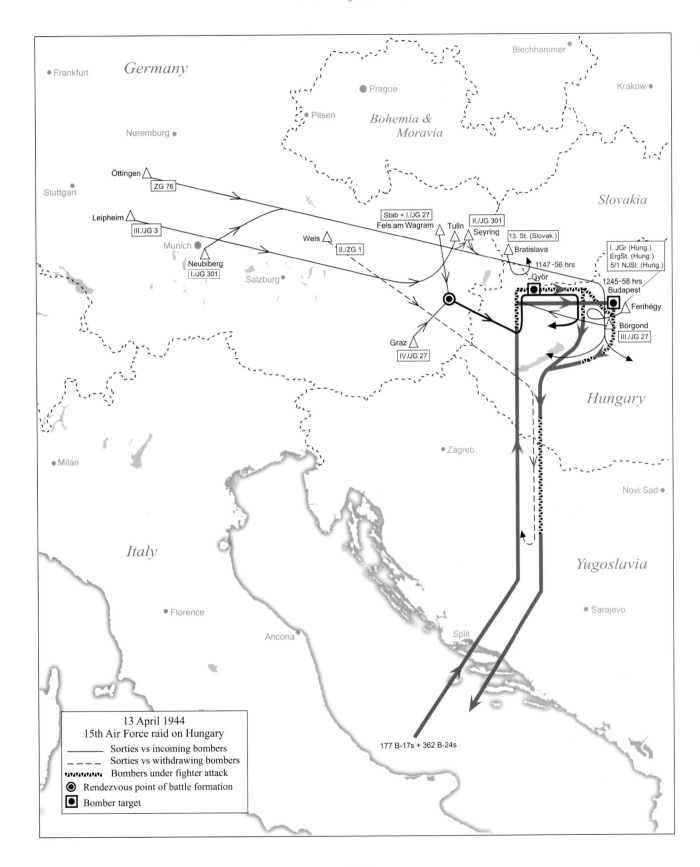

Germany

Frankfurt

Nuremburg

Stuttgart

Öttingen
ZG 76

Leipheim
III./JG 3

Munich

Neubiberg
I./JG 301

Salzburg

Wels
II./ZG 1

Graz
IV./JG 27

Bohemia &
Moravia

Prague

Pilsen

Blechhammer

Krakow

Slovakia

Stab + I./JG 27
Fels am Wagram

Tulln
Seyring

II./JG 301

13. St. (Slovak.)
Bratislava

1147-56 hrs

Györ

I. JGr (Hung.)
ErgSt. (Hung.)
5/1 NJSt. (Hung.)

1245-58 hrs
Budapest

Ferihégy

Börgond
III./JG 27

Hungary

Zagreb

Novi Sad

Italy

Milan

Florence

Ancona

Split

Yugoslavia

Sarajevo

177 B-17s + 362 B-24s

13 April 1944
15th Air Force raid on Hungary

———— Sorties vs incoming bombers
- - - - Sorties vs withdrawing bombers
▼▲▼▲▼ Bombers under fighter attack
◉ Rendezvous point of battle formation
◨ Bomber target

scrambled from Tulln at 1355 hours in a Bf 109G-6/U4 (MK 108 3-cm engine cannon, two MG 131s) with eight Bf 109s to attack a heavy bomber formation approaching the Augsburg–München area from the northwest. At 1455 hours, I sighted several Fortress Pulks with escorts hanging above them over and west of the Ammersee. The heavies had been heading for München [Munich], but turned left over the Ammersee and headed toward Augsburg. I immediately attacked the leading Pulk with all of my aircraft and scored an immediate shootdown. I then made a second attack on the same Pulk with just my wingman who had a gun stoppage. I saw effective hits on two B-17s, but they did not go down. I made a

third attack from the high rear on the left rear outside B-17, closed to 200 metres and fired all of my remaining ammo in one long burst. After I exited, I saw the B-17 dive, trailing black smoke, leaving the protection of its formation and disappearing in cumulus clouds at 3,000 metres. I could not follow because of my duties as a Gruppenkommandeur. I made a situation report to Division and then landed on Bad Wörishofen at 1530 hours due to low fuel. My wingman, Uffz. Mächtele, witnessed the combat.

Major Walther Dahl, Gruppenkommandeur
Stab III./JG 3 Udet

15 April

8th Air Force Mission #303: 616 fighters (3 P-38 FGs, 7 P-47 FGs, 6 P-51 FGs) strafe 26 airfields in C and W Germany – lose 33-2-34, claim 18-1-6 (air), 40-0-29 (ground).

Sixteen 8th and 9th Fighter Command groups executed a mass strafing mission to 26 airfields in Germany in mediocre weather. The I. Jagdkorps could do no better than scramble the duty Staffeln to defend their own airfields. Of the 133 fighters to take off, only 33 made contact; all of these were from the two

operational JG 11 Gruppen and Sturmstaffel 1. Many of the pilots' claims for P-38s got lost in the verification system, but 11 P-38s failed to return from the mission. American losses totalled 35 fighters, most to the airfield Flak. JG 11 lost five KIA, two WIA and 19 fighters, and III./JG 11 had to be taken off operations for rebuilding. The I. Jagdkorps claimed a success as only two fighters on the ground were lost to the strafers.

Mechanics pose on the wing of a Sturmstaffel 1 Fw 190A-7 at Salzwedel in April. *(Smith)*

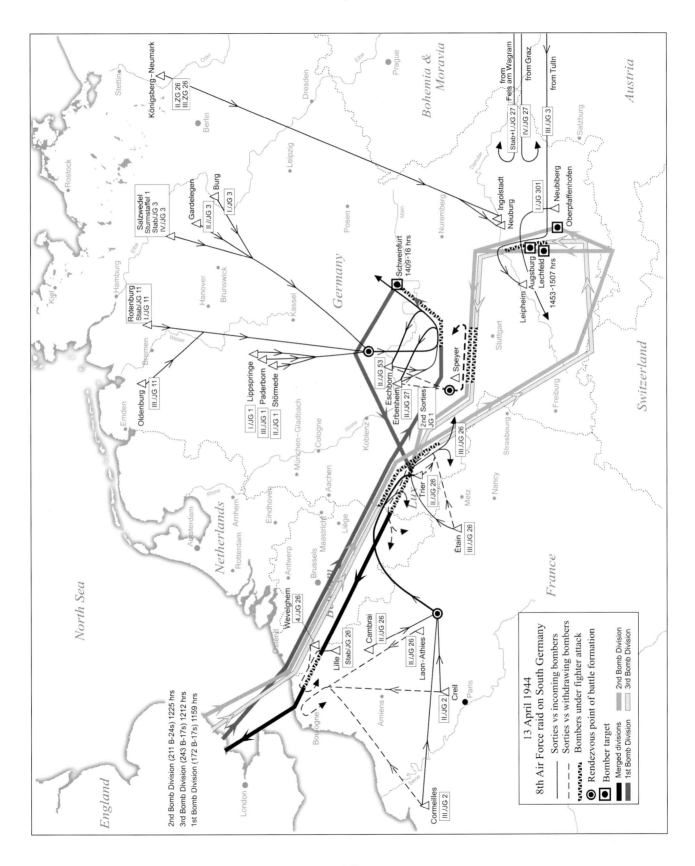

13 April 1944
8th Air Force raid on South Germany

2nd Bomb Division (211 B-24s) 1225 hrs
3rd Bomb Division (243 B-17s) 1212 hrs
1st Bomb Division (172 B-17s) 1159 hrs

Sorties vs incoming bombers
Sorties vs withdrawing bombers
Bombers under fighter attack
Rendezvous point of battle formation
Bomber target
Merged divisions
1st Bomb Division
2nd Bomb Division
3rd Bomb Division

Luftwaffe defensive activity vs. 8th Air Force – 13 April 1944

Unit	Type	Gruppe up			Gruppe down		Claims	Losses				
		Base	No	Time	Base	Time		Dest	Dam	KIA	MIA	WIA
vs. incoming stream												
Luftflotte Reich												
I. Jagdkorps			*412									
Jagddivision 1:												
Stab/JG 3	Bf 109G	Salzwedel	2	1245	Salzwedel	~1430	2 B-17	0	0	0	0	0
I./JG 3	Bf 109G	Burg	15	1245	Burg	~1430	0	5	1	1	0	0
II./JG 3	Bf 109G	Gardelegen	17	1248	Eschborn	1452	2 B-17	1	3	0	0	0
IV./JG 3	Bf 109G	Salzwedel	24	1245	Gießen	1440	3 B-17	3	0	0	0	0
II./ZG 26	Me 410A	Königsberg–Neumark		1325	Ingolstadt, Neuburg	1540	n/c	0	0	0	0	0
III./ZG 26	Bf 110G	Königsberg–Neumark	12	1325	Ingolstadt, Neuburg	1540	n/c	0	0	0	0	0
Sturmstaffel 1	Fw 190A	Salzwedel	9	1245	Wertheim	1440	3 B-17	1	1	1	0	0
Jagddivision 2:												
Stab/JG 11	Fw 190A	Rotenburg	3	1245	Rotenburg?	~1415	0	0	0	0	0	0
I./JG 11	Fw 190A	Rotenburg	17	1245	Wiesbaden	~1445	1 P-51	5	1	2	0	1
III./JG 11	Fw 190A	Oldenburg	12	1245	Oldenburg?	~1415	0	2	0	0	0	0
Jagddivision 3:												
I./JG 1	Fw 190A	Lippspringe	24	1310	Frankfurt area	~1430	2 B-17	0	0	0	0	0
II./JG 1	Fw 190A	Störmede	10	1249	Frankfurt area	1410	1 B-17	0	0	0	0	0
III./JG 1	Bf 109G	Paderborn	20	1253	Frankfurt area	~1430	0	0	0	0	0	0
Abschfü Mittelrhein:												
II./JG 27	Bf 109G	Erbenheim	16	1246	Gießen	1355	0	4	0	0	0	2
II./JG 53	Bf 109G	Eschborn	10	1249	Eschborn	~1400	2 B-17	6	1	1	0	1
Luftflotte 3												
II. Jagdkorps												
Jagddivision 4:												
II./JG 26	Fw 190A	Cambrai-Sud		1209	Laon–Athies, Trier, Juvincourt	~1400	1 B-17, 1 P-47	2	1	1	0	1
III./JG 26	Bf 109G	Etain		1212	Etain, Speyerdorf	1350	5 B-17	4	0	0	0	1
Jagddivision 5:												
II./JG 2	Bf 109G	Creil		1209	Creil	~1400	0	0	2	0	0	1
III./JG 2	Fw 190A	Cormeilles		1209	Cormeilles	~1400	0	3	2	1	0	2
vs. withdrawing stream												
Luftflotte Reich												
I. Jagdkorps												
Jagddivision 1:												
I./JG 3	Bf 109G	Burg	4	1458	Burg	~1630	0	0	0	0	0	0
IV./JG 3	Bf 109G	Salzwedel	15	1610	Salzwedel	~1630	0	0	0	0	0	0
Jagddivision 3:												
Abschfü Mittelrhein:												
I./JG 1	Fw 190A	Erbenheim	5	1513	Lippspringe?	~1630	0	3	1	2	0	1
	Fw 190A	Erbenheim	1	1539	Lippspringe?	~1630	0	0	0	0	0	0
II./JG 1	Fw 190A	Erbenheim		1545	Erbenheim	1614	1 B-17	2	0	0	0	1
III./JG 1	Bf 109G	Erbenheim	2	1539	Paderborn?	~1630	0	2	2	2	0	0
	Bf 109G	Eschborn	1	1525	Paderborn?	~1630	0	1	0	0	0	1
II./JG 3	Bf 109G	Eschborn		1700	Eschborn	1740	0	0	0	0	0	0

Luftwaffe defensive activity vs. 8th Air Force – 13 April 1944 Continued

Unit	Type	Gruppe up			Gruppe down		Claims	Losses				
		Base	No	Time	Base	Time		Dest	Dam	KIA	MIA	WIA
II./JG 27	Bf 109G	Erbenheim	2	1502	Erbenheim	~1630	0	0	0	0	0	0
	Bf 109G	Erbenheim	3	1515	Erbenheim	~1630	0	0	0	0	0	0
	Bf 109G	Erbenheim	9	1606	Erbenheim	1645	0	0	0	0	0	0
II./JG 53	Bf 109G	Eschborn	11	1510	Eschborn	~1630	1 B-17	0	0	0	0	0
Jagddivision 7:												
III./JG 3	Bf 109G	Tulln (A)	8	1355	Leipheim, Bad Wörishofen	~1600	1 B-17	0	0	0	0	0
I./JG 301	Bf 109G	Neubiberg	11	1352	Neubiberg	~1530	1 P-51	0	0	0	0	0
Jafü Ostmark:												
Stab/JG 27	Bf 109G	Fels am Wagram	4	1420	Fels am Wagram	~1600	0	0	0	0	0	0
I./JG 27	Bf 109G	Fels am Wagram	10	1420	Fels am Wagram	~1600	0	1	0	0	0	1
IV./JG 27	Bf 109G	Graz	6	1325	Graz	~1600	0	0	0	0	0	0
II./ZG 1	Bf 110G	Wels		~1430	Wels	~1630	1 B-24	0	0	0	0	0
Luftflotte 3												
II. Jagdkorps												
Jagddivision 4:												
Stab/JG 26	Fw 190A	Lille–Nord		1600	Lille–Nord	1720	1 B-17	0	0	0	0	0
4./JG 26	Fw 190A	Wevelghem		~1600	Wevelghem	~1720	0	0	1	0	0	0
II./JG 26	Fw 190A	Trier		~1530	Cambrai–Sud	~1630	0	0	0	0	0	0
III./JG 26	Bf 109G	Etain		~1500	Etain	~1630	1 P-38	0	0	0	0	0
Jagddivision 5:												
II./JG 2	Bf 109G	Creil		1547	Creil	~1630	0	0	0	0	0	0
III./JG 2	Fw 190A	Cormeilles		1547	Cormeilles	~1630	1 B-17	0	0	0	0	0

*412 total sorties by I. JK vs. incoming + withdrawing streams

18 April

8th Air Force Mission #306: 733 of 776 HBs (all BDs) bomb aviation targets in Berlin area, TOT 1423-44 – lose 19-0-204, claim 13-5-6. Escort of 3 P-38 FGs, 6 P-47 FGs, 6 P-51 FGs (634 sorties) claims 4-0-1, loses 5-3-28.

The 8th AF bombed a number of targets in the Berlin area in poor weather that kept most of the Luftwaffe on the ground. Of the 96 single-engine fighters to sortie, 73 made contact. These were in the Jagddivision 1 Gefechtsverband, formed around JG 3 and commanded by its Kommodore, Major Friedrich-Karl Müller. Müller found a hole in the escort and led a spectacular attack on one 3rd BD combat wing. One Gruppe, IV./JG 3, was credited with 14 B-17s and was rewarded by being designated as the first Sturmgruppe. Müller was commended in the day's war communiqué. The Americans wrote off 19 bombers and eight escorts; the Luftwaffe lost eight KIA, one WIA and nine fighters.

19 April

8th Air Force Mission #308: 744 of 772 HBs (all BDs) bomb Kassel aviation targets, airfields C Germany – claim 1-0-4, lose 5-1-150. Escort of 3 P-38 FGs, 9 P-47 FGs, 6 P-51 FGs (697 sorties) claims 16-1-2, loses 2-0-9.

A large 8th AF raid on Kassel showed clearly the trend that the air war was taking. Bad weather kept Jagddivision 7 down, and three of the principal north German Gruppen were off operations – II./JG 11 and III./JG 11 for rebuilding, and III./JG 54 for re-equipment. The I. Jagdkorps scrambled 208 single-engine fighters, but only 96 were credited with combat sorties. Many of the rest were deterred from approaching the bomber stream by a strong, unbroken escort screen, and the formations that did come close were quickly broken up by the American fighters. The Americans wrote off only six bombers and two escorts. The Luftwaffe lost 14 KIA, six WIA and 24 fighters.

Luftwaffe defensive activity – 15 April 1944

Unit	Type	Gruppe up			Gruppe down		Claims	Losses				
		Base	No	Time	Base	Time		Dest	Dam	KIA	MIA	WIA
Luftflotte Reich												
I. Jagdkorps			133									
Jagddivision 1:												
I./JG 3	Bf 109G	Burg	12	1027	Burg	~1130	n/c	0	0	0	0	0
II./JG 3	Bf 109G	Gardelegen	14	1326	Gardelegen	~1430	n/c	0	0	0	0	0
IV./JG 3	Bf 109G	Salzwedel	18	1320	Salzwedel	~1430	n/c	0	0	0	0	0
I./JG 302	Bf 109G	Jüterbog	7	1355	Jüterbog	~1430	n/c	0	0	0	0	0
II./JG 302	Bf 109G	Ludwigslust	8	1330	Ludwigslust	~1430	n/c	0	0	0	0	0
NJGr 10	Fw 190A	Werneuchen	5	1342	Werneuchen	~1430	n/c	0	0	0	0	0
Sturmstaffel 1	Fw 190A	Salzwedel		1320	Salzwedel	~1430	0	1	0	0	0	0
Jagddivision 2:												
Stab/JG 11	Fw 190A	Oldenburg	2	1310	Oldenburg	~1430	0	1	0	1	0	0
I./JG 11	Fw 190A	Rotenburg	9	1310	Rotenburg	~1430	2 P-38, 1 P-47*	5	1	2	0	1
	Fw 190A	Rotenburg	10	1350	Rotenburg	~1430	0	0	0	0	0	0
III./JG 11	Fw 190A	Oldenburg	9	1310	Oldenburg	~1430	1 P-38**	8	0	2	0	1
Jagddivision 3:												
I./JG 1	Fw 190A	Lippspringe	6	1414	Lippspringe	1504	a/f protection	0	0	0	0	0
II./JG 1	Fw 190A	Störmede	16	1330	Störmede	1507	n/c	0	0	0	0	0
III./JG 1	Bf 109G	Paderborn	6	1405	Paderborn	~1500	n/c	0	0	0	0	0
Abschfü Mittelrhein:												
II./JG 27	Bf 109G	Erbenheim		1335	Erbenheim	1445	n/c	0	0	0	0	0
Jagddivision 7:												
III./JG 3	Bf 109G	Bad Wörishofen		1040	Bad Wörishofen	1050	n/c	0	0	0	0	0

*I./JG 11: + 2 P-38, 1 P-47 claims undocumented   **III./JG 11: + 6 P-38 claims undocumented

22 April

8th Air Force Mission #311: 779 of 803 HBs (all BDs) bomb Hamm rail yards, TOT 1849-1938 – lose 15-15-197, claim 20-6-8. Escort of 3 P-38 FGs, 10 P-47 FGs, 6 P-51 FGs (859 sorties) claims 34-2-9, loses 13-1-22.

Weather forced the 8th AF to delay its planned raid on Hamm until late evening. The commanders of the German defence correctly deduced the target area and concentrated their forces, but were unable to make much headway against the preliminary Allied fighter sweeps and close escort. III./JG 1 was hit extremely hard, losing a dozen Bf 109s and seven pilots. The only noteworthy success for I. Jagdkorps was Major Heinz Bär's 200th victory claim, which made him a hero to the Luftwaffe and the news media only a few months after he had narrowly escaped courtmartial for insubordination.

II. Jagdkorps had been reduced to three Gruppen – I./JG 2 was in Italy, II./JG 26 was resting in southern France, and III./JG 26 had been sent to Neubiberg to reinforce the Munich area for Hitler's birthday – and violated its usual policy by scrambling them early against the sweeps. This early mission downed two 9th AF P-47s and one RAF Mustang for the loss of two fighters and pilots; it was a statistical success, but another loss in the war of attrition.

The day ended with a major air victory for the Luftwaffe, albeit for IX. Fliegerkorps of the bomber arm rather than the RLV force. II./KG 51 specialised in Ju 88 hit-and-run raids on England by night. It contained one Staffel of Me 410s to fend off RAF night fighters. When it became apparent that the B-24s of the 2nd AD would not reach England until after dark, this Staffel was authorised to follow the B-24s back to their bases and attack them as they landed. The number of B-24s shot down or destroyed after landing is estimated to be 14, for the loss of two Me 410s and their crews. The 8th AF drew the proper lesson and never again scheduled such a late mission.

Luftwaffe defensive activity – 18 April 1944

Unit	Type	Gruppe up			Gruppe down		Claims	Losses				
		Base	No	Time	Base	Time		Dest	Dam	KIA	MIA	WIA
Luftflotte Reich												
I. Jagdkorps			144									
Jagddivision 1:												
Stab//JG 3	Bf 109G	Salzwedel		~1320	Salzwedel	~1500	3 B-17	0	0	0	0	0
I./JG 3	Bf 109G	Burg		1315	Burg, Schwerin	~1500	1 B-17, 1 P-38, 1 P-51	2	2	2	0	0
II./JG 3	Bf 109G	Gardelegen		1317	Gardelegen	1510	2 B-17	3	1	3	0	0
IV.(Sturm)/JG 3	Bf 109G	Salzwedel		1320	Salzwedel	1515	13 B-17, 1 B-17 HSS	1	0	1	0	0
II./JG 302	Bf 109G	Ludwigslust		~1315	Ludwigslust	~1500	1 B-17	0	0	0	0	0
Sturmstaffel 1	Fw 190A	Salzwedel	9	1320	Helmstedt	1505	2 B-17, 1 P-51	1	0	0	0	0
II./ZG 26	Me 410A	Königsberg–Neumark		1402	Königsberg–Neumark	1614	0	1	0	2	0	0
III./ZG 26	Bf 110G	Königsberg–Neumark	13	~1400	Königsberg–Neumark	~1600	n/c	0	0	0	0	0
Jagddivision 2:												
I./JG 11	Fw 190A	Rotenburg		~1530	Rotenburg	~1630	1 B-24	0	0	0	0	0
Jagddivision 3:												
Abschfü Mittelrhein:												
II./JG 1	Fw 190A	Erbenheim	24	1251	Erbenheim	~1400	n/c	1	0	0	0	1
Jagddivision 7:												
III./JG 3	Bf 109G	Bad Wörishofen		1440	Bad Wörishofen	1525	n/c	0	0	0	0	0
III./JG 26	Bf 109G	Neubiberg		1450	Neubiberg	1535	n/c	0	0	0	0	0

Luftwaffe defensive activity – 19 April 1944

Unit	Type	Gruppe up			Gruppe down		Claims	Losses				
		Base	No	Time	Base	Time		Dest	Dam	KIA	MIA	WIA
Luftflotte Reich												
I. Jagdkorps			220									
Jagddivision 1:												
Stab//JG 3	Bf 109G	Salzwedel		~0930	Salzwedel	~1115	0	0	0	0	0	0
I./JG 3	Bf 109G	Burg		0930	Burg	~1115	1 P-51	2	0	0	0	2
II./JG 3	Bf 109G	Gardelegen		0935	Gardelegen	1115	1 B-17, 2 P-51	0	0	0	0	0
IV.(Sturm)/JG 3	Bf 109G	Salzwedel		0930	Brunswick, Magdeburg–Ost	1130	2 B-17	2	0	1	0	0
I./JG 302	Bf 109G	Jüterbog		~0930	Jüterbog	~1115	0	2	0	1	0	0
II./JG 302	Bf 109G	Ludwigslust		~0930	Ludwigslust	~1115	0	2	0	2	0	0
Sturmstaffel 1	Fw 190A	Salzwedel		0944	Berlin–Staaken	1135	n/c	0	0	0	0	0
II./ZG 26	Me 410A	Königsberg–Neumark		0955	Königsberg–Neumark	1150	n/c	0	0	0	0	0
Jagddivision 2:												
I./JG 11	Fw 190A	Rotenburg		~0900	Rotenburg	~1030	0	1	0	0	0	0
Jagddivision 3:												
I./JG 1	Fw 190A	Lippspringe		0910	Göttingen	1055	0	5	1	3	0	2
II./JG 1	Fw 190A	Störmede	29	0905	Störmede	~1045	1 B-17	1	3	1	0	0
III./JG 1	Bf 109G	Paderborn		0915	Paderborn	~1045	1 P-51	0	0	0	0	0
II./JG 27	Bf 109G	Lippspringe	12	0900	Lippspringe?	~1045	1 B-17	6	0	4	0	2
II./JG 53	Bf 109G	Paderborn	12	0900	Paderborn?	~1045	3 B-17	2	0	1	0	0
II./JG 2	Bf 109G	?		~0900	?	~1045	0	1	0	1	0	0

This Luftwaffe success thus proved to be unique. The Americans lost 15 bombers over Europe and another 15 to crashes or crash-landings in the UK, most attributable to the handful of Me 410s. Escort losses totalled one RAF and 14 USAAF fighters. The RLV force had scrambled 243 single-engine fighters, of which 182 were credited with combat sorties, and lost 18 KIA, seven WIA and 30 aircraft. The IX. Fliegerkorps raiders lost two KIA, two MIA and two Me 410s.

Major Günther Specht, the II./JG 11 Kommandeur, shows off his new Bf 109G 'AS', with a DB 605AS high-altitude engine, at Wunstorf in April. His Gruppe was the first to receive the type. Recognition points are the small air intake in front of the cockpit and a silica gel capsule visible inside the corner of the first canopy side panel. Specht's personal marking, the 'flying pencil', is clearly visible. *(Bundesarchiv 676-7975A-37)*

COMBAT REPORT[3]
22 April 1944

One Liberator destroyed from 6,000 metres at 2008 hours, PQ JQ, 8–9 km N of Ahlen
[Bär's victim was Lt. Spaven's 458th Bomb Group B-24: DC]

I took off at 1953 hours in Fw 190A-7 'Red 23' (two MG 151/20, two MG 131) with Obfw. Schuhmacher against a lone Liberator flying northwest of the airfield, dropping smoke canisters as target markers. I assumed that the aircraft was a pathfinder. The four engines of the Liberator were running smoothly. I began my attack from behind and fired from 400 to 100 metres, at which the Liberator immediately jettisoned its bombs. Four crewmen bailed out shortly thereafter. Bright flames and light-coloured smoke poured from the fuselage. The Liberator dove to the left and broke up in the air. The wreckage fell to the ground north of Ahlen. The victory was witnessed by Obfw. Schuhmacher in the air and by II./JG 1 personnel on the ground.

Major Heinz Bär, Gruppenkommandeur
Stab II./JG 1

---

23 April

15th Air Force: 171 of 222 B-17s bomb Wiener Neustadt a/i, TOT 1426-40 – lose 2, claim 9-1-0. 170 of 219 B-24s bomb Bad Vöslau a/f, TOT 1414-47 – lose 5, claim 16-8-8. 140 of 159 B-24s bomb Schwechat a/i, TOT 1444-50 – lose 3, claim 0. 31 of 38 B-24s bomb Wiener Neustadt a/f, TOT 1439 – lose 2, claim 1-0-2. Escort of 202 P-38s (3 FGs), 52 P-47s (1 FG), 41 P-51s (1 FG) claims 26-6-16, loses 3 P-38s, 4 P-51s.

The 15th AF flew a maximum-strength mission to four

Luftwaffe defensive activity – 22 April 1944

Unit	Type	Gruppe up			Gruppe down		Claims	Losses				
		Base	No	Time	Base	Time		Dest	Dam	KIA	MIA	WIA
Luftflotte Reich												
I. Jagdkorps			193									
Jagddivision 1:												
Stab/JG 3	Bf 109G	Salzwedel		1820	Salzwedel	2030	3 B-24	0	0	0	0	0
I./JG 3	Bf 109G	Burg	23	1830	Burg	~2000	3 P-38	3	0	1	0	1
II./JG 3	Bf 109G	Sachau	14	1830	Sachau	2030	0	0	0	0	0	0
IV.(Sturm)/JG 3	Bf 109G	Salzwedel	27	1830	Salzwedel, Lippstadt, Kassel–Rothwesten	2030	2 B-24	1	0	0	0	0
Sturmstaffel 1	Fw 190A	Salzwedel	8	1837	Salzwedel	2015	0	0	0	0	0	0
Jagddivision 2:												
Stab/JG 11	Bf 109G	Rotenburg	3	1745	Rotenburg	~1930	n/c	0	0	0	0	0
I./JG 11	Fw 90A	Rotenburg	24	1745	Rotenburg	~1930	n/c	0	0	0	0	0
II./NJG 3	Ju 88C	Stade		?	Stade	?	shadower	1	0	3	0	0
LBeob St 2	Ju 88C	Stade		?	Stade	?	shadower	1	0	2	0	0
Jagddivision 3:												
I./JG 1	Fw 190A	Lippspringe	24	1751	Gütersloh, Dortmund	2003	2 B-17, 1 P-47	4	3	1	0	2
II./JG 1	Fw 190A	Störmede	24	1751	Störmede	1915	2 B-17, 2 P-47	4	1	1	0	1
	Fw 190A	Störmede	2	1953	Störmede	2020	1 B-24	0	0	0	0	0
III./JG 1	Bf 109G	Paderborn	25	1705	Paderborn	~1900	1 P-51	12	3	7	0	2
Abschfü Mittelrhein:												
II./JG 27	Bf 109G	Erbenheim	16	1852	Erbenheim	1950	0	1	1	0	0	1
II./JG 53	Bf 109G	Eschborn	8	1853	Eschborn	~2000	0	0	0	0	0	0
Luftflotte 3			50									
IX. Fliegerkorps:												
II./KG 51	Me 410A	Soesterberg		2055	Soesterberg	2400	1 B-17, 7 B-24	2	0	2	2	0
II. Jagdkorps												
Jagddivision 4:												
I./JG 26	Fw 190A	Florennes, Denain		1708	Bonn–Hangelar, Florennes	1903	2 P-47	0	2	0	0	0
2nd sorties	Fw 190A	Florennes		~2000	Florennes	~2115	1 B-24	0	0	0	0	0
4./JG 26	Fw 190A	Wevelghem		1708	Bonn–Hangelar, Florennes	~1900	0	0	0	0	0	0
2nd sorties	Fw 190A	Florennes		~2000	Wevelghem	~2115	0	1	0	1	0	0
Jagddivision 5:												
II./JG 2	Bf 109G	Creil	14	~1700	Metz	~1830	1 Mustang	2	0	2	0	0
III./JG 2	Fw 190A	Cormeilles		~1700	Metz	~1830	0	0	0	0	0	0

aviation targets in Austria. Jagddivision 7 and its subordinate Jafü in Austria, Hungary and Silesia scrambled 174 fighters in beautiful weather that allowed 169 to make contact. The Luftwaffe fighter units still in northern Italy attacked the incoming stream, and five Croatian Macchi MC 202s tackled the withdrawing B-24s. Results were mediocre, owing primarily to a newly strengthened escort. The first

15th AF P-51 group flew its first mission today; it claimed 15 Axis fighters for the loss of four Mustangs. The defences benefited from the presence of III./JG 26, which had been moved from the Channel coast to Munich for Hitler's birthday. It was highly experienced against Mustangs, having battled them for close to a year over its home territory, and claimed two, in addition to three bombers. The Americans lost

Axis defensive activity – 23 April 1944

Unit	Type	Gruppe up			Gruppe down		Claims	Losses				
		Base	No	Time	Base	Time		Dest	Dam	KIA	MIA	WIA
Luftflotte Reich												
I. Jagdkorps			174									
Jagddivision 7:												
III./JG 3	Bf 109G	Bad Wörishofen	24	1255	Wels	1440	0	1	2	0	0	1
III./JG 26	Bf 109G	Neubiberg	30	1305	Fels am Wagram, Wien–Seyring	1450	2 B-17, 1 B-24, 2 P-51	1	0	0	1	0
II./ZG 76	Bf 110G	Ansbach	20	1245	Ansbach	~1500	1 P-38, 1 P-51	3	1	4	0	1
ErprKdo 25	Bf 110G, Me 210	Augsburg?		1255	Augsburg?	1535	0	2	1	0	2	1
Jafü Ostmark:												
Stab/JG 27	Bf 109G	Fels am Wagram	4	1240	Fels am Wagram	1450	0	0	0	0	0	0
I./JG 27	Bf 109G	Fels am Wagram	31	1240	Fels am Wagram	1425	1 B-17, 2 B-24	2	0	2	0	0
IV./JG 27	Bf 109G	Graz	23	1242	Graz	~1430	0	3	2	2	0	1
VbdFhr Schule	Bf 109G	Fels am Wagram	—	1240	Fels am Wagram	1425	1 B-24	0	0	0	0	0
6./NJG 101	Do 217N	Parndorf		1340	Parndorf	1539	0	0	0	0	0	0
I./SG 152	Fw 190F	Prossnitz	14	1345	Prossnitz	~1530	1 B-24	1	0	1	0	0
JGr (Croatia)	MC 202	Lucko	5	~1330	Lucko	~1500	1 B-24	2	0	0	0	0
Abschfü Ungarn:												
III./JG 27	Bf 109G	Börgönd (H)	22	1230	Börgönd (H)	~1415	1 B-24, 2 P-51	1	0	1	0	0
Luftflotte 2												
Jafü Oberitalien:												
Stab/JG 77	Bf 109G	Povoletto		1230	Povoletto, Laibach	1340	0	0	0	0	0	0
I./JG 77	Bf 109G	Lavariano		1230	Lavariano, Laibach	1340	1 B-24	0	1	0	0	0

12 bombers to all causes and three P-38s in addition to the four P-51s. The Axis forces lost at least 13 KIA and MIA, four WIA and 16 fighters.

24 April – South German aviation industry (see map)

8th Air Force Mission #315: 268 of 281 1st BD B-17s bomb Landsberg a/f, Oberpfaffenhofen a/i, Erding a/f, TOT 1334-1402h – lose 27-0-112; 229 of 243 3rd BD B-17s bomb Friedrichshafen a/i, TOT 1316-20h – lose 9-0-119; 219 of 230 2nd BD B-24s bomb Gablingen, Leipheim a/fs, TOT 1343h – lose 4-1-26. Total losses include 14 interned in Switzerland. Total bomber claims 20-1-36. Escort of 3 P-38 FGs, 10 P-47 FGs, 6 P-51 FGs (867 sorties) claims 70-6-2, loses 17-1-30.

The 8th AF raided aviation targets in the Munich and Friedrichshafen areas. A 15th AF raid on Romania diverted no Reich defenders, and the I. Jagdkorps deduced the 8th AF target area and scrambled 318 single-engine and 34 twin-engine fighters, of which

247 and 26 made contact. The escort force of 19 groups was unusually strong, and the result was some exceptionally heavy air combat that lasted more than an hour. The defenders did very well, aided by the presence again today of III./JG 26, which claimed 17 B-17s, of which 10 were confirmed, and two P-51s, which were unconfirmed for lack of witnesses. The Gruppe sustained no losses. The Americans wrote off 41 bombers, including 14 which flew to Switzerland and internment, and 18 fighters. Losses to the RLV force were also very high: 43 KIA, 13 WIA and 66 aircraft.

25 April

8th Air Force Mission #317: 31 of 199 2nd BD B-24s bomb Mannheim rail yard – lose 5-0-26, claim 0. 263 of 355 1st BD + 3rd BD B-17s bomb French airfields – lose 2-0-62, claim 0. Escort of 3 P-38 FGs, 6 P-47 FGs, 6 P-51 FGs (719 sorties) claims 5-0-1, loses 2-2-6.

The 8th AF ordered a mission to Mannheim and several

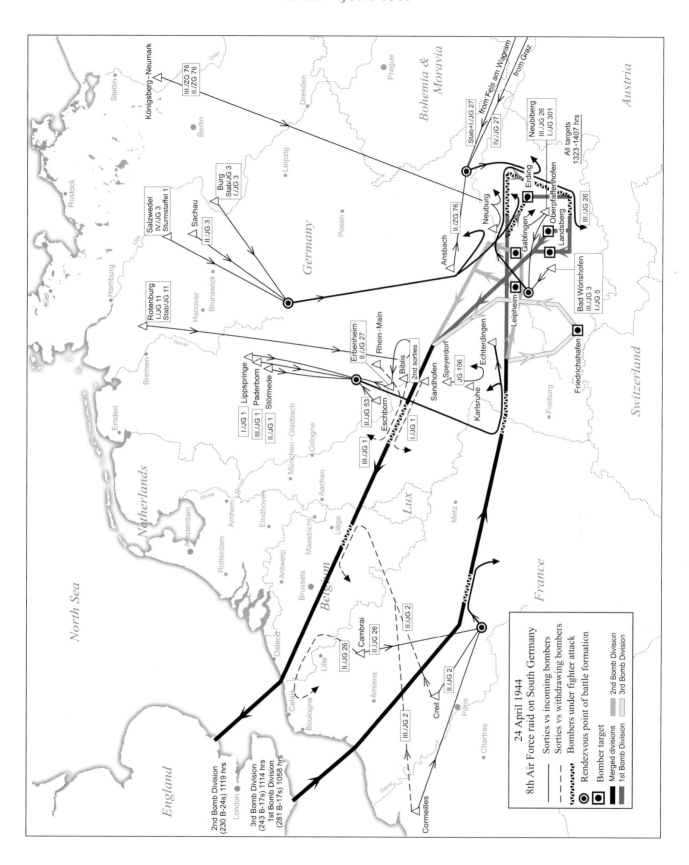

24 April 1944
8th Air Force raid on South Germany

Sorties vs incoming bombers
Sorties vs withdrawing bombers
Bombers under fighter attack
Rendezvous point of battle formation

Merged divisions   2nd Bomb Division
1st Bomb Division   3rd Bomb Division

Bomber target

2nd Bomb Division (230 B-24s) 1119 hrs
3rd Bomb Division (243 B-17s) 1114 hrs
1st Bomb Division (281 B-17s) 1058 hrs

All targets 1323–1407 hrs

Luftwaffe defensive activity – 24 April 1944

Unit	Type	Gruppe up			Gruppe down		Claims	Losses (—: included with 1st sortie)				
		Base	No	Time	Base	Time		Dest	Dam	KIA	MIA	WIA
vs. incoming stream												
Luftflotte Reich												
I. Jagdkorps			*350									
Jagddivision 1:												
Stab/JG 3	Bf 109G	Burg	4	1205	Burg?	~1400	3 B-17	0	0	0	0	0
I./JG 3	Bf 109G	Burg	16	1205	Burg?	~1400	1 B-17, 1 P-51	5	0	4	0	0
II./JG 3	Bf 109G	Sachau	16	1202	Sachau?	~1400	1 B-17, 1 B-17 HSS	4	1	2	0	0
IV.(Sturm)/JG 3	Bf 109G	Salzwedel	29	1158	Bad Wörishofen	1420	6 B-17, 3 B-17 HSS**	3	0	2	0	0
II./ZG 26	Bf 110G	Königsberg–Neumark	27	1207	Neuburg	~1430	0	0	1	0	0	0
III./ZG 26	Bf 110G	Königsberg–Neumark	14	1207	München–Riem, Neuburg, Aibling	~1430	1 P-51***	4	6	8	0	0
Sturmstaffel 1	Fw 190A	Salzwedel	9	1158	Neuburg/Donau	1401	0	1	0	0	0	1
Jagddivision 2:												
Stab/JG 11	Bf 109G	Rotenburg	4	1240	Rotenburg	~1400	0	0	2	0	0	0
I./JG 11	Fw 190A	Rotenburg	28	1240	Rotenburg	~1400	2 P-51	11	5	6	0	1
10./JG 11	Fw 190A	Rotenburg		1240	Rotenburg	~1400	0	0	0	0	0	0
Jagddivision 3:												
I./JG 1	Fw 190A	Lippspringe	20	1138	Mannheim–Sandhofen, Karlsruhe	1420	0	0	0	0	0	0
II./JG 1	Fw 190A	Störmede	15	1135	Echterdingen	~1415	1 B-17	2	1	0	0	2
III./JG 1	Bf 109G	Paderborn	18	1142	Rhein–Main	~1415	0	0	1	0	0	0
Abschfü Mittelrhein:												
II./JG 27	Bf 109G	Erbenheim	8	1157	various	~1345	0	4	0	3	0	0
II./JG 53	Bf 109G	Eschborn	8	1158	various	~1345	0	2	0	0	0	0
Jagddivision 7:												
III./JG 3	Bf 109G	Bad Wörishofen	20	1220	München–Riem	1355	2 B-17, 1 P-51****	7	3	4	0	2
I./JG 5	Bf 109G	Bad Wörishofen	12	1310	München–Riem	~1430	1 B-17	1	0	1	0	0
III./JG 26	Bf 109G	Neubiberg		1240	Neubiberg	~1420	7 B-17*****	0	0	0	0	0
I./JG 301	Bf 109G	Neubiberg	12	1310	München–Riem	1355	0	7	1	3	0	3
JG 106	Bf 109G	Lachen–Speyerdorf	5	1212	Biblis	~1330	0	1	3	1	0	1
II./ZG 76	Bf 110G	Ansbach	7	1305	Ansbach	~1500	0	0	0	0	0	0
Jafü Ostmark:												
Stab/JG 27	Bf 109G	Fels am Wagram	4	1230	Pocking	1435	0	0	0	0	0	0
I./JG 27	Bf 109G	Fels am Wagram	19	1230	Pocking	1435	0	4	0	2	0	1
IV./JG 27	Bf 109G	Graz	16	1225	Graz	~1430	2 B-17, 3 P-51	4	0	3	0	0
VbdFhr Schule	Bf 109G	Fels am Wagram		1230	Pocking	1435	1 B-17 HSS	4	0	3	0	1
Luftflotte 3												
II. Jagdkorps												
Jagddivision 4:												
II./JG 26	Fw 190A	Cambrai		1106	Cambrai	1230	0	0	0	0	0	0
Jagddivision 5:												
II./JG 2	Bf 109G	Creil		1106	Creil	1230	0	2	0	1	0	1
III./JG 2	Fw 190A	Cormeilles		1106	Cormeilles	1230	0	0	0	0	0	0

Luftwaffe defensive activity – 24 April 1944 Continued

Unit	Type	Gruppe up			Gruppe down		Claims	Losses (—: included with 1st sortie)				
		Base	No	Time	Base	Time		Dest	Dam	KIA	MIA	WIA
vs. withdrawing sream:												
Luftflotte Reich												
I. Jagdkorps												
Jagddivision 2:												
I./JG 11	Fw 190A	Rotenburg		~1430	Rotenburg	~1600	1 P-47	0	0	0	0	0
Jagddivision 3:												
I./JG 1	Fw 190A	Mannheim–Sandhofen	11	1425	Mannheim–Sandhofen	1555	1 B-17, 1 P-47	0	0	0	0	0
	Fw 190A	Langendiebach		1700	Lippspringe	1737	0	0	0	0	0	0
III./JG 1	Bf 109G	Rhein–Main	2	1440	Paderborn?	~1600	0	0	0	0	0	0
Abschfü MItteIrheiп:												
II./JG 27	Bf 109G	Göppingen	7	1445	Erbenheim?	~1615	1 B-17	0	0	0	0	0
	Bf 109G	Biblis	1	1457	Erbenheim?	~1630	0	0	0	0	0	0
II./JG 53	Bf 109G	Biblis	3	1454	Eschborn?	~1630	0	0	0	0	0	0
JG 106	Bf 109G	Biblis	4	1449	Biblis	~1630	0	—	—	—	—	—
Luftflotte 3												
II. Jagdkorps												
Jagddivision 4:												
II./JG 26	Fw 190A	Cambrai		~1500	Cambrai	~1630	0	0	0	0	0	0
Jagddivision 5:												
II./JG 2	Bf 109G	Creil		~1500	Creil	~1630	1 B-17, 1 B-24	—	—	—	—	—
III./JG 2	Fw 190A	Cormeilles		~1630	Cormeilles	~1800	0	0	0	0	0	0

*350 total I. JK sorties vs. incoming + withdrawing streams **III./JG 3: + 3 B-17, 6 B-17 HSS claims unconfirmed (unwitnessed) ***III./ZG 26: + 7 P-51 claims undocumented ****IV./JG 3: + 1 B-17, 3 B-17 HSS claims unconfirmed (unwitnessed) *****III./JG 26: + 7 B-17, 2 P-51 claims unconfirmed (unwitnessed)

The Sturmstaffel 1 pilots disperse after posing for a unit picture on 29 April, shortly before the unit was disbanded. According to Oskar Bösch (far right), only four of the 15 men in the group photo survived the war. *(Mombeek)*

Uffz. Maximowitz returns from a Sturmstaffel mission after a close call, probably on 29 April. A shell has penetrated the fuselage decking above the tactical number 'White 10'; another has fragmented the 'Scheuklappe' armoured canopy glass, which probably saved his life. *(Smith)*

airfields in France in bad weather. The II. Jagdkorps scrambled 33 fighters from II./JG 26, which had returned from its rest in southern France, and the theatre's two JG 2 Gruppen; 30 made contact with the enemy. III./JG 2 encountered a wing of Spitfires and apparently downed two and forced a third to crash-land, although no claims have survived. The Spitfire pilots claimed six Fw 190s, but German records clearly indicate that only two went down; one pilot survived. II./JG 26 and II./JG 2 reached the B-24s, and the former unit filed one claim, which was not confirmed, although it matches a known crash. The three Gruppen lost two KIA, one WIA and four fighters. As no II. Jagdkorps mission times are available, the mission list is somewhat tentative.

26 April

8th Air Force Mission #319: 238 2nd BD B-24s target Paderborn, 0 bomb – lose 0-0-18, claim 0. 344 of 351 1st BD + 3rd BD B-17s bomb Brunswick – lose 0-2-121, claim 0. Escort of 2 P-38 FGs, 7 P-47 FGs, 4 P-51 FGs (554 sorties) claims 0, loses 5-1-10.

An 8th AF mission to the Brunswick area found a solid cloud deck. The B-17s of the 1st and 3rd BDs bombed blind on the signals of their pathfinders; the B-24s of the 2nd BD, which still had no pathfinders, brought their bombs back to England. Jagddivision 1 scrambled 97 fighters to defend Berlin and their own airfields; after patrolling for an hour, they were ordered to land. This they did safely, a notable accomplishment given the poor blind flying skills of most Luftwaffe fighter pilots.

27 April

8th Air Force Mission #322: 476 of 596 HBs (all BDs) bomb V-weapon sites in Calais and Cherbourg areas – lose 4-2-252, claim 0. Escort of 1 P-38 FG, 5 P-47 FGs, 1 P-51 FG (357 sorties) claims 0, loses 2-0-9.

8th Air Force Mission #323: 471 of 486 HBs (all BDs) bomb 6 airfields and rail yards in western occupied zone – lose 4-4-84, claim 0. Escort of 3 P-38 FGs, 6 P-47 FGs, 4 P-51 FGs (543 sorties) claims 3-0-1, loses 4-0-3.

The 8th AF turned its attention to tactical targets: V-weapon sites on the coast and various railroad centres in the interior of France. The II. Jagdkorps scrambled its four available Jagdgruppen, plus the JG 2 Stabsschwarm – I./JG 26 was en route to southern France for a rest, but III./JG 26 returned from Munich just in time for this mission. None of the German fighters reached the bombers. All were engaged by P-47s, which killed Major Kurt Ubben, the JG 2 Kommodore, and two other pilots, injured two and shot down five Bf 109s and Fw 190s, for the loss of three Thunderbolts.

29 April

8th Air Force Mission #327: 628 of 679 HBs (all BDs) bomb Berlin, TOT 1116-54 – lose 63-2-432, claim 73-26-34. Escort of 3 P-38 FGs, 8 P-47 FGs, 6 P-51 FGs (814 sorties) claims 16-6-9, loses 13-1-30.

The 8th AF scheduled a full-strength mission to the centre of Berlin. Weather conditions and a shortage of pathfinder aircraft forced the three bomb divisions to fly the mission in trail; the 12 combat wings took 38 minutes to cross the city. The I. Jagdkorps determined the target early from the usual clues of time, direction and size of the stream and managed one of the best defensive efforts in some time. The standard RLV tactics worked well. Although the 41 twin-engine fighters avoided the bombers and their escorts as ordered, 271 of the 336 Bf 109s and Fw 190s that took off made contact. The Gefechtsverbände of the three north German Jagddivisionen all made effective attacks on the incoming stream. Eight of the Sturmstaffel's B-17 claims were confirmed after its last independent mission before being absorbed in the new Sturmgruppe, IV.(Sturm)/JG 3 – the Staffel was renamed 11.(Sturm)/JG 3 on 8 May. The escorts spent much of their time chasing back and forth along the bomber stream seeking the elusive German fighters.

Luftwaffe defensive activity – 25 April 1944

Unit	Type	Gruppe up			Gruppe down		Claims	Losses				
		Base	No	Time	Base	Time		Dest	Dam	KIA	MIA	WIA
Luftflotte 3												
II. Jagdkorps			33									
Jagddivision 4:												
II./JG 26	Fw 190A	Cambrai		?	Cambrai	?	1 B-24	2	0	1	0	0
Jagddivision 5:												
II./JG 2	Bf 109G	Creil		?	Creil	?	0	1	0	1	0	0
III./JG 2	Fw 190A	Cormeilles		?	Cormeilles	?	0	1	0	0	0	1

Luftwaffe defensive activity – 26 April 1944

Unit	Type	Gruppe up			Gruppe down		Claims	Losses				
		Base	No	Time	Base	Time		Dest	Dam	KIA	MIA	WIA
Luftflotte Reich												
I. Jagdkorps			97									
Jagddivision 1:												
I./JG 3	Bf 109G	Burg	12	0846	Burg	~1000	a/f protection	0	0	0	0	0
II./JG 3	Bf 109G	Sachau	15	0848	Sachau	~1000	a/f protection	0	0	0	0	0
IV.(Sturm)/JG 3	Bf 109G	Salzwedel	19	0851	Salzwedel	~1000	a/f protection	0	0	0	0	0
I./JG 302	Bf 109G	Jüterbog		~0845	Jüterbog	~1000	0	0	0	0	0	0
II./JG 302	Bf 109G	Ludwigslust	9	0847	Ludwigslust	~1000	0	0	0	0	0	0
Sturmstaffel 1	Fw 190A	Salzwedel	19	0851	Salzwedel	~1000	a/f protection	0	0	0	0	0
Jagddivision 3:												
Abschfü Mittelrhein:												
II./JG 27	Bf 109G	Erbenheim	9	0832	Erbenheim	~1000	0	0	0	0	0	0
II./JG 53	Bf 109G	Eschborn	10	0833	Eschborn	~1000	0	0	0	0	0	0

Luftwaffe defensive activity – 27 April 1944

Unit	Type	Gruppe up			Gruppe down		Claims	Losses				
		Base	No	Time	Base	Time		Dest	Dam	KIA	MIA	WIA
Luftflotte 3												
II. Jagdkorps												
Jagddivision 4:												
II./JG 26	Fw 190A	Cambrai		~1630	Laoni	~1800	2 P-47	0	1	0	0	0
2nd sorties	Fw 190A	Laon		~1830	Cambrai	~1930	0	1	0	1	0	0
III./JG 26	Bf 109G	Etain		1639	Laon?	1723	0	2	0	1	0	0
2nd sorties	Bf 109G	Laon?		~1900	Etain	~2100	0	0	1	0	0	1
Jagddivision 5:												
Stab/JG 2	Fw 190A	Cormeilles		~1630	Cormeilles	~1800	0	1	0	1	0	0
II./JG 2	Bf 109G	Creil		~1630	Creil	~1800	0	0	0	0	0	0
III./JG 2	Fw 190A	Cormeilles		~1630	Cormeilles	~1800	1 P-47	1	0	0	0	1

Luftwaffe defensive activity – 29 April 1944

Unit	Type	Gruppe up			Gruppe down		Claims	Losses (—: included with 1st sortie)				
		Base	No	Time	Base	Time		Dest	Dam	KIA	MIA	WIA
vs. incoming stream												
Luftflotte Reich												
I. Jagdkorps			275									
Jagddivision 1:												
Stab/JG 3	Bf 109G	Salzwedel	2	1010	Salzwedel	~1145	1 B-17	0	0	0	0	0
I./JG 3	Bf 109G	Burg	12	1000	Burg	~1145	2 B-17	1	2	1	0	1
II./JG 3	Bf 109G	Sachau	21	0952	Sachau	~1130	5 B-17	4	0	2	0	0
IV.(Sturm)/JG 3	Bf 109G	Salzwedel	25	1010	Salzwedel, Stendal	1150	4 B-17	3	0	1	0	0
I./JG 302	Bf 109G	Jüterbog	11	0956	Jüterbog	~1150	3 B-17, 2 P-51	1	0	1	0	0
II./JG 302	Bf 109G	Ludwigslust	8	1000	Ludwigslust	~1150	0	0	0	0	0	0
II./ZG 26	Me 410A	Königsberg–Neumark		1040	Königsberg–Neumark	1245	n/c	0	0	0	0	0
III./ZG 26	Bf 110G	Königsberg–Neumark	11	1035	Königsberg–Neumark	1255	n/c	0	0	0	0	0
Sturmstaffel 1	Fw 190A	Salzwedel	13	1010	Salzwedel	~1200	8 B-17	2	3	0	0	0
JaSta Erla	Bf 109G	Delitzsch		~1040	Delitzsch	~1230	1 B-17	0	0	0	0	0
LBeob St 1	?	Neuruppin		1045	Neuruppin	1237	1 B-17 (shadower)	0	0	0	0	0
Jagddivision 2:												
Stab/JG 11	Bf 109G	Rotenburg	3	1011	Rotenburg	~1200	0	0	0	0	0	0
I./JG 11	Fw 190A	Rotenburg	29	1011	Rotenburg	1200	12 B-24	4	3	1	0	1
II./JG 11	Bf 109G	Wunstorf	29	1010	Wunstorf	~1200	2 P-38, 1 P-51*	6	1	4	0	1
Jagddivision 3:												
I./JG 1	Fw 190A	Lippspringe	22	0948	Brunswick	1115	3 B-17	1	0	0	0	1
II./JG 1	Fw 190A	Störmede	25	0945	Störmede, Quedlinburg	1127	2 B-17, 2 B-24, 2 P-47	2	1	2	0	0
III./JG 1	Bf 109G	Paderborn	12	0947	Paderborn	~1115	0	1	0	0	0	0
Abschfü Mittelrhein:												
St/JGvbV	Bf 109G	Erbenheim	1	0930	Erbenheim	~1130	1 B-17	0	0	0	0	0
II./JG 27	Bf 109G	Erbenheim	10	0930	Erbenheim	~1130	1 B-17	0	0	0	0	0
II./JG 53	Bf 109G	Eschborn	11	0930	Eschborn, Völkenrode	1135	2 B-17	1	0	0	0	1
vs. withdrawing stream												
Luftflotte Reich												
I. Jagdkorps			75									
Jagddivision 1:												
I./JG 1	Fw 190A	Salzwedel?		~1245	Salzwedel?	~1345	2 B-24	0	0	0	0	0
II./JG 1	Fw 190A	Salzwedel	3	1245	Salzwedel?	~1345	1 B-17	0	0	0	0	0
III./JG 1	Bf 109G	Sachau	3	1350	Sachau	~1430	0	0	0	0	0	0
Stab/JG 3	Bf 109G	Burg		~1230	Burg	~1400	0	0	0	0	0	0
I./JG 3	Bf 109G	Burg	5	1237	Burg	~1400	1 B-24	0	0	0	0	0
II./JG 3	Bf 109G	Sachau	7	1232	Sachau	~1400	0	0	0	0	0	0
IV.(Sturm)/JG 3	Bf 109G	Salzwedel	12	1235	Salzwedel	1330	1 B-24**	—	—	—	—	—
Jagddivision 2:												
Stab/JG 11	Bf 109G	Rotenburg	3	1301	Rotenburg	~1430	1 B-24	0	0	0	0	0
I./JG 11	Fw 190A	Rotenburg	10	1301	Rotenburg	~1430	1 B-24 HSS	0	0	0	0	0
	Fw 190A	Wunstorf	4	1230	Wunstorf	~1430	0	0	0	0	0	0
II./JG 11	Bf 109G	Wunstorf	8	1250	Wunstorf	~1430	4 B-24	0	0	0	0	0
III./JG 11	Bf 109G	Oldenburg	5	1420	Oldenburg	1459	n/c	0	0	0	0	0
II./JG 53	Bf 109G	Wunstorf	7	1258	Wunstorf	~1430	0	0	0	0	0	0
III./NJG 3	Bf 110G	Stade		~1300	Stade	~1500	1 B-17	0	0	0	0	0

Luftwaffe defensive activity – 29 April 1944 Continued

Unit	Type	Gruppe up			Gruppe down		Claims	Losses (—: included with 1st sortie)				
		Base	No	Time	Base	Time		Dest	Dam	KIA	MIA	WIA
Jagddivision 3:												
Abschfü Mittelrhein:												
II./JG 27?	Bf 109G	Erbenheim		~1300	Erbenheim	~1430	0	0	0	0	0	0
II./JG 53	Bf 109G	Eschborn		~1300	Eschborn	~1430	0	0	0	0	0	0
Luftflotte 3												
II. Jagdkorps												
Jagddivision 4:												
II./JG 26	Fw 190A	Juvincourt		1300	Juvincourt	1424	2 B-17	0	0	0	0	0
Jagddivision 5:												
III./JG 2	Fw 190A	Cormeilles		~1330	Cormeilles	~1450	n/c	1	0	0	0	0

*II./JG 11: + 4 P-51 claims undocumented, 1 P-51 claim unconfirmed (unwitnessed) **IV./JG 3: + 3 B-17 HSS, 7 B-24 HSS claims unconfirmed (unwitnessed)

Luftwaffe defensive activity – 30 April 1944

Unit	Type	Gruppe up			Gruppe down		Claims	Losses				
		Base	No	Time	Base	Time		Dest	Dam	KIA	MIA	WIA
Luftflotte 3												
II. Jagdkorps												
Jagddivision 5:												
II./JG 2	Bf 109G	Creil		~1100	Creil	~1230	2 B-17	6	0	3	0	2
III./JG 2	Fw 190A	Cormeilles		~1100	Cormeilles	~1230	1 B-17, 1 P-51	10	0	6	0	2

Seventy-five fighters flew second sorties against the withdrawing bombers and scored heavily against loose formations and stragglers, while sustaining minimal losses. A total of 65 bombers and 14 escorts were written off; the I. Jagdkorps lost only 12 KIA, five WIA and 27 fighters.

PILOT'S ACCOUNT[4]
29 April 1944

At 0700 hours, we were alerted of a big assembly over Great Yarmouth. After breakfast our alert status tightened, and at 1010 hours, we scrambled from Salzwedel with IV./JG 3. At about 1030 hours, we met other units of JD 1 over Magdeburg at 6,000 metres and formed a large Gefechtsverband. Shortly before 1100 hours, we sighted a large mass of B-17s at our altitude, with many P-51s above. As our escorts engaged Mustangs and our other fighters tried to attack our Sturmstaffel head on, 190s approached the B-17s from the high rear, facing tremendous firepower from all sides. First we used our 13 mm [machine guns], then our 20 mm [cannon]

and, at the very last moment, our 30 mm [cannon], which made our ships deadly weapons. Our Staffel achieved 13 Abschüsse without a single total loss – only four aircraft had minor damage. It was a great day for us, but there were others that cost us deadly losses.

Lt. Richard Franz, Sturmstaffel 1

Armourers load W.Gr. 21 rockets on a Fw 190A-8/R6 of the JG 26 Geschwaderstab at Lille–Vendeville in May. *(Bundesarchiv 674-7772-28a)*

30 April

8th Air Force Mission #329: 284 of 295 HBs (all BDs) bomb 1 V-weapon site and 2 French airfields – lose 1-0-20, claim 3-0-6. Escort of 3 P-47 FGs, 6 P-47 FGs, 6 P-51 FGs (644 sorties) claims 18-1-5, loses 5-1-11.

The 8th AF rested from its exertions on the 29th with a low-strength raid to three French targets, which were defended by the II. Jagdkorps. Of the three Jagddivision 4 Jagdgruppen, I./JG 26 was returning from a brief rest in southern France and was not operational. II./JG 26 and III./JG 26 were kept on the ground, for unknown reasons. The defence was left to the two Jagddivision 5 Jagdgruppen, II./JG 2 and III./JG 2, which paid a heavy price for their valiant efforts. They were beset by the sweeping P-47s and P-51s and lost nine KIA, four WIA and 16 fighters. Few reached the bombers, which lost only one. The escorts lost six crashed or scrapped, most due to ground fire.

May 1944

The USSTAF continued its war of attrition against the Jagdwaffe and, at mid-month, added a new strategic target to its list, one that was truly critical to Germany's war machine: the petroleum industry. Few options were available to the defenders in the Reich. The basic tactical formation was the Gefechtsverband. After the weak Abschnittsführer Mittelrhein at Frankfurt gave up its two Jagdgruppen to Jagddivision 7, each I. Jagdkorps Jagddivision, plus Jafü Ostmark, controlled one Gefechtsverband, for a total of five. Each had at least four Jagdgruppen. One of these was a 'light' Gruppe of Bf 109s equipped with new high-altitude engines; its mission was to hold off the escorts to facilitate bomber attacks by the 'heavy' Gruppen of either Fw 190s or Bf 109s with gun pods.

For the RLV commanders, the pattern was clear. Their equipment, tactics and control procedures were sufficient to allow them to punish any bomber formation caught without escort. But bombers which were fully shielded by escorts were almost invulnerable to fighter attack. Although isolated bomber wings could always be savaged, bomber losses as a percentage of sorties flown continued to drop.

The RLV force desperately needed revolutionary new weapons and tactics. The Sturmgruppen would be effective bomber destroyers, but were not yet ready for service and were equipped with unwieldy, heavy fighters as vulnerable to the escorts as the twin-engine Zerstörer. They would thus require special escort by the light fighters. Two revolutionary new fighters that began arriving in the RLV force in small numbers showed more promise. The jet-propelled Me 262 and the rocket-powered Me 163 were available in large enough quantities to allow service evaluation. Service test squadrons Erprobungskommando 262 (ErprKdo 262) and ErprKdo 16 were established to introduce the Me 262 and Me 163 to combat and develop tactics for their use.

Fighter pilot losses in the Reich were now exceeding the supply from the training schools. Galland's recommendations for making up the shortfall included returning all fit fighter pilots serving in staff positions to operational posts, making 80–100 instructors available for combat duty and transferring some qualified night fighter pilots to day units. The experience level in the RLV force continued to drop. Bolstering the force quickly with competent commanders and pilots could only be done by taking complete Gruppen from the combat fronts. In mid-May, Galland and Schmid obtained Göring's permission to transfer II./JG 5 and IV./JG 54 from the Eastern Front to I. Jagdkorps. These were the last Gruppen to be obtained from the east; the few Jagdgruppen remaining in Italy would all be withdrawn to the Reich over the next few months.

On 25 May, the Luftwaffe High Command took an even more drastic step to reinforce I. Jagdkorps: 11 Jagdgruppen on the eastern and southern fronts were ordered to surrender one complete Jagdstaffel each – one-third of their combat strength – to the RLV force. Several of the transferred Staffeln, notably 2./JG 51, 12./JG 51, 4./JG 52 and 2./JG 54, provided much-needed boosts to their new Jagdgruppen. The others were quickly chewed up with no noticeable effect on the efficiency of their new host units.

The continuing struggle against ever-increasing odds cost the German home defences 276 fighter pilots and 487 fighters in May. The German fighter arm lost 25 per cent of its pilots and 50 per cent of its aircraft during the month. Despite strenuous efforts to build up the Jagdwaffe, the number of fighter pilots on duty had dropped from 2395 to 2283 since the beginning of the year. Losses so far in 1944 totalled 2262 pilots or about 100 per cent of average strength.

Luftwaffe defensive activity – 1 May 1944

Unit	Type	Gruppe up			Gruppe down		Claims	Losses				
		Base	No	Time	Base	Time		Dest	Dam	KIA	MIA	WIA
Luftflotte Reich												
I. Jagdkorps			97									
Jagddivision 2:												
I./JG 11	Fw 190A	Rotenburg		1710	Rotenburg	1752	n/c	0	0	0	0	0
II./JG 11	Bf 109G	Wunstorf	21	1717	Wunstorf	1828	n/c	0	0	0	0	0
Jagddivision 3:												
I./JG 1	Fw 190A	Lippspringe		~1710	Lippspringe	~1830	0	1	0	0	0	0
II./JG 1	Fw 190A	Störmede	24	1710	Rhein–Main	1905	0	0	0	0	0	0
	Fw 190A	Paderborn		1744	Erbenheim	1825	0	0	0	0	0	0
III./JG 1	Bf 109G	Paderborn		~1710	Rhein–Main	~1830	0	0	0	0	0	0
Abschfü Mittelrhein:												
Stab/JGzbV	Bf 109G	Erbenheim		~1700	Erbenheim	~1830	0	1	0	0	0	1
II./JG 27	Bf 109G	Erbenheim		~1700	Erbenheim	~1830	0	2	0	1	0	1
II./JG 53	Bf 109G	Eschborn		1700	Eschborn	1912	0	2	1	0	0	1
Luftflotte 3												
II. Jagdkorps			26									
Jagddivision 4:												
I./JG 26	Fw 190A	Denain		0849	Charleville	0942	0	0	0	0	0	0
	Fw 190A	Denain		~1700	Denain	~1830	0	0	0	0	0	0
II./JG 26	Fw 190A	Cambrai		~1700	Cambrai	~1830	0	1	0	0	0	1
III./JG 26	Bf 109G	Etain		0862	Etain	0925	0	0	0	0	0	0
	Bf 109G	Etain		1703	Hagenau	1920	1 P-51	0	0	0	0	0
Jagddivision 5:												
II./JG 2	Bf 109G	Creil		~1800	Creil	~1930	0	0	0	0	0	0
III./JG 2	Fw 190A	Cormeilles		~1800	Cormeilles	~1930	0	0	0	0	0	0

1 May

8th Air Force Mission #332: 130 of 531 HBs (all BDs) target 23 French V-weapon sites, bomb 3 – lose 0-3-54, claim 0. Escort of 3 P-47 FGs, 2 P-51 FGs (209 sorties) claims 0, loses 0.

8th Air Force Mission #333: 328 of 386 HBs (all BDs) bomb 7 rail yards in western occupied zone – lose 3-1-116, claim 0. Escort of 3 P-38 FGs, 6 P-47 FGs, 4 P-51 FGs (558 sorties) claims 6-0-3, loses 3-0-5.

The 8th AF attempted to raid a number of V-weapon sites in the morning, but most of the bombers had to abort because of bad weather. II. Jagdkorps scrambled small formations that did not make contact. Later in the day, individual bomb wings attacked a number of railroad yards in the occupied zone. The RLV force scrambled 123 defenders, but fewer than 50 were credited with combat sorties. Jagddivision 3 put up two combat formations. These could not penetrate the escorts sweeping to the east of the bombers: JG 1 apparently avoided combat,

while the small Jagdabschnitt Mittelrhein Verband lost one KIA, three WIA and five Bf 109s to the P-51s, without gaining any successes. II. Jagdkorps scrambled all five of its Jagdgruppen to seek out targets of opportunity. Most spent their time in the air evading the escort, but III./JG 26 claimed two P-51s (one confirmed) without loss. The Americans wrote off six bombers and three escorts to all causes.

4 May

8th Air Force Mission #328: 360 1st BD B-17s, 231 2nd BD B-24s target Berlin + Brunswick, recalled; 40 1st BD B-17s bomb Bergen airfield as t/o – total losses 0-1-15, claim 0. Escort of 1 P-38 FG, 3 P-47 FGs, 6 P-51 FGs (516 sorties) claims 9-2-6, loses 3-5-9.

Even at the height of spring, atmospheric conditions kept the 8th AF from carrying out many of its missions as planned. Today, heavy clouds at altitude forced the recall of a major mission to Berlin and Brunswick. 268

Luftwaffe defensive activity – 4 May 1944

Unit	Type	Gruppe up			Gruppe down		Claims	Losses				
		Base	No	Time	Base	Time		Dest	Dam	KIA	MIA	WIA
Luftflotte Reich												
I. Jagdkorps			197									
Jagddivision 1:												
I./JG 3	Bf 109G	Burg		~0945	Burg	~1130	n/c	1	0	1	0	0
II./JG 3	Bf 109G	Sachau		~0945	Sachau	~1130	n/c	1	0	0	0	0
IV.(Sturm)/JG 3	Bf 109G	Salzwedel		0946	Salzwedel	1200	0	0	0	0	0	0
Sturmstafffel 1	Fw 190A	Salzwedel		0950	Salzwedel, Staaken	1129	n/c	0	0	0	0	0
III./ZG 26	Bf 110G	Königsberg–Neumark	13	1045	Königsberg–Neumark	1135	n/c	0	0	0	0	0
Jagddivision 2:												
I./JG 11	Fw 190A	Rotenburg	10	0953	Rotenburg	~1130	2 P-47	1	0	1	0	0
II.JG 11	Bf 109G	Wunstorf	26	0939	Wunstorf	1119	n/c	0	0	0	0	0
III./JG 11	Fw 190A	Oldenburg		~0945	Oldenburg	~1130	1 P-47	2	0	1	0	0
Jagddivision 3:												
I./JG 1	Fw 190A	Lippspringe		~0945	Lippspringe	~1130	0	0	0	0	0	0
II./JG 1	Fw 190A	Störmede	30	0922	Störmede	1112	1 P-51	1	2	1	0	0
III./JG 1	Bf 109G	Paderborn		0932	Paderborn	~1115	0	1	1	1	0	0
Abschfü Mittelrhein:												
II./JG 27?	Bf 109G	Erbenheim		~0930	Erbenheim	~1115	0	0	0	0	0	0
II./JG 53	Bf 109G	Eschborn		0928	Eschborn	1120	0	1	0	0	0	0
Luftflotte 3												
II. Jagdkorps			71									
Jagddivision 4:												
I./JG 26	Fw 190A	Wevelghem		0922	Wevelghem	1042	0	0	0	0	0	0
	Fw 190A	Denain		0924	Denain	1035	0	0	0	0	0	0
II./JG 26	Fw 190A	Cambrai		0922	Cambrai	1038	0	0	0	0	0	0
III./JG 26?	Bf 109G	Etain		~0920	Etain	~1040	0	0	0	0	0	0

COMBAT REPORT[5]
8 May 1944

One Liberator shot from formation from 6,800 metres at 1007 hours, PQ FA, Celle-Gifhorn
One Liberator shot from formation from 6,800 metres at 1014 hours, PQ FA-9, N of Braunschweig
[Neither claim confirmed – crashes not witnessed: DC]

I scrambled from Salzwedel in a Bf 109G-6/U4 (one MK 108, two MG 151/20, two MG 131) at 0841 hours versus incoming heavy bombers. At 1000 hours, the Gefechtsverband sighted 80 B-24s and 40 B-17s north of Braunschweig [Brunswick]. At 1007 hours, I led the Gruppe in a closed-formation frontal attack on a Pulk of 40 B-24s.

Firing from 1,000 down to 200 metres, I hit a bomber on the right side of the formation in the right wing between the engines. Large parts flew off, and the bomber went into a right spin into a solid cloud bank. The combat was witnessed by the Kommodore, Major Müller. My own airplane sustained no damage. I assembled the Gruppe in a left turn and made a frontal attack on the same Pulk. I fired from 1,000 to 200 metres and hit a B-24 in the right wing root. It flamed brightly and dived away, trailing dark smoke. The combat was witnessed by Lt. Weik.

Hptm. Wilhelm Moritz, Gruppenkommandeur
Stab IV./JG 3 Udet

Luftwaffe defensive activity – 7 May 1944

Unit	Type	Gruppe up				Gruppe down		Claims	Losses				
		Base	No	Time		Base	Time		Dest	Dam	KIA	MIA	WIA
Luftflotte Reich													
I. Jagdkorps			28										
Jagddivision 1:													
I./JG 302	Bf 109G	Jüterbog–Damm		~0930		Jüterbog–Damm	~1100	0	0	0	0	0	0
II./ZG 26	Me 410A	Königsberg–Neumark	28	1010		Königsberg–Neumark	1215	n/c	0	0	0	0	0
III./ZG 26	Bf 110G	Königsberg–Neumark		~1010		Königsberg–Neumark	~1215	n/c	0	0	0	0	0
Jagddivision 2:													
I./JG 11?	Fw 190A	Rotenburg		~0930		Rotenburg	~1030	n/c	0	0	0	0	0
III./JG 11?	Fw 190A	Oldenburg		~0930		Oldenburg	~1030	n/c	0	0	0	0	0
Jagddivision 3:													
Abschfü Mittelrhein:													
II./JG 27?	Bf 109G	Erbenheim		~0930		Erbenheim	~1030	0	0	0	0	0	0
II./JG 53	Bf 109G	Eschborn		0931		Eschborn	1018	n/c	0	0	0	0	0
Luftflotte 3													
II. Jagdkorps			81										
Jagddivision 4:													
I./JG 26	Fw 190A	Denain		0700		Laon–Athies	~0730	transfer	0	0	0	0	0
	Fw 190A	Laon–Athies		0900		Laon–Athies	1030	0	3	0	2	0	1
II./JG 26	Fw 190A	Cambrai–Epinoy		0653		Laon–Athies	0715	transfer	0	0	0	0	0
	Fw 190A	Laon–Athies		0904		Laon–Athies	1027	0	1	0	0	0	0
III./JG 26?	Bf 109G	Etain		0855		Etain	0950	0	0	0	0	0	0
Jagddivision 5:													
I./JG 2	Fw 190A	Cormeilles		~0900		Cormeilles	~1030	2 P-38, 1 B-26	0	1	0	0	0
II./JG 2	Bf 109G	Creil		~0900		Creil	~1030	0	1	0	1	0	0

Major Wilhelm Moritz, here seen as a Hauptmann, was a pre-war pilot and served in several Zerstörer and fighter units from 1939–1944. In April 1944, he became Gruppenkommandeur of IV./JG 3 and led it through its conversion to the first Sturmgruppe. He was relieved in December and, after a rest period, led a training unit and then, for the last month of the war, II./JG 4. He was considered an outstanding formation leader, a strength not necessarily reflected in his victory total of 44, which included 12 heavy bombers. *(Author's collection)*

Luftwaffe defensive activity – 8 May 1944

Unit	Type	Gruppe up			Gruppe down		Claims	Losses (—: included with 1st sortie)				
		Base	No	Time	Base	Time		Dest	Dam	KIA	MIA	WIA
Luftflotte Reich												
I. Jagdkorps			400									
Jagddivision 1:												
Stab/JG 3	Bf 109G	Salzwedel		0842	Salzwedel	~1030	1 B-24	1	0	0	0	0
2nd sorties	Bf 109G	Salzwedel		~1130	Salzwedel	~1300	1 B-17, 1 P-51	—	0	0	0	0
I./JG 3	Bf 109G	Burg		0845	Burg	~1030	1 B-17	1	1	1	0	1
II./JG 3	Bf 109G	Sachau		0842	Sachau	~1030	4 B-17, 1 B-24	4	2	2	0	0
IV.(Sturm)/JG 3	Bf 109G	Salzwedel		0842	Salzwedel	1040	4 B-24, 1 B-24 HSS	3	1	1	0	0
2nd sorties	Bf 109G	Salzwedel	10	1127	Salzwedel, Hannover	1250	3 B-17	0	1	0	0	1
I./JG 302	Bf 109G	Jüterbog–Damm		~0845	Jüterbog–Damm	~1030	0	0	0	0	0	0
II./JG 302	Bf 109G	Salzwedel		~0845	Salzwedel	~1030	0	2	0	2	0	0
Sturmstaffel 1	Fw 190A	Salzwedel	7	0845	Halberstadt, others	1028	7 B-24	0	0	0	0	0
Jagddivision 2:												
Stab/JG 11	Bf 109G	Rotenburg		~0900	Rotenburg	~1030	0	1	0	0	0	0
I./JG 11	Fw 190A	Rotenburg		-0900	Rotenburg	~1030	5 B-17	4	1	3	0	0
2nd sorties	Fw 190A	Rotenburg		1100	Rotenburg	~1200	0	0	0	0	0	0
3rd sorties	Fw 190A	Rotenburg	10	1145	Rotenburg	~1300	1 P-51	0	0	0	0	0
II./JG 11	Bf 109G	Wunstorf		0900	Wunstorf, Rotenburg	1045	1 B-24	6	1	2	0	2
2nd sorties	Bf 109G	Wunstorf, Rotenburg		1140	Wunstorf, Burg	1245	2 P-38, 1 P-47	0	0	0	0	0
III./JG 11	Fw 190A	Oldenburg		-0900	Oldenburg	~1015	2 B-17, 1 P-47	2	1	1	0	0
2nd sorties	Fw 190A	Oldenburg		1030	Oldenburg	~1115	1 B-17	0	0	0	0	0
3rd sorties	Fw 190A	Oldenburg		1145	Oldenburg	~1300	1 B-17	0	0	0	0	0
10./JG 11	Fw 190A	Aalborg		~0830	Aalborg	~1000	0	1	0	0	0	0
Jagddivision 3:												
Stab/JG 1	Fw 190A	Lippspringe		~0835	Lippspringe	~1000	2 B-17, 1 P-47	0	0	0	0	0
2nd sorties	Fw 190A	Lippspringe		~1130	Lippspringe	~1300	0	0	0	0	0	0
I./JG 1	Fw 190A	Lippspringe		~0835	various	~1000	3 B-24,1 P-51, 1 B-24 HSS	6	2	5	0	2
2nd sorties	Fw 190A	various		~1130	Lippspringe	~1300	0	0	0	0	0	0
II./JG 1	Fw 190A	Störmede		0836	Gütersloh, others	~1000	1 B-17, 4 B-24	1	3	0	0	2
2nd sorties	Fw 190A	Various		~1130	Störmede	~1300	0	0	0	0	0	0
2nd sorties	Fw 190A	Wunstorf	2	1142	Störmede	~1300	1 P-51	0	0	0	0	0
III./JG 1	Bf 109G	Paderborn		0840	various	~1000	0	5	1	3	0	0
2nd sorties	Bf 109G	various		~1130	Paderborn	~1300	1 B-17	1	0	0	0	1
Abschfü Mittelrhein:												
II./JG 27	Bf 109G	Erbenheim		0850	Erbenheim	~1030	0	5	0	3	0	0
II./JG 53	Bf 109G	Eschborn		0848	Volkenröde	1030	1 B-24	5	1	2	0	1
2nd sorties	Bf 109G	Volkenröde		1120	Paderborn	1205	0	0	0	0	0	0
Luftflotte 3												
II. Jagdkorps												
Jagddivision 4:												
I./JG 26	Fw 190A	Denain		0946	Athies	1036	0	0	0	0	0	0
4./JG 26	Fw 190A	Wevelghem		0932	Athies	1016	1 P-47	0	0	0	0	0
II./JG 26	Fw 190A	Cambrai–Epinoy		0838	Cambrai–Epinoy	1053	1 P-47	1	0	0	0	1
III./JG 26	Bf 109G	Etain		~0930	Etain	~1100	0	1	0	0	0	1
Jagddivision 5:												
I./JG 2	Fw 190A	Cormeilles		~0930	Cormeilles	~1100	1 P-38	0	0	0	0	0
II./JG 2	Bf 109G	Creil		~0930	Creil	~1100	0	1	1	0	0	0

COMBAT REPORT[6]
8 May 1944

One B-17 Fortress shot down from 6,000 metres at 1212 hours, PQ FT-1, NW of Nienburg

At 1127 hours, we scrambled from Salzwedel on our second mission. I led the Gruppe with 10 aircraft in a Bf 109G-6/U4 (one MK 108, two MG 151/20, two MG 131). We climbed through the clouds, assembled over Hannover at 4,000 metres and sought to locate the enemy 4-engine formations ourselves, since we received no radio report. In the area NW of Nienburg (PQ FT-1), we saw a large enemy 4-engine formation with a strong fighter escort flying at about 6,500 metres. Below them was a single Kette of Boeing Fortresses. We attacked this Kette from the front, and I observed hits in the fuselage and both right engines. I fired from 400 to 150 metres. Large pieces flew away immediately, and the aircraft broke away sharply to the left, on fire. I made another attack from the rear, without observing any great effect from my fire. The aircraft I hit on my first pass dove in steep spirals and exploded at 2,000 metres. I observed five parachutes. Air witnesses were Major Müller (Kommodore) and Fw. Schäfer (10.St). I received 10 hits in my right wing and crash-landed S of Uelzen at about 1220 hours.

Lt. Hans Weik, Staffelkapitän
10./JG 3 Udet

fighters from the three north German Jagddivisionen and Jagddivision 4 were scrambled, but only 87 made contact – exclusively with the escorts, four of which were confirmed shot down. Most units avoided both the bombers and their screen; one disgusted Sturmgruppe pilot recorded the mission in his logbook as a 'propaganda flight over Berlin'. American losses were one B-17 scrapped and eight escorts written off. The Luftwaffe lost five KIA and eight fighters.

7 May
8th Air Force Mission #342: 553 of 600 1st BD + 3rd BD B-17s bomb Berlin – lose 8-2-265, claim 0; 312 of 322 2nd BD B-24s bomb Münster and Osnabrück – lose 1-1-22, claim 1-0-0. Escort of 3 P-38 FGs, 4 P-47 FGs, 5 P-51 FGs (754 sorties) claims 0, loses 4-1-9.

8th Air Force Mission #343: 29 of 67 3rd BD B-24s bomb Liège rail yard – lose 0, claim 0. Escort of 1 P-47 FG, 1 P-51 FG (75 sorties) claims 0, loses 0.

The 8th AF attempted another raid on Berlin. This time, the force was led by Pathfinders, and the centre of the city was bombed through cloud to great effect. Few I. Jagdkorps fighters were ordered off the ground. Only the bad-weather fighters of I./JG 302 scored a possible success; one B-17 was claimed, but no confirmation has been found. The two Zerstörergruppen at Königsberg–Neumark were scrambled, but as no holes in the escort were found, they were ordered not to approach the bombers. All of the 12 bombers and five fighters the Americans wrote off were attributed to Flak and mechanical problems.

Two new B-24 groups attempted to raid the Liège rail yards and drew a response of sorts from the II. Jagdkorps. Two or three Jagdgruppen flew inland to form a battle formation. They missed the bombers, but had several encounters with tactical units, which the Luftwaffe typically did not engage during this period of the war. Three Focke-Wulfs and pilots were shot down by 2nd TAF Spitfires, which were apparently unharmed. The day's only confirmed Luftwaffe victories were scored by I./JG 2, which claimed one 9th AF B-26 and two P-38s without loss.

8 May
8th Air Force Mission #344: 742 of 807 HBs (all BDs) bomb Berlin and Brunswick, TOT 1100 + 1004 – lose 36-8-197, claim 76-16-16. Escort of 3 P-38 FGs, 5 P-47 FGs, 6 P-51 FGs (729 sorties) claims 55-4-20, loses 13-2-4.

8th Air Force Mission #345: 149 of 164 HBs (all BDs) bomb 2 French V-weapon sites, Brussels rail yard – lose 5-1-58, claim 0. Escort of 2 P-47 FGs (97 sorties) claims 0, loses 0.

The 8th AF mounted another strong raid on Berlin and Brunswick using Pathfinder guidance. Weather conditions over Germany reduced the number of areas suitable for the formation of the RLV Gefechtsverbände, but did not unduly hinder operations. JD 7 and the two Zerstörergeschwader did not take part, but the Bf 109s and Fw 190s of Jagddivisionen 1, 2 and 3 flew 400 sorties, 358 of which made contact. The JD 1 Gefechtsverband (JG 3) did not form up properly, but its individual Gruppen flew successful missions, as did the JD 2 Gefechtsverband

Luftwaffe defensive activity – 9 May 1944

Unit	Type	Gruppe up			Gruppe down		Claims	Losses				
		Base	No	Time	Base	Time		Dest	Dam	KIA	MIA	WIA
Luftflotte Reich												
I. Jagdkorps			114									
Jagddivision 1:												
Stab/JG 3?	Bf 109G	Salzwedel		~0900	Salzwedel	~1030	n/c	0	0	0	0	0
I./JG 3	Bf 109G	Burg		0855	Nürnberg	~1030	n/c	0	0	0	0	0
II./JG 3?	Bf 109G	Sachau		~0900	Sachau	~1030	n/c	0	0	0	0	0
IV.(Sturm)/JG 3	Bf 109G	Salzwedel		0847	Salzwedel	1032	n/c	0	0	0	0	0
11.(Sturm)/JG 3	Fw 190A	Salzwedel		0850	Salzwedel	~1030	n/c	0	0	0	0	0
II./ZG 26	Me 410	Königsberg–Neumark		0905	Königsberg–Neumark	1200	n/c	0	0	0	0	0
Jagddivision 2:												
Stab/JG 11?	Bf 109G	Rotenburg		~0900	Rotenburg	~1030	n/c	0	0	0	0	0
I./JG 11	Fw 190A	Rotenburg		~0900	Rotenburg	~1030	n/c	0	0	0	0	0
II./JG 11	Bf 109G	Wunstorf, Hustedt		0902	Burg	1020	n/c	0	0	0	0	0
III./JG 11	Fw 190A	Oldenburg		~0900	Oldenburg	~1030	n/c	0	0	0	0	0
Jagddivision 3:												
Stab/JG 1?	Fw 190A	Lippspringe		~0900	Lippspringe	~1030	n/c	0	0	0	0	0
I./JG 1	Fw 190A	Lippspringe		~0900	Lippspringe	~1030	n/c	0	0	0	0	0
II./JG 1	Fw 190A	Störmede		0834	Erbenheim	1030	n/c	0	0	0	0	0
III./JG 1	Bf 109G	Paderborn		~0900	Paderborn	~1030	n/c	0	0	0	0	0
Abschfü Mittelrhein:												
II./JG 27	Bf 109G	Erbenheim		~0845	Erbenheim	~1045	n/c	0	0	0	0	0
II./JG 53	Bf 109G	Eschborn		0840	Eschborn	1037	n/c	0	0	0	0	0
Luftflotte 3												
II. Jagdkorps												
Jagddivision 4:												
I./JG 26	Fw 190A	Denain		0700	Florennes	~0730	transfer	0	0	0	0	0
	Fw 190A	Florennes		0849	Mönchen–Gladbach	1010	1 P-51	3	0	2	0	1
4./JG 26?	Fw 190A	Wevelghem		~0845	Wevelghem	~1015	0	0	0	0	0	0
II./JG 26	Fw 190A	Cambrai-Epinoy		0630	Florennes	0700	transfer	0	0	0	0	0
	Fw 190A	Florennes		0855	Deelen, Trier	1015	2 B-24, 1 P-51	2	1	0	0	1
III./JG 26	Bf 109G	Etain		0845	Etain	1025	0	1	0	0	0	0
Jagddivision 5:												
I./JG 2	Fw 190A	Cormeilles		~0845	Cormeilles	~1015	2 P-38	0	0	0	0	0
II./JG 2	Bf 109G	Creil		~0845	Creil	~1015	0	1	0	0	0	1

(JG 11) and the JD 3 Gefechtsverband (JG 1). The fighter pilots were under great pressure to obtain results, and some flew three missions: the second versus the withdrawing stream, and the third against stragglers. Sturmstaffel 1 flew its last mission today before its absorption into IV.(Sturm)/JG 3. It took off with this Gruppe, but remained some distance away from it and, when the B-24s were spotted, was able to circle behind the leading Pulk, attack it from the rear and down seven Liberators. This major mission cost the 8th AF 44 bombers and 15 escorts; the I. Jagdkorps lost 25 KIA, 10 WIA and 48 fighters.

Part of the 8th AF joined the 9th AF and 2nd TAF in attacking tactical targets in the occupied zone. Defending against these raids gave II. Jagdkorps all it could handle. An attempt was made to concentrate the three JG 26 Gruppen and one or both JG 2 Gruppen over Juvincourt, but all were involved in combats with the sweeping escorts before rendezvous could be effected. Three American fighters were claimed, for the loss of two WIA and three fighters. The 8th AF wrote off six bombers to all causes on this mission.

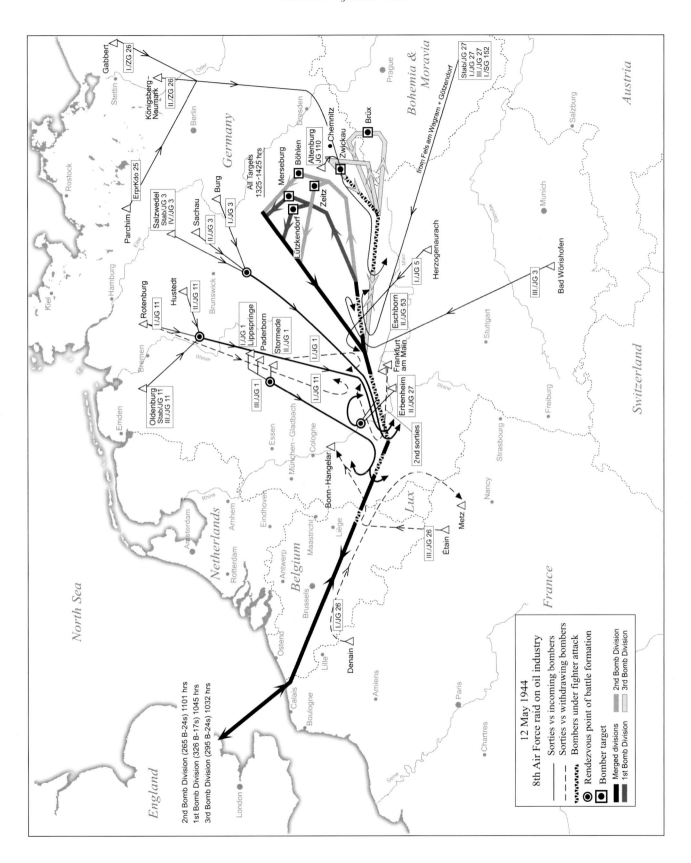

Gabbert

I./ZG 26

II./ZG 26

Königsberg–Neumark

Stettin

Rostock

ErprKdo 25

Parchim

Salzwedel Stab/JG 3 IV./JG 3

Sachau

II./JG 3

Burg

I./JG 3

Berlin

Germany

Oder

Elbe

Dresden

Chemnitz

Prague

Bohemia & Moravia

Brüx

Altenburg JG 110

Böhlen

Zwickau

Zwickau

Merseburg

All Targets 1325-1425 hrs

Zeitz

Lützkendorf

from Fels am Wagram + Götzendorf

Stab/JG 27 I./JG 27 III./JG 27 I./SG 152

Austria

Salzburg

Munich

Herzogenaurach

I./JG 5

Main

III./JG 3

Bad Wörishofen

Hamburg

Kiel

Rotenburg I./JG 11

Hustedt

II./JG 11

Brunswick

Weser

Lippspringe

Paderborn

I./JG 1

Stormede II./JG 1

I./JG 1

Frankfurt am Main

Eschborn II./JG 53

Danube

Stuttgart

Freiburg

Switzerland

Bremen

Emden

Oldenburg Stab/JG 11 III./JG 11

III./JG 11

Rhine

I./JG 11

Erbenheim II./JG 27

Rhine

München–Gladbach

Essen

Cologne

2nd sorties

Bonn–Hangelar

Netherlands

Amsterdam

Rotterdam

Arnhem

Eindhoven

Maastricht

Liège

Belgium

Antwerp

Brussels

Lux

Metz

Nancy

Strasbourg

III./JG 26

Étain

I./JG 26

Denain

Ostend

Lille

Boulogne

Calais

Amiens

Paris

Chartres

France

North Sea

England

2nd Bomb Division (265 B-24s) 1101 hrs
1st Bomb Division (326 B-17s) 1045 hrs
3rd Bomb Division (295 B-24s) 1032 hrs

London

Seine

12 May 1944
8th Air Force raid on oil industry

———— Sorties vs incoming bombers
– – – – Sorties vs withdrawing bombers
〰〰〰 Bombers under fighter attack
◉ Rendezvous point of battle formation
◉ ▣ Bomber target
Merged divisions
1st Bomb Division
2nd Bomb Division
3rd Bomb Division

Luftwaffe defensive activity – 10 May 1944

Unit	Type	Gruppe up			Gruppe down		Claims	Losses				
		Base	No	Time	Base	Time		Dest	Dam	KIA	MIA	WIA
Luftflotte Reich												
I. Jagdkorps			175									
Jagddivision 3:												
Abschfü Mittelrhein:												
II./JG 53	Bf 109G	Eschborn		0830	Eschborn	1012	n/c	1	0	0	0	0
Jagddivision 7:												
III./JG 3	Bf 109G	Bad Wörishofen	24	~1030	Wels	~1200	2 B-17, 1 B-24	2	1	2	0	1
I./JG 5	Bf 109G	Neubiberg		~1030	Wels?	~1200	1 B-17, 1 P-38, 1 Mosquito	1	0	1	0	0
I./JG 53	Bf 109G	Neubiberg		1000	Wien–Götzendorf	1120	transfer	0	0	0	0	0
Jafü Ostmark:												
Stab/JG 27	Bf 109G	Fels am Wagram		~0945	Fels am Wagram	~1130	1 B-17	0	0	0	0	0
I./JG 27	Bf 109G	Fels am Wagram		0945	Fels am Wagram	1135	4 B-17, 1 B-24	3	1	2	0	0
2nd sorties	Bf 109G	Fels am Wagram		1055	Wien–Aspern	1155	0	0	0	0	0	0
IV./JG 27	Bf 109G	Steinamanger		~1030	Steinamanger	~1200	2 B-24, 1 P-38	3	0	2	0	0
2nd sorties	Bf 109G	Steinamanger		1225	Steinamanger	~1345	0	1	0	1	0	0
I./JG 302	Bf 109G	Wien–Seyring		~1030	Wien–Seyring	~1200	3 B-24	0	0	0	0	0
I./SG 152	Fw 190G	Prossnitz		~1030	Prossnitz	~1200	1 B-24	?	?	?	?	?
2nd sorties	Fw 190G	Prossnitz		~1230	Prossnitz	~1345	1 B-24	?	?	?	?	?
VFhr Schule	Bf 109G	Fels am Wagram		~0945	Fels am Wagram	~1130	1 B-17	0	0	0	0	0
Luftflotte 2												
Jafü Oberitalien:			32									
Stab/JG 77	Bf 109G	Povoletto		1158	Povoletto	1315	1 P-38	1	1	0	0	0
I./JG 77	Bf 109G	Lavariano		1158	Lavariano	1315	1 B-24, 2 P-38	0	3	0	0	0

9 May

8th Air Force Mission #325: 802 of 823 HBs (all BDs) bomb 13 airfields and rail yards in western occupied

Oblt. Waldemar Radener (II./JG 26) leads his 7. Staffel in Fw 190A-7 'Brown 4' in early May. Its rudder shows 20 victory bars. Uffz. Gerhard Langhammer turned this airplane over in a bomb crater while landing on Epinoy on 12 May. (Sy)

zone – lose 6-1-117, claim 0. Escort of 1 P-38 FG, 5 P-47 FGs, 6 P-51 FGs (668 sorties) claims 3-0-1, loses 7-1-1.

The 8th AF and the Allied Expeditionary Air Force (AEAF), which commanded the 9th US Air Force and the RAF's 2nd TAF, began a systematic bomber and fighter-bomber campaign against rail yards and Luftwaffe bases in France and Belgium in preparation for D-Day. Responding to the approach of the heavy bombers, I. Jagdkorps ordered the three north German Jagddivisionen to scramble their Gefechtsverbände and fly south, but recalled them when they reached the II. Jagdkorps boundary. The defence against the full-strength raid on 13 airfields and rail yards was left to about 100 JG 2 and JG 26 fighters. They did as well as could be expected, claiming two bombers and four escorts for the loss of two KIA, three WIA and seven fighters.

Luftwaffe defensive activity – 11 May 1944

Unit	Type	Gruppe up				Gruppe down		Claims	Losses				
		Base	No	Time		Base	Time		Dest	Dam	KIA	MIA	WIA
Luftflotte Reich													
I. Jagdkorps			131										
Jagddivision 1:													
Stab/JG 3?	Bf 109G	Salzwedel		~1800		Salzwedel	~2000	0	0	0	0	0	0
I./JG 3	Bf 109G	Burg		1800		Burg	2005	0	1	0	0	0	0
II./JG 3?	Bf 109G	Sachau		~1800		Sachau	~1930	0	0	0	0	0	0
IV.(Sturm)/JG 3	Bf 109G	Salzwedel		1800		Salzwedel	2000	0	2	0	0	0	0
11.(Sturm)/JG 3	Fw 190A	Salzwedel		~1800		Salzwedel	~1930	0	1	0	0	0	1
III./JG 302	Bf 109G	Völkenrode		~1800		Völkenrode	~1930	0	1	1	1	0	0
Jagddivision 2:													
Stab/JG 11?	Bf 109G	Rotenburg		~1800		Rotenburg	~1930	n/c	0	0	0	0	0
I./JG 11	Fw 190A	Rotenburg		~1800		Rotenburg	~1930	n/c	1	1	0	0	0
II./JG 11	Bf 109G	Wunstorf		~1800		Burg	~1930	n/c	0	0	0	0	0
III./JG 11	Fw 190A	Oldenburg		~1800		Oldenburg	~1930	n/c	0	2	0	0	0
Jagddivision 3:													
Stab/JG 1	Bf 109G	Paderborn		~1700		Paderborn	~1830	0	1	0	1	0	0
I./JG 1	Fw 190A	Lippspringe		~1700		Lippspringe	~1830	0	0		0	0	0
II./JG 1	Fw 190A	Störmede		~1700		Erbenheim	~1830	0	1	0	0	0	0
III./JG 1	Bf 109G	Paderborn		~1700		Paderborn	~1830	0	4	4	1	0	1
Abschfü Mittelrhein:													
Stab/JG zbV	Bf 109G	Erbenheim				Erbenheim	~1700	0	0	0	0	0	0
2nd sorties	Bf 109G	Erbenheim		~1720		Diedenhofen	~1900	0	0	0	0	0	0
II./JG 27	Bf 109G	Frbenheim		1520		Erbenheim	~1700	0	0	0	0	0	0
2nd sorties	Bf 109G	Erbenheim		1720		Diedenhofen	~1900	1 B-17 HSS	0	0	0	0	0
II./JG 53	Bf 109G	Eschborn		1520		Eschborn	1628	0	0	0	0	0	0
2nd sorties	Bf 109G	Eschborn		1720		Diedenhofen	1910	2 B-17	1	0	1	0	0
Jagddivision 7:													
III./JG 3	Bf 109G	Bad Wörishofen	22	1520		Bad Wörishofen	~1700	0	0	0	0	0	0
2nd sortues	Bf 109G	Bad Wörishofen	20	1820		Bad Wörishofen	~1930	1 P-51	4	0	2	0	0
I./JG 5	Bf 109G	Neubiberg		~1820		Neubiberg	~2000	1 B-17, 3 P51	0	0	0	0	0
Luftflotte 3													
II. Jagdkorps													
Jagddivision 4:													
I./JG 26	Fw 190A	Denain		~0700		Metz	~0800	transfer	0	0	0	0	0
	Fw 190A	Metz		1310		Etain	1550	2 P-47	1	0	0	0	0
2nd sorties	Fw 190A	Etain		1850		Metz	1935	0	0	0	0	0	0
II./JG 26	Fw 190A	Cambrai–Epinoy		0705		Metz	0809	transfer	0	0	0	0	0
	Fw 190A	Metz		1315		Villaroche, Orléans	1419	2 B-24	2	0	0	0	2
III./JG 26	Bf 109G	Etain		~1300		Etain	~1430	0	0	2	0	0	0
Jagddivision 5:													
I./JG 2	Fw 190A	Cormeilles		~1300		Cormeilles	~1430	0	3	0	1	1	1
II./JG 2	Bf 109G	Creil		~1300		Creil	~1430	0	1	1	0	0	0
III./JG 2	Fw 190A	Cormeilles		~1300		Cormeilles	~1430	0	1	0	1	0	0

10 May

15th Air Force: 174 of 207 B-17s, 126 of 160 B-24s bomb Wiener Neustadt Bf 109 factory, TOT 1058-1210 – lose 22. 102 of 117 B-24s bomb Wiener Neustadt airfield, TOT 1142-48 – lose 7. Escort of 168 P-38s (3 FGs), 48 P-47s (1 FG), 48 P-51s (1 FG) claims 15-1-20, loses 3 P-38s.

The 15th AF sent nearly 400 bombers to bomb the important Wiener Neustadt Bf 109 plant. Partial escort was provided by one P-47, three P-38 and two P-51 groups. The Austrian defences now included I./JG 302, which had transferred from Jüterbog near Berlin. The Messerschmitts were largely successful in evading the escort and attacked the bombers from all directions. The Messerschmitt factory was hit, but at a cost of 29 bombers, 8 per cent of those dispatched; three P-38s were also lost. The I. Jagdkorps scrambled 175 fighters, of which 156 made contact; a few of these were on second sorties against the withdrawing stream. The last contact was by 32 Bf 109s of the Stab and I./JG 77 from northern Italy, which were credited with one B-24 and three P-38s, for the loss of one Messerschmitt, but no casualties. German losses totalled at least eight KIA, one WIA and 12 fighters.

11 May

8th Air Force Mission #350: 254 of 364 2nd BD + 3rd BD B-24s bomb 9 French rail yards, TOT 1519-25 – lose 8-3-47, claim 0. Escort of 3 P-38 FGs, 4 P-47 FGs, 4 P-51 FGs (536 sorties) claims 3-0-2, loses 5-1-10.

8th Air Force Mission #351: 547 of 609 1st BD + 3rd BD B-17s bomb 11 rail yards in western occupied zone, TOT 1811-47 – lose 8-1-172, claim 0. Escort of 2 P-38 FGs, 4 P-47 FGs, 5 P-51 FGs (471 sorties) claims 11-0-4, loses 4-0-0.

The 8th AF flew two missions to French and Belgian rail yards and airfields. The RLV units scrambled 251 fighters. Most of those from I. Jagdkorps were ordered to land when the targets became obvious, but a few pilots became involved with the leading bombers and sweeping escorts. One was Obst. Walter Oesau, the JG 1 Kommodore, who was shot down and killed by P-38s. Oesau had been a highly respected combat veteran and one of the few consistently successful Gefechtsverband leaders; his loss was impossible to fill. The five II. Jagdkorps Gruppen all apparently made contact, but with limited success. The two American forces wrote off 20 bombers and 10 escorts from all causes; the Luftwaffe lost nine pilots KIA or MIA, five WIA and 25 fighters.

12 May – Central German oil industry (see map)

8th Air Force Mission #353: 258 of 295 3rd BD B-17s bomb Zwickau a/i, Brüx o/i, TOT 1338-1413h – lose 41-1-162, 0 claims recorded; 314 of 326 1st BD B-17s bomb Merseburg, Lützkendorf o/i, TOT 1348-1408h – lose 2-3-189, 0 claims recorded; 242 of 265 2nd BD B-24s bomb Zeitz, Böhlen o/i, TOT 1402-1410h – lose 3-5-61, 0 claims recorded. 8th FC escort of 3 P-38 FGs, 6 P-47 FGs, 8 P-51 FGs (657 sorties) claims 61-1-11, loses 7-0-13; 9th FC escort of 3 P-38 FGs, 2 P-51 FGs (219 sorties) claims 7-0-0, loses 3-0-0.

Albert Speer and Germany's war economists had long dreaded an Allied air campaign against German synthetic oil production. The USSTAF began such a campaign today with an 8th AF attack on five refineries and one aircraft factory in central Germany. The bombers crossed the coast in a single stream headed southeast, turned east south of Koblenz and split south of Frankfurt to head for its various targets. They drew the full and undivided attention of the RLV force. The I. Jagdkorps ordered all of its controllers to scramble their fighters, assemble them in their usual Gefechtsverbände and head them to Frankfurt. Jafü Ostmark first ordered its Gruppen toward an incoming 15th AF formation, but when that went elsewhere, these fighters also headed for Frankfurt. The RLV controllers in the Reich succeeded for the first time in concentrating all of their day fighters in a single combat area. Twenty-two Jagdgruppen containing 475 single-engine fighters and three Zerstörergruppen with 40 twin-engine fighters sortied; this was the largest defensive mission of the entire strategic air war.

The defenders found the bomber stream to be highly concentrated and primarily well escorted. Of the six Gefechtsverbände, only two, those of JD 1 (JG 3) and JD 2 (JG 11), found an unescorted stretch and were able to make repeated firing passes by Gruppen to close range before the belated arrival of the P-51s. There was only one interception in any of the target areas. ZG 26 had scrambled all 40 of its Me 410s from Königsberg-Neumark and was well placed to attack some unescorted bombers heading for a target of opportunity, Chemnitz. It claimed five bombers for the loss of four Zerstörer and most of their crews, all to bomber gunfire. Most of the Bf 109 and Fw 190 pilots had been fought out before the stream broke up into smaller, more vulnerable units, and their exhaustion was so great that fewer than a hundred

Luftwaffe defensive activity – 12 May 1944

Unit	Type	Gruppe up			Gruppe down		Claims		Losses				
		Base	No	Time	Base	Time			Dest	Dam	KIA	MIA	WIA
vs. incoming stream													
Luftflotte Reich													
I. Jagdkorps			415										
Jagddivision 1:													
Stab/JG 3	Bf 109G	Salzwedel		1123	Salzwedel	~1300	3 B-17		0	0	0	0	0
I./JG 3	Bf 109G	Burg		1115	Burg	~1300	1 B-17 HSS, 2 P-51		2	1	0	0	1
II./JG 3	Bf 109G	Sachau		1120	Frankfurt area	~1300	10 B-17, 1 B-17 HSS		5	0	1	0	1
IV.(Sturm)/JG 3	Bf 109G	Salzwedel		1123	Frankfurt area	1245	6 B-17, 2 B-17 HSS		3	1	0	0	0
11.(Sturm)/JG 3	Fw 190A	Salzwedel		~1125	Frankfurt area	~1300	2 B-17		1	0	0	0	1
I./JG 110	Fw 190A	Zwickau		~1130	Zwickau	~1300	0		2	0	0	0	2
I./ZG 26	Me 410A	Gabbert		~1130	Gabbert	~1330	0		0	0	0	0	0
II./ZG 26	Me 410A	Königsberg–Neumark		~1130	Königsberg–Neumark	~1330	1 B-17		5	1	4	0	3
ErprKdo 25	Me 410A	Parchim		~1130	Parchim	~1300	0		1	0	2	0	0
Jagddivision 2:													
Stab/JG 11	Bf 109G	Oldenburg		~1130	Oldenburg	~1300	1 B-17		1	0	0	0	0
I./JG 11	Fw 190A	Rotenburg		~1130	Rotenburg	~1300	4 B-17		2	1	0	1	1
II./JG 11	Bf 109G	Hustedt		~1130	Frankfurt area	~1300	1 P-47, 1 P-51		11	1	2	0	5
III./JG 11	Fw 190A	Oldenburg		~1130	Oldenburg	~1300	5 B-17		4	0	0	0	0
Jagddivision 3:													
I./JG 1	Fw 190A	Lippspringe		1113	Lippspringe	~1230	0		0	0	0	0	0
II./JG 1	Fw 190A	Störmede	21	1113	Mannheim–Sandhofen	~1245	2 B-24, 1 P-47		5	2	5	0	0
III./JG 1	Bf 109G	Paderborn		1113	Paderborn	~1230	0		2	1	1	0	0
Abschfü Mittelrhein:													
II./JG 27	Bf 109G	Erbenheim, Merzhausen		1138	Erbenheim, Altenburg	1323	1 B-17, 1 B-17 HSS		5	0	1	0	1
II./JG 53	Bf 109G	Eschborn		1130	Eschborn, Langendiebach	1243	3 B-17		6	2	1	0	2
Jagddivision 7:													
III./JG 3	Bf 109G	Bad Wörishofen	22	1122	Frankfurt area	~1300	0		4	2	4	0	0
I./JG 5	Bf 109G	Herzogenaurach		~1115	Frankfurt area	~1245	3 P-47		1	0	1	0	0
Jafü Ostmark:													
Stab/JG 27	Bf 109G	Fels am Wagram		1107	Frankfurt area	~1300	3 B-17, 1 B-17 HSS		0	0	0	0	0
I./JG 27	Bf 109G	Fels am Wagram		1105	Gelnhausen	1250	3 B-17, 1 P-51, 1 B-17 HSS		9	5	0	0	5
III./JG 27	Bf 109G	Götzendorf		1105	Götzendorf	~1300	4 B-17, 2 B-17 HSS		4	2	3	0	1
I./SG 152	Fw 190G	Prossnitz		~1105	Prossnitz	~1300	0		2	0	0	0	2
VFhr Schule	Bf 109G	Fels am Wagram		~1105	Fels am Wagram	~1300	0		1	1	0	0	1
vs. withdrawing stream													
Luftflotte Reich													
I. Jagdkorps			51										
Jagddivision 1:													
I./ZG 26	Me 410A	Gabbert		~1400	Gabbert	~1600	2 B-24		0	0	0	0	0
II./ZG 26	Me 410A	Königsberg–Neumark		1300	Erfurt–Bindersleben	1555	1 B-17		0	0	0	0	0
Jagddivision 2:													
I./JG 11	Fw 190A	Rotenburg		~1430	Rotenburg	~1600	0		0	0	0	0	0

Luftwaffe defensive activity – 12 May 1944 Continued

Unit	Type	Gruppe up			Gruppe down		Claims	Losses				
		Base	No	Time	Base	Time		Dest	Dam	KIA	MIA	WIA
Jagddivision 3:												
I./JG 1	Fw 190A	Lippspringe		~1430	Lippspringe	~1530	2 B-24	7	2	1	0	2
Abschfü Mittelrhein:												
Various units	Bf 109G,	Frankfurt area	51	1430	Frankfurt area	~1600	3 B-17	3	0	1	0	2
2nd sorties	Fw 190A											
Jagddivision 7:												
I./JG 301	Bf 109G	Holzkirchen		1333	Holzkirchen	1355	n/c	0	0	0	0	0
	Bf 109G	Holzkirchen		1444	Holzkirchen	1554	0	0	0	0	0	0
Luftflotte 3												
II. Jagdkorps												
Jagddivision 4:												
I./JG 26	Fw 190A	Denain		1422	Metz	1519	n/c	0	2	0	0	0
III./JG 26	Bf 109G	Etain		1510	Bonn–Hangelar	1630	1 B-17, 2 B-17 HSS	2	1	1	0	1

could fly second sorties against the withdrawing bombers. They flew in small, improvised formations and sought out stragglers. The II. Jagdkorps could not neglect its obligation to defend the Channel coast, but sent two Gruppen inland to await the withdrawing stream. Only one of these, III./JG 26, found the bombers and made a fairly effective attack.

Aided by good weather and the absence of aerial defenders over the targets, the bombardiers had an exceptionally good day. The post-mission evaluation that evening rated results at three of the refineries as 'very good', at one as 'good' and at only one as 'fair'. The USAAF wrote off 55 bombers and 10 escorts on the mission; the Luftwaffe lost 29 KIA or MIA, 31 WIA and 88 fighters.

In the author's opinion, this was the worst single day of the war for Germany. It was the true tipping point, leaving Germany with no chance of a reversal of fortune and leading irrevocably to its final defeat. Five synthetic oil refineries, all absolutely crucial to the successful prosecution of the war, were reached and heavily bombed. The RLV force put up its largest day fighter force ever; I. Jagdkorps command-and-control procedures worked perfectly; and the bombers still could not be stopped. All that the Americans had to do was keep up the campaign they had now begun (not necessarily a given), and German defeat was inevitable.

PILOT'S ACCOUNT[7]
12 May 1944

The Gruppe [I./JG 11] scrambled 15–18 Fw 190s from Hannover–Rotenburg, flew south to our rendezvous point over the Steinhuder Meer and then to the south. Hptm. Rolf Hermichen led the main *Keil* [wedge]. I led the *Deckungskeil* [protection wedge] behind and below. We sighted a large B-17 formation at 6,400 metres over Giessen, covered by Thunderbolts above and to the side. II./JG 11 Bf-109s took on the escort, while the Fw 190s made a frontal attack. My 2. Staffel attacked the lower B-17 Pulk, which was flying in very close formation. Its machine-gun turrets put up a murderous defensive fire. A B-17G loomed up in my gunsight. I gave it a full blast with my machine guns, but my cannon shots dropped below it. We came nearer, and at least two bombers exploded. Then wupp … wupp … through the wall of explosive fire and the Pulk we went, finding ourselves below and behind it. As we re-formed to the side, we were hit by Thunderbolts. My wingman and I turned flaps-down with four of them. After gaining in the turn, we injected MW-50 and pulled away. The Gruppe lost one KIA and one WIA. Hptm. Hermichen bailed out OK, but was taken off combat duty, and the Kapitän of the 3. Staffel, Oblt. König, took over the Gruppe. It was a successful day, with seven B-17 shootdowns confirmed. [The Gruppe was attacked by 56th Fighter Group P-47s: DC]

Oblt. Fritz Engau, Staffelkapitän   2./JG 11

Luftwaffe defensive activity – 13 May 1944

Unit	Type	Gruppe up			Gruppe down		Claims	Losses				
		Base	No	Time	Base	Time		Dest	Dam	KIA	MIA	WIA
Luftflotte Reich												
I. Jagdkorps			253									
Jagddivision 1:												
Stab/JG 3?	Bf 109G	Salzwedel		~1315	Salzwedel	~1500	0	0	0	0	0	0
I./JG 3	Bf 109G	Burg		~1315	Burg	~1500	1 P-51	3	2	1	0	0
II./JG 3	Bf 109G	Sachau	20	1315	Sachau, others	~1500	1 B-17, 1 P-51	5	1	0	0	2
IV.(Sturm)/JG 3	Bf 109G	Salzwedel		1251	Salzwedel	~1430	1 B-17	1	1	1	0	0
11.(Sturm)/JG 3	Fw 190A	Salzwedel		~1250	Salzwedel	~1430	3 B-17	0	0	0	0	0
II./JG 302	Bf 109G	Salzwedel		~1300	Salzwedel	~1430	0	5	0	1	0	3
II./ZG 26	Me 410A	Königsberg–Neumark		1105	Königsberg–Neumark	1305	0	0	0	0	0	0
	Me 410A	Königsberg–Neumark		1315	Königsberg–Neumark	~1515	0	6	0	7	0	2
Jagddivision 2:												
Stab/JG 11	Bf 109G	Oldenburg		~1230	Oldenburg	~1415	1 P-47	0	0	0	0	0
I./JG 11	Fw 190A	Rotenburg		~1230	Rotenburg	~1415	0	3	3	1	0	1
II./JG 11	Bf 109G	Hustedt		~1230	Hustedt	~1415	0	0	1	0	0	0
III./JG 11	Fw 190A	Oldenburg		~1230	Oldenburg	~1415	1 B-24, 2 P-47	7	1	1	0	1
10./JG 11	Fw 190A	Aalborg–West		~1200	Aalborg–West	~1330	0	1	1	1	0	0
11./JG 11	Fw 190A	Lister		~1200	Lister	~1330	0	1	0	1	0	0
ErprKdo 16	Me 163B	Bad Zwischenahn	1	~1230	Bad Zwischenahn	~1300	0	0	0	0	0	0
Jagddivision 3:												
I./JG 1	Fw 190A	Lippspringe		1220	Lippspringe	~1415	1 P-47	1	1	1	0	0
II./JG 1	Fw 190A	Störmede	16	1222	Störmede	~1415	1 P-47, 1 P-51	0	1	0	0	0
III./JG 1	Bf 109G	Paderborn		1220	Stade	~1415	0	1	0	1	0	0
Abschü Mittelrhein:												
II./JG 27	Bf 109G	Merzhausen		1208	Erbenheim	~1400	1 B-17	1	0	0	0	0
II./JG 53	Bf 109G	Eschborn		0643	Biblis	0703	transfer	0	0	0	0	0
	Bf 109G	Biblis		1204	Neumünster, Neustadt–Glewe	1417	0	2	2	2	0	0
Jagddivision 7:												
III./JG 3	Bf 109G	Bad Wörishofen		~1230	Burg	~1400	0	1	1	0	0	0
2nd sorties	Bf 109G	Burg	6	~1430	Bad Wörishofen	~1600	n/c	0	0	0	0	0
I./JG 5	Bf 109G	Herzogenaurach		~1230	Burg	~1400	0	0	0	0	0	0
2nd sorties	Bf 109G	Burg		~1430	Herzogenaurach	~1600	n/c	0	0	0	0	0

COMBAT REPORT[8]
12 May 1944

One B-17 Fortress shot down from 6,500 metres at 1230 hours PQ PR, NE of Frankfurt/Main
One B-17 Fortress shot down from 6,500 metres at 1237 hours PQ PS, NE of Frankfurt/Main

I scrambled from Salzwedel in a Bf 109G-6/U4 (one MK 108, two MG 151/20, two MG 131) as leader of the Gruppe to intercept an incoming enemy formation. The Gefechtsverband assembled over the Brocken and flew, first at 240° and then 270°, toward the incoming formation. We flew at 7,000 metres and at 1225 hours sighted large enemy 4-mot Verbände on an easterly course, coming directly toward us. We attacked the second Verband immediately. I attacked a Boeing Fortress on the right side of the formation and obtained hits in the fuselage and the left wing. I then observed explosions and flames in the nose section. The airplane immediately fell away in flames. Several burning parts of the aircraft fell off. The airplane crashed at 1230 hours in Planquadrant PR, NE of Frankfurt. I observed several parachutes.

After the first pass, I pulled away to the right and flew parallel to the Verband. After a 180° course reversal at 1237 hours, I resumed my attack on the Verband, which had split apart somewhat after our first attack. I attacked a Boeing Fortress high on the left side of the enemy formation. I observed 3-centimetre hits in the fuselage, which immediately caught on fire. The aircraft lost altitude and exploded completely about 100 metres below the Verband. While I was pulling away from this attack, an air gunner hit my cockpit and right side of the fuselage. The oxygen equipment failed, so I had to land on Frankfurt/M at 1245 hours.

Lt. Hans Weik, Staffelkapitän
10.(Sturm)/JG 3 Udet

13 May
8th Air Force Mission #355: 691 of 749 HBs (all BDs) bomb Tutow aviation industry, Osnabrück rail yard, Stettin t/o – lose 12-0-144, claim 11-2-0. 8th FC escort of 3 P-38 FGs, 4 P-47 FGs, 7 P-51 FGs (737 sorties) claims 47-3-13, loses 5-1-12. 9th FC escort (370 sorties) claims 11-1-3, loses 4.

The USSTAF scheduled an immediate follow-up to the successful 12 May attack. The 8th AF targeted refineries in Poland, but the weather did not cooperate, and targets of opportunity were bombed. I. Jagdkorps scrambled 228 single-engine and 25 twin-engine fighters, but of the three Gefechtsverbände that reached the bombers, only the JD 1 formation (JG 3) could evade the escorts and make a modestly successful attack. Most combats were with the escorts, which were everywhere. II./ZG 26, flying alone, was decimated by Mustangs, losing six Me 410s, seven KIA and two WIA. One of the Luftwaffe's technical innovations, the rocket-powered Me 163 fighter, made its combat debut today – a scoreless sortie by Major Wolfgang Späte, the ErprKdo 16 commander. The Americans wrote off only 12 bombers and 10 escorts; the Germans lost a total of 18 KIA, nine WIA and 38 aircraft.

COMBAT REPORT[9]
13 May 1944

One P-51 rammed from 6,000 metres at 1338 hours in PQ SA-SB, Kieler Bucht
[Bindseil's victim was Capt. Frank Cutler (KIA), 352nd Fighter Group: DC]

After Sitzbereitschaft, I took off at 1222 hours in Fw 190A-8 'Yellow 10' (two MG 151/20, two MG 131) as a 6. Staffel *Schwarmflieger* [wingman] in the II./JG 1 formation. After sighting a bomber Verband, we made *Feindberührung* [enemy contact] with P-47s and P-51s over the Kieler Bucht. The Gruppe was attacked from all sides and above, and individual combats developed. I flew as the last in our formation and was attacked by a Mustang from the left rear side. I immediately banked left. The Mustang approached to ramming distance and started its own left turn. So as not to be shot, I immediately chopped the throttle to fall behind the Mustang. My propeller hit its right stabiliser and vertical tail. I immediately opened the throttle to strengthen the ramming effect. The right stabiliser and parts of the vertical tail flew off. The Mustang dropped almost straight down. I dove after it and gave it a full salvo. It crashed into the Kieler Bucht. Since I had been forced away from my formation, my victory was not witnessed, but Uffz. Wurl and Uffz. Golinger noted my prop was 'not normal' in the air. After landing it was noted that the tip of one blade was ripped off and the other two tips were bent forward and twisted.

Fw. Alfred Bindseil   6./JG 1

Luftwaffe defensive activity – 19 May 1944

Unit	Type	Gruppe up			Gruppe down		Claims	Losses				
		Base	No	Time	Base	Time		Dest	Dam	KIA	MIA	WIA
Luftflotte Reich												
I. Jagdkorps			451									
Jagddivision 1:												
Stab/JG 3?	Bf 109G	Salzwedel		1214	Salzwedel	~1400	0	0	0	0	0	0
I./JG 3	Bf 109G	Burg		1214	Burg	1405	4 P-51	5	4	3	0	3
II./JG 3	Bf 109G	Sachau		1224	Sachau, others	~1415	2 B-17, 1 P-51	7	3	1	0	3
IV.(Sturm)/JG 3	Fw 190A	Salzwedel		1225	Salzwedel	1430	1 B-17	1	0	1	0	0
2nd sorties	Fw 190A	Salzwedel		1440	Salzwedel	~1600	2 B-17	2	1	1	0	1
II./JG 102	Bf 109G	Zerbst		~1230	Zerbst	~1400	0	1	0	1	0	0
II./JG 302	Bf 109G	Salzwedel		~1230	Salzwedel	~1415	0	1	0	1	0	0
Jagddivision 2:												
Stab/JG 11	Bf 109G	Oldenburg		~1140	Oldenburg	~1315	0	1	0	0	1	0
I./JG 11	Fw 190A	Rotenburg		~1140	Rotenburg	~1315	5 B-24*	1	0	1	0	0
2nd sorties	Fw 190A	Rotenburg	10	~1430	Rotenburg	~1600	1 B-24 HSS**	0	2	0	0	0
II./JG 11	Bf 109G	Hustedt		~1140	Hustedt	~1315	1 P-47, 1 P-51	7	3	2	0	1
2nd sorties	Bf 109G	Hustedt		~1430	Hustedt	~1600	0	0	0	0	0	0
III./JG 11	Fw 190A	Oldenburg		~1140	Oldenburg	~1315	0	3	1	0	0	0
2nd sorties	Fw 190A	Oldenburg		~1430	Oldenburg	~1600	2 B-17	0	0	0	0	0
Jagddivision 3:												
I./JG 1	Fw 190A	Lippspringe		1142	Lippspringe	1315	1 B-24, 1 B-24 HSS	4	2	1	0	1
II./JG 1	Fw 190A	Störmede	21	1140	Störmede	~1315	1 B-24, 4 P-47	3	0	2	0	0
III./JG 1	Bf 109G	Paderborn		1140	Stade	~1315	0	0	0	0	0	0
2nd sorties	Bf 109G	Stade		~1430	Paderborn	~1600	1 P-51	1	0	1	0	0
Abschfü Mittelrhein:												
Stab/JG zbV	Bf 109G	Ansbach		~0930	Paderborn	~1030	transfer	0	0	0	0	0
	Bf 109G	Paderborn		~1140	Ansbach	~1215	0	0	1	1	0	0
II./JG 27	Bf 109G	Merzhausen		0939	Paderborn	1032	transfer	0	0	0	0	0
	Bf 109G	Paderborn		1140	Merzhausen	~1215	0	5	1	2	0	1
II./JG 53	Bf 109G	Biblis		0942	Paderborn	1025	transfer	0	0	0	0	0
2nd sorties	Bf 109G	Paderborn	23	1105	Wunstorf	1215	0	6	0	3	0	1
Jagddivision 7:												
III./JG 3	Bf 109G	Bad Wörishofen	22	1135	Brunswick area	~1330	1 B-24***	2	1	0	0	0
2nd sorties	Bf 109G	Brunswick area		~1430	Bad Wörishofen	~1600	0	0	0	0	0	0
I./JG 5	Bf 109G	Herzogenaurach		1135	Herzogenaurach	~1330	0	1	1	1	0	0
III./JG 54	Fw 190A	Landau		~1130	Landau	~1330	4 B-24, 1 P-38****	5	1	1	1	3
Jafü Ostmark:												
Stab/JG 27	Bf 109G	Fels am Wagram		1139	Magdeburg–Ost	1340	2 B-24, 1 P-51, 1 B-24 HSS	2	1	1	0	0
I./JG 27	Bf 109G	Fels am Wagram		1145	Magdeburg–Ost, Gardelegen	1333	2 B-24, 2 P-47, 1 B-24 HSS, 1 P-51	5	2	1	1	1
III./JG 27	Bf 109G	Götzendorf		~1145	Götzendorf	~1330	1 B-24, 1 B-24 HSS	4	1	1	0	2
IV./JG 27	Bf 109G	Steinamanger (H)		~1145	Steinamanger (H)	~1330	2 P-47,1 P-51	1	1	1	0	0

*I/JG 11: + 1 B-24, 1 B-24 claims unconfirmed (unwitnessed) [first sortie]

**I/JG 11: + 2 B-17, 1 B-17 HSS claims undocumented, 2 B-17 claims unconfirmed (unwitnessed) [second sortie]

***III/JG 3: + 1 B-24, 1 B-24 HSS claims undocumented, 4 B-24 HSS claims unconfirmed (unwitnessed)

****III/JG 54: + 4 B-24, 2 P-38 claims unconfirmed (unwitnessed)

19 May

8th Air Force Mission #358: 818 of 888 HBs (all BDs) bomb Berlin, Kiel port area, Brunswick aviation industry – lose 28-2-353, claim 0. 8th FC escort of 3 P-38 FGs, 4 P-47 FGs, 7 P-51 FGs (700 sorties) claims 70-0-23, loses 19-2-15. 9th FC escort (264 sorties) claims 4-0-6, loses 3.

The target priorities of the Americans shifted with bewildering frequency. The Combined Bomber Offensive had ended on 1 April, and the USSTAF would now report to SHAEF (Supreme Headquarters, Allied Expeditionary Force) until the success of the invasion of the Continent was assured. It thus had some responsibility for tactical targets, but it retained some flexibility to continue the strategic campaign. Instead of concentrating on the oil industry, a known bottleneck, it returned today to the 'old' targets of Berlin and Brunswick. The I. Jagdkorps responded with its maximum force of 447 single-engine fighters. The Zerstörer were either stood down or scrambled under orders to avoid the escorts. The fortunes of the six Gefechtsverbände were mixed. The Verbände of JD 1, JD 2, JD 3 and Jafü Ostmark were based on full Geschwader, had Höhengruppen (high-altitude Gruppen) permanently assigned to ward off the escorts and had a greater chance of success. The Dachs Verband (Badger Formation) from Abschnittsführer Mittelrhein comprised only a command Schwarm and two Bf 109 Gruppen and was frequently driven to ground by the escorts if it could not join up with a larger formation. The JD 7 Verband also had only two Bf 109 Gruppen, but was dominated by the aggressive Major Walther Dahl and his III./JG 3 and usually found a way to reach the bombers and claim victories. JD 7 was bolstered today by III./JG 54, which had been off operations to convert to Fw 190s. It adopted Dahl's tactics and claimed eight B-24s – only four of which were confirmed – for the loss of five Fw 190s. The USAAF wrote off 30 bombers and 24 escorts today; the Luftwaffe lost 30 KIA or MIA, 17 WIA and 68 fighters.

The II. Jagdkorps did not respond to this major raid on the Reich. It was conserving its forces for the coming invasion, against which it was to play a major role, and was in fact sending its six Jagdgruppen to southern France one at a time for rest, relaxation and restoration.

COMBAT REPORT[10]
19 May 1944

One B-24 shot down from 6,500 metres at 1245 hours in PQ FQ-GQ-FR-GR, nr Quakenbrück
One P-47 shot down from 500–800 metres at 1255 hours in PQ GS-GT-HS-HT, nr Nienburg-Wunstorf (Steinhuder Meer)

I scrambled with the Gruppe at 1140 hours in Fw 190A-8 'Red 24' (two MG 151/20, two MG 131) after Sitzbereitschaft. We were ordered to assemble with I./JG 1 and III./JG 1 over Paderborn at 1,000 metres and fly to Porta Westfalica, reaching 7,000–8,000 metres. The Verband reached the ordered area in a climb and was then ordered to fly 340°. After several course changes, we sighted the bomber stream and engaged in combat in PQ FQ-6, course east. The planned attack on the bomber Verband fell apart as the Gruppe became involved in combat with the escorts, which were flying southeast. The Verband pressed to the east, and I was able to reform the Gruppe and lead a head-on formation attack. I attacked the B-24 flying second from the outer left in a tight Pulk from the low front, firing from 500 down to 100 metres. The B-24 flamed immediately with a bright plume and pulled out of the Verband. As I pulled away, its tail broke off and the bomber exploded. I was then involved with four P-47s in the area of Minden. After I had turned with them down to 1,200 metres, I escaped and was attacked by five more P-47s to 800 metres. My airplane spun out of a steep turn, whereupon I saw below me a Fw 190 [wingman Gefr. Stuckenbrock] being chased by two P-47s. I regained control and made a rear attack, firing a long burst down to 30 metres, at which the two Thunderbolts exploded in the air. Gefr. Stuckenbrock and Uffz. Wurl witnessed the B-24 attack; its crash was not seen. Stuckenbrock saw both P-47s crash; Wurl saw one.

Oblt. Georg-Peter Eder
Stab II./JG 1

Luftwaffe defensive activity – 20 May 1944

Unit	Type	Gruppe up			Gruppe down		Claims	Losses				
		Base	No	Time	Base	Time		Dest	Dam	KIA	MIA	WIA
Luftflotte 3												
II. Jagdkorps												
Jagddivision 4:												
I./JG 26	Fw 190A	Lille–Vendeville	23	0940	Venlo	1059	2 P-51	0	0	0	0	0
2. + 3./JG 26	Fw 190A	Denain		0940	Metz, Vogelsang	1120	transfer	1	0	0	0	1
4./JG 26	Fw 190A	Wevelghem		0940	Metz	1045	transfer	0	0	0	0	0
III./JG 26	Bf 109G	Nancy	22	~0940	Nancy, Trier	~1030	n/c	0	0	0	0	0
Jagddivision 5:												
I./JG 2	Fw 190A	Cormeilles		0930	Cormeilles	~1100	2 P-38	1	1	1	0	0
II./JG 2	Bf 109G	Creil		0930	Creil	~1100	0	1	0	0	0	1

Luftwaffe defensive activity – 22 May 1944

Unit	Type	Gruppe up			Gruppe down		Claims	Losses				
		Base	No	Time	Base	Time		Dest	Dam	KIA	MIA	WIA
Luftflotte Reich												
I. Jagdkorps			184									
Jagddivision 1:												
I./JG 3	Bf 109G	Burg		1223	Burg	1423	n/c	0	0	0	0	0
IV.(Sturm)/JG 3	Fw 190A	Salzwedel		1225	Salzwedel	~1415	0	1	0	0	0	1
II./ZG 26	Me 410A	Königsberg–Neumark		1300	Königsberg–Neumark	1455	n/c	0	0	0	0	0
Jagddivision 2:												
I./JG 11	Fw 190A	Rotenburg		1207	Rotenburg	~1345	2 P-47	5	0	2	0	2
II./JG 11	Bf 109G	Hustedt	15	1213	Hustedt	1350	0	0	0	0	0	0
III./JG 11	Fw 190A	Oldenburg		1207	Oldenburg	~1345	4 P-38*	1	0	0	0	1
Jagddivision 3:												
I./JG 1	Fw 190A	Lippspringe		1148	Lüneburg	1340	0	0	2	0	0	0
II./JG 1	Fw 190A	Störmede	18	1146	Störmede	~1330	1 P-38	0	2	0	0	0
III./JG 1	Bf 109G	Oldenburg		1145	Oldenburg	~1330	0	1	3	1	0	1

**III/JG 11: + 4 B-17, 1 P-38, 1 P-51 claims undocumented

20 May

8th Air Force Mission #359: 638 HBs (all BDs) target 6 rail yards and airfields in the western occupied zone, 288 bomb 4 targets – lose 2-8-114, claim 0. 8th FC escort of 3 P-38 FGs, 4 P-47 FGs, 7 P-51 FGs (657 sorties) claims 2-0-1, loses 4-0-5. 9th FC escort (296 sorties) claims 0, loses 0.

After several days of bad weather, the 8th AF scheduled a short-range raid on tactical targets in the occupied zone. II. Jagdkorps followed its frequent practice of ordering some of its units inland; whether to facilitate a concentrated attack on bombers returning from a deep-penetration raid or simply to clear its most vulnerable airfields is unknown. Its four Jagdgruppen were fully occupied by the escorts, against which they had some success; however, they did not reach the bombers.

Back in the Reich, command of the currently leaderless JGzbV (*Jagdgeschwader zur besonderen Verwendung*; Fighter Wing for Special Applications) was awarded to Major Dahl. This unit was a Geschwaderstab without permanently assigned Gruppen. It had been established originally to command the independent JD 7 Jagdgruppen, but had recently been leading the two Gruppen of the Dachs Verband. The Abschnittsführer

Mittelrhein would now give these two Gruppen back to JD 7, and Dahl would control five Jagdgruppen in the air. According to Dahl's memoir, he was promised even more responsibility in the near future. The coming Allied invasion would cue the immediate transfer of most I. Jagdkorps Gruppen to the invasion front. Those remaining in the Reich were to be commanded by Dahl.

Uffz. Willi Unger sits on the wing of his 12. (Sturm)/JG 3 Fw 190A-8 'Yellow 17' at Barth on 20 May. This entire Staffel of IV.(Sturm)/JG 3 was equipped with rearward-firing 21-cm rocket launcher tubes. These were unsuited for the tactics intended for the Gruppe and were soon removed. *(Crow)*

COMBAT REPORT[11]
20 May 1944

One Mustang destroyed from 7,500 metres at 1050 hours, PQ MM, Bocholt-Roermond [Kiefner's victim was a 355th Fighter Group P-51: DC]

At 0940 hours, the Gruppe scrambled versus an enemy bomber formation. I flew in a Fw 190A-8 (two MG 151/20s and two MG 131s) as an element leader in the 1. Staffel Schwarm. At 1030 hours, we sighted three heavily escorted B-17 Pulks in PQ QK. We flew toward the sun to put ourselves in a favourable position to attack. After the fighter escort had left, we planned to overtake the rear Pulk and attack it from the front. However, it made a left turn to the northwest. We were then attacked by new escorts coming from the front and high rear. We turned toward a Schwarm of Mustangs. With my wingman, I attacked the right

outer machine from the rear and slightly above. I fired from about 80 metres. With my first salvo, I saw good strikes in the centre of the fuselage and the right wing. The enemy machine immediately burst into flames, fell over its right wing and dove straight down, trailing pieces. I could not observe the crash owing to a continuous cloud deck. The battle was witnessed by Uffz. Oltmanns, Ofhr. Söffing and Uffz. Wyrich.

Oblt. Georg Kiefner
1./JG 26

Left: Lt. Georg Kiefner, Kapitän of the 1. Staffel of I./JG 26, and his Fw 190A8 'White 5' (W. Nr. 171079) on 24 June, the day he received it. *(Kiefner)*

22 May
8th Air Force Mission #361: 294 of 342 1st BD + 3rd BD B-17s bomb Kiel port area, TOT 1300-08 – lose 5-1-209, claim 0. 94 of 96 2nd BD B-24s bomb Siracourt V-weapon site, TOT 1124 – lose 0-0-1, claim 0. Escort of 3 P-38 FGs, 2 P-47 FGs, 7 P-51 FGs (568 sorties) claims 22-4-8, loses 7-3-4.

A raid on Kiel by a small force of 8th AF B-17s elicited only a *pro forma* response from the I. Jagdkorps. 184 fighters were scrambled, but only 101 from JG 1, JG 11 and IV.(Sturm)/JG 3 were credited with combat sorties. Only III./JG 11, which flew alone today, had a successful mission. For the loss of one Fw 190A, whose pilot survived without injury, the Gruppe claimed four B-17s, five P-38s and one P-51. Most of the claims disappeared in the system, however, and the unit was credited only with four P-38s. The USAAF wrote off six bombers and 10 escorts; the Luftwaffe lost three KIA, five WIA and eight fighters.

Luftwaffe defensive activity – 23 May 1944

Unit	Type	Gruppe up			Gruppe down		Claims	Losses				
		Base	No	Time	Base	Time		Dest	Dam	KIA	MIA	WIA
Luftflotte Reich												
I. Jagdkorps												
Jagddivision 1:												
I./JG 3	Bf 109G	Burg		0846	Burg	0935	n/c	0	0	0	0	0
II./JG 3	Bf 109G	Sachau		0847	Sachau	0943	n/c	0	0	0	0	0
IV.(Sturm)/JG 3?	Bf 109G	Salzwedel		~0845	Salzwedel	~0930	n/c	0	0	0	0	0
Jagddivision 2:												
I./JG 11	Fw 190A	Rotenburg		~0845	Salzwedel	~0930	transfer	0	0	0	0	0
II./JG 11	Bf 109G	Wunstorf		~0845	Salzwedel	~0930	transfer	0	0	0	0	0
III./JG 11	Fw 190A	Oldenburg		~0845	Salzwedel	~0930	transfer	0	0	0	0	0
Jagddivision 3:												
I./JG 1	Fw 190A	Lippspringe		~0845	Salzwedel, Burg	~0930	transfer	0	0	0	0	0
II./JG 1	Fw 190A	Störmede	18	~0845	Salzwedel	~0930	transfer	0	0	0	0	0
III./JG 1	Bf 109G	Paderborn		~0845	Salzwedel, Burg	~0930	transfer	0	0	0	0	0
Abschfü Mittelrhein:												
II./JG 27?	Bf 109G	Erbenheim		~0845	Erbenheim	~1030	n/c	0	0	0	0	0
II./JG 53	Bf 109G	Öttingen		0842	Öttingen	1030	n/c	0	0	0	0	0
Jagddivision 7:												
Stab/JG zbV	Bf 109G	Ansbach		0835	Ansbach	1030	n/c	0	0	0	0	0
III./JG 3	Bf 109G	Bad Wörishofen	20	0845	Bad Wörishofen	1025	n/c	0	0	0	0	0
III./JG 54	Fw 190A	Illesheim	21	~0845	Illesheim	~1030	n/c	0	0	0	0	0
Luftflotte 3												
II. Jagdkorps												
Jagddivision 4:												
III./JG 26	Bf 109G	Nancy?	27	0833	Strasbourg	0952	0	1	0	1	0	0
Jagddivision 5:												
I./JG 2	Fw 190A	Boissy–le–Bois		0903	Boissy–le–Bois	1000	n/c	0	0	0	0	0

23 May

8th Air Force Mission #364: 814 of 1045 HBs (all BDs) bomb 13 French rail yards and airfields, TOT 0827-0925 – lose 3-3-83, claim 0. 8th FC escort of 3 P-38 FGs, 4 P-47 FGs, 7 P-51 FGs (562 sorties) claims 0, loses 0-1-2. 9th FC escort (644 sorties) claims 0, loses 4.

The 8th AF dispatched a record 1,045 heavy bombers against railroad yards in central France and western Germany. The time and size of the mission apparently fooled the I. Jagdkorps completely, and it transferred most of its fighters to Burg and Salzwedel to defend Berlin or the oil targets in the Leipzig area. The air defence was left to a single II. Jagdkorps Gruppe, III./JG 26, which scrambled 27 Bf 109s from Nancy. It was vectored to a B-17 formation near Colmar, but a planned frontal attack was prudently broken off with the approach of the Mustang escort. One Messerschmitt was downed with its pilot in the ensuing combat. The flying Luftwaffe ended the day scoreless. The few American losses were credited to the Flak (an arm of the Luftwaffe) and operational causes.

24 May – vs. 8th Air Force

8th Air Force Mission #367: 517 of 616 1st BD + 3rd BD B-17s bomb Berlin, TOT 1051-1113 – lose 33-1-256, claim 0. 400 of 490 2nd BD + 3rd BD B-24s bomb 4 French airfields, TOT 0850 – lose 0-0-33, claim 0. 8th FC escort of 3 P-38 FGs, 4 P-47 FGs, 7 P-51 FGs (602 sorties) claims 33-7-6, loses 10-1-6. 9th FC escort (351 sorties) claims 0, loses 6.

Luftwaffe defensive activity vs 8th Air Force – 24 May 1944

Unit	Type	Gruppe up			Gruppe down		Claims	Losses				
		Base	No	Time	Base	Time		Dest	Dam	KIA	MIA	WIA
Luftflotte Reich												
I. Jagdkorps			286									
Jagddivision 1:												
I./JG 1	Fw 190A	Salzwedel		0940	Lippspringe	~1140	2 B-17	0	1	0	0	0
II./JG 1	Fw 190A	Salzwedel	10	0940	Störmede	~1140	1 B-17	0	0	0	0	0
III./JG 1	Bf 109G	Salzwedel		0940	Paderborn	~1140	1 B-17, 1 P-38	1	0	0	0	0
Stab/JG 3	Bf 109G	Salzwedel		~0940	Salzwedel	~1140	1 B-17	0	0	0	0	0
I./JG 3	Bf 109G	Burg	17	0943	Jüterbog	1147	1 B-17, 1 P-38, 2 P-51	3	0	2	0	0
II./JG 3	Bf 109G	Sachau	20	0940	Sachau	~1140	1 B-17	2	2	1	0	0
IV.(Sturm)/JG 3	Fw 190A	Salzwedel		0941	Salzwedel	1212	5 B-17**	1	1	0	0	0
II./JG 302	Bf 109G	Salzwedel		0940	Salzwedel	~1140	3 B-17	1	0	1	0	0
I./ZG 26	Me 410A	Königsberg–Neumark	*31	0940	Königsberg–Neumark	1215	0	0	0	0	0	0
II./ZG 26	Me 410A	Königsberg–Neumark	—	1020	Königsberg–Neumark	1222	0	1	0	2	0	0
Jagddivision 2:												
I./JG 11	Fw 190A	Rotenburg	10	~0940	Rotenburg	~1130	1 B-17***	3	0	2	0	0
II./JG 11	Bf 109G	Wunstorf		~0940	Wunstorf	~1130	0****	9	0	3	1	2
III./JG 11	Fw 190A	Oldenburg		~0940	Oldenburg	~1130	4 B-17*****	0	2	0	0	0
Jagddivision 7:												
Stab/JG zbV	Bf 109G	Ansbach		0948	Ansbach	~1130	0	1	0	1	0	0
III./JG 3	Bf 109G	Ansbach		0948	Ansbach	1140	0	2	1	1	0	0
I./JG 5	Bf 109G	Neubiberg		~0940	Neubiberg	~1130	0	0	0	0	0	0
II./JG 27	Bf 109G	Öttingen, Unterschlauersbach		0945	Unterschlauersbach	~1130	1 P-51	2	2	1	0	1
II./JG 53	Bf 109G	Öttingen		~0945	Öttingen	~1130	0	1	2	1	0	0
III./JG 54	Fw 190A	Illesheim		0942	Salzwedel	1157	7 B-24, 1 P-51******	4	0	2	0	2
Luftflotte 3 (total losses for day shown)												
II. Jagdkorps												
Jagddivision 4:												
I./JG 26	Fw 190A	Denain		1050	Denain	1215	1 P-47	1	1	1	0	0
4./JG 26	Fw 190A	Wevelghem		1045	Metz	~1215	0	0	1	0	0	0
III./JG 26	Bf 109G	Nancy		1045	Nancy	1250	0	0	1	0	0	0
Jagddivision 5:												
I./JG 2	Fw 190A	Cormeilles, Boissy–le–Bois		1035	Cormeilles, Boissy–le–Bois	1128	0	1	1	0	0	0
II./JG 2	Bf 109G	Creil		~1035	Chamant	~1130	0	3	1	0	0	2

*31 total sorties by ZG 26

**IV.(Sturm)/JG 3: + 2 P-51 claims undocumented, 4 B-17 HSS, 1 P-38 claims unconfirmed (unwitnessed)

***I/JG 11: + 1 B-17 claim undocumented, 3 B-17 HSS claims unconfirmed (unwitnessed)

****II/JG 11: + 1 B-17 claim undocumented, 2 P-51 claims unconfirmed (unwitnessed)

*****II/JG 11: + 1 B-17 claim undocumented, 2 B-17 HSS claims unconfirmed (unwitnessed)

******III/JG 54: + 3 B-17 HSS claims unconfirmed (unwitnessed)

Axis defensive activity vs. 15th Air Force – 24 May 1944

Unit	Type	Gruppe up			Gruppe down		Claims	Losses				
		Base	No	Time	Base	Time		Dest	Dam	KIA	MIA	WIA
Luftflotte Reich												
I. Jagdkorps			111									
Jagddivision 7:												
Jafü Ostmark:												
Stab/JG 27	Bf 109G	Fels am Wagram		0912	Fels am Wagram	1030	3 B-24	0	0	0	0	0
I./JG 27	Bf 109G	Fels am Wagram		0915	Fels am Wagram	1033	4 B-24, 1 P-51*	2	0	1	0	0
III./JG 27	Bf 109G	Götzendorf		~0915	Götzendorf	~1030	10 B-24, 1 B-24 HSS**	6	0	4	0	0
IV./JG 27	Bf 109G	Agram (Y)		~0915	Agram (Y)	~1030	2 B-17, 1 B-24***	3	1	1	0	1
I./JG 302	Bf 109G	Wien–Seyring	30	~0916	Wien–Seyring	~1020	4 B-24, 1 B-24 HSS****	7	0	0	0	2
II./ZG 1	Bf 110G	Wels	35	~1100	Wels	~1230	2 P-38	1	2	0	0	1
II./SG 152	Fw 190G	Prossnitz		~1100	Prossnitz	~1230	2 B-24	0	0	0	0	0
Abschfü Ungarn:												
101/1 JSt (Hungary)	Bf 109G	Veszprém	13	1100	Veszprém	~1230	1 B-17, 3 B-24, 1 P-51	2	6	2	0	0
Luftflotte 2												
Jafü Oberltalien:			24									
Stab/JG 77	Bf 109G	Ferrara	3	0935	Ferrara	1045	0	0	0	0	0	0
II./JG 77	Bf 109G	Ferrara		0935	Ferrara	1045	1 P-38	2	0	0	?	?

*I./JG 27: + 1 B-24, 2 B-24 HSS claims undocumented, 4 B-24 claims unconfirmed (unwitnessed)

**III./JG 27: + 3 B-24 claims undocumented, 1 B-24 claims unconfirmed (unwitnessed)   ***IV./JG 27: + 2 B-24 claims unconfirmed (unwitnessed)

****I./JG 302: + 5 B-24, 2 P-51 claims unconfirmed (unwitnessed)

Luftwaffe defensive activity – 25 May 1944

Unit	Type	Gruppe up			Gruppe down		Claims	Losses				
		Base	No	Time	Base	Time		Dest	Dam	KIA	MIA	WIA
Luftflotte Reich												
I. Jagdkorps												
Jagddivision 3:												
I./JG 1	Fw 190A	Lippspringe		0815	Lippspringe	~1015	0	1	1	0	0	1
II./JG 1	Fw 190A	Störmede		0815	Echterdingen, Illesheim	~1015	n/c	0	0	0	0	0
III./JG 1	Bf 109G	Paderborn		0815	Paderborn	~1015	2 P-51	1	2	1	0	0
Jagddivision 7:												
Stab/JG zbV	Bf 109G	Ansbach		0828	Ansbach	1030	n/c	0	0	0	0	0
III./JG 3	Bf 109G	Ansbach	16	0827	Ansbach	1015	n/c	0	0	0	0	0
III./JG 54	Fw 190A	Illesheim		~0830	Illesheim	~1030	0	1	0	0	0	0
Luftflotte 3												
II. Jagdkorps												
Jagddivision 4:												
I./JG 26	Fw 190A	Denain		~0800	Metz	~0930	0	1	0	1	0	0
4./JG 26	Fw 190A	Wevelghem		0654	Metz	0740	transfer	0	0	0	0	0
	Fw 190A	Metz		0747	Metz	0846	0	0	0	0	0	0
III./JG 26	Bf 109G	Nancy		0800	Nancy	0920	1 P-47	5	2	2	0	1
Jagddivision 5:												
I./JG 2	Fw 190A	Cormeilles		~0845	Cormeilles	~1045	1 B-24, 4 P-38	2	1	2	0	0
II./JG 2	Bf 109G	Creil		~0845	Creil	~1045	0	0	0	0	0	0

Luftwaffe defensive activity – 27 May 1944

Unit	Type	Gruppe up			Gruppe down		Claims	Losses				
		Base	No	Time	Base	Time		Dest	Dam	KIA	MIA	WIA
Luftflotte Reich												
I. Jagdkorps												
Jagddivision 7:			89									
Stab/JG zbV	Bf 109G	Ansbach		1120	Ansbach	~1300	0	0	0	0	0	0
III./JG 3	Bf 109G	Ansbach	21	1126	Ansbach	~1300	1 B-17	6	1	3	0	3
I./JG 5	Bf 109G	Herzogenaurach		~1130	Herzogenaurach	~1300	2 B-17*	7	5	7	0	5
II./JG 27	Bf 109G	Unterschlauersbach		~1130	Unterschlauersbach	~1300	1 P-51	6	3	3	0	0
II./JG 53	Bf 109G	Öttingen	16	1120	Öttingen	~1330	2 B-17, 1 P-51	4	1	1	0	1
III./JG 54	Fw 190A	Illesheim		~1130	Illesheim	~1300	5 B-17, 1 P-51**	5	0	1	0	4
I./JG 301	Bf 109G	Holzkirchen		1235	Holzkirchen	1421	n/c	0	0	0	0	0
Luftflotte 3												
II. Jagdkorps			84									
Jagddivision 4:												
I./JG 26	Fw 190A	Denain		1017	Laon–Athies	1200	0	1	1	0	0	0
	Fw 190A	Cambrai–Epinoy	2	1415	Cambrai–Epinoy	~1500	0	1	0	1	0	0
4./JG 26	Fw 190A	Wevelghem		~1030	Wevelghem	~1200	0	0	0	0	0	0
III./JG 26	Bf 109G	Nancy	15	0935	Nancy, Tavaux	1140	0	0	0	0	0	0
Jagddivision 5:												
I./JG 2	Fw 190A	Cormeilles		~1030	Cormeilles	~1200	0	0	2	0	0	0
II./JG 2	Bf 109G	Creil		~1030	Creil	~1200	0	0	1	0	0	0

*I./JG 5: + 4 P-51 claims unconfirmed (unwitnessed)

**III./JG 54: + 4 B-17 claims unconfirmed (unwitnessed)

The 8th AF dispatched 616 B-17s to bomb Berlin and, as part of the pre-invasion preparations, sent 490 B-24s to bomb the airfields of JG 2. This history is not intended to cover the activity of the tactical air forces, but 450 9th Air Force B-26s and A-20s bombed other airfields as well as coastal defences and V-1 sites, which was a typical day's activity on the Channel coast. Also typically, the II. Jagdkorps ignored most of this action in the name of force conservation. The two operational JG 26 Gruppen were sent inland to help the Berlin defenders, but only one encounter was reported, in which one 9th AF P-47 was downed without loss. Over the course of the day, one JG 26 and four JG 2 aircraft were shot down, but details are lacking.

The principal 8th AF target, Berlin, was deduced properly today by the I. Jagdkorps, but only 254 Bf 109s and Fw 190s were available to the defenders; the Jafü Ostmark fighters were tied down in Austria. As usual on Berlin raids, the JD 2 Verband (JG 11) struck first. Next came the JD 1 Verband, which today contained JD 3's JG 1 (which had overnighted on Salzwedel) in addition to JG 3 and totalled 150

fighters. The newly enlarged JD 7 Verband reached the bombers as they were leaving the target. The defensive concentration was thus almost perfect, but escort coverage was also very good, and bomber crews noted that the tactic of many of the defenders was 'one pass and away'. The day's losses totalled 34 B-17s and 17 escorts for the 8th AF, and at least 19 KIA and MIA, seven WIA and 36 fighters for the Luftwaffe in northern Europe.

24 May – vs. 15th Air Force
15th Air Force: 128 of 137 B-17s bomb Vienna-Atzgerdorf Bf 109 factory, TOT 1051-1113 – lose 3, claim 0. 329 of 598 B-24s bomb 4 Austrian airfields, TOT 1013-50 – lose 17, claim 0. Escort of 89 P-38s (2 FGs), 38 P-47s (1 FG), 66 P-51s (2 FGs) claims 34-9-11, loses 2 P-38s, 2 P-51s.

The USSTAF succeeded in conducting a rare combined mission today. The 15th AF dispatched its B-17 wing to a major Vienna Bf 109 factory, while its B-24s bombed four Austrian airfields. The 15th Fighter Command had received a second P-51 group, but one P-38 group did not fly today, so the escort

Luftwaffe defensive activity – 28 May 1944

Unit	Type	Gruppe up			Gruppe down		Claims	Losses				
		Base	No	Time	Base	Time		Dest	Dam	KIA	MIA	WIA
Luftflotte Reich												
I. Jagdkorps			333									
Jagddivision 1:												
Stab/JG 3	Bf 109G	Salzwedel		~1310	Salzwedel?	~1500	1 B-17	0	0	0	0	0
I./JG 3	Bf 109G	Burg	8	1315	Aschersleben, Burg, Halle, others	1510	0*	6	2	1	0	3
II./JG 3	Bf 109G	Sachau		1310	Zwolle, Sachau, others	1440	2 B-17**	3	1	0	0	1
IV./JG 3	Fw 190A	Salzwedel		1305	Salzwedel	~1500	0	2	0	1	0	0
II./JG 302	Bf 109G	Salzwedel		~1305	Salzwedel	~1500	0	1	0	0	0	1
I./ZG 26	Me 410A	Königsberg–Neumark		1245	Zerbst	1555	1 B-17, 1 P-51	2	1	?	?	?
II./ZG 26	Me 410A	Königsberg–Neumark		1335	Königsberg–Neumark	1515	0	0	1	1	0	0
LBeob St 1	Ju 88C	Neuruppin	1	~1300	?	?	shadower	1	0	3	0	0
Jafü Oberschlesien:												
3./JGr Ost	Fw 190A	Liegnitz		~1330	Liegnitz	~1530	1 B-17	0	0	0	0	0
Jagddivision 2:												
I./JG 11	Fw 190A	Rotenburg		~1305	Rotenburg	~1500	4 B-17, 1 P-51	4	1	2	0	0
II./JG 11	Bf 109G	Hustedt	16	1307	Salzwedel, others	1445	4 P-51	3	1	1	0	0
III./JG 11	Fw 190A	Oldenburg		~1307	Oldenburg	~1500	5 B-17, 2 P-51	1	3	1	0	0
Jagddivision 3:												
I./JG 1	Fw 190A	Lippspringe		~1305	Lippspringe	~1500	7 B-17***	4	3	2	0	1
II./JG 1	Fw 190A	Störmede	16	1305	10 airfields	~1500	2 B-17****	1	1	0	0	1
III./JG 1	Bf 109G	Paderborn		1305	Paderborn	~1500	0	0	1	0	0	1
	Bf 109G	Paderborn	4	1518	Paderborn	1530	1 P-51	2	0	1	0	1
Jagddivision 7:												
Stab/JG zbV	Bf 109G	Ansbach		1345	Ansbach	~1500	0	0	0	0	0	0
III./JG 3	Bf 109G	Ansbach		1345	Ansbach	~1500	0	3	0	1	0	2
I./JG 5	Bf 109G	Herzogenaurach		~1305	Herzogenaurach	~1500	0	3	0	2	0	1
II./JG 27	Bf 109G	Unterschlauersbach		~1305	Unterschlauersbach	~1500	0	6	0	3	0	0
II./JG 53	Bf 109G	Öttingen	12	1232	Öttingen	~1500	0	1	2	0	0	1
III./JG 54	Fw 190A	Landau		~1305	Landau	~1500	1 P-38	1	1	0	0	0
Jafü Ostmark:												
Stab/JG 27	Bf 109G	Fels am Wagram		1258	Fels am Wagram	~1445	0	0	0	0	0	0
I./JG 27	Bf 109G	Fels am Wagram		1255	various	1500	1 B-17	2	2	2	0	0
III./JG 27	Bf 109G	Götzendorf		~1255	Götzendorf	~1445	6 B-17*****	3	1	1	0	1
IV./JG 27	Bf 109G	Steinamanger (H)		~1255	Steinamanger (H)	~1445	1 P-51	1	1	1	0	0

*I./JG 3: + 4 P-51 claims unconfirmed (unwitnessed)

**II./JG 3: + 3 B-17 HSS claims unconfirmed (unwitnessed)

***I./JG 1: + 8 B-17 HSS claims unconfirmed (unwitnessed)

****II./JG 1: + 2 B-17, 4 B-17 HSS claims unconfirmed (unwitnessed)

*****III./JG 27: + 2 B-17 claims undocumented, 5 B-17 claims unconfirmed (unwitnessed)

force totalled five groups, still not enough for full escort. Awaiting them were 135 Bf 109s from the JG 27 Stab, three JG 27 Gruppen, I./JG 302 (a former *Wilde Sau* unit) and 35 Bf 110s from II./ZG 1. Together, these made up the standard Jafü Ostmark Gefechtsverband. Also seeing action today were the operational Staffel of the training unit I./SG 152 and one Bf 109 Staffel from the Hungarian home defences. One Luftwaffe unit in Italy apparently took a swipe at the formation as it headed north. The defenders did well, although not as well as their 37 confirmed victory claims would imply: 20 bombers and four escorts failed to return to their Italian bases. The German and Hungarian defenders lost eight KIA, four WIA and 23 aircraft.

25 May

8th Air Force Mission #370: 326 of 406 HBs (all BDs) bomb 22 rail yards, airfields and coastal gun positions in France and Belgium, TOT ca. 0836 – lose 4-1-145, claim 0. 8th FC escort of 3 P-38 FGs, 4 P-47 FGs, 6 P-51 FGs (604 sorties) claims 13-2-3, loses 12-0-15. 9th FC escort (207 sorties) claims 0, loses 0.

The 8th AF continued its campaign against airfields, railroad yards and coastal defences in France. As an experiment, the bombers were split into small formations to maximise the number of targets struck in a single morning. The II. Jagdkorps had some

success against the escorts, but only one bomber is known to have been downed by a Luftwaffe fighter. The only I. Jagdkorps unit to make contact was JG 1, which became involved with some P-51s. The 8th AF wrote off five bombers and 12 escorts on this mission; the Luftwaffe lost six KIA, two WIA and 11 fighters.

27 May

8th Air Force Mission #373: 930 of 1126 HBs (all BDs) bomb 10 rail yards in E France and SW Germany, TOT 1259-1320, 2 coastal gun positions in France – lose 24-2-205, claim 0. 8th FC escort of 4 P-38 FGs, 4 P-47 FGs, 7 P-51 FGs (710 sorties) claims 35-1-5, loses 7-2-8. 9th FC escort (425 sorties) claims 4-0-0, loses 1.

The 8th AF and the two tactical air forces in the UK attacked numerous rail yards in France and southwestern Germany; the USAAF alone flew more than 3,000 sorties. The II. Jagdkorps scrambled its fighters and sent them inland. They were vectored to various locations, but the real if unstated goal of these missions was to keep out of the Allies' way. The I. Jagdkorps was hampered by weather conditions that grounded three of its Jagddivisionen, but mounted a serious if small-scale effort against the bombers: 173 single-engine and 32 twin-engine sorties were flown, all of which made contact. The twin-engine unit remains unknown, but the single-engine fighters represented the full strength of the JGzbV and its five

Luftwaffe defensive activity vs. 15th Air Force – 29 May 1944

Unit	Type	Gruppe up			Gruppe down		Claims	Losses				
		Base	No	Time	Base	Time		Dest	Dam	KIA	MIA	WIA
Luftflotte Reich												
I. Jagdkorps												
Jagddivision 7:												
Jafü Ostmark:			101									
Stab/JG 27	Bf 109G	Fels am Wagram		0900	Fels am Wagram	1040	2 B-24	2	0	2	0	0
I./JG 27	Bf 109G	Fels am Wagram		0900	Fels am Wagram	1025	3 B-24	1	0	1	0	0
III./JG 27	Bf 109G	Götzendorf		~0855	Götzendorf	~1030	1 B-24*	0	0	0	0	0
IV./JG 27	Bf 109G	Agram (Y)		~0855	Agram (Y)	~1030	2 P-51	1	0	1	0	0
I./JG 302	Bf 109G	Wien–Seyring		~0900	Wien–Seyring	~1030	3 B-24**	1	0	1	0	0
II./ZG 1	Bf 110G	Wels		~0900	Wels	~1100	5 B-24, 3 P-51	13	1	17	1	7
Luftflotte 2												
Jafü Oberitalien:												
II./JG 77	Bf 109G	Lavariano		1045	Lavariano	1230	8 B-24	2	1	0	1	0

*III./JG 27: + 2 B-24 claims undocumented, 2 B-24 HSS claims unconfirmed (unwitnessed)

**I./JG 302: + 4 B-24 HSS claims unconfirmed (unwitnessed)

Luftwaffe defensive activity vs. 8th Air Force – 29 May 1944

Unit	Type	Gruppe up			Gruppe down		Claims	Losses (–included with 1st sortie)				
		Base	No	Time	Base	Time		Dest	Dam	KIA	MIA	WIA
Luftflotte Reich												
I. Jagdkorps			275									
Jagddivision 1:												
Stab/JG 3	Bf 109G	Salzwedel		~1100	Salzwedel	~1230	0	1	0	1	0	0
I./JG 3	Bf 109G	Burg		1055	Burg	1210	0	1	3	0	0	0
II./JG 3	Bf 109G	Sachau		1052	Stargard?	1240	4 B-24	3	0	2	0	1
IV.(Sturm)/JG 3	Fw 190A	Salzwedel	6	~1100	Salzwedel	~1230	0	2	0	1	0	0
2nd sorties	Fw 190A	Salzwedel		~1300	Salzwedel	~1430	0	0	0	0	0	0
I./ZG 26	Me 410A	Königsberg–Neumark		1115	Königsberg–Neumark	1255	4 B-24*	4	1	5	0	3
2nd sorties	Me 410A	Königsberg–Neumark		~1330	Königsberg–Neumark	~1530	1 B-24, 2 P-51	—	—	—	—	—
II./ZG 26	Me 410A	Königsberg–Neumark		1120	Königsberg–Neumark	1320	4 B-24	0	1	1	0	0
2nd sorties	Me 410A	Königsberg–Neumark		~1345	Königsberg–Neumark	~1530	1 B-24	—	—	—	—	—
Jafü Oberschlesien:												
1./JGr Ost	Fw 190A	Liegnitz	12	~1230	Liegnitz	~1400	3 B-17, 1 P-51	7	1	5	0	3
4./JGr Ost	Bf 109G	Liegnitz		~1230	Liegnitz	~1400	0	2	0	1	0	1
Jagddivision 2:												
I./JG 11	Fw 190A	Rotenburg		~1100	Stettin, others	~1300	3 B-17, 1 B-24	5	0	3	0	1
II./JG 11	Bf 109G	Hustedt	19	1057	Hustedt, others	1255	3 P-51	4	1	1	0	1
III./JG 11	Fw 190A	Oldenburg		~1100	Oldenburg, others	~1300	2 B-24**	7	1	1	0	0
IV./NJG 3	Ju 88C	Kastrup		1422	Kastrup	1505	0	0	0	0	0	0
Jagddivision 3:												
I./JG 1	Fw 190A	Lippspringe		~1100	Lippspringe	~1300	1 B-17	1	1	0	0	0
II./JG 1	Fw 190A	Störmede	20	1101	Cottbus, others	~1300	6 B-17	2	5	1	0	2
III./JG 1	Bf 109G	Paderborn		~1100	Paderborn	~1300	0	1	2	1	0	0
Jagddivision 7:												
Stab/JG zbV?	Bf 109G	Ansbach		~1100	Ansbach	~1300	0	0	0	0	0	0
III./JG 3	Bf 109G	Ansbach	13	1100	Ansbach, Dresden, others	~1300	2 B-17***	0	0	0	0	0
II./JG 27	Bf 109G	Unterschlauersbach		~1100	Unterschlauersbach	~1300	0	0	0	0	0	0
II./JG 53	Bf 109G	Öttingen		~1100	Öttingen	~1300	1 B-17	1	0	0	0	0
III./JG 54	Fw 190A	Illesheim		~1100	Illesheim	~1300	0	0	0	0	0	0
Luftflotte 3												
II. Jagdkorps												
Jagddivision 4:												
I./JG 26	Fw 190A	Denain	17	0845	Metz–Frescaty	0927	transfer	0	0	0	0	0
	Fw 190A	Metz–Frescaty		~1300	Denain	~1430	0	0	0	0	0	0
4./JG 26	Fw 190A	Wevelghem		0835	Metz–Frescaty	0942	transfer	0	0	0	0	0
	Fw 190A	Metz–Frescaty		1310	Wevelghem	1415	0	0	0	0	0	0
III./JG 26	Bf 109G	Nancy		~1300	Nancy	~1430	0	2	0	1	0	0
I./JG 105	Bf 109G	Bourges		?	Bourges	?	0	1	0	0	0	0

*I./ZG 26: + 3 B-24 claims unconfirmed (unwitnessed)

**III./JG 11: + 2 P-47 claims undocumented, 2 B-17 HSS claims unconfirmed (unwitnessed)

***III./JG 3: + 1 B-17 claim undocumented, 4 B-17 HSS claims unconfirmed (unwitnessed)

Jagdgruppen, now under the control of Jagddivision 7. Major Dahl returned early with a bad radio, but the rest of his large force had some success, marked by the high claims typical of Dahl's forces, while sustaining serious losses. The 8th AF wrote off a total of 26 bombers and 10 escorts; the Luftwaffe lost 16 KIA, 13 WIA and 30 fighters.

28 May

8th Air Force Mission #377: 806 of 1282 HBs (all BDs) bomb 25 German oil and aviation targets; 58 of 59 1st BD B-17s glide-bomb Cologne rail yard, TOT 1302-1442 – lose 32-1-210, claim 37-29-24. 8th FC escort of 4 P-38 FGs, 4 P-47 FGs, 7 P-51 FGs (697 sorties) claims 27-1-6, loses 9-3-11. 9th FC escort (527 sorties) claims 33-0-10, loses 5.

Buoyed by a favourable weather forecast, the USSTAF ordered the 8th AF to fly a maximum-strength raid to a number of oil refineries and aircraft factories in central Germany. The three bomb divisions formed into a single stream of well over 1,000 bombers and headed due east, in the direction of Berlin and Brunswick. The I. Jagdkorps responded to this provocation by ordering all of its Bf 109s and Fw 190s to scramble and rendezvous in the Magdeburg area; they numbered 330, of which 258 made contact. Fifteen Zerstörer also took off under their usual restrictions; 10 of them made contact. The fighters of JD 1, JD 2, JD 3 and JD 7 formed a single large Gefechtsverband, but were able to find only a few weak areas in the huge escort screen, today comprising 697 8th FC and 527 9th FC fighters, even after the bomber wings split up to hit their multiple targets. Although the Jafü Ostmark Verband was also ordered to Magdeburg, it did not find the large Gefechtsverband, but was directed to a choice target, a B-17 combat wing that had lost its place 'in line' due to a form-up error and had flown the entire mission without escort. This one wing lost 15 of the 33 bombers written off; 17 escorts were also lost. The I. Jagdkorps lost 23 KIA, 14 WIA and 50 airplanes.

29 May – vs. 8th Air Force

8th Air Force Mission #377: 888 of 993 HBs (all BDs) bomb 12 oil and aviation targets in Poland and E Germany, TOT 1209-1304 – lose 34-3-327, claim 62-37-29. 8th FC escort of 4 P-38 FGs, 4 P-47 FGs, 7 P-51 FGs (673 sorties) claims 39-1-5, loses 10-0-9. 9th FC escort (592 sorties) claims 1-0-0, loses 2.

The USSTAF mounted another combined attack on the oil and aviation industries. The 8th Air Force attempted

to split the northern defences by sending its B-17s to attack aviation targets in eastern Germany, while its B-24s flew in a separate stream along the Baltic coast, bombing the Pölitz refinery and Tutow aviation targets. The German response was late but severe; 307 single-engine and 54 twin-engine fighters eventually sortied. Twenty 2nd BD B-24s were written off, most over the Baltic to an attack by the JD 1 Verband, which comprised JG 3, JG 11 and ZG 26. The north German Zerstörer were credited with 10 B-24s and two P-51s. The RLV fighters left in central Germany, reinforced by the *Einsatzstaffel* [operational squadron] of the training unit JGr Ost, were directed to the B-17s, 17 of which failed to return to England. For the day, the 8th AF wrote off 37 bombers and 12 escorts. The Luftwaffe forces opposing them lost 24 KIA, 12 WIA and 44 aircraft; the JGr Ost formation was almost wiped out.

29 May – vs. 15th Air Force

15th Air Force: 166 of 168 B-17s, 139 of 155 B-24s bomb Wollersdorf (A) airfield, TOT 0942-1013 – lose 7, claim 18-5-1. 104 of 112 B-24s bomb Wiener Neustadt aircraft factory, TOT 1010-12 – lose 2, claim 5-1-0. 126 of 148 B-24s bomb Atzgersdorf aircraft factory, TOT 1031-38 – lose 9, claim 5-3-0. Escort of 135 P-38s (3 FGs), 134 P-51s (2 FGs) claims 32-6-8, loses 4 P-38s, 4 P-51s.

The 15th AF was sent to bomb factories and airfields in the Vienna area. Its main target, the Wiener Neustadt Messerschmitt factory, was severely damaged. The Jafü Ostmark fighters were pressed hard by the five escort groups, but II./JG 77 was scrambled from its base in northern Italy against the withdrawing B-24s and was credited with eight, most probably stragglers that went into the 15th AF books as 'missing'. A total of 19 bombers and eight escorts were lost. The defending Bf 109 units lost five KIA, one MIA and seven fighters; II./ZG 1 lost 18 KIA and MIA, seven WIA and 13 Bf 110s to the Mustangs and was temporarily wiped off the Jafü Ostmark organisation chart.

30 May – vs. 8th Air Force

8th Air Force Mission #380: 919 of 928 HBs (all BDs) bomb 9 aviation targets in Germany, 3 rail yards in western occupied zone – lose 12-3-201, claim 8-5-1. 8th FC escort of 4 P-38 FGs, 4 P-47 FGs, 7 P-51 FGs (672 sorties) claims 50-3-2, loses 9-2-7. 9th FC escort (637 sorties) claims 8-0-2, loses 3.

In the absence of any directive from SHAEF to focus

Luftwaffe defensive activity vs. 8th Air Force – 30 May 1944

Unit	Type	Gruppe up			Gruppe down		Claims	Losses				
		Base	No	Time	Base	Time		Dest	Dam	KIA	MIA	WIA
Luftflotte Reich												
I. Jagdkorps			185									
Jagddivision 1:												
I./JG 3	Bf 109G	Burg		0956	Burg	~1200	0	5	1	2	0	1
II./JG 3	Bf 109G	Sachau		1000	Sachau	1210	1 B-17, 1 P-51	1	2	0	0	0
IV.(Sturm)/JG 3	Fw 190A	Salzwedel	3	0930	Salzwedel, Burg	1205	1 B-17 HSS	0	0	0	0	0
I./ZG 26	Me 410A	Königsberg–Neumark	13	0955	Königsberg–Neumark	~1200	1 P-51*	7	0	10	0	1
II./ZG 26	Me 410A	Königsberg–Neumark		1037	Königsberg–Neumark	1208	0	0	0	0	0	0
Jagddivision 2:												
I./JG 11	Fw 190A	Rotenburg		~1000	Reinsehlen	~1200	0	2	1	2	0	0
II./JG 11	Bf 109G	Hustedt		1000	Hustedt	~1200	3 P-51	3	7	0	0	1
III./JG 11	Fw 190A	Reinsehlen		~1000	Reinsehlen	~1200	1 B-24**	9	2	0	0	0
Jagddivision 3:												
I./JG 1	Fw 190A	Lippspringe		~1000	Lippspringe	~1200	0	4	0	2	0	1
II./JG 1	Fw 190A	Störmede	14	0958	Störmede	~1200	1 P-51	1	5	1	0	0
III./JG 1	Bf 109G	Paderborn		~1000	Paderborn	~1200	1 P-51	3	2	1	0	1
Jagddivision 7:												
III./JG 3	Bf 109G	Ansbach	12	1050	Ansbach	~1230	3 B-17***	4	0	0	0	4
II./JG 27	Bf 109G	Unterschlauersbach		~1030	Unterschlauersbach	~1230	0	2	1	0	0	2
II./JG 53	Bf 109G	Öttingen		~1030	Öttingen	~1230	2 B-17	0	0	0	0	0
Luftflotte 3												
II. Jagdkorps												
Jagddivision 4:												
I./JG 26	Fw 190A	Denain		0719	Trier	0807	transfer	0	0	0	0	0
	Fw 190A	Trier		1020	Metz–Frescaty	1145	0	0	3	0	0	0
4./JG 26	Fw 190A	Wevelghem		~0715	Trier	~0800	transfer	0	0	0	0	0
	Fw 190A	Trier		~1015	Wevelghem	~1200	0	0	0	0	0	0
III./JG 26	Bf 109G	Nancy		1015	Nancy	1130	0	0	0	0	0	0
Jagddivision 5:												
I./JG 2	Fw 190A	Cormeilles		~1030	Cormeilles	~1200	1 P-51	0	0	0	0	0

*I./ZG 26: + 1 P-51 claim undocumented, 1 B-17 claim unconfirmed (unwitnessed)

**III./JG 11: + 1 B-24 claim undocumented, 1 B-24 HSS claim unconfirmed (unwitnessed)

***III./JG 3: + 2 B-17 claims undocumented, 2 B-17 claims unconfirmed (unwitnessed)

exclusively on tactical targets, the USSTAF took advantage of good spring weather to order another combined mission, the purpose of which was to continue whittling down the Luftwaffe fighter force. The 8th AF was sent to aviation factories and airfields in Germany and several rail yards in the western occupied zone. The I. Jagdkorps scrambled the four Gefechtsverbände based in Germany, but these contained only 171 single-engine fighters and had little effect. I./ZG 26 put up 13 of its new Me 410s. Ten made contact, and seven of them were shot down. II. Jagdkorps ordered some of its fighters inland to attack cripples, but found few opportunities. The Americans wrote off 15 bombers and 14 escorts. The I. Jagdkorps lost 18 KIA, 11 WIA and as many as 41 aircraft (the data conflict).

30 May – vs. 15th Air Force

15th Air Force: 166 of 168 B-17s, 134 of 147 B-24s bomb Wels (A) airfield, TOT 1038-47; 101 of 112 B-24s bomb Wels aircraft factory, TOT 1036-42; 194 of 222 B-24s bomb 4 Wiener Neustadt aircraft factories, TOT 1026-38 – lose 5, claim 8-3-2. Escort of 137 P-38s (3 FGs), 95 P-51s (2 FGs) claims 3-0-0, loses 1 P-51.

The 15th Air Force revisited Austrian aircraft plants and airfields. The Bf 109s of JG 27 and the Hungarians were up, the latter flying for the first time as a full Gruppe, the Pumas. Only a handful of JG 27 Messerschmitts made determined attacks on the bombers, which lost only five to all causes. In addition, one escort failed to return to Italy. The Hungarians made no contact at all, blaming poor ground control. One operational training unit Bf 109 crashed with its pilot. Other than three damaged JG 27 Bf 109s, no other Axis fighter losses or pilot casualties are known.

PILOT'S ACCOUNT[12]
30 May 1944

At 0930 hours, Uffz. K.-H. Schmidt and I scrambled from Salzwedel. It was not a *Gruppeneinsatz* [Gruppe mission], as our Gruppe [IV.(Sturm)/JG 3] had suffered heavy losses in men and machines in previous missions. We flew up-armoured Fw 190A-7s; my tactical number was 'White 10'. South of Berlin at 6,000–7,000 metres, we encountered several B-17 formations. While turning in for a frontal attack, I lost altitude and fell somewhat behind. I was attacked by a P-51 and received several hits in my right wing. Since at this altitude I had no chance in a dogfight in my heavy machine, I made a half-roll and steep dive and escaped. The P-51 probably could not follow my quick movement. At my high speed, I could only pull out at 2,000 metres using my elevator trim. My right aileron was out, and I could only make left turns. I had to land on Magdeburg–Burg with my last drops of fuel, keeping the airplane level with the rudder. After a very fortunate landing, I found more strikes in the fuselage. I was forbidden to fly it further, so returned to Salzwedel by train.

Uffz. Günther Ehrlich
11. (Sturm)/JG 3

31 May

8th Air Force Mission #382: 356 of 1029 HBs (1st BD + 2nd BD; 3rd BD recalled) bomb 9 rail yards and airfields in W Germany and western occupied zone – lose 1-1-105, claim 0. 8th FC escort of 4 P-38 FGs, 4 P-47 FGs, 7 P-51 FGs (682 sorties) claims 5-1-3, loses 3-0-4. 9th FC escort (647 sorties) claims 0, loses 0.

A full-strength 8th AF raid on rail yards and airfields in western Germany and the occupied zone found the II. Jagdkorps hunkered down on its bases – Jagddivision 4 reported that 1,000 Allied aircraft had flown overhead, which was an accurate estimate of the formation's strength. The raid did not achieve its aims: it did not bring the Luftwaffe up in force, and bad weather over the targets forced two–thirds of the bombers to abandon their missions. Only II./JG 1 made contact, to its detriment. This Gruppe lost three KIA, one WIA and five Fw 190s; its counterclaim for one Thunderbolt was not confirmed.

Luftwaffe defensive activity vs. 15th Air Force – 30 May 1944

Unit	Type	Gruppe up			Gruppe down		Claims	Losses				
		Base	No	Time	Base	Time		Dest	Dam	KIA	MIA	WIA
Luftflotte Reich												
I. Jagdkorps												
Jagddivision 7												
Jafü Ostmark:			57									
Stab/JG 27	Bf 109G	Fels am Wagram		0940	Fels am Wagram	~1140	0	0	0	0	0	0
I./JG 27	Bf 109G	Fels am Wagram		0940	Fels am Wagram	~1140	0	0	3	0	0	0
III./JG 27	Bf 109G	Götzendorf		~0940	Götzendorf	~1140	1 B-24*	0	0	0	0	0
IV./JG 27	Bf 109G	Agram (Y)		~0940	Agram (Y)	~1140	1 B-24	0	0	0	0	0
I./JG 107	Bf 109G	Markersdorf		~0940	Markersdorf	~1100	0	1	0	1	0	0
II./ZG 76	Me 410A	Prague		~0900	Prague	~1200	0	0	1	0	0	0
Abschü Ungarn:												
101 JGr (Hungary)	Bf 109G	Veszprém	32	1043	Veszprém	~1230	n/c	0	0	0	0	0

*III./JG 27: + 2 B-24 claims unconfirmed (unwitnessed)

Luftwaffe defensive activity – 31 May 1944

Unit	Type	Gruppe up			Gruppe down		Claims	Losses				
		Base	No	Time	Base	Time		Dest	Dam	KIA	MIA	WIA
Luftflotte Reich												
I. Jagdkorps												
Jagddivision 3:												
I./JG 1	Fw 190A	Lippspringe		1830	Lippspringe	~2000	0	0	1	0	0	0
II./JG 1	Fw 190A	Störmede	12	1829	Störmede	~2000	0*	5	3	3	0	1
III./JG 1	Bf 109G	Paderborn		1830	Paderborn	~2000	0	0	2	0	0	0

*II./JG 1: + 1 P-47 claim undocumented

June 1944

The Luftwaffe commanders knew the significance of the looming cross-Channel invasion and planned to send most of the I. Jagdkorps Jagdgruppen west to help drive the invaders back into the sea as soon as word of the landings reached Berlin. The initial plan called for the reinforcements to be employed in an escort and air superiority role. However, as the invasion approached, it became clear that the available ground attack strength was insufficient, and that some of the fighters would have to function as fighter-bombers, despite their pilots' lack of training for this role. Thus about half of the fighters were to join II. Jagdkorps; the others, II. Fliegerkorps, a ground attack command. No aspect of the reinforcement went according to plan; the Luftwaffe failed yet another critical mission. The reasons for the failure are many and need not be discussed here.

Seventeen Jagdgruppen and four Geschwaderstäbe left the Reich for the *Invasionsfront* [invasion front] in the first wave. Their absence was, of course, disastrous for the Reich-based RLV forces. By the evening of 7 June, only the five ex-*Wilde Sau* Gruppen, with one Stab, and five Zerstörergruppen, with two Stäbe, remained operational in Germany. They were given a partial reprieve by SHAEF's need to employ the 8th AF over the beachhead, but in mid-June the 8th rejoined the 15th AF and RAF BC in the strategic campaign, hammering the Reich continuously.

Although Jagdgruppen began returning from the Invasionsfront to the Reich before the end of June, only IV.(Sturm)/JG 3 rejoined the I. Jagdkorps order of battle immediately; the rest had to be taken off operations for rebuilding. II./JG 27 had not gone to France, but had remained in the Reich as an assembly Gruppe for Bf 109 pilots, which in the original plan were to be sent to France as individuals instead of in rebuilt units. It was given a new role: it received new Bf 109G-6/AS fighters and returned to RLV operations as the high-altitude Gruppe in Jagddivision 8 (the upgraded Jafü Ostmark). These were the only two reinforcements Schmid's I. Jagdkorps received in June.

Above: Obfw. Günther Fink of ErprKdo 25 in the cockpit of Fw 190A-8 'Green 3' at Parchim in June or July. It is equipped with the SG 116 apparatus, which comprised three 30-mm single-shot recoilless cannon mounted behind the cockpit, firing upward. After the Fw 190 flew beneath a heavy bomber, a photocell, visible beneath the cockpit, was to trigger the cannon sequentially. In an exhibition flight for General Galland, the cannon fired simultaneously, destroying the Fw 190. A photograph from this roll was captioned incorrectly in *The Luftwaffe over Germany*. *(Fletcher)*

Above: A Bf 109G-6 of the II./JG 3 Stabsschwarm prepares to take off from Evreux on a bombing mission shortly after D-Day. The photo is technically out of place in a history of the RLV, but does show the airplane as it looked when it left Germany for France in June. JG 3, an experienced RLV unit, was totally unsuited for the fighter-bomber role it was first given, and the three Bf 109 Gruppen that remained on the Invasionsfront were quickly converted to the 'air superiority' mission. *(Bundesarchiv 493-3362-27a)*

Below: Uffz. Willi Maximowitz of 11. (Sturm)/JG 3 taxies his Fw 190A-8/R2 'Black 8' into its revetment at Dreux during the one week that IV.(Sturm)/JG 3 spent on the Invasionsfront. It was 13 June before Berlin came to its senses and returned the newly designated, newly equipped Sturmgruppe to Germany and the RLV force. You can see the Geschwader emblem and white fuselage band, the Gruppe's black cowling and 'wave' bar, and the 'eagle's wing' on the fuselage to mask exhaust stains. *(Bundesarchiv 493-3362-5a)*

The size of the RLV day fighter force in the Reich had peaked in early 1944. Its strength dropped dramatically after D-Day when most Luftflotte Reich fighter units were transferred to Luftflotte 3, tripling the latter's establishment strength. The Invasionsfront became a bottomless pit for Luftwaffe aircraft and aircrew. By 30 June, Luftflotte 3 fighter strength was down to 37 per cent of establishment, and only 49 per cent of these were operational. Luftflotte Reich had 254 operational fighters; Luftflotte 3,216.

2 June

15th Air Force: 130 B-17s, bomb Debreczen (H) rail yard, continue to Russia (FRANTIC mission) – lose 2, claim 0. 258 B-24s bomb 4 Hungarian rail yards – lose 1, claim 0. Escort of 70 P-51s (1 FG), FRANTIC escort of 70 P-51s (1FG) claims 0, loses 0.

The first shuttle mission to the Soviet Union, and the only one by the 15th AF, was flown today. Shuttle missions, codenamed Operation FRANTIC, were begun with high hopes. Both the 8th and the 15th Air Forces were to attack eastern targets which were normally beyond their range before landing on airfields that had been prepared in the Soviet Union after long and hard negotiations. The target of this mission was a relatively innocuous Hungarian rail yard. No RLV fighters are known to have defended against this raid. JG 52, an Eastern Front Geschwader, claimed two B-24s, but details are lacking.

The 8th AF was now flying tactical missions exclusively; this would continue until 15 June. On D-Day, 6 June, Luftflotte 3 became a tactical air organisation, and its II. Jagdkorps was no longer considered part of the RLV force. Confrontations between the 8th AF and Luftflotte 3 fighters over the Normandy Invasionsfront during this period were not part of the strategic air war, and few of these battles are covered in this book.

9 June

15th Air Force: 292 of 500 B-17s + B-24s bomb targets in Munich area – lose 17, claim 0. Escort claims 19-2-2, loses 1 P-47.

The 15th AF concentrated its attention on the Reich, while the 8th AF was occupied in Normandy. Given that nearly all of the fighters of Jagddivision 7 and Jafü Ostmark had transferred to the Invasionsfront, today's raid on Munich met resistance of unexpected effectiveness from the 128 single-engine and 43 Zerstörer (twin-engine fighters) that sortied. Italian fighters and the three Luftwaffe Jagdgruppen still in Italy, now concentrated in the north, attacked the north-bound stream, stripping away much of the escort, and later made a low-strength attack on the withdrawing bombers. I./JG 302, currently the heart of the Austrian air defences, had just been reinforced from the Eastern Front with 12./JG 51, which was redesignated 4./JG 302 and named the Gruppe Höhenstaffel (high-altitude protection Staffel). The three original Staffeln made a closed-formation attack on the bomber steam west of Vienna, while 4./JG 302 sparred with the escorting P-51s. The ex-*Wilde Sau* Gruppe flew a successful, loss-free mission, claiming 16 B-24s and one P-51, although only six claims were confirmed – the 10 claims for bombers cut from formation and the P-51 claim were held up for lack of witnesses to their final destruction. American losses to all causes totalled 16 B-24s, one B-17 and one P-47; the Axis forces lost five KIA or MIA, six WIA and 13 fighters.

13 June

15th Air Force: 597 B-17s + B-24s bomb targets in Munich area – lose 19, claim 0. Escort claims 20-1-7, loses 2 P-38s.

A return trip to Munich by the 15th AF was met by a smoke screen which blanketed most of the targets, as well as greater aerial resistance than was available on the 9th: 180 fighters and 46 Zerstörer sortied. The German and Italian fighters in northern Italy nibbled at the incoming and withdrawing streams, but the main damage was done by three Gruppen that had not previously been available to Jagddivision 7: the ex-*Wilde Sau* Gruppen II./JG 300 and III./JG 300, and the Zerstörergruppe I./ZG 76, newly equipped with Me 410s. The day's scoring honours went to the last-named Gruppe, which claimed eight B-24s; five claims were confirmed. The Americans lost 19 bombers and two escorts. The 15th FC had now added a 3rd P-51 group to its order of battle. The 48 additional Mustangs had a noticeable effect on the efficiency of the screen, and Axis casualties went up; losses were approximately 19 KIA, five WIA and 23 fighters.

Axis defensive activity – 9 June 1944

Unit	Type	Gruppe up			Gruppe down		Claims	Losses				
		Base	No	Time	Base	Time		Dest	Dam	KIA	MIA	WIA
Luftflotte Reich												
I. Jagdkorps												
Jagddivision 7:												
Jafü Ostmark:			81									
I./JG 302	Bf 109G	Wien–Seyring	38	0825	Wien–Seyring	1125	6 B-24**	0	0	0	0	0
II./ZG 1	Bf 110G	Wels	43	~0830	Wels	~1130	1 P-51	0	0	0	0	0
Luftflotte 2												
Jafü Oberitalien:			*90									
I./JG 4	Bf 109G	Lavariano	—	~0830	Lavariano	~1000	1 B-17, 1 B-24	1	0	0	0	1
III./JG 53	Bf 109G	Maniago	—	0830	Maniago	~1000	0	0	0	0	0	0
2nd sorties	Bf 109G	Maniago		~1100	Maniago	~1230	2 B-24	2	0	0	1	1
Stab/JG 77	Bf 109G	Ferrara	4	~1100	Ferrara	~1230	1 B-24	0	0	0	0	0
I./JG 77	Bf 109G	Bologna	12	~0830	Bologna	~1000	1 P-47, 1 P-51	4	3	1	1	0
2nd sorties	Bf 109G	Bologna	4	~1100	Bologna	~1230	0	0	0	0	0	0
II./JG 77	Bf 109G	Poggio–Renatico, Ferrara	—	~0830	Poggio–Renatico, Ferrara	~1000	3 B-24***	6	2	2	0	4
1° Gr. Ca. (Italy)	MC 205, G 55	Udine	—	~1100	Udine	~1230	2 B-24	0	0	0	0	0

*Jafü Oberitalien scrambled 90 fighters total on first sorties.

**I./JG 302: +10 B-24 HSS, 1 P-51 claims unconfirmed (unwitnessed)

***II./JG 77: + 1 B-24, 2 B-24 HSS claims unconfirmed (unwitnessed)

14 June

15th Air Force: 384 B-17s + B-24s bomb Hungarian, Czech, Yugoslav oil targets – lose 5, claim 0. Escort claims 18-3-6, loses 5 P-38s.

The 15th AF targeted six refineries in three countries. The defenders were unable to repeat their recent successes. The Axis fighters in Italy could not reach the bomber stream. Jafü Ostmark put up 80 interceptors from I./JG 302 and the two ZG 76 Gruppen, both now flying Me 410s. I./JG 302 claimed one P-38, and II./ZG 76 claimed three B-17s; none of these claims were confirmed. The Hungarian Puma group was kept from the bombers by the P-38s of the 14th FG, and after a massive dogfight, five Lightnings and one Messerschmitt and pilot went down. These were the only American escort losses; five bombers were lost to all causes. The Luftwaffe lost six KIA, two WIA and nine aircraft.

15 June

8th Air Force Mission #414: 992 of 1,361 HBs (all BDs) bomb tactical targets in France, 208 bomb Hannover-Misburg refinery, various targets in Germany – lose 2-3-376, claim 0. Escort (509 sorties) claims 5-0-5, loses 4-1-?.

The 8th AF returned to the strategic air war over the Reich with a raid by 208 B-17s on a refinery and other targets in the Hannover area, while the rest of the 1,200 bombers available bombed bridges and airfields in the invasion zone. The I. Jagdkorps had no operational fighters in northern Germany and did not oppose the raid on Hannover. On the Invasionsfront, however, one II. Jagdkorps Geschwader did make a rare successful attack on a heavy bomber formation. Although these bombers were attacking France and not Germany, it is perhaps appropriate to cover this combat here. All of JG 26 (the Stab and three Gruppen), supplemented by III./JG 54, were ordered to fly an early-morning sweep west of Caen. In the air, their orders were changed to an attack on a stream of

Axis defensive activity – 13 June 1944

Unit	Type	Gruppe up			Gruppe down		Claims	Losses				
		Base	No	Time	Base	Time		Dest	Dam	KIA	MIA	WIA
Luftflotte Reich												
I. Jagdkorps			113									
Jagddivision 7:												
I./JG 300	Bf 109G	Bonn–Hangelar		~0800	Neubiberg	~0900	transfer	0	0	0	0	0
	Bf 109G	Neubiberg		~1000	Neubiberg	~1130	1 B-24	4	1	1	0	0
II./JG 300	Fw 190A	Rheine		~0800	Rhein–Main	~0900	transfer	0	0	0	0	0
	Fw 190A	Rhein–Main	13	0952	Rhein–Main	~1130	0***	5	2	2	0	3
Jafü Ostmark:												
I./JG 302	Bf 109G	Wien–Götzendorf		0830	Wien–Götzendorf	1050	2 B-24, 1 P-38****	2	0	2	0	0
II./ZG 1	Bf 110G	Wels	*46	~0830	Wels	~1100	1 B-24	1	0	2	0	0
Stab/ZG 76	Me 410A	Wien–Seyring	—	~0830	Wien–Seyring	~1100	0	1	0	2	0	0
I./ZG 76	Me 410A	Wien–Seyring	—	~0830	Wien–Seyring	~1100	5 B-24*****	4	3	6	0	2
ErgSt/ZG 76	Me 410A	Wien–Seyring	—	~0830	Wien–Seyring	~1130	0	1	0	2	0	0
Luftflotte 2												
Jafü Oberitalien:			**113									
I./JG 4	Bf 109G	Lavariano	—	0900	Lavariano	~1030	1 B-24	1	0	0	1	0
III./JG 53	Bf 109G	Maniago	—	0830	Maniago	~1030	2 B-24, 1 P-47	2	0	2	0	0
Stab/JG 77	Bf 109G	Ferrara	2	0911	Ferrara	~1030	n/c	0	0	0	0	0
I./JG 77	Bf 109G	Bologna	—	1100	Bologna	1220	n/c	0	0	0	0	0
II./JG 77	Bf 109G	Poggio–Renatico, Ferrara	—	0830	Poggio–Renatico, Ferrara	~1030	2 B-24, 1 B-24 HSS	1	0	0	0	0
1° Gr. Ca. (It)	MC 205, G 55	Reggio Emilia	—	0830	Aviano	~1030	0	1	0	0	0	0

*46 Zerstörer sorties total   **113 fighters scrambled from Italy.   ***II./JG 300: + 5 B-24 claims undocumented

**** I./JG 302: + 1 B-24 HSS, 1 P-51 claim unconfirmed (unwitnessed)   ***** I./ZG 76:+ 3 B-24 HSS claims unconfirmed (unwitnessed)

B-24s just crossing the French coast. II./JG 26 fended off the Mustangs, claiming one (unconfirmed) for the loss of two Focke-Wulfs, one MIA and one WIA. Obstlt. Josef 'Pips' Priller, the Geschwaderkommodore, downed a 492nd BG B-24 for his 100th Western Front victory; it crashed on the beachhead. The rest of the Geschwader split up and attacked other parts of the stream, claiming two B-24s (one confirmed) and one B-17 shot from formation for the loss of one Messerschmitt; its pilot was injured.

16 June

15th Air Force: 439 B-17s + B-24s bomb Vienna refineries – lose 10, claim 0. 155 B-24s bomb Bratislava refinery – lose 4, claim 0. Escort claims 40-4-8, loses 7 P-38s, 1 P-51.

The 15th AF bombed refineries in Vienna and Bratislava.

The Axis fighters in Italy did not make an appearance, and the American escort reached the target areas at full strength. The B-24s bombing Bratislava lost only four to II./ZG 76 from Prague, but their escort was attacked savagely by the Hungarian Pumas, which were credited with seven P-38s and one P-51. A Slovak Bf 109 squadron scrambled, but apparently circled Bratislava, their capital, without attacking the bombers. Vienna was defended by Jagddivision 8, newly formed from Jafü Ostmark, which called on its own I./JG 302, II./ZG 1 and I./ZG 76, and Jagddivision 7's I./JG 300, now operational at full strength. The rocket attacks by the ZG 76 Me 410s, not previously seen in strength in this theatre, made a great impression on the bomber crews. The Americans lost a total of 14 bombers and eight escorts. From its 171 single-engine and 55 twin-engine sorties, the defenders lost 17 KIA or MIA, seven WIA and 23 aircraft.

Axis defensive activity – 14 June 1944

Unit	Type	Gruppe up			Gruppe down		Claims	Losses				
		Base	No	Time	Base	Time		Dest	Dam	KIA	MIA	WIA
Luftflotte Reich												
I. Jagdkorps												
Jagddivision 7:												
IV.(Sturm)/JG 3	Fw 190A	Dreux		0710	München–Riem	1715	transfer	0	0	0	0	0
I./JG 300	Bf 109G	Merzhausen	30	~1530	Herzogenaurach	1700	transfer	0	0	0	0	0
Jafü Ostmark:												
I./JG 302	Bf 109G	Wien–Götzendorf		~1100	Wien–Götzendorf	~1230	0	1	0	0	0	0
Stab/ZG 76	Me 410A	Wien–Seyring	*50	~1100	Wien–Seyring	~1230	0	0	0	0	0	0
I./ZG 76	Me 410A	Wien–Seyring	—	~1100	Wien–Seyring	~1230	0**	2	1	4	0	2
II./ZG 76	Me 410A	Fels am Wagram	12	~1100	Fels am Wagram	~1230	0	2	1	1	0	0
Abschfü Ungarn:												
101 JGr (Hungary)	Bf 109G	Veszprém	32	~1100	Veszprém	~1230	5 P-38***	3	0	1	0	0
Luftflotte 2												
Jafü Oberitalien:												
Stab/JG 77	Bf 109G	Lagnasco		1048	Lagnasco	~1200	0	0	0	0	0	0
II./JG 77	Bf 109G	Lavariano		~1100	Lavariano	~1200	0	1	0	0	0	0

*50 ZG 76 sorties total   ** II./ZG 76: + 3 B-17 claims unconfirmed (unwitnessed)   ***101 JGr: + 4 P-38, 2 B-24 claims unconfirmed

Luftwaffe defensive activity – 15 June 1944

Unit	Type	Gruppe up			Gruppe down		Claims	Losses (all losses for day included)				
		Base	No	Time	Base	Time		Dest	Dam	KIA	MIA	WIA
Luftflotte 3												
II. Jagdkorps												
Jagddivision 5:												
Stab/JG 26	Fw 190A	Guyancourt	2	~0610	Guyancourt	~0745	1 B-24	0	0	0	0	0
I./JG 26	Fw 190A	Boissy–le–Bois		0610	Guyancourt	0730	1 B-17 HSS	0	0	0	0	0
II./JG 26	Fw 190A	Guyancourt		~0610	Guyancourt	~0745	0*	2	0	0	1	1
III./JG 26	Bf 109G	Villacoublay–Nord		0618	Villacoublay–Nord	0745	1 B-24**	1	0	0	0	1
III./JG 54	Fw 190A	Villacoublay–Sud		~0610	Villacoublay–Sud	~0745	0	0	0	0	0	0

*II./JG 26: + 1 P-51 claim unconfirmed (unwitnessed)   **III./JG 26: + 1 B-24 HSS claim unconfirmed (unwitnessed)

Lt. Manfred Dieterle, Kapitän of the 2. Staffel of I./JG 300, sits on his Bf 109G-6 'Red 1' at Herzogenaurach in June. It is still equipped with dampers over its exhausts for night missions. (Rosch)

Axis defensive activity – 16 June 1944

Unit	Type	Gruppe up			Gruppe down		Claims	Losses				
		Base	No	Time	Base	Time		Dest	Dam	KIA	MIA	WIA
Luftflotte Reich												
I. Jagdkorps			166									
Jagddivision 7:												
I./JG 300	Bf 109G	Herzogenaurach	28	1010	Herzogenaurach	~1200	1 B-24*	2	0	0	0	1
II./ZG 1	Bf 110G	Wels		~1000	Wels	~1200	0	1	0	1	0	1
II./ZG 76	Me 410A	Prag–Kbely, Ruzlò		~0930	Prag–Kbely, Ruzlò	~1200	3 B-24	4	1	8	0	0
Jagddivision 8:												
I./JG 302	Bf 109G	Wien–Götzendorf		0855	Wien–Götzendorf	1105	6 B-24, 1 P-38**	8	1	0	1	2
Stab/ZG 76?	Me 410A	Wien–Seyring		~0900	Wien–Seyring	~1100	0	0	0	0	0	0
I./ZG 76	Me 410A	Wien–Seyring		~0900	Wien–Seyring	~1100	1 B-24***	2	1	2	0	1
13. JSt (Slav)	Bf 109G	Piestany		0920	Piestany	~1100	0	0	0	0	0	0
Abschfü Ungarn:												
101 JGr (Hungary)	Bf 109G	Veszprém	28	0904	Veszprém	~1100	7 P-38, 1 P-51	6	7	5	0	2

*I./JG 300: + 1 B-24 claim udocumented , 2 B-24 claims unconfirmed (unwitnessed) **I./JG 302: + 1 B-24, 4 B-24 HSS, 2 P-51 claims unconfirmed (unwitnessed)
***I./ZG 76: + 6 B-24, 1 P-51 claims unconfirmed (unwitnessed)

Luftwaffe defensive activity – 20 June 1944

Unit	Type	Gruppe up			Gruppe down		Claims	Losses (all losses for day included)				
		Base	No	Time	Base	Time		Dest	Dam	KIA	MIA	WIA
Luftflotte Reich												
I. Jagdkorps			167									
Jagddivision 1:												
III./JG 300	Bf 109G	Jüterbog	42	0746	Jüterbog, Stettin	0945	1 B-24, 2 P-51**	13	2	4	1	5
2nd sorties	Bf 109G	Stettin	4	1000	Jüterbog	1100	1 B-24, 1 P-51	0	0	0	0	0
I./ZG 26	Me 410A	Königsberg–Neumark	*52	0750	Königsberg–Neumark	1010	5 B-24***	4	1	4	0	2
	Me 410A	Königsberg–Neumark	—	0930	Königsberg–Neumark	1015	0	0	0	0	0	0
II./ZG 26	Me 410A	Königsberg–Neumark	—	0755	Königsberg–Neumark	1000	20 B-24****	8	3	5	2	12
Jagddivision 7:												
I./JG 300	Bf 109G	Herzogenaurach	30	0730	Herzogenaurach	~0930	2 P-51*****	5	1	3	0	0
II./JG 300	Fw 190A	Unterschlauersbach	20	0730	Unterschlauersbach	~0930	3 B-17	1	2	1	0	0
Jagddivision 8:												
II./ZG 76	Me 410A	Prag–Kbely	28	~0730	Prague-Kbely	~1000	0	3	0	6	0	0

*52 ZG 26 sorties total **III./JG 300: + 4 B-24 claims unconfirmed (unwitnessed) ***I./ZG 26: + 1 B-24 claim unconfirmed (unwitnessed)
****II./ZG 26: + 6 B-24, 2 P-51 claims unconfirmed (unwitnessed) *****I./JG 300: + 1 B-24, 1 P-51 claims undocumented, 2 B-17 claims unconfirmed (unwitnessed)

18 June

8th Air Force Mission #421: 1213 of 1378 HBs (all BDs) bomb 18 strategic targets (primarily oil) in N Germany – lose 11-1-337, claim 0. Escort (585 sorties) claims 0, loses 0-1-?

The 8th AF returned to strategic bombing in full force, sending 1,378 bombers to targets in Hamburg, Hannover and Bremen. No Luftwaffe fighters were seen; all were grounded by bad weather, and the 12 bomber losses were all credited to the Flak.

Luftwaffe defensive activity – 21 June 1944

Unit	Type	Gruppe up			Gruppe down		Claims	Losses				
		Base	No	Time	Base	Time		Dest	Dam	KIA	MIA	WIA
Luftflotte Reich												
I. Jagdkorps			134									
Jagddivision 1:												
III./JG 300	Bf 109G	Jüterbog	23	0814	Jüterbog	~1030	4 B-17, 1 B-24	4	1	1	1	1
I./ZG 26	Me 410A	Königsberg–Neumark		~0820	Königsberg–Neumark	~1030	1 B-17*	2	1	4	0	1
II./ZG 26	Me 410A	Königsberg–Neumark		0820	Königsberg–Neumark	0940	3 B-17	9	5	9	0	12
LBeob St 1	?	?		~1100	?	~1300	1 B-24** (shadower)	0	0	0	0	0
Jagddivision 7:												
I./JG 300	Bf 109G	Herzogenaurach		0841	Herzogenaurach	~1040	1 B-17, 2 B-24, 1 B-24 HSS	5	1	1	0	2
II./JG 300	Fw 190A	Unterschlauersbach	28	~0840	Unterschlauersbach	~1040	2 B-17, 2 B-24***	2	0	1	0	1
Jagddivision 8:												
I./ZG 76	Me 410	Wien–Seyring		~0840	Wien–Seyring	~1040	0	0	2	0	0	0
II./ZG 76	Me 410	Prag–Kbely		~0840	Prag–Kbely	~1040	2 B-24, 2 P-51	5	2	7	0	5
Luftflotte 6												
Jagdabschnittsfü 6:			25									
StabsSt/JG 51	Bf 109G	Orscha		~1200	Orscha	~1300	0	0	0	0	0	0
I./JG 51	Bf 109G	Orscha		~1200	Orscha	~1300	1 B-17, 1 P-51	0	0	0	0	0
III./JG 51	Bf 109G	Bobruisk		~1200	Bobruisk	~1300	0	1	0	1	0	0

*I./ZG 26: + 1 B-17, 1 B-17 HSS claim unconfirmed (unwitnessed)

**Luft Beob St 1: + 1 B-17 claim unconfirmed (unwitnessed)

***II./JG 300: + 2 B-24, 1 P-51 cllaims undocumented, 1 B-17, 7 B-24, 1 B-24 HSS claims unconfirmed (unwitnessed)

20 June
8th Air Force Mission #425: 1,252 of 1,402 HBs (all BDs) bomb 15 strategic targets (primarily oil) in N Germany and Poland, TOT 0852-0952 – lose 48-3-759, claim 12-3-8. Escort (637 sorties) claims 38-2-19, loses 6-0-?.

The 8th AF kept up the pressure on the weakened RLV force by sending 1,400 bombers and 600 escorts against oil and industrial targets in Germany and Poland. The 53 fighters and 62 Zerstörer making contact out of 167 scrambling performed creditably against this armada. The three bomb divisions flew independently; the two flying the greatest distance drew all of the defenders' attention. The 2nd BD crossed Schleswig–Holstein, flew up the Baltic Sea and turned back to bomb Pölitz. The Jagddivision 1 Gefechtsverband, now comprising I./ZG 26 and II./ZG 26, escorted by III./JG 300, was directed north and found the B-24s in a strung-out formation, escorted by only one P-51 group. The Bf 109 escort Gruppe attacked the Mustangs, at high cost to itself, and allowed the Me 410s to attack the Liberators repeatedly before the relief group of P-51s arrived to punish the Zerstörer, 12 of which were shot down or crash-landed

back at their Königsberg–Neumark base. Thirteen B-24s went down immediately or broke from formation to head for sanctuary in Sweden. The 2nd BD lost a total of 34 B-24s on the mission. The JD 1 Verband claimed 38; 27 of these claims were confirmed on the most successful mission ever flown by the Me 410s.

I. Jagdkorps directed the two JD 7 Gruppen, I./JG 300 and II./JG 300, and the only JD 8 Gruppe in range, II./ZG 76, to Magdeburg to attack part of the 3rd BD. The B-17s were well escorted, and claims for only three B-17s and two P-51s were confirmed. The Americans sustained the surprisingly high loss of 54 bombers and 15 escorts during the day, but the bomber loss amounted to only 4 per cent of those given mission credit. The I. Jagdkorps lost 26 KIA or MIA, 19 WIA and 34 aircraft. This too was a heavy loss – 30 per cent of the aircraft given sortie credit – and was totally unsustainable.

21 June
8th Air Force Mission #428: 145 of 163 3rd BD B-17s bomb Ruhland oil refinery, proceed to USSR (FRANTIC); 965 of 1,071 HBs (all BDs) bomb 12 industrial and city

targets in Berlin area, TOT 0957-1032 – lose 45-2-508, claim 29-23-22. Escort (1,269 sorties) claims 20-0-10, loses 4-2-?.

The 8th AF mounted another full-strength mission to Germany. The bombers executed a complex flight plan in which Berlin was attacked from all directions. This mass of bombers effectively screened an attack on the Ruhland oil installation south of Berlin by two wings of 3rd BD B-17s that proceeded east to Russia after bombing. The I. Jagdkorps scrambled the same six Gruppen as the previous day, at somewhat greater strength (151 fighters and 61 Zerstörer, of which 100 and 51 made contact), but had little success. The Ruhland bombers were unopposed until they were crossing Poland, where they were intercepted by Eastern Front units – the JG 51 Stabsstaffel, I./JG 51, and III./JG 51. One B-17 and one P-51 were shot down. The latter crash-landed smoothly and was found to contain a map showing its landing ground, Poltava, which was previously unknown to the Germans – this airfield had been built specifically for the American FRANTIC missions. An attack on the airfield that night by 180 He 111s and Ju 88s destroyed 43 B-17s and 15 P-51s on the ground. American enthusiasm for these shuttle flights waned, never to be restored. Aside from the Ruhland force, the Americans wrote off 47 bombers, most to the fierce Berlin Flak, and six escorts. The I. Jagdkorps lost 24 KIA or MIA, 22 WIA and 27 aircraft.

24 June

8th Air Force Mission #438: 306 of 340 1st BD + 3rd BD B-17s bomb Bremen oil targets – lose 1-0-105, claim 0. Escort (251 sorties) claims 0, loses 0.

The 8th AF sent a small B-17 force to Bremen. No interception was made; according to the I. Jagdkorps war diary, the weather was too bad to allow take-offs.

26 June

15th Air Force: 660 B-17s + B-24s bomb 6 Vienna oil targets, 1 aircraft factory, 1 rail yard, TOT ca. 0945 – lose 38, claim 0. Escort (260 sorties) claims 32-0-17, loses 2 P-38s, 2 P47s, 2 P-51s.

The 15th AF took a break from its ongoing campaign against the Ploesti petroleum complex to test the southern RLV defences with a major mission to six refineries, hydrogenation plants and oil depots in the Vienna area. Jagddivision 8 mounted a full-strength defensive effort utilising its own fighters, those of Jagddivision 7 and the air defence units of Hungary and Slovakia. A total of 203 fighters and 117 Zerstörer sortied; 168 plus 72 made contact. The Hungarian Pumas struck first as the stream crossed their base, claiming five aircraft for the loss of three KIA. The bombers then clipped a corner of Slovakia, which scrambled its most combat-worthy squadron. Its eight Bf 109s downed a B-24, for the only Slovak victory over an American airplane for the war, while losing six planes and three pilots. II./ZG 76 attacked alone from Prague, drawing most of the escorts to itself. The remaining German units formed two loose Gefechtsverbände. The JD 7 formation made a nicely co-ordinated attack and wrought great havoc on a B-24 wing caught making a wide turn, downing 18. The JD 8 formation came upon the well-escorted main force and barely dented it. All airborne fighters were then directed to the Neusiedler See, where they downed a few more Allied aircraft, which then had to get past JG 77 in Italy; these Messerschmitts claimed a final two B-24s. The day's losses for the 15th AF totalled 38 bombers – almost 6 per cent of those given mission credit – and six escorts. The Axis lost 43 KIA or MIA, 11 WIA and 41 fighters, 17 per cent of those given sortie credit, on what was nevertheless a successful day.

27 June

15th Air Force: 113 B-17s + B-24s bomb Budapest rail yard – lose 4, claim 0. Escort claims 20-2-11, loses 2 P-51s.

The 15th AF split its bombers, with most bombing Yugoslavia. When it became obvious that a small stream was heading for Budapest, Jagddivision 8 scrambled the fighters that were available in its own sector: 45 single-engine and 53 twin-engine fighters, of which 27 and 34 made contact. The Hungarian Bf 109s flew alone, which left only one Luftwaffe Bf 109 group, I./JG 302, to shield the vulnerable Zerstörer while carrying out its principal mission, attacking the bombers. The Me 410s of ZG 76 seem to have avoided the American escorts (and the bombers as well), but the slow Bf 110s of II./ZG 1 were treated harshly by the American Mustangs – at least nine went down, and every crewman on these nine planes became a casualty. The Budapest raiders lost four bombers and two escorts; Jagddivision 8 lost 24 KIA or MIA, 10 WIA and 23 aircraft.

Axis defensive activity – 26 June 1944

Unit	Type	Gruppe up			Gruppe down		Claims	Losses				
		Base	No	Time	Base	Time		Dest	Dam	KIA	MIA	WIA
Luftflotte Reich												
I. Jagdkorps			203									
Jagddivision 1:												
III./JG 300	Bf 109G	Jüterbog		0905	Jüterbog	~1000	n/c	0	1	0	0	0
Jagddivision 7:												
I./JG 300	Bf 109G	Herzogenaurach	33	0820	Herzogenaurach	~1010	7 B-24**	4	2	1	1	1
II./JG 300	Fw 190A	Unterschlauersbach	28	0820	Unterschlauersbach	~1010	8 B-24, 3 B-24 HSS***	6	5	3	0	1
II./ZG 1	Bf 110G	Wels	27	~0815	Wels	~1015	4 B-24	4	2	5	0	2
II./ZG 76	Me 410A	Prag–Kbely	46*	~0815	Prag–Kbely	~1030	2 B-24, 1 P-38, 1 P-51	4	1	7	0	3
Jagddivision 8:												
I./JG 302	Bf 109G	Wien–Götzendorf	44	0830	Deutsch–Brod, Deutsch–Wagram	1045	3 B-24, 2 P-51, 1 B-24 HSS****	6	1	3	0	2
7./ZG 26	Me 410A	Wien–Seyring		~0815	Wien–Seyring	~1030	3 B-24	0	0	0	0	0
Stab/ZG 76	Me 410A	Wien–Seyring		~0815	Wien–Seyring	~1030	1 B-17	0	0	0	0	0
I./ZG 76	Me 410A	Wien–Seyring		~0815	Wien–Seyring	~1030	2 B-17, 1 B-24*****	8	1	17	0	1
13. JSt (Slov)	Bf 109G	Piestany	8	0840	Piestany	~1000	1 B-24	6	2	3	0	1
Abschfü Ungarn:												
101 JGr (Hungary)	Bf 109G	Veszprém	30	0830	Veszprém	~1000	3 B-24, 1 P-38, 1 P-51	3	0	3	0	0
Luftflotte 2												
Jafü Oberitalien:												
Stab/JG 77	Bf 109G	Maniago	4	1006	Laibach, Görz	~1200	0	0	0	0	0	0
I./JG 77	Bf 109G	Maniago	14	~1000	Maniago?	~1130	0	0	1	0	0	0
II./JG 77	Bf 109G	Maniago		0955	Lavariano	1153	0******	0	0	0	0	0

*46 sorties total for ZG 76   **I./JG 300: + 5 B-24 claims unconfirmed (unwitnessed)   ***II./JG 300: + 3 B-24, 1 B-24 HSS claims unconfirmed (unwitnessed)

****I./JG 302: + 1 B-17 HSS, 2 B-24 HSS, 1 P-51 claims unconfirmed (unwitnessed)   *****I./ZG 76: + 1 B-17, 2 B-24 claims unconfirmed (unwitnessed)

******II./JG 77: + 2 B-24 claims unconfirmed (unwitnessed)

Axis defensive activity – 27 June 1944

Unit	Type	Gruppe up			Gruppe down		Claims	Losses				
		Base	No	Time	Base	Time		Dest	Dam	KIA	MIA	WIA
Luftflotte Reich												
I. Jagdkorps			45									
Jagddivision 8:												
I./JG 302	Bf 109G	Wien–Götzendorf		0905	Wien–Götzendorf	~1115	2 B-17*	7	0	4	0	0
II./ZG 1	Bf 110G	Wels		~0900	Wels	~1115	2 B-17	8	1	10	0	7
7./ZG 26	Me 410A	Wien–Seyring		~0915	Wien–Seyring	~1145	0	1	0	0	2	0
Stab/ZG 76	Me 410A	Wien–Seyring		~0915	Wien–Seyring	~1145	0	2	0	4	0	0
I./ZG 76	Me 410A	Wien–Seyring		~0915	Wien–Seyring	~1145	0	2	2	2	0	3
II./ZG 76	Me 410A	Wien–Seyring		0910	Wien–Seyring	1145	1 P-51	3	0	2	0	0
Abschfü Ungarn:												
101 JGr (Hungary)	Bf 109G	Veszprém	24		Veszprém		2 B-17, 1 B-24, 1 P-51	0	0	0	0	0

*I./JG 302: + 3 B-17, 2 B-17 HSS claims undocumented

PILOT'S ACCOUNT[13]
26 June 1944

At 0834 hours, I./JG 302 scrambled from Wien–Götzendorf to intercept heavy bombers targeting the Moosbierbaum hydrogenation plant. It was my first combat sortie. The 1. Staffel put up 10 Bf 109s. I was a wingman on the far right of the formation. We rendezvoused with Me 410s from Wien. [The controller] Rosenkavalier attempted to guide us to an attack on the lead Pulk, but the turn was too tight, and the escort was too strong. My Rottenführer and I could not keep up on the turn. I was hit by an unseen P-51, spun out, recovered near the ground and landed on Deutsch–Wagram at 0934 hours. The Gruppe claimed four B-24s and three P-51s shot down and three B-24s shot from formation while losing three pilots killed.

Uffz. Willi Reschke
1./JG 302

Obfw. Willi Reschke joined the Luftwaffe in 1941 at the age of 19 and was fortunate enough to receive extensive flight training, including an instrument course. He joined 1./JG 302, a *Wilde Sau* unit, in June 1944 and flew with it and JG 301 for the rest of the war. One of the most successful late-war RLV pilots, Reschke claimed 27 victories, including 20 heavy bombers, in about 70 missions. He was shot down 8 times, bailed out 4 times and was wounded once. He was awarded the Knight's Cross in April 1945. *(Author's collection)*

29 June

8th Air Force Mission #447: 705 of 1150 HBs (all BDs) bomb Böhlen refinery, 18 industrial targets in Leipzig area, TOT 0856-0931 – lose 15-4-391, claim 0. Escort (674 sorties) claims 34-0-9, loses 3-0-?.

The 8th AF flew a full-scale mission to the Böhlen refinery and other strategic targets in the Leipzig area. The I. Jagdkorps was able to scramble only 72 fighters and 37 Zerstörer, of which 48 and 27 made contact. Only I./JG 300 and II./JG 300, the JD 7 single-engine Gruppen, were able to form up for a proper attack, and this small formation was quickly scattered by the Mustangs. The problems of the other three airborne Gruppen were blamed on the controller. Although evidence for 11 B-17 and five P-51 claims by JG 300 has been found, only those for two B-17s and one P 51 are known to have been confirmed. The Americans wrote off 19 bombers and three escorts from all causes; the I. Jagdkorps lost 11 KIA, seven WIA and 18 fighters.

30 June

15th Air Force: targets Blechhammer refinery, diverted owing to weather. 118 B-17s + B-24s bomb t/os in Austria, Hungary, Yugoslavia – lose 7, claim 0. Escort claims 5-1-2, loses 1 P-51.

The 15th AF's planned raid on the Blechhammer refinery complex was spoiled by the weather, and its bombers hit targets in Austria, Hungary and Yugoslavia. The forces up under the command of Jagddivision 8 totalled 87 fighters and 72 Zerstörer, of which 52 and 30 made contact. The Zerstörer were put in position to make one of their last successful attacks of the war; 11 of their B-24 claims were confirmed. The Hungarian Pumas had three B-24 claims confirmed, apparently for some of the same targets. The Croatian Air Force scrambled six fighters and lost five for no successes. I./JG 4 was up from northern Italy on a mission whose purpose remains obscure; it lost three Bf 109s to P-51s and claimed nothing. The Americans lost seven bombers and one escort to all causes. The Axis forces lost at least seven KIA or MIA, four WIA and 12 aircraft.

Luftwaffe defensive activity – 29 June 1944

Unit	Type	Gruppe up			Gruppe down		Claims	Losses				
		Base	No	Time	Base	Time		Dest	Dam	KIA	MIA	WIA
Luftflotte Reich												
I. Jagdkorps			109									
Jagddivision 1:												
III./JG 300	Bf 109G	Jüterbog	*72	0810	Jüterbog	~1030	1 B-17***	3	1	1	0	1
I./ZG 26	Me 410A	Königsberg–Neumark	**37	~0800	Königsberg–Neumark	~1030	0	2	1	3	0	1
II./ZG 26	Me 410A	Königsberg–Neumark		0805	Magdeburg–Ost	1018	0	0	3	0	0	1
Jagddivision 7:												
I./JG 300	Bf 109G	Herzogenaurach	23	0805	Herzogenaurach	~1000	1 B-17, 1 P-51****	8	3	4	0	3
II./JG 300	Fw 190A	Unterschlauersbach		0820	Unterschlauersbach	~1000	0*****	6	2	3	0	1

*72 JG 300 sorties total   **37 ZG 26 sorties total   ***III./JG 300: +1 B-17 claim not documented   ****I./JG 300: +1 B-17, 4 P-51 claims unconfirmed (unwitnessed)
*****II./JG 300: + 7 B-17 claims not documented

Axis defensive activity – 30 June 1944

Unit	Type	Gruppe up			Gruppe down		Claims	Losses				
		Base	No	Time	Base	Time		Dest	Dam	KIA	MIA	WIA
Luftflotte Reich												
I. Jagdkorps												
Jagddivision 8:												
I./JG 302	Bf 109G	Wien–Götzendorf	50	0757	Tapolca	1015	1 P-38	1	1	1	0	1
II./ZG 1	Bf 110G	Wels		~0800	Wels	~1030	4 B-24	?	?	?	?	?
Stab/ZG 76	Me 410A	Wien–Seyring		~0800	Wien–Seyring	~1030	1 B-24	0	0	0	0	0
I./ZG 76	Me 410A	Wien–Seyring		~0800	Wien–Seyring	~1030	3 B-24	1	2	1	0	1
II./ZG 76	Me 410A	Prag–Kbely		~0800	Prag–Kbely	~1030	1 B-17, 2 B-24	1	0	1	0	1
JGr (Croatia)	MC 202, MC 205	Pleso	6	~0800	Pleso	~0930	0	5	0	0	0	0
Abschfü Ungarn:												
101 JGr (Hungary)	Bf 109G	Veszprém		0845	Veszprém	~1030	3 B-24	1	0	1	0	1
Luftflotte 2												
Jafü Oberitalien:												
I./JG 4	Bf 109G	Lavariano		?	Lavariano	?	0	3	0	0	3	0

Notes
[1] Bär Gefechtsbericht, BA-MA RL 10/483.
[2] Dahl Gefechtsbericht, NARA T-971 roll 11.
[3] Bär Gefechtsbericht, BA-MA RL 10/483.
[4] Franz correspondence with author, 2003.
[5] Moritz Gefechtsbericht, BA-MA RL 10/584.
[6] Weik Gefechtsbericht, in private collection.
[7] Engau correspondence with author, 2001.
[8] Weik Gefechtsbericht, in private collection.
[9] Bindsell Gefechtsbericht, BA-MA RL 10/483.
[10] Eder Gefechtsbericht, in private collection.
[11] Kiefner correspondence with author, 1999.
[12] Ehrlich correspondence with author, 2002.
[13] Reschke correspondence with author, 2001.

CHAPTER 7

JULY – SEPTEMBER 1944

July 1944

The strength of the Luftflotte Reich day fighter force remained low throughout the month. The Americans gave the defenders little respite, although the 8th Air Force in England was called on to fly tactical missions from time to time, and the 15th Air Force in Italy, which had peaked at half the size of the 8th AF, had responsibilities in Italy and the Balkans. The days on which both the 8th and 15th AF targeted the Reich were especially punishing. Of the 10 missions intercepted in the second half of the month, the average number of I. Jagdkorps fighters to make contact with enemy aircraft was 75. More bombers were lost to Flak than to fighters, and fewer than 2 per cent of the bombers dispatched per mission were being lost. The Zerstörer units, which had promised such great hope for Reich defence in late 1943, were withdrawn from the RLV force by the end of July. One Zerstörergruppe was converting to Me 262 jet fighters; others were retraining in Bf 109s. The Invasionsfront Jagdgruppen that were withdrawn to the Reich for rebuilding were for the most part sent back to France; only I./JG 3 remained in Germany, joining Jagddivision 2. The return of Jagdgruppen from the other combat fronts continued at a slow pace; one Gruppe, III./JG 53, was added to Jagddivision 2 after transferring from Italy.

Novel tactics or weapons offered the only hopes of regaining air superiority over the Reich. Only one tactical innovation showed promise – the *Sturmtaktik*, an attack on bomber formations to close range from the rear by tight formations of *Sturmböcke* [attack billy goats], specially armed and armoured Fw 190s. Sturmstaffel 1 had proven the technique in the spring, but the first full-strength Jagdgruppe, IV.(Sturm)/JG 3, was delayed by an idiotic sojourn in Normandy and did not enter combat as a Sturmgruppe until 7 July. A

second Sturmgruppe, II.(Sturm)/JG 4, was formed quickly by renaming a superfluous Zerstörergruppe, but its conversion would prove lengthy.

The Luftwaffe did possess two novel weapons that deserved to be called *Wunderwaffen*: the rocket-powered Me 163 and the jet-propelled Me 262. The former entered operations in low strength before the end of the month; it would prove to be a technical dead end. The latter, a truly revolutionary weapon, was embroiled in both politics and technical problems, and the date of its entry into the Reich defence force could not even be foreseen.

2 July

15th Air Force: 52 of 176 B-17s, 420 of 472 B-24s bomb Budapest oil, rail targets, airfield, TOT 1017-1112h – lose 4 B-17s, 11 B-24s, claim 23-3-7. Escort of 113 15th AF P-38s (2 FGs), 150 15th AF P-51s (3 FGs), parts of 2 8th AF P-51 FGs claims 33-3-9, loses 9 P51s.

I. Jagdkorps scrambled a total of 117 fighters and 84 Zerstörer against the 15th AF; 64 and 17 of these made contact. Jagddivision 1 (JD 1) turned its aircraft over to the Silesian controller in case the bombers headed in that direction, but withdrew them without making contact. Jagddivision 8 (JD 8) attempted to form a single Gefechtsverband as the bombers headed due north from Italy, scrambling 28 II./JG 27 Bf 109s, 39 I./JG 302 Bf 109s, 20 Hungarian Bf 109s, 22 II./ZG 1 Bf 110s and 20 I./ZG 76 Me 410s. When the bomber stream turned due east for Budapest, the large defensive formation was unable to form up properly. II./JG 27 attacked the bombers alone and was punished severely by the P-51s for no successes. The rest of the Axis fighters were ordered to meet the withdrawing stream south of Lake Balaton, where I./JG 302 and the Hungarian fighters scored heavily against a formation of B-24s. I./ZG 76 did well against the B-17 wing. The Americans wrote off 15 bombers and nine escorts to all causes. The Axis forces lost 17 KIA or MIA, eight WIA and 30 aircraft.

6 July

8th Air Force Mission #455: 229 of 262 2nd BD B-24s bomb Kiel shipyards – lose 3-1-105, claim 0. Escort of 3 P-51 FGs (168 sorties) claims 0, loses 1. The rest of the 8th AF bombs Pas de Calais V-1 sites, Paris bridges (tactical mission) – lose 0-2-270. Escort claims 15-1-2, loses 4-0-?.

2nd BD B-24s bombed the Kiel shipyards, while the rest of the 8th AF attacked targets in the Invasion Zone. Jagddivision 1 scrambled 122 fighters and 38 Zerstörer against the B-24s, but none made contact in bad weather.

7 July – 8th Air Force attack on oil targets (see map)

8th Air Force Mission #458: 337 of 373 2nd BD B-24s bomb Lützkendorf, Halle o/i, Aschersleben o/i, TOT 0921-0940h – lose 28-1-126; 252 of 303 3rd BD B-17s bomb Böhlen, Merseburg o/i, TOT 1000-1013h – lose 2-0-112; 350 of 453 1st BD B-17s bomb Leipzig o/i, TOT 0945-1008h – lose 7-2-152. Bomber claims total 39-5-10.

Escort of 15 FGs (756 sorties) claims 75-1-19, loses 6-1-?.

Favourable weather allowed the USSTAF to order a rare joint mission for the 8th and 15th AFs, both against oil targets. I. Jagdkorps was forced to split its small fighter force: Jagddivisionen 1 and 7 opposed the 8th, and Jagddivision 8 the 15th AF; a total of 291 fighters and 83 Zerstörer were scrambled, of which 253 and 63 made contact. JD 7 had a new weapon to deploy: the first Sturmgruppe, IV.(Sturm)/JG 3, which flew as part of Major Dahl's JG 300 Gefechtsverband. The Sturmgruppe was directed unerringly to a B-24 wing that was out of position and unescorted, and shot down 19 Liberators (some shared with other units) with its specially armed and armoured Fw 190A-8/R2s in a devastating three-minute attack from the rear in close formation. JG 300 also claimed a large number of B-24s in conventional attacks, but it was clear to the Luftwaffe High Command that the Sturmangriff was an effective tactic against vulnerable parts of the bomber stream. The 8th AF wrote off 40 bombers and seven escorts on this mission; the hardest hit B-24 group, the 492nd BG, was disbanded. I. Jagdkorps lost 19 KIA, 22 WIA and 50 aircraft against the 8th AF.

Axis defensive activity – 2 July 1944

Unit	Type	Gruppe up			Gruppe down		Claims	Losses				
		Base	No	Time	Base	Time		Dest	Dam	KIA	MIA	WIA
Luftflotte Reich												
I. Jagdkorps			201									
Jagddivision 1:												
III./JG 300	Bf 109G	Jüterbog	30	0922	Jüterbog	~1115	n/c	1	2	0	0	0
I./ZG 26	Me 410A	Königsberg–Neumark	14	0923	Königsberg–Neumark	1140	n/c	0	0	0	0	0
II./ZG 26	Me 410A	Königsberg–Neumark	26	0921	Königsberg–Neumark	1140	n/c	0	0	0	0	0
LBeob St 1	Ju 88	Brieg	2	1033	Brieg	1230	n/c	0	0	0	0	0
Jagddivision 8:												
II./JG 27	Bf 109G	Fels am Wagram	28	0919	Fels am Wagram	~1100	0	8	1	2	0	5
I./JG 302	Bf 109G	Wien–Götzendorf	39	0935	various	1120	13 B-24, 1 P-51	10	2	9	1	2
2nd sorties	Bf 109G	various		1130	Wien–Götzendorf	1240	1 B-17	0	0	0	0	0
II./ZG 1	Bf 110G	Wels	22	0852	Wels	~1100	0	1	1	0	2	0
I./ZG 76	Me 410A	Wien–Seyring	20	0920	Wien–Seyring	~1130	6 B-17	1	0	0	0	0
Abschfü Ungarn:												
101 JGr (Hungary)	Bf 109G	Veszprém	20	0941	Veszprém	~1130	1 B-17, 6 B-24, 1 P-38, 4 P-51	9	0	3	0	1

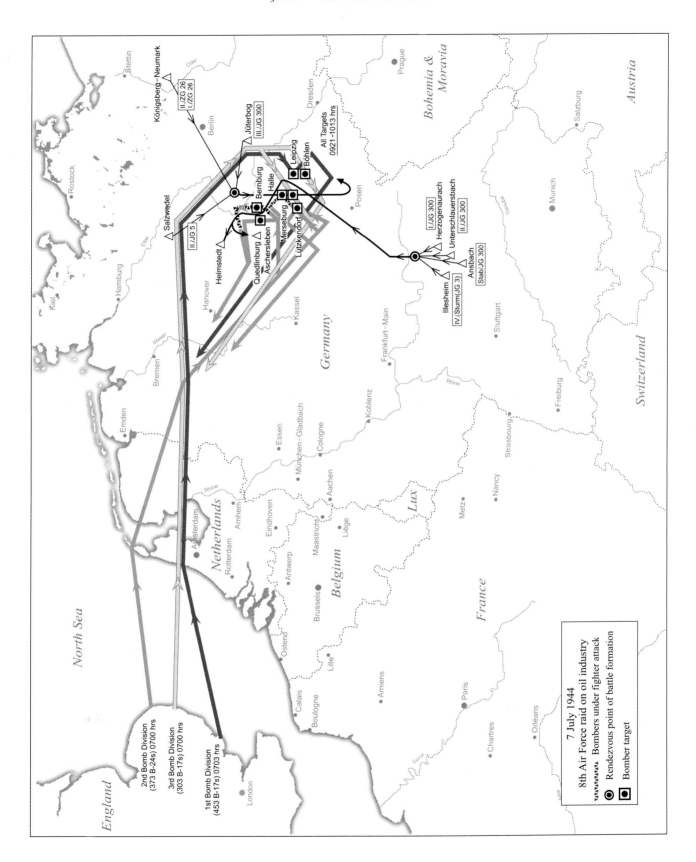

PILOT'S ACCOUNT[1]
7 July 1944

The *Sturmangriff* was a close-formation attack on a heavy bomber formation from the rear at the same level to closest range. When strength permitted, the Gruppe flew in two broad vees. The rear *Deckungsstaffel* [cover Staffel – formerly 2./JG 51] was 1,500 metres back and higher up. The formation was usually guided by *Y-Führung*. Early attempts by the controller to put the formation into the best attack position failed; the *Verbandsführer* [formation leader] was later given a free hand to direct the attack after sighting the enemy – Moritz was good at it and used his influence to get his own way. Tanks were dropped at the last minute. After the turn-in for the approach, the leader assigned targets by Staffeln. Altitudes were adjusted as needed. From 1,000 metres to firing took about 1½ minutes. The leader ordered 'Open fire!' by [shouting] 'Pauke, Pauke!' [beat the kettledrums]. Usually 400 metres for 2-cm, 200 metres for 3-cm fire in short bursts, but our ammo was usually consumed in one pass. Most defenders opened fire at 600 metres, using tracer. Our *Sturmböcke* were very resistant to this fire. Our break-away by an *Abschwung* was up to the individual pilots, based on the effect of the attack. Second passes were very rare; I made only one and then was out of ammo.

Today's was the first fully successful *Sturmjäger* attack. We downed an entire squadron of B-24s. The news called it '*Blitzluftschlacht* [Lightning Air Battle] *von Oschersleben*'.

Lt. Walter Hagenah
10.(Sturm)/JG 3

Lt. Walter Hagenah, a successful Sturmgruppe pilot. He joined I./JG 3 on the Eastern Front after completing fighter pilot training in 1942, returned to the Reich with this Gruppe and then transferred to IV./JG 3 as it converted to the Sturmgruppe role. He succeeded Lt. Hans Weik as Staffelkapitän of 10.(Sturm)/JG 3 in July 1944 and, from September that year, was a student and instructor before joining III./JG 7 in March 1945 to fly Me 262s. On 10 April, he downed a P-51 with R4M rockets for his last victory. *(Author's collection)*

PILOT'S ACCOUNT[2]
7 July 1944

I scrambled from Bad Wörishofen or Herzogenaurach – I don't remember which – [Herzogenaurach – DC] in Bf 109G-6 (411464) 'Yellow 14'. We flew north in the JG 300 *Gefechtsverband*. My Staffel formed the *Höhenschutz* [high-altitude protection]. We were hit by a heavy Flak barrage over Leipzig and split in all directions like a spreading fan. Who wants to be shot down by their own Flak? As I recall, Jagddivision 7 had problems passing control to Jagddivision 1. The Flak could not distinguish between friendly and enemy formations, which were arriving over the target at the same time.

After we reassembled, the American escort fighters engaged us in heavy air battles, which led to heavy losses on our part. My crate was one of those hit. Bailing out proved to be very difficult – the canopy probably was jammed by the shellfire. I pressed against it with all my strength, and suddenly it flew away. I tumbled into the air and pulled the ripcord, which did not let me down. Several swings of the pendulum, then I hit the ground near the crater formed by my airplane, on the left bank of the Elbe. Living through the last few minutes had drained my nerves. The air battles continued overhead. A nearby bush gave me shade. My body was soaking wet from sweat. I returned to my unit by train. The Gruppenkommandeur sent me a flask of champagne, which my comrades and I drained quickly.

Lt. Günther Sinnecker
3./JG 300

Lt. Günther Sinnecker, a *Wilde Sau* pilot in II./JG 302 from September 1943. He transferred to I./JG 300 when his former Gruppe disbanded in June 1944 and survived the war in that unit. *(Sinnecker)*

PILOT'S ACCOUNT[3]
7 July 1944

III./JG 300 scrambled from Jüterbog at 0830 hours and again escorted Major Kogler's Me 410s in the Thüringen area. At 0930 hours, my Stabsstaffel (six Bf 109s) was ordered to ward off P-38s, which were flying west and apparently never saw us. I was now separated from our main formation and led an attack on about 20 withdrawing B-24s in the Leipzig–Halle–Halberstadt area. We hit the heavies from an empty sky. Their tail gunners opened fire from 200 metres – too late. In a few seconds we had reached ramming distance, the gunners were silenced, and the sky was filled with columns of fire and parachutes.

In three minutes, my target exploded in the air, and I was sitting behind another. The defensive fire was very strong, but there were no enemy fighters, so our backs were free. By the fifth minute, my next target crashed to earth in flames. I also witnessed the victory of an Unteroffizier in my Stabsstaffel – I no longer recall his name.

My fighter's effective fire on the bombers left 20–25 parachutes in the air. Since I had ammunition left, I made a second pass with my wingman, Uffz.

Franzel Knoll, and brought down a third bomber – three in less than 11 minutes.

The other four Messerschmitts had already left the battlefield for lack of fuel and ammunition, so we had to return alone. My nerves and strength were apparently exhausted, and when I reached our home field, I forgot to lower my landing gear. So my score read three shootdowns for one belly-landed Me.

Oblt. Kurt Gabler, Staffelkapitän
8./JG 300

Oxen tow 'White 1', a III./JG 300 Bf 109G-6/AS, at Jüterbog. Animals frequently replaced tractors for this duty in the last year of the war. (Rosch)

Luftwaffe defensive Activity vs. 8th Air Force – 7 July 1944

Unit	Type	Gruppe up			Gruppe down		Claims	Losses				
		Base	No	Time	Base	Time		Dest	Dam	KIA	MIA	WIA
Luftflotte Reich												
I. Jagdkorps			*374									
Jagddivision 1:												
II./JG 5	Bf 109G	Salzwedel	34	0820	Salzwedel	~1000	0**	10	1	2	0	4
III./JG 300	Bf 109G	Jüterbog	37	0829	Jüterbog	~1000	1 B-17, 4 B-24, 1 P-51***	13	1	4	0	3
I./ZG 26	Me 410A	Königsberg–Neumark	15	0825	Königsberg–Neumark	~1045	1 B-24****	0	2	0	0	0
II./ZG 26	Me 410A	Königsberg–Neumark	27	0821	Königsberg–Neumark	1053	2 B-24, 1 P-38	6	2	5	0	4
LBeob St 1	Ju 88	Neuruppin	3	0848	Neuruppin	~1100	shadowers	0	0	0	0	0
Jagddivision 7:												
IV.(Sturm)/JG 3	Fw 190A	Illesheim	44	0820	Helmstedt, Quedlinburg	1010	26 B-24, 1 B-24 HSS	8	2	6	0	1
Stab/JG 300	Fw 190A	Ansbach	2	0820	Quedlinburg	1010	3 B-24	0	1	0	0	0
I./JG 300	Bf 109G	Herzogenaurach	32	0820	Herzogenaurach	~1000	1 B-17, 1 P-51*****	9	2	2	0	6
II./JG 300	Fw 190A	Unterschlauersbach	24	0820	Unterschlauersbach	~1000	8 B-24, 1 B-24 HSS******	4	4	0	0	4

*374 total sorties vs. 8th and 15th Air Forces   ** II./JG 5: + 1 B-24, 1 P-51 claims unconfirmed (unwitnessed)   *** III./JG 300: + 1 B-24, 1 P-51 claims unconfirmed (unwitnessed)

****I./ZG 26: + 1 B-24 HSS, 2 P-38 claims unconfirmed (unwitnessed)   *****I./JG 300: + 3 B-24 claims unconfirmed (unwitnessed)

******II./JG 300: + 1 B-24 claim undocumented; 4 B-24, 2 P-38 claims unconfirmed (unwitnessed)

7 July – 15th Air Force attack on oil targets (see map)

15th Air Force: 162 of 189 B-17s, 289 of 366 B-24s bomb Odertal, Blechhammer oil targets, TOT 1047-1132 – lose 10 B-17s, 17 B-24s, claim 35-11-4. 96 of 111 B-24s bomb Agram without air opposition. 132 of 146 P-38s, 175 of 206 P-51s (all FGs) escort all legs, claim 14-0-4, lose 1 P-38, 2 P-51s.

Today's main targets for the 15th AF were the hydrogenation plants at Odertal and Blechhammer, in the southeastern tip of Silesia. The five JD 8 Gruppen were up in time, but could only make stern attacks on the bombers as they continued due north past Budapest. The target area was defended by the operational training unit Jagdgruppe Ost, which put up all of its serviceable fighters. On their second sorties against the withdrawing bombers, I./JG 302 and the Hungarians found unescorted B-24 Pulks and made effective attacks. The 15th AF lost 27 bombers and three fighters on the mission; according to the latest research, the Axis lost only six KIA or MIA, nine WIA and 15 fighters, but failed to prevent significant damage to two of their most important oil installations.

Axis defensive activity vs. 15th Air Force – 7 July 1944

Unit	Type	Gruppe up			Gruppe down		Claims	Losses (—: included with 1st sortie)				
		Base	No	Time	Base	Time		Dest	Dam	KIA	MIA	WIA
vs. incoming stream:												
Luftflotte Reich												
I. Jagdkorps												
Jagddivision 8:												
II./JG 27	Bf 109G	Moosbierbaum	8	0828	Moosbierbaum	~1030	0	1	0	1	0	0
I./JG 302	Bf 109G	Götzendorf	27	0832	Götzendorf	~1030	1 B-17	4	1	1	1	2
II./ZG 1	Bf 110G	Wels	20	0825	Wels	~1030	2 B-17, 1 B-24	2	0	2	0	2
I./ZG 76	Me 410A	Malacky	18	0837	Malacky	~1030	1 P-51	0	0	0	0	0
Abschü Ungarn:												
101 JGr (Hungary)	Bf 109G	Veszprém	16	~0830	Veszprém	~1000	0	2	0	0	0	1
Jafü Oberschlesien:												
1.+3./JGr Ost	Fw 190A	Liegnitz	17	1025	Liegnitz	~1200	2 B-24	2	1	0	0	1
2.+4./JGr Ost	Bf 109G	Wiedengut	24	1027	Wiedengut	~1240	2 B-24, 1 P-51, 1 B-24 HSS	2	1	1	0	2
vs. withdrawing stream:												
Luftflotte Reich												
I. Jagdkorps												
Jagddivision 8:												
II./JG 27	Bf 109G	Moosbierbaum	4	0954	Moosbierbaum	~1130	n/c	—	—	—	—	—
	Bf 109G	Moosbierbaum	4	1135	Moosbierbaum	~1230	0	—	—	—	—	—
I./JG 302	Bf 109G	Götzendorf	12	1139	Götzendorf	1245	3 B-24*	—	—	—	—	—
Abschü Ungarn:												
101 JGr (Hungary)	Bf 109G	Veszprém	10	~1130	Veszprém	~1230	1 B-17, 5 B-24, 1 B-24 HSS, 3 P-38	2	0	0	0	1

* I./JG 302: + 3 B-24 HSS claims unconfirmed (unwitnessed)

8 July

15th Air Force: 158 of 166 B-17s, 383 of 429 B-24s bomb Vienna oil, rail targets, airfield, Veszprém (H) airfield, TOT 1036-1115h – lose 5 B-17s, 13 B-24s, claim 26-4-2. 116 of 133 P-38s (3 FGs), 93 of 97 P-51s (2 FGs) escort and sweep, claim 28-4-11, lose 2 P-38s, 2 P-51s.

The RLV commanders expected a follow-up raid on Silesia and moved most of the JD 7 fighters to Hörsching and Wels in Austria, where they refuelled and took off to the north, in the wrong direction to defend the day's targets. Radio problems forced them to abort the mission; a few I./JG 300 Bf 109s were found by the oncoming Mustangs, which downed one. The true targets for the 15th AF were oil installations and airfields in the Vienna area. The five JD 8 Gruppen made independent interceptions, with varying results. One P-38 group sweeping the Vienna area spotted the 16 I./ZG 76 Me 410s climbing to attack and fell on them in a perfect bounce which downed nine Zerstörer and killed 13 of their crewmen. The Gruppe was taken off operations and replaced by II./ZG 76 from Prague. I./JG 302 downed seven B-24s and one B-17, at a high cost to itself. The Americans lost 18 bombers and four escorts to all causes, but the defenders flew an ineffective mission: of the 187 fighters and 59 Zerstörer put up, only 47 and 12 made contact; these lost 15 KIA, six WIA and 17 aircraft.

About 30 of our Bf 109G-6s scrambled from Wien–Götzendorf at 1000 hours, led by Hptm. Heinrich Wurzer, Kapitän of the 1. Staffel. Rosenkavalier [the Jagddivision 8 controller: DC] reported that the bomber formations were approaching from the southwest and would pass to the east of Viennese airspace. We thus contacted the enemy and engaged in combat over the Neusiedler See, east of Vienna and near Pressburg [Bratislava]. Despite the enemy's numerical superiority, the Gruppe fought an heroic battle.

We first intercepted a B-24 Pulk. B-24s were much more desirable targets than B-17s, because they would go down after one attack. B-17s would often stay in formation after the attacker had exhausted his ammo.

The air battles took place in part over our own airfield. Our ground personnel thus could witness the mission of their Jagdgruppe, making this a special day in the unit's history. Our airfield could have been bombed, but through good luck – or perhaps the field's good camouflage – it was not.

Other units involved today were II./JG 27 from Fels am Wagram, II./ZG 1 from Wels and I./ZG 76 from Seyring. I./JG302 claimed six B-24 downed and three HSS [shot from formation], plus two B-17 downed and one HSS, between 1030 and 1120 hours. Hptm. Wurzer claimed one B-24 downed and one HSS, but was hit in the arm and belly-landed near the airfield. He was off operations for a long time. Three other pilots were badly injured, and one was killed.

Uffz. Willi Reschke
1./JG 302

13 July

8th Air Force Mission #471: 908 of 1,043 HBs (all BDs) bomb Munich through cloud – lose 10-10-316, claim 11-4-8. 543 of 609 fighters (13 FGs) escorts claim 2-1-2, lose 5-1-?.

A full-strength bad-weather raid on Munich by the 8th AF brought an exceptionally disorganised response by I. Jagdkorps, which sortied 141 fighters and 40 Zerstörer, but managed to put only one Gruppe, I./JG 300 with 20 Bf 109s, into firm contact with the Americans. The other JD 7 units were either waiting in Austria or were sent in that direction to oppose a 15th AF raid which never left Italian airspace. The Gruppen of the JG 300 Gefechtsverband spent the evening moving to new bases as ordered by Reichsmarschall Göring after Allied radio threatened Major Dahl, the JG 300 Kommodore, by name. I./JG 300 lost four KIA, one WIA, five Bf 109s destroyed and six damaged on its mission. At least eight JG 300 machines were damaged on their transfer flights. The 8th AF wrote off 20 bombers and six fighters during the day, most to Flak.

14 July

15th Air Force: 161 of 167 B-17s, 268 of 331 B-24s bomb Hungarian oil targets, one rail yard – lose 3 B-17s, 3 B-24s, claim 0. 149 P-38s (3 FGs), 141 P-51s (3 FGs) dispatched on escort claim 6-2-3, lose 6 P-38s.

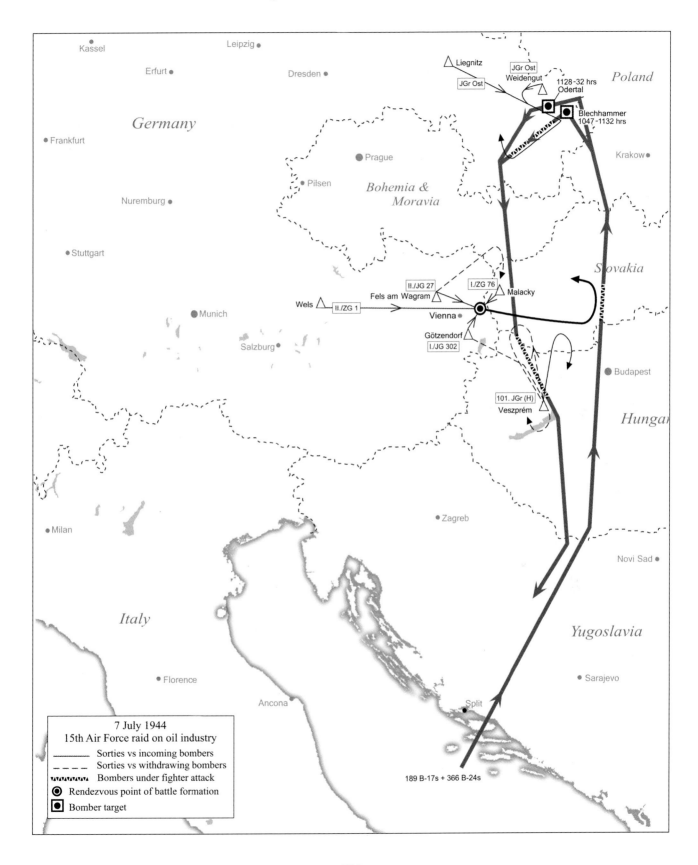

Kassel

Leipzig

Liegnitz

JGr Ost

Weidengut

JGr Ost

Erfurt

Dresden

Poland

1128-32 hrs
Odertal

Blechhammer
1047-1132 hrs

Germany

Frankfurt

Prague

Krakow

Bohemia &
Moravia

Pilsen

Nuremburg

Stuttgart

Slovakia

II./JG 27

I./ZG 76

Fels am Wagram

Malacky

Wels

II./ZG 1

Vienna

Munich

Götzendorf

I./JG 302

Budapest

Salzburg

101. JGr (H)

Veszprém

Hungar

Zagreb

Novi Sad

Italy

Milan

Yugoslavia

Florence

Sarajevo

Ancona

Split

7 July 1944
15th Air Force raid on oil industry

—————— Sorties vs incoming bombers
– – – – – Sorties vs withdrawing bombers
▼▼▼▼▼▼▼ Bombers under fighter attack
◉ Rendezvous point of battle formation
▣ Bomber target

189 B-17s + 366 B-24s

The 15th AF paid another visit to the Budapest refineries. JD 8 scrambled 69 fighters and 40 Zerstörer, of which 57 and 21 were credited with combat sorties. The JG 300 Stabsschwarm and IV.(Sturm)/JG 3 were ordered up from their new Memmingen base, but were too slow to reach the Austrian Verband and were returned to base. II./ZG 76 was ordered to abort its mission owing to the strength of the Allied escort. The other Axis fighters were unable to reach the bombers, but took part in several notable battles with the P-38 escorts. II./JG 27 claimed three, for a loss of two Bf 109s; II./ZG 1 claimed four, while losing a single Bf 110; the Hungarians claimed two, for no losses. Axis losses totalled three KIA and eight aircraft; the Americans lost six bombers and six Lightnings.

Axis defensive activity – 8 July 1944

Unit	Type	Gruppe up			Gruppe down		Claims	Losses				
		Base	No	Time	Base	Time		Dest	Dam	KIA	MIA	WIA
Luftflotte Reich												
I. Jagdkorps			246									
Jagddivision 7:												
I./JG 300	Bf 109G	Hörsching		~1030	Herzogenaurach	~1200	0	1	0	0	0	0
Jagddivision 8:												
II./JG 27	Bf 109G	Fels am Wagram		~0930	Fels am Wagram	~1130	1 B-24, 1 P-51	3	2	1	0	0
I./JG 302	Bf 109G	Götzendorf	30	0940	Götzendorf	1130	1 B-17, 7 B-24	4	3	1	0	4
II./ZG 1	Bf 110G	Wels	*59	~0930	Wels	~1130	0	0	0	0	0	0
I./ZG 76	Me 410A	Malacky	16	~0930	Malacky	~1130	1 P-38	9	0	13	0	2
Abschfü Ungarn:												
101 JGr (Hungary)	Bf 109G	Veszprém		~0930	Veszprém	~1130	0	0	0	0	0	0

*59 total Zerstörer sorties

Axis defensive activity – 13 July 1944

Unit	Type	Gruppe up			Gruppe down		Claims	Losses				
		Base	No	Time	Base	Time		Dest	Dam	KIA	MIA	WIA
Luftflotte Reich												
I. Jagdkorps			181									
Jagddivision 1:												
II./JG 5	Bf 109G	Salzwedel	32	1050	Salzwedel	~1200	n/c	3	0	0	0	0
II./JG 300	Bf 109G	Unterschlauersbach		~1025	Unterschlauersbach	~1200	n/c	1	0	0	0	0
III./JG 300	Bf 109G	Jüterbog	25	1025	Jüterbog	~1200	n/c	0	1	0	0	0
Jagddivision 7:												
I./JG 300	Bf 109G	Herzogenaurach	29	0955	Herzogenaurach	~1130	2 B-17*	5	6	4	0	1
Jagddivision 8:												
IV.(Sturm)/JG 3	Fw 190A	Götzendorf		1006	Götzendorf	~1130	1 B-17	0	0	0	0	0
II./JG 27	Bf 109G	Fels am Wagram	29	1014	Fels am Wagram	~1130	n/c	1	2	0	0	0
I./JG 302	Bf 109G	Götzendorf	32	1006	Götzendorf	~1130	n/c	1	0	1	0	0
II./ZG 1	Bf 110	Wels	22	0918	Wels	~1130	n/c	0	0	0	0	0
II./ZG 76	Me 410	Seyring	10	1018	Seyring	~1200	n/c	0	0	0	0	0

**I./JG 300: + 5 B-17, 2 P-51 claims filed, believed rejected

Luftwaffe defensive activity – 14 July 1944

Unit	Type	Gruppe up			Gruppe down		Claims	Losses				
		Base	No	Time	Base	Time		Dest	Dam	KIA	MIA	WIA
Luftflotte Reich												
I. Jagdkorps			109									
Jagddivision 7:												
IV.(Sturm)/JG 3	Fw 190A	Memmingen		0900	Memmingen	1035	n/c	0	0	0	0	0
Stab/JG 300	Fw 190A	Memmingen		0910	Memmingen	1020	n/c	0	0	0	0	0
Jagddivision 8:												
II./JG 27	Bf 109G	Fels am Wagram, Moosbierbaum	25	0853	Fels am Wagram, Moosbierbaum	~1030	3 P-38	2	1	1	0	0
I./JG 302	Bf 109G	Götzendorf	30	0910	Steinamanger	1055	0	5	0	2	0	0
II./ZG 1	Bf 110G	Wels, Raffelding	21	0828	Wels, Raffelding	~1030	4 P-38	1	0	0	0	0
II./ZG 76	Me 410A	Wien–Seyring	24	0916	Wien–Seyring	~1030	0	0	0	0	0	0
Abschfü Ungarn:												
101 JGr (Hungary)	Bf 109G	Veszprém	14	0915	Veszprém	~1100	2 P-38	0	0	0	0	0

16 July – vs. 8th Air Force

8th Air Force Mission #476: 984 of 1,087 HBs (all BDs) bomb Munich, Stuttgart, Saarbrücken through cloud – lose 11-5-202, claim 2-3-2. 623 of 712 fighters (15 FGs) escorts claim 0, lose 3-1-5.

The USSTAF sent its two air forces to Munich and Vienna and successfully split the defences. I. Jagdkorps scrambled a total of 217 fighters and 45 Zerstörer, but only 68 and 21 made contact. JD 1 sent its two Bf 109 Gruppen south to reinforce JD 7 in defence of Munich, but bad weather permitted only low-strength attacks. The 8th AF wrote off 16 bombers and four fighters, most to Flak. The defenders lost six KIA, four WIA and 12 fighters.

16 July – vs. 15th Air Force

15th Air Force: 130 of 150 B-17s, 237 of 346 B-24s bomb oil, aviation targets in Vienna area, TOT 1000-35 – lose 6 B-17s, 10 B-24s, claim 16-13-0. 146 P-38s (3 FGs), 194 P-51s (4 FGs) dispatched on escort and sweep, claim 23-3-7, lose 2 P-38s, 3 P-51s.

Jagddivision 8 led the defence against the 15th AF. I./JG 302 had a good day against the Liberators, claiming 12 and one P-38 (5 B-24s confirmed) for the loss of three Bf 109s and pilots. The attack of II./ZG 1 was broken up by Mustangs, which downed four Bf

110s. The desperate Zerstörer crews claimed three P-51s. The Americans lost 16 bombers and five fighters to all causes; the defenders lost 11 KIA or MIA, two WIA and nine aircraft.

18 July – vs. 8th Air Force

8th Air Force Mission #481: 650 of 750 B-17s (1st BD + 3rd BD) bomb Kiel, Peenemünde – lose 3-0-85, claim 0. 419 of 496 fighters (11 FGs) escorts claim 21-0-12, lose 3-1-5.

The USSTAF ordered another joint mission. I. Jagdkorps put up a total of 228 fighters and 90 Zerstörer, of which 209 and 31 made contact. The 8th AF B-17s flew to north Germany and bombed a Kiel refinery and the Peenemünde rocket experimental station. The bomber crews did not see a single German fighter and lost three B-17s to all causes. The defenders, III./JG 300 and the two ZG 26 Gruppen, were engulfed by Mustangs and lost 20 KIA + MIA, seven WIA and 24 Bf 109s and Me 410s while claiming three P-51s. In addition, the Me 262 combat evaluation unit, Erprobungskommando 262, lost its commander on the unit's first combat mission.

18 July – vs. 15th Air Force

15th Air Force: 79 of 167 B-17s, 67 of 456 B-24s bomb Manzell jet engine factory, Memmingen a/f, TOT 1046-1134 – lose 16 B-17s, claim 26-7-2. 148 P-38s (3 FGs), 224

P-51s (4 FGs) dispatched on escort, claim 40-2-16, lose 6 P-51s.

The 15th AF targeted the Manzell Dornier factory near Friedrichshafen, but much of the formation abandoned the mission or sought out alternate targets owing to bad weather. Most of the JD 7 Jagdgruppen flew together as the JG 300 Gefechtsverband, and its Sturmgruppe, IV. (Sturm)/JG 3, found an isolated, strung-out B-17 Pulk and made repeated stern attacks until driven off by P-51s. The Gruppe's escort Staffel, 2./JG 51, joined in attacking the bombers, but should have stuck to its own task – the Mustangs downed 12 of the Sturmjäger for the loss of three. The Sturmgruppe and its escort Staffel were credited with 34 B-17s. These were from the 483rd BG, which lost 14 and was awarded the Distinguished Unit Citation for the mission. The two JG 300 Gruppen fought the main American formation near Friedrichshafen. The two JD 8 Bf 109 Gruppen were scrambled late and

I./ZG 26 Me 410s at Königsberg–Neumark in the summer of 1944. *(Petrick)*

contributed little; there is no evidence that the two JD 8 Zerstörergruppen were employed at all. American losses totalled 16 B-17s and six P-51s. The defenders lost 17 KIA, 10 WIA and 28 fighters.

Luftwaffe defensive activity vs. 8th Air Force – 16 July 1944

Unit	Type	Gruppe up			Gruppe down		Claims	Losses (—: included with 1st sortie)				
		Base	No	Time	Base	Time		Dest	Dam	KIA	MIA	WIA
Luftflotte Reich												
I. Jagdkorps			*262									
Jagddivision 1:												
II./JG 5	Bf 109G	Salzwedel	27	~0730	Herzogenaurach	~0815	transfer	0	0	0	0	0
III./JG 300	Bf 109G	Jüterbog	24	~0730	Herzogenaurach	~0815	transfer	0	0	0	0	0
Jagddivision 7:												
IV.(Sturm)/JG 3	Fw 190A	Memmingen, Illesheim	44	0830	Holzkirchen	1030	n/c	4	2	1	0	1
II./JG 5	Bf 109G	Herzogenaurach	27	0830	Herzogenaurach	~1000	0	0	2	0	0	0
Stab/JG 300	Fw 190A	Memmingen	2	0830	Memmingen	~1000	n/c	0	0	0	0	0
I./JG 300	Bf 109G	Bad Wörishofen	28	0830	Bad Wörishofen	~1000	n/c	0	0	0	0	0
II./JG 300	Fw 190A	Holzkirchen	34	0830	Holzkirchen	~1000	1 B-17**	5	1	4	0	1
2nd sorties	Fw 190A	Holzkirchen		~1030	Holzkirchen	~1130	1 B-17	—	—	—	—	—
III./JG 300	Bf 109G	Herzogenaurach	24	0830	Herzogenaurach, Landshut	1000	0***	3	3	1	0	2
2nd sorties	Bf 109G	Herzogenaurach		~1030	Herzogenaurach	~1130	1 B-17	—	—	—	—	—

*262 sorties total vs. 8th and 15th Air Forces

**II./JG 300: + 4 B-17 claims filed, believed rejected

***I./JG 300: + 6 B-17 claims filed, believed rejected

Axis defensive activity vs. 15th Air Force – 16 July 1944

Unit	Type	Gruppe up			Gruppe down		Claims	Losses				
		Base	No	Time	Base	Time		Dest	Dam	KIA	MIA	WIA
Luftflotte Reich												
I. Jagdkorps												
Jagddivision 8:												
II./JG 27	Bf 109G	Fels am Wagram	17	0907	Fels am Wagram	~1030	0	2	0	2	0	0
I./JG 302	Bf 109G	Götzendorf	26	0915	Götzendorf, Steinamanger	1035	5 B-24*	3	0	3	0	0
II./ZG 1	Bf 110G	Wels	22	0915	Wels	~1030	3 P-51	4	1	0	6	2
II./ZG 76	Me 410A	Wien–Seyring	21	0921	Wien–Seyring	~1030	0	0	2	0	0	0
Abschfü Ungarn:												
101 JGr (Hungary)	Bf 109G	Veszprém	15	0910	Veszprém	~1030	1 B-17, 3 B-24	0	0	0	0	0

* I/JG 302: + 2 B-24, 5 B-24 HSS, 1 P-38 claims unconfirmed (unwitnessed)

Luftwaffe defensive activity vs. 8th Air Force – 18 July 1944

Unit	Type	Gruppe up			Gruppe down		Claims	Losses				
		Base	No	Time	Base	Time		Dest	Dam	KIA	MIA	WIA
Luftflotte Reich												
I. Jagdkorps			*318									
Jagddivision 1:												
III./JG 300	Bf 109G	Jüterbog	25	0800	Jüterbog	1000	0**	8	1	3	1	2
	Bf 109G	Jüterbog	2	1145	Jüterbog	~1300	1 Mosquito	0	0	0	0	0
I./ZG 26	Me 410A	Königsberg–Neumark	15	0810	Königsberg–Neumark	~1000	1 P-51	8	1	9	0	1
II./ZG 26	Me 410A	Königsberg–Neumark	25	0811	Königsberg–Neumark	0955	2 P-51	8	3	7	0	4
ErprKdo 25	He 177	Finow	4	0832	Finow	~1000	0	0	0	0	0	0
	Ju 88	Finow	4	0832	Finow	~1000	0	0	0	0	0	0
ErprKdo 262	Me 262A	Lechfeld	?		Lechfeld	?	0	1	0	1	0	0
LBeob St 1	Ju 88	Neuruppin	6	0810	Neuruppin	~1000	shadowers	0	0	0	0	0

*318 total sorties vs. 8th and 15th Air Forces   **III./JG 300: + 2 B-17, 2 P-51 claims undocumented

Luftwaffe defensive activity vs. 15th Air Force – 18 July 1944

Unit	Type	Gruppe up			Gruppe down		Claims	Losses				
		Base	No	Time	Base	Time		Dest	Dam	KIA	MIA	WIA
Luftflotte Reich												
I. Jagdkorps												
Jagddivision 7:												
IV.(Sturm)/JG 3	Fw 190A	Memmingen	45	0925	Memmingen	~1130	34 B-17, 2 P-51	12	1	7	0	5
I./JG 300	Bf 109G	Bad Wörishofen	35	0925	Bad Wörishofen	~1130	2 P-51	7	0	3	0	3
II./JG 300	Fw 190A	Holzkirchen	29	0925	Holzkirchen	~1130	4 B-17, 1 P-38, 2 P-51	5	0	5	0	0
Jagddivision 8:												
II./JG 27	Bf 109G	Fels am Wagram	18	0941	Fels am Wagram	~1140	1 P-51	2	0	2	0	0
I./JG 302	Bf 109G	Götzendorf	24	0931	Neubiberg, Kaufbeuren	1140	0*	2	0	0	0	2
II./ZG 1	Bf 110	Wels	19	1007	Wels	~1200	n/c	0	0	0	0	0
II./ZG 76	Me 410	Seyring	19	1000	Seyring	~1200	n/c	0	0	0	0	0

*I./JG 302: + 1 B-24, 1 P-51 claim undocumented

19 July – vs. 8th and 15th Air Forces

8th Air Force Mission #482: 1,082 of 1,242 HBs (all BDs) bomb industrial targets in W and SW Germany – lose 17-4-347, claim 6-4-4. 670 of 761 fighters (all 15 FGs) escorts claim 17-0-4, lose 7-1-7.

15th Air Force: 141 B-17s, 342 B-24s dispatched to bomb industrial targets in Munich area 90 min after 8th AF, TOT 1114-47 – lose 22 HBs, all to Flak, claim 0. 146 P-38s (3 FGs), 196 P-51s (4 FGs) dispatched on escort and sweep, claim 7-0-1, lose 5 P-38s.

The summer weather allowed the USSTAF to order another joint mission – this time to the same general area of southern and southwestern Germany. The 15th AF times on target were a nominal 90 minutes after the 8th AF to catch the defenders on the ground. Although the JD 1 Zerstörergruppen were no longer to be used except in special circumstances, the Division had sent its two Bf 109 Gruppen south the previous night, so the defenders were reasonably well concentrated. A total of 184 fighters and 40 Zerstörer were scrambled; 110 and 0 made contact. The American plan worked well. The 8th AF bombers saw some opposition, writing off 21 (plus eight escorts) to all causes, while the bomber crews of the 15th AF saw no fighters, while losing 22 bombers to Flak. The sweeping 15th AF escorts caught the defenders that were still up against the 8th AF and a few that were attempting to fly 2nd sorties. The defenders lost 11 KIA, five WIA and 23 fighters to the two American forces; five 15th AF P-38s went down. 1./JG 400, the first operational Me 163 combat unit, flew its first mission today, without result.

20 July – vs. 8th Air Force

8th Air Force Mission #484: 1,077 of 1,172 HBs (all BDs) bomb oil and industrial targets in central Germany, TOT 1110-1204 – lose 19-1-372, claim 11-9-7. 476 of 542 fighters (all FGs) escort, claim 6-1-4, lose 8-2-12.

Today's joint mission sent the 8th AF to the critical oil targets in central Germany. This drew the powerful JD 7 Gefechtsverband north, leaving only the weakened JD 8, now comprising only two Bf 109 and one carefully utilised Me 410 Gruppen to oppose the 15th AF. A total of 183 fighters and 40 Zerstörer were scrambled; 133 and 1 made contact. The Jagddivision 7 Verband, comprising the Stab and three Gruppen of JG 300, IV.(Sturm)/JG 3 and II./JG 5, made an effective but costly attack on the 8th AF, which wrote off 20 bombers and 10 escorts to all causes. JD 7 lost seven KIA, five WIA and 18 fighters.

20 July – vs. 15th Air Force

15th Air Force: 140 B-17s, 360 B-24s dispatched to bomb Memmingen a/f, Friedrichshafen a/i, TOT 1055-1105 – lose 13 B-24s, claim 4-0-0. 141 P-38s (3 FGs), 202 P-51s (4 FGs) dispatched on escort, claim 15-0-3, lose 2 P-38s.

The 15th AF raid on southwestern Germany went according to the USSTAF plan. The 15th AF escorts chased the JD 8 Bf 109s to ground. II./JG 27 claimed two P 38s (one confirmed), while I./JG 302 was held scoreless. The Germans lost three KIA, two WIA and five Bf 109s. In addition to the two P 38s, the 15th AF lost 13 B-24s, none to the Luftwaffe. The *Aeronautica Nazionale Repubblicana* (Fascist Italian Air Force) was more effective, making two attacks on the bomber stream over Udine – against both the outgoing and returning streams – and downing two B 24s for the loss of two KIA and four fighters.

21 July – vs. 8th Air Force

8th Air Force Mission #485: 980 of 1,110 HBs (all BDs) bomb aviation and ball-bearing targets in S and SW Germany – lose 31-3-262, claim 10-2-0. 706 of 795 fighters (all FGs) escorts claim 6-0-1, lose 8-3-5.

The two American strategic air forces were sent to widely dispersed areas: the 8th AF to southern and southwestern Germany, and the 15th AF to Czechoslovakia. The I. Jagdkorps was growing weaker by the day. Only 138 fighters and 38 Zerstörer were scrambled; 77 and 0 were credited with making contact. Apparently only the three Bf 109 Gruppen of the RLV force based in Germany closed with the 8th AF; they were credited with three B-24s. The 8th AF wrote off 34 bombers and 11 fighters, most to Flak; the small defensive force lost four KIA, three WIA and 11 fighters.

Luftwaffe defensive activity vs. 8th and 15th Air Forces – 19 July 1944

Unit	Type	Gruppe up			Gruppe down		Claims	Losses (—: included with 1st sortie)				
		Base	No	Time	Base	Time		Dest	Dam	KIA	MIA	WIA
Luftflotte Reich												
I. Jagdkorps			224									
Jagddivision 1:												
I./JG 3	Bf 109G	Gütersloh	2	1053	Gütersloh	1243	0	0	0	0	0	0
III./JG 300	Bf 109G	Jüterbog	2	1104	Jüterbog	~1230	n/c	0	0	0	0	0
I./JG 302	Bf 109G	Gütersloh	2	1518	Gütersloh	1650	n/c	0	0	0	0	0
Jagddivision 2:												
1./JG 400	Me 163A	Wittmundhafen	1	1630	Wittmundhafen	1655	0	0	0	0	0	0
Jagddivision 7:												
IV.(Sturm)/JG 3	Fw 190A	Memmingen	12	0810	Memmingen	~1030	4 B-17	2	0	2	0	0
II./JG 5	Bf 109G	Herzogenaurach	21	0810	Herzogenaurach	~1030	1 B-17	5	2	2	0	1
2nd sorties	Bf 109G	various JD 7 a/fs	2	1015	Herzogenaurach	~1130	n/c	0	0	0	0	0
Stab./JG 300	Fw 190A	Bad Wörishofen		~1030	Bad Wörishofen	~1200	1 P-38	0	0	0	0	0
I./JG 300	Bf 109G	Bad Wörishofen	26	0810	Bad Wörishofen	~1030	1 B-17	3	1	1	0	1
2nd sorties	Bf 109G	various JD 7 a/fs	8	1015	Bad Wörishofen	~1130	n/c	0	0	0	0	0
II./JG 300	Fw 190A	Holzkirchen	11	0810	Holzkirchen	~1030	1 B-17, 3 P-51	6	1	3	0	0
2nd sorties	Fw 190A	Holzkirchen	5	1015	Holzkirchen	~1200	1 P-38	—	—	—	—	—
III./JG 300	Bf 109G	Herzogenaurach	21	0810	Crailsheim	1033	2 B-17, 1 P-51	1	1	0	0	1
Jagddivision 8:												
II./JG 27	Bf 109G	Fels am Wagram	20	0840	Fels am Wagram	~1000	1 P-51	1	3	1	0	0
I./JG 302	Bf 109G	Götzendorf	27	0828	Neubiberg, München–Riem	1000	3 B-17*	5	0	2	0	2
2nd sorties	Bf 109G	München–Riem, various JD 7 a/fs	11	1015	Götzendorf	~1200	0	—	—	—	—	—
II./ZG 76	Me 410A	Wien–Seyring	21	0845	Prag–Gbell	~1030	0	0	2	0	0	0

*I./JG 302: + 1 B-17 claim undocumented; 4 B-17, 3 B-17 HSS claims unconfirmed (unwitnessed)

Luftwaffe defensive activity vs. 8th Air Force – 20 July 1944

Unit	Type	Gruppe up			Gruppe down		Claims	Losses (—: included with 1st sortie)				
		Base	No	Time	Base	Time		Dest	Dam	KIA	MIA	WIA
Luftflotte Reich												
I. Jagdkorps			*223									
Jagddivision 1:												
I./JG 3	Bf 109	Gütersloh	2	1815	Gütersloh	1935	n/c	0	0	0	0	0
I./ZG 26	Me 410	Königsberg–Neumark	6	1053	Königsberg–Neumark	1258	n/c	0	0	0	0	0
II./ZG 26	Me 410	Königsberg–Neumark	15	1050	Königsberg–Neumark	~1230	n/c	0	0	0	0	0
LBeob St 1	Ju 88	Neuruppin	1	1010	Neuruppin	~1200	shadower	0	0	0	0	0
	Ju 88	Neuruppin	2	1117	Neuruppin	~1300	shadowers	0	0	0	0	0
Jagddivision 7:												
IV.(Sturm)/JG 3	Fw 190A	Memmingen	13	0945	Memmingen	~1130	8 B-17	3	0	3	0	0
2nd sorties	Fw 190A	Memmingen		1150	Marienbad	1345	0	—	—	—	—	—
II./JG 5	Bf 109G	Herzogenaurach	21	0955	Herzogenaurach	~1130	1 B-17	4	3	3	0	1
Stab/JG 300	Fw 190A	Bad Wörishofen		~0940	Bad Wörishofen	~1130	0	0	0	0	0	0
I./JG 300	Bf 109G	Bad Wörishofen	24	0945	Bad Wörishofen	~1130	1 B-24 HSS**	1	1	0	0	0
II./JG 300	Fw 190A	Holzkirchen	11	0945	Holzkirchen	~1145	11 B-17	4	1	1	0	1
III./JG 300	Bf 109G	Bad Wörishofen	24	0958	Jüterbog	1210	3 B-17, 2 P-51	6	0	0	0	3

*223 total sorties vs. 8th and 15th Air Forces   **I./JG 300: + 2 B-17 claims undocumented

Axis defensive activity vs. 15th Air Force – 20 July 1944

Unit	Type	Gruppe up			Gruppe down		Claims	Losses				
		Base	No	Time	Base	Time		Dest	Dam	KIA	MIA	WIA
Luftflotte Reich												
I. Jagdkorps												
Jagddivision 8:												
II./JG 27	Bf 109G	Fels am Wagrm	20	0951	Fels am Wagrm	~1130	1 P-38	3	2	2	0	1
I./JG 302	Bf 109G	Götzendorf	20	0941	Neubiberg, Kaufbeuren	~1130	0	2	1	1	0	1
II//ZG 76	Me 410	Wien–Seyring	14	0941	Wien–Seyring	~1130	n/c	0	0	0	0	0
Luftflotte 2												
Jafü Oberitalien:												
1° Gr. Ca.	MC 205	Vicenza	10	1305	Vicenza	~1430	0	2	0	1	0	0
(Italy)	G 55	Vicenza	12	1305	Vicenza	~1430	0	2	0	1	0	0
2° Gr. Ca. (Italy)	Bf 109G	Villafranca	4	~0900	Villafranca	~1000	2 B-24	0	0	0	0	0

Luftwaffe defensive activity vs. 8th Air Force – 21 July 1944

Unit	Type	Gruppe up			Gruppe down		Claims	Losses				
		Base	No	Time	Base	Time		Dest	Dam	KIA	MIA	WIA
Luftflotte Reich												
I. Jagdkorps			*176									
Jagddivision 1:												
I./JG 3	Bf 109G	Gütersloh	2	1738	Gütersloh	1920	n/c	1	0	0	0	0
II./JG 5	Bf 109G	Jüterbog	4	0905	Jüterbog	~1100	0	1	1	1	0	1
III./JG 300	Bf 109G	Jüterbog	17	0905	Jüterbog	~1100	3 B-24, 1 B-24 HSS**	3	0	1	0	1
I./JG 400	Me 163	Brandis	1	1212	Brandis	1220	n/c	0	0	0	0	0
I./ZG 26	Me 410	Königsberg–Neumark	5	0951	Königsberg–Neumark	~1200	n/c	0	0	0	0	0
II./ZG 26	Me 410	Königsberg–Neumark	10	0951	Königsberg–Neumark	~1200	n/c	0	0	0	0	0
LBeob St 1	Me 410	Neuruppin	1	1149	Neuruppin	1313	shadower	0	0	0	0	0
	Ju 88	Neuruppin	1	1149	Neuruppin	1313	shadower	0	0	0	0	0
Jagddivision 7:												
IV.(Sturm)/JG 3	Fw 190A	Memmingen		?	Memmingen	?	0	0	1	0	0	0
Stab/JG 300	Fw 190A	Bad Wörishofen		?	Bad Wörishofen	?	0	1	0	0	0	0
I./JG 300	Bf 109G	Bad Wörishofen	22	0935	Bad Wörishofen	~1100	0***	7	0	1	0	2
II./JG 300	Fw 190A	Holzkirchen		?	Holzkirchen	?	0	0	0	0	0	0

*176 total sorties vs. 8th and 15th Air Forces

**III./JG 300: + 1 B-24 claim unconfirmed (unwitnessed); 5 B-24, 1 P-51 claims undocumented

***I./JG 300: + 1 B-24, 2 P-51 claims undocumented

21 July – vs. 15th Air Force

15th Air Force: 166 B-17s, 357 B-24s dispatched to bomb Brüx (Cz) synthetic fuel plant, TOT 1113-1208 – lose 6 B-17s, 4 B-24s, claim 4-4-1. 142 P-38s (3 FGs), 238 P 51s (4 FGs) dispatched on escort, claim 4-0-5, lose 1 P-38, 2 P-51s.

The southern front of the Reich was defended by a variety of forces today. The two JD 8 Bf 109 Gruppen made an aggressive attack over Salzburg, claiming 13 B-17s and two P-38s, of which seven B-17 claims were confirmed. Bomber crewmen observed II./ZG 76 Me 410s lobbing rockets, but the Zerstörer did not close with the formation and escaped without claims or losses. The Americans also claimed to see some Fw 190s. These may have been from the two JD 7 Fw 190 Gruppen; no evidence of their activity has been found in the Luftwaffe records. Jafü Oberitalien in northern Italy again scrambled one of its few Jagdgruppen, today II./JG 77, against part of the bomber stream. The Bf 109 pilots claimed one B-24 without loss. It has to be assumed that this was in response to a special plea from the strapped Jagddivision 8 to the equally resource-poor Axis force in Italy, but it must be stated that these bombers may actually have been targeting an Italian rail yard rather than Brüx. The 15th AF lost 10 bombers and three fighters today to all causes; Jagddivision 8 lost two KIA, one WIA and three Bf 109s.

25 July

15th Air Force: 167 B-17s, 351 B-24s dispatched to bomb Linz tank factory, TOT 1110-44 – lose 3 B-17s, 17 B-24s, claim 54-10-10. 74 P-38s (2 FGs), 154 P 51s (3 FGs) dispatched on escort, claim 12-1-5, lose 2 P-51s.

The 15th AF kept up the strategic pressure, while the 8th AF helped the US Army in its efforts to break out of Normandy. Today, the 15th AF targeted the Hermann Göring Panzer factory in Linz. I. Jagdkorps had been rested for a few days, but its strength had not recovered; it scrambled only 134 fighters and 54 Zerstörer, of which 79 and 0 were credited with making contact. JD 1 sent its fighters and Zerstörer toward Silesia, in case the bombers went that way. The JD 7 fighters, less the resting IV.(Sturm)/JG 3, reinforced the JD 8 Gruppen over Vienna. The impromptu Gefechtsverband, shielded effectively from the escorts by II./JG 27, attacked the B-24s of the 461st BG with great élan. The bomber crews reported that Me 410s were among the most aggressive of the attackers. These could only have been from II./ZG 76, the only Zerstörergruppe in the area, which scrambled 23 aircraft. This proved to be the last successful bomber interception by the Zerstörer, but ironically, the JD 8 controller was overheard by the Allies ordering the Gruppe to stay away from Vienna until the escorts had left, and the German records credit it with no combat sorties or victory claims. The attackers were apparently a few 'wild hares' among the Zerstörer. The Americans lost 20 bombers and two fighters on the mission. The Axis effort – which included one Italian squadron flying from Vienna – cost 11 KIA, three WIA and 21 fighters.

26 July

15th Air Force: 162 B-17s, 263 B-24s dispatched to bomb aviation targets in Vienna area, TOT 1110-29, + Albanian oil storage facility – lose 11 B-17s, 7 B-24s, claim 20-5-4. 133 P-38s (3 FGs), 233 P-51s (4 FGs) up on escort or returning from FRANTIC mission to Soviet Union, claim 25-3-9, lose 3 P-38s, 3 P-51s.

The 15th AF returned to Vienna. The RLV force was able to scramble 109 fighters and 54 Zerstörer, of which 79 and 0 received sortie credit. As on the previous day, JD 1 sent its fighters and Zerstörer toward Silesia to protect its refineries. The two Zerstörergruppen typically returned from such fruitless missions by way of a 'victory parade' over Berlin, to the humiliation of the Me 410 crews who were under orders to avoid combat with the enemy under most circumstances. The JD 7 fighters headed toward Vienna to join JD 8, which was also helped out today by the Hungarians. Today's target was an isolated B-17 Pulk. The Americans lost 18 bombers and six fighters on the mission; the Axis, six KIA or MIA, five WIA and 18 fighters. ErprKdo 262 filed the first Me 262 victory claim, for a RAF Mosquito reconnaissance aircraft, but that airplane made it back to base with structural damage.

Luftwaffe defensive activity vs. 15th Air Force – 21 July 1944

Unit	Type	Gruppe up			Gruppe down		Claims	Losses (—: included with 1st sortie)				
		Base	No	Time	Base	Time		Dest	Dam	KIA	MIA	WIA
Luftflotte Reich												
I. Jagdkorps												
Jagddivision 8:												
II./JG 27	Bf 109G	Fels am Wagram	22	0949	Fels am Wagram	~1130	2 B-17*	1	1	0	0	1
2nd sorties	Bf 109G	Bierbaum	10	1240	Bierbaum	~1300	0**	—	—	—	—	—
I./JG 302	Bf 109G	Götzendorf	25	0935	Götzendorf	~1130	5 B-17***	3	0	1	0	1
2nd sorties	Bf 109G	Bierbaum	4	1252	Götzendorf	~1400	0	—	—	—	—	—
II./ZG 76	Me 410A	Novy Dvor	15	0947	Novy Dvor	~1130	0	0	0	0	0	0
Luftflotte 2												
Jafü Oberitalien:												
II./JG 77	Bf 109G	Ghedi I		~0900	Ghedi I	~1030	1 B-24	0	1	0	0	0

*II./JG 27: + 1 P-38 claim unconfirmed (unwitnessed)

**II./JG 27: + 1 B-24 HSS claim unconfirmed (unwitnessed) [2nd sortie]

***I./JG 302: + 2 B-17 claims undocumented; 4 B-17 HSS, 1 P-38 claims unconfirmed (unwitnessed)

Axis defensive activity – 25 July 1944

Unit	Type	Gruppe up			Gruppe down		Claims	Losses				
		Base	No	Time	Base	Time		Dest	Dam	KIA	MIA	WIA
Luftflotte Reich												
I. Jagdkorps			213									
Jagddivision 1:												
III./JG 300	Bf 109G	Jüterbog	17	~1000	Stubendorf	1135	n/c	0	0	0	0	0
I./ZG 26	Me 410A	Königsberg–Neumark	*31	0950	Königsberg–Neumark	1210	n/c	0	0	0	0	0
II./ZG 26	Me 410A	Königsberg–Neumark	—	1015	Königsberg–Neumark	1220	n/c	1	1	0	0	2
Jagddivision 7:												
Stab/JG 300	Fw 190A	Bad Wörishofen	—	~1000	Bad Wörishofen	~1130	1 B-24	0	0	0	0	0
I./JG 300	Bf 109G	Bad Wörishofen	19	1000	Bad Wörishofen	~1130	7 B-24**	2	1	0	0	0
II./JG 300	Fw 190A	Holzkirchen	13	1000	Holzkirchen	~1130	7 B-24***	2	1	1	0	1
Jagddivision 8:												
II./JG 27	Bf 109G	Fels am Wagram	21	0950	Fels am Wagram	~1130	3 P-51****	6	2	4	1	0
I./JG 302	Bf 109G	Götzendorf	26	0940	Götzendorf	~1130	0*****	10	2	4	0	2
II./ZG 76	Me 410A	Wien–Seyring	23	0956	Wien–Seyring	~1200	n/c	1	0	0	0	0
2° Gr. Ca. (Italy)	Bf 109G	Wien–Tulln	13	~1030	Villafranca	~1230	0	1	0	1	0	0
Abschfü Ungarn:												
101 JGr	Bf 109G	Veszprém	11	1020	Veszprém	~1200	n/c	0	0	0	0	0
(Hungary)	Bf 109G	Veszprém	2	1430	Veszprém	~1530	n/c	0	0	0	0	0
Luftflotte 2												
Jafü Oberitalien:												
2° Gr. Ca. (Italy)	Bf 109G	Villafranca	13	0820	Wien–Tulln	1010	transfer	0	0	0	0	0

*31 total ZG 26 sorties   **I./JG 300: + 2 B-24 claims undocumented; 3 B-24 HSS claims unconfirmed (unwitnessed)

***II./JG 300: + 3 B-24 claims undocumented   ****II./JG 27: + 1 P-51 claim undocumented; 2 P-51 claims unconfirmed (unwitnessed)

*****I./JG 302: + 7 B-24 claims unconfirmed (unwitnessed)

Luftwaffe defensive activity – 26 July 1944

Unit	Type	Gruppe up			Gruppe down		Claims	Losses				
		Base	No	Time	Base	Time		Dest	Dam	KIA	MIA	WIA
Luftflotte Reich												
I. Jagdkorps			163									
Jagddivision 1:												
III./JG 300	Bf 109G	Jüterbog	17	~1015	Stubendorf	~1200	n/c	0	0	0	0	0
I./ZG 26	Me 410A	Königsberg–Neumark	*54	1010	Königsberg–Neumark	1214	n/c	0	0	0	0	0
II./ZG 26	Me 410A	Königsberg–Neumark	—	1005	Königsberg–Neumark	1220	n/c	0	1	0	0	0
Jagddivision 7:												
Stab/JG 300	Fw 190A	Bad Wörishofen		~0945	Bad Wörishofen	~1145	0**	0	0	0	0	0
I./JG 300	Bf 109G	Bad Wörishofen	21	0945	Bad Wörishofen	~1145	4 B-17, 1 P-38, 1 P-51	1	1	0	0	0
II./JG 300	Fw 190A	Holzkirchen	20	0945	Holzkirchen	~1145	8 B-17	9	0	4	0	4
ErprKdo 262	Me 262A	Lechfeld		?	Lechfeld	?	1 Mosquito	0	0	0	0	0
Jagddivision 8:												
II./JG 27	Bf 109G	Fels am Wagram, Bierbaum	17	0946	Malacky	1210	1 P-38	5	0	0	0	0
I./JG 302	Bf 109G	Götzendorf	25	0956	Malacky	1210	3 B-17	2	0	0	1	1
II./ZG 76	Me 410A	Wien–Seyring	20	1017	Wien–Seyring	~1230	n/c	0	1	0	0	0
Abschfü Ungarn:												
101 JGr (Hung)	Bf 109G	Veszprém	15	1007	Veszprém	1215	1 B-24	1	0	1	0	0

*54 total Zerstörer sorties   **Stab/JG 300: + 1 B-17 claim unconfirmed (unwitnessed)

27 July

15th Air Force: 109 B-17s, 319 B-24s dispatched to bomb Budapest ordnance factory, TOT 0930-1012 – lose 9 B-24s, claim 0. 133 P-38s (2 FGs), 233 P 51s (3 FGs) dispatched on escort, claim 14-0-4, lose 3 P-51s.

The 15th AF kept up the pressure with an attack on the important Manfred Weiss Armament Works in Budapest. The dwindling RLV force scrambled 99 fighters and 20 Zerstörer, of which 60 and 0 were credited with making contact. Jagddivision 1 sent its fighters and Zerstörer to Silesia, as had become the custom, but the JD 8 controller identified the target early and got maximum support not only from JD 7 but the Hungarian Jagdgruppe. Two Verbände were formed: the Hungarians joined the two JD 8 Bf 109 Gruppen, but these attracted the attention of the escorts and were dispersed early. The JD 7 Verband found an unescorted Pulk of 455th BG B-24s and pummeled it. The Americans lost nine bombers and three fighters; the Axis lost five KIA or MIA and nine fighters.

28 July

8th Air Force Mission #501: 714 of 786 B-17s (1st BD + 3rd BD) bomb Merseburg–Leuna, Leipzig o/i – lose 7-1-233, claim 1-2-1. 386 of 454 fighters (9 FGs) escort, claim 4-1-1, lose 2-0-3.

The 15th AF bombed Ploesti today, outside the scope of this study. But the 8th AF returned to the strategic campaign against the Reich with an attack by its B-17s on the Merseburg–Leuna petroleum complex. I. Jagdkorps was able to send up only 131 fighters and 26 Zerstörer, of which 40 and 0 made contact with this raid against Germany's single most important target. Two Jagdgruppen had returned from the Invasionsfront and were now operational in Jagddivision 2, but this division's controllers, possibly out of practice in handling day fighters, were unable to put them into contact with the bomber stream. The closest thing to a highlight for the defenders was the first full-scale operational mission for one of the Luftwaffe's 'wonder weapons', the rocket-powered Me 163. 1./JG 400 put up seven fighters from its new Brandis base, chosen for its proximity to Leuna, but did not close with the bombers. Several escort pilots observed them carefully, resulting in an excellent tactical notice that circulated quickly within the 8th AF. The 8th AF wrote off eight bombers and two fighters to all causes; I. Jagdkorps lost four KIA, two WIA and eight fighters, including three of the 'last four' of II./JG 300, which was withdrawn to rebuild.

29 July

8th Air Force Mission #503: 603 of 657 B-17s (1st BD + 3rd BD) bomb Merseburg–Leuna, other oil targets – lose 15-1-349, claim 0; 445 of 473 2nd BD B-24s bomb Bremen oil targets – lose 2-0-96, claim 0. 535 of 605 fighters (12 FGs) escort, claim 21-2-3, lose 7-0-7.

The 8th AF B-17s returned to Merseburg–Leuna, to find I. Jagdkorps somewhat better prepared than the day before. The Luftwaffe scrambled 138 fighters and 25 Zerstörer, of which 86 and 25 were recorded as making contact; these Zerstörer cannot be identified, however, and the number in contact is probably an error. The RLV commanders ignored the B-24s attacking Bremen and concentrated on the B-17s

targeting Leuna. The Jagdgruppen had only modest success, with the exception of IV.(Sturm)/JG 3, which returned to duty as a replacement for II./JG 300 in the JD 7 Gefechtsverband and downed 10 B-17s and one P-51 – most of these victories went into the books of 2./JG 51, which was serving as the Sturmgruppe's 4th Staffel, but had not yet been redesignated. The Americans wrote off 18 bombers and seven fighters to all causes; the Luftwaffe lost 13 KIA or MIA, four WIA and 24 fighters.

30 July

15th Air Force: 136 B-17s, 298 B-24s dispatched to bomb Budapest aviation targets – lose 2 B-17s, 3 B-24s, claim 0. 119 P-38s (2 FGs), 203 P-51s (3 FGs) dispatched on escort, claim 4-0-2, lose 1 P-38, 1 P-51.

The 15th AF returned to Budapest, while the 8th AF had the day off. The RLV force scrambled 76 fighters, of which 56 made contact. The records show that no Zerstörer took off; bookkeeping had caught up with reality. Only a weak JD 7 Verband reached the bomber

Axis defensive activity – 27 July 1944

Unit	Type	Gruppe up			Gruppe down		Claims	Losses				
		Base	No	Time	Base	Time		Dest	Dam	KIA	MIA	WIA
Luftflotte Reich												
I. Jagdkorps			119									
Jagddivision 1:												
III./JG 300	Bf 109G	Jüterbog	20	~0900	Stubendorf	~1045	n/c	0	0	0	0	0
I./ZG 26	Me 410A	Königsberg–Neumark	*20	~0900	Königsberg–Neumark	~1045	n/c	0	0	0	0	0
II./ZG 26	Me 410A	Königsberg–Neumark	—	0855	Königsberg–Neumark	1045	n/c	0	1	0	0	0
Jagddivision 7:												
Stab/JG 300	Fw 190A	Bad Wörishofen	—	~0815	?	~1015	0	1	0	0	0	0
I./JG 300	Bf 109G	Bad Wörishofen	19	0815	various Hungarian a/fs	~1015	3 B-24	1	1	1	0	0
II./JG 300	Fw 190A	Holzkirchen	15	0830	various Hungarian a/fs	~1015	11 B-24	4	0	1	0	0
Jagddivision 8:												
II./JG 27	Bf 109G	Fels am Wagram, Bierbaum	13	0817	Fels am Wagram, Bierbaum	~1000	1 P-51	2	0	2	0	0
I./JG 302	Bf 109G	Götzendorf	27	0830	Götzendorf	~1000	0*	1	1	0	1	0
Abschfü Ungarn:												
101 JGr (Hungary)	Bf 109G	Veszprém	11	0835	Veszprém	~1000	4 B-24, 2 P-51	0	0	0	0	0

*20 total Zerstörer sorties   **I./JG 302: + 2 P-51 claims unconfirmed (unwitnessed)

stream, downing three B-17s and a possible P-38. JD 8 did not make contact. The Hungarians were able to scramble only four Bf 109s to defend their own capital; these downed two straggling B-24s. The Americans lost five bombers and two fighters to all causes; the Axis, one KIA, two WIA and three fighters.

31 July

8th Air Force Mission #507: 1,097 of 1,191 HBs (all BDs) bomb Munich industry, Ludwigshafen chemical plant – lose 16-0-517, claim 0. 474 of 556 fighters (11 FGs) escort, claim 0-1-0, lose 3-0-9.

The USSTAF whipsaw process sent the 8th AF B-17s to Munich, while the B-24s bombed Ludwigshafen. The 15th AF returned to Romania, outside this history. Jagddivision 7 scrambled 35 fighters against the 8th AF – IV.(Sturm)/JG 3 and I./JG 300 – but they were forced to land at Landsberg after two hours of futile attempts to penetrate the cloud deck. The 8th AF lost 16 bombers and three fighters to Flak and operational causes; Jagddivision 7 apparently sustained no losses.

Luftwaffe defensive activity – 28 July 1944

Unit	Type	Gruppe up				Gruppe down		Claims	Losses				
		Base	No	Time		Base	Time		Dest	Dam	KIA	MIA	WIA
Luftflotte Reich													
I. Jagdkorps			157										
Jagddivision 1:													
I./JG 400	Me 163	Brandis	2	0940		Brandis	0950	0	0	0	0	0	0
	Me 163	Brandis	1	0944		Brandis	~1000	0	0	0	0	0	0
I./ZG 26	Me 410A	Königsberg–Neumark	11	0910		Königsberg–Neumark	~1050	n/c	0	0	0	0	0
II./ZG 26	Me 410A	Königsberg–Neumark	6	0912		Königsberg–Neumark	1052	n/c	0	0	0	0	0
Erpr St 25	He 177	Finow	4	0856		Finow	~1030	n/c	0	0	0	0	0
	Ju 88	Finow	3	0928		Finow	~1030	n/c	0	0	0	0	0
Jagddivision 2:													
I./JG 3	Bf 109G	Gütersloh	34	0941		Burg	1050	n/c	0	5	0	0	0
III./JG 53	Bf 109G	Bad Lippspringe	31	0855		Salzwedel, Brunswick, Bad Lippspringe	~1050	n/c	0	0	0	0	0
7./JG 53	Bf 109G	Paderborn	13	0855		Paderborn	~1055	n/c	0	0	0	0	0
Jagddivision 7:													
I./JG 300	Bf 109G	Bad Wörishofen	15	0855		Bad Wörishofen	~1045	1 B-17, 1 P-51*	0	1	0	0	0
II./JG 300	Fw 190A	Holzkirchen	4	0850		Holzkirchen	~1045	0**	3	1	3	0	0
Jagddivision 8:													
II./JG 27	Bf 109G	Fels am Wagram	13	0840		Fels am Wagram	~1030	0	1	0	0	0	0
I./JG 302	Bf 109G	Götzendorf	19	0831		Götzendorf	~1100	1 B-17, 1 P-51	4	0	1	0	2

*I./JG 300: + 1 B-17 claim undocumented   **II./JG 300: + 1 B-17 claim undocumented

Luftwaffe defensive activity – 29 July 1944

Unit	Type	Gruppe up			Gruppe down		Claims	Losses				
		Base	No	Time	Base	Time		Dest	Dam	KIA	MIA	WIA
Luftflotte Reich												
I. Jagdkorps			163									
Jagddivision 1:												
I./JG 3	Bf 109G	Burg	22	0912	Leipzig–Delitzsch	1050	n/c	0	0	0	0	0
	Bf 109G	Gütersloh	2	1815	Burg	1935	n/c	0	0	0	0	0
III./JG 300	Bf 109G	Jüterbog	17	0910	Jüterbog	~1045	2 B-17	7	0	5	0	1
I./JG 400	Me 163	Brandis	6	?	Brandis	?	0	0	1	0	0	0
I./ZG 26	Me 410A	Königsberg–Neumark	2	0842	Königsberg–Neumark	~1045	shadowers	0	0	0	0	0
	Me 410A	Königsberg–Neumark	2	0927	Königsberg–Neumark	~1130	n/c	0	0	0	0	0
II./ZG 26	Me 410A	Königsberg–Neumark	16	0930	Königsberg–Neumark	~1130	n/c	0	0	0	0	0
Erpr St 25	He 177	Finow	4	0937	Finow	~1130	n/c	0	0	0	0	0
	Ju 88	Finow	3	0955	Finow	~1130	n/c	0	0	0	0	0
Jagddivision 2:												
II./JG 5	Bf 109G	Werl	15	0934	Werl	~1100	0	0	0	0	0	0
	Bf 109G	Störmede	10	0942	Störmede	~1100	0	0	0	0	0	0
III./JG 53	Bf 109G	Bad Lippspringe	12	0933	Bad Lippspringe	~1100	0	3	0	0	0	1
Jagddivision 7:												
IV.(Sturm)/JG 3	Fw 190A	Schwaighofen	14	0920	Herzogenaurach	1100	10 B-17, 1 P-51	2	0	1	0	0
Stab/JG 300	Fw 190A	Herzogenaurach	—	~0900	Herzogenaurach	~1100	0	0	0	0	0	0
I./JG 300	Bf 109G	Herzogenaurach	17	0955	Herzogenaurach	~1100	1 B-17, 1 P-51 1 B-17 HSS*	7	2	2	1	2
Jagddivision 8:												
II./JG 27	Bf 109G	Fels am Wagram	15	0908	Fels am Wagram	~1100	1 P-51	2	2	1	1	0
I./JG 302	Bf 109G	Götzendorf	16	0853	Götzendorf	~1100	4 B-17	3	1	1	1	0

*I./JG 300: + 2 B-17 HSS claims unconfirmed (unwitnessed); 1 P-51 claim undocumented

Axis defensive activity – 30 July 1944

Unit	Type	Gruppe up			Gruppe down		Claims	Losses				
		Base	No	Time	Base	Time		Dest	Dam	KIA	MIA	WIA
Luftflotte Reich												
I. Jagdkorps			76									
Jagddivision 7:												
IV.(Sturm)/JG 3	Fw 190A	Schwaighofen	22	0910	Wiener Neustadt, Neubiberg, Parndorf	1115	3 B-17	1	1	0	0	2
I./JG 300	Bf 109G	Bad Wörishofen	12	0915	Wien–Seyring	~1115	0	1	0	1	0	0
ErprKdo 262	Me 262A	Lechfeld		?	Lechfeld	?	0	1	0	0	0	0
Jagddivision 8:												
II./JG 27	Bf 109G	Fels am Wagram		0910	Fels am Wagram	~1115	n/c	0	1	0	0	0
I./JG 302	Bf 109G	Götzendorf		?	Götzendorf	?	n/c	0	1	0	0	0
Abschfü Ungarn:												
101 JGr (Hungary)	Bf 109G	Veszprém	4	0830	Veszprém	~1115	2 B-24	0	0	0	0	0

August 1944

On 1 August, the operational day fighter strength of Luftflotte Reich comprised seven single-engine Jagdgruppen. These had all been expanded to four Staffeln, each with an establishment strength of 16 fighters. Skilled pilots for these units were hard to find. Replacement pilots were either green trainees or transfers from disbanded bomber, reconnaissance and transport units. None of these men had more than rudimentary fighter pilot skills, and the fuel shortage prevented much training, even in the combat units. An eighth combat Gruppe was added to the I. Jagdkorps order of battle on 4 August by redesignating ErprKdo 25 as Jagdgruppe 10. I./JG 77 arrived from Italy for service in the RLV, but would require time to re-equip and train. I./JG 4 soon followed, but was slated for service on the Invasionsfront, although that front was collapsing. There was little good news for the RLV force. On the positive side, Me 262s of ErprKdo 262 shot down a reconnaissance Mosquito on 8 August, and a B-17 on 15 August, the first heavy bomber victory for the jets. As of 9 August there were two operational Sturmgruppen; Major Dahl obtained up-armoured Fw 190A-8s for his II./JG 300, and without a day off operations it entered the I. Jagdkorps order of battle as II.(Sturm)/JG 300. A third Sturmgruppe, II.(Sturm)/JG 4, was in training.

Luftwaffe fuel supplies were now so tight that defensive fighter operations were the only flights allowed to continue without restriction. Weather and other reconnaissance was cut back, and bombers were limited to 'decisive missions'. The Reich air defences can be said to have reached a critical state by mid-August, matching Germany's overall war situation. I. Jagdkorps was shooting down fewer than 2 per cent of the American bombers that formed an aluminium curtain over the daytime Reich. RLV operational strength was dealt a blow by a *Führerbefehl* [Hitler's order] that rebuilt Invasionsfront Jagdgruppen would have to return to the western front cauldron rather than remain in the Reich. Furthermore, JG 6 and JG 76, two new Jagdgeschwader created from old Zerstörergruppen, were also to be sent to France. The strength of the RLV force would never again reach the level needed to have any significant effect on the Allied bombing campaign. There was no hope for equality in numbers, but it was believed that technical innovations could turn the tide. The Germans experimented with many novel weapons. With hindsight, it is obvious that only the Me 262 offered any chance of reversing Germany's fortunes. To take advantage of its unique qualities would require more decisiveness and discipline than the Luftwaffe High Command had yet exhibited. At any rate, August found the Me 262 not yet ready for operational service.

3 August – vs. 15th Air Force

15th Air Force: 157 B-17s, 446 B-24s dispatched to bomb Friedrichshafen industrial area, Immenstadt rail yards, TOT 1111-13 – lose 3 B-17s, 8 B-24s, claim 7-12-0. 136 P-38s (3 FGs), 217 P-51s (4 FGs) dispatched on escort, claim 11-0-2, lose 1 P-51.

The day's joint raids by the USSTAF were separated enough in time that the small RLV force could be employed against both in turn, but could sortie only 102 single-engine fighters, of which 72 contacted the enemy. The 15th AF raid on targets in the Friedrichshafen area brought another noteworthy but expensive success for the Sturmgruppe. Jagddivision 7 formed a battle formation from two Gruppen: 19 IV.(Sturm)/JG 3 Fw 190s from Schongau, escorted by 17 I./JG 300 Bf 109s from Bad Wörishofen. A third Gruppe, III./JG 53, sortied on its first RLV mission, but failed to locate either its own fighters or the bombers. Major Moritz, leading the Gefechtsverband, did not reach the bomber stream until it had finished bombing and re-formed for its return to Italy, but then headed for the weakest link of the chain. The 465th BG was flying in two boxes. Against orders, the second

I./JG 4 Bf 109G-14 'White 10' (W. Nr. 166224), abandoned at Nogent–le–Roi during the August retreat from France. The '97' marked on its rudder is probably in green. *(Rosch)*

Hptm. Wilhelm Moritz leads the Fw 190A-8/R2s of his IV.(Sturm)/JG 3 to the take-off point at Schongau in August. His Kommandeur's machine has lost its distinctive Geschwader and Gruppe markings. 'Black 12' of the 11th Staffel still has its black cowl and 'eagle's wing' (fuselage exhaust stain masking). *(Bundesarchiv 736-180-16)*

had dropped back to cover a straggling B-24 and was now 15 miles behind the main formation, and unescorted. Moritz led the Sturmgruppe up from the undercast and attacked the bombers from the low rear. The Sturmböcke made a single pass and then broke in all directions. The I./JG 300 Bf 109s apparently followed the Fw 190s through the bombers, but made no claims and were out of position when 325th FG Mustangs responded to the bombers' calls for help. The P-51s fell on the Focke-Wulfs, shooting down nine, as well as a Messerschmitt. Seven German pilots were KIA or MIA. Their single pass had, however, brought down eight of the fragile B-24s.

3 August – vs. 8th Air Force
8th Air Force Mission #512: 450 of 672 HBs (from all BDs) bomb oil + rail targets near French-German border – lose 6-1-160, claim 4-1-1. ~350 fighters (8 FGs) escort, claim 6-0-0, lose 6-?-?.

In the afternoon, the 8th AF sent a moderate-sized formation to bomb rail targets in the Strasbourg region. The RLV commanders got more units up than had faced the morning raid, but the force was tiny, and results were meager. III./JG 53 was caught emerging from the undercast by 355th FG P-51s and was quickly engaged in dogfights that punished both units. IV.(Sturm)/JG 3 flew another successful mission, claiming four B-17s. The 8th AF lost seven bombers and five fighters; I. Jagdkorps lost two KIA, one WIA and eight fighters.

4 August
8th Air Force Mission #514: 1,186 of 1,307 HBs (all BDs) bomb strategic targets in northern and eastern Germany – lose 15-9-404, claim 1-4-2. 800 of 883 fighters (all 15 FGs) escort, claim 68-1-10, lose 16-3-12.

The experience of I. Jagdkorps today fit into what would become a common pattern. It scrambled 166 single-engine fighters and 11 Zerstörer; 84 single-engine fighters were credited with contact. The 8th AF bombed Hamburg and Peenemünde. The Jagddivision 8 fighters in Austria were completely out of range. The heavy Sturmböcke of IV.(Sturm)/JG 3 scrambled from Schongau, but ran low on fuel and had to return to base. The four Jagdgruppen that did approach the bombers were savaged by the escorts and lost 18 KIA or MIA, five WIA and at least 24 fighters. Bf 110 night fighters were involved as well, possibly inadvertently, and lost three KIA and two aircraft. The Bf 109 and Fw 190 pilots claimed victories over seven escorts and four B-17s, but of the 19 escorts and 24 bombers lost or scrapped on return to England, the USAAF credited only two fighters and one bomber to German fighters. Overclaiming was not limited to one side, of course; the American escorts received credit for downing 68 German fighters.

5 August
8th Air Force Mission #519: 543 of 1,171 HBs (all BDs) bomb strategic targets in northern and central Germany, TOT 1242-56 – lose 13-3-492, claim 3-1-3. 583 of 658 fighters (14 FGs) escort, claim 29-1-9, lose 6-3-13.

The 8th AF targeted a number of targets in northern and central Germany. By transferring one Gruppe from Vienna to Jüterbog and ordering another to fly a maximum-range mission, I. Jagdkorps put six Jagdgruppen near the enemy, but at no greater strength than the previous day: 130 single-engine fighters and eight Zerstörer were scrambled; 89 single-engine fighters made contact. They were dispersed easily by the escorts, losing 14 KIA or MIA, 10 WIA and 26 fighters. The Americans wrote off 16 bombers and nine fighters to all causes.

6 August

8th Air Force Mission #524: 905 of 1,095 HBs (all BDs) bomb strategic targets in northern and central Germany, TOT 1145-1301 – lose 24-4-531, claim 0-4-5. 713 of 740 fighters (all 15 FGs) escort, claim 31-2-7, lose 8-2-3.

The 8th AF made successful visual attacks on oil and other strategic targets. I. Jagdkorps responded in maximum strength, scrambling 184 single-engine fighters and 14 Zerstörer, of which 127 and 1 made contact. Jagddivisionen 1 and 7 each put up a Gefechtsverband led by a Geschwader Stabsschwarm; that of JD 1 comprised only light Bf 109 Gruppen, while the JD 7 contained a newly-redesignated Fw 190 Sturmgruppe, II.(Sturm)/JG 300, in addition to the original IV./(Sturm)/JG 3, escorted (in theory) by several Bf 109 Gruppen. Their efforts were in vain: eight claims were apparently confirmed, for losses of at least 14 KIA, six WIA and 35 aircraft. The USAAF wrote off 28 bombers and 10 fighters, primarily to Flak.

Luftwaffe defensive activity vs. 15th Air Force – 3 August 1944

Unit	Type	Gruppe up			Gruppe down		Claims	Losses				
		Base	No	Time	Base	Time		Dest	Dam	KIA	MIA	WIA
Luftflotte Reich												
I. Jagdkorps			*102									
Jagddivision 2:												
III./JG 53	Bf 109G	Bad Lippspringe		1100	Karlsruhe	1315	0	0	0	0	0	0
Jagddivision 7:												
IV.(Sturm)/JG 3	Fw 190A	Schongau	19	1035	Schongau	1155	17 B-24	9	1	5	1	1
I./JG 300	Bf 109G	Bad Wörishofen	17	1035	Bad Wörishofen	~1200	0	1	0	1	0	0

*102 total sorties vs. 8th and 15th Air Forces

Luftwaffe defensive activity vs. 8th Air Force – 3 August 1944

Unit	Type	Gruppe up			Gruppe down		Claims	Losses				
		Base	No	Time	Base	Time		Dest	Dam	KIA	MIA	WIA
Luftflotte Reich												
I. Jagdkorps												
Jagddivision 1:												
I./JG 3	Bf 109G	Burg		1400	Bayreuth	1615	n/c	0	0	0	0	0
II./JG 5	Bf 109G	Salzwedel	31	~1345	Salzwedel	~1545	0	1	0	0	0	0
III./JG 300	Bf 109G	Jüterbog	16	1345	Jüterbog	~1545	0	1	3	0	0	0
Jagddivision 2:												
III./JG 53	Bf 109G	Bad Lippspringe		1349	Karlsruhe	1545	1 B-17, 4 P-51*	4	4	2	0	1
Jagddivision 7:												
IV.(Sturm)/JG 3	Fw 190A	Schongau	9	1515	Schongau	~1630	4 B-17	1	0	0	0	0
I./JG 300	Bf 109G	Bad Wörishofen	11	1430	Bad Wörishofen	~1600	0	1	2	0	0	0

*III./JG 53: + 1 B-17 claim undocumented; 1 B-17, 1 B-17 HSS claim unconfirmed (unwitnessed)

Luftwaffe defensive activity – 4 August 1944

Unit	Type	Gruppe up			Gruppe down		Claims	Losses				
		Base	No	Time	Base	Time		Dest	Dam	KIA	MIA	WIA
Luftflotte Reich												
I. Jagdkorps			177									
Jagddivision 1:												
I./JG 3	Bf 109G	Burg	31	1157	Burg, Bayreuth	1405	2 P-51	7	2	5	0	2
	Bf 109G	Burg	9	1508	Burg	~1630	n/c	0	0	0	0	0
II./JG 5	Bf 109G	Sachau	25	1206	Sachau	~1430	1 B-17, 2 P-47*	5	0	1	2	1
	Bf 109G	Sachau	3	1505	Sachau	~1630	n/c	0	0	0	0	0
I./JG 300	Bf 109G	Staaken	5	1514	Wörishofen	~1600	n/c	0	0	0	0	0
III./JG 300	Bf 109G	Jüterbog	9	1152	Jüterbog	~1400	0	1	0	0	1	0
	Bf 109G	Jüterbog	3	1459	Jüterbog	~1600	n/c	0	0	0	0	0
LBeob St 1	Me 410	Königsberg–Neumark	3	1152	Königsberg–Neumark	~1400	shadowers	0	0	0	0	0
	Me 410	Königsberg–Neumark	1	1415	Königsberg–Neumark	~1600	shadower	0	0	0	0	0
Jagddivision 2:												
JGr 10	Ju 88	Paderborn	3	0928	Paderborn	~1100	n/c	0	0	0	0	0
III./JG 53	Bf 109G	Bad Lippspringe	9	1152	Karlsruhe	~1330	2 P-47**	11	1	5	4	2
	Bf 109G	Stade	4	1522	Stade	~1630	n/c	0	0	0	0	0
	Bf 109G	Rotenburg	4	1522	Rotenburg	~1630	0	0	0	0	0	0
7./JG 53	Bf 109G	Paderborn	7	1155	Paderborn	~1330	0***	0	0	0	0	0
IV./NJG 1	Bf 110G	Grove	1	1245	Grove	~1445	shadower?	0	0	0	0	0
	Bf 110G	Grove	1	1415	Grove	~1600	shadower?	0	0	0	0	0
	Bf 110G	Grove		~1500	Grove	~1630	0	2	0	3	0	0
	He 219	Grove	1	1539	Grove	~1630	shadower?	0	0	0	0	0
II./NJG 3	Ju 88	Grove	4	1405	Grove	~1600	n/c	0	0	0	0	0
Jagddivision 7:												
IV.(Sturm)/JG 3	Fw 190A	Schongau	17	1230	Schongau	1400	n/c	0	0	0	0	0
I./JG 300	Bf 109G	Bad Wörishofen	14	1225	Bad Wörishofen, Staaken	~1400	n/c	0	0	0	0	0
ErprKdo 262	Me 262A	Lechfeld		1127	Lechfeld	1215	n/c	0	0	0	0	0

*II./JG 5: + 2 B-17 claims unconfirmed (unwitnessed)   **III./JG 53: + 1 P-51 claim undocumented   ***7./JG 53: + 1 P-47 claim undocumented

7 August

15th Air Force: 137 B-17s, 360 B-24s dispatched to bomb Blechhammer synthetic oil refineries, TOT 1100-31 – lose 13, claim 6-8-1. 117 P-38s (3 FGs), 238 P-51s (4 FGs) dispatched on escort, claim 22-0-3, lose 3 P-38s, 1 P-51.

The 15th AF mounted a major raid on the Blechhammer oil targets, in the far southeastern corner of the Reich. I. Jagdkorps made no attempt to employ Jagddivision 7, but Jagddivision 8 was able to position its German and Hungarian Jagdgruppen over Lake Balaton to meet the incoming stream. The Americans covered this favourite rendezvous point with sweeping fighters and scattered the Axis formations. Jagdgruppe Ost, the usual defender of targets in Silesia, was bolstered today with two famous Eastern Front Jagdgruppen, II./JG 52 and III./JG 52, which were now based in nearby Cracow owing to the approach of the battle lines from the east. They too were fought off by American P-38s and P-51s. The withdrawing bomber stream faced one more attack, by the two Austrian Jagdgruppen on a second sortie, but this too was ineffective. The day proved to be a disaster for the Axis defenders, who lost seven KIA, eight WIA and 20 fighters; claims for five bombers and three fighters were confirmed. American losses to all causes totalled 13 bombers and four fighters.

Luftwaffe defensive activity – 5 August 1944

Unit	Type	Gruppe up			Gruppe down		Claims	Losses				
		Base	No	Time	Base	Time		Dest	Dam	KIA	MIA	WIA
Luftflotte Reich												
I. Jagdkorps			138									
Jagddivision 1:												
I./JG 3	Bf 109G	Burg	24	1103	Burg, Brunswick	1240	2 P-38, 1 P-51	6	3	5	0	1
II./JG 5	Bf 109G	Sachau	22	1100	Sachau	~1230	0	8	2	4	2	2
III./JG 300	Bf 109G	Jüterbog	11	1053	Jüterbog	~1230	0**	4	1	1	0	4
	Bf 109G	Jüterbog	2	1522	Jüterbog	~1630	0	0	0	0	0	0
I./JG 400	Me 163	Brandis	4	1301	Brandis	~1320	n/c	0	0	0	0	0
LBeob St 1	Me 410	Königsberg–Neumark	4	1138	Königsberg–Neumark	~1330	n/c	0	0	0	0	0
Jagddivision 2:												
JGr 10	Ju 88	Stade	3	0928	Stade	~1100	n/c	0	0	0	0	0
III./JG 53	Bf 109G	Bad Lippspringe	16	1052	Bad Lippspringe	1150	n/c	0	0	0	0	0
	Bf 109G	Bad Lippsprlnye	*14	1316	Bad Lippspringe	~1430	2 B-24	3	2	0	0	1
	Bf 109G	Stade	4	1522	Bad Lippspringe	~1700	n/c	0	0	0	0	0
7./JG 53	Bf 109G	Paderborn	6	1032	Paderborn	~1200	n/c	0	0	0	0	0
	Bf 109G	Paderborn	—	1316	Paderborn	~1430	0***	0	0	0	0	0
Jagddivision 7:												
IV.(Sturm)/JG 3	Fw 190A	Schongau		~1100	Schongau	~1230	n/c	1	0	1	0	0
Jagddivision 8:												
II./JG 27	Bf 109G	Fels am Wagram	24	1120	Schongau	~1330	1 P-51	4	3	1	0	2
I./JG 302	Bf 109G	Götzendorf	13	1106	Götzendorf	~1300	1 B-17	0	0	0	0	0

*14 total sorties III./JG 53 + 7./JG 53   **III./JG 300: + 1 P-51 claim undocumented   ***7./JG 53: + 1 B-24 claim undocumented

9 August

8th Air Force Mission #533: all BDs dispatched to strategic targets in SE Germany – weather forces recall; 520 of 824 bomb t/os in western Europe, TOT 1024-1134 – lose 18-4-377, claim 1-1-1. 735 of 847 fighters (all 15 FGs) escort, claim 39-0-14, lose 3-7-?.

15th Air Force: 430 B-17s + B-24s bomb strategic targets in Hungary and Yugoslavia – lose 2 B-24s, claim 0. Escort claims 0, loses 2 P-51s.

Bad weather prompted a late recall of an 8th AF mission to southeastern Germany; many bombers dropped on targets of opportunity in western Germany. The escort plan was disrupted enough to permit the first successful Sturmangriff by the new Sturmgruppe, II.(Sturm)/JG 300, which filed the only RLV claims to be confirmed. All other attacks were broken up by the escorts, which punished mainly the two heavy Fw 190 Gruppen. Several of the escorting Bf 109 Gruppen broke away quickly and sustained light losses. I. Jagdkorps scrambled 119 fighters (92 made contact) and lost 14 KIA, five WIA and 25 aircraft. The Americans wrote off 22 bombers and 10 fighters to all causes.

15th AF bombers dispatched to Hungarian targets reported no encounters with enemy aircraft, although 13 of the 33 Axis fighters scrambled were credited with combat sorties.

14 August

8th Air Force Mission #552: 688 of 730 1st BD + 3rd BD B-17s bomb oil + aviation targets in SW Germany – lose 2-1-252, claim 0. 256 of 292 P-51s escort, claim 10-0-11, lose 1-0-0.

A raid on various targets in southwestern Germany by the 8th AF B-17s was harried only slightly by I. Jagdkorps, which reported one small-scale attack on the bombers (seven combat sorties) from the 57 scrambled. One KIA, one WIA and three fighters were lost; no claims were confirmed. This raid cost the Americans three bombers and one fighter. Most of the escorts' combats and successes were against Luftflotte 3 fighters up on tactical missions.

Luftwaffe defensive activity – 6 August 1944

Unit	Type	Gruppe up			Gruppe down		Claims	Losses				
		Base	No	Time	Base	Time		Dest	Dam	KIA	MIA	WIA
Luftflotte Reich												
I. Jagdkorps			198									
Jagddivision 1:												
I./JG 3	Bf 109G	Burg	21	1023	Burg, Brunswick	~1230	0	5	0	4	0	0
	Bf 109G	Burg	6	1245	Burg	~1400	n/c	0	0	0	0	0
	Bf 109G	Burg	4	1330	Burg	~1500	n/c	0	0	0	0	0
Stab/JG 4	Bf 109G	Sachau	2	1024	Sachau	~1230	0	1	0	0	0	1
II./JG 5	Bf 109G	Sachau	13	1027	Sachau	~1230	0	2	0	?	?	?
	Bf 109G	Sachau	4	1336	Sachau	~1500	0	0	0	0	0	0
III./JG 300	Bf 109G	Jüterbog	15	1015	Jüterbog	~1230	2 P-51*	9	2	2	0	1
	Bf 109G	Jüterbog	1	1335	Jüterbog	~1500	n/c	0	0	0	0	0
	Bf 109G	Jüterbog	2	1547	Jüterbog	~1700	n/c	0	0	0	0	0
LBeob St 1	Me 410	Königsberg–Neumark	3	1033	Königsberg–Neumark	~1200	n/c	0	0	0	0	0
	Me 410	Königsberg–Neumark	1	1317	Königsberg–Neumark	?	shadower	1	0	?	?	?
Jagddivision 2:												
III./JG 53	Bf 109G	Lippspringe, Paderborn	13	0958	Lippspringe, Paderborn	~1130	0	3	2	2	0	2
Jagddivision 7:												
IV.(Sturm)/JG 3	Fw 190A	Schongau		~1045	Schongau	~1300	0	0	1	0	0	0
Stab/JG 300	Fw 190A	Bad Wörishofen	4	1048	Bad Wörishofen	~1130	n/c	0	0	0	0	0
I./JG 300	Bf 109G	Bad Wörishofen	17	1045	Bad Wörishofen	~1300	0**	2	0	1	0	0
II.(Sturm)/JG 300	Fw 190A	Holzkirchen	24	1045	Wörishofen	~1300	6 B-17	9	0	4	0	2
ErprKdo 262	Me 262A	Lechfeld		1002	Lechfeld	1021	n/c	0	0	0	0	0
Jagddivision 8:												
II./JG 27	Bf 109G	Fels am Wagram	22	1045	Stendal	~1245	0	3	1	1	0	0
I./JG 302	Bf 109G	Götzendorf	14	1035	Götzendorf	~1245	0	0	1	?	?	?

*III./JG 300: + 1 B-17, 1 P-51 claims undocumented   **I./JG 300: + 2 B-17, 2 P-51 claims undocumented

Axis defensive activity – 7 August 1944

Unit	Type	Gruppe up			Gruppe down		Claims	Losses				
		Base	No	Time	Base	Time		Dest	Dam	KIA	MIA	WIA
Luftflotte Reich												
I. Jagdkorps			98									
Jagddivision 8:												
II./JG 27	Bf 109G	Fels am Wagram, Bierbaum	17	0835	Götzendorf	~1100	0	0	0	0	0	0
2nd sorties	Bf 109G	Götzendorf	9	1210	Fels am Wagram	~1330	1 B-17, 1 P-38	2	3	1	0	1
I./JG 302	Bf 109G	Götzendorf	13	0845	Götzendorf	~1100	0	0	0	0	0	0
2nd sorties	Bf 109G	Götzendorf	6	1207	Götzendorf	~1330	1 B-24	4	0	1	0	3
Abschfü Ungarn:												
101 JGr (Hungary)	Bf 109G	Veszprém	19	0850	Veszprém	~1100	2 P-51	8	0	2	0	1
Jafü Oberschlesien:												
II./JG 52	Bf 109G	Cracow		~1030	Cracow	~1230	1 B-24	0	0	0	0	0

Axis defensive activity – 7 August 1944 Continued

Unit	Type	Gruppe up			Gruppe down		Claims	Losses				
		Base	No	Time	Base	Time		Dest	Dam	KIA	MIA	WIA
III./JG 52	Bf 109G	Cracow		~1030	Cracow	~1230	0	3	0	2	0	1
1.+3./JGr Ost	Fw 190A	Liegnitz	4	1105	Liegnitz	~1230	2 B-24	0	0	0	0	0
	Bf 109G	Liegnitz	8	1105	Liegnitz	~1230	0	0	0	0	0	0
2.+4./JGr Ost	Bf 109G	Weidengut	17	1105	Weidengut	~1230	0	3	2	1	0	2
9./NJG 7	Ju 88	Brieg	1	1040	Brieg	~1240	shadower	0	0	0	0	0

Luftwaffe defensive activity – 9 August 1944

Unit	Type	Gruppe up			Gruppe down		Claims	Losses				
		Base	No	Time	Base	Time		Dest	Dam	KIA	MIA	WIA
Luftflotte Reich												
I. Jagdkorps			119									
Jagddivision 1:												
I./JG 3	Bf 109G	Burg	17	0925	Leipheim, Gablingen	1120	0	6	2	2	0	1
II./JG 5	Bf 109G	Salzwedel		~0930	Salzwedel	~1115	0	3	1	2	0	0
III./JG 300	Bf 109G	Sachau	9	0924	Sachau	~1115	0	0	0	0	0	0
Jagddivision 2:												
III./JG 53	Bf 109G	Bad Lippspringe		~0930	Bad Lippspringe	~1115	0	0	0	0	0	0
Jagddivision 7:												
IV.(Sturm)/JG 3	Fw 190A	Schongau	32	0940	Schongau, Lechfeld	1135	0*	10	2	8	0	4
Stab/JG 300	Fw 190A	Holzkirchen	1	1105	Holzkirchen	1255	0	0	0	0	0	0
I./JG 300	Bf 109G	Bad Wörishofen	12	0935	Bad Wörishofen, Oettingen	~1115	0**	1	0	0	0	0
II.(Sturm)/JG 300	Fw 190A	Holzkirchen	24	0935	Bad Wörishofen, Darmstadt	~1115	10 B-17***	5	1	2	0	0

*IV.(Sturm)/JG 3: + 2 B-17 claims undocumented   **I./JG 300: + 1 P-51 claim undocumented   ***II.(Sturm)/JG 300: + 4 B-17 claims unconfirmed (unwitnessed)

Luftwaffe defensive activity – 14 August 1944

Unit	Type	Gruppe up			Gruppe down		Claims	Losses				
		Base	No	Time	Base	Time		Dest	Dam	KIA	MIA	WIA
Luftflotte Reich												
I. Jagdkorps			57									
Jagddivision 1:												
I./JG 400	Me 163	Brandis	6	~1100	Brandis	~1130	0	0	0	0	0	0
Jagddivision 7:												
IV.(Sturm)/JG 3	Fw 190A	Schongau	20	1045	Schongau, Lechfeld	~1300	0	2	1	0	0	1
Stab/JG 300	Fw 190A	Holzkirchen	2	1100	Holzkirchen	1300	0	0	0	0	0	0
I./JG 300	Bf 109G	Bad Wörishofen	12	1100	Bad Wörishofen, Oettingen	~1300	0	0	0	0	0	0
II.(Sturm)/JG 300	Fw 190A	Holzkirchen	20	1045	Bad Wörishofen, Darmstadt	~1300	0*	1	1	1	0	0

*II.(Sturm)/JG 300: + 1 B-17, 1 B-17 HSS claims undocumented

15 August

8th Air Force Mission #554: 877 of 932 HBs (all BDs) bomb airfields in Germany and the Low Countries, TOT 1051-1207 – lose 16-2-156, claim 13-3-2. 393 of 443 fighters escorts, claim 14-0-1, lose 5.

An 8th AF raid on German airfields was met by the most effective resistance seen in some time. I. Jagdkorps put up 135 fighters (84 with contact) in two Gefechtsverbände. That of JD 7 contained both of the Sturmgruppen and a dedicated high-altitude protection Gruppe and made an effective Sturmangriff, sustaining modest losses. Its initial claims were high, but 15 B-17 shootdowns were ultimately confirmed. The JD 1 Gefechtsverband lacked high-altitude protection, but made a closed attack on an unescorted B-24 formation before the P-51s found it; 10 B-24 claims were confirmed. The new Me 262 jet fighter claimed its first bomber, a straggling B-17. For the day, the RLV force lost 10 KIA, four WIA and 23 fighters; the Americans wrote off 13 B-17s, five B-24s and five escort fighters.

PILOT'S ACCOUNT[5]
15 August 1944

At about 1100 hours, I led 25–30 II./JG 5 Bf 109s up from Sachau. We met Major Götz and III./JG 53 over the Müritzsee. The Jagddivision 1 controller (Major Herrmann) ordered us to fly southwest, toward Kassel. After about 45 minutes, we were ordered to turn northwest. We crossed the Rhein and a broad green plain that we later decided was in the Netherlands. We were now in a clear high-pressure weather front. Suddenly we saw a Liberator formation flying in the direction of England. I learned later that it had bombed a target in northern Germany. It was without fighter protection, probably because it was so close to home. Major Götz, the formation leader, ordered an immediate attack, and several bombers were quickly set on fire. One machine sheered off to the right, and I went after it. I chased it for a kilometre, its tail gunner firing all the time. I held my fire until I reached 100 metres and fired first with the MGs and then with the cannon. Parts of the tail broke off immediately; then the right engine began to smoke. As I raced past the bomber, the first men were beginning to bail out. Then the Lightnings arrived. My fuel was low, and I did not take part in this dogfight, but landed on an airfield near Havelte. While approaching the airfield cross, I jumped out and dove into a ditch, saving myself from the strafing Lightnings.

Long after the war, I met a crewman from the Liberator I shot down. It was 'True Love' from the 466th Bomb Group's 786th Bomb Squadron.

Lt. Ernst Scheufele
6./JG 5

Luftwaffe defensive activity – 15 August 1944

Unit	Type	Gruppe up			Gruppe down		Claims	Losses				
		Base	No	Time	Base	Time		Dest	Dam	KIA	MIA	WIA
Luftflotte Reich												
I. Jagdkorps			135									
Jagddivision 1:												
I./JG 3	Bf 109G	Burg		1105	Burg, Quakenbrück	1300	0	0	1	0	0	0
II./JG 5	Bf 109G	Gardelegen?	25	1100	Gardelegen?, Havel	~1300	1 B-24*	8	0	1	0	1
III./JG 53	Bf 109G	Sachau		1100	Sachau, Steenwijk	~1300	4 B-24	3	2	2	0	1
III./JG 300	Bf 109G	Jüterbog	22	1100	Jüterbog	~1300	3 B-24**	2	3	1	0	0
Jagddivision 7:												
IV.(Sturm)/JG 3	Fw 190A	Schongau	13	1014	Schongau, Lechfeld	~1230	9 B-17	3	1	1	0	1
Stab/JG 300	Fw 190A	Wörishofen	6	0948	Mainz–Finthen	1155	3 B-17	0	1	0	0	0
I./JG 300	Bf 109G	Wörishofen	19	0935	Wörishofen, Darmstadt	1210	0	7	1	5	0	1
II.(Sturm)/JG 300	Fw 190A	Holzkirchen	17	1014	Mainz–Finthen	1232	3 B-17***	0	2	0	0	0
ErprKdo 262	Me 262A	Lechfeld	2	1254	Echterdingen	1350	1 B-17	0	0	0	0	0

*II./JG 5: + 3 B-24 claims unconfirmed (unwitnessed)   **III./JG 300: + 2 B-24 claims unconfirmed (unwitnessed)

***II.(Sturm)/JG 300: + 3 B-17 claims undocumented; 3 B-17 HSS claims unconfirmed (unwitnessed)

Lt. Ernst Scheufele. an experienced fighter pilot on the Arctic Sea front, led 6./JG 5 on the Invasionsfront and in the RLV force. When II./JG 5 was renamed IV./JG 4 in October, Scheufele became Staffelkapitän of 14./JG 4. He was shot down by American antiaircraft fire and taken prisoner on 3 December. *(Scheufele)*

PILOT'S ACCOUNT[6]
15 August 1944

This was the first mission in I./JG 300 for the four of us who had just returned from *Fühlungshalter* [contact keeper] duty in Italy. Our Staffel comprised two Schwärme today. We were to meet 110s and 410s near Miltenberg and escort them. We reached the rendezvous point at 8,000 metres and saw nothing but a large number of Mustangs. We were expecting ca. 60 Lightnings to come in from the west, but the controller had said nothing about Mustangs. Our formation split up. We pulled up into the sun and broke in all directions. I used the methanol injection, and the 109 shot up like an elevator. A few turns enabled me to lose the P-51s. I then lost altitude quickly in a steep sideslip and was soon at 1,000 metres. Now flying northwest, I saw four aircraft that looked like Fw 190s from the Sturmgruppe – but it was not my lucky day! They were Thunderbolts with their huge engines. They banked toward me, and all I could do was dive. As soon as I saw them straighten out to aim, I let my crate sideslip or skid, always banking slightly. The main thing was to remain at a sharp angle for several seconds without actually banking into a turn. The tactic was effective: the shells being fired in my direction sprayed the sky around my Me. In the end, the Amis turned away to strafe a train. My crate had taken a few strikes in the tail, but flew well, and I landed my 'Black 4' at Darmstadt. After minor repairs and refueling, it was declared ready for take-off. In the meantime, I had telephoned my parents in Bensheim and told them I would be coming by – this was strictly forbidden, of course. Their joy was great. I made several low passes over our house and saw my mother, father and sister before returning to Bad Wörishofen. Of our eight aircraft, six had now landed; one had belly-landed elsewhere, and Reinhold Fackenthal was missing. That evening, the Adjutant called me. A totally burnt-out Bf 109 with its pilot had been located near Lohr am Main. Some burnt fragments of a letter were found; these were all we had to identify the body. It was Reinhold Fackenthal. I had lost a wonderful comrade, one day after our return from Italy.

Uffz. Berthold Wendler
3./JG 300

16 August

8th Air Force Mission #556: 976 of 1,090 HBs (all BDs) bomb oil + aviation targets in C Germany, TOT 1052-1135 – lose 23-2-269, claim 0. 612 of 692 fighters (all FGs) escort and sweep, claim 32-1-4, lose 3-1-11.

15th Air Force: 89 B-24s bomb Friedrichshafen chemical plant – lose 2, claim 0. Escorts claim 0, lose 0 (no air opposition).

The 8th AF made a maximum-strength raid on strategic targets in central Germany. I. Jagdkorps scrambled 121 fighters, of which 77 made contact.

Luftwaffe defensive activity – 16 August 1944

Unit	Type	Gruppe up			Gruppe down		Claims	Losses				
		Base	No	Time	Base	Time		Dest	Dam	KIA	MIA	WIA
Luftflotte Reich												
I. Jagdkorps			122									
Jagddivision 1:												
I./JG 3	Bf 109G	Borkheide		~0915	Borkheide	~1115	2 P-51	6	2	4	0	1
II./JG 5	Bf 109G	Salzwedel		~0915	Salzwedel	~1115	1 P-51	2	0	2	0	0
II./JG 27	Bf 109G	Rhein–Main?	22	0855	Rhein–Main?	~1100	0	6	3	2	0	2
III./JG 53	Bf 109G	Sachau		~0915	Sachau	~1115	1 B-24	2	0	0	0	0
III./JG 300	Bf 109G	Jüterbog	12	0910	Jüterbog	~1115	0	4	0	2	1	0
I./JG 400	Me 163B	Brandis	5	~1045	Brandis	~1115	0*	2	0	1	0	0
Jagddivision 7:												
IV.(Sturm)/JG 3	Fw 190A	Schongau	9	0900	Schongau	1100	4 B-17	2	0	1	0	1
Stab/JG 300	Fw 190A	Langendiebach?		~0900	Langendiebach?	~1040	0	0	0	0	0	0
I./JG 300	Bf 109G	Langendiebach	5	0857	Langendiebach	1040	0**	1	0	0	1	0
II.(Sturm)/JG 300	Fw 190A	Langendiebach	8	0900	Langendiebach	~1040	2 B-17	0	0	0	0	0
I./JG 302	Bf 109G	Langendiebach	16	0858	Langendiebach, Nordhausen	1040	4 B-17	2	1	0	0	1

*I./JG 400: + 3 B-17 claims unconfirmed (unwitnessed)   **I./JG 300: + 1 P-51 claim undocumented

Five rocket-powered Me 163s attacked the B-17 stream and claimed three, for the loss of two fighters and one pilot. None of the crashes were witnessed and therefore could not be confirmed; this would be a recurring problem for these high-speed, limited-endurance craft. The rest of the defending fighters formed their two Gefechtsverbände and searched for poorly defended stretches of the stream. These were hard to find. Claims for 11 bombers and three fighters were confirmed; the conventional German fighters lost 14 KIA or MIA, five WIA and 27 fighters. The Americans wrote off 25 bombers and four fighters.

The 15th AF bombed the important Friedrichshafen chemical complex and reported no encounters with Axis fighters; in fact, none were sortied against them.

PILOT'S ACCOUNT[7]
16 August 1944

I./JG 302 had moved to Langendiebach the previous evening, anticipating another attack from the west. A strong bomber force was reported in the morning, and we scrambled at 0858 hours in the direction of Halle. We formed a *Gefechtsverband* with a JG 300

Höhengruppe and IV.(Sturm)/JG 3. We met the bombers near Kassel. The escorts were numerous, but kept a respectful distance, flying past to stay between us and the bombers. The JG 300 Gruppe recognised this tactic and attacked the Mustangs. Conditions were now favourable for the two heavy Gruppen to attack the bombers. Tracers from the bombers' guns passed the attacking fighters in a stream of fire that made our pilots feel that they were under a shower. In these seconds, our nerves were stretched to the limit. The tension broke when a target was found in the Revi's lighted cross and we pressed the firing buttons. Our own aircraft vibrated slightly under the hammering of our guns. Since we used the same angle of attack on almost all of our attacks on bomber Pulks, the procedure had become routine.

My 1. Staffel was the first *Angriffskeil* [attack wedge] in the Gruppe formation. Although this was my first mission since a recent injury, I was very experienced in the procedure. I first silenced the tail gunner with my two MG 131s, then aimed at a wing root and inner engine. The strikes formed a good pattern, without showing much of an effect, and I fired with all barrels up to a distance of about 50 metres before breaking away in a tight *Abschwung* [split-S] to the left, planning to make another attack on the B-17 as quickly as possible. As I took my last turn toward the bomber formation, I saw that my B-17 – also in a left turn – had left its formation. A new attack showed an immediate effect, and it dove away with an ever-lengthening smoke plume. The B-17 was still under control; a crash became inevitable at about 4,000 metres. I trailed the diving machine in order to observe the exact crash site. I passed the bomber and then saw it crash southeast of Kassel at the edge of a forest.

I had lost much altitude while preoccupied with the B-17 and was now in great danger. A quick glance behind me revealed the belly of a Mustang, and behind it, another. Since my speed had dropped to match the Boeing, I pulled up in a steep left turn, attempting at the same time to gain some speed and get out of this ticklish situation. As soon as I got a little height, I attempted to escape at lowest altitude, using every bit of forest. To my great joy, I could see after a while that I was no longer being followed.

I landed at Nordhausen at 1040 hours and, after completing my roll-out, saw an officer striding quickly up to my machine. I learned later that he was the airfield commandant. He ordered me to take off immediately as there were bombers overhead, and he did not want to make his field a target. But after two hours in the air, my airplane had to be refuelled, and as the servicing personnel were not close by, I could not get away for Langendiebch until 1220 hours.

Our attack today was successful. While the JG 300 Höhengruppe held off the escort, IV.(Sturm)/JG 3 downed four B-17s, as did our I./JG 302, at the cost to us of two Bf 109s and one badly injured pilot who never returned to the Gruppe.

Uffz. Willi Reschke
1./JG 302

Axis defensive activity – 20 August 1944

Unit	Type	Gruppe up			Gruppe down		Claims	Losses				
		Base	No	Time	Base	Time		Dest	Dam	KIA	MIA	WIA
Luftflotte Reich												
I. Jagdkorps			224									
Jagddivision 1:												
I./JG 3	Bf 109G	Borkheide	11	0912	Borkheide	1130	n/c	0	0	0	0	0
III./JG 53	Bf 109G	Mörtitz	26	0910	Mörtitz	1045	n/c	0	0	0	0	0
III./JG 300	Bf 109G	Jüterbog	14	0913	Jüterbog	1030	n/c	0	0	0	0	0
Jagddivision 7:												
IV.(Sturm)/JG 3	Fw 190A	Schongau		0855	Schongau	1055	n/c	0	0	0	0	0
I./JG 300	Bf 109G	Biblis		0900	Bad Wörishofen	~1100	n/c	0	0	0	0	0
II.(Sturm)/JG 300	Fw 190A	Holzkirchen		~0900	Holzkirchen	~1100	n/c	0	0	0	0	0
Jagddivision 8:												
II./JG 27	Bf 109G	Fels am Wagram	17	0834	Fels am Wagram	~1045	0	0	0	0	0	0
I./JG 302	Bf 109G	Götzendorf	17	0847	Götzendorf	~1045	1 B-17*	2	0	2	0	0
Abschfü Ungarn:												
101 JGr (Hungary)	Bf 109G	Veszprém	27	0845	Veszprém	~1030	0	?	?	?	?	?
2nd sorties	Bf 109G	Veszprém	20	1215	Veszprém	~1345	0	?	?	?	?	?
Jafü Oberschlesien:												
1.+3./JGr Ost	Fw 190A	Liegnitz	8	1050	Liegnitz	1212	n/c	0	0	0	0	0
2.+4./JGr Ost	Bf 109G	Weidengut	10	1050	Weidengut	1212	n/c	0	0	0	0	0

*I./JG 302: + 1 B-17, 1 B-17 HSS claims undocumented; 2 B-17, 1 B-24 claims unconfirmed (unwitnessed)

20 August

15th Air Force: 140 B-17s, 342 B-24s dispatched to bomb oil, aviation, rail targets in Czechoslovakia, Hungary, Poland – lose 3, claim 0. 35 P-38s (1 FG), 213 P-51s (4 FGs) dispatched on escort, claim 0, lose 0.

The 15th AF completed its campaign against Ploesti on the 19th and returned to strategic targets in the territory defended by Luftflotte Reich. A major raid to Czechoslovakia, Hungary, and Poland resulted in the smallest losses yet sustained on a deep-penetration raid: seven bombers and no fighters. I. Jagdkorps ordered 224 fighters up, but only 22 made contact, all from Jagddivision 8, whose I./JG 302 claimed six bombers (one confirmed) for the loss of two formation leaders. The Hungarian Pumas flew two missions, but their combats resulted in no known claims or losses. The Allied radio intercept service heard the Silesian controller attempt to direct the fighters from Jagddivision 1 and JGr Ost to the Czech and Polish targets, but these had to be recalled before reaching the targeted areas. This was a most unsuccessful day for the RLV forces, even though the only Axis losses known to the author are the two I./JG 302 Bf 109s and pilots.

21 August

15th Air Force: 102 B-24s dispatched to bomb Hungarian airfield – lose 1, claim 0. 46 P-51s (1 FG) dispatched to escort and strafe, claim 1, lose 0.

The only 15th AF formation to penetrate Luftwaffe Reich territory bombed the Hajdúböszörmeny airfield, home to the Hungarian Me 210 squadron. These aircraft now served as light bombers, and the attack was thus of some use to the approaching Red Army. I. Jagdkorps assumed that the raid would be larger and scrambled 183 fighters, of which 30 made contact – I./JG 302 and the Hungarian Pumas. Known Axis casualties totalled one KIA and three Bf 109s. I./JG 302 claimed two B-24s, but these were not confirmed for lack of witnesses. Due to luck or good intelligence, most of the RLV force spent the night on airfields quite close to the route that a much larger American force would take on the following day.

22 August – Viennese and Silesian oil targets (see map)

15th Air Force: 267 of 324 B-24s bomb Vienna o/i, TOT 1015-17 – lose 10, claim 37-8-5; 100 of 124 B-24s bomb

Blechhammer synthetic oil plant, TOT 1144-51 – lose 13, claim 2-2-0; 135 of 168 B-17s bomb Odertal synthetic oil plant, TOT 1134-52 – lose 5, claim 7-1-0. Escort of 91 P-38s, 261 P-51s (all FGs) claims 14-0-5, loses 4.

The 15th AF flew a full-strength mission to the oil refineries at Blechhammer, Odertal and Vienna, and the underground oil storage facility at Lobau. The RLV commanders had prepositioned most of their units for just such a contingency and scrambled 222 fighters (116 with contact) – nine Jagdgruppen, the operational training unit Jagdgruppe Ost and the Hungarian Pumas, which were now down to the strength of a single Staffel. Jagddivision 8 directed the fighters in Austria (JD 7 and JD 8) in attacks on both the incoming and withdrawing streams. Jafü Schlesien attempted to control its own JGr Ost, plus four JD 1 Gruppen in the Silesian target area. Hard fighting brought fairly good results despite a heavy escort, indicating the crucial importance of defensive numbers. The 15th AF lost 28 bombers and four escorts to all causes; the Axis lost only four KIA, nine WIA and 21 fighters. Of these, the Hungarians lost one KIA and Bf 109; their accumulated losses now forced them to withdraw from the strategic battlefield for a month.

PILOT'S ACCOUNT[8]
22 August 1944

I./JG 302, which was now down to half-establishment strength, received a welcome reinforcement from IV.(Sturm)/JG 3, I./JG 300 and II.(Sturm)/JG 300. The four Jagdgruppen scrambled from Wien–Götzendorf and Wien–Seyring at 0900 hours and were ordered by Rosenkavalier to fly southeast into Hungarian airspace. Our Gefechtsverband contacted the enemy near Pápa, north of Lake Balaton. They were B-24 Pulks, surrounded by a strong escort of P-38s and P-51s. While our own escort Gruppe [I./JG 300] attacked the American escorts, we had to punch through their formation to reach the bombers. We were strong enough to do this. Some of the bomber crews were obviously unprepared for such a massive attack as we could see several B-24s attempt to jettison their bombs.

IV.(Sturm)/JG 3 formed the leading attack wedge. Their attack caused several B-24s to fall away in flames. I was flying on the far left side of our own formation, and during the breakthrough to the

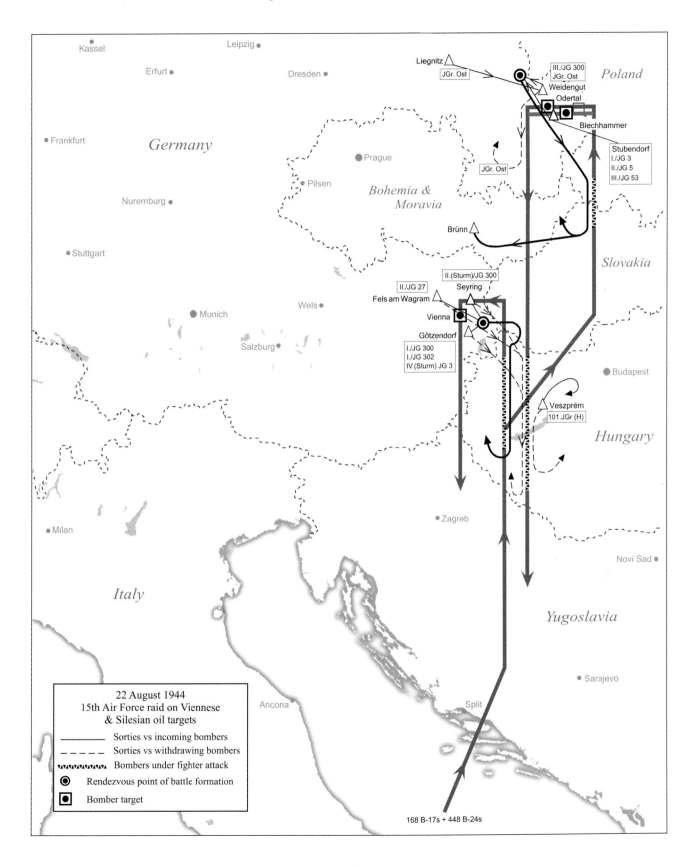

22 August 1944
15th Air Force raid on Viennese
& Silesian oil targets

———— Sorties vs incoming bombers

— — — — Sorties vs withdrawing bombers

ᴠᴠᴠᴠᴠᴠᴠᴠᴠᴠᴠ Bombers under fighter attack

◉ Rendezvous point of battle formation

▣ Bomber target

168 B-17s + 448 B-24s

Axis defensive activity – 21 August 1944

Unit	Type	Gruppe up			Gruppe down		Claims	Losses				
		Base	No	Time	Base	Time		Dest	Dam	KIA	MIA	WIA
Luftflotte Reich												
I. Jagdkorps			183									
Jagddivision 1:												
I./JG 3	Bf 109G	Borkheide	15	0927	Weidengut, Stubendorf	1110	n/c	0	0	0	0	0
II./JG 5	Bf 109G	Sachau	18	1000	Weidengut, Stubendorf	1136	n/c	0	0	0	0	0
III./JG 53	Bf 109G	Mörtitz	20	0927	Weidengut, Stubendorf	1124	n/c	0	0	0	0	0
III./JG 300	Bf 109G	Juterbog	20	0930	Weidengut, Stubendorf	1111	n/c	0	0	0	0	0
Jagddivision 7:												
IV.(Sturm)/JG 3	Fw 190A	Schongau		~0900	Götzendorf	~1030	transfer	0	0	0	0	0
I./JG 300	Bf 109G	Bad Wörishofen		~0900	Götzendorf	~1030	transfer	0	0	0	0	0
II.(Sturm)/JG 300	Fw 190A	Holzkirchen		0855	Wien-Seyring	1030	transfer	0	0	0	0	0
Jagddivision 8:												
II./JG 27	Bf 109G	Fels am Wagram	16	0844	Fels am Wagram	~1000	0	1	0	0	0	0
I./JG 302	Bf 109G	Götzendorf	14	0855	Götzendorf	~1000	0*	1	0	0	0	0
Abschfü Ungarn:												
101 JGr (Hungary)	Bf 109G	Veszprém	17	0910	Veszprém	~1000	0	1	0	1	0	0

*1./JG 302: + 2 B-24 claims unconfirmed (unwitnessed)

bombers my wingman, Ogfr. Angermann, and I were engaged by P-51s. We had long since dropped our tanks, and at this altitude – above 7,000 metres – the Bf 109G-6 gave its best performance, equal to that of the P-51. We were held back only by our numerical inferiority. We worked hard to keep our Rotte together. In such air battles – fighter against fighter – minutes seemed like hours, and instinctive reactions were required. We had learned to judge success by mere survival, and, in fact, we reached Götzendorf in good shape and landed at 1015 hours.

Since this battle had taken place not far from Götzendorf, most of our fighters landed there. The fighters were immediately refuelled and made ready for the next mission. At 1225 hours, the mixed formation received its orders. The battle zone was not far from the earlier one. We were to attack a B-17 formation on its way back to Italy. Entirely in contrast to the previous mission, these B-17 Pulks were escorted by only a few fighters, so our attack could be carried out without much hindrance. The attack wedges had already been formed. I flew in the first wedge and had already reached firing position – 800 metres – when I saw a Fw 190 flying on my left side, quite close. After making eye contact, the pilot raised his hand and pointed forward; we both had the same

target and opened fire on the B-17 at the same time. Both of its wings quickly showed the effect of our fire. As soon as our attack began, black points began dropping from the machine; it was the crew. Shortly afterward, the B-17, still in formation, blew apart under the massive fire of the two fighters. This, for me, was a unique experience, never to be repeated in future missions. After landing on Götzendorf, I learned that the Fw 190 pilot was Oblt. Horst Haase, Kapitän of 16.(Sturm)/JG 3. We congratulated each other on our success, which was then apportioned according to rank.

This was the last mission for I./JG 302 in Hungarian airspace, although we did not know this at the time. It was another mission carried out with dogged determination; again, the pilots fought bravely and successfully. For the day, the Gruppe claimed one B-17, three B-24s and one P-38 destroyed, and one B-17 and one B-24 shot from formation. My own claim was credited as a 'final destruction', which was worth little. Our losses today were bearable. My Staffelkapitän was injured, but after a stay in hospital was able to return to the Gruppe.

Uffz. Willi Reschke
1./JG 302

23 August

15th Air Force: 133 of 204 B-24s bomb Markersdorf a/f, TOT 1225-43 – lose 10, claim 25-14-7; 255 bombers strike Vienna oil, aviation targets – lose 2, claim 0. Escort of 94 P-38s, 215 P 51s (all FGs) claims 20-0-3, lose 1.

The 15th AF returned to Blechhammer, Odertal and Vienna to find a much weaker defence. I. Jagdkorps scrambled 96 fighters; 50 made contact. The only significant success was scored by IV.(Sturm)/JG 3, which located a Pulk flying alone to a secondary target and shot down eight 451st BG B-24s and damaged eight others in a classic closed-formation rear Sturmangriff. The Luftwaffe lost 13 KIA or MIA and 19 fighters; the Americans lost 12 bombers and one fighter.

A B-24 from the 15th Air Force's 451st Bomb Group, 725th Bomb Squadron, after being set on fire by a IV.(Sturm)/JG 3 Sturmangriff while bombing Austria on 23 August. It was photographed from the squadron's only surviving B24. (USAAF)

24 August

8th Air Force Mission #568: 1,213 of 1,319 HBs (all BDs) bomb oil + aviation targets in C Germany, TOT 1130-1300 – lose 26-5-547, claim 10-3-4. 626 of 739 fighters (all FGs) escort, claim 10-0-1, lose 4-0-3.

15th Air Force: 158 of 167 B-17s bomb Pardubice (Cz) a/f, TOT 1229-33 – lose 2, claim 0; 110 of 117 B-24s bomb Pardubice (Cz) refinery, TOT 1218-21 – lose 10, claim 29-12-10; 204 of 233 B-24s strike Vienna oil, misc rail targets – lose 1, claim 0. Escort of 105 P-38s, 215 P-51s (all FGs) claims 10-0-1, loses 0.

Simultaneous raids by both American strategic air forces forced I. Jagdkorps to split its small force: JD 1 against the 8th AF, JD 7 and JD 8 against the 15th AF. 223 fighters were scrambled; only 99 made contact. Some missions against the incoming raids were recalled early, for reasons that remain obscure, but most Gruppen were able to fly second sorties against the withdrawing streams. Two Jagdgruppen flew their most productive RLV missions today: III./JG 53, the lone representative of its Geschwader in the Reich,

Axis defensive activity vs. 15th Air Force – 22 August 1944

Unit	Type	Gruppe up			Gruppe down		Claims	Losses (—: included with 1st sortie)				
		Base	No	Time	Base	Time		Dest	Dam	KIA	MIA	WIA
vs. incoming stream												
Luftflotte Reich												
I. Jagdkorps			*222									
Jagddivision 8:												
IV. (Sturm)/JG 3	Fw 190A	Götzendorf	18	0855	Götzendorf	1100	8 B-24	1	6	0	0	1
II./JG 27	Bf 109G	Fels am Wagram, Bierbaum	19	0845	Fels am Wagram, Bierbaum	~1030	0	0	0	0	0	0
I./JG 300	Bf 109G	Götzendorf	11	0855	Götzendorf	1050	0**	0	0	0	0	0
II.(Sturm)/JG 300	Fw 190A	Seyring	21	0850	Seyring	1000	3 B-24, 2 P-38***	9	0	0	0	3
I./JG 302	Bf 109G	Götzendorf	13	0853	Götzendorf	1015	3 B-24, 1 P-38	1	1	0	0	1
Abschfü Ungarn:												
101 JGr (Hungary)	Bf 109G	Veszprém	12	0909	Veszprém	~1030	n/c	1	1	1	0	0
Jafü Oberschlesien:												
I./JG 3	Bf 109G	Stubendorf	10	0957	Stubendorf, Weidengut	1200	1 P-51	4	1	2	0	1
II./JG 5	Bf 109G	Stubendorf	11	0957	Stubendorf	~1200	0	1	1	0	0	1
III./JG 53	Bf 109G	Stubendorf	16	0957	Brünn	~1200	1 P-51	0	0	0	0	0
III./JG 300	Bf 109G	Weidengut	18	0957	Weidengut	~1200	1 P-51****	0	1	0	0	0
1.+3./JGr Ost	Fw 190A	Liegnitz	6	1028	Weidengut	1130	0.	0	0	0	0	0
2.+4./JGr Ost	Bf 109G	Weidengut	16	1025	Weidengut	1130	0	1	0	0	0	1
vs. withdrawing stream												
Luftflotte Reich												
I. Jagdkorps												
Jagddivision 8:												
IV.(Sturm)/JG 3	Fw 190A	Götzendorf	1	1210	Götzendorf	~1315	1 B-17	0	0	0	0	0
II./JG 27	Bf 109G	Fels am Wagram	13	1207	Fels am Wagram	~1315	1 B-17*****	1	2	0	0	0
I./JG 300	Bf 109G	Götzendorf	3	1210	Götzendorf	~1315	1 B-17	2	2	1	0	1
II.(Sturm)/JG 300	Fw 190A	Seyring		~1215	Seyring	~1315	1 B-24	—	—	—	—	—
I./JG 302	Bf 109G	Götzendorf	5	1215	Götzendorf	1307	1 B-17******	—	—	—	—	—
Abschfü Ungarn:												
101 JGr (Hungary)	Bf 109G	Veszprém	10	1230	Veszprém	~1330	2 B-24	—	—	—	—	—
Jafü Oberschlesien:												
JGr Ost	Bf 109G	Weidengut	11	1204	Weidengut	1230	n/c	0	0	0	0	0

*222 total sorties vs. incoming and withdrawing streams

**I./JG 300: + 1 B-24, 1 P-51 claims undocumented; 1 B-24 HSS claims unconfirmed (unwitnessed)

***I./JG 300: + 2 B-24 claims undocumented; 1 B-24, 2 P-38 claims unconfirmed (unwitnessed)

****III./JG 300: + 1 P-51 claim undocumented

*****II./JG 27: + 2 B-17, 1 P-51 claims unconfirmed (unwitnessed)

******I./JG 302: + 1 B-17 claims unconfirmed (unwitnessed)

Luftwaffe defensive activity – 23 August 1944

Unit	Type	Gruppe up			Gruppe down		Claims	Losses				
		Base	No	Time	Base	Time		Dest	Dam	KIA	MIA	WIA
Luftflotte Reich												
I. Jagdkorps			96									
Jagddivision 1:												
I./JG 3	Bf 109G	Borkheide	7	1100	Hörsching	1300	n/c	0	0	0	0	0
II./JG 5	Bf 109G	Salzwedel	9	~1100	Salzwedel	~1300	n/c	2	0	0	0	0
III./JG 53	Bf 109G	Sachau	5	~1100	Sachau	~1300	n/c	0	0	0	0	0
III./JG 300	Bf 109G	Jüterbog	18	~1100	Jüterbog	~1300	n/c	1	0	0	0	0
Jagddivision 7:												
Stab/JG 300	Fw 190A	Holzkirchen	2	1102	Götzendorf	1255	1 P-51*	0	0	0	0	0
IV.(Sturm)/JG 3	Fw 190A	Schongau	17	1055	Schongau	1225	8 B-24	6	3	5	1	0
I./JG 300	Bf 109G	Bad Wörishofen	6	1055	Bad Wörishofen	1250	n/c	0	0	0	0	0
II.(Sturm)/JG 300	Fw 190A	Holzkirchen	15	1055	Holzkirchen	1255	2 P-51**	7	0	5	0	0
Jagddivision 8:												
II./JG 27	Bf 109G	Fels am Wagram		1145	Fels am Wagram	~1330	0***	3	1	2	0	0

*Stab/JG 300: + 1 P-51 claim unconfirmed (unwitnessed)

**II.(Sturm)/JG 300: + 1 P-51 claim unconfirmed (unwitnessed)

***II./JG 27: + 1 B-24 claim unconfirmed (unwitnessed)

Luftwaffe defensive activity vs. 8th Air Force – 24 August 1944

Unit	Type	Gruppe up			Gruppe down		Claims	Losses				
		Base	No	Time	Base	Time		Dest	Dam	KIA	MIA	WIA
Luftflotte Reich												
I. Jagdkorps			*223									
Jagddivision 1:												
I./JG 3	Bf 109G	Borkheide		1009	Borkheide, Pretsch	1200	0**	1	0	0	0	0
II./JG 5	Bf 109G	Salzwedel		~1000	Salzwedel, Havel	~1200	0	3	1	1	0	1
III./JG 53	Bf 109G	Mörtitz		1005	Stade	~1200	6 B-17	4	2	1	0	3
2nd sorties	Bf 109G	Stade		1320	Mörtitz	~1400	0	0	0	0	0	0
III./JG 300	Bf 109G	Jüterbog	15	1007	Jüterbog	1205	2 B-17***	0	0	0	0	0
2nd sorties	Bf 109G	Jüterbog		1305	Jüterbog	~1400	0	1	0	0	0	0
I./JG 400	Me 163B	Brandis	8	1200	Brandis	1215	2 B-17****	1	1	1	0	0
2nd sorties	Me 163B	Brandis		1230	Brandis	1245	1 B-17	0	0	0	0	0

*223 total sorties vs. 8th and 15th Air Forces

**I./JG 3: + 1 B-17 claim undocumented

***III./JG 300: + 1 B-17, 2 B-17 HSS claims unconfirmed (unwitnessed)

****I./JG 400: + 1 B-17 claim unconfirmed (unwitnessed)

with six B-17 shootdowns, and I./JG 400, the only Me 163 unit, which claimed four B-17s (three confirmed) on two missions. The Luftwaffe lost eight KIA, 10 WIA and 26 fighters; the two American air forces wrote off 44 bombers and four fighters.

25 August

8th Air Force Mission #570: 1,219 of 1,308 HBs (all BDs) bomb oil + aviation targets, Luftwaffe experimental stations in N and E Germany – lose 18-3-312, claim 0. 629 of 708 fighters (13 FGs) escort, claim 11-2-3, lose 7-0-7.

15th Air Force: 168 B-17s, 169 B-24s dispatched to aviation targets in Czechoslovakia – lose 2, claim 0. Escort of 102 P-38s, 216 P-51s (all 7 FGs) claims 12-1-2, loses 1.

The two USSTAF air forces flew another joint mission. The response by I. Jagdkorps was notably ineffective. The 137 fighters to scramble were split as before: JD 1 against the 8th AF, JD 7 and JD 8 against the 15th AF. Only 53 made contact, and only one claim was confirmed: a P-38 by III./JG 53, out of three it filed. The Luftwaffe lost at least 20 KIA or MIA, three WIA and 30 fighters. The ground attack training unit I./SG 152 was the hardest hit, losing nine pilots and as many as 13 Fw 190s to marauding P-38s and P-51s in the vicinity of their Prostejov airfield. The two American air forces wrote off 23 bombers and eight fighters, nearly all due to Flak.

26 August

8th Air Force Mission #576: 505 of 588 1st BD B-17s + 2nd BD B-24s HBs bomb oil + chemical industry targets in W Germany – lose 10-0-144, claim 0. 413 of 451 fighters (8 FGs) escort, claim 0, lose 3-1-0.

The 8th AF sent two of its bomb divisions to strategic targets in western Germany, while the 15th AF feinted toward the Reich before sending part of its force to assist the Romanian Army, which was now trying to expel the Wehrmacht from its country. Jagddivisionen 7 and 8 were tied down by the feint, and of the 64 JD 1 fighters that sortied against the 8th AF, only four made contact. One of these, a III./JG 53 Bf 109, was shot down. The 8th AF wrote off 10 bombers and four fighters, none attributed to Luftwaffe fighters. No RLV mission list has been included for this date.

27 August

8th Air Force Mission #583: 1,203 HBs (all BDs) dispatched to targets in Berlin area; recalled owing very high cloud, 199 bomb t/os – lose 3-2-73, claim 0. 505 of 545 fighters (9 FGs) escort, claim 1-0-0, lose 10-2-19.

15th Air Force: 160 B-17s, 421 B-24s dispatched to Blechhammer oil synthesis plants, communications targets – lose 9, claim 0. Escort of 94 P-38s, 211 P-51s (all 7 FGs) claims 0, loses 0 – 4 enemy aircraft seen; none encountered.

The 8th AF ordered a full-strength mission to the Berlin area, but it was recalled over northern Germany owing to high cloud over the targets and encountered no German fighters. The 15th AF went back to the Reich with a raid on the Silesian oil targets and returned to Italy reporting the sighting of only four unaggressive Axis fighters during the mission. Allied Intelligence heard what was interpreted as typical signals traffic from the five JD 7 and JD 8 Jagdgruppen, but these were in the process of transferring to Jagddivision 1 airfields in central Germany; the skies over southern Germany and Austria were being conceded temporarily to the Americans. As no defensive mission was flown, no mission list is included.

28 August

15th Air Force: 160 B-17s, 437 B-24s dispatched to Moosbierbaum (A) oil synthesis and chemical plants, misc targets Hungary – lose 4, claim 0. Escort of 104 P-38s, 193 P-51s (all 7 FGs) claims 5-0-0, loses 2.

The 15th AF dispatched a full-strength mission to Austria and Hungary. The 8th AF did not make an appearance, allowing Jagddivision 1 to send its newly strengthened force to defend the south. Only 64 fighters could be scrambled. Control was passed to Jagddivision 8, which could do little good with the fighters: only 34 made contact, and only one claim, a P-51 by IV.(Sturm)/JG 3, was confirmed. The Luftwaffe lost only one fighter and no pilots; the 15th AF lost four bombers and two fighters to all causes.

29 August

15th Air Force: 168 B-17s, 431 B-24s dispatched to oil, ordnance, rail targets Czechoslovakia and Hungary – lose 15, claim 0. Escort of 109 P-38s, 185 P-51s (all 7 FGs) claims 5-0-2, loses 3.

Luftwaffe defensive activity vs. 15th Air Force – 24 August 1944

Unit	Type	Gruppe up			Gruppe down		Claims	Losses				
		Base	No	Time	Base	Time		Dest	Dam	KIA	MIA	WIA
Luftflotte Reich												
I. Jagdkorps												
Jagddivision 7:												
IV.(Sturm)/JG 3	Fw 190A	Schongau	13	0900	Schongau	1050	n/c	0	0	0	0	0
2nd sorties	Fw 190A	Schongau	5	1200	Schongau	1350	2 B-24	1	1	1	0	1
Stab/JG 300	Fw 190A	Holzkirchen		0900	Hörsching, Seyring	1030	n/c	0	0	0	0	0
2nd sorties	Fw 190A	Hörsching, Seyring		~1200	Holzkirchen	~1330	0	0	0	0	0	0
I./JG 300	Bf 109G	Bad Wörishofen	11	0900	Seyring	1030	n/c	0	0	0	0	0
2nd sorties	Bf 109G	Seyring	4	1140	Bad Wörishofen	~1330	1 B-24*	3	0	0	0	2
II.(Sturm)/JG 300	Fw 190A	Holzkirchen	11	0900	Seyring	~1030	n/c	0	0	0	0	0
2nd sorties	Fw 190A	Seyring	9	~1200	Holzkirchen	~1330	1 B-24**	5	0	1	0	1
Jagddivision 8:												
II./JG 27	Bf 109G	Fels am Wagram	15	0936	Fels am Wagram	~1030	n/c	0	0	0	0	0
2nd sorties	Bf 109G	Fels am Wagram	15	1130	Fels am Wagram	~1330	1 B-24, 1 P-51***	3	0	1	0	0
I./JG 302	Bf 109G	Götzendorf	15	0926	Götzendorf	1041	n/c	0	0	0	0	0
2nd sorties	Bf 109G	Götzendorf	12	1157	Götzendorf		2 B-24****	4	0	2	0	2

*I./JG 300: + 1 B-24 HSS claim unconfirmed (unwitnessed)

**II./JG 300: + 2 B-24 claims undocumented; 1 B-24 HSS claim unconfirmed (unwitnessed)

***II./JG 27: + 2 P-51 claims unconfirmed (unwitnessed)

****I./JG 302: + 1 P-51 claim unconfirmed (unwitnessed)

Luftwaffe defensive activity vs. 8th Air Force – 25 August 1944

Unit	Type	Gruppe up			Gruppe down		Claims	Losses				
		Base	No	Time	Base	Time		Dest	Dam	KIA	MIA	WIA
Luftflotte Reich												
I. Jagdkorps			*137									
Jagddivision 1:												
I./JG 3	Bf 109G	Borkheide		1043	Neuruppin	1245	0	2	1	1	1	0
II./JG 5	Bf 109G	Salzwedel		~1045	Salzwedel	~1230	0	4	0	3	0	0
III./JG 53	Bf 109G	Mörtitz		~1045	Mörtitz	~1230	1 P-38**	2	2	0	0	2
III./JG 300	Bf 109G	Jüterbog	12	1042	Jüterbog	~1230	0**	4	1	3	0	0

*137 total sorties vs. 8th and 15th Air Forces

**III./JG 53: + 2 P-38 claims undocumented

***III./JG 300: + 1 P-51 claim undocumented

The 8th AF was again grounded by bad weather in England. The 15th AF sent another full-strength mission to Austria and Hungary, and Jagddivision 1 again sent the entire conventional RLV force south to meet them. This totalled only 89 Bf 109s and Fw 190s, of which 65 were credited with combat sorties, but the mission went quite well. A single Gefechtsverband was formed comprising the two Sturmgruppen, six high-altitude protection Gruppen and one conventional bomber interception Gruppe, I./JG 302, which was down to its last three fighters. A shadower in a Fw 190 told the JD 8 controller of one B-17 Pulk – the 2nd BG – that was in poor formation and apparently unescorted. The formation leaders were given the appropriate orders. The protection Gruppen climbed to counter the escorts, while the other fighters played their accustomed roles: the two Sturmgruppen made closed-formation attacks from the rear, while the three I./JG 302 Messerschmitts attacked the flanks from out of the undercast. The escorting P-51s were too far in front to intervene immediately, so the protection fighters were able to join in the attacks on the bombers. Nine B-17s went down in this attack, along with a B-24 with mechanical problems that had joined

the B-17 stream for protection. German casualties were amazingly light: one KIA, four WIA and nine fighters shot down or lost to operational causes. The Americans lost 15 bombers and three fighters to all causes. The RLM confirmed 20 claims for B-17s destroyed or shot from formation. The overclaiming can be understood as the result of the large number of units (seven) claiming the same aircraft and the enthusiasm of the pilots who had not had this much success in some time.

Luftwaffe defensive activity vs. 15th Air Force – 25 August 1944

Unit	Type	Gruppe up			Gruppe down		Claims	Losses				
		Base	No	Time	Base	Time		Dest	Dam	KIA	MIA	WIA
Luftflotte Reich												
I. Jagdkorps												
Jagddivision 7:												
IV.(Sturm)/JG 3	Fw 190A	Schongau	12	0900	Götzendorf	1055	n/c	0	0	0	0	0
2nd sorties	Fw 190A	Götzendorf	8	1142	Schongau	1300	0	2	1	2	0	0
I./JG 300	Bf 109G	Bad Wörishofen		0900	Seyring, Götzendorf	~1100	n/c	0	0	0	0	0
2nd sorties	Bf 109G	Seyring, Götzendorf	9	1152	Bad Wörishofen	~1300	0	1	1	0	0	0
II.(Sturm)/JG 300	Fw 190A	Holzkirchen		0900	Seyring	~1100	n/c	0	0	0	0	0
2nd sorties	Fw 190A	Götzendorf	1	1142	Holzkirchen	~1300	0	1	0	1	0	0
Jagddivision 8:												
II./JG 27	Bf 109G	Fels am Wagram		?	Fels am Wagram	?	0	1	0	0	0	1
I./JG 302	Bf 109G	Götzendorf	9	?	Götzendorf	?	n/c	0	0	0	0	0
2nd sorties	Bf 109G	Götzendorf	8	?	Götzendorf	?	0	0	0	0	0	0
Jafü Oberschlesien:												
JGr Ost	Bf 109G	Wiedengut	8	1120	Wiedengut	1155	n/c	0	0	0	0	0
I./SG 152	Fw 190F	Prossnitz		~1100	Prossnitz	~1200	0	13	?	9	?	?

Luftwaffe defensive activity – 28 August 1944

Unit	Type	Gruppe up			Gruppe down		Claims	Losses				
		Base	No	Time	Base	Time		Dest	Dam	KIA	MIA	WIA
Luftflotte Reich												
I. Jagdkorps												
Jagddivision 1:			64									
I./JG 3	Bf 109G	Borkheide	9	0947	Borkheide, Deutsch–Brod	1200	0	0	1	0	0	0
IV.(Sturm)/JG 3	Fw 190A	Jüterbog	16	0948	Jüterbog	1155	1 P-51*	0	1	0	0	0
II./JG 27	Bf 109G	Borkheide	12	0945	Borkheide	1200	0	0	0	0	0	0
III./JG 53	Bf 109G	Mörtitz	4	0950	Mörtitz	1155	n/c	0	0	0	0	0
Stab/JG 300	Fw 190A	Jüterbog	—	0945	Wien–Aspern	1155	0**	0	0	0	0	0
I./JG 300	Bf 109G	Mörtitz		?	Esperstedt	?	transfer	0	0	0	0	0
II.(Sturm)/JG 300	Fw 190A	Jüterbog	10	0948	Jüterbog	1212	0	0	0	0	0	0
III./JG 300	Bf 109G	Jüterbog	13	0948	Jüterbog	1130	0	1	1	0	0	0
I./JG 302	Bf 109G	Leeuwarden		?	Mörtitz	?	transfer	0	0	0	0	0

* IV.(Sturm)/JG 3: + 1 B-24 claim undocumented
**Stab/JG 300: + 1 P-51 claim undocumented

Luftwaffe defensive activity – 29 August 1944

Unit	Type	Gruppe up			Gruppe down		Claims	Losses				
		Base	No	Time	Base	Time		Dest	Dam	KIA	MIA	WIA
Luftflotte Reich												
I. Jagdkorps												
Jagddivision 1:			89									
I./JG 3	Bf 109G	Borkheide	8	0903	various	1130	0*	2	1	0	0	0
IV.(Sturm)/JG 3	Fw 190A	Juterbog	15	0905	Markersdorf	1105	4 B-17	1	3	1	0	0
II./JG 5	Bf 109G	Jüterbog	11	0905	Jüterbog	1120	0	1	1	0	0	0
II./JG 27	Bf 109G	Borkheide	12	0908	Borkheide	1120	1 B-17**	0	0	0	0	0
III./JG 53	Bf 109G	Mörtitz	20	0905	Mörtitz	1110	6 B-17	2	1	0	0	1
Stab/JG 300	Fw 190A	Jüterbog	—	0905	Markersdorf	1120	1 B-17***	0	0	0	0	0
I./JG 300	Bf 109G	Mörtitz	4	0905	Mörtitz	1115	2 B-17****	1	0	0	0	1
II.(Sturm)/JG 300	Fw 190A	Jüterbog	9	0906	Jüterbog	1110	3 B-17, 1 B-17 HSS	1	0	0	0	1
III./JG 300	Bf 109G	Jüterbog	7	0907	Jüterbog	1115	1 B-17, 1 B-17 HSS	1	1	0	0	1
I./JG 302	Bf 109G	Mörtitz	3	0911	Mörtitz	1120	0*****	0	1	0	0	0

*I./JG 3: + 1 B-17 HSS claim unconfirmed (unwitnessed)
**II./JG 27: + 1 B-17 HSS claim unconfirmed (unwitnessed)
***Stab/JG 300: + 1 B-17 claim undocumented
****I./JG 300: + 2 B-17 HSS claim unconfirmed (unwitnessed)
*****I./JG 302: + 1 B-17 HSS claim unconfirmed (unwitnessed)

September 1944

The fervent hope of the Allies that the war in Europe could be ended in 1944 was dashed when the offensives of both the Soviets and the Anglo-Americans ground to a halt as their armies ran out of supplies roughly along Germany's pre-war borders. This respite allowed the Wehrmacht to build up its border defences enough to make them impervious to attack in an autumn or winter campaign. Could the Luftwaffe use this period to rebuild its strength? The airplane production programme had succeeded amazingly well. The number of types in production had been ruthlessly slashed, and factory dispersal and the widespread use of forced labour permitted September 1944 to become the peak month of the war for fighter production: 4103 were built, and 3013 were accepted by the Luftwaffe.

These thousands of new fighters needed pilots and fuel. The attrition of the previous year had permanently eroded the quality of the fighter arm, despite efforts to cull experienced pilots from disbanded bomber, transport and reconnaissance units and accelerate the training of brand-new pilots. But the most critical problem for the German defences was fuel. Small synthetic fuel plants proved surprisingly easy to build and repair once the Nazi regime assigned them its highest priority, but oil also remained the USSTAF's highest priority, and the relentless bombing campaign did not allow the restoration of any fuel reserve. I. Jagdkorps needed to force at least a temporary halt to the bombing to allow German industry some time for recovery.

Two Luftwaffe fighter generals proposed one-time operations intended to cause such high casualties that the Americans would have to curtail their strategic bombing campaign to prepare counter-measures, which had, in fact, happened after the second Schweinfurt raid in October 1943. The first proposal was by Generalmajor Galland, the General of the Fighter Arm. He called it *der große Schlag* (the Big Blow). This was to be a greater-than-maximum effort against the day bombers, using an interception force 10 times larger than anything seen since D-Day. I. Jagdkorps would lead the operation with 2,000 day fighters in 11 battle formations. It was hoped that 400–500 bombers could be downed for a loss of 400 fighters and 100–150 pilots. Galland's office drew up the plan in detail. The units back from the Invasionsfront were not to rejoin the RLV order of battle in a piecemeal fashion, but would have to be husbanded until the right moment. Galland's authority extended to operational training, and he kept the rebuilding Jagdgruppen under his tight control. Little documentation survives, but apparently Galland had at least the tacit approval of the Luftwaffe Chief of Staff. It is obvious today that Galland's plan was excessively optimistic. It expected too much of the pilots whose mean level of skill had dropped markedly in the previous year. But the RLV commanders at least had a definite goal toward which to work.

The second plan, by Oberst Hajo Herrmann, a former bomber pilot now in command of Jagddivision 1, was much more radical: a full air fleet of ram fighters. When initially proposed, it stood no chance, given Hitler's antipathy toward suicidal tactics, but it would be brought up again in 1945.

The strength of the RLV day fighter force was to remain low while Galland trained his reserve. Jagddivision 1 in Berlin took command of all of the operational Jagdgruppen, which were now concentrated to defend the critical oil targets in central Germany. The two, soon to be three, Sturmgruppen, were to be the principal weapon against the bombers. Each was to be protected from US escorts by one or more conventional fighter Gruppen. The ex-*Wilde Sau* Geschwader JG 300 and JG 301 were to take key roles in the RLV day force. JG 301 received new models of

A Me 410 of I./ZG 26, photographed at Prowehren on 2 September as ZG 26 was being rebuilt for the last time with heavy fighters before it was renamed JG 6 and converted to Bf 109s. *(Crow)*

the Fw 190A which were fully equipped for operations in poor weather. It was intended to build up both Geschwader to the new establishment strength of four Gruppen, each of four 16-fighter Staffeln. They contained enough instrument-rated pilots to be considered bad-weather units and were expected to operate in all weather conditions.

This short-term plan was stalled on 17 September by Operation MARKET-GARDEN, the Anglo-American airborne invasion of the Netherlands. As on D-Day, the RLV force was ordered to send many of its units to the battle front to help stem the threat on the ground. It took two weeks to stabilise the front, during which period Jagddivision 1, the active air defence command, was reduced to five Jagdgruppen and had to ignore the 8th Air Force's strategic raids. The 15th Air Force was already being ignored; Jagddivisionen 7 and 8, the defenders of southern Germany and Austria, had lost their day fighters at the end of August.

11 September – Oil targets (see map)

8th Air Force Mission #623: 333 of 384 3rd BD B-17s bomb Ruhland, Böhlen, Brüx, Chemnitz o/i, TOT 1227-1328h – lose 16-3-94, claim 12-16-1; 321 of 351 1st BD B-17s bomb Merseburg, Lützkendorf o/i, TOT 1140-1250 – lose 13-2-106, claim 1-1-2; 362 of 396 2nd BD B 24s bomb Misburg, Magdeburg o/i, TOT 1228-1244h – lose 10-2-179, claim 4-8-1. 663 of 715 fighters (all 15 FGs) escort, claim 115-7-23, lose 17-8-18.

During the first 10 days of September, I. Jagdkorps was struggling to fit the battered Jagdgruppen returning from the collapsed Invasionsfront into its order of battle and ignored several raids by the American strategic air forces. However, on the 11th, a major attack by the 8th AF on the central German synthetic oil plants brought the largest response by the RLV force since D-Day. I. Jagdkorps scrambled all 12 of its Jagdgruppen – 355 fighters. The plan was to form three *Gefechtsverbände* [battle formations], each anchored by a Sturmgruppe. Only two battle formations were assembled; the largest, commanded by Major Dahl of JG 300, wound up containing two of the Sturmgruppen, IV.(Sturm)/JG 3 and II./(Sturm)/JG 300, escorted by I./JG 76 and I./JG 300. These Gruppen were separated by P-51s before making an attack, but IV./(Sturm)/JG 3 found the 92nd BG in a vulnerable position and blasted the rear of its box. Eight B-17s went down immediately; four more crashed or crash-landed behind Allied lines. Dahl's

Obfw. Willi Unger in front of 'Red 8' of IV.(Sturm)/JG 3 after returning from a September mission. He is carrying his scarf, which he has used to staunch the flow of blood from a minor wound. Note the 'whites of their eyes' insignia above his jacket pocket, a distinction allowed Sturmgruppe pilots. *(Crow)*

Stabsschwarm also made a successful attack, but the rest of his Gefechtsverband sustained high losses and claimed only a few victories.

The second battle formation was formed around the new II.(Sturm)/JG 4 and III./JG 4, both flying their first RLV missions. They were led today by Major Specht and his JG 11 Stabsschwarm and were directed to the low box of the second 3rd BD combat wing, which was far behind the rest of its formation and unescorted. After one III./JG 4 Staffel and the Sturmgruppe made single passes, 11 B-17s of the perpetually unlucky

Obstlt. Walther Dahl, Kommodore of JG 300, celebrates his 75th victory on 11 September beside his suitably decorated Fw 190A-8. *(Rosch)*

Luftwaffe defensive activity – 11 September 1944

Unit	Type	Gruppe up			Gruppe down		Claims	Losses (—: included with 1st sortie)				
		Base	No	Time	Base	Time		Dest	Dam	KIA	MIA	WIA
vs. incoming stream												
Luftflotte Reich												
I. Jagdkorps												
Jagddivision 1:			*355									
I./JG 3	Bf 109G	Borkheide		~1030	Borkheide	~1230	0	2	0	1	0	0
IV.(Sturm)/JG 3	Fw 190A	Schafstädt		1045	Schafstädt, Burg	1230	13 B-17	7	0	2	1	1
II.(Sturm)/JG 4	Fw 190A	Welzow		~1030	Welzow	~1230	18 B-17, 5 B-17 HSS	23	2	12	0	4
III./JG 4	Bf 109G	Alteno		1030	Alteno, Plauen	1300	6 B-17, 4 B-17 HSS, 1 P-51, 1 Spitfire**	27	4	9	0	5
JGr 10	Fw 190A	Parchim		~1030	Parchim	~1230	0	4	0	3	0	1
Stab/JG 11	Fw 190A	Alteno?		~1030	Alteno?	~1230	1 P-51	1	0	0	0	0
II./JG 27	Bf 109G	Finsterwalde		1030	Finsterwalde	~1230	0	6	1	6	0	0
III./JG 53	Bf 109G	Mörtitz		1040	Mörtitz	~1240	4 B-24, 1 B-24 HSS	7	2	3	0	2
I./JG 76	Bf 109G	Gahro		~1040	Gahro	~1240	2 P-51***	13	6	6	1	7
Stab/JG 300	Fw 190A	Erfurt–Bindersleben	4	1040	Erfurt–Bindersleben	1315	2 B-17, 1 B-17 HSS	0	0	0	0	0
I./JG 300	Bf 109G	Esperstedt	32	1050	Esperstedt	~1250	0	6	5	0	1	1
II.(Sturm)/JG300	Fw 190A	Erfurt–Bindersleben		1040	Erfurt–Bindersleben	1315	5 P-51****	12	1	9	1	2
III./JG 300	Bf 109G	Jüterbog		~1045	Jüterbog	~1230	1 B-24*****	3	1	1	0	0
I./JG 400	Me 163	Brandis	7	1236	Brandis	1250	1 B-17	0	0	0	0	0
vs. withdrawing stream:												
Luftflotte Reich												
I. Jagdkorps												
Jagddivision 1:												
II.(Sturm)/JG300	Fw 190A	Erfurt–Bindersleben		~1300	Erfurt–Bindersleben	~1400	1 B-24	—	—	—	—	—

*355 total sorties vs. incoming and withdrawing streams **III./JG 4: + 2 B-17, 1 P-51, 1 Spitfire claims unconfirmed (unwitnessed)

***I./JG 76: + 3 P-51 claims unconfirmed (unwitnessed) ****II.(Sturm)/JG 300: + 1 B-17, 1 B-24, 3 P-51 claims undocumented; 3 P-51 claims unconfirmed (unwitnessed)

*****III./JG 300: + 1 B-24, 1 P-51 claims undocumented; 1 B-24 claim unconfirmed (unwitnessed)

100th BG fell to earth; three more crashed in France or in England. The JG 4 pilots were then punished by the escorts and ended the day with losses of 21 KIA, nine WIA and 42 fighters; their first mission had cost them half of their strength.

The other conventional I. Jagdkorps Gruppen flew independent missions; few had any success. The most unconventional Luftwaffe unit, I./JG 400, flew a full-strength mission with seven Me 163s, and claimed one success, a B-17 shot down near the rocket fighters' Brandis base, for no losses. The mission as a whole demonstrated the utter inadequacy of conventional RLV tactics and equipment. The USAAF wrote off 46 bombers and 25 fighters to all causes. The Luftwaffe lost around 56 pilots KIA or MIA and 23 WIA. Of the 305 fighters to make contact with the enemy, 111 were destroyed – a calamitous 36 per cent loss rate.

Pilots of I./JG 5 are briefed by the 'weather frog' prior to a mission from Wunstorf in September after the unit's return from the Invasionsfront. From left: meteorological officer, unknown (holding map), 3. StaKa Oblt. Jahn, 4. StaKa Oblt. Faber (light jacket), 2. StaKa Oblt. Weil, 1. StaKa Oblt. Gerlach, unknown, unknown, Uffz. Fuhrmann (holding map), I. Gruppenkommandeur Major Theodor Weissenberger. *(Crow)*

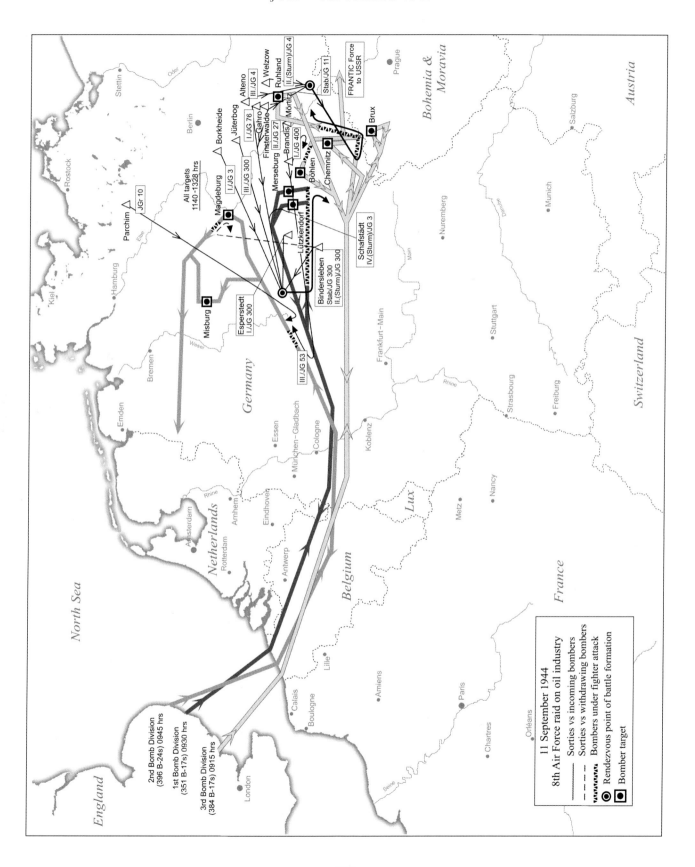

11 September 1944
8th Air Force raid on oil industry

Sorties *vs* incoming bombers
Sorties *vs* withdrawing bombers
Bombers under fighter attack
Rendezvous point of battle formation
Bomber target

2nd Bomb Division (396 B-24s) 0945 hrs
1st Bomb Division (351 B-17s) 0930 hrs
3rd Bomb Division (384 B-17s) 0915 hrs

All targets 1140 -1328 hrs

12 September

8th Air Force Mission #626: 813 of 888 HBs (all BDs) bomb oil targets in C Germany – lose 35-5-304, claim 27-14-12. 579 of 662 fighters (14 FGs) escort, claim 54-2-8, lose 12-2-10.

15th Air Force: 168 B-17s, 377 B-24s dispatched to aviation factories and airfields in Munich area – lose 13, claim 0. Escort of 112 P-38s, 213 P-51s (all 7 FGs) claims 0, loses 1. Jets + 20 s/e fighters sighted, but no encounters reported.

The central German oil targets were again targeted by the 8th AF. Luftflotte Reich ordered a full-strength mission, but only 190 fighters could take part, owing to the previous day's losses. The fighters of I. Jagdkorps and II. Jagdkorps assembled in three Gefechtsverbände, which were intended to hit the bombers inbound, in the target area, and on withdrawal. I. Jagdkorps provided two of the battle formations. The first contained II.(Sturm)/JG 4, escorted by III./JG 4 and I./JG 76. They met the incoming 1st BD stream near Magdeburg. Most of the formation was able to make one pass through the B-17s before the arrival of Mustangs. It claimed 27 B-17s and two P-51s, but lost 16 KIA, four WIA, 13 Bf 109s and seven Fw 190s. Its most likely target was the 351st BG, which lost nine B-17s. This second mission for the Sturmgruppe cost it its Kommandeur, Obstlt. Hans-Günther von Kornatzki.

The second I. Jagdkorps Gefechtsverband was led by Major Dahl and the JG 300 Stabsschwarm and

The wing guns of Fw. Konrad 'Pitt' Bauer's II.(Sturm)/JG 300 Fw 190A-8 'Red 3' are foresighted in September on Erfurt–Bindersleben. Bauer is standing on the right. *(Rosch)*

contained all three JG 300 Gruppen, I./JG 3, IV.(Sturm)/JG 3, II./JG 27 and III./JG 53. Too large for control by one man, it broke up before reaching the bombers, but two successful attacks were the result. IV.(Sturm)/JG 3 approached the 1st BD stream north of Berlin, found the 306th BG out of position and quickly downed five B-17s. The senior Sturmgruppe lost three KIA, two WIA and seven Fw 190s.

Dahl led the rest of his formation toward the 3rd BD stream, but did not reach it until the combat wings had separated and bombed their individual targets. Dahl chose to attack the bombers leaving Magdeburg. A rear attack by II.(Sturm)/JG 300, combined with a frontal pass by III./JG 53, cost the 493rd BG eight B-17s immediately; three more crash-landed in France or England.

The third Gefechtsverband comprised three II. Jagdkorps Fw 190 Gruppen: I./JG 2, I./JG 11 and I./JG 77. These were ordered to attack the withdrawing bombers, but while still heading for the stream, they were bounced north of Frankfurt by two 9th AF P-51 flights, plus a few 8th AF Mustang pilots on withdrawal escort. Twenty-nine Fw 190s were shot down, carrying 14 pilots to their deaths; 13 pilots survived with injuries.

Of the 147 I. Jagdkorps and II. Jagdkorps fighters to contact 8th (and 9th) Air Force aircraft, 78 were shot down, a loss of 53 per cent of the force. Forty-two pilots were KIA or MIA, and 17 were WIA. The 8th AF wrote off 40 bombers and 16 fighters from all causes. The 15th AF was also up today and made a successful attack on a Munich jet engine factory, but the RLV force made no serious attempt to intercept the southern intruders.

Fw. Wolfgang 'Lumpi' Hundsdorfer sits in his I./JG 300 Bf 109-14/AS 'Red 10' at Esperstedt. *(Rosch)*

Luftwaffe defensive activity – 12 September 1944

Unit	Type	Gruppe up			Gruppe down		Claims	Losses				
		Base	No	Time	Base	Time		Dest	Dam	KIA	MIA	WIA
vs. incoming stream												
Luftflotte Reich												
I. Jagdkorps												
Jagddivision 1:			*190									
I./JG 3	Bf 109G	Borkheide		~1000	Borkheide	~1200	0**	3	0	0	0	2
IV.(Sturm)/JG 3	Fw 190A	Schafstädt		0950	Finsterwalde, Warnemünde	1210	7 B-17	7	3	3	0	2
II.(Sturm)/JG 4	Fw 190A	Welzow		0950	Welzow	~1200	6 B-17***	8	1	4	0	1
III./JG 4	Bf 109G	Alteno		0950	Alteno, Stendal	1150	3 B-17, 1 P-51****	9	1	7	1	2
II./JG 27	Bf 109G	Finsterwalde		0953	Finsterwalde	~1200	0*****	4	2	2	0	0
III./JG 53	Bf 109G	Mörtitz		~1000	various	~1200	4 B-17, 1 P-51	3	0	2	0	1
I./JG 76	Bf 109G	Gahro		~1000	Gahro	~1200	5 B-17	6	1	4	0	2
Stab/JG 300	Fw 190A	Erfurt–Bindersleben		~0950	Erfurt–Bindersleben	~1150	0	0	0	0	0	0
I./JG 300	Bf 109G	Esperstedt	20	0950	Esperstedt	~1150	1 B-17******	2	2	1	0	1
II.(Sturm)/JG300	Fw 190A	Erfurt–Bindersleben		0955	Erfurt–Bindersleben	~1150	4 B-17*******	5	0	3	0	1
III./JG 300	Bf 109G	Jüterbog	30	~0950	Jüterbog	~1150	0********	2	0	1	0	1
vs. withdrawal:												
Luftflotte Reich												
I. Jagdkorps												
Jagddivision 1:												
III./JG 4	Bf 109G	Alteno		~1200	Alteno	~1330	0	—	—	—	—	—
Luftflotte 3												
II. Jagdkorps												
Jagddivison 5:												
I.JG 2	Fw 190A	Merzhausen		~1200	Merzhausen	~1330	1 P-51	9	0	7	1	0
I./JG 11	Fw 190A	Gelnhausen		~1200	Gelnhausen	~1330	4 P-51*********	7	1	2	0	2
I./JG 77	Bf 109G	Babenhausen		~1200	Babenhausen	~1330	1 P-51	13	0	4	0	2

*190 total JD 1 sorties vs. incoming and withdrawing streams   **I./JG 3: + 2 B-17 HSS claims unconfirmed (unwitnessed)

***II.(Sturm)/JG 4: + 8 B-17 claims unconfirmed (unwitnessed)   ****III./JG 4: + 3 B-17, 1 P-51 claims unconfirmed (unwitnessed)

*****II./JG 27: + 1 P-51 claim unconfirmed (unwitnessed)   ******I./JG 300: + 1 P-51 claim undocumented

*******II.(Sturm)/JG300: + 1 P-51 claim undocumented; 6 B-17 claims unconfirmed (unwitnessed)

********III./JG 300: + 3 P-51 claims undocumented   *********I./JG 11: + 2 P-51 claims unconfirmed (unwitnessed)

13 September

8th Air Force Mission #628: 790 of 1,026 HBs (all BDs) bomb oil and industrial targets in S Germany, TOT 1108-55 – lose 15-7-406, claim 1-0-0. 542 of 603 fighters (14 FGs) escort and strafe, claim 33-0-4, lose 10-1-9.

15th Air Force dispatches 400 B-24s, 168 B-17s to bomb Silesian and Polish oil synthesis and chemical plants – lose 26, claim 0 (no encounters with e/a). Escort of 108 P-38s, 210 P-51s claims 2-0-0, loses 1.

The USSTAF made its third attack on the oil industry in three days. The 15th AF bombed the Odertal and Blechhammer refineries without aerial opposition, while the 8th returned to its central German targets. I. Jagdkorps attacked the latter force, but could only scramble 137 fighters, and of these, only 63 made contact. One Gruppe was off operations owing to high recent losses; others were grounded or failed to make contact owing to bad weather. The Gruppe formations that reached the bomber stream were, without exception, broken up by the escorts. I. Jagdkorps lost 12 KIA, seven WIA and 18 fighters for its futile efforts. The two American air forces did have to write off 48 bombers and 12 fighters, but nearly all of these were lost to Flak or operational accidents.

Luftwaffe defensive activity – 13 September 1944

Unit	Type	Gruppe up			Gruppe down		Claims	Losses				
		Base	No	Time	Base	Time		Dest	Dam	KIA	MIA	WIA
Luftflotte Reich												
I. Jagdkorps												
Jagddivision 1:			137									
I./JG 3	Bf 109G	Borkheide		~1130	Borkheide	~1300	1 P-47, 1 P-51	6	2	5	0	0
III./JG 4	Bf 109G	Alteno	7	1045	Alteno, Erfurt	1330	n/c	0	0	0	0	0
II./JG 27	Bf 109G	Finsterwalde		1105	Finsterwalde	1130	n/c	0	0	0	0	0
III./JG 53	Bf 109G	Mörtitz		~1130	Mörtitz	~1300	0	1	0	1	0	0
I./JG 76	Bf 109G	Gahro		~1130	Gahro	~1300	0	6	0	5	0	1
Stab/JG 300	Fw 190A	Erfurt–Bindersleben		1046	Erfurt–Bindersleben	1250	0*	0	0	0	0	0
I./JG 300	Bf 109G	Esperstedt	26	1035	Esperstedt	~1245	1 B-17, 1 P-51**	5	6	1	0	6
II.(Sturm)/JG 300	Fw 190A	Erfurt–Bindersleben		~1045	Erfurt–Bindersleben	~1245	0***	0	0	0	0	0
I./JG 400	Me 163	Brandis	9	?	Brandis	?	n/c	0	0	0	0	0
ErprKdo 262	Me 262	Lärz		1055	Lärz	1142	n/c	0	0	0	0	0

*Stab/JG 300: + 1 B-17, 1 B-17 HSS claims undocumented

**I./JG 300: + 1 B-17, 4 P-51 claims undocumented; 1 B-17 HSS, 1 P-51 claims unconfirmed (unwitnessed)

***II.(Sturm)/JG300: + 1 P-51 claim undocumented

PILOT'S ACCOUNT[9]
13 September 1944

Twenty-six I./JG 300 Bf 109G-14/AS's scrambled from Esperstedt at 1040 hours on a beautiful, cloudless autumn day. The Gruppe flew high cover for the JG 300 Gefechtsverband. We flew north and were at 8,000 metres when we met the B-17s at the same altitude, with their escort 1,000 metres above them. We were seen well before we could make an attack. Our Gruppe was quickly split up by a superior number of P-51s. There were no clouds into which we could escape. Fw. Bernd Schreiber's Schwarm, in which I flew, was attacked by 11 Mustangs. The Messerschmitt of one of my comrades exploded. I then fought alone with four Mustangs for about 30 minutes. I shot one down, but was eventually forced to crash-land in my 'Yellow 3', which overturned. I was badly injured and regained consciousness in hospital, where I remained until the next February.

Nine I./JG 300 aircraft returned to base after this mission. Eight pilots were killed or injured. Eight Bf 109s were declared operational for the following day.

Fhj.-Uffz. Robert Jung   3./JG 300

18 September

8th Air Force Mission #640: 107 of 110 3rd BD B-17s drop supplies to Warsaw insurgents, continue to Russia (FRANTIC VII) – lose 1-0-7, claim 0. Escort of 137 or 150 P-51s (2 FGs) claims 4-0-0, loses 2-0-0.

On the 17th, Operation MARKET-GARDEN, the Allied attempt to force the lower Rhine, brought another crushing blow to the strength of the RLV force. I. Jagdkorps was ordered to send five of its operational Jagdgruppen to the new Invasionsraum, leaving the aerial defence of the Reich to one Geschwader Stab, the three Sturmgruppen, one high-altitude escort Gruppe and the small Me 262 and Me 163 fighter units. No viable attack formation could be assembled from this mixture of units. Most of the 8th AF would be tied down for a few days with tactical missions, but on the 18th, 100 B-17s were sent to Warsaw on the last FRANTIC mission. The OKL War Diary recorded 24 sorties on Reich defence, but these were not flown by I. Jagdkorps, but by Eastern Front units, two JG 51 Gruppen that were temporarily based in the Warsaw area. Far outnumbered by the Mustang escort, the fighters of the Mölders Geschwader were saved from destruction when the P-51s had to break off owing to low fuel; the Germans lost two KIA and

Fhj-Obfw. Lothar Födrich of II.(Sturm)/JG 300 stands in front of his Fw 190A-8/R2 'Yellow 12' at Finsterwalde. *(Rosch)*

one WIA and managed to bring down one B-17. No RLV mission list has been included for this date.

27 September

8th Air Force Mission #650: 1,103 of 1,192 HBs (all BDs) bomb strategic targets in W Germany, TOT 1020-47 – lose 27-8-348, claim 5-3-0. 640 of 678 fighters (all 15 FGs) escort, claim 31-0-6, lose 2-1-6.

The battle lines in north Germany and the Netherlands had again stabilised, and several Jagdgruppen returned to bases in central Germany to resume the air defence task. Today, I. Jagdkorps ordered Jagddivision 1 up in force against an 8th AF raid on small hydrogenation (petroleum from coal) plants along the Rhine. Jagddivision 1 scrambled 121 fighters; 111 made contact. The three Sturmgruppen flew in a single Gefechtsbverband, escorted by only the JG 300 Stab and First Gruppe. The controllers

found one B-24 Pulk badly out of position and unescorted after a succession of navigation errors, and positioned the compact Fw 190 formation for an immediate Sturmangriff. The three Sturmgruppen attacked in quick succession, and within five minutes, the Liberator formation, containing the 445th BG, had been reduced to seven airplanes; 25 crashed immediately, while five more dropped back to crash- or force-land in France or England, saved from total destruction by the lack of German pursuit. Many fighters were able to make two passes before the P-51s arrived and broke up the attacks. The German fighters returned to their bases short of 18 KIA or MIA, nine WIA and 31 aircraft, but the pilots jubilantly proclaimed their success: claims for 70 B-24s downed or shot from formation were apparently allowed. The true American loss of 35 bombers was bad enough, but most bomber crews flying the mission saw no enemy fighters at all. The 445th BG, however, had to write off 28 B-24s, the greatest single-mission loss for any bomber group in the war.

PILOT'S ACCOUNT[10]
27 September 1944

IV.(Sturm)/JG 3 flew its mission in a Gefechtsverband with other RLV units against incoming American bomber formations. Our attack formation was in the form of a wedge, led by our Kommandeur, Hptm. Wilhelm Moritz. The four Staffeln of the Gruppe were positioned to the left and right. Ground control led the Gefechtsverband to the vicinity of the enemy formation by radio commands. Once the enemy was sighted, the formation leader was to plan and execute the attack. As Führer of the 15. Staffel, I was in a good tactical position and attacked a Kette of B-24 Liberators. Just as in our first Sturmangriff over Oschersleben on 7 July, my attack was made in three quick stages: I first fired at the fuselage to hit the gun positions and the cockpit; I then tried to set two engines on one side on fire. With these two engines burning, control was lost almost immediately: an aircraft hit this way lost its flight stability and dove in a spiral over the burning wing. It happened like that today: I first attacked the left B-24 in the Kette, then the right and finally the lead aircraft, approaching to ramming distance. I then pulled up in a steep turn and observed all three burning B-24s descending in spirals, with pieces of their wings near the burning engines breaking off.

The film from my gun camera showed the effect of my fire on all three B-24s in frightful detail. The hit location and effect were graphed and analysed by weapon calibre and ammunition type. The most punishing damage was caused by the two Mk 108 3-cm cannon, which owing to their low-muzzle velocity should only be fired from 400 metres. The trajectories of the two 2-cm MG 151/20 cannon were much straighter. The cannon could only be fired in pairs. I opened fire against bombers with the 2-cm cannon first and from 400 metres to ramming distance with all four guns, firing in very short bursts. This was most important, as I was being thrown about by the turbulence of the bomber's evasive movements and its propellor wake.

[Romm's victims were 445th Bomb Group B-24s: DC]

Lt. Oskar Romm, Staffelkapitän
15. (Sturm)/JG 3

Lt. Oskar Romm had a varied career as a fighter pilot. He was posted to JG 51 on the Eastern Front on completion of his training in September 1942 and was commissioned and awarded the Knight's Cross after a successful tour. He transferred to IV.(Sturm)/JG 3 in June 1944 for RLV duty and shot down eight heavy bombers before transferring to other units for short periods. He rejoined IV.(Sturm)/JG 3, now on the Eastern Front, in January 1945 and became Gruppenkommandeur in February. A severe injury in April ended his flying. *(Author's collection)*

PILOT'S ACCOUNT[11]
27 September 1944

II.(Sturm)/JG 4 flew its first missions in August with four Staffeln of 11 aircraft each. The missions of 11 and 13 September cost us 38 pilots, including the Gruppenkommandeur. The 6. and 8. Staffeln had to be grounded. The 5. Staffel was rebuilt with replacements; the 7. with survivors of the other two. Twenty aircraft flew today's mission in two attack wedges, with Oblt. Othmar Zehart, today's formation leader, in the middle. After we scrambled from Welzow and joined the other Sturmgruppen and one high-altitude Gruppe of Bf 109s, the Jagddivision 1 controller ordered us to make numerous course changes to avoid the escorts and finally led us to an unescorted Pulk of Liberators. We flew from behind into the stream and split up to attack individual bombers. Whoever was not shot down was expected to shoot down a bomber or ram it. After passing through the formation we could see bombers crashing … Ten or 12 bombers exploded in the air, even though they had already dropped their bombs. After our single passes, we attempted to escape in split-S manœuvres, but the Mustangs arrived and hit us hard. We returned to base alone. A wheel and its support fell off when I lowered my landing gear, and I had to make a belly landing. Eleven machines failed to return; seven pilots, including Zehart, were killed or missing, and three more were injured. I do not know how many of our claims were confirmed. I have lost all of my records. Our gun camera film was confiscated by the victorious powers, and I never saw mine again.

Oblt. Werner Vorberg
5.(Sturm)/JG 4

PILOT'S ACCOUNT[12]
27 September 1944

II.(Sturm)/JG 300 scrambled about 30 Fw 190s from Finsterwalde at 1000 hours. As I recall, the sky was overcast and we were led up through the clouds by the *Y-Führung* [blind flying apparatus]. The controller then sent us in several directions. We were above the clouds, so could not check our position on the ground, and as we were alone in our cockpits, we could not really follow our maps, so we did not know exactly where we were. But our course was generally to the west. The controller now became agitated and told us to expect enemy contact. Which proved correct. We saw a large Pulk of Liberators ahead, flying away from us. They quickly became larger as we approached.

Suddenly several of the 'fat cars' began to burn and plunge down in fire and smoke – even before we had fired a single shot. A Jagdgruppe ahead of us had already begun the attack. The sky was immediately filled with parachutes and wreckage, and we were flying right into it. My Staffelkapitän and I were testing the new [EZ 40] gyroscopic gunsight, which allowed me to open fire at greater-than-normal range. Short bursts from my six guns chewed into its left wing and set both its engines on fire. The bomber lurched downward. I set my sight on a nearby bomber that was already smoking. My fire caused it to erupt in bright flames, which streamed to the rear as I hurtled past. I saw the bomber roll over on its back and start down. I circled the two descending Liberators in a shallow

descending spiral. I wanted to confirm both their crashes, as a double shootdown was something exceptional in 1944. I was forced to dodge parachutes and falling wreckage, shutting my eyes at times. I quickly approached the cloud deck, through which 15 plumes of smoke emerged. I pulled up somewhat and passed through the clouds. I could now see the ground, but could no longer distinguish my victims. Burning wreckage and parachutes were everywhere. As I hurtled over the ground at 100 metres, airmen ran in all directions, some raising their hands in an apparent attempt to surrender to me. I could not recognise any landmarks and had no idea where I was.

Suddenly I spotted a yellow-nosed fighter hurtling toward me almost head-on. It was unmistakably a P-51B. We passed each other, and each broke around hard to confront each other again, just like a tournament from the Middle Ages. As we blazed away, my Focke-Wulf took hits in the tail, and my rudder pedals decreased in effectiveness. I then ran out of ammunition and had to evade by skidding and yawing, despite poor rudder control. We repeated these passes five or six times before I snapped into a dive and attempted to escape at tree-top height, counting on my camouflage for protection. This was apparently successful as the P-51 pilot pulled up slightly and could not find me again.

I landed on Langensalza at 1130 hours, drenched in sweat. My fin had a few bullet holes, and the rudder covering was ripped, but there was no serious damage. I was back on my regular base, Erfurt–Bindersleben, by 1215 hours. This was the most eventful day in my career as a fighter pilot. 'Red 19', my personal airplane, had served me well. It was not a heavily armoured *Sturmbock* but a standard Fw 190A-8 with four MG 151/20 2-cm machine cannon and two MG 131 heavy machine guns. I had nicknamed it *Kölle alaaf!* [Cologne lives!] in the dialect of my hometown. [Schröder's victims were 445th Bomb Group B-24s: DC]

Uffz. Ernst Schröder
5.(Sturm)/JG 300

28 September
8th Air Force Mission #652: 972 of 1,049 HBs (all BDs) bomb oil targets and ordnance factories in C Germany, TOT 1234-1312 – lose 34-2-463, claim 10-7-5. 646 of 724 fighters (all 15 FGs) escorts claim 26-1-13, lose 7-1-7.

Luftwaffe defensive activity – 27 September 1944

Unit	Type	Gruppe up			Gruppe down		Claims	Losses				
		Base	No	Time	Base	Time		Dest	Dam	KIA	MIA	WIA
Luftflotte Reich												
I. Jagdkorps												
Jagddivision 1:			121									
IV.(Sturm)/JG 3	Fw 190A	Alteno		1000	Zwickau	1140	19 B-24	6	3	0	0	5
II.(Sturm)/JG 4	Fw 190A	Welzow		1000	Welzow	~1145	22 B-24, 2 P-51, 15 B-24 HSS	11	2	5	2	3
Stab/JG 300	Fw 190A	Finsterwalde		1000	Finsterwalde	~1145	0	0	0	0	0	0
I./JG 300	Bf 109G	Gahro	36	1000	Gahro	~1145	0*	5	0	4	0	0
II.(Sturm)/JG 300	Fw 190A	Finsterwalde		1000	Finsterwalde	~1145	12 B-24, 1 P-51, 2 B-24 HSS**	9	2	7	0	1

*I./JG 300: + 2 B-24 undocumented; 2 P-51 unconfirmed (unwitnessed)

**II.(Sturm)/JG300: + 1 B-24, 1 P-51 undocumented; 5 B-24, 2 B-24 HSS, 4 P-51 unconfirmed (unwitnessed)

Luftwaffe defensive activity – 28 September 1944

Unit	Type	Gruppe up			Gruppe down		Claims	Losses				
		Base	No	Time	Base	Time		Dest	Dam	KIA	MIA	WIA
Luftflotte Reich												
I. Jagdkorps												
Jagddivision 1:			96									
IV.(Sturm)/JG 3	Fw 190A	Alteno		1120	Alteno	1345	9 B-17	6	2	5	0	0
II.(Sturm)/JG 4	Fw 190A	Welzow		1105	Welzow	~1300	4 B-17, 2 P-38, 2 B-17 HSS	11	3	5	0	4
Stab/JG 300	Fw 190A	Finsterwalde		1057	Quedlinburg	1300	3 B-17	0	0	0	0	0
I./JG 300	Bf 109G	Gahro		1120	Brandenburg-Briest	1335	0	6	6	3	0	3
II.(Sturm)/JG300	Fw 190A	Finsterwalde		1120	Finsterwalde	~1300	7 B-17, 1 P-51	5	1	2	0	1
I./JG 400	Me 163	Brandis	6	?	Brandis	?	0	0	0	0	0	0

An 8th AF raid on the central German oil targets brought up the same conventional RLV units as the previous day, with the same tactical plan, a mass attack by a single Gefechtsverband led by Major Dahl. The number of German fighters to sortie was reduced to 96 by the previous day's losses; 82 made contact. No vulnerable bomber Pulk was found, but a quick attack on the 303rd BG's low squadron was successful despite the bombers' tight formation. The attack was broken up by the 479th Fighter Group, which claimed the last victories by 8th AF P-38s before these were replaced entirely by P-51s. The 303rd BG lost 11 of the 40 bombers that the Americans wrote off after the mission; eight escorts were also lost. Jagddivision 1 lost 15 KIA, eight WIA and 28 conventional fighters. I./JG 400 scrambled six Me 163s, which operated alone – each now with its own controller – but their attacks resulted in no reportable results.

Notes

1 Hagenah correspondence with A. Price, 1980.

2 Sinnecker correspondence with author, 2004.

3 Gabler correspondence with author, 1990.

4 Reschke correspondence with author, 2001.

5 Scheufele correspondence with author, 1999.

6 Wendler correspondence with author, 2000.

7 *Jagdgeschwader 301/302 'Wilde Sau'*, Motorbuch Verlag, p. 118.

8 *Jagdgeschwader 301/302 'Wilde Sau'*, Motorbuch Verlag, p. 124.

9 Jung correspondence with author, 2000.

10 *The Kassel Mission Reports*, privately printed, p. 16.

11 *The Kassel Mission Reports*, privately printed, p. 16.

12 Schröder correspondence with author, 2000.

CHAPTER 8

OCTOBER – DECEMBER 1944

October 1944

For the first time in the war, all of Germany's air defences reported to a single headquarters, Luftflotte Reich. Its principal operational commands were I. Jagdkorps, covering the Reich itself, and II. Jagdkorps (through Luftwaffenkommando West, the downgraded Luftflotte 3), covering the western battle area. The map below shows the new Jagddivision boundaries. Note that the collapsing battle lines had eliminated the western, eastern and southern boundaries. The month provided an unbroken series of disappointments for the air defences. They were fated to remain quantitatively inferior to the Allies. The USSTAF had finally reached its full size and outnumbered the Luftwaffe by 5 or 10 to one on any given mission. Galland's *grosse Schlag* ('Big Blow') was intended to even the odds, and planning continued for this one-shot mission. In practice, this meant keeping depleted units non-

operational until they could be built up to full establishment strength, which kept the daily availability figures lower than they could have been.

The shortage of aviation fuel did not yet affect operations, although it had nearly strangled the pilot training program. The Jagdgruppen received trained replacement pilots from disbanded bomber units during the autumn, but these men were a decidedly mixed blessing. They were all instrument rated, giving them an advantage over typical German fighter pilots, but generally lacked elementary fighter pilot skills, and operational training in the combat units to provide them with these skills had been cut back severely.

There were still hopes that the Luftwaffe could regain its qualitative edge over the western Allies. Day fighter production rates remained high throughout the autumn, but the types produced were nearly all obsolescent Bf 109Gs and Fw 190As. There were a few

A III./JG 77 Bf 109K-4, probably 'Blue 11', at Neuruppin in October or November. JG 77 was in Galland's reserve, but never joined the RLV force. *(Mol)*

Alfred Nitsch (III./JG 77) in Bf 109K-4 'Blue 3' (W. Nr. 330177) at Neuruppin in October or November. *(Mol)*

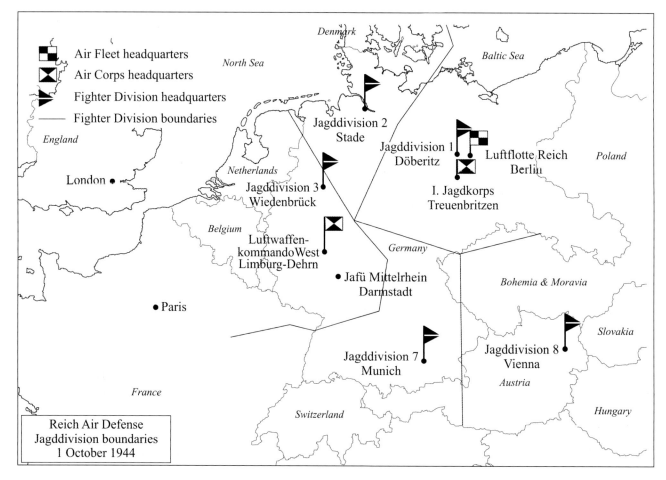

Reich Air Defense
Jagddivision boundaries
1 October 1944

improved Bf 109Ks and Fw 190Ds coming out, but Luftwaffe hopes rested in its two revolutionary new types – the rocket-propelled Me 163 and the jet-engine Me 262. The Me 163 was killing its own pilots at a shocking rate, and would prove to be a technical dead end, but the Me 262 was a true war-winner – or at least a war-extender. The Me 262 fighter programme had been stalled for several months by Hitler's demand that the jet be employed exclusively as a bomber, but *der Führer* had at last been won over. The first Me 262 fighter unit of Gruppe strength, Kommando Nowotny, entered operations from Achmer, but it did not fulfill the hopes placed in it, apparently due to the technical incompetence of the unit's commander, Major Walter Nowotny, and a strange lack of follow-through by Generalmajor Adolf Galland, who tolerated the lethargic performance of Nowotny, one of Galland's worst appointments.

Internal politics within the Luftwaffe proved especially pernicious during this period. The problems on the fighter side were watched carefully by

the bomber side, which had gained great influence on Göring's RLM staff. A plan existed to form new fighter units by redesignating bomber units, absorbing not only their pilots but their ground staffs. Jagdgeschwader 7 had been formed in August from Kampfgeschwader 1, but had yet to receive aircraft or a mission. The renumbering of bomber units as fighter units displeased the former bomber pilots on Göring's staff, and the next such change was handled differently. On 1 October, Kampfgeschwader 54 was renamed Kampfgeschwader (Jagd) 54 [KG(J) 54]. It was to remain a bomber wing, but would be re-equipped with fighters and operate in a conventional fighter role. The unit would continue to be supervised by the General of the Bomber Arm, Generalmajor Dietrich Peltz, and would be subordinated for operations to IX. Fliegerkorps, a bomber headquarters, rather than I. Jagdkorps. Furthermore, it was to be the first complete Geschwader equipped with Me 262 fighters. The arguments used to justify moving bomber pilots into Me 262 fighters – instrument

Hauptmann, later Major, Walter Nowotny. One of the most successful of the younger fighter pilots who entered service after the war began, his phenomenal career on the Eastern Front ended in November 1943 when he was grounded after his 256th air victory, for which he became the eighth member of the Wehrmacht to receive the Oak Leaves with Swords and Diamonds to the Knight's Cross. He was chosen to command the unit which would introduce the Me 262 jet fighter to combat and was killed on 8 November 1944 in combat with P-51s. (Author's collection)

Generalmajor Dietrich Peltz, one of the most controversial Luftwaffe commanders. A bomber pilot, he commanded successively larger bomber units, was promoted to general at the age of 29 and was awarded the Oak Leaves with Swords to the Knight's Cross. His career took a startling turn in October 1944 when he was named commander of II. Jagdkorps, which contained all of the fighters on the Western Front. He was responsible for planning Operation BODENPLATTE, which destroyed the fighter force beyond any hope of rebuilding, and was then given command of IX. Fliegerkorps (Jagd), which contained all of the Luftwaffe's Me 262 fighters. In March 1945, he was promoted to command the RLV force, the position he held at the end of the war. (Author's collection)

training and twin-engine experience – had some validity, but ignored certain basic differences between fighter and bomber pilots: The latter tended to be older, more conservative, slower to react and unwilling or unable to make the wild manœuvres necessary for survival in skies dominated by the Allies. Leaving bomber-as-fighter units in the bomber chain of command was a stunning insult to the entire Fighter Arm, especially to its General and champion, Adolf Galland, and to the commanders who had built the RLV into a formidable combined-arms force in a very short time.

A combination of bad weather and low operational strength forced Luftflotte Reich to ignore all eleven 8th Air Force raids from 13 October to 2 November. The situation was even worse in the south, which was short of defensive units. During this same period, only two 15th Air Force raids were intercepted, while eight were not. Fortunately for the Reich, the pervasive autumn overcast forced most bombs to be dropped blindly through clouds. The putative targets of these raids were just that, targets, and are therefore indicated in this book's tables. They were rarely damaged seriously in what amounted to area bombing raids.

3 October

8th Air Force Mission #662: 995 of 1,095 HBs (all BDs) target industrial areas and airfields in S and W Germany – lose 3-3-282, claim 0. 699 of 753 fighters (all 15 FGs) escort, claim 0, lose 4-2-10.

A full-strength 8th AF raid on Cologne, Hamm and Kassel on 2 October was ignored completely by Luftflotte Reich, which was moving the Jagdgruppen temporarily attached to Jagddivision 3 for the defence of Arnhem back to their home organisations. This meant that JG 1, JG 3, JG 4 and JG 11 could possibly return to RLV duty, but today only 93 fighters, probably all from JG 300, were scrambled against another full-strength 8th AF raid; none made contact with Allied aircraft.

5 October

8th Air Force Mission #665: 935 of 1,090 HBs (all BDs) target Cologne, Rheine, Münster industrial areas, rail yards, airfields – lose 9-5-353, claim 0. 675 of 733 fighters (15 FGs) escort, claim 1, lose 5-0-4.

The RLV response to the 8th AF raid on the 5th duplicated that of the 3rd: 80 JG 300 fighters were scrambled, but none made contact with Allied aircraft.

6 October – North German industrial targets (see map)

8th Air Force Mission #667: 1,200 of 1,271 HBs (all BDs) bomb various oil and industrial targets + airfields in N

Lt. Paul Kolster (I./JG300) sits on the sill of his usual Bf 109G-14 'Red 18' in late 1944. *(Rosch)*

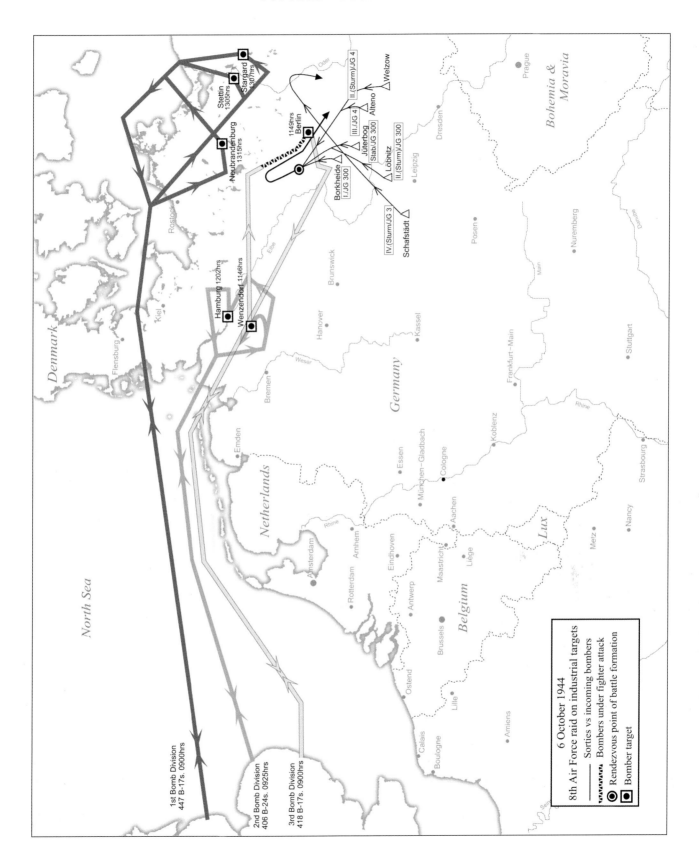

Stargard
1307hrs

Stettin
1305hrs

Neubrandenburg
1315hrs

II.(Sturm)/JG 4

Welzow

III./JG 4

Alteno

1149hrs
Berlin

Jüterbog
Stab/JG 300

II.(Sturm)/JG 300

Löbnitz

Leipzig

Borkheide
1./JG 300

IV.(Sturm)/JG 3

Schafstädt

Dresden

Prague

*Bohemia &
Moravia*

Posen

Nuremberg

Hamburg 1202hrs

Wenzendorf 1146hrs

Germany

Brunswick

Hanover

Kassel

Bremen

Weser

Elbe

Rhine

Main

Stuttgart

Rostock

Kiel

Flensburg

Denmark

North Sea

Emden

Netherlands

Amsterdam

Rotterdam

Arnhem

Eindhoven

Essen

München–Gladbach

Cologne

Koblenz

Frankfurt–Main

Rhine

Aachen

Maastricht

Liège

Lux

Antwerp

Ostend

Belgium

Brussels

Lille

Ostend

Metz

Nancy

Strasbourg

Calais

Boulogne

Amiens

1st Bomb Division
447 B-17s. 0900hrs

2nd Bomb Division
406 B-24s. 0925hrs

3rd Bomb Division
418 B-17s. 0900hrs

**6 October 1944
8th Air Force raid on industrial targets**

— Sorties vs incoming bombers
⌐⌐⌐ Bombers under fighter attack
◉ Rendezvous point of battle formation
▣ Bomber target

Germany, TOT 1146-1315 – lose 19-1-395, 3rd BD claim 3-9-5. 699 of 764 fighters (15 FGs) escort, claim 19-1-8, lose 4-2-13.

Today's 8th AF raid appeared to be heading for the central German oil targets and brought a full-strength response from the newly reinforced Jagddivision 1. 127 defensive sorties were flown, of which 77 made contact. All three Sturmgruppen flew the mission. II.(Sturm)/JG 4 and II.(Sturm)/JG 300 were protected by the high-altitude Staffeln of their own Geschwader, while IV.(Sturm)/JG 3 flew its mission alone, without any high-altitude escort. It was dispersed by P-51s before reaching the bombers, but the other two Sturmgruppen reported great success. Twenty bombers were in fact written off, most as a result of the Sturmangriffe, and six American escorts were also lost. Luftwaffe losses were modest, amounting to 13 KIA, three WIA and 20 fighters.

7 October – Oil industry and Kassel (see map)

8th Air Force Mission #667: 1,401 of 1,422 HBs (all BDs) bomb 7 oil installations + Kassel armour plant, TOT 1218-1340 – lose 40-3-701, claim 11-13-10. 521 of 900 fighters (15 8th AF FGs + 2 9th AF FGs) escort, claim 29-0-4, lose 11-2-7.

15th Air Force dispatches 722 B-24s, 206 B-17s to bomb Vienna synthetic oil plants, Györ airfield – lose 16, claim 0 (no air opposition. Escort of 162 P-38s, 251 P-51s claims 1, loses 2.

The USSTAF responded to the increased strength exhibited by the RLV force on the 6th by ordering a joint raid by both of its air forces. The RLV

Fw 190A-8/R2 'Red 11' of II.(Sturm)/JG 300, jacked up for maintenance at Löbnitz. This was usually the aircraft of Ofhr. Harry Piel, but Ernst Schröder bailed out of it on 11 November after he was unable to land it in the darkness. *(Crow)*

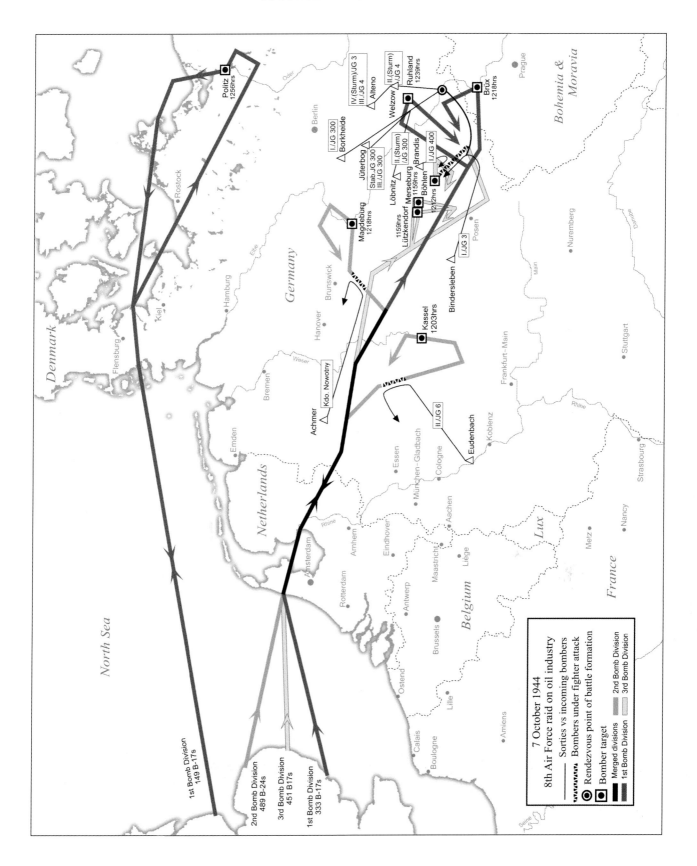

7 October 1944
8th Air Force raid on oil industry

Sorties vs incoming bombers
Bombers under fighter attack
Rendezvous point of battle formation
Bomber target
Merged divisions
1st Bomb Division
2nd Bomb Division
3rd Bomb Division

Politz 1256hrs
IV.(Sturm)/JG 3
III./JG 4
Alteno
II.(Sturm)/JG 4
Welzow
Ruhland 1239hrs
Brüx 1218hrs
I./JG 300
Borkheide
Jüterbog
Stab.JG 300
III./JG 300
II.(Sturm)/JG 300
Löbnitz
Lützkendorf 1159hrs
Brandis
Merseburg 1159hrs
Böhlen 1212hrs
I./JG 400
Magdeburg 1218hrs
I./JG 3
Bindersleben
Kassel 1203hrs
Kdo. Nowotny
Achmer
II./JG 6
Eudenbach

1st Bomb Division
149 B-17s
2nd Bomb Division
489 B-24s
3rd Bomb Division
451 B17s
1st Bomb Division
333 B-17s

North Sea
Denmark
Germany
Netherlands
Belgium
Lux
France
Bohemia & Moravia

Prague
Berlin
Oder
Rostock
Hamburg
Kiel
Flensburg
Elbe
Brunswick
Hanover
Weser
Bremen
Emden
Amsterdam
Rotterdam
Rhine
Arnhem
Eindhoven
Maastricht
Liège
Antwerp
Brussels
Ostend
Lille
Calais
Boulogne
Amiens
Seine
Nancy
Metz
Strasbourg
Stuttgart
Nuremberg
Main
Danube
Posen
Frankfurt-Main
Koblenz
Cologne
München-Gladbach
Essen
Aachen
Rhine

commanders ignored the 15th AF and concentrated their strength against the 8th, which, again, threatened the vulnerable oil industry. 113 fighters were scrambled; 80 made contact. I. Jagdkorps ordered its piston-engine units to form a single Gefechtsverband comprising the three Sturmgruppen escorted by four Bf 109 Gruppen. The Verbandsführer Major Dahl had to abort, but the Gruppen performed their roles well, downing 12 B-17s in a mass attack near Leipzig.

The small Me 262 and Me 163 units made their greatest efforts to date. Kommando Nowotny claimed three B-24s, for the loss of one KIA, one WIA and four Me 262s. 1./JG 400 claimed one or two B-17s for the loss of two pilots and five Me 163s.

Jagddivision 3 apparently scrambled its remaining tactical Gruppen against the large B-24 force raiding Kassel; data are sparse. Most JD 3 formations seem to have been dispersed by 9th AF fighters, and only one B-24 was claimed. The day's results for the RLV force fell into the usual pattern: only the Sturmtaktik achieved worthwhile results, and then only if the Sturmgruppen had an opportunity to attack poorly escorted formations. The 8th AF wrote off 43 bombers to all causes; all 16 15th AF losses were attributable to Flak and operational reasons. The Americans lost 15 fighters, a negligible percentage of the sorties flown. Jagddivision 1 losses were tolerable today, totalling 12 KIA or MIA, five WIA and 28 fighters.

A line-up of Fw 190A-8/R2s of II.(Sturm)/JG 300 on Löbnitz. *(Rosch)*

Luftwaffe defensive activity – 3 October 1944

Unit	Type	Gruppe up			Gruppe down		Claims	Losses				
		Base	No	Time	Base	Time		Dest	Dam	KIA	MIA	WIA
Luftflotte Reich												
I. Jagdkorps			93									
Jagddivision 1:												
I./JG 300	Bf 109G	Gahro		1045	Gahro	1230	n/c	0	0	0	0	0
II.(Sturm)/JG300	Fw 190A	Finsterwalde		1045	Finsterwalde	~1230	n/c	0	0	0	0	0
III./JG 300	Bf 109G	Jüterbog		1050	Jüterbog	~1230	n/c	0	0	0	0	0

Luftwaffe defensive activity – 5 October 1944

Unit	Type	Gruppe up			Gruppe down		Claims	Losses				
		Base	No	Time	Base	Time		Dest	Dam	KIA	MIA	WIA
Luftflotte Reich												
I. Jagdkorps			80									
Jagddivision 1:												
I./JG 300	Bf 109G	Gahro		1130	Borkheide	1330	n/c	0	2	0	0	0
II.(Sturm)/JG300	Fw 190A	Löbnitz		~1130	Löbnitz	~1330	n/c	1	1	0	0	0

Luftwaffe defensive activity – 6 October 1944

Unit	Type	Gruppe up			Gruppe down		Claims	Losses				
		Base	No	Time	Base	Time		Dest	Dam	KIA	MIA	WIA
Luftflotte Reich												
I. Jagdkorps			127									
Jagddivision 1:												
IV.(Sturm)/JG 3	Fw 190A	Schafstädt		1150	Schafstädt, Luckau, Alteno	1315	0	4	2	4	0	0
II.(Sturm)/JG 4	Fw 190A	Welzow, Alteno		1038	Welzow, Alteno	~1240	9 B-17, 6 B-17 HSS	10	1	7	0	3
III./JG 4	Bf 109G	Alteno		1040	Alteno	1230	1 B-17*	5	1	2	0	0
Stab/JG 300	Fw 190A	Jüterbog		1040	Jüterbog	1231	1 B-17	0	0	0	0	0
I./JG 300	Bf 109G	Borkheide	33	1045	Borkheide, Finsterwalde	1245	0**	0	0	0	0	0
II.(Sturm)/JG 300	Fw 190A	Löbnitz		1040	Löbnitz, Jüterbog	1240	0***	1	1	0	0	0

*III./JG 4: + 3 B-17, 1 P-51 claims undocumented, 3 B-17, 1 P-51 claims unconfirmed (unwitnessed)

**I./JG 300: + 1 P-51 claim undocumented

***II.(Sturm)/JG 300: + 5 B-17, 4 B-17 HSS claims undocumented

COMBAT REPORT[1]
7 October 1944

One Boeing B-17 shot down from 8,000 metres at 1206 hours, PQ LC/LD – MC/MD

I scrambled from Alteno at 1055 hours in a Fw 190A-8 (four MG 151/20) as a Kettenführer in the Gruppe Gefechtsverband. At 1155 hours, we sighted ca. 300 Boeing Fortresses and 80–100 escorts southwest of Halle in PQ LD-6. At 1206 hours and 8,000 metres altitude, our Gruppe made an attack on a Pulk of ca. 30 Boeing Fortresses from directly behind them. I was positioned on the right and gained firing position on the high right rear Fortress. I fired short bursts at the enemy aircraft from 400 down to 50 metres. I saw shells hit the left inner engine, fuselage, right wing and both right engines. Parts of the engines and right wing flew off. The right wing gave off dark smoke and burst into flames. The Boeing dove to the right and began to spin, smoking and burning on the right side. I myself was hit in the oil tank by two enemy fighters and was therefore unable to see the crash. Uffz. Glässen, one of my wingmen, and Fhj.-Fw. Angres witnessed the combat. We saw no chutes.
    I landed on Jüterbog-Waldlager at 1240 hours.

Fhj.-Obfw. Willi Unger
15.(Sturm)/JG 3

Luftwaffe defensive activity – 7 October 1944

Unit	Type	Gruppe up			Gruppe down		Claims	Losses				
		Base	No	Time	Base	Time		Dest	Dam	KIA	MIA	WIA
Luftflotte Reich												
I. Jagdkorps			113									
Jagddivision 1:												
I./JG 3	Bf 109G	Bindersleben, Borkheide		1108	Bindersleben, Borkheide	1242	0	1	0	1	0	0
IV.(Sturm)/JG 3	Fw 190A	Alteno, Luckau		1100	Alteno, Jüterbog	1240	6 B-17, 2 B-17 HSS	0	0	0	0	0
II.(Sturm)/JG 4	Fw 190A	Welzow		1100	Welzow	~1230	3 B-17, 1 B-17 HSS*	3	3	2	0	1
III./JG 4	Bf 109G	Alteno		1100	Alteno	1250	0**	3	0	1	0	1
Stab/JG 300	Fw 190A	Jüterbog		1100	Jüterbog	~1250	1 P-51	0	0	0	0	0
I./JG 300	Bf 109G	Borkheide		1100	Borkheide	1235	0***	3	2	1	0	0
II.(Sturm)/JG 300	Fw 190A	Löbnitz		1050	Löbnitz	~1250	0****	3	1	1	1	0
III./JG 300	Bf 109G	Jüterbog		1050	Jüterbog, Delitzsch	~1250	0*****	4	1	2	0	1
I./JG 400	Me 163B	Brandis		1230	Brandis	1250	1 B-17, 1 B-17 HSS	5	1	2	0	1
Jagddivision 2:												
Kdo Nowotny	Me 262A	Achmer, Hesepe		1240	Achmer, Hesepe	1323	2 B-24******	2	0	1	0	1
2nd sorties	Me 262A	Achmer, Hesepe		1345	Achmer, Hesepe	~1430	0	2	0	0	0	0
Jagddivision 3:												
II./JG 6	Fw 190A	Eudenbach		~1100	Eudenbach	~1230	1 B-24	2	1	0	0	0

*II.(Sturm)/JG 4: + 2 B-17 claims undocumented; 1 B-17 claim unconfirmed (unwitnessed)

**III./JG 4: + 1 B-17 claim undocumented

***I./JG 300: + 1 P-51 claim undocumented; 1 P-51 claim unconfirmed (unwitnessed)

****II.(Sturm)/JG 300: + 4 B-17, 4 B-17 HSS, 1 P-51 claims undocumented; 1 B-17 claim unconfirmed (unwitnessed)

*****III./JG 300: + 2 B-17, 3 B-17 HSS claims undocumented; 1 P-47 claim unconfirmed (unwitnessed)

******Kdo Nowotny: + 1 B-24 claim undocumented; 1 B-24 claim unconfirmed (unwitnessed)

12 October

8th Air Force Mission #674: 511 of 552 2nd BD B-24s + 3rd BD B-17s bomb Bremen a/i and Osnabrück rail yard, TOT 1135-53 – lose 3-1-126, claim 0. 483 of 514 escorts (11 FGs) claim 18-3-1, lose 5.

15th Air Force dispatches 160 P-51s (3 FGs) to strafe Danube traffic, Hungarian airfield – claim 14-0-3, lose 2.

After ignoring 8th AF raids on the 9th and 11th and a 15th AF raid on the 11th, Luftflotte Reich attempted to attack the American bombers today. A large weather front over central and eastern Germany kept the I. Jagdkorps fighters on the ground until it was too late to make contact. Kommando Nowotny did scramble a few Me 262s as conditions permitted, but found only escorts; one claim for a P-51 was confirmed. The II. Jagdkorps Gruppen were ordered to scramble, form up into Verbände and make the interception. These tactical units had never been given such a mission, and the few experienced pilots still on strength had not faced the heavies since D-Day. Only JG 26 was able to form up in a semblance of a Geschwader formation, and this soon broke up in the clouds. The American escorts found them quickly, and the Geschwader returned to its bases short of 12 fighters; six pilots were KIA, three MIA and two bailed out WIA. These were only combat losses reported by Luftflotte Reich for the time of the raid. Oberst Josef Priller, the JG 26 Kommodore, claimed the only Geschwader victory, a P-51 from the 357th FG. The Americans did write off four bombers and four fighters to other causes. Luftflotte Reich scrambled 457 fighters during the day, but only 83 – probably all from JG 26 and the jet unit – were credited with contacting the enemy.

An interesting, unpublished photograph of Fw 190A-8s in flight, obtained from the album of a JG 26 pilot and possibly showing I./JG 26 aircraft, although the camouflage is much darker than was customary for this unit. The indistinct identity markings are noteworthy, and the spirals on the spinners date the photograph as post D-Day. *(Stumpf)*

13 October

15th Air Force dispatches 621 B-24s, 250 B-17s to bomb Blechhammer, TOT 1955-1141; Vienna o/i TOT 1128-1149 – lose 27, claims unknown. Escort of 173 P-38s, 235 P51s claims 0, loses 6.

The only aerial opposition to this major 15th AF attack on oil targets in Silesia and Austria came from a ground attack training unit, IV./SG 151, flying Fw 190F-8s from Prossnitz. The small Focke-Wulf formation never reached the bombers and lost one KIA to the escorts, which were otherwise engaged in strafing rail targets.

16 October

15th Air Force dispatches 553 B-24s, 216 B-17s, targeting Brüx oil targets, Czech and Austrian ordnance plants – lose 15-?-?, claims unknown. Escort of 167 P-38s, 232 P-51s claims 17-1-6, loses 0.

The 15th AF scheduled a full-strength long-range mission to several important Czech targets. This air force had only half the number of escort units of the larger 8th AF and may have appeared especially vulnerable today as it came within range of the Jagddivision 1 bases in central Germany. The RLV force reacted in maximum strength: 455 sorties were flown, of which 223 made contact. Two Sturmgruppen were among the 10 Jagdgruppen scrambled, but results were extremely disappointing. The bombers split into small formations to bomb a number of targets, confusing the ground controllers. What was worse, the 400 US escorts seemed to leave no holes in their coverage. Only five victory claims are known to have been filed, and none were confirmed. Fifteen American bombers, and no escorts, were lost to all causes. Jagddivision 1 lost 10 KIA, three WIA and 17 fighters.

17 October

8th Air Force Mission #681: 1,250 of 1,338 HBs (all BDs) target Cologne area – lose 4-4-486, claim 0. 774 of 811 escorts (all 15 FGs) claim 0, lose 1.

15th Air Force dispatches 429 B-24s + 168 B-17s, targets Blechhammer oil industry, Hungarian and Austrian rail yards – lose 18, claim 0. Escort of 161 P-38s, 214 P51s claims 4, loses 1.

The USSTAF scheduled another joint mission by its two air forces. 1,250 8th AF bombers pummelled

Luftwaffe defensive activity – 12 October 1944

Unit	Type	Gruppe up			Gruppe down		Claims	Losses				
		Base	No	Time	Base	Time		Dest	Dam	KIA	MIA	WIA
Luftflotte Reich												
I. Jagdkorps			457									
Jagddivision 1:												
II.(Sturm)/JG 4	Fw 190A	Gahro		1117	Gahro	~1230	n/c	0	0	0	0	0
III./JG 4	Bf 109G	Alteno	~1117	Alteno	~1230	n/c	0	0	0	0	0
I./JG 300	Bf 109G	Borkheide		1120	Borkheide	·1230	n/c	1	1	0	0	0
II.(Sturm)/JG300	Fw 190A	Löbnitz		1120	Löbnitz	~1230	n/c	0	0	0	0	0
III./JG 300	Bf 109G	Jüterbog		1120	Jüterbog, Delitzsch	~1230	n/c	0	0	0	0	0
IV./JG 300	Bf 109G	Reinsdorf		1120	Brandis	~1230	n/c	0	0	0	0	0
Jagddivision 2:												
Kdo Nowotny	Me 262A	Achmer		1035	Wesermunde	1150	1 P-51*	0	2	0	0	0
LwKdo West												
II. Jagdkorps												
Jagddivision 5:												
Stab/JG 26	Fw 190A	Krefeld		~1030	Krefeld	~1215	1 P-51	0	0	0	0	0
I./JG 26	Fw 190A	Krefeld	22	1028	Krefeld, Dortmund, Hildesheim	1215	0	3	0	1	2	0
II./JG 26	Fw 190A	Kirchhellen		1040	Kirchhellen	1254	0	5	1	3	1	1
III./JG 26	Bf 109G	Lette, Bönninghardt		1035	Lette, Hildesheim, Bönninghardt	1210	0**	4	0	2	0	2

*Kdo. Nowotny: + 1 P-51 claim unconfirmed (unwitnessed)   **III./JG 26: + 1 P-51 claim undocumented

Luftwaffe defensive activity – 16 October 1944

Unit	Type	Gruppe up			Gruppe down		Claims	Losses				
		Base	No	Time	Base	Time		Dest	Dam	KIA	MIA	WIA
Luftflotte Reich												
I. Jagdkorps			455									
Jagddivision 1:												
I./JG 3	Bf 109G	Erfurt		1122	Erfurt	1243	0*	2	0	1	0	0
II./JG 3	Bf 109G	Alpenstedt		1115	Alpenstedt	1320	0**	4	1	4	0	1
IV.(Sturm)/JG 3	Fw 190A	Schafstädt		1120	Schafstädt, Frankfurt/Oder	1340	0	1	2	1	0	0
I./JG 4	Bf 109G	Gahro		1120	Gahro	~1315	0***	1	3	0	0	1
III./JG 4	Bf 109G	Alteno		1120	Alteno	~1315	0	2	0	1	0	0
II./JG 5	Bf 109G	Salzwedel		~1120	Salzwedel	~1315	0****	3	7	2	0	1
I./JG 300	Bf 109G	Borkheide		1115	Borkheide	~1315	0	0	3	0	0	0
II.(Sturm)/JG 300	Fw 190A	Löbnitz		1115	Löbnitz	~1315	0	1	0	0	0	0
III./JG 300	Bf 109G	Jüterbog		1115	Jüterbog	~1315	0	2	0	0	0	0
IV./JG 300	Bf 109G	Reinsdorf		1115	Reinsdorf	~1315	0	1	1	1	0	0

*I./JG 3: + 2 P-51 claims unconfirmed (unwitnessed)

**II./JG 3: + 1 P-51 claim undocumented

***I./JG 4: + 1 P-51 claim unconfirmed (unwitnessed)

****II./JG 5: + 1 P-51 claim unconfirmed (unwitnessed)

Cologne through clouds. This area-bombing raid, although infuriating to the men of the Luftwaffe and the citizens of Cologne, had to be ignored by Luftflotte Reich, which could only afford to defend critical targets. The day's major target for the 15th AF, the Blechhammer-Süd/IG Farben oil synthesis plant, certainly qualified as critical, but the defensive effort was pathetic. 17 sorties were flown, and all were credited with making contact, but the unit involved reported no claims or losses, and cannot be identified. The Allied Signals Intercept service in Italy reported that the Vienna controller constantly ordered his fighters away from the oncoming bombers until there was no longer time to land and refuel for an attack on the withdrawing stream. He – and they – was obviously looking for unescorted Pulks, which could not be found. The 19 aircraft lost by the 15th AF were all chalked up to Flak and operational causes. As noted, the RLV force reported no claims or losses on what proved to be its last mission in October.

November 1944

November was the peak month of the American air offensive against German oil production, although most bombs had to be dropped blindly through the autumn overcast. The 8th AF flew 13 missions against petroleum facilities; the 15th AF, 12. Production dropped to 31 per cent of the monthly average in the spring of 1944. The RLV forces had one of their least effective months: only five 8th AF missions and two 15th AF missions were intercepted by Luftflotte Reich piston-engine units.

Two entire Geschwader left the RLV force at mid-month. JG 27 was moved to northwestern Germany and given a single mission: protection of the jet bases in the area, which now contained I./KG 51, with Me 262 bombers, and Kommando Sperling, with Ar 234 reconnaissance aircraft. The second Geschwader, JG 4, was ordered to transfer to LwKdo West bases in the Frankfurt–Darmstadt area, where it was to specialise in hunting Allied fighter-bombers. The Geschwader's short tour in the RLV force thus came to an abrupt end. Generalmajor Galland was informed on 20 November that all but two of the piston-engine RLV day fighter Geschwader would soon be transferred to the west for offensive operations. The 'Big Blow', *der grosse Schlag*, never an official operation, was thus effectively cancelled.

Uffz. Friedrich Zenk (IV./JG 4, ex-II./JG 5) poses on his Bf 109G-14/AS 'White 4', nicknamed 'Christel', on Finsterwalde. This was long after JG 4 had left the RLV force. Photos of the Geschwader from that brief period are scarce; this photo shows the typical appearance of IV./JG 4 Bf 109G-14s. *(Mombeek)*

After the death of its Kommandeur, Kommando Nowotny was withdrawn from operations, redesignated III./JG 7, and sent to Bavaria for more training. It shared its base with III./EJG 2, a Me 262 conversion training unit that had evolved from ErprKdo 262. The two units were forbidden to attack large Allied formations, but were permitted to intercept reconnaissance aircraft. These small-scale missions are outside the scope of this study.

Galland continued to tinker with the organisation of JG 7, which was destined to become the only jet fighter Geschwader in the traditional fighter chain of command. He obtained a full Gruppe of trained fighter pilots for the Geschwader by renaming II./JG 3 as I./JG 7. The old I./JG 7, which was having a hard time converting its ex-bomber pilots to conventional fighters, was renamed II./JG 7; the old II./JG 7 became II./JG 3. Galland appointed Oberst Johannes Steinhoff as Kommodore of the all-jet Geschwader. Steinhoff wore the Knight's Cross with Oak Leaves and Swords and had commanded JG 77 on the Mediterranean Front for 19 months. Steinhoff's record promised both combat and leadership skills; it was not clear how much he had left to offer after five years of continuous service.

Oberst Johannes Steinhoff. A successful fighter pilot and combat commander on all fronts, he was named the first Kommodore of JG 7, the jet fighter Geschwader, but was relieved at the end of 1944. He joined JV 44, Galland's 'Jet Unit of the Aces', in March and scored six victories in the Me 262. On April 18, 1945, his heavily loaded fighter crashed on take-off and burst into flames. He survived with severe burns that kept him in hospital until 1947. *(Author's collection)*

1 November

8th Air Force Mission #696: 317 of 323 HBs (all BDs) target Gelsenkirchen synthetic oil plants, W German rail bridge – lose 0-0-56, claim 0. 286 of 321 escorts (9 FGs) claim 2-0-0, lose 1-1-1.

A small 8th AF raid in bad weather was opposed by four Kommando Nowotny Me 262s, which were kept from the bombers by the close escort of P-47s and P-51s. One Me 262 was shot down; its pilot bailed out and survived. One P-51 was also shot down; its pilot was killed.

2 November

8th Air Force Mission #698: 1,100 of 1,174 HBs (all BDs) target Merseburg/Leuna, other central German synthetic oil plants, Bielefeld rail targets, TOT 1203-54h – lose 40-2-583, claim 36-35-27. 873 of 968 escorts (all 15 FGs + 1 FG 9th AF P-38s) claim 102-6-25, lose 16-0-0.

A full-strength 8th AF raid following a straight-line course to the oil targets in central Germany provoked a strong defensive effort by the I. Jagdkorps. JG 300 and JG 301 were stood down, but Gefechtsverbände were formed around JG 3, JG 4 and JG 27. The first two had the typical organisation of a Sturmgruppe escorted by several light Gruppen, while JG 27, which was operating as a full Geschwader for the first time in the war, contained only light Gruppen. The two Sturmgruppen were guided to vulnerable bomber Pulks by the experienced 1. Jagddivision controllers and made effective attacks – IV.(Sturm)/JG 3 on the 91st BG, II.(Sturm)/JG 4 on the 457th BG – before the American escorts broke through the Bf 109 escorts and took their revenge. JG 27 was unable to make any headway against the bombers before being driven to ground by P-51s; its losses today were the greatest of any day of the war. The jet and rocket fighters were up, but the jets of Kommando Nowotny were burdened with WGr 21 mortar tubes – there was still a dispute over their best armament against bombers – and could not reach the bombers, although they did claim three escorts for the loss of one jet fighter and pilot. One III./JG 54 Staffel had the mission of protecting the jets' take-offs and landings with its new Fw 190D9s, and the five fighters it scrambled from Achmer downed two B-17s without loss, outshining the jets. I./JG 400 scrambled five Me 163s from Brandis, but since this was the only rocket fighter base and was in the day's target area, it was blanketed by sweeping P-

Luftwaffe defensive activity – 1 November 1944

Unit	Type	Gruppe up			Gruppe down		Claims	Losses				
		Base	No	Time	Base	Time		Dest	Dam	KIA	MIA	WIA
Luftflotte Reich												
I. Jagdkorps												
Jagddivision 2:												
Kdo Nowotny	Me 262A	Achmer	4	~1330	Achmer	~1430	1 P-51	1	0	0	0	0

Luftwaffe defensive activity – 2 November 1944

Unit	Type	Gruppe up			Gruppe down		Claims*	Losses				
		Base	No	Time	Base	Time		Dest	Dam	KIA	MIA	WIA
Luftflotte Reich												
I. Jagdkorps												
Jagddivision 1:												
Stab/JG 3	Bf 109G	Erfurt–Bindersleben		1130	Erfurt–Bindersleben	1230	0	1	0	0	0	0
I./JG 3	Bf 109G	Erfurt–Bindersleben		1130	Erfurt–Bindersleben	~1330	1 B-17, 1 P-47, 2 P-51	11	5	4	0	5
II./JG 3	Bf 109G	Alpenstedt		1135	Alpenstedt, Burg	1250	1 B-17, 1 P-51	17	8	11	0	2
IV.(Sturm)/JG 3	Fw 190A	Schafstädt		1135	Schafstädt	1323	27 B-17	20	4	11	0	4
Stab/JG 4	Fw 190A	Welzow		~1140	Welzow	~1330	3 B-17	1	0	0	0	0
I./JG 4	Bf 109G	Finsterwalde	30	~1140	Finsterwalde	~1330	4 B-17	4	5	0	0	2
II.(Sturm)/JG 4	Fw 190A	Welzow	15	~1140	Welzow	~1330	12 B-17	10	4	5	1	3
III./JG 4	Bf 109G	Alteno	30	1140	Alteno	1330	0	5	1	3	0	2
IV./JG 4	Bf 109G	Finsterwalde	30	~1140	Finsterwalde	~1330	3 B-17	6	0	5	0	1
Stab/JG 27	Bf 109G	Riesa–Canitz		~1200	Riesa–Canitz	~1330	0	0	0	0	0	0
I./JG 27	Bf 109G	Riesa–Canitz		1130	Riesa–Canitz, Pomßen	1308	2 P-51	25	1	11	0	0
II./JG 27	Bf 109G	Riesa–Canitz, Pomßen		~1200	Riesa–Canitz, Pomßen	~1330	1 P-51	3	2	1	0	2
III./JG 27	Bf 109K	Großenhain		~1200	Großenhain	~1330	2 P-51	8	0	5	0	4
IV./JG 27	Bf 109G	Pomßen		~1200	Pomßen	~1330	3 P-51	17	4	10	0	5
I./JG 400	Me 163B	Brandis	5	1216	Brandis	1234	0	4	0	3	0	1
Jagddivision 2:												
III./JG 54	Fw 190D	Achmer	3	~1130	Achmer	~1230	1 B-17	0	0	0	0	0
	Fw 190D	Achmer	2	~1300	Achmer	~1430	1 B-17	0	0	0	0	0
Kdo. Nowotny	Me 262A	Achmer		~1200	Achmer	~1300	2 P-47, 1 P-51	1	1	1	0	0

* No claims confirmed from this date to end of war – claims tabulated in the book from this point are those known filed and in apparent good order.

51s, and the Mustangs and leading B-17s downed four of the rocket fighters, killing three pilots. I./JG 400 could report no success and was unable to fly another mission in this strength for four months. After the mission, the 8th AF wrote off 42 bombers, most owing to the two successful Sturmangriffe, as well as 16 escorts. I. Jagdkorps lost 71 KIA or MIA, 31 WIA and 133 fighters. The day was an unmitigated disaster for I. Jagdkorps. It had scrambled 490 fighters, of which 305 made contact. 133 of these were shot down: a loss of 44 per cent. On 6 November, victory claims being

processed for this mission totalled 52 for the fighters and 30 for the Flak. At the Führer conference on that date, Hitler studied these data and made it clear that he had lost all confidence in the Jagdwaffe; that it was '… insanity to go on producing the aircraft … [when] the hope of decimating the enemy with a mass deployment is not realistic'. Although it did not become clear for two more weeks, Galland's planned 'Big Blow' and any hope for a massive victory by the RLV force died at that moment.

PILOT'S ACCOUNT[2]
2 November 1944

This was my first mission since my head injury on 20 August. My Staffelkapitän, Oblt. Gerth, asked me if I was ready to fly and, when I told him I was, assigned me to be his wingman. We were told that we would be defending the Leuna synthetic oil plant. It was a cold morning, with dark clouds on the horizon. Eight of us scrambled from Schafstädt at 1135 hours, joined the rest of Moritz's Gruppe and headed northwest. We sighted the bomber stream and, at 1230 hours, were led to a B-17 Pulk near Halle that had no visible escort. We turned in 1,000 metres behind it. As always, we came under heavy fire as soon as the tail gunners saw us, but held our own fire until we were only 400 metres away. Oblt. Gerth and I each downed a bomber. We had been briefed to reassemble to the right of the bombers after the first attack. Just as I formed up on Oblt. Gerth's wing, the cry came, 'Indianer!' Red-nosed Mustangs were diving on us. We were outnumbered and lost any idea of a second attack. Oblt. Gerth disappeared at this time, and I am sure he was hit by the Mustangs. I myself escaped in a maximum speed spiral dive. I entered a solid cloud deck, and as I came out of it, I was approaching the ground – fast – and I had to pull on the stick with both hands. I applied all the muscle I had to pull back the stick. I pulled up just in time, narrowly missing chimneys and roofs as I levelled off. I had lost the Mustangs, but nearly killed myself in the process. My canopy was completely iced up, and I could see only through the electrically heated windshield. The area around the refinery looked like a battlefield, with numerous explosions and B-17s crashing all around. After the ice cleared, I landed on Quedlinburg, refuelled and flew back to Schafstädt. Although we

had downed a number of bombers, our Staffel had lost three pilots, including our Staffelkapitän. [Bösch's victim was a 91st Bomb Group B-17: DC]

Uffz. Oskar Bösch
14.(Sturm)/JG 3

Fw. Oskar Bösch in a photograph taken at flight school in March. Bösch volunteered for the Sturmstaffel direct from training and finished the war in IV. (Sturm)/JG 3. *(Bösch)*

4 November

8th Air Force Mission #700: 768 of 890 HBs (all BDs) target Hamburg, Hannover, other oil targets – lose 5-0-192, claim 0. 768 of 890 escorts (15 8th AF FGs + 1 FG 9th AF P51s) claim 0-0-1, lose 2-2-0.

15th Air Force dispatches 598 B-24s + 217 B-17s, targets Regensburg oil storage facility, various industrial areas – lose 4, claim 1-1-2. Escort of 192 P-38s, 252 P-51s claims 0, loses 0.

Apart from a skirmish between Kommando Nowotny and some 8th AF escorts, Luftflotte Reich ignored both American air forces, even though they were attacking oil targets. However, the *2º Gruppo Caccia* (2nd Fighter Group) of the *Aeronautica Nazionale Repubblicana* (ANR – the Italians still allied with Germany) scrambled six Bf 109Gs against the withdrawing 15th AF, caught seven isolated B-24s and downed two certain and one probable, for the loss of one crash-landed Messerschmitt.

Axis defensive activity vs. 8th and 15th US Air Forces – 4 November 1944

Unit	Type	Gruppe up			Gruppe down		Claims	Losses				
		Base	No	Time	Base	Time		Dest	Dam	KIA	MIA	WIA
Luftflotte Reich												
I. Jagdkorps												
Jagddivision 2:												
Kdo Nowotny	Me 262A	Achmer		~1230	Achmer	~1330	1 P-47	3	0	0	1	0
Luftflotte 2												
Jafü Oberitalien:												
2° Gr. Caccia	Bf 109G	Villafranca, Ghedi	27	1000	Aviano	1045	transfer	0	0	0	0	0
(Italy)	Bf 109G	Aviano	6	~1200	Aviano	1310	2 B-24	1	0	0	0	0

Axis defensive activity – 5 November 1944

Unit	Type	Gruppe up			Gruppe down		Claims	Losses				
		Base	No	Time	Base	Time		Dest	Dam	KIA	MIA	WIA
Luftflotte Reich												
I. Jagdkorps												
Jagddivision 1:												
II./JG 3	Bf 109G	Alpenstedt		1115	Alpenstedt	1250	n/c	1	0	1	0	0
IV.(Sturm)/JG 3	Fw 190A	Schafstädt		1110	Schafstädt	1250	n/c	0	0	0	0	0
III./JG 4	Bf 109G	Alteno		1153	Alteno	1259	n/c	0	0	0	0	0
Stab/JG 300	Fw 190A	Jüterbog		~1110	Jüterbog	~1245	1 B-17	0	0	0	0	0
I./JG 300	Bf 109G	Borkheide		1110	Borkheide	1245	n/c	0	1	0	0	0
II.(Sturm)/JG 300	Fw 190A	Löbnitz		1110	Löbnitz	~1245	n/c	0	0	0	0	0
III./JG 300	Bf 109G	Jüterbog		1120	Jüterbog	~1245	n/c	0	0	0	0	0
IV./JG 300	Bf 109G	Reinsdorf		~1110	Reinsdorf	~1245	n/c	0	0	0	0	0
Jagddivision 8:												
I./JG 53	Bf 109G	Veszprém		~1300	Veszprém	~1430	n/c	0	0	0	0	0
101 JGr	Bf 109G	Veszprém		~1300	Veszprém	~1430	4 B-24, 1 P-51	5	?	4	0	?
(Hungary)												

5 November

15th Air Force dispatches 516 B-24s + 217 B-17s, targets Vienna–Florisdorf refinery – lose 5, claim 1-1-2. Escort of 192 P-38s, 252 P-51s claims 10, loses 2.

Luftflotte Reich ignored a large 8th AF raid on rail yards, but attempted to defend the Vienna–Florisdorf refinery against the largest raid that the 15th AF ever dispatched against a single target. JG 3 and JG 300 were scrambled too late from their German bases and failed to make contact. The defence was left to seven Bf 109 squadrons flying from Veszprém, the principal Hungarian fighter base: the three Staffeln of the low-strength I./JG 53, which failed to make contact, and four Hungarian squadrons, which made a co-ordinated attack on 500 bombers from a staggered formation and claimed four B-24s and one P-51 for the loss of five Bf 109s and four pilots KIA. The B-24 group involved, the 461st BG, claimed 1-1-2 Messerschmitts and apparently lost no bombers. The 15th AF's losses totalled five bombers, one P-38 and one P-51, which collided with a Hungarian Bf 109.

6 November

8th Air Force Mission #704: 1,088 of 1,131 HBs (all BDs) target oil industry in W Germany – lose 5-0-228, claim 0. 722 of 802 escorts (all 15 FGs) claim 4, lose 5-1-?.

15th Air Force dispatches 554 B-24s + 220 B-17s, targets Vienna refineries, ordnance plant – lose 7, claim 0. Escort of 175 P-38s, 227 P-51s claims 4-2-1, loses 0.

Luftflotte Reich ignored a large-scale 8th AF bad-weather raid on the oil industry, although American escorts did encounter Kommando Nowotny jets and II. Jagdkorps and Jagddivision 3 tactical fighters. The RLV organisation attempted to field a respectable defence against the 15th AF, with even less success than on the previous day. Jagddivision 8 was reinforced with II./JG 51, which had spent most of 1944 battling partisans in the Balkans. Ten Staffeln scrambled from Veszprém and reached the bombers, but according to the American report did not attack aggressively and were driven off by one escort group, which claimed four Messerschmitts. II./JG 51 claimed one P-38, but lost two pilots KIA and a Staffelkapitän WIA. I./JG 53 made contact but reported no results. The Hungarians made no claims and lost one formation leader, who crashed due to an oxygen malfunction, and his wingman, who followed him into the ground. The Hungarian fighters were sent to the fast-approaching Eastern Front the next day to battle the Red Army and Air Force and were never again ordered up against a USAAF formation.

8 November

8th Air Force Mission #705: 290 of 690 1st BD B-17s + 2nd BD B-24s target Merseburg–Leuna o/i, Rheine rail yard – lose 3-0-100, claim 0. 799 of 890 escorts (all 15 FGs) claim 4-5-?, lose 11-2-?.

An 8th AF raid on Rheine was opposed by Kommando Nowotny, which did not reach the bombers on two missions but claimed one P-47 and three P-51s while losing its Kommandeur and three Me 262s. This proved to be Kommando Nowotny's last combat. Two III./JG 54 Staffeln, which had the mission of guarding the jets' Achmer and Hesepe airfields, also got involved and downed another P-47.

16 November

15th Air Force dispatches 513 B-24s + 208 B-17s, to attack Munich, Innsbruck rail yards – lose 6, claim 0. Escort of 183 P-38s, 220 P-51s claims 8-2-2, loses 1.

Luftflotte Reich did not attempt to intercept a large 15th AF raid on southern Germany. However, the *2º Gruppo Caccia* of the ANR in northern Italy made one of its infrequent forays against the withdrawing formations. Two squadrons each scrambled eight Bf 109Gs and, in separate combats, claimed four B-17s and two P-51s for

the loss of two KIA in their Messerschmitts. The Americans lost six bombers and one P-51 to all causes.

21 November

8th Air Force Mission #720: 1,149 of 1,291 HBs (all BDs) target Merseburg, Hamburg, Osnabrück o/i, TOT 1134-1154 – lose 25-8-567, claim 1-0-1. 858 of 964 escorts (15 FGs) claim 68-7-22, lose 15-?-?.

I. Jagdkorps attempted a full-scale defence against a bad-weather 8th AF raid on several important oil targets. Most Jagdgruppen were held on the ground until it was too late to intercept the bombers prior to bombing; apparently the I. Jagdkorps commander hoped either that the rain pelting their bases would stop or that the Americans would turn back. Most of the Luftwaffe formations emerged from the overcast sky to find the P-51s waiting for them. Some units reached the bombers, but all paid a heavy price. I./JG 1 claimed 12 B-17s and three P-51s, but lost 15 KIA or MIA, five WIA and 28 Fw 190s (half its strength) on its first mission since returning to the RLV force. III./JG 4 claimed one B17 and two P-51s, but lost one KIA, four WIA and eight Bf 109s on its last RLV mission before joining the rest of JG 4 in II. Jagdkorps on the western front. Several Jagddivision 3 Gruppen attempted to attack the withdrawing bombers, without noteworthy success. JG 300 and JG 301, the two 'bad-weather' Geschwader, had no more luck than their weather-challenged comrades. The Americans wrote off 33 bombers and 15 fighters after the mission; few of these were lost to Luftwaffe fighters, which, in contrast, lost 40 KIA or MIA, 24 WIA and 86 fighters.

Uffz. Heinz Bake sits on the wing of his IV.(Sturm)/JG 3 Fw 190A-8/R2 'Sturmbock' with his crew chief at Störmede in late November or early December. *(Smith)*

Axis defensive activity – 6 November 1944

Unit	Type	Gruppe up			Gruppe down		Claims	Losses				
		Base	No	Time	Base	Time		Dest	Dam	KIA	MIA	WIA
Luftflotte Reich												
I. Jagdkorps												
Jagddivision 2:												
Kdo Nowotny	Me 262A	Achmer		1045	Achmer	~1145	1 P-51	2	2	0	0	1
Jagddivision 8:												
II./JG 51	Bf 109G	Veszprém		~1130	Veszprém	~1300	1 P-38	3	1	2	0	1
I./JG 53	Bf 109G	Veszprém		~1130	Veszprém	~1300	0	1	0	0	0	0
101 JGr (Hungary)	Bf 109G	Veszprém		~1130	Veszprém	~1300	0	2	?	2	0	?

Luftwaffe defensive activity – 8 November 1944

Unit	Type	Gruppe up			Gruppe down		Claims	Losses				
		Base	No	Time	Base	Time		Dest	Dam	KIA	MIA	WIA
Luftflotte Reich												
I. Jagdkorps												
Jagddivision 2:												
III./JG 54	Fw 190D	Achmer, Hesepe		~0945	Achmer, Hesepe	~1110	1 P-47	0	0	0	0	0
2nd sorties	Fw 190D	Achmer, Hesepe		~1230	Achmer, Hesepe	~1345	0	0	0	0	0	0
Kdo Nowotny	Me 262A	Hesepe	2	~0945	Achmer	~1100	1 P-47	0	1	0	0	0
	Me 262A	Achmer	1	~0945	Achmer	~1100	1 P-51	0	0	0	0	0
2nd sorties	Me 262A	Achmer	3	~1230	Achmer	n/a	2 P-51	3	0	1	0	0

Axis defensive activity – 16 November 1944

Unit	Type	Gruppe up			Gruppe down		Claims	Losses				
		Base	No	Time	Base	Time		Dest	Dam	KIA	MIA	WIA
Luftflotte 2												
Jafü Oberitalien:												
2° Gr. Caccia	Bf 109G	Aviano	8	1200	Aviano	~1300	1 B-17, 2 P-51	0	0	0	0	0
(Italy)	Bf 109G	Aviano	8	~1245	Aviano	~1400	3 B-17	2	0	2	0	0

Fw. Eberhard Gzik of I./JG 300 sits on the cockpit sill of his Bf 109G-10 'Red 2' at Borkheide in the autumn. The fuselage band is rust-red, standard for the Geschwader at the time. The aircraft bears the name 'Rita'. *(Prien)*

PILOT'S ACCOUNT[3]
21 November 1944

Our Gruppe had just rejoined the Reich defence after rebuilding. Exactly four pilots in my 4. Staffel had flown missions as flight leaders; all of the others were young comrades who had just finished an abbreviated course at the fighter school. This morning the 'dicke Autos' [fat cars] were reported heading for Berlin. The weather was not at all 'fighter friendly': poor visibility and an almost solid cloud deck. Hptm. Ehlers led our 57 Fw 190s up from Greifswald at 1042 hours. We assembled under the cloud deck and were sent south in close formation through the layer to rendezvous with a Gruppe of 80 Bf 109s. The 4. Staffel as usual was at the rear of the formation. After an hour without sighting a single bomber, I spotted the contrails of fighters paralleling our course, about 1,000 metres above. I warned Hptm. Ehlers, 'Indians above us!' only to be told curtly to shut up and keep radio silence. I was then taken by surprise by Mustangs attacking directly from our rear, hidden by our own contrails. We were constrained by our tight formation. The Gruppe broke up and was chased as far south as Erfurt. My 'Red 1' was hit in a dogfight with the Mustangs, but I was fortunately able to make a smooth belly landing near Gotha in my burning Focke-Wulf and could walk away without injury.

Of the 57 aircraft to take off, 26 were shot down; 15 pilots lost their lives. The 4. Staffel suffered the worst. Eight of its 14 aircraft were shot down; four pilots were killed. Once again, it was made clear that, although the Luftwaffe could still put a useful number of aircraft into the air, its losses were ever increasing. For many of our young pilots, some only 19 years old, their first mission proved to be their last. They were nothing but cannon fodder, as was the rest of the fighter force.

Lt. Gerhard Hanf
Staffelkapitän, 4./JG 1

PILOT'S ACCOUNT[4]
21 November 1944

This was to be the first mission for JG 301 after three months off operations to rebuild. It was now equipped entirely with Fw 190A-8s and Fw 190A-9s and concentrated on airfields near Berlin. The bomber stream stretched west of Kassel, and JG 301 received the take-off order after it became clear that its target was the Merseburg–Bitterfeld industrial area. It soon became obvious that we had been ordered up too late. We were to assemble south of Gardelegen. The leading bombers were already south of us, and it would be hard to reach the ordered 8,000 metres in time to attack the stream; we wound up trailing it.

Visibility was only fair; there was no continuous cloud deck, but many clouds at various altitudes. We had just sighted the enemy south of Magdeburg when I./JG 301 and II./JG 301 were struck by a large P-51 formation. Casualties were high, especially among the inexperienced new pilots; the II./JG 301 Kommandeur was among the dead. III./JG 301, which was flying somewhat lower, avoided the attention of the Mustangs and continued on course in close formation. We soon saw bomber contrails, and Hptm. Fulda attempted to lead the formation in a head-on attack. Not only were the pilots of the Gruppe inexperienced in this tactic, the angle of attack was too great for any but the leading pilots to follow Fulda. A few pilots, including myself, broke away from the Gruppe and attempted a more familiar rear attack from slightly above. My heavy armament did the job, and both inner engines of my target quickly burst into flames; the bomber dropped from the formation trailing heavy smoke. The American escorts then approached from all directions. We broke off the attack on the bombers and fought for our lives. I lost my wingman, but escaped and landed on Burg near Magdeburg after almost two hours in the air.

Fw. Willi Reschke
10./JG 301

Luftwaffe defensive activity – 21 November 1944

Unit	Type	Gruppe up			Gruppe down		Claims	Losses				
		Base	No	Time	Base	Time		Dest	Dam	KIA	MIA	WIA
Luftflotte Reich												
I. Jagdkorps												
Jagddivision 1:												
I./JG 1	Fw 190A	Greifswald	57	1042	Greifswald, Gotha	1240	10 B-17, 3 P-51, 2 B-17 HSS	28	7	11	4	5
IV.(Sturm)/JG 3	Fw 190A	Störmede	49	1215	Störmede	1315	0	0	1	0	0	0
I./JG 4	Bf 109G	Darmstadt–Griesheim		~1100	Darmstadt–Griesheim	~1200	0	2	1	0	0	0
III./JG 4	Bf 109K	Erfurt	23	1100	Erfurt, Esperstedt	1155	1 B-17, 2 P-51	8	0	1	0	4
Stab/JG 300	Fw 190A	Löbnitz	*178	1030	Jüterbog	1225	0	0	0	0	0	0
I./JG 300	Bf 109G	Borkheide	—	1030	Borkheide	1225	0	4	8	2	0	1
II.(Sturm)/JG 300	Fw 190A	Löbnitz	—	1030	Löbnitz	1225	0	2	2	0	0	0
III./JG 300	Bf 109G	Jüterbog	—	1030	Jüterbog	1225	1 B-17, 1 P-47, 1 P-51	1	0	0	0	0
IV./JG 300	Bf 109G	Reinsdorf	—	1038	Reinsdorf	1225	0	4	5	2	0	2
I./JG 301	Fw 190A	Salzwedel	**155	1055	Salzwedel, Magdeburg–Ost	1250	2 P-51	13	8	8	0	4
II./JG 301	Fw 190A	Sachau	—	~1055	Sachau	~1150	2 P-51	10	3	3	1	3
III./JG 301	Fw 190A	Stendal	—	1055	Stendal, Burg	1150	1 B-17	0	3	0	0	1
Jagddivision 3:												
I./JG 3	Bf 109G	Werl	35	1213	Werl	1315	0	1	0	0	0	0
III./JG 26	Bf 109K	Plantlünne	33	1214	Plantlünne	1330	1 P-51	0	0	0	0	0
I./JG 27	Bf 109G	Rheine		0950	Rheine	1000	0	1	0	0	1	0
II./JG 27	Bf 109G	Hopsten		1037	Hopsten	~1200	0	7	1	3	2	1
IV./JG 54	Fw 190A	Hopsten		~1040	Hopsten	~1200	0	5	0	2	0	3

*178 total JG 300 sorties   **155 total JG 301 sorties

22 November

15th Air Force dispatches 468 B-24s + 214 B-17s, targets Munich rail yards, bomb numerous communications targets and targets of opportunity – lose 13, claim 0-0-1. Escort of 179 P-38s, 157 P-51s claims 0, loses 1.

Various 15th AF bomber and escort formations were tracked by small Luftwaffe formations that did not close with the Americans, a fairly common phenomenon that cannot be documented from the existing German records. Several jets did pass through a P-38 formation, after which one 14th FG Lightning turned up missing. The Luftwaffe unit involved cannot be identified.

26 November

8th Air Force Mission #725: 1,037 of 1,137 HBs (all BDs) target Misburg o/i, TOT 1137-1219; Bielefeld rail viaduct, TOT 1209-1238; Hamm rail yard – lose 34-8-299, claim 16-11-11. 668 of 732 fighters (15 FGs) escort, claim 114-3-31, lose 9-2- 0.

The 8th AF dispatched another large-scale bad-weather raid to the central German oil installations. The I. Jagdkorps ordered a large-scale defensive effort. The RLV bases were clear at ground level. Although none of the Sturmgruppen was ordered to participate, six other Jagdgruppen got up in time to form two Gefechtsverbände and reach the bombers prior to bombing. One formation was led by the JG 301 Kommodore and contained the three JG 301 Gruppen, all freshly equipped with Fw 190s. It was directed to an unescorted B-24 Pulk and downed 21 Liberators, most from the 491st BG, before Mustangs arrived to begin a slaughter of the green Focke-Wulf pilots. The other Verband, led by the JG 1 Kommodore and comprising I./JG 1, II./JG 1 and III./JG 6, downed a few more B-24s before P-51s could put an end to their attacks. Nine Jagddivision 3 Gruppen were also scrambled against the bomber streams, but could not get through the escorts and accomplished little. The Americans wrote off 42 bombers and 11 escorts after the mission, a high number for the period, but Luftflotte Reich suffered the ruinous loss of 62 KIA or MIA, 32 WIA and 122 fighters.

This poor copy print shows I./JG 1 taking off from Greifswald in November. Order of take-off is Stab, 3., 2., 1., 4. Staffel. *(Berger)*

Aircraft of I./JG 1, possibly photographed at Greifswald in November. Note the absence of RLV bands. *(Mol)*

PILOT'S ACCOUNT[5]
26 November 1944

The morning fog burnt off, and the first reports came in of an enemy formation over the Deutsche Bucht. 30-minute readiness was followed by 15-minute readiness, at which the aircraft were taxied to their take-off positions. The 120 Fw 190A-8s and Fw 190A-9s of the Geschwader waited for the take-off order; for III./JG 301, this came at 1140 hours. After take-off, the Gruppe climbed while flying due west to Planquadrat FC, where we met the rest of the Geschwader. The message came over our headsets, 'Fat Cars with many Indians approaching the area Hannover–Brunswick; increase speed and climb to 7,500 metres.' After closing up, the Geschwader was given a new course of 240°. Soon we could see the broad contrails of the bomber Pulks on the horizon; not to be overlooked were the numerous thin streams from the escorts. After a few minutes, escort fighters passed us to the left, quite a distance away. Major Aufhammer gave the order, 'Drop tanks!'

The P-51s were not ready for an attack at this moment. They were probably surprised to see such a strong German fighter formation directly in front of them. But the situation changed very quickly. I./JG 301 and most of II./JG 301 were soon involved in heavy combat. Many pilots of the Geschwader were not prepared for combat with enemy fighters; some of the Schwarmführer [flight leaders] were retrained bomber pilots, and most of the wingmen were youngsters right out of fighter pilot training.

The air battles quickly spread over the entire area between Hannover and Brunswick and were conducted with mutual bitterness. III./JG 301, which was designated a 'heavy Gruppe' and was expected always to attack the bombers, escaped the American fighters and found itself behind a B24 Pulk, which was then attacked from directly to the rear and 500 metres above. We had formed our attack wedges on the approach. Each wedge contained two flights echeloned back to left and right and was led by two experienced Schwarmführer who had flown with I./JG 302 in southern Germany. During the attack, the rear aircraft in the wedges moved up almost into line abreast formation, so that each wingman became an attacker. The first seconds of the attack stretched our nerves almost to the breaking point. The pilot behind his control stick, with thumb and index finger on the weapon buttons, could not avoid glancing over the Revi at the bomber. Despite the incoming tracers he had to find the nerves to hold down his fire to a range of 400 metres. At this point, the tension broke. Individual tactics differed among the pilots. Some first tried to knock out the gun turrets; others fired at the two inner engines.

Holes appeared in the Liberator formation during the first attack. Burning bombers and pieces crashed below. The radio conversation in such situations can scarcely be repeated. But the pilots of III./JG 301 understood the order to form up for a second attack on the remains of the bomber Pulk. After the second attack there were only a handful of Liberators, some damaged, still holding their course. The magazines of many fighters were now empty, but there were still

the escorts to contend with. These almost always showed up after an attack on the bombers. We were always in an inferior position, from which it was not easy to escape in one piece. After such an air battle there was no attempt to re-form the Geschwader. Some machines could reach their home fields, but most had to make intermediate landings on strange fields. When all of the survivors had reported in, it was determined that 26 pilots were killed or remained missing; 13 had survived with severe injuries. These were the heaviest one-day losses JG 301 ever sustained; on its first two missions since returning to combat, the Geschwader lost 60 pilots – half its strength.

Fw. Willi Reschke
10./JG 301

Luftwaffe defensive activity – 26 November 1944

Unit	Type	Gruppe up			Gruppe down		Claims	Losses				
		Base	No	Time	Base	Time		Dest	Dam	KIA	MIA	WIA
Luftflotte Reich												
I. Jagdkorps												
Jagddivision 1:												
Stab/JG 1	Fw 190A	Greifswald		~1120	Greifswald	~1300	0*	1	0	1	0	0
I./JG 1	Fw 190A	Greifswald	32	1120	Greifswald	~1300	6 B-24	2	3	1	0	0
II./JG 1	Fw 190A	Tutow		~1120	Tutow	~1300	9 B-24	12	1	10	0	3
III./JG 6	Bf 109G	Schwerin–Gorries	40	~1120	Schwerin–Gorries	~1300	1 B-24, 1 P-51	12	2	6	0	6
Stab/JG 301	Fw 190A	Stendal		~1140	Stendal	~1315	0**	1	0	1	0	0
I./JG 301	Fw 190A	Salzwedel		1149	Salzwedel, Hildesheim	1316	3 B-17, 12 B-24, 3 P-51	19	2	13	0	3
II./JG 301	Fw 190A	Sachau		~1140	Sachau	~1315	4 B-17, 14 B-24, 4 P-51	20	3	9	0	6
III./JG 301	Fw 190A	Stendal		1140	Stendal	1319	37 B-24, 3 P-51	11	9	4	0	5
Jagddivision 3:												
I./JG 3	Bf 109G	Paderborn		~1030	Paderborn	~1200	0	5	2	3	0	0
I./JG 26	Fw 190A	Fürstenau	5	1024	Fürstenau, Varrelbusch	1200	1 P-51	0	0	0	0	0
III./JG 26	Bf 109K	Plantlünne		~1030	Plantlünne	~1200	1 P-47	1	1	1	0	1
I./JG 27	Bf 109G	Rheine		1010	Rheine, Paderborn	1210	1 P-51	8	1	2	0	1
II./JG 27	Bf 109G	Hopsten		1015	Hopsten	~1200	0**	6	4	2	0	4
III./JG 27	Bf 109K	Großenhain		~1015	Großenhain	~1200	0***	11	4	3	1	2
IV./JG 27	Bf 109G	Achmer		~1015	Achmer	~1200	0****	9	4	3	0	1
IV./JG 54	Fw 190A	Vörden		~1015	Vörden	~1200	0*****	4	1	2	0	0

*Stab/JG 1: + 1 B-17 claim undocumented

**Stab/JG 301: + 1 B-17 claim undocumented

***II./JG 27: + 1 P-51 claim undocumented

****III./JG 27: + 1 P-51 claim undocumented

*****IV./JG 27: + 2 B-17, 1 P-47, 4 P-51 claims undocumented

27 November

8th Air Force Mission #727: 483 of 530 HBs (all BDs) target Bingen and Offenburg rail yards, TOT 1216-1247 – lose 0-0-69, claim 0 (no air opposition). 267 of 277 fighters (5 FGs) escorts claim 0, lose 3-1-0. 460 of 493 fighters (10 FGs) dispatched to bomb and strafe 4 oil centres in north and central Germany, claim 98-4-11, lose 12-0-0.

The 8th AF mounted a successful spoof raid in which 10 fighter groups flew above the overcast on a course and in a formation simulating a bomber raid on the central German oil targets. Only one of these groups carried bombs. I. Jagdkorps was fooled completely and ordered a maximum-strength interception. JG 300 and JG 301 emerged from the overcast to find only Mustangs and Thunderbolts, which slaughtered the hapless pilots of the two Geschwader that now formed the heart of the RLV force, costing them 27 KIA or MIA, 13 WIA and 50 fighters. In the meantime, the heavy bombers, escorted by the five remaining 8th AF fighter groups, bombed two west German rail yards without encountering a single Luftwaffe fighter. II. Jagdkorps was ordered to intercept the withdrawing bombers and scrambled seven of its Gruppen, but the reduced escort was sufficient to keep them from the bombers and cost the tactical units 10 KIA, six WIA and 30 fighters. For the day, the Americans wrote off 16 fighters and no bombers; Luftflotte Reich lost a total of 37 KIA or MIA, 19 WIA and 80 fighters.

30 November

8th Air Force Mission #731: 1,219 of 1,281 HBs (all BDs) target Merseburg, Böhlen, other oil targets (B-17s – TOT 1306-1437), Neunkirchen and Homburg rail yards (B-24s – TOT 1239-1255) – lose 29-12-616, claim 0 (no air opposition). 895 of 972 8th AF fighters (15 FGs) + 98 9th AF P-38s + 18 9th AF P-51s escort, claim 4-2-0, lose 3-2-0.

RM Göring ordered Luftflotte Reich to defend against yet another 8th AF maximum-strength raid on the central German oil targets, despite continued bad weather and its recent heavy losses. JG 301 was kept on the ground, and only two JG 300 Gruppen scrambled. Results were predictable. The bad-weather fighters never reached the bombers and lost three KIA, two WIA and nine fighters, some to the escorts and some in bad-weather bailouts. The Americans wrote off five fighters and 41 bombers for operational reasons and Flak damage. It is worth noting that Flak was now a much greater hazard to American bombers than were the Luftwaffe fighters. Many 88-mm dual-purpose artillery units had been withdrawn from the contracting battle fronts and concentrated in antiaircraft batteries around the Reich's high-priority strategic targets.

Lt. Karl Spenst stands in front of a 'Black 10', his usual II.(Sturm)/JG 300 Fw 190A-8, on 27 November. He has adopted the Berlin bear as his emblem. (Rosch)

Luftwaffe defensive activity – 27 November 1944

Unit	Type	Gruppe up			Gruppe down		Claims	Losses				
		Base	No	Time	Base	Time		Dest	Dam	KIA	MIA	WIA
Luftflotte Reich												
I. Jagdkorps												
Jagddivision 1:												
I./JG 1	Fw 190A	Greifswald		~1150	Greifswald	~1350	0	0	1	0	0	0
II./JG 1	Fw 190A	Tutow		~1150	Tutow	~1350	0	1	0	0	0	0
Stab/JG 300	Fw 190A	Löbnitz		1155	Jüterbog	1352	0	0	0	0	0	0
I./JG 300	Bf 109G	Borkheide		1150	Borkheide	~1350	0	9	1	3	0	0
II.(Sturm)/JG 300	Fw 190A	Löbnitz		1150	Löbnitz	~1350	2 P-51	12	2	6	1	4
III./JG 300	Bf 109G	Jüterbog		1150	Jüterbog	~1350	3 P-51	12	0	7	0	4
IV./JG 300	Bf 109G	Reinsdorf		1150	Reinsdorf	~1350	1 P-51	3	1	1	0	1
Stab/JG 301	Fw 190A	Stendal		~1150	Stendal	~1350	0	1	0	1	0	0
I./JG 301	Fw 190A	Salzwedel		1154	Salzwedel	~1350	0	8	3	4	0	4
II./JG 301	Fw 190A	Sachau		~1150	Sachau	~1350	0	4	0	4	0	0
Jagddivision 3:												
I./JG 3	Bf 109G	Paderborn		~1115	Paderborn	~1315	0	3	3	0	0	0
IV.(Sturm)/JG 3	Fw 190A	Störmede		1116	Störmede, Wunstorf	1315	0	1	2	0	0	0
I./JG 26	Fw 190A	Fürstenau	5	1105	Fürstenau	1240	0	1	0	0	0	1
III./JG 26	Bf 109K	Plantlünne		1105	Plantlünne	1205	0*	6	0	2	0	2
I./JG 27	Bf 109G	Rheine		1100	Rheine, Hopsten	1220	0**	0	0	0	0	0
II./JG 27	Bf 109G	Hopsten		~1100	Hopsten	~1230	0	0	2	0	0	0
III./JG 27	Bf 109K	Großenhain		~1100	Großenhain	~1230	0	4	0	3	0	0
IV./JG 27	Bf 109G	Achmer		~1100	Achmer	~1230	0***	11	1	2	0	2
IV./JG 54	Fw 190A	Vörden		~1100	Vörden	~1230	0	4	1	3	0	1

*III./JG 26: + 2 P-51 claims undocumented

**I./JG 27: + 1 P-51 claim undocumented

***IV./JG 27: + 1 P-47, 2 P-51 claims undocumented

Luftwaffe defensive activity – 30 November 1944

Unit	Type	Gruppe up			Gruppe down		Claims	Losses				
		Base	No	Time	Base	Time		Dest	Dam	KIA	MIA	WIA
Luftflotte Reich												
I. Jagdkorps												
Jagddivision 1:												
I./JG 300	Bf 109G	Borkheide	9	1230	Borkheide	~1330	0	5	2	2	0	1
II.(Sturm)/JG 300	Fw 190A	Löbnitz		1245	Löbnitz	~1345	0	4	3	1	0	1

December 1944

Luftflotte Reich piston-engine fighters could accomplish next to nothing against the USSTAF, given the Americans' enormous quantitative and qualitative superiority. The basic tactical formation, the Gefechtsverband, had been devised to put a large number of fighters into contact with weak parts of the bomber streams. It was now clear that it was too slow to form up and too vulnerable during this process. In the Sturmgruppe-based Verbände, the Bf 109 escorts were unable to protect the heavy Fw 190 assault fighters for an entire mission. Galland's office issued a circular stating that the bombers were henceforth to be attacked by single, fast-climbing Jagdgruppen using hit-and-run methods, thus reverting to the tactics of mid-1943.

Erasing the quantitative deficit was beyond hope. The Luftwaffe still planned to restore qualitative superiority with jet and rocket fighters, but these were extremely slow to reach full operational status. There were now five Me 262 fighter Gruppen, all in south-western Germany, where they were allowed to shadow 15th AF bomber streams without attacking them. Training of the ex-bomber pilots of the three KG(J) 54 Gruppen was proceeding very slowly. The two operational I. Jagdkorps jet fighter units, III./JG 7 and III./EJG 2, were now attacking single reconnaissance aircraft with success. No jet fighters were in position to attack the huge 8th AF streams coming from England. Jagdgeschwader 7 continued to fail operational readiness inspections, and before the end of the year, Galland removed Steinhoff from command and promoted Major Theodor Weissenberger to the position. The single Gruppe containing rocket-propelled Me 163 fighters, I./JG 400, was well positioned, but struggled constantly to find enough rocket fuel to fly missions at all. The future of the rocket fighters was dim, but the Luftwaffe high command had plans for a full Me 163 Geschwader, and Galland even named its Kommodore.

In mid-December JG 1, JG 3 and JG 11 transferred from Jagddivision 1 to Jagddivision 3 or II. Jagdkorps and flew to bases near the western German border. They were needed for Hitler's last great offensive in the west, Operation WACHT AM RHEIN (Watch on the Rhine), the Battle of the Ardennes, known to the Allies as the Battle of the Bulge. They would become tactical fighters and never return to Jagddivision 1,

the principal RLV operational command, which now contained only JG 300, JG 301 and I./JG 400. Galland stated in his postwar interrogation, 'With the Ardennes offensive, the history of the organised air defence of the Reich comes to an end.'

Oberleutnant, later Major, Theodor Weissenberger. A Bf 110 and Bf 109 pilot on the Northern Front with an initial reputation for indiscipline, he commanded I./JG 5 and II./JG 5 on various fronts in 1944, adding to his reputation as a combat leader with each posting. He trained on the Me 262 in late 1944, became Gruppenkommandeur of I./JG 7 in November and succeeded Steinhoff as JG 7 Kommodore in late December, leading the unit until the end of the war. He was credited with eight victories (seven B-17s and a P-51) while flying the Me 262. *(Author's collection)*

2 December

8th Air Force Mission #734: 277 of 455 HBs (1st BD + 2nd BD) target Oberlahnstein, Bingen rail yards – lose 11-0-4, claim 2-1-2. 569 of 604 fighters (11 FGs) escort and sweep, claim 32-2-6, lose 4-2.

I. Jagdkorps declined the opportunity to defend the Silesian oil targets from a 15th AF attack and ordered three Geschwader formations up against an 8th AF attack on west German rail yards. The JG 1 and JG 301 Kommodoren were unable to assemble their Gefechtsverbände and were soon recalled to base. JG 3 formed properly and was guided to a B-24 Pulk. As I./JG 3 and II./JG 3 fought off the escorts, IV.(Sturm)/JG 3 made a classic Sturmangriff that downed nine 392nd BG Liberators. The escorts, primarily 56th FG P-47s, then downed 25 fighters, costing the Geschwader 16 KIA or MIA and seven WIA for the loss of one Thunderbolt and pilot. For the day, the 8th AF wrote off 34 bombers and six fighters; I. Jagdkorps lost 25 KIA or MIA, eight WIA and 36 fighters. The days of the Sturmangriff were numbered. Only one more Sturmangriff would be made by a Gefechtsverband with the standard mid-1944 configuration of one Fw 190 Sturmgruppe escorted by two or more Bf 109 Begleitgruppen.

5 December

8th Air Force Mission #738: 427 of 451 1st BD + 3rd BD B-17s target Berlin/Tegel ordnance works, TOT 1043-1123; 120 of 135 2nd BD B-24s target Munich rail yard – lose 12-0-179, claim 0. 811 of 901 fighters (15 FGs) escort, claim 91-7-28, lose 17-2.

RAF Bomber Command dispatches 385 Halifaxes, 100 Lancasters, 12 Mosquitos to bomb Soest rail yards, escorted by Fighter Command Spitfires + Mustangs – claim 0, lose 2 Halifaxes (none to fighters), 1 Spitfire.

The 8th AF sent its B-17s to bomb the important Tegel ammunition works in Berlin, while the B-24s were sent to the Munich rail yards. The JG 1, JG 300 and JG 301 Gefechtsverbände all formed up and headed for Berlin, a higher-priority target, but all were dispersed by the Berlin Flak and/or American escorts before reaching the bombers. JG 1 lost 26 KIA or MIA, 15 WIA and 51 fighters on what proved to be its worst day of the war. The Americans wrote off 12 bombers and 19 escorts. The situation was desperate enough for Luftflotte Reich to send up I./KG 51, a pure Me 262 bomber unit and thus never in the RLV force, with orders to attack the escorts. The bomber pilots had no luck against the escorts, but did claim one B-17 without loss.

RAF Bomber Command ordered a large force of its heavy bombers to bomb the Soest rail yards by day, shielded from the attention of Jagddivision 1 by the American raid on Berlin. II. Jagdkorps and Jagddivision 3 could not pass up a chance to attack an RAF bomber formation and sent up seven Jagdgruppen. These could not penetrate the heavy screen of RAF Spitfires and Mustangs, however, and lost eight KIA, four WIA and 14 fighters while downing one Spitfire. Luftflotte Reich lost 56 KIA or MIA, 23 WIA and 94 fighters against the two Allied bomber forces while claiming seven B-17s, 31 P-51s and three Spitfires. The confirmation process broke down before any of these claims made it through the system, but it appears that only one bomber and 11 fighters were in fact shot down by Luftwaffe fighters; the claims are only an indication of the intensity of the fighting.

6 December

15th Air Force dispatches 545 B-24s + 257 B-17s to bomb communications targets in Austria, Hungary, Yugoslavia in support of Soviets – lose 4, claim 7-3-1. Escort of 102 P-38s, 123 P-51s claims 1, loses 1.

Luftflotte Reich ignored both the 8th AF and 15th AF today: the first owing to bad weather and high recent losses; the second for lack of resources in the area. However, one 15th AF B-24 group, the 464th, lost four bombers in an attack that exemplified the unpredictability and constant danger of the European skies. II./JG 51, an Ostfront Bf 109 Gruppe, broke from the clouds and attacked a circling Pulk from the rear. The Gruppe made several more attacks before P-38s arrived and chased the Messerschmitts away, downing one. The B-24 gunners were slow to respond, but on their return to Foggia claimed 7-1-3 Messerschmitts, very close to the actual losses of five fighters and four pilots. Crews from neighboring B-24 units, which drove off attacks on themselves and sustained no losses, blamed inattention by the 464th BG crews for the debacle. No information on the II./JG 51 mission times, base or controller is available and therefore no mission list is included for this date.

Luftwaffe defensive activity – 2 December 1944

Unit	Type	Gruppe up			Gruppe down		Claims	Losses				
		Base	No	Time	Base	Time		Dest	Dam	KIA	MIA	WIA
Luftflotte Reich												
I. Jagdkorps												
Jagddivision 1:												
Stab/JG 1	Fw 190A	Greifswald	4	1222	Greifswald	~1330	n/c	0	0	0	0	0
I./JG 1	Fw 190A	Greifswald	29	1222	Greifswald	1351	n/c	0	4	0	0	0
II./JG 1	Fw 190A	Tutow		1230	Tutow	~1330	n/c	0	0	0	0	0
III./JG 1	Bf 109G	Anklam		1230	Anklam	~1330	n/c	0	3	0	0	0
Stab/JG 3	Fw 190A	Paderborn		1140	Paderborn	~1320	0	1	0	0	1	0
I./JG 3	Bf 109G	Paderborn	16	1140	Paderborn	~1320	2 B-24, 1 P-47	11	3	8	0	3
III./JG 3	Bf 109G	Schachten		1115	Schachten	~1320	1 B-24, 1 P-47	6	2	4	0	2
IV.(Sturm)/JG 3	Fw 190A	Störmede		1130	Störmede	1318	22 B-24	8	5	4	0	2
Stab/JG 300	Fw 190A	Löbnitz		~1130	Jüterbog	~1330	n/c	0	0	0	0	0
I./JG 300	Bf 109G	Borkheide	18	~1130	Borkheide	~1330	0	2	1	2	0	0
II.(Sturm)/JG 300	Fw 190A	Löbnitz		1132	Löbnitz	~1330	n/c	0	0	0	0	0
III./JG 300	Bf 109G	Jüterbog	37	~1130	Jüterbog	1345	n/c	0	0	0	0	0
Stab/JG 301	Fw 190A	Stendal		~1140	Stendal	~1340	n/c	0	0	0	0	0
I./JG 301	Fw 190A	Salzwedel		~1140	Salzwedel	~1340	n/c	0	0	0	0	0
II./JG 301	Fw 190A	Sachau		~1140	Sachau	~1340	n/c	0	0	0	0	0
III./JG 301	Fw 190A	Stendal		1140	Stendal	1344	n/c	0	0	0	0	0
Jagddivision 2:												
III./JG 27	Bf 109G	Achmer		1115	Achmer	1210	0	0	0	0	0	0
LwKdo West												
II. Jagdkorps												
Jafü Mittelrhein:												
I./JG 4	Bf 109G	Finsterwalde		~1200	Finsterwalde	~1400	2 P-51	6	1	5	0	1
III./JG 4	Bf 109G	Biblis		1130	Biblis	1328	n/c	0	1	0	0	0
IV./JG 4	Bf 109G	Finsterwalde		~1200	Finsterwalde	~1400	0	2	1	1	0	0

12 December

RAF Bomber Command: 136 of 140 No. 3 Group Lancasters target Witten steel plant, TOT 1402-11 – lose 8, claim 5-0-1. 79 of 90 No. 11 Group Mustang escorts claim 5-2-5, lose 1.

Luftflotte Reich ignored raids by the two American air forces, but ordered Jagddivision 3 to send fighters up against an RAF Bomber Command day raid – these were always considered easier targets, and attacking them was good for morale. Two Bf 109 Gruppen, I/JG 3 and IV/JG 27, were scrambled. They made independent approaches below the solid cloud deck; both found the small Lancaster formation entirely without escort and made several damaging passes before the tardy arrival of RAF Mustangs, which had probably been battling two other JG 27 Gruppen in the area. Nine Messerschmitts were shot down, killing five pilots, but not until eight Lancasters had gone down.

PILOT'S ACCOUNT[6]
12 December 1944

The 20 Bf 109G-14s of IV./JG 27 took off at 1230 hours into cloudy skies, assembled in a great circuit over our Achmer field and flew beneath the continuous cloud deck on a southwestern course toward the reported bomber formation. Over the Ruhr, the clouds thinned enough so that we could get our bearings. Hptm. Heinz Dudeck, the Kommandeur, split the formation into Staffeln and ordered each Staffel and the Stabsschwarm to fly through the 2,500-metre thick cloud deck independently and assemble above it. We climbed in tight spirals and emerged to see a mixed Liberator-Lancaster formation [sic] in the distance. Making use of the irregular upper surface of the cloud deck for cover, Hptm. Dudeck brought the Stabsschwarm in behind a spread-apart Lancaster formation so that each pilot had an enemy plane in front of him. I came under heavy fire and fired back at my bomber's turret. I then fired at the right wing until both of its engines caught on fire, but continued to run. Then I fired a long burst at the fuselage with all weapons. There was a sudden explosion between the two starboard engines. The bomber exploded in a gigantic fireball, from which I was showered with a cloud of wreckage. With a burst of thunder, my canopy flew away, and I could see a hole in my right wing. But the engine ran completely normally, and the 'Beule' ['Bump' – the Bf 109G] reacted normally to all the controls, although the wind howled painfully in my ears. I dove through the clouds and saw a lone Bf 109, which I called over the radio without getting an answer. I nevertheless formed up on him, and we flew together to Achmer. After landing, I discovered that my departing canopy had taken my radio antenna with it. The missing canopy and hole in the wing left my mechanic shaking his head.

Obfw. Heinrich Bartels [the leading Experte in the Gruppe] had landed before me and came up to me in the command post. 'Was that you in "Chevron 4", who flew through the exploding four-engine? I'll write you an eyewitness report right now. Congratulations on the victory!' It was my first. The Gruppe adjutant wanted to open some brandy, but the staff doctor forbade it. We were nonetheless in a good mood. Bartels came back with his report and awarded me a special recognition. From now on I would be allowed to call him 'Hein'.

There were many reasons for congratulations on this day. We had shot down a number of bombers, most significantly the 'Expertenmaschine' in the lead, after which the formation jettisoned its bombs and missed its target. And all of Hptm. Dudeck's planes had returned to Achmer. In those December days that was extraordinary.

Fhr. Gottfried Zils
Stab IV./JG 27

17 December

15th Air Force dispatches 464 B-24s + 194 B-17s to attack Moravska–Ostrava, Blechhammer oil targets, rail targets in S Germany – lose 20, claim 20-2-1. Escort of 201 P-38s + 227 P-51s claims 23-3-6, loses 5.

Jagddivision 1 was required to reinforce II. Jagdkorps and Jagddivision 3 for the Ardennes offensive, leaving it with only two Jagdgeschwader, JG 300 and JG 301, to conduct RLV missions by day. JG 300 was used to spring a nasty surprise on the 15th Air Force, whose attacks on the Silesian synthetic oil plants had rarely encountered serious air opposition. Today, JG 300 put its 'bad weather' credentials to the test by scrambling from its bases in central Germany, forming up and flying southeast in almost unbroken cloud to intercept an unescorted part of the B-24 stream before it dropped its bombs. II.(Sturm)/JG 300 made a Sturmangriff from the rear, assisted by III./JG 300 from the flanks. At least 15 B-24s went down under this attack, most from the 461st BG. The escorts then arrived, and the slaughter of the German fighters began. JG 300 lost 20 KIA, five WIA and 40 fighters. The Americans lost a total of 20 bombers and five escorts.

Fw 190A-8 'Roter Hahn' {red rooster] of II.(Sturm)/JG 300, photographed in Germany in late 1944. Fw. Hannes Thies abandoned it on Holzkirchen on 30 April 1945. *(Crow)*

18 December

15th Air Force dispatches 430 B-24s + 225 B-17s to attack Moravska–Ostrava, Blechhammer, Odertal, Vienna oil targets – lose 19-?-?, claim 2-1-4. Escort of 212 P-38s + 227 P-51s claims 1, loses 0.

The RLV units were rested today. 8th AF attacks on communications and tactical targets in western Germany were entirely unopposed in the air. A 15th AF B-17 formation targeting the Silesian oil targets

Luftwaffe defensive activity – 5 December 1944

Unit	Type	Gruppe up			Gruppe down		Claims	Losses				
		Base	No	Time	Base	Time		Dest	Dam	KIA	MIA	WIA
Luftflotte Reich												
I. Jagdkorps												
Jagddivision 1:												
Stab/JG 1	Fw 190A	Greifswald	4	1015	Greifswald	~1200	0	0	0	0	0	0
I./JG 1	Fw 190A	Greifswald	38	1017	Greifswald	~1200	8 P-51	20	4	5	2	11
II./JG 1	Fw 190A	Tutow		~1015	Tutow	~1200	6 P-51	18	0	12	2	3
III./JG 1	Bf 109G	Anklam		1016	Anklam	~1200	1 P-51	13	1	3	2	1
I./JG 3	Bf 109G	Paderborn		~1200	Paderborn	~1330	0	2	0	2	0	0
Stab/JG 11	Fw 190A	Wunstorf	4	1210	Wunstorf	~1245	3 P-51	0	0	0	0	0
Stab/JG 300	Fw 190A	Löbnitz		1010	Jüterbog	~1200	2 B-17, 1 P-51	0	0	0	0	0
I./JG 300	Bf 109G	Borkheide		1010	Borkheide	~1200	0	0	8	0	0	0
II.(Sturm)/JG 300	Fw 190A	Löbnitz		1010	Löbnitz	~1200	0	3	1	1	0	2
III./JG 300	Bf 109G	Mark Zwuschen		1010	Mark Zwuschen	~1200	1 B-17, 1 P-51	0	0	0	0	0
IV./JG 300	Bf 109G	Reinsdorf		1010	Reinsdorf	~1200	1 P-51	1	2	1	0	0
Stab/JG 301	Fw 190A	Stendal		~1000	Stendal	~1130	2 P-51	2	0	0	0	0
I./JG 301	Fw 190A	Salzwedel		1003	Salzwedel, Prenzlau	1130	1 P-51	4	1	4	0	1
II./JG 301	Fw 190A	Sachau		~1000	Sachau	~1130	1 B-17, 4 P-51	7	0	7	0	0
III./JG 301	Fw 190A	Stendal		~1000	Stendal	~1130	1 B-17, 3 P-51	10	2	5	2	2
Jagddivision 3:												
I./JG 26	Fw 190A	Fürstenau	5	1325	Fürstenau	1345	1 B-17	0	0	0	0	0
I./JG 27	Bf 109G	Rheine		1055	Rheine	~1215	1 Spitfire	2	2	1	0	0
II./JG 27	Bf 109G	Hopsten		~1100	Hopsten	~1215	1 Spitfire	5	0	3	0	1
III./JG 27	Bf 109K	Großenhain		1055	Großenhain	1215	0	1	0	0	0	0
IV./JG 27	Bf 109G	Achmer		1055	Achmer, Wunstorf	1210	1 Spitfire	3	0	2	0	1
IV./JG 54	Fw 190A	Vörden		~1100	Vörden	~1230	0	1	0	1	0	0
I./KG 51	Me 262	Hopsten	7	1105	Hopsten	1220	1 B-17	0	0	0	0	0
LwKdo West												
II. Jagdkorps												
Jafü Mittelrhein:												
III./JG 4	Bf 109G	Biblis		~1100	Biblis	~1230	0	1	1	0	0	1
IV./JG 4	Bf 109G	Finsterwalde		~1100	Finsterwalde	~1230	0	1	2	1	0	0

Luftwaffe defensive activity – 12 December 1944

Unit	Type	Gruppe up			Gruppe down		Claims	Losses				
		Base	No	Time	Base	Time		Dest	Dam	KIA	MIA	WIA
Luftflotte Reich												
I. Jagdkorps												
Jagddivision 3:												
I./JG 3	Bf 109G	Paderborn		1230	Paderborn	~1430	13 Lancaster, 1 Mustang	5	1	4	0	0
I./JG 27	Bf 109G	Rheine		1310	Rheine	1430	1 Mustang	3	1	1	0	1
III./JG 27	Bf 109G	Hesepe		~1230	Hesepe	~1430	1 Mustang	0	0	0	0	0
IV./JG 27	Bf 109G	Achmer	20	1230	Achmer	1434	5 Lancaster, 3 Lancaster HSS	1	0	0	0	0

Luftwaffe defensive activity – 17 December 1944

Unit	Type	Gruppe up			Gruppe down		Claims	Losses				
		Base	No	Time	Base	Time		Dest	Dam	KIA	MIA	WIA
Luftflotte Reich												
I. Jagdkorps												
Jagddivision 1:												
Jafü Oberschlesien:												
Stab/JG 300	Fw 190A	Jüterbog		1045	Jüterbog	~1230	0	1	0	0	0	0
I./JG 300	Bf 109G	Borkheide		1030	Borkheide	~1230	0	2	4	0	0	0
II.(Sturm)/JG 300	Fw 190A	Löbnitz		1045	Löbnitz	~1230	22 B-24, 1 P-38	13	1	8	0	2
III./JG 300	Bf 109G	Jüterbog		1030	Jüterbog	~1230	10 B-24, 1 P-51	9	5	3	0	1
IV./JG 300	Bf 109G	Reinsdorf	23	1035	Reinsdorf	~1230	1 B-17, 1 P-38, 1 P-51	15	1	9	0	2

was attacked by a number of eastern front fighters (to date unidentified), but was able to fight them off, apparently without the aid of escorts, for the loss of four Fortresses. Fifteen 15th AF B-24s also failed to return; most of these were victims of Flak.

23 December

8th Air Force Mission #757: 403 of 423 HBs (all BDs) bomb communications centres and rail targets behind Ardennes battle area, TOT 1223-1252 – lose 1-0-196, claim 0. 592 of 636 fighters (12 FGs) escort and sweep, claim 69-1-18, lose 7-1.

RAF Bomber Command dispatches 27 No. 8 Group Lancasters, 3 Mosquitoes to bomb Cologne/Gremberg rail yard – lose 7, claim 0. No escort.

Bad weather grounded the Luftwaffe in northern Europe for several days, while the lack of defensive forces in southern Europe allowed the 15th AF to continue its raids unmolested. Improved weather over the Ardennes allowed the tactical air forces of both sides to sortie in great numbers today. The 8th AF sent a small force of bombers to attack communications targets behind the battle lines. Numerous fighters swept ahead of the bomber stream to take care of any possible attackers; many of their 69 victims were in fact tactical fighters with no intention of tackling the American heavy bombers, although some were given that task. The 9th AF medium bombers saw their most furious aerial opposition of the war, but only those Jagdgruppen known to have encountered heavy bombers or their escorts are listed in the mission table; they lost five KIA, five MIA, four POW, three WIA and 29 fighters. The only heavy bombers sustaining severe losses belonged to RAF Bomber

Command's No. 8 Pathfinder Group, which dispatched 27 unescorted Lancasters and three Mosquitoes to bomb a Cologne rail yard through cloud. The cloud cleared, and the vulnerable bombers were attacked by a small II./JG 26 formation flying their first mission in 'long nose' Fw 190D-9s. These had been sweeping the Ardennes looking for Allied fighter-bombers when six were directed to the new target. They expended all of their ammunition on the British bombers and retired unscathed; six Lancasters and one Mosquito went down.

24 December

8th Air Force Mission #760: 1,884 of 2,046 HBs (all BDs) bomb communications centres and airfields in W Germany, TOT 1415-1514 – lose 12-23-487, claim 18-5-1. 813 of 853 (13 FGs) escorts claim 74-1-20, lose 10-2.

RAF Bomber Command dispatches 248 Halifaxes, 79 Lancasters, 11 Mosquitoes of No. 4, 6, 8 Groups to bomb Düsseldorf and Mühlheim airfields in good visibility – lose 4 Halifaxes, 2 Lancasters, claim 0. Details of escort unknown.

The weather over both England and the north European continent was clear enough for flying, and the 8th Air Force dispatched its greatest number of sorties of the war against communications centres and airfields believed to be supporting the German offensive. RAF Bomber Command sent 338 bombers in daylight to the same types of target. The huge armada became the top priority objective for all I. Jagdkorps and II. Jagdkorps fighters. Two experienced RLV units, IV.(Sturm)/JG 3 and III./JG 301, claimed successful attacks on B-17 boxes, but most Gruppen, piloted almost entirely by novices, were easily

Luftwaffe defensive activity – 23 December 1944

Unit	Type	Gruppe up			Gruppe down		Claims	Losses				
		Base	No	Time	Base	Time		Dest	Dam	KIA	MIA	WIA
Luftflotte Reich												
I. Jagdkorps												
Jagddivision 3:												
III./JG 1	Fw 190A	Rheine	12	1126	Rheine	~1300	1 B-17, 1 B-17 HSS	4	3	0	0	1
II./JG 26	Fw 190D	Nordhorn	19	1150	Nordhorn, Gütersloh	1320	6 Lancaster, 1 Mosquito, 1 P-51	2	0	0	1	1
I./JG 27	Bf 109G	Rheine		~1110	Rheine	~1310	0	2	2	0	0	0
II./JG 27	Bf 109G	Hopsten		1111	Hopsten, Bensheim	1311	1 B-17 HSS	2	1	2	0	0
III./JG 27	Bf 109K	Großenhain		~1110	Großenhain	~1310	3 P-47	3	4	0	1*	0
IV./JG 27	Bf 109G	Achmer		~1110	Achmer	~1310	1 P-47, 2 P-51	3	1	1	0	0
IV./JG 54	Fw 190A	Vörden		~1110	Vörden	~1310	0	3	0	1	2	0
LwKdo West												
II. Jagdkorps												
Jafü Mittelrhein:												
I./JG 4	Bf 109G	Darmstadt-Griesheim		~1100	Darmstadt–Griesheim	~1230	1 Spitfire	3	3	0	0	1
II.(Sturm)/JG 4	Fw 190A	Babenhausen		~1100	Babenhausen	~1230	0	7	3	1	5**	0

*III./JG 27: MIA are POW.   **II.(Sturm)/JG 4: MIA include 3 POW.

Luftwaffe defensive activity – 24 December 1944

Unit	Type	Gruppe up			Gruppe down		Claims	Losses				
		Base	No	Time	Base	Time		Dest	Dam	KIA	MIA	WIA
Luftflotte Reich												
I. Jagdkorps												
Jagddivision 3:												
Stab/JG 1	Fw 190A	Twente	4	1111	Twente	~1300	1 P-51	1	0	1	0	0
I./JG 1	Fw 190A	Twente	19	1111	Twente, Köln–Wahn	1245	1 B-17 HSS, 7 B-24	4	0	0	0	1
II./JG 1	Fw 190A	Drope		~1110	Drope	~1300	0	3	2	1	0	1
III./JG 1	Bf 109G	Rheine		1108	Rheine	~1300	1 P-51	8	1	3	1	2
I./JG 3	Bf 109G	Paderborn	12	~1100	Paderborn	~1300	1 P-51	6	1	2	1	1
III./JG 3	Bf 109G	Bad Lippspringe		1055	Bad Lippspringe	~1300	0	1	2	1	0	0
IV.(Sturm)/JG 3	Fw 190A	Gütersloh	20	1108	Gütersloh, Köln–Wahn	1205	1 B-24, 5 P-47, 1 P-51	10	1	2	6*	0

*IV.(Sturm)/JG 3: MIA include 2 POW.

dispersed by the American escorts. For the day, the Americans wrote off 35 heavy bombers, at least six to fighter attack, and 12 escorts. The RAF lost six bombers, none to Luftwaffe fighters, although III./JG 1 apparently attempted to reach them. Luftflotte Reich lost at least 17 pilots KIA, five POW, 10 WIA and 40 fighters in missions against Allied heavy bombers. These numbers are almost certainly low, as the surviving data become sketchier and less reliable toward the end of the war: for example, no losses are known for JG 301, which was heavily engaged.

25 December

8th Air Force Mission #761: 388 of 422 2nd BD B-24s + 3rd BD B-17s bomb communications centres and railroad bridges west of the Rhine, TOT 1136-1157 – lose 5-4-128, claim 3-1-4. 432 of 460 (12 FGs) escorts claim 46-6-8, lose 9-3.

The 8th AF took advantage of continued good

weather on Christmas Day to dispatch two divisions to bomb tactical targets west of the Rhine. Jagddivision 1 stood down, but Jagddivision 3 attempted to form a Gefechtsverband from six Gruppen with great experience against the heavies – I./JG 1, II./JG 1, III./JG 1, I./JG 3, II./JG 3 and IV.(Sturm)/JG 3 – led by the JG 1 Kommodore. The Verband could not be assembled due to the omnipresent P-51s, but I./JG 1 and the Sturmgruppe were in shape to make concentrated attacks when they reached B-24 boxes and downed six of the nine bombers that had to be written off. Twelve American escorts were also lost. The mission against the heavy bombers cost Jagddivision 3 10 KIA, six MIA, two POW, five WIA and 33 fighters. The II. Jagdkorps fighters and the rest of Jagddivision 3 were engaged in missions over the battlefield. They also sustained losses to the 8th AF escorts; these have not been included in this compilation.

26 December
8th Air Force Mission #762: 128 of 151 2nd BD B-24s + 3rd BD B-17 bomb rail targets in Ardennes battle area – lose 0-0-30, claim 0-0-1. 321 of 336 (9 FGs) escorts claim

'Yellow 2', the 6.(Sturm)/JG 300 Fw 190A-8/R2 of Fw. Hubert Engst, who bailed out of it successfully on 24 December. *(Rosch)*

11-0-0, lose 2-1.
    15th Air Force dispatches 320 B-24s + 164 B-17s to attack Blechhammer, Odertal, Oswiecim oil targets – lose 24, claim 0. Escort of 203 P-38s and 238 P-51s claims 3, loses 1.

The weather had closed in again, but the 8th AF sent a small force to attack rail targets behind the battle zone. No Luftwaffe fighter approached the bombers; the 11 claimed by the escorts were all engaged in tactical missions. The 15th AF added Oswiecim (Auschwitz) to its list of eastern oil targets. Its raid to Poland and Silesia today lost as many as 24 bombers, most to Flak, but some possibly to Eastern Front fighters as yet unidentified.

31 December
8th Air Force Mission #772: 1,259 of 1,327 HBs (all BDs) bomb various oil industry, rail, communications targets

– lose 27-6-366, claim 26-9-16. 721 of 785 (15 FGs) escorts claim 61.5-2-5, lose 10-1.

During the last week of December, I. Jagdkorps ignored the missions that the 8th AF flew to tactical targets near the Ardennes battlefield. Today, the Americans resumed the strategic air war with a full-strength raid on numerous targets throughout Germany, and I. Jagdkorps responded with all of the forces that it had. JG 300 and JG 301 had been rebuilt to approximately full strength and were scrambled against the bomber streams. Following the new guidelines, the seven Gruppen did not attempt to form Gefechtsverbände but sought to evade the escorts and make independent attacks on the bombers. This new tactic proved surprisingly successful, and many of the 33 bombers and 11 escorts that were written off were lost to the fighters. The two RLV Geschwader paid a heavy price, as usual, losing 26 KIA or MIA, nine WIA and 62 fighters. The Jagdgruppen of the two tactical commands were ordered to keep away from the bomber streams. They flew their typical battlefront missions and returned to find preliminary orders for a full-strength mission to be flown the following morning.

Luftwaffe defensive activity – 31 December 1944

Unit	Type	Gruppe up			Gruppe down		Claims	Losses				
		Base	No	Time	Base	Time		Dest	Dam	KIA	MIA	WIA
Luftflotte Reich												
I. Jagdkorps												
Jagddivision 1:												
I./JG 300	Bf 109G	Borkheide	35	1050	Borkheide	~1230	0	1	2	1	0	0
II.(Sturm)/JG 300	Fw 190A	Löbnitz	19	1050	Löbnitz	~1230	10 B-17, 1 P-51	14	2	7	0	2
III./JG 300	Bf 109G	Jüterbog	20	1048	Jüterbog	~1230	2 B-17, 1 B-17 HSS	6	1	2	0	0
IV./JG 300	Bf 109G	Reinsdorf	16	1050	Reinsdorf	~1230	1 B-17	1	3	0	0	0
I./JG 301	Fw 190A	Salzwedel		~1050	Salzwedel	~1230	?	4	3	1	0	3
II./JG 301	Fw 190A	Sachau		~1050	Sachau	~1230	?	12	0	7	0	1
III./JG 301	Fw 190A	Stendal		1050	Stendal, Lüneburg	1210	1 B-24. 2 P-51	14	2	7	1	3

Notes

[1] Unger Gefechtsbericht, in private collection.

[2] Bösch correspondence with author, 1997.

[3] Hanf correspondence with author, 1995.

[4] *Jägerblatt 94/5*, p. 58.

[5] *Jägerblatt 94/5*, p. 58.

[6] *Jägerblatt 85/1*, p. 25.

CHAPTER 9

JANUARY – MAY 1945

January 1945

Events in January left little hope that the Luftwaffe day fighter force would ever regain a prominent role in the defence of Germany. The month began with Operation BODENPLATTE on the western battlefront, which cost II. Jagdkorps one-third of its fighters, most of which had been obtained from the RLV force for the Ardennes offensive. I. Jagdkorps concentrated its few operational units in the Berlin area to defend the critical central German oil targets. Jagdgruppen trickling back from the Western Front were withheld from operations for rebuilding. The 8th AF bombed communications targets in western Germany for two weeks (2–13 January) without opposition from the RLV force.

The Soviet winter offensive began on 12 January. The Red Army advanced from the Vistula River to the Oder, well within Germany proper, in two weeks. Twenty fighter Gruppen were withdrawn from the west and sent east to counter the Soviet juggernaut. These included all of the Gruppen of JG 1, JG 3 and JG 11, the most senior of the home defence Geschwader.

These never returned to the RLV force, which retained only the two former *Wilde Sau* Geschwader, JG 300 and JG 301, and the jet and rocket units as its day fighter components. Of these, only seven Jagdgruppen were fully operational – four in JG 300 and three in JG 301. On 14 January, these reported 311 fighters on strength, of which 225 were fit for operations. This minuscule force stood in opposition to the two largest American air forces. In January, the 8th AF had an average strength of 2,700 bombers and 1,200 fighters; the 15th AF, 1,170 bombers and 630 fighters. The ground organisation of the 8th AF had grown so huge that an attempt was made to streamline it by eliminating an entire command level. The 8th Fighter Command was abolished, and each of its five-group fighter wings was assigned to one of the three bomb divisions, which were renamed air divisions.

Göring reorganised his fighter defences on 26

A new Fw 190D-9 (right) heads a line-up of Focke-Wulfs captured by the Soviets in East Prussia in 1945. They were supposedly incorporated into the Red Air Force as a combat squadron. (Rosch)

January. The I. Jagdkorps was disbanded, and command of the Reich day fighters was given to the IX. Fliegerkorps (Jagd), under Generalmajor Peltz. Three Reich Jagddivisionen were retained to control the night fighters. A new unit, Fliegerdivision 9 (Jagd), was established to finish the job of converting bomber pilots to fighter pilots for the Kampfgeschwader (Jagd). The rest of the fighter command organisation also saw major changes: II. Jagdkorps was disbanded, and three new Fliegerdivisionen, 14, 15 and 16, were established to command all of the units on the western front – mostly fighter Gruppen, but including reconnaissance and night ground assault units – under Luftwaffenkommando West (LwKdo West), command of which was given to Beppo Schmid.

Adolf Galland lost his position as General of the Fighter Arm and was put under house arrest. As he remained one of Hitler's favourites, he was eventually given the authority to establish a jet Staffel and operate it independently, entirely apart from the new fighter command structure. The new unit, Jagdverband 44 (Fighter Unit 44; JV 44), did not become operational until April, even though Galland hand-picked its staff and its pilots were almost all decorated combat veterans. It was assigned to LwKdo West and was thus kept outside Peltz's reach, fulfilling Hitler's promise.

1 January

8th Air Force Mission #774: 732 of 850 HBs (all 3 Air Divisions [ADs]) target oil installations and bridges in western Germany, TOT 1143-1318 – lose 8-11-177, claim 6-0-2. 651 of 725 fighters (15 FGs) escort, claim 17-1-1, lose 2-1-?.

___

The full strength of II. Jagdkorps – 900 fighters and fighter-bombers – took part in Generalmajor Peltz's Operation BODENPLATTE, a morning attack on Allied tactical airfields behind the Ardennes battlefront. Although the mission achieved complete tactical surprise, it was much less successful than hoped, and 214 Luftwaffe pilots, including 19 irreplaceable formation leaders, were killed, taken prisoner or remained missing. Any last faint hope of rebuilding the Jagdwaffe died with this mission.

The sacrifice of the tactical fighters had no immediate effect on the strategic air war. USSTAF celebrated New Year's Day by sending the 8th AF to the oil installations in northern and central Germany. Four JG 300 Gruppen, three JG 301 Gruppen and the

Fw 190A-8 'Green 5' of Stab I./JG 1 after a hard landing on Herzogenaurach. *(Crow)*

low-strength III./JG 7 were scrambled, but most of the interceptors were dispersed by the escorts. A few JG 301 Fw 190s reached a small 1st Air Division (1st AD) B-17 formation dropping Window 80 km (50 miles) ahead of the main stream. The JG 301 fighters made a co-ordinated attack; I./JG 301 drew the P-51 escort away to the north, while the other two Gruppen attacked the B-17s from the rear and downed six. The small RLV force also claimed one P-51 probable victory, while losing 10 KIA, seven WIA and 34 fighters.

14 January

8th Air Force Mission #792: 345 of 376 3rd AD B-17s, 326 of 348 2nd AD B-24s bomb central German oil targets, TOT 1244-1328; 176 of 187 1st AD B-17s bomb Cologne highway bridges, TOT 1338-44 – lose 7-5-293, claim 31-9-7. 761 of 860 fighters (15 FGs) escort and sweep, claim 155-0-25, lose 11-5-?.

___

Today's rare unlimited visibility prompted the Americans to send two air divisions to bomb synthetic petroleum plants in central Germany. These small targets could only be located and hit in clear weather. The raid brought a full-scale response from the RLV defences. In an attempt at co-ordination, the I. Jagdkorps controller ordered III./JG 7 to draw off the escorts to allow the Fw 190s of II.(Sturm)/JG 300 and JG 301 to reach the bombers. JG 301 was met head-on by P-51s while still climbing and was unable to reach the bombers in strength. JG 300 did make a successful attack, but at a heavy price. Its Sturmgruppe made a

Luftwaffe defensive activity – 1 January 1945

Unit	Type	Gruppe up			Gruppe down		Claims	Losses				
		Base	No	Time	Base	Time		Dest	Dam	KIA	MIA	WIA
Luftflotte Reich												
I. Jagdkorps												
Jagddivision 1:												
III./JG 7	Me 262A	Brandenburg–Briest		~1130	Brandenburg–Briest	~1230	0	3	1	1	0	0
I./JG 300	Bf 109G	Borkheide	23	1050	Borkheide	~1230	0	7	2	2	0	0
II.(Sturm)/JG 300	Fw 190A	Löbnitz	17	1050	Hessisch–Lichtenau	1230	0	2	1	0	0	0
III./JG 300	Bf 109G	Mark Zwuschen	20	1105	Mark Zwuschen	~1230	0	5	0	1	0	0
IV./JG 300	Bf 109G	Reinsdorf	17	1100	Reinsdorf	~1230	0	5	0	3	0	1
Stab/JG 301	Fw 190A	Salzwedel		~1045	Salzwedel	~1215	0	1	0	0	0	0
I./JG 301	Fw 190A	Salzwedel		~1045	Salzwedel	~1215	0	4	1	2	0	1
II./JG 301	Fw 190A	Salzwedel		~1045	Salzwedel	~1215	1 B-17	1	0	1	0	0
III./JG 301	Fw 190A	Stendal		1102	Stendal	~1215	3 B-17	6	5	0	0	5

Luftwaffe defensive activity – 14 January 1944

Unit	Type	Gruppe up			Gruppe down		Claims	Losses				
		Base	No	Time	Base	Time		Dest	Dam	KIA	MIA	WIA
Luftflotte Reich												
I. Jagdkorps												
Jagddivision 1:												
III. I./JG 7	Me 262A	Brandenburg–Briest		~1200	Brandenburg–Briest	~1300	0*	2	0	2	0	0
	Me 262A	Parchim	2	1232	Lärz	n/a	0	2	0	1	0	0
I./JG 300	Bf 109G	Borkheide		1142	Borkheide	~1300	1 B-17, 1 P-51	9	1	5	0	1
II.(Sturm)/JG 300	Fw 190A	Löbnitz	31	1115	Hessisch–Lichtenau	~1300	21 B-17	16	0	3	2	3
III./JG 300	Bf 109G	Mark Zwuschen, Jüterbog		1140	Mark Zwuschen, Jüterbog	~1300	2 B-17, 2 P-51	18	2	10	1	2
IV./JG 300	Bf 109G	Reinsdorf	28	1135	Reinsdorf	~1300	2 B-17, 1 P-47, 1 P-51	17	1	11	0	3
Stab/JG 301	Fw 190A	Welzow?		~1140	Welzow?	~1300	0	1	1	1	0	1
I./JG 301	Fw 190A	Finsterwalde		~1140	Finsterwalde	~1300	1 B-17	10	1	5	0	6
II./JG 301	Fw 190A	Welzow?		~1140	Welzow?	~1300	1 B-17	10	0	9	0	1
III./JG 301	Fw 190A	Alteno		1150	Königsberg–Neumark	1315	1 P-47, 1 P-51	5	1	4	0	2

*III./JG 7: 1 B-17 claim undocumented

successful Sturmangriff on a vulnerable part of the 3rd AD stream and downed nine 390th BG B-17s before the heavy Fw 190s and their escorting Bf 109s were swarmed over by Mustangs. In only 10 minutes, the Geschwader lost 32 KIA, seven WIA and 56 aircraft to a single P-51 group, the 357th FG, which was awarded a Distinguished Unit Citation for this mission. III./JG 7 (the only jet Gruppe near full operational status) and the two piston-engine RLV Geschwader lost 54 pilots KIA or MIA, 19 WIA and 90 fighters. Many II. Jagdkorps fighters also became involved with the 8th AF, but mostly as unwilling participants, attacked on their tactical missions by the 761 fighters flying sweeps and escorts along the route of the bombers. II. Jagdkorps lost 52 KIA and 17 WIA, many to the 8th AF escorts, as described in the pilot's account below, but also to their more frequent opponents: Allied tactical fighters, antiaircraft fire and other battlefield hazards. The 106 fatalities suffered by the Jagdwaffe made this one of its worst days of the war.

PILOT'S ACCOUNT[1]
14 January 1945

After two weeks of bad weather, the overcast lifted a little. It was still hazy; horizontal visibility was not good, and vertically one could see to the ground only in a small circle. We were given the mission of ground support for our troops, together with other fighter units. We were ordered to fly at an altitude where we could be seen by the ground forces. This meant that we would be facing a 20- to 30-fold superiority in the air, which we could no longer deal with; we had lost too many of our pilots with high victory scores.

We reached the airspace over the battle area at 8,500 metres and saw a formation of fighter-bombers, flying east, beneath us. No other aircraft could be seen owing to the haze, so this enemy formation would be attacked. As we were passing about 2,000 metres above this formation, I heard over the radio, 'Attention! Small brothers beneath us!' (This was the codeword for our own fighters.) They were Bf 109s. We had almost made a fatal error by bouncing them from above without a clear identification, but we knew that there were strong Allied formations in this area.

We needed to regain altitude quickly, as we saw a formation of Thunderbolts that had been missed in the haze. We wanted to be able to use our superior climbing and turning ability. We soon reached the height for an attack and approached the enemy formation from a superior position. I was keeping an eye on Major Hackl to the left of me, to maintain enough distance for the required flight manœuvres, when I suddenly saw a string of tracers between us, coming from behind and above. Before I could react, my plane was hit in the fuselage, wings and cockpit. A shell hit the armour plate behind my head and destroyed part of the Plexiglas canopy. All that was left was a long shard over my head. Another hit the left side of the instrument panel and destroyed two instruments. All of this without injury to me. Several small splinters from the canopy ripped holes in my leather jacket.

I immediately jerked the stick forward to escape the hail of fire and then pulled it into my belly with all my strength while advancing the throttle all the way. The Fw 190D-9 climbed straight up. When I had escaped the battle, I could see below me to my left a Mustang with a red/white chequer-board pattern on its lower cowling, flying past me to the left. My speed was still great enough for me to make a steep left bank and pull up about 15–20 metres behind the Mustang. I saw that the pilot was looking down to the left, since he was expecting my machine to stall out and dive. Since I was right behind him, I opened fire, but my first salvo went beneath his machine. I pulled the stick with both hands to bank as tightly as possible, and the Mustang disappeared beneath my engine. When it became visible again, I could see large holes in its fuselage and wings: it had been hit by several rounds. The pilot made a quick turn to the right to dive away. I was still behind him and firing. He crossed through my cone of fire several times and dove away. I could see that his propeller was slowing down, probably due to engine damage. In order not to ram him or overtake him to let him get behind me, I made a left turn, keeping my eyes out for Major Hackl. I thus lost sight of the Mustang, but could see three crash sites on the ground. Major Hackl had also shot down a Mustang (he had a gun camera) and could later confirm the crash of my Mustang.

Since my Fw 190D had sustained battle damage, I dove to low altitude and headed for Münster, which had a large landing area, a well-equipped fire service for crash landings and a workshop ready to make quick repairs.

There is one side story to tell. I reported to the control room and was told to sit down and discuss my damage with the maintenance officer. I had to have my shoulders shaken to stay awake. I did not even remove my radio harness. Later, when I took off my helmet, I saw that it was full of hair. It probably had fallen out from shock when I was hit. The helmet was not damaged, and I had no head injuries.

I can still remember clearly what went through my head when the shells hit my cockpit and I jammed the stick forward to escape the fire. To fly as the Kommandeur's wingman is no life insurance policy (as I was told): one can also be shot down! I believe that in such situations it is crucial not to give up and not to accept a seemingly unavoidable fate.

[Mittag's and Hackl's victims were 78th Fighter Group P-51s: DC]

Gefr. Wilhelm Mittag
Stab II./JG 26

A Me 410B-2/U4 (W. Nr. 710458), abandoned alongside a Munich autobahn and photographed by the Allies in May. The airplane had probably served previously with II./ZG 26, the only unit to take the hated BK 5 5cm cannon into combat. *(Crow)*

A clean Fw 190D, probably from JG 26, abandoned at Schleswig in May. *(Permann)*

17 January

8th Air Force Mission #798: 665 of 700 HBs (all ADs) bomb Hamburg, Harburg oil industry – lose 9-1-151, claim 0. 320 of 362 fighters (11 FGs) escort and sweep, claim 0, lose 7-1-?.

While struggling to rebuild their strength after the 14th, JG 300 and JG 301 put up a few fighters on 15–18 July, losing several to 8th AF escorts. III./JG 7 was now up to strength in pilots, aircraft and jet fuel and could put up small intercept formations on a regular basis. Hit-and-run attacks from the rear could rarely be headed off by the American escorts. One such attack today apparently downed a straggling B-17; mission details remain unknown.

20 January

8th Air Force Mission #801: 664 of 772 HBs (all ADs) target Sterkrade oil industry, various rail yards – lose 4-7-115, claim 0. 426 of 455 fighters (8 FGs) escort and sweep, claim 2-0-0, lose 3-0-?.

15th Air Force: 170 B-17s + 190 B-24s target Linz, Salzburg rail yards, Regensburg oil storage – lose 15, claims unknown. P-38s + 209 P-51s escorts claim 4, lose 1.

Small formations from III./JG 7 and the jet

Luftwaffe defensive activity – 20 January 1945

Unit	Type	Gruppe up			Gruppe down		Claims	Losses				
		Base	No	Time	Base	Time		Dest	Dam	KIA	MIA	WIA
Luftflotte Reich												
I. Jagdkorps												
Jagddivision 1:												
III./JG 7	Me 262A	Briest, Lechfeld		1130	Briest, Lechfeld, Neuburg	1220	0	0	0	0	0	0
I./JG 300	Bf 109G	Borkheide		1203	Borkheide	~1300	0	0	0	0	0	0
II.(Sturm)/JG 300	Fw 190A	Löbnitz		1203	Hessisch–Lichtenau	~1230	0	0	0	0	0	0
III./JG 300	Bf 109G	Mark Zwuschen		1203	Mark Zwuschen	~1230	1 P-51	4	0	0	0	2
IV./JG 300	Bf 109G	Reinsdorf		1203	Reinsdorf	~1230	0	0	0	0	0	0
Stab/JG 301	Fw 190A	Welzow?		~1230	Sagan, others	~1330	transfer	0	0	0	0	0
I./JG 301	Fw 190A	Finsterwalde		~1230	Sagan, others	~1330	transfer	2	0	2	0	0
II./JG 301	Fw 190A	Welzow?		~1230	Sagan, others	~1330	transfer	1	0	1	0	0
III./JG 301	Fw 190A	Alteno		~1230	Sagan, others	~1330	transfer	1	0	1	0	0
III./EJG 2	Me 262A	Lechfeld		~1230	Lechfeld	~1330	0	1	0	1	0	0

A wrecked Fw 190A-8 of 8.(Sturm)/JG 300, photographed at Bayreuth in the spring of 1945. The airplane, formerly in the charge of JG 10, shows the remains of that unit's snake insignia on the fuselage. *(Crow)*

conversion unit III./EJG 2 were up today, with no known success and the loss of one pilot. JG 300 was scrambled late against the 8th AF and avoided most contact – one P-51 was claimed, for the loss of four Bf 109s and two injured pilots. JG 301 became embroiled with 15th AF B-17s attacking Regensburg; whether this was a deliberate interception or an inadvertent encounter during a transfer flight to the Eastern Front is not known. The Mustang escort shot down and killed four Focke-Wulf pilots, for the loss of one of their own. By the end of the day, the two piston-engine Geschwader had temporarily left the RLV force. They were ordered to fly fighter-bomber missions against the advancing Red Army; this assignment lasted only one week.

February 1945

The top priority for IX Fliegerkorps (Jagd) was to increase the number of operational Me 262 fighter Geschwader. The JG 7 Geschwaderstab and First

Gruppe joined III./JG 7 on operations by the end of the month, but the bomber-as-fighter units continued to have a tough time, with only I./KG(J) 54 joining the order of battle. Training flights were always hazardous: on 15 February, III./KG(J) 54 lost one jet to a patrolling Mustang, and two more were damaged making quick landings. Peltz suggested to Chief-of-Staff Koller during the month that all of KG(J) 54 should withdraw to Austria to oppose the 15th Air Force, while the next two ex-bomber Geschwader in

A Me 262A abandoned at an airbase, probably Herzogenaurach. The checkered tail band indicates that the jet had previously belonged to one of the bomber units converted to fighters, probably KG(J) 6. *(Crow)*

Luftwaffe defensive activity – 3 February 1945

Unit	Type	Gruppe up			Gruppe down		Claims	Losses				
		Base	No	Time	Base	Time		Dest	Dam	KIA	MIA	WIA
Luftflotte Reich												
IX. Fliegerkorps (Jagd):												
III./JG 7	Me 262A	Brandenburg–Briest		~1030	Brandenburg–Briest	~1130	0*	0	0	0	0	0
	Me 262A	Lechfeld		1454	Lechfeld	1605	0	0	0	0	0	0

*III./JG 7: 5 B-17, 1 B-24, 3 P-47, 1 P-51 claims undocumented

the pipeline, KG(J) 6 and KG(J) 27, were sent east for seasoning. Koller concurred, and the order was recorded in the OKL war diary, but it was never carried out.

The ground infrastructure supporting jet fighters now shot to the top of the USSTAF target list. The 15th AF had continued its role in the strategic air war, even though the RLV force had ignored it for months, with a consequent decrease in mentions by this history. The 15th AF struck a major blow against the jets in an unopposed 16 February raid on the Regensburg Me 262 factory and the jet airfields in the Munich area. III./KG(J) 54 lost 16 Me 262s on the ground. KG(J) 55 was hit even harder, losing at least 23 Me 262s, and never came close to entering operations.

3 February

8th Air Force Mission #817: 1,370 of 1,437 HBs bomb Berlin city centre (1st AD + 3rd AD B-17s), Magdeburg synthetic oil targets (2nd AD B-24s), TOT 1102-1310 – lose 23-6-339, claim 0. 885 of 948 fighters (15 FGs) escort and sweep, claim 21-1-7, lose 8-2-?.

The first test of the new RLV command-and-control organisation came today and resulted in the most humiliating defeat of the war for the German air defences. Although JG 300 and JG 301 had returned to their RLV bases after brief duty against the Soviets, Generalmajor Peltz kept all of his fighters but III./JG 7 on the ground during the 8th AF's most destructive raid on Berlin's city centre. The B-17s of the 1st and 3rd Air Divisions flattened the government quarter, damaging the RLM (Reich Air Ministry) headquarters, the OKW (Armed Forces High Command) headquarters, the Reich Chancellery, the Propaganda Ministry and the Gestapo headquarters. Fires raged over an area of two square miles. The other 8th AF bombers, 2nd AD B-24s, paid a return visit to the Magdeburg synthetic oil plant, also unopposed in the air. 32

USAAF bombers and 10 fighters were written off after the mission; most were lost to the highly concentrated Berlin Flak, and a few to the usual operational causes – collision and mechanical failure. Several references state that III./JG 7 claimed as many as five B-17s, one B-24, three P-47s and one P-51 without loss. However, the 8th AF mission report clearly states that only two Luftwaffe fighters, Bf 109s, were encountered, and no mention of a combat with jets has been located in a search of 8th AF unit histories.

9 February

8th Air Force Mission #824: 1,200 of 1,296 HBs (all ADs) target numerous oil targets, TOT 1134-1333 – lose 8-4-133, claim 0-1-2. 809 of 871 fighters (15 FGs) escort, claim 24-3-8, lose 5-2-?.

The 8th AF flew a maximum-strength mission – 1,296 bombers took off – against the central German oil targets and railroad viaducts, the latter now considered choke points in Germany's stressed transportation system. The bombers flew in six task forces, three of which encountered German fighters. Peltz

American soldiers pose on Fw 190A-9 'Yellow 17' (W. Nr. 380374) of I./JG 301 at Pilsen, Czechoslovakia. *(Crow)*

ordered up the only two operational jet fighter Gruppen, III./JG 7 and I./KG(J) 54, as well as six weak piston-engine Jagdgruppen, with fewer than 100 Bf 109s and Fw 190s.

The Americans noted that the JG 7 fighters bounced the escorts aggressively, presumably to facilitate attacks on the bombers by the rest of the fighters, but there was no coordinated attack. The battle formation containing the piston-engine fighters was broken up by P51s and never reached the bombers in strength, but did an adequate job of evading the Mustangs, losing only six pilots KIA or MIA, five WIA and 16 aircraft, while claiming two B-24s and two P-51s. III./JG 7 claimed four B-17s and one P-51, without loss. KG(J) 54 succeeded in reaching the bombers and shot down at least one B17, while claiming four, but then became easy prey for the P-51s, whose pilots noted the ex-bomber pilots' wide turns and tentative tactics and shot down four of the jets while colliding with a fifth. The collision killed both an American pilot and the KG(J) 54 Kommodore. The other casualties included almost the entire I./KG(J) 54 Stabsschwarm. IX. Fliegerkorps (Jagd) losses totalled nine KIA or MIA, six WIA and 21 fighters.

14 February

8th Air Force Mission #830: 1,293 of 1,377 HBs (all ADs) target several oil & rail targets, TOT 1152-1332 – lose 7-8-188, claim 1-0-0. 881 of 962 fighters (15 FGs) escort and sweep, claim 10-0-3, lose 7-2-?.

Me 262A-1 'White 7' (W. Nr. 110376) of 7./EJG 2 was left at Neubiberg in May. Its pilot was Fw. Böckl. This airplane was a veteran of 1944 service in Kommando Nowotny. (Crow)

The RLV fighters were ordered up to oppose a full-strength 8th AF raid on a variety of targets, including Dresden. Peltz scrambled 78 conventional fighters from JG 300, 68 from JG 301 and a small number of Me 262s from I./JG 7, III./JG 7 and KG(J) 54. Although the jet pilots claimed at least three B-17s for no recorded losses, no jet attacks were noted by the Americans, who summarised the Luftwaffe reaction as "strikingly weak and almost entirely ineffective". The only successful attack was made by a handful of Fw 190s, probably from JG 301, which caught an isolated B-17 squadron circling to make a second bomb run and shot down one B-17, severely damaging a second; the claimants are not known. IX Fliegerkorps (Jagd) lost a total of 10 pilots KIA or MIA, three WIA and 15 aircraft.

21 February

8th Air Force Mission #839: 1,219 of 1,262 HBs (all ADs) target Nuremberg rail yard – lose 0-1-361, claim 0. 743 of 792 fighters (13 8th AF + 2 9th AF FGs) escort and sweep, claim 0, lose 7-0-?.

A full-strength raid by the 8th AF on the important Nuremberg rail yard was met by III./JG 7, which was fended off effectively by 479th FG P-51s; neither side sustained casualties.

22 February – Operation CLARION

8th Air Force Mission #841: 1,372 of 1,428 HBs (all ADs) bomb numerous communications targets, from 10,000 feet (3.05 km) if no antiaircraft defences – lose 7-0-97, claim 0-0-1. 817 of 862 fighters (15 FGs) escort and sweep, claim 4-2-18, lose 13-1-?.

The USSTAF ordered Operation CLARION, an all-out attack on road and rail communications, which were judged to be near collapse. Both the 8th and 15th Air Forces flew full-strength missions. The 8th AF ordered visual bombing from 10,000 feet (3.05 km) for those targets with no known flak defences. Peltz's response was to keep his piston-engine fighters well dispersed on the ground, while scrambling 32 Me 262s from the Stab, First and Third Gruppen of JG 7 versus the 8th AF; the 15th AF was unopposed. Interception was attempted in the Stendal–Salzwedel area, but no more than two B17s were shot down before every Me 262 Schwarm was involved with Mustangs. Four P-51s were shot down, for the loss of two jet pilots KIA, one WIA and nine Me 262s.

Luftwaffe defensive activity – 9 February 1945

Unit	Type	Gruppe up			Gruppe down		Claims	Losses				
		Base	No	Time	Base	Time		Dest	Dam	KIA	MIA	WIA
Luftflotte Reich												
IX. Fliegerkorps (Jagd):												
II./JG 3	Bf 109G	Alperstedt	16	1135	Alperstedt	~1230	0	0	2	0	0	0
III./JG 7	Me 262A	Brandenburg–Briest		~1130	Brandenburg–Briest	~1230	4 B-17, 1 P-51	0	0	0	0	0
I./JG 300	Bf 109G	Borkheide	25	1135	Borkheide	~1230	0	4	1	2	0	2
II.(Sturm)/JG 300	Fw 190A	Löbnitz		1135	Löbnitz	~1230	2 B-24	1	0	0	0	0
III./JG 300	Bf 109G	Mark Zwuschen, Jüterbog	18	1135	Mark Zwuschen, Jüterbog	~1230	2 P-51	7	3	2	0	1
I./JG 301	Fw 190A	Finsterwalde		1135	Finsterwalde	~1230	0	1	0	0	0	1
II./JG 301	Fw 190A	Welzow	8	1135	Welzow	~1230	0	3	0	0	2	1
I./KG(J) 54	Me 262A	Giebelstadt	18	1130	Giebelstadt	~1230	3 B-17, 1 B-17 HSS	5	1	3	0	1
III./EJG 2	Me 262A	Lechfeld		~1130	Lechfeld	~1230	0	0	0	0	0	0

Luftwaffe defensive activity – 14 February 1945

Unit	Type	Gruppe up			Gruppe down		Claims	Losses				
		Base	No	Time	Base	Time		Dest	Dam	KIA	MIA	WIA
Luftflotte Reich												
IX. Fliegerkorps (Jagd):		144										
I./JG 7	Me 262A	Kaltenkirchen	2	~1130	Kaltenkirchen	~1230	0	0	0	0	0	0
III./JG 7	Me 262A	Brandenburg–Briest	6	~1130	Brandenburg–Briest	~1230	3 B-17	0	0	0	0	0
I./JG 300	Bf 109G	Borkheide	*78	1100	Borkheide	~1230	0	2	3	1	0	0
II.(Sturm)/JG 300	Fw 190A	Löbnitz	—	1100	Löbnitz	~1230	1 P-51	5	3	4	0	1
III./JG 300	Bf 109G	Mark Zwuschen, Jüterbog	—	1100	Mark Zwuschen, Jüterbog	~1230	0	3	1	2	0	0
IV./JG 300	Bf 109K	Reinsdorf	—	1100	Reinsdorf	~1230	0	0	0	0	0	0
I./JG 301	Fw 190A	Finsterwalde	**68	~1100	Finsterwalde	~1230	0	1	1	1	0	0
II./JG 301	Fw 190D	Welzow	—	~1100	Welzow	~1230	0	3	0	1	1	1
IV./JG 301	Bf 109G	Gahro	—	~1100	Gahro	~1230	0	1	0	0	0	1
I./KG(J) 54	Me 262A	Giebelstadt	3	1430	Giebelstadt	1530	0	0	0	0	0	0

*78 JG 300 sorties total   **68 JG 301 sorties total

24 February
8th Air Force Mission #845: 1,055 of 1,114 HBs (all ADs) attack oil & rail targets – lose 2-2-226, claim 0. 557 of 592 fighters (11 FGs) escort and sweep, claim 0, lose 11-0-?.

The USSTAF's pounding of areas containing industrial and communications targets continued. Today's raid by the 8th AF brought up III./JG 7 to defend the central German oil targets; one B-17 and one P-51 were claimed, for no losses. The operational training unit I./EJG 2 provided the only defence of north Germany, losing one Bf 109G and pilot for no claims.

25 February
8th Air Force Mission #847: 1,157 of 1,197 HBs (all ADs) bomb tank factory, jet airfields, oil depots, rail targets – lose 5-3-363, claim 0. 704 of 755 fighters (15 FGs) escort and sweep, claim 21-0-4, lose 8-1-?

Luftwaffe defensive activity – 21 February 1945

Unit	Type	Gruppe up			Gruppe down		Claims	Losses				
		Base	No	Time	Base	Time		Dest	Dam	KIA	MIA	WIA
Luftflotte Reich												
IX. Fliegerkorps (Jagd):												
III./JG 7	Me 262A	Brandenburg–Briest, Parchim		1200	Brandenburg–Briest, Parchim	1300	0	0	0	0	0	0
	Me 262A	Brandenburg–Briest, Parchim		1430	Parchim, Weimar–Nord	1530	0	0	0	0	0	0

Luftwaffe defensive activity – 22 February 1945

Unit	Type	Gruppe up			Gruppe down		Claims	Losses				
		Base	No	Time	Base	Time		Dest	Dam	KIA	MIA	WIA
Luftflotte Reich												
IX. Fliegerkorps (Jagd):			32									
Stab/JG 7	Me 262A	Brandenburg–Briest	*32	~1140	Brandenburg–Briest	~1245	0	2	0	0	0	1
I./JG 7	Me 262A	Oranienburg	—	1139	Oranienburg, Kaltenkirchen	1245	2 P-51	0	2	0	0	0
III./JG 7	Me 262A	Parchim, Lechfeld	—	1141	Parchim, Ütersen; Lechfeld	1245	2 B-17, 1 P-51	6	7	1	0	0
I./KG(J) 54	Me 262A	Giebelstadt	4	?	Giebelstadt	?	0	0	0	0	0	0
III./KG(J) 54	Me 262A	Neuburg/Donau		?	Neuburg/Donau	?	0	1	0	1	0	0

*32 JG 7 sorties total

Luftwaffe defensive activity – 24 February 1945

Unit	Type	Gruppe up			Gruppe down		Claims	Losses				
		Base	No	Time	Base	Time		Dest	Dam	KIA	MIA	WIA
Luftflotte Reich												
IX. Fliegerkorps (Jagd):												
III./JG 7	Me 262A	Parchim, Lechfeld?		?	Parchim, Lechfeld?	?	1 B-17, 1 P-51	0	0	0	0	0
I./EJG 2	Bf 109G	Ludwigslust?		?	Perleberg	?	0	1	0	1	0	0

The 8th AF flew a maximum-strength mission against a variety of targets. The entire RLV force was scrambled against it, to little effect. JG 300 and JG 301 had been ordered to fly ground-attack missions for Luftflotte 6, but a single clattering teletype message returned them to RLV duty in Luftflotte Reich, without any change of bases. JG 300 claimed one B-17 and one P-51, for no losses. Of the three JG 301 Gruppen, the First was split up by P-51s on take-off from Salzwedel and lost four pilots killed; the Second was kept from the bombers by the P-51s; and the Third followed its leader back to base when he had to abort, not making contact with the enemy. Of the jet units, no JG 7 claims or losses are known, while the bad luck of KG(J) 54 continued. Jets from its First and Second Gruppen were hit by P-51s as they scrambled from Giebelstadt and Kitzingen and lost four KIA, one WIA and four Me 262s. A handful of Fw 190D-9s from JG 2, a western front tactical unit, were scrambled against some nearby B-24s returning from Aschaffenburg, but were overwhelmed by the escorts and lost two pilots for no known claims. Luftflotte Reich losses totaled 11 KIA or MIA, three WIA and 20 fighters.

Luftwaffe defensive activity – 25 February 1945

Unit	Type	Gruppe up			Gruppe down		Claims	Losses				
		Base	No	Time	Base	Time		Dest	Dam	KIA	MIA	WIA
Luftflotte Reich												
IX. Fliegerkorps (Jagd):			234									
III./JG 7	Me 262A	Brandenburg–Briest, Parchim	10	1045	Brandenburg–Briest, Parchim	1115	0	0	0	0	0	0
I./JG 300	Bf 109G	Borkheide	*224	~1000	Borkheide	~1100	1 P-51	0	0	0	0	0
II.(Sturm)/JG 300	Fw 190A	Löbnitz	—	~1000	Löbnitz	~1100	1 B-17	0	0	0	0	0
I./JG 301	Fw 190A	Salzwedel	—	~1000	Salzwedel	~1100	0	5	0	4	0	0
II./JG 301	Fw 190D	Welzow	—	~1000	Welzow	~1100	1 P-51	1	0	1	0	0
III./JG 301	Fw 190D	Stendal	—	~1000	Stendal	~1100	n/c	0	0	0	0	0
I./KG(J) 54	Me 262A	Giebelstadt		~1000	Giebelstadt	~1030	0	1	2	1	0	1
II./KG(J) 54	Me 262A	Kitzingen	16	~1000	Kitzingen	~1030	0	3	0	2	0	1
III./EJG 2	Me 262A	Lechfeld		~1030	Lechfeld	~1130	0	1	0	1	0	0
Luftwaffenkdo West												
Fliegerdivision 14:												
I./JG 2	Fw 190D	Nidda		?	Nidda	?	0	5	2	0	1	0
III./JG 2	Fw 190D	Ettinghausen		?	Ettinghausen	?	0	4	3	1	0	1

*224 JG 300 + JG 301 sorties total

March 1945

Reliable primary sources on the Luftwaffe are scarce for the last months of the war, for reasons that are detailed in the author's previous book. As stated there, the historian is forced to resort to secondary, often conflicting sources. The best result to be hoped for is a self-consistent narrative and an accurate 'big picture'. Major gaps and uncertainties will be pointed out in the daily mission summaries.

In March, Me 262s from the few fully operational jet fighter units (primarily the Stabsschwarm and the First and Third Gruppen of JG 7) sortied against almost every 8th AF raid, some 15th AF raids, plus a few RAF BC day raids. In most cases, the jets could penetrate the escort screen for one rear pass at a bomber box; they became vulnerable if they tried to turn, either for another attack on the bombers or to battle the escorts.

Although the standard Me 262 armament of four MK 108 30-mm cannon was effective against bombers at short range, efforts were made to find something with greater range and destructive power. Unsuccessful experiments were conducted with aerial bombs and old WGr 21 mortar shells. In February, the evaluation unit tried R4M rockets, which were already

in production as antitank weapons. Some of these small (55 mm diameter) impact-fused rockets were quickly converted from armour piercing to high explosive warheads, and simple wooden racks holding 12 rockets side by side were fabricated for the Me 262. Firing tests began on 8 March and were so successful that production was given top priority. The Me 262

'White 14' in a line-up of II./JG 300 Fw 190A-8s at Löbnitz in March. The Geschwader flew a few airfield protection sorties, but little else, in the last months of the war. *(Rosch)*

armed with 24 R4M unguided rockets became the war's most lethal weapon system against heavy bombers.

The last two conventional RLV units, JG 300 and JG 301, were ordered up as fuel permitted, but a few costly missions reduced their strength to such an extent that by the end of the month the survivors were being used only to screen the jets' airfields. For the rest of the war they were used mainly in support of the ground forces, although they remained on the IX. Fliegerkorps (Jagd) order of battle.

Operations of the tactical Jagdgeschwader on the battle fronts were restricted greatly by the availability of fuel. Fighter units began to be disbanded, with the best pilots transferring to other fighter units. Other men deemed worthy of protection went to the Flak arm, especially the railroad Flak; the rest went to the paratroops or the nearest infantry unit. The most desirable posting was to a jet unit. These were so overwhelmed with transfer requests that the standards were raised; only pilots with a Knight's Cross or a German Cross in Gold could be accepted.

1 March

8th Air Force Mission #857: 1,209 of 1,228 HBs (all ADs) target rail yards in central & southern Germany – claim 0, lose 0-3-30. 460 of 488 fighters (9 FGs) escort, claim 3-0-1, lose 7-2-?.

15th Air Force: 222 B-17s + 516 B-24s target Moosbierbaum oil industry – claim unknown, lose 20. 194 P-38s + 224 P-51s escort, claim 7-1-0, lose 3.

The month's first jet casualties came today. Eight I./KG(J) 54 Me 262s on a training mission were bounced by Mustangs and lost two aircraft and pilots, while claiming one P-51 and one bomber. A single source credits a III./JG 301 Ta 152H with a Mustang, a rare victory for this rarest of the Luftwaffe's conventional fighters. In the south, the unpredictable Hungarians were stirred to action against the 15th Air Force. Six Pumas sortied from Veszprém against a damaged B-24 returning alone to Italy and downed it.

2 March

8th Air Force Mission #859: 1,167 of 1,232 HBs (all ADs) target tank factory, 3 synthetic oil plants, TOT 1000-1103 – lose 14-1-166, claim 8-3-11. 713 of 774 fighters (15 FGs) escort, claim 66.5-6-20, lose 13-2-?.

III./JG 7 was given the day off to train; every other

A JG 300 Fw 190A-9 at Löbnitz in March in simplified late-war markings with no identification numbers or fuselage bands. *(Crow)*

operational RLV unit was ordered up against a full-strength 8th AF raid on the central German synthetic fuel plants. I./KG(J) 54 scrambled 14 Me 262s, which were bounced by a flight of sweeping P-51s. Only two of the German pilots pressed on with their mission. They shot down one bomber and one P-51, but both were then shot down and killed by Mustangs. The two jet operational training units – III./EJG 2 (for the fighters) and I./EKG(J) 1 (for the bombers-as-fighters) – were up early to train and lost one pilot without affecting the main action. JG 300 and JG 301 each sortied for the last time in full four-Gruppe strength – a total of 198 Bf 109s and Fw 190s took off – and in the absence of any Me 262s to divert the P-51s, their leaders had to look for weak spots in the escort coverage. By luck or good direction, II.(Sturm)/JG 300 found itself in the rear of the leading 3rd AD combat wing and made a closed-formation assault attack that downed four 385th BG B-17s before the P-51s arrived. JG 301 was not so fortunate, even with the brand-new Ta 152s of III./JG 301 flying high cover for the battle formation. The Geschwader was apparently delayed in forming up by the cloud cover and was split up by P-51s before reaching the bombers. Small groups of Fw 190s were able to reach the 1st AD and 2nd AD and downed at least three B-17s and B-24s. At least four P-51s were shot down in the wide-ranging air combats, but the Bf 109s and Fw 190s suffered grievous losses in return. JG 300, JG 301 and JGr 10 lost 24 pilots KIA, five MIA, 10 WIA and 48 aircraft destroyed. The new IV./JG 301, which had been slow to join operations, lost eight pilots killed; this was its first and last RLV mission.

Axis Defensive Activity — 1 March

Unit	Type	Gruppe up			Gruppe down		Claims	Losses				
		Base	No	Time	Base	Time		Dest	Dam	KIA	MIA	WIA
Luftflotte Reich												
IX. Fliegerkorps (Jagd):												
III./JG 301	Ta 152H	Sachau		?	Sachau	?	1 P-51	0	0	0	0	0
I./KG(J) 54	Me 262A	Giebelstadt	8	1135	Giebelstadt	1240	1 B-24,1 P-51	2	0	2	0	1
Luftflotte 4												
I. Jagdkorps												
Fliegerführer 102 (Hungary):												
101 JGr (Hungary)	Bf 109G	Veszprém	6	1430	Veszprém	~1530	1 B-24	0	1	0	0	0

Luftwaffe defensive activity – 2 March 1945

Unit	Type	Gruppe up			Gruppe down		Claims	Losses				
		Base	No	Time	Base	Time		Dest	Dam	KIA	MIA	WIA
Luftflotte Reich												
IX. Fliegerkorps (Jagd):			198									
JGr 10	Fw 190A	Redlin		~1010	Redlin	~1100	0	2	2	0	2	0
I./JG 300	Bf 109G	Borkheide		~0930	Borkheide	~1100	1 P-51	0	0	0	0	0
II.(Sturm)/JG 300	Fw 190A	Löbnitz	31	~0930	Löbnitz	~1100	5 B-17	8	0	3	1	0
III./JG 300	Bf 109G	Jüterbog		~0930	Jüterbog	~1100	0	7	1	2	0	3
IV./JG 300	Bf 109K	Reinsdorf		~0930	Reinsdorf	~1100	0	3	1	2	0	1
I./JG 301	Fw 190A	Salzwedel		~1010	Finsterwalde	~1130	0	4	1	1	2	0
II./JG 301	Fw 190D	Stendal		1015	Welzow	~1130	1 B-17	9	2	8	0	1
III./JG 301	Ta 152H	Stendal	12	~1010	Stendal	~1130	0	0	0	0	0	0
	Fw 190A	Stendal	12	~1010	Stendal	~1130	1 B-17	0	0	0	0	0
IV./JG 301	Bf 109G	Stendal, Gardelegen		~1010	Stendal, Gardelegen	~1130	0	15	5	8	0	5
I./KG(J) 54	Me 262A	Giebelstadt	14	0837	Giebelstadt	0943	0	4	0	3	0	1
III./EJG 2	Me 262A	Lechfeld		1035	Lechfeld	1112	0	0	0	0	0	0
I./EKG(J) 1	Me 262A	Ansbach		~0830	Ansbach	~0930	0	1	0	1	0	0

Luftwaffe defensive activity – 3 March 1945

Unit	Type	Gruppe up			Gruppe down		Claims	Losses				
		Base	No	Time	Base	Time		Dest	Dam	KIA	MIA	WIA
Luftflotte Reich												
IX. Fliegerkorps (Jagd):			29									
Stab/JG 7	Me 262A	Brandenburg–Briest	3	0945	Brandenburg–Briest	1045	0	0	0	0	0	0
III./JG 7	Me 262A	Brandenburg–Briest, Parchim, Lechfeld	26	0945	Brandenburg–Briest, Parchim, Lechfeld, Hagenow	1045	5 B-17, 4 B-24, 2 P-47, 1 P-51	2	2	1	0	0

3 March

8th Air Force Mission #861: 1,069 of 1,102 HBs (all ADs) attack numerous oil targets, TOT 1034-1126 – lose 9-2-207, claim 2-2-4. 684 of 754 fighters (15 FGs) escort and sweep, claim 4-0-8, lose 8-1-?.

III./JG 7 returned to battle with an impressive performance. Twenty-nine Me 262s scrambled from several airfields in the Berlin area to counter yet another 8th AF raid on the central German oil targets. The jet pilots did not attempt mass attacks, but quickly broke up into flights of three or four aircraft that attacked the combat boxes from the rear in echelon formation, almost in trail. In response, a bomber gunner hit one jet in the cockpit; it dove to the ground with its dead pilot. The jet pilots were careful to keep up their speed, flying from one box to the next and not being drawn into fighter combat. As many as nine B-17s and B-24s were shot down on the most successful jet mission to date. There was only the one German combat loss, plus one jet lost and several damaged with technical failures. P-51 pilots claimed six damaged Me 262s; apparently all of them reached base.

14 March

15th Air Force: 245 B-17s + 613 B-24s bomb Austrian + Czech rail yards, Hungarian oil installation – lose 7, claims unknown. 200 P-38s + 234 P-51s escort, claim 20-1-2, lose 4.

Both USSTAF air forces flew maximum-strength missions against oil, rail and communications targets. Ten III./JG 300 Bf 109s scrambled from Jüterbog to protect the Hannover airfield. They were swarmed over by Mustangs and lost half of their number. Three III./JG 7 Me 262s bounced a pair of Mustangs and claimed them both; no matching losses have been located. In the south, a flight of Hungarian ground-attack Fw 190Fs lost four of their number to 15th AF Mustangs, while apparently downing one P-51. As they were not on an intercept mission, this combat has not been included on the mission list.

15 March

8th Air Force Mission #889: 1,310 of 1,353 HBs (all ADs) bomb Zossen army headquarters, several rail yards – lose 9-2-340, claim 0. 764 of 833 fighters (15 FGs) escort and sweep, claim 1-0-0, lose 4-6-?.

The USSTAF again sent both air forces against oil, rail and communications targets; in addition, the 8th AF bombed the German army headquarters at Zossen in support of the Soviet offensive. III./JG 7 and III./EJG 2 were directed against the bombers and claimed eight. The 8th AF lost seven B-17s and two B-24s, but reported no encounters with jets. It is possible that some bombers reported as blown up by antiaircraft fire were instead hit by R4M rockets, the most potent air-to-air weapon of the war. Several Me 262s may have been lost, but no pilot casualties are known. II./JG 301 scrambled 12 fighters to protect its airfields and claimed one B-17; II./JG 400 scrambled nine Me 163s and lost three of its rocket fighters for no known successes. One of these fighters was downed by an 8th AF P-51, in the last USAAF fighter combat with Me 163s.

16 March

15th Air Force: 228 B-17s + 582 B-24s bomb Vienna oil installations, Austrian rail yards – lose 9, claim 0. 207 P-38s + 225 P-51s escort, claim 4-0-0, lose 4.

The 15th Air Force executed a massive raid on Austrian strategic targets, while the RLV force restricted its activity to airfield defence and attacks on reconnaissance aircraft. 15th AF Mustangs claimed several Axis fighters. Their units are unknown to the author, and no mission list has been prepared.

18 March

8th Air Force Mission #894: 1,184 of 1,329 HBs (all ADs) bomb Berlin railroad stations, tank plants – lose 13-15-714, claim 7-1-1. ? of 733 P-51s (14 FGs) escort, claim 14-0-4, lose 6-1-4.

The 8th AF made a full-strength visual attack on Berlin rail yards and tank factories in support of the Soviets. More than 37 jets took to the air in response. Me 262s of the JG 7 Stab and Third Gruppe flew their most successful mission to date, aided by hazy cloud and R4M rockets. Numerous attacks from the rear of the bomber boxes and at least one head-on attack downed six B-17s for the loss of one KIA, one severely injured Staffelkapitän and two Me 262s. These attacks made a deep impression on the Americans, who knew nothing of the efforts of another Gruppe, I./JG 7, which flew a disastrous mission. Its base was shrouded in a low overcast, and the efforts of its one instrument-rated pilot were insufficient to assemble the unit. One Staffelkapitän collided with his wingman, killing both

Luftwaffe defensive activity – 14 March 1945

Unit	Type	Gruppe up			Gruppe down		Claims	Losses				
		Base	No	Time	Base	Time		Dest	Dam	KIA	MIA	WIA
Luftflotte Reich												
IX. Fliegerkorps (Jagd):												
III./JG 7	Me 262A	Brandenburg–Briest	3	0945	Brandenburg–Briest	1045	2 P-51	0	0	0	0	0
III./JG 300	Bf 109G	Esperstedt	10	1345	Esperstedt	1430	0	7	0	4	0	2

Luftwaffe defensive activity – 15 March 1945

Unit	Type	Gruppe up			Gruppe down		Claims	Losses				
		Base	No	Time	Base	Time		Dest	Dam	KIA	MIA	WIA
Luftflotte Reich												
IX. Fliegerkorps (Jagd):												
III./JG 7	Me 262A	Brandenburg–Briest		~1430	Brandenburg–Briest	~1530	2 B-17, 5 B-24	4?	0	0	0	0
II./JG 301	Fw 190D	Stendal	12	~1430	Stendal	~1530	1 B-17	0	0	0	0	0
II./JG 400	Me 163B	Bad Zwischenahn	9	~1445	Bad Zwischenahn	~1515	0	3	0	1	0	1
III./EJG 2	Me 262A	Lechfeld		~1430	Lechfeld	~1530	1 B-17	0	0	0	0	0

Luftwaffe defensive activity – 18 March 1945

Unit	Type	Gruppe up			Gruppe down		Claims	Losses				
		Base	No	Time	Base	Time		Dest	Dam	KIA	MIA	WIA
Luftflotte Reich												
IX. Fliegerkorps (Jagd):			46									
Stab/JG 7	Me 262A	Brandenburg–Briest	3	~1030	Brandenburg–Briest	~1200	3 B-17	0	0	0	0	0
I./JG 7	Me 262A	Kaltenkirchen	2	~1030	Kaltenkirchen	~1200	0*	0	0	0	0	0
	Me 262A	Kaltenkirchen	11	1224	Kaltenkirchen	~1245	0	4	?	3	0	0
III./JG 7	Me 262A	Brandenburg–Briest, Lechfeld	21	1030	Brandenburg–Briest, Lechfeld	1205	13 B-17, 3 P-51	3	0	1	0	1
III./EJG 2	Me 262A	Lechfeld		~1030	Lechfeld	~1200	2 P-51	0	0	0	0	0

*I./JG 7: 2 B-17 claims undocumented

men, and several other aircraft apparently had to crash-land. The Gruppenkommandeur did record two B-17 shootdowns in his logbook, but these claims were not processed.

19 March

8th Air Force Mission #896: 1,224 of 1,273 HBs (all ADs) target central German industry, rail yards, airfields – lose 6-6-125, claim 1-1-2. 623 of 675 P-51s (13 FGs) escort and support, claim 40-2-17, lose 10-0-?.

15th Air Force: 242 B-17s + 611 B-24s bomb south German rail yards – lose 2, claim 0. 194 P-38s + 241 P-51s escort, claim 1-0-0, lose 5.

The USSTAF dispatched both of its air forces to a variety of targets in central and southern Germany. IX. Fliegerkorps (Jagd) countered by scrambling every operational RLV unit: jets from JG 7, KG(J) 54 and III./EJG 2; rocket fighters from JG 400; and piston-engine fighters from JG 300 and JG 301. Once again, III./JG 7 scored the day's most notable victory. The Gruppe attacked in larger formations than before: three waves, each of about a dozen jets, in line abreast. Four B-17s were downed with R4M rockets; Mustangs were then able to catch some of the jets and downed two, killing both pilots. The successes of the other RLV units were minor. I./JG 7 Me 262s lost one plane to a P-51 while claiming one certain B-17 and one probable.

I./KG(J) 54 also claimed one certain B-17 and one probable. It lost no jets in the air, but B-24 bombs destroyed or damaged 11 of III./KG(J) 54's 16 jets on the ground at Neuburg. III./EJG 2 damaged one P-51. The two conventional Geschwader stayed close to their airfields, but did claim one B-17. 8th AF P-51s reported several heavy engagements with Fw 190Ds and Bf 109s; as these were tactical fighters from JG 26 and JG 27, these battles had no effect on the strategic air war.

20 March

8th Air Force Mission #898: 418 of 451 HBs (from all ADs) bomb various Hamburg area targets – lose 4-1-63, claim 6-3-5. 338 of 355 P-51s (10 FGs) escort and strafe, claim 4-0-8, lose 2-0-?.

15th Air Force: 245 B-17s + 600 B-24s bomb oil distribution targets in southern Germany and Austria – lose 4, claim 0. 195 P-38s + 244 P-51s escort, claim 2-1-1, lose 1.

The USSTAF sent the 15th AF to southern Germany and Austria in full strength and a reduced force of 8th AF bombers to Hamburg. I. Fliegerkorps in the south sent several of its tactical units, including the renowned II./JG 52, up against the 15th AF. Their presence was noted by the American crews, but little is known about their successes and losses. IX. Fliegerkorps (Jagd) scrambled fighters from I./JG 7, III./JG 7 and JG 300 versus the 8th AF. The two jet Gruppen claimed nine certain B-17s and B-24s for the loss of two KIA, one WIA and four Me 262s, but the Americans wrote off only five bombers to all causes. Attacks of the two Gruppen on the same part of the bomber stream may have resulted in duplicate claims.

21 March

8th Air Force Mission #901: 1,353 of 1,408 HBs (all ADs) bomb 13 jet airfields – lose 1-1-189, claim 3-3-3. 751 of 806 P-51s (14 FGs) escort and sweep, claim 9-0-2, lose 9-2-?.

15th Air Force: 240 B-17s + 538 B-24s bomb 8 Austrian oil targets & rail yards, Neuburg jet factory – lose 4, claim 0. 194 P-38s + 232 P-51s escort, claim 1, lose 0.

The 15th AF bombed a number of targets in Austria and southern Germany and reported seeing one Me 262. The 8th AF bombed 13 known and suspected jet fighter bases, reflecting the Americans' concern for the jets' increasing effectiveness. The JG 7 Stabsschwarm and four Me 262 Gruppen – I./JG 7,

III./JG 7, I./KG(J) 54 and III./EJG 2 – strove to reach the bombers, while JG 300 scrambled a few fighters to protect airfields. Most of the known successes can be credited to JG 7's Stab and Third Gruppe. Their principal target was the 3rd AD stream. Five B-17s were lost to the jets, and a sixth to collision. III./JG 7 lost two KIA, two WIA and four Me 262s. I./JG 7 claimed two B17s, for no losses. III./EJG 2 claimed one B-24 and one P-38, possibly from the 15th AF, while I./KG(J) 54 lost one pilot for no known claims.

22 March

8th Air Force Mission #906: 1,301 of 1,331 HBs (all ADs) bomb military encampments & airfields, TOT 1146-1345 – lose 1-4-257, claim 0. 632 of 662 P-51s (14 FGs) escort, claim 14-1-4, lose 3-1-?.

15th Air Force: 169 B-17s + 574 B-24s bomb Ruhland oil synthesis plant, Austrian and Czech oil and rail targets – lose 21, claim 1-3-0. 198 P-38s + 231 P-51s escort, claim 5-1-5, lose 0.

The 15th AF B-24s bombed several oil and rail targets in Austria and Czechoslovakia without seeing the Luftwaffe. The 15th AF B-17 wing was sent to a frequent 8th AF target, the Ruhland synthetic fuel plant 120 km (75 miles) south of Berlin – a 2,300 km (1,400 mile) round trip for the Italy-based crews – and encountered the newly aggressive jets for the first time. Three 15th AF P-51 groups and an 8th AF group that was sweeping the Berlin area were unable to prevent the initial attack by the JG 7 Stabsschwarm and Third Gruppe, which on their initial pass through the Flak barrage to get at the bombers shot down six

Me 262A (W.Nr. 170071) of III./EJG 2, an operational training unit that joined combat in the last months of the war. Its pilot was the Gruppenkommandeur, Major Erich Hohagen. The airplane was abandoned in southern Germany. *(Crow)*

Luftwaffe defensive activity – 19 March 1945

Unit	Type	Gruppe up			Gruppe down		Claims	Losses				
		Base	No	Time	Base	Time		Dest	Dam	KIA	MIA	WIA
Luftflotte Reich												
IX. Fliegerkorps (Jagd):			76									
I./JG 7	Me 262A	Kaltenkirchen		1500	Kaltenkirchen	~1600	1 B-17	1	0	0	0	0
III./JG 7	Me 262A	Brandenburg–Briest, Lechfeld, Parchim	33	1321	Brandenburg–Briest, Lechfeld, Parchim	1420	4 B-17, 1 P-51, 1 B-17 HSS	2	4	2	0	0
JG 300	Bf 109G	various	24	?	various	?	0	0	0	0	0	0
JG 301	Fw 190A	various		?	various	?	1 B-17	0	0	0	0	0
I./JG 400	Me 163B	Brandis	1	?	Brandis	?	0	0	0	0	0	0
I./KG(J) 54	Me 262A	Giebelstadt	12	?	Giebelstadt	?	1 B-17	0	1	0	0	0
III./EJG 2	Me 262A	Lechfeld		1215	Brandis	1300	0	0	0	0	0	0

Luftwaffe defensive activity – 20 March 1945

Unit	Type	Gruppe up			Gruppe down		Claims	Losses				
		Base	No	Time	Base	Time		Dest	Dam	KIA	MIA	WIA
Luftflotte Reich												
IX. Fliegerkorps (Jagd):			45									
I./JG 7	Me 262A	Kaltenkirchen	13	1545	Kaltenkirchen	1700	1 B-17	1	1	1	0	0
III./JG 7	Me 262A	Brandenburg–Briest, Lechfeld, Parchim	18	1546	Brandenburg–Briest, Lechfeld, Parchim	1646	7 B-17, 1 B-24, 1 B-17 HSS	2	4	1	0	1
1JG 300	Bf 109G	various	18	?	various	?	0	0	0	0	0	0
Luftflotte 4												
I. Fliegerkorps												
Fliegerführer 102 (Hungary):												
II./JG 52	Bf 109G	Veszprém		1345	Veszprém	1425	0*	0	0	0	0	0

*II./JG 52: + 1 P-51 claim unwitnessed

Luftwaffe defensive activity – 21 March 1945

Unit	Type	Gruppe up			Gruppe down		Claims	Losses				
		Base	No	Time	Base	Time		Dest	Dam	KIA	MIA	WIA
Luftflotte Reich												
IX. Fliegerkorps (Jagd):			39									
Stab/JG 7	Me 262A	Brandenburg–Briest		~0905	Brandenburg–Briest	~1005	2 B-17	0	0	0	0	0
I./JG 7	Me 262A	Kaltenkirchen		0905	Kaltenkirchen	1010	2 B-17	0	0	0	0	0
III./JG 7	Me 262A	Brandenburg–Briest, Parchim	21	0905	Brandenburg–Briest, Parchim, Stendal, Brandis	1005	9 B-17, 1 B-24, 1 P-51	4	4	2	0	2
2JG 300	Bf 109G	various	8	?	various	?	0	1	0	1	0	0
I./KG(J) 54	Me 262A	Giebelstadt	10	~0905	Giebelstadt	~1005	0	1	0	1	0	0
III./EJG 2	Me 262A	Lechfeld		1130	Brandis	1215	1 B-24, 1 P-38	0	0	0	0	0

483rd BG B-17s. Mustangs then chased the jets away, downing three. Meanwhile the 8th AF bombed tactical targets and KG(J) 54 airfields. The other jet units were apparently scrambled against the 8th AF, but did not reach the bombers. These units made no known claims and lost three fighters.

23 March

8th Air Force Mission #908: 1,244 of 1,276 HBs (all ADs) bomb rail targets in western and central Germany – lose 7-3-273, claim 0. 469 of 499 P-51s (14 FGs) escort and sweep, claim 1-0-0, lose 3-1-?.

15th Air Force: 171 B-17s + 541 B-24s bomb Ruhland oil synthesis plant, Austrian tank factory, Austrian and Czech oil and rail targets – lose 9, claim 1-3-0. 203 P-38s + 237 P-51s escort, claim 0, lose 1.

RAF Bomber Command: 128 No. 1 & No. 5 Gp. Lancasters bomb Bremen and Bad Oeynhausen bridges – lose 2-0-1, claim 0. No. 11 Gp. Mustangs escort, claims 1-0-0, lose 0.

All three of the Allied heavy bomber forces made daylight raids on the shrinking Reich. IX Fliegerkorps (Jagd) ignored the 8th AF as it bombed tactical targets in support of Field Marshal Montgomery's massive Rhine crossing, Operation VARSITY, which was scheduled for the next day. A small number of JG 7 Stabsschwarm and Third Gruppe Me 262s were sent to Ruhland and Chemnitz, which were being revisited by the 15th AF, and claimed two B24s. Part of RAF Bomber Command attacked similar targets. This tempting bomber force was not ignored: I./JG 7 Me 262s shot down two Lancasters and forced a Halifax to crash-land. An RAF Mustang downed one of the jets.

24 March

8th Air Force Mission #911: 1,714 of 1,749 HBs (all ADs) bomb airfields in western and northwestern Germany – lose 5-1-124, claim 1-0-0. 1,297 of 1,375 P-51s (15 FGs) escort and support, claim 53-0-2, lose 9-1-?.

15th Air Force: 169 B-17s + 527 B-24s bomb Neuburg jet factory, Berlin tank engine factory, Czech rail yard – lose 13, claim 8-5-0. 203 P-38s + 237 P-51s escort, claim 8-3-6, lose 5.

Stab/JG 7, III./JG 7 and III./EJG 2 defended the Daimler-Benz tank factory in Berlin, which was bombed today by the 15th AF on its longest-ever mission, a round trip of some 2,400 km (1,500 miles). Close escort by the Mustangs and a hail of fire from the

B-17 gunners forced the jets to keep their distance. The Me 262s downed only two bombers and three P-51s, which was a source of great pride for the 15th AF, and Distinguished Unit Citations for the 332nd FG and the 483rd BG. The intense combat resulted in excessive claims by both sides. The Italy-based aircrews were credited with 16-9-6 of the jets. JG 7 claimed 10 B17s, for a loss of four Me 262s and four injured pilots. III./EJG 2 claimed one B-24 and one P51 for no losses.

The 8th AF supported Montgomery's Rhine crossing directly, with airfield bombings and supply drops. The four JG 300 Gruppen were ordered west to attack the bridgeheads. Allied fighters tore II.(Sturm)/JG 300 apart, killing 15 Fw 190 pilots. The agile Bf 109s of the other three Gruppen escaped the area with light losses, but the Sturmgruppe was finished, and the Geschwader flew no more major missions as a battle formation.

PILOT'S ACCOUNT[2]
24 March 1945

Although I had returned from the hospital in February, I was not ordered up on a mission until today. The 'young hares' were obviously being saved for the ramming mission. But it was otherwise in my case. I received mission orders along with my Gruppe. The Americans had crossed the Rhine near Wesel and had established a bridgehead on the right side of the river. Our orders read that all operational aircraft were to be employed against the large supporting formations of enemy fighters and bombers.

JG 300 took off from Thuringia under orders first to do battle, and then to seek out and land at any suitable airfield in the western Reich. Our Gruppe took off at 1420 hours and flew in the direction of the Ruhr. We contacted the enemy flying at about 6,000 metres. That was unusual. We believed (incorrectly) that they were there not so much as bomber escorts but as fighter-bombers. But they were waiting for us. We could see that we were far outnumbered by the Mustangs.

We immediately sought to split up our formation so that we would have to deal with small numbers of the enemy in their combat units. But that worked both ways. My Rottenflieger [wingman] Obfw. Seibert and I were quickly alone with seven Mustangs. The outcome of the combat was predictable. Obfw. Seibert was the first of us to go down, but he was able

Luftwaffe defensive activity – 22 March 1945

Unit	Type	Gruppe up			Gruppe down		Claims	Losses				
		Base	No	Time	Base	Time		Dest	Dam	KIA	MIA	WIA
Luftflotte Reich												
IX. Fliegerkorps (Jagd):			51									
Stab/JG 7	Me 262A	Brandenburg–Briest		~1215	Brandenburg–Briest	~1320	2 B-17	0	0	0	0	0
III./JG 7	Me 262A	Brandenburg–Briest, Parchim	25	1218	Brandenburg–Briest, Parchim, Pretzsch	1326	10 B-17, 1 P-51	3	0	3	0	0
JG 300	Bf 109G	various	12	?	various	?	0	0	0	0	0	0
I./KG(J) 54	Me 262A	Giebelstadt	6	~1235	Giebelstadt	~1330	0	2	0	1	0	1
III./EJG 2	Me 262A	Lechfeld	3	0935	Lechfeld	1035	0	0	0	0	0	0
	Me 262A	Lechfeld		~1215	Lechfeld	~1315	0	1	0	1	0	0

Luftwaffe defensive activity – 23 March 1945

Unit	Type	Gruppe up			Gruppe down		Claims	Losses				
		Base	No	Time	Base	Time		Dest	Dam	KIA	MIA	WIA
Luftflotte Reich												
IX. Fliegerkorps (Jagd):			64									
Stab/JG 7	Me 262A	Brandenburg–Briest		?	Brandenburg–Briest	?	2 B-24	0	0	0	0	0
I./JG 7	Me 262A	Kaltenkirchen	9	0935	Kaltenkirchen	1045	2 Lancaster, 1 Halifax	1	0	1	0	0
2nd sorties	Me 262A	Kaltenkirchen	5	1532	Kaltenkirchen	1635	0	0	0	0	0	0
III./JG 7	Me 262A	Brandenburg–Briest		~1100	Brandenburg–Briest	~1200	0	0	1	0	0	1
JG 300	Bf 109G	various	45	?	various	?	0	0	0	0	0	0
JG 301	Bf 109G	various	10	?	various	?	0	0	0	0	0	0

to bail out. He was attacked by a Mustang as he hung in his chute and was severely wounded. Later in the hospital he lay beside me – unconscious. In the night – I slept little – orderlies came and rolled his bed from the room. To my question they replied that he was being moved. The next morning I learned that Seibert had died from the wounds he had received while parachuting.

Returning to my story, my last air battle lasted for eight to 10 minutes. My engine was hit, and the propeller began to spin freely. Since I had only a little altitude, I pulled up, threw the Messerschmitt into a left bank, released the canopy and loosened my seat harness. I pushed the control stick forward only a few centimetres and was hurled from my seat. I exited without hitting the tail, my chute opened, and a glance beneath showed that the ground was very close. I was grateful that I was able to climb after I was hit.

I was slightly injured when I struck the ground on the eastern edge of Bad Sassendorf, several kilometres from Soest. That was the end of my war. I had survived.

Fahnenjunker-Uffz. Robert Jung
3./JG 300

25 March
8th Air Force Mission #913: 243 of 1,009 B-24s (2nd AD only) bomb oil depots – lose 4-5-19, claim 2-4-9. 223 of 242 P-51s (5 FGs) escort, claim 4-0-3, lose 0.

Worsening weather forced the recall of the two 8th AF B-17 divisions, leaving the 2nd AD B-24s to proceed alone with the briefed attack on oil targets. A mixed formation from III./JG 7 and the Stab and First Gruppe of KG(J) 54 caught an isolated 448th BG squadron and downed four Liberators. III./JG 7, which was rapidly wearing down, lost four pilots killed: one on take-off, one in combat near the bombers and two while landing.

Luftwaffe defensive activity – 24 March 1945

Unit	Type	Gruppe up			Gruppe down		Claims	Losses				
		Base	No	Time	Base	Time		Dest	Dam	KIA	MIA	WIA
Luftflotte Reich												
IX. Fliegerkorps (Jagd):			62									
Stab/JG 7	Me 262A	Brandenburg–Briest		~1130	Brandenburg–Briest	~1230	1 B-17	0	0	0	0	0
I./JG 7	Me 262A	Kaltenkirchen		~0900	Kaltenkirchen	~1000	1 Tempest	0	0	0	0	0
	Me 262A	Brandenburg–Briest	2	~1130	Brandenburg–Briest	~1230	1 P-38, 2 P-51	0	0	0	0	0
III./JG 7	Me 262A	Brandenburg–Briest, Parchim		0930	Brandenburg–Briest, Parchim	~1100	0	0	0	0	0	0
2nd sorties	Me 262A	Brandenburg–Briest, Brandis	31	1150	Brandenburg–Briest, Brandis	1300	9 B-17, 1 B-17 HSS	4	0	0	0	4
I./JG 300	Bf 109G	Mörtitz		1420	Mörtitz	~1600	1 P-51	5	0	3	0	1
II.(Sturm)/JG 300	Fw 190A	Löbnitz	32	1420	Löbnitz	~1600	2 P-51	19	0	15	2	1
III./JG 300	Bf 109G	Jüterbog	15	1420	Jüterbog	~1600	0	0	0	0	0	0
IV./JG 300	Bf 109K	Reinsdorf	15	1420	Reinsdorf	~1600	1 P-51	3	0	1	1	1
III./EJG 2	Me 262A	Lechfeld		1117	Lechfeld	1220	1 B-24, 1 P-51	0	0	0	0	0

Luftwaffe defensive activity – 25 March 1945

Unit	Type	Gruppe up			Gruppe down		Claims	Losses				
		Base	No	Time	Base	Time		Dest	Dam	KIA	MIA	WIA
Luftflotte Reich												
IX. Fliegerkorps (Jagd):			33									
I./JG 7	Me 262A	Kaltenkirchen		~1410	Kaltenkirchen	~1430	0*	0	0	0	0	0
III./JG 7	Me 262A	Brandenburg–Briest, Parchim, Brandis	23	0945	Brandenburg–Briest, Parchim, Brandis	1109	5 B-24, 3 P-51, 1 B-24 HSS	5	1	4	0	0
I./JG 300	Bf 109G	Mörtitz	3	~0645	Mörtitz	~0730	1 P-51	1	0	1	0	0
Stab/KG(J) 54	Me 262A	Giebelstadt		~0945	Giebelstadt	~1100	0	0	0	0	0	0
I./KG(J) 54	Me 262A	Giebelstadt		~0945	Giebelstadt	~1100	0	2	0	2	0	0

*I./JG 7: 1 B-17 claim undocumented

Luftwaffe defensive activity – 28 March 1945

Unit	Type	Gruppe up			Gruppe down		Claims	Losses				
		Base	No	Time	Base	Time		Dest	Dam	KIA	MIA	WIA
Luftflotte Reich												
IX. Fliegerkorps (Jagd):												
I./JG 7	Me 262A	Kaltenkirchen		?	Kaltenkirchen	?	1 B-17, 2 P-51	0	0	0	0	0

Luftwaffe defensive activity – 30 March 1945

Unit	Type	Gruppe up			Gruppe down		Claims	Losses				
		Base	No	Time	Base	Time		Dest	Dam	KIA	MIA	WIA
Luftflotte Reich												
IX. Fliegerkorps (Jagd):			76									
I./JG 7	Me 262A	Kaltenkirchen	8	1300	Kaltenkirchen	1400	1 B-17, 3 P-51	3	4	0	0	0
	Me 262A	Kaltenkirchen	2	~1310	Kaltenkirchen	~1400	1 Mosquito	1	0	1	0	0
III./JG 7	Me 262A	Brandenburg–Briest, others?	17	~1300	Brandenburg–Briest, others?	~1400	3 B-17	1	0	0	0	1
	Me 262A	Brandenburg–Briest, Parchim	2	1413	Brandenburg–Briest, Parchim	1439	0	0	0	0	0	0
	Me 262A	Brandenburg–Briest, Brandis	2	1553	Brandenburg–Briest, Brandis	1640	0	0	0	0	0	0

Luftwaffe defensive activity – 31 March 1945

Unit	Type	Gruppe up			Gruppe down		Claims	Losses				
		Base	No	Time	Base	Time		Dest	Dam	KIA	MIA	WIA
Luftflotte Reich												
IX. Fliegerkorps (Jagd):												
Stab/JG 7	Me 262A	Brandenburg–Briest		~0930	Brandenburg–Briest	~1030	1 B-17	0	0	0	0	0
I./JG 7	Me 262A	Kaltenkirchen	12	~0830	Kaltenkirchen	~0930	6 Lancaster	0	0	0	0	0
III./JG 7	Me 262A	Brandenburg–Briest, Parchim, Brandis	15	0835	Brandenburg–Briest, Parchim, Brandis	0940	7 Lancaster	0	0	0	0	0
	Me 262A	Brandenburg–Briest, others?		~0930	Brandenburg–Briest, others?	~1030	2 B-17	0	0	0	.0	0
II./KG(J) 6	Bf 109K	Prague–Klecan		~1400	Prague–Klecan	~1500	0	15	0	4	0	6
I./KG(J) 54	Me 262A	Giebelstadt		~1015	Giebelstadt	~1045	0	2	0	1	0	0
NSFK Standorte 15	Me 262A	Buchen	1	~0845	Buchen	~1015	1 Lancaster, 1 Halifax	0	0	0	0	0

28 March
8th Air Force Mission #917: 891 of 965 1st AD + 3rd AD B-17s target Berlin, Hannover armament factories – lose 2-5-199, claim 0. 345 of 390 P-51s (8 FGs) escort, claim 0, lose 0-2-?.

I./JG 7 managed to scramble several jets despite bad weather and reached an unescorted 1st AD B-17 Pulk as it left Berlin. The fighters downed two bombers, badly damaged a third and escaped unscathed.

30 March
8th Air Force Mission #918: 1,320 of 1,402 HBs (all ADs) bomb U-Boat targets – lose 5-3-547, claim 0-1-3. 852 of 899 fighters (15 FGs) escort and sweep, claim 7-0-8, lose 4-0-?.

The weather cleared sufficiently to allow the 8th Air Force to fly a full-scale raid on U-boat shipyards in Hamburg, Bremen and Wilhelmshaven. The approach routes to the closely spaced coastal targets were guarded by large numbers of Mustangs, and most of the 31 JG 7 jets that reached the area were headed off; however, the force claimed four B-17s, three P-51s and one Mosquito. One German pilot was killed, and a second lost a leg after he hit his airplane's tail when bailing out. Other jets were shot down or crash-landed without injury to their pilots.

31 March
8th Air Force Mission #920: 1,302 of 1,348 HBs (all ADs) target benzol plants, refinery and tank factory – lose 5-4-149, claim 3-3-1. 847 of 889 fighters (15 FGs) escort, claim 6-0-8, lose 4-0-?.

15th Air Force: 168 B-17s + 455 B-24s target Linz rail station, various other targets – lose 6, claims unknown. 189 P-38s + 223 P-51s escort, claim 35-1-4, lose 10.

RAF Bomber Command: 361 Lancasters, 100 Halifaxes, 8 Mosquitoes of No. 1, No. 6, No. 8 Groups attack Hamburg U-boat yards through cloud – lose 11, claim 4. Escort unknown.

As the weather closed in again, the 8th AF raided central Germany against light opposition, bombing mainly secondary targets, while 469 RAF BC aircraft made a day raid on the Blohm und Voss U-boat yard in Hamburg. All serviceable JG 7 aircraft were ordered up against the RAF bombers. The last formation in the bomber stream, from No. 6 Group (RCAF), had missed rendezvous with its fighter cover and had continued the mission without escort. The hurriedly scrambled jets found the vulnerable Canadians and streaked in on them from the rear. The turrets of the Canadian bombers could not track them. Eleven Lancasters and Halifaxes were lost on the mission. A few were hit by Flak; most were downed by jet pilots, including one civilian test pilot from the Nazi Flying Corps. Apparently, no jets were lost to the RCAF bombers; two KG(J) 54 jets were shot down, probably by 9th AF P-47s, but no JG 7 losses have been confirmed on this or a later mission this day which claimed a few B-17s and P-51s.

The 15th Air Force bombers hit the main rail station in Linz, while its fighters swept over central Europe on their most successful 1945 mission. Ten P-38s and P-51s were lost for claims of 35 Bf 109s and Fw 190s. It cannot be determined whether any of these Axis fighters had been ordered to attack the bombers or were just trying to stay out of the way. One large battle took place just north of Prague and decimated II./KG(J) 6, which had had to settle for Bf 109s instead of Me 262s. The Gruppe lost at least four KIA, including the Kommandeur, six WIA and 15 Bf 109s, and was disbanded shortly thereafter. The 31st FG, the Mustang group responsible for this massacre, returned to Italy without loss.

April–May 1945

By now the Luftwaffe was a totally spent force. None of its activities could have the slightest effect on Germany's imminent defeat. It had proven ineffective in defence of the Army, the industrial base and the civilian population. Headquarters and combat units were disbanded daily. The survivors moved to stay ahead of the advancing Allied armies, becoming less able to function with each move. The jet units were nevertheless up every day, and on most days the claims of the jet pilots still exceeded their losses. The USSTAF was about out of strategic targets, but its commanders worried about the 'jet menace' and devoted thousands of tons of bombs to tearing up jet airfields and the shells of jet aircraft production facilities.

I./JG 7 was the last Me 262 Gruppe to join IX. Fliegerkorps (Jagd) at full strength. JV 44, Galland's unit, set up shop in Bavaria, but it had only the strength of an enlarged Staffel and operated outside the formal Reich defence organisation.

The many late-war Luftwaffe research programmes did produce a second jet fighter that entered operations in the last month of the war – the He 162 Volksjäger ('People's Fighter'). The product of a politically favoured crash programme, the small single-engine jet suffered from several dangerous design flaws. Half-trained 'Flying Hitler Youth' originally were to fly it, but the irrationality of this plan became obvious even to the dedicated Nazis in the Luftwaffe High Command, and the airplane was instead assigned to JG 1, which could no longer obtain sufficient replacement Fw 190s owing to the destruction of its factories and the Reich's transportation infrastructure. I./JG 1 did fly a few He 162 missions in the last weeks of the war, but these were against RAF tactical aircraft, and are outside the scope of this narrative.

The combat units remaining in the RLV force soldiered on during April with ever-decreasing effectiveness. Production facilities fell to the Allies, or at least fell into ruins, and the ability of the transportation system to distribute the remaining stocks withered away. As the Allies advanced into the Reich from all sides, the flying units continued to retreat, and their ability to fly often depended on the fuel and ammunition that could be located in the immediate vicinity of their new bases. The Allied heavy bombers flew their last bombing missions on 25–26 April. The last Luftwaffe combat missions were flown against the advancing Allied and Soviet armies and their tactical air fleets.

The officers of the Wehrmacht were released from their personal oaths of service to Adolf Hitler by his 30 April suicide, and many began to consider how to

I./JG 1 He 162s and vehicles awaiting surrender to the British at Leck. (*Strasen via Roba*)

distance their units from the Soviets and surrender to the Western Allies. The mobility of the Luftwaffe gave it great freedom in this regard, and the war ended fairly painlessly for many of its officers and men. The rest of the Wehrmacht was quick to follow suit: large-scale surrenders began on 2 May on the Italian front, followed on 4 May by the northwestern front. The German High Command surrendered unconditionally on the 7th, and Victory in Europe Day (V-E Day) was declared on the 8th.

4 April
8th Air Force Mission #926: 960 of 1,431 HBs (all ADs) bomb Kiel shipyard, north German airfields – lose 10-3- 184, claim 6-4-6. 812 of 866 fighters (15 FGs) escort, claim 24-0-24, lose 4-0-?.

The jets operated in full strength against an 8th AF raid on the Kiel shipyards and several airfields in northern Germany – more than 40 combat sorties were flown. Eight III./JG 7 jets took off from Parchim directly beneath the Mustang screen. They reached the thick overcast safely, but, when emerging, the Kommandeur was shot down and badly injured. His men evaded the Mustangs in the clouds and attacked the very combat box that had targeted Parchim. Four B-24s exploded or broke apart when hit by R4M rockets; a fifth reached England with severe damage.

He 162A-2 'White 4' (W.Nr. 120097) of 1./JG/1, photographed at Kassel–Rothwesten in the summer of 1945. (*Crow*)

Me 262A-1a (W. Nr. 111857) of JV 44, devoid of unit or aircraft ID markings — Innsbruck–Hötting, Austria, summer 1945. *(Crow)*

Other JG 7 flights cruised across northern Germany looking for vulnerable bombers, while squadrons of P-51s attempted to head them off. JG 7 pilots claimed as many as a dozen victories today, but the Geschwader sustained serious losses: four pilots were killed and another injured. The other operational jet units were also active. III./EJG 2 claimed a P-51, without loss. I./KG(J) 54 claimed two B-17s for no losses that have been traced, but its cumulative losses had been so severe that it withdrew in a few days to Prague's Rusin airfield.

JV 44 claimed its first victory during a 15th AF raid on Munich. One Rotte scrambled from München–Riem and approached a squadron of P-38s head-on. The German wingman collided with his target, which crashed. His own aircraft was only lightly damaged, and he returned to Riem without incident.

COMBAT REPORT[3]
4 April 1945

I took off from Parchim on a mission against incoming heavy bombers. Before we took off, enemy fighters were reported over the field at 8,000 metres. Their altitude was probably overestimated, as from their sound they were much closer. I now think that these fighters were waiting for us at 400 metres above the 9–10/10 cloud deck. In 1 1/2 circuits over the field I assembled seven aircraft beneath the clouds; others were visible behind us. I pulled up through a thin spot in the clouds and immediately saw four aircraft with elliptical wings (undoubtedly Thunderbolts) above me in the sun to my left. I banked steeply toward them; I could not turn away due to my inferior speed. The Thunderbolts turned away sharply to come onto an opposing course. While trying to follow them, I saw four Mustangs chasing a lone 262. I did not want to fire my rockets, as this would have set a bad example for the rest of the Gruppe. While trying to distance myself from the Mustangs, I saw above me to my right four more Mustangs, diving. I turned away beneath them, but was caught from behind and received heavy fire. Defensive movements – climbing, diving, or speeding up – were impossible due to the nearness of the ground. I was now being chased by eight Mustangs. While attempting to dive into the clouds, I received my first hit. I attempted to salvo my rockets while between the clouds. Two Mustangs followed me at some distance. My rockets would not come loose. While I worked on the switch, my cockpit filled with thick smoke. I received more hits and saw that my left wing was on fire. The flames were already reaching the cockpit. After a short defensive manœuvre, I decided to bail out. I left the aircraft at 700 km/h [435 mph], without hitting the tail. I saw immediately that my parachute was ripped and my right leg was tangled up in the harness and cords. I believed that the parachute bag had come loose from the harness. Since I was very near the ground, I pulled the ripcord anyway and observed to my astonishment that the chute opened after it pulled sharply on my leg. I was attached to the chute only by the left harness strap. I landed in a freshly ploughed field with one thigh and my left arm tangled in the cords. I could not get loose immediately and was dragged 20 metres [65 feet] into a barbed-wire fence. Two Mustangs fired at me while I was in the barbed wire. I stayed still while I was in their field of vision, but as they circled for a second attack, I ran 25 steps from my chute and hid in a furrow. They kept firing at the chute, but their fire was badly off target. Finally, they flew away, probably because of Flak fire from Redlin (I had landed very near the airfield).

I received first aid from the crew of a radar station and medical treatment from the Jagdgruppe 10 doctor.

[Sinner was shot down by 339th Fighter Group P-51s: DC]

Major Rudolf Sinner, Gruppenkommandeur
Stab III./JG 7

Major Rudolf Sinner was a fighter unit leader who began the war in the Flak arm and did not join the flying Luftwaffe until 1940. He commanded four Bf 109 and Fw 190 Jagdgruppen in succession before taking over the first fully operational Me 262 Gruppe, III./JG 7, on 1 January 1945. He was shot down by P-51s on 4 April with injuries severe enough to keep him from returning to the war. (Author's collection)

A JV 44 Me 262A-1a left on Innsbruck–Hötting in May. The airplane in the background is a Ju 87D-3 from a night ground-attack unit. (USAAF)

5 April

8th Air Force Mission #928: 1,039 of 1,358 HBs (all ADs) bomb south German ordnance deports, rail yards, airfields – lose 10-4-119, claim 0. 606 of 662 fighters (12 FGs) escort, claim 1-0-3, lose 1-0-?.

Most of the jet units were employed against a large 8th AF raid on targets in southern Germany. No information is available for I./JG 7, and III./EJG 2 failed to make contact, but III./JG 7 downed at least one bomber, I./KG(J) 54 claimed two, and JV 44 claimed its first. It was in fact responsible for one B-17 crashing immediately and two being written off on their return to England. Only one Me 262 is known to have been shot down today.

7 April – Operation WERWOLF (see map)

8th Air Force Mission #931: 503 of 529 3rd AD B-17s bomb Kaltenkirchen, Parchim a/fs, Buchen ordnance depot, Güstrow ammo dump, TOT 1325-1441 – lose 14-0-117, claim 26-10-10; 322 of 340 2nd AD B24s bomb Hamburg ammunition plants, TOT 1256-1322 – lose 3-1-44, claim 14-2-6; 432 of 442 1st AD B-17s bomb north German ordnance depot, airfields, TOT 1519-1604 – lose 0-0-27, claim 0-0-1. 830 of 898 escorts (15 FGs) claim 64-1-15, lose 5-2-?.

The 8th AF sent its three air divisions against a large number of airfields and ordnance targets in northern Germany. In addition to the jet units, a novel Bf 109 unit – *Sonderkommando* [Special Command] *Elbe* – was scrambled in Operation WERWOLF [Werewolf]. This unit had been conceived in January. Its half-trained pilots were to be sent aloft to ram American bombers in Bf 109s provided with high-altitude engines and

Luftwaffe defensive activity – 4 April 1945

Unit	Type	Gruppe up			Gruppe down		Claims	Losses				
		Base	No	Time	Base	Time		Dest	Dam	KIA	MIA	WIA
Luftflotte Reich												
IX. Fliegerkorps (Jagd):			49									
Stab/JG 7	Me 262A	Brandenburg–Briest	*30	0910	Brandenburg–Briest	~1010	1 B-17	2	0	2	0	0
I./JG 7	Me 262A	Brandenburg–Briest, Burg	—	0910	Brandenburg–Briest, Burg	~1010	1 B-17, 1 P-47, 1 P-51	0	0	0	0	0
III./JG 7	Me 262A	Brandenburg–Briest, Lärz	—	0910	Brandenburg–Briest, Lärz	~1010	5 B-24	3	5	2	0	0
	Me 262A	Parchim	8	0912	Parchim	1000	0	1	0	0	0	1
I./KG(J) 54	Me 262A	Zerbst	14	0900	Zerbst	~1000	2 B-17	0	0	0	0	0
III./EJG 2	Me 262A	Lechfeld		1455	Lechfeld	1530	1 P-51	0	0	0	0	0
Luftwaffenkdo West												
7. Jagddivision:												
JV 44	Me 262A	München–Riem	2	1100	München–Riem	1200	1 P-38	0	1	0	0	0

*JG 7: 30 Stab, I., III./JG 7 aircraft scramble 0910 hours

Luftwaffe defensive activity – 5 April 1945

Unit	Type	Gruppe up			Gruppe down		Claims	Losses				
		Base	No	Time	Base	Time		Dest	Dam	KIA	MIA	WIA
Luftflotte Reich												
IX. Fliegerkorps (Jagd):												
I./JG 7	Me 262A	Brandenburg–Briest		1130	Brandenburg–Briest	1225	0	0	0	0	0	0
III./JG 7	Me 262A	Brandenburg–Briest, Parchim , Lärz	10	~1115	Brandenburg–Briest, Parchim , Lärz	~1215	1 B-17	0	0	0	0	0
I./KG(J) 54	Me 262A	Zerbst	16	~1115	Zerbst	~1215	2 HBs	1	1	?	?	?
III./EJG 2	Me 262A	Lechfeld		0955	Lechfeld	1025	0	0	0	0	0	0
	Me 262A	Lechfeld		1105	Lechfeld	1120	0	0	0	0	0	0
Luftwaffenkdo West												
7. Jagddivision:												
JV 44	Me 262A	München–Riem	5	1115	München–Riem	1215	1 B-17*	1	0	0	0	0
	Me 262A	München–Riem		1545	München–Riem	1635	0*	0	0	0	0	0

*JV 44: + 2 P-51 claims undocumented

metal propellers and stripped of superfluous equipment such as radio transmitters and guns in excess of one. The shortage of aviation fuel and American air supremacy over Germany left these young men with no chance to become fully qualified fighter pilots, and they responded in some numbers to a call for volunteers in early March. Elbe's proponents argued that the shock effect of a mass ramming attack would deflate American morale and result in a pause in the bombing campaign, but the Luftwaffe chief-of-staff was not as enthusiastic, and the number of pilots was limited to about 200. After a brief training course, the pilots were split up among seven airfields and waited for mission orders. When these came, 188 Bf 109s had been declared operational, but only 143 took off, and many others returned early due to maintenance defects and pilot inadequacies. Those that carried out the mission did surprisingly well: 14 3rd AD and 2nd AD heavy bombers were lost to ramming attacks, and another seven crash-landed on the Continent or were scrapped on their return to England. Elbe casualties were less than expected: 24 pilots were KIA, eight were

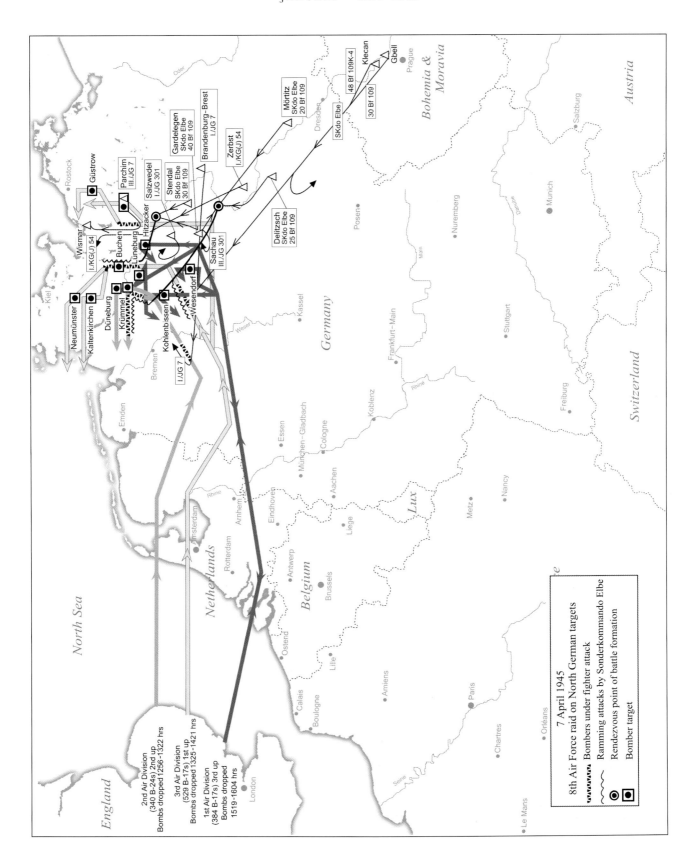

Gbell

Klecan

48 Bf 109K-4

30 Bf 109

Mörtitz
SKdo Elbe
20 Bf 109

SKdo Elbe

Bohemia &
Moravia

Prague

Austria

Gardelegen
SKdo Elbe
40 Bf 109

Brandenburg-Brest
I./JG 7

Salzburg

Stendal
SKdo Elbe
30 Bf 109

Zerbst
I./KG(J) 54

Dresden

Güstrow

Parchim
III./JG 7

Salzwedel
I./JG 301

Rostock

Delitzsch
SKdo Elbe
25 Bf 109

Posen

Oder

Wismar

Buchen

Hitzacker

Lüneburg

Sachau
III./JG 301

Munich

Nuremberg

I./KG(J) 54

Kiel

Neumünster

Kaltenkirchen

Düneburg

Krümmel

Wesendorf

Kohlenbissen

Kassel

Main

Frankfurt-Main

Germany

I./JG 7

Bremen

Weser

Stuttgart

Switzerland

Emden

Essen

München-Gladbach

Cologne

Koblenz

Freiburg

Rhine

North Sea

Netherlands

Amsterdam

Arnhem

Eindhoven

Aachen

Lux

Metz

Nancy

Danube

Rhine

Rotterdam

Belgium

Antwerp

Brussels

Liège

Ostend

Lille

Calais

Boulogne

Amiens

Paris

Seine

England

2nd Air Division
(340 B-24s) 2nd up
Bombs dropped 1256-1322 hrs

3rd Air Division
(529 B-17s) 1st up
Bombs dropped 1325-1421 hrs

1st Air Division
(384 B-17s) 3rd up
Bombs dropped
1519-1604 hrs

London

Chartres

Orléans

Le Mans

7 April 1945
8th Air Force raid on North German targets

△ Bombers under fighter attack

〰〰〰 Ramming attacks by Sonderkommando Elbe

◉ Rendezvous point of battle formation

■ Bomber target

Luftwaffe defensive activity – 7 April 1945

Unit	Type	Gruppe up				Gruppe down		Claims	Losses				
		Base	No	Time		Base	Time		Dest	Dam	KIA	MIA	WIA
Luftflotte Reich													
IX. Fliegerkorps (Jagd):													
I./JG 7	Me 262A	Brandenburg–Briest, Oranienburg	*15	~1200		Brandenburg–Briest, Oranienburg	~1300	1 B-24, 1 P-51	0	0	0	0	0
	Me 262A	Brandenburg–Briest	—	1455		Brandenburg–Briest	1545	0	0	0	0	0	0
III./JG 7	Me 262A	Parchim	44	1150		Wismar, Hustedt	1245	1 B-17, 2 P-51	0	0	0	0	0
I./JG 301	Bf 109G	Salzwedel		1115		Salzwedel	~1300	0	2	0	2	0	0
III./JG 301	Bf 109G	Sachau		1115		Sachau	~1300	0	1	0	1	0	0
I./KG(J) 54	Me 262A	Zerbst	15	~1200		Zerbst	~1300	4 B-17	1	0	0	0	1
Skdo Elbe	Bf 109K	Delitzsch	25	1115		Delitzsch	~1300	13 B-17, 5 B-24**	45**	3**	24**	8**	13**
	Bf 109G	Gardelegen	40	1115		Gardelegen	~1300	—	—	—	—	—	—
	Bf 109	Mörtitz	20	1115		Mörtitz	~1300	—	—	—	—	—	—
	Bf 109G	Sachau	20	1115		Sachau	1250	—	—	—	—	—	—
	Bf 109	Stendal	30	1115		Stendal	~1300	—	—	—	—	—	—
	Bf 109K	Prague–Klecan	48	1120		Prague–Klecan	1215-1300	—	—	—	—	—	—
	Bf 109	Prague–Gbell	30	1120		Prague–Gbell	1215-1300	—	—	—	—	—	—

*III./JG 7 sorties total 15

**Skdo Elbe claims and losses are totals; 8 MIA include 2 POW.

taken prisoner or remained MIA, and five returned with injuries. Forty-five Bf 109s were shot down or destroyed during their ramming attacks.

The Elbe pilots had been told that they would be

Aircraft of IV./JG 4, abandoned in Czechoslovakia in May. In the foreground is Bf 109G-6/U2 'White 7'; next is Bf 109G-14 'White 1'. *(Crow)*

protected from American fighters by Me 262s, but there is no evidence that the jet pilots knew anything of this. Their doctrine called for them to attack bombers, not fighters, and this is what they did today. Fifty-nine jets from JG 7 and I./KG(J) 54 were scrambled. JG 7 pilots claimed two B-17s, one B-24 and three P-51s, for no known losses. I./KG(J) 54 reported four victories over B-17s and lost one Me 262 to a B-17 gunner. JG 301 flew its first RLV mission in several weeks, and may in fact have been given escort responsibilities, but the data are lacking. The scale of events overwhelmed the efforts of this unit. One I./JG 301 Fw 190D collided with a B-17; the Geschwader lost three Focke-Wulfs and pilots.

The 8th AF lost 17 bombers today, the greatest loss on a bombing mission since 3 February; 189 more bombers returned to base with damage. The USAAF claimed that the large number of aerial collisions was coincidental and specifically denied that any deliberate ramming had taken place. The sacrifices of the Elbe youths were thus not acknowledged by the Americans and certainly did not affect their morale, as Elbe's commanders had hoped. The organisation was quickly disbanded; the surviving pilots returned to their previous units or were allowed to volunteer for other special operations.

PILOT'S ACCOUNT[4]
7 April 1945

After a night in which most of us got little sleep in anticipation of the things to come, we were awakened and told that after our daily routine of washing and shaving we were all to assemble in the breakfast room for a special last meal and a further surprise. The tables were set up in a square pattern, and in the middle sat some highly decorated officers in gala uniforms with Knight's Crosses around their necks. They were there to set us a luminous example; however, I saw none of them climb into a crate later to go with us. We were told that the listening service had determined that a strong bomber formation, accompanied by many fighter escorts, was on its way. They would probably come in over northern Germany. The assembly point for the ram fighters was thus to be Magdeburg. From there we would be guided to the bomber stream. The importance of maintaining a tight formation at all costs was stressed.

My friend Ogfr. Horst Seidel and I had decided to fly together, as it was left up to the pilots to choose their formations. Of course, comrades who had known each other for a long time usually flew together. We now went to the aircraft dispersals, where I selected a Me 109K-4 with an auxiliary tank which held 300 litres of gasoline, more than enough for the mission. Unfortunately, Horst's machine had no auxiliary tank. The refuelling crews were now driving from plane to plane, filling their tanks. Our attempts to find an auxiliary tank for Horst failed.

I had noticed that the canopy of my K-4 still contained a *Gallandhaube* [armoured glass headrest], and I demanded its immediate removal, as I feared that it would hit me in the neck when the canopy was jettisoned. My wishes were immediately complied with. We nervously smoked cigarettes and walked around our aircraft to confirm that they were in shape to fly, as the mechanics had already reported.

It was going on 1100 hours when the loudspeakers announced a higher state of readiness. Cockpit readiness was ordered immediately. Horst and I exchanged last handshakes. I gave away my last cigarettes to the mechanics as they tightened my parachute harness and my shoulder and leg straps, and plugged the radio cord into my helmet. They plugged the oxygen line into my mask and checked the seal. I heard a march over the radio and found that I could only receive, not transmit. Then silence.

A mechanic climbed onto my right wing and inserted the starting crank into the engine. A green flare shot up; this was the signal for the ram fighters to take off as quickly as possible. I closed and bolted the canopy, switched on both magnetos, sprayed some gasoline into the aspirator and pulled the stick into my belly. These were all automatic movements. After the mechanics had given the starter the required number of turns, they signalled for me to start the engine – but nothing. The mechanics walked the prop backwards, and we tried again. The engine coughed, but did not run. It started on the third try. I let it warm up a little and checked both magnetos. All seemed to be in order, so Horst and I taxied to the take-off point, where we could see that we were the last to get off. I quickly set the flaps at 15 degrees, checked the trim, gave a last salute to the ground crews and gave it full throttle. The tail lifted; I put on opposite rudder to prevent a ground loop. When I had enough speed, I pulled the stick back slowly and lifted into the air. I raised the landing gear, checking for the green lamps and the indicator pins in the wings. I closed the flaps, throttled back and glanced to the right to see that Horst was there. After turning on the Revi and charging the gun, I circled the field once, saw no more aircraft and set a course directly for Hannover. I did this because of Horst's lack of an auxiliary tank. Chasing the others toward Magdeburg would have used too much fuel, and there was no telling when we would contact the enemy. If I had been a coward, I had enough fuel to fly home.

Now ground control reported in. More march music: I can still hear the *Horst-Wessel-Lied*, the *Deutschlandlied* and the *Badenweilermarsch* today. Suddenly a woman's voice reported in, calling us 'werewolves of the air' and exhorting us to think of Dresden and the other bombed cities, and the civilians dead in the carpet bombings. 'Save the Homeland' and similar slogans. I was, however, thinking of other things – my future tactics. I wanted to make my attack with the sun absolutely at my back, so that the bombers would recognise me late, or perhaps not at all.

During our solo flight, we were overtaken only once by a Me 109 flying at high speed at over 10,000 metres. This was the only interruption. We were miserably cold at our high altitude. We had been in the air for some time and were getting ever closer to the combat zone. We searched the heavens restlessly in all directions, especially behind and below us. Our thoughts were circling around one point: how would this day end for us? Would we survive, or would our machines wedge into the bombers and take us to a deadly crash? Or, since the bomber would surely fly violent defensive movements, would we explode in a fireball with it? Would we be able to escape our aircraft and land with our parachutes, or would we be lucky enough to make emergency landings in our disabled machines? The announced number of about 1,300 bombers and up to 800 fighter escorts would have a fiery reception for us in any case.

Then, in the distance to the northwest, we saw flashes, rapidly increasing in frequency – and there they were. They were approaching in a long, stretched-out formation, and not in the dreaded tight combat boxes. The escort fighters were flying in front. Approaching from the east and very easy to see were our comrades, with huge condensation trails behind them. As we were at about the same altitude, I looked behind Horst's aircraft and saw the same treacherous contrails. I immediately lost some altitude; Horst followed me. After flying over Hannover, I jettisoned my auxiliary tank. It was still partly full, and would have added a gigantic risk – we were not Kamikazes and had no thoughts of suicide.

Now we tightened our little formation, raised our hand in a final greeting and waggled our wings. This was the sign that we had bombers in a favourable attack position beneath us. I half-rolled my mill onto its back and dove sideways toward the bombers with increasing speed. The first one that I targeted sheered away, and I left it alone; it had probably already jettisoned its bombs and was already trailing a smoke plume. Unseen, or in any case noticed too late, I approached another bomber from the sun. It was flying at ca. 6,000 metres. No defensive reaction; no defensive fire. It flew straight and level through the skies. At about 300 metres from my goal, I shut off the automatic propeller-pitch mechanism and manually screwed the blades to their finest pitch. I forced the throttle past the emergency stop and aimed the fighter with its howling and overwinding engine at the right side of my target's tail assembly. The propeller, turning edge-on at maximum speed, was like a circular saw with many sharp teeth.

The moment before the hitting the Fortress I estimated that I had at least 200 km/h excess speed. The tail gunner must have seen the approaching disaster at the last moment, for he dropped his guns and put his hands over his face. The impact came with such violence that I immediately lost consciousness; I probably hit my head against the reflector sight. When I came to, I saw with horror that my Messerschmitt did not respond to stick movements, and the canopy was smeared with oil. I pulled out the magneto knob to prevent a possible engine fire. My altitude was not obvious, but I suspected that I was near crashing. I pulled the plug from my helmet, took a deep breath of oxygen through the mask, loosened the seat belts, pulled the lever to release the canopy and thought, 'Now begins your first parachute jump!' But to my horror the canopy did not fly off; it must have been jammed by the collision with the Fortress. With all my strength I now pressed my back against the canopy. Nothing happened! Panic at the thought of crashing into the ground while still alive came over me, and I pushed with new force. Suddenly there was a rattle of bullets hitting the left side of the canopy and cockpit. The shattered canopy flew away, and I was sucked from the cockpit. My right shoulder hit the tail, and my right arm twisted painfully out of its socket. My collarbone was also broken, but this would be discovered later. An enemy fighter had pursued me and had shot down his defenseless victim, thereby saving my life. Somersaulting through the air, I felt like fainting again, but pulled the ripcord with my left hand right before passing out.

What followed next I know only from the descriptions of others. My 'saviour' or another Mustang hero opened fire on me and put 19 holes in my parachute, as counted later on the ground. I was hanging lifelessly and I am certain that the Ami thought that the 'bandit', as they called us, was dead. I do not think badly of him today, because he had saved my life, after all. I came to near the ground, saw that I was approaching a large meadow and a farmhouse and passed out again before hitting the ground. I lay there for two hours; the farmer either thought I was dead or was an Ami to be afraid of. My memory only returned when I got up, unzipped my flying suit and put on my peaked cap, which was folded inside my suit. He and his wife took me into their house and treated my many injuries.

In the meantime, air battles continued to rage in the skies. Everyone was so alarmed by the screaming engines and crashing aircraft that they stayed inside.

Not until late in the day was I taken to the nearest field hospital at Schwarmstedt, two kilometres away. There, my wounds were simply sewn up, leaving much embedded shrapnel to be removed at a later date. I was able to report my victory by telephone to Major Köhnke, the Elbe commander, but the car that was supposedly sent for me never arrived, and I was taken prisoner by the British two days later after they had shelled the hospital.

The body of my friend and wingman, Ogfr. Seidel, was discovered some weeks after the end of the war on the southern edge of the Ostenholzer Moor. His parachute was unopened, and the circumstances of his death remain unknown.

Uffz. Werner Zell, Sonderkommando Elbe

Uffz. Werner Zell. A typical volunteer for Sonderkommando Elbe, Zell completed his elementary pilot training in June 1944, but never received enough fighter training for a posting to an operational unit. On 7 April, Zell succeeded in ramming his targeted B-17, but was badly injured in the collision, consequent bailout and strafing by American fighters. He was captured by the British Army in his hospital bed on 10 April. *(Zell)*

8 April

8th Air Force Mission #932: 1,103 of 1,173 HBs (all ADs) bomb jet engine factory, ordnance depot, rail targets, airfields – lose 9-1-152, claim 0. 763 of 794 fighters (14 FGs) escort, claim 3-0-0, lose 1-1-?.

Jet airfields were of personal interest to the commanders and aircrew of the USSTAF and RAF Bomber Command and were bombed at every opportunity. Parchim, the base for I./JG 1 and its He 162s and a dispersal base for JG 7, was bombed today and put out of action for a week. Luftwaffe data are sketchy, but all of the operational jet units were up. As many as eight heavy bombers, one P-38 and two P-51s were claimed. Known losses total two Me 262s destroyed in combat and five Me 262s damaged or destroyed in crash-landings.

9 April

8th Air Force Mission #935: 1,215 of 1,252 HBs (all ADs) bomb central German oil storage facility, ammunition plant, south German jet airfields – lose 7-3-61, claim 0. 812 of 848 fighters (15 FGs) escorts claim 1-1-4, lose 5-2-?.

RAF Bomber Command: 57 No. 5 Group Lancasters bomb Hamburg oil storage facility, U-Boat shelters – lose 2, claim 0. No. 11 Gp. Mustangs escort claims 0, lose 0.

It was now time for the jet airfields in southern Germany to take a pounding. Six of JV 44's Me 262s were badly damaged on Brandenburg–Briest. JV 44 scrambled only one jet to meet this attack, without

Me 262A-1a 'White 1' of JV 44, one of the oldest Me 262s still in service at war's end. It carries early mottled tail camouflage, the narrow yellow fuselage band unique to Erprobungskommando 262 and Kommando Nowotny, which was disbanded on 2 Dec 44, and a white 'S' (not seen here) denoting later service in a school unit – Innsbruck–Hötting, Austria, 29 May. *(Crow)*

Luftwaffe defensive activity – 8 April 1945

Unit	Type	Gruppe up			Gruppe down		Claims	Losses				
		Base	No	Time	Base	Time		Dest	Dam	KIA	MIA	WIA
Luftflotte Reich												
IX. Fliegerkorps (Jagd):												
I./JG 7	Me 262A	Brandenburg–Briest,	15	?	Brandenburg–Briest,	?	1 Lancaster, 1 P-38 [F-5]	0	0	0	0	0
III./JG 7	Me 262A	Parchim		?	Parchim	?	2 P-51	1	0	0	0	0
I./KG(J) 54	Me 262A	Zerbst	14	?	Zerbst	?	3 B-17	0	4	0	0	0
III./EJG 2	Me 262A	Lechfeld		1150	Lechfeld	~1250	0	0	0	0	0	0
Luftwaffenkdo West												
7. Jagddivision:												
JV 44	Me 262A	München–Riem		1542	München–Riem	1644	4 B-24	1	1	0	0	0

Luftwaffe defensive activity – 9 April 1945

Unit	Type	Gruppe up			Gruppe down		Claims	Losses				
		Base	No	Time	Base	Time		Dest	Dam	KIA	MIA	WIA
Luftflotte Reich												
IX. Fliegerkorps (Jagd):												
I./JG 7	Me 262A	Brandenburg–Briest,	*29	?	Brandenburg–Briest,	?	1 P-51, 3 Lancaster	1	0	1	0	0
III./JG 7	Me 262A	Parchim, Lärz	—	1725	Parchim, Lärz	1835	1 P-47, 1 Lancaster	0	0	0	0	0
I./KG(J) 54	Me 262A	Zerbst	15	?	Zerbst	?	n/c	0	0	0	0	0
III./EJG 2	Me 262A	Lechfeld	2	0945	Lechfeld	1020	2 B-26	1	0	0	0	0
Luftwaffenkdo West												
7. Jagddivision:												
JV 44	Me 262A	München–Riem	1	1720	München–Riem	1803	0	0	0	0	0	0

*JG 7 sorties total 29

success. In the north, JG 7 went after RAF Lancasters bombing Hamburg, shooting down two, while III./EJG 2 was directed to a medium bomber formation and shot down two B-26s. Two jets and at least one pilot were lost.

10 April

8th Air Force Mission #938: 1,232 of 1,315 HBs (all ADs) bomb Oranienburg army HQ, north German jet airfields, TOT 1436-1541 – lose 19-4-254, claim 17-4-12. 868 of 905 fighters (14 FGs) escort and support, claim 10.5-0-13, lose 8-0-?.

The 8th AF dispatched a full-strength raid to one army headquarters and eight north German airfields suspected of harbouring jets. IX. Fliegerkorps (Jagd) scrambled 63 Me 262s on what proved to be the high point of Luftwaffe jet activity. The 1st AD and 3rd AD streams were both attacked in the Berlin area by Me 262s, which swept in from 6 o'clock high, level or low

either individually or in small groups. The jet pilots claimed 16 B-17s and, a little later, two P-47s and six P-51s while fighting through the escorts to find somewhere to land while their own bases were under attack. JG 7 and KG(J) 54 lost at least six pilots KIA (including three Staffelkapitäne) and four WIA, and as many as 27 Me 262s, although this number is uncertain. An unknown number of jets were destroyed on their bases, all of which were now unserviceable. JG 7 and KG(J) 54 were ordered to withdraw to the south. The Stab of KG(J) 54 made it to Fürstenfeldbruck near Munich, but the other north German units wound up in the Prague area.

According to some sources, I./JG 400 flew a mission, sending up a single Me 163 that downed a straggling B-17 or Lancaster with the *Jägerfaust* (Hunter's Fist) weapon, which comprised 10 vertically mounted 50-mm gun barrels in the wing roots, triggered by a photocell. If true, this was either the ninth or tenth, and last, victory for the Me 163.

Luftwaffe defensive activity – 10 April 1945

Unit	Type	Gruppe up			Gruppe down		Claims	Losses				
		Base	No	Time	Base	Time		Dest	Dam	KIA	MIA	WIA
Luftflotte Reich												
IX. Fliegerkorps (Jagd):			63									
I./JG 7	Me 262A	Oranienburg	15	1415	Oranienburg	~1500	11 B-17	3+	0	2	0	0
III./JG 7	Me 262A	Parchim, Lärz	24	1400	Parchim, Lärz, Alt–Lönnewitz	1508	1 B-17, 4 P-51, 3 P-47	6+	0	2	0	2
	Me 262A	Lärz	2	1430	Köthen	1533	1 P-51	1	0	1	0	0
	Me 262A	Alt–Lönnewitz	1	1546	Alt–Lönnewitz	1641	0	0	0	0	0	0
Stab/JG 301	Ta 152H	Sachau	4	1913	Sachau	2045	1 P-47	0	0	0	0	0
I./JG 400	Me 193B	Brandis	1	?	Brandis	?	1 Lancaster	0	0	0	0	0
I./KG(J) 54	Me 262A	Zerbst	21	1400	Zerbst	~1500	4 B-17, 1 B-24, 1 P-51, 1 B-17 HSS	4	6	2	0	2
Luftwaffenkdo West												
7. Jagddivision:												
JV 44	Me 262A	München–Riem		1032	München–Riem	1138	1 P-47	0	0	0	0	0

PILOT'S ACCOUNT[5]
10 April 1945

The day began as a sunny spring morning with a bright blue sky. More than 2,000 enemy aircraft would soon be heading for Germany, opposed by the 63 operational jet fighters of JG 7 and KG(J) 54. As the bomber stream crossed the English coast at noon, we were called to cockpit readiness. My 3. Staffel had seven turbos ready! At 1340 hours, the controller reported that the enemy formation was approaching Osnabrück. After climbing to 7,000 metres, the three air divisions split up and headed for different jet airfields. I scrambled from Oranienburg at 1415 hours in my 'Yellow 1' with the rest of I./JG 7, leading my seven Me 262s. We were directed to climb to 8,000 metres over Oranienburg to meet heavies coming from the northwest. Escorts were patrolling above like a swarm of hornets. To get through them to the bombers, I led my Staffel on a zig-zag course to 10,000 metres and brought them behind the bombers in a broad curve. We then attacked the Flying Fortresses from above. We were so much faster than the heavies that I had worked out a special tactic to attack them. A formation of several hundred bombers stretches to a length of several kilometres, even in tight formation. To make several long, curving approaches seemed senseless. To minimise our exposure to defensive fire from the machine gun turrets, while using as little fuel as possible, and because there were plenty of targets, I decided to 'surf' over the bomber stream: diving from 1,000 metres above, seeking out a bomber on the far left or right, firing a short burst at the inner engine, pulling up at least 200 metres over the machine in case it drops suddenly and then making the next attack. Such a 'ride' allows you to obtain several shootdowns in one pass. Firing at the inner engine or between the two engines shows an immediate effect because this is where the fuel tanks are. I did not understand the attack tactics of many other pilots who attacked a close formation of such 'flying fortresses' from the side, below or the front. Only if you fly in the direction of the bomber stream and attack from above, can you moderate somewhat the effect of their concentrated firepower. Although the bomber gunners could fire at us effectively from 700 metres, we had to close to 300 metres for our four MK 108 cannon to be effective.

I saw Oranienburg in flames, thought of Hamburg and attacked the bombers in a rage. I fired at the huge tail of the nearest B-17. The 3-cm shells separated it from the fuselage like a power saw and it fell below. I made an Abschwung [split-S] to attack the Pulk below. I hit the next B-17 between the two right engines, and before I side-slipped over the wing, I could see the name 'Henn's Revenge' [303rd BG: DC] in large letters beneath the cockpit. Because the fatally hit bomber already filled my windscreen, I pulled up sharply to avoid a collision. The B-17s had by now dropped their loads and pressed on stoically to the east, surrounded by Flak bursts. One split from the formation trailing thick smoke and turned north. At first I wanted to give it the coup de grâce, but when I got nearer, I saw that a shell had torn the skin off the starboard side from the cockpit to aft of the wing. Because the fate of the machine was sealed, I made a broad circle around it, not wanting to fire at the defenceless crew. The co-pilot was hanging out the front in his harness; the crew was assembled in the fuselage preparing to bail out; the weapons were unmanned. While pulling away, I saw nine chutes.I now approached my 3rd victim; its wing attracted my tracers like a magnet. The 3-cm incendiary and AP rounds hit the engines with immense force. The B-17 tilted up, showing a huge hole in the wing, and dived away in flames. As I lined up on my 4th victim, I saw on its tail a large triangle with a stenciled 'U'. After I hit the inner engine of the Fortress, large pieces whirled through the air; then the wing ripped off. I later learned that this B-17 was named 'Moonlight Mission' [457th BG: DC] and that most of the crew had bailed out before it exploded at 5,000 metres.

I was now out of ammunition and searched the sky for my comrades. My ride over the bombers had lost them. Suddenly shells hit my left wing, leaving a trail to the leading turbine ring. As I pulled to the right to avoid the fire, a Mustang swept past, firing from all barrels. A glance at my instruments showed I was at 8,200 metres, and my left engine was failing … The only saving clouds were far below … Reaching them, I looked around … At any moment the engine could explode and the wing could rip off … I decided to bail out, but got tangled up in various cords. I tore myself loose with a strength arising from a fear of death and fell free until very near the ground … I picked up a ride to Berlin with a truckload of soldiers, visited my girlfriend's mother, was told that the war was lost and reached Oranienburg at 2200 hours. I was looking forward to relaxing in my room with a bottle of cognac, but it was gone – the *Spiess* [senior NCO] had already gone through my things, and the *Leichenfledderer* [corpse looters] had drunk to my memory with my own cognac. I was now taken off operations; my ankles were so badly bruised that I could not use the rudder pedals.

[Schuck was shot down by Lt. Peterburs of the 20th Fighter Group: DC]

Oblt. Walter Schuck, Staffelkapitän
3./JG 7

Oblt. Walter Schuck, here shown as an Oberfeldwebel, joined JG 5 in April 1942 and became one of the top-scoring pilots in JG 5, the Arctic Ocean Geschwader, receiving the Knight's Cross with Oak Leaves. In early 1945, he volunteered for jets and made his first Me 262 flight on 20 March. He was obviously a quick study, and Major Weissenberger gave him command of 3./JG 7 on 26 March. On 10 April, he downed four B-17s before his Me 262 was hit by a P-51. Schuck bailed out, but sprained both ankles upon landing and did not return to active service. He claimed 206 victories, including eight in the Me 262, in over 500 combat missions. *(Author's collection)*

Luftwaffe defensive activity – 17 April 1945

Unit	Type	Gruppe up				Gruppe down		Claims	Losses				
		Base	No	Time		Base	Time		Dest	Dam	KIA	MIA	WIA
Luftflotte Reich													
IX. Fliegerkorps (Jagd):			48										
I./JG 7	Me 262A	Prague–Rusin		~1430		Prague–Rusin, Saatz	~1530	4 B-17	5	0	4	1	0
II./JG 7	Me 262A	Prague–Rusin		~1430		Prague–Rusin	~1530	0	1	0	1	0	0
III./JG 7	Me 262A	Alt–Lönnewitz		~1330		Prague–Rusin	~1400	transfer	1	0	1	0	0
	Me 262A	Prague–Rusin		~1430		Prague–Rusin	~1530	4 B-17, 1 P-38	1	0	0	1	0
I./KG(J) 54	Me 262A	Prague–Rusin		1430		Prague–Rusin	~1530	1 B-17	0	0	0	0	0
II./KG(J) 54	Me 262A	Prague–Rusin		~1430		Prague–Rusin	~1530	n/c	0	0	0	0	0
III./EJG 2	Me 262A	Lechfeld		1330		Lechfeld	1400	1 B-26	0	0	0	0	0
Luftwaffenkdo West													
7. Jagddivision:													
JV 44	Me 262A	München–Riem	7	1334		München–Riem	1415	2 B-17	1	0	0	0	0

Luftwaffe defensive activity – 19 April 1945

Unit	Type	Gruppe up				Gruppe down		Claims	Losses				
		Base	No	Time		Base	Time		Dest	Dam	KIA	MIA	WIA
Luftflotte Reich													
IX. Fliegerkorps (Jagd):			42										
I./JG 7	Me 262A	Prague–Rusin		~1200		Prague–Rusin	~1300	4 B-17	1	0	0	0	0
III./JG 7	Me 262A	Prague–Rusin		~1200		Prague–Rusin	~1300	1 B-17	1	0	0	0	1
I./KG(J) 54	Me 262A	Prague–Rusin		~1200		Prague–Rusin	~1300	0	1	0	1	0	0
II./KG(J) 54	Me 262A	Prague–Rusin		~1200		Prague–Rusin	~1300	n/c	0	0	0	0	0
III./EJG 2	Me 262A	Lechfeld		0948		Lechfeld	1018	1 B-26, 1 P-51	0	0	0	0	0
Luftwaffenkdo West													
7. Jagddivision:													
JV 44	Mc 262A	München–Riem	3	?		München–Riem	?	1 P-51	0	0	0	0	0

17 April

8th Air Force Mission #957: 981 of 1,054 HBs (all ADs) bomb Dresden, Czech rail targets – lose 8-1-177, claim 1-0-1. 756 of 816 fighters (15 FGs) escort, claim 13-0-5, lose 17-?-?.

The 8th AF searched out targets in eastern Germany and Czechoslovakia. I./JG 7, II./JG 7, III./JG 7, I./KG(J) 54 and JV 44 jets were up (48 from the IX. Fliegerkorps (Jagd) units) and reported a number of victories, but only two B-17s are known to have been lost to the jets: one to JG 7 and one (by collision) to JV 44. These were the last 1st AD aircraft lost to the Luftwaffe. The number of jets lost is uncertain, but an entire 1./JG 7 Schwarm was shot down by Mustangs while landing, with only the Kapitän surviving.

19 April

8th Air Force Mission #961: 585 of 609 1st AD + 3rd AD B-17s bomb numerous rail targets, TOT 1049-1243 – lose 5-0-40, claim 6-1-2. 486 of 584 fighters (11 FGs) escort and sweep, claim 12-0-3, lose 2-3-?.

The 8th AF targeted a number of rail yards. A surviving Luftwaffe document states that 42 fighters were up in defense, claiming seven certain and five probable victories for a loss of four aircraft destroyed, five missing and three damaged – not all of these losses can be corroborated today. JG 7 flew its last large-scale mission and downed five 3rd AD B-17s, the last heavy bombers to fall to the German jets. I./KG(J) 54 joined JG 7 over Bohemia, while III./EJG 2 and JV 44 attacked B-26s in the south. Other Luftwaffe activity included the formal disbanding of the

A 9./JG 7 Me 262A-1a (W. Nr. 501221) after being shot down by PFC R. V. Caputo at Kloetze, Germany, on about 21 April. This aircraft has been associated with Obfw. Hermann Buchner, but according to his memoir, Buchner was in a ground convoy during this period. (Rosch)

immobile I./JG 400 at Brandis, just as American tanks appeared on the airfield.

25 April

8th Air Force Mission #968: 554 of 589 HBs (1st AD + 2nd AD) bomb southeastern German and Czech airfields and rail targets – lose 6-4-200, claim 0. 539 of 584 fighters (11 FGs) escort and sweep, claim 1-1-0, lose 1-0-?.

The US Army met the Soviet Army at Torgau on the Elbe, splitting the dying Reich into northern and southern portions, while two Soviet army groups encircled Berlin and Adolf Hitler. There were no industrial targets left, but if airfields and rail targets can be classed as 'strategic', the 8th AF flew its last strategic mission today. IX. Fliegerkorps (Jagd) flew 15 sorties and apparently claimed eight B-17s southwest of Prague, but the USAAF blamed their six B-17 losses on antiaircraft fire. RAF BC flew its last strategic mission that night; the 15th AF flew small missions on 26 April and 1 May, without encountering the Luftwaffe. Jet operations from Prague were now restricted by the fuel supply. When missions could be flown, they were directed against the approaching Red Army. JV 44, the only jet unit in southern Germany, flew its last missions against American tactical bombers and fighter-bombers.

Me 262A-1a 'White 3' (W.Nr. 500071) of 9./JG 7, photographed after force-landing out of fuel at Zürich–Dubendorf in Switzerland on 25 April. The pilot, Fhr. Hans-Guido Mütke, was interned for the brief remainder of the war. The airplane displays the blue-red Geschwader identification band, but lacks the famous 'running wolf' badge. (Bundesarchiv 141-2492)

Luftwaffe defensive activity – 25 April 1945

Unit	Type	Gruppe up			Gruppe down		Claims	Losses				
		Base	No	Time	Base	Time		Dest	Dam	KIA	MIA	WIA
Luftflotte Reich												
IX. Fliegerkorps (Jagd):			**13**									
I./JG 7	Me 262A	Prague–Rusin		?	Prague–Rusin	?	6 B-17	0	0	0	0	0
III./JG 7	Me 262A	Prague–Rusin		?	Prague–Rusin	?	0	1	0	0	1	0
III./KG(J) 6	Me 262A	Prague–Rusin		?	Prague–Rusin	?	2 B-17	1	0	1	0	0
Luftwaffenkdo West												
7. Jagddivision:												
JV 44	Me 262A	München–Riem	13	1711	München–Riem	~1800	2 P-51	0	0	0	0	0

Notes

[1] Mittag correspondence with author, 2002.

[2] Jung correspondence with author, 2000.

[3] Sinner Gefechtsbericht, in private collection.

[4] Zell correspondence with author, 2000.

[5] *Abschuss!*, Helios, p. 210.

Surrendered Bf 109s and Fw 190s lined up at Copenhagen in the spring of 1946. *(Stafford)*

CHAPTER 10

SUMMARY AND CONCLUSIONS

The successes and failures of the Luftwaffe day fighter arm – and, more specifically, that large part that was responsible for defending the Reich – have been discussed in detail in this book's companion volume. There were a few operational successes: the RAF was driven to abandon day bombing in 1939, forcing the British into a night campaign that absorbed resources on both sides but took years to have any real effect. And the RLV day fighters shot down B-17s and B-24s at an unsustainable rate in late 1943 and forced a brief slowdown in the American air campaign until the long-range escort fighters that were in the pipeline became operational. There were several technical and tactical innovations that could be considered successes. Strategically, however, the RLV force and the Jagdwaffe were utter failures.

This book has taken a quantitative, statistical approach to covering the campaign. To complete it, new summary tables have been prepared for this chapter. They present the author's best estimates of some critical data for the American strategic air campaign and the German defence. It is well known that data for the Luftwaffe are fragmentary, owing to damaging bomber raids on its Berlin headquarters and an order by its high command to destroy all unit records as total defeat approached. But the Americans also did the historian no favours. The men of the 8th and 15th Air Forces abandoned Europe in mid-1945 without preparing comprehensive statistical summaries of their efforts. Fortunately, Roger Freeman, a British historian who formed indelibly fond impressions of the Americans while growing up near a B-17 base, researched the 8th Air Force unit records in the American and British archives exhaustively in the 1960s and wrote a definitive three-volume history of the 8th in the 1970s and early 1980s, coining the term 'The Mighty Eighth' in the process. Anyone who attempts to write about the European daylight air campaign owes Roger Freeman a debt of gratitude. The 'Forgotten Fifteenth' Air Force did not attract a Roger Freeman, and no complete history of the 15th has ever been written. The present author dug into the American and British archives for enough data on the 15th to tell his own story, but blank spaces in the following tables show where he failed in his search.

Table A, 'Luftwaffe Day Fighter strength and losses on Reich defence missions, by quarters', was compiled from two major sources. Strengths are taken from a well-known USSBS document in the USAFHRA, 'German Order of Battle: Statistics as of Quarter Years, for the Period of 1 Aug 1939 to 10 Jan 1945', using data for those units that were part of the day RLV organisation. Losses are taken from the author's own research by tallying the fighter losses of Luftflotte Reich, Luftflotte 3 and (infrequently) Luftflotten 4 and 6 on day RLV missions. Some explanation of the table is in order:

TO & E strength: The Tables of Organisation and Equipment (TO & E) are the sacred writ governing the existence of every military unit, describing its organisation and detailing its authorised strength in personnel and equipment, which increased several times for the units of the Jagdwaffe. The Gruppen began the war with three 12-fighter Staffeln and a four-fighter Stabsschwarm. The standard Geschwader had three Gruppen, plus its own Stabsschwarm, for a total of 128 fighters. During the war the Staffeln were increased to 16 fighters, the Gruppen to four Staffeln, and the Geschwader to four Gruppen, for an ultimate authorised strength of 276 fighters.

Aircraft on hand: The number of fighters on inventory in the unit. This was almost always less than the TO & E strength; after heavy operations, much less.

Aircraft available: The number of serviceable fighters, i.e., those cleared to fly missions, in the unit at a given time. This number was reported up the chain of command at the end of each day's operations. It could vary greatly over the course of any single day, and its use for statistical purposes can be misleading. However, it does reflect the efficiency of a given unit's supply and maintenance functions.

% TO & E on hand: This is an attempt to show in a single number the success of the Luftwaffe supply organisation in keeping the units up to strength in aircraft. From 1942 to 1944, this number drops from 100 per cent to 60–70 per cent for Luftflotte Reich and to 30–40 per cent for Luftflotte 3, which had the additional responsibility of defending the western occupied zone against the Allied tactical air forces.

Dest: aircraft destroyed; in the Luftwaffe, any airplane damaged 60 per cent or more was considered 'destroyed' and written off the books. The Luftwaffe's 'destroyed' is thus equivalent to the Allies' 'destroyed', plus 'Category E damage'.

Dam: aircraft damaged less than 60 per cent; repairable in the unit or at upper-echelon repair facilities.

KIA and WIA are self-explanatory; MIA are aircrew permanently lost, not simply those who had failed to return at the end of a day's operations. For statistical purposes they can be considered KIA.

% Dest per quarter: this is the ratio of Jagdwaffe aircraft destroyed in a quarter-year to the aircraft on hand at the end of the quarter; it is intended to be a single-figure estimate for aircraft turnover in the front-line units from combat losses. It assumes that the tabulated on-hand figure is an adequate approximation for the average number on hand during the quarter. This column bears careful study. Luftflotte Reich's losses shot up from 50 per cent to 100 per cent in the first quarter of 1944, when it lost air superiority over the Reich. The vulnerability of certain aircraft types is borne out by the figures. Losses of Bf 110 Zerstörer were 250 per cent for this quarter. Its successor, the Me 410, sustained 150 per cent losses in the next quarter.

TABLE A
Luftwaffe day fighter strength and losses on Reich defence missions, by quarters

Quarter	Command + fighter type	TO & E strength	Aircraft on hand	Aircraft available	% TO & E on hand	Losses on day RLV missions					% Dest per quarter
						Dest	Dam	KIA	MIA	WIA	
4th Quarter	Lw Bfh Mitte	164	184	150	112.2	2	1	2	0	0	1.1
1942	Bf 109	40	45	31	112.5	0	0	0	0	0	0.0
	Fw 190	124	139	119	136.3	2	1	2	0	0	1.4
	Luftflotte 3	308	300	229	97.4	33	16	15	4	4	11.0
	Bf 109	34	41	30	136.7	3	1	0	0	0	7.3
	Fw 190	274	259	199	94.5	30	15	15	4	4	11.5
1st Quarter	Lw Bfh Mitte	260	185	138	71.2	27	13	8	4	8	11.3
1943	Bf 109	124	109	84	87.9	10	3	1	1	1	9.2
	Fw 190	136	76	54	55.9	11	3	3	1	1	14.4
	Bf 110 (N)	—	—	—	—	6	7	4	2	6	—
	Luftflotte 3	213	280	209	131.4	21	5	9	2	5	7.5
	Bf 109	17	56	42	329.4	9	3	5	0	2	16.1
	Fw 190	196	224	167	114.3	12	2	4	2	3	5.4
2nd Quarter	Lw Bfh Mitte	552	404	304	73.2	64	58	17	9	28	14.9
1943	Bf 109	352	259	193	73.6	45	39	10	6	24	17.4
	Fw 190	200	145	111	72.5	15	18	5	1	4	10.3
	Bf 110 (N)	—	—	—	—	4	1	2	2	0	—
	Luftflotte 3	364	336	248	92.3	61	31	17	9	21	18.2
	Bf 109	148	129	96	87.2	20	8	4	2	6	15.5
	Fw 190	216	207	152	95.8	41	23	13	7	15	19.8

Quarter	Command + fighter type	TO & E strength	Aircraft on hand	Aircraft available	% TO & E on hand	Losses on day RLV missions					% Dest per quarter
						Dest	Dam	KIA	MIA	WIA	
3rd Quarter	Lw Bfh Mitte	1,128	906	599	80.3	207	98	55	21	70	21.0
1943	Bf 109	708	518	346	73.1	111	50	16	15	34	21.4
	Fw 190	132	125	67	94.7	73	44	21	2	27	58.4
	Bf 110 (Z)	196	188	157	95.1	2	1	0	2	0	1.1
	Me 410	80	58	29	72.5	4	0	4	0	1	6.9
	Ju 88	12	17	0	141.7	0	0	0	0	0	0.0
	Bf 110 (N)	—	—	—	—	17	3	14	2	8	—
	Luftflotte 3	460	328	200	71.3	113	89	52	5	51	33.8
	Bf 109	136	102	62	75.0	36	30	19	2	13	35.3
	Fw 190	280	187	117	66.8	75	57	32	3	35	40.1
	Bf 110 (Z)	44	39	21	88.6	0	0	0	0	0	0.0
	Bf 110 (N)	—	—	—	—	2	2	1	0	3	—
4th Quarter	Luftflotte Reich	1,160	758	548	65.3	461	211	263	20	193	58.4
1943	Bf 109	672	441	317	65.6	219	117	78	12	66	49.7
	Fw 190	212	121	92	57.1	116	42	51	4	37	95.9
	Bf 110 (Z)	236	179	125	69.9	82	25	88	0	62	45.8
	Me 410	40	17	14	42.5	26	17	31	0	14	152.9
	Ju 88	—	—	—	—	6	2	10	3	5	—
	Do 217	—	—	—	—	1	0	2	0	1	—
	Bf 110 (N)	—	—	—	—	11	8	3	1	8	—
	Luftflotte 3	388	237	148	61.1	92	39	45	2	29	36.2
	Bf 109	108	97	61	89.8	55	15	25	1	18	56.7
	Fw 190	280	140	87	50.0	31	21	17	1	7	22.1
	Bf 110 (N)	—	—	—	—	6	3	3	0	4	—
	Luftflotte 2	—	—	—	—	2	1	0	0	1	—
	Bf 109	—	—	—	—	2	1	0	0	1	—
1st Quarter	Luftflotte Reich	1,296	949	643	73.2	1,094	461	560	29	332	102.8
1944	Bf 109	796	606	416	76.1	563	228	223	21	140	83.0
	Fw 190	292	233	163	79.8	226	148	105	7	63	97.0
	Bf 110 (Z)	124	66	49	53.2	172	55	130	0	88	260.6
	Me 410	84	44	15	52.3	24	15	22	1	15	56.8
	Ju 88	—	—	—	—	46	7	35	0	16	—
	Do 217	—	—	—	—	4	0	2	0	2	—
	Bf 110 (N)	—	—	—	—	58	8	43	0	8	—
	Luftflotte 3	364	134	92	36.8	159	72	85	5	52	115.7
	Bf 109	136	61	38	44.8	74	36	37	2	31	121.3
	Fw 190	228	73	54	32.0	81	32	46	3	20	111.0
	Bf 110 (N)	—	—	—	—	4	4	2	0	1	—
	Luftflotte 2	—	—	—	—	15	5	4	4	3	—
	Bf 109	—	—	—	—	15	5	4	4	3	—

Quarter	Command + fighter type	TO & E strength	Aircraft on hand	Aircraft available	% TO & E on hand	Losses on day RLV missions					% Dest per quarter
						Dest	Dam	KIA	MIA	WIA	
2nd Quarter	Luftflotte Reich	908	619	336	68.2	1,165	386	658	23	331	188.2
1944	Bf 109	416	299	170	69.4	675	204	309	11	172	225.8
	Fw 190	192	149	88	77.6	300	117	123	3	74	201.3
	Bf 110 (Z)	160	87	32	54.3	57	23	64	5	24	65.5
	Me 410	108	74	40	68.5	109	40	146	4	60	147.3
	Me 163	32	10	6	31.3	0	0	0	0	0	0.0
	Me 210	—	—	—	—	14	2	8	0	1	—
	Ju 88	—	—	—	—	3	0	8	0	0	—
	MC 202	—	—	—	—	7	0	0	0	0	—
	Luftflotte 3	1,300	485	233	37.3	113	43	48	5	30	22.9
	Bf 109	724	307	152	42.4	41	16	15	0	16	13.4
	Fw 190	576	178	81	30.9	70	27	31	3	14	39.3
	Me 410	—	—	—	—	2	0	2	2	0	
	Luftflotte 2	—	—	—	—	46	19	9	14	9	—
	Bf 109	—	—	—	—	37	15	6	14	7	—
	MC 205	—	—	—	—	7	0	3	0	2	—
	G 50 bis	—	—	—	—	2	2	0	0	0	—
	MS 406	—	—	—	—	0	2	0	0	0	—
3rd Quarter	I. Jagdkorps	2,140	1,323	844	61.8	849	265	420	40	235	60.8
1944	Bf 109	1,040	722	456	69.4	571	182	228	24	154	79.4
	Fw 190	980	555	352	56.6	228	63	150	8	64	41.1
	Me 163	68	23	14	33.8	3	2	2	0	0	13.0
	Me 262	52	23	22	44.2	2	0	1	0	0	8.7
	Bf 110 (Z)	—	—	—	—	8	2	2	8	2	—
	Me 410	—	—	—	—	35	16	34	0	15	—
	Bf 110 (N)	—	—	—	—	2	0	3	0	0	—
	II. Jagdkorps	904	307	216	34.0	68	1	13	1	4	22.1
	Bf 109	548	182	136	33.2	13	0	4	0	2	7.1
	Fw 190	356	125	80	35.1	55	1	9	1	2	44.0
	Luftflotte 2	—	—	—	—	4	1	2	0	0	—
	Bf 109	—	—	—	—	0	1	0	0	0	—
	MC 205	—	—	—	—	2	0	1	0	0	—
	G 55	—	—	—	—	2	0	1	0	0	—
4th Quarter	I. Jagdkorps	916	609	319	66.4	833	242	315	47	148	136.8
1944	Bf 109	340	224	121	65.9	397	124	132	9	55	177.2
	Fw 190	384	275	164	71.6	411	114	179	37	90	149.4
	Me 163	108	91	22	84.2	9	1	2	0	1	9.9
	Me 262	84	19	12	22.6	16	3	2	1	2	84.2
	II. Jagdkorps	2,352	1,206	833	51.3	36	13	14	8	7	3.0
	Bf 109	1,372	622	397	45.3	21	9	9	0	6	3.4
	Fw 190	980	584	436	59.6	15	4	5	8	1	2.6
	Luftflotte 2	—	—	—	—	3	0	2	0	0	—
	Bf 109	—	—	—	—	3	0	2	0	0	—

Quarter	Command + fighter type	TO & E strength	Aircraft on hand	Aircraft available	% TO & E on hand	Losses on day RLV missions					% Dest per quarter
						Dest	Dam	KIA	MIA	WIA	
1st Quarter	IX. Fliegerkorps (Jagd)	—	—	—	—	334	72	180	11	75	—
1945	Bf 109	—	—	—	—	140	23	66	1	32	—
	Fw 190	—	—	—	—	122	14	67	10	25	—
	Me 163	—	—	—	—	3	0	1	0	1	—
	Me 262	—	—	—	—	69	35	46	0	17	—
	Luftwaffenkdo West	—	—	—	—	9	5	1	1	1	—
	Bf 109	—	—	—	—	0	0	0	0	0	—
	Fw 190	—	—	—	—	9	5	1	1	1	—
	Luftflotte 4	—	—	—	—	0	1	0	0	0	—
	Bf 109	—	—	—	—	0	1	0	0	0	—
2nd Quarter	IX. Fliegerkorps (Jagd)	—	—	—	—	86	19	47	11	20	—
1945	Bf 109	—	—	—	—	48	3	27	8	13	—
	Fw 190	—	—	—	—	0	0	0	0	0	—
	Me 262	—	—	—	—	38	16	20	3	7	—
	Luftwaffenkdo West	—	—	—	—	3	2	0	0	0	—
	Bf 109	—	—	—	—	0	0	0	0	0	—
	Fw 190	—	—	—	—	0	0	0	0	0	—
	Me 262	—	—	—	—	3	2	0	0	0	—

Table B, 'Reich defence force missions vs. the US 8th Air Force', presents the author's best estimates of monthly totals of sorties, victory claims and losses by Luftflotte Reich and Luftflotte 3 on missions against the 8th Air Force. These have been pulled together from many sources; effective sorties (those coming into contact with the enemy) were especially hard to come by, but are believed good to ±10 per cent. These were needed to estimate the percentage of defending fighters lost per effective sortie, which was a sustainable 8 per cent for Luftflotte Reich (then Lw Bfh Mitte) through 1943, but rose to a disastrous 22 per cent in 1944. Losses by the RLV force against the 8th Air Force totalled 5,015 airplanes and 2,717 aircrew. These losses included both combat losses and those sustained on combat missions but not in combat.

Special mention of victory claims will be made here. It is the author's contention that while 'losses' are real – broken hardware on the ground – 'claims' are only notional – by definition, a matter of opinion. The proper metrics for evaluating combat performance in a given air campaign are thus the two sides' losses, not their victory claims. Yet, during the war, victory claims had legitimate uses beyond mere propaganda. Victory claims were a widely used measure of a unit's effectiveness. Given the chance to score, the best fighter units had the most victory claims. Skilful upper-level commanders knew this and gave their better units

greater opportunities by assigning them the most critical tasks. Ironically, these superior units often had a higher percentage of invalid claims than lesser units, but that's the nature of the fighter pilot: the best ones were highly aggressive and self-confident, leading to victory claims that later evaluation could not substantiate.

Post-war interest in victory claims and their accuracy remains high. Other researchers have compared the claims of individual pilots with enemy losses to calculate an 'overclaim rate' for those pilots. Similar estimates have been made for some combat units (Allied fighter groups and German Jagdgruppen). It would be of interest to extend such estimates to entire air forces and campaigns. Tables B–E contain sufficient data to permit claim accuracy ratios to be estimated for the RLV force versus 8th and 15th Air Force bombers and fighters (separately) as well as for both the 8th and 15th Air Force versus the RLV force. Figures for losses specifically to enemy aircraft were required for the calculations; these had to be distinguished from other causes. Details of how these figures were obtained are found in the discussion for Table C. Losses of 8th Air Force fighters after D-Day could not be split between strategic and tactical missions, and the RLV claim accuracy ratio versus fighters was not calculated past May 1944. Summarising the Table B results, the overclaim ratio versus bombers was 1.39; versus fighters, 0.97. Claims versus fighters were thus 'perfect', proving that the Luftwaffe confirmation process worked well when the number of claims was relatively small and crashes could be found and counted.

TABLE B
Reich defence force missions vs. the US 8th Air Force

Month	Luftflotte Reich (Luftwaffenbefehlshaber Mitte)								Luftflotte 3 (Luftwaffenkommando West)								RLV claims/	RLV claims/
	Sorties		Claims			Own Losses		% Dest./ Sortie	Sorties		Claims			Own losses		% Dest./ Sortie	HB loss	Ftr loss
	Total (est.)	Eff. (est.)	HBs Dest.	HBs HSS	Ftrs	Dest.	KIA + MIA		Total (est.)	Eff. (est.)	HBs Dest.	HBs HSS	Ftrs	Dest.	KIA + MIA			
Sep 42	60	60	0	0	0	2	2	3.3	120	110	4	0	0	2	1	1.8	2.00	0.00
Oct 42	0	0	0	0	0	0	0	0	305	265	10	1	1	10	6	3.8	1.25	1.00
Nov 42	0	0	0	0	0	0	0	0	250	250	8	0	0	8	6	3.2	0.80	0.00
Dec 42	30	30	2	0	0	0	0	0	452	380	18	1	0	9	5	2.4	1.06	---
TOTAL 42	90	90	2	0	0	2	0	1.9	1,127	1,005	40	2	1	29	18	2.9	1.08	1.00
Jan 43	60	50	8	0	0	7	4	14.0	170	150	23	0	0	5	1	3.3	1.72	0.00
Feb 43	237	189	21	0	0	12	5	6.3	185	155	10	0	0	4	2	2.6	1.48	0.00
Mar 43	467	275	19	0	0	8	6	2.9	600	437	16	0	0	13	5	3.0	1.94	0.00
Apr 43	217	165	16	3	0	5	1	3.0	371	296	16	0	0	12	6	4.1	1.14	0.00
May 43	585	461	50	0	0	23	11	5.0	711	617	52	0	2	31	14	5.0	2.12	0.50
Jun 43	950	735	76	1	1	35	14	4.8	544	358	24	0	9	17	6	4.7	1.28	1.25
Jul 43	1,661	1,262	94	5	9	83	35	6.6	759	614	38	6	7	25	8	4.1	1.67	1.78
Aug 43	1,237	762	80	14	0	49	14	6.5	1,102	910	26	0	4	40	24	4.4	1.22	0.57
Sep 43	690	468	34	9	3	43	23	9.2	1,597	1,133	55	2	6	49	23	4.3	1.93	0.90
Oct 43	3,333	2,204	226	14	10	166	103	7.5	389	304	21	2	1	23	13	7.6	1.78	0.92
Nov 43	2,286	1,396	92	3	42	151	91	10.8	352	287	18	0	3	18	7	6.3	2.08	0.88
Dec 43	1654	1,094	102	2	26	121	89	11.1	514	474	47	1	13	41	25	8.7	2.26	0.66
TOTAL 43	13,377	9,061	818	51	91	703	396	7.8	7,294	5,735	346	11	45	278	134	4.8	1.66	0.85
Jan 44	2,942	1,308	127	19	41	218	158	17.0	996	617	65	8	24	46	25	7.5	1.38	1.14
Feb 44	2,348	1,806	218	22	63	344	191	19.0	1,523	1,145	53	4	20	52	26	4.5	1.59	1.20
Mar 44	2,464	1,425	267	17	71	354	202	24.8	1,094	641	23	0	9	70	43	10.9	1.63	1.48
Apr 44	3,487	2,283	261	13	62	370	206	16.2	670	572	38	0	13	72	39	11.9	0.95	0.55
May 44	4,172	2,562	241	18	96	478	217	18.7	1,100	796	5	2	23	48	19	6.0	1.17	1.17
Jun 44	410	311	51	1	8	80	61	25.7	82	62	2	1	0	3	1	4.8	0.83	--
Jul 44	1,338	700	109	5	20	186	86	26.3	0	0	0	0	0	0	0	0	1.36	--
Aug 44	1,227	712	67	0	21	202	102	28.4	0	0	0	0	0	0	0	0	1.10	--
Sep 44	854	663	153	30	21	237	129	35.7	45	45	0	0	6	29	14	64.4	1.12	--
Oct 44	783	161	24	10	2	50	25	31.0	86	79	0	0	1	12	9	15.2	0.67	--
Nov 44	1,883	1,557	152	2	55	439	215	28.2	0	0	0	0	0	0	0	0	3.04	--
Dec 44	1,368	1,134	91	9	74	278	157	24.5	180	166	0	0	6	24	13	14.5	3.25	--
TOTAL 44	23,276	14,622	1,761	146	534	3,234	1,749	22.1	5,776	4,123	186	15	102	356	189	8.6	1.28	*1.01
Jan 45	520	450	32	0	8	133	60	29.6	0	0	0	0	0	0	0	0	0.65	--
Feb 45	841	547	17	1	9	57	31	10.4	30	30	0	0	0	9	2	30.0	1.21	--
Mar 45	884	737	112	3	29	126	82	21.2	0	0	0	0	0	0	0	0	1.78	--
Apr 45	571	471	84	1	23	86	56	17.6	47	40	7	0	5	2	0	5.0	1.26	--
TOTAL 45	2,816	2,205	245	5	69	402	229	18.1	77	70	7	0	5	11	2	15.7	1.27	--
GRAND TOTAL	39,559	25,978	2826	202	694	4341	2374	16.7	14,274	10,933	579	28	153	674	343	6.2	1.39	*0.97

*through May 44

Table C, '8th Air Force missions opposed by the Reich defence force', is the American counterpart to Table B. All data except the loss breakdown are taken directly from Freeman, whose mission lists allow a split between strategic missions (this book's scope) and tactical missions. Freeman's losses do not indicate their causes, and the present study required losses to enemy aircraft to be stated explicitly. These were obtained from an official document, *Army Air Forces Statistical Digest: World War II*, prepared in December 1945 by the AAF Office of Statistical Control in Washington, DC. Monthly losses are given there and attributed to enemy aircraft, antiaircraft or other causes. Since it is stated that these are operational losses, it is assumed that 'other causes' are 'operational non-combat', including take-off and landing accidents, collisions, and weather and mechanical losses. Strategic and tactical missions are combined. As the number of 8th AF tactical missions was relatively small, and total losses on these missions were available from Freeman, the 'enemy aircraft/antiaircraft fire/other causes' split for bomber losses was obtained by ratio and subtracted from the *Statistical Digest* numbers; the results were entered in Table C. As stated previously, this was not possible for fighter losses after May 1944. One caveat: many lost bombers were reported by the units as FTR, or failed to return, and the reason for their loss was unknown until (or unless) returning POWs could be interviewed. There is no indication that the Office of Statistical Control used any post-war data, and yet it reports no missing

bombers. How they were accounted for is unclear; this author's rationale for using the *Digest* numbers is that they come from an official government publication, and no better substitute is known. One encouraging fact is that the *Digest's* loss totals agree closely with those in Freeman.

The 8th Air Force lost 4,184 heavy bombers on missions opposed by the RLV force and 845 bombers (not tabulated in this book) on missions that were not. On missions opposed by the RLV force, 58.5 per cent were lost to enemy aircraft, 30.5 per cent to antiaircraft fire and 10.9 per cent to other causes. 1,578 escort fighters were lost on missions opposed by the RLV force; the causes of these losses were not broken down.

The last Table C column presents the ratio of 8th AF victory claims to RLV losses. Data for the RLV force lumps combat losses with operational non-combat losses, so the number of losses shown is high, resulting in a ratio that is artificially low. The statistical nature of the data does not permit claims by bombers to be separated from claims by fighters, so we are left with one ratio for the entire air force; this varied significantly with time. In 1943, with few escorts for the first half of the year, the overclaim ratio averaged 3.74. During 1944, when the escorts took on most of the job of combating the Luftwaffe, the ratio was 1.55, a strong indication that claims by fighter pilots were much more accurate than those by bomber gunners. The grand average for the war was 2.03.

TABLE C
8th Air Force missions opposed by the Reich defence force

Month	Heavy bombers								US escort fighters							US claims/
	Sorties		Claims	Losses to				% lost/	Sorties	Claims	Losses to				% lost/	RLV loss
	total	eff.		e/a	Flak	other	total	sortie			e/a	Flak	other	total	sortie	
Sep 42	93	52	16	2	0	0	2	3.8	0	0	0	0	0	0	0	4.00
Oct 42	264	138	44	8	0	2	10	7.2	31	0	1	0	0	1	3.2	4.40
Nov 42	307	200	42	10	3	3	16	8.0	0	0	0	0	0	0	0	5.25
Dec 42	363	172	106	17	0	0	17	9.9	0	0	0	0	0	0	0	3.42
TOTAL 42	1,027	562	208	37	3	5	45	8.0	31	0	1	0	0	1	3.2	3.92
Jan 43	321	241	46	18	3	2	23	9.5	0	0	0	0	0	0	0	3.83
Feb 43	344	190	63	21	3	0	24	12.6	0	0	0	0	0	0	0	3.93
Mar 43	802	613	142	18	4	6	28	4.6	0	0	0	0	0	0	0	6.76
Apr 43	428	352	135	28	1	0	29	8.2	0	0	0	0	0	0	0	7.94
May 43	1,489	1,186	349	48	13	14	75	6.3	339	5	4	0	0	4	1.2	6.56
Jun 43	1,750	1,122	280	78	12	0	90	8.0	522	12	8	0	1	9	3.3	5.38
Jul 43	2,829	1,612	514	79	29	31	139	8.6	486	37	9	0	0	9	1.9	4.76
Aug 43	2,352	1,733	401	87	20	14	121	7.0	1,412	57	7	0	5	12	0/8	5.14
Sep 43	2,834	1,999	255	46	30	30	106	5.3	1,720	36	10	0	5	15	0.9	3.16
Oct 43	2,222	1,892	729	139	38	17	194	10.3	1,649	74	12	0	0	12	0.7	4.24
Nov 43	3,582	2,431	131	53	25	43	121	5.0	2,619	101	51	1	0	52	2.0	1.37
Dec 43	5,102	4,004	208	85	65	52	202	5.0	3,791	92	59	0	0	59	1.6	1.85
TOTAL 43	24,055	17,375	3,253	700	243	209	1,152	6.6	12,538	414	160	1	11	172	1.4	3.74
Jan 44	5,932	4,583	497	139	27	45	211	4.6	5,825	223	57	6	23	86	1.5	2.73
Feb 44	7,441	6,392	282	170	81	31	282	4.4	8,452	358	69	13	23	105	1.2	1.61
Mar 44	7,830	6,036	341	178	112	28	318	5.3	10,113	435	54	46	79	179	1.8	1.83
Apr 44	10,191	8,245	345	314	78	1	393	4.8	12,096	416	136	41	13	190	1.6	1.72
May 44	16,741	12,805	145	211	122	13	346	2.7	18,213	559	102	57	38	197	1.1	1.34
Jun 44	5,147	4,059	29	112	10	0	122	3.0	3,089	97	—	—	—	19	0.6	1.51
Jul 44	9,449	8,382	80	80	75	25	180	2.1	5,730	152	—	—	—	59	1.0	1.26
Aug 44	10,448	8,577	32	61	110	24	195	2.3	6,352	250	—	—	—	75	1.2	1.40
Sep 44	5,286	4,684	60	137	32	10	179	3.8	3,382	289	—	—	—	61	1.8	1.20
Oct 44	5,430	5,042	14	36	41	10	87	1.7	3,664	67	—	—	—	35	1.0	1.31
Nov 44	8,447	7,451	53	50	111	10	171	2.3	7,425	396	—	—	—	88	1.2	1.02
Dec 44	5,399	4,894	54	28	71	10	109	2.2	4,629	378	—	—	—	69	1.5	1.43
TOTAL 44	97,741	81,150	1,932	1,516	870	207	2,593	3.2	88,970	3,620	—	—	—	1,163	1.3	1.55
Jan 45	3,233	2,908	37	49	3	0	52	1.8	2,040	174	—	—	—	22	0.6	1.59
Feb 45	9,111	8,666	1	14	52	10	76	0.9	5,782	80	—	—	—	67	1.2	1.23
Mar 45	18,925	17,418	37	63	74	15	152	0.9	10,374	226	—	—	—	101	1.0	2.09
Apr 45	10,149	8,983	70	72	32	10	114	1.3	6,457	129	—	—	—	52	0.8	2.26
TOTAL 45	41,418	37,975	145	198	161	35	394	1.0	24,653	609	—	—	—	242	1.0	1.82
GRAND TOTAL	164,241	137,082	5,538	2,451	1,277	456	4,184	3.0	126,192	4,643	—	—	—	1,578	1.3	2.03

Table D, 'Reich defence force missions vs. the US 15th Air Force', is the equivalent of Table B for missions in the southern Reich and Hungary. The main difference from Table B is the result of the scarcity of 15th Air Force mission data, especially for missions outside the Reich and Hungary (i.e., to Italy, southern France and the Balkans), which outnumbered those to the territory defended by the RLV force. There was no way to split out the losses that were within our scope from the totals in the *Statistical Digest* once missions to Ploesti became the top priority of the 15th. The calculation of overclaim ratios for the RLV force thus stops at May 1944. The overclaim ratio versus bombers was 1.94; versus fighters, 2.06. Both of these numbers are quite a bit higher than those

calculated against the 8th Air Force. Losses by the RLV force (Luftflotte Reich, with some support from Luftflotten 2 and 4) against the 15th Air Force totalled 815 airplanes and 487 aircrew. These losses included both combat losses and those sustained on combat missions, but not in combat. More than 2,000 Luftwaffe pilots and air gunners were killed on day RLV duty in 1944. What did this mean to the men themselves? Fewer than 1,000 were in the combat units at any given time. Very few unit rosters came through the 1945 bonfires, but several surviving pilots kept their own rosters, which show that the odds of a pilot escaping death or serious injury on late-war duty in Luftflotte Reich were about one in 10.

TABLE D
Reich defence force missions vs. the US 15th Air Force

Month	Luftflotte Reich (Luftwaffenbefehlshaber Mitte)								Luftflotte 2 or Luftflotte 4								RLV claims/	RLV claims/
	Sorties		Claims			Own Losses		% Dest./	Sorties		Claims			Own losses		% Dest./	HB loss	Ftr loss
	Total (est.)	Eff. (est.)	HBs Dest.	HBs HSS	Ftrs	Dest.	KIA + MIA	Sortie	Total (est.)	Eff. (est.)	HBs Dest.	HBs HSS	Ftrs	Dest.	KIA + MIA	Sortie		
Oct 43	176	68	9	2	0	1	0	1.5	0	0	0	0	0	0	0	0	0.90	0.00
Nov 43	147	64	15	0	0	8	2	12.5	0	0	0	0	0	0	0	0	1.36	0.00
Dec 43	165	90	21	2	0	10	10	11.1	58	58	1	0	0	2	0	3.4	1.83	0.00
TOTAL 43	488	222	45	4	0	19	12	8.6	58	58	1	0	0	2	0	3.4	1.39	0.00
Jan 44	218	104	3	0	15	2	2	1.9	58	34	0	0	4	4	5	11.8	---	2.11
Feb 44	836	619	107	10	5	75	34	12.1	71	71	12	1	0	6	1	8.5	1.70	0.50
Mar 44	194	103	21	0	0	12	8	11.6	162	66	4	1	1	5	2	7.6	1.67	0.50
Apr 44	1,105	887	73	1	19	77	48	8.7	264	255	10	0	4	19	11	7.4	1.93	4.60
May 44	591	407	64	2	12	51	40	12.5	74	66	9	0	4	5	1	7.6	3.48	3.20
Jun 44	997	669	82	4	25	122	111	18.2	273	221	15	1	3	22	11	10.0	--	--
Jul 44	1,833	966	164	2	43	173	96	17.9	46	36	3	0	0	4	2	11.1	--	--
Aug 44	1,294	517	81	2	13	113	50	21.9	0	0	0	0	0	0	0	0	--	--
Oct 44	455	223	0	0	0	17	10	7.6	0	0	0	0	0	0	0	0	--	--
Nov 44	244	84	5	0	2	12	9	14.3	22	22	6	0	2	3	2	13.6	--	--
Dec 44	87	87	33	0	4	40	20	47.7	0	0	0	0	0	0	0	0	--	--
TOTAL 44	7,854	4,666	633	21	138	694	428	14.9	970	771	59	3	18	68	35	8.8	*2.08	*2.06
Mar 45	196	140	17	1	7	32	12	22.9	26	26	1	0	0	0	0	0.0	--	--
GRAND TOTAL	8,538	5,028	695	26	145	745	452	14.8	1,054	855	61	3	18	70	35	8.2	*1.94	*2.06

*through May 1944

Table E, '15th Air Force missions opposed by the Reich defence force', suffers from sparse data. Published 15th AF bomber claims are known to be incomplete, and the RLV force losses, which contain operational non-combat losses, are high, so the 15th AF claim/RLV loss ratio is artificially low. Nevertheless, here it is: 2.35, higher than that of the 8th. Since the Jagdwaffe overclaim ratios in the south are also high, it is interesting to speculate on a common cause. Jagddivisionen 7 and 8 held inferior positions in the Luftflotte Reich organisation until mid-1944. The men of the 15th Air Force always resented their subordinate position to their 'big brothers' in the 8th (the survivors still do). Is it possible that the high number of claims filed by both the Germans and the Americans in the south were an attempt to call attention to their underappreciated efforts? This is one of many questions that a study of these tables can prompt. Despite the aforementioned gaps in the data, the tables will allow for some new and meaningful conclusions to be drawn about the most intense air action the world is ever likely to see.

TABLE E
15th Air Force missions opposed by the Reich defence force

| Month | Heavy Bombers | | | | | | | | US Escort Fighters | | | | | | | US claims/ |
| | Sorties | | Claims | Losses to | | | | % lost/ | Sorties | Claims | Losses to | | | | % lost/ | RLV Loss |
	total	eff.		e/a	Flak	other	total	sortie			e/a	Flak	other	total	sortie	
Oct 43	115	115	0	10	0	0	10	8.7	0	0	0	0	0	0	0	0.00
Nov 43	139	112	56	11	0	0	11	9.8	72	0	0	0	0	0	0	7.00
Dec 43	178	161	--	12	0	0	12	7.5	40	0	0	0	0	0	0	0.00
TOTAL 43	432	388	>56	33	0	0	33	8.5	112	0	0	0	0	0	0	*7.00
Jan 44	134	122	0	0	0	0	0	0.0	180	7	9	0	0	9	5.0	0.00
Feb 44	891	641	188	70	7	7	84	13.1	504	14	10	0	0	10	2.0	2.49
Mar 44	599	415	28	12	5	6	23	5.5	235	2	2	0	0	2	0.9	1.67
Apr 44	2,558	2,394	179	43	26	10	79	3.3	946	114	5	2	6	13	1.4	3.05
May 44	2,449	1,989	36	21	44	7	72	3.6	958	84	5	5	6	16	1.7	2.14
Jun 44	2,966	2,758	--	--	--	--	104	3.8	1,920	154	--	--	--	25	1.3	--
Jul 44	6,726	5,717	208	--	--	--	195	3.4	4,204	225	--	--	--	56	1.3	2.45
Aug 44	5,239	5,009	113	--	--	--	104	2.1	3,212	100	--	--	--	18	0.6	1.88
Oct 44	769	769	--	--	--	--	15	2.0	399	17	0	0	0	0	0.0	--
Nov 44	2,835	2,530	2	--	--	--	22	0.9	1,693	22	--	--	--	3	0.2	1.61
Dec 44	658	658	20	--	--	--	20	3.0	428	23	--	--	--	5	1.2	1.08
TOTAL 44	25,824	23,002	>774	--	--	--	718	3.1	14,679	762	--	--	--	157	1.1	**2.27
Mar 45	6,068	6,068	10	--	--	--	82	1.4	3,447	78	--	--	--	29	0.8	2.75
GRAND TOTAL	32,324	29,458	>840	--	--	--	833	2.8	18,238	840	--	--	--	186	1.0	***2.35

*omits Dec 43

**omits Jun 44, Oct 44

***omits Dec 43, Jun 44, Oct 44

TABLE OF EQUIVALENT RANKS

Luftwaffe – United States Army Air Forces – Royal Air Force

LUFTWAFFE Title	LUFTWAFFE Abbr.	USAAF Title	USAAF Abbr.	RAF Title	RAF Abbr.
Commissioned officers					
Reichsmarschall	RM.	–	–	–	–
Generalfeldmarschall	GFM.	General (5 star)	Gen.	Marshal of the RAF	
Generaloberst	Genobst.	General (4 star)	Gen.	Air Chief Marshal	ACM.
General der Flieger	Gen. der Flg.	Lieutenant General	LGen.	Air Marshal	AM.
Generalleutnant	Genlt.	Major General	MGen.	Air Vice Marshal	AVM.
Generalmajor	Genmaj.	Brigadier General	BGen.	Air Commodore	Air Cdre.
Oberst	Obst.	Colonel	Col.	Group Captain	Gp. Capt.
Oberstleutnant	Obstlt.	Lieutenant Colonel	LCol.	Wing Commander	Wing Cdr.
Major	Maj.	Major	Maj.	Squadron Leader	Sqd. Ldr.
Hauptmann	Hptm.	Captain	Capt.	Flight Lieutenant	Flt. Lt.
Oberleutnant	Oblt.	First Lieutenant	1st Lt.	Flying Officer	Flg. Off.
Leutnant	Lt.	Second Lieutenant	2nd Lt.	Pilot Officer	Plt. Off.
Warrant officers					
Stabsfeldwebel	Stabsfw.	Flight Officer	Flt. Off.	Warrant Officer	Wt. Off.
Oberfähnrich	Ofhr. [sr. ofc. candidate]	–	–	–	–
Noncommissioned officers					
Oberfeldwebel	Obfw.	Master Sergeant	MSgt.	Flight Sergeant	Flt. Sgt.
Fähnrich	Fhr. [officer candidate]	–	–	–	–
Fahnenjunker	Fhj. [officer candidate]	–	–	–	–
Feldwebel	Fw.	Technical Sergeant	TSgt.	Sergeant	Sgt.
Unterfeldwebel	Ufw.	Sergeant	Sgt.	–	–
Unteroffizier	Uffz.	Corporal	Cpl.	Corporal	Cpl.
Enlisted men					
Hauptgefreiter	Hptgfr.	–	–	–	
Obergefreiter	Ogfr.	–	–	Leading Aircraftman	LAC.
Gefreiter	Gefr.	Private 1st Class	PFC.	Aircraftman 1st Cl.	AC.
Flieger	Flg.	Private	Pvt.	Aircraftman 2nd Cl.	AC.

GLOSSARIES

Abbreviations

AEAF: Allied Expeditionary Air Force
a/f: airfield
a/i: aviation industry
ASR: Air-Sea Rescue
CBO: Combined Bomber Offensive – the USAAF and RAF joint strategic bombing campaign
CO: commanding officer
DOW: died of wounds
e/a: enemy aircraft
ETO: European Theatre of Operations
FTR: failed to return
IFF: Identification – Friend from Foe
IP: Initial Point, from which a bomber formation maintained a steady course to its target
KIA: killed in action
KIFA: killed in a flying accident
MIA: missing in action
MTO: Mediterranean Theatre of Operations
NCO: non-commissioned officer
o/i: oil (petroleum) industry
POW: prisoner of war
PFF: Pathfinder Force.
PRU: photo reconnaissance unit
RAF: Royal Air Force
RCAF: Royal Canadian Air Force
TAF: (RAF) Tactical Air Force
t/o: target of opportunity
TOT: Time on target
USAAF: US Army Air Forces
USSTAF: US Strategic Air Forces – the 8th and 15th Air Forces; commanded by Gen. Spaatz from England
WIA: wounded in action

Aviation terms

(#-#-#): (destroyed-damaged beyond economical repair [Cat E]-repairable damage) aircraft losses (by Allies)
(#-#-#): (destroyed-probable-damaged) aircraft claims (by Allies)
Split-S: a half-roll followed by a dive that results in a reversal of direction and the loss of a great deal of altitude; a common means of breaking off combat
TacR: tactical reconnaissance
Vic: a vee-shaped formation of three aircraft

German terms

Abschuss: 'shootdown' – an air victory
Abschussmeldung: victory report
Abschwung: split-S; a half-roll followed by a dive
Alarmeinheit: 'alarm unit' – a small unit drawn from a training school or aircraft factory for air defence
Alarmstart: scramble; a rapid take-off for an intercept mission
ASM (Anerkennung später möglich): 'confirmation of (victory claim) later possible'; a claim neither admitted or rejected by the RLM victory evaluation staff
Benito: Allied code name for *Y-Führung* (q.v.)
Blitzverlegung: rapid transfer of a unit's flying component
Casino: pilots' mess
dicke Autos: 'fat cars' – Luftwaffe code designation for Allied heavy bombers
Egon: Erstling long-range control procedure – a method of ground control utilising the Erstling IFF device. In service from mid-1944
Einsatzstaffel: operational Staffel (of a training unit)
Endausbildungsstaffel: operational training squadron
endgültige Vernichtung (eV): final destruction; the shootdown of a bomber already separated from its formation
Erprobungskommando (ErprKdo): test unit; tested new weapons or aircraft before they were cleared for full operational service
Ergänzungsgruppe (ErgGr): advanced training group
Ergänzungsstaffel (ErgSt): advanced training squadron
Experte: a fighter pilot proficient in aerial combat; the Allied 'ace'
Feindberührung: enemy contact; required in order for a Jagdwaffe pilot to receive credit for a combat mission
Flak (Fliegerabwehrkanone): antiaircraft artillery
Fliegerdivision (FD): air division – a higher command containing several types of flying units

Fliegerkorps (FK): air corps – a higher command containing several types of flying units; usually contained one or more Fliegerdivisionen

Flugbuch: aircrewman's logbook

Flugmeldedienst: Aircraft Reporting Service

Flugwachen: ground observers

Flugzeugführer: pilot

freie Jagd (pl. **freie Jagden**): 'free hunt' – a fighter sweep without ground control

Fühlungshalter: contact keeper; an airborne reporter whose mission was to radio information about enemy bomber formations to ground control

Führer (pl. **Führer**)· leader

Führungsstaffel: command squadron

Führungsverband: command formation

Gefechtsstand: command post

Gefechtsverband: battle formation; two or more Jagdgruppen and/or Zerstörergruppen airborne under a single commander

General der Jagdflieger (GdJ): General of the Fighter Arm; a staff position in the Luftwaffe general staff. Werner Mölders and Adolf Galland were the most prominent holders of the position

Generalluftzeugmeister: Director of the Office of Air Armament; the RLM post responsible for all aspects of aircraft development and production. Prominent holders of the position were Ernst Udet, and, after his suicide, Erhard Milch.

Geschwader: wing (pl. **Geschwader**) – the largest mobile, homogeneous Luftwaffe flying unit

Geschwader-Adjutant: wing adjutant; responsible for the administration of a Geschwader

Geschwadergruppe: wing commodore's group; a fixed but unofficial grouping of two or three Staffeln under the operational command of a Kommodore

Geschwaderkommodore: wing commodore – usually a Major, Oberstleutnant or Oberst in rank

Geschwaderstab: wing staff; sometimes refers to a flight under the command of the Kommodore

GFB (Gefechtsbericht): combat report; the form a pilot or unit commander used to report victory claims and other significant mission details

Gruppe (Gr): group (pl. **Gruppen**) – the basic Luftwaffe combat and administrative unit

Gruppenkommandeur: group commander – usually a Hauptmann, Major or Oberstleutnant in rank

Heer: army – refers to the German Army

Herausschuss (HSS): 'shootout'—the separation of a bomber from its combat formation

Höhengruppe: high-altitude group

Höhenstaffel: high-altitude squadron

Holzauge: 'woodeneye' – a spotter; the last airplane or the top cover unit of a formation

Ia: a unit staff officer responsible for operations and logistics – sometimes flew missions

Indianer: Indians – Luftwaffe code designation for enemy fighters

Industrieschutzstaffel (or **-schwarm**): industry protection squadron or flight – based at aircraft production facilities and dedicated to their defence; commanded by Luftwaffe officers and staffed primarily by test pilots

Invasionsfront: (Normandy) invasion front

Invasionsraum: (Normandy) invasion lodgment area

Jabojagd: fighter-bomber hunt

Jabostaffel: fighter-bomber squadron

Jagdabschnitt: fighter sector; an independent command smaller than a Jafü

Jagdbomber (Jabo): fighter-bomber

Jagddivision (JD): fighter division; an upper-level headquarters that administered the fighter units based within its geographic area and controlled the fighters airborne above it

Jagdflieger: fighter pilot(s)

Jagdfliegerführer (Jafü): fighter command/control unit or its commander. The Jafü originated as administrative units, but quickly gained operational control responsibilities. Their control functions were surrendered to the larger Jagddivisionen in 1944, and most of the Jafü were disbanded

Jagdgeschwader (JG): fighter wing, commanding three or four Gruppen. The authorised strength of a three-Gruppe Geschwader after the reorganisation of 1 October 1943 was 208 aircraft

Jagdgeschwader zur besondere Verwendung (JGzbV): fighter wing for special applications; a headquarters established in Jagddivision 7 to control several independent Jagdgruppen

Jagdgruppe (JGr): fighter group, containing three or four Staffeln. The authorised strength of a Jagdgruppe was originally 40 aircraft; this was upped to 68 after 1 October 1943.

Jagdlehrerüberprüfungsgruppe (JLÜberprGr): fighter pilot instructor training group

Jagdstaffel: fighter squadron, containing 12 or 16 aircraft (three or four Schwärme of four aircraft)

Jagdverband (JV): fighter unit – a Gruppe-sized fighter formation; used only by Genlt. Galland's JV 44

Jagdvorstoss: fighter strike

Jagdwaffe: fighter arm or fighter force

Jäger: originally, a hunter– beginning in World War I, also a fighter pilot

Jägerführung: fighter ground control

Jägerstab: Fighter Staff – established in March 1944 under Karl-Otto Saur in Speer's Armaments Ministry to set production goals and maximise fighter production

Kanalfront: (English) Channel Front

Kanalgeschwader: the Geschwader serving on the English Channel (JG 2 and JG 26)

Kanaljäger: fighter pilot(s) based near the Channel

Kapitän: 'captain'; a command position rather than a rank

Katschmarek: a slang term for wingman – originally a derogatory term for a dim-witted infantry recruit

Kette: flight of three aircraft; the basic tactical unit for fighters until Mölders' 1939 reforms when it was replaced by the four-fighter Schwarm; it remained the basic unit of bomber formations

Kommandeur: 'commander'; a command position rather than a rank

Kommando, Kommandoführer: detachment; detachment leader

Kommodore: 'commodore'; a command position rather than a rank

Kriegstagebuch (KTB): unit war diary

Luftbeobachterstaffel (LBeobSt): air observation squadron – 'shadowed' Allied bomber formations

Luftflotte (LF): air fleet; a mixed-equipment force corresponding to a numbered American Air Force

Luftgaukommando (Luftgau, pl. Luftgaue): air force administrative area; a fixed geographic region of the Reich that commanded various aviation resources

Luftwaffe: 'Air Force' – refers to the German Air Force of the Third Reich (1935-45)

Luftwaffen Befehlshaber Mitte (Lw Bfh Mitte): the German air defence command in the mid-war period; superseded by Luftflotte Reich

Möbelwagen: furniture vans, Luftwaffe slang for heavy bombers

Nachtjagdgeschwader (NJG): night fighter wing

Nachtjagdgruppe (NJGr): night fighter group

Nachwuchs: 'new growth' – the late-war crop of pilot trainees

Oberbefehlshaber der Luftwaffe (ObdL): Supreme Commander of the Luftwaffe (Reichsmarschall Göring)

Oberkommando des Heeres (OKH): the (German) Army High Command

Oberkommando der Luftwaffe (OKL): the Luftwaffe High Command; controlled most of the military aspects of German aviation from its establishment in February 1944

Oberkommando der Wehrmacht (OKW): the (German) Armed Forces High Command

Oesau: JG 1's honor title; commemorated Oberst Walter Oesau, KIA 11 May 1944

Ostfront: Eastern Front

Planquadrant (PQ): map coordinates, esp. from the Luftwaffe fighter coordinates system (see map p.8)

Pulk: 'bunch' or 'herd' – Luftwaffe slang for one or more combat boxes of heavy bombers

Reich: 'empire' – Hitler's Germany was 'the Third Reich'

Reichsjägerwelle: Reich Fighter Frequency, a comprehensive running commentary on each air raid; broadcast on a common radio frequency to all defenders

Reichsluftfahrtministerium (RLM): German Air Ministry; Göring's headquarters that controlled all aspects of German aviation

Reichsluftverteidigung (RLV): 'aerial defence of the Reich' – the German air defences

Reichsverteidigung: 'defence of the Reich' – a general term for the defensive forces in the German homeland, including fighter units, antiaircraft units, ground control units and the civil defence organisation

Richthofen: JG 2's honour title; commemorated Manfred von Richthofen, the famous World War I ace

Rotte: tactical element of two aircraft

Rottenflieger: wingman; the second man in a Rotte

Rottenführer: leader of an element of two aircraft

Schlageter: JG 26's honour title; commemorated Albert Leo Schlageter, a nationalist martyr of the interwar period

Schlachtflieger: ground-attack aircraft or unit

Schlachtgeschwader (SG): ground-attack wing

Schnellkampfgeschwader (SKG): fast bomber wing

Schwarm: flight of four aircraft (pl. **Schwärme**); the basic unit of all Jagdwaffe tactical formations from 1939 to 1945 when it was replaced in some units by the Kette

Schwarmführer: flight leader

Schwarzemann: 'black man' –groundcrewman, so called because of their black coveralls

Sitzbereitschaft: 'seated readiness' – cockpit readiness; the highest form of alert, with pilots seated in their cockpits for immediate take-off

Sonderkommando: special command – used for Sonderkommando Elbe, a ramming unit

Stab: staff

Stabsschwarm: staff flight

Staffel (St): squadron (pl. **Staffeln**)

Staffelführer: squadron leader (temporary or probationary)

Staffelkapitän: squadron leader – usually a Leutnant, Oberleutnant or Hauptmann

Sturmbock: 'assault billy goat' or 'assault battering ram'; the heavily armed and armoured Fw 190 variants used by the Sturmgruppen

Sturmgruppe: assault group; a unit whose mission was to attack bomber formations in close formation from the rear to extremely close range

Sturmjäger: assault pilot, pilots, fighter or fighters

Sturmstaffel: assault squadron; Sturmstaffel 1 was an experimental unit used to develop the Sturmtaktik

Sturmtaktik: assault tactics; the tactics adopted by the Sturmgruppen

TO (Technischer Offizier): a unit engineering officer, sometimes flew missions

Udet: JG 3's honour title; commemorated Genobst. Ernst Udet, who committed suicide on 17 Nov 1941

Werfergruppe: (rocket) launcher Gruppe; a fighter group equipped with WGr 21 rocket mortar tubes

Wehrmacht: armed forces – refers to the German Armed Forces

Werkenummer (W. Nr.): aircraft serial number

Wilde Sau: 'Wild Sow' – procedure for using single-engine fighters to engage night bombers over the target; also, the units involved

Verband: formation

Verbandsführer: formation leader; the leader of a Staffel, Gruppe, Geschwader or Gefechtsverband in the air

Viermot: 'four-engine' – Luftwaffe slang for Allied heavy bomber

VNE (Vernichtung nicht erwiesen): 'destruction (of aircraft) not proven'; a claim not accepted by the RLM victory evaluation staff for lack of a crash location or crash witness

Y-Führung: Y-Control – ground-control procedure requiring two fighters with FuG 16ZY radios, one for transmitting location and the other for receiving orders

Zerstörer: 'destroyer' (heavy fighter) – Bf 110 or Me 410 twin-engine fighter

Zerstörergeschwader (ZG): heavy fighter wing

Zerstörergruppe (ZGr): heavy fighter group

NOTES ON SOURCES

Archives

The principal archives consulted were:

Bundesarchiv-Militärarchiv, Freiburg im Breisgau, Germany (BA-MA)

National Archives of the UK (formerly Public Records Office), Kew, England (PRO)

National Archives & Records Administration of the United States, Washington, DC (NARA)

USAF Historical Research Agency, Maxwell AFB, AL (USAFHRA)

Archival sources for German documents

The following primary sources were utilised throughout:

Air Directorate of Intelligence (section K) (ADI(K) reports: a wide variety of intelligence summaries of Luftwaffe operations and equipment, plus very useful POW interrogations (PRO).

BA-MA files: These contain various operational orders, technical notes and fragmentary data from many units. Relevant Kreigstagebücher (war diaries) from only three combat units are present:
    III./ZG 26: RL 10/256, 10/257, 10/565 (4 Oct 43–30 Sep 44)
    II./JG 1: RL 10/482, 10/483 (29 Dec 42–6 Jun 44)
    I./JG 26: RL 10/258, 10/259 (5 Oct 44-8 May 45)

BA-MA maps: The record group Kart 44 contains daily I. Jagdkorps mission maps for 1944 titled 'Einsatz der Fliegendenverbände – Luftlage (eig. u. feindl. Luftwaffen)'. There are many missing, including those for entire months, but those on hand contain the best data on unit mission strengths and, when no Flugbücher for the unit are available, take-off times.

Deutsche Dienststelle (WAST), Berlin: German personnel bureau records that include circumstances of loss for fatalities. Files were closed to private researchers for years; abstracted for me by A. Abendroth.

Luftwaffen-Personalamt L.P. (A)5(V) Abschüsse-Tagebücher: RLM daily victory claim worksheets (microfilm obtained from BA-MA). The data, with recent additions, are available on the Internet at http://www.lesbutler.ip3.co.uk/tony/tonywood.htm, thanks to Tony Wood.

Meldungen über Flugzeugverluste bei den fl. Verbänden (BA-MA RL 2 III/XXX): 'tally sheets' summarising daily losses; especially useful for 1944.

Ob.d.L. Gen. Q. Gen. 6. Abt. Flugzeugunfälle und Verluste bei den Verbänden (täglich): OKL daily aircraft loss lists (microfilm obtained from the Imperial War Museum, London). An authoritative reference for the dates included; unfortunately, the entire year 1944 is missing.

ULTRA transcripts released in the 1970s and published by Clearwater on microfilm in ca. 1988 were studied in detail. Signal groups declassified recently (DEFE, HW-5) were accessed in the PRO with the help of enthusiasts.

The Luftwaffe records that survived the 1945 bonfires were captured by the Allies. After sifting through these for technical nuggets and information useful in the Cold War, the Americans and British returned most of the original material to Germany in the 1960s. Some has appeared in the German archives; much remains inaccessible. Copies were made for the Allied archives; these have suffered from poor indexing and preservation, but specific record groups at the USAFHRA and the NARA were valuable resources for this study.

The USAFHRA contains the files of the German Air Force Historical Project, known informally as the Karlsruhe Project. In the 1950s, the USAF Historical Division hired a number of retired Luftwaffe officers to write historical studies of the Luftwaffe General Staff and various aspects of the air war. Many of these 'USAF Historical Studies' were published by Arno Press. However, those studies covering the Reichsluftverteidigung, which had no apparent relevance to the Cold War, were not published, and are available to the researcher today only as poor-quality microfilm, and, as of recently, as computer scans which, unfortunately, are not much better. The studies of the RLV (microfilm HRA K1026) were written by Genlt. Josef Schmid and Generalmajor Walter Grabmann and can be considered authoritative, especially as the authors had access to the I. Jagdkorps War Diaries, which survive on microfilm up to 20 May 1944 (HRA K1028). Other supporting documents are available in this same set of microfilm rolls.

The NARA wound up with the files of the OKL Genst. 8. Abteilung [General Staff Historical Branch], known as the von Rohden Collection. These contain historical studies and varied back-up material. Especially useful for this book was a set of pilot Abschussmeldungen [shootdown reports] and Gefechtsberichte [combat reports] (NARA T-971, roll 11).

Published sources

General histories:

Boiten & MacKenzie, *Nachtjagd War Diaries*

Boog, *et al.*, *Die Deutsche Luftwaffenführung; Das Deutsche Reich und der Zweite Weltkrieg, Band 7*

Craven & Cate, *The Army Air Forces in World War II, Vols. I–III.*

Corum & Muller, *The Luftwaffe's Way of War: German Air Force Doctrine 1911–1945*

Davis, *Carl A. Spaatz and the Air War in Europe*

Davis, *Bombing the European Axis Powers*

McFarland & Newton, *To Command the Sky*

Middlebrook & Everitt, *The Bomber Command War Diaries*

Price, *Battle over the Reich*

Prien, *et al.*, *Die Jagdfliegerverbände der Deutschen Luftwaffe, Teile 7, 10/I-IV*

USSBS, *Over-all Report (European Air War)*

Westermann, *Flak*

Campaign and battle histories:

25 Jul 1943: Middlebrook

17 Aug 1943: Middlebrook

10 Oct 1943: Hawkins

6 Mar 1944: Ethell & Price

22 Apr 1944: McLachlan

28 May 1944: de Jong

2 Mar 1945: Kassak

7 Apr 1945: Wier

Oil Campaign: Girbig, *... mit Kurs auf Leuna.*

Luftwaffe Defeat 1944–45: Girbig, *Start im Morgengrauen*; Price, *Last Year of the Luftwaffe*; Rose, *Radikaler Luftkampf.*

Unit histories:

JG 1: Mombeek; Prien, *et al.*

JG 2: Federl; Weal

JG 3: Prien, *et al.*

JG 4: Mombeek

JG 5: Girbig

JG 7: Boehme

JG 11: Prien, *et al.*

JG 26: Caldwell; Priller

JG 27: Prien, *et al.*; Ring & Girbig

JG 51: Aders & Held

JG 53: Prien, *et al.*

JG 54: Urbanke

JG 77: Prien, *et al.*

JG 300: Lorant & Goyat

JG 301/302: Reschke

JV 44: Forsyth

Jasta Helgoland: Marshall

KG(J) 54: Dierich

I./NJG 2: Rökker

NJG 6: Kock

SKdo Elbe: Alsdorf

Sturmstaffel 1: Mombeek

ZG 1: Vasco

Pilot documents

Flugbücher [logbooks], *Leistungsbücher* [achievement books], *Abschussmeldungen* [shootdown reports] and/or *Gefechtsberichte* [combat reports] from the following pilots and radiomen were used: Alfred Ambs, Balthazar Aretz, Heinz Bär, Helmut Beckmann, Hans Berger, Kuno von Bieberstein, Josef Bigge, Alfred Bindseil, Gerhard Bitter, Hans-Eberhard Blume, Wolfgang Brunner, Wendelin Brüse, Fritz Buchholz, Hermann Buchner, Walter Büdde, Eberhard Burath, Heinz Claus, Siegfried Conrad, Peter Crump, Walther Dahl, Willi Desinger, Manfred Dieterle, Gottfried Dietze, Josef Dobnig, Erich Doll, Herbert Dosch, Peter Düttmann, Georg-Peter Eder, Günther Eggebrecht, Günther Ehrlich, Günther Eilhardt, Franz Eisenach, Xaver Ellenrieder, Fritz Engau, Christlieb Fenger, Richard Franz, Wilhelm Freuwörth, Oskar Fromberg, Kurt Gabler, Wilhelm-Ferdinand Galland, Franz Gapp, Fritz Gehrmann, Adolf Glunz, Heinz Gomann, Albert Greiner, Arthur Gross, Hans-Georg Güthenke, Eberhard Gzik, Heinrich Haeffner, Walter Hagenah, Martin Hain, Willi Hallenberger, Alfred Hammer, Gerhard Hanf, Rudolf Haninger, Heinz Hanke, Herbert Harff, Gottfried Hauss, Karl Dieter Hecker, Hans Heitmann, Werner Held, Hans Herrmann, Heinrich Heuser, Walter Hoeckner, Werner Hoffmann, Höllinger, Heinz Hommes, Erich Homrighausen, Erich Hondt, Heinrich Janssen, Alois Job, Robert Jung, Otto Kammerdiener, Johannes Kaufmann, Josef Keil, Heinz Kemethmüller, Georg Kiefner, Rüdiger Kirchmayr, Hans Klaffenbach, Otto Kleinert, Herbert Knefel, Walter Köhne, Helmut Konrad, Hans Kornatz, Willi Kotuczek, Ewald Kraas, Wolfgang Kretschmer, Josef Kunz, Paul Kustusch, Erwin Laskowski, Wilhelm Latka, Ernst Laube, Erich Leie, Wilhelm Lemke, Helmut Lennartz, Erwin Leykauf, Hermann Litzinger, Wolfgang Löhe, Walter Loos, Ewald Lübben, Karl-Martin Lueg-Althoff, Heinz Lüpertz, Hans Maximow, Wilhelm Mayer, Karl-Heinz Messer, Albin Meyer, Klaus Mietusch, Wilhelm Mittag, Wilhelm Moritz, Willi Morzinek, Fritz R. G. Müller, H. Müller, Hans-Hermann Müller, Karl-Johann Müller, Siegfried Müller, Theo Nau, Rudolf Nielinger, Josef Niesmann, Walter Oesau, Oppelmayer, Wilhelm Philipp, Wolfgang Polster, Josef Priller, Othmar Raab, Willi Reschke, Ernst Richter, Gustav Rödel, Oskar Romm, Rudorffer, Siegfried Rudschinat, Helmut Ruschen, Heinrich Sannemann, Gerd Schaedle, Eduard Schallmoser, Rudolf Scheibe, Kurt Schellenberger, Ernst Scheufele, Kurt Schiebeler, Heinrich Schiemert, Jan Schild, Adalbert Schlarb, Otto Schmid, Heinz Schmidt, Dieter Schmidt-Barbo, Karl Schmitz, Emil-Rudolf Schnoor, Gerhard Schöpfel, Ernst Schröder, Werner Schroer, Walter Schuck, Erich Schwarz, Heinz Schwarz, Günther Seeger, Günther Sinnecker, Rudolf Sinner, Georg Spies, Franz Stadler, Hermann Staiger, Otto Stammberger, Heinrich Staniwoga, Heinz Stege, Franz Steiner, Karl-Heinz von den Steinen, Johannes Steinhoff, Alfred Surau, Kurt Tangermann, Horst Teich, Ekkehard Tichy, Winand Ubber, Albert Ullrich, Werner Ulrich, Fritz Ungar, Willi Unger, Kurt Ventzke, Werner Vorberg, Gerhard Waag, Hans Waldmann, Hans Weik, Helmut Weinbrenner, Theodor Weissenberger, Berthold Wendler, Hans-Georg Wennekers, Wilhelm Westhoff, Gerd Wiegand, August Wiing, Witgens, Günther Wolf, Walter Wolfrum, Karl Wünsch, Werner Zell, Helmut Ziems, Gottfried Zils, Herbert Zimmer and Paul Zorner.

Allied sources

8th Air Force: The principal source for basic mission data is Freeman's *Mighty Eighth War Diary*. This is supplemented from unit histories and mission folders from the USAFHRA and PRO. Bomb squadron, bomb group, fighter squadron and fighter group histories provide much detail. The mission folders supply additional detail, including TOTs (times on target), which Freeman frequently omits, and the bomber tracks and times needed for the mission maps. Fighter group mission details are also found in Miller, *Fighter Units & Pilots of the 8th Air Force*.

15th Air Force: Its only published history is Rust's *Fifteenth Air Force Story*, a 64-page softback that was excellent for its time and purpose, but did not meet the needs of the present study. Mission reports from the USAFHRA and PRO were thus vital for the work, especially the INTOPS reports, which combined US operational details with intelligence on enemy activity in single concise reports. Published bomber and fighter group unit histories were also important; fortunately, all seven fighter groups are the subjects of recently written histories.

Monthly statistics for both the 8th and 15th Air Forces can be found in the *Army Air Forces Statistical Digest: World War II*, which the USAFHRA has made available in PDF format on their website (http://www.afhra.af.mil/). These confirmed Freeman's data for the 8th Air Force and helped flesh out the data for the 15th. Especially useful was the sorting of losses by cause. After some creative bookkeeping to split out losses on non-strategic, non-Reich missions, it was possible to estimate the overall accuracy of victory claims by the RLV force against the bombers and fighters of the two US air forces, results that were certainly not expected when the research for this book began.

Aircrew losses are found in the Missing Aircrew Reports (MACRs) in the NARA. These reports were initiated at the unit level when an airplane failed to return from a mission, and their folders continued to grow as more information was obtained. The NARA sells them on microfiche. They are now available from Footnote.com (http://www.footnote.com/) as JPGs, a much more convenient format, for a membership fee. The MACR contents for 8th Air Force losses have been summarised in Andrews & Adams, *The Mighty Eighth Combat Chronology*. This reference proved useful for quickly identifying crash sites. No similar summary is available for the 15th AF. Furthermore, it has been estimated that up to 20 per cent of that air force's losses cannot be found in the NARA's MACRs; these were either never prepared or have vanished.

Fighter claims are covered in Olynyk, *USAAF (European Theater) and (Mediterranean Theater) Credits for the Destruction of Enemy Aircraft in Air-to-Air Combat in World War 2*. Olynyk has documented his work so thoroughly that his books can be considered primary references. Bomber gunner claims were never put through a formal confirmation process; the USAAF command used them for their propaganda and morale value.

BIBLIOGRAPHY

Aders, Gebhard, *History of the German Night Fighter Force 1917–1945*, Jane's, London, 1979.

Aders, Gebhard, and Werner Held, *Jagdgeschwader 51 'Mölders'*, Motorbuch Verlag, Stuttgart, 1985.

Ailing, Charles, *A Mighty Fortress: Lead Bomber over Europe*, Casemate, Havertown PA, 2002.

Air Ministry, *The Rise and Fall of the German Air Force: History of the Luftwaffe in World War II*, HMSO, London, 1948.

Alsdorf, Dietrich, *Auf den Spuren des Elbe-Kommandos Rammjäger*, Podzun-Pallas-Verlag, Berstadt, Germany, 2001.

Andrews, Paul, and William Adams, *The Mighty Eighth Combat Chronology: Heavy Bomber and Fighter Activities 1942–1945*, Eighth Air Force Memorial Museum Foundation, Warrenton, VA, 1997.

Anonymous, *The Kassel Mission Reports: Highest Group Loss in 8th Air Force History*, privately published, n.d.

Anonymous, *Ultra and the History of the USSAFE versus the German Air Force*, University Publications, Frederick MD, 1980.

Anonymous, *ULTRA – Main Series of Signals Conveying Intelligence to Allied Commands*, Clearwater Publishing, New York, ca. 1988 [104 microfilm rolls].

Anonymous, *The Flight of the Vulgar Vultures: 455th Bomb Group (H) 1943–1945*, privately published, 1991.

Anonymous, *Defenders of Liberty: 2nd Bombardment Group/Wing 1918–1993*, Turner Publishing, Paducah, KY, 1996.

Arnold, H. H., *Global Mission*, Harper & Brothers, New York, 1949.

Beale, Nick, Ferdinando D'Amico and Gabriele Velentini, *Air War Italy 1944–45*, Airlife, Shrewsbury, England, 1996.

Bekker, Cajus, *The Luftwaffe War Diaries*, Doubleday, Garden City, NY, 1964.

von Below, Nicolaus, *At Hitler's Side: The Memoirs of Hitler's Luftwaffe Adjutant 1937–1945*, Greenhill, London, 2001.

Bergström, Christer, *Graf & Grislawski: A Pair of Aces*, Eagle Editions, Hamilton MT, 2003.

Blake, Steve, *Adorimini: A History of the 82nd Fighter Group*, 82nd FG History Inc., Boise, ID, 1992.

Blake, Steve, *The Pioneer Mustang Group*, Schiffer, Altglen, PA, 2008.

Blakebrough, Ken, *The Fireball Outfit: The 457th Bombardment Group in the Skies over Europe*, Aero Publishers, Fallbrook, CA, 1968.

Blue, Allen, *The Fortunes of War*, Aero Publishers, Fallbrook, CA, 1967.

Blyth, Kenneth, *Cradle Crew*, Sunflower University Press, Manhattan, KS, 1997.

Blyth, Kenneth, *Who Shot Down Eq-Queenie?*, Fenestra Books, Tucson, AZ, 2004.

Boehm-Tettelbach, Karl, *Als Flieger in der Hexenküche*, v. Hase & Koehler Verlag, Mainz, Germany, 1981.

Boehme, Manfred, *JG 7: The World's First Jet Fighter Unit 1944/1945*, Schiffer Military History, Atglen, PA, 1992.

Bohnstedt, D. L., and B. J. Bohnstedt, *460th Bomb Group History*, Taylor Publishing, Dallas, TX, 1996.

Boiten, Theo, and Martin Bowman, *Battles with the Luftwaffe*, HarperCollins, London, 2001.

Boiten, Theo, *Nachtjagd: The Night Fighter vs. Bomber War over the Third Reich*, The Crowood Press, Ramsbury, England, 1997.

Boiten, Theo, *Nachtjagd War Diaries: An Operational History of the German Night Fighter Force in the West, Vol. 1 Sept 1939–Mar 1944*, Red Kite, Surrey, England, 2007.

Boiten, Theo and Roderick MacKenzie, *Nachtjagd War Diaries: An Operational History of the German Night Fighter Force in the West, Vol. 2 Apr 1944–May 1945*, Red Kite, Surrey, England, 2009.

Boog, Horst, *Die deutsche Luftwaffenführung 1935–1945*, Deutsche Verlags-Anstalt, Stuttgart, 1982.

Boog, Horst, *et al.*, *Germany and the Second World War, Vol. VI – The Global War: Widening of the Conflict into a World War and the Shift of the Initiative 1941–1943*, Clarendon Press, Oxford, England, 2001.

Boog, Horst, *et al.*, *Das Deutsche Reich und der Zweite Weltkrieg, Band 7 – Das Deutsche Reich in der Defensive*, Deutsche Verlags-Anstalt, Stuttgart, Germany, 2001.

Bracke, Gerhard, *Gegen vielfache Übermacht*, Motorbuch Verlag, Stuttgart, Germany, 1977.

Buchner, Hermann, *Stormbird*, Hikoki Publications, Aldershot, England, 2000.

Budraß, Lutz, *Flugzeugindustrie und Luftrüstung in Deutschland 1918–1945*, Droste Verlag, Düsseldorf, Germany, 1998.

Budrass, Lutz, Jonas Scherner, and Jochen Streb, "Demystifying the German 'Armaments Miracle' during World War II: New Insights from the Annual Audits of German Aircraft Producers", Economic Growth Center, Yale University, New Haven, CT, January 2005.

Caldwell, Donald, *JG 26: Top Guns of the Luftwaffe*, Orion Books, New York, 1991.

Caldwell, Donald, *The JG 26 War Diary Volume One: 1939–1942*, Grub Street, London, 1996.

Caldwell, Donald, *The JG 26 War Diary Volume Two: 1943–1945*, Grub Street, London, 1998.

Caldwell, Donald, and Richard R. Muller, *The Luftwaffe over Germany: Defense of the Reich*, Greenhill Books, London, 2007.

Conversino, Mark. J., *Fighting with the Soviets: The Failure of Operation FRANTIC, 1944–1945*, University Press of Kansas,

Lawrence, KS, 1997.

Cooper, Matthew, *The German Air Force 1933–1945*, Jane's, London, 1981.

Copp, DeWitt, *Forged in Fire*, Doubleday, New York, 1982.

Corum, James S., *The Luftwaffe: Creating the Operational Air War*, University Press of Kansas, Manhattan, KS, 1997.

Corum, James S., and Richard R. Muller, *The Luftwaffe's Way of War: German Air Force Doctrine 1911–1945*, Nautical & Aviation, Baltimore, MD, 1998.

Craven, Wesley, and James Cate, *The Army Air Forces in World War II: Vol. I, Plans and Early Operations*, University of Chicago Press, Chicago, IL, 1948.

Craven, Wesley, and James Cate, *The Army Air Forces in World War II: Vol. II, Europe: Torch to Pointblank*, University of Chicago Press, Chicago, IL, 1949.

Craven, Wesley, and James Cate, *The Army Air Forces in World War II: Vol. III, Europe: Argument to V-E Day*, University of Chicago Press, Chicago, IL, 1951.

Craven, Wesley, and James Cate, *The Army Air Forces in World War II: Vol. VI, Men and Planes*, Office of Air Force History, Washington, DC, 1983.

Dahl, Walther, *Rammjäger*, Orion Verlag, Heusenstamm, Germany, 1961.

Davis, Richard G., *Carl A. Spaatz and the Air War in Europe*, Center for Air Force History, Washington, DC, 1993.

Davis, Richard G., *Bombing the European Axis Powers: A Historical Digest of the Combined Bomber Offensive, 1939–1945*, Air University Press, Maxwell AFB, AL, 2006.

Deist, Wilhelm, *et al.*, *Das Deutsche Reich und der Zweite Weltkrieg, Band I: Ursachen und Voraussetzungen der deutschen Kriegspolitik*, DVA, Stuttgart, Germany, 1979.

de Jong, Ivo, *Mission 376: Battle over the Reich 28 May 1944*, Hikoki Publications, Crowborough, England, 2003.

de Zeng, Henry L. IV, and Douglas G. Stankey, *Bomber Units of the Luftwaffe 1933–1945 Volume 1*, Ian Allan Publishing, Hersham, England, 2007.

de Zeng, Henry L. IV, and Douglas G. Stankey, *Bomber Units of the Luftwaffe 1933–1945 Volume 2*, Ian Allan Publishing, Hersham, England, 2008.

Dickfeld, Adolf, *Footsteps of the Hunter*, J. J. Fedorowicz Publishing, Winnipeg, Canada, 1993.

Dierich, Wolfgang. *Kampfgeschwader 'Edelweiß': The History of a German Bomber Unit 1939–1945*, Ian Allan, London, 1975.

Doolittle, James, *I Could Never Be So Lucky Again*, Bantam Books, New York, 1991.

Engau, Fritz, *Frontal durch die Bomberpulks*, Hoppe Verlag, Graz, Austria, 1997.

Ethell, Jeffrey, and Alfred Price, *The German Jets in Combat*, Jane's, London, 1979.

Ethell, Jeffrey, and Alfred Price, *Target Berlin – Mission 250: 6 March 1944*, Jane's, London, 1981.

Federl, Christian, *Jagdgeschwader 2 'Richthofen'*, VDM Heinz Nickel, Zweibrücken, Germany, 2006.

Foreman, John, and S. E. Harvey, *Me 262 Combat Diary*, Air Research Publications, Surrey, England, 1990.

Foreman, John, *Fighter Command War Diaries Vol 3: Jan 1942–June 1943*, Air Research Publications, Surrey, England, 2001.

Foreman, John, *Fighter Command War Diaries Vol 4: Jul 1943–June 1944*, Air Research Publications, Surrey, England, 2001.

Foreman, John, Johannes Matthews & Simon Parry, *Luftwaffe Night Fighter Combat Claims 1939–1945*, Red Kite, Walton-on-Thames, Surrey, England, 2004.

Forsyth, Robert, *JV 44: The Galland Circus*, Classic Publications, West Sussex, England, 1996,

Forsyth, Robert, and Eddie Creek, *Jagdwaffe: Defending the Reich 1943–1944*, Ian Allan, Surrey, England, 2004.

Forsyth, Robert, *Jagdwaffe: Defending the Reich 1944–1945*, Ian Allan, Surrey, England, 2005.

Franks, Norman, *RAF Fighter Command Losses of WW II Vol. 2: 1942–1943*, Midland Publishing Ltd, Leicester, England, 1998.

Franks, Norman, *RAF Fighter Command Losses of WW II Vol. 3: 1944–1945*, Midland Publishing Ltd, Leicester England, 2000.

Frappé, Jean-Bernard, *La Luftwaffe face au débarquement allié: 6 juin au 31 août 1944*, Editions Heimdal, Bayeux, France, 1999.

Freeman, Roger, *The Mighty Eighth*, Doubleday, Garden City, New York, 1970.

Freeman, Roger, *Mighty Eighth War Diary*, Jane's, London, 1981.

Freeman, Roger, *Mighty Eighth War Manual*, Jane's, London, 1984.

Friedrich, Jörg, *Der Brand: Deutschland im Bombenkrieg 1940–1945*, Propyläen, Munich, Germany, 2002.

Fry, Garry, and Jeffrey Ethell, *Escort to Berlin: The 4th Fighter Group in World War II*, Arco, New York, 1980.

Galland, Adolf, *Die Ersten und die Letzten*, Franz Schneekluth, Darmstadt, Germany, 1953.

Galland, Adolf, *The First and the Last*, Henry Holt, New York, 1954.

Girbig, Werner, *Start im Morgengrauen*, Motorbuch Verlag, Stuttgart, Germany, 1975.

Girbig, Werner, *Jagdgeschwader 5 'Eismeerjäger'*, Motorbuch Verlag, Stuttgart, Germany, 1976.

Girbig, Werner, *… mit Kurs auf Leuna: Die Luftoffensive gegen die Triebstoffindustrie und der deutsche Abwehreinsatz 1944–1945*, Motorbuch Verlag, Stuttgart, Germany, 1980.

Gobrecht, Harry, *Might in Flight: Daily Diary of the Eighth Air Force's Hell's Angels, 303rd Bombardment Group (H)*, 303rd Bomb Group Association, San Clemente, CA, 1997.

Gomann, Heinz, *Und über uns der Himmel: Fliegergeschichten vom JG 26*, Kurt Vowinckel Verlag, Berg am See, Germany, 1996.

Green, William, *The Warplanes of the Third Reich*, Doubleday, New York, 1972.

Häberlen, Klaus, *Davongekommen: Als Kampfflieger über den Fronten*, VDM Heinz Nickel, Zweibrücken, Germany, 2001.

Hammel, Eric, *Air War Europa: America's Air War against Germany in Europe and North Africa 1942–1945*, Pacifica Press, Pacifica, CA, 1994.

Hannig, Norbert, *Luftwaffe Fighter Ace: From the Eastern Front to the Defence of the Homeland*, Grub Street, London, 2004.

Hastings, Max, *Bomber Command*, Dial Press/James Wade, New York, 1979.

Hastings, Max, *Armageddon: The Battle for Germany, 1944–1945*, Knopf, New York, 2004.

Havelaar, Marion, and William Hess, *The Ragged Irregulars of Bassingbourn: The 91st Bombardment Group in World War II*, Schiffer Publishing, Atglen, PA, 1995.

Hawkins, Ian, *Münster: The Way It Was*, Robinson Typographics, Anaheim, CA, 1984.

Held, Werner, *Reichsverteidigung – Die deutsche Tagjagd 1943–1945*, Podzun-Pallas-Verlag, Friedberg, Germany, 1988.

Herrmann, Hajo, *Eagle's Wings*, Motorbooks International, Osceola, WI, 1991.

Hess, William, *Zemke's Wolfpack: The 56th Fighter Group in World War*

II, Motorbooks International, Osceola, WI, 1992.

Hess, William, *German Jets vs. the US Army Air Force*, Specialty Press, North Branch, MN, 1996.

Hess, William, *Hell in the Heavens: Ill-Fated 8th Air Force Bomb Group Missions*, Specialty Press, North Branch, MN, 2000.

Hess, William, *354th Fighter Group*, Osprey, Oxford, England, 2002.

Hess, William, *B-17 Flying Fortress Units of the MTO*, Osprey, Oxford, England, 2003.

Hoseason, James, *The 1,000 Day Battle*, Gillingham Publications, Lowestoft, England, 1979.

Irving, David, *The Rise and Fall of the Luftwaffe: The Life of Field Marshal Erhard Milch*, Little, Brown & Co., Boston, 1973.

Irving, David, *Hitler's War*, Viking, New York, 1977.

Irving, David, *Göring: A Biography*, Morrow, New York, 1989.

Jansen, Ab A., *Wespennest Leeuwarden Deel 2: okt 1942–okt 1943*, Hollandia BV, Baarn, NL, 1976.

Jansen, Ab A., *Wespennest Leeuwarden Deel 3: nov 1943–mei 1945*, Hollandia BV, Baarn, NL, 1977.

Jansen, Ab A., *Sporen an de Hemel Deel 1: jan 1943–sep 1943*, Hollandia BV, Baarn, NL, 1979.

Jansen, Ab A., *Sporen an de Hemel Deel 2: sep 1943–jan 1944*, Hollandia BV, Baarn, NL, 1979.

Jansen, Ab A., *Sporen an de Hemel Deel 3: jan 1944–apr 1945*, Hollandia BV, Baarn, NL, 1980.

Johnson, Charles, *The History of the Hell Hawks*, Southcoast Typesetting, Anaheim, CA, 1975.

Jung, Robert, *Auf verlorenem Posten: Die Geschichte eines jungen Jagdfliegers*, privately published, 1994.

Kassak, Peter, *An Ordinary Day in 1945*, Stratus, Sandomierz, Poland, 2005.

Kay, Antony L., and J. Richard Smith, *German Aircraft of the Second World War*, Naval Institute Press, Annapolis, MD, 2002.

Knoke, Heinz, *I Flew for the Führer*, Henry Holt, New York, 1953.

Kock, Werner, *Das Kriegstagebuch des Nachtjagdgeschwaders 6*, privately printed, 1996.

Lay, Jr., Beirne, "Smashing the Luftwaffe's Nest", in *The 100 Best True Stories of World War II*, Wise & Co., New York, 1945.

Lay, Jr., Beirne, and Sy Bartlett, *Twelve O'Clock High!*, Harper & Brothers, New York, 1948.

Lorant, Jean-Yves, and Richard Goyat, *Jagdgeschwader 300 'Wilde Sau' Vol. 1: June 1943–Sep 1944*, Eagle Editions, Hamilton, MT, 2005.

Lorant, Jean-Yves, and Richard Goyat, *Jagdgeschwader 300 'Wilde Sau' Vol. 2: Sep 1944–May 1945*, Eagle Editions, Hamilton, MT, 2007.

MacDonald, Charles, *The Mighty Endeavor: American Armed Forces in the European Theater in World War II*, Oxford University Press, New York, 1969.

Manuel, Frank E., *Scenes from the End: The Last Days of World War II in Europe*, Steerforth Press, South Royalton, VT, 2000.

Marshall, Francis, *Sea Eagles: The Messerschmitt Bf 109T*, Air Research Publications, Surrey, England, 1993.

McFarland, Stephen L., and Wesley Phillips Newton, *To Command the Sky: The Battle for Air Superiority over Germany, 1942–1944*, Smithsonian Institution Press, Washington, DC, 1991.

McLachlan, Ian, *Night of the Intruders: First-Hand Accounts Chronicling the Slaughter of Homeward Bound USAAF Mission 311*, Patrick Stephens, Sparkford, England, 1994.

Mehner, Kurt, and Reinhard Teuber, *Die Luftwaffe 1939–1945*, Militär-Verlag Klaus D. Patzwall, Norderstedt, Germany, 1996.

Meilinger, Philip S., ed., *The Paths of Heaven: The Evolution of Airpower Theory*, Air University Press, Maxwell AFB, AL, 1997.

Merrick, Ken, *By Day and by Night: The Bomber War in Europe, 1939–1945*, Ian Allan, London, 1989.

Mets, David R., *Master of Airpower: Gen. Carl A. Spaatz*, Presidio, Novato, CA, 1988.

Michulec, Robert, and Donald Caldwell, *Adolf Galland*, Stratus, Sandomierz, Poland, 2003.

Middlebrook, Martin, *The Battle of Hamburg: Allied Bomber Forces against a German City in 1943* [25 Jul 43], Chas. Scribner's Sons, New York, 1980.

Middlebrook, Martin, *The Schweinfurt–Regensburg Mission* [17 Aug 43], Chas. Scribner's Sons, New York, 1983.

Middlebrook, Martin, and Chris Everitt, *The Bomber Command War Diaries: An Operational Reference Book, 1939–1945*, Penguin, New York, 1990.

Miller, Kent, *Fighter Units & Pilots of the 8th Air Force September 1942–May 1945 Vol. 1: Day-to-Day Operations – Fighter Group Histories*, Schiffer Military History, Altglen, PA, 2001.

Mombeek, Eric, *Defending the Reich: The History of Jagdgeschwader 1 'Oesau'*, JAC Publications, Norwich, England, 1992.

Mombeek, Eric, *Sturmjäger: Zur Geschichte des Jagdgeschwaders 4 und der Sturmstaffel 1: Band 1*, privately published, 1997.

Mombeek, Eric, *Sturmjäger: Zur Geschichte des Jagdgeschwaders 4 und der Sturmstaffel 1: Band 2*, privately published, n.d.

Mombeek, Eric, *Defenders of the Reich: Jagdgeschwader 1 Volume 2: 1943*, Classic Publications, Surrey, England, 2001.

Mombeek, Eric, *Defenders of the Reich: Jagdgeschwader 1 Volume 3: 1944–1945*, Classic Publications, Surrey, England, 2003.

Muller, Richard, *The German Air War in Russia*, Nautical & Aviation, Baltimore, MD, 1992.

Murray, Williamson, *Luftwaffe*, Nautical & Aviation, Baltimore, MD, 1985.

Murray, Williamson, ed., *German Military Effectiveness*, Nautical & Aviation, Baltimore, MD, 1992.

Neulen, Hans Werner, *In the Skies of Europe: Air Forces Allied to the Luftwaffe*, Crowood Press, Wiltshire, England, 1998.

Obermaier, Ernst, *Die Ritterkreuzträger der Luftwaffe 1939–1945 Band I: Jagdflieger*, Verlag Dieter Hoffmann, Mainz, Germany, 2nd Edition, 1989.

O'Connell, Dan, *Messerschmitt Me 262: The Production Log 1941–1945*, Ian Allan, Hersham, Surrey, England, 2005.

Olmsted, Merle, *The 357th over Europe: The 357th Fighter Group in World War II*, Phalanx Pulishing, St. Paul, MN, 1994.

Olmsted, Merle, *To War with the Yoxford Boys*, Eagle Editions, Hamilton, MT, 2004.

Olynyk, Frank, *USAAF (European Theater) Credits for the Destruction of Enemy Aircraft in Air-to-Air Combat in World War 2*, privately published, Aurora, OH, 1987.

Olynyk, Frank, *USAAF (Mediterranean Theater) Credits for the Destruction of Enemy Aircraft in Air-to-Air Combat* in *World War 2*, privately published, Aurora, OH, 1987.

Overy, R. J., *Göring: The 'Iron Man'*, Routledge & Kegan Paul, London, 1984.

Overy, R. J., *War and Economy in the Third Reich*, Clarendon Press, Oxford, England, 1994.

Overy, R. J., *Why the Allies Won*, W. W. Norton, New York, 1996.

Parker, Danny, *To Win the Winter Sky: Air War over the Ardennes, 1944–1945*, Combined Books, Conshohocken, PA, 1994.

Price, Alfred, *Battle over the Reich*, Charles Scribner's Sons, New York, 1973.

Price, Alfred, *Blitz on Britain, 1939–1945*, Ian Allan, London, 1977.

Price, Alfred, *Instruments of Darkness: The History of Electronic Warfare*, Charles Scribner's Sons, New York, 1978.

Price, Alfred, *Last Year of the Luftwaffe: May 1944 to May 1945*, Motorbooks International, Osceola, WI, 1991.

Prien, Jochen, and Peter Rodeike, *Jagdgeschwader 1 und Jagdgeschwader 11, Einsatz in der Reichsverteidigung von 1939 bis 1945 Teil 1: 1939–1943*, Struve-Druck, Eutin, Germany, n.d.

Prien, Jochen, and Peter Rodeike, *Jagdgeschwader 1 und Jagdgeschwader 11: Einsatz in der Reichsverteidigung von 1939 bis 1945 Teil 2: 1944*, Struve-Druck, Eutin, Germany, n.d.

Prien, Jochen, and Peter Rodeike, *Jagdgeschwader 1 und 11: Einsatz in der Reichsverteidigung von 1939 bis 1945 Teil 3: 1944-45*, Struve-Druck, Eutin, Germany, n.d.

Prien, Jochen, and Gerhard Stemmer, *Messerschmitt Bf 109 im Einsatz beim Stab und I./JG 3: 1938-1945*, Struve-Druck, Eutin, Germany, n.d.

Prien, Jochen, and Gerhard Stemmer, *Messerschmitt Bf 109 im Einsatz beim II./Jagdgeschwader 3: 1940–1945*, Struve-Druck, Eutin, Germany, 1996.

Prien, Jochen, and Gerhard Stemmer, *Messerschmitt Bf 109 im Einsatz beim III./Jagdgeschwader 3: 1940–1945*, Struve-Druck, Eutin, Germany, 1996.

Prien, Jochen, *IV./JG 3: Chronik einer Jagdgruppe 1943–1945*, Struve-Druck, Eutin, Germany, n.d.

Prien, Jochen, et al., *Messerschmitt Bf 109 im Einsatz beim Stab und I./JG 27*, Struve-Druck, Eutin, Germany, n.d.

Prien, Jochen, et al., *Messerschmitt Bf 109 im Einsatz beim II./Jagdgeschwader 27*, Struve-Druck, Eutin, Germany, n.d.

Prien, Jochen, et al., *Messerschmitt Bf 109 im Einsatz beim III./JG 27 und IV./JG 27*, Struve-Druck, Eutin, Germany, 1995.

Prien, Jochen, *'Pik-As': Geschichte des Jagdgeschwaders 53 Teil 3*, Struve-Druck, Eutin, Germany, 1991.

Prien, Jochen, *Geschichte des Jagdgeschwaders 77 Teil 4: 1944–1945*, Struve-Druck, Eutin, Germany, n.d.

Prien, Jochen, et al., *Die Jagdfliegerverbände der Deutschen Luftwaffe 1934 bis 1945 Teil 7: Heimatverteidigung und Einsatz im Westen 1 Jan. bis 31 Dez. 1942*, Struve-Druck, Eutin, Germany, n.d.

Prien, Jochen, et al., *Die Jagdfliegerverbände der Deutschen Luftwaffe 1934 bis 1945 Teil 10/I: Reichsverteidigung 1943 – 1.1. bis 31.12.1943*, Struve-Druck, Eutin, Germany, n.d.

Prien, Jochen, et al., *Die Jagdfliegerverbände der Deutschen Luftwaffe 1934 bis 1945 Teil 10/II: Reichsverteidigung 1943 – 1.1. bis 31.12.1943*, Struve-Druck, Eutin, Germany, n.d.

Prien, Jochen, et al., *Die Jagdfliegerverbände der Deutschen Luftwaffe 1934 bis 1945 Teil 10/III: Reichsverteidigung 1943 – 1.1. bis 31.12.1943*, Struve-Druck, Eutin, Germany, n.d.

Prien, Jochen, et al., *Die Jagdfliegerverbände der Deutschen Luftwaffe 1934 bis 1945 Teil 10/IV: Einsatz im Westen 1943 – 1.1. bis 31.12.1943*, Struve-Druck, Eutin, Germany, n.d.

Priller, Josef, *JG 26: Geschichte eines Jagdgeschwaders*, Kurt Vowinckel, Heidelberg, Germany, 1956.

Probert, Henry, *Bomber Harris: His Life and Times*, Greenhill, London, 2001.

Punka, György, *Messerschmitt Me 210/410 in Action*, Squadron/Signal, Carrollton, TX, 1994.

Punka, György, *Hungarian Aces of World War II*, Osprey, Oxford, England, 2002.

Rajlich, Jiri, et al., *Slovakian and Bulgarian Aces of World War II*, Osprey, Oxford, England, 2004.

Renner, W., *Wilhelm-Ferdinand Galland*, Hans Arens Verlag, Berlin, 1943.

Reschke, Willi, *Jagdgeschwader 301/302 'Wilde Sau'*, Motorbuch Verlag, Stuttgart, Germany, 1998.

Richards, Denis, *The Hardest Victory: RAF Bomber Command in the Second World War*, W. W. Norton, New York, 1994.

Rieckhoff, Herbert Joachim, *Trumpf oder Bluff? 12 Jahre deutsche Luftwaffe*, Interavia, Geneva, Switzerland, 1945.

Ring, Hans, and Werner Girbig, *Jagdgeschwader 27*, Motorbuch Verlag, Stuttgart, Germany, 1971.

Rökker, Heinz, *I. Gruppe Nachtjagdgeschwader 2*, VDM Heinz Nickel, Zweibrücken, Germany, 1997.

Rose, Arno, *Radikaler Luftkampf*, Motorbuch Verlag, Stuttgart, Germany, 1977.

Rust, Kenn, *Fifteenth Air Force Story*, Historical Aviation Album, Temple City, CA, 1976

Savic, Dravan, and Boris Ciglic, *Croatian Aces of World War 2*, Osprey, Oxford, England, 2002.

Schliephake, Hanfried, *The Birth of the Luftwaffe*, Henry Regnery Company, Chicago, IL, 1971.

Schramm, Percy, ed., *Kriegstagebuch des Oberkommandos der Wehrmacht 1943 Band 2 (III/6)*, Bernard und Graefe, Munich, Germany, 1982.

Schreier, Hans, *JG 52: Das erfolgreichste Jagdgeschwader des II. Weltkrieges*, Kurt Vowinckel Verlag, Berg am See, Germany, 1990.

Schuck, Walter, *Abschuss! Von der Me 109 zur Me 262: Erinnerungen an die Luftkämpfe beim Jagdgeschwader 5 und 7*, Helios Verlags- und Buchvertriebsgesellschaft, Aachen, Germany, 2007.

Shepherd, D., *Of Men and Wings: the First 100 Missions of the 449th Bombardment Group*, Norfield, Panama City, FL, 1996.

Sloan, John, *The Route as Briefed: the History of the 92nd Bombardment Group 1942–1945*, Argus Press, Cleveland, OH, 1946.

Smith, J. Richard, and Eddie Creek, *Me 262: Volume 2*, Classic Publications, Crowborough, England, 1998.

Smith, J. Richard, and Eddie Creek, *Me 262: Volume 3*, Classic Publications, Crowborough, England, 2000.

Smith, J. Richard, and Eddie Creek, *Me 262: Volume 4*, Classic Publications, Crowborough, England, 2000.

Smith, Jack, *Mustangs and Unicorns: A History of the 359th FG*, Pictorial Histories, Missoula, MT, 1997.

Speer, Albert, *Inside the Third Reich*, Macmillan, New York, 1970.

Steinhoff, Johannes, *Messerschmitts over Sicily*, Nautical & Aviation, Baltimore, MD, 1987.

Stern, D. G., *The 483rd Bomb Group (H)*, Turner Publishing, Paducah, KY, 1994.

Stiles, Bert, *Serenade to the Big Bird*, W. W. Norton, New York, 1952.

Strong, Russell, *First over Germany: A History of the 306th Bombardment Group*, privately published, Charlotte, NC, 1990.

Suchenwirth, Richard, *Command and Leadership in the German Air Force*, Arno Press, New York, 1971.

Swanborough, Gordon, and William Green, *The Focke-Wulf Fw 190*, Arco, New York, 1976.

Terraine, John, *A Time for Courage: The Royal Air Force in the European War*, Macmillan, New York, 1985.

Thom, Walter, *The Brotherhood of Courage: The History of the 305th Bombardment Group (H) in World War II*, privately published, 1986.

Tessin, Georg, *Verbände und Truppen der deutschen Wehrmacht und Waffen-SS im Zweiten Weltkrieg: Band 14*, Biblio Verlag, Osnabrück, Germany, 1980.

Thomas, Chris, and Christopher Shores, *The Typhoon & Tempest Story*, Arms & Armour Press, London, 1988.

Urbanke, Axel, *Green Hearts: First in Combat with the Dora-9*, Eagle Editions Ltd, Hamilton MT, 1997.

United States Army Air Forces, *Target Germany*, Simon and Schuster, New York, 1943.

United States Army Air Forces, *Statistical Digest: World War II*, AAF Office of Statistical Control, Washington, DC, 1945.

United States Strategic Bombing Survey, *Over-all Report (European Air War)*, Government Printing Office, Washington, DC (1945).

United States Strategic Bombing Survey, *The Defeat of the German Air Force*, Government Printing Office, Washington, DC (1947).

Vajda, Ferenc A., and Peter Dancy, *German Aircraft Industry and Production*, SAE, Warrendale, PA, 1998.

van Ishoven, Armand, *Messerschmitt Bf 109 at War*, Charles Scribner's Sons, New York, 1977.

Vasco, John, *The Sting of the Luftwaffe: Schnellkampfgeschwader 210 and Zerstörergeschwader 1 'Wespengeschwader' in World War II*, Schiffer Publishing, Altglen, PA, 2001.

Weal, John, *Jagdgeschwader 2 'Richthofen'*, Osprey, Oxford, England, 2000.

Weal, John, *Luftwaffe Sturmgruppen*, Osprey, Oxford, England, 2005.

Webster, Charles, and Noble Frankland, *The Strategic Air Offensive against Germany, 1939–1945, Volume I: Preparation*, HMSO, London, 1961.

Wegmann, G., *"Das Oberkommando der Wehrmacht gibt bekannt …" Band 2*, Biblio Verlag, Osnabrück, Germany, 1982.

Weinberg, Gerhard, ed., *Hitler and His Generals: Military Conferences 1942–1945*, Enigma Books, New York, 2003.

Weir, Adrian, *The Last Flight of the Luftwaffe: The Fate of Schulungslehrgang Elbe, 7 April 1945*, Arms & Armour Press, London, 1997.

Wells, Mark K., *Courage and Air Warfare: The Allied Aircrew Experience in the Second Word War*, Frank Cass, London, 1995.

Westermann, Edward B., *Flak: German Anti-Aircraft Defenses, 1914–1945*, University Press of Kansas, Manhattan, KS, 2001.

Williams, David P., *Day Fighters: Hunters of the Reich*, Cerberus, Bristol, England, 2002.

Wood, Tony, and Bill Gunston, *Hitler's Luftwaffe*, Salamander, London, n.d.

Woodward, Ellis, *Flying School: Combat Hell*, American Literary Press, Baltimore, MD, 1998.

Ziegler, Mano, *Rocket Fighter: The Story of the Messerschmitt Me 163*, Arms & Armour Press, London, 1976.

INDEX

Staffeln

LOCATIONS
Airfields

Cities, military and industrial targets

PERSONNEL

German